Investments

Investments

ELEVENTH EDITION

ZVI BODIE

Boston University

ALEX KANE

University of California, San Diego

ALAN J. MARCUS

Boston College

INVESTMENTS, ELEVENTH EDITION

Published by McGraw-Hill Education, 2 Penn Plaza, New York, NY 10121. Copyright © 2018 by McGraw-Hill Education. All rights reserved. Printed in the United States of America. Previous editions © 2014, 2011, and 2009. No part of this publication may be reproduced or distributed in any form or by any means, or stored in a database or retrieval system, without the prior written consent of McGraw-Hill Education, including, but not limited to, in any network or other electronic storage or transmission, or broadcast for distance learning.

Some ancillaries, including electronic and print components, may not be available to customers outside the United States.

This book is printed on acid-free paper.

2 3 4 5 6 7 8 9 LWI 21 20 19 18

ISBN 978-1-259-27717-7
MHID 1-259-27717-8

Executive Brand Manager: *Chuck Synovec*
Senior Product Developer: *Noelle Bathurst*
Marketing Manager: *Trina Maurer*
Core Content Project Manager: *Kathryn D. Wright*
Senior Assessment Content Project Manager: *Kristin Bradley*
Media Content Project Manager: *Karen Jozefowicz*
Senior Buyer: *Laura Fuller*
Senior Designer: *Matt Diamond*
Lead Content Licensing Specialist: *Beth Thole*
Cover Image: © *marigold_88*
Compositor: *SPi Global*
Printer: *LSC Communications*

All credits appearing on page or at the end of the book are considered to be an extension of the copyright page.

Library of Congress Cataloging-in-Publication Data

Names: Bodie, Zvi, author. | Kane, Alex, 1942- author. | Marcus, Alan J., author.
Title: Investments / Zvi Bodie, Boston University, Alex Kane, University of
    California, San Diego, Alan J. Marcus, Boston College.
Description: Eleventh edition. | New York, NY : McGraw-Hill Education, [2018]
Identifiers: LCCN 2017013354 | ISBN 9781259277177 (alk. paper)
Subjects: LCSH: Investments. | Portfolio management.
Classification: LCC HG4521 .B564 2018 | DDC 332.6—dc23
LC record available at https://lccn.loc.gov/2017013354

The Internet addresses listed in the text were accurate at the time of publication. The inclusion of a website does not indicate an endorsement by the authors or McGraw-Hill Education, and McGraw-Hill Education does not guarantee the accuracy of the information presented at these sites.

About the Authors

ZVI BODIE
Boston University

Zvi Bodie is the Norman and Adele Barron Professor of Management at Boston University. He holds a PhD from the Massachusetts Institute of Technology and has served on the finance faculty at the Harvard Business School and MIT's Sloan School of Management. Professor Bodie has published widely on pension finance and investment strategy in leading professional journals. In cooperation with the Research Foundation of the CFA Institute, he has recently produced a series of Webcasts and a monograph entitled *The Future of Life Cycle Saving and Investing*.

ALEX KANE
University of California, San Diego

Alex Kane is professor of finance and economics at the Graduate School of International Relations and Pacific Studies at the University of California, San Diego. He has been visiting professor at the Faculty of Economics, University of Tokyo; Graduate School of Business, Harvard; Kennedy School of Government, Harvard; and research associate, National Bureau of Economic Research. An author of many articles in finance and management journals, Professor Kane's research is mainly in corporate finance, portfolio management, and capital markets, most recently in the measurement of market volatility and pricing of options.

ALAN J. MARCUS
Boston College

Alan Marcus is the Mario J. Gabelli Professor of Finance in the Carroll School of Management at Boston College. He received his PhD in economics from MIT. Professor Marcus has been a visiting professor at the Athens Laboratory of Business Administration and at MIT's Sloan School of Management and has served as a research associate at the National Bureau of Economic Research. Professor Marcus has published widely in the fields of capital markets and portfolio management. His consulting work has ranged from new-product development to provision of expert testimony in utility rate proceedings. He also spent two years at the Federal Home Loan Mortgage Corporation (Freddie Mac), where he developed models of mortgage pricing and credit risk. He currently serves on the Research Foundation Advisory Board of the CFA Institute.

Brief Contents

Brief Contents

Contents

Contents

Contents

Contents

Contents

Contents

Contents

Contents

Preface

The past three decades witnessed rapid and profound change in the investments industry as well as a financial crisis of historic magnitude. The vast expansion of financial markets during this period was due in part to innovations in securitization and credit enhancement that gave birth to new trading strategies. These strategies were in turn made feasible by developments in communication and information technology, as well as by advances in the theory of investments.

Yet the financial crisis also was rooted in the cracks of these developments. Many of the innovations in security design facilitated high leverage and an exaggerated notion of the efficacy of risk transfer strategies. This engendered complacency about risk that was coupled with relaxation of regulation as well as reduced transparency, masking the precarious condition of many big players in the system. Of necessity, our text has evolved along with financial markets and their influence on world events.

Investments, Eleventh Edition, is intended primarily as a textbook for courses in investment analysis. Our guiding principle has been to present the material in a framework that is organized by a central core of consistent fundamental principles. We attempt to strip away unnecessary mathematical and technical detail, and we have concentrated on providing the intuition that may guide students and practitioners as they confront new ideas and challenges in their professional lives.

This text will introduce you to major issues currently of concern to all investors. It can give you the skills to assess watershed current issues and debates covered by both the popular media and more-specialized finance journals. Whether you plan to become an investment professional, or simply a sophisticated individual investor, you will find these skills essential, especially in today's rapidly evolving environment.

Our primary goal is to present material of practical value, but all three of us are active researchers in financial economics and find virtually all of the material in this book to be of great intellectual interest. The capital asset pricing model, the arbitrage pricing model, the efficient markets hypothesis, the option-pricing model, and the other centerpieces of modern financial research are as much intellectually engaging subjects as they are of immense practical importance for the sophisticated investor.

In our effort to link theory to practice, we also have attempted to make our approach consistent with that of the CFA Institute. In addition to fostering research in finance, the CFA Institute administers an education and certification program to candidates seeking designation as a Chartered Financial Analyst (CFA). The CFA curriculum represents the consensus of a committee of distinguished scholars and practitioners regarding the core of knowledge required by the investment professional.

Many features of this text make it consistent with and relevant to the CFA curriculum. Questions adapted from past CFA exams appear at the end of nearly every chapter, and references are listed at the end of the book. Chapter 3 includes excerpts from the "Code of Ethics and Standards of Professional Conduct" of the CFA Institute. Chapter 28, which discusses investors and the investment process, presents the CFA Institute's framework for systematically relating investor objectives and constraints to ultimate investment policy. End-of-chapter problems also include questions from test-prep leader Kaplan Schweser.

In the Eleventh Edition, we have continued our systematic presentation of Excel spreadsheets that will allow you to explore concepts more deeply. These spreadsheets, available in Connect and on the student resources site (**www.mhhe.com/Bodie11e**), provide a taste of the sophisticated analytic tools available to professional investors.

UNDERLYING PHILOSOPHY

While the financial environment is constantly evolving, many basic *principles* remain important. We believe that fundamental principles should organize and motivate all study and that attention to these few central ideas can simplify the study of otherwise difficult material. These principles are crucial to understanding the securities traded in financial markets and in understanding new securities that will be introduced in the future, as well as their effects on global markets. For this reason, we have made this book thematic, meaning we never offer rules of thumb without reference to the central tenets of the modern approach to finance.

The common theme unifying this book is that *security markets are nearly efficient,* meaning most securities are usually priced appropriately given their risk and return attributes. Free lunches are rarely found in markets as competitive as the financial market. This simple observation is, nevertheless, remarkably powerful in its implications for the design of investment strategies; as a result, our discussions of strategy are always guided by the implications of the efficient markets hypothesis. While the degree of market efficiency is, and always will be, a matter of debate (in fact we devote a full chapter to the behavioral challenge to the efficient market hypothesis), we hope our discussions throughout the book convey a good dose of healthy skepticism concerning much conventional wisdom.

Distinctive Themes

Investments is organized around several important themes:

1. The central theme is the **near-informational-efficiency of well-developed security markets,** such as those in the United States, and the general awareness that competitive markets do not offer "free lunches" to participants.

   A second theme is the **risk–return trade-off.** This too is a no-free-lunch notion, holding that in competitive security markets, higher expected returns come only at a price: the need to bear greater investment risk. However, this notion leaves several questions unanswered. How should one measure the risk of an asset? What should be the quantitative trade-off between risk (properly measured) and expected return? The approach we present to these issues is known as *modern portfolio theory,* which is another organizing principle of this book. Modern portfolio theory focuses on the techniques and implications of *efficient diversification,* and we devote considerable attention to the effect of diversification on portfolio risk as well as the implications of efficient diversification for the proper measurement of risk and the risk–return relationship.

2. This text places great emphasis on **asset allocation.** We prefer this emphasis for two important reasons. First, it corresponds to the procedure that most individuals actually follow. Typically, you start with all of your money in a bank account, only then considering how much to invest in something riskier that might offer a higher expected return. The logical step at this point is to consider risky asset classes, such as stocks, bonds, or real estate. This is an asset allocation decision. Second, in most cases, the asset allocation choice is far more important in determining overall investment performance than is the set of security selection decisions. Asset allocation is the primary determinant of the risk–return profile of the investment portfolio, and so it deserves primary attention in a study of investment policy.

3. This text offers a **broad and deep treatment of futures, options, and other derivative security markets.** These markets have become both crucial and integral to the financial universe. Your only choice is to become conversant in these markets—whether you are to be a finance professional or simply a sophisticated individual investor.

NEW IN THE ELEVENTH EDITION

The following is a guide to changes in the Eleventh Edition. This is not an exhaustive road map, but instead is meant to provide an overview of substantial additions and changes to coverage from the last edition of the text.

Chapter 1 The Investment Environment
This chapter contains additional discussions of corporate governance, particularly activist investors and corporate control.

Chapter 3 How Securities Are Traded
We have updated this chapter and included new material on trading venues such as dark pools.

Chapter 5 Risk, Return, and the Historical Record
This chapter has been updated and substantially streamlined. The material on the probability distribution of security returns has been reworked for greater clarity, and the discussion of long-run risk has been simplified.

Chapter 7 Optimal Risky Portfolios
The material on risk sharing, risk pooling, and time diversification has been extensively rewritten with a greater emphasis on intuition.

Chapter 8 Index Models
We have reorganized and rewritten this chapter to improve the flow of the material and provide more insight into the links between index models, factor models, and the distinction between diversifiable and systematic risk.

Chapter 9 The Capital Asset Pricing Model
We have simplified the development of the CAPM. The relations between the assumptions underlying the model and

their implications are now more explicit. The links between the CAPM and the index model are also more fully explored.

Chapter 10 Arbitrage Pricing Theory and Multifactor Models of Risk and Return

This chapter has been substantially rewritten. The derivation of the APT has been streamlined, with greater emphasis on intuition. The extension of the APT from portfolios to individual assets is now also more explicit. Finally, the relation between the CAPM and the APT has been further clarified.

Chapter 11 The Efficient Market Hypothesis

We have added new material pertaining to insider information and trading to this chapter.

Chapter 13 Empirical Evidence on Security Returns

Increased attention is given to tests and interpretations of multifactor models of risk and return and the implications of these tests for the importance of extra-market hedging demands.

Chapter 14 Bond Prices and Yields

This chapter includes new material on sovereign credit default swaps and the relationship between swap prices and credit spreads in the bond market.

Chapter 18 Equity Valuation Models

This chapter includes new material on the practical problems entailed in using DCF security valuation models, in particular, the problems entailed in estimating the terminal value of an investment, and the appropriate response of value investors to these problems.

Chapter 24 Portfolio Performance Evaluation

We have added new material to clarify the circumstances in which each of the standard risk-adjusted performance measures, such as alpha, the Sharpe and Treynor measures, and the information ratio, will be of most relevance to investors.

Chapter 25 International Diversification

This chapter also has been extensively rewritten. There is now a sharper focus on the benefits of international diversification. However, we have retained previous material on political risk in an international setting.

ORGANIZATION AND CONTENT

The text is composed of seven sections that are fairly independent and may be studied in a variety of sequences. Because there is enough material in the book for a two-semester course, clearly a one-semester course will require the instructor to decide which parts to include.

Part One is introductory and contains important institutional material focusing on the financial environment.

We discuss the major players in the financial markets, provide an overview of the types of securities traded in those markets, and explain how and where securities are traded. We also discuss in depth mutual funds and other investment companies, which have become an increasingly important means of investing for individual investors. Perhaps most important, we address how financial markets can influence all aspects of the global economy, as in 2008.

The material presented in Part One should make it possible for instructors to assign term projects early in the course. These projects might require the student to analyze in detail a particular group of securities. Many instructors like to involve their students in some sort of investment game, and the material in these chapters will facilitate this process.

Parts Two and Three contain the core of modern portfolio theory. Chapter 5 is a general discussion of risk and return, making the general point that historical returns on broad asset classes are consistent with a risk–return trade-off and examining the distribution of stock returns. We focus more closely in Chapter 6 on how to describe investors' risk preferences and how they bear on asset allocation. In the next two chapters, we turn to portfolio optimization (Chapter 7) and its implementation using index models (Chapter 8).

After our treatment of modern portfolio theory in Part Two, we investigate in Part Three the implications of that theory for the equilibrium structure of expected rates of return on risky assets. Chapter 9 treats the capital asset pricing model and Chapter 10 covers multifactor descriptions of risk and the arbitrage pricing theory. Chapter 11 covers the efficient market hypothesis, including its rationale as well as evidence that supports the hypothesis and challenges it. Chapter 12 is devoted to the behavioral critique of market rationality. Finally, we conclude Part Three with Chapter 13 on empirical evidence on security pricing. This chapter contains evidence concerning the risk–return relationship, as well as liquidity effects on asset pricing.

Part Four is the first of three parts on security valuation. This part treats fixed-income securities—bond pricing (Chapter 14), term structure relationships (Chapter 15), and interest-rate risk management (Chapter 16). **Parts Five and Six** deal with equity securities and derivative securities. For a course emphasizing security analysis and excluding portfolio theory, one may proceed directly from Part One to Part Four with no loss in continuity.

Finally, **Part Seven** considers several topics important for portfolio managers, including performance evaluation, international diversification, active management, and practical issues in the process of portfolio management. This part also contains a chapter on hedge funds.

Distinctive Features

This book contains several features designed to make it easy for students to understand, absorb, and apply the concepts and techniques presented.

CONCEPT CHECKS

A unique feature of this book! These self-test questions and problems found in the body of the text enable the students to determine whether they've understood the preceding material. Detailed solutions are provided at the end of each chapter.

the corporation is their original investment. Unlike owners of unincorporated businesses, whose creditors can lay claim to the personal assets of the owner (house, car, furniture), corporate shareholders may at worst have worthless stock. They are not personally liable for the firm's obligations.

✓ Concept Check **2.3**

a. If you buy 100 shares of IBM stock, to what are you entitled?

b. What is the most money you can make on this investment over the next year?

c. If you pay $150 per share, what is the most money you could lose over the year?

NUMBERED EXAMPLES

are integrated throughout chapters. Using the worked-out solutions to these examples as models, students can learn how to solve specific problems step-by-step as well as gain insight into general principles by seeing how they are applied to answer concrete questions.

Example 4.2 Fees for Various Classes

The table below lists fees for different classes of the Dreyfus High Yield Fund in 2016. Notice the trade-off between the front-end loads versus 12b-1 charges in the choice between Class A and Class C shares. Class I shares are sold only to institutional investors and carry lower fees.

	Class A	Class C	Class I
Front-end load	0–4.5%[a]	0	0
Back-end load	0	0–1%[b]	0%[b]
12b-1 fees[c]	0.25%	1.0%	0%
Expense ratio	0.7%	0.7%	0.7%

[a]Depending on size of investment.
[b]Depending on years until holdings are sold.
[c]Including service fee.

WORDS FROM THE STREET BOXES

Short articles and financial coverage adapted from business periodicals, such as *The Wall Street Journal,* are included in boxes throughout the text. The articles are chosen for real-world relevance and clarity of presentation.

What Level of Risk Is Right for You?

No risk, no reward. Most people intuitively understand that they have to bear some risk to achieve an acceptable return on their investment portfolios.

But how much risk is right for you? If your investments turn sour, you may put at jeopardy your ability to retire, to pay for your kid's college education, or to weather an unexpected need for cash. These worst-case scenarios focus our attention on how to manage our exposure to uncertainty.

Assessing—and quantifying—risk aversion is, to put it mildly, difficult. It requires confronting at least these two big questions.

First, how much investment risk can you afford to take? If you have a steady high-paying job, for example, you have greater ability to withstand investment losses. Conversely, if you are close to retirement, you have less ability to adjust your lifestyle in response to bad investment outcomes.

Second, you need to think about your personality and decide how much risk you can tolerate. At what point will you be unable to sleep at night?

To help clients quantify their risk aversion, many financial firms have designed quizzes to help people determine whether they are conservative, moderate, or aggressive investors. These quizzes try to get at clients' attitudes toward risk and their capacity to absorb investment losses.

Here is a sample of the sort of questions these quizzes tend to pose to shed light on an investor's risk tolerance.

MEASURING YOUR RISK TOLERANCE

Circle the letter that corresponds to your answer.

1. The stock market fell by more than 30% in 2008. If you had been holding a substantial stock investment in that year, which of the following would you have done?
   a. Sold off the remainder of your investment before it had the chance to fall further.
   b. Stayed the course with neither redemptions nor purchases.
   c. Bought more stock, reasoning that the market is now cheaper and therefore offers better deals.

2. The value of one of the funds in your 401(k) plan (your primary source of retirement savings) increased 30% last year. What

4. At the end of the month, you find yourself:
   a. Short of cash and impatiently waiting for your next paycheck.
   b. Not overspending your salary, but not saving very much.
   c. With a comfortable surplus of funds to put into your savings account.

5. You are 30 years old and enrolling in your company's retirement plan, and you need to allocate your contributions across 3 funds: a money market account, a bond fund, and a stock fund. Which of these allocations sounds best to you?
   a. Invest everything in a safe money-market fund.
   b. Split your money evenly between the bond fund and stock fund.
   c. Put everything into the stock fund, reasoning that by the time you retire the year-to-year fluctuations in stock returns will have evened out.

6. You are a contestant on Let's Make a Deal, and have just won $1,000. But you can exchange the winnings for two random payoffs. One is a coin flip with a payoff of $2,500 if the coin comes up heads. The other is a flip of two coins with a payoff of $6,000 if both coins come up heads. What will you do?
   a. Keep the $1,000 in cash.
   b. Choose the single coin toss.
   c. Choose the double coin toss.

7. Suppose you have the opportunity to invest in a start-up firm. If the firm is successful, you will multiply your investment by a factor of ten. But if it fails, you will lose everything. You think the odds of success are around 20%. How much would you be willing to invest in the start-up firm?
   a. Nothing
   b. 2 months' salary
   c. 6 months' salary

8. Now imagine that to buy into the start-up you will need to borrow money. Would you be willing to take out a $10,000 loan to make the investment?

EXCEL APPLICATIONS

The Eleventh Edition features Excel Spreadsheet Applications with Excel questions. A sample spreadsheet is presented in the text with an interactive version available in Connect and on the student resources site at **www.mhhe .com/Bodie11e.**

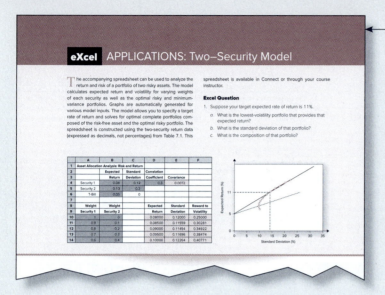

eXcel APPLICATIONS: Two—Security Model

The accompanying spreadsheet can be used to analyze the return and risk of a portfolio of two risky assets. The model calculates expected return and volatility for varying weights of each security as well as the optimal risky and minimum-variance portfolios. Graphs are automatically generated for various model inputs. The model allows you to specify a target rate of return and solves for optimal complete portfolios composed of the risk-free asset and the optimal risky portfolio. The spreadsheet is constructed using the two-security return data (expressed as decimals, not percentages) from Table 7.1. This spreadsheet is available in Connect or through your course instructor.

Excel Question

1. Suppose your target expected rate of return is 11%.
   a. What is the lowest-volatility portfolio that provides that expected return?
   b. What is the standard deviation of that portfolio?
   c. What is the composition of that portfolio?

EXCEL EXHIBITS

Selected exhibits are set as Excel spreadsheets, and the accompanying files are available in Connect and on the student resources site at **www.mhhe .com/Bodie11e.**

	A	B	C	D	E	F
1	Year	Implicit Probability	HPR (decimal)	Squared Deviation	Gross Return = 1 + HPR	Wealth Index*
2	1	0.20	−0.1189	0.0196	0.8811	0.8811
3	2	0.20	−0.2210	0.0586	0.7790	0.6864
4	3	0.20	0.2869	0.0707	1.2869	0.8833
5	4	0.20	0.1088	0.0077	1.1088	0.9794
6	5	0.20	0.0491	0.0008	1.0491	1.0275
7	Arithmetic average	= AVERAGE(C2:C6)	0.0210			
8	Expected HPR	SUMPRODUCT(B2:B6, C2:C6)	0.0210			
9	Variance	SUMPRODUCT(B2:B6, D2:D6)		0.0315		
10	Standard deviation	SQRT(D9)		0.1774		
11	Standard deviation	STDEV.P(C2:C6)		0.1774		
12	Std dev (df = 4)	SQRT(D9*5/4)		0.1983		
13	Std dev (df = 4)	STDEV.S(C2:C6)		0.1983		
14	Geometric avg return	F6^(1/5)−1				0.0054
15						
16	* The wealth index is the cumulative value of $1 invested at the beginning of the sample period.					

Spreadsheet 5.2

Time series of holding-period returns

PROBLEM SETS

PROBLEM SETS
1. The Fisher equation tells us that the real interest rate approximately equals the nominal rate minus the inflation rate. Suppose the inflation rate increases from 3% to 5%. Does the Fisher equation imply that this increase will result in a fall in the real rate of interest? Explain.
2. You've just stumbled on a new dataset that enables you to compute historical rates of return on U.S. stocks all the way back to 1880. What are the advantages and disadvantages in using these data to help estimate the expected rate of return on U.S. stocks over the coming year?
3. You are considering two alternative two-year investments: You can invest in a risky asset with a positive risk premium and returns in each of the two years that will be identically distributed and

We strongly believe that practice in solving problems is critical to understanding investments, so each chapter provides a good variety of problems. Select problems and algorithmic versions are assignable within Connect.

EXAM PREP QUESTIONS

Practice questions for the CFA® exams provided by Kaplan Schweser, A Global Leader in CFA® Education, are available in selected chapters for additional test practice. Look for the Kaplan Schweser logo. Learn more at **www.schweser.com.**

5. Characterize each company in the previous problem as underpriced, overpriced, or pr priced.
6. What is the expected rate of return for a stock that has a beta of 1.0 if the expected return market is 15%?
   a. 15%.
   b. More than 15%.
   c. Cannot be determined without the risk-free rate.
7. Kaskin, Inc., stock has a beta of 1.2 and Quinn, Inc., stock has a beta of .6. Which of the foll statements is *most* accurate?
   a. The expected rate of return will be higher for the stock of Kaskin, Inc., than that of Quin
   b. The stock of Kaskin, Inc., has more total risk than the stock of Quinn, Inc.
   c. The stock of Quinn, Inc., has more systematic risk than that of Kaskin, Inc.
8. You are a consultant to a large manufacturing corporation that is considering a project wi wing net aft

CFA PROBLEMS

We provide several questions adapted for this text from past CFA examinations in applicable chapters. These questions represent the kinds of questions that professionals in the field believe are relevant to the "real world." Located at the back of the book is a listing of each CFA question and the level and year of the CFA exam it was included in for easy reference.

1. Given $100,000 to invest, what is the expected risk premium in dollars of investing in equities versus risk-free T-bills (U.S. Treasury bills) based on the following table?

Action	Probability	Expected Return
Invest in equities	0.6	$50,000
	0.4	−$30,000
Invest in risk-free T-bill	1.0	$ 5,000

2. Based on the scenarios below, what is the expected return for a portfolio with the following return profile?

	Bear Market	Normal Market	Bull Market
Probability	0.2	0.3	0.5
Rate of return	−25%	10%	24%

Use the following scenario analysis for Stocks X and Y to answer CFA Problems 3 through 6 (round to the nearest percent).

	Bear Market	Normal Market	Bull Market
Probability	0.2	0.5	0.3
Stock X	−20%	18%	50%
Stock Y	−15%	20%	10%

3. What are the expected rates of return for Stocks X and Y?

4. What are the standard deviations of returns on Stocks X and Y?

5. Assume that of your $10,000 portfolio, you invest $9,000 in Stock X and $1,000 in Stock Y. What is the expected return on your portfolio?

6. Probabilities for three states of the economy and probabilities for the returns on a particular stock in each state are shown in the table below.

State of Economy	Probability of Economic State	Stock Performance	Probability of Stock Performance in Given Economic State

EXCEL PROBLEMS

Selected chapters contain problems, denoted by an icon, specifically linked to Excel templates that are available in Connect and on the student resource site at **www.mhhe.com/Bodie11e.**

49.50	800	51.50	100
49.25	500	54.75	300
49.00	200	58.25	100
48.50	600		

a. If a market buy order for 100 shares comes in, at what price will it be filled?
b. At what price would the next market buy order be filled?
c. If you were a security dealer, would you want to increase or decrease your inventory of this stock?

9. You are bullish on Telecom stock. The current market price is $50 per share, and you have $5,000 of your own to invest. You borrow an additional $5,000 from your broker at an interest rate of 8% per year and invest $10,000 in the stock.

a. What will be your rate of return if the price of Telecom stock goes up by 10% during the next year? The stock currently pays no dividends.
b. How far does the price of Telecom stock have to fall for you to get a margin call if the maintenance margin is 30%? Assume the price fall happens immediately.

10. You are bearish on Telecom and decide to sell short 100 shares at the current market price of $50 per share.

a. How much in cash or securities must you put into your brokerage account if the broker's initial margin requirement is 50% of the value of the short position?
b. How high can the price of the stock go before you get a margin call if the maintenance margin is 30% of the value of the short position?

E-INVESTMENTS EXERCISES

The Federal Reserve Bank of St. Louis has information available on interest rates and economic conditions. Its *Monetary Trends* page (**https://research.stlouisfed.org/datatrends/mt/**) contains graphs and tables with information about current conditions in the capital markets. Find the most recent issue of *Monetary Trends* and answer these questions.

1. What is the professionals' consensus forecast for inflation for the next two years? (Use the *Federal Reserve Bank of Philadelphia* line on the graph for *Measures of Expected Inflation* to answer this.)
2. What do consumers expect to happen to inflation over the next two years? (Use the *University of Michigan* line on the graph to answer this.)
3. Have real interest rates increased, decreased, or remained the same over the last two years?
4. What has happened to short-term nominal interest rates over the last two years? What about long-term nominal interest rates?
5. How do recent U.S. inflation and long-term interest rates compare with those of the other countries listed?
6. What are the most recently available levels of 3-month and 10-year yields on Treasury securities?

E-INVESTMENTS BOXES

These exercises provide students with simple activities to enhance their experience using the Internet. Easy-to-follow instructions and questions are presented so students can utilize what they have learned in class and apply it to today's data-driven world.

McGraw-Hill Connect®
Learn Without Limits

Connect is a teaching and learning platform that is proven to deliver better results for students and instructors.

Connect empowers students by continually adapting to deliver precisely what they need, when they need it, and how they need it, so your class time is more engaging and effective.

73% of instructors who use **Connect** require it; instructor satisfaction **increases** by 28% when **Connect** is required.

Connect's Impact on Retention Rates, Pass Rates, and Average Exam Scores

Using **Connect** improves retention rates by **19.8%**, passing rates by **12.7%**, and exam scores by **9.1%**.

Analytics

Connect Insight®

Connect Insight is Connect's new one-of-a-kind visual analytics dashboard that provides at-a-glance information regarding student performance, which is immediately actionable. By presenting assignment, assessment, and topical performance results together with a time metric that is easily visible for aggregate or individual results, Connect Insight gives the user the ability to take a just-in-time approach to teaching and learning, which was never before available. Connect Insight presents data that helps instructors improve class performance in a way that is efficient and effective.

Impact on Final Course Grade Distribution

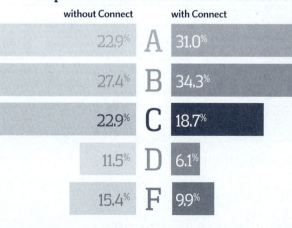

Adaptive

THE ADAPTIVE READING EXPERIENCE
DESIGNED TO TRANSFORM THE WAY STUDENTS READ

> More students earn **A's** and **B's** when they use McGraw-Hill Education **Adaptive** products.

SmartBook®

Proven to help students improve grades and study more efficiently, SmartBook contains the same content within the print book, but actively tailors that content to the needs of the individual. SmartBook's adaptive technology provides precise, personalized instruction on what the student should do next, guiding the student to master and remember key concepts, targeting gaps in knowledge and offering customized feedback, and driving the student toward comprehension and retention of the subject matter. Available on tablets, SmartBook puts learning at the student's fingertips—anywhere, anytime.

> Over **8 billion questions** have been answered, making McGraw-Hill Education products more intelligent, reliable, and precise.

www.mheducation.com

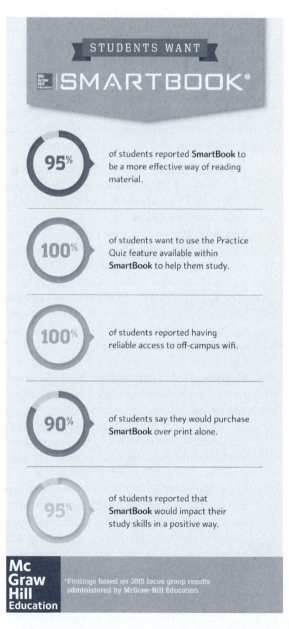

STUDENTS WANT SMARTBOOK®

95% of students reported SmartBook to be a more effective way of reading material.

100% of students want to use the Practice Quiz feature available within SmartBook to help them study.

100% of students reported having reliable access to off-campus wifi.

90% of students say they would purchase SmartBook over print alone.

95% of students reported that SmartBook would impact their study skills in a positive way.

Mc Graw Hill Education

*Findings based on 2015 focus group results administered by McGraw-Hill Education

Supplements

connect.mheducation.com

INSTRUCTOR LIBRARY

The Connect Instructor Library is your repository for additional resources to improve student engagement in and out of class. You can select and use any asset that enhances your lecture. The Connect Instructor Library includes all of the instructor supplements for this text.

- **Solutions Manual** Updated by Nicholas Racculia, Saint Vincent College, in close collaboration with the authors, this Manual provides detailed solutions to the end-of-chapter problem sets.
- **Test Bank** Prepared by John Farlin, Ohio Dominican University, and Andrew Lynch, Mississippi State University, the Test Bank has been revised to improve the quality of questions. Each question is ranked by level of difficulty, which allows greater flexibility in creating a test and also provides a rationale for the solution. The test bank is available as downloadable Word files, and tests can also be created online within McGraw-Hill's Connect or through TestGen.
- **Computerized TestGen Test Bank** TestGen is a complete, state-of-the-art test generator and editing application software that allows instructors to quickly and easily select test items from McGraw-Hill's test bank content. The instructors can then organize, edit, and customize questions and answers to rapidly generate tests for paper or online administration. Questions can include stylized text, symbols, graphics, and equations that are inserted directly into questions using built-in mathematical templates. TestGen's random generator provides the option to display different text or calculated number values each time questions

are used. With both quick-and-simple test creation and flexible and robust editing tools, TestGen is a complete test generator system for today's educators.

- **Instructor's Manual** Prepared by Nicholas Racculia, the Manual has been revised and improved for this edition. Each chapter includes a Chapter Overview, Learning Objectives, and Presentation of Material.
- **PowerPoint Presentation** These presentation slides, also prepared by Nicholas Racculia, contain figures and tables from the text, key points, and summaries in a visually stimulating collection of slides that you can customize to fit your lecture.

STUDENT STUDY CENTER

The Connect Student Study Center is the place for students to access additional resources. The Student Study Center:

- Offers students quick access to the recommended study tools, Excel files and templates, a listing of related websites, lectures, eBooks, and more.
- Provides instant practice material and study questions, easily accessible on the go.

Students can also access the text resources at **www.mhhe. com/Bodie11e**.

STUDENT PROGRESS TRACKING

Connect keeps instructors informed about how each student, section, and class is performing, allowing for more productive use of lecture and office hours. The progress-tracking function enables you to:

- View scored work immediately and track individual or group performance with assignment and grade reports.

- Access an instant view of student or class performance relative to learning objectives.
- Collect data and generate reports required by many accreditation organizations, such as the AACSB and AICPA.

MCGRAW-HILL CUSTOMER CARE CONTACT INFORMATION

At McGraw-Hill, we understand that getting the most from new technology can be challenging. That's why our services don't stop after you purchase our products. You can e-mail our product specialists 24 hours a day to get product training online. Or you can search our knowledge bank of frequently asked questions on our support website.

For customer support, call **800-331-5094** or visit **www.mhhe.com/support**. One of our technical support analysts will be able to assist you in a timely fashion.

Acknowledgments

Throughout the development of this text, experienced instructors have provided critical feedback and suggestions for improvement. These individuals deserve a special thanks for their valuable insights and contributions. The following instructors played a vital role in the development of this and previous editions of *Investments*:

J. Amanda Adkisson
Texas A&M University

Sandro Andrade
University of Miami at Coral Gables

Tor-Erik Bakke
University of Wisconsin

Richard J. Bauer Jr.
St. Mary's University

Scott Besley
University of Florida

John Binder
University of Illinois at Chicago

Paul Bolster
Northwestern University

Phillip Braun
University of Chicago

Leo Chan
Delaware State University

Charles Chang
Cornell University

Kee Chaung
SUNY Buffalo

Ludwig Chincarini
Pomona College

Stephen Ciccone
University of New Hampshire

James Cotter
Wake Forest University

L. Michael Couvillion
Plymouth State University

Anna Craig
Emory University

Elton Daal
University of New Orleans

David C. Distad
University of California at Berkeley

Craig Dunbar
University of Western Ontario

David Durr
Murray State University

Bjorn Eaker
Duke University

John Earl
University of Richmond

Michael C. Ehrhardt
University of Tennessee at Knoxville

Venkat Eleswarapu
Southern Methodist University

David Ellis
Babson College

Andrew Ellul
Indiana University

John Farlin
Ohio Dominican University

John Fay
Santa Clara University

Greg Filbeck
University of Toledo

James Forjan
York College of Pennsylvania

David Gallagher
University of Technology, Sydney

Jeremy Goh
Washington University

Richard Grayson
Loyola College

John M. Griffin
Arizona State University

Weiyu Guo
University of Nebraska at Omaha

Mahmoud Haddad
Wayne State University

Greg Hallman
University of Texas at Austin

Robert G. Hansen
Dartmouth College

Joel Hasbrouck
New York University

Andrea Heuson
University of Miami

Eric Higgins
Drexel University

Shalom J. Hochman
University of Houston

Stephen Huffman
University of Wisconsin at Oshkosh

Eric Hughson
University of Colorado

Delroy Hunter
University of South Florida

A. James Ifflander
A. James Ifflander and Associates

Robert Jennings
Indiana University

George Jiang
University of Arizona

Richard D. Johnson
Colorado State University

Susan D. Jordan
University of Kentucky

Acknowledgments

G. Andrew Karolyi
Ohio State University

Ajay Khorana
Georgia Institute of Technology

Anna Kovalenko
Virginia Tech University

Josef Lakonishok
University of Illinois at Champaign/Urbana

Malek Lashgari
University of Hartford

Dennis Lasser
Binghamton SUNY

Hongbok Lee
Western Illinois University

Bruce Lehmann
University of California at San Diego

Jack Li
Northeastern University

Larry Lockwood
Texas Christian University

Christopher K. Ma
Texas Tech University

Anil K. Makhija
University of Pittsburgh

Davinder Malhotra
Philadelphia University

Steven Mann
University of South Carolina

Deryl W. Martin
Tennessee Technical University

Jean Masson
University of Ottawa

Ronald May
St. John's University

William McDonald
University of Notre Dame

Rick Meyer
University of South Florida

Bruce Mizrach
Rutgers University at New Brunswick

Mbodja Mougoue
Wayne State University

Kyung-Chun (Andrew) Mun
Truman State University

Carol Osler
Brandeis University

Gurupdesh Pandner
DePaul University

Don B. Panton
University of Texas at Arlington

Dimitris Papanikolaou
Northwestern University

Dilip Patro
Rutgers University

Robert Pavlik
Southwest Texas State

Marianne Plunkert
University of Colorado at Denver

Jeffrey Pontiff
Boston College

Andrew Prevost
Ohio University

Herbert Quigley
University of the District of Columbia

Nicholas Racculia
Saint Vincent College

Murli Rajan
University of Scranton

Speima Rao
University of Southwestern Louisiana

Rathin Rathinasamy
Ball State University

William Reese
Tulane University

Craig Rennie
University of Arkansas

Maurico Rodriquez
Texas Christian University

Leonard Rosenthal
Bentley College

Anthony Sanders
Ohio State University

Gary Sanger
Louisiana State University

James Scott
Missouri State University

Don Seeley
University of Arizona

John Settle
Portland State University

Edward C. Sims
Western Illinois University

Robert Skena
Carnegie Mellon University

Steve L. Slezak
University of North Carolina at Chapel Hill

Keith V. Smith
Purdue University

Patricia B. Smith
University of New Hampshire

Ahmad Sohrabian
California State Polytechnic University–Pomona

Eileen St. Pierre
University of Northern Colorado

Laura T. Starks
University of Texas

Mick Swartz
University of Southern California

Manuel Tarrazo
University of San Francisco

Steve Thorley
Brigham Young University

Ashish Tiwari
University of Iowa

Jack Treynor
Treynor Capital Management

Charles A. Trzincka
SUNY Buffalo

Yiuman Tse
Binghamton SUNY

Joe Ueng
University of St. Thomas

Gopala Vasuderan
Suffolk University

Joseph Vu
DePaul University

Qinghai Wang
Georgia Institute of Technology

Richard Warr
North Carolina State University

Simon Wheatley
University of Chicago

Marilyn K. Wiley
Florida Atlantic University

James Williams
California State University at Northridge

Michael Williams
University of Denver

Tony R. Wingler
University of North Carolina at Greensboro

Guojun Wu
University of Michigan

Hsiu-Kwang Wu
University of Alabama

Geungu Yu
Jackson State University

Thomas J. Zwirlein
University of Colorado at Colorado Springs

Edward Zychowicz
Hofstra University

Acknowledgments

For granting us permission to include many of its examination questions in the text, we are grateful to the CFA Institute.

In addition, we would like to thank the dedicated experts who have helped with updates to our instructor materials and online content in Connect and LearnSmart, including Marc-Anthony Isaacs, Nicholas Racculia, Mishal Rawaf, Matthew Will, Andrew Lynch, Gregory Besharov, and John Farlin. Their efforts are much appreciated as they will help both students and instructors.

Much credit is due to the development and production team at McGraw-Hill Education: our special thanks go to Noelle Bathurst, Senior Product Developer; Chuck Synovec, Executive Brand Manager and Director; Kathryn Wright, Core Project Manager; Kristin Bradley, Assessment Project Manager; Trina Maurer, Senior Marketing Manager; Dave O'Donnell, Marketing Specialist; Laura Fuller, Senior Buyer; and Matt Diamond, Designer.

Finally, we thank Judy, Hava, and Sheryl, who contribute to the book with their support and understanding.

Zvi Bodie
Alex Kane
Alan J. Marcus

The Investment Environment

AN INVESTMENT IS the *current* commitment of money or other resources in the expectation of reaping *future* benefits. For example, an individual might purchase shares of stock anticipating that the future proceeds from the shares will justify both the time that her money is tied up as well as the risk of the investment. The time you will spend studying this text (not to mention its cost) also is an investment. You are forgoing either current leisure or the income you could be earning at a job in the expectation that your future career will be sufficiently enhanced to justify this commitment of time and effort. While these two investments differ in many ways, they share one key attribute that is central to all investments: You sacrifice something of value now, expecting to benefit from that sacrifice later.

This text can help you become an informed practitioner of investments. We will focus on investments in securities such as stocks, bonds, or options and futures contracts, but much of what we discuss will be useful in the analysis of any type of investment. The text will provide you with background in the organization of various securities markets; will survey the valuation and risk-management principles useful in particular markets, such as those for bonds or stocks; and will introduce you to the principles of portfolio construction.

Broadly speaking, this chapter addresses three topics that will provide a useful perspective for the material that is to come later. First, before delving into the topic of "investments," we consider the role of financial assets in the economy. We discuss the relationship between securities and the "real" assets that actually produce goods and services for consumers, and we consider why financial assets are important to the functioning of a developed economy.

Given this background, we then take a first look at the types of decisions that confront investors as they assemble a portfolio of assets. These investment decisions are made in an environment where higher returns usually can be obtained only at the price of greater risk and in which it is rare to find assets that are so mispriced as to be obvious bargains. These themes—the risk–return trade-off and the efficient pricing of financial assets—are central to the investment process, so it is worth pausing for a brief discussion of their implications as we begin the text. These implications will be fleshed out in much greater detail in later chapters.

We provide an overview of the organization of security markets as well as the various players that participate in those markets. Together, these introductions should give you a feel for who the major participants are in the securities markets as well as

(continued)

the setting in which they act. Finally, we discuss the financial crisis that began playing out in 2007 and peaked in 2008. The crisis dramatically illustrated the connections between the financial system and the "real" side of the economy. We look at the origins of the crisis and the lessons that may be drawn about systemic risk. We close the chapter with an overview of the remainder of the text.

1.1 Real Assets versus Financial Assets

The material wealth of a society is ultimately determined by the productive capacity of its economy, that is, the goods and services its members can create. This capacity is a function of the **real assets** of the economy: the land, buildings, machines, and knowledge that can be used to produce goods and services.

In contrast to real assets are **financial assets** such as stocks and bonds. Such securities are no more than sheets of paper or, more likely, computer entries, and they do not contribute directly to the productive capacity of the economy. Instead, these assets are the means by which individuals in well-developed economies hold their claims on real assets. Financial assets are claims to the income generated by real assets (or claims on income from the government). If we cannot own our own auto plant (a real asset), we can still buy shares in Ford or Toyota (financial assets) and thereby share in the income derived from the production of automobiles.

While real assets generate net income to the economy, financial assets simply define the allocation of income or wealth among investors. Individuals can choose between consuming their wealth today or investing for the future. If they choose to invest, they may place their wealth in financial assets by purchasing various securities. When investors buy these securities from companies, the firms use the money so raised to pay for real assets, such as plant, equipment, technology, or inventory. So investors' returns on securities ultimately come from the income produced by the real assets that were financed by the issuance of those securities.

The distinction between real and financial assets is apparent when we compare the balance sheet of U.S. households, shown in Table 1.1, with the composition of national wealth in the United States, shown in Table 1.2. Household wealth includes financial assets such as bank accounts, corporate stock, or bonds. However, these securities, which are financial assets of households, are *liabilities* of the issuers of the securities. For example, a bond that you treat as an asset because it gives you a claim on interest income and repayment of principal from Toyota is a liability of Toyota, which is obligated to make these payments to you. Your asset is Toyota's liability. Therefore, when we aggregate over all balance sheets, these claims cancel out, leaving only real assets as the net wealth of the economy. National wealth consists of structures, equipment, inventories of goods, and land.[1]

Concept Check 1.1

Are the following assets real or financial?

a. Patents

b. Lease obligations

c. Customer goodwill

d. A college education

e. A $5 bill

[1]You might wonder why real assets held by households in Table 1.1 amount to $30,979 billion, while total real assets in the domestic economy (Table 1.2) are far larger, at $64,747 billion. A big part of the difference reflects the fact that real assets held by firms, for example, property, plant, and equipment, are included as *financial* assets of the household sector, specifically through the value of corporate equity and other stock market investments. Similarly, Table 1.2 includes assets of noncorporate businesses. Finally, there are some differences in valuation methods. For example, equity and stock investments in Table 1.1 are measured by market value, whereas plant and equipment in Table 1.2 are valued at replacement cost.

Assets	$ Billion	% Total	Liabilities and Net Worth	$ Billion	% Total
Real assets			**Liabilities**		
Real estate	$ 25,276	25.0%	Mortgages	$ 9,711	9.6%
Consumer durables	5,241	5.2	Consumer credit	3,533	3.5
Other	463	0.5	Bank and other loans	975	1.0
Total real assets	$ 30,979	30.6%	Other	291	0.3
			Total liabilities	$ 14,510	14.3%
Financial assets					
Deposits	$ 10,693	10.6%			
Life insurance reserves	1,331	1.3			
Pension reserves	20,972	20.7			
Corporate equity	13,311	13.1			
Equity in noncorporate business	10,739	10.6			
Mutual fund shares	8,119	8.0			
Debt securities	4,200	4.1			
Other	962	0.9			
Total financial assets	$ 70,327	69.4	Net worth	86,796	85.7
Total	$101,306	100.0%		$101,306	100.0%

Table 1.1

Balance sheet of U.S. households
Note: Column sums may differ from total because of rounding error.
Source: *Flow of Funds Accounts of the United States,* Board of Governors of the Federal Reserve System, March 2016.

Assets	$ Billion
Commercial real estate	$17,269
Residential real estate	31,643
Equipment and intellectual property	8,104
Inventories	2,492
Consumer durables	5,240
Total	$64,747

Note: Column sums may differ from total because of rounding error.
Source: *Flow of Funds Accounts of the United States,* Board of Governors of the Federal Reserve System, March 2016.

Table 1.2

Domestic net worth

We will focus almost exclusively on financial assets. But you shouldn't lose sight of the fact that the successes or failures of the financial assets we choose to purchase ultimately depend on the performance of the underlying real assets.

1.2   Financial Assets

It is common to distinguish among three broad types of financial assets: fixed income, equity, and derivatives. **Fixed-income** or **debt securities** promise either a fixed stream of income or a stream of income determined by a specified formula. For example, a corporate bond typically would promise that the bondholder will receive a fixed amount of interest each year. Other so-called floating-rate bonds promise payments that depend on current interest rates. For example, a bond may pay an interest rate that is fixed at 2 percentage points above the rate paid on U.S. Treasury bills. Unless the borrower is declared bankrupt, the payments on these securities are either fixed or determined by formula. For this reason, the investment performance of debt securities typically is least closely tied to the financial condition of the issuer.

Nevertheless, fixed-income securities come in a tremendous variety of maturities and payment provisions. At one extreme, the *money market* refers to debt securities that are short term, highly marketable, and generally of very low risk, for example, U.S. Treasury bills or bank certificates of deposit (CDs). In contrast, the fixed-income *capital market* includes long-term securities such as Treasury bonds, as well as bonds issued by federal agencies, state and local municipalities, and corporations. These bonds range from very safe in terms of default risk (e.g., Treasury securities) to relatively risky (e.g., high-yield or "junk" bonds). They also are designed with extremely diverse provisions regarding payments provided to the investor and protection against the bankruptcy of the issuer. We will take a first look at these securities in Chapter 2 and undertake a more detailed analysis of the debt market in Part Four.

Unlike debt securities, common stock, or **equity,** in a firm represents an ownership share in the corporation. Equityholders are not promised any particular payment. They receive any dividends the firm may pay and have prorated ownership in the real assets of the firm. If the firm is successful, the value of equity will increase; if not, it will decrease. The performance of equity investments, therefore, is tied directly to the success of the firm and its real assets. For this reason, equity investments tend to be riskier than investments in debt securities. Equity markets and equity valuation are the topics of Part Five.

Finally, **derivative securities** such as options and futures contracts provide payoffs that are determined by the prices of *other* assets such as bond or stock prices. For example, a call option on a share of Intel stock might turn out to be worthless if Intel's share price remains below a threshold or "exercise" price such as $30 a share, but it can be quite valuable if the stock price rises above that level.[2] Derivative securities are so named because their values derive from the prices of other assets. For example, the value of the call option will depend on the price of Intel stock. Other important derivative securities are futures and swap contracts. We will treat these in Part Six.

Derivatives have become an integral part of the investment environment. One use of derivatives, perhaps the primary use, is to hedge risks or transfer them to other parties. This is done successfully every day, and the use of these securities for risk management is so commonplace that the multitrillion-dollar market in derivative assets is routinely taken for granted. Derivatives also can be used to take highly speculative positions, however. Every so often, one of these positions blows up, resulting in well-publicized losses of hundreds of millions of dollars. While these losses attract considerable attention, they are in fact the exception to the more common use of such securities as risk management tools. Derivatives will continue to play an important role in portfolio construction and the financial system. We will return to this topic later in the text.

Investors and corporations regularly encounter other financial markets as well. Firms engaged in international trade regularly transfer money back and forth between dollars and other currencies. In London alone, nearly $2 trillion dollars of currency is traded each day.

---

[2]A call option is the right to buy a share of stock at a given exercise price on or before the option's expiration date. If the market price of Intel remains below $30 a share, the right to buy for $30 will turn out to be valueless. If the share price rises above $30 before the option expires, however, the option can be exercised to obtain the share for only $30.

Investors also might invest directly in some real assets. For example, dozens of commodities are traded on exchanges such as the New York Mercantile Exchange or the Chicago Board of Trade. You can buy or sell corn, wheat, natural gas, gold, silver, and so on.

Commodity and derivative markets allow firms to adjust their exposure to various business risks. For example, a construction firm may lock in the price of copper by buying copper futures contracts, thus eliminating the risk of a sudden jump in the price of its raw materials. Wherever there is uncertainty, investors may be interested in trading, either to speculate or to lay off their risks, and a market may arise to meet that demand.

1.3   Financial Markets and the Economy

We stated earlier that real assets determine the wealth of an economy, while financial assets merely represent claims on real assets. Nevertheless, financial assets and the markets in which they trade play several crucial roles in developed economies. Financial assets allow us to make the most of the economy's real assets.

The Informational Role of Financial Markets

Stock prices reflect investors' collective assessment of a firm's current performance and future prospects. When the market is more optimistic about the firm, its share price will rise. That higher price makes it easier for the firm to raise capital and therefore encourages investment. In this manner, stock prices play a major role in the allocation of capital in market economies, directing capital to the firms and applications with the greatest perceived potential.

Do capital markets actually channel resources to the most efficient use? At times, they appear to fail miserably. Companies or whole industries can be "hot" for a period of time (think about the dot-com bubble that peaked in 2000), attract a large flow of investor capital, and then fail after only a few years. The process seems highly wasteful.

But we need to be careful about our standard of efficiency. No one knows with certainty which ventures will succeed and which will fail. It is therefore unreasonable to expect that markets will never make mistakes. The stock market encourages allocation of capital to those firms that appear *at the time* to have the best prospects. Many smart, well-trained, and well-paid professionals analyze the prospects of firms whose shares trade on the stock market. Stock prices reflect their collective judgment.

You may well be skeptical about resource allocation through markets. But if you are, then take a moment to think about the alternatives. Would a central planner make fewer mistakes? Would you prefer that Congress make these decisions? To paraphrase Winston Churchill's comment about democracy, markets may be the worst way to allocate capital except for all the others that have been tried.

Consumption Timing

Some individuals are earning more than they currently wish to spend. Others, for example, retirees, spend more than they currently earn. How can you shift your purchasing power from high-earnings to low-earnings periods of life? One way is to "store" your wealth in financial assets. In high-earnings periods, you can invest your savings in financial assets such as stocks and bonds. In low-earnings periods, you can sell these assets to provide funds for your consumption needs. By so doing, you can "shift" your consumption over the course of your lifetime, thereby allocating your consumption to periods that provide the greatest satisfaction. Thus, financial markets allow individuals to separate decisions concerning current consumption from constraints that otherwise would be imposed by current earnings.

Allocation of Risk

Virtually all real assets involve some risk. When Toyota builds its auto plants, for example, it cannot know for sure what cash flows those plants will generate. Financial markets and the diverse financial instruments traded in those markets allow investors with the greatest taste for risk to bear that risk, while other, less risk-tolerant individuals can, to a greater extent, stay on the sidelines. For example, if Toyota raises the funds to build its auto plant by selling both stocks and bonds to the public, the more optimistic or risk-tolerant investors can buy shares of its stock, while the more conservative ones can buy its bonds. Because the bonds promise to provide a fixed payment, the stockholders bear most of the business risk but reap potentially higher rewards. Thus, capital markets allow the risk that is inherent to all investments to be borne by the investors most willing to bear that risk.

This allocation of risk also benefits the firms that need to raise capital to finance their investments. When investors are able to select security types with the risk-return characteristics that best suit their preferences, each security can be sold for the best possible price. This facilitates the process of building the economy's stock of real assets.

Separation of Ownership and Management

Many businesses are owned and managed by the same individual. This simple organization is well suited to small businesses and, in fact, was the most common form of business organization before the Industrial Revolution. Today, however, with global markets and large-scale production, the size and capital requirements of firms have skyrocketed. For example, at the end of 2015 General Electric listed on its balance sheet about $57 billion of property, plant, and equipment and total assets of $493 billion. Corporations of such size simply cannot exist as owner-operated firms. GE actually has more than half a million stockholders with an ownership stake in the firm proportional to their holdings of shares.

Such a large group of individuals obviously cannot actively participate in the day-to-day management of the firm. Instead, they elect a board of directors that in turn hires and supervises the management of the firm. This structure means that the owners and managers of the firm are different parties. This gives the firm a stability that the owner-managed firm cannot achieve. For example, if some stockholders decide they no longer wish to hold shares in the firm, they can sell their shares to other investors, with no impact on the management of the firm. Thus, financial assets and the ability to buy and sell those assets in the financial markets allow for easy separation of ownership and management.

How can all of the disparate owners of the firm, ranging from large pension funds holding hundreds of thousands of shares to small investors who may hold only a single share, agree on the objectives of the firm? Again, the financial markets provide some guidance. All may agree that the firm's management should pursue strategies that enhance the value of their shares. Such policies will make all shareholders wealthier and allow them all to better pursue their personal goals, whatever those goals might be.

Do managers really attempt to maximize firm value? It is easy to see how they might be tempted to engage in activities not in the best interest of shareholders. For example, they might engage in empire building or avoid risky projects to protect their own jobs or overconsume luxuries such as corporate jets, reasoning that the cost of such perquisites is largely borne by the shareholders. These potential conflicts of interest are called **agency problems** because managers, who are hired as agents of the shareholders, may pursue their own interests instead.

Several mechanisms have evolved to mitigate potential agency problems. First, compensation plans tie the income of managers to the success of the firm. A major part of the total compensation of top executives is often in the form of shares or stock options, which means that the managers will not do well unless the stock price increases, benefiting shareholders. (Of course, we've learned that overuse of options can create its own agency problem. Options can create an incentive for managers to manipulate information to prop up a stock price temporarily, giving them a chance to cash out before the price returns to a level reflective of the firm's true prospects. More on this shortly.) Second, while boards of directors have sometimes been portrayed as defenders of top management, they can, and in recent years, increasingly have, forced out management teams that are underperforming. Third, outsiders such as security analysts and large institutional investors such as mutual funds or pension funds monitor the firm closely and make the life of poor performers at the least uncomfortable. Such large investors today hold about half of the stock in publicly listed firms in the U.S.

Finally, bad performers are subject to the threat of takeover. If the board of directors is lax in monitoring management, unhappy shareholders in principle can elect a different board. They can do this by launching a *proxy contest* in which they seek to obtain enough proxies (i.e., rights to vote the shares of other shareholders) to take control of the firm and vote in another board. Historically, this threat was usually minimal. Shareholders who attempt such a fight have to use their own funds, while management can defend itself using corporate coffers.

However, in recent years, the odds of a successful proxy contest have increased along with the rise of so-called activist investors. These are large and deep-pocketed investors, often hedge funds, that identify firms they believe to be mismanaged in some respect. They buy large positions in shares of those firms and then campaign for slots on the board of directors and/or for specific reforms. One estimate is that since the end of 2009, about 15% of the firms in the S&P 500 have faced an activist campaign and that activists have taken share positions in about half of the firms included in the S&P 500. In 2014, nearly three-quarters of proxy votes were won by dissidents.[3]

Aside from proxy contests, the real takeover threat is from other firms. If one firm observes another underperforming, it can acquire the underperforming business and replace management with its own team. The stock price should rise to reflect the prospects of improved performance, which provides an incentive for firms to engage in such takeover activity.

Example 1.1   Activist Investors and Corporate Control

Here are a few of the better known activist investors, along with a sample of their recent initiatives.

- Carl Icahn: One of the earliest and most combative of activist investors. Challenged Apple to increase cash distributions to investors.
- William Ackman, Pershing Square: Took large positions in JCPenney, Valeant Pharmaceuticals, and Kraft Foods with a view toward influencing management practice.
- Nelson Peltz, Trian: Sought board seats on DuPont. Pushed for it to split up into more highly focused corporations.
- Dan Loeb, Third Point: Tried to get Sony to spin off its entertainment units.
- Jeff Smith, Starboard Value: Pushed for Staples and Office Depot to merge. Ultimately, the firms did attempt to combine, but the merger was blocked by the federal government on antitrust grounds.

---

[3]"An Investor Calls," *The Economist,* February 7, 2015.

Corporate Governance and Corporate Ethics

We've argued that securities markets can play an important role in facilitating the deployment of capital resources to their most productive uses. But market signals will help to allocate capital efficiently only if investors are acting on accurate information. We say that markets need to be *transparent* for investors to make informed decisions. If firms can mislead the public about their prospects, then much can go wrong.

Despite the many mechanisms to align incentives of shareholders and managers, the three years from 2000 through 2002 were filled with a seemingly unending series of scandals that collectively signaled a crisis in corporate governance and ethics. For example, the telecom firm WorldCom overstated its profits by at least $3.8 billion by improperly classifying expenses as investments. When the true picture emerged, it resulted in the largest bankruptcy in U.S. history, at least until Lehman Brothers smashed that record in 2008. The next-largest U.S. bankruptcy was Enron, which used its now-notorious "special-purpose entities" to move debt off its own books and similarly present a misleading picture of its financial status. Unfortunately, these firms had plenty of company. Other firms such as Rite Aid, HealthSouth, Global Crossing, and Qwest Communications also manipulated and misstated their accounts to the tune of billions of dollars. And the scandals were hardly limited to the United States. Parmalat, the Italian dairy firm, claimed to have a $4.8 billion bank account that turned out not to exist. These episodes suggest that agency and incentive problems are far from solved.

Other scandals of that period included systematically misleading and overly optimistic research reports put out by stock market analysts. (Their favorable analysis was traded for the promise of future investment banking business, and analysts were commonly compensated not for their accuracy or insight, but for their role in garnering investment banking business for their firms.) Additionally, initial public offerings were allocated to corporate executives as a quid pro quo for personal favors or the promise to direct future business back to the manager of the IPO.

What about the auditors who were supposed to be the watchdogs of the firms? Here too, incentives were skewed. Recent changes in business practice had made the consulting businesses of these firms more lucrative than the auditing function. For example, Enron's (now-defunct) auditor Arthur Andersen earned more money consulting for Enron than by auditing it; given Arthur Andersen's incentive to protect its consulting profits, we should not be surprised that it, and other auditors, were overly lenient in their auditing work.

In 2002, in response to the spate of ethics scandals, Congress passed the Sarbanes-Oxley Act to tighten the rules of corporate governance. For example, the act requires corporations to have more independent directors, that is, more directors who are not themselves managers (or affiliated with managers). The act also requires each CFO to personally vouch for the corporation's accounting statements, provides for an oversight board to oversee the auditing of public companies, and prohibits auditors from providing various other services to clients.

1.4   The Investment Process

An investor's *portfolio* is simply his collection of investment assets. Once the portfolio is established, it is updated or "rebalanced" by selling existing securities and using the proceeds to buy new securities, by investing additional funds to increase the overall size of the portfolio, or by selling securities to decrease the size of the portfolio.

Investment assets can be categorized into broad asset classes, such as stocks, bonds, real estate, commodities, and so on. Investors make two types of decisions in constructing their portfolios. The **asset allocation** decision is the choice among these broad asset classes, while the **security selection** decision is the choice of which particular securities to hold *within* each asset class.

"Top-down" portfolio construction starts with asset allocation. For example, an individual who currently holds all of his money in a bank account would first decide what proportion of the overall portfolio ought to be moved into stocks, bonds, and so on. In this way, the broad features of the portfolio are established. For example, while the average annual return on the common stock of large firms since 1926 has been better than 11% per year, the average return on U.S. Treasury bills has been less than 4%. On the other hand, stocks are far riskier, with annual returns (as measured by the Standard & Poor's 500 index) that have ranged as low as –46% and as high as 55%. In contrast, T-bills are effectively risk-free: You know what interest rate you will earn when you buy them. Therefore, the decision to allocate your investments to the stock market or to the money market where Treasury bills are traded will have great ramifications for both the risk and the return of your portfolio. A top-down investor first makes this and other crucial asset allocation decisions before turning to the decision of the particular securities to be held in each asset class.

Security analysis involves the valuation of particular securities that might be included in the portfolio. For example, an investor might ask whether Merck or Pfizer is more attractively priced. Both bonds and stocks must be evaluated for investment attractiveness, but valuation is far more difficult for stocks because a stock's performance usually is far more sensitive to the condition of the issuing firm.

In contrast to top-down portfolio management is the "bottom-up" strategy. In this process, the portfolio is constructed from securities that seem attractively priced without as much concern for the resultant asset allocation. Such a technique can result in unintended bets on one or another sector of the economy. For example, it might turn out that the portfolio ends up with a very heavy representation of firms in one industry, from one part of the country, or with exposure to one source of uncertainty. However, a bottom-up strategy does focus the portfolio on the assets that seem to offer the most attractive investment opportunities.

1.5   Markets Are Competitive

Financial markets are highly competitive. Thousands of intelligent and well-backed analysts constantly scour securities markets searching for the best buys. This competition means that we should expect to find few, if any, "free lunches," securities that are so underpriced that they represent obvious bargains. This no-free-lunch proposition has several implications. Let's examine two.

The Risk–Return Trade-Off

Investors invest for anticipated future returns, but those returns rarely can be predicted precisely. There will almost always be risk associated with investments. Actual or realized returns will almost always deviate from the expected return anticipated at the start of the investment period. For example, in 1931 (the worst calendar year for the market since 1926), the S&P 500 index fell by 46%. In 1933 (the best year), the index gained 55%. You can be sure that investors did not anticipate such extreme performance at the start of either of these years.

Naturally, if all else could be held equal, investors would prefer investments with the highest expected return.[4] However, the no-free-lunch rule tells us that all else cannot be held equal. If you want higher expected returns, you will have to pay a price in terms of accepting higher investment risk. If higher expected return can be achieved without bearing extra risk, there will be a rush to buy the high-return assets, with the result that their prices will be driven up. Individuals considering investing in the asset at the now-higher price will find the investment less attractive. Its price will continue to rise until expected return is no more than commensurate with risk. At this point, investors can anticipate a "fair" return relative to the asset's risk, but no more. Similarly, if returns were independent of risk, there would be a rush to sell high-risk assets and their prices would fall. The assets would get cheaper (improving their expected future rates of return) until they eventually were attractive enough to be included again in investor portfolios. We conclude that there should be a **risk–return trade-off** in the securities markets, with higher-risk assets priced to offer higher expected returns than lower-risk assets.

Of course, this discussion leaves several important questions unanswered. How should one measure the risk of an asset? What should be the quantitative trade-off between risk (properly measured) and expected return? One would think that risk would have something to do with the volatility of an asset's returns, but this guess turns out to be only partly correct. When we mix assets into diversified portfolios, we need to consider the interplay among assets and the effect of diversification on the risk of the entire portfolio. *Diversification* means that many assets are held in the portfolio so that the exposure to any particular asset is limited. The effect of diversification on portfolio risk, the implications for the proper measurement of risk, and the risk–return relationship are the topics of Part Two. These topics are the subject of what has come to be known as *modern portfolio theory*. The development of this theory brought two of its pioneers, Harry Markowitz and William Sharpe, Nobel Prizes.

Efficient Markets

Another implication of the no-free-lunch proposition is that we should rarely expect to find bargains in the security markets. We will spend all of Chapter 11 examining the theory and evidence concerning the hypothesis that financial markets process all available information about securities quickly and efficiently, that is, that the security price usually reflects all the information available to investors concerning its value. According to this hypothesis, as new information about a security becomes available, its price quickly adjusts so that at any time, the security price equals the market consensus estimate of the value of the security. If this were so, there would be neither underpriced nor overpriced securities.

One interesting implication of this "efficient market hypothesis" concerns the choice between active and passive investment-management strategies. **Passive management** calls for holding highly diversified portfolios without spending effort or other resources attempting to improve investment performance through security analysis. **Active management** is the attempt to improve performance either by identifying mispriced securities or by timing the performance of broad asset classes—for example, increasing one's commitment to stocks when one is bullish on the stock market. If markets are efficient and prices reflect all relevant information, perhaps it is better to follow passive strategies instead of spending resources in a futile attempt to outguess your competitors in the financial markets.

---

[4]The "expected" return is not the return investors believe they necessarily will earn, or even their most likely return. It is instead the result of averaging across all possible outcomes, recognizing that some outcomes are more likely than others. It is the average rate of return across possible economic scenarios.

If the efficient market hypothesis were taken to the extreme, there would be no point in active security analysis; only fools would commit resources to actively analyze securities. Without ongoing security analysis, however, prices eventually would depart from "correct" values, creating new incentives for experts to move in. Therefore, even in environments as competitive as the financial markets, we may observe only *near-efficiency*, and profit opportunities may exist for especially diligent and creative investors. In Chapter 12, we examine such challenges to the efficient market hypothesis, and this motivates our discussion of active portfolio management in Part Seven. More important, our discussions of security analysis and portfolio construction generally must account for the likelihood of nearly efficient markets.

1.6   The Players

From a bird's-eye view, there would appear to be three major players in the financial markets:

1. **Firms are net demanders of capital.** They raise capital now to pay for investments in plant and equipment. The income generated by those real assets provides the returns to investors who purchase the securities issued by the firm.

2. **Households typically are net suppliers of capital.** They purchase the securities issued by firms that need to raise funds.

3. **Governments can be borrowers or lenders,** depending on the relationship between tax revenue and government expenditures. Since World War II, the U.S. government typically has run budget deficits, meaning that its tax receipts have been less than its expenditures. The government, therefore, has had to borrow funds to cover its budget deficit. Issuance of Treasury bills, notes, and bonds is the major way that the government borrows funds from the public. In contrast, in the latter part of the 1990s, the government enjoyed a budget surplus and was able to retire some outstanding debt.

Corporations and governments do not sell all or even most of their securities directly to individuals. For example, about half of all stock is held by large financial institutions such as pension funds, mutual funds, insurance companies, and banks. These financial institutions stand between the security issuer (the firm) and the ultimate owner of the security (the individual investor). For this reason, they are called *financial intermediaries*. Similarly, corporations do not market their own securities to the public. Instead, they hire agents, called investment bankers, to represent them to the investing public. Let's examine the roles of these intermediaries.

Financial Intermediaries

Households want desirable investments for their savings, yet the small (financial) size of most households makes direct investment difficult. A small investor seeking to lend money to businesses that need to finance investments doesn't advertise in the local newspaper to find a willing and desirable borrower. Moreover, an individual lender would not be able to diversify across borrowers to reduce risk. Finally, an individual lender is not equipped to assess and monitor the credit risk of borrowers.

For these reasons, **financial intermediaries** have evolved to bring the suppliers of capital (investors) together with the demanders of capital (primarily corporations and the federal government). These financial intermediaries include banks, investment companies, insurance companies, and credit unions. Financial intermediaries issue their own securities to raise funds to purchase the securities of other corporations.

For example, a bank raises funds by borrowing (taking deposits) and lending that money to other borrowers. The spread between the interest rates paid to depositors and the rates charged to borrowers is the source of the bank's profit. In this way, lenders and borrowers do not need to contact each other directly. Instead, each goes to the bank, which acts as an intermediary between the two. The problem of matching lenders with borrowers is solved when each comes independently to the common intermediary.

Financial intermediaries are distinguished from other businesses in that both their assets and their liabilities are overwhelmingly financial. Table 1.3 presents the aggregated balance sheet of commercial banks, one of the largest sectors of financial intermediaries. Notice that the balance sheet includes only very small amounts of real assets. Compare Table 1.3 to the aggregated balance sheet of the nonfinancial corporate sector in Table 1.4, for which real assets are about half of all assets. The contrast arises because intermediaries simply move funds from one sector to another. In fact, the primary social function of such intermediaries is to channel household savings to the business sector.

Other examples of financial intermediaries are investment companies, insurance companies, and credit unions. All these firms offer similar advantages in their intermediary role. First, by pooling the resources of many small investors, they are able to lend considerable sums to large borrowers. Second, by lending to many borrowers, intermediaries achieve significant diversification, so they can accept loans that individually might be too risky. Third, intermediaries build expertise through the volume of business they do and can use economies of scale and scope to assess and monitor risk.

Investment companies, which pool and manage the money of many investors, also arise out of economies of scale. Here, the problem is that most household portfolios are not

Assets	$ Billion	% Total	Liabilities and Net Worth	$ Billion	% Total
Real assets			**Liabilities**		
Equipment and premises	$ 111.9	0.8%	Deposits	$11,349.4	76.2%
Other real estate	13.2	0.1	Debt and other borrowed funds	1,038.1	7.0
Total real assets	$ 125.2	0.8%	Federal funds and repurchase agreements	259.4	1.7
			Other	563.7	3.8
			Total liabilities	$13,210.6	88.7%
Financial assets					
Cash	$ 1,686.4	11.3%			
Investment securities	3,425.4	23.0			
Loans and leases	8,060.9	54.1			
Other financial assets	553.0	3.7			
Total financial assets	$13,725.7	92.2%			
Other assets					
Intangible assets	$ 350.4	2.4%			
Other	692.1	4.6			
Total other assets	$ 1,042.5	7.0%	Net worth	$ 1,682.8	11.3%
Total	$14,893.4	100.0%		$14,893.4	100.0%

Table 1.3

Balance sheet of FDIC-insured commercial banks and savings institutions
Note: Column sums may differ from total because of rounding error.
Source: Federal Deposit Insurance Corporation, **www.fdic.gov**, March 2016.

Assets	$ Billion	% Total	Liabilities and Net Worth	$ Billion	% Total
Real assets			**Liabilities**		
Equipment and intellectual property	$ 6,713	17.0%	Bonds and mortgages	$ 6,046	15.3%
Real estate	12,485	31.6	Bank loans	948	2.4
Inventories	2,219	5.6	Other loans	1,103	2.8
Total real assets	$21,417	54.2%	Trade debt	1,969	5.0
			Other	6,636	16.8
			Total liabilities	$16,702	42.3%
Financial assets					
Deposits and cash	$ 992	2.5%			
Marketable securities	955	2.4			
Trade and consumer credit	2,719	6.9			
Other	13,418	34.0			
Total financial assets	$18,084	45.8%	*Net worth*	$22,799	57.7%
Total	$39,501	100.0%		$39,501	100.0%

Table 1.4

Balance sheet of U.S. nonfinancial corporations
Note: Column sums may differ from total because of rounding error.
Source: *Flow of Funds Accounts of the United States,* Board of Governors of the Federal Reserve System, March 2016.

large enough to be spread across a wide variety of securities. In terms of brokerage fees and research costs, purchasing one or two shares of many different firms is very expensive. Mutual funds have the advantage of large-scale trading and portfolio management, while participating investors are assigned a prorated share of the total funds according to the size of their investment. This system gives small investors advantages they are willing to pay for via a management fee to the mutual fund operator.

Investment companies also can design portfolios specifically for large investors with particular goals. In contrast, mutual funds are sold in the retail market, and their investment philosophies are differentiated mainly by strategies that are likely to attract a large number of clients.

Like mutual funds, *hedge funds* also pool and invest the money of many clients. But they are open only to institutional investors such as pension funds, endowment funds, or wealthy individuals. They are more likely to pursue complex and higher-risk strategies. They typically keep a portion of trading profits as part of their fees, whereas mutual funds charge a fixed percentage of assets under management.

Economies of scale also explain the proliferation of analytic services available to investors. Newsletters, databases, and brokerage house research services all engage in research to be sold to a large client base. This setup arises naturally. Investors clearly want information, but with small portfolios to manage, they do not find it economical to personally gather all of it. Hence, a profit opportunity emerges: A firm can perform this service for many clients and charge for it.

Investment Bankers

Just as economies of scale and specialization create profit opportunities for financial intermediaries, so do these economies create niches for firms that perform specialized services for businesses. Firms raise much of their capital by selling securities such as stocks and

Separating Commercial Banking from Investment Banking

Until 1999, the Glass-Steagall Act had prohibited banks in the United States from both accepting deposits and underwriting securities. In other words, it forced a separation of the investment and commercial banking industries. But when Glass-Steagall was repealed, many large commercial banks began to transform themselves into "universal banks" that could offer a full range of commercial and investment banking services. In some cases, commercial banks started their own investment banking divisions from scratch, but more frequently they expanded through merger. For example, Chase Manhattan acquired J.P. Morgan to form JPMorgan Chase. Similarly, Citigroup acquired Salomon Smith Barney to offer wealth management, brokerage, investment banking, and asset management services to its clients. Most of Europe had never forced the separation of commercial and investment banking, so their giant banks such as Credit Suisse, Deutsche Bank, HSBC, and UBS had long been universal banks. Until 2008, however, the stand-alone investment banking sector in the U.S. remained large and apparently vibrant, including such storied names as Goldman Sachs, Morgan-Stanley, Merrill Lynch, and Lehman Brothers.

But the industry was shaken to its core in 2008, when several investment banks were beset by enormous losses on their holdings of mortgage-backed securities. In March, on the verge of insolvency, Bear Stearns was merged into JPMorgan Chase. On September 14, 2008, Merrill Lynch, also suffering steep mortgage-related losses, negotiated an agreement to be acquired by Bank of America. The next day, Lehman Brothers entered into the largest bankruptcy in U.S. history, having failed to find an acquirer able and willing to rescue it from its steep losses. The next week, the only two remaining major

independent investment banks, Goldman Sachs and Morgan Stanley, decided to convert from investment banks to traditional bank holding companies. In doing so, they became subject to the supervision of national bank regulators such as the Federal Reserve and the far tighter rules for capital adequacy that govern commercial banks. The firms decided that the greater stability they would enjoy as commercial banks, particularly the ability to fund their operations through bank deposits and access to emergency borrowing from the Fed, justified the conversion. These mergers and conversions marked the effective end of the independent investment banking industry—but not of investment banking. Those services are now supplied by the large universal banks.

Today, the debate about the separation between commercial and investment banking that seemed to have ended with the repeal of Glass-Steagall has come back to life. The Dodd-Frank Wall Street Reform and Consumer Protection Act places new restrictions on bank activities. For example, the Volcker Rule, named after former chairman of the Federal Reserve Paul Volcker, prohibits banks from "proprietary trading," that is, trading securities for their own accounts, and restricts their investments in hedge funds or private equity funds. The rule is meant to limit the risk that banks can take on. While the Volcker Rule is far less restrictive than Glass-Steagall had been, they both are motivated by the belief that banks enjoying Federal guarantees should be subject to limits on the sorts of activities in which they can engage. Proprietary trading is a core activity for investment banks, so limitations on this activity for commercial banks reintroduces a separation between their business models.

---

bonds to the public. Because these firms do not do so frequently, however, **investment bankers** that specialize in such activities can offer their services at a cost below that of maintaining an in-house security issuance division. In this role, they are called *underwriters*.

Investment bankers advise the issuing corporation on the prices it can charge for the securities issued, appropriate interest rates, and so forth. Ultimately, the investment banking firm handles the marketing of the security in the **primary market,** where new issues of securities are offered to the public. Later, investors can trade previously issued securities among themselves in the so-called **secondary market.**

For most of the last century, investment banks and commercial banks in the U.S. were separated by law. While those regulations were effectively eliminated in 1999, the industry known as "Wall Street" was until 2008 still comprised of large, independent investment banks such as Goldman Sachs, Merrill Lynch, and Lehman Brothers. But that stand-alone model came to an abrupt end in September 2008, when all the remaining major U.S. investment banks were absorbed into commercial banks, declared bankruptcy, or reorganized as commercial banks. The nearby box presents a brief introduction to these events.

Venture Capital and Private Equity

While large firms can raise funds directly from the stock and bond markets with help from their investment bankers, smaller and younger firms that have not yet issued securities to the public do not have that option. Start-up companies rely instead on bank loans and investors who are willing to invest in them in return for an ownership stake in the firm. The equity investment in these young companies is called **venture capital (VC).** Sources of venture capital are dedicated venture capital funds, wealthy individuals known as *angel investors,* and institutions such as pension funds.

Most venture capital funds are set up as limited partnerships. A management company starts with its own money and raises additional capital from limited partners such as pension funds. That capital may then be invested in a variety of start-up companies. The management company usually sits on the start-up company's board of directors, helps recruit senior managers, and provides business advice. It charges a fee to the VC fund for overseeing the investments. After some period of time, for example, 10 years, the fund is liquidated and proceeds are distributed to the investors.

Venture capital investors commonly take an active role in the management of a start-up firm. Other active investors may engage in similar hands-on management but focus instead on firms that are in distress or firms that may be bought up, "improved," and sold for a profit. Collectively, these investments in firms that do not trade on public stock exchanges are known as **private equity** investments.

1.7   The Financial Crisis of 2008

This chapter has laid out the broad outlines of the financial system, as well as some of the links between the financial side of the economy and the "real" side in which goods and services are produced. The financial crisis of 2008 illustrated in a painful way the intimate ties between these two sectors. We present in this section a capsule summary of the crisis, attempting to draw some lessons about the role of the financial system as well as the causes and consequences of what has become known as *systemic risk*. Some of these issues are complicated; we consider them briefly here but will return to them in greater detail later in the text once we have more context for analysis.

Antecedents of the Crisis

In early 2007, most observers thought it inconceivable that within two years, the world financial system would be facing its worst crisis since the Great Depression. At the time, the economy seemed to be marching from strength to strength. The last significant macroeconomic threat had been from the implosion of the high-tech bubble in 2000–2002. But the Federal Reserve responded to an emerging recession by aggressively reducing interest rates. Figure 1.1 shows that Treasury bill rates dropped drastically between 2001 and 2004, and the LIBOR rate, which is the interest rate at which major money-center banks lend to each other, fell in tandem.[5] These actions appeared to have been successful, and the recession was short-lived and mild.

By mid-decade the economy was apparently healthy once again. Although the stock market had declined substantially between 2001 and 2002, Figure 1.2 shows that it reversed direction just as dramatically beginning in 2003, fully recovering all of its post-tech-meltdown losses within a few years. Of equal importance, the banking sector seemed healthy. The spread between the LIBOR rate (at which banks borrow from each other) and the Treasury-bill rate (at which the U.S. government borrows), a common measure of credit risk in the banking sector (often referred to as the *TED spread*[6]), was

---

[5]LIBOR stands for London Interbank Offer Rate. It is a rate charged in an interbank lending market outside of the U.S. (largely centered in London). The rate is typically quoted for 3-month loans.

[6]TED stands for Treasury–Eurodollar spread. The Eurodollar rate in this spread is in fact LIBOR.

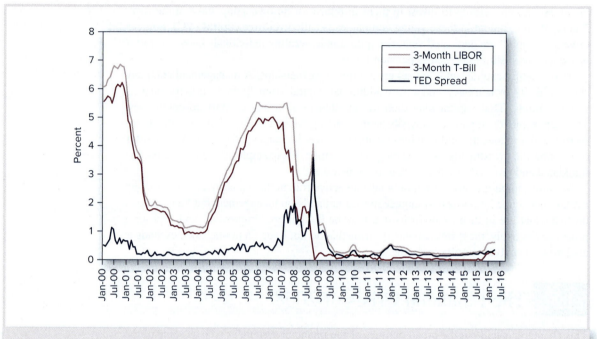

Figure 1.1 Short-term LIBOR and Treasury-bill rates and the TED spread

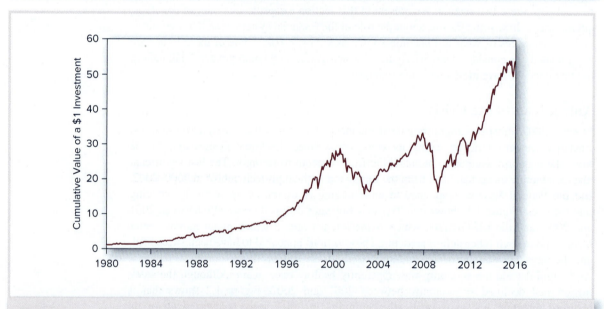

Figure 1.2 Cumulative returns on the S&P 500 index

only around .25% in early 2007 (see the bottom curve in Figure 1.1), suggesting that fears of default or "counterparty" risk in the banking sector were extremely low.

Indeed, the apparent success of monetary policy in this recession, as well as in the last 30 years more generally, had engendered a new term, the "Great Moderation," to describe the fact that recent business cycles—and recessions in particular—seemed so mild

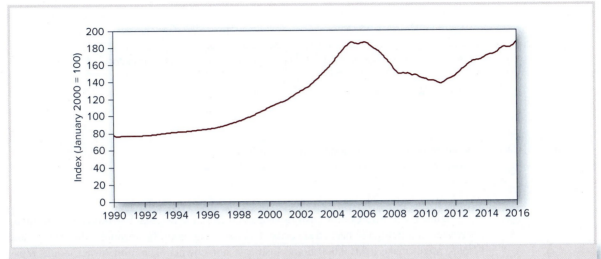

Figure 1.3 The Case-Shiller index of U.S. housing prices

compared to past experience. Some observers wondered whether we had entered a golden age for macroeconomic policy in which the business cycle had been tamed.

The combination of dramatically reduced interest rates and an apparently stable economy fed a historic boom in the housing market. Figure 1.3 shows that U.S. housing prices began rising noticeably in the late 1990s and accelerated dramatically after 2001 as interest rates plummeted. In the 10 years beginning in 1997, average prices in the U.S. approximately tripled.

But the newfound confidence in the power of macroeconomic policy to reduce risk, the impressive recovery of the economy from the high-tech implosion, and particularly the housing price boom following the aggressive reduction in interest rates may have sown the seeds for the debacle that played out in 2008. On the one hand, the Fed's policy of reducing interest rates had resulted in low yields on a wide variety of investments, and investors were hungry for higher-yielding alternatives. On the other hand, low volatility and optimism about macroeconomic prospects encouraged greater tolerance for risk in the search for these higher-yielding investments. Nowhere was this more evident than in the exploding market for securitized mortgages. The U.S. housing and mortgage finance markets were at the center of a gathering storm.

Changes in Housing Finance

Prior to 1970, most mortgage loans would come from a local lender such as a neighborhood savings bank or credit union. A homeowner would borrow funds for a home purchase and repay the loan over a long period, commonly 30 years. A typical thrift institution would have as its major asset a portfolio of these long-term home loans, while its major liability would be the accounts of its depositors. This landscape began to change when Fannie Mae (FNMA, or Federal National Mortgage Association) and Freddie Mac (FHLMC, or Federal Home Loan Mortgage Corporation) began buying mortgage loans from originators and bundling them into large pools that could be traded like any other financial asset. These pools, which were essentially claims on the underlying mortgages, were soon dubbed mortgage-backed securities, and the process was called **securitization.** Fannie and Freddie quickly became the behemoths of the mortgage market, between them buying around half of all mortgages originated by the private sector.

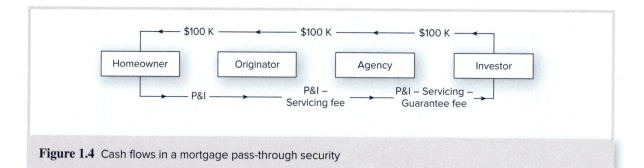

Figure 1.4 Cash flows in a mortgage pass-through security

Figure 1.4 illustrates how cash flows passed from the original borrower to the ultimate investor in a mortgage-backed security. The loan originator, for example, the savings and loan, might make a $100,000 home loan to a homeowner. The homeowner would repay principal and interest (P&I) on the loan over 30 years. But then the originator would sell the mortgage to Freddie Mac or Fannie Mae and recover the cost of the loan. The originator could continue to service the loan (collect monthly payments from the homeowner) for a small servicing fee, but the loan payments net of that fee would be passed along to the agency. In turn, Freddie or Fannie would pool the loans into mortgage-backed securities and sell the securities to investors such as pension funds or mutual funds. The agency (Fannie or Freddie) typically would guarantee the credit or default risk of the loans included in each pool, for which it would retain a guarantee fee before passing along the rest of the cash flow to the ultimate investor. Because the mortgage cash flows were passed along from the homeowner to the lender to Fannie or Freddie to the investor, the mortgage-backed securities were also called *pass-throughs*.

Until the last decade, the vast majority of securitized mortgages were held or guaranteed by Freddie Mac or Fannie Mae. These were low-risk *conforming* mortgages, meaning that eligible loans for agency securitization couldn't be too big, and homeowners had to meet underwriting criteria establishing their ability to repay the loan. For example, the ratio of loan amount to house value could be no more than 80%. But securitization gave rise to a new market niche for mortgage lenders: the "originate to distribute" (versus originate to hold) business model.

Whereas conforming loans were pooled almost entirely through Freddie Mac and Fannie Mae, once the securitization model took hold, it created an opening for a new product: securitization by private firms of *nonconforming* "subprime" loans with higher default risk. One important difference between the government agency pass-throughs and these so-called private-label pass-throughs was that the investor in the private-label pool would bear the risk that homeowners might default on their loans. Thus, originating mortgage brokers had little incentive to perform due diligence on the loan *as long as the loans could be sold to an investor.* These investors, of course, had no direct contact with the borrowers, and they could not perform detailed underwriting concerning loan quality. Instead, they relied on borrowers' credit scores, which steadily came to replace conventional underwriting.

A strong trend toward low-documentation and then no-documentation loans, entailing little verification of a borrower's ability to carry a loan, soon emerged. Other subprime underwriting standards quickly deteriorated. For example, allowed leverage on home loans (as measured by the loan-to-value ratio) rose dramatically. By 2006, the majority of subprime borrowers purchased houses by borrowing the *entire* purchase price!

When housing prices began falling, these loans were quickly "underwater," meaning that the house was worth less than the loan balance, and many homeowners decided to walk away from their loans.

Adjustable-rate mortgages (ARMs) also grew in popularity. These loans offered borrowers low initial or "teaser" interest rates, but these rates eventually would reset to current market interest yields, for example, the Treasury bill rate plus 3%. Many of these borrowers "maxed out" their borrowing capacity at the teaser rate, yet, as soon as the loan rate was reset, their monthly payments would soar, especially if market interest rates had increased.

Despite these obvious risks, the ongoing increase in housing prices over the last decade seemed to lull many investors into complacency, with a widespread belief that continually rising home prices would bail out poorly performing loans. But starting in 2004, the ability of refinancing to save a loan began to diminish. First, higher interest rates put payment pressure on homeowners who had taken out adjustable-rate mortgages. Second, as Figure 1.3 shows, housing prices peaked by 2006, so homeowners' ability to refinance a loan using built-up equity in the house declined. Mortgage default rates began to surge in 2007, as did losses on mortgage-backed securities. The crisis was ready to shift into high gear.

Mortgage Derivatives

One might ask: Who was willing to buy all of these risky subprime mortgages? Securitization, restructuring, and credit enhancement provide a big part of the answer. New risk-shifting tools enabled investment banks to carve out AAA-rated securities from original-issue "junk" loans. Collateralized debt obligations, or CDOs, were among the most important and eventually damaging of these innovations.

CDOs were designed to concentrate the credit (i.e., default) risk of a bundle of loans on one class of investors, leaving the other investors in the pool relatively protected from that risk. The idea was to prioritize claims on loan repayments by dividing the pool into senior versus junior slices, called *tranches*. The senior tranches had first claim on repayments from the entire pool. Junior tranches would be paid only after the senior ones had received their cut.[7] For example, if a pool were divided into two tranches, with 70% of the pool allocated to the senior tranche and 30% allocated to the junior one, the senior investors would be repaid in full as long as 70% or more of the loans in the pool performed, that is, as long as the default rate on the pool remained below 30%. Even with pools composed of risky subprime loans, default rates above 30% seemed extremely unlikely, and thus senior tranches were frequently granted the highest (i.e., AAA) rating by the major credit rating agencies, Moody's, Standard & Poor's, and Fitch. Large amounts of AAA-rated securities were thus carved out of pools of low-rated mortgages. (We will describe CDOs in more detail in Chapter 14.)

Of course, we know now that these ratings were wrong. The senior-subordinated structure of CDOs provided far less protection to senior tranches than investors anticipated. When housing prices across the entire country began to fall in unison, defaults in all regions increased, and the hoped-for benefits from spreading the risks geographically never materialized.

Why had the rating agencies so dramatically underestimated credit risk in these subprime securities? First, default probabilities had been estimated using historical data from an unrepresentative period characterized by a housing boom and an uncommonly

---

[7]CDOs and related securities are sometimes called *structured products*. "Structured" means that original cash flows are sliced up and reapportioned across tranches according to some stipulated rule.

prosperous and recession-free macroeconomy. Moreover, the ratings analysts had extrapolated historical default experience to a new sort of borrower pool—one without down payments, with exploding-payment loans, and with low- or no-documentation loans (often called *liar loans*). Past default experience was largely irrelevant given these profound changes in the market. Moreover, the power of cross-regional diversification to minimize risk engendered excessive optimism.

Finally, agency problems became apparent. The ratings agencies were paid to provide ratings by the issuers of the securities—not the purchasers. They faced pressure from the issuers, who could shop around for the most favorable treatment, to provide generous ratings.

 Concept Check **1.2**

> When Freddie Mac and Fannie Mae pooled mortgages into securities, they guaranteed the underlying mortgage loans against homeowner defaults. In contrast, there were no guarantees on the mortgages pooled into subprime mortgage-backed securities, so investors were the ones to bear the credit risk. Were either of these arrangements necessarily a better way to manage and allocate default risk?

Credit Default Swaps

In parallel to the CDO market, the market in *credit default swaps* also exploded in this period. A credit default swap, or CDS, is in essence an insurance contract against the default of one or more borrowers. (We will describe these in more detail in Chapter 14.) The purchaser of the swap pays an annual premium (like an insurance premium) for protection from credit risk. Credit default swaps became an alternative method of credit enhancement, seemingly allowing investors to buy subprime loans and insure their safety. But in practice, some swap issuers ramped up their exposure to credit risk to unsupportable levels, without sufficient capital to back those obligations. For example, the large insurance company AIG alone sold more than $400 billion of CDS contracts on subprime mortgages.

The Rise of Systemic Risk

By 2007, the financial system displayed several troubling features. Many large banks and related financial institutions had adopted an apparently profitable financing scheme: borrowing short term at low interest rates to finance holdings in higher-yielding, long-term illiquid assets,[8] and treating the interest rate differential between their assets and liabilities as economic profit. But this business model was precarious: By relying primarily on short-term loans for their funding, these firms needed to constantly refinance their positions (i.e., borrow additional funds as the loans matured), or else face the necessity of quickly selling off their less-liquid asset portfolios, which would be difficult in times of financial stress. Moreover, these institutions were highly leveraged and had little capital as a buffer against losses. Large investment banks on Wall Street in particular had sharply increased leverage, which added to an underappreciated vulnerability to refunding requirements—especially

---

[8]*Liquidity* refers to the speed and the ease with which investors can realize the cash value of an investment. Illiquid assets, for example, real estate, can be hard to sell quickly, and a quick sale may require a substantial discount from the price at which the asset could be sold in an unrushed situation.

if the value of their asset portfolios came into question. Even small portfolio losses could drive their net worth negative, at which point no one would be willing to renew outstanding loans or extend new ones.

Another source of fragility was widespread investor reliance on "credit enhancement" through products like CDOs. Many of the assets underlying these pools were illiquid, hard to value, and highly dependent on forecasts of future performance of other loans. In a widespread downturn, with rating downgrades, these assets would prove difficult to sell.

This new financial model was brimming with **systemic risk,** a potential breakdown of the financial system when problems in one market spill over and disrupt others. When lenders such as banks have limited capital and are afraid of further losses, they may rationally choose to hoard their capital instead of lending it to customers such as small firms, thereby exacerbating funding problems for their customary borrowers.

The Shoe Drops

By fall 2007, housing price declines were widespread (Figure 1.3), mortgage delinquencies increased, and the stock market entered its own free fall (Figure 1.2). Many investment banks, which had large investments in mortgages, also began to totter.

The crisis peaked in September 2008. On September 7, the giant federal mortgage agencies Fannie Mae and Freddie Mac, both of which had taken large positions in subprime mortgage–backed securities, were put into conservatorship. (We will have more to say on their travails in Chapter 2.) The failure of these two mainstays of the U.S. housing and mortgage finance industries threw financial markets into a panic. By the second week of September, it was clear that both Lehman Brothers and Merrill Lynch were on the verge of bankruptcy. On September 14, Merrill Lynch was sold to Bank of America, again with the benefit of government brokering and protection against losses. The next day, Lehman Brothers, which was denied equivalent treatment, filed for bankruptcy protection. Two days later, on September 17, the government reluctantly lent $85 billion to AIG, reasoning that its failure would have been highly destabilizing to the banking industry, which was holding massive amounts of its credit guarantees (i.e., CDS contracts). The next day, the Treasury unveiled its first proposal to spend $700 billion to purchase "toxic" mortgage-backed securities.

A particularly devastating fallout of the Lehman bankruptcy was on the "money market" for short-term lending. Lehman had borrowed considerable funds by issuing very short-term debt, called commercial paper. Among the major customers in commercial paper were money market mutual funds, which invest in short-term, high-quality debt of commercial borrowers. When Lehman faltered, the Reserve Primary Money Market Fund, which was holding large amounts of (AAA-rated!) Lehman commercial paper, suffered investment losses that drove the value of its assets below $1 per share.[9] Fears spread that other funds were similarly exposed, and money market fund customers across the country rushed to withdraw their funds. The funds in turn rushed out of commercial paper into safer and more liquid Treasury bills, essentially shutting down short-term financing markets.

The freezing up of credit markets was the end of any dwindling possibility that the financial crisis could be contained to Wall Street. Larger companies that had relied on

---

[9]Money market funds typically bear very little investment risk and can maintain their asset values at $1 per share. Investors view them as near substitutes for checking accounts. Until this episode, no other retail fund had "broken the buck."

the commercial paper market were now unable to raise short-term funds. Banks similarly found it difficult to raise funds. (Look back to Figure 1.1, where you will see that the TED spread, a measure of bank insolvency fears, skyrocketed in 2008.) With banks unwilling or unable to extend credit to their customers, thousands of small businesses that relied on bank lines of credit also became unable to finance their normal business operations. Capital-starved companies were forced to scale back their own operations precipitously. The unemployment rate rose rapidly, and the economy was in its worst recession in decades. The turmoil in the financial markets had spilled over into the real economy, and Main Street had joined Wall Street in a bout of protracted misery.

The crisis was not limited to the United States. Housing markets throughout the world fell, and many European banks had to be rescued by their governments, which were themselves heavily in debt. As the cost of the bank bailouts mounted, the ability of these governments to repay their own debts came into doubt. In this way, the banking crisis spiraled into a sovereign debt crisis.

Greece was the hardest hit. Its government debt of about $460 billion was considerably more than its annual GDP. In 2011 it defaulted on debts totaling around $130 billion. Despite a series of rescue packages from the European Union, the European Central Bank, and the International Monetary Fund, it was still on shaky ground in 2016.

The Dodd-Frank Reform Act

The crisis engendered many calls for reform of Wall Street. These eventually led to the passage in 2010 of the Dodd-Frank Wall Street Reform and Consumer Protection Act, which proposes several mechanisms to mitigate systemic risk.

The act calls for stricter rules for bank capital, liquidity, and risk management practices, especially as banks become larger and their potential failure would be more threatening to other institutions. With more capital supporting banks, the potential for one insolvency to trigger another could be contained. In addition, when banks have more capital, they have less incentive to ramp up risk, as potential losses will come at their own expense and not the FDIC's.

Dodd-Frank also attempts to limit the risky activities in which banks can engage. The so-called Volcker Rule, named after former chairman of the Federal Reserve Paul Volcker, prohibits banks from trading for their own accounts and limits total investments in hedge funds or private equity funds.

The act also addresses incentive issues. Among these are proposals to force employee compensation to reflect longer-term performance. For example, public companies must set "claw-back provisions" to take back executive compensation if it was based on inaccurate financial statements. The motivation is to discourage excessive risk-taking by large financial institutions in which big bets can be wagered with the attitude that a successful outcome will result in a big bonus while a bad outcome will be borne by the company, or worse, the taxpayer.

The incentives of the bond rating agencies are also a sore point. Few are happy with a system that has the ratings agencies paid by the firms they rate. The act creates an Office of Credit Ratings within the Securities and Exchange Commission to oversee the credit rating agencies.

It is still too early to know which, if any, of these reforms will stick. The implementation of Dodd-Frank is still subject to considerable interpretation by regulators, and the act is still under attack by some members of Congress. But the crisis surely has made clear the essential role of the financial system in the functioning of the real economy.

1.8   Outline of the Text

The text has seven parts, which are fairly independent and may be studied in a variety of sequences. Part One is an introduction to financial markets, instruments, and trading of securities. This part also describes the mutual fund industry.

Parts Two and Three contain the core of what has come to be known as "modern portfolio theory." We start in Part Two with a general discussion of risk and return and the lessons of capital market history. We then focus more closely on how to describe investors' risk preferences and progress to asset allocation, efficient diversification, and portfolio optimization.

In Part Three, we investigate the implications of portfolio theory for the equilibrium relationship between risk and return. We introduce the capital asset pricing model, its implementation using index models, and more advanced models of risk and return. This part also treats the efficient market hypothesis as well as behavioral critiques of theories based on investor rationality and closes with a chapter on empirical evidence concerning security returns.

Parts Four through Six cover security analysis and valuation. Part Four is devoted to debt markets and Part Five to equity markets. Part Six covers derivative assets, such as options and futures contracts.

Part Seven is an introduction to active investment management. It shows how different investors' objectives and constraints can lead to a variety of investment policies. This part discusses the role of active management in nearly efficient markets and considers how one should evaluate the performance of managers who pursue active strategies. It also shows how the principles of portfolio construction can be extended to the international setting and examines the hedge fund industry.

SUMMARY

1. Real assets create wealth. Financial assets represent claims to parts or all of that wealth. Financial assets determine how the ownership of real assets is distributed among investors.

2. Financial assets can be categorized as fixed income, equity, or derivative instruments. Top-down portfolio construction techniques start with the asset allocation decision—the allocation of funds across broad asset classes—and then progress to more specific security-selection decisions.

3. Competition in financial markets leads to a risk–return trade-off, in which securities that offer higher expected rates of return also impose greater risks on investors. The presence of risk, however, implies that actual returns can differ considerably from expected returns at the beginning of the investment period. Competition among security analysts also promotes financial markets that are nearly informationally efficient, meaning that prices reflect all available information concerning the value of the security. Passive investment strategies may make sense in nearly efficient markets.

4. Financial intermediaries pool investor funds and invest them. Their services are in demand because small investors cannot efficiently gather information, diversify, and monitor portfolios. The financial intermediary sells its own securities to the small investors. The intermediary invests the funds thus raised, uses the proceeds to pay back the small investors, and profits from the difference (the spread).

5. Investment banking brings efficiency to corporate fundraising. Investment bankers develop expertise in pricing new issues and in marketing them to investors. By the end of 2008,

all the major stand-alone U.S. investment banks had been absorbed into commercial banks or had reorganized themselves into bank holding companies. In Europe, where universal banking had never been prohibited, large banks had long maintained both commercial and investment banking divisions.

6. The financial crisis of 2008 showed the importance of systemic risk. Systemic risk can be limited by transparency that allows traders and investors to assess the risk of their counterparties; capital requirements to prevent trading participants from being brought down by potential losses; frequent settlement of gains or losses to prevent losses from accumulating beyond an institution's ability to bear them; incentives to discourage excessive risk taking; and accurate and unbiased analysis by those charged with evaluating security risk.

KEY TERMS		
investment	security selection	primary market
real assets	security analysis	secondary market
financial assets	risk–return trade-off	venture capital (VC)
fixed-income (debt) securities	passive management	private equity
equity	active management	securitization
derivative securities	financial intermediaries	systemic risk
agency problem	investment companies	
asset allocation	investment bankers	

PROBLEM SETS

1. Financial engineering has been disparaged as nothing more than paper shuffling. Critics argue that resources used for *rearranging* wealth (i.e., bundling and unbundling financial assets) might be better spent on *creating* wealth (i.e., creating real assets). Evaluate this criticism. Are any benefits realized by creating an array of derivative securities from various primary securities?

2. Why would you expect securitization to take place only in highly developed capital markets?

3. What is the relationship between securitization and the role of financial intermediaries in the economy? What happens to financial intermediaries as securitization progresses?

4. Although we stated that real assets constitute the true productive capacity of an economy, it is hard to conceive of a modern economy without well-developed financial markets and security types. How would the productive capacity of the U.S. economy be affected if there were no markets in which to trade financial assets?

5. Firms raise capital from investors by issuing shares in the primary markets. Does this imply that corporate financial managers can ignore trading of previously issued shares in the secondary market?

6. Suppose housing prices across the world double.

   a. Is society any richer for the change?

   b. Are homeowners wealthier?

   c. Can you reconcile your answers to (*a*) and (*b*)? Is anyone worse off as a result of the change?

7. Lanni Products is a start-up computer software development firm. It currently owns computer equipment worth $30,000 and has cash on hand of $20,000 contributed by Lanni's owners. For each of the following transactions, identify the real and/or financial assets that trade hands. Are any financial assets created or destroyed in the transaction?

   a. Lanni takes out a bank loan. It receives $50,000 in cash and signs a note promising to pay back the loan over 3 years.

   b. Lanni uses the cash from the bank plus $20,000 of its own funds to finance the development of new financial planning software.

c. Lanni sells the software product to Microsoft, which will market it to the public under the Microsoft name. Lanni accepts payment in the form of 2,500 shares of Microsoft stock.

d. Lanni sells the shares of stock for $50 per share and uses part of the proceeds to pay off the bank loan.

8. Reconsider Lanni Products from the previous problem.

   a. Prepare its balance sheet just after it gets the bank loan. What is the ratio of real assets to total assets?

   b. Prepare the balance sheet after Lanni spends the $70,000 to develop its software product. What is the ratio of real assets to total assets?

   c. Prepare the balance sheet after Lanni accepts the payment of shares from Microsoft. What is the ratio of real assets to total assets?

9. Examine the balance sheet of commercial banks in Table 1.3.

   a. What is the ratio of real assets to total assets?

   b. What is the ratio of real assets to total assets for nonfinancial firms (Table 1.4)?

   c. Why should this difference be expected?

10. Consider Figure 1A, which describes an issue of American gold certificates.

   a. Is this issue a primary or secondary market transaction?

   b. Are the certificates primitive or derivative assets?

   c. What market niche is filled by this offering?

Figure 1A A gold-backed security

11. Discuss the advantages and disadvantages of the following forms of managerial compensation in terms of mitigating agency problems, that is, potential conflicts of interest between managers and shareholders.

   a. A fixed salary.

   b. Stock in the firm that must be held for five years.

   c. A salary linked to the firm's profits.

12. Oversight by large institutional investors or creditors is one mechanism to reduce agency problems. Why don't individual investors in the firm have the same incentive to keep an eye on management?

13. Give an example of three financial intermediaries and explain how they act as a bridge between small investors and large capital markets or corporations.

14. The average rate of return on investments in large stocks has outpaced that on investments in Treasury bills by about 8% since 1926. Why, then, does anyone invest in Treasury bills?

15. What are some advantages and disadvantages of top-down versus bottom-up investing styles?

16. You see an advertisement for a book that claims to show how you can make $1 million with no risk and with no money down. Will you buy the book?

17. Why do financial assets show up as a component of household wealth, but not of national wealth? Why do financial assets still matter for the material well-being of an economy?

18. Wall Street firms have traditionally compensated their traders with a share of the trading profits that they generated. How might this practice have affected traders' willingness to assume risk? What is the agency problem this practice engendered?

19. What reforms to the financial system might reduce its exposure to systemic risk?

SOLUTIONS TO CONCEPT CHECKS

1. *a.* Real

   b. Financial

   c. Real

   d. Real

   e. Financial

2. The central issue is the incentive and ability to monitor the quality of loans when originated as well as over time. Freddie and Fannie clearly had incentive to monitor the quality of conforming loans that they had guaranteed, and their ongoing relationships with mortgage originators gave them opportunities to evaluate track records over extended periods of time. In the subprime mortgage market, the ultimate investors in the securities (or the CDOs backed by those securities), who were bearing the credit risk, should not have been willing to invest in loans with a disproportionate likelihood of default. If they properly understood their exposure to default risk, then the (correspondingly low) prices they would have been willing to pay for these securities would have imposed discipline on the mortgage originators and servicers. The fact that they were willing to hold such large positions in these risky securities suggests that they did not appreciate the extent of their exposure. Maybe they were led astray by overly optimistic projections for housing prices or by biased assessments from the credit-reporting agencies. In principle, either arrangement for default risk could have provided the appropriate discipline on the mortgage originators; in practice, however, the informational advantages of Freddie and Fannie probably made them the better "recipients" of default risk. The lesson is that information and transparency are some of the preconditions for well-functioning markets.

Asset Classes and Financial Instruments

2

YOU LEARNED IN Chapter 1 that the process of building an investment portfolio usually begins by deciding how much money to allocate to broad classes of assets, such as safe money market securities or bank accounts, longer term bonds, stocks, or even asset classes like real estate or precious metals. This process is called *asset allocation.* Within each class the investor then selects specific assets from a more detailed menu. This is called *security selection.*

Each broad asset class contains many specific security types, and the many variations on a theme can be overwhelming. Our goal in this chapter is to introduce you to the important features of broad classes of securities. Toward this end, we organize our tour of financial instruments according to asset class.

Financial markets are traditionally segmented into **money markets** and **capital markets.** Money market instruments include short-term, marketable, liquid, low-risk debt securities. Money market instruments sometimes are called *cash equivalents,* or just *cash* for short. Capital markets, in contrast, include longer term and riskier securities. Securities in the capital market are much more diverse than those found within the money market. For this reason, we will subdivide the capital market into four segments: longer term bond markets, equity markets, and the derivative markets for options and futures.

We first describe money market instruments. We then move on to debt and equity securities. We explain the structure of various stock market indexes in this chapter because market benchmark portfolios play an important role in portfolio construction and evaluation. Finally, we survey the derivative security markets for options and futures contracts.

2.1 The Money Market

The money market is a subsector of the fixed-income market. It consists of very short-term debt securities that usually are highly marketable. Table 2.1 lists outstanding volume in 2015 for some of the major instruments in this market. Many of these securities trade in large denominations and so are out of the reach of individual investors. Money

Table 2.1

Major components of
the money market

	$ Billion
Federal funds and repurchase agreements	$3,748
Small-denomination time deposits and savings deposits*	8,991
Large-denomination time deposits†	1,865
Treasury bills	1,527
Commercial paper	1,120
Money market mutual funds	2,716

*Small-denomination time deposits are less than $100,000.
†Large-denomination time deposits are greater than $100,000.
Sources: *Flow of Funds Accounts of the United States,* Board of Governors of the Federal Reserve System,
March 2016.

market funds, however, are easily accessible to small investors. These mutual funds pool the resources of many investors and purchase a wide variety of money market securities on their behalf.

Treasury Bills

U.S. *Treasury bills* (T-bills, or just bills, for short) are the most marketable of all money market instruments. T-bills represent the simplest form of borrowing: The government raises money by selling bills to the public. Investors buy the bills at a discount from the stated maturity value. At the bill's maturity, the government pays the investor the face value of the bill. The difference between the purchase price and ultimate maturity value constitutes the investor's earnings.

T-bills are issued with initial maturities of 4, 13, 26, or 52 weeks. Individuals can purchase T-bills directly, at auction, or on the secondary market from a government securities dealer. T-bills are highly liquid; that is, they are easily converted to cash and sold at low transaction cost and with not much price risk. Unlike most other money market instruments, which sell in minimum denominations of $100,000, T-bills sell in minimum denominations of only $100, although $10,000 denominations are far more common. The income earned on T-bills is exempt from all state and local taxes, another characteristic distinguishing them from other money market instruments.

Figure 2.1 is a partial listing of T-bill rates. Rather than providing prices of each bill, the financial press reports yields based on those prices. You will see yields corresponding to both bid and ask prices. The **ask price** is the price you would have to pay to buy a T-bill from a securities dealer. The **bid price** is the slightly lower price you would receive if you wanted to sell a bill to a dealer. The **bid–ask spread** is the difference in these prices, which is the dealer's source of profit. (Notice in Figure 2.1 that the bid *yield* is higher than the ask yield. This is because prices and yields are inversely related.)

The first two yields in Figure 2.1 are reported using the *bank-discount method.* This means that the bill's discount from its maturity or face value is "annualized" based on a 360-day year, and then reported as a percentage of face value. For example, for the highlighted bill maturing on October 27, 2016, days to maturity are 171 and the yield under the column labeled "ASKED" is given as .340%. This means that a dealer was willing to sell the bill at a discount from face value of .340% × (171/360) = .1615%. So a bill with $10,000 face value could be purchased for $10,000 × (1 − .001615) = $9,983.85.

TREASURY BILLS

MATURITY	DAYS TO MAT	BID	ASKED	CHG	ASKED YIELD
July 14, 2016	66	0.155	0.145	0.005	0.148
September 1, 2016	115	0.233	0.223	0.000	0.226
October 27, 2016	171	0.350	0.340	0.000	0.345
December 8, 2016	213	0.348	0.338	0.005	0.344
April 27, 2017	353	0.503	0.493	0.002	0.502

Figure 2.1 Treasury bill yields

Source: Compiled from data obtained from *The Wall Street Journal Online*, May 9, 2016.

Similarly, on the basis of the bid yield of .350%, a dealer would be willing to purchase the bill for $10,000 × (1 − .00350 × 171/360) = $9,983.375.

The bank discount method for computing yields has a long tradition, but it is flawed for at least two reasons. First, it assumes that the year has only 360 days. Second, it computes the yield as a fraction of par value rather than of the price the investor paid to acquire the bill.[1] An investor who buys the bill for the ask price and holds it until maturity will see her investment grow over 171 days by a multiple of $10,000/$9,983.85 = 1.001618, for a gain of .1618%. Annualizing this gain using a 365-day year results in a yield of .1618% × 365/171 = .345%, which is the value reported in the last column under "ASKED YIELD." This last value is called the Treasury-bill's *bond-equivalent yield.*

Certificates of Deposit

A **certificate of deposit,** or CD, is a time deposit with a bank. Time deposits may not be withdrawn on demand. The bank pays interest and principal to the depositor only at the end of the fixed term of the CD. CDs issued in denominations greater than $100,000 are usually negotiable, however; that is, they can be sold to another investor if the owner needs to cash in the certificate before its maturity date. Short-term CDs are highly marketable, although the market significantly thins out for maturities of 3 months or more. CDs are treated as bank deposits by the Federal Deposit Insurance Corporation, so they are currently insured for up to $250,000 in the event of a bank insolvency.

Commercial Paper

Large, well-known companies often issue their own short-term unsecured debt notes rather than borrow directly from banks. These notes are called **commercial paper.** Very often, commercial paper is backed by a bank line of credit, which gives the borrower access to cash that can be used (if needed) to pay off the paper at maturity.

[1]Both of these "errors" were dictated by computational simplicity in precomputer days. It is easier to compute percentage discounts from a round number such as par value rather than purchase price. It is also easier to annualize using a 360-day year, because 360 is an even multiple of so many numbers.

Commercial paper maturities range up to 270 days, but most often, commercial paper is issued with a maturity of less than 1 or 2 months. Usually, it is issued in multiples of $100,000. Therefore, small investors can invest in commercial paper only indirectly, via money market mutual funds.

Commercial paper is considered to be a fairly safe asset, because a firm's condition presumably can be monitored and predicted over a term as short as 1 month.

While most commercial paper is issued by nonfinancial firms, in recent years there was a sharp increase in *asset-backed commercial paper* issued by financial firms such as banks. This was short-term commercial paper typically used to raise funds for the institution to invest in other assets, most notoriously, subprime mortgages. These assets were in turn used as collateral for the commercial paper—hence the label "asset backed." This practice led to many difficulties starting in the summer of 2007 when the subprime mortgagors began defaulting. The banks found themselves unable to issue new commercial paper to refinance their positions as the old paper matured.

Bankers' Acceptances

A **banker's acceptance** starts as an order to a bank by a bank's customer to pay a sum of money at a future date, typically within 6 months. At this stage, it is similar to a postdated check. When the bank endorses the order for payment as "accepted," it assumes responsibility for ultimate payment to the holder of the acceptance. At this point, the acceptance may be traded in secondary markets like any other claim on the bank. Bankers' acceptances are considered very safe assets because traders can substitute the bank's credit standing for their own. They are used widely in foreign trade where the creditworthiness of one trader is unknown to the trading partner. Acceptances sell at a discount from the face value of the payment order, just as T-bills sell at a discount from par value.

Eurodollars

Eurodollars are dollar-denominated deposits at foreign banks or foreign branches of American banks. By locating outside the United States, these banks escape regulation by the Federal Reserve. Despite the tag "Euro," these accounts need not be in European banks, although that is where the practice of accepting dollar-denominated deposits outside the United States began.

Most Eurodollar deposits are for large sums, and most are time deposits of less than 6 months' maturity. A variation on the Eurodollar time deposit is the Eurodollar certificate of deposit, which resembles a domestic bank CD except that it is the liability of a non-U.S. branch of a bank, typically a London branch. The advantage of Eurodollar CDs over Eurodollar time deposits is that the holder can sell the asset to realize its cash value before maturity. Eurodollar CDs are considered less liquid and riskier than domestic CDs, however, and thus offer higher yields. Firms also issue Eurodollar bonds, which are dollar-denominated bonds outside the U.S., although bonds are not a money market investment because of their long maturities.

Repos and Reverses

Dealers in government securities use **repurchase agreements,** also called "repos" or "RPs," as a form of short-term, usually overnight, borrowing. The dealer sells government securities to an investor on an overnight basis, with an agreement to buy back those securities the next day at a slightly higher price. The increase in the price is the overnight interest. The dealer thus takes out a 1-day loan from the investor, and the securities serve as collateral.

A *term repo* is essentially an identical transaction, except that the term of the implicit loan can be 30 days or more. Repos are considered very safe in terms of credit risk because the loans are backed by the government securities. A *reverse repo* is the mirror image of a repo. Here, the dealer finds an investor holding government securities and buys them, agreeing to sell them back at a specified higher price on a future date.

Federal Funds

Just as most of us maintain deposits at banks, banks maintain deposits of their own at a Federal Reserve bank. Each member bank of the Federal Reserve System, or "the Fed," is required to maintain a minimum balance in a reserve account with the Fed. The required balance depends on the total deposits of the bank's customers. Funds in the bank's reserve account are called **federal funds,** or *fed funds.* At any time, some banks have more funds than required at the Fed. Other banks, primarily big banks in New York and other financial centers, tend to have a shortage of federal funds. In the federal funds market, banks with excess funds lend to those with a shortage. These loans, which are usually overnight transactions, are arranged at a rate of interest called the *federal funds rate.*

Although the fed funds market arose primarily as a way for banks to transfer balances to meet reserve requirements, today the market has evolved to the point that many large banks use federal funds in a straightforward way as one component of their total sources of funding. Therefore, the fed funds rate is simply the rate of interest on very short-term loans among financial institutions. While most investors cannot participate in this market, the fed funds rate commands great interest as a key barometer of monetary policy.

Brokers' Calls

Individuals who buy stocks on margin borrow part of the funds to pay for the stocks from their broker. The broker in turn may borrow the funds from a bank, agreeing to repay the bank immediately (on call) if the bank requests it. The rate paid on such loans is usually about 1% higher than the rate on short-term T-bills.

The LIBOR Market

The **London Interbank Offered Rate (LIBOR)** is the rate at which large banks in London are willing to lend money among themselves. This rate, which is quoted on dollar-denominated loans, has become the premier short-term interest rate quoted in the European money market, and it serves as a reference rate for a wide range of transactions. For example, a corporation might borrow at a floating rate equal to LIBOR plus 2%.

LIBOR interest rates may be tied to currencies other than the U.S. dollar. For example, LIBOR rates are widely quoted for transactions denominated in British pounds, yen, euros, and so on. There is also a similar rate called EURIBOR (European Interbank Offered Rate) at which banks in the euro zone are willing to lend euros among themselves.

LIBOR is a key reference rate in the money market, and many trillions of dollars of loans and derivative assets are tied to it. Therefore, the 2012 scandal involving the fixing of LIBOR deeply shook these markets. The nearby box discusses those events.

Yields on Money Market Instruments

Although most money market securities are low risk, they are not risk-free. The securities of the money market promise yields greater than those on default-free T-bills, at

The LIBOR Scandals

LIBOR was designed initially as a survey of interbank lending rates but soon became a key determinant of short-term interest rates with far-reaching significance. More than $500 trillion of derivative contracts have payoffs tied to it, and hundreds of trillions of dollars of loans and bonds with floating interest rates linked to LIBOR are currently outstanding. LIBOR is quoted for loans in five currencies (U.S. dollar, yen, euro, British pound, and Swiss franc) and for seven maturities ranging from a day to a year, although 3 months is the most common.

However, LIBOR is not a rate at which actual transactions occur; instead, it is just a survey of "estimated" borrowing rates, and this has made it vulnerable to tampering. Several large banks are asked to report the rate at which they *believe* they can borrow in the interbank market. Outliers are trimmed from the sample of responses, and LIBOR is calculated as the average of the mid-range estimates.

Over time, several problems surfaced. First, it appeared that banks understated the rates at which they claimed they could borrow in an effort to make themselves look financially stronger. Other surveys that asked for estimates of the rates at which *other* banks could borrow resulted in higher values. Moreover, LIBOR did not seem to reflect current market conditions. A majority of LIBOR submissions were unchanged from day to day even when other interest rates fluctuated, and

LIBOR spreads showed surprisingly low correlation with other measures of credit risk. Even worse, once the market came under scrutiny, it emerged that participating banks were colluding to manipulate their LIBOR submissions to enhance profits on their derivatives trades. Traders used e-mails and instant messages to tell each other whether they wanted to see higher or lower submissions. Members of this informal cartel essentially set up a "favor bank" to help each other move the survey average up or down depending on their trading positions.

To date, over $5 billion of fines have been paid, among them, Deutsche Bank ($2.5 billion), UBS ($1.5 billion), Royal Bank of Scotland ($612 million), and Barclays ($450 million). But government fines may be only the beginning. A federal appeals court in 2016 ruled that private lawsuits involving antitrust violations may proceed. Customers who borrowed funds at an interest rate tied to LIBOR argue that they were harmed by the collusion of participating banks to coordinate rates.

Several reforms have been suggested. The British Bankers Association, which until recently ran the LIBOR survey, yielded responsibility for LIBOR to British regulators. LIBOR quotes in less active currencies and maturities, where collusion is easier, have been eliminated. More substantive proposals would replace the survey rate with one based on actual, verifiable, transactions—that is, real loans among banks.

least in part because of greater relative riskiness. In addition, many investors require more liquidity; thus they will accept lower yields on securities such as T-bills that can be quickly and cheaply sold for cash. Figure 2.2 shows that bank CDs, for example, consistently have paid a premium over T-bills. Moreover, that premium increased with economic crises

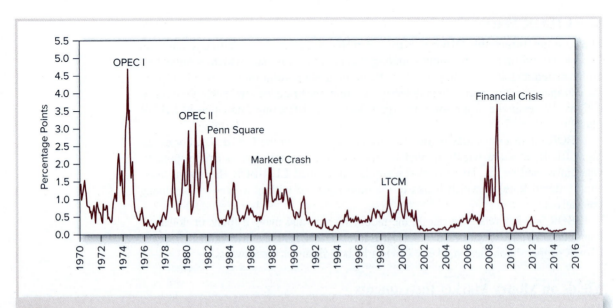

Figure 2.2 The spread between 3-month CD and Treasury bill rates

Money Market Funds and the Credit Crisis of 2008

Money market funds are mutual funds that invest in the short-term debt instruments that comprise the money market. They are required to hold only short-maturity debt of the highest quality: The average maturity of their holdings must be maintained at less than 3 months. Their biggest investments tend to be in commercial paper, but they also hold sizable fractions of their portfolios in certificates of deposit, repurchase agreements, and Treasury securities. Because of this very conservative investment profile, money market funds typically experience extremely low price risk. Investors for their part usually acquire check-writing privileges with their funds and often use them as a close substitute for a bank account. This is feasible because the funds almost always maintain share value at $1.00 and pass along all investment earnings to their investors as interest.

Until 2008, only one fund had "broken the buck," that is, suffered losses large enough to force value per share below $1. But when Lehman Brothers filed for bankruptcy protection on September 15, 2008, several funds that had invested heavily in its commercial paper suffered large losses. The next day, the Reserve Primary Fund, the oldest money market fund, broke the buck when its value per share fell to only $.97.

The realization that money market funds were at risk in the credit crisis led to a wave of investor redemptions similar to a run on a bank. Fearing further outflows, the U.S. Treasury announced that it would make federal insurance available to money market funds willing to pay an insurance fee. This program would thus be similar to FDIC bank insurance. With the federal insurance in place, the outflows were quelled.

However, the turmoil in Wall Street's money market funds had already spilled over into "Main Street." Fearing further investor redemptions, money market funds had become afraid to commit funds even over short periods, and their demand for commercial paper had effectively dried up. Firms throughout the economy had come to depend on those markets as a major source of short-term finance to fund expenditures ranging from salaries to inventories. Further breakdown in the money markets would have had an immediate crippling effect on the broad economy.

To end the panic and stabilize the money markets, the federal government decided to guarantee investments in money market funds. The guarantee did, in fact, calm investors and end the run, but it put the government on the hook for a potential liability of up to $3 trillion—the assets held in money market funds at the time.

U.S. regulators have since approved a series of reforms to reduce the risks of runs on these funds. Institutional money market funds (those servicing institutions rather than private investors) are required to "float" the prices of their shares based on the value of their assets rather than maintain a fixed $1 value per share. This limits the incentive during a crisis for investors to compete to be the first to withdraw funds while share prices are maintained at a nonsustainable level of $1. In addition, funds will have the authority to either limit redemptions or impose redemption fees of up to 2% if a fund's assets fall by more than 30%. Finally, the rules call for enhanced transparency, with greater disclosure of asset values, portfolio composition, and liquidity.

---

such as the energy price shocks associated with the two OPEC disturbances, the failure of Penn Square bank, the stock market crash in 1987, the collapse of Long Term Capital Management in 1998, and the financial crisis of 2008–2009. If you look back to Figure 1.1 in Chapter 1, you'll see that the TED spread, the difference between the LIBOR rate and Treasury bills, also peaked during periods of financial stress.

Money market funds are mutual funds that invest in money market instruments and have become major sources of funding to that sector. The nearby box discusses the fallout of the credit crisis of 2008 on those funds.

2.2 The Bond Market

The bond market is composed of longer term borrowing or debt instruments than those that trade in the money market. This market includes Treasury notes and bonds, corporate bonds, municipal bonds, mortgage securities, and federal agency debt.

These instruments are sometimes said to comprise the *fixed-income capital market,* because most of them promise either a fixed stream of income or a stream of income that is determined according to a specific formula. In practice, these formulas can result in a flow of income that is far from fixed. Therefore, the term *fixed income* is probably not fully appropriate. It is simpler and more straightforward to call these securities either debt instruments or bonds.

Treasury Notes and Bonds

The U.S. government borrows funds in large part by selling **Treasury notes** and **Treasury bonds.** T-notes are issued with maturities ranging up to 10 years, while bonds are issued with maturities ranging from 10 to 30 years. Both notes and bonds may be issued in increments of $100 but far more commonly trade in denominations of $1,000. Both notes and bonds make semiannual interest payments called *coupon payments,* a name derived from precomputer days, when investors would literally clip coupons attached to the bond and present a coupon to receive the interest payment.

Figure 2.3 is a listing of Treasury issues. The bid price of the highlighted note, which matures in May 2019, is 99.8125. (This is the decimal version of 99104/128. The minimum *tick size,* or price increment in the Treasury-bond market, is generally 1/128 of a point.) Although bonds are typically traded in denominations of $1,000 par value, prices are quoted as a percentage of par. Thus, the bid price should be interpreted as 99.8125% of par, or $988.125 for the $1,000 par value bond. Similarly, the ask price at which the bond could be sold to a dealer is 99.8281% of par, or $998.281. The −.0859 change means that the closing price on this day fell by .0859% of par value (equivalently, by 11/128 of a point) from the previous day's close. Finally, the yield to maturity based on the ask price is .933%.

The **yield to maturity** reported in the last column is calculated by determining the semiannual yield and then doubling it, rather than compounding it for two half-year periods. This use of a simple interest technique to annualize means that the yield is quoted on an annual percentage rate (APR) basis rather than as an effective annual yield. The APR method in this context is also called the *bond equivalent yield.* We discuss the yield to maturity in more detail in Part Four.

 Concept Check **2.1**

What were the bid price, ask price, and yield to maturity of the 2% August 2025 Treasury bond displayed in Figure 2.3? What was its ask price the previous day?

LISTING OF TREASURY ISSUES

MATURITY	COUPON	BID	ASKED	CHG	ASKED YLD TO MAT
May 15, 2018	1.000	100.3984	100.4141	−0.0859	0.791
May 15, 2019	0.875	99.8125	99.8281	−0.0859	0.933
Feb 15, 2021	7.875	130.5781	130.5938	−0.2656	1.225
Aug 15, 2025	2.000	102.2813	102.2969	−0.3438	1.730
May 15, 2030	6.250	152.3984	152.4609	−0.7969	1.950
Nov 15, 2041	3.125	111.7891	111.8203	−0.8750	2.496
May 15, 2046	2.500	97.9922	98.0234	−0.9063	2.595

Figure 2.3 Listing of Treasury bonds and notes

Source: Compiled from data obtained from *The Wall Street Journal Online,* May 16, 2016.

Inflation-Protected Treasury Bonds

The best place to start building an investment portfolio is at the least risky end of the spectrum. Around the world, governments of many countries, including the United States, have issued bonds that are linked to an index of the cost of living in order to provide their citizens with an effective way to hedge inflation risk.

In the United States, inflation-protected Treasury bonds are called TIPS (Treasury Inflation Protected Securities). The principal amount on these bonds is adjusted in proportion to increases in the Consumer Price Index. Therefore, they provide a constant stream of income in real (inflation-adjusted) dollars. Yields on TIPS bonds should be interpreted as real or inflation-adjusted interest rates. We return to TIPS bonds in more detail in Chapter 14.

Federal Agency Debt

Some government agencies issue their own securities to finance their activities. These agencies usually are formed to channel credit to a particular sector of the economy that Congress believes might not receive adequate credit through normal private sources.

The major mortgage-related agencies are the Federal Home Loan Bank (FHLB), the Federal National Mortgage Association (FNMA, or Fannie Mae), the Government National Mortgage Association (GNMA, or Ginnie Mae), and the Federal Home Loan Mortgage Corporation (FHLMC, or Freddie Mac). The FHLB borrows money by issuing securities and lends this money to savings and loan institutions to be lent in turn to individuals borrowing for home mortgages.

Although the debt of federal agencies was never explicitly insured by the federal government, it had long been assumed that the government would assist an agency nearing default. Those beliefs were validated when Fannie Mae and Freddie Mac encountered severe financial distress in September 2008. With both firms on the brink of insolvency, the government stepped in, putting them both into conservatorship and assigning the Federal Housing Finance Agency to run the firms; however, it did in fact agree to make good on the firm's bonds.

International Bonds

Many firms borrow abroad and many investors buy bonds from foreign issuers. In addition to national capital markets, there is a thriving international capital market, largely centered in London.

A *Eurobond* is a bond denominated in a currency other than that of the country in which it is issued. For example, a dollar-denominated bond sold in Britain would be called a Eurodollar bond. Similarly, investors might speak of Euroyen bonds, yen-denominated bonds sold outside Japan. Because the European currency is called the euro, the term Eurobond may be confusing. It is best to think of them simply as international bonds.

In contrast to bonds that are issued in foreign currencies, many firms issue bonds in foreign countries but in the currency of the investor. For example, a Yankee bond is a dollar-denominated bond sold in the United States by a non-U.S. issuer. Similarly, Samurai bonds are yen-denominated bonds sold in Japan by non-Japanese issuers.

Municipal Bonds

Municipal bonds are issued by state and local governments. They are similar to Treasury and corporate bonds except that their interest income is exempt from federal income taxation. The interest income also is usually exempt from state and local taxation in the

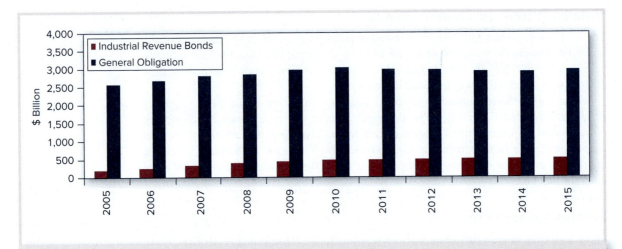

Figure 2.4 Tax-exempt debt outstanding

Source: *Flow of Funds Accounts of the United States,* Board of Governors of the Federal Reserve System, March, 2016.

issuing state. Capital gains taxes, however, must be paid on "munis" when the bonds mature or if they are sold for more than the investor's purchase price.

General obligation bonds are backed by the "full faith and credit" (i.e., the taxing power) of the issuer, while *revenue bonds* are issued to finance particular projects and are backed either by the revenues from that project or by the particular municipal agency operating the project. Typical issuers of revenue bonds are airports, hospitals, and turnpike or port authorities. Obviously, revenue bonds are riskier in terms of default than general obligation bonds. Figure 2.4 plots outstanding amounts of both types of municipal securities.

An *industrial development bond* is a revenue bond that is issued to finance commercial enterprises, such as the construction of a factory that can be operated by a private firm. In effect, these private-purpose bonds give the firm access to the municipality's ability to borrow at tax-exempt rates, and the federal government limits the amount of these bonds that may be issued.[2]

Like Treasury bonds, municipal bonds vary widely in maturity. A good deal of the debt issued is in the form of short-term *tax anticipation notes,* which raise funds to pay for expenses before actual collection of taxes. Other municipal debt is long term and used to fund large capital investments. Maturities range up to 30 years.

The key feature of municipal bonds is their tax-exempt status. Because investors pay neither federal nor state taxes on the interest proceeds, they are willing to accept lower yields on these securities.

An investor choosing between taxable and tax-exempt bonds must compare after-tax returns on each bond. An exact comparison requires a computation of after-tax rates of return that explicitly accounts for taxes on income and realized capital gains. In practice, there is a simpler rule of thumb. If we let t denote the investor's combined federal plus local marginal tax bracket and $r_{taxable}$ denote the total before-tax rate of return available

---

[2]A warning, however: Although interest on industrial development bonds usually is exempt from federal tax, it can be subject to the alternative minimum tax if the bonds are used to finance projects of for-profit companies.

on taxable bonds, then $r_{taxable}(1 - t)$ is the after-tax rate available on those securities.[3] If this value exceeds the rate on municipal bonds, r_{muni}, the investor does better holding the taxable bonds. Otherwise, the tax-exempt municipals provide higher after-tax returns.

One way to compare bonds is to determine the interest rate on taxable bonds that would be necessary to provide an after-tax return equal to that of municipals. To derive this value, we set after-tax yields equal and solve for the **equivalent taxable yield** of the tax-exempt bond. This is the rate a taxable bond must offer to match the after-tax yield on the tax-free municipal.

$$r_{taxable}(1 - t) = r_{muni} \tag{2.1}$$

or

$$r_{taxable} = r_{muni}/(1 - t) \tag{2.2}$$

Thus the equivalent taxable yield is simply the tax-free rate divided by $1 - t$. Table 2.2 presents equivalent taxable yields for several municipal yields and tax rates.

This table frequently appears in the marketing literature for tax-exempt mutual bond funds because it demonstrates to high-tax-bracket investors that municipal bonds offer highly attractive equivalent taxable yields. Each entry is calculated from Equation 2.2. If the equivalent taxable yield exceeds the actual yields offered on taxable bonds, the investor is better off after taxes holding municipal bonds. Notice that the equivalent taxable interest rate increases with the investor's tax bracket; the higher the bracket, the more valuable the tax-exempt feature of municipals. Thus high-tax-bracket investors tend to hold municipals.

We also can use Equation 2.1 or 2.2 to find the tax bracket at which investors are indifferent between taxable and tax-exempt bonds. The cutoff tax bracket is given by solving Equation 2.2 for the tax bracket at which after-tax yields are equal. Doing so, we find that

$$\text{Cutoff tax bracket} = 1 - \frac{r_{muni}}{r_{taxable}} \tag{2.3}$$

Thus the yield ratio $r_{muni}/r_{taxable}$ is a key determinant of the attractiveness of municipal bonds. The higher the yield ratio, the lower the cutoff tax bracket, and the more individuals will prefer to hold municipal debt.

Figure 2.5 plots the ratio of 20-year municipal debt yields to the yield on Baa-rated corporate debt. The default risk of these corporate and municipal bonds may be comparable,

Marginal Tax Rate	Tax-Exempt Yield				
	1%	2%	3%	4%	5%
20%	1.25%	2.50%	3.75%	5.00%	6.25%
30	1.43	2.86	4.29	5.71	7.14
40	1.67	3.33	5.00	6.67	8.33
50	2.00	4.00	6.00	8.00	10.00

Table 2.2

Equivalent taxable yields corresponding to various tax-exempt yields

[3]An approximation to the combined federal plus local tax rate is just the sum of the two rates. For example, if your federal tax rate is 28% and your state rate is 5%, your combined tax rate would be approximately 33%. A more precise approach would recognize that state taxes are deductible at the federal level. You owe federal taxes only on income net of state taxes. Therefore, for every dollar of income, your after-tax proceeds would be $(1 - t_{federal}) \times (1 - t_{state})$. In our example, your after-tax proceeds on each dollar earned would be $(1 - .28) \times (1 - .05) = .684$, which implies a combined tax rate of $1 - .684 = .316$, or 31.6%.

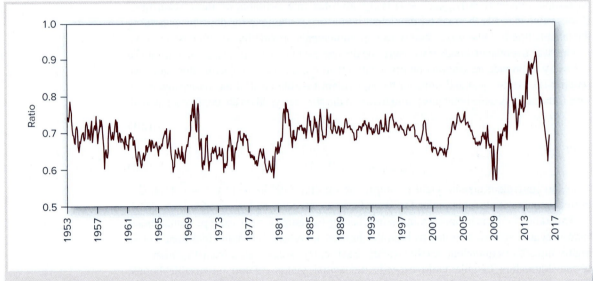

Figure 2.5 Ratio of yields on municipal debt to corporate Baa-rated debt

Source: Authors' calculations, using data from **www.federalreserve.gov/releases/h15/data.htm**.

but certainly will fluctuate over time. For example, the sharp run-up in the ratio in 2011 probably reflects increased concern at the time about the precarious financial condition of several states and municipalities, leading to higher credit spreads on their bonds.

Example 2.1   Taxable versus Tax-Exempt Yields

Figure 2.5 shows that for most of the last 30 years, the ratio of tax-exempt to taxable yields fluctuated around .70. What does this imply about the cutoff tax bracket above which tax-exempt bonds provide higher after-tax yields? Equation 2.3 shows that an investor whose tax bracket (federal plus local) exceeds $1 - .70 = .30$, or 30%, will derive a greater after-tax yield from municipals. As we pointed out, however, it is difficult to control precisely for differences in the risks of these bonds, so the cutoff tax bracket must be taken as approximate.

 Concept Check **2.2**

Suppose your tax bracket is 30%. Would you prefer to earn a 6% taxable return or a 4% tax-free return? What is the equivalent taxable yield of the 4% tax-free yield?

Corporate Bonds

Corporate bonds are the means by which private firms borrow money directly from the public. These bonds are similar in structure to Treasury issues—they typically pay semiannual coupons over their lives and return the face value to the bondholder at maturity. They differ most importantly from Treasury bonds in degree of risk. Default risk is a real consideration in the purchase of corporate bonds, and Chapter 14 discusses this issue in considerable detail. For now, we distinguish only among *secured bonds,* which have specific collateral backing them in the event of firm bankruptcy; unsecured bonds, called *debentures,* which have no collateral; and *subordinated debentures,* which have a lower priority claim to the firm's assets in the event of bankruptcy.

Corporate bonds sometimes come with options attached. *Callable bonds* give the firm the option to repurchase the bond from the holder at a stipulated call price. *Convertible bonds* give the bondholder the option to convert each bond into a stipulated number of shares of stock. These options are treated in more detail in Chapter 14.

Mortgages and Mortgage-Backed Securities

Because of the explosion in mortgage-backed securities, almost anyone can invest in a portfolio of mortgage loans, and these securities have become a major component of the fixed-income market. As described in Chapter 1, a *mortgage-backed security* is either an ownership claim in a pool of mortgages or an obligation that is secured by such a pool. Most pass-throughs have traditionally been comprised of *conforming mortgages,* which means that the loans must satisfy certain underwriting guidelines (standards for the creditworthiness of the borrower) before they may be purchased by Fannie Mae or Freddie Mac. In the years leading up to the financial crisis, however, a large amount of *subprime mortgages,* that is, riskier loans made to financially weaker borrowers, were bundled and sold by "private-label" issuers. Figure 2.6 illustrates the explosive growth of both agency and private-label mortgage-backed securities, at least until the crisis.

In an effort to make housing more affordable to low-income households, Fannie and Freddie had been encouraged to buy subprime mortgage securities. As we saw in Chapter 1, these loans turned out to be disastrous, with trillion-dollar losses spread among banks, hedge funds and other investors, and Freddie and Fannie, which lost billions of dollars on the subprime mortgage pools they had purchased. You can see from Figure 2.6 that starting in 2007, the market in private-label mortgage pass-throughs began to shrink rapidly.

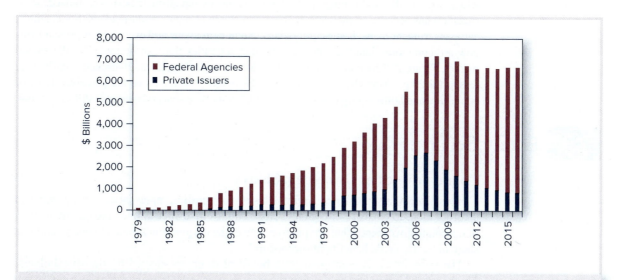

Figure 2.6 Mortgage-backed securities outstanding

Source: *Flow of Funds Accounts of the United States,* Board of Governors of the Federal Reserve System, March 2016.

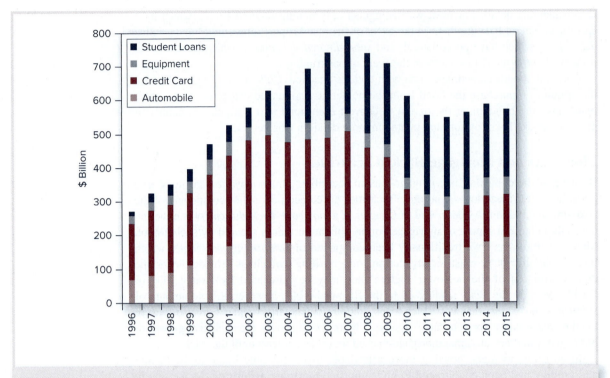

Figure 2.7 Asset-backed securities outstanding

Source: The Securities & Industry and Financial Markets Association, **www.sifma.org**.

Despite these troubles, few believe that securitization itself will cease, although practices in this market are likely to remain far more conservative than in previous years, particularly with respect to the credit standards that must be met by the ultimate borrower. Indeed, securitization has become an increasingly common staple of many credit markets. For example, car loans, student loans, home equity loans, credit card loans, and even debt of private firms now are commonly bundled into pass-through securities that can be traded in the capital market. Figure 2.7 documents the rapid growth of nonmortgage asset–backed securities, at least until 2007. After the financial crisis, the market contracted as the perceived risks of credit card and home equity loans skyrocketed, but the asset-backed market is still substantial.

2.3 | Equity Securities

Common Stock as Ownership Shares

Common stocks, also known as *equity securities* or **equities,** represent ownership shares in a corporation. Each share of common stock entitles its owner to one vote on any matters of corporate governance that are put to a vote at the corporation's annual meeting and to a share in the financial benefits of ownership.[4]

The corporation is controlled by a board of directors elected by the shareholders. The board, which meets only a few times each year, selects managers who actually run

[4]A corporation sometimes issues two classes of common stock, one bearing the right to vote, the other not. Because of its restricted rights, the nonvoting stock might sell for a lower price.

the corporation on a day-to-day basis. Managers have the authority to make most business decisions without the board's specific approval. The board's mandate is to oversee the management to ensure that it acts in the best interests of shareholders.

The members of the board are elected at the annual meeting. Shareholders who do not attend the annual meeting can vote by *proxy,* empowering another party to vote in their name. Management usually solicits the proxies of shareholders and normally gets a vast majority of these proxy votes. Thus, management usually has considerable discretion to run the firm as it sees fit—without daily oversight from the equityholders who actually own the firm.

We noted in Chapter 1 that such separation of ownership and control can give rise to "agency problems," in which managers pursue goals not in the best interests of shareholders. However, there are several mechanisms that alleviate these agency problems. Among these are compensation schemes that link the success of the manager to that of the firm; oversight by the board of directors as well as outsiders such as security analysts, creditors, or large institutional investors; the threat of a proxy contest in which unhappy shareholders attempt to replace the current management team; or the threat of a takeover by another firm.

The common stock of most large corporations can be bought or sold freely on one or more stock exchanges. A corporation whose stock is not publicly traded is said to be private. In most privately held corporations, the owners of the firm also take an active role in its management. Therefore, takeovers are generally not an issue.

Characteristics of Common Stock

The two most important characteristics of common stock as an investment are its **residual claim** and **limited liability** features.

Residual claim means that stockholders are the last in line of all those who have a claim on the assets and income of the corporation. In a liquidation of the firm's assets the shareholders have a claim to what is left after all other claimants such as the tax authorities, employees, suppliers, bondholders, and other creditors have been paid. For a firm not in liquidation, shareholders have claim to the part of operating income left over after interest and taxes have been paid. Management can either pay this residual as cash dividends to shareholders or reinvest it in the business to increase the value of the shares.

Limited liability means that the most shareholders can lose in the event of failure of the corporation is their original investment. Unlike owners of unincorporated businesses, whose creditors can lay claim to the personal assets of the owner (house, car, furniture), corporate shareholders may at worst have worthless stock. They are not personally liable for the firm's obligations.

 Concept Check **2.3**

a. If you buy 100 shares of IBM stock, to what are you entitled?

b. What is the most money you can make on this investment over the next year?

c. If you pay $150 per share, what is the most money you could lose over the year?

Stock Market Listings

Figure 2.8 presents key trading data for a small sample of stocks traded on the New York Stock Exchange. The NYSE is one of several markets in which investors may buy or sell shares of stock. We will examine these markets in detail in Chapter 3.

NAME	SYMBOL	CLOSE	NET CHG	VOLUME	52 WK HIGH	52 WK LOW	DIV	YIELD	P/E	YTD %CHG
Gap	GPS	21.81	0.14	4,948,832	40.64	21.11	0.92	4.22	9.82	–11.70
Gartner	IT	95.91	–1.50	587,975	97.98	77.80	....	....	46.33	5.74
GATX	GMT	44.23	0.03	407,499	57.93	33.53	1.60	3.62	8.90	3.95
Gazit-Globe	GZT	9.24	0.22	2,616	13.22	7.15	....	....	2.70	2.88
GCP Applied Technologies	GCP	22.45	–0.43	399,787	22.99	14.47	....	....	39.47	12.25
Genco Shipping&Trading	GNK	0.65	–0.12	276,030	7.85	0.45	....	....	....dd	–55.09
Gener8 Maritime	GNRT	7.02	–0.27	100,083	14.82	4.81	....	....	3.11	–25.71
Generac Holdings	GNRC	34.82	0.03	318,868	43.75	26.29	....	....	35.17	16.96
General Cable	BGC	15.35	–0.65	851,418	21.31	6.21	0.72	4.69	....dd	14.30
General Dynamics	GD	142.97	–0.47	1,375,410	153.76	121.61	3.04	2.13	15.39	4.08
General Electric	GE	29.87	–0.25	26,458,696	32.05	19.37	0.92	3.08	30.68	–4.11

Figure 2.8 Listing of stocks traded on the New York Stock Exchange

Source: Compiled from data from *The Wall Street Journal Online*, May 10, 2016.

To interpret Figure 2.8, consider the highlighted listing for General Electric. The table provides the ticker symbol (GE), the closing price of the stock ($29.87), and its change (−$.25) from the previous trading day. About 26.5 million shares of GE traded on this day. The listing also provides the highest and lowest price at which GE has traded in the last 52 weeks. The .92 value in the Dividend column means that the last quarterly dividend payment was $.23 per share, which is consistent with annual dividend payments of $.23 × 4 = $.92. This corresponds to an annual dividend yield (i.e., annual dividend per dollar paid for the stock) of .92/29.87 = .0308, or 3.08%.

The dividend yield is only part of the return on a stock investment. It ignores prospective **capital gains** (i.e., price increases) or losses. Low-dividend firms presumably offer greater prospects for capital gains, or investors would not be willing to hold these stocks in their portfolios. If you scan Figure 2.8, you will see that dividend yields vary widely across companies.

The P/E ratio, or **price–earnings ratio,** is the ratio of the current stock price to last year's earnings per share. The P/E ratio tells us how much stock purchasers must pay per dollar of earnings that the firm generates. For GE, the ratio of price to earnings is 30.68. The P/E ratio also varies widely across firms. Where the dividend yield and P/E ratio are not reported in Figure 2.8, the firms have zero dividends, or zero or negative earnings. We shall have much to say about P/E ratios in Chapter 18. Finally, we see that GE's stock price has decreased by 4.11% since the beginning of the year.

Preferred Stock

Preferred stock has features similar to both equity and debt. Like a bond, it promises to pay to its holder a fixed amount of income each year. In this sense, preferred stock is similar to an infinite-maturity bond, that is, a perpetuity. It also resembles a bond in that it does not convey voting power regarding the management of the firm. Preferred stock is an equity investment, however. The firm retains discretion to make the dividend payments to the preferred stockholders; it has no contractual obligation to pay those dividends. Instead, preferred dividends are usually *cumulative;* that is, unpaid dividends cumulate and must be paid in full before any dividends may be paid to holders of common stock. In contrast, the firm does have a contractual obligation to make the interest payments on the debt. Failure to make these payments sets off corporate bankruptcy proceedings.

Preferred stock also differs from bonds in terms of its tax treatment for the firm. Because preferred stock payments are treated as dividends rather than interest, they are not tax-deductible expenses for the firm. This disadvantage is somewhat offset by the fact that corporations may exclude 70% of dividends received from domestic corporations in the computation of their taxable income. Preferred stocks therefore make desirable fixed-income investments for some corporations.

Even though preferred stock ranks after bonds in terms of the priority of its claims to the assets of the firm in the event of corporate bankruptcy, it often sells at lower yields than corporate bonds. Presumably, this reflects the value of the 70% dividend exclusion, because the higher risk of preferred stock would tend to result in higher yields than those offered by bonds. Individual investors, who cannot use the tax exclusion, generally will find preferred stock yields unattractive relative to those on other available assets.

Preferred stock is issued in variations similar to those of corporate bonds. It may be callable by the issuing firm, in which case it is said to be *redeemable*. It also may be convertible into common stock at some specified conversion ratio. Adjustable-rate preferred stock is another variation that, like adjustable-rate bonds, ties the dividend to current market interest rates.

Depositary Receipts

American Depositary Receipts, or ADRs, are certificates traded in U.S. markets that represent ownership in shares of a foreign company. Each ADR may correspond to ownership of a fraction of a foreign share, one share, or several shares of the foreign corporation. ADRs were created to make it easier for foreign firms to satisfy U.S. security registration requirements. They are the most common way for U.S. investors to invest in and trade the shares of foreign corporations.

2.4   Stock and Bond Market Indexes

Stock Market Indexes

The daily performance of the Dow Jones Industrial Average is a staple portion of the evening news report. Although the Dow is the best-known measure of the performance of the stock market, it is only one of several indicators. Other more broadly based indexes are computed and published daily. In addition, several indexes of bond market performance are widely available.

The ever-increasing role of international trade and investments has made indexes of foreign financial markets part of the general news as well. Thus foreign stock exchange indexes such as the Nikkei Average of Tokyo and the Financial Times index of London are fast becoming household names.

Dow Jones Industrial Average

The Dow Jones Industrial Average (DJIA) of 30 large, "blue-chip" corporations has been computed since 1896. Its long history probably accounts for its preeminence in the public mind. (The average covered only 20 stocks until 1928.)

Originally, the DJIA was calculated as the average price of the stocks included in the index. Thus, one would add up the prices of the 30 stocks in the index and divide by 30. The percentage change in the DJIA would then be the percentage change in the average price of the 30 shares.

This procedure means that the percentage change in the DJIA measures the return (excluding dividends) on a portfolio that invests one share in each of the 30 stocks in the index. The value of such a portfolio (holding one share of each stock in the index) is the sum of the 30 prices. Because the percentage change in the *average* of the 30 prices is the same as the percentage change in the *sum* of the 30 prices, the index and the portfolio have the same percentage change each day.

Because the Dow corresponds to a portfolio that holds one share of each component stock, the investment in each company in that portfolio is proportional to the company's share price. Therefore, the Dow is called a **price-weighted average.**

Example 2.2   Price-Weighted Average

Consider the data in Table 2.3 for a hypothetical two-stock version of the Dow Jones Average. Let's compare the changes in the value of the portfolio holding one share of each firm and the price-weighted index. Stock ABC starts at $25 a share and increases to $30. Stock XYZ starts at $100, but falls to $90.

Portfolio:	Initial value = $25 + $100 = $125
	Final value = $30 + $90 = $120
	Percentage change in portfolio value = −5/125 = −.04 = −4%
Index:	Initial index value = (25 + 100)/2 = 62.5
	Final index value = (30 + 90)/2 = 60
	Percentage change in index = −2.5/62.5 = −.04 = −4%

The portfolio and the index have identical 4% declines in value.

Notice that price-weighted averages give higher-priced shares more weight in determining performance of the index. For example, although ABC increased by 20%, while XYZ fell by only 10%, the index dropped in value. This is because the 20% increase in ABC represented a smaller price gain ($5 per share) than the 10% decrease in XYZ ($10 per share). The "Dow portfolio" has four times as much invested in XYZ as in ABC because XYZ's price is four times that of ABC. Therefore, XYZ dominates the average. We conclude that a high-price stock can dominate a price-weighted average.

Table 2.3

Data to construct stock price indexes

Stock	Initial Price	Final Price	Shares (million)	Initial Value of Outstanding Stock ($ million)	Final Value of Outstanding Stock ($ million)
ABC	$ 25	$30	20	$500	$600
XYZ	100	90	1	100	90
Total				$600	$690

You might wonder why the DJIA is now (in late 2016) at a level of about 19,000 if it is supposed to be the average price of the 30 stocks in the index. The DJIA no longer equals the average price of the 30 stocks because the averaging procedure is adjusted whenever a stock splits or pays a stock dividend of more than 10%, or when one company in the group of 30 industrial firms is replaced by another. When these events occur, the divisor used to compute the "average price" is adjusted so as to leave the index unaffected by the event.

Example 2.3   Splits and Price-Weighted Averages

Suppose XYZ were to split two for one so that its share price fell to $50. We would not want the average to fall, as that would incorrectly indicate a fall in the general level of market prices. Following a split, the divisor must be reduced to a value that leaves the average unaffected. Table 2.4 illustrates this point. The initial share price of XYZ, which was $100 in Table 2.3, falls to $50 if the stock splits at the beginning of the period. Notice that the number of shares outstanding doubles, leaving the market value of the total shares unaffected.

We find the new divisor as follows. The index value before the stock split = 125/2 = 62.5. We must find a new divisor, d, that leaves the index unchanged after XYZ splits and its price falls to $50. Therefore, we solve for d in the following equation:

$$\frac{\text{Price of ABC} + \text{Price of XYZ}}{d} = \frac{25 + 50}{d} = 62.5$$

which implies that the divisor must fall from its original value of 2.0 to a new value of 1.20.

Because the split changes the price of stock XYZ, it also changes the relative weights of the two stocks in the price-weighted average. Therefore, the return of the index is affected by the split.

At period-end, ABC will sell for $30, while XYZ will sell for $45, representing the same negative 10% return it was assumed to earn in Table 2.3. The new value of the price-weighted average is (30 + 45)/1.20 = 62.5, the same as its value at the start of the year; therefore, the rate of return is zero, rather than the −4% return that we calculated in the absence of a split.

The split reduces the relative weight of XYZ because its initial price is lower; because XYZ is the poorer performing stock, the performance of the average is higher. This example illustrates that the implicit weighting scheme of a price-weighted average is somewhat arbitrary, being determined by the prices rather than by the outstanding market values (price per share times number of shares) of the shares in the average.

Table 2.4

Data to construct stock price indexes after a stock split

Stock	Initial Price	Final Price	Shares (million)	Initial Value of Outstanding Stock ($ million)	Final Value of Outstanding Stock ($ million)
ABC	$25	$30	20	$500	$600
XYZ	50	45	2	100	90
Total				$600	$690

In the same way that the divisor is updated for stock splits, if one firm is dropped from the average and another firm with a different price is added, the divisor has to be updated to leave the average unchanged by the substitution. By 2016, the divisor for the Dow Jones Industrial Average had fallen to a value of about .146.

Because the Dow Jones averages are based on small numbers of firms, care must be taken to ensure that they are representative of the broad market. As a result, the composition of the average is changed every so often to reflect changes in the economy. Table 2.5 presents the composition of the Dow industrials in 1928 as well as its composition as of mid-2016. The table presents striking evidence of the changes in the U.S. economy in the last 85 years. Many of the "bluest of the blue chip" companies in 1928 no longer exist, and the industries that were the backbone of the economy in 1928 have given way to some that could not have been imagined at the time.

Dow Industrials in 1928	Current Dow Companies	Ticker Symbol	Industry	Year Added to Index
Wright Aeronautical	3M	MMM	Diversified industrials	1976
Allied Chemical	American Express	AXP	Consumer finance	1982
North American	Apple	AAPL	Electronic equipment	2015
Victor Talking Machine	Boeing	BA	Aerospace and defense	1987
International Nickel	Caterpillar	CAT	Construction	1991
International Harvester	Chevron	CVX	Oil and gas	2008
Westinghouse	Cisco Systems	CSCO	Construction	1991
Texas Gulf Sulphur	Coca-Cola	KO	Beverages	1987
General Electric	DuPont	DD	Chemicals	1935
American Tobacco	ExxonMobil	XOM	Oil and gas	1928
Texas Corp	General Electric	GE	Diversified industrials	1907
Standard Oil (NJ)	Goldman Sachs	GS	Investment banking	2013
Sears Roebuck	Home Depot	HD	Home improvement retailers	1999
General Motors	Intel	INTC	Semiconductors	1999
Chrysler	IBM	IBM	Computer services	1979
Atlantic Refining	Johnson & Johnson	JNJ	Pharmaceuticals	1997
Paramount Publix	JPMorgan Chase	JPM	Banking	1991
Bethlehem Steel	McDonald's	MCD	Restaurants	1985
General Railway Signal	Merck	MRK	Pharmaceuticals	1979
Mack Trucks	Microsoft	MSFT	Software	1999
Union Carbide	Nike	NKE	Apparel	2013
American Smelting	Pfizer	PFE	Pharmaceuticals	2004
American Can	Procter & Gamble	PG	Household products	1932
Postum Inc.	Travelers	TRV	Insurance	2009
Nash Motors	UnitedHealth Group	UNH	Health insurance	2012
American Sugar	United Technologies	UTX	Aerospace	1939
Goodrich	Verizon	VZ	Telecommunications	2004
Radio Corp	Visa	V	Electronic payments	2013
Woolworth	Wal-Mart	WMT	Retailers	1997
U.S. Steel	Walt Disney	DIS	Broadcasting and entertainment	1991

Table 2.5

Companies included in the Dow Jones Industrial Average: 1928 and 2016

 Concept Check **2.4**

Suppose the price of XYZ in Table 2.3 increases to $110, while ABC falls to $20. Find the percentage change in the price-weighted average of these two stocks. Compare that to the percentage return of a portfolio holding one share in each company.

The Standard & Poor's 500 Index

The Standard & Poor's Composite 500 (S&P 500) stock index represents an improvement over the Dow Jones Averages in two ways. First, it is a more broadly based index of 500 firms. Second, it is a **market-value-weighted index.** In the case of the firms XYZ and ABC in Example 2.2, the S&P 500 would give ABC five times the weight given to XYZ because the market value of its outstanding equity is five times larger, $500 million versus $100 million.

The S&P 500 is computed by calculating the total market value of the 500 firms in the index and the total market value of those firms on the previous day of trading. The percentage increase in the total market value from one day to the next represents the increase in the index. The rate of return of the index equals the rate of return that would be earned by an investor holding a portfolio of all 500 firms in the index in proportion to their market values, except that the index does not reflect cash dividends paid by those firms.

Actually, most indexes today use a modified version of market-value weights. Rather than weighting by total market value, they weight by the market value of *free float,* that is, by the value of shares that are freely tradable among investors. For example, this procedure does not count shares held by founding families or governments. These shares are effectively not available for investors to purchase. The distinction is more important in Japan and Europe, where a higher fraction of shares are held in such non-traded portfolios.

Example 2.4   Value-Weighted Indexes

To illustrate how value-weighted indexes are computed, look again at Table 2.3. The final value of all outstanding stock in our two-stock universe is $690 million. The initial value was $600 million. Therefore, if the initial level of a market-value-weighted index of stocks ABC and XYZ were set equal to an arbitrarily chosen starting value such as 100, the index value at year-end would be $100 \times (690/600) = 115$. The increase in the index reflects the 15% return earned on a portfolio consisting of those two stocks held in proportion to outstanding market values.

Unlike the price-weighted index, the value-weighted index gives more weight to ABC. Whereas the price-weighted index fell because it was dominated by higher-price XYZ, the value-weighted index rises because it gives more weight to ABC, the stock with the higher total market value.

Note also from Tables 2.3 and 2.4 that market-value-weighted indexes are unaffected by stock splits. The total market value of the outstanding XYZ stock decreases from $100 million to $90 million regardless of the stock split, thereby rendering the split irrelevant to the performance of the index.

 Concept Check **2.5**

Reconsider companies XYZ and ABC from Concept Check 2.4. Calculate the percentage change in the market-value-weighted index. Compare that to the rate of return of a portfolio that holds $500 of ABC stock for every $100 of XYZ stock (i.e., an index portfolio).

A nice feature of both market-value-weighted and price-weighted indexes is that they reflect the returns to straightforward portfolio strategies. If one were to buy shares in each component firm in the index in proportion to its outstanding market value, the value-weighted index would perfectly track capital gains on the underlying portfolio. Similarly, a price-weighted index tracks the returns on a portfolio comprised of an equal number of shares of each firm.

Investors today can easily buy market indexes for their portfolios. One way is to purchase shares in mutual funds that hold shares in proportion to their representation in the S&P 500 or another index. These **index funds** yield a return equal to that of the index and so provide a low-cost passive investment strategy for equity investors. Another approach is to purchase an *exchange-traded fund,* or ETF, which is a portfolio of shares that can be bought or sold as a unit, just as one can buy or sell a single share of stock. Available ETFs range from portfolios that track extremely broad global market indexes all the way to narrow industry indexes. We discuss both mutual funds and ETFs in detail in Chapter 4.

Other U.S. Market-Value Indexes

The New York Stock Exchange publishes a market-value-weighted composite index of all NYSE-listed stocks, in addition to subindexes for industrial, utility, transportation, and financial stocks. These indexes are even more broadly based than the S&P 500. NASDAQ computes a Composite index of more than 3,000 firms traded on the NASDAQ market. The NASDAQ 100 is a subset of the larger firms in the Composite Index, but it accounts for a large fraction of its total market capitalization.

The ultimate U.S. equity index so far computed is the Wilshire 5000 index of the market value of essentially all actively traded stocks in the U.S. At one point, it included more than 5,000 stocks, but today, there are fewer than 4,000 stocks in the index. A similar comprehensive index is published by CRSP (the Center for Research in Security Prices at the University of Chicago).

Equally Weighted Indexes

Market performance is sometimes measured by an equally weighted average of the returns of each stock in an index. Such an averaging technique, by placing equal weight on each return, corresponds to an implicit portfolio strategy that invests equal dollar values in each stock. This is in contrast to both price weighting (which requires equal numbers of shares of each stock) and market-value weighting (which requires investments in proportion to outstanding value).

Unlike price- or market-value-weighted indexes, equally weighted indexes do not correspond to buy-and-hold portfolio strategies. Suppose that you start with equal dollar investments in the two stocks of Table 2.3, ABC and XYZ. Because ABC increases in value by 20% over the year while XYZ decreases by 10%, your portfolio no longer is equally weighted. It is now more heavily invested in ABC. To reset the portfolio to equal weights, you would need to rebalance: Sell off some ABC stock and/or purchase more XYZ stock. Such rebalancing would be necessary to align the return on your portfolio with that on the equally weighted index.

Foreign and International Stock Market Indexes

Development in financial markets worldwide includes the construction of indexes for these markets. Among these are the Nikkei (Japan), FTSE (U.K.; pronounced "footsie"), DAX (Germany), Hang Seng (Hong Kong), and TSX (Canada).

Regional Indexes		Countries	
Developed Markets	**Emerging Markets**	**Developed Markets**	**Emerging Markets**
EAFE (Europe, Australia, Far East)	Emerging Markets (EM)	Australia	Brazil
Europe	EM Asia	Austria	Chile
European Monetary Union (EMU)	EM Far East	Belgium	China
Far East	EM Latin America	Canada	Colombia
Kokusai (World excluding Japan)	EM Eastern Europe	Denmark	Czech Republic
Nordic countries	EM Europe	Finland	Egypt
North America	EM Europe and Middle East	France	Greece
Pacific		Germany	Hungary
World		Hong Kong	India
World excluding U.S.		Ireland	Indonesia
		Israel	Korea
		Italy	Malaysia
		Japan	Mexico
		Netherlands	Peru
		New Zealand	Philippines
		Norway	Poland
		Portugal	Russia
		Singapore	South Africa
		Spain	Taiwan
		Sweden	Thailand
		Switzerland	Turkey
		U.K.	
		U.S.	

Table 2.6

Sample of MSCI stock indexes
Source: MSCI, **www.msci.com**.

A leader in the construction of international indexes has been MSCI (Morgan Stanley Capital International), which computes dozens of country indexes and several regional indexes. Table 2.6 presents many of the indexes computed by MSCI.

Bond Market Indicators

Just as stock market indexes provide guidance concerning the performance of the overall stock market, several bond market indicators measure the performance of various categories of bonds. The three most well-known indexes are those of Merrill Lynch, Barclays, and the Citi Broad Investment Grade Bond Index. Figure 2.9 shows the components of the U.S. fixed-income market in 2016.

The major problem with bond market indexes is that true rates of return on many bonds are difficult to compute because the infrequency with which the bonds trade makes reliable up-to-date prices difficult to obtain. In practice, some prices must be estimated from bond-valuation models. These "matrix" prices may differ from true market values.

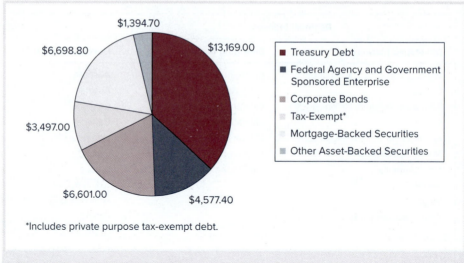

*Includes private purpose tax-exempt debt.

Figure 2.9 The U.S. fixed-income market (values in $ billions)

Source: *Flow of Funds Accounts of the United States: Flows & Outstandings,* Board of Governors of the Federal Reserve System, March 2016.

2.5   Derivative Markets

Futures, options, and related derivatives contracts provide payoffs that depend on the values of other variables such as commodity prices, bond and stock prices, interest rates, or market index values. For this reason, these instruments sometimes are called **derivative assets:** Their values *derive from* the values of other assets. These assets are also called **contingent claims** because their payoffs are contingent on the value of other values.

Options

A **call option** gives its holder the right to purchase an asset for a specified price, called the **exercise** or **strike price,** on or before a specified expiration date. For example, a July call option on IBM stock with an exercise price of $150 entitles its owner to purchase IBM stock for a price of $150 at any time up to and including the expiration date in July. Each option contract is for the purchase of 100 shares. However, quotations are made on a per-share basis. The holder of the call need not exercise the option; it will be profitable to exercise only if the market value of the asset that may be purchased exceeds the exercise price.

When the market price exceeds the exercise price, the option holder may "call away" the asset for the exercise price and reap a payoff equal to the difference between the stock price and the exercise price. Otherwise, the option will be left unexercised. If not exercised before the expiration date of the contract, the option simply expires and no longer has value. Calls therefore provide greater profits when stock prices increase and thus represent bullish investment vehicles.

In contrast, a **put option** gives its holder the right to *sell* an asset for a specified exercise price on or before a specified expiration date. A July put on IBM with an exercise price of $150 thus entitles its owner to sell IBM stock to the put writer at a price of $150 at any time before expiration in July, even if the market price of IBM is lower than $150. Whereas profits on call options increase when the asset increases in value, profits on put options

Expiration	Strike	Call	Put
June	145	6.60	1.57
June	150	3.31	3.30
June	155	1.27	6.53
July	145	7.73	2.58
July	150	4.43	4.42
July	155	2.28	7.30

Table 2.7

Prices of stock options on IBM, May 10, 2016

Note: IBM stock on this day was $149.97.
Source: Compiled from data downloaded from Yahoo! Finance, May 10, 2016.

increase when the asset value falls. The put is exercised only if its holder can deliver an asset worth less than the exercise price in return for the exercise price.

Table 2.7 presents prices of IBM options on May 10, 2016. The price of IBM shares on this date was $149.97. The first two columns give the expiration month and exercise (or strike) price for each option. We have included listings for call and put options with exercise prices of $145, $150, and $155 per share and with expiration dates in June and July 2016.

For example, the July 2016 expiration call with an exercise price of $150 last traded at $4.43, meaning that an option to purchase one share of IBM at an exercise price of $150 sold for $4.43. Each option *contract* (on 100 shares) therefore cost $443.

Notice that the prices of call options decrease as the exercise price increases. For example, the July expiration call with exercise price $155 costs only $2.28. This makes sense, because the right to purchase a share at a higher price is less valuable. Conversely, put prices increase with the exercise price. The right to sell IBM at a price of $150 in July costs $4.42, while the right to sell at $155 costs $7.30.

Option prices also increase with time until expiration. Clearly, one would rather have the right to buy IBM for $150 at any time until July rather than at any time until June. Not surprisingly, this shows up in a higher price for the longer expiration options. For example, the call with exercise price $150 expiring in July sells for $4.43 compared to only $3.31 for the June call.

 Concept Check **2.6**

What would be the profit or loss per share to an investor who bought the June 2016 expiration IBM call option with exercise price $150 if the stock price at the expiration date is $157? What about a purchaser of the put option with the same exercise price and expiration?

Futures Contracts

A **futures contract** calls for delivery of an asset (or in some cases, its cash value) at a specified delivery or maturity date for an agreed-upon price, called the futures price, to be paid at contract maturity. The *long position* is held by the trader who commits to purchasing the asset on the delivery date. The trader who takes the *short position* commits to delivering the asset at contract maturity.

Table 2.8

Corn futures prices
on the Chicago
Mercantile Exchange,
May 10, 2016

Maturity Date	Futures Price
July 2016	$3.81
September 2016	3.83
December 2016	3.88
March 2017	3.96
May 2017	4.02
July 2017	4.07

Source: **www.cmegroup.com**.

Table 2.8 presents corn futures contracts on the Chicago Mercantile Exchange on May 10, 2016. Each contract calls for delivery of 5,000 bushels of corn. The first entry is for the nearest term or "front" contract, with maturity in July 2016. The futures price for delivery in May was $3.81 per bushel.

The trader holding the long position profits from price increases. Suppose that at contract maturity, corn is selling for $3.83 per bushel. The long position trader who entered the contract at the futures price of $3.81 on May 10 would pay the previously agreed-upon $3.81 for each bushel of corn, which at contract maturity would be worth $3.83.

Because each contract calls for delivery of 5,000 bushels, the profit to the long position would equal $5,000 \times (\$3.83 - \$3.81) = \$1,000$. Conversely, the short position must deliver 5,000 bushels for the previously agreed-upon futures price. The short position's loss equals the long position's profit.

The right to purchase the asset at an agreed-upon price, as opposed to the obligation, distinguishes call options from long positions in futures contracts. A futures contract *obliges* the long position to purchase the asset at the futures price; the call option, in contrast, *conveys the right* to purchase the asset at the exercise price. The purchase will be made only if it yields a profit.

Clearly, a holder of a call has a better position than the holder of a long position on a futures contract with a futures price equal to the option's exercise price. This advantage, of course, comes only at a price. Call options must be purchased; futures contracts are entered into without cost. The purchase price of an option is called the *premium*. It represents the compensation the purchaser of the call must pay for the ability to exercise the option only when it is profitable to do so. Similarly, the difference between a put option and a short futures position is the right, as opposed to the obligation, to sell an asset at an agreed-upon price.

SUMMARY

1. Money market securities are very short-term debt obligations. They are usually highly marketable and have relatively low credit risk. Their low maturities and low credit risk ensure minimal capital gains or losses. These securities trade in large denominations, but they may be purchased indirectly through money market funds.

2. Much of U.S. government borrowing is in the form of Treasury bonds and notes. These are coupon-paying bonds usually issued at or near par value. Treasury notes and bonds are similar in design to coupon-paying corporate bonds.

3. Municipal bonds are distinguished largely by their tax-exempt status. Interest payments (but not capital gains) on these securities are exempt from federal income taxes. The equivalent taxable yield offered by a municipal bond equals $r_{muni}/(1 - t)$, where r_{muni} is the municipal yield and t is the investor's tax bracket.

4. Mortgage pass-through securities are pools of mortgages sold in one package. Owners of pass-throughs receive the principal and interest payments made by the borrowers. The originator that issued the mortgage merely services it and "passes through" the payments to the purchasers of the mortgage. A federal agency may guarantee the payments of interest and principal on

mortgages pooled into its pass-through securities, but these guarantees are absent in private-label pass-throughs.

5. Common stock is an ownership share in a corporation. Each share entitles its owner to one vote on matters of corporate governance and to a prorated share of the dividends paid to shareholders. Stock, or equity, owners are the residual claimants on the income earned by the firm.

6. Preferred stock usually pays fixed dividends for the life of the firm; it is a perpetuity. A firm's failure to pay the dividend due on preferred stock, however, does not precipitate corporate bankruptcy. Instead, unpaid dividends simply cumulate. Variants of preferred stock include convertible and adjustable-rate issues.

7. Many stock market indexes measure the performance of the overall market. The Dow Jones averages, the oldest and best-known indicators, are price-weighted indexes. Today, many broad-based, market-value-weighted indexes are computed daily. These include the Standard & Poor's 500 stock index, the NYSE index, the NASDAQ index, the Wilshire 5000 index, and indexes of many non-U.S. stock markets.

8. A call option is a right to purchase an asset at a stipulated exercise price on or before an expiration date. A put option is the right to sell an asset at some exercise price. Calls increase in value while puts decrease in value as the price of the underlying asset increases.

9. A futures contract is an obligation to buy or sell an asset at a stipulated futures price on a maturity date. The long position, which commits to purchasing, gains if the asset value increases while the short position, which commits to delivering, loses.

KEY TERMS

money market	London Interbank Offered	price–earnings ratio
capital markets	Rate (LIBOR)	preferred stock
ask price	Treasury notes	price-weighted average
bid price	Treasury bonds	market-value-weighted index
bid–ask spread	yield to maturity	index funds
certificate of deposit	municipal bonds	derivative assets
commercial paper	equivalent taxable yield	(or contingent claims)
banker's acceptance	equities	call option
Eurodollars	residual claim	exercise (or strike) price
repurchase agreements	limited liability	put option
federal funds	capital gains	futures contract

KEY EQUATIONS

Equivalent taxable yield: $\dfrac{r_{muni}}{1 - \text{tax rate}}$, where r_{muni} is the rate on tax-free municipal debt

Cutoff tax rate (for indifference to taxable versus tax-free bonds): $1 - \dfrac{r_{muni}}{r_{taxable}}$

PROBLEM SETS

1. In what ways is preferred stock like long-term debt? In what ways is it like equity?

2. Why are money market securities sometimes referred to as "cash equivalents"?

3. Which of the following *correctly* describes a repurchase agreement?

   a. The sale of a security with a commitment to repurchase the same security at a specified future date and a designated price.

   b. The sale of a security with a commitment to repurchase the same security at a future date left unspecified, at a designated price.

   c. The purchase of a security with a commitment to purchase more of the same security at a specified future date.

4. What would you expect to happen to the spread between yields on commercial paper and Treasury bills if the economy were to enter a steep recession?

5. What are the key differences between common stock, preferred stock, and corporate bonds?

6. Why are high-tax-bracket investors more inclined to invest in municipal bonds than low-bracket investors?

7. Turn back to Figure 2.3 and look at the Treasury bond maturing in November 2041.

   a. How much would you have to pay to purchase one of these bonds?
   b. What is its coupon rate?
   c. What is the yield to maturity of the bond?

8. Suppose investors can earn a return of 2% per 6 months on a Treasury note with 6 months remaining until maturity. What price would you expect a 6-month maturity Treasury bill to sell for?

9. Find the after-tax return to a corporation that buys a share of preferred stock at $40, sells it at year-end at $40, and receives a $4 year-end dividend. The firm is in the 30% tax bracket.

10. Turn to Figure 2.8 and look at the listing for General Dynamics.

    a. How many shares could you buy for $5,000?
    b. What would be your annual dividend income from those shares?
    c. What must be General Dynamics' earnings per share?
    d. What was the firm's closing price on the day before the listing?

11. Consider the three stocks in the following table. P_t represents price at time t, and Q_t represents shares outstanding at time t. Stock C splits two for one in the last period.

	P_0	Q_0	P_1	Q_1	P_2	Q_2
A	90	100	95	100	95	100
B	50	200	45	200	45	200
C	100	200	110	200	55	400

   a. Calculate the rate of return on a price-weighted index of the three stocks for the first period ($t = 0$ to $t = 1$).
   b. What must happen to the divisor for the price-weighted index in year 2?
   c. Calculate the rate of return for the second period ($t = 1$ to $t = 2$).

12. Using the data in the previous problem, calculate the first-period rates of return on the following indexes of the three stocks:

    a. A market-value-weighted index.
    b. An equally weighted index.

13. An investor is in a 30% tax bracket. If corporate bonds offer 9% yields, what must municipals offer for the investor to prefer them to corporate bonds?

14. Find the equivalent taxable yield of a short-term municipal bond currently offering yields of 4% for tax brackets of (a) zero, (b) 10%, (c) 20%, and (d) 30%.

15. What problems would confront a mutual fund trying to create an index fund tied to an equally weighted index of a broad stock market?

16. Which security should sell at a greater price?

    a. A 10-year Treasury bond with a 4% coupon rate versus a 10-year T-bond with a 5% coupon.
    b. A 3-month expiration call option with an exercise price of $40 versus a 3-month call on the same stock with an exercise price of $35.
    c. A put option on a stock selling at $50, or a put option on another stock selling at $60 (all other relevant features of the stocks and options may be assumed to be identical).

17. Look at the futures listings for the corn contract in Table 2.8. Suppose you buy one contract for March 2017 delivery. If the contract closes in March at a level of 4.06, what will your profit be?

18. Turn back to Table 2.7 and look at the IBM options. Suppose you buy a June 2016 expiration call option with exercise price $150.

   a. Suppose the stock price in June is $152. Will you exercise your call? What is the profit on your position?
   b. What if you had bought the June call with exercise price $145?
   c. What if you had bought a June put with exercise price $155?

19. Why do call options with exercise prices greater than the price of the underlying stock sell for positive prices?

20. Both a call and a put currently are traded on stock XYZ; both have strike prices of $50 and expirations of 6 months. What will be the profit to an investor who buys the call for $4 in the following scenarios for stock prices in 6 months? What will be the profit in each scenario to an investor who buys the put for $6?

   a. $40
   b. $45
   c. $50
   d. $55
   e. $60

21. Explain the difference between a put option and a short position in a futures contract.

22. Explain the difference between a call option and a long position in a futures contract.

---

1. A firm's preferred stock often sells at yields below its bonds because

   a. Preferred stock generally carries a higher agency rating.
   b. Owners of preferred stock have a prior claim on the firm's earnings.
   c. Owners of preferred stock have a prior claim on a firm's assets in the event of liquidation.
   d. Corporations owning stock may exclude from income taxes most of the dividend income they receive.

CFA®
PROBLEMS

2. A municipal bond carries a coupon of 6.75% and is trading at par. What is the equivalent taxable yield to a taxpayer in a combined federal plus state 34% tax bracket?

3. Which is the *most risky* transaction to undertake in the stock index option markets if the stock market is expected to increase substantially after the transaction is completed?

   a. Write a call option.
   b. Write a put option.
   c. Buy a call option.
   d. Buy a put option.

4. Short-term municipal bonds currently offer yields of 4%, while comparable taxable bonds pay 5%. Which gives you the higher after-tax yield if your tax bracket is:

   a. Zero
   b. 10%
   c. 20%
   d. 30%

5. The coupon rate on a tax-exempt bond is 5.6%, and the rate on a taxable bond is 8%. Both bonds sell at par. At what tax bracket (marginal tax rate) would an investor be indifferent between the two bonds?

SOLUTIONS TO CONCEPT CHECKS

1. The bid price of the bond is 102.2813% of par, or $1,022.813. The asked price is 102.2969 or $1022.969. This asked price corresponds to a yield of 1.730%. The ask price decreased .3438 from its level yesterday, so the ask price then must have been 102.6407, or $1,026.407.

2. A 6% taxable return is equivalent to an after-tax return of $6(1 - .30) = 4.2\%$. Therefore, you would be better off in the taxable bond. The equivalent taxable yield of the tax-free bond is $4/(1 - .30) = 5.71\%$. So a taxable bond would have to pay a 5.71% yield to provide the same after-tax return as a tax-free bond offering a 4% yield.

3. *a.* You are entitled to a prorated share of IBM's dividend payments and to vote in any of IBM's stockholder meetings.

    b. Your potential gain is unlimited because IBM's stock price has no upper bound.

    c. Your outlay was $150 \times 100 = \$15,000$. Because of limited liability, this is the most you can lose.

4. The price-weighted index increases from 62.5 [i.e., $(100 + 25)/2$] to 65 [i.e., $(110 + 20)/2$], a gain of 4%. An investment of one share in each company requires an outlay of $125 that would increase in value to $130, for a return of 4% (i.e., 5/125), which equals the return to the price-weighted index.

5. The market-value-weighted index return is calculated by computing the increase in the value of the stock portfolio. The portfolio of the two stocks starts with an initial value of $100 million + $500 million = $600 million and falls in value to $110 million + $400 million = $510 million, a loss of 90/600 = .15, or 15%. The index portfolio return is a weighted average of the returns on each stock with weights of ⅙ on XYZ and ⅚ on ABC (weights proportional to relative investments). Because the return on XYZ is 10%, while that on ABC is −20%, the index portfolio return is ⅙ × 10% + ⅚ × (−20%) = −15%, equal to the return on the market-value-weighted index.

6. The payoff to the call option is $7 per share at expiration. The option cost is $3.31 per share. The dollar profit is therefore $3.69. The put option expires worthless. Therefore, the investor's loss is the cost of the put, or $3.30.

How Securities Are Traded

3

THIS CHAPTER WILL provide you with a broad introduction to the many venues and procedures available for trading securities in the United States and international markets. We will see that trading mechanisms range from direct negotiation among market participants to fully automated computer crossing of trade orders.

The first time a security trades is when it is issued to the public. Therefore, we begin with a look at how securities are first marketed to the public by investment bankers, the midwives of securities. We turn next to a broad survey of how already-issued securities may be traded among investors, focusing on the differences among dealer markets, electronic markets, and specialist markets. With this background, we consider specific trading arenas such as the New York Stock Exchange, NASDAQ, and several all-electronic markets. We compare the mechanics of trade execution and the impact of cross-market integration of trading.

We then turn to the essentials of some specific types of transactions, such as buying on margin and short-selling stocks. We close the chapter with a look at some important aspects of the regulations governing security trading, including insider trading laws, and the role of security markets as self-regulating organizations.

3.1 How Firms Issue Securities

Firms regularly need to raise new capital to help pay for their many investment projects. Broadly speaking, they can raise funds either by borrowing money or by selling shares in the firm. Investment bankers are generally hired to manage the sale of these securities in what is called a **primary market** for newly issued securities. Once these securities are issued, however, investors might well wish to trade them among themselves. For example, you may decide to raise cash by selling some of your shares in Apple to another investor. This transaction would have no impact on the total outstanding number of Apple shares. Trades in existing securities take place in the so-called **secondary market.**

Shares of *publicly listed* firms trade continually in markets such as the New York Stock Exchange or the NASDAQ Stock Market. There, any investor can choose to buy shares for his or her portfolio. These companies are also called *publicly traded, publicly owned,* or just *public companies.* Other firms, however, are *private corporations,* whose shares are held by small numbers of managers and investors. Ownership stakes in the firm are still proportional to share ownership, but those shares do not trade in public exchanges. While many private firms are relatively young companies that have not yet chosen to make their shares generally available to the public, others may be more established firms that are still largely owned by the company's founders or families, and others may simply have decided that private organization is preferable.

Privately Held Firms

A privately held company is owned by a relatively small number of shareholders. Privately held firms have fewer obligations to release financial statements and other information to the public. This saves money and frees the firm from disclosing information that might be helpful to its competitors. Some firms also believe that eliminating requirements for quarterly earnings announcements gives them more flexibility to pursue long-term goals free of shareholder pressure.

When private firms wish to raise funds, they sell shares directly to institutional or wealthy investors in a **private placement.** Rule 144A of the SEC allows them to make these placements without preparing the extensive and costly registration statements required of a public company. While this is attractive, shares in privately held firms do not trade in secondary markets such as a stock exchange (although large financial institutions can trade unregistered securities among themselves), and this greatly reduces their liquidity and presumably reduces the prices that investors will pay for them. *Liquidity* has many specific meanings, but generally speaking, it refers to the ability to buy or sell an asset at a fair price on short notice. Investors demand price concessions to buy illiquid securities.

Until recently, private firms were allowed to have only up to 499 shareholders. This limited their ability to raise large amounts of capital from a wide base of investors. Thus, almost all of the largest companies in the U.S. have been public corporations.

As firms increasingly chafed against the informational requirements of going public, federal regulators came under pressure to loosen the constraints entailed by private ownership. The JOBS (Jumpstart Our Business Startups) Act, which was signed into law in 2012, increased the number of shareholders a company may have before being required to register its common stock with the SEC and file public reports from 500 to 2,000. The act also loosened rules limiting the degree to which private firms could market their shares to the public.

Some firms have set up computer networks to enable holders of private-company stock to trade among themselves. However, unlike the public stock markets regulated by the SEC, these networks require little disclosure of financial information and provide correspondingly little oversight of the operations of the market. Skeptics worry that investors in these markets cannot obtain a clear view of the firm, the interest among other investors in the firm, or the process by which trades in the firm's shares are executed.

Publicly Traded Companies

When a private firm decides that it wishes to raise capital from a wide range of investors, it may decide to *go public.* This means that it will sell its securities to the general public and allow those investors to freely trade those shares in established securities markets. This first issue of shares to the general public is called the firm's **initial public offering,** or **IPO.** Later, the firm may go back to the public and issue additional shares. A *seasoned equity offering* is the sale of additional shares in firms that already are publicly traded. For example, a sale by Apple of new shares of stock would be considered a seasoned new issue.

Public offerings of both stocks and bonds typically are marketed by investment bankers who in this role are called **underwriters.** More than one investment banker usually markets the securities. A lead firm forms an underwriting syndicate of other investment bankers to share the responsibility for the stock issue.

Investment bankers advise the firm regarding the terms on which it should attempt to sell the securities. A preliminary registration statement must be filed with the Securities and Exchange Commission (SEC), describing the issue and the prospects of the company. When the statement is in final form and accepted by the SEC, it is called the **prospectus.** At this point, the price at which the securities will be offered to the public is announced.

In a typical underwriting arrangement, the investment bankers purchase the securities from the issuing company and then resell them to the public. The issuing firm sells the securities to the underwriting syndicate for the public offering price less a spread that serves as compensation to the underwriters. This procedure is called a *firm commitment.* In addition to the spread, the investment banker also may receive shares of common stock or other securities of the firm. Figure 3.1 depicts the relationships among the firm issuing the security, the lead underwriter, the underwriting syndicate, and the public.

Shelf Registration

An important innovation was introduced in 1982 when the SEC approved Rule 415 for seasoned offerings, which allows firms to register securities and gradually sell them to the public for three years following the initial registration. Because the securities are

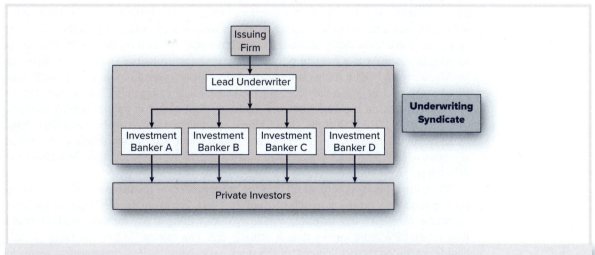

Figure 3.1 Relationships among a firm issuing securities, the underwriters, and the public

already registered, they can be sold on short notice, with little additional paperwork. Moreover, they can be sold in small amounts without incurring substantial flotation costs. The securities are "on the shelf," ready to be issued, which has given rise to the term *shelf registration.*

Concept Check **3.1**

Why does it make sense for shelf registration to be limited in time?

Initial Public Offerings

Investment bankers manage the issuance of new securities to the public. Once the SEC has commented on the registration statement and a preliminary prospectus has been distributed to interested investors, the investment bankers organize *road shows* in which they travel around the country to publicize the imminent offering. These road shows serve two purposes. First, they generate interest among potential investors and provide information about the offering. Second, they provide information to the issuing firm and its underwriters about the price at which they will be able to market the securities. Large investors communicate their interest in purchasing shares of the IPO to the underwriters; these indications of interest are called a *book,* and the process of polling potential investors is called *bookbuilding.* The book provides valuable information to the issuing firm because institutional investors often will have useful insights about the market demand for the security as well as the prospects of the firm and its competitors. Investment bankers frequently revise both their initial estimates of the offering price of a security and the number of shares offered based on feedback from the investing community.

Why do investors truthfully reveal their interest in an offering to the investment banker? Might they be better off expressing little interest, in the hope that this will drive down the offering price? Truth is the better policy in this case because truth telling is rewarded. Shares of IPOs are allocated across investors in part based on the strength of each investor's expressed interest in the offering. If a firm wishes to get a large allocation when it is optimistic about the security, it needs to reveal its optimism. In turn, the underwriter needs to offer the security at a bargain price to these investors to induce them to participate in bookbuilding and share their information. Thus, IPOs commonly are underpriced compared to the price at which they could be marketed. Such underpricing is reflected in price jumps that occur on the date when the shares are first traded in public security markets. The September 2014 IPO of the giant Chinese e-commerce firm Alibaba was a fairly typical example of underpricing. The company issued about 320 million shares to the public at a price of $68. The stock price closed that day at $93.89, a bit more than 38% above the offering price.

While the explicit costs of an IPO tend to be around 7% of the funds raised, such underpricing should be viewed as another cost of the issue. For example, if Alibaba had sold its shares for the $93.89 that investors obviously were willing to pay for them, its IPO would have raised 38% more money than it actually did. The money "left on the table" in this case far exceeded the explicit cost of the stock issue. Nevertheless, underpricing seems to be a universal phenomenon. Figure 3.2 presents average first-day returns on IPOs of stocks across the world. The results consistently indicate that IPOs are marketed to investors at attractive prices.

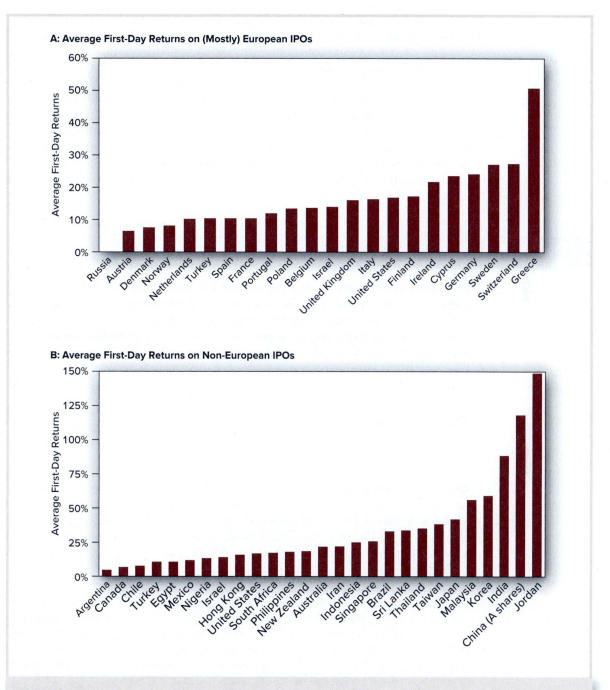

Figure 3.2 Average first-day returns on IPOs from around the world

Source: Professor Jay Ritter, **https://site.warrington.ufl.edu/ritter/ipo-data/**, 2016.

   Pricing of IPOs is not trivial and not all IPOs turn out to be underpriced. Some do poorly after issue. Facebook's 2012 IPO was a notable disappointment. Within a week of its IPO, Facebook's share price was 15% below the $38 offer price, and five months later, its shares were selling at about half the offer price. (In the end, however, those who held on to their shares profited; by mid-2016, the share price was around $120.) Other IPOs cannot even be fully sold to the market. Underwriters left with unmarketable securities are forced to sell them at a loss on the secondary market. Therefore, the investment banker bears price risk for an underwritten issue.

Interestingly, despite their typically attractive first-day returns, IPOs have been poor long-term investments. Professor Jay Ritter, a leading expert in the field, has calculated the returns to a hypothetical investor buying equal amounts of each U.S. IPO between 1980 and 2014 at the close of trading on the first day the stock is listed and holding each position for three years. That portfolio underperforms the broad U.S. stock market on average by 17.8% for three-year holding periods and underperforms "style-matched" portfolios of firms with comparable size and ratio of book value to market value by 6.3%.[1]

3.2   How Securities Are Traded

Financial markets develop to meet the needs of particular traders. Consider what would happen if organized markets did not exist. Any household wishing to invest in some type of financial asset would have to find others wishing to sell. Soon, venues where interested traders could meet would become popular. Eventually, financial markets would emerge from these meeting places. Thus, a pub in old London called Lloyd's launched the maritime insurance industry. A Manhattan curb on Wall Street became synonymous with the financial world.

Types of Markets

We can differentiate four types of markets: direct search markets, brokered markets, dealer markets, and auction markets.

Direct Search Markets   A *direct search market* is the least organized market. Buyers and sellers must seek each other out directly. An example of a transaction in such a market is the sale of a used refrigerator where the seller advertises for buyers in a local newspaper or on Craigslist. Such markets are characterized by sporadic participation and nonstandard goods. Firms would find it difficult to profit by specializing in such an environment.

Brokered Markets   The next level of organization is a *brokered market.* In markets where trading in a good is active, brokers find it profitable to offer search services to buyers and sellers. A good example is the real estate market, where economies of scale in searches for available homes and for prospective buyers make it worthwhile for participants to pay brokers to help them conduct the searches. Brokers in particular markets develop specialized knowledge on valuing assets traded in that market.

The *primary market,* where new issues of securities are offered to the public, is another example of a brokered market. In the primary market, investment bankers who market a firm's securities to the public act as brokers; they seek investors to purchase securities directly from the issuing corporation.

---

[1]Ritter's Web site contains a wealth of information and data about IPOs: **http://bear.warrington.ufl.edu/ritter/ ipodata.htm**.

Dealer Markets   When trading activity in a particular type of asset increases, **dealer markets** arise. Dealers specialize in various assets, purchase these assets for their own accounts, and later sell them for a profit from their inventory. The spreads between dealers' buy (or "bid") prices and sell (or "ask") prices are a source of profit. Dealer markets save traders on search costs because market participants can easily look up the prices at which they can buy from or sell to dealers. A fair amount of market activity is required before dealing in a market is an attractive source of income. Most bonds trade in over-the-counter dealer markets.

Auction Markets   The most integrated market is an **auction market,** in which all traders converge at one place (either physically or "electronically") to buy or sell an asset. The New York Stock Exchange (NYSE) is an example of an auction market. An advantage of auction markets over dealer markets is that one need not search across dealers to find the best price for a good. If all participants converge, they can arrive at mutually agreeable prices and save the bid–ask spread.

Notice that both over-the-counter dealer markets and stock exchanges are secondary markets. They are organized for investors to trade existing securities among themselves.

Concept Check **3.2**

Many assets trade in more than one type of market. What types of markets do the following trade in?

a. Used cars

b. Paintings

c. Rare coins

Types of Orders

Before comparing alternative trading practices and competing security markets, it is helpful to begin with an overview of the types of trades an investor might wish to have executed in these markets. Broadly speaking, there are two types of orders: market orders and orders contingent on price.

Market Orders   Market orders are buy or sell orders that are to be executed immediately at current market prices. For example, our investor might call her broker and ask for the market price of Facebook. The broker might report back that the best **bid price** is $118.34 and the best **ask price** is $118.36, meaning that the investor would need to pay $118.36 to purchase a share, and could receive $118.34 a share if she wished to sell some of her own holdings of Facebook. The **bid–ask spread** in this case is $.02. So an order to buy 100 shares "at market" would result in purchase at $118.36, and an order to "sell at market" would be executed at $118.34.

This simple scenario is subject to a few potential complications. First, the posted price quotes actually represent commitments to trade up to a specified number of shares. If the market order is for more than this number of shares, the order may be filled at multiple prices. For example, if the ask price is good for orders up to 300 shares and the investor wishes to purchase 500 shares, it may be necessary to pay a slightly higher price for the last 200 shares. Figure 3.3 shows the average *depth* of the markets for shares of stock (i.e., the total number of shares offered for trading at the best bid and ask prices). Notice that depth is considerably higher for the large stocks in the S&P 500 than for the smaller stocks that constitute the Russell 2000 index. Depth is considered another component of liquidity. Second, another trader may beat our investor to the quote, meaning that her order would then be executed at a worse price. Finally, the best price quote may change before her order arrives, again causing execution at a price different from the one quoted at the moment of the order.

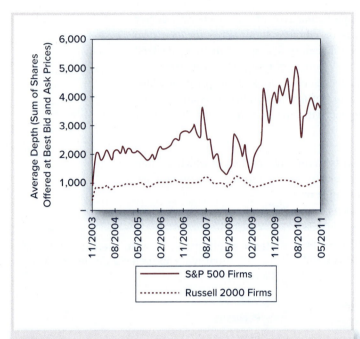

Figure 3.3 Average market depth for large (S&P 500) and small (Russell 2000) firms

Source: James J. Angel, Lawrence E. Harris, and Chester Spatt, "Equity Trading in the 21st Century," *Quarterly Journal of Finance* 1 (2011), pp. 1–53; Knight Capital Group.

Price-Contingent Orders   Investors also may place orders specifying prices at which they are willing to buy or sell a security. A limit buy order may instruct the broker to buy some number of shares if and when Facebook may be obtained *at or below* a stipulated price. Conversely, a limit sell instructs the broker to sell if and when the stock price rises *above* a specified limit. A collection of **limit orders** waiting to be executed is called a *limit order book.*

Figure 3.4 is a portion of the limit order book for shares in Facebook taken from the BATS exchange (one of several electronic exchanges; more on these shortly). Notice that the best orders are at the top of the list: the offers to buy at the highest price and to sell at the lowest price. The buy and sell orders at the top of the list—$118.34 and $118.36—are called the *inside quotes;* they are the highest buy and lowest sell orders. The inside spread at this time was only 2 cents. Note, however, that order sizes at the inside quotes can be fairly small. Therefore, investors interested in larger trades face an *effective* spread greater than the nominal one because they cannot execute their entire trades at the inside price quotes.

Concept Check 3.3

What type of trading order might you give to your broker in each of the following circumstances?

a. You want to buy shares of Facebook to diversify your portfolio. You believe the share price is approximately at the "fair" value, and you want the trade done quickly and cheaply.

b. You want to buy shares of Facebook, but you believe that the current stock price is too high given the firm's prospects. If the shares could be obtained at a price 5% lower than the current value, you would like to purchase shares for your portfolio.

c. You believe your shares of Facebook are already priced generously, and you are inclined to sell them. But there is a chance that price fluctuations might result in a short-lived increase of a few dollars per share. If the share price were to rise by $4 you are convinced that it would be greatly overpriced and you would want to sell it immediately.

Trading Mechanisms

An investor who wishes to buy or sell shares will place an order with a brokerage firm. The broker charges a commission for arranging the trade on the client's behalf. Brokers have several avenues by which they can execute that trade, that is, find a buyer or seller and arrange for the shares to be exchanged.

Facebook, Inc. (FB) - NasdaqGS ⭐ **Watchlist**

118.34 ↓ 1.47 (1.23%)   1:13PM EDT - Nasdaq Real Time Price

Order Book

Top of Book

Bid		Ask	
Price	**Size**	**Price**	**Size**
118.34	200	118.36	300
118.33	700	118.37	300
118.32	900	118.38	300
118.31	400	118.39	500
118.30	400	118.40	500

Figure 3.4 A portion of the limit order book for Facebook on the BATS Market, May 16, 2016

Source: BATS Market, May 16, 2016.

Broadly speaking, there are three trading systems employed in the United States: over-the-counter dealer markets, electronic communication networks, and specialist markets. Electronic trading is by far the most prevalent, but the best-known markets such as NASDAQ or the New York Stock Exchange actually use a variety of trading procedures, so before you delve into specific markets, it is useful to understand the basic operation of each type of trading system.

Dealer Markets   Roughly 35,000 securities trade on the **over-the-counter (OTC) market.** Thousands of brokers register with the SEC as security dealers. Dealers quote prices at which they are willing to buy or sell securities. A broker then executes a trade by contacting a dealer listing an attractive quote.

Before 1971, all OTC quotations were recorded manually and published daily on so-called pink sheets. In 1971, the National Association of Securities Dealers introduced its Automatic Quotations System, or NASDAQ, to link brokers and dealers in a computer network where price quotes could be displayed and revised. Dealers could use the network to display the bid price at which they were willing to purchase a security and the ask price at which they were willing to sell. The difference in these prices, the bid–ask spread, was the source of the dealer's profit. Brokers representing clients could examine quotes over the computer network, contact the dealer with the best quote, and execute a trade.

As originally organized, NASDAQ was more of a price-quotation system than a trading system. While brokers could survey bid and ask prices across the network of dealers in the search for the best trading opportunity, actual trades required direct negotiation (often over the phone) between the investor's broker and the dealer in the security. However, as we will see, NASDAQ is no longer a mere price quotation system. While dealers still post bid and ask prices over the network, what is now called the **NASDAQ Stock Market** allows for electronic execution of trades, and the vast majority of trades are executed electronically.

Electronic Communication Networks (ECNs)   **Electronic communication networks (ECNs)** allow participants to post market and limit orders over computer networks. The limit-order book is available to all participants. An example of such an order book from BATS, one of the leading ECNs, appears in Figure 3.4. Orders that can be "crossed," that is, matched against another order, are executed automatically without requiring the intervention of a broker. For example, an order to buy a share at a price of $50 or lower will be immediately executed if there is an outstanding ask price of $50. Therefore, ECNs are true trading systems, not merely price-quotation systems.

ECNs offer several advantages. Direct crossing of trades without using a broker-dealer system eliminates the bid–ask spread that otherwise would be incurred. Instead, trades are automatically crossed at a modest cost, typically less than a penny per share. ECNs are attractive as well because of the speed with which a trade can be executed. Finally, these systems offer investors considerable anonymity in their trades.

Specialist Markets   Specialist systems have been largely replaced by electronic communication networks, but as recently as two decades ago, they were still the dominant means by which stocks were traded. In these systems, exchanges such as the NYSE assign responsibility for managing the trading in each security to a **specialist.** Brokers wishing to buy or sell shares for their clients direct the trade to the specialist's post on the floor of the exchange. While each security is assigned to only one specialist, each specialist firm makes a market in many securities. The specialist maintains the limit order book of all outstanding unexecuted limit orders. When orders can be executed at market prices, the specialist executes, or "crosses," the trade. The highest outstanding bid price and the lowest outstanding ask price "win" the trade.

Specialists are also mandated to maintain a "fair and orderly" market when the book of limit buy and sell orders is so thin that the spread between the highest bid price and lowest ask price becomes too wide. In this case, the specialist firm would be expected to offer to buy and sell shares from its own inventory at a narrower bid–ask spread. In this role, the specialist serves as a dealer in the stock and provides liquidity to other traders. In this context, liquidity providers are those who stand willing to buy securities from or sell securities to other traders.

3.3   The Rise of Electronic Trading

When first established, NASDAQ was primarily an over-the-counter dealer market and the NYSE was a specialist market. But today both are primarily electronic markets. These changes were driven by an interaction of new technologies and new regulations. New regulations allowed brokers to compete for business, broke the hold that dealers once had on information about best-available bid and ask prices, forced integration of markets, and allowed securities to trade in ever-smaller price increments (called *tick sizes*). Technology made it possible for traders to rapidly compare prices across markets and direct their trades to the markets with the best prices. The resulting competition drove down the cost of trade execution to a tiny fraction of its level just a few decades ago.

In 1975, fixed commissions on the NYSE were eliminated, which freed brokers to compete for business by lowering their fees. In that year also, Congress amended the Securities Exchange Act to create the National Market System to at least partially centralize trading across exchanges and enhance competition among different market makers. The idea was to implement centralized reporting of transactions as well as a centralized price quotation system to give traders a broader view of trading opportunities across markets.

The aftermath of a 1994 scandal at NASDAQ turned out to be a major impetus in the further evolution and integration of markets. NASDAQ dealers were found to be colluding to maintain wide bid–ask spreads. For example, if a stock was listed at $30 bid–$30½ ask, a retail client who wished to buy shares from a dealer would pay $30½ while a client who wished to sell shares would receive only $30. The dealer would pocket the ½-point spread as profit. Other traders may have been willing to step in with better prices (e.g., they may have been willing to buy shares for $30⅛ or sell them for $30⅜), but those better quotes were not made available to the public, enabling dealers to profit from artificially wide spreads at the public's expense. When these practices came to light, an antitrust lawsuit was brought against NASDAQ.

In response to the scandal, the SEC instituted new order-handling rules. Published dealer quotes now had to reflect limit orders of customers, allowing them to effectively compete with dealers to capture trades. As part of the antitrust settlement, NASDAQ agreed to integrate quotes from ECNs into its public display, enabling the electronic exchanges to also compete for trades. Shortly after this settlement, the SEC adopted Regulation ATS (Alternative Trading Systems), giving ECNs the right to register as stock exchanges. Not surprisingly, they captured an ever-larger market share, and in the wake of this new competition, bid–ask spreads narrowed.

Even more dramatic narrowing of trading costs came in 1997, when the SEC allowed the minimum tick size to fall from one-eighth of a dollar to one-sixteenth. Not long after, in 2001, "decimalization" allowed the tick size to fall to 1 cent. Bid–ask spreads again fell dramatically. Figure 3.5 shows estimates of the "effective spread" (the cost of a transaction) during three distinct time periods defined by the minimum tick size. Notice how dramatically effective spread falls along with the minimum tick size.

Technology was also changing trading practices. The first ECN, Instinet, was established in 1969. By the 1990s, exchanges around the world were rapidly adopting fully electronic trading systems. Europe led the way in this evolution, but eventually American exchanges followed suit. The National Association of Securities Dealers (NASD) spun off the NASDAQ Stock Market as a separate entity in 2000, which quickly evolved into a centralized limit-order matching system—effectively a large ECN. The NYSE acquired the electronic Archipelago Exchange in 2006 and renamed it NYSE Arca.

In 2005, the SEC adopted Regulation NMS (for National Market System), which was fully implemented in 2007. The goal was to link exchanges electronically, thereby creating, in effect, one integrated electronic market. The regulation required exchanges to honor quotes of other exchanges when they could be executed automatically. An exchange that could not handle a quote electronically would be labeled a "slow market" under Reg NMS and could be ignored by other market participants. The NYSE, which was still devoted to the specialist system, was particularly at risk of being passed over, and in response to this pressure, it moved aggressively toward automated execution of trades. Electronic trading networks and the integration of markets in the wake of Reg NMS made it much easier for exchanges around the world to compete; the NYSE lost its effective monopoly in the trading of its own listed stocks, and by the end of the decade, its share in the trading of NYSE-listed stocks fell from about 75% to 25%.

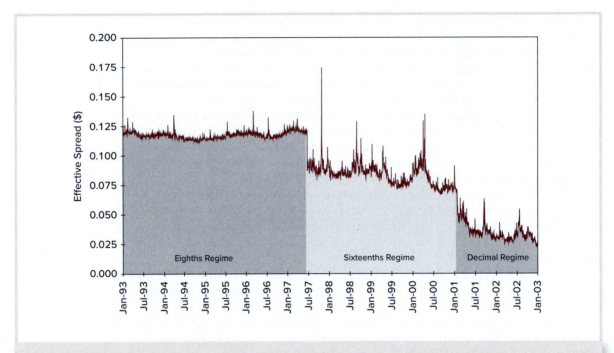

Figure 3.5 The effective spread (measured in dollars per share) fell dramatically as the minimum tick size fell (value-weighted average of NYSE-listed shares)

Source: Tarun Chordia, Richard Roll, and Avanidhar Subrahmanyam, "Liquidity and Market Efficiency," *Journal of Financial Economics* 87 (2008), 249–268.

While specialists still exist, trading today is overwhelmingly electronic, at least for stocks. Bonds are still traded in more traditional dealer markets. In the U.S., the share of electronic trading in equities rose from about 16% in 2000 to over 80% by the end of the decade. In the rest of the world, the dominance of electronic trading is even greater.

3.4 U.S. Markets

The NYSE and the NASDAQ Stock Market remain the best-known U.S. stock markets. But electronic communication networks have steadily increased their market share. Figure 3.6 shows the comparative trading volume of NYSE-listed shares on the NYSE and NASDAQ as well as on the major ECNs, namely, BATS, NYSE Arca, and Direct Edge. (Since this study was published, BATS and Direct Edge merged, creating one of the world's largest stock exchanges, called BATS Global Markets.) The "Other" category, which exceeds 30%, includes so-called dark pools, which we will discuss shortly.

NASDAQ

The NASDAQ Stock Market lists around 3,000 firms. It has steadily introduced ever-more sophisticated trading platforms, which today handle the great majority of its trades. Its NASDAQ Market Center consolidates NASDAQ's previous electronic markets into one integrated system. NASDAQ merged in 2007 with OMX, a Swedish-Finnish company that controls seven Nordic and Baltic stock exchanges to form NASDAQ OMX Group.

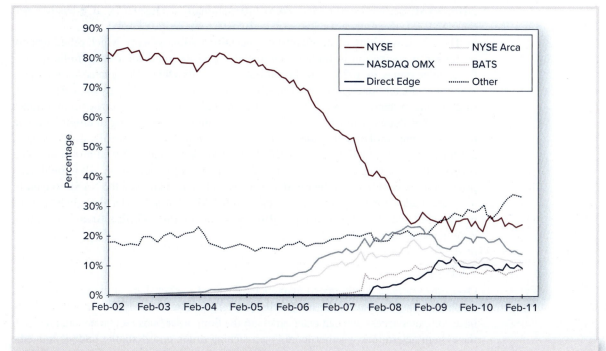

Figure 3.6 Market share of trading in NYSE-listed shares

Source: James J. Angel, Lawrence E. Harris, and Chester Spatt, "Equity Trading in the 21st Century," *Quarterly Journal of Finance* 1 (2011), 1–53.

In addition to maintaining the NASDAQ Stock Market, it also maintains several stock markets in Europe as well as an options and futures exchange in the U.S.

NASDAQ has three levels of subscribers. The highest, level 3 subscribers, are registered market makers. These are firms that make a market in securities, maintain inventories of securities, and post bid and ask prices at which they are willing to buy or sell shares. Level 3 subscribers can enter and change bid–ask quotes continually and have the fastest execution of trades. They profit from the spread between bid and ask prices.

Level 2 subscribers receive all bid and ask quotes but cannot enter their own quotes. They can see which market makers are offering the best prices. These subscribers tend to be brokerage firms that execute trades for clients but do not actively deal in stocks for their own account.

Level 1 subscribers receive only inside quotes (i.e., the best bid and ask prices), but do not see how many shares are being offered. These subscribers tend to be investors who are not actively buying or selling but want information on current prices.

The New York Stock Exchange

The NYSE is the largest U.S. **stock exchange** as measured by the market value of listed stocks. Daily trading volume on the NYSE is about a billion shares. In 2006, the NYSE merged with the Archipelago Exchange to form a publicly held company called the NYSE Group, and then in 2007, it merged with the European exchange Euronext to form NYSE Euronext. The firm acquired the American Stock Exchange in 2008, which was renamed NYSE Amex and focuses on small firms. NYSE Arca is the firm's electronic communications network, and this is where the bulk of exchange-traded funds trade. In

2013, NYSE Euronext was purchased by InternationalExchange (ICE). ICE has retained the NYSE Euronext name.

The NYSE was long committed to its specialist trading system, which relied heavily on human participation in trade execution. It began its transition to electronic trading for smaller trades in 1976 with the introduction of its DOT (Designated Order Turnaround), and later SuperDOT systems, which could route orders directly to the specialist. In 2000, the exchange launched Direct+, which could automatically cross smaller trades (up to 1,099 shares) without human intervention, and in 2004, it began eliminating the size restrictions on Direct+ trades. The change of emphasis dramatically accelerated in 2006 with the introduction of the NYSE Hybrid Market, which allowed brokers to send orders either for immediate electronic execution or to the specialist, who could seek price improvement from another trader. The Hybrid system allowed the NYSE to qualify as a fast market for the purposes of Regulation NMS, but still offer the advantages of human intervention for more complicated trades. In contrast, NYSE's Arca marketplace is fully electronic.

ECNs

Over time, more fully automated markets have gained market share at the expense of less automated ones, in particular, the NYSE. Brokers that have an affiliation with an ECN have computer access and can enter orders in the limit order book. As orders are received, the system determines whether there is a matching order, and if so, the trade is immediately crossed.

Originally, ECNs were open only to other traders using the same system. But following the implementation of Reg NMS, ECNs began listing limit orders on other networks. Traders could use their computer systems to sift through the limit order books of many ECNs and instantaneously route orders to the market with the best prices. Those cross-market links have become the impetus for one of the more popular strategies of so-called high-frequency traders, which seek to profit from even small, transitory discrepancies in prices across markets. Speed is obviously of the essence here, and ECNs compete in terms of the speed they can offer. **Latency** refers to the time it takes to accept, process, and deliver a trading order. For example, BATS, one of the biggest ECNs, advertises latency times of around 200 microseconds (i.e., .0002 second).

3.5 New Trading Strategies

The marriage of electronic trading mechanisms with computer technology has had far-ranging impacts on trading strategies and tools. *Algorithmic trading* delegates trading decisions to computer programs. *High frequency trading* is a special class of algorithmic trading in which computer programs initiate orders in tiny fractions of a second, far faster than any human could process the information driving the trade. Much of the market liquidity that once was provided by brokers making a market in a security has been displaced by these high-frequency traders. But when high-frequency traders abandon the market, as in the so-called flash crash of 2010, liquidity can likewise evaporate in a flash. *Dark pools* are trading venues that preserve anonymity, but also affect market liquidity. We will address these emerging issues later in this section.

Algorithmic Trading

Algorithmic trading is the use of computer programs to make trading decisions. Well more than half of all equity volume in the U.S. is believed to be initiated by computer

The Flash Crash of May 2010

At 2:42 New York time on May 6, 2010, the Dow Jones Industrial Average was already down about 300 points for the day. The market was demonstrating concerns about the European debt crisis, and nerves were already on edge. Then, in the next 5 minutes, the Dow dropped an *additional* 600 points. And only 20 minutes after that, it had recovered most of those 600 points. Besides the staggering intraday volatility of the broad market, trading in individual shares and ETFs was even more disrupted. The iShares Russell 1000 Value fund temporarily fell from $59 a share to 8 cents. Shares in the large consulting company Accenture, which had just sold for $38, traded at 1 cent only a minute or two later. At the other extreme, price quotes for Apple and Hewlett-Packard momentarily increased to over $100,000. These markets were clearly broken.

The causes of the flash crash are still debated. An SEC report issued after the trade pointed to a $4 billion sale of market index futures contracts by a mutual fund. As market prices began to tumble, many algorithmic trading programs withdrew from the markets, and those that remained became net sellers, further pushing down equity prices. As more and more of these algorithmic traders shut down, liquidity in these markets evaporated: Buyers for many stocks simply disappeared.

Finally, trading was halted for a short period. When it resumed, buyers decided to take advantage of many severely depressed stock prices, and the market rebounded almost as quickly as it had crashed. Given the intraday turbulence and the clearly distorted prices at which some trades had been executed, the NYSE and NASDAQ decided to cancel all trades that were executed more than 60% away from a "reference price" close to the opening price of the day. Almost 70% of those canceled trades involved ETFs.

The SEC has since approved experimentation with new circuit breakers to halt trading for 5 minutes in large stocks that rise or fall by more than 10% in a 5-minute period. The idea is to prevent trading algorithms from moving share prices quickly before human traders have a chance to determine whether those prices are moving in response to fundamental information.

The flash crash highlighted the fragility of markets in the face of huge variation in trading volume created by algorithmic traders. The potential for these high-frequency traders to withdraw from markets in periods of turbulence remains a concern, and many observers are not convinced that we are protected from future flash crashes.

algorithms. Many of these trades exploit very small discrepancies in security prices and entail numerous and rapid cross-market price comparisons that are well suited to computer analysis. These strategies would not have been feasible before decimalization of the minimum tick size.

Some algorithmic trades attempt to exploit very short-term trends (as short as a few seconds or less) as new information about a firm, or, more controversially, about the intentions of other traders, becomes available. Others use versions of *pairs trading* in which normal price relations between pairs (or larger groups) of stocks seem temporarily disrupted and offer small profit opportunities as they move back into alignment. Still others attempt to exploit discrepancies between stock prices and prices of stock-index futures contracts.

Some algorithmic trading involves activities akin to traditional market making. The traders seek to profit from the bid–ask spread by buying a stock at the bid price and rapidly selling it at the ask price before the price can change. While this mimics the role of a market maker who provides liquidity to other traders in the stock, these algorithmic traders are not registered market makers and so do not have an affirmative obligation to maintain both bid and ask quotes. If they abandon a market during a period of turbulence, the shock to market liquidity can be disruptive. This seems to have been a problem during the flash crash of May 6, 2010, when the stock market encountered extreme volatility, with the Dow Jones Industrial Average falling by 1,000 points before recovering around 600 points in intraday trading. The nearby box discusses this amazing and troubling episode.

High-Frequency Trading

It is easy to see that many algorithmic trading strategies require extremely rapid trade initiation and execution. **High-frequency trading** is a subset of algorithmic trading that relies on computer programs to make extremely rapid decisions. High-frequency traders compete for trades that offer very small profits. But if those opportunities are numerous enough, they can accumulate to big money.

We pointed out that one high-frequency strategy entails a sort of market making, attempting to profit from the bid–ask spread. Another relies on cross-market arbitrage, in which even tiny price discrepancies across markets allow the firm to buy a security at one price and simultaneously sell it at a slightly higher price. The competitive advantage in these strategies lies with the firms that are quickest to identify and execute these profit opportunities. There is a tremendous premium on being the first to "hit" a bid or ask price.

Trade execution times for high-frequency traders are now measured in milliseconds, even microseconds. This has induced trading firms to "co-locate" their trading centers next to the computer systems of the electronic exchanges. When execution or latency periods are less than a millisecond, the extra time it takes for a trade order to travel from a remote location to a New York exchange would be enough to make it nearly impossible to win the trade.

To understand why co-location has become a key issue, consider this calculation. Even light can travel only 186 miles in 1 millisecond, so an order originating in Chicago transmitted at the speed of light would take almost 5 milliseconds to reach New York. But ECNs today claim latency periods considerably less than 1 millisecond, so an order from Chicago could not possibly compete with one launched from a co-located facility.

In some ways, co-location is a new version of an old phenomenon. Think about why, even before the advent of the telephone, so many brokerage firms originally located their headquarters in New York: They were "co-locating" with the NYSE so that their brokers could bring trades (on foot!) to the exchange quickly and efficiently. Today, trades are transmitted electronically, but competition among traders for fast execution means that the need to be near the market (now embodied in computer servers) remains.

Dark Pools

Many large traders seek anonymity. They fear that if others see them executing a large buy or sell program, their intentions will become public and prices will move against them. This is a particular concern with large orders that will be executed over time using several trades. Very large trades (called **blocks,** usually defined as a trade of more than 10,000 shares) traditionally were brought to "block houses," brokerage firms specializing in matching block buyers and sellers. Part of the expertise of block brokers is in identifying traders who might be interested in a large purchase or sale if given an offer. These brokers discreetly arrange large trades out of the public eye, and so avoid moving prices against their clients.

Block trading today has been displaced to a great extent by **dark pools,** private trading systems in which participants can buy or sell large blocks of securities without showing their hand. Limit orders are not visible to the general public as they would be on a conventional exchange, and traders' identities can also be kept private. Trades are not reported until after they are crossed, which limits the vulnerability to other traders anticipating one's trading program.

Many large traders gravitate toward dark pools because it makes them less vulnerable to high-frequency traders. They want a trading venue where other traders find it more difficult to infer their trading intentions and trade in front of them. However, this ideal has not always been realized. In 2011, Pipeline LLC, which operated a dark pool, was accused of enabling high-frequency traders to participate in its market and to gauge the intentions of other participants in the pool. Similarly, in 2014, Barclays was accused of misrepresenting the level of high-frequency trading in a dark pool that it operated. There are lingering concerns regarding the extent to which dark pools provide the protections from other traders that they are purportedly designed to offer.

Dark pools are somewhat controversial because they contribute to the fragmentation of markets. When many orders are removed from the consolidated limit order book, there are fewer orders left to absorb fluctuations in demand for the security, and the public price may no longer be "fair" in the sense that it reflects all the potentially available information about security demand.

Another approach to dealing with large trades is to split them into many small trades, each of which can be executed on electronic markets, attempting to hide the fact that the total number of shares ultimately to be bought or sold is large. This trend has led to rapid decline in average trade size, which today is less than 300 shares.

Bond Trading

In 2006, the NYSE obtained regulatory approval to expand its bond-trading system to include the debt issues of any NYSE-listed firm. Until then, each bond needed to be registered before listing, and such a requirement was too onerous to justify listing most bonds. In conjunction with these new listings, the NYSE has expanded its electronic bond-trading platform, which is now called NYSE Bonds and is the largest centralized bond market of any U.S. exchange.

Nevertheless, the vast majority of bond trading occurs in the OTC market among bond dealers, even for bonds that are actually listed on the NYSE. This market is a network of bond dealers such as Merrill Lynch (now part of Bank of America), Salomon Smith Barney (a division of Citigroup), and Goldman Sachs that is linked by a computer quotation system. However, because these dealers do not carry extensive inventories of the wide range of bonds that have been issued to the public, they cannot necessarily offer to sell bonds from their inventory to clients or even buy bonds for their own inventory. They may instead work to locate an investor who wishes to take the opposite side of a trade. In practice, however, the corporate bond market often is quite "thin," in that there may be few investors interested in trading a specific bond at any particular time. As a result, the bond market is subject to a type of liquidity risk, for it can be difficult to sell one's holdings quickly if the need arises.

3.6   Globalization of Stock Markets

Figure 3.7 shows that NYSE-Euronext is by far the largest equity market as measured by the total market value of listed firms. All major stock markets today are effectively electronic.

Securities markets have come under increasing pressure in recent years to make international alliances or mergers. Much of this pressure is due to the impact of electronic trading. To a growing extent, traders view stock markets as computer networks that link them to other traders, and there are increasingly fewer limits on the securities around the world that they can trade. Against this background, it becomes more important for exchanges to provide the cheapest and most efficient mechanism by which trades can be executed and cleared. This argues for global alliances that can facilitate the nuts and bolts of cross-border trading and benefit from economies of scale. Exchanges feel that they eventually need to offer 24-hour global markets and platforms that allow trading of different security types, for example, both stocks and derivatives. Finally, companies want to be able to go beyond national borders when they wish to raise capital.

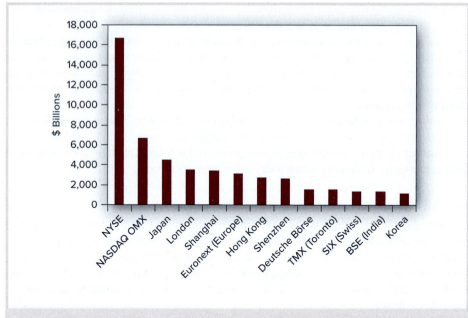

Figure 3.7 The biggest stock markets in the world by domestic market capitalization in 2015

Source: World Federation of Exchanges, 2016.

These pressures have resulted in a broad trend toward market consolidation. In the U.S., the NYSE merged with the Archipelago ECN in 2006, and in 2008 it acquired the American Stock Exchange. In Europe, Euronext was formed by the merger of the Paris, Brussels, Lisbon, and Amsterdam exchanges and shortly thereafter purchased Liffe, the derivatives exchange based in London. The NYSE Group and Euronext merged in 2007, and was itself acquired by ICE in 2013.

NASDAQ acquired Instinet (which operated another major ECN, INET) in 2005 and the Boston Stock Exchange in 2007. It merged with OMX, which operates seven Nordic and Baltic stock exchanges, to form NASDAQ OMX Group in 2007.

In the derivatives market, the Chicago Mercantile Exchange acquired the Chicago Board of Trade in 2007 and the New York Mercantile Exchange in 2008, thus moving almost all futures trading in the U.S. onto one exchange. In 2008, Eurex took over International Securities Exchange (ISE), to form a major options exchange.

3.7   Trading Costs

Part of the cost of trading a security is obvious and explicit. Your broker must be paid a commission. Individuals may choose from two kinds of brokers: full-service or discount brokers. Full-service brokers who provide a variety of services often are referred to as account executives or financial consultants.

Besides carrying out the basic services of executing orders, holding securities for safekeeping, extending margin loans, and facilitating short sales, brokers routinely provide information and advice relating to investment alternatives.

Full-service brokers usually depend on a research staff that prepares analyses and fore-casts of general economic as well as industry and company conditions and often makes specific buy or sell recommendations. Some customers take the ultimate leap of faith and allow a full-service broker to make buy and sell decisions for them by establishing a *discretionary account.* In this account, the broker can buy and sell prespecified securi-ties whenever deemed fit. (The broker cannot withdraw any funds, though.) This action requires an unusual degree of trust on the part of the customer, for an unscrupulous broker can "churn" an account, that is, trade securities excessively with the sole purpose of gen-erating commissions.

Discount brokers, on the other hand, provide "no-frills" services. They buy and sell securities, hold them for safekeeping, offer margin loans, facilitate short sales, and that is all. The only information they provide about the securities they handle is price quo-tations. Discount brokerage services have become increasingly available in recent years. Many banks, thrift institutions, and mutual fund management companies now offer such services to the investing public as part of a general trend toward the creation of one-stop "financial supermarkets." Stock trading fees have fallen steadily over the last decade, and discount brokerage firms such as Schwab, E*Trade, or TD Ameritrade now offer commis-sions below $10.

In addition to the explicit part of trading costs—the broker's commission—there is an implicit part—the dealer's bid–ask spread. Sometimes the broker is also a dealer in the security being traded and charges no commission but instead collects the fee entirely in the form of the bid–ask spread. Another implicit cost of trading that some observers would distinguish is the price concession an investor may be forced to make for trading in quanti-ties greater than those associated with the posted bid or ask price.

3.8 Buying on Margin

When purchasing securities, investors have easy access to a source of debt financing called *broker's call loans.* The act of taking advantage of broker's call loans is called *buying on margin.*

Purchasing stocks on margin means the investor borrows part of the purchase price of the stock from a broker. The **margin** in the account is the portion of the purchase price contributed by the investor; the remainder is borrowed from the broker. The brokers in turn borrow money from banks at the call money rate to finance these purchases; they then charge their clients that rate (defined in Chapter 2), plus a service charge for the loan. All securities purchased on margin must be maintained with the brokerage firm in street name, for the securities are collateral for the loan.

The Board of Governors of the Federal Reserve System limits the extent to which stock purchases can be financed using margin loans. The current initial margin requirement is 50%, meaning that at least 50% of the purchase price must be paid for in cash, with the rest borrowed.

Example 3.1 Margin

The percentage margin is defined as the ratio of the net worth, or the "equity value," of the account to the market value of the securities. To demonstrate, suppose an inves-tor initially pays $6,000 toward the purchase of $10,000 worth of stock (100 shares at

$100 per share), borrowing the remaining $4,000 from a broker. The initial balance sheet looks like this:

Assets		Liabilities and Owners' Equity	
Value of stock	$10,000	Loan from broker	$4,000
		Equity	6,000

The initial percentage margin is

$$\text{Margin} = \frac{\text{Equity in account}}{\text{Value of stock}} = \frac{\$6,000}{\$10,000} = .60, \text{ or } 60\%$$

If the price declines to $70 per share, the account balance becomes:

Assets		Liabilities and Owners' Equity	
Value of stock	$7,000	Loan from broker	$4,000
		Equity	3,000

The assets in the account fall by the full decrease in the stock value, as does the equity. The percentage margin is now

$$\text{Margin} = \frac{\text{Equity in account}}{\text{Value of stock}} = \frac{\$3,000}{\$7,000} = .43, \text{ or } 43\%$$

If the stock value in Example 3.1 were to fall below $4,000, owners' equity would become negative, meaning the value of the stock is no longer sufficient collateral to cover the loan from the broker. To guard against this possibility, the broker sets a *maintenance margin.* If the percentage margin falls below the maintenance level, the broker will issue a *margin call,* which requires the investor to add new cash or securities to the margin account. If the investor does not act, the broker may sell securities from the account to pay off enough of the loan to restore the percentage margin to an acceptable level.

Example 3.2   Maintenance Margin

Continuing the scenario presented in Example 3.1, suppose the maintenance margin is 30%. How far could the stock price fall before the investor would get a margin call?

Let P be the price of the stock. The value of the investor's 100 shares is then $100P$, and the equity in the account is $100P - \$4,000$. The percentage margin is $(100P - \$4,000)/100P$. The price at which the percentage margin equals the maintenance margin of .3 is found by solving the equation

$$\frac{100P - 4,000}{100P} = .3$$

which implies that $P = \$57.14$. If the price of the stock were to fall below $57.14 per share, the investor would get a margin call.

eXcel APPLICATIONS: Buying on Margin

The following Excel spreadsheet, available in Connect or through your course instructor, makes it easy to analyze the impacts of different margin levels and the volatility of stock prices. It also allows you to compare return on investment for a margin trade with a trade using no borrowed funds.

Excel Questions

1. Suppose you buy 100 shares of stock initially selling for $50, borrowing 25% of the necessary funds from your broker (i.e., the initial margin on your purchase is 25%). You pay an interest rate of 8% on margin loans.

   a. How much of your own money do you invest? How much do you borrow from your broker?

   b. What will be your rate of return for the following stock prices at the end of a 1-year holding period? (i) $40; (ii) $50; (iii) $60.

2. Repeat Question 1 assuming your initial margin was 50%. How does margin affect the risk and return of your position?

	A	B	C	D	E	F	G	H
1								
2			Action or Formula	Ending	Return on		Ending	Return with
3			for Column B	St Price	Investment		St Price	No Margin
4	Initial Equity Investment	$10,000.00	Enter data		−41.60%			−18.80%
5	Amount Borrowed	$10,000.00	(B4/B10) − B4	$20.00	−121.60%		$20.00	−58.80%
6	Initial Stock Price	$50.00	Enter data	25.00	−101.60%		25.00	−48.80%
7	Shares Purchased	400	(B4/B10) − B6	30.00	−81.60%		30.00	−38.80%
8	Ending Stock Price	$40.00	Enter data	35.00	−61.60%		35.00	−28.80%
9	Cash Dividends During Hold Per.	$0.60	Enter data	40.00	−41.60%		40.00	−18.80%
10	Initial Margin Percentage	50.00%	Enter data	45.00	−21.60%		45.00	−8.80%
11	Maintenance Margin Percentage	30.00%	Enter data	50.00	−1.60%		50.00	1.20%
12				55.00	18.40%		55.00	11.20%
13	Rate on Margin Loan	8.00%	Enter data	60.00	38.40%		60.00	21.20%
14	Holding Period in Months	6	Enter data	65.00	58.40%		65.00	31.20%
15			B13 − B14	70.00	78.40%		70.00	41.20%
16	Return on Investment		B4	75.00	98.40%		75.00	51.20%
17	Capital Gain on Stock	−$4,000.00	B7* (B8 − B6)	80.00	118.40%		80.00	61.20%
18	Dividends	$240.00	B7* B9					
19	Interest on Margin Loan	$400.00	B5* (B14/12)* B13					
20	Net Income	−$4,160.00	B17 + B18 − B19			LEGEND:		
21	Initial Investment	$10,000.00	B4			Enter data		
22	Return on Investment	−41.60%	B20/B21			Value calculated		

 Concept Check **3.4**

Suppose the maintenance margin in Example 3.2 is 40%. How far can the stock price fall before the investor gets a margin call?

Why do investors buy securities on margin? They do so when they wish to invest an amount greater than their own money allows. Thus, they can achieve greater upside potential, but they also expose themselves to greater downside risk.

To see how, let's suppose an investor is bullish on FinCorp stock, which is selling for $100 per share. An investor with $10,000 to invest expects FinCorp to go up in price by 30% during the next year. Ignoring any dividends, the expected rate of return would be 30% if the investor invested $10,000 to buy 100 shares.

Table 3.1

Illustration of buying stock on margin

Change in Stock Price	End-of-Year Value of Shares	Repayment of Principal and Interest*	Investor's Rate of Return
30% increase	$26,000	$10,900	51%
No change	20,000	10,900	−9
30% decrease	14,000	10,900	−69

*Assuming the investor buys $20,000 worth of stock, borrowing $10,000 of the purchase price at an interest rate of 9% per year.

But now assume the investor borrows another $10,000 from the broker and invests it in FinCorp, too. The total investment would be $20,000 (for 200 shares). Assuming an interest rate on the margin loan of 9% per year, what will the investor's rate of return be (again ignoring dividends) if the stock price increases 30% by year's end?

The 200 shares will be worth $26,000. Paying off $10,900 of principal and interest on the margin loan leaves $15,100 (i.e., $26,000 − $10,900). The rate of return in this case will be

$$\frac{\$15,100 - \$10,000}{\$10,000} = 51\%$$

The investor has parlayed a 30% rise in the stock's price into a 51% rate of return on the $10,000 investment.

Doing so, however, magnifies the downside risk. Suppose that, instead of going up by 30%, the stock price drops by 30% to $70 per share. In that case, the 200 shares will be worth $14,000, and the investor is left with $3,100 after paying off the $10,900 of principal and interest on the loan. The result is a disastrous return of

$$\frac{\$3,100 - \$10,000}{\$10,000} = -69\%$$

Table 3.1 summarizes the possible results of these hypothetical transactions. If there is no change in the stock price, the investor loses 9%, the cost of the loan.

 Concept Check **3.5**

Suppose that in the FinCorp example, the investor borrows only $5,000 at the same interest rate of 9% per year. What will the rate of return be if the stock price increases by 30%? If it falls by 30%? If it remains unchanged?

3.9 Short Sales

Normally, an investor would first buy a stock and later sell it. With a short sale, the order is reversed. First, you sell and then you buy the shares. In both cases, you begin and end with no shares.

Table 3.2

Cash flows from purchasing versus short-selling shares of stock

Purchase of Stock		
Time	**Action**	**Cash Flow***
0	Buy share	− Initial price
1	Receive dividend, sell share	Ending price + Dividend
Profit = (Ending price + Dividend) − Initial price		

Short Sale of Stock		
Time	**Action**	**Cash Flow***
0	Borrow share; sell it	+ Initial price
1	Repay dividend and buy share to replace the share originally borrowed	− (Ending price + Dividend)
Profit = Initial price − (Ending price + Dividend)		

*A negative cash flow implies a cash *outflow*.

A **short sale** allows investors to profit from a decline in a security's price. An investor borrows a share of stock from a broker and sells it. Later, the short-seller must purchase a share of the same stock in order to replace the one that was borrowed. This is called *covering the short position*. Table 3.2 compares stock purchases to short sales.[2]

The short-seller anticipates the stock price will fall, so that the share can be purchased later at a lower price than it initially sold for; if so, the short-seller will reap a profit. Short-sellers must not only replace the shares but also pay the lender of the security any dividends paid during the short sale.

In practice, the shares loaned out for a short sale are typically provided by the short-seller's brokerage firm, which holds a wide variety of securities of its other investors in street name (i.e., the broker holds the shares registered in its own name on behalf of the client). The owner of the shares need not know that the shares have been lent to the short-seller. If the owner wishes to sell the shares, the brokerage firm will simply borrow shares from another investor. Therefore, the short sale may have an indefinite term. However, if the brokerage firm cannot locate new shares to replace the ones sold, the short-seller will need to repay the loan immediately by purchasing shares in the market and turning them over to the brokerage house to close out the loan.

Finally, exchange rules require that proceeds from a short sale must be kept on account with the broker. The short-seller cannot invest these funds to generate income, although large or institutional investors typically will receive some income from the proceeds of a short sale being held with the broker. Short-sellers also are required to post margin (cash or collateral) with the broker to cover losses should the stock price rise during the short sale.

[2]*Naked short-selling* is a variant on conventional short-selling. In a naked short, a trader sells shares that have not yet been borrowed, assuming that the shares can be acquired in time to meet any delivery deadline. While naked short-selling is prohibited, enforcement has been spotty, as many firms have engaged in it based on their "reasonable belief" that they will be able to acquire the stock by the time delivery is required. Now the SEC is requiring that short-sellers make firm arrangements for delivery before engaging in the sale.

Example 3.3   Short Sales

To illustrate the mechanics of short-selling, suppose you are bearish (pessimistic) on Dot Bomb stock, and its market price is $100 per share. You tell your broker to sell short 1,000 shares. The broker borrows 1,000 shares either from another customer's account or from another broker.

The $100,000 cash proceeds from the short sale are credited to your account. Suppose the broker has a 50% margin requirement on short sales. This means you must have other cash or securities in your account worth at least $50,000 that can serve as margin on the short sale. Let's say that you have $50,000 in Treasury bills. Your account with the broker after the short sale will then be:

Assets		Liabilities and Owners' Equity	
Cash	$100,000	Short position in Dot Bomb stock (1,000 shares owed)	$100,000
T-bills	50,000	Equity	50,000

Your initial percentage margin is the ratio of the equity in the account, $50,000, to the current value of the shares you have borrowed and eventually must return, $100,000:

$$\text{Percentage margin} = \frac{\text{Equity}}{\text{Value of stock owed}} = \frac{\$50,000}{\$100,000} = .50$$

Suppose you are right and Dot Bomb falls to $70 per share. You can now close out your position at a profit. To cover the short sale, you buy 1,000 shares to replace the ones you borrowed. Because the shares now sell for $70, the purchase costs only $70,000.[3] Because your account was credited for $100,000 when the shares were borrowed and sold, your profit is $30,000: The profit equals the decline in the share price times the number of shares sold short.

Like investors who purchase stock on margin, a short-seller must be concerned about margin calls. If the stock price rises, the margin in the account will fall; if margin falls to the maintenance level, the short-seller will receive a margin call.

Example 3.4   Margin Calls on Short Positions

Suppose the broker has a maintenance margin of 30% on short sales. This means the equity in your account must be at least 30% of the value of your short position at all times. How much can the price of Dot Bomb stock rise before you get a margin call?

Let P be the price of Dot Bomb stock. Then the value of the shares you must pay back is $1,000P$ and the equity in your account is $150,000 - 1,000P$. Your short position margin ratio is Equity/Value of stock $= (150,000 - 1,000P)/1,000P$. The critical value of P is thus

$$\frac{\text{Equity}}{\text{Value of shares owed}} = \frac{150,000 - 1,000P}{1,000P} = .3$$

[3]Notice that when buying on margin, you borrow a given amount of dollars from your broker, so the amount of the loan is independent of the share price. In contrast, when short-selling, you borrow a given number of *shares*, which must be returned. Therefore, when the price of the shares changes, the value of the loan also changes.

This Excel spreadsheet model was built using Example 3.3 for Dot Bomb. The model allows you to analyze the effects of returns, margin calls, and different levels of initial and maintenance margins. The model also includes a sensitivity analysis for ending stock price and return on investment.

Excel Questions

1. Suppose you sell short 100 shares of stock initially selling for $100 a share. Your initial margin requirement is 50% of the value of the stock sold. You receive no interest on the funds placed in your margin account.

a. How much do you need to contribute to your margin account?

b. Assuming the stock pays no dividends, what will be your rate of return for the following stock prices at the end of a 1-year holding period? (i) $90; (ii) $100; (iii) $110.

2. Repeat Question 1(b) but now assume that the stock pays dividends of $2 per share at year-end. What is the relationship between the total rate of return on the stock and the return to your short position?

	A	B	C	D	E
1					
2			Action or Formula	Ending	Return on
3			for Column B	St Price	Investment
4	Initial Investment	$50,000.00	Enter data		60.00%
5	Initial Stock Price	$100.00	Enter data	$170.00	−140.00%
6	Number of Shares Sold Short	1,000	(B4/B9)/B5	160.00	−120.00%
7	Ending Stock Price	$70.00	Enter data	150.00	−100.00%
8	Cash Dividends per Share	$0.00	Enter data	140.00	−80.00%
9	Initial Margin Percentage	50.00%	Enter data	130.00	−60.00%
10	Maintenance Margin Percentage	30.00%	Enter data	120.00	−40.00%
11				110.00	−20.00%
12	**Return on Short Sale**			100.00	0.00%
13	Capital Gain on Stock	$30,000.00	B6* (B5 − B7)	90.00	20.00%
14	Dividends Paid	$0.00	B8 * B6	80.00	40.00%
15	Net Income	$30,000.00	B13 − B14	70.00	60.00%
16	Initial Investment	$50,000.00	B4	60.00	80.00%
17	Return on Investment	60.00%	B15/B16	50.00	100.00%
18				40.00	120.00%
19	**Margin Positions**			30.00	140.00%
20	Margin Based on Ending Price	114.29%	(B4 + (B5 * B6) − B14 − (B6 * B7)) / (B6 * B7)	20.00	160.00%
21				10.00	180.00%
22	Price for Margin Call	$115.38	(B4 + (B5 * B6) − B14) / (B6 * (1 + B10))		
23					LEGEND:
24					Enter data
25					Value calculated

which implies that $P = \$115.38$ per share. If Dot Bomb stock should *rise* above $115.38 per share, you will get a margin call, and you will either have to put up additional cash or cover your short position by buying shares to replace the ones borrowed.

✓ Concept Check **3.6**

a. Construct the balance sheet if Dot Bomb in Example 3.4 goes up to $110.

b. If the short position maintenance margin in the Dot Bomb example is 40%, how far can the stock price rise before the investor gets a margin call?

Short-Selling Comes Under Fire—Again

Short-selling has long been viewed with suspicion, if not outright hostility. England banned short sales for a good part of the 18th century. Napoleon called short-sellers enemies of the state. In the U.S., short-selling was widely viewed as contributing to the market crash of 1929, and in 2008, short-sellers were blamed for the collapse of the investment banks Bear Stearns and Lehman Brothers. With share prices of other financial firms tumbling in September 2008, the SEC instituted a temporary ban on short-selling of nearly 1,000 of those firms. Similarly, the Financial Services Authority, the financial regulator in the U.K., prohibited short sales on about 30 financial companies, and Australia banned shorting altogether.

The rationale for these bans is that short sales put downward pressure on share prices that in some cases may be unwarranted: Stories abound of investors who first put on a short sale and then spread negative rumors about the firm to drive down its price. More often, however, shorting is a legitimate bet that a share price is too high and is due to fall. Nevertheless, during the market stresses of late 2008, the widespread feeling was that even if short positions were legitimate, regulators should do what they could to prop up the affected institutions.

Hostility to short-selling may well stem from confusion between bad news and the bearer of that news. Short-selling allows investors whose analysis indicates a firm is overpriced to take action on that belief—and to profit if they are correct. Rather than *causing* the stock price to fall, shorts may be *anticipating* a decline in the stock price. Their sales simply force the market to reflect the deteriorating prospects of troubled firms sooner than it might have otherwise. In other words, short-selling is part of the process by which the full range of information and opinion—pessimistic as well as optimistic—is brought to bear on stock prices.

For example, short-sellers took large (negative) positions in firms such as WorldCom, Enron, and Tyco even before these firms were exposed by regulators. In fact, one might argue that these emerging short positions helped regulators identify the previously undetected scandals. And in the end, Lehman and Bear Stearns were brought down by their very real losses on their mortgage-related investments—not by unfounded rumors.

Academic research supports the conjecture that short sales contribute to efficient "price discovery." For example, the greater the demand for shorting a stock, the lower its future returns tend to be; moreover, firms that attack short-sellers with threats of legal action or bad publicity tend to have especially poor future returns.* Short-sale bans may in the end be nothing more than an understandable, but nevertheless misguided, impulse to "shoot the messenger."

*See, for example, C. Jones and O. A. Lamont, "Short Sale Constraints and Stock Returns," *Journal of Financial Economics,* November 2002, pp. 207–39; or O. A. Lamont, "Go Down Fighting: Short Sellers vs. Firms," *Review of Asset Pricing Studies,* 2012, pp. 1–30.

Short-selling periodically comes under attack, particularly during times of financial stress when share prices fall. The last few years have been no exception to this rule. For example, following the 2008 financial crisis, the SEC voted to restrict short sales in stocks that decline by at least 10% on a given day, allowing them to be shorted on that day and the next only at a price greater than the highest bid price across national stock markets. The nearby box examines the controversy surrounding short sales in greater detail.

3.10　Regulation of Securities Markets

Trading in securities markets in the United States is regulated by a myriad of laws. The major governing legislation includes the Securities Act of 1933 and the Securities Exchange Act of 1934. The 1933 act requires full disclosure of relevant information relating to the issue of new securities. This is the act that requires registration of new securities and issuance of a prospectus that details the financial prospects of the firm. SEC approval of a prospectus or financial report is not an endorsement of the security as a good investment. The SEC cares only that the relevant facts are disclosed; investors must make their own evaluation of the security's value.

The 1934 act established the Securities and Exchange Commission to administer the provisions of the 1933 act. It also extended the disclosure principle of the 1933 act by requiring periodic disclosure of relevant financial information by firms with already-issued securities on secondary exchanges.

The 1934 act also empowers the SEC to register and regulate securities exchanges, OTC trading, brokers, and dealers. While the SEC is the administrative agency responsible for broad oversight of the securities markets, it shares responsibility with other regulatory agencies. The Commodity Futures Trading Commission (CFTC) regulates trading in futures markets, while the Federal Reserve has broad responsibility for the health of the U.S. financial system. In this role, the Fed sets margin requirements on stocks and stock options and regulates bank lending to security market participants.

The Securities Investor Protection Act of 1970 established the Securities Investor Protection Corporation (SIPC) to protect investors from losses if their brokerage firms fail. Just as the Federal Deposit Insurance Corporation provides depositors with federal protection against bank failure, the SIPC ensures that investors will receive securities held for their account in street name by a failed brokerage firm up to a limit of $500,000 per customer. The SIPC is financed by levying an "insurance premium" on its participating, or member, brokerage firms.

Security trading also is subject to state laws, known generally as *blue sky laws* because they are intended to give investors a clearer view of investment prospects. Varying state laws were somewhat unified when many states adopted portions of the Uniform Securities Act, which was enacted in 1956.

The 2008 financial crisis also led to regulatory changes, some of which we detailed in Chapter 1. The Financial Stability Oversight Council (FSOC) was established by the Dodd-Frank Wall Street Reform and Consumer Protection Act to monitor the stability of the U.S. financial system. It is largely concerned with risks arising from potential failures of large, interconnected banks, but its voting members are the chairpersons of the main U.S. regulatory agencies, and therefore the FSOC serves a broader role to connect and coordinate key financial regulators.

Self-Regulation

In addition to government regulation, the securities market exercises considerable self-regulation. The most important overseer in this regard is the Financial Industry Regulatory Authority (FINRA), which is the largest nongovernmental regulator of all securities firms in the United States. FINRA was formed in 2007 through the consolidation of the National Association of Securities Dealers (NASD) with the self-regulatory arm of the New York Stock Exchange. It describes its broad mission as the fostering of investor protection and market integrity. It examines securities firms, writes and enforces rules concerning trading practices, and administers a dispute-resolution forum for investors and registered firms.

The community of investment professionals provides another layer of self-regulation. For example, the CFA Institute has developed standards of professional conduct that govern the behavior of members with the Chartered Financial Analysts designation, commonly referred to as CFAs. The nearby box presents a brief outline of those principles.

The Sarbanes-Oxley Act

The scandals of 2000–2002 centered largely on three broad practices: allocations of shares in initial public offerings, tainted securities research and recommendations put out to the public, and, probably most important, misleading financial statements and accounting

Excerpts from CFA Institute Standards of Professional Conduct

I. Professionalism

- Knowledge of law. Members must understand, have knowledge of, and comply with all applicable laws, rules, and regulations including the Code of Ethics and Standards of Professional Conduct.
- Independence and objectivity. Members shall maintain independence and objectivity in their professional activities.
- Misrepresentation. Members must not knowingly misrepresent investment analysis, recommendations, or other professional activities.

II. Integrity of Capital Markets

- Non-public information. Members must not exploit material non-public information.
- Market manipulation. Members shall not attempt to distort prices or trading volume with the intent to mislead market participants.

III. Duties to Clients

- Loyalty, prudence, and care. Members must place their clients' interests before their own and act with reasonable care on their behalf.
- Fair dealing. Members shall deal fairly and objectively with clients when making investment recommendations or taking actions.
- Suitability. Members shall make a reasonable inquiry into a client's financial situation, investment experience, and investment objectives prior to making appropriate investment recommendations.
- Performance presentation. Members shall attempt to ensure that investment performance is presented fairly, accurately, and completely.
- Confidentiality. Members must keep information about clients confidential unless the client permits disclosure.

IV. Duties to Employers

- Loyalty. Members must act for the benefit of their employer.
- Compensation. Members must not accept compensation from sources that would create a conflict of interest with their employer's interests without written consent from all involved parties.
- Supervisors. Members must make reasonable efforts to detect and prevent violation of applicable laws and regulations by anyone subject to their supervision.

V. Investment Analysis and Recommendations

- Diligence. Members must exercise diligence and have reasonable basis for investment analysis, recommendations, or actions.
- Communication. Members must distinguish fact from opinion in their presentation of analysis and disclose general principles of investment processes used in analysis.

VI. Conflicts of Interest

- Disclosure of conflicts. Members must disclose all matters that reasonably could be expected to impair their objectivity or interfere with their other duties.
- Priority of transactions. Transactions for clients and employers must have priority over transactions for the benefit of a member.

VII. Responsibilities as Member of CFA Institute

- Conduct. Members must not engage in conduct that compromises the reputation or integrity of the CFA Institute or CFA designation.

practices. The Sarbanes-Oxley Act, often called SOX, was passed by Congress in 2002 in response to these problems. Among the key reforms are:

- Creation of the Public Company Accounting Oversight Board to oversee the auditing of public companies.
- Rules requiring independent financial experts to serve on audit committees of a firm's board of directors.
- CEOs and CFOs must now personally certify that their firms' financial reports "fairly represent, in all material respects, the operations and financial condition of the company," and are subject to personal penalties if those reports turn out to be misleading. Following the letter of the rules may still be necessary, but it is no longer sufficient accounting practice.

- Auditors may no longer provide several other services to their clients. This is intended to prevent potential profits on consulting work from influencing the quality of their audit.
- The Board of Directors must be composed of independent directors and hold regular meetings of directors in which company management is not present (and therefore cannot impede or influence the discussion).

More recently, there has been a fair amount of pushback on Sarbanes-Oxley. Many observers believe that the compliance costs associated with the law are too onerous, especially for smaller firms, and that heavy-handed regulatory oversight is giving foreign locales an undue advantage over the United States when firms decide where to list their securities. Moreover, the efficacy of single-country regulation is being tested in the face of increasing globalization and the ease with which funds can move across national borders.

Insider Trading

Regulations also prohibit insider trading. It is illegal for anyone to transact in securities and thus profit from **inside information,** that is, private information held by officers, directors, or major stockholders that has not yet been divulged to the public. But the definition of insiders can be ambiguous. While it is obvious that the chief financial officer of a firm is an insider, it is less clear whether the firm's biggest supplier can be considered an insider. Yet a supplier may deduce the firm's near-term prospects from significant changes in orders. This gives the supplier a unique form of private information, yet the supplier is not technically an insider. These ambiguities plague security analysts, whose job is to uncover as much information as possible concerning the firm's expected prospects. The dividing line between legal private information and illegal inside information can be fuzzy.

The SEC requires officers, directors, and major stockholders to report all transactions in their firm's stock. The idea is to track any implicit vote of confidence or no confidence made by insiders.

Insiders *do* exploit their knowledge. Three forms of evidence support this conclusion. First, there have been well-publicized convictions of principals in insider trading schemes.

Second, there is considerable evidence of "leakage" of useful information to some traders before any public announcement of that information. For example, share prices of firms announcing dividend increases (which the market interprets as good news concerning the firm's prospects) commonly increase in value a few days *before* the public announcement of the increase. Clearly, some investors are acting on the good news before it is released to the public. Share prices still rise substantially on the day of the public release of good news, however, indicating that insiders, or their associates, have not fully bid up the price of the stock to the level commensurate with the news.

A third form of evidence on insider trading has to do with returns earned on trades by insiders. Researchers have examined the SEC's summary of insider trading to measure the performance of insiders. In one of the best known of these studies, Jaffee[4] examined the abnormal return of stocks over the months following purchases or sales by insiders. For months in which insider purchasers of a stock exceeded insider sellers of the stock by three or more, the stock had an abnormal return in the following 8 months of about 5%. Moreover, when insider sellers exceeded insider buyers, the stock tended to perform poorly.

---

[4]Jeffrey E. Jaffee, "Special Information and Insider Trading," *Journal of Business* 47 (July 1974).

SUMMARY

1. Firms issue securities to raise the capital necessary to finance their investments. Investment bankers market these securities to the public on the primary market. Investment bankers generally act as underwriters who purchase the securities from the firm and resell them to the public at a markup. Before the securities may be sold to the public, the firm must publish an SEC-approved prospectus that provides information on the firm's prospects.

2. Already-issued securities are traded on the secondary market, that is, on organized stock markets; on the over-the-counter market; and occasionally, for very large trades, through direct negotiation. Brokerage firms holding licenses to trade on security exchanges sell their services to individuals, charging commissions for executing trades on their behalf.

3. Trading may take place in dealer markets, via electronic communication networks, or in specialist markets. In dealer markets, security dealers post bid and ask prices at which they are willing to trade. Brokers for individuals execute trades at the best available prices. In electronic markets, the existing book of limit orders provides the terms at which trades can be executed. Mutually agreeable offers to buy or sell securities are automatically crossed by the computer system operating the market.

4. NASDAQ was traditionally a dealer market in which a network of dealers negotiated directly over sales of securities. The NYSE was traditionally a specialist market. Today, however, trading in both markets is overwhelmingly electronic.

5. Buying on margin means borrowing money from a broker to buy more securities than can be purchased with one's own money alone. By buying securities on margin, an investor magnifies both the upside potential and the downside risk. If the equity in a margin account falls below the required maintenance level, the investor will get a margin call from the broker.

6. Short-selling is the practice of selling securities that the seller does not own. The short-seller borrows the securities sold through a broker and may be required to cover the short position at any time on demand. The cash proceeds of a short sale are kept in escrow by the broker, and the broker usually requires that the short-seller deposit additional cash or securities to serve as margin (collateral).

7. Securities trading is regulated by the Securities and Exchange Commission, by other government agencies, and through self-regulation of the exchanges. Many of the important regulations have to do with full disclosure of relevant information concerning the securities in question. Insider trading rules also prohibit traders from attempting to profit from inside information.

KEY TERMS

primary market	ask price	stock exchanges
secondary market	bid–ask spread	latency
private placement	limit order	algorithmic trading
initial public offering (IPO)	over-the-counter (OTC)	high-frequency trading
underwriters	market	blocks
prospectus	NASDAQ Stock Market	dark pools
dealer markets	electronic communication	margin
auction market	networks (ECNs)	short sale
bid price	specialist	inside information

PROBLEM SETS

1. What are the differences among a stop-loss order, a limit sell order, and a market order?

2. Why have average trade sizes declined in recent years?

3. How do margin trades magnify both the upside potential and the downside risk of an investment position?

4. A market order has:

   a. Price uncertainty but not execution uncertainty.
   b. Both price uncertainty and execution uncertainty.
   c. Execution uncertainty but not price uncertainty.

5. Where would an illiquid security in a developing country *most likely* trade?

   a. Broker markets.
   b. Electronic crossing networks.
   c. Electronic limit-order markets.

6. Dée Trader opens a brokerage account and purchases 300 shares of Internet Dreams at $40 per share. She borrows $4,000 from her broker to help pay for the purchase. The interest rate on the loan is 8%.

   a. What is the margin in Dée's account when she first purchases the stock?
   b. If the share price falls to $30 per share by the end of the year, what is the remaining margin in her account? If the maintenance margin requirement is 30%, will she receive a margin call?
   c. What is the rate of return on her investment?

7. Old Economy Traders opened an account to short sell 1,000 shares of Internet Dreams from the previous problem. The initial margin requirement was 50%. (The margin account pays no interest.) A year later, the price of Internet Dreams has risen from $40 to $50, and the stock has paid a dividend of $2 per share.

   a. What is the remaining margin in the account?
   b. If the maintenance margin requirement is 30%, will Old Economy receive a margin call?
   c. What is the rate of return on the investment?

8. Consider the following limit-order book for a share of stock. The last trade in the stock occurred at a price of $50.

Limit Buy Orders		Limit Sell Orders	
Price	Shares	Price	Shares
$49.75	500	$50.25	100
49.50	800	51.50	100
49.25	500	54.75	300
49.00	200	58.25	100
48.50	600		

   a. If a market buy order for 100 shares comes in, at what price will it be filled?
   b. At what price would the next market buy order be filled?
   c. If you were a security dealer, would you want to increase or decrease your inventory of this stock?

9. You are bullish on Telecom stock. The current market price is $50 per share, and you have $5,000 of your own to invest. You borrow an additional $5,000 from your broker at an interest rate of 8% per year and invest $10,000 in the stock.

   a. What will be your rate of return if the price of Telecom stock goes up by 10% during the next year? The stock currently pays no dividends.
   b. How far does the price of Telecom stock have to fall for you to get a margin call if the maintenance margin is 30%? Assume the price fall happens immediately.

10. You are bearish on Telecom and decide to sell short 100 shares at the current market price of $50 per share.

   a. How much in cash or securities must you put into your brokerage account if the broker's initial margin requirement is 50% of the value of the short position?
   b. How high can the price of the stock go before you get a margin call if the maintenance margin is 30% of the value of the short position?

11. Suppose that Xtel currently is selling at $20 per share. You buy 1,000 shares using $15,000 of your own money, borrowing the remainder of the purchase price from your broker. The rate on the margin loan is 8%.

   a. What is the percentage increase in the net worth of your brokerage account if the price of Xtel *immediately* changes to: (i) $22; (ii) $20; (iii) $18? What is the relationship between your percentage return and the percentage change in the price of Xtel?

   b. If the maintenance margin is 25%, how low can Xtel's price fall before you get a margin call?

   c. How would your answer to (b) change if you had financed the initial purchase with only $10,000 of your own money?

   d. What is the rate of return on your margined position (assuming again that you invest $15,000 of your own money) if Xtel is selling *after 1 year* at: (i) $22; (ii) $20; (iii) $18? What is the relationship between your percentage return and the percentage change in the price of Xtel? Assume that Xtel pays no dividends.

   e. Continue to assume that a year has passed. How low can Xtel's price fall before you get a margin call?

12. Suppose that you sell short 1,000 shares of Xtel, currently selling for $20 per share, and give your broker $15,000 to establish your margin account.

   a. If you earn no interest on the funds in your margin account, what will be your rate of return after one year if Xtel stock is selling at: (i) $22; (ii) $20; (iii) $18? Assume that Xtel pays no dividends.

   b. If the maintenance margin is 25%, how high can Xtel's price rise before you get a margin call?

   c. Redo parts (a) and (b), but now assume that Xtel also has paid a year-end dividend of $1 per share. The prices in part (a) should be interpreted as ex-dividend, that is, prices after the dividend has been paid.

13. Here is some price information on Marriott:

	Bid	Ask
Marriott	69.95	70.05

   You have placed a stop-loss order to sell at $70. What are you telling your broker? Given market prices, will your order be executed?

14. Here is some price information on FinCorp stock. Suppose that FinCorp trades in a dealer market.

Bid	Ask
55.25	55.50

   a. Suppose you have submitted an order to your broker to buy at market. At what price will your trade be executed?

   b. Suppose you have submitted an order to sell at market. At what price will your trade be executed?

   c. Suppose you have submitted a limit order to sell at $55.62. What will happen?

   d. Suppose you have submitted a limit order to buy at $55.37. What will happen?

15. You've borrowed $20,000 on margin to buy shares in Ixnay, which is now selling at $40 per share. Your account starts at the initial margin requirement of 50%. The maintenance margin is 35%. Two days later, the stock price falls to $35 per share.

   a. Will you receive a margin call?

   b. How low can the price of Ixnay shares fall before you receive a margin call?

16. On January 1, you sold short one round lot (i.e., 100 shares) of Four Sisters stock at $21 per share. On March 1, a dividend of $2 per share was paid. On April 1, you covered the short sale by buying the stock at a price of $15 per share. You paid 50 cents per share in commissions for each transaction. What is the value of your account on April 1?

1. FBN Inc. has just sold 100,000 shares in an initial public offering. The underwriter's explicit fees were $70,000. The offering price for the shares was $50, but immediately upon issue, the share price jumped to $53.

   a. What is your best guess as to the total cost to FBN of the equity issue?
   b. Is the entire cost of the underwriting a source of profit to the underwriters?

2. If you place a stop-loss order to sell 100 shares of stock at $55 when the current price is $62, how much will you receive for each share if the price drops to $50?

   a. $50.
   b. $55.
   c. $54.87.
   d. Cannot tell from the information given.

3. Specialists on the New York Stock Exchange do all of the following *except:*

   a. Act as dealers for their own accounts.
   b. Execute limit orders.
   c. Help provide liquidity to the marketplace.
   d. Act as odd-lot dealers.

E-INVESTMENTS EXERCISES

Several factors must be considered when choosing a brokerage firm to execute your trades. There are also a wide range of services claiming to objectively evaluate these firms. However, many are actually sponsored by the brokerage firms themselves.

Go to the Web site **www.consumersearch.com/online-brokers/reviews** and read the information provided under "Ratings of Sources." Search for Barron's best online broker's survey. There you can find general information as well as details on offerings, costs, and so on. Suppose that you have $10,000 to invest and want to put it in a non-IRA account.

1. Are all of the brokerage firms suitable if you want to open a cash account? Are they all suitable if you want a margin account?

2. Choose two of the firms listed. Assume that you want to buy 100 shares of LLY stock using a market order. If the order is filled at $75 per share, how much will the commission be for the two firms if you place an online order?

3. Are there any maintenance fees associated with the account at either brokerage firm?

4. Now assume that you have a margin account and the balance is $5,000. Find the interest rate you would pay if you borrowed money to buy the stock on margin.

✅ SOLUTIONS TO CONCEPT CHECKS

1. Limited-time shelf registration was introduced because its cost savings outweighed the disadvantage of slightly less up-to-date disclosures. Allowing unlimited shelf registration would circumvent "blue sky" laws that ensure proper disclosure as the financial circumstances of the firm change over time.

2. *a.* Used cars trade in dealer markets (used-car lots or auto dealerships) and in direct search markets when individuals advertise in local newspapers or on the Web.

   b. Paintings trade in broker markets when clients commission brokers to buy or sell art for them, in dealer markets at art galleries, and in auction markets.

   c. Rare coins trade in dealer markets in coin shops, but they also trade in auctions and in direct search markets when individuals advertise they want to buy or sell coins.

3. *a.* You should give your broker a market order. It will be executed immediately and is the cheapest type of order in terms of brokerage fees.

   b. You should give your broker a limit-buy order, which will be executed only if the shares can be obtained at a price about 5% below the current price.

   c. You should give your broker a limit-sell order, which will be executed if the share price rises above the level at which you are convinced that the firm is overvalued.

4. Solving

$$\frac{100P - \$4,000}{100P} = .4$$

   yields $P = \$66.67$ per share.

5. The investor will purchase 150 shares, with a rate of return as follows:

Year-End Change in Price	Year-End Value of Shares	Repayment of Principal and Interest	Investor's Rate of Return
30%	$19,500	$5,450	40.5%
No change	15,000	5,450	−4.5
−30%	10,500	5,450	−49.5

6. *a.* Once Dot Bomb stock goes up to $110, your balance sheet will be:

Assets		Liabilities and Owner's Equity	
Cash	$100,000	Short position in Dot Bomb	$110,000
T-bills	50,000	Equity	40,000

   b. Solving

$$\frac{\$150,000 - 1,000P}{1,000P} = .4$$

   yields $P = \$107.14$ per share.

Mutual Funds and Other Investment Companies

4

THE PREVIOUS CHAPTER introduced you to the mechanics of trading securities and the structure of the markets in which securities trade. Commonly, however, individual investors do not trade securities directly for their own accounts. Instead, they direct their funds to investment companies that purchase securities on their behalf. The most important of these financial intermediaries are open-end investment companies, more commonly known as mutual funds, to which we devote most of this chapter. We also touch briefly on other types of investment companies such as unit investment trusts, hedge funds, and closed-end funds.

We begin the chapter by describing and comparing the various types of investment companies available to investors. We then examine the functions of mutual funds, their investment styles and policies, and the costs of investing in these funds. Next we take a first look at the investment performance of these funds. We consider the impact of expenses and turnover on net performance and examine the extent to which performance is consistent from one period to the next. In other words, will the mutual funds that were the best *past* performers be the best *future* performers? Finally, we discuss sources of information on mutual funds, and we consider in detail the information provided in Morningstar's mutual fund reports.

4.1 Investment Companies

Investment companies are financial intermediaries that collect funds from individual investors and invest those funds in a potentially wide range of securities or other assets. Pooling of assets is the key idea behind investment companies. Each investor has a claim to the portfolio established by the investment company in proportion to the amount invested. These companies thus provide a mechanism for small investors to "team up" to obtain the benefits of large-scale investing.

Investment companies perform several important functions for their investors:

1. *Record keeping and administration.* Investment companies issue periodic status reports, keeping track of capital gains distributions, dividends, investments, and redemptions, and they may reinvest dividend and interest income for shareholders.

2. *Diversification and divisibility.* By pooling their money, investment companies enable investors to hold fractional shares of many different securities. They can act as large investors even if any individual shareholder cannot.

3. *Professional management.* Investment companies can support full-time staffs of security analysts and portfolio managers who attempt to achieve superior investment results for their investors.

4. *Lower transaction costs.* Because they trade large blocks of securities, investment companies can achieve substantial savings on brokerage fees and commissions.

While all investment companies pool assets of individual investors, they also need to divide claims to those assets among those investors. Investors buy shares in investment companies, and ownership is proportional to the number of shares purchased. The value of each share is called the **net asset value (NAV).** Net asset value equals assets minus liabilities expressed on a per-share basis:

$$\text{Net asset value} = \frac{\text{Market value of assets} - \text{Liabilities}}{\text{Shares outstanding}}$$

Example 4.1   Net Asset Value

Consider a mutual fund that manages a portfolio of securities worth $120 million. Suppose the fund owes $4 million to its investment advisers and another $1 million for rent, wages due, and miscellaneous expenses. The fund has 5 million shares outstanding.

$$\text{Net asset value} = \frac{\$120 \text{ million} - \$5 \text{ million}}{5 \text{ million shares}} = \$23 \text{ per share}$$

 Concept Check **4.1**

Consider these data from the March 2016 balance sheet of Vanguard's Growth and Income Fund. What was the net asset value of the fund?

Assets:	$5,986.0 million
Liabilities:	$118.5 million
Shares:	148.36 million

4.2   Types of Investment Companies

In the United States, investment companies are classified by the Investment Company Act of 1940 as either unit investment trusts or managed investment companies. The portfolios of unit investment trusts are essentially fixed and thus are called "unmanaged." In contrast, managed companies are so named because securities in their investment portfolios are continually bought and sold: The portfolios are managed. Managed companies are further classified as either closed-end or open-end. Open-end companies are what we commonly call mutual funds.

Unit Investment Trusts

Unit investment trusts are pools of money invested in a portfolio that is fixed for the life of the fund. To form a unit investment trust, a sponsor, typically a brokerage firm, buys a portfolio of securities that are deposited into a trust. It then sells shares, or "units," in the trust, called *redeemable trust certificates.* All income and payments of principal from the portfolio are paid out by the fund's trustees (a bank or trust company) to the shareholders.

There is little active management of a unit investment trust because once established, the portfolio composition is fixed; hence these trusts are referred to as *unmanaged.* Trusts tend to invest in relatively uniform types of assets; for example, one trust may invest in municipal bonds, another in corporate bonds. The uniformity of the portfolio is consistent with the lack of active management. The trusts provide investors a vehicle to purchase a pool of one particular type of asset that can be included in an overall portfolio as desired.

Sponsors of unit investment trusts earn their profit by selling shares in the trust at a premium to the cost of acquiring the underlying assets. For example, a trust that has pur-chased $5 million of assets may sell 5,000 shares to the public at a price of $1,030 per share, which (assuming the trust has no liabilities) represents a 3% premium over the net asset value of the securities held by the trust. The 3% premium is the trustee's fee for establishing the trust.

Investors who wish to liquidate their holdings of a unit investment trust may sell the shares back to the trustee for net asset value. The trustees can either sell enough securities from the asset portfolio to obtain the cash necessary to pay the investor, or they may instead sell the shares to a new investor (again at a slight premium to net asset value). Unit investment trusts have steadily lost market share to mutual funds in recent years. Assets in such trusts declined from $105 billion in 1990 to only $94 billion in 2016.

Managed Investment Companies

There are two types of managed companies: closed-end and open-end. In both cases, the fund's board of directors, which is elected by shareholders, hires a management com-pany to manage the portfolio for an annual fee that typically ranges from .2% to 1.25% of assets. In many cases the management company is the firm that organized the fund. For example, Fidelity Management and Research Corporation sponsors many Fidelity mutual funds and is responsible for managing the portfolios. It assesses a management fee on each Fidelity fund. In other cases, a mutual fund will hire an outside portfolio manager. For example, Vanguard has hired Wellington Management as the investment adviser for its Wellington Fund. Most management companies have contracts to manage several funds.

Open-end funds stand ready to redeem or issue shares at their net asset value (although both purchases and redemptions may involve sales charges). When investors in open-end funds wish to "cash out" their shares, they sell them back to the fund at NAV. In contrast, **closed-end funds** do not redeem or issue shares. Investors in closed-end funds who wish to cash out must sell their shares to other investors. Shares of closed-end funds are traded on organized exchanges and can be purchased through brokers just like other

FUND	NAV	MKT PRICE	PREM/ DISC %	52-WEEK MKT RETURN %
Gabelli Div & Inc Tr (GDV)	21.18	18.77	−11.38	−8.49
Gabelli Equity Trust (GAB)	5.83	5.54	−4.97	−7.25
General Amer Investors(GAM)	37.67	30.83	−18.16	−11.73
Guggenheim Enh Eq Inc (GPM)	8.30	7.55	−9.04	−4.55
Guggenheim Enh Eq Strat (GGE)	17.08	15.31	−10.36	−3.47
Guggenheim EW Enh Eq Inc (GEQ)	17.97	15.98	−11.07	−12.85
J Hancock Tx-Adv Div Inc (HTD)	25.46	23.62	−7.23	19.68
Liberty All-Star Equity (USA)	5.93	5.01	−15.51	−8.39

Figure 4.1 Closed-end mutual funds

Source: Data compiled from *The Wall Street Journal Online*, May 24, 2016.

common stock; their prices, therefore, can differ from NAV. In early 2016, about $261 billion of assets were held in closed-end funds.

Figure 4.1 is a listing of closed-end funds. The first column gives the name and ticker symbol of the fund. The next two columns give the fund's most recent net asset value and closing share price. The premium or discount in the next column is the percentage difference between price and NAV: (Price − NAV)/NAV. Notice that these funds are all selling at discounts to NAV (indicated by negative differences). Finally, the 52-week return based on the percentage change in share price plus dividend income is presented in the last column.

The common divergence of price from net asset value, often by wide margins, is a puzzle that has yet to be fully explained. To see why this is a puzzle, consider a closed-end fund that is selling at a discount from net asset value. If the fund were to sell all the assets in the portfolio, it would realize proceeds equal to net asset value. The difference between the market price of the fund and the fund's NAV would represent the per-share increase in the wealth of the fund's investors. Moreover, fund premiums or discounts tend to dissipate over time, so funds selling at a discount receive a boost to their rate of return as the discount shrinks. Pontiff estimates that a fund selling at a 20% discount would have an expected 12-month return more than 6% greater than funds selling at net asset value.[1]

Interestingly, while many closed-end funds sell at a discount from net asset value, the prices of these funds when originally issued are often above NAV. This is a further puzzle, as it is hard to explain why investors would purchase these newly issued funds at a premium to NAV when the shares tend to fall to a discount shortly after issue.

In contrast to closed-end funds, the price of open-end funds cannot fall below NAV, because these funds stand ready to redeem shares at NAV. The offering price will exceed NAV, however, if the fund carries a **load.** A load is, in effect, a sales charge. Load funds are sold by securities brokers and directly by mutual fund groups.

Unlike closed-end funds, open-end mutual funds do not trade on organized exchanges. Instead, investors simply buy shares from and liquidate through the investment company at net asset value. Thus, the number of outstanding shares of these funds changes daily.

Other Investment Organizations

Some intermediaries are not formally organized or regulated as investment companies but nevertheless serve similar functions. Three of the more important are commingled funds, real estate investment trusts, and hedge funds.

Commingled Funds   Commingled funds are partnerships of investors that pool funds. The management firm that organizes the partnership, for example, a bank or insurance company, manages the funds for a fee. Typical partners in a commingled fund might be trust or retirement accounts with portfolios much larger than those of most individual investors, but still too small to warrant managing on a separate basis.

---

[1]Jeffrey Pontiff, "Costly Arbitrage: Evidence from Closed-End Funds," *Quarterly Journal of Economics* 111 (November 1996), pp. 1135–51.

Commingled funds are similar in form to open-end mutual funds. Instead of shares, though, the fund offers *units,* which are bought and sold at net asset value. A bank or insurance company may offer an array of different commingled funds, for example, a money market fund, a bond fund, and a common stock fund.

Real Estate Investment Trusts (REITs)   A REIT is similar to a closed-end fund. REITs invest in real estate or loans secured by real estate. Besides issuing shares, they raise capital by borrowing from banks and issuing bonds or mortgages. Most of them are highly leveraged, with a typical debt ratio of 70%.

There are two principal kinds of REITs. *Equity trusts* invest in real estate directly, whereas *mortgage trusts* invest primarily in mortgage and construction loans. REITs generally are established by banks, insurance companies, or mortgage companies, which then serve as investment managers to earn a fee.

Hedge Funds   Like mutual funds, **hedge funds** are vehicles that allow private investors to pool assets to be invested by a fund manager. Unlike mutual funds, however, hedge funds are commonly structured as private partnerships and thus subject to only minimal SEC regulation. They typically are open only to wealthy or institutional investors. Many require investors to agree to initial "lock-ups," that is, periods as long as several years in which investments cannot be withdrawn. Lock-ups allow hedge funds to invest in illiquid assets without worrying about meeting demands for redemption of funds. Moreover, because hedge funds are only lightly regulated, their managers can pursue investment strategies involving, for example, heavy use of derivatives, short sales, and leverage; such strategies typically are not open to mutual fund managers.

Hedge funds by design are empowered to invest in a wide range of investments, with various funds focusing on derivatives, distressed firms, currency speculation, convertible bonds, emerging markets, merger arbitrage, and so on. Other funds may jump from one asset class to another as perceived investment opportunities shift.

Hedge funds enjoyed great growth in the last several years, with assets under management ballooning from about $50 billion in 1990 to about $3 trillion in 2016. We devote all of Chapter 26 to these funds.

4.3   Mutual Funds

Mutual funds are the common name for open-end investment companies. This is the dominant investment company today, accounting for 87% of investment company assets. Assets under management in the U.S. mutual fund industry were approximately $15.7 trillion in early 2016, with approximately the same amount held in non-U.S. funds.

Investment Policies

Each mutual fund has a specified investment policy, which is described in the fund's prospectus. For example, money market mutual funds hold the short-term, low-risk instruments of the money market (see Chapter 2 for a review of these securities), while bond funds hold fixed-income securities. Some funds have even more narrowly defined mandates. For example, some bond funds will hold primarily Treasury bonds, others primarily mortgage-backed securities.

Management companies manage a family, or "complex," of mutual funds. They organize an entire collection of funds and then collect a management fee for operating them.

By managing a collection of funds under one umbrella, these companies make it easy for investors to allocate assets across market sectors and to switch assets across funds while still benefiting from centralized record keeping. Some of the most well-known management companies are Fidelity, Vanguard, Barclays, and T. Rowe Price. Each offers an array of open-end mutual funds with different investment policies. In 2016, there were about 8,000 mutual funds in the U.S., which were offered by more than 800 fund complexes.

Funds are commonly classified by investment policy into one of the following groups: money market funds, equity funds, sector funds, bond funds, international funds, balanced funds, asset allocation and flexible funds, and index funds.

Money Market Funds   These funds invest in money market securities such as commercial paper, repurchase agreements, or certificates of deposit. The average maturity of these assets tends to be a bit more than 1 month. Money market funds usually offer check-writing features and net asset value is fixed at $1 per share,[2] so there are no tax implications such as capital gains or losses associated with redemption of shares.

Equity Funds   Equity funds invest primarily in stock, although they may, at the portfolio manager's discretion, also hold fixed-income or other types of securities. Equity funds commonly will hold between 4% and 5% of total assets in money market securities to provide the liquidity necessary to meet potential redemption of shares.

Stock funds are traditionally classified by their emphasis on capital appreciation versus current income. Thus, *income funds* tend to hold shares of firms with consistently high dividend yields. *Growth funds* are willing to forgo current income, focusing instead on prospects for capital gains. While the classification of these funds is couched in terms of income versus capital gains, in practice, the more relevant distinction concerns the level of risk these funds assume. Growth stocks, and therefore growth funds, are typically riskier and respond more dramatically to changes in economic conditions than do income funds.

Sector Funds   Some equity funds, called *sector* funds, concentrate on a particular industry. For example, Fidelity markets dozens of "select funds," each of which invests in a specific industry such as biotechnology, utilities, energy, or telecommunications. Other funds specialize in securities of particular countries.

Bond Funds   As the name suggests, these funds specialize in the fixed-income sector. Within that sector, however, there is considerable room for further specialization. For example, various funds will concentrate on corporate bonds, Treasury bonds, mortgage-backed securities, or municipal (tax-free) bonds. Indeed, some municipal bond funds invest only in bonds of a particular state (or even city!) to satisfy the investment desires of residents of that state who wish to avoid local as well as federal taxes on interest income. Many funds also specialize by maturity, ranging from short-term to intermediate to long-term, or by the credit risk of the issuer, ranging from very safe to high-yield, or "junk," bonds.

International Funds   Many funds have an international focus. *Global funds* invest in securities worldwide, including the United States. In contrast, *international funds* invest in securities of firms located outside the United States. *Regional funds* concentrate

[2]The Words from the Street box in Chapter 2 (see section 2.1) noted that money market funds are able to maintain NAV at $1.00 because they invest in short-maturity debt of the highest quality with minimal price risk. In only the rarest circumstances have any funds incurred losses large enough to drive NAV below $1.00. In September 2008, however, Reserve Primary Fund, the nation's oldest money market fund, "broke the buck" when it suffered losses on its holding of Lehman Brothers commercial paper and its NAV fell to $.97.

on a particular part of the world, and *emerging market funds* invest in companies of developing nations.

Balanced Funds   Some funds are designed to be candidates for an individual's entire investment portfolio. These balanced funds hold both equities and fixed-income securities in relatively stable proportions. *Life-cycle funds* are balanced funds in which the asset mix can range from aggressive (primarily marketed to younger investors) to conservative (directed at older investors). Static allocation life-cycle funds maintain a stable mix across stocks and bonds, while *targeted-maturity funds* gradually become more conservative as the investor ages.

Many balanced funds are in fact **funds of funds.** These are mutual funds that primarily invest in shares of other mutual funds. Balanced funds of funds invest in equity and bond funds in proportions suited to their investment goals.

Asset Allocation and Flexible Funds   These funds are similar to balanced funds in that they hold both stocks and bonds. However, asset allocation funds may dramatically vary the proportions allocated to each market in accord with the portfolio manager's forecast of the relative performance of each sector. Hence these funds are engaged in market timing and are not designed to be low-risk investment vehicles.

Index Funds   An index fund tries to match the performance of a broad market index. The fund buys shares in securities included in a particular index in proportion to each security's representation in that index. For example, the Vanguard 500 Index Fund is a mutual fund that replicates the composition of the Standard & Poor's 500 stock price index. Because the S&P 500 is a value-weighted index, the fund buys shares in each S&P 500 company in proportion to the market value of that company's outstanding equity. Investment in an index fund is a low-cost way for small investors to pursue a passive investment strategy—that is, to invest without engaging in security analysis. More than 20% of equity funds in 2016 were indexed. Of course, index funds can be tied to nonequity indexes as well. For example, Vanguard offers a bond index fund and a real estate index fund.

Table 4.1 breaks down the number of mutual funds by investment orientation. Sometimes a fund name describes its investment policy. For example, Vanguard's GNMA fund invests in mortgage-backed securities, the Municipal Intermediate fund invests in intermediate-term municipal bonds, and the High-Yield Corporate bond fund invests in large part in speculative grade, or "junk," bonds with high yields. However, names of common stock funds often reflect little or nothing about their investment policies. Examples are Vanguard's Windsor and Wellington funds.

How Funds Are Sold

Mutual funds are generally marketed to the public either directly by the fund underwriter or indirectly through brokers acting on behalf of the underwriter. Direct-marketed funds are sold through the mail, various offices of the fund, over the phone, or, more so, over the Internet. Investors contact the fund directly to purchase shares.

About half of fund sales today are distributed through a sales force. Brokers or financial advisers receive a commission for selling shares to investors. (Ultimately, the commission is paid by the investor. More on this shortly.) Investors who rely on their broker's advice to select their mutual funds should be aware that this advice may suffer from a conflict of interest if the broker receives compensation for directing the sale to a particular fund.

Table 4.1

U.S. mutual funds by investment classification

	Assets ($ billion)	% of Total Assets	Number of Funds
Equity funds			
Capital appreciation focus	$ 1,843	11.8%	1,345
World/international	2,102	13.4	1,487
Total return	4,203	26.9	1,932
Total equity funds	$ 8,148	52.1%	4,764
Bond funds			
Investment grade	$ 1,513	9.7%	622
High yield	326	2.1	240
World	432	2.8	371
Government	266	1.7	192
Multisector	284	1.8	156
Single-state municipal	160	1.0	319
National municipal	434	2.8	254
Total bond funds	$ 3,412	21.8%	2,154
Hybrid (bond/stock) funds	$ 1,337	8.5%	717
Money market funds			
Taxable	$ 2,500	16.0%	336
Tax-exempt	255	1.6	145
Total money market funds	$ 2,755	17.6%	481
Total	$15,652	100.0%	8,116

Note: Column sums subject to rounding error.
Source: Investment Company Institute, *2016 Investment Company Fact Book.*

Many funds also are sold through "financial supermarkets" that sell shares in funds of many complexes. Instead of charging customers a sales commission, the broker splits management fees with the mutual fund company. Another advantage is unified record keeping for all funds purchased from the supermarket, even if the funds are offered by different complexes. On the other hand, many contend that these supermarkets result in higher expense ratios because mutual funds pass along the costs of participating in these programs in the form of higher management fees.

4.4   Costs of Investing in Mutual Funds

Fee Structure

An individual investor choosing a mutual fund should consider not only the fund's stated investment policy and past performance but also its management fees and other expenses. Comparative data on virtually all important aspects of mutual funds are available on Morningstar's Web site at **www.morningstar.com.** You should be aware of four general classes of fees.

Operating Expenses   Operating expenses are the costs incurred by the mutual fund in operating the portfolio, including administrative expenses and advisory fees paid to the investment manager. These expenses, usually expressed as a percentage of total assets under management, may range from .2% to 2%. Shareholders do not receive an explicit bill for these operating expenses; however, the expenses periodically are deducted from the assets of the fund. Shareholders pay for these expenses through the reduced value of the portfolio.

The simple average of the expense ratio of all equity funds in the U.S. was 1.31% in 2015. But larger funds tend to have lower expense ratios, so the average expense ratio weighted by assets under management is considerably smaller, .68%. Not surprisingly, the average expense ratio of actively managed funds is considerably higher than that of indexed funds, .84% versus .11% (weighted by assets under management).

In addition to operating expenses, many funds assess fees to pay for marketing and distribution costs. These charges are used primarily to pay the brokers or financial advisers who sell the funds to the public. Investors can avoid these expenses by buying shares directly from the fund sponsor, but many investors are willing to incur these distribution fees in return for the advice they may receive from their broker.

Front-End Load   A front-end load is a commission or sales charge paid when you purchase the shares. These charges, which are used primarily to pay the brokers who sell the funds, may not exceed 8.5%, but in practice they are rarely higher than 6%. *Low-load funds* have loads that range up to 3% of invested funds. *No-load funds* have no front-end sales charges. Loads effectively reduce the amount of money invested. For example, each $1,000 paid for a fund with a 6% load results in a sales charge of $60 and fund investment of only $940. You need cumulative returns of 6.4% of your net investment (60/940 = .064) just to break even.

Back-End Load   A back-end load is a redemption, or "exit," fee incurred when you sell your shares. Typically, funds that impose back-end loads start them at 5% or 6% and reduce them by 1 percentage point for every year the funds are left invested. Thus an exit fee that starts at 6% would fall to 4% by the start of your third year. These charges are known more formally as "contingent deferred sales loads."

12b-1 Charges   The Securities and Exchange Commission allows the managers of so-called 12b-1 funds to use fund assets to pay for distribution costs such as advertising, promotional literature including annual reports and prospectuses, and, most important, commissions paid to brokers who sell the fund to investors. These **12b-1 fees** are named after the SEC rule that permits use of these plans. Funds may use 12b-1 charges instead of, or in addition to, front-end loads to generate the fees with which to pay brokers. As with operating expenses, investors are not explicitly billed for 12b-1 charges. Instead, the fees are deducted from the assets of the fund. Therefore, 12b-1 fees (if any) must be added to operating expenses to obtain the true annual expense ratio of the fund. The SEC requires that all funds include in the prospectus a consolidated expense table that summarizes all relevant fees. The 12b-1 fees are limited to 1% of a fund's average net assets per year.[3]

Many funds offer "classes" that represent ownership in the same portfolio of securities, but with different combinations of fees. Typically, Class A shares have front-end loads and a small 12b-1 fee, often around .25%. Class C shares rely on larger 12b-1 fees, commonly 1%, and often charge a modest back-end load. Class I shares are sold to institutional investors. These are sometimes called class Y shares and carry no loads or 12b-1 fees.[4]

---

[3]The maximum 12b-1 charge for the sale of the fund is .75%. However, an additional service fee of .25% of the fund's assets also is allowed for personal service and/or maintenance of shareholder accounts.

[4]Many funds used to market Class B shares as well. These shares had higher expense ratios, particularly higher back-end loads. However, if an investor held Class B shares for a long enough duration, typically 6-8 years, the shares would convert into Class A shares. Class B shares have become increasingly less common in recent years.

Example 4.2   Fees for Various Classes

The table below lists fees for different classes of the Dreyfus High Yield Fund in 2016. Notice the trade-off between the front-end loads versus 12b-1 charges in the choice between Class A and Class C shares. Class I shares are sold only to institutional investors and carry lower fees.

	Class A	Class C	Class I
Front-end load	0–4.5%[a]	0	0
Back-end load	0	0–1%[b]	0%[b]
12b-1 fees[c]	0.25%	1.0%	0%
Expense ratio	0.7%	0.7%	0.7%

[a]Depending on size of investment.
[b]Depending on years until holdings are sold.
[c]Including service fee.

Each investor must choose the best combination of fees. Obviously, pure no-load no-fee funds distributed directly by the mutual fund group are the cheapest alternative, and these will often make most sense for knowledgeable investors. However, as we have noted, many investors are willing to pay for financial advice, and the commissions paid to advisers who sell these funds are the most common form of payment. Alternatively, investors may choose to hire a fee-only financial manager who charges directly for services instead of collecting commissions. These advisers can help investors select portfolios of low- or no-load funds (as well as provide other financial advice). Independent financial planners have become increasingly important distribution channels for funds in recent years.

If you do buy a fund through a broker, the choice between paying a load and paying 12b-1 fees will depend primarily on your expected time horizon. Loads are paid only once for each purchase, whereas 12b-1 fees are paid annually. Thus, if you plan to hold your fund for a long time, a one-time load may be preferable to recurring 12b-1 charges.

Fees and Mutual Fund Returns

The rate of return on an investment in a mutual fund is measured as the increase or decrease in net asset value plus income distributions such as dividends or distributions of capital gains expressed as a fraction of net asset value at the beginning of the investment period. If we denote the net asset value at the start and end of the period as NAV_0 and NAV_1, respectively, then

$$\text{Rate of return} = \frac{NAV_1 - NAV_0 + \text{Income and capital gain distributions}}{NAV_0}$$

For example, if a fund has an initial NAV of $20 at the start of the month, makes income distributions of $.15 and capital gain distributions of $.05, and ends the month with NAV of $20.10, the monthly rate of return is computed as

$$\text{Rate of return} = \frac{\$20.10 - \$20.00 + \$.15 + \$.05}{\$20.00} = .015, \text{ or } 1.5\%$$

Notice that this measure of the rate of return ignores any commissions such as front-end loads paid to purchase the fund.

On the other hand, the rate of return is affected by the fund's expenses and 12b-1 fees. This is because such charges are periodically deducted from the portfolio, which reduces net asset value. Thus the investor's rate of return equals the gross return on the underlying portfolio minus the total expense ratio.

Example 4.3   Fees and Net Returns

To see how expenses can affect rate of return, consider a fund with $100 million in assets at the start of the year and with 10 million shares outstanding. The fund invests in a portfolio of stocks that provides no income but increases in value by 10%. The expense ratio, including 12b-1 fees, is 1%. What is the rate of return for an investor in the fund?

The initial NAV equals $100 million/10 million shares = $10 per share. In the absence of expenses, fund assets would grow to $110 million and NAV would grow to $11 per share, for a 10% rate of return. However, the expense ratio of the fund is 1%. Therefore, $1 million will be deducted from the fund to pay these fees, leaving the portfolio worth only $109 million and NAV equal to $10.90. The rate of return on the fund is only 9%, which equals the gross return on the underlying portfolio minus the total expense ratio.

Fees can have a big effect on performance. Table 4.2 considers an investor who starts with $10,000 and can choose among three funds that all earn an annual 12% return on investment before fees but have different fee structures. The table shows the cumulative amount in each fund after several investment horizons. Fund A has total operating expenses of .5%, no load, and no 12b-1 charges. This might represent a low-cost producer like Vanguard. Fund B has no load but has 1% in management expenses and .5% in 12b-1 fees. This level of charges is fairly typical of actively managed equity funds. Finally, Fund C has 1% in management expenses, has no 12b-1 charges, but assesses an 8% front-end load on purchases.

Note the substantial return advantage of low-cost Fund A. Moreover, that differential is greater for longer investment horizons.

	Cumulative Proceeds (All Dividends Reinvested)		
	Fund A	Fund B	Fund C
Initial investment*	$10,000	$10,000	$ 9,200
5 years	17,234	16,474	15,502
10 years	29,699	27,141	26,123
15 years	51,183	44,713	44,018
20 years	88,206	73,662	74,173

Table 4.2

Impact of costs on investment performance

*After front-end load, if any.
Notes:
1. Fund A is no-load with .5% expense ratio.
2. Fund B is no-load with 1.5% expense ratio.
3. Fund C has an 8% load on purchases and a 1% expense ratio.
4. Gross return on all funds is 12% per year before expenses.

✔ Concept Check **4.2**

The Equity Fund sells Class A shares with a front-end load of 4% and Class B shares with 12b-1 fees of .5% annually as well as back-end load fees that start at 5% and fall by 1% for each full year the investor holds the portfolio (until the fifth year). Assume the rate of return on the fund portfolio net of operating expenses is 10% annually. What will be the value of a $10,000 investment in Class A and Class B shares if the shares are sold after (a) 1 year, (b) 4 years, and (c) 10 years? Which fee structure provides higher net proceeds at the end of each investment horizon?

Although expenses can have a big impact on net investment performance, it is sometimes difficult for the investor in a mutual fund to measure true expenses accurately. This is because of the practice of paying for some expenses in **soft dollars.** A portfolio manager earns soft-dollar credits with a brokerage firm by directing the fund's trades to that broker. On the basis of those credits, the broker will pay for some of the mutual fund's expenses, such as databases, computer hardware, or stock-quotation systems. The soft-dollar arrangement means that the stockbroker effectively returns part of the trading commission to the fund. Purchases made with soft dollars are not included in the fund's expenses, so funds with extensive soft-dollar arrangements may report artificially low expense ratios to the public. However, the fund may have paid its broker needlessly high commissions to obtain its soft-dollar "rebate." The impact of the higher trading commission shows up in net investment performance rather than the reported expense ratio.

4.5   Taxation of Mutual Fund Income

Investment returns of mutual funds are granted "pass-through status" under the U.S. tax code, meaning that taxes are paid only by the investor in the mutual fund, not by the fund itself. The income is treated as passed through to the investor as long as the fund meets several requirements, most notably that virtually all income is distributed to shareholders. A fund's short-term capital gains, long-term capital gains, and dividends are passed through to investors as though the investor earned the income directly.

The pass-through of investment income has one important disadvantage for individual investors. If you manage your own portfolio, you decide when to realize capital gains and losses on any security; therefore, you can time those realizations to efficiently manage your tax liabilities. When you invest through a mutual fund, however, the timing of the sale of securities from the portfolio is out of your control, which reduces your ability to engage in tax management.[5]

A fund with a high portfolio turnover rate can be particularly "tax inefficient." **Turnover** is the ratio of the trading activity of a portfolio to the assets of the portfolio. It measures the fraction of the portfolio that is "replaced" each year. For example, a $100 million portfolio with $50 million in sales of some securities and purchases of other

---

[5]An interesting problem that an investor needs to be aware of derives from the fact that capital gains and dividends on mutual funds are typically paid out to shareholders once or twice a year. This means that an investor who has just purchased shares in a mutual fund can receive a capital gain distribution (and be taxed on that distribution) on transactions that occurred long before he or she purchased shares in the fund. This is particularly a concern late in the year when such distributions typically are made.

securities would have a turnover rate of 50%. High turnover means that capital gains or losses are being realized constantly, and therefore that the investor cannot time the realizations to manage his or her overall tax obligation.

Turnover rates in equity funds in the last decade have typically been around 50% when weighted by assets under management. By contrast, a low-turnover fund such as an index fund may have turnover as low as 2%, which is both tax-efficient and economical with respect to trading costs.

 Concept Check **4.3**

> An investor's portfolio currently is worth $1 million. During the year, the investor sells 500 shares of FedEx at a price of $160 per share and 3,200 shares of Cisco at a price of $25 per share. The proceeds are used to buy 1,000 shares of IBM at $160 per share.
>
> a. What is the portfolio turnover rate?
>
> b. If the shares in FedEx originally were purchased for $140 each and those in Cisco were purchased for $20, and the investor's tax rate on capital gains income is 20%, how much extra will the investor owe on this year's taxes as a result of these transactions?

4.6   Exchange-Traded Funds

Exchange-traded funds (ETFs), first introduced in 1993, are offshoots of mutual funds that allow investors to trade index portfolios just as they do shares of stock. The first ETF was the "spider," a nickname for SPDR, or Standard & Poor's Depository Receipt, which is a unit investment trust holding a portfolio matching the S&P 500 Index. Unlike mutual funds, which can be bought or sold only at the end of the day when NAV is calculated, investors can trade spiders throughout the day, just like any other share of stock. Spiders gave rise to many similar products such as "diamonds" (based on the Dow Jones Industrial Average, ticker DIA), "cubes" (based on the NASDAQ 100 index, ticker QQQ), and "WEBS" (World Equity Benchmark Shares, which are shares in portfolios of foreign stock market indexes). By 2016, about $2.1 trillion was invested in 1,600 U.S. ETFs. Table 4.3, Panel A, presents some of the major sponsors of ETFs, and Panel B gives a very small flavor of the types of funds offered.

Figure 4.2 shows the rapid growth in the ETF market since 1998. Until 2008, most ETFs were required to track specified indexes, and ETFs tracking broad indexes still dominate the industry. However, there are dozens of industry-sector ETFs, and as Figure 4.2 makes clear, a significant number of commodity, bond, and international ETFs. Figure 4.3 shows that ETFs have captured a significant portion of the assets under management in the investment company universe.

Barclays Global Investors was long the market leader in the ETF market, using the product name iShares. Since Barclays's 2009 merger with BlackRock, iShares has operated under the BlackRock name. The firm sponsors ETFs for several dozen equity index funds, including many broad U.S. equity indexes, broad international and single-country funds, and U.S. and global industry sector funds. BlackRock also offers several bond ETFs and a few commodity funds such as ones for gold and silver. For more information on these funds, go to **www.iShares.com**.

A. ETF Sponsors

Sponsor	Product Name
BlackRock	iShares
StateStreet	Select Sector SPDRs (S&P Depository Receipts: "spiders")
Vanguard	Vanguard ETF

B. Sample of ETF Products

Name	Ticker	Index Tracked
Broad U.S. indexes		
Spiders	SPY	S&P 500
Diamonds	DIA	Dow Jones Industrials
Cubes	QQQ	NASDAQ 100
iShares Russell 2000	IWM	Russell 2000
Total Stock Market (Vanguard)	VTI	Wilshire 5000
Industry indexes		
Energy Select Spider	XLE	S&P 500 energy companies
iShares Energy Sector	IYE	Dow Jones energy companies
Financial Sector Spider	XLF	S&P 500 financial companies
iShares Financial Sector	IYF	Dow Jones financial companies
International indexes		
WEBS United Kingdom	EWU	MSCI U.K. Index
WEBS France	EWQ	MSCI France Index
WEBS Japan	EWJ	MSCI Japan Index

Table 4.3

ETF sponsors and products

More recently, a variety of new ETF products have been devised. Among these are leveraged ETFs, with daily returns that are a targeted *multiple* of the returns on an index, and inverse ETFs, which move in the opposite direction to an index. Another recent innovation is the actively managed ETF that, like actively managed mutual funds, attempts to outperform passive indexes. However, until recently, these funds have had to report portfolio holdings on a daily basis, which makes it easy for competitors to take advantage of their buying and selling programs. This requirement has severely limited the growth of this segment of the market. In 2014, however, the SEC gave permission to Eaton Vance to offer an actively managed "nontransparent" ETF that is required to report its portfolio composition only once each quarter, the same frequency at which mutual funds disclose their portfolio holdings. Other companies such as BlackRock have also indicated interest in sponsoring nontransparent ETFs. At the end of 2015, there were 134 actively managed ETFs registered with the SEC.

Other even more exotic variations are so-called synthetic ETFs such as exchange-traded notes (ETNs) or exchange-traded vehicles (ETVs). These are nominally debt securities, but with payoffs linked to the performance of an index. Often that index measures the performance of an illiquid and thinly traded asset class, so the ETF gives the investor the opportunity to add that asset class to his or her portfolio. However, rather than invest in those assets directly, the ETF achieves this exposure by entering a "total return swap" with

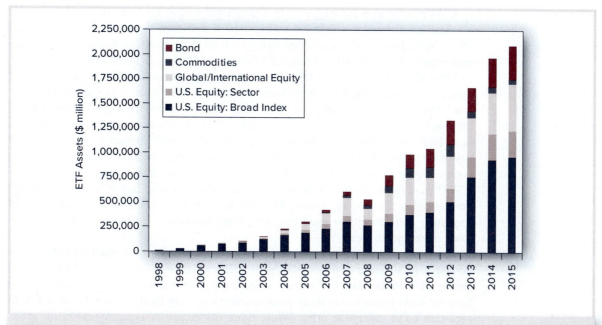

Figure 4.2 Growth of U.S. ETFs over time

Source: Investment Company Institute, *2016 Investment Company Fact Book.*

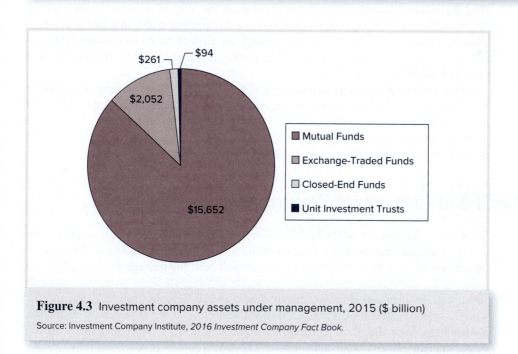

Figure 4.3 Investment company assets under management, 2015 ($ billion)

Source: Investment Company Institute, *2016 Investment Company Fact Book.*

an investment bank in which the bank agrees to pay the ETF the return on the index in exchange for a relatively fixed fee. These have become controversial, as the ETF is then exposed to risk that in a period of financial stress the investment bank will be unable to fulfill its obligation, leaving investors without the returns they were promised.

ETFs offer several advantages over conventional mutual funds. First, as we just noted, a mutual fund's net asset value is quoted—and therefore, investors can buy or sell their shares in the fund—only once a day. In contrast, ETFs trade continuously. Moreover, like other shares, but unlike mutual funds, ETFs can be sold short or purchased on margin.

ETFs also offer a potential tax advantage over mutual funds. When large numbers of mutual fund investors redeem their shares, the fund must sell securities to meet the redemptions. This can trigger capital gains taxes, which are passed through to and must be paid by the remaining shareholders. In contrast, when small investors wish to redeem their position in an ETF, they simply sell their shares to other traders, with no need for the fund to sell any of the underlying portfolio. Large investors can exchange their ETF shares for shares in the underlying portfolio; this form of redemption also avoids a tax event.

ETFs are often cheaper than mutual funds. Investors who buy ETFs do so through brokers rather than buying directly from the fund. Therefore, the fund saves the cost of marketing itself directly to small investors. This reduction in expenses may translate into lower management fees.

There are some disadvantages to ETFs, however. First, while mutual funds can be bought at no expense from no-load funds, ETFs must be purchased from brokers for a fee. In addition, because ETFs trade as securities, their prices can depart from NAV, at least for short periods, and these price discrepancies can easily swamp the cost advantage that ETFs otherwise offer. While those discrepancies typically are quite small, they can spike unpredictably when markets are stressed. Chapter 3 briefly discussed the so-called flash crash of May 6, 2010, when the Dow Jones Industrial Average fell by 583 points in *seven minutes,* leaving it down nearly 1,000 points for the day. Remarkably, the index recovered more than 600 points in the next 10 minutes. In the wake of this incredible volatility, the stock exchanges canceled many trades that had gone off at what were viewed as distorted prices. Around one-fifth of all ETFs changed hands on that day at prices less than one-half of their closing price, and ETFs accounted for about two-thirds of all canceled trades.

At least two problems were exposed in this episode. First, when markets are not working properly, it can be hard to measure the net asset value of the ETF portfolio, especially for ETFs that track less liquid assets. And, reinforcing this problem, some ETFs may be supported by only a very small number of dealers. If they drop out of the market during a period of turmoil, prices may swing wildly.

4.7   Mutual Fund Investment Performance: A First Look

We noted earlier that one of the benefits of mutual funds for the individual investor is the ability to delegate management of the portfolio to investment professionals. The investor retains control over the broad features of the overall portfolio through the asset allocation decision: Each individual chooses the percentages of the portfolio to invest in bond funds versus equity funds versus money market funds, and so forth, but can leave the specific security selection decisions within each investment class to the managers of each fund. Shareholders hope that these portfolio managers can achieve better investment performance than they could obtain on their own.

What is the investment record of the mutual fund industry? This seemingly straightforward question is deceptively difficult to answer because we need a standard against which to evaluate performance. For example, we clearly would not want to compare the investment performance of an equity fund to the rate of return available in the money market. The vast differences in the risk of these two markets dictate that year-by-year as well as average performance will differ considerably. We would expect to find that equity funds outperform money market funds (on average) as compensation to investors for the extra risk incurred in equity markets. How then can we determine whether mutual fund portfolio managers are performing up to par *given* the level of risk they incur? In other words, what is the proper benchmark against which investment performance ought to be evaluated?

Measuring portfolio risk properly and using such measures to choose an appropriate benchmark is far from straightforward. We devote all of Parts Two and Three of the text to issues surrounding the proper measurement of portfolio risk and the trade-off between risk and return. In this chapter, therefore, we will satisfy ourselves with a first look at the question of fund performance by using only very simple performance benchmarks and ignoring the more subtle issues of risk differences across funds. However, we will return to this topic in Chapter 11, where we take a closer look at mutual fund performance after adjusting for differences in the exposure of portfolios to various sources of risk.

Here we use as a benchmark for the performance of equity fund managers the rate of return on the Wilshire 5000 index. Recall from Chapter 2 that this is a value-weighted index of essentially all actively traded U.S. stocks. The performance of the Wilshire 5000 is a useful benchmark with which to evaluate professional managers because it corresponds to a simple passive investment strategy: Buy all the shares in the index in proportion to their outstanding market value. Moreover, this is a feasible strategy for even small investors, because the Vanguard Group offers an index fund (its Total Stock Market Portfolio) designed to replicate the performance of the Wilshire 5000 index. Using the Wilshire 5000 index as a benchmark, we may pose the problem of evaluating the performance of mutual fund portfolio managers this way: How does the typical performance of actively managed equity mutual funds compare to the performance of a passively managed portfolio that simply replicates the composition of a broad index of the stock market?

Casual comparisons of the performance of the Wilshire 5000 index versus that of professionally managed mutual funds reveal disappointing results for active managers. Figure 4.4 shows that the average return on diversified equity funds was below the return on the Wilshire index in 27 of the 45 years from 1971 to 2015. The average annual return on the index was 12.1%, which was 1% greater than that of the average mutual fund.[6]

This result may seem surprising. After all, it would not seem unreasonable to expect that professional money managers should be able to outperform a very simple rule such as "hold an indexed portfolio." As it turns out, however, there may be good reasons to expect such a result. We explore them in detail in Chapter 11, where we discuss the efficient market hypothesis.

Of course, one might argue that there are good managers and bad managers, and that good managers can, in fact, consistently outperform the index. To test this notion, we ask whether managers with good performance in one year are likely to repeat that performance in a following year. Is superior performance in any particular year due to luck, and therefore random, or due to skill, and therefore consistent from year to year?

To answer this question, we can examine the performance of a large sample of equity mutual fund portfolios, divide the funds into two groups based on total investment return, and ask: "Do funds with investment returns in the top half of the sample in one period continue to perform well in a subsequent period?"

---

[6]Of course, actual funds incur trading costs while indexes do not, so a fair comparison between the returns on actively managed funds versus those on a passive index should first reduce the return on the Wilshire 5000 by an estimate of such costs. Vanguard's Total Stock Market Index portfolio, which tracks the Wilshire 5000, charges an expense ratio of less than .10%, and, because it engages in little trading, incurs low trading costs. Therefore, it would be reasonable to reduce the returns on the index by about .15%. This reduction would not erase the difference in average performance.

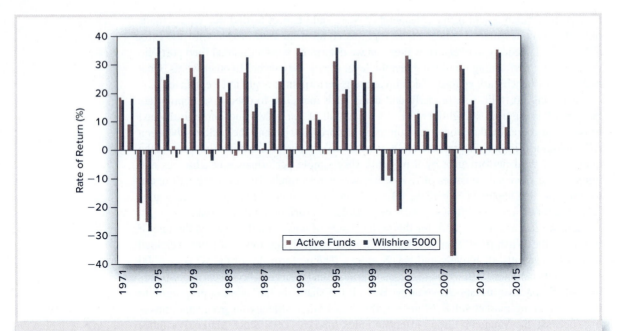

Figure 4.4 Rates of return on actively managed equity funds versus Wilshire 5000 index, 1971–2015

Source: For Wilshire returns, see **www.wilshire.com**. For active fund returns, see *SPIVA U.S. Scorecard*, S&P Dow Jones Indices Research.

Table 4.4 presents such an analysis from a study by Malkiel.[7] The table shows the fraction of "winners" (i.e., top-half performers) in each year that turn out to be winners or losers in the following year. If performance were purely random from one period to the next, there would be entries of 50% in each cell of the table, as top- or bottom-half performers would be equally likely to perform in either the top or bottom half of the sample in the following period. On the other hand, if performance were due entirely to skill, with no randomness, we would expect to see entries of 100% on the diagonals and entries of 0% on the off-diagonals: Top-half performers would all remain in the top half, while bottom-half

Table 4.4

Consistency of investment results

Initial Period Performance	Successive Period Performance	
	Top Half	**Bottom Half**
A. 1970s		
Top half	65.1%	34.9%
Bottom half	35.5	64.5
B. 1980s		
Top half	51.7	48.3
Bottom half	47.5	52.5

Source: Burton G. Malkiel, "Returns from Investing in Equity Mutual Funds 1971–1991," *Journal of Finance* 50 (June 1995), pp. 549–72.

[7]Burton G. Malkiel, "Returns from Investing in Equity Mutual Funds 1971–1991," *Journal of Finance* 50 (June 1995), pp. 549–72.

performers similarly would all remain in the bottom half. In fact, looking at the 1970s data in Panel A, the table shows that 65.1% of initial top-half performers fall in the top half of the sample in the following period, while 64.5% of initial bottom-half performers fall in the bottom half in the following period. This evidence is consistent with the notion that at least part of a fund's performance is a function of skill as opposed to luck, so that relative performance tends to persist from one period to the next.[8]

On the other hand, this relationship does not seem stable across different sample periods. While initial-year performance predicts subsequent-year performance in the 1970s (Panel A), the pattern of persistence in performance virtually disappears in the 1980s (Panel B). To summarize, the evidence that performance is consistent from one period to the next is suggestive, but it is inconclusive.

Other studies suggest that there is little performance persistence among professional managers, and if anything, bad performance is more likely to persist than good performance.[9] This makes some sense: It is easy to identify fund characteristics that will result in consistently poor investment performance, notably high expense ratios, and high turnover ratios with associated trading costs. It is far harder to identify the secrets of successful stock picking. (If it were easy, we would all be rich!) Thus the consistency we do observe in fund performance may be due in large part to the poor performers. This suggests that the real value of past performance data is to avoid truly poor funds, even if identifying the future top performers is still a daunting task.

 Concept Check **4.4**

> Suppose you observe the investment performance of 400 portfolio managers and rank them by investment returns during the year. Twenty percent of all managers are truly skilled, and therefore always fall in the top half, but the others fall in the top half purely because of good luck. What fraction of this year's top-half managers would you expect to be top-half performers next year?

4.8   Information on Mutual Funds

The first place to find information on a mutual fund is in its prospectus. The Securities and Exchange Commission requires that the prospectus describe the fund's investment objectives and policies in a concise "Statement of Investment Objectives" as well as in lengthy discussions of investment policies and risks. The fund's investment adviser and its portfolio manager are also described. The prospectus also presents the costs associated with purchasing shares in the fund in a fee table. Sales charges such as front-end and back-end loads as well as annual operating expenses such as management fees and 12b-1 fees are detailed in the fee table.

Funds provide information about themselves in two other sources. The Statement of Additional Information (SAI), also known as Part B of the prospectus, includes a list of the securities in the portfolio at the end of the fiscal year, audited financial statements, a list of the directors and officers of the fund (as well as their personal investments in the fund),

---

[8]Another possibility is that performance consistency is due to variation in fee structure across funds. We return to this possibility in Chapter 11.

[9]See for example, Mark M. Carhart, "On Persistence in Mutual Fund Performance," *Journal of Finance* 52 (1997), 57–82. Carhart's study also addresses survivorship bias, the tendency for better-performing funds to stay in business and thus remain in the sample. We return to his study in Chapter 11.

and data on brokerage commissions paid by the fund. However, unlike the fund prospectus, investors do not receive the SAI unless they specifically request it; one industry joke is that SAI stands for "something always ignored." The fund's annual report also includes portfolio composition and financial statements, as well as a discussion of the factors that influenced fund performance over the last reporting period.

With thousands of funds to choose from, it can be difficult to find and select the fund that is best suited for a particular need. Several publications now offer "encyclopedias" of mutual fund information to help in the search process. Morningstar's Web site, **www.morningstar.com,** is an excellent source of information, as is Yahoo!'s site, **finance.yahoo.com/funds.** The Investment Company Institute (**www.ici.org**), the national association of mutual funds, closed-end funds, and unit investment trusts, publishes an annual *Directory of Mutual Funds* that includes information on fees as well as phone numbers to contact funds. To illustrate the range of information available about funds, we consider Morningstar's report on Fidelity's Magellan Fund, reproduced in Figure 4.5.

The table on the left labeled "Performance" first shows the fund's quarterly returns in the last few years, and just below that, returns over longer periods. You can compare returns to two benchmarks (the Russell 1000 and the S&P 500) in the rows labeled +/− Bmark, as well as its percentile rank within its comparison (or "Mstar category") group (funds with a large growth stock orientation). The middle column provides data on fees and expenses, as well as several measures of the fund's risk and return characteristics. (We will discuss these measures in Part Two of the text.) The fund has provided good returns compared to risk in the last three years, earning it a 4-star rating, but its 10-year performance has been disappointing. Of course, we are all accustomed to the disclaimer that "past performance is not a reliable measure of future results," and this is presumably true as well of Morningstar's star ratings. Consistent with this disclaimer, past results have little predictive power for future performance, as we saw in Table 4.4.

More data on the performance of the fund are provided in the graph near the top of the figure. The line graph compares the growth of $10,000 invested in the fund versus its first benchmark over the last 10 years. Below the graph are boxes for each year that depict the relative performance of the fund for that year. The shaded area on the box shows the quartile in which the fund's performance falls relative to other funds with the same objective. If the shaded band is at the top of the box, the firm was a top quartile performer in that period, and so on. The table below the bar charts presents historical data on the year-by-year performance of the fund.

Below the table, the "Portfolio Analysis" table shows the asset allocation of the fund, and then Morningstar's well-known style box. In this box, Morningstar evaluates style along two dimensions: One dimension is the size of the firms held in the portfolio as measured by the market value of outstanding equity; the other dimension is a value/growth measure. Morningstar defines *value stocks* as those with low ratios of market price per share to various measures of value. It puts stocks on a growth-value continuum based on the ratios of stock price to the firm's earnings, book value, sales, cash flow, and dividends. Value stocks are those with a low price relative to these measures of value. In contrast, *growth stocks* have high ratios, suggesting that investors in these firms must believe that the firm will experience rapid growth to justify the prices at which the stocks sell. In Figure 4.5, the shaded box shows that the Magellan Fund tends to hold larger firms (top row) and growth stocks (right column).

Finally, the tables in the right column provide information on the current composition of the portfolio. You can find the fund's 20 "Top Holdings" there as well as the weighting of the portfolio across various sectors of the economy.

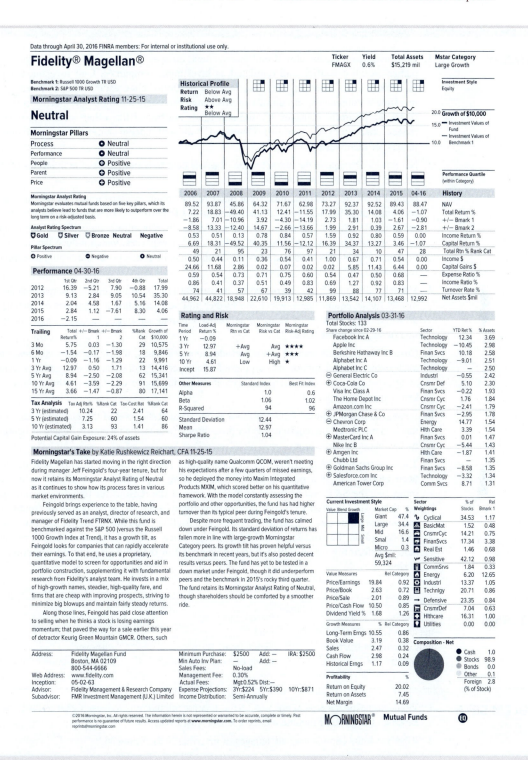

Figure 4.5 Morningstar report

Source: Morningstar Mutual Funds, © 2016 Morningstar, Inc.

SUMMARY

1. Unit investment trusts, closed-end management companies, and open-end management companies are all classified and regulated as investment companies. Unit investment trusts are essentially unmanaged in the sense that the portfolio, once established, is fixed. Managed investment companies, in contrast, may change the composition of the portfolio as deemed fit by the portfolio manager. Closed-end funds are traded like other securities; they do not redeem shares for their investors. Open-end funds will redeem shares for net asset value at the request of the investor.

2. Net asset value equals the market value of assets held by a fund minus the liabilities of the fund divided by the shares outstanding.

3. Mutual funds free the individual from many of the administrative burdens of owning individual securities and offer professional management of the portfolio. They also offer advantages that are available only to large-scale investors, such as discounted trading costs. On the other hand, funds are assessed management fees and incur other expenses, which reduce the investor's rate of return. Funds also eliminate some of the individual's control over the timing of capital gains realizations.

4. Mutual funds are often categorized by investment policy. Major policy groups include money market funds; equity funds, which are further grouped according to emphasis on income versus growth or specialization by sector; bond funds; international funds; balanced funds; asset allocation funds; and index funds.

5. Costs of investing in mutual funds include front-end loads, which are sales charges; back-end loads, which are redemption fees or, more formally, contingent-deferred sales charges; fund operating expenses; and 12b-1 charges, which are recurring fees used to pay for the expenses of marketing the fund to the public.

6. Income earned on mutual fund portfolios is not taxed at the level of the fund. Instead, as long as the fund meets certain requirements for pass-through status, the income is treated as being earned by the investors in the fund.

7. The average rate of return of the average equity mutual fund in the last four decades has been below that of a passive index fund holding a portfolio to replicate a broad-based index like the S&P 500 or Wilshire 5000. Some of the reasons for this disappointing record are the costs incurred by actively managed funds, such as the expense of conducting the research to guide stock-picking activities, and trading costs due to higher portfolio turnover. The record on the consistency of fund performance is mixed. In some sample periods, the better-performing funds continue to perform well in the following periods; in other sample periods they do not.

KEY TERMS

investment company	closed-end fund	12b-1 fees
net asset value (NAV)	load	soft dollars
unit investment trust	hedge fund	turnover
open-end fund	funds of funds	exchange-traded funds (ETFs)

PROBLEM SETS

1. Would you expect a typical open-end fixed-income mutual fund to have higher or lower operating expenses than a fixed-income unit investment trust? Why?

2. What are some comparative advantages of investing in the following?
   a. Unit investment trusts.
   b. Open-end mutual funds.
   c. Individual stocks and bonds that you choose for yourself.

3. Open-end equity mutual funds find it necessary to keep a significant percentage of total invest-ments, typically around 5% of the portfolio, in very liquid money market assets. Closed-end funds do not have to maintain such a position in "cash equivalent" securities. What difference between open-end and closed-end funds might account for their differing policies?

4. Balanced funds, life-cycle funds, and asset allocation funds all invest in both the stock and bond markets. What are the differences among these types of funds?

5. Why can closed-end funds sell at prices that differ from net asset value while open-end funds do not?

6. What are the advantages and disadvantages of exchange-traded funds versus mutual funds?

7. An open-end fund has a net asset value of $10.70 per share. It is sold with a front-end load of 6%. What is the offering price?

8. If the offering price of an open-end fund is $12.30 per share and the fund is sold with a front-end load of 5%, what is its net asset value?

9. The composition of the Fingroup Fund portfolio is as follows:

Stock	Shares	Price
A	200,000	$35
B	300,000	40
C	400,000	20
D	600,000	25

The fund has not borrowed any funds, but its accrued management fee with the portfolio manager currently totals $30,000. There are 4 million shares outstanding. What is the net asset value of the fund?

10. Reconsider the Fingroup Fund in the previous problem. If during the year the portfolio manager sells all of the holdings of stock D and replaces it with 200,000 shares of stock E at $50 per share and 200,000 shares of stock F at $25 per share, what is the portfolio turnover rate?

11. The Closed Fund is a closed-end investment company with a portfolio currently worth $200 million. It has liabilities of $3 million and 5 million shares outstanding.

   a. What is the NAV of the fund?
   b. If the fund sells for $36 per share, what is its premium or discount as a percent of net asset value?

12. Corporate Fund started the year with a net asset value of $12.50. By year-end, its NAV equaled $12.10. The fund paid year-end distributions of income and capital gains of $1.50. What was the (pretax) rate of return to an investor in the fund?

13. A closed-end fund starts the year with a net asset value of $12.00. By year-end, NAV equals $12.10. At the beginning of the year, the fund was selling at a 2% premium to NAV. By the end of the year, the fund is selling at a 7% discount to NAV. The fund paid year-end distributions of income and capital gains of $1.50.

   a. What is the rate of return to an investor in the fund during the year?
   b. What would have been the rate of return to an investor who held the same securities as the fund manager during the year?

14. a. Impressive Fund had excellent investment performance last year, with portfolio returns that placed it in the top 10% of all funds with the same investment policy. Do you expect it to be a top performer next year? Why or why not?
   b. Suppose instead that the fund was among the poorest performers in its comparison group. Would you be more or less likely to believe its relative performance will persist into the following year? Why?

15. Consider a mutual fund with $200 million in assets at the start of the year and 10 million shares outstanding. The fund invests in a portfolio of stocks that provides dividend income at the end of the year of $2 million. The stocks included in the fund's portfolio increase in price by 8%, but no securities are sold and there are no capital gains distributions. The fund charges 12b-1 fees of 1%, which are deducted from portfolio assets at year-end. What is the fund's net asset value at the start and end of the year? What is the rate of return for an investor in the fund?

16. The New Fund had average daily assets of $2.2 billion last year. The fund sold $400 million worth of stock and purchased $500 million during the year. What was its turnover ratio?

17. If New Fund's expense ratio (see the previous problem) was 1.1% and the management fee was .7%, what were the total fees paid to the fund's investment managers during the year? What were other administrative expenses?

18. You purchased 1,000 shares of the New Fund at a price of $20 per share at the beginning of the year. You paid a front-end load of 4%. The securities in which the fund invests increase in value by 12% during the year. The fund's expense ratio is 1.2%. What is your rate of return on the fund if you sell your shares at the end of the year?

19. Loaded-Up Fund charges a 12b-1 fee of 1.0% and maintains an expense ratio of .75%. Economy Fund charges a front-end load of 2% but has no 12b-1 fee and an expense ratio of .25%. Assume the rate of return on both funds' portfolios (before any fees) is 6% per year. How much will an investment in each fund grow to after:

    a. 1 year?
    b. 3 years?
    c. 10 years?

20. City Street Fund has a portfolio of $450 million and liabilities of $10 million.

    a. If 44 million shares are outstanding, what is net asset value?
    b. If a large investor redeems 1 million shares, what happens to the (i) portfolio value, (ii) shares outstanding, and (iii) NAV?

21. The Investments Fund sells Class A shares with a front-end load of 6% and Class B shares with 12b-1 fees of .5% annually as well as back-end load fees that start at 5% and fall by 1% for each full year the investor holds the portfolio (until the fifth year). Assume the portfolio rate of return net of operating expenses is 10% annually. If you plan to sell the fund after 4 years, are Class A or Class B shares the better choice for you? What if you plan to sell after 15 years?

22. You are considering an investment in a mutual fund with a 4% load and an expense ratio of .5%. You can invest instead in a bank CD paying 6% interest.

    a. If you plan to invest for 2 years, what annual rate of return must the fund portfolio earn for you to be better off in the fund than in the CD? Assume annual compounding of returns.
    b. How does your answer change if you plan to invest for 6 years? Why does your answer change?
    c. Now suppose that instead of a front-end load the fund assesses a 12b-1 fee of .75% per year. What annual rate of return must the fund portfolio earn for you to be better off in the fund than in the CD? Does your answer in this case depend on your time horizon?

23. Suppose that every time a fund manager trades stock, transaction costs such as commissions and bid–ask spreads amount to .4% of the value of the trade. If the portfolio turnover rate is 50%, by how much is the total return of the portfolio reduced by trading costs?

24. You expect a tax-free municipal bond portfolio to provide a rate of return of 4%. Management fees of the fund are .6%. What fraction of portfolio income is given up to fees? If the management fees for an equity fund also are .6%, but you expect a portfolio return of 12%, what fraction of portfolio income is given up to fees? Why might management fees be a bigger factor in your

investment decision for bond funds than for stock funds? Can your conclusion help explain why unmanaged unit investment trusts tend to focus on the fixed-income market?

25. Suppose you observe the investment performance of 350 portfolio managers for 5 years and rank them by investment returns during each year. After 5 years, you find that 11 of the funds have investment returns that place the fund in the top half of the sample in each and every year of your sample. Such consistency of performance indicates to you that these must be the funds whose managers are in fact skilled, and you invest your money in these funds. Is your conclusion warranted?

E-INVESTMENTS EXERCISES

Go to **www.morningstar.com**. In the Morningstar Tools section, click on the link for the *Mutual Fund Screener.* Set the criteria you desire, then click on the *Show Results* tab. If you get no funds that meet all of your criteria, choose the criterion that is least important to you and relax that constraint. Continue the process until you have several funds to compare.

1. Examine all of the views available in the drop-down box menu (*Snapshot, Performance, Portfolio,* and *Nuts and Bolts*) to answer the following questions:

   a. Which fund has the best expense ratio?

   b. Which funds have the lowest Morningstar Risk rating?

   c. Which fund has the best 3-year return? Which has the best 10-year return?

   d. Which fund has the lowest turnover ratio? Which has the highest?

   e. Which fund has the longest manager tenure? Which has the shortest?

   f. Do you need to eliminate any of the funds from consideration due to a minimum initial investment that is higher than you are capable of making?

2. Based on what you know about the funds, which one do you think would be the best one for your investment?

3. Select up to five funds that are of the most interest to you. Click on the button that says *Score These Results.* Customize the criteria listed by indicating their importance to you. Examine the score results. Does the fund with the highest score match the choice you made in part 2?

✔ SOLUTIONS TO CONCEPT CHECKS

1. $\text{NAV} = \dfrac{\$5,986.0 - \$118.5}{148.36} = \$39.55$

2. The net investment in the Class A shares after the 4% commission is $9,600. If the fund earns a 10% return, the investment will grow after n years to $\$9,600 \times (1.10)^n$. The Class B shares have no front-end load. However, the net return to the investor after 12b-1 fees will be only 9.5%. In addition, there is a back-end load that reduces the sales proceeds by a percentage equal to (5 − years until sale) until the fifth year, when the back-end load expires.

Horizon	Class A Shares $\$9,600 \times (1.10)^n$	Class B Shares $\$10,000 \times (1.095)^n \times (1 - \text{Percentage exit fee})$
1 year	$10,560	$10,000 \times (1.095) \times (1 - .04) = \$10,512$
4 years	$14,055	$10,000 \times (1.095)^4 \times (1 - .01) = \$14,233$
10 years	$24,900	$10,000 \times (1.095)^{10} = \$24,782$

For a very short horizon such as 1 year, the Class A shares are the better choice. The front-end and back-end loads are equal, but the Class A shares don't have to pay the 12b-1 fees. For moderate horizons such as 4 years, the Class B shares dominate because the front-end load of the Class A shares is more costly than the 12b-1 fees and the now-smaller exit fee. For long horizons of 10 years or more, Class A again dominates. In this case, the one-time front-end load is less expensive than the continuing 12b-1 fees.

3. *a.* Turnover = $160,000 in trades per $1 million of portfolio value = 16%.
   b. Realized capital gains are $20 × 500 = $10,000 on FedEx and $5 × 3,200 = $16,000 on Cisco. The tax owed on the capital gains is therefore .20 × $26,000 = $5,200.

4. Twenty percent of the managers are skilled, which accounts for .2 × 400 = 80 of those managers who appear in the top half. There are 120 slots left in the top half, and 320 other managers, so the probability of an unskilled manager "lucking into" the top half in any year is 120/320, or .375. Therefore, of the 120 lucky managers in the first year, we would expect .375 × 120 = 45 to repeat as top-half performers next year. Thus, we should expect a total of 80 + 45 = 125, or 62.5%, of the better initial performers to repeat their top-half performance.

Risk, Return, and the Historical Record

CASUAL OBSERVATION AND formal research both suggest that investment risk is as important to investors as expected return. While we have theories about the relationship between risk and expected return that would prevail in rational capital markets, there is no theory about the levels of risk we should find in the marketplace. We can at best estimate from historical experience the level of risk that investors are likely to confront.

This situation is to be expected because prices of investment assets fluctuate in response to news about the fortunes of corporations, as well as to macroeconomic developments. There is no theory about the frequency and importance of such events; hence we cannot determine a "natural" level of risk.

Compounding this difficulty is the fact that neither expected returns nor risk are directly observable. We observe only *realized* rates of return. These provide noisy estimates of the expected returns and risk that investors actually anticipated.

Moreover, in learning from an historical record, we face what has become known as the "black swan" problem.[1] No matter how long the historical record, there is never a guarantee that it exhibits the worst (and best) that nature can throw at us in the future.

In this chapter, we present the essential tools for estimating expected returns and risk from the historical record and consider implications for future investments. We begin with interest rates and investments in safe assets and examine the history of risk-free investments in the U.S. over the last 90 years. Moving to risky assets, we begin with scenario analysis of risky investments and the data inputs necessary to conduct it. With this in mind, we develop the statistical tools needed to make inferences from historical time series of portfolio returns. We present several empirical estimates of risk and return and consider as well the incidence of extreme events that investors confront.

---

[1]Black swans are a metaphor for highly improbable—but highly impactful—events. Until the discovery of Australia, Europeans, having observed only white swans, believed that a black swan was outside the realm of reasonable possibility or, in statistical jargon, an extreme "outlier" relative to their "sample" of observations. See Nassim N. Taleb, *The Black Swan: The Impact of the Highly Improbable* (New York: Random House, 2010).

5.1   Determinants of the Level of Interest Rates

The level of interest rates is perhaps the most important macroeconomic factor to consider in one's investment analysis. Forecasts of interest rates directly determine expected returns in the fixed-income market. If your expectation is that rates will increase by more than the consensus view, you will want to shy away from longer term fixed-income securities. Similarly, increases in interest rates tend to be bad news for the stock market. Thus, a superior technique to forecast interest rates would be of immense value to an investor attempting to determine the best asset allocation for his or her portfolio.

Unfortunately, forecasting interest rates is one of the most notoriously difficult parts of applied macroeconomics. Nonetheless, we do have a good understanding of the fundamental factors that determine the level of interest rates:

1. The supply of funds from savers, primarily households.
2. The demand for funds from businesses to be used to finance investments in plant, equipment, and inventories (real assets or capital formation).
3. The government's net demand for funds as modified by actions of the Federal Reserve Bank.
4. The expected rate of inflation.

We begin by distinguishing real from nominal interest rates.

Real and Nominal Rates of Interest

An interest rate is a promised rate of return denominated in some unit of account (dollars, yen, euros, or even purchasing power units) over some time period (a month, a year, 20 years, or longer). Thus, when we say the interest rate is 5%, we must specify both the unit of account and the time period. Even if an interest rate is risk-free for one unit of account and time period, it will not be risk-free for other units or periods. For example, interest rates that are absolutely safe in dollar terms will be risky when evaluated in terms of purchasing power because of inflation uncertainty.

To illustrate, consider a (nominal) risk-free interest rate. Suppose that one year ago you deposited $1,000 in a 1-year bank deposit guaranteeing a rate of interest of 10%. You are about to collect $1,100 in cash. What is the real return on your investment? That depends on what your money can buy today relative to what you *could* buy a year ago. The consumer price index (CPI) measures purchasing power by averaging the prices of goods and services in the consumption basket of an average urban family of four.

Suppose the rate of inflation (the percent change in the CPI, denoted by i) is running at $i = 6\%$. So a loaf of bread that cost $1 last year might cost $1.06 this year. Last year you could buy 1,000 loaves with your funds. After investing for a year, you can buy $1,100/\$1.06 = 1,038$ loaves. The rate at which your purchasing power has increased is therefore 3.8%.

Part of your interest earnings have been offset by the reduction in the purchasing power of the dollars you will receive at the end of the year. With a 10% interest rate, after you net out the 6% reduction in the purchasing power of money, you are left with a net increase in purchasing power of almost 4%. Thus we need to distinguish between a **nominal interest rate**—the growth rate of your money—and a **real interest rate**—the growth rate of your purchasing power.

More precisely, we find the proportional increase in purchasing power by dividing the growth of invested funds by the growth of prices. If we call r_{nom} the nominal interest rate, r_{real} the real rate, and i the inflation rate, then we conclude

$$1 + r_{real} = \frac{1 + r_{nom}}{1 + i} = \frac{1.10}{1.06} = 1.038 \tag{5.1}$$

A common approximation to this relation is

$$r_{real} \approx r_{nom} - i \tag{5.2}$$

In words, the real rate of interest is the nominal rate reduced by the loss of purchasing power resulting from inflation.

The exact relationship in Equation 5.1 can be rearranged to

$$r_{real} = \frac{r_{nom} - i}{1 + i} \tag{5.3}$$

which shows that the approximation rule (Equation 5.2) overstates the real rate by the factor $1 + i$.

Example 5.1   Approximating the Real Rate

If the nominal interest rate on a 1-year CD is 8%, and you expect inflation to be 5% over the coming year, then using the approximation formula, you expect the real rate of interest to be r_{real} = 8% − 5% = 3%. Using the exact formula, the real rate is $r_{real} = \frac{.08 - .05}{1 + .05} =$ .0286, or 2.86%. Therefore, the approximation rule overstates the expected real rate by .14% (14 basis points). The approximation rule is more exact for small inflation rates and is perfectly exact for continuously compounded rates. We discuss further details in the next section.

Conventional fixed income investments, for example, bank certificates of deposit, promise a *nominal* rate of interest. However, because future inflation is uncertain, the real rate of return that you will earn is risky even if the nominal rate is risk-free.[2] Thus you can only infer the *expected* real rate on these investments by adjusting the nominal rate for your expectation of the rate of inflation.

The Equilibrium Real Rate of Interest

Although there are many different interest rates economywide (as many as there are types of debt securities), these rates tend to move together, so economists frequently talk as if there were a single representative rate. Three basic factors—supply, demand, and government actions—determine the *real* interest rate. The nominal interest rate is the real rate plus the expected rate of inflation.

Figure 5.1 shows a downward-sloping demand curve and an upward-sloping supply curve. On the horizontal axis, we measure the quantity of funds, and on the vertical axis, we measure the real rate of interest.

---

[2]You can lock in the real rate for a desired maturity from inflation-indexed bonds issued by the U.S. Treasury, called TIPS. (See Chapter 14 for a fuller discussion.) The difference between TIPS yields and yields on comparable nominal Treasury bonds provides an estimate of the market's expectation of future inflation.

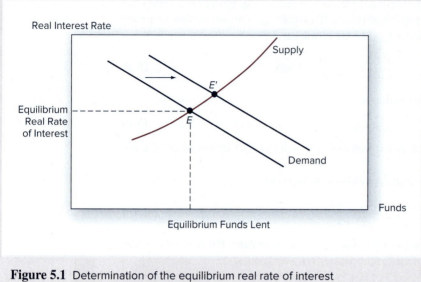

Figure 5.1 Determination of the equilibrium real rate of interest

The supply curve slopes up from left to right because the higher the real interest rate, the greater the supply of household savings. The assumption is that at higher real interest rates households will choose to postpone some current consumption and set aside or invest more of their disposable income for future use.

The demand curve slopes down from left to right because the lower the real interest rate, the more businesses will want to invest in physical capital. Assuming that businesses rank projects by the expected real return on invested capital, firms will undertake more projects the lower the real interest rate on the funds needed to finance those projects.

Equilibrium is at the point of intersection of the supply and demand curves, point E in Figure 5.1.

The government and the central bank (the Federal Reserve) can shift these supply and demand curves either to the right or to the left through fiscal and monetary policies. For example, consider an increase in the government's budget deficit. This increases the government's borrowing demand and shifts the demand curve to the right, which causes the equilibrium real interest rate to rise to point E'. The Fed can offset such a rise through an expansionary monetary policy, which will shift the supply curve to the right.

Thus, although the fundamental determinants of the real interest rate are the propensity of households to save and the expected profitability of investment in physical capital, the real rate can be affected as well by government fiscal and monetary policies.

The Equilibrium Nominal Rate of Interest

Equation 5.2 tells us that the nominal rate of return on an asset is approximately equal to the real rate plus inflation. Because investors should be concerned with real returns—their increase in purchasing power—we would expect higher nominal interest rates when inflation is higher. This higher nominal rate is necessary to maintain the expected real return offered by an investment.

Irving Fisher (1930) argued that the nominal rate ought to increase one-for-one with expected inflation, $E(i)$. The so-called Fisher hypothesis is

$$r_{nom} = r_{real} + E(i) \tag{5.4}$$

The Fisher hypothesis implies that when real rates are stable, changes in nominal rates ought to predict changes in inflation rates. This prediction has been debated and empirically investigated with mixed results. It is difficult to definitively test the hypothesis because the equilibrium real rate also changes unpredictably over time. Although the data do not strongly support the Fisher equation, nominal interest rates seem to predict inflation as well as alternative methods, in part because we are unable to forecast inflation well with any method.

 Concept Check **5.1**

a. Suppose the real interest rate is 3% per year and the expected inflation rate is 8%. According to the Fisher hypothesis, what is the nominal interest rate?

b. Suppose the expected inflation rate rises to 10%, but the real rate is unchanged. What happens to the nominal interest rate?

Taxes and the Real Rate of Interest

Tax liabilities are based on *nominal* income and the tax rate determined by the investor's tax bracket. Congress recognized the resultant "bracket creep" (when nominal income grows due to inflation and pushes taxpayers into higher brackets) and mandated index-linked tax brackets in the Tax Reform Act of 1986.

However, index-linked tax brackets do not provide relief from the effect of inflation on the taxation of savings. Given a tax rate (t) and a nominal interest rate, r_{nom}, the after-tax interest rate is $r_{nom}(1 - t)$. The real after-tax rate is approximately the after-tax nominal rate minus the inflation rate:

$$r_{nom}(1 - t) - i = (r_{real} + i)(1 - t) - i = r_{real}(1 - t) - it \qquad (5.5)$$

Equation 5.5 tells us that, because you pay taxes on even the portion of interest earnings that is merely compensation for inflation, your after-tax real return falls by the tax rate times the inflation rate. If, for example, you are in a 30% tax bracket and your investments provide a nominal return of 12% while inflation runs at 8%, your before-tax real rate is approximately 4%, and you *should*, in an inflation-protected tax system, net an after-tax real return of 4%(1 − .3) = 2.8%. But the tax code does not recognize that the first 8% of your return is only compensation for inflation—not real income. Your after-tax nominal return is 12%(1 − .3) = 8.4%, so your after-tax real interest rate is only 8.4% − 8% = .4%. As predicted by Equation 5.5, your after-tax real return has fallen by $it = 8\% \times .3 = 2.4\%$.

5.2 Comparing Rates of Return for Different Holding Periods

Consider an investor who seeks a safe investment, say, in U.S. Treasury securities. We observe zero-coupon Treasury securities with several different maturities. Zero-coupon bonds, discussed more fully in Chapter 14, are sold at a discount from par value and provide their entire return from the difference between the purchase price and the ultimate repayment of par value.[3] Given the price, $P(T)$, of a Treasury bond with $100 par value

---

[3] The U.S. Treasury issues T-bills, which are pure discount (or zero-coupon) securities with maturities of up to 1 year. However, financial institutions create zero-coupon Treasury bonds called Treasury strips with maturities up to 30 years by buying coupon-paying T-bonds, "stripping" off the coupon payments, and selling claims to the coupon payments and final payment of face value separately. See Chapter 14 for further details.

and maturity of T years, we calculate the total risk-free return available for a horizon of T years as the percentage increase in the value of the investment.

$$r_f(T) = \frac{100}{P(T)} - 1 \qquad (5.6)$$

For $T = 1$, Equation 5.6 provides the risk-free rate for an investment horizon of 1 year.

Example 5.2   Annualized Rates of Return

Suppose prices of zero-coupon Treasuries with $100 face value and various maturities are as follows. We find the total return of each security by using Equation 5.6:

Horizon, T	Price, $P(T)$	$[100/P(T)] - 1$	Total Return for Given Horizon
Half-year	$97.36	100/97.36 − 1 = 0.0271	$r_f(0.5) = 2.71\%$
1 year	$95.52	100/95.52 − 1 = 0.0469	$r_f(1)\ \ = 4.69\%$
25 years	$23.30	100/23.30 − 1 = 3.2918	$r_f(25) = 329.18\%$

Not surprisingly, longer horizons in Example 5.2 provide greater total returns. How should we compare returns on investments with differing horizons? This requires that we express each *total* return as a *rate* of return for a common period. We typically express all investment returns as an **effective annual rate (EAR),** defined as the percentage increase in funds invested over a 1-year horizon.

For a 1-year investment, the EAR equals the total return, $r_f(1)$, and the gross return, $(1 + \text{EAR})$, is the terminal value of a $1 investment. For investments that last less than 1 year, we compound the per-period return for a full year. For the 6-month bill in Example 5.2, we compound 2.71% half-year returns over two semiannual periods to obtain a terminal value of $1 + \text{EAR} = (1.0271)^2 = 1.0549$, implying that EAR = 5.49%.

For investments longer than a year, the convention is to express the EAR as the annual rate that would compound to the same value as the actual investment. For example, the investment in the 25-year bond in Example 5.2 grows by its maturity by a factor of 4.2918 (i.e., $1 + 3.2918$), so its EAR is found by solving

$$(1 + \text{EAR})^{25} = 4.2918$$
$$1 + \text{EAR} = 4.2918^{1/25} = 1.0600$$

In general, we can relate EAR to the total return, $r_f(T)$, over a holding period of length T by using the following equation:

$$1 + \text{EAR} = \left[1 + r_f(T)\right]^{1/T} \qquad (5.7)$$

We illustrate with an example.

Example 5.3   Effective Annual Rate versus Total Return

For the 6-month Treasury in Example 5.2, $T = \frac{1}{2}$, and $1/T = 2$. Therefore,

$$1 + \text{EAR} = 1.0271^2 = 1.0549 \text{ and EAR} = 5.49\%$$

For the 25-year Treasury in Example 5.2, $T = 25$. Therefore,

$$1 + \text{EAR} = 4.2918^{1/25} = 1.060 \text{ and EAR} = 6.0\%$$

Annual Percentage Rates

Annualized rates on short-term investments (by convention, $T < 1$ year) often are reported using simple rather than compound interest. These are called **annual percentage rates, or APRs.** For example, the APR corresponding to a monthly rate such as that charged on a credit card is reported as 12 times the monthly rate. More generally, if there are n compounding periods in a year, and the per-period rate is $r_f(T)$, then the APR $= n \times r_f(T)$. Conversely, you can find the per-period rate from the APR as $r_f(T) = $ APR$/n$, or equivalently, as $T \times$ APR.

Using this procedure, the APR of the 6-month bond in Example 5.2 with a 6-month rate of 2.71% is $2 \times 2.71 = 5.42\%$. To generalize, note that for short-term investments of length T, there are $n = 1/T$ compounding periods in a year. Therefore, the relationship among the compounding period, the EAR, and the APR is

$$1 + \text{EAR} = [1 + r_f(T)]^n = [1 + r_f(T)]^{1/T} = [1 + T \times \text{APR}]^{1/T} \tag{5.8}$$

Equivalently,

$$\text{APR} = \frac{(1 + \text{EAR})^T - 1}{T}$$

Example 5.4   EAR versus APR

In Table 5.1 we use Equation 5.8 to find the APR corresponding to an EAR of 5.8% with various compounding periods. Conversely, we find values of EAR implied by an APR of 5.8%.

Continuous Compounding

It is evident from Table 5.1 (and Equation 5.8) that the difference between APR and EAR grows with the frequency of compounding. This raises the question: How far will these two rates diverge as the compounding frequency continues to grow? Put differently, what is the limit of $[1 + T \times \text{APR}]^{1/T}$, as T gets ever smaller? As T approaches zero, we effectively approach *continuous compounding (CC)*, and the relation of EAR to the

Compounding Period	T	$r_f(T)$	EAR $= [1+r_f(T)]^{1/T}-1 = 0.058$ APR $= [(1+\text{EAR})^T-1]/T$	$r_f(T)$	APR $= r_f(T) \times (1/T) = 0.058$ EAR $= (1+\text{APR} \times T)^{(1/T)}-1$
1 year	1.0000	0.0580	0.05800	0.0580	0.05800
6 months	0.5000	0.0286	0.05718	0.0290	0.05884
1 quarter	0.2500	0.0142	0.05678	0.0145	0.05927
1 month	0.0833	0.0047	0.05651	0.0048	0.05957
1 week	0.0192	0.0011	0.05641	0.0011	0.05968
1 day	0.0027	0.0002	0.05638	0.0002	0.05971
Continuous			$r_{cc} = \ln(1 + \text{EAR}) = 0.05638$		EAR $= \exp(r_{cc}) - 1 = 0.05971$

Table 5.1

Annual percentage rates (APR) and effective annual rates (EAR). In the first set of columns, we hold the equivalent annual rate (EAR) fixed at 5.8% and find APR for each holding period. In the second set of columns, we hold APR fixed at 5.8% and solve for EAR.

eXcel
Please visit us at
www.mhhe.com/Bodie11e

annual percentage rate, denoted by r_{cc} for the continuously compounded case, is given by the exponential function

$$1 + \text{EAR} = \exp(r_{cc}) = e^{r_{cc}} \qquad\qquad (5.9)$$

where e is approximately 2.71828.

To find r_{cc} from the effective annual rate, we solve Equation 5.9 for r_{cc} as follows:

$$\ln(1 + \text{EAR}) = r_{cc}$$

where $\ln(\bullet)$ is the natural logarithm function, the inverse of $\exp(\bullet)$. Both the exponential and logarithmic functions are available in Excel and are called EXP($\bullet$) and LN($\bullet$), respectively.

Example 5.5   Continuously Compounded Rates

The continuously compounded annual percentage rate, r_{cc}, that provides an EAR of 5.8% is 5.638% (see Table 5.1). This is virtually the same as the APR for daily compounding. But for less frequent compounding, for example, semiannually, the APR necessary to provide the same EAR is noticeably higher, 5.718%. With less frequent compounding, a higher APR is necessary to provide an equivalent effective return.

While continuous compounding may at first seem to be a mathematical nuisance, working with such rates can sometimes simplify calculations of expected return and risk. For example, given a continuously compounded rate, the total return for any period T, $r_{cc}(T)$, is simply $\exp(T \times r_{cc})$.[4] In other words, the total return scales up in direct proportion to the time period, T. This is far simpler than working with the exponents that arise using discrete period compounding. As another example, look again at Equation 5.1. There, the relationship between the real interest rate r_{real}, the nominal rate r_{nom}, and the inflation rate i, $r_{\text{real}} \approx r_{\text{nom}} - i$, was only an approximation, as demonstrated by Equation 5.3. But if we express all rates as continuously compounded, then Equation 5.1 is exact,[5] that is, $r_{cc}(\text{real}) = r_{cc}(\text{nominal}) - i_{cc}$.

 Concept Check **5.2**

A bank offers two alternative interest schedules for a savings account of $100,000 locked in for 3 years: (a) a monthly rate of 1%; and (b) an annually, continuously compounded rate, r_{cc}, of 12%. Which alternative should you choose?

5.3   Bills and Inflation, 1926–2015

Financial time series often begin in July 1926, the starting date of a widely used return database from the Center for Research in Security Prices at the University of Chicago.

---

[4]This follows from Equation 5.9. If $1 + \text{EAR} = e^{r_{cc}}$, then $(1 + \text{EAR})^T = e^{r_{cc}T}$.

[5]$$1 + r(\text{real}) = \frac{1 + r(\text{nominal})}{1 + \text{inflation}}$$

$$\Rightarrow \ln[1 + r(\text{real})] = \ln\left(\frac{1 + r(\text{nominal})}{1 + \text{inflation}}\right) = \ln[1 + r(\text{nominal})] - \ln(1 + \text{inflation})$$

$$\Rightarrow r_{cc}(\text{real}) = r_{cc}(\text{nominal}) - i_{cc}$$

	Average Annual Rates			Standard Deviation		
	T-Bills	**Inflation**	**Real T-Bill**	**T-Bills**	**Inflation**	**Real T-Bill**
All months	3.46	3.00	0.56	3.12	4.07	3.81
First half	1.04	1.68	−0.29	1.29	5.95	6.27
Recent half	4.45	3.53	0.90	3.11	2.89	2.13

Table 5.2

Statistics for T-bill rates, inflation rates, and real rates, 1926–2015

Sources: *Annual rates of return from rolling over 1-month T-bills:* Kenneth French; *annual inflation rates:* Bureau of Labor Statistics.

Table 5.2 summarizes the history of returns on 1-month U.S. Treasury bills, the inflation rate, and the resultant real rate. You can find the entire post-1926 history of the monthly rates of these series in Connect (link to the material for Chapter 5).

The first set of columns of Table 5.2 lists average annual rates for three periods. The average interest rate over the more recent portion of our history, 1952–2015 (essentially the post-war period), 4.45%, was noticeably higher than in the earlier portion, 1.04%. The reason is inflation, the main driver of T-bill rates, which also had a noticeably higher average value, 3.53%, in the later portion of the sample than in the earlier period, 1.68%. Nevertheless, nominal interest rates in the recent period were still high enough to leave a higher average real rate, .90%, compared with a negative 29 basis points (−.29%) for the earlier period.

Figure 5.2 shows why we divide the sample period at 1952. After that year, inflation is far less volatile, and, probably as a result, the nominal interest rate tracks the inflation rate with far greater precision, resulting in a far more stable real interest rate. This shows up as the dramatic reduction in the standard deviation of the real rate documented in the last column of Table 5.2. Whereas the standard deviation is 6.27% in the early part of the

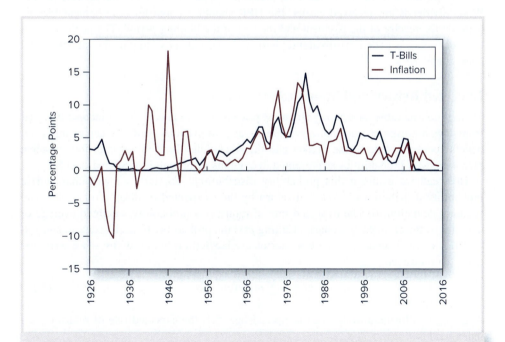

Figure 5.2 Interest and inflation rates, 1926–2015

sample, it is only 2.13% in the later portion. The lower standard deviation of the real rate in the post-1952 period reflects a similar decline in the standard deviation of the inflation rate. We conclude that the Fisher relation appears to work far better when inflation is itself more predictable and investors can more accurately gauge the nominal interest rate they require to provide an acceptable real rate of return.

5.4   Risk and Risk Premiums

Holding-Period Returns

You are considering investing in a stock-index fund. The fund currently sells for $100 per share. With an investment horizon of 1 year, the realized rate of return on your investment will depend on (a) the price per share at year's end and (b) the cash dividends you will collect over the year.

Suppose the price per share at year's end is $110 and cash dividends over the year amount to $4. The realized return, called the *holding-period return,* or HPR (in this case, the holding period is 1 year), is defined as

$$\text{HPR} = \frac{\text{Ending price of a share} - \text{Beginning price} + \text{Cash dividend}}{\text{Beginning price}} \tag{5.10}$$

Here we have

$$\text{HPR} = \frac{\$110 - \$100 + \$4}{\$100} = .14, \text{ or } 14\%$$

This definition of the HPR treats the dividend as paid at the end of the holding period. When dividends are received earlier, the HPR should account for reinvestment income between the receipt of the payment and the end of the holding period. The percent return from dividends is called the **dividend yield,** and so dividend yield plus the rate of capital gains equals HPR.

Expected Return and Standard Deviation

There is considerable uncertainty about the price of a share plus dividend income one year from now, however, so you cannot be sure about your eventual HPR. We can quantify our beliefs about the state of the market and the stock-index fund in terms of four possible scenarios, with probabilities as presented in columns A through E of Spreadsheet 5.1.

How can we evaluate this probability distribution? To start, we will characterize probability distributions of rates of return by their expected or mean return, $E(r)$, and standard deviation, σ. The expected rate of return is a probability-weighted average of the rates of return in each scenario. Calling $p(s)$ the probability of each scenario and $r(s)$ the HPR in each scenario, where scenarios are labeled or "indexed" by s, we write the expected return as

$$E(r) = \sum_s p(s)r(s) \tag{5.11}$$

Applying this formula to the data in Spreadsheet 5.1, the expected rate of return on the index fund is

$$E(r) = (.25 \times .31) + (.45 \times .14) + [.25 \times (-.0675)] + [.05 \times (-.52)] = .0976$$

	A	B	C	D	E	F	G	H	I
1									
2									
3	Purchase Price =		$100			T-Bill Rate =	0.04		
4									
5							Squared		Squared
6	State of the		Year-End	Cash		Deviations	Deviations	Excess	Deviations
7	Market	Probability	Price	Dividends	HPR	from Mean	from Mean	Returns	from Mean
8	Excellent	0.25	126.50	4.50	0.3100	0.2124	0.0451	0.2700	0.0451
9	Good	0.45	110.00	4.00	0.1400	0.0424	0.0018	0.1000	0.0018
10	Poor	0.25	89.75	3.50	−0.0675	−0.1651	0.0273	−0.1075	0.0273
11	Crash	0.05	46.00	2.00	−0.5200	−0.6176	0.3815	−0.5600	0.3815
12	Expected Value (mean)	SUMPRODUCT(B8:B11, E8:E11) =			0.0976				
13	Variance of HPR			SUMPRODUCT(B8:B11, G8:G11) =			0.0380		
14	Standard Deviation of HPR			SQRT(G13) =			0.1949		
15	Risk Premium			SUMPRODUCT(B8:B11, H8:H11) =			0.0576		
16	Standard Deviation of Excess Return			SQRT(SUMPRODUCT(B8:B11, I8:I11)) =					0.1949

Spreadsheet 5.1

Scenario analysis of holding-period return of the stock-index fund

Spreadsheet 5.1 shows that this sum can be evaluated easily in Excel, using the SUMPRODUCT function, which first calculates the products of a series of number pairs, and then sums the products. Here, the number pair is the probability of each scenario and the rate of return.

The variance of the rate of return (σ^2) is a measure of volatility. It measures the dispersion of possible outcomes around the expected value. Volatility is reflected in deviations of actual returns from the mean return. In order to prevent positive deviations from canceling out with negative deviations, we calculate the expected value of the *squared* deviations from the expected return. The higher the dispersion of outcomes, the higher will be the average value of these squared deviations. Therefore, variance is a natural measure of uncertainty. Symbolically,

$$\sigma^2 = \sum_s p(s)[r(s) - E(r)]^2 \tag{5.12}$$

Therefore, in our example

$$\sigma^2 = .25(.31 - .0976)^2 + .45\,(.14 - .0976)^2 + .25(-.0675 - .0976)^2$$
$$+ .05(-.52 - .0976)^2 = .0380$$

This value is calculated in cell G13 of Spreadsheet 5.1 using the SUMPRODUCT function.

When we calculate variance, we square deviations from the mean and therefore change units. To get back to original units, we calculate the standard deviation as the square root of variance. Standard deviation is calculated in cell G14 as

$$\sigma = \sqrt{.0380} = .1949 = 19.49\%$$

Clearly, what would trouble potential investors in the index fund is the downside risk of a crash or poor market, not the upside potential of a good or excellent market. The standard deviation of the rate of return does not distinguish between good or bad surprises; it treats both simply as deviations from the mean. Still, as long as the probability distribution is more or less symmetric about the mean, σ is a reasonable measure of risk. In the special case where we can assume that the probability distribution is normal—represented by the well-known bell-shaped curve—$E(r)$ and σ completely characterize the distribution.

Excess Returns and Risk Premiums

How much, if anything, would you invest in the index fund? First, you must ask how much of an expected reward is offered for the risk involved in investing in stocks.

We measure the reward as the difference between the *expected* HPR on the index stock fund and the **risk-free rate,** that is, the rate you would earn in risk-free assets such as T-bills, money market funds, or the bank. We call this difference the **risk premium** on common stocks. The risk-free rate in our example is 4% per year, and the expected index fund return is 9.76%, so the risk premium on stocks is 5.76% per year. The difference in any particular period between the *actual* rate of return on a risky asset and the actual risk-free rate is called the **excess return.** Therefore, the risk premium is the expected value of the excess return, and the standard deviation of the excess return is a measure of its risk. (See Spreadsheet 5.1 for these calculations.)

Notice that the risk premium on risky assets is a real quantity. The expected rate on a risky asset equals the risk-free rate plus a risk premium. That risk premium is incremental to the risk-free rate and therefore makes for the same addition whether we state the risk-free rate in real or nominal terms.

The degree to which investors are willing to commit funds to stocks depends on their **risk aversion.** Investors are risk averse in the sense that, if the risk premium were zero, they would not invest any money in stocks. In theory, there must always be a positive risk premium on stocks in order to induce risk-averse investors to hold the existing supply of stocks instead of placing all their money in risk-free assets.

As a general rule, when evaluating the risk premium, the maturity of the risk-free rate should match the investment horizon. Investors with long maturities will view the rate on long-term safe bonds as providing the benchmark risk-free rate. To properly consider a long-term investment, therefore, we should begin with the relevant real, risk-free rate. In practice, however, excess returns are usually stated relative to one-month T-bill rates. This is because most discussions refer to short-term investments.

Although the scenario analysis in Spreadsheet 5.1 illustrates the concepts behind the quantification of risk and return, you may still wonder how to get a more realistic estimate of $E(r)$ and σ for common stocks and other types of securities. Here, history has insights to offer. Analysis of the historical record of portfolio returns makes use of a variety of statistical concepts and tools, and so we first turn to a preparatory discussion.

 Concept Check **5.3**

You invest $27,000 in a corporate bond selling for $900 per $1,000 par value. Over the coming year, the bond will pay interest of $75 per $1,000 of par value. The price of the bond at the end of the year will depend on the level of interest rates prevailing at that time. You construct the following scenario analysis:

Interest Rates	Probability	Year-End Bond Price
Higher	0.2	$850
Unchanged	0.5	915
Lower	0.3	985

Your alternative investment is a T-bill that yields a sure rate of return of 5%. Calculate the HPR for each scenario, the expected rate of return, and the risk premium on your investment. What is the expected end-of-year dollar value of your investment?

5.5   Time Series Analysis of Past Rates of Return

Time Series versus Scenario Analysis

In a forward-looking scenario analysis, we determine a set of relevant scenarios and associated investment rates of return, assign probabilities to each, and conclude by computing the risk premium (reward) and standard deviation (risk) of the proposed investment. In contrast, asset return histories come in the form of time series of realized returns that do not explicitly provide investors' original assessments of the probabilities of those returns; we observe only dates and associated HPRs. We must infer from this limited data the probability distributions from which these returns might have been drawn or, at least, the expected return and standard deviation.

Expected Returns and the Arithmetic Average

When we use historical data, we treat each observation as an equally likely "scenario." So if there are n observations, we substitute equal probabilities of $1/n$ for each $p(s)$ in Equation 5.11. The expected return, $E(r)$, is then estimated by the arithmetic average of the sample rates of return:

$$E(r) = \sum_{s=1}^{n} p(s)r(s) = \frac{1}{n} \sum_{s=1}^{n} r(s) \qquad (5.13)$$

$$= \text{Arithmetic average of historic rates of return}$$

Example 5.6   Arithmetic Average and Expected Return

To illustrate, Spreadsheet 5.2 presents a (very short) time series of hypothetical holding-period returns for the S&P 500 index over a 5-year period. We treat each HPR of the $n = 5$ observations in the time series as an equally likely annual outcome during the sample years and assign it an equal probability of 1/5, or .2. Column B in Spreadsheet 5.2 therefore uses .2 as probabilities, and Column C shows the annual HPRs. Applying Equation 5.13 (using Excel's SUMPRODUCT function) to the time series in Spreadsheet 5.2 demonstrates that adding up the products of probability times HPR amounts to taking the arithmetic average of the HPRs (compare cells C7 and C8).

Example 5.6 illustrates the logic for the wide use of the arithmetic average in investments. If the time series of historical returns fairly represents the true underlying probability distribution, then the arithmetic average return from a historical period provides a forecast of the investment's expected future HPR.

The Geometric (Time-Weighted) Average Return

The arithmetic average provides an unbiased estimate of the *expected* future return. But what does the time series tell us about the *actual* performance of a portfolio over the *past* sample period? Let's continue Example 5.6 using its very short sample period just to illustrate. We will present results for meaningful sample periods later in the chapter.

	A	B	C	D	E	F
1	Year	Implicit Probability	HPR (decimal)	Squared Deviation	Gross Return = 1 + HPR	Wealth Index*
2	1	0.20	−0.1189	0.0196	0.8811	0.8811
3	2	0.20	−0.2210	0.0586	0.7790	0.6864
4	3	0.20	0.2869	0.0707	1.2869	0.8833
5	4	0.20	0.1088	0.0077	1.1088	0.9794
6	5	0.20	0.0491	0.0008	1.0491	1.0275
7	Arithmetic average	= AVERAGE(C2:C6)	0.0210			
8	Expected HPR	SUMPRODUCT(B2:B6, C2:C6)	0.0210			
9	Variance	SUMPRODUCT(B2:B6, D2:D6)		0.0315		
10	Standard deviation	SQRT(D9)		0.1774		
11	Standard deviation	STDEV.P(C2:C6)		0.1774		
12	Std dev (df = 4)	SQRT(D9*5/4)		0.1983		
13	Std dev (df = 4)	STDEV.S(C2:C6)		0.1983		
14	Geometric avg return	F6^(1/5)−1				0.0054
15						
16	* The wealth index is the cumulative value of $1 invested at the beginning of the sample period.					

Spreadsheet 5.2

Time series of holding-period returns

Column F in Spreadsheet 5.2 shows the investor's "wealth index" from investing $1 in an S&P 500 index fund at the beginning of the first year. Wealth in each year increases by the "gross return," that is, by the multiple $(1 + HPR)$, shown in column E. The wealth index is the cumulative value of $1 invested at the beginning of the sample period. The value of the wealth index at the end of the fifth year, $1.0275, is the terminal value of the $1 investment, which implies a *5-year* holding-period return of 2.75%.

An intuitive measure of performance over the sample period is the (fixed) annual HPR that would compound over the period to the same terminal value obtained from the sequence of actual returns in the time series. Denote this rate by g, so that

$$\text{Terminal value} = (1 + r_1) \times (1 + r_2) \times \ldots \times (1 + r_5) = 1.0275$$

$$(1 + g)^n = \text{Terminal value} = 1.0275 \text{ (cell F6 in Spreadsheet 5.2)} \tag{5.14}$$

$$g = \text{Terminal value}^{1/n} - 1 = 1.0275^{1/5} - 1 = .0054 = .54\% \text{ (cell F14)}$$

Practitioners call g the *time-weighted* (as opposed to dollar-weighted) average return to emphasize that each past return receives an equal weight in the process of averaging. This distinction is important because investment managers often experience significant changes in funds under management as investors purchase or redeem shares. Rates of return obtained during periods when the fund is large have a greater impact on final value than rates obtained when the fund is small. We discuss this distinction in Chapter 24 on portfolio performance evaluation.

Notice that the geometric average return in Spreadsheet 5.2, .54%, is less than the arithmetic average, 2.1%. The greater the volatility in rates of return, the greater the discrepancy between arithmetic and geometric averages. If returns come from a normal distribution, the expected difference is exactly half the variance of the distribution, that is,

$$E[\text{Geometric average}] = E[\text{Arithmetic average}] - \tfrac{1}{2}\sigma^2 \tag{5.15}$$

(A warning: To use Equation 5.15, you must express returns as decimals, not percentages.) When returns are approximately normal, Equation 5.15 will be a good approximation.[6]

The discrepancy between the geometric and arithmetic average arises from the asymmetric effect of positive and negative rates of returns on the terminal value of the portfolio. Example 5.7 illustrates this effect.

Example 5.7   Geometric versus Arithmetic Average

Suppose you have a rate of return of −20% in year 1 and 20% in year 2. The arithmetic average is 0. Yet each dollar invested for two years will grow to only .80 × 1.20 = $.96, *less* than the dollar you started with, implying a negative geometric average return. Your positive HPR in year 2 is applied to a smaller investment base than the negative HPR incurred in year 1. To break even after losing 20% in year 1, you would have needed a rate of return of 25% in year 2.

Now suppose that the order of the rates of return were switched, so that your HPRs were 20% in year 1 and −20% in year 2. Again, your arithmetic average return is zero, but you still end up with only $.96 (= 1.20 × .80). In this case, the loss in year 2 is applied to a bigger investment base than the gain in year 1, resulting in a larger dollar loss. In either case, the geometric average is less than the arithmetic one.

 Concept Check **5.4**

> You invest $1 million at the beginning of 2020 in an S&P 500 stock-index fund. If the rate of return in 2020 is −40%, what rate of return in 2021 will be necessary for your portfolio to recover to its original value?

Variance and Standard Deviation

When thinking about risk, we are interested in the likelihood of deviations of actual outcomes from the *expected* return. Because we cannot directly observe expectations, we calculate variance by averaging squared deviations from our *estimate* of the expected return, the arithmetic average, $\bar{r}$. Adapting Equation 5.12 for historic data, we again use equal probabilities for each observation and use the sample average in place of the unobservable $E(r)$.

$$\text{Variance} = \text{Expected value of squared deviations}$$
$$\sigma^2 = \sum p(s)[r(s) - E(r)]^2$$

---

[6]We measure historical performance over a particular sample period by the *geometric* average but estimate expected future performance from that same sample using the *arithmetic* average. The question naturally arises: If the same sample were to recur in the future, performance would be measured by the *geometric* average, so isn't that the best estimator of expected return? Surprisingly, the answer is no. Future results will always contain both positive and negative surprises compared to prior expectations. When compounded, a run of positive surprises has greater impact on final wealth than a run of equal-sized negative ones. Because of this asymmetry, the sample geometric average is actually a downward-biased estimate of the future average return drawn from the same distribution. The bias turns out to be half the variance, and thus using the arithmetic average corrects for this bias.

Using historical data with n observations, we could *estimate* variance as

$$\hat{\sigma}^2 = \frac{1}{n} \sum_{s=1}^{n} [r(s) - \bar{r}]^2 \tag{5.16}$$

where $\hat{\sigma}$ replaces σ to denote that it is an estimate.

Example 5.8   Variance and Standard Deviation

Take another look at Spreadsheet 5.2. Column D shows the squared deviation from the arithmetic average, and cell D9 gives the variance as .0315. This is the sum of the product of the probability of each outcome across our five observations (because these are historical estimates, we take each outcome as equally likely) times the squared deviation of that outcome. Finally, the standard deviation given in cell D10, .1774, is the square root of the variance.

The variance estimate from Equation 5.16 is biased downward, however. The reason is that we have taken deviations from the sample arithmetic average, $\bar{r}$, instead of the unknown, true expected value, $E(r)$, and so have introduced an estimation error. Its effect on the estimated variance is sometimes called a *degrees of freedom* bias. We can eliminate the bias by multiplying the arithmetic average of squared deviations by the factor $n/(n-1)$. The variance and standard deviation then become

$$\hat{\sigma}^2 = \left(\frac{n}{n-1}\right) \times \frac{1}{n} \sum_{s=1}^{n} [r(s) - \bar{r}]^2 = \frac{1}{n-1} \sum_{s=1}^{n} [r(s) - \bar{r}]^2$$

$$\hat{\sigma} = \sqrt{\frac{1}{n-1} \sum_{s=1}^{n} [r(s) - \bar{r}]^2} \tag{5.17}$$

Cell D13 shows the unbiased estimate of standard deviation, .1983, which is higher than the .1774 value obtained in cell D11. In Excel, the function STDEV.P calculates standard deviation without any correction for degrees of freedom (consistent with Equation 5.16) while the function STDEV.S applies the correction (consistent with Equation 5.17). For large samples, the distinction is usually not important: $n/(n-1)$ is close to 1, and the adjustment for degrees of freedom becomes trivially small.

Mean and Standard Deviation Estimates from Higher-Frequency Observations

Do more frequent observations lead to more accurate estimates? The answer to this question is surprising: Observation frequency has no impact on the accuracy of estimates of expected return. It is the *duration* of a sample time series (as opposed to the *number* of observations) that improves accuracy.

Ten annual returns provide as accurate an estimate of the expected rate of return as 120 monthly returns. Because the average monthly return must be consistent with the average annual returns, the additional intra-year observations provide no additional information about mean return. A longer sample, for example, a 100-year return, *does* provide a more accurate estimate of the mean return than a 10-year return, *provided* the probability distribution of returns remains unchanged over the 100 years. This suggests a rule: Use the longest sample that you still believe comes from the same return distribution. Unfortunately, in practice, old data may be less informative. Are return data from the 19th century relevant to estimating expected returns in the 21st century? Quite possibly not, implying that we face severe limits to the accuracy of our estimates of mean returns.

In contrast to the mean, the accuracy of estimates of the standard deviation can be made more precise by increasing the number of observations. This is because the more frequent observations give us more information about the distribution of deviations from the average. Thus, we can improve the accuracy of estimates of SD by using more frequent observations.

Estimates of standard deviation begin with the variance. When monthly returns are uncorrelated from one month to another, monthly variances simply add up. Thus, when the variance is the same every month, the variance of annual returns is 12 times the variance of monthly returns:[7] $\sigma_A^2 = 12\sigma_M^2$. In general, the T-month variance is T times the 1-month variance. Consequently, standard deviation grows at the rate of $\sqrt{T}$; for example, the standard deviation of annual returns is related to the standard deviation of monthly returns by $\sigma_A = \sqrt{12}\,\sigma_M$. While the mean and variance grow in direct proportion to time, SD grows at the rate of square root of time.

The Reward-to-Volatility (Sharpe) Ratio

Investors presumably are interested in the expected *excess* return they can earn by replacing T-bills with a risky portfolio, as well as the risk they would thereby incur. Even if the T-bill rate is not constant, we still know with certainty what nominal rate we will earn in any period if we purchase a bill and hold it to maturity. Other investments typically entail accepting some risk in return for the prospect of earning more than the safe T-bill rate. Investors price risky assets so that the risk premium will be commensurate with the risk of that expected *excess* return, and hence it's best to measure risk by the standard deviation of excess, not total, returns.

The importance of the trade-off between reward (the risk premium) and risk (as measured by standard deviation or SD) suggests that we measure the attraction of a portfolio by the ratio of its risk premium to the SD of its excess returns. This reward-to-volatility measure was first used extensively by William Sharpe and hence is commonly known as the *Sharpe ratio*. It is widely used to evaluate the performance of investment managers.

$$\text{Sharpe ratio} = \frac{\text{Risk premium}}{\text{SD of excess return}} \tag{5.18}$$

Example 5.9   Sharpe Ratio

Take another look at Spreadsheet 5.1. The scenario analysis for the proposed investment in the stock-index fund resulted in a risk premium of 5.76% and standard deviation of excess returns of 19.49%. This implies a Sharpe ratio of .30, a value roughly in line with the historical performance of stock-index funds. We will see that while the Sharpe ratio is an adequate measure of the risk–return trade-off for diversified portfolios (the subject of this chapter), it is inadequate when applied to individual assets such as shares of stock.

---

[7]When returns are uncorrelated, we do not have to worry about covariances among them. Therefore, the variance of the sum of 12 monthly returns (i.e., the variance of the annual return) is the sum of the 12 monthly variances. If returns are correlated across months, annualizing is more involved and requires adjusting for the structure of serial correlation.

Concept Check **5.5**

Using the annual returns for years 3–5 in Spreadsheet 5.2,

a. Compute the arithmetic average return.

b. Compute the geometric average return.

c. Compute the standard deviation of returns.

d. Compute the Sharpe ratio, assuming the risk-free rate was 6% per year.

5.6   The Normal Distribution

The bell-shaped **normal distribution** appears naturally in many applications. For example, the heights and weights of newborns, the lifespans of many consumer items such as light bulbs, and many standardized test scores are well described by the normal distribution. Variables that are the end result of multiple random influences tend to exhibit a normal distribution, for example, the error of a machine that aims to fill containers with exactly 1 gallon of liquid. By the same logic, because rates of return are affected by a multiplicity of unanticipated factors, they also might be expected to be at least approximately normally distributed.

To see why the normal curve is "normal," consider a newspaper stand that turns a profit of $100 on a good day and breaks even on a bad day, with equal probabilities of .5. Thus, the mean daily profit is $50 dollars. We can build a tree that compiles all the possible outcomes at the end of any period. Here is an **event tree** showing outcomes after 2 days:

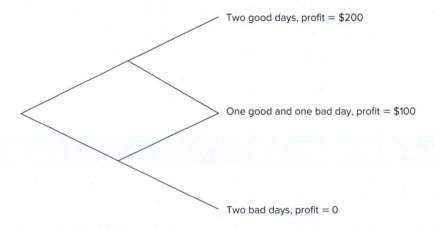

Notice that 2 days can produce three different outcomes and, in general, n days can produce $n + 1$ possible outcomes. The most likely 2-day outcome is "one good and one bad day," which can happen in two ways (first a good day, or first a bad day). The probability of this outcome is .5. Less likely are the two extreme outcomes (both good days or both bad days) with probability .25 each.

What is the distribution of profits at the end of 200 days? There are 201 possible outcomes and, again, the midrange outcomes are the most likely because there are more sequences that lead to them. While only one sequence can result in 200 consecutive bad days, an enormous number of sequences of good and bad days result in 100 good days and 100 bad days. Therefore, midrange outcomes are far more likely than are either extremely good or extremely bad outcomes, just as described by the familiar bell-shaped curve.

Figure 5.3 shows a graph of the normal curve with mean of 10% and standard deviation of 20%. A smaller SD means that possible outcomes cluster more tightly around the mean, while a higher SD implies more diffuse distributions. The likelihood of realizing any particular outcome when sampling from a normal distribution is fully determined by the number of standard deviations that separate that outcome from the mean. Put differently, the normal distribution is completely characterized by two parameters, the mean and SD.

Investment management is far more tractable when rates of return can be well approximated by the normal distribution. First, the normal distribution is symmetric, that is, the probability of any positive deviation above the mean is equal to that of a negative deviation of the same magnitude. Absent symmetry, the standard deviation is an incomplete measure of risk. Second, the normal distribution belongs to a special family of distributions characterized as "stable" because of the following property: When assets with normally distributed returns are mixed to construct a portfolio, the portfolio return also is normally distributed. Third, scenario analysis is greatly simplified when only two parameters (mean and SD) need to be estimated to obtain the probabilities of future scenarios. Fourth, when constructing portfolios of securities, we must account for the statistical dependence of returns across securities. Generally, such dependence is a complex, multilayered relationship. But when securities are normally distributed, the statistical relation between returns can be summarized with a single correlation coefficient.

How closely must actual return distributions fit the normal curve to justify its use in investment management? Clearly, the normal curve cannot be a perfect description of reality. For example, actual returns cannot be less than −100%, which the normal distribution would not rule out. But this does not mean that the normal curve cannot still be useful. A similar issue arises in many other contexts. For example, birth weight is typically evaluated in comparison to a normal curve of newborn weights, although no baby is born with a negative weight. The normal distribution still is useful here because the SD of the weight

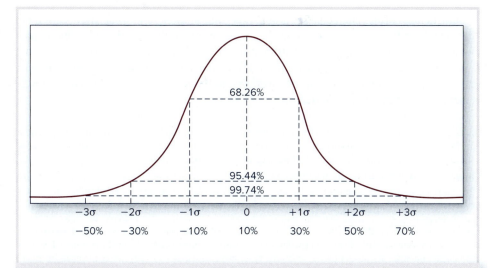

Figure 5.3 The normal distribution with mean 10% and standard deviation 20%.

is small relative to its mean, and the predicted likelihood of a negative weight would be too trivial to matter.[8] In a similar spirit, we must identify criteria to determine the adequacy of the normality assumption for rates of return.

Example 5.10   Normal Distribution Function in Excel

Suppose the monthly rate of return on the S&P 500 is approximately normally distributed with a mean of 1% and standard deviation of 6%. What is the probability that the return on the index in any month will be negative? We can use Excel's built-in functions to quickly answer this question. The probability of observing an outcome less than some cutoff according to the normal distribution function is given as NORM.DIST(cutoff, mean, standard deviation, TRUE).[9] In this case, we want to know the probability of an outcome below zero, when the mean is 1% and the standard deviation is 6%, so we compute NORM.DIST(0, 1, 6, TRUE) = .4338. We could also use Excel's built-in *standard* normal function, NORM.S.DIST, which uses a mean of 0 and a standard deviation of 1, and ask for the probability of an outcome 1/6 of a standard deviation below the mean: NORM.S.DIST(−1/6, TRUE) = .4338.

 Concept Check **5.6**

What is the probability that the return on the index in Example 5.10 will be below −15%?

5.7   Deviations from Normality and Alternative Risk Measures

As we noted earlier (but you can't repeat it too often!), normality of excess returns hugely simplifies portfolio selection. Normality assures us that standard deviation is a complete measure of risk and, hence, the Sharpe ratio is a complete measure of portfolio performance. Unfortunately, deviations from normality of asset returns are potentially significant and dangerous to ignore.

Statisticians often characterize probability distributions by what they call their "moments," and deviations from normality may be discerned by calculating the higher moments of return distributions. The nth central moment of a distribution of excess returns, R, is estimated as the average value of $(R − \overline{R})^n$. The first moment ($n = 1$) is necessarily zero (the average deviation from the sample average must be zero). The second moment ($n = 2$) is the estimate of the variance of returns, $\hat{\sigma}^2$.[10]

---

[8]In fact, the standard deviation is 511 grams while the mean is 3,958 grams. A negative weight would therefore be 7.74 standard deviations below the mean, and according to the normal distribution would have probability of only 4.97×10^{-15}. The issue of negative birth weight clearly isn't a *practical* concern.

[9]In older versions of Excel, this function is NORMDIST(cutoff, mean, standard deviation).

[10]For distributions that are symmetric about the average, as is the case for the normal distribution, all odd moments ($n = 1, 3, 5, \ldots$) have expectations of zero. For the normal distribution, the expectations of all higher even moments ($n = 4, 6, \ldots$) are functions *only* of the standard deviation, σ. For example, the expected fourth moment ($n = 4$) is $3\sigma^4$, and for $n = 6$, it is $15\sigma^6$. Thus, for normally distributed returns the standard deviation, σ, provides a complete measure of risk, and portfolio performance may be measured by the Sharpe ratio. For other distributions, however, asymmetry may be measured by the higher odd moments. Larger even moments (in excess of those consistent with the normal distribution), combined with large, negative odd moments, indicate higher probabilities of extreme negative outcomes.

A measure of asymmetry called **skew** is the ratio of the average *cubed* deviations from the sample average, called the third moment, to the cubed standard deviation:

$$\text{Skew} = \text{Average}\left[\frac{(R - \bar{R})^3}{\hat{\sigma}^3}\right] \tag{5.19}$$

Cubing deviations maintains their sign (the cube of a negative number is negative). When a distribution is "skewed to the right," as is the dark curve in Figure 5.4A, the extreme positive values, when cubed, dominate the third moment, resulting in a positive skew. When a distribution is "skewed to the left," the cubed extreme negative values dominate, and skew will be negative.

When the distribution is positively skewed (skewed to the right), the standard deviation overestimates risk, because extreme positive surprises (which do not concern investors) nevertheless increase the estimate of volatility. Conversely, and more important, when the distribution is negatively skewed, the SD will underestimate risk.

Another potentially important deviation from normality, **kurtosis,** concerns the likelihood of extreme values on either side of the mean at the expense of a smaller likelihood of moderate deviations. Graphically speaking, when the tails of a distribution are "fat," there is more probability mass in the tails of the distribution than predicted by the normal distribution. That extra probability is taken at the expense of "slender shoulders," that is, there is less probability mass near the center of the distribution. Figure 5.4B superimposes a "fat-tailed" distribution on a normal distribution with the same mean and SD. Although symmetry is still preserved, the SD will underestimate the likelihood of extreme events: large losses as well as large gains.

Kurtosis measures the degree of fat tails. We use deviations from the

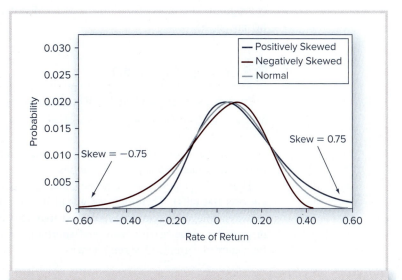

Figure 5.4A Normal and skewed distributions (mean = 6%, SD = 17%)

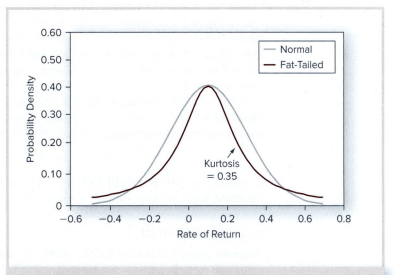

Figure 5.4B Normal and fat-tailed distributions (mean = .1, SD = .2)

average raised to the *fourth* power (the fourth moment of the distribution), scaled by the fourth power of the SD,

$$\text{Kurtosis} = \text{Average}\left[\frac{(R - \overline{R})^4}{\hat{\sigma}^4}\right] - 3 \tag{5.20}$$

We subtract 3 in Equation 5.20 because the expected value of the ratio for a normal distribution is 3. Thus, this formula for kurtosis uses the normal distribution as a benchmark: The kurtosis for the normal distribution is, in effect, defined as zero, so kurtosis above zero is a sign of fatter tails. The kurtosis of the distribution in Figure 5.4B, which has visible fat tails, is .35.

 Concept Check **5.7**

Estimate the skew and kurtosis of the five holding period returns in Spreadsheet 5.2.

Notice that both skew and kurtosis are pure numbers. They do not change when annualized from higher frequency observations.

Higher frequency of extreme negative returns may result from negative skew and/or kurtosis (fat tails). Therefore, we would like a risk measure that indicates vulnerability to extreme negative returns. We discuss four such measures that are most frequently used in practice: value at risk, expected shortfall, lower partial standard deviation, and the frequency of extreme (3-sigma) returns.

Value at Risk

The **value at risk** (denoted **VaR** to distinguish it from *Var*, the abbreviation for variance) is the loss corresponding to a very low percentile of the entire return distribution, for example, the 5th or 1st percentile return. VaR is actually written into regulation of banks and closely watched by risk managers. It is another name for the *quantile* of a distribution. The quantile, *q*, of a distribution is the value below which lie *q*% of the possible values. Thus the median is *q* = 50th quantile. Practitioners commonly estimate the 1% VaR, meaning that 99% of returns will exceed the VaR, and 1% of returns will be worse. Therefore, the 1% VaR may be viewed as the cut-off separating the 1% worst-case future scenarios from the rest of the distribution.

When portfolio returns are normally distributed, the VaR is fully determined by the mean and SD of the distribution. Recalling that −2.33 is the first percentile of the standard normal distribution (with mean = 0 and SD = 1), the VaR for a normal distribution is

$$\text{VaR}(1\%, \text{normal}) = \text{Mean} - 2.33\text{SD}$$

To obtain a sample estimate of VaR, we sort the observations from high to low. The VaR is the return at the 1st percentile of the sample distribution.[11]

Expected Shortfall

When we assess tail risk by looking at the 1% worst-case scenarios, the VaR is the most optimistic measure of bad-case outcomes as it takes the highest return (smallest loss) of all these cases. In other words, it tells you the investment loss at the first percentile of the

---

[11]Almost always, 1% of the number of observations will not be an integer; in this case we must interpolate between the observation just above the first percentile and the observation just below.

return distribution, but it ignores the magnitudes of potential losses even further out in the tail. A more informative view of downside exposure would focus instead on the *expected* loss given that we find ourselves in one of the worst-case scenarios. This value, unfortunately, has two names: either **expected shortfall (ES)** or **conditional tail expectation (CTE)**; the latter emphasizes that this expectation is conditioned on being in the left tail of the distribution. ES is the more commonly used terminology. Using a sample of historical returns, we would estimate the 1% expected shortfall by identifying the worst 1% of all observations and taking their average.[12]

Lower Partial Standard Deviation and the Sortino Ratio

The use of standard deviation as a measure of risk when the return distribution is non-normal presents two problems: (1) The asymmetry of the distribution suggests we should look at negative outcomes separately, and (2) because an alternative to a risky portfolio is a risk-free investment, we should look at deviations of returns from the risk-free rate rather than from the sample average, that is, at negative *excess* returns.

A risk measure that addresses these issues is the **lower partial standard deviation (LPSD)** of excess returns, which is computed like the usual standard deviation, but using only "bad" returns. Specifically, it uses only negative deviations from the risk-free rate (rather than negative deviations from the sample average), squares those deviations to obtain an analog to variance, and then takes the square root to obtain a "left-tail standard deviation." The LPSD is therefore the square root of the average squared deviation, *conditional* on a negative excess return. Notice that this measure ignores the frequency of negative excess returns; that is, portfolios with the same average squared negative excess returns will yield the same LPSD regardless of the relative frequency of negative excess returns.

Practitioners who replace standard deviation with this LPSD typically also replace the Sharpe ratio (the ratio of average excess return to standard deviation) with the ratio of average excess returns to LPSD. This variant on the Sharpe ratio is called the **Sortino ratio.**

Relative Frequency of Large, Negative 3-Sigma Returns

Here we concentrate on the relative frequency of large, negative returns compared with those frequencies in a normal distribution with the same mean and standard deviation. Extreme returns are often called *jumps,* as the stock price makes a big sudden movement. We compare the fraction of observations with returns 3 or more standard deviations below the mean to the relative frequency of negative 3-sigma returns in the corresponding normal distribution.

This measure can be quite informative about downside risk but, in practice, is most useful for large samples observed at a high frequency. Observe from Figure 5.3 that the relative frequency of returns that are 3 standard deviations or more below the mean in a standard normal distribution is only 0.13%, that is, 1.3 observations per 1,000. Thus in a small sample, it is hard to obtain a representative outcome, one that reflects true statistical expectations of extreme events.

---

[12]A formula for the ES in the case of normally distributed returns is given in Jonathan Treussard, "The Non-monotonicity of Value-at-Risk and the Validity of Risk Measures over Different Horizons," *IFCAI Journal of Financial Risk Management,* March 2007. The formula is

$$\text{ES} = \frac{1}{.05} \exp(\mu)N[-\sigma - F(.95)] - 1$$

where μ is the mean of the continuously compounded returns, σ is the SD, $N(\bullet)$ is the cumulative standard normal, and F is its inverse. It should be noted, however, that estimates of VaR and ES from historical samples, while unbiased, are subject to large estimation errors because they are estimated from a small number of extreme returns.

5.8   Historic Returns on Risky Portfolios

We can now apply the analytical tools worked out in previous sections to look at the historic performance of several important portfolios.

We begin by comparing the performance of Treasury bills, Treasury bonds, and a diversified portfolio of U.S. stocks. T-bills are widely considered the least risky of all assets. There is essentially no risk that the U.S. government will fail to honor its commitments to these investors, and their short maturities means that their prices are relatively stable. Long-term U.S. Treasury bonds are also certain to be repaid, but the prices of these bonds fluctuate as interest rates vary, so they impose meaningful risk. Finally, common stocks are the riskiest of the three groups of securities. As a part-owner of the corporation, your return will depend on the success or failure of the firm.

Our stock portfolio is the broadest possible U.S. equity portfolio, including all stocks listed on the NYSE, AMEX, and NASDAQ. We shall denote it as "the U.S. market index." Because larger firms play a greater role in the economy, this index is a value-weighted portfolio and therefore dominated by the large-firm corporate sector. The monthly data series include excess returns on these stocks from July 1926 to June 2016, a sample period spanning 90 years. The annual return series comprise full-year returns from 1927–2015.

Figure 5.5 is a frequency distribution of annual returns on these three portfolios. The greater volatility of stock returns compared to T-bill or T-bond returns is immediately apparent. Compared to stock returns, the distribution of T-bond returns is far more concentrated in the middle of the distribution, with far fewer outliers. The distribution of T-bill returns is even tighter. More to the point, the spread of the T-bill distribution does not

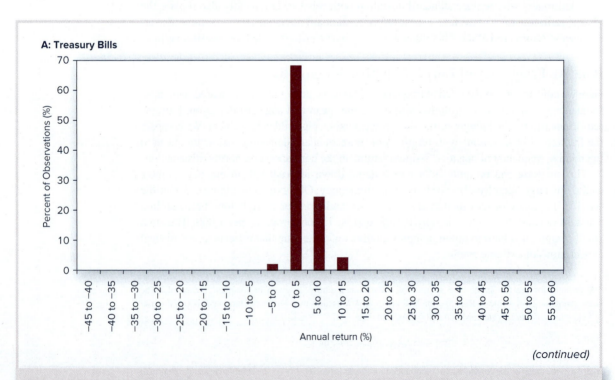

(continued)

Figure 5.5 Frequency distribution of annual returns on U.S. Treasury bills, Treasury bonds, and common stocks

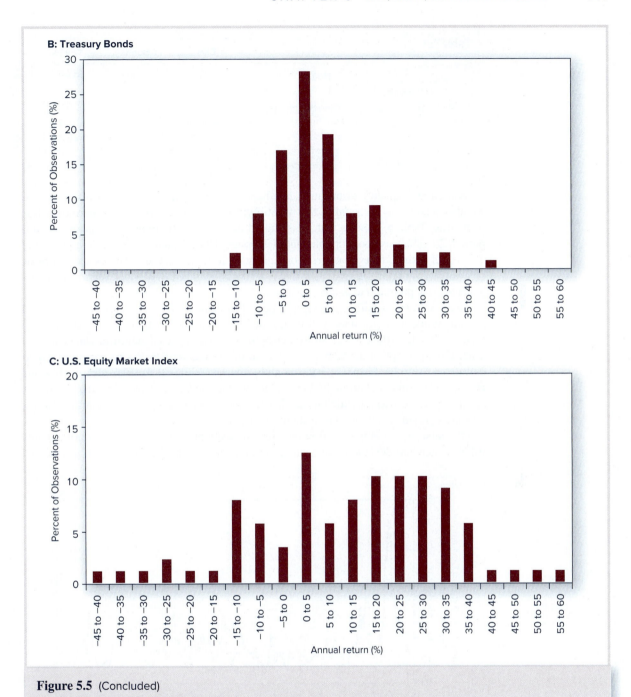

Figure 5.5 (Concluded)

reflect risk but rather changes in the risk-free rate over time.[13] Anyone buying a T-bill knows exactly what the (nominal) return will be when the bill matures, so variation in the return is not a reflection of risk over that short holding period.

[13]You might wonder about the negative T-bill rates that show up in the frequency distribution in Figure 5.5. T-bills did not make their debut until the 1940s. For earlier dates, commercial paper is used as the closest approximation to short-term risk-free rates. In a few instances they were issued slightly above par and thus yielded slightly negative rates.

Table 5.3		T-Bills	T-Bonds	Stocks
Risk and return of investments in major asset classes, 1926–2015	Average	3.47%	6.00%	11.77%
	Risk premium	N/A	2.53	8.30
	Standard deviation	3.13	10.02	20.28
	Max	14.71	40.36	57.53
	Min	−0.02	−14.90	−44.04

While the frequency distribution is a handy visual representation of investment risk, we also need a way to quantify that volatility; this is provided by the standard deviation of returns. Table 5.3 shows that the standard deviation of the return on stocks over this period, 20.28%, was about double that of T-bonds, 10.02%, and more than 6 times that of T-bills. Of course, that greater risk brought with it greater reward. The excess return on stocks (i.e., the return in excess of the T-bill rate) averaged 8.30% per year, providing a generous risk premium to equity investors.

Table 5.3 uses a fairly long sample period to estimate the average level of risk and reward. While averages may well be useful indications of what we might expect going forward, we nevertheless should expect both risk and expected return to fluctuate over time. Figure 5.6 plots the standard deviation of the market's excess return in each year calculated from the 12 most recent monthly returns. While market risk clearly ebbs and flows, aside from its abnormally high values during the Great Depression, there does not seem to be any obvious trend in its level. This gives us more confidence that historical risk estimates provide useful guidance about the future.

Of course, as we emphasized in the previous sections, unless returns are normally distributed, standard deviation is not sufficient to measure risk. We also need to think about

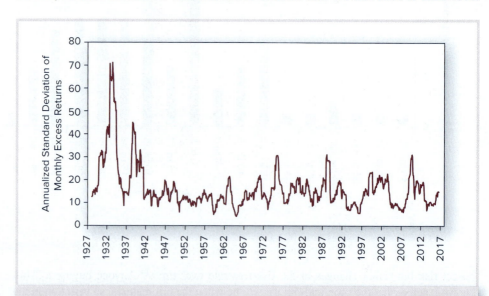

Figure 5.6 Annualized standard deviation of the monthly excess return on the market index portfolio

Source: Authors' calculations using data from Prof. Kenneth French's Web site: **http://mba.tuck.dartmouth.edu/pages/faculty/ken.french/data_library.html.**

"tail risk," that is, our exposure to unlikely but very large outcomes in the left tail of the probability distributions. Figure 5.7 provides some evidence of this exposure. It shows a frequency distribution of *monthly* excess returns on the market index since 1926. The first bar in each set shows the historical frequency of excess returns falling within each range, while

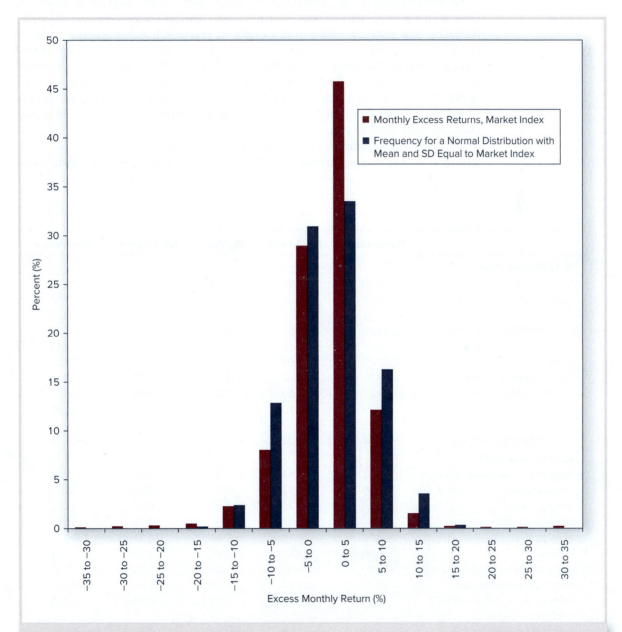

Figure 5.7 Frequency distribution of monthly excess returns on the market index (the first bar in each set) versus predicted frequency from a normal distribution with matched mean and standard deviation (the second bar in each set)

Source: This frequency distribution is for monthly excess returns on the market index, obtained from Prof. Kenneth French's Web site, **http://mba.tuck.dartmouth.edu/pages/faculty/ken.french/data_library.html.** The returns are expressed as continuously compounded rates, as these are most appropriate for comparison with the normal distribution.

the second bar shows the frequencies that we *would* observe if these returns followed a normal distribution with the same mean and variance as the actual empirical distribution. You can see here some evidence of a fat-tailed distribution: The actual frequencies of extreme returns, both high and low, are higher than would be predicted by the normal distribution.

Further evidence on the distribution of excess equity returns is given in Table 5.4. Here, we use monthly data on both the market index and, for comparison, several "style" portfolios. You may remember from Chapter 4, Figure 4.5, that the performance of mutual funds is commonly evaluated relative to other funds with similar investment "styles." (See the Morningstar style box in Figure 4.5.) Style is defined along two dimensions: size (do the funds invest in large cap or small cap firms?) and value vs. growth. Firms with high ratios of market value to book value are viewed as "growth firms" because, to justify their high prices relative to current book values, the market must anticipate rapid growth.

The use of style portfolios as a benchmark for performance evaluation traces back to influential papers by Eugene Fama and Kenneth French, who extensively documented

	Market Index	Big/Growth	Big/Value	Small/Growth	Small/Value
A. 1926–June 2016					
Mean excess return (annualized)	08.30	7.98	11.67	8.79	15.56
Standard deviation (annualized)	18.64	18.50	24.62	26.21	28.36
Sharpe ratio	0.45	0.43	0.47	0.34	0.55
Lower partial SD (annualized)	19.49	18.57	22.78	25.92	25.98
Skew	0.20	−0.10	1.70	0.70	2.19
Kurtosis	7.77	5.55	19.05	7.83	22.21
VaR (1%) actual (monthly) returns	−13.95	−14.68	−19.53	−20.59	−20.47
VaR (1%) normal distribution	−11.87	−11.80	−15.63	−16.92	−17.87
% of monthly returns more than 3 SD below mean	0.94%	0.75%	0.94%	0.75%	0.57%
Expected shortfall (monthly)	−20.14	−20.33	−24.30	−25.02	−25.76
B. 1952–June 2016					
Mean excess return (annualized)	7.52	7.18	9.92	7.05	13.34
Standard deviation (annualized)	14.89	15.54	15.95	22.33	18.42
Sharpe ratio	0.50	0.46	0.62	0.32	0.72
Lower partial SD (annualized)	16.51	15.67	16.01	23.79	19.36
Skew	−0.52	−0.36	−0.29	−0.36	−0.35
Kurtosis	1.90	1.81	2.26	2.17	3.48
VaR (1%) actual (monthly) returns	−10.80	−10.90	−11.94	−16.93	−15.21
VaR (1%) normal distribution	−9.37	−9.84	−9.89	−14.41	−11.26
% of monthly returns more than 3 SD below mean	0.66%	0.66%	0.80%	0.93%	1.19%
Expected shortfall (monthly)	−18.85	−17.99	−21.30	−24.66	−28.33

Table 5.4

Statistics for monthly excess returns on the market index and four "style" portfolios

Sources: Authors' calculations using data from Prof. Kenneth French's Web site: **http://mba.tuck.dartmouth.edu/pages/faculty/ken.french/data_library.html**.

that firm size and the book value-to-market value ratio predict average returns; these patterns have since been corroborated in stock exchanges around the world.[14] A high book-to-market (B/M) ratio is interpreted as an indication that the value of the firm is driven primarily by assets already in place, rather than the prospect of high future growth. These are called "value" firms. In contrast, a low book-to-market ratio is typical of firms whose market value derives mostly from ample growth opportunities. Realized average returns, other things equal, historically have been higher for value firms than for growth firms and for small firms than for large ones. The Fama-French database includes returns on portfolios of U.S. stocks sorted by size (Big; Small) and by B/M ratios (High; Medium; Low).[15]

Following the Fama-French classifications, we drop the medium B/M portfolios and identify firms ranked in the top 30% of B/M ratio as "value firms" and firms ranked in the bottom 30% as "growth firms." We split firms into above and below median levels of market capitalization to establish subsamples of small versus large firms. We thus obtain four comparison portfolios: Big/Growth, Big/Value, Small/Growth, and Small/Value.

Table 5.4, Panel A, presents results using monthly data for the full sample period, July 1926–June 2016. The top two lines show the annualized average excess return and standard deviation of each portfolio. The broad market index outperformed T-bills by an average of 8.30% per year, with a standard deviation of 18.64%, resulting in a Sharpe ratio (third line) of 8.30/18.64 = .45. In line with the Fama-French analysis, small/value firms had the highest average excess return and the best risk–return trade-off with a Sharpe ratio of .55. However, Figure 5.5 warns us that actual returns may have fatter tails than the normal distribution, so we need to consider risk measures beyond just the standard deviation. The table therefore also presents several measures of risk that are suited for non-normal distributions.

Several of these other measures actually do not show meaningful departures from the symmetric normal distribution. Skew is generally near zero; if downside risk were substantially grater than upside potential, we would expect skew to be generally negative, which it is not. Along the same lines, the lower partial standard deviation is generally quite close to the conventional standard deviation. Finally, while the actual 1% VaR of these portfolios are uniformly higher than the 1% VaR that would be predicted from normal distributions with matched means and standard deviations, the differences between the empirical and predicted VaR statistics are not large. By this metric as well, the normal appears to be a decent approximation to the actual return distribution.

However, there is other evidence suggesting fat tails in the return distributions of these portfolios. To begin, note that kurtosis (the measure of the "fatness" of both tails of the distribution) is uniformly high. Investors are, of course, concerned with the lower (left) tail of the distribution; they do not lose sleep over their exposure to extreme good returns! Unfortunately, these portfolios suggest that the left tail of the return distribution is over-represented compared to the normal. If excess returns were normally distributed, then only .13% of them would fall more than 3 standard deviations below the mean. In fact, the actual incidence of excess returns below that cutoff are at least a few multiples of .13% for each portfolio.

The expected shortfall (ES) estimates show why VaR is only an incomplete measure of downside risk. ES in Table 5.4 is the average excess return of those observations that fall

---

[14]This literature began in earnest with their 1992 publication: "The Cross Section of Expected Stock Returns," *Journal of Finance* 47, 427–465.

[15]We use the Fama-French data to construct Figures 5.4 and 5.5 and Tables 5.3 and 5.4. The database is available at: **http://mba.tuck.dartmouth.edu/pages/faculty/ken.french/data_library.html.**

in the extreme left tail, specifically, those that fall below the 1% VaR. By definition, this value must be worse than the VaR, as it averages among all the returns that are below the 1% cutoff. Because it uses the actual returns of the "worst-case outcomes," ES is by far a better indicator of exposure to extreme events.

Figure 5.2 showed us that the post-war years (more accurately, the years after 1951) have been far more predictable, at least with respect to interest rates. This suggests that it may be instructive to examine stock returns in the post-1951 period as well to see if risk and return characteristics for equity investments have changed meaningfully in the more recent period. The relevant statistics are given in Panel B of Table 5.4. Perhaps not surprisingly in light of the history of inflation and interest rates, the more recent period is in fact less risky. Standard deviation for all five portfolios is noticeably lower in recent years, and kurtosis, our measure of fat tails, drops dramatically. VaR also falls. While the number of excess returns that are more than 3 SD below the mean changes inconsistently, because SD is lower in this period, those negative returns are also less dramatic: Expected shortfall generally is lower in the latter period.

The frequency distribution in Figure 5.5 and the statistics in Table 5.4 for the market index as well as the style portfolios tell a reasonably consistent story. There is some, admittedly inconsistent, evidence of fat tails, so investors should not take normality for granted. On the other hand, extreme returns are in fact quite uncommon, especially in more recent years. The incidence of returns on the market index in the post-1951 period that are worse than 3 SD below the mean is .66%, compared to a prediction of .13% for the normal distribution. The "excess" rate of extreme bad outcomes is thus only .53%, or about once in 187 months (15½ years). So it is not unreasonable to accept the simplification offered by normality as an acceptable approximation as we think about constructing and evaluating our portfolios.

A Global View of the Historical Record

As financial markets around the world grow and become more transparent, U.S. investors look to improve diversification by investing internationally. Foreign investors that traditionally used U.S. financial markets as a safe haven to supplement home-country investments also seek international diversification to reduce risk. The question arises as to how historical U.S. experience compares with that of stock markets around the world.

Figure 5.8 shows a century-plus-long history (1900–2015) of average excess returns in 20 stock markets. The mean annual excess return across these countries was 7.40% and the median was 6.50%. The United States is roughly in the middle of the pack, with a historical risk premium of 7.55%. Similarly, the standard deviation of returns in the U.S. (not shown) was just a shade below the median volatility in these other countries. So the U.S. performance has been pretty much consistent with international experience. We might tentatively conclude that the characteristics of historical returns in the U.S. also can serve as a rough indication of the risk–return trade-off in a wider range of countries.

Of course, we've seen that there is tremendous variability in year-by year returns, and this makes even long-term average performance a very noisy estimate of future returns. There is an ongoing debate as to whether the historical U.S. average risk-premium of large stocks over T-bills of 8.30% (Table 5.4) is a reasonable forecast for the long term. This debate centers around two questions: First, do economic factors that prevailed over that historic period (1926–2015) adequately represent those that may prevail over the forecasting horizon? Second, is average performance from the available history a good yardstick for long-term forecasts? We will return to these questions again later in the text.

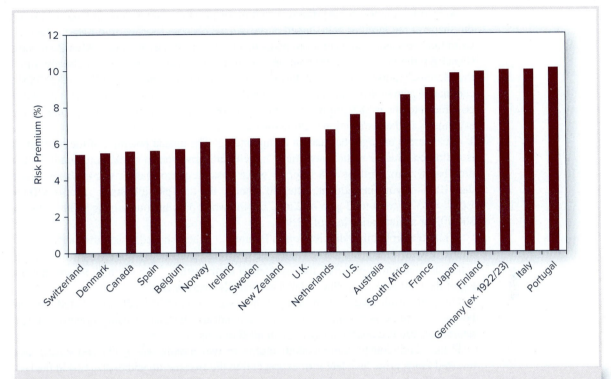

Figure 5.8 Average excess returns in 20 countries, 1900–2015

Note: The data for Germany omit the hyperinflation years 1922 and 1923.
Source: Authors' calculations using data from E. Dimson, P. R. Marsh, and M. Staunton, *Triumph of the Optimists: 101 Years of Global Investment Returns* (Princeton, NJ: Princeton University Press, 2002), with updates kindly provided by *Triumph's* authors.

5.9   Normality and Long-Term Investments*

Based on historical experience, it may be reasonable to treat short-term stock returns as approximately described by a symmetric normal distribution. But even if that is so, long-term performance cannot be normal. If r_1 and r_2 are the returns in two periods, and each have the same normal distribution, then the *sum* of the returns, $r_1 + r_2$, would be normal. But the two-period compound return is not the sum of the two returns. Instead, invested funds would compound to $(1 + r_1)(1 + r_2)$, which is *not* normal. This is more than a theoretical point. The shape of the distribution changes noticeably as the investment horizon extends.

To illustrate, suppose that you invest $100 in a stock with an expected monthly return of 1%. But there is dispersion around the expected value: With equal probability, the actual return in any month will exceed the mean by 2% (for a return of 1% + 2% = 3%), or fall short by 2% (for a return of 1% − 2% = −1%). These two possible monthly returns, −1% or 3%, are thus symmetrically distributed around the 1% mean. Now let's look at the distribution of the portfolio value at the end of several investment horizons. Figure 5.9 shows the results.

*The material in this section addresses important and ongoing debates about risk and return, but it is more challenging. It may be skipped in shorter courses without impairing the ability to understand later chapters.

After 6 months (Panel A), the distribution of possible values is beginning to take on the shape of the familiar bell-shaped curve. As we observed earlier, mid-range values are more likely because there are more paths that take us to these outcomes. After 20 months (Panel B), the bell-shaped distribution is even more obvious, but there is already a hint that extremely good cumulative returns (with possible stock prices extending to $180 for a cumulative gain of 80%) are more prevalent than extremely poor ones (notice that the worst possible outcome is $82, implying a total loss of only 18%). After 40 months (Panel C), the asymmetry in the distribution is pronounced.

This pattern emerges because of compounding. The upside potential of the investment is unlimited. But no matter how many months in a row you lose 1%, your funds cannot drop below zero, so there is a floor on worst-possible performance: you can't lose more than 100% of your investment. After 40 months, the best possible stock value is $100 × 1.03^{40} = $326, for a total gain of 226%, but the worst possible outcome is $100 × $.99^{40}$ = $66.90, for a cumulative loss of 33.1%.

While the probability distribution in Figure 5.9 is bell-shaped, it is a distinctly "asymmetric bell" with a positive skew, and the distribution is clearly not normal. In fact, the actual distribution approaches the **lognormal distribution.** "Lognormal" means that the log of the final portfolio value, $\ln(W_T)$ is normally distributed.

Does this result invalidate the simplifying assumption of normally distributed returns? Fortunately, there is a simple fix to this conundrum. Instead of using effective annual returns, we can use continuously compounded returns.

If the continuously compounded returns in two months are $r_{cc}(1)$ and $r_{cc}(2)$, then invested funds grow by a factor of $\exp[r_{cc}(1)]$ in the first month and $\exp[r_{cc}(2)]$ in the second month, where exp( ) is the exponential function. The total growth in the investment is thus $\exp[r_{cc}(1)] \times \exp[r_{cc}(2)] = \exp[r_{cc}(1) + r_{cc}(2)]$. In other words, the total two-month return expressed as a continuously compounded rate is the sum of the one-month returns. Therefore, if the monthly returns are normal, then the multi-month returns will also be normal.[16] Thus, by using continuously compounded rates, even long-term returns can be described by the normal distribution. Moreover, if returns have the same distribution in each month, then the expected two-month return is just twice the expected one-month return, and if returns over time are uncorrelated, then the variance of the two-month return is also twice that of the one-month return.[17]

We can generalize from this example to arbitrary investment horizons, which we will call T. If the expected per-period continuously compounded return is called $E(r_{cc})$, then the expected cumulative return after an investment of T periods is $E(r_{cc})T$, and the expected final value of the portfolio is $E(W_T) = W_0 \exp[E(r_{cc})T]$. The variance of the cumulative return is also proportional to the time horizon: $\text{Var}(r_{cc}T) = T\text{Var}(r_{cc})$. Therefore, the standard deviation grows in proportion to the square root of the time horizon:

$$SD(r_{cc}\, T) = \sqrt{T\, Var(r_{cc})} = \sigma\sqrt{T}$$

Short-Run versus Long-Run Risk

Our results on the risk and return of investments over different time horizons appear to offer a mitigation of investment risk in the long run: Because expected return increases

[16] By the way, notice that if we take the log of the cumulative return, we get $\ln[\exp[r_{cc}(1) + r_{cc}(2)] = r_{cc}(1) + r_{cc}(2)$, which is normally distributed. So if the continuously compounded return is normally distributed, the final value of the portfolio will be lognormally distributed.

[17] A warning: The variance of the effective annual return is not exactly equal to that of the continuously compounded return. If σ^2 is the variance of the continuously compounded return and μ is its mean, then the variance of the effective annual rate when returns are lognormally distributed is:

$$\text{Var}(r) = \exp[2(\mu + \tfrac{1}{2}\sigma^2)] \times [\exp(\sigma^2) - 1]$$

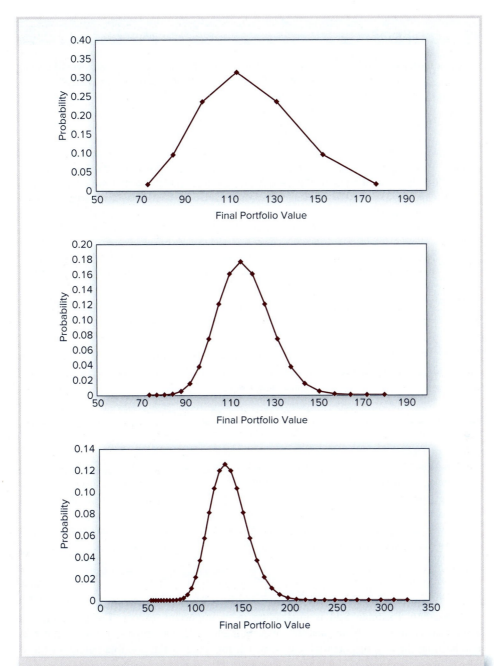

Figure 5.9 Frequency distribution of final portfolio value after different number of months. Initial investment = $100. In any month, portfolio value will increase by 3% or fall by 1% with equal probability.

with horizon at a faster rate than standard deviation, the expected return of a long-term risky investment becomes ever larger relative to its standard deviation. Does this mean that investments are less risky when horizons are longer? To see why many people believe so, consider the following example.

Example 5.11   Investment Risk in the Short Run and the Long Run

Suppose that investment returns are independent from year to year with an expected continuously compounded rate of return of .05, and a standard deviation of $\sigma = .30$. Let's look at the properties of the investment at horizons of 1, 10, and 30 years. These are laid out in Table 5.5. The mean average annual return is 5% regardless of the horizon, but the mean cumulative return rises in direct proportion to T. The standard deviation of the cumulative return rises in proportion to the square root of T.

Next, we look at the probability that the cumulative return will be negative, in other words, that the investor will suffer a loss. For the 1-year investor to suffer a loss, the actual return must be .05 below the mean. This implies a return that is $.05/.3 = .167$ standard deviations below the mean return. Assuming normality, the probability of such an outcome is .434. (See Example 5.10 for an example of how to compute this probability.) For the 10-year investor, the mean cumulative continuously compounded return is .500 and the standard deviation is .949. Therefore, the investor will suffer losses only if the actual 10-year return is $.500/.949 = .527$ standard deviations below the expected value. The probability of this outcome is only .299. The probability of a loss after 30 years is even lower, .181. As the horizon expands, mean return increases faster than standard deviation and therefore the probability of a loss steadily shrinks.

Table 5.5

Investment risk at different horizons

	Investment Horizon			
	1	10	30	Comment
Mean total return	0.050	0.500	1.500	$= 0.05^*T$
Mean average return	0.050	0.050	0.050	$= 0.05$
Std dev total return	0.300	0.949	1.643	$= 0.30^*\sqrt{T}$
Probability return < 0	0.434	0.299	0.181	assuming normal distribution
1% VaR total return	−0.648	−1.707	−2.323	continuously compounded return
Implies final wealth relative of:	0.523	0.181	0.098	=exp(VaR total return)
0.1% VaR total return	−0.877	−2.432	−3.578	continuously compounded return
Implies final wealth relative of:	0.416	0.088	0.028	=exp(VaR total return)

A warning: Example 5.11 is misleading in an important respect. The probability of a shortfall is an incomplete measure of investment risk. This probability does not take into account the size of potential losses, which for some of the possible outcomes (however unlikely they may be), amount to near ruin. The worst-case scenarios for the 30-year investment are far worse than for the 1-year investment. We can see this point vividly by comparing the VaR of the investment at different horizons.

Table 5.5 shows that the 1% VaR after one year entails a continuously compounded cumulative loss of .648, implying that each dollar invested will fall almost in half, specifically to $e^{-.648} = .523$. This value is called the "wealth relative" of the investment (i.e., it is the final value of the portfolio as a fraction of initially invested funds). The 1% VaR after 30 years is far worse: It implies a wealth relative of .098, less than one-fifth the value of the 1-year VaR. Thus, while the *probability* of losses falls as the investment horizon lengthens, the *magnitude* of potential losses grows. The comparison is even more extreme when we look at the 0.1% VaR.

A better way to quantify the risk of a long-term investment would be to calculate the market price of insuring it against a loss. An insurance premium must take into account both the probability of possible losses and the magnitude of these losses. We show in later chapters how the fair market price of this sort of portfolio insurance can be estimated from option-pricing models. Contrary to any intuition that a longer horizon reduces risk, the value of portfolio insurance increases dramatically with the investment horizon. And these policies would not come cheap: For example, for reasonable parameters, a 25-year policy would cost about 30% of the initial portfolio value.

Despite this, many observers hold on to the view that investment risk is less pertinent to long-term investors. A typical demonstration relies on the fact that the standard deviation (or range of likely outcomes) of *annualized* returns is lower for longer-term horizons. But the demonstration is silent on the range of *total* returns.

Forecasts for the Long Haul

We use arithmetic averages to forecast future rates of return because they are unbiased estimates of expected rates over equivalent holding periods. But the arithmetic average of short-term returns can be misleading when used to forecast long-term cumulative returns. This is because sampling errors in the estimate of expected return will have asymmetric impact when compounded over long periods. Positive sampling variation will compound to greater upward errors than negative variation.

Jacquier, Kane, and Marcus show that an unbiased forecast of total return over long horizons requires compounding at a weighted average of the arithmetic and geometric historical averages.[18] The proper weight applied to the geometric average equals the ratio of the length of the forecast horizon to the length of the estimation period. For example, if we wish to forecast the cumulative return for a 25-year horizon from a 90-year history, an unbiased estimate would be to compound at a rate of

$$\text{Geometric average} \times \frac{25}{90} + \text{Arithmetic average} \times \frac{(90 - 25)}{90}$$

This correction would take about .5% off the historical arithmetic average risk premium on large stocks and almost 2% off the arithmetic average premium of small stocks. A forecast for the next 90 years would require compounding at only the geometric average, and for longer horizons at an even lower number. The forecast horizons that are relevant for current investors would depend on their investment horizons.

[18]Eric Jacquier, Alex Kane, and Alan J. Marcus, "Geometric or Arithmetic Means: A Reconsideration," *Financial Analysts Journal,* November/December 2003.

SUMMARY

1. The economy's equilibrium level of real interest rates depends on the willingness of households to save, as reflected in the supply curve of funds, and on the expected profitability of business investment in plant, equipment, and inventories, as reflected in the demand curve for funds. It depends also on government fiscal and monetary policy.

2. The nominal rate of interest is the equilibrium real rate plus the expected rate of inflation. In general, we can directly observe only nominal interest rates; from them, we must infer expected real rates, using inflation forecasts. Assets with guaranteed nominal interest rates are risky in real terms because the future inflation rate is uncertain.

3. The equilibrium expected rate of return on any security is the sum of the equilibrium real rate of interest, the expected rate of inflation, and a security-specific risk premium.

4. Investors face a trade-off between risk and expected return. Historical data confirm our intuition that assets with low degrees of risk should provide lower returns on average than do those of higher risk.

5. Historical rates of return over the last century in other countries suggest the U.S. history of stock returns is not an outlier compared to other countries.

6. Historical returns on stocks exhibit somewhat more frequent large negative deviations from the mean than would be predicted from a normal distribution. The lower partial standard deviation (LPSD), skew, and kurtosis of the actual distribution quantify the deviation from normality.

7. Widely used measures of tail risk are value at risk (VaR) and expected shortfall or, equivalently, conditional tail expectations. VaR measures the loss that will be exceeded with a specified probability such as 1% or 5%. Expected shortfall (ES) measures the expected rate of return conditional on the portfolio falling below a certain value. Thus, 1% ES is the expected value of the outcomes that lie in the bottom 1% of the distribution.

8. Investments in risky portfolios *do not* become safer in the long run. On the contrary, the longer a risky investment is held, the greater the risk. The basis of the argument that stocks are safe in the long run is the fact that the probability of an investment shortfall becomes smaller. However, probability of shortfall is a poor measure of the safety of an investment. It ignores the magnitude of possible losses.

KEY TERMS

nominal interest rate	excess return	expected shortfall (ES)
real interest rate	risk aversion	conditional tail expectation
effective annual rate (EAR)	normal distribution	(CTE)
annual percentage rate (APR)	event tree	lower partial standard
dividend yield	skew	deviation (LPSD)
risk-free rate	kurtosis	Sortino ratio
risk premium	value at risk (VaR)	lognormal distribution

KEY EQUATIONS

Arithmetic average of n returns: $(r_1 + r_2 + \cdots + r_n)/n$

Geometric average of n returns: $[(1 + r_1)(1 + r_2) \cdots (1 + r_n)]^{1/n} - 1$

Continuously compounded rate of return, $r_{cc} = \ln(1 + \text{Effective annual rate})$

Expected return: $\sum [\text{prob(Scenario)} \times \text{Return in scenario}]$

Variance: $\sum [\text{prob(Scenario)} \times (\text{Deviation from mean in scenario})^2]$

Standard deviation: $\sqrt{\text{Variance}}$

Sharpe ratio: $\dfrac{\text{Portfolio risk premium}}{\text{Standard deviation of excess return}} = \dfrac{E(r_P) - r_f}{\sigma_P}$

Real rate of return: $\dfrac{1 + \text{Nominal return}}{1 + \text{Inflation rate}} - 1$

Real rate of return (continuous compounding): $r_{\text{nominal}} - \text{Inflation rate}$

PROBLEM SETS

1. The Fisher equation tells us that the real interest rate approximately equals the nominal rate minus the inflation rate. Suppose the inflation rate increases from 3% to 5%. Does the Fisher equation imply that this increase will result in a fall in the real rate of interest? Explain.

2. You've just stumbled on a new dataset that enables you to compute historical rates of return on U.S. stocks all the way back to 1880. What are the advantages and disadvantages in using these data to help estimate the expected rate of return on U.S. stocks over the coming year?

3. You are considering two alternative two-year investments: You can invest in a risky asset with a positive risk premium and returns in each of the two years that will be identically distributed and

uncorrelated, or you can invest in the risky asset for only one year and then invest the proceeds in a risk-free asset. Which of the following statements about the first investment alternative (compared with the second) are true?

a. Its two-year risk premium is the same as the second alternative.
b. The standard deviation of its two-year return is the same.
c. Its annualized standard deviation is lower.
d. Its Sharpe ratio is higher.
e. It is relatively more attractive to investors who have lower degrees of risk aversion.

4. You have $5,000 to invest for the next year and are considering three alternatives:

a. A money market fund with an average maturity of 30 days offering a current yield of 6% per year.
b. A 1-year savings deposit at a bank offering an interest rate of 7.5%.
c. A 20-year U.S. Treasury bond offering a yield to maturity of 9% per year.

What role does your forecast of future interest rates play in your decisions?

5. Use Figure 5.1 in the text to analyze the effect of the following on the level of real interest rates:

a. Businesses become more pessimistic about future demand for their products and decide to reduce their capital spending.
b. Households are induced to save more because of increased uncertainty about their future Social Security benefits.
c. The Federal Reserve Board undertakes open-market purchases of U.S. Treasury securities in order to increase the supply of money.

6. You are considering the choice between investing $50,000 in a conventional 1-year bank CD offering an interest rate of 5% and a 1-year "Inflation-Plus" CD offering 1.5% per year plus the rate of inflation.

a. Which is the safer investment?
b. Can you tell which offers the higher expected return?
c. If you expect the rate of inflation to be 3% over the next year, which is the better investment? Why?
d. If we observe a risk-free nominal interest rate of 5% per year and a risk-free real rate of 1.5% on inflation-indexed bonds, can we infer that the market's expected rate of inflation is 3.5% per year?

7. Suppose your expectations regarding the stock price are as follows:

State of the Market	Probability	Ending Price	HPR (including dividends)
Boom	0.35	$140	44.5%
Normal growth	0.30	110	14.0
Recession	0.35	80	−16.5

Use Equations 5.11 and 5.12 to compute the mean and standard deviation of the HPR on stocks.

8. Derive the probability distribution of the 1-year HPR on a 30-year U.S. Treasury bond with an 8% coupon if it is currently selling at par and the probability distribution of its yield to maturity a year from now is as follows:

State of the Economy	Probability	YTM
Boom	0.20	11.0%
Normal growth	0.50	8.0
Recession	0.30	7.0

For simplicity, assume the entire 8% coupon is paid at the end of the year rather than every 6 months.

9. Determine the standard deviation of a random variable q with the following probability distribution:

Value of q	Probability
0	0.25
1	0.25
2	0.50

10. The continuously compounded annual return on a stock is normally distributed with a mean of 20% and standard deviation of 30%. With 95.44% confidence, we should expect its actual return in any particular year to be between which pair of values? (*Hint:* Look again at Figure 5.4.)

    a. −40.0% and 80.0%
    b. −30.0% and 80.0%
    c. −20.6% and 60.6%
    d. −10.4% and 50.4%

11. Using historical risk premiums from Table 5.4 over the 1926–2016 period as your guide, what would be your estimate of the expected annual HPR on the Big/Value portfolio if the current risk-free interest rate is 3%?

12. Visit Professor Kenneth French's data library website: **http://mba.tuck.dartmouth.edu/pages/faculty/ken.french/data_library.html** and download the monthly returns of "6 portfolios formed on size and book-to-market (2 × 3)." Choose the value-weighted series for the period from January 1930–December 2016 (1,020 months). Split the sample in half and compute the average, SD, skew, and kurtosis for each of the six portfolios for the two halves. Do the six split-halves statistics suggest to you that returns come from the same distribution over the entire period?

13. During a period of severe inflation, a bond offered a nominal HPR of 80% per year. The inflation rate was 70% per year.

    a. What was the real HPR on the bond over the year?
    b. Compare this real HPR to the approximation $r_{real} \approx r_{nom} - i$.

14. Suppose that the inflation rate is expected to be 3% in the near future. Using the historical data provided in this chapter, what would be your predictions for:

    a. The T-bill rate?
    b. The expected rate of return on the Big/Value portfolio?
    c. The risk premium on the stock market?

15. An economy is making a rapid recovery from steep recession, and businesses foresee a need for large amounts of capital investment. Why would this development affect real interest rates?

16. You are faced with the probability distribution of the HPR on the stock market index fund given in Spreadsheet 5.1 of the text. Suppose the price of a put option on a share of the index fund with exercise price of $110 and time to expiration of 1 year is $12.

    a. What is the probability distribution of the HPR on the put option?
    b. What is the probability distribution of the HPR on a portfolio consisting of one share of the index fund and a put option?
    c. In what sense does buying the put option constitute a purchase of insurance in this case?

17. Take as given the conditions described in the previous problem, and suppose the risk-free interest rate is 6% per year. You are contemplating investing $107.55 in a 1-year CD and simultaneously buying a call option on the stock market index fund with an exercise price of $110 and expiration of 1 year. What is the probability distribution of your dollar return at the end of the year?

18. Consider these long-term investment data:

    • The price of a 10-year $100 par value zero-coupon inflation-indexed bond is $84.49.
    • A real-estate property is expected to yield 2% per quarter (nominal) with a SD of the (effective) quarterly rate of 10%.
        a. Compute the annual rate of return on the real (i.e., inflation-indexed) bond.
        b. Compute the continuously compounded annual risk premium on the real-estate investment.
        c. Use the formula in footnote 17 and Excel's Solver or Goal Seek to find the standard deviation of the continuously compounded annual excess return on the real-estate investment.
        d. What is the probability of loss or shortfall after 10 years?

1. Given $100,000 to invest, what is the expected risk premium in dollars of investing in equities versus risk-free T-bills (U.S. Treasury bills) based on the following table?

Action	Probability	Expected Return
Invest in equities	0.6	$50,000
	0.4	−$30,000
Invest in risk-free T-bill	1.0	$ 5,000

2. Based on the scenarios below, what is the expected return for a portfolio with the following return profile?

	Bear Market	Normal Market	Bull Market
Probability	0.2	0.3	0.5
Rate of return	−25%	10%	24%

Use the following scenario analysis for Stocks X and Y to answer CFA Problems 3 through 6 (round to the nearest percent).

	Bear Market	Normal Market	Bull Market
Probability	0.2	0.5	0.3
Stock X	−20%	18%	50%
Stock Y	−15%	20%	10%

3. What are the expected rates of return for Stocks X and Y?

4. What are the standard deviations of returns on Stocks X and Y?

5. Assume that of your $10,000 portfolio, you invest $9,000 in Stock X and $1,000 in Stock Y. What is the expected return on your portfolio?

6. Probabilities for three states of the economy and probabilities for the returns on a particular stock in each state are shown in the table below.

State of Economy	Probability of Economic State	Stock Performance	Probability of Stock Performance in Given Economic State
Good	0.3	Good	0.6
		Neutral	0.3
		Poor	0.1
Neutral	0.5	Good	0.4
		Neutral	0.3
		Poor	0.3
Poor	0.2	Good	0.2
		Neutral	0.3
		Poor	0.5

What is the probability that the economy will be neutral *and* the stock will experience poor performance?

7. An analyst estimates that a stock has the following probabilities of return depending on the state of the economy:

State of Economy	Probability	Return
Good	0.1	15%
Normal	0.6	13
Poor	0.3	7

What is the expected return of the stock?

✅ SOLUTIONS TO CONCEPT CHECKS

1. *a.* $1 + r_{nom} = (1 + r_{real})(1 + i) = (1.03)(1.08) = 1.1124$
   $r_{nom} = 11.24\%$

   b. $1 + r_{nom} = (1.03)(1.10) = 1.133$
   $r_{nom} = 13.3\%$

2. *a.* $EAR = (1 + .01)^{12} - 1 = .1268 = 12.68\%$

   b. $EAR = e^{.12} - 1 = .1275 = 12.75\%$

   Choose the continuously compounded rate for its higher EAR.

3. Number of bonds bought is $27,000/900 = 30$

Interest Rates	Probability	Year-End Bond Price	HPR	End-of-Year Value
Higher	0.2	$850	$(75 + 850)/900 - 1 = 0.0278$	$(75 + 850)30 = \$27,750$
Unchanged	0.5	915	0.1000	$29,700
Lower	0.3	985	0.1778	$31,800
Expected rate of return			0.1089	
Expected end-of-year dollar value				$29,940
Risk premium			0.0589	

4. $(1 + \text{Required rate})(1 - .40) = 1$

   Required rate $= .667$, or 66.7%

5. *a.* Arithmetic return $= (1/3)(.2869) + (1/3)(.1088) + (1/3)(0.0491) = .1483 = 14.83\%$

   b. Geometric average $= (1.2869 \times 1.1088 \times 1.0491)^{1/3} - 1 = .1439 = 14.39\%$

   c. Standard deviation $= 12.37\%$

   d. Sharpe ratio $= (14.83 - 6.0)/12.37 = .71$

6. The probability of a more extreme bad month, with return below -15%, is much lower: NORM. DIST($-15,1,6$, TRUE) $= .00383$. Alternatively, we can note that -15% is 16/6 standard deviations below the mean return, and use the standard normal function to compute NORM.S.DIST($-16/6$) $= .00383$.

7. If the probabilities in Spreadsheet 5.2 represented the true return distribution, we would use Equations 5.19 and 5.20 to obtain: Skew $= 0.0931$; Kurtosis $= -1.2081$. However, in this case, the data in the table represent a (short) historical sample, and correction for degrees-of-freedom bias is required (in a similar manner to our calculations for standard deviation). You can use Excel functions to obtain: SKEW(C2:C6) $= 0.1387$; KURT(C2:C6) $= -0.2832$.

Capital Allocation to Risky Assets

6

PORTFOLIO CONSTRUCTION IS commonly—and very properly—viewed as comprising two broad tasks: (1) the allocation of the overall portfolio to safe assets such as a money-market account or Treasury bills versus to risky assets such as shares of stock and (2) the determination of the composition of the risky portion of the complete portfolio. The first step, in which you determine the proportion of your overall portfolio to devote to risky versus risk-free assets, is called the *capital allocation decision,* and that is where we will begin our tour of what is known as *portfolio theory.*

Of course, one cannot rationally make a capital allocation decision without knowing the properties of the risky portfolio, specifically its risk premium and volatility, but we will start by assuming that investors are aware of acceptable candidate risky portfolios and have a sense of their properties. For now, you can think of that risky portfolio as one that might be offered by a mutual fund company, or even better, as a stock market index fund. We will devote a lot of attention in the next two chapters to how such portfolios might be constructed.

The optimal capital allocation will depend in part on the risk–return trade-off offered by the risky portfolio. But it will also depend on the investor's attitude toward risk, so we need a way to measure and describe risk aversion. Therefore, we will show how risk aversion can be captured by a "utility function" that investors can use to rank portfolios with different expected returns and levels of risk. By choosing the overall portfolio with the highest utility score, investors optimize their trade-off between risk and return; that is, they achieve the optimal allocation of capital to risky versus risk-free assets.

The utility model also reveals the appropriate objective function for the construction of an optimal *risky* portfolio, and thus explains how an investment management industry can construct portfolios that are acceptable to investors with highly diverse preferences without knowing each of them and, specifically, their tolerance for risk, personally.

6.1   Risk and Risk Aversion

In Chapter 5 we introduced the concepts of the holding-period return (HPR) and the excess rate of return over the risk-free rate. We also discussed estimation of the **risk premium** (the *expected* excess return) and the standard deviation of the excess return, which we use as the measure of portfolio risk. We demonstrated these concepts with a scenario analysis of a specific risky portfolio (Spreadsheet 5.1). To emphasize that bearing risk typically must be accompanied by a reward in the form of a risk premium, we first differentiate between speculation and gambling.

Risk, Speculation, and Gambling

One definition of *speculation* is "the assumption of considerable investment risk to obtain commensurate gain." By "considerable risk" we mean that the risk is sufficient to affect the decision. By "commensurate gain" we mean a positive risk premium, that is, an expected return greater than the risk-free alternative.

To gamble is "to bet or wager on an uncertain outcome." The central difference between gambling and speculation is the lack of "commensurate gain." A gamble is the assumption of risk for enjoyment of the risk itself, whereas speculation is undertaken *in spite of* the risk involved because one perceives a favorable risk–return trade-off. To turn a gamble into a speculative venture requires an adequate risk premium to compensate risk-averse investors for the risks they bear. Hence, *risk aversion and speculation are consistent.* Notice that a risky investment with a risk premium of zero, sometimes called a **fair game,** amounts to a gamble because there is no expected gain to compensate for the risk entailed. A risk-averse investor will reject gambles, but not necessarily speculative positions.

In some cases, a gamble may *appear* to be speculation. Suppose two investors disagree sharply about the future exchange rate of the U.S. dollar against the British pound. They may choose to bet on the outcome: Paul will pay Mary $100 if the value of £1 exceeds $1.40 one year from now, whereas Mary will pay Paul if the pound is worth less than $1.40. There are only two relevant outcomes: (1) the pound will exceed $1.40, or (2) it will fall below $1.40. If both Paul and Mary agree on the probabilities of the two possible outcomes, and if neither party anticipates a loss, it must be that they assign $p = .5$ to each outcome. In that case the expected profit to both is zero and each has entered one side of a gambling prospect.

What is more likely, however, is that Paul and Mary assign different probabilities to the outcome. Mary assigns it $p > .5$, whereas Paul's assessment is $p < .5$. They perceive, subjectively, two different prospects. Economists call this case of differing beliefs "heterogeneous expectations." In such cases, investors on each side of a financial position see themselves as speculating rather than gambling.

 Concept Check **6.1**

Assume that dollar-denominated T-bills in the United States and pound-denominated bills in the United Kingdom offer equal yields to maturity. Both are short-term assets, and both are free of default risk. Neither offers investors a risk premium. However, a U.S. investor who holds U.K. bills is subject to exchange rate risk, because the pounds earned on the U.K. bills eventually will be exchanged for dollars at the future exchange rate. Is the U.S. investor engaging in speculation or gambling?

Risk Aversion and Utility Values

Historical returns on various asset classes, analyzed in a mountain of empirical studies, leave no doubt that risky assets command a risk premium. This implies that most investors are risk averse.

Investors who are **risk averse** reject investment portfolios that are fair games or worse. Risk-averse investors consider only risk-free or speculative prospects with positive risk premiums. Loosely speaking, a risk-averse investor "penalizes" the expected rate of return of a risky portfolio by a certain percentage (or penalizes the expected profit by a dollar amount) to account for the risk involved. The greater the risk, the larger the penalty. We believe that most investors would accept this view from simple introspection, but we discuss the question more fully in Appendix A of this chapter.

To illustrate the issues we confront when choosing among portfolios with varying degrees of risk, suppose the risk-free rate is 5% and that an investor is comparing the three alternative risky portfolios shown in Table 6.1. The risk premiums and degrees of risk (standard deviation, SD) represent the properties of low-risk short-term bonds (L), medium-risk long-term bonds (M), and higher-risk large stocks (H). Accordingly, these portfolios offer progressively higher risk premiums to compensate for greater risk. How might investors choose among them?

Intuitively, a portfolio is more attractive when its expected return is higher and its risk is lower. But when risk increases along with return, the most attractive portfolio is not obvious. How can investors quantify the rate at which they are willing to trade off return against risk?

We will assume that each investor can assign a welfare, or **utility,** score to competing portfolios on the basis of the expected return and risk of those portfolios. Higher utility values are assigned to portfolios with more attractive risk–return profiles. Portfolios receive higher utility scores for higher expected returns and lower scores for higher volatility. Many particular "scoring" systems are reasonable. One function that has been employed by both financial theorists and the CFA Institute assigns a portfolio with expected return $E(r)$ and variance of returns σ^2 the following utility score:

$$U = E(r) - \frac{1}{2} A\sigma^2 \qquad (6.1)$$

where U is the utility value and A is an index of the investor's risk aversion. The factor of ½ is just a scaling convention. To use Equation 6.1, rates of return must be expressed as decimals rather than percentages. Notice that the portfolio in question here will potentially serve as the investor's overall or complete portfolio. Hence, assuming normality, standard deviation is the appropriate measure of risk.

Equation 6.1 is consistent with the notion that utility is enhanced by high expected returns and diminished by high risk. Notice that risk-free portfolios (with variance = 0) receive a utility score equal to their (known) rate of return, because they receive no penalty for risk. The extent to which the variance of risky portfolios lowers utility depends on A,

Portfolio	Risk Premium	Expected Return	Risk (SD)
L (low risk)	2%	7%	5%
M (medium risk)	4	9	10
H (high risk)	8	13	20

Table 6.1

Available risky portfolios (risk-free rate = 5%)

the investor's degree of risk aversion. More risk-averse investors (who have larger values of A) penalize risky investments more severely. Investors choosing among competing investment portfolios will select the one providing the highest utility level. The Words from the Street box later in this section discusses some techniques that financial advisers use to gauge the risk aversion of their clients.

Example 6.1   Evaluating Investments by Using Utility Scores

Consider three investors with different degrees of risk aversion: $A_1 = 2$, $A_2 = 3.5$, and $A_3 = 5$, all of whom are evaluating the three portfolios in Table 6.1. Because the risk-free rate is assumed to be 5%, Equation 6.1 implies that all three investors would assign a utility score of .05 to the risk-free alternative. Table 6.2 presents the utility scores that would be assigned by each investor to each portfolio. The portfolio with the highest utility score for each investor appears as the bold entry in each row. Notice that the high-risk portfolio, H, would be chosen only by the investor with the lowest degree of risk aversion, $A_1 = 2$, while the low-risk portfolio, L, would be passed over even by the most risk-averse of our three investors. All three portfolios beat the risk-free alternative for the investors with levels of risk aversion given in the table.

We can interpret the utility score of *risky* portfolios as a **certainty equivalent rate** of return. The certainty equivalent is the rate that a risk-free investment would need to offer to provide the same utility score as the risky portfolio. In other words, it is the rate that, if earned with certainty, would provide a utility score equal to that of the portfolio in question. The certainty equivalent rate of return is a natural way to compare the utility values of competing portfolios.

A portfolio can be desirable only if its certainty equivalent return exceeds that of the risk-free alternative. If an investor is sufficiently risk averse, he will assign any risky portfolio, even one with a positive risk premium, a certainty equivalent rate of return below the risk-free rate and will reject the portfolio. At the same time, a less risk-averse investor may assign the same portfolio a certainty equivalent rate greater than the risk-free rate and thus will prefer it to the risk-free alternative. If the risk premium is zero or negative to begin with, any downward adjustment to utility only makes the portfolio look worse. Its certainty equivalent rate will be below that of the risk-free alternative for any risk-averse investor.

Investor Risk Aversion (A)	Utility Score of Portfolio L [$E(r) = 0.07$; $\sigma = 0.05$]	Utility Score of Portfolio M [$E(r) = 0.09$; $\sigma = 0.10$]	Utility Score of Portfolio H [$E(r) = 0.13$; $\sigma = 0.20$]
2.0	$0.07 - \frac{1}{2} \times 2 \times 0.05^2 = 0.0675$	$0.09 - \frac{1}{2} \times 2 \times 0.1^2 = 0.0800$	$\mathbf{0.13 - \frac{1}{2} \times 2 \times 0.2^2 = 0.09}$
3.5	$0.07 - \frac{1}{2} \times 3.5 \times 0.05^2 = 0.0656$	$\mathbf{0.09 - \frac{1}{2} \times 3.5 \times 0.1^2 = 0.0725}$	$0.13 - \frac{1}{2} \times 3.5 \times 0.2^2 = 0.06$
5.0	$0.07 - \frac{1}{2} \times 5 \times 0.05^2 = 0.0638$	$\mathbf{0.09 - \frac{1}{2} \times 5 \times 0.1^2 = 0.0650}$	$0.13 - \frac{1}{2} \times 5 \times 0.2^2 = 0.03$

Table 6.2

Utility scores of alternative portfolios for investors with varying degrees of risk aversion

✔️ Concept Check **6.2**

A portfolio has an expected rate of return of 20% and standard deviation of 30%. T-bills offer a safe rate of return of 7%. Would an investor with risk-aversion parameter $A = 4$ prefer to invest in T-bills or the risky portfolio? What if $A = 2$?

In contrast to risk-averse investors, **risk-neutral** investors (with $A = 0$) judge risky prospects solely by their expected rates of return. The level of risk is irrelevant to the risk-neutral investor, meaning that there is no penalty for risk. For this investor, a portfolio's certainty equivalent rate is simply its expected rate of return.

A **risk lover** (for whom $A < 0$) is happy to engage in fair games and gambles; this investor adjusts the expected return *upward* to take into account the "fun" of confronting the prospect's risk. Risk lovers will always take a fair game because their upward adjustment of utility for risk gives the fair game a certainty equivalent that exceeds the alternative of the risk-free investment.

We can depict the individual's trade-off between risk and return by plotting the characteristics of portfolios that would be equally attractive on a graph with axes measuring the expected value and standard deviation of portfolio returns. Figure 6.1 plots the characteristics of one portfolio, denoted *P.*

Portfolio *P,* which has expected return $E(r_P)$ and standard deviation σ_P, is preferred by risk-averse investors to any portfolio in quadrant IV because its expected return is equal to or greater than any portfolio in that quadrant and its standard deviation is equal to or smaller than any portfolio in that quadrant. Conversely, any portfolio in quadrant I dominates portfolio *P* because its expected return is equal to or greater than *P*'s and its standard deviation is equal to or less than *P*'s.

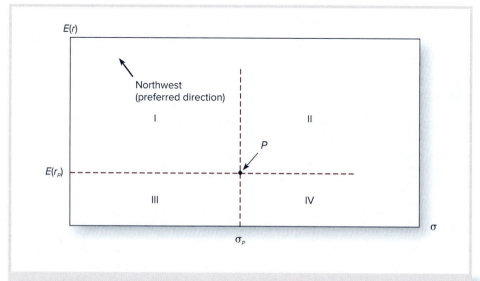

Figure 6.1 The trade-off between risk and return of a potential investment portfolio, *P*

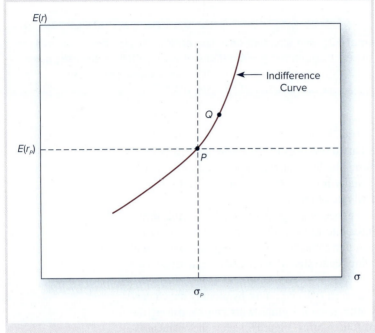

Figure 6.2 The indifference curve

This is the mean-standard deviation, or equivalently, the **mean-variance (M-V) criterion.** It can be stated as follows: portfolio A dominates B if

$$E(r_A) \geq E(r_B)$$

and

$$\sigma_A \leq \sigma_B$$

and at least one inequality is strict (to rule out indifference between the two portfolios).

In the expected return–standard deviation plane in Figure 6.1, the preferred direction is northwest, because in this direction we simultaneously increase the expected return *and* decrease the volatility of the rate of return. Any portfolio that lies northwest of *P* is superior to it.

What can be said about portfolios in quadrants II and III? Their desirability, compared with *P*, depends on the degree of the investor's risk aversion.

Suppose an investor identifies all portfolios that are equally attractive as portfolio *P*. Starting at *P*, an increase in standard deviation lowers utility; it must be compensated for by an increase in expected return. Thus, point *Q* in Figure 6.2 is equally desirable to this investor as *P*. Investors will be equally attracted to portfolios with high risk and high expected returns as to portfolios with lower risk but lower expected returns. These equally preferred portfolios will lie in the mean–standard deviation plane on a curve called the **indifference curve,** which connects all portfolio points with the same utility value (Figure 6.2).

To determine some of the points that appear on the indifference curve, examine the utility values of several possible portfolios for an investor with $A = 4$, presented in Table 6.3. Note that each portfolio offers identical utility, because the portfolios with higher expected return also have higher risk (standard deviation).

 Concept Check **6.3**

a. How will the indifference curve of a less risk-averse investor compare to the indifference curve drawn in Figure 6.2?

b. Draw both indifference curves passing through point *P*.

Table 6.3		
Utility values of possible portfolios for investor with risk aversion, $A = 4$		

Expected Return, $E(r)$	Standard Deviation, σ	Utility = $E(r) - \frac{1}{2} A\sigma^2$
0.10	0.200	$0.10 - 0.5 \times 4 \times 0.04 = 0.02$
0.15	0.255	$0.15 - 0.5 \times 4 \times 0.065 = 0.02$
0.20	0.300	$0.20 - 0.5 \times 4 \times 0.09 = 0.02$
0.25	0.339	$0.25 - 0.5 \times 4 \times 0.115 = 0.02$

What Level of Risk Is Right for You?

No risk, no reward. Most people intuitively understand that they have to bear some risk to achieve an acceptable return on their investment portfolios.

But how much risk is right for you? If your investments turn sour, you may put at jeopardy your ability to retire, to pay for your kid's college education, or to weather an unexpected need for cash. These worst-case scenarios focus our attention on how to manage our exposure to uncertainty.

Assessing—and quantifying—risk aversion is, to put it mildly, difficult. It requires confronting at least these two big questions.

First, how much investment risk can you afford to take? If you have a steady high-paying job, for example, you have greater ability to withstand investment losses. Conversely, if you are close to retirement, you have less ability to adjust your lifestyle in response to bad investment outcomes.

Second, you need to think about your personality and decide how much risk you can tolerate. At what point will you be unable to sleep at night?

To help clients quantify their risk aversion, many financial firms have designed quizzes to help people determine whether they are conservative, moderate, or aggressive investors. These quizzes try to get at clients' attitudes toward risk and their capacity to absorb investment losses.

Here is a sample of the sort of questions these quizzes tend to pose to shed light on an investor's risk tolerance.

MEASURING YOUR RISK TOLERANCE

Circle the letter that corresponds to your answer.

1. The stock market fell by more than 30% in 2008. If you had been holding a substantial stock investment in that year, which of the following would you have done?
   a. Sold off the remainder of your investment before it had the chance to fall further.
   b. Stayed the course with neither redemptions nor purchases.
   c. Bought more stock, reasoning that the market is now cheaper and therefore offers better deals.
2. The value of one of the funds in your 401(k) plan (your primary source of retirement savings) increased 30% last year. What will you do?
   a. Move your funds into a money market account in case the price gains reverse.
   b. Sit tight and do nothing.
   c. Put more of your assets into that fund, reasoning that its value is clearly trending upward.
3. How would you describe your non-investment sources of income (for example, your salary)?
   a. Highly uncertain
   b. Moderately stable
   c. Highly stable

4. At the end of the month, you find yourself:
   a. Short of cash and impatiently waiting for your next paycheck.
   b. Not overspending your salary, but not saving very much.
   c. With a comfortable surplus of funds to put into your savings account.
5. You are 30 years old and enrolling in your company's retirement plan, and you need to allocate your contributions across 3 funds: a money market account, a bond fund, and a stock fund. Which of these allocations sounds best to you?
   a. Invest everything in a safe money-market fund.
   b. Split your money evenly between the bond fund and stock fund.
   c. Put everything into the stock fund, reasoning that by the time you retire the year-to-year fluctuations in stock returns will have evened out.
6. You are a contestant on Let's Make a Deal, and have just won $1,000. But you can exchange the winnings for two random payoffs. One is a coin flip with a payoff of $2,500 if the coin comes up heads. The other is a flip of two coins with a payoff of $6,000 if both coins come up heads. What will you do?
   a. Keep the $1,000 in cash.
   b. Choose the single coin toss.
   c. Choose the double coin toss.
7. Suppose you have the opportunity to invest in a start-up firm. If the firm is successful, you will multiply your investment by a factor of ten. But if it fails, you will lose everything. You think the odds of success are around 20%. How much would you be willing to invest in the start-up?
   a. Nothing
   b. 2 months' salary
   c. 6 months' salary
8. Now imagine that to buy into the start-up you will need to borrow money. Would you be willing to take out a $10,000 loan to make the investment?
   a. No
   b. Maybe
   c. Yes

SCORING YOUR RISK TOLERANCE

For each question, give yourself one point if you answered (a), two points if you answered (b), and three points for a (c). The higher your total score, the greater is your risk tolerance, or equivalently, the lower is your risk aversion.

Estimating Risk Aversion

How can we estimate the levels of risk aversion of individual investors? A number of methods may be used. The questionnaire in the nearby box is of the simplest variety and, indeed, can distinguish only between high (conservative), medium (moderate), or low (aggressive) levels of the coefficient of risk aversion. More complex questionnaires, allowing subjects to pinpoint specific levels of risk aversion coefficients, ask would-be investors to choose from various sets of hypothetical lotteries.

Access to the investment accounts of active investors would provide observations of how portfolio composition changes over time. Coupling this information with estimates of the risk and return of these positions would in principle allow us to infer investors' risk aversion coefficients.

Finally, researchers track the behavior of groups of individuals to obtain average degrees of risk aversion. These studies range from observed purchase of insurance policies to labor supply and aggregate consumption behavior.

6.2   Capital Allocation across Risky and Risk-Free Portfolios

History shows us that long-term bonds have been riskier investments than Treasury bills and that stocks have been riskier still. On the other hand, the riskier investments have offered higher average returns. Investors, of course, do not make all-or-nothing choices from these investment classes. They can and do construct their portfolios using securities from all asset classes. Some of the portfolio may be in risk-free Treasury bills, some in high-risk stocks.

The most straightforward way to control the risk of the portfolio is through the fraction of the portfolio invested in Treasury bills or other safe money market securities versus what is invested in risky assets. Most investment professionals consider such broad asset allocation decisions the most important part of portfolio construction. Consider this statement by John Bogle, made when he was chairman of the Vanguard Group of Investment Companies:

> The most fundamental decision of investing is the allocation of your assets: How much should you own in stock? How much should you own in bonds? How much should you own in cash reserves? . . . That decision [has been shown to account] for an astonishing 94% of the differences in total returns achieved by institutionally managed pension funds. . . . There is no reason to believe that the same relationship does not also hold true for individual investors.[1]

Therefore, we start our discussion of the risk–return trade-off available to investors by examining the most basic asset allocation choice: how much of the portfolio should be placed in risk-free money market securities versus other risky asset classes.

We denote the investor's portfolio of risky assets as P and the risk-free asset as F. We assume for the sake of illustration that the risky component of the investor's overall

---

[1]John C. Bogle, *Bogle on Mutual Funds* (Burr Ridge, IL: Irwin Professional Publishing, 1994), p. 235.

portfolio comprises two mutual funds, one invested in stocks and the other invested in long-term bonds. For now, we take the composition of the risky portfolio as given and focus only on the allocation between it and risk-free securities. In the next chapter, we ask how best to determine the composition of the risky portfolio.

When we shift wealth from the risky portfolio to the risk-free asset, we do not change the relative proportions of the various risky assets within the risky portfolio. Rather, we reduce the relative weight of the risky portfolio as a whole in favor of risk-free assets.

For example, assume that the total market value of an initial portfolio is $300,000, of which $90,000 is invested in the Ready Asset money market fund, a risk-free asset for practical purposes. The remaining $210,000 is invested in risky securities—$113,400 in equities ($E$) and $96,600 in long-term bonds (B). The equities and bond holdings comprise "the" risky portfolio, 54% in E and 46% in B:

$$E: \quad w_E = \frac{113,400}{210,000} = .54$$

$$B: \quad w_B = \frac{96,600}{210,000} = .46$$

The weight of the risky portfolio, P, in the **complete portfolio,** including risk-free *and* risky investments, is denoted by y:

$$y = \frac{210,000}{300,000} = .7 \text{ (risky assets)}$$

$$1 - y = \frac{90,000}{300,000} = .3 \text{ (risk-free assets)}$$

The weights of each asset class in the *complete* portfolio are, therefore, as follows:

$$E: \quad \frac{\$113,400}{\$300,000} = .378$$

$$B: \quad \frac{\$96,600}{\$300,000} = .322$$

$$\text{Risky portfolio} = E + B = .700$$

The risky portfolio makes up 70% of the complete portfolio.

Example 6.2   The Risky Portfolio

Suppose the owner of this portfolio wishes to decrease risk by reducing the allocation to the risky portfolio from $y = .7$ to $y = .56$. The risky portfolio would then total only $.56 \times \$300,000 = \$168,000$, requiring the sale of $42,000 of the original $210,000 of risky holdings, with the proceeds used to purchase more shares in Ready Asset (the money market fund). Total holdings in the risk-free asset will increase to $300,000 × (1 − .56) = $132,000, the original holdings plus the new contribution to the money market fund:

$$\$90,000 + \$42,000 = \$132,000$$

The key point, however, is that the proportions of each asset in the risky portfolio remain unchanged. Because the weights of E and B in the risky portfolio are .54 and .46, respectively, we sell .54 × $42,000 = $22,680 of E and .46 × $42,000 = $19,320 of B. After the sale, the proportions of each asset in the risky portfolio are in fact unchanged:

$$E: \quad w_E = \frac{113,400 - 22,680}{210,000 - 42,000} = .54$$

$$B: \quad w_B = \frac{96,600 - 19,320}{210,000 - 42,000} = .46$$

Therefore, rather than thinking of our risky holdings as E and B separately, it is better to view our holdings as if they were in a single fund that holds equities and bonds in fixed proportions. In this sense, we may treat the risky fund as a single risky asset, that asset being a particular bundle of securities. As we shift in and out of safe assets, we simply alter our holdings of that bundle of securities commensurately.

With this simplification, we turn to the desirability of reducing risk by changing the risky/risk-free asset mix, that is, reducing risk by decreasing the proportion y. As long as we do not alter the weights of each security within the risky portfolio, the probability distribution of the rate of return on the risky portfolio remains unchanged by the asset reallocation. What will change is the probability distribution of the rate of return on the *complete* portfolio that consists of the risky asset and the risk-free asset.

 Concept Check **6.4**

What will be the dollar value of your position in equities (E), and its proportion in your overall portfolio, if you decide to hold 50% of your investment budget in Ready Asset?

6.3   The Risk-Free Asset

By virtue of its power to tax and control the money supply, only the government can issue default-free bonds. Even the default-free guarantee by itself is not sufficient to make the bonds risk-free in real terms. The only risk-free asset in real terms would be a perfectly price-indexed bond. Moreover, even a default-free perfectly indexed bond would offer a guaranteed real return to an investor only if the maturity of the bond is identical to the investor's desired holding period. Even indexed bonds are subject to interest rate risk, because real interest rates change unpredictably through time. When future real rates are uncertain, so is the future price of indexed bonds.

Nevertheless, it is common practice to view Treasury bills as "the" **risk-free asset.** Their short-term nature makes their prices insensitive to interest rate fluctuations. Indeed, an investor can lock in a short-term nominal return by buying a bill and holding it to maturity. Moreover, inflation uncertainty over the course of a few weeks, or even months, is negligible compared with the uncertainty of stock market returns.

In practice, most investors use a broad range of money market instruments as a risk-free asset. All the money market instruments are virtually free of interest rate risk because of their short maturities and are fairly safe in terms of default or credit risk.

Money market funds hold, for the most part, three types of securities—Treasury bills, other Treasury and U.S. agency securities, and repurchase agreements. The yields to maturity on nongovernment money market securities are always somewhat higher than those of T-bills with comparable maturity. Still, we saw in Chapter 2, Figure 2.2, that these yield spreads over T-bills are generally small, despite an occasional spike during periods of financial stress.

While the portfolio composition of money market funds changes over time, in the last few years, T-bills have made up only about 20% of their portfolios.[2] Nevertheless, the risk of blue-chip short-term investments is minuscule compared with that of most other assets such as long-term corporate bonds, common stocks, or real estate. Hence we treat money market funds as the most easily accessible risk-free asset for most investors.

6.4   Portfolios of One Risky Asset and a Risk-Free Asset

In this section, we examine the risk–return combinations available to investors once the properties of the risky portfolio have been determined. This is the "technical" part of capital allocation. In the next section we address the "personal" part of the problem—the individual's choice of the best risk–return combination from the feasible set.

Suppose the investor has already decided on the composition of the risky portfolio, P. Now the concern is with capital allocation, that is, the proportion of the investment budget, y, to be allocated to P. The remaining proportion, $1 - y$, is to be invested in the risk-free asset, F.

Denote the risky rate of return of P by r_P, its expected rate of return by $E(r_P)$, and its standard deviation by σ_P. The rate of return on the risk-free asset is denoted as r_f. In our numerical example, we will assume that $E(r_P) = 15\%$, $\sigma_P = 22\%$, and the risk-free rate is $r_f = 7\%$. Thus the risk premium on the risky asset is $E(r_P) - r_f = 8\%$.

With a proportion, y, in the risky portfolio, and $1 - y$ in the risk-free asset, the rate of return on the *complete* portfolio, denoted C, is r_C where

$$r_C = yr_P + (1 - y)r_f \tag{6.2}$$

Taking the expectation of this portfolio's rate of return,

$$E(r_C) = yE(r_P) + (1 - y)r_f$$
$$= r_f + y[E(r_P) - r_f] = 7 + y(15 - 7) \tag{6.3}$$

This result has a nice interpretation: The base rate of return for any portfolio is the risk-free rate. In addition, the portfolio is *expected* to earn a proportion, y, of the risk premium of the risky portfolio, $E(r_P) - r_f$.

---

[2]See **http://www.icifactbook.org/**, Section 4 of Data Tables.

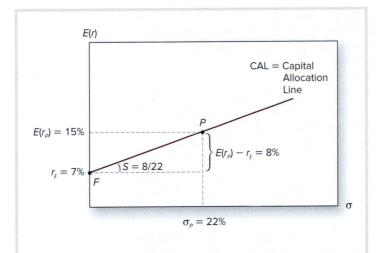

Figure 6.3 The investment opportunity set with a risky asset and a risk-free asset in the expected return–standard deviation plane

With a proportion y in a risky asset, the standard deviation of the complete portfolio is the standard deviation of the risky asset multiplied by the weight, y, of the risky asset in that portfolio.[3] Because the standard deviation of the risky portfolio is $\sigma_P = 22\%$,

$$\sigma_C = y\sigma_P = 22y \qquad (6.4)$$

which makes sense because the standard deviation of the complete portfolio is proportional to both the standard deviation of the risky asset and the proportion invested in it. In sum, the expected return of the complete portfolio is $E(r_C) = r_f + y[E(r_P) - r_f] = 7 + 8y$ and the standard deviation is $\sigma_C = 22y$.

The next step is to plot the portfolio characteristics (with various choices for y) in the expected return–standard deviation plane in Figure 6.3. The risk-free asset, F, appears on the vertical axis because its standard deviation is zero. The risky asset, P, is plotted with a standard deviation of 22%, and expected return of 15%. If an investor chooses to invest solely in the risky asset, then $y = 1.0$, and the complete portfolio is P. If the chosen position is $y = 0$, then $1 - y = 1.0$, and the complete portfolio is the risk-free portfolio, F.

What about the more interesting midrange portfolios where y lies between 0 and 1? These portfolios will graph on the straight line connecting points F and P. The slope of that line is rise/run = $[E(r_P) - r_f]/\sigma_P$, which in this case equals 8/22.

Increasing the fraction of the overall portfolio invested in the risky asset increases expected return at a rate of $15\% - 7\% = 8\%$, according to Equation 6.3. It also increases portfolio standard deviation at the rate of 22%, according to Equation 6.4. The extra return per extra risk is thus $8/22 = .36$.

To derive the exact equation for the straight line between F and P, we rearrange Equation 6.4 to find that $y = \sigma_C/\sigma_P$, and we substitute for y in Equation 6.3 to describe the expected return–standard deviation trade-off:

$$E(r_C) = r_f + y[E(r_P) - r_f]$$
$$= r_f + \frac{\sigma_C}{\sigma_P}[E(r_P) - r_f] = 7 + \frac{8}{22}\sigma_C \qquad (6.5)$$

Thus, the expected return of the complete portfolio as a function of its standard deviation is a straight line, with intercept r_f and slope

$$S = \frac{E(r_P) - r_f}{\sigma_P} = \frac{8}{22} \qquad (6.6)$$

---

[3]This is an application of a basic rule from statistics: If you multiply a random variable by a constant, the standard deviation is multiplied by the same constant. In our application, the random variable is the rate of return on the risky asset, and the constant is the fraction of that asset in the complete portfolio. We will elaborate on the rules for portfolio return and risk in the following chapter.

Figure 6.3 graphs the *investment opportunity set,* which is the set of feasible expected return and standard deviation pairs of all portfolios resulting from different values of *y.* The graph is a straight line originating at r_f and going through the point labeled *P.*

This straight line is called the **capital allocation line (CAL).** It depicts all the risk–return combinations available to investors. The slope of the CAL, denoted *S,* equals the increase in the expected return of the complete portfolio per unit of additional standard deviation—in other words, incremental return per incremental risk. The slope, the **reward-to-volatility ratio,** is usually called the **Sharpe ratio** (see Chapter 5), after William Sharpe, who first used it extensively.

A portfolio equally divided between the risky asset and the risk-free asset, that is, where $y = .5$, will have an expected rate of return of $E(r_C) = 7 + .5 \times 8 = 11\%$, implying a risk premium of 4%, and a standard deviation of $\sigma_C = .5 \times 22 = 11\%$. It will plot on the line *FP* midway between *F* and *P.* The Sharpe ratio is $S = 4/11 = .36$, precisely the same as that of portfolio *P.*

What about points on the CAL to the right of portfolio *P*? If investors can borrow at the (risk-free) rate of $r_f = 7\%$, they can construct portfolios that may be plotted on the CAL to the right of *P.*

 Concept Check **6.5**

Can the Sharpe (reward-to-volatility) ratio, $S = [E(r_C) - r_f]/\sigma_C$, of any combination of the risky asset and the risk-free asset be different from the ratio for the risky asset taken alone, $[E(r_P) - r_f]/\sigma_P$, which, in this case, is .36?

Example 6.3   Leverage

Suppose the investment budget is $300,000 and our investor borrows an additional $120,000, investing the total available funds in the risky asset. This is a *levered* position in the risky asset, financed in part by borrowing. In that case

$$y = \frac{420,000}{300,000} = 1.4$$

and $1 - y = 1 - 1.4 = -.4$, reflecting a short (borrowing) position in the risk-free asset. Rather than lending at a 7% interest rate, the investor borrows at 7%. The distribution of the portfolio rate of return still exhibits the same reward-to-volatility ratio:

$$E(r_C) = 7\% + (1.4 \times 8\%) = 18.2\%$$

$$\sigma_C = 1.4 \times 22\% = 30.8\%$$

$$S = \frac{E(r_C) - r_f}{\sigma_C} = \frac{18.2 - 7}{30.8} = .36$$

As one might expect, the levered portfolio has a higher standard deviation than does an unlevered position in the risky asset.

Clearly, nongovernment investors cannot borrow at the risk-free rate. The risk of a borrower's default leads lenders to demand higher interest rates on loans. Therefore, the nongovernment investor's borrowing cost will exceed the lending rate of $r_f = 7\%$. Suppose the borrowing rate is $r_f^B = 9\%$. Then in the borrowing range, the Sharpe ratio, the slope of the CAL, will be

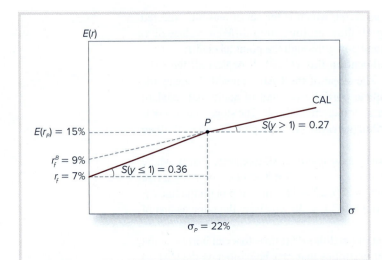

Figure 6.4 The opportunity set with differential borrowing and lending rates

$[E(r_P) - r_f^B]/\sigma_P = 6/22 = .27$. The CAL will therefore be "kinked" at point P, as shown in Figure 6.4. To the left of P the investor is lending at 7%, and the slope of the CAL is .36. To the right of P, where $y > 1$, the investor is borrowing at 9% to finance extra investments in the risky asset, and the slope is .27.

In practice, borrowing to invest in the risky portfolio is straightforward if you have a margin account with a broker. All you have to do is tell your broker that you want to buy "on margin." Margin purchases may not exceed 50% of the purchase value. Therefore, if your net worth in the account is $300,000, the broker is allowed to lend you up to $300,000 to purchase additional stock.[4] You would then have $600,000 on the asset side of your account and $300,000 on the liability side, resulting in $y = 2.0$.

 Concept Check **6.6**

Suppose that there is an upward shift in the expected rate of return on the risky asset, from 15% to 17%. If all other parameters remain unchanged, what will be the slope of the CAL for $y \leq 1$ and $y > 1$?

6.5   Risk Tolerance and Asset Allocation

We have shown how to find the CAL, the graph of all feasible risk–return combinations available for capital allocation. The investor confronting the CAL now must choose one optimal complete portfolio, C, from the set of feasible choices. This choice entails a trade-off between risk and return. Individual differences in risk aversion lead to different capital allocation choices even when facing an identical opportunity set (i.e., a risk-free rate and Sharpe ratio). In particular, more risk-averse investors will choose to hold less of the risky asset and more of the risk-free asset.

The expected return on the complete portfolio is given by Equation 6.3: $E(r_C) = r_f + y[E(r_P) - r_f]$. Its variance is, from Equation 6.4, $\sigma_C^2 = y^2\sigma_P^2$. Investors choose the allocation to the risky asset, y, that maximizes their utility function as given by Equation 6.1: $U = E(r) - \frac{1}{2}A\sigma^2$. As the allocation to the risky asset increases (higher y), expected return increases, but so does volatility, so utility can increase or decrease. Table 6.4 shows utility

---

[4]Margin purchases require the investor to maintain the securities in a margin account with the broker. If the value of the securities falls below a "maintenance margin," a "margin call" is sent out, requiring a deposit to bring the net worth of the account up to the appropriate level. If the margin call is not met, regulations mandate that some or all of the securities be sold by the broker and the proceeds used to reestablish the required margin. See Chapter 3, Section 3.8, for further discussion.

Table 6.4

Utility levels for various positions in risky assets (y) for an investor with risk aversion A = 4

(1) y	(2) E(r_C)	(3) σ_C	(4) U = E(r) − ½Aσ²
0	0.070	0	0.0700
0.1	0.078	0.022	0.0770
0.2	0.086	0.044	0.0821
0.3	0.094	0.066	0.0853
0.4	0.102	0.088	0.0865
0.5	0.110	0.110	0.0858
0.6	0.118	0.132	0.0832
0.7	0.126	0.154	0.0786
0.8	0.134	0.176	0.0720
0.9	0.142	0.198	0.0636
1.0	0.150	0.220	0.0532

levels corresponding to different values of y. Initially, utility increases as y increases, but eventually it declines.

Figure 6.5 is a plot of the utility function from Table 6.4. The graph shows that utility is highest at y = .41. When y is less than .41, investors are willing to assume more risk to increase expected return. But at higher levels of y, risk is higher, and additional allocations to the risky asset are undesirable—beyond this point, further increases in risk dominate the increase in expected return and reduce utility.

To solve the utility maximization problem more generally, we write the problem as follows:

$$\max_{y} U = E(r_C) - \tfrac{1}{2}A\sigma_C^2 = r_f + y\left[E(r_P) - r_f\right] - \tfrac{1}{2}Ay^2\sigma_P^2$$

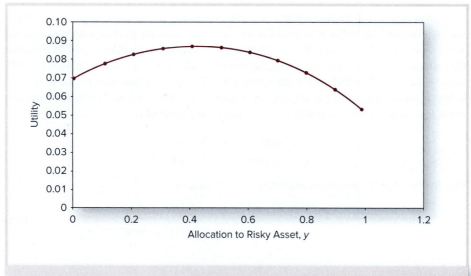

Figure 6.5 Utility as a function of allocation to the risky asset, y

Students of calculus will recognize that the maximization problem is solved by setting the derivative of this expression to zero. Doing so and solving for y gives us the optimal position for risk-averse investors in the risky asset, y^*, as follows:[5]

$$y^* = \frac{E(r_P) - r_f}{A\sigma_P^2} \tag{6.7}$$

This solution shows that the optimal position in the risky asset is *inversely* proportional to the level of risk aversion and the level of risk (as measured by the variance) and directly proportional to the risk premium offered by the risky asset.

Example 6.4   Capital Allocation

Using our numerical example [$r_f = 7\%$, $E(r_P) = 15\%$, and $\sigma_P = 22\%$], and expressing all returns as decimals, the optimal solution for an investor with a coefficient of risk aversion $A = 4$ is

$$y^* = \frac{.15 - .07}{4 \times .22^2} = .41$$

In other words, this particular investor will invest 41% of the investment budget in the risky asset and 59% in the risk-free asset. As we saw in Figure 6.5, this is the value of y at which utility is maximized.

With 41% invested in the risky portfolio, the expected return and standard deviation of the complete portfolio are

$$E(r_C) = 7 + [.41 \times (15 - 7)] = 10.28\%$$
$$\sigma_C = .41 \times 22 = 9.02\%$$

The risk premium of the complete portfolio is $E(r_C) - r_f = 3.28\%$, which is obtained by taking on a portfolio with a standard deviation of 9.02%. Notice that $3.28/9.02 = .36$, which is the reward-to-volatility (Sharpe) ratio of any complete portfolio given the parameters of this example.

A graphical way of presenting this decision problem is to use indifference curve analysis. To illustrate how to build an indifference curve, consider an investor with risk aversion $A = 4$ who currently holds all her wealth in a risk-free portfolio yielding $r_f = 5\%$. Because the variance of such a portfolio is zero, Equation 6.1 tells us that its utility value is $U = .05$. Now we find the expected return the investor would require to maintain the *same* level of utility when holding a risky portfolio, say, with $\sigma = 1\%$. We use Equation 6.1 to find how much $E(r)$ must increase to compensate for the higher value of σ:

$$U = E(r) - \tfrac{1}{2} \times A \times \sigma^2$$
$$.05 = E(r) - \tfrac{1}{2} \times 4 \times .01^2$$

This implies that the necessary expected return increases to

$$\text{Required } E(r) = .05 + \tfrac{1}{2} \times A \times \sigma^2 \tag{6.8}$$
$$= .05 + \tfrac{1}{2} \times 4 \times .01^2 = .0502$$

---

[5]The derivative with respect to y equals $E(r_P) - r_f - yA\sigma_P^2$. Setting this expression equal to zero and solving for y yields Equation 6.7.

σ	A = 2		A = 4	
	U = 0.05	U = 0.09	U = 0.05	U = 0.09
0	0.0500	0.0900	0.050	0.090
0.05	0.0525	0.0925	0.055	0.095
0.10	0.0600	0.1000	0.070	0.110
0.15	0.0725	0.1125	0.095	0.135
0.20	0.0900	0.1300	0.130	0.170
0.25	0.1125	0.1525	0.175	0.215
0.30	0.1400	0.1800	0.230	0.270
0.35	0.1725	0.2125	0.295	0.335
0.40	0.2100	0.2500	0.370	0.410
0.45	0.2525	0.2925	0.455	0.495
0.50	0.3000	0.3400	0.550	0.590

Table 6.5

Spreadsheet calculations of indifference curves (Entries in columns 2–4 are expected returns necessary to provide specified utility value.)

We can repeat this calculation for other levels of σ, each time finding the value of $E(r)$ necessary to maintain $U = .05$. This process will yield all combinations of expected return and volatility with utility level of .05; plotting these combinations gives us the indifference curve.

We can readily generate an investor's indifference curves using a spreadsheet. Table 6.5 contains risk–return combinations with utility values of .05 and .09 for two investors, one with $A = 2$ and the other with $A = 4$. The plot of these indifference curves appears in Figure 6.6. Notice that the intercepts of the indifference curves are at .05 and .09, exactly the certainty equivalent returns corresponding to the two curves.

Any investor would prefer a portfolio on the higher indifference curve with a higher certainty equivalent return (utility). Portfolios on higher indifference curves offer a higher expected return for any given level of risk. For example, both indifference curves for $A = 2$ have the same shape, but for any level of volatility, a portfolio on the curve with utility of .09 offers an expected return 4% greater than the corresponding portfolio on the lower curve, for which $U = .05$.

Figure 6.6 demonstrates that more risk-averse investors have steeper indifference curves than less risk-averse investors. Steeper curves mean that investors require a greater increase in expected return to compensate for an increase in portfolio risk.

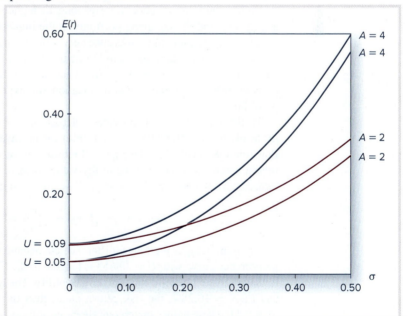

Figure 6.6 Indifference curves for $U = .05$ and $U = .09$ with $A = 2$ and $A = 4$

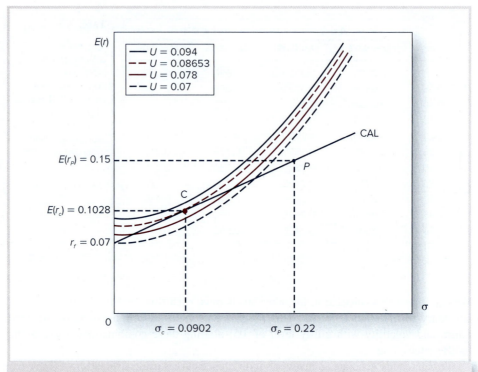

Figure 6.7 Finding the optimal complete portfolio by using indifference curves

Higher indifference curves correspond to higher levels of utility. The investor thus attempts to find the complete portfolio on the highest possible indifference curve. When we superimpose plots of indifference curves on the investment opportunity set represented by the capital allocation line as in Figure 6.7, we can identify the *highest possible* indifference curve that still touches the CAL. That curve is tangent to the CAL, and the tangency point corresponds to the standard deviation and expected return of the optimal complete portfolio.

To illustrate, Table 6.6 provides calculations for four indifference curves (with utility levels of .07, .078, .08653, and .094) for an investor with $A = 4$. Columns 2–5 use Equation 6.8 to calculate the expected return that must be paired with the standard deviation in column 1 to provide the utility value corresponding to each curve. Column 6 uses Equation 6.5 to calculate $E(r_C)$ on the CAL for the standard deviation σ_C in column 1:

$$E(r_C) = r_f + \left[E(r_P) - r_f\right]\frac{\sigma_C}{\sigma_P} = 7 + [15 - 7]\frac{\sigma_C}{22}$$

Figure 6.7 graphs the four indifference curves and the CAL. The graph reveals that the indifference curve with $U = .08653$ is tangent to the CAL; the tangency point corresponds to the complete portfolio that maximizes utility. The tangency point occurs at $\sigma_C = 9.02\%$ and $E(r_C) = 10.28\%$, the risk–return parameters of the optimal complete portfolio with $y^* = 0.41$. These values match our algebraic solution using Equation 6.7.

We conclude that the choice for y^*, the fraction of overall investment funds to place in the risky portfolio, is determined by risk aversion (the slope of indifference curves) and the Sharpe ratio (the slope of the opportunity set).

Table 6.6

Expected returns on four indifference curves and the CAL (Investor's risk aversion is $A = 4$.)

σ	U = 0.07	U = 0.078	U = 0.08653	U = 0.094	CAL
0	0.0700	0.0780	0.0865	0.0940	0.0700
0.02	0.0708	0.0788	0.0873	0.0948	0.0773
0.04	0.0732	0.0812	0.0897	0.0972	0.0845
0.06	0.0772	0.0852	0.0937	0.1012	0.0918
0.08	0.0828	0.0908	0.0993	0.1068	0.0991
0.0902	0.0863	0.0943	0.1028	0.1103	0.1028
0.10	0.0900	0.0980	0.1065	0.1140	0.1064
0.12	0.0988	0.1068	0.1153	0.1228	0.1136
0.14	0.1092	0.1172	0.1257	0.1332	0.1209
0.18	0.1348	0.1428	0.1513	0.1588	0.1355
0.22	0.1668	0.1748	0.1833	0.1908	0.1500
0.26	0.2052	0.2132	0.2217	0.2292	0.1645
0.30	0.2500	0.2580	0.2665	0.2740	0.1791

 Concept Check **6.7**

a. If an investor's coefficient of risk aversion is $A = 3$, how does the optimal asset mix change? What are the new values of $E(r_C)$ and σ_C?

b. Suppose that the borrowing rate, $r_f^B = 9\%$ is greater than the lending rate, $r_f = 7\%$. Show graphically how the optimal portfolio choice of some investors will be affected by the higher borrowing rate. Which investors will *not* be affected by the borrowing rate?

Non-Normal Returns

In the foregoing analysis, we implicitly assumed normality of returns by treating standard deviation as the appropriate measure of risk. But as we discussed in Chapter 5, departures from normality could result in extreme losses with far greater likelihood than would be plausible under a normal distribution. These exposures, which are typically measured by value at risk (VaR) or expected shortfall (ES), also would be important to investors.

Therefore, an appropriate extension of our analysis would be to present investors with forecasts of VaR and ES. Taking the capital allocation from the normal-based analysis as a benchmark, investors facing fat-tailed distributions might consider reducing their allocation to the risky portfolio in favor of an increase in the allocation to the risk-free vehicle.

Probabilities of moderate outcomes in finance can be readily assessed from experience because of the high relative frequency of such observations. Extreme negative values are blissfully rare, but for that very reason, accurately assessing their probabilities is virtually impossible.

Nevertheless, "black swans," those rare but high-impact events that can result in drastic security returns, clearly concern investors. We will see ample evidence of their concern when we look at empirical evidence on the pricing of options in Chapter 21.

6.6   Passive Strategies: The Capital Market Line

The CAL is derived with the risk-free and "the" risky portfolio, *P*. Determination of the assets to include in *P* may result from a passive or an active strategy. A **passive strategy** describes a portfolio decision that avoids *any* direct or indirect security analysis.[6] At first blush, a passive strategy would appear to be naïve. As will become apparent, however, forces of supply and demand in large capital markets may make such a strategy the reasonable choice for many investors.

In Chapter 5, we presented a compilation of the history of rates of return on different portfolios. The data are available at Professor Kenneth French's Web site, **mba.tuck .dartmouth.edu/pages/faculty/ken.french/data_library.html**. We can use these data to examine various passive strategies.

A natural candidate for a passively held risky asset would be a well-diversified portfolio of common stocks such as the "U.S. Market" described in Chapter 5. Because a passive strategy requires that we devote no resources to acquiring information on any individual stock or group of stocks, we must follow a "neutral" diversification strategy. One way is to select a diversified portfolio of stocks that mirrors the value of the corporate sector of the U.S. economy. This results in a portfolio in which, for example, the proportion invested in Microsoft stock will be the ratio of Microsoft's total market value to the market value of all listed stocks.

Table 6.7 summarizes the performance of the U.S. Market portfolio over the 90-year period 1926–2015, as well as for four subperiods. The table shows the average return for the portfolio, the annual return realized by rolling over 1-month T-bills for the same period, as well as the resultant average excess return (risk premium) and its standard deviation. The Sharpe ratio was .40 for the overall period, 1926–2015. In other words, stock markct investors enjoyed a .40% average excess return over the T-bill rate for every 1% of standard deviation.

But the risk–reward trade-off we infer from the historical data is far from precise. This is because the excess return on the market portfolio is so variable, with an annual standard deviation of 20.59%. With such high year-by-year volatility, it is no surprise that the reward-to-risk trade-off was also highly variable. The Sharpe ratios across subperiods vary

Period	Average Annual Returns		U.S. Equity Market		
	U.S. Equity Market	1-Month T-Bills	Excess Return	Standard Deviation	Sharpe Ratio
1926–2015	11.77	3.47	8.30	20.59	0.40
1992–2015	10.79	2.66	8.13	18.29	0.44
1970–1991	12.87	7.54	5.33	18.20	0.29
1948–1969	14.14	2.70	11.44	17.67	0.65
1926–1947	9.25	0.91	8.33	27.99	0.30

Table 6.7

Average annual return on stocks and 1-month T-bills; standard deviation and Sharpe ratio of stocks over time

---

[6]By "indirect security analysis" we mean the delegation of that responsibility to an intermediary such as a professional money manager.

by more than a factor of 2, ranging from .29 to .65. The lesson here is that we should be very humble when we use historical data to forecast future returns. Returns and the risk–return trade-off are extremely difficult to predict, and we can have only a loose sense of what that trade-off will be in coming periods.

We call the capital allocation line provided by 1-month T-bills and a broad index of common stocks the **capital market line (CML).** A passive strategy generates an investment opportunity set that is represented by the CML.

How reasonable is it for an investor to pursue a passive strategy? We cannot answer such a question without comparing the strategy to the costs and benefits accruing to an active portfolio strategy. Some thoughts are relevant even at this point, however.

First, the alternative active strategy is not free. Whether you choose to invest the time and cost to acquire the information needed to generate an optimal active portfolio of risky assets, or whether you delegate the task to a professional who will charge a fee, constitution of an active portfolio is more expensive than a passive one. Passive management entails only negligible costs to purchase T-bills and very modest management fees to either an exchange-traded fund or a mutual fund company that operates a market index fund. Vanguard, for example, operates several index portfolios. One, the 500 Index Fund, tracks the S&P 500. It purchases shares of the firms comprising the S&P 500 in proportion to the market values of the outstanding equity of each firm, and therefore essentially replicates the S&P 500 index. It has one of the lowest operating expenses (as a percentage of assets) of all mutual stock funds precisely because it requires minimal managerial effort. Whereas the S&P 500 is primarily an index of large, high-capitalization (large cap) stocks, another Vanguard index fund, the Total Stock Market Index Fund, is more inclusive and provides investors with exposure to the entire U.S. equity market, including small- and mid-cap stocks as well as growth and value stocks. It is nearly identical to what we have called the U.S. Market Index.

A second reason to pursue a passive strategy is the free-rider benefit. If there are many active, knowledgeable investors who quickly bid up prices of undervalued assets and force down prices of overvalued assets (by selling), we have to conclude that at any time most assets will be fairly priced. Therefore, a well-diversified portfolio of common stock will be a reasonably fair buy, and the passive strategy may not be inferior to that of the average active investor. (We will elaborate on this argument and provide a more comprehensive analysis of the relative success of passive strategies in later chapters.) As we saw in Chapter 4, passive index funds have actually outperformed most actively managed funds in the past decades and investors are increasingly responding to the lower costs and better performance of index funds by directing their investments into these products.

To summarize, a passive strategy involves investment in two passive portfolios: virtually risk-free short-term T-bills (or, alternatively, a money market fund) and a fund of common stocks that mimics a broad market index. The capital allocation line representing such a strategy is called the *capital market line.* Historically, based on 1926 to 2015 data, the passive risky portfolio offered an average risk premium of 8.3% and a standard deviation of 20.59%, resulting in a reward-to-volatility ratio of .40.

Passive investors allocate their investment budgets among instruments according to their degree of risk aversion. We can use our analysis to deduce a typical investor's risk-aversion parameter. From Table 1.1 in Chapter 1, we estimate that approximately 68.7% of net worth is invested in a broad array of risky assets.[7] We assume this portfolio has the

---

[7]We include in the risky portfolio the following entries from Table 1.1 of Chapter 1: real assets ($30,979 billion), half of pension reserves ($10,486 billion), corporate and noncorporate equity ($24,050 billion), and half of mutual fund shares ($4,060 billion). This portfolio sums to $69,575 billion, which is 68.7% of household net worth ($101,306 billion).

same reward–risk characteristics that the U.S. equity market has exhibited since 1926, as documented in Table 6.7. Substituting these values in Equation 6.7, we obtain

$$y^* = \frac{E(r_M) - r_f}{A\sigma_M^2} = \frac{.083}{A \times .2059^2} = .687$$

which implies a coefficient of risk aversion of

$$A = \frac{.083}{.687 \times .2059^2} = 2.85$$

Of course, this calculation is highly speculative. We have assumed that the average investor holds the naïve view that historical average rates of return and standard deviations are the best estimates of expected rates of return and risk, looking to the future. To the extent that the average investor takes advantage of contemporary information in addition to simple historical data, our estimate of $A = 2.85$ would be an unjustified inference. Nevertheless, a broad range of studies, taking into account the full range of available assets, places the degree of risk aversion for the representative investor in the range of 2.0 to 4.0.[8]

 Concept Check **6.8**

Suppose that expectations about the U.S. equity market and the T-bill rate are the same as they were in 2016, but you find that a greater proportion is invested in T-bills today than in 2016. What can you conclude about the change in risk tolerance over the years since 2016?

[8]See, for example, I. Friend and M. Blume, "The Demand for Risky Assets," *American Economic Review* 64 (1974); or S. J. Grossman and R. J. Shiller, "The Determinants of the Variability of Stock Market Prices," *American Economic Review* 71 (1981).

SUMMARY

1. Speculation is the undertaking of a risky investment for its risk premium. The risk premium has to be large enough to compensate a risk-averse investor for the risk of the investment.

2. A fair game is a risky prospect that has a zero risk premium. It will not be undertaken by a risk-averse investor.

3. Investors' preferences toward the expected return and volatility of a portfolio may be expressed by a utility function that is higher for higher expected returns and lower for higher portfolio variances. More risk-averse investors will apply greater penalties for risk. We can describe these preferences graphically using indifference curves.

4. The desirability of a risky portfolio to a risk-averse investor may be summarized by the certainty equivalent value of the portfolio. The certainty equivalent rate of return is a value that, if received with certainty, would yield the same utility as the risky portfolio.

5. Shifting funds from the risky portfolio to the risk-free asset is the simplest way to reduce risk. Other methods involve diversification of the risky portfolio and hedging. We take up these methods in later chapters.

6. T-bills provide a perfectly risk-free asset in nominal terms only. Nevertheless, the standard deviation of real rates on short-term T-bills is small compared to that of other assets such as long-term bonds and common stocks, so for the purpose of our analysis we consider T-bills as the risk-free asset. Money market funds hold, in addition to T-bills, short-term relatively safe

obligations such as repurchase agreements or bank CDs. These entail some default risk, but again, the additional risk is small relative to most other risky assets. For convenience, we often refer to money market funds as risk-free assets.

7. An investor's risky portfolio (the risky asset) can be characterized by its reward-to-volatility or Sharpe ratio, $S = [E(r_P) - r_f]/\sigma_P$. This ratio is also the slope of the CAL, the line that, when graphed, goes from the risk-free asset through the risky asset. All combinations of the risky asset and the risk-free asset lie on this line. Other things equal, an investor would prefer a steeper-sloping CAL, because that means higher expected return for any level of risk. If the borrowing rate is greater than the lending rate, the CAL will be "kinked" at the point of the risky asset.

8. The investor's degree of risk aversion is characterized by the slope of his or her indifference curve. Indifference curves show, at any level of expected return and risk, the required risk premium for taking on one additional percentage point of standard deviation. More risk-averse investors have steeper indifference curves; that is, they require a greater risk premium for taking on more risk.

9. The optimal position, y^*, in the risky asset, is proportional to the risk premium and inversely proportional to the variance and degree of risk aversion:

$$y^* = \frac{E(r_P) - r_f}{A\sigma_P^2}$$

Graphically, this portfolio represents the point at which the indifference curve is tangent to the CAL.

10. A passive investment strategy disregards security analysis, targeting instead the risk-free asset and a broad portfolio of risky assets such as the S&P 500 stock portfolio. If in 2016 investors took the mean historical return and standard deviation of the S&P 500 as proxies for its expected return and standard deviation, then the values of outstanding assets would imply a degree of risk aversion of about $A = 2.85$ for the average investor. This is in line with other studies, which estimate typical risk aversion in the range of 2.0 through 4.0.

risk premium	risk lover	capital allocation line (CAL)	**KEY TERMS**
fair game	mean-variance (M-V)	reward-to-volatility or Sharpe	
risk averse	criterion	ratio	
utility	indifference curve	passive strategy	
certainty equivalent rate	complete portfolio	capital market line (CML)	
risk neutral	risk-free asset		

Utility score: $U = E(r) - \frac{1}{2}A\sigma^2$ **KEY EQUATIONS**

Optimal allocation to risky portfolio: $y^* = \dfrac{E(r_P) - r_f}{A\sigma_P^2}$

1. Which of the following choices best completes the following statement? Explain. An investor   **PROBLEM SETS**
with a higher degree of risk aversion, compared to one with a lower degree, will most prefer investment portfolios

   a. with higher risk premiums.
   b. that are riskier (with higher standard deviations).
   c. with lower Sharpe ratios.
   d. with higher Sharpe ratios.

2. Which of the following statements are true? Explain.

    a. A lower allocation to the risky portfolio reduces the Sharpe (reward-to-volatility) ratio.
    b. The higher the borrowing rate, the lower the Sharpe ratios of levered portfolios.
    c. With a fixed risk-free rate, doubling the expected return and standard deviation of the risky portfolio will double the Sharpe ratio.
    d. Holding constant the risk premium of the risky portfolio, a higher risk-free rate will increase the Sharpe ratio of investments with a positive allocation to the risky asset.

3. What do you think would happen to the expected return on stocks if investors perceived higher volatility in the equity market? Relate your answer to Equation 6.7.

4. Consider a risky portfolio. The end-of-year cash flow derived from the portfolio will be either $70,000 or $200,000 with equal probabilities of .5. The alternative risk-free investment in T-bills pays 6% per year.

    a. If you require a risk premium of 8%, how much will you be willing to pay for the portfolio?
    b. Suppose that the portfolio can be purchased for the amount you found in (a). What will be the expected rate of return on the portfolio?
    c. Now suppose that you require a risk premium of 12%. What is the price that you will be willing to pay?
    d. Comparing your answers to (a) and (c), what do you conclude about the relationship between the required risk premium on a portfolio and the price at which the portfolio will sell?

5. Consider a portfolio that offers an expected rate of return of 12% and a standard deviation of 18%. T-bills offer a risk-free 7% rate of return. What is the maximum level of risk aversion for which the risky portfolio is still preferred to T-bills?

6. Draw the indifference curve in the expected return–standard deviation plane corresponding to a utility level of .05 for an investor with a risk aversion coefficient of 3. (*Hint:* Choose several possible standard deviations, ranging from 0 to .25, and find the expected rates of return providing a utility level of .05. Then plot the expected return–standard deviation points so derived.)

7. Now draw the indifference curve corresponding to a utility level of .05 for an investor with risk aversion coefficient $A = 4$. Comparing your answer to Problem 6, what do you conclude?

8. Draw an indifference curve for a risk-neutral investor providing utility level .05.

9. What must be true about the sign of the risk aversion coefficient, A, for a risk lover? Draw the indifference curve for a utility level of .05 for a risk lover.

For Problems 10 through 12: Consider historical data showing that the average annual rate of return on the S&P 500 portfolio over the past 90 years has averaged roughly 8% more than the Treasury bill return and that the S&P 500 standard deviation has been about 20% per year. Assume these values are representative of investors' expectations for future performance and that the current T-bill rate is 5%.

10. Calculate the expected return and variance of portfolios invested in T-bills and the S&P 500 index with weights as follows:

W_{bills}	W_{index}
0	1.0
0.2	0.8
0.4	0.6
0.6	0.4
0.8	0.2
1.0	0

11. Calculate the utility levels of each portfolio of Problem 10 for an investor with $A = 2$. What do you conclude?

12. Repeat Problem 11 for an investor with $A = 3$. What do you conclude?

Use these inputs for Problems 13 through 19: You manage a risky portfolio with an expected rate of return of 18% and a standard deviation of 28%. The T-bill rate is 8%.

13. Your client chooses to invest 70% of a portfolio in your fund and 30% in an essentially risk-free money market fund. What is the expected value and standard deviation of the rate of return on his portfolio?

14. Suppose that your risky portfolio includes the following investments in the given proportions:

Stock A	25%
Stock B	32%
Stock C	43%

What are the investment proportions of your client's overall portfolio, including the position in T-bills?

15. What is the reward-to-volatility (Sharpe) ratio (S) of your risky portfolio? Your client's?

16. Draw the CAL of your portfolio on an expected return–standard deviation diagram. What is the slope of the CAL? Show the position of your client on your fund's CAL.

17. Suppose that your client decides to invest in your portfolio a proportion y of the total investment budget so that the overall portfolio will have an expected rate of return of 16%.

   a. What is the proportion y?
   b. What are your client's investment proportions in your three stocks and the T-bill fund?
   c. What is the standard deviation of the rate of return on your client's portfolio?

18. Suppose that your client prefers to invest in your fund a proportion y that maximizes the expected return on the complete portfolio subject to the constraint that the complete portfolio's standard deviation will not exceed 18%.

   a. What is the investment proportion, y?
   b. What is the expected rate of return on the complete portfolio?

19. Your client's degree of risk aversion is $A = 3.5$.

   a. What proportion, y, of the total investment should be invested in your fund?
   b. What is the expected value and standard deviation of the rate of return on your client's optimized portfolio?

20. Look at the data in Table 6.7 on the average excess return of the U.S. equity market and the standard deviation of that excess return. Suppose that the U.S. market is your risky portfolio.

   a. If your risk-aversion coefficient is $A = 4$ and you believe that the entire 1926–2015 period is representative of future expected performance, what fraction of your portfolio should be allocated to T-bills and what fraction to equity?
   b. What if you believe that the 1970–1991 period is representative?
   c. What do you conclude upon comparing your answers to (*a*) and (*b*)?

21. Consider the following information about a risky portfolio that you manage and a risk-free asset: $E(r_P) = 11\%$, $\sigma_P = 15\%$, $r_f = 5\%$.

   a. Your client wants to invest a proportion of her total investment budget in your risky fund to provide an expected rate of return on her overall or complete portfolio equal to 8%. What proportion should she invest in the risky portfolio, P, and what proportion in the risk-free asset?
   b. What will be the standard deviation of the rate of return on her portfolio?
   c. Another client wants the highest return possible subject to the constraint that you limit his standard deviation to be no more than 12%. Which client is more risk averse?

22. Investment Management Inc. (IMI) uses the capital market line to make asset allocation recommendations. IMI derives the following forecasts:

   • Expected return on the market portfolio: 12%

- Standard deviation on the market portfolio: 20%
- Risk-free rate: 5%

Samuel Johnson seeks IMI's advice for a portfolio asset allocation. Johnson informs IMI that he wants the standard deviation of the portfolio to equal half of the standard deviation for the market portfolio. Using the capital market line, what expected return can IMI provide subject to Johnson's risk constraint?

For Problems 23 through 26: Suppose that the borrowing rate that your client faces is 9%. Assume that the equity market index has an expected return of 13% and standard deviation of 25%, that $r_f = 5\%$, and that your fund has the parameters given in Problem 21.

23. Draw a diagram of your client's CML, accounting for the higher borrowing rate. Superimpose on it two sets of indifference curves, one for a client who will choose to borrow, and one for a client who will invest in both the index fund and a money market fund.

24. What is the range of risk aversion for which a client will neither borrow nor lend, that is, for which $y = 1$?

25. Solve Problems 23 and 24 for a client who uses your fund rather than an index fund.

26. What is the largest percentage fee that a client who currently is lending ($y < 1$) will be willing to pay to invest in your fund? What about a client who is borrowing ($y > 1$)?

For Problems 27 through 29: You estimate that a passive portfolio, for example, one invested in a risky portfolio that mimics the S&P 500 stock index, yields an expected rate of return of 13% with a standard deviation of 25%. You manage an active portfolio with expected return 18% and standard deviation 28%. The risk-free rate is 8%.

27. Draw the CML and your funds' CAL on an expected return–standard deviation diagram.

   a. What is the slope of the CML?

   b. Characterize in one short paragraph the advantage of your fund over the passive fund.

28. Your client ponders whether to switch the 70% that is invested in your fund to the passive portfolio.

   a. Explain to your client the disadvantage of the switch.

   b. Show him the maximum fee you could charge (as a percentage of the investment in your fund, deducted at the end of the year) that would leave him at least as well off investing in your fund as in the passive one. (*Hint:* The fee will lower the slope of his CAL by reducing the expected return net of the fee.)

29. Consider again the client in Problem 19 with $A = 3.5$.

   a. If he chose to invest in the passive portfolio, what proportion, *y,* would he select?

   b. Is the fee (percentage of the investment in your fund, deducted at the end of the year) that you can charge to make the client indifferent between your fund and the passive strategy affected by his capital allocation decision (i.e., his choice of *y*)?

CFA® PROBLEMS

Use the following data in answering CFA Problems 1–3:

Utility Formula Data

Investment	Expected Return, $E(r)$	Standard Deviation, σ
1	0.12	0.30
2	0.15	0.50
3	0.21	0.16
4	0.24	0.21

$U = E(r) - \frac{1}{2}A\sigma^2$, where $A = 4$

1. On the basis of the utility formula above, which investment would you select if you were risk averse with $A = 4$?

2. On the basis of the utility formula above, which investment would you select if you were risk neutral?

3. The variable (A) in the utility formula represents the:

   a. Investor's return requirement.
   b. Investor's aversion to risk.
   c. Certainty equivalent rate of the portfolio.
   d. Preference for one unit of return per four units of risk.

Use the following graph to answer CFA Problems 4 and 5.

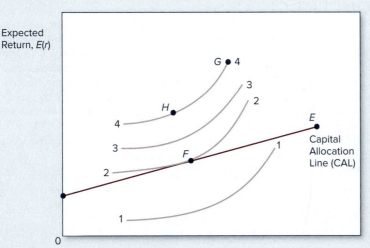

4. Which indifference curve represents the greatest level of utility that can be achieved by the investor?

5. Which point designates the optimal portfolio of risky assets?

6. Given $100,000 to invest, what is the expected risk premium in dollars of investing in equities versus risk-free T-bills on the basis of the following table?

Action	Probability	Return
Invest in equities	0.6	$50,000
	0.4	−$30,000
Invest in risk-free T-bills	1.0	$ 5,000

7. The change from a straight to a kinked capital allocation line is a result of the:

   a. Reward-to-volatility (Sharpe) ratio increasing.
   b. Borrowing rate exceeding the lending rate.
   c. Investor's risk tolerance decreasing.
   d. Increase in the portfolio proportion of the risk-free asset.

8. You manage an equity fund with an expected risk premium of 10% and an expected standard deviation of 14%. The rate on Treasury bills is 6%. Your client chooses to invest $60,000 of her portfolio in your equity fund and $40,000 in a T-bill money market fund. What is the expected return and standard deviation of return on your client's portfolio?

9. What is the reward-to-volatility (Sharpe) ratio for the *equity fund* in CFA Problem 8?

✓ SOLUTIONS TO CONCEPT CHECKS

1. The investor is taking on exchange rate risk by investing in a pound-denominated asset. If the exchange rate moves in the investor's favor, the investor will benefit and will earn more from the U.K. bill than the U.S. bill. For example, if both the U.S. and U.K. interest rates are 5%, and the current exchange rate is $1.40 per pound, a $1.40 investment today can buy 1 pound, which can be invested in England at a certain rate of 5%, for a year-end value of 1.05 pounds. If the year-end exchange rate is $1.50 per pound, the 1.05 pounds can be exchanged for $1.05 \times $1.50 = $1.575 for a rate of return in dollars of $1 + r = $1.575/$1.40 = 1.125$, or $r = 12.5\%$, more than is available from U.S. bills. Therefore, if the investor expects favorable exchange rate movements, the U.K. bill is a speculative investment. Otherwise, it is a gamble.

2. For the $A = 4$ investor the utility of the risky portfolio is

$$U = .20 - (\tfrac{1}{2} \times 4 \times .3^2) = .02$$

while the utility of bills is

$$U = .07 - (\tfrac{1}{2} \times 4 \times 0) = .07$$

The investor will prefer bills to the risky portfolio. (Of course, a mixture of bills and the portfolio might be even better, but that is not a choice here.)

For the less risk-averse investor with $A = 2$, the utility of the risky portfolio is

$$U = .20 - (\tfrac{1}{2} \times 2 \times .3^2) = .11$$

while the utility of bills is again .07. The less risk-averse investor prefers the risky portfolio.

3. The less risk-averse investor has a shallower indifference curve. An increase in risk requires less increase in expected return to restore utility to the original level.

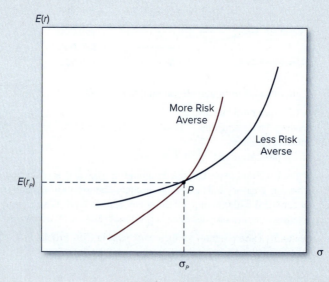

4. Holding 50% of your invested capital in Ready Assets means that your investment proportion in the risky portfolio is reduced from 70% to 50%.

   Your risky portfolio is constructed to invest 54% in E and 46% in B. Thus the proportion of E in your overall portfolio is $.5 \times 54\% = 27\%$, and the dollar value of your position in E is $300,000 \times .27 = \$81,000$.

5. In the expected return–standard deviation plane all portfolios that are constructed from the same risky and risk-free funds (with various proportions) lie on a line from the risk-free rate through the risky fund. The slope of the CAL (capital allocation line) is the same everywhere; hence the reward-to-volatility (Sharpe) ratio is the same for all of these portfolios. Formally, if you invest a proportion, y, in a risky fund with expected return $E(r_P)$ and standard deviation σ_P, and the remainder, $1 - y$, in a risk-free asset with a sure rate r_f, then the portfolio's expected return and standard deviation are

$$E(r_C) = r_f + y\left[E(r_P) - r_f\right]$$
$$\sigma_C = y\sigma_P$$

and therefore the Sharpe ratio of this portfolio is

$$S_C = \frac{E(r_C) - r_f}{\sigma_C} = \frac{y\left[E(r_P) - r_f\right]}{y\sigma_P} = \frac{E(r_P) - r_f}{\sigma_P}$$

which is independent of the proportion y.

6. The lending and borrowing rates are unchanged at $r_f = 7\%$, $r_f^B = 9\%$. The standard deviation of the risky portfolio is still 22%, but its expected rate of return on the risky portfolio increases from 15% to 17%.

   The slope of the two-part CAL is

$$\frac{E(r_P) - r_f}{\sigma_P} \text{ for the lending range}$$

$$\frac{E(r_P) - r_f^B}{\sigma_P} \text{ for the borrowing range}$$

   Thus, in both cases, the slope increases: from 8/22 to 10/22 for the lending range and from 6/22 to 8/22 for the borrowing range.

7. *a.* The parameters are $r_f = .07$, $E(r_P) = .15$, $\sigma_P = .22$. An investor with a degree of risk aversion A will choose a proportion y in the risky portfolio of

$$y = \frac{E(r_P) - r_f}{A\sigma_P^2}$$

   With the assumed parameters and with $A = 3$ we find that

$$y = \frac{.15 - .07}{3 \times .0484} = .55$$

   When the degree of risk aversion decreases from the original value of 4 to the new value of 3, investment in the risky portfolio increases from 41% to 55%. Accordingly, both the expected return and standard deviation of the optimal portfolio increase:

$$E(r_C) = .07 + (.55 \times .08) = .114 \text{ (before: .1028)}$$
$$\sigma_C = .55 \times .22 = .121 \text{ (before: .0902)}$$

   b. All investors whose degree of risk aversion is such that they would hold the risky portfolio in a proportion equal to 100% or less ($y \leq 1.00$) are lending rather than borrowing, and so are unaffected by the borrowing rate. The individuals just at the dividing line separating lenders from borrowers are the ones who choose to hold exactly 100% of their assets in the risky portfolio ($y = 1$). We can solve for the degree of risk aversion of these "cut off" investors from the parameters of the investment opportunities:

$$y = 1 = \frac{E(r_P) - r_f}{A\sigma_P^2} = \frac{.08}{.0484\,A}$$

which implies

$$A = \frac{.08}{.0484} = 1.65$$

Any investor who is more risk tolerant (i.e., $A < 1.65$) would choose to borrow *if* the borrowing rate were 7%. These are the investors who are affected by the higher borrowing rate. For borrowers,

$$y = \frac{E(r_P) - r_f^B}{A\sigma_P^2}$$

Suppose, for example, an investor has $A = 1.1$. If $r_f = r_f^B = 7\%$, this investor would have chosen to invest in the risky portfolio:

$$y = \frac{.08}{1.1 \times .0484} = 1.50$$

which means that the investor would have borrowed an amount equal to 50% of her own investment capital, placing all the proceeds in the risky portfolio. But at the higher borrowing rate, $r_f^B = 9\%$, the investor will choose to borrow less and put less in the risky asset. In this case,

$$y = \frac{.06}{1.1 \times .0484} = 1.13$$

and "only" 13% of her investment capital will be borrowed. Graphically, the line from r_f to the risky portfolio shows the CAL for lenders. The dashed part of the line originating at r_f *would* be relevant if the borrowing rate equaled the lending rate. When the borrowing rate exceeds the lending rate, the CAL is kinked at the point corresponding to the risky portfolio.

The following figure shows indifference curves of two investors. The steeper indifference curve portrays the more risk-averse investor, who chooses portfolio C_0, which involves lending. This investor's choice is unaffected by the borrowing rate. The more risk-tolerant investor is portrayed by the shallower-sloped indifference curves. If the lending rate equaled the borrowing rate, this investor would choose portfolio C_1 on the dashed part of the CAL. When the borrowing rate is higher, this investor instead chooses portfolio C_2 (in the borrowing range of the kinked

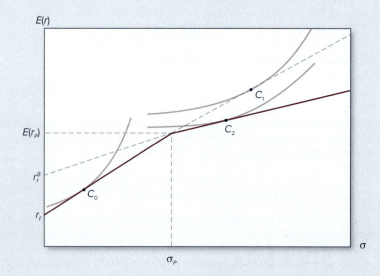

CAL), which involves less borrowing than before. This investor is hurt by the increase in the borrowing rate.

8. If all the investment parameters remain unchanged, the only reason for an investor to decrease the investment proportion in the risky asset is an increase in the degree of risk aversion. If you think that this is unlikely, then you have to reconsider your faith in your assumptions. Perhaps the U.S. equity market is not a good proxy for the optimal risky portfolio. Perhaps investors expect a higher real rate on T-bills.

APPENDIX A: Risk Aversion, Expected Utility, and the St. Petersburg Paradox

We digress in this appendix to examine the rationale behind our contention that investors are risk averse. Recognition of risk aversion as central in investment decisions goes back at least to 1738. Daniel Bernoulli, one of a famous Swiss family of distinguished mathematicians, spent the years 1725 through 1733 in St. Petersburg, where he analyzed the following coin-toss game. To enter the game one pays an entry fee. Thereafter, a coin is tossed until the *first* head appears. The number of tails, denoted by n, that appears until the first head is tossed is used to compute the payoff, $\$R$, to the participant, as

$$R(n) = 2^n$$

The probability of no tails before the first head ($n = 0$) is 1/2 and the corresponding payoff is $2^0 = \$1$. The probability of one tail and then heads ($n = 1$) is $1/2 \times 1/2$ with payoff $2^1 = \$2$, the probability of two tails and then heads ($n = 2$) is $1/2 \times 1/2 \times 1/2$, and so forth.

The following table illustrates the probabilities and payoffs for various outcomes:

Tails	Probability	Payoff = $ $R(n)$	Probability × Payoff
0	1/2	$1	$1/2
1	1/4	$2	$1/2
2	1/8	$4	$1/2
3	1/16	$8	$1/2
⋮	⋮	⋮	⋮
n	$(1/2)^{n+1}$	2^n	$1/2

The expected payoff is therefore

$$E(R) = \sum_{n=0}^{\infty} \Pr(n)R(n) = \tfrac{1}{2} + \tfrac{1}{2} + \cdots = \infty$$

The evaluation of this game is called the "St. Petersburg Paradox." Although the expected payoff is infinite, participants obviously will be willing to purchase tickets to play the game only at a finite, and possibly quite modest, entry fee.

Bernoulli resolved the paradox by noting that investors do not assign the same value per dollar to all payoffs. Specifically, the greater their wealth, the less their "appreciation" for each extra dollar. We can make this insight mathematically precise by assigning a welfare or utility value to any level of investor wealth. Our utility function should increase as wealth is higher, but each extra dollar of wealth should increase utility by progressively smaller amounts.[9] (Modern economists would say that investors exhibit "decreasing

---

[9]This utility is similar in spirit to the one that assigns a satisfaction level to portfolios with given risk and return attributes. However, the utility function here refers not to investors' satisfaction with alternative portfolio choices but only to the subjective welfare they derive from different levels of wealth.

marginal utility" from an additional payoff dollar.) One particular function that assigns a subjective value to the investor from a payoff of $R,$ which has a smaller value per dollar the greater the payoff, is the function $\ln(R)$ where ln is the natural logarithm function. If this function measures utility values of wealth, the subjective utility value of the game is indeed finite, equal to .693.[10] The certain wealth level necessary to yield this utility value is $2.00, because $\ln(2.00) = .693$. Hence the certainty equivalent value of the risky payoff is $2.00, which is the maximum amount that this investor will pay to play the game.

Von Neumann and Morgenstern adapted this approach to investment theory in a complete axiomatic system in 1946. Avoiding unnecessary technical detail, we restrict ourselves here to an intuitive exposition of the rationale for risk aversion.

Imagine two individuals who are identical twins, except that one of them is less fortunate than the other. Peter has only $1,000 to his name, while Paul has a net worth of $200,000. How many hours of work would each twin be willing to offer to earn one extra dollar? It is likely that Peter (the poor twin) has more essential uses for the extra money than does Paul. Therefore, Peter will offer more hours. In other words, Peter derives a greater personal welfare or assigns a greater "utility" value to the 1,001st dollar than Paul does to the 200,001st. Figure 6A.1 depicts graphically the relationship between wealth and the utility value of wealth that is consistent with this notion of decreasing marginal utility.

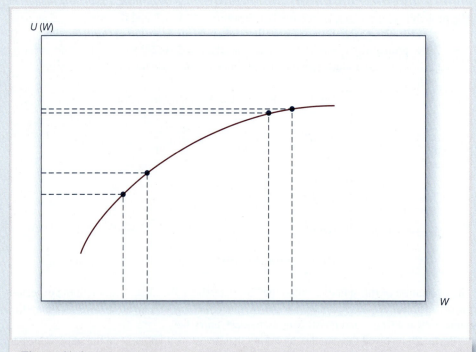

Figure 6A.1 Utility of wealth with a log utility function

---

[10]If we substitute the "utility" value, $\ln(R)$, for the dollar payoff, $R,$ to obtain an expected utility value of the game (rather than expected dollar value), we have, calling $V(R)$ the expected utility,

$$V(R) = \sum_{n=0}^{\infty} \Pr(n) \ln[R(n)] = \sum_{n=0}^{\infty} (1/2)^{n+1} \ln(2^n) = .693$$

Individuals have different rates of decrease in their marginal utility of wealth. What is constant is the *principle* that the per-dollar increment to utility decreases with wealth. Functions that exhibit the property of decreasing per-unit value as the number of units grows are called concave. A simple example is the log function, familiar from high school mathematics. Of course, a log function will not fit all investors, but it is consistent with the risk aversion that we assume for all investors.

Now consider the following simple prospect:

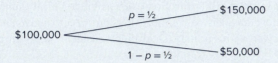

This is a fair game in that the expected profit is zero. Suppose, however, that the curve in Figure 6A.1 represents the investor's utility value of wealth, assuming a log utility function. Figure 6A.2 shows this curve with numerical values marked.

Figure 6A.2 shows that the loss in utility from losing $50,000 exceeds the gain from winning $50,000. Consider the gain first. With probability $p = .5$, wealth goes from $100,000 to $150,000. Using the log utility function, utility goes from $\ln(100,000) = 11.51$ to $\ln(150,000) = 11.92$, the distance G on the graph. This gain is $G = 11.92 - 11.51 = .41$. In expected utility terms, then, the gain is $pG = .5 \times .41 = .21$.

Now consider the possibility of coming up on the short end of the prospect. In that case, wealth goes from $100,000 to $50,000. The loss in utility, the distance L on the graph, is $L = \ln(100,000) - \ln(50,000) = 11.51 - 10.82 = .69$. Thus the loss in expected utility terms is $(1 - p)L = .5 \times .69 = .35$, which exceeds the gain in expected utility from the possibility of winning the game.

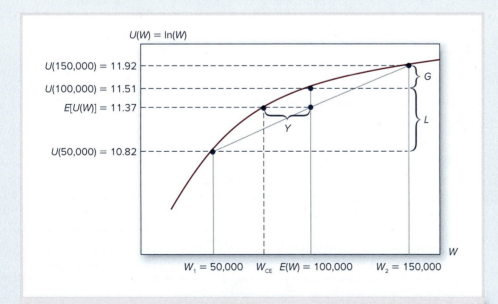

Figure 6A.2 Fair games and expected utility

We compute the expected utility from the risky prospect:

$$E[U(W)] = pU(W_1) + (1 - p)U(W_2)$$
$$= \tfrac{1}{2}\ln(50{,}000) + \tfrac{1}{2}\ln(150{,}000) = 11.37$$

If the prospect is rejected, the utility value of the (sure) $100,000 is $\ln(100{,}000) = 11.51$, greater than that of the fair game (11.37). Hence the risk-averse investor will reject the fair game.

Using a specific investor utility function (such as the log utility function) allows us to compute the certainty equivalent value of the risky prospect to a given investor. This is the amount that, if received with certainty, she would consider equally attractive as the risky prospect.

If log utility describes the investor's preferences toward wealth outcomes, then Figure 6A.2 can also tell us what is, for her, the dollar value of the prospect. We ask, What sure level of wealth has a utility value of 11.37 (which equals the expected utility from the prospect)? A horizontal line drawn at the level 11.37 intersects the utility curve at the level of wealth W_{CE}. This means that

$$\ln(W_{CE}) = 11.37$$

which implies that

$$W_{CE} = e^{11.37} = \$86{,}681.87$$

W_{CE} is therefore the certainty equivalent of the prospect. The distance Y in Figure 6A.2 is the penalty, or the downward adjustment, to the expected profit that is attributable to the risk of the prospect.

$$Y = E(W) - W_{CE} = \$100{,}000 - \$86{,}681.87 - \$13{,}318.13$$

This investor views $86,681.87 for certain as being equal in utility value as $100,000 at risk. Therefore, she would be indifferent between the two.

✓ Concept Check 6A.1

Suppose the utility function is $U(W) = \sqrt{W}$.

a. What is the utility level at wealth levels $50,000 and $150,000?

b. What is expected utility if p still equals .5?

c. What is the certainty equivalent of the risky prospect?

d. Does this utility function also display risk aversion?

e. Does this utility function display more or less risk aversion than the log utility function?

PROBLEMS:
APPENDIX A

1. Suppose that your wealth is $250,000. You buy a $200,000 house and invest the remainder in a risk-free asset paying an annual interest rate of 6%. There is a probability of .001 that your house will burn to the ground and its value will be reduced to zero. With a log utility of end-of-year wealth, how much would you be willing to pay for insurance (at the beginning of the year)? (Assume that if the house does not burn down, its end-of-year value still will be $200,000.)

2. If the cost of insuring your house is $1 per $1,000 of value, what will be the certainty equivalent of your end-of-year wealth if you insure your house at:

   a. ½ its value.
   b. Its full value.
   c. 1½ times its value.

SOLUTIONS TO CONCEPT CHECK

A.1.   a. $U(W) = \sqrt{W}$

   $U(50,000) = \sqrt{50,000} = 223.61$

   $U(150,000) = 387.30$

   b. $E(U) = (.5 \times 223.61) + (.5 \times 387.30) = 305.45$

   c.   We must find W_{CE} that has utility level 305.45. Therefore

   $$\sqrt{W_{CE}} = 305.45$$
   $$W_{CE} = 305.45^2 = \$93,301$$

   d.   Yes. The certainty equivalent of the risky venture is less than the expected outcome of $100,000.

   e.   The certainty equivalent of the risky venture to this investor is greater than it was for the log utility investor considered in the text. Hence this utility function displays less risk aversion.

APPENDIX B: Utility Functions and Risk Premiums

The utility function of an individual investor allows us to measure the subjective value the individual would place on a dollar at various levels of wealth. Essentially, a dollar in bad times (when wealth is low) is more valuable than a dollar in good times (when wealth is high).

Suppose that all investors hold the risky S&P 500 portfolio. Then, if the portfolio value falls in a worse-than-expected economy, all investors will, albeit to different degrees, experience a "low-wealth" scenario. Therefore, the equilibrium value of a dollar in the low-wealth economy would be higher than the value of a dollar when the portfolio performs better than expected. This observation helps explain why an investment in a stock portfolio (and hence in individual stocks) has a risk premium that appears to be so high and results in probability of shortfall that is so low. Despite the low probability of underperforming, stocks still do not dominate the lower-return risk-free bond, because if an investment shortfall should transpire, it will coincide with states in which the marginal value of an extra dollar is high.

Does revealed behavior of investors demonstrate risk aversion? Looking at prices and past rates of return in financial markets, we can answer with a resounding yes. With remarkable consistency, riskier bonds are sold at lower prices than are safer ones with otherwise similar characteristics. Riskier stocks also have provided higher average rates of return over long periods of time than less risky assets such as T-bills. For example, over the 1926 to 2015 period, the average rate of return on the S&P 500 portfolio exceeded the T-bill return by around 8% per year.

It is abundantly clear from financial data that the average, or representative, investor exhibits substantial risk aversion. For readers who recognize that financial assets are priced to compensate for risk by providing a risk premium and at the same time feel the urge for some gambling, we have a constructive recommendation: Direct your gambling impulse to investment in financial markets. As Von Neumann once said, "The stock market is a casino with the odds in your favor." A small risk-seeking investment may provide all the excitement you want with a positive expected return to boot!

Optimal Risky Portfolios

THE INVESTMENT DECISION can be viewed as a top-down process: (1) *capital allocation* between the risky portfolio and risk-free assets, (2) *asset allocation* within the risky portfolio across broad asset classes (e.g., U.S. stocks, international stocks, and long-term bonds), and (3) *security selection* of individual assets within each asset class.

Capital allocation, as we saw in Chapter 6, determines the investor's exposure to risk. The optimal capital allocation is determined by risk aversion as well as expectations for the risk–return trade-off of the investor's risky portfolio.

In principle, asset allocation and security selection are technically identical; both aim at identifying the optimal risky portfolio, specifically, the combination of risky assets that provides the best risk–return trade-off or, equivalently, the highest Sharpe ratio. In practice, however, asset allocation and security selection are typically separated into two steps, in which the broad outlines of the portfolio are established first (asset allocation), while details concerning specific securities are filled in later (security selection). After we show how the optimal risky portfolio may be constructed, we will consider the costs and benefits of pursuing this two-step approach.

We begin by illustrating the potential gains from simple diversification into many assets. We then turn to *efficient* diversification, starting with

an investment menu of only two risky assets, then adding the risk-free asset, and finally, incorporating the entire universe of available risky securities. We learn how diversification can reduce risk without affecting expected returns. This accomplished, we re-examine the rationale for the portfolio construction hierarchy: capital allocation, followed by asset allocation, followed by security selection. Finally, we offer insight into the power of diversification by drawing an analogy between it and the workings of the insurance industry.

The portfolios we discuss in this and the following chapters presume a short-term horizon—even if the overall investment horizon is long, portfolio composition can be rebalanced or updated almost continuously. For these short horizons, the assumption of normality is sufficiently accurate to describe holding-period returns, and we will be concerned only with portfolio means and variances.

In Appendix A, we demonstrate how construction of the optimal risky portfolio can easily be accomplished with Excel. Appendix B provides a review of portfolio statistics with emphasis on the intuition behind covariance and correlation measures. Even if you have had a good quantitative methods course, it may be well worth skimming.

7.1   Diversification and Portfolio Risk

Suppose your portfolio is composed of only one stock, say, Digital Computer Corp. What would be the sources of risk to this "portfolio"? You might think of two broad sources of uncertainty. First, there is the risk that comes from conditions in the general economy, such as the business cycle, inflation, interest rates, and exchange rates. None of these macroeconomic factors can be predicted with certainty, and all affect the rate of return on Digital stock. In addition to these macroeconomic factors, there are firm-specific influences, such as Digital's success in research and development and personnel changes. These factors affect Digital without noticeably affecting other firms in the economy.

Now consider a naïve **diversification** strategy, in which you include additional securities in your portfolio. For example, place half your funds in ExxonMobil and half in Digital. What should happen to portfolio risk? To the extent that the firm-specific influences on the two stocks differ, diversification should reduce portfolio risk. For example, when oil prices fall, hurting ExxonMobil, computer prices might rise, helping Digital. The two effects are offsetting and stabilize portfolio return.

But why end diversification at only two stocks? If we diversify into many more securities, we continue to spread out our exposure to firm-specific factors, and portfolio volatility should continue to fall. Ultimately, however, even with a large number of stocks, we cannot avoid risk altogether because virtually all securities are affected by the common macroeconomic factors. For example, if all stocks are affected by the business cycle, we cannot avoid exposure to business cycle risk no matter how many stocks we hold.

When all risk is firm-specific, as in Figure 7.1, Panel A, diversification can reduce risk to arbitrarily low levels. The reason is that with all risk sources independent, the exposure to any particular source of risk is reduced to a negligible level. Risk reduction by spreading exposure across many independent risk sources is sometimes called the

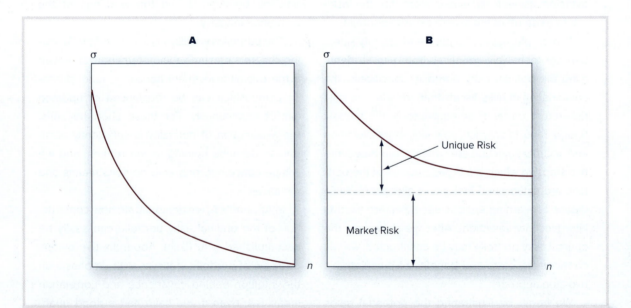

Figure 7.1 Portfolio risk as a function of the number of stocks in the portfolio. *Panel A:* All risk is firm specific. *Panel B:* Some risk is systematic, or marketwide.

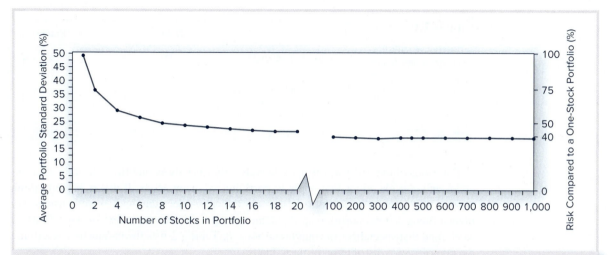

Figure 7.2 Portfolio diversification. The average standard deviation of returns of portfolios composed of only one stock was 49.2%. The average portfolio risk fell rapidly as the number of stocks included in the portfolio increased. In the limit, portfolio risk could be reduced to only 19.2%.

Source: Meir Statman, "How Many Stocks Make a Diversified Portfolio?" *Journal of Financial and Quantitative Analysis* 22 (September 1987).

insurance principle because of the notion that an insurance company depends on such diversification when it writes many policies insuring against many independent sources of risk, each policy being a small part of the company's overall portfolio. (We discuss the insurance principle in more detail in Section 7.5.)

When common sources of risk affect all firms, however, even extensive diversification cannot eliminate risk. In Figure 7.1, Panel B, portfolio standard deviation falls as the number of securities increases, but it cannot be reduced to zero. The risk that remains even after extensive diversification is called **market risk,** risk that is attributable to marketwide risk sources. Such risk is also called **systematic risk,** or **nondiversifiable risk.** In contrast, the risk that *can* be eliminated by diversification is called **unique risk, firm-specific risk, nonsystematic risk,** or **diversifiable risk.**

This analysis is borne out by empirical studies. Figure 7.2 shows the effect of portfolio diversification, using data on NYSE stocks.[1] The figure shows the average standard deviation of equally weighted portfolios constructed by selecting stocks at random as a function of the number of stocks in the portfolio. On average, portfolio risk does fall with diversification, but the power of diversification to reduce risk is limited by systematic or common sources of risk.

7.2   Portfolios of Two Risky Assets

In the last section we considered naïve diversification using equally weighted portfolios of several securities. It is time now to study *efficient* diversification, whereby we construct risky portfolios to provide the lowest possible risk for any given level of expected return.

---

[1]Meir Statman, "How Many Stocks Make a Diversified Portfolio?" *Journal of Financial and Quantitative Analysis* 22 (September 1987).

Table 7.1

Descriptive statistics for two mutual funds

	Debt	Equity
Expected return, $E(r)$	8%	13%
Standard deviation, σ	12%	20%
Covariance, $\text{Cov}(r_D, r_E)$	72	
Correlation coefficient, ρ_{DE}		0.30

Portfolios of two risky assets are relatively easy to analyze, and they illustrate the principles and considerations that apply to portfolios of many assets. It makes sense to think about a two-asset risky portfolio as an asset allocation decision, and so we consider two mutual funds, a bond portfolio specializing in long-term debt securities, denoted D, and a stock fund that specializes in equity securities, E. Table 7.1 lists the parameters describing the rate-of-return distribution of these funds.

A proportion denoted by w_D is invested in the bond fund, and the remainder, $1 - w_D$, denoted w_E, is invested in the stock fund. The rate of return on this portfolio, r_p, will be[2]

$$r_p = w_D r_D + w_E r_E \tag{7.1}$$

where r_D is the rate of return on the debt fund and r_E is the rate of return on the equity fund.

The expected return on the portfolio is a weighted average of expected returns on the component securities with portfolio proportions as weights:

$$E(r_p) = w_D E(r_D) + w_E E(r_E) \tag{7.2}$$

The variance of the two-asset portfolio is

$$\sigma_p^2 = w_D^2 \sigma_D^2 + w_E^2 \sigma_E^2 + 2 w_D w_E \text{Cov}(r_D, r_E) \tag{7.3}$$

Our first observation is that the variance of the portfolio, unlike the expected return, is *not* a weighted average of the individual asset variances. To understand the formula for the portfolio variance more clearly, recall that the covariance of a variable with itself is the variance of that variable; that is

$$
\begin{aligned}
\text{Cov}(r_D, r_D) &= \sum_{\text{scenarios}} \text{Pr(scenario)}[r_D - E(r_D)][r_D - E(r_D)] \\
&= \sum_{\text{scenarios}} \text{Pr(scenario)}[r_D - E(r_D)]^2 \\
&= \sigma_D^2
\end{aligned}
\tag{7.4}
$$

Therefore, another way to write the variance of the portfolio is

$$\sigma_p^2 = w_D w_D \text{Cov}(r_D, r_D) + w_E w_E \text{Cov}(r_E, r_E) + 2 w_D w_E \text{Cov}(r_D, r_E) \tag{7.5}$$

In words, the variance of the portfolio is a weighted sum of covariances, and each weight is the product of the portfolio proportions of the pair of assets in the covariance term.

Table 7.2 shows how portfolio variance can be calculated from a spreadsheet. Panel A of the table shows the *bordered* covariance matrix of the returns of the two mutual funds. The bordered matrix is the covariance matrix with the portfolio weights for each fund

[2]See Appendix B of this chapter for a review of portfolio statistics.

A. Bordered Covariance Matrix		
Portfolio Weights	w_D	w_E
w_D	$\text{Cov}(r_D, r_D)$	$\text{Cov}(r_D, r_E)$
w_E	$\text{Cov}(r_E, r_D)$	$\text{Cov}(r_E, r_E)$
B. Border-Multiplied Covariance Matrix		
Portfolio Weights	w_D	w_E
w_D	$w_D w_D \text{Cov}(r_D, r_D)$	$w_D w_E \text{Cov}(r_D, r_E)$
w_E	$w_E w_D \text{Cov}(r_E, r_D)$	$w_E w_E \text{Cov}(r_E, r_E)$
$w_D + w_E = 1$	$w_D w_D \text{Cov}(r_D, r_D) + w_E w_D \text{Cov}(r_E, r_D)$	$w_D w_E \text{Cov}(r_D, r_E) + w_E w_E \text{Cov}(r_E, r_E)$
Portfolio variance	$w_D w_D \text{Cov}(r_D, r_D) + w_E w_D \text{Cov}(r_E, r_D) + w_D w_E \text{Cov}(r_D, r_E) + w_E w_E \text{Cov}(r_E, r_E)$	

Table 7.2

Computation of portfolio variance from the covariance matrix

placed on the borders, that is, along the first row and column. To find portfolio variance, multiply each element in the covariance matrix by the pair of portfolio weights in its row and column borders. Add up the resultant terms, and you have the formula for portfolio variance given in Equation 7.5.

We perform these calculations in Panel B, which is the *border-multiplied* covariance matrix: Each covariance has been multiplied by the weights from the row and the column in the borders. The bottom line of Panel B confirms that the sum of all the terms in this matrix (which we obtain by adding up the column sums) is indeed the portfolio variance in Equation 7.5.

This procedure works because the covariance matrix is symmetric around the diagonal, that is, $\text{Cov}(r_D, r_E) = \text{Cov}(r_E, r_D)$. Thus each covariance term appears twice.

This technique for computing the variance from the border-multiplied covariance matrix is general; it applies to any number of assets and is easily implemented on a spreadsheet. Concept Check 7.1 asks you to try the rule for a three-asset portfolio. Use this problem to verify that you are comfortable with this concept.

 Concept Check **7.1**

a. First confirm for yourself that our simple rule for computing the variance of a two-asset portfolio from the bordered covariance matrix is consistent with Equation 7.3.

b. Now consider a portfolio of three funds, X, Y, Z, with weights w_X, w_Y, and w_Z. Show that the portfolio variance is

$$w_X^2 \sigma_X^2 + w_Y^2 \sigma_Y^2 + w_Z^2 \sigma_Z^2 + 2w_X w_Y \, \text{Cov}(r_X, r_Y)$$
$$+ \, 2w_X w_Z \, \text{Cov}(r_X, r_Z) + 2w_Y w_Z \, \text{Cov}(r_Y, r_Z)$$

Equation 7.3 reveals that variance is reduced if the covariance term is negative. But even if the covariance term is positive, the portfolio standard deviation is *still* less than the weighted average of the individual security standard deviations, unless the two securities are perfectly positively correlated.

To see this, notice that the covariance can be computed from the correlation coefficient, ρ_{DE}, as

$$Cov(r_D, r_E) = \rho_{DE}\sigma_D\sigma_E \tag{7.6}$$

Therefore,

$$\sigma_p^2 = w_D^2\sigma_D^2 + w_E^2\sigma_E^2 + 2w_Dw_E\sigma_D\sigma_E\rho_{DE} \tag{7.7}$$

Other things equal, portfolio variance is higher when ρ_{DE} is higher. In the case of perfect positive correlation, $\rho_{DE} = 1$, the right-hand side of Equation 7.7 is a perfect square and simplifies to

$$\sigma_p^2 = (w_D\sigma_D + w_E\sigma_E)^2 \tag{7.8}$$

or

$$\sigma_p = w_D\sigma_D + w_E\sigma_E \tag{7.9}$$

Therefore, the standard deviation of the portfolio with perfect positive correlation is just the weighted average of the component standard deviations. In all other cases, the correlation coefficient is less than 1, making the portfolio standard deviation *less* than the weighted average of the component standard deviations.

A hedge asset has *negative* correlation with the other assets in the portfolio. Equation 7.7 shows that such assets will be particularly effective in reducing total risk. Moreover, Equation 7.2 shows that expected return is unaffected by correlation between returns. Therefore, other things equal, we will always prefer to add to our portfolios assets with low or, even better, negative correlation with our existing position.

Because the portfolio's expected return is the weighted average of its component expected returns, whereas its standard deviation is less than the weighted average of the component standard deviations, *portfolios of less than perfectly correlated assets always offer some degree of diversification benefit.* The lower the correlation between the assets, the greater the gain in efficiency.

How low can portfolio standard deviation be? The lowest possible value of the correlation coefficient is -1, representing perfect negative correlation. In this case, Equation 7.7 simplifies to

$$\sigma_p^2 = (w_D\sigma_D - w_E\sigma_E)^2 \tag{7.10}$$

and the portfolio standard deviation is

$$\sigma_p = \text{Absolute value } (w_D\sigma_D - w_E\sigma_E) \tag{7.11}$$

When $\rho = -1$, a perfectly hedged position can be obtained by choosing the portfolio proportions to solve

$$w_D\sigma_D - w_E\sigma_E = 0$$

The solution to this equation is

$$w_D = \frac{\sigma_E}{\sigma_D + \sigma_E}$$

$$w_E = \frac{\sigma_D}{\sigma_D + \sigma_E} = 1 - w_D \tag{7.12}$$

These weights drive the standard deviation of the portfolio to zero.

Example 7.1   Portfolio Risk and Return

We can apply this analysis to the bond and stock funds whose properties were summarized in Table 7.1. Using these data, the formulas for the expected return, variance, and standard deviation of the portfolio as a function of the portfolio weights are

$$E(r_p) = 8w_D + 13w_E$$
$$\sigma_p^2 = 12^2 w_D^2 + 20^2 w_E^2 + 2 \times 12 \times 20 \times .3 \times w_D w_E$$
$$= 144 w_D^2 + 400 w_E^2 + 144 w_D w_E$$
$$\sigma_p = \sqrt{\sigma_p^2}$$

We can experiment with different portfolio proportions to observe the effect on portfolio expected return and variance. Suppose we change the proportion invested in bonds. The effect on expected return is tabulated in Table 7.3, column 3, and plotted in Figure 7.3. When the proportion invested in debt varies from zero to 1 (so that the proportion in equity varies from 1 to zero), the portfolio expected return goes from 13% (the stock fund's expected return) to 8% (the expected return on bonds).

What happens when $w_D > 1$ and $w_E < 0$? In this case, portfolio strategy would call for selling the equity fund short and investing the proceeds of the short sale in the debt fund. This will decrease the expected return of the portfolio. For example, when $w_D = 2$ and $w_E = -1$, expected portfolio return falls to $E(r_p) = 2 \times 8 + (-1) \times 13 = 3\%$. At this point, the value of the bond fund in the portfolio is twice the net worth of the account. This extreme position is financed in part by short-selling stocks equal in value to the portfolio's net worth.

Table 7.3

Expected return and standard deviation with various correlation coefficients

w_D	w_E	$E(r_p)$	Portfolio Standard Deviation for Given Correlation			
			$\rho = -1$	$\rho = 0$	$\rho = 0.30$	$\rho = 1$
0.00	1.00	13.00	20.00	20.00	20.00	20.00
0.10	0.90	12.50	16.80	18.04	18.40	19.20
0.20	0.80	12.00	13.60	16.18	16.88	18.40
0.30	0.70	11.50	10.40	14.46	15.47	17.60
0.40	0.60	11.00	7.20	12.92	14.20	16.80
0.50	0.50	10.50	4.00	11.66	13.11	16.00
0.60	0.40	10.00	0.80	10.76	12.26	15.20
0.70	0.30	9.50	2.40	10.32	11.70	14.40
0.80	0.20	9.00	5.60	10.40	11.45	13.60
0.90	0.10	8.50	8.80	10.98	11.56	12.80
1.00	0.00	8.00	12.00	12.00	12.00	12.00
			Minimum Variance Portfolio			
		w_D	0.6250	0.7353	0.8200	—
		w_E	0.3750	0.2647	0.1800	—
		$E(r_p)$	9.8750	9.3235	8.9000	—
		σ_p	0.0000	10.2899	11.4473	—

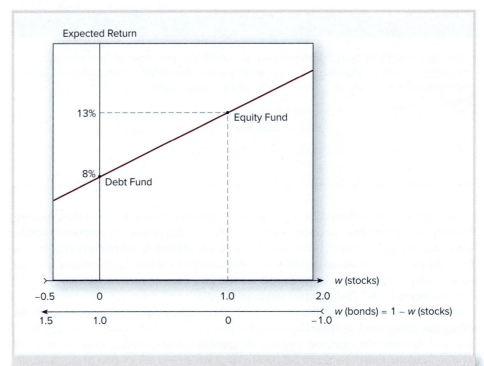

Figure 7.3 Portfolio expected return as a function of investment proportions

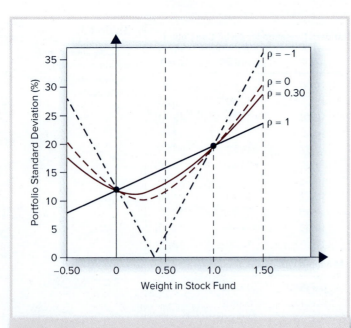

Figure 7.4 Portfolio standard deviation as a function of investment proportions

The reverse happens when $w_D < 0$ and $w_E > 1$. This strategy calls for selling the bond fund short and using the proceeds to finance additional purchases of the equity fund.

Of course, varying investment proportions also has an effect on portfolio standard deviation. Table 7.3 presents portfolio standard deviations for different portfolio weights calculated from Equation 7.7 using the assumed value of the correlation coefficient, .30, as well as other values of ρ. Figure 7.4 shows the relationship between standard deviation and portfolio weights. Look first at the solid curve for $\rho_{DE} = .30$. The graph shows that as the portfolio weight in the equity fund increases from zero to 1, portfolio standard deviation first falls with the initial diversification from bonds into stocks, but then rises again as the portfolio becomes heavily concentrated in stocks, and again is undiversified. This pattern will generally hold as long as the correlation coefficient between the funds is not too high.[3] For a pair of assets

[3] As long as $\rho < \sigma_D/\sigma_E$, volatility will initially fall when we start with all bonds and begin to move into stocks.

with a large positive correlation of returns, the portfolio standard deviation will increase monotonically from the low-risk asset to the high-risk asset. Even in this case, however, there is a positive (if small) benefit from diversification.

What is the minimum level to which portfolio standard deviation can be held? For the parameter values stipulated in Table 7.1, the portfolio weights that solve this minimization problem turn out to be[4]

$$w_{\text{Min}}(D) = .82$$
$$w_{\text{Min}}(E) = 1 - .82 = .18$$

This minimum-variance portfolio has a standard deviation of

$$\sigma_{\text{Min}} = [(.82^2 \times 12^2) + (.18^2 \times 20^2) + (2 \times .82 \times .18 \times 72)]^{1/2} = 11.45\%$$

as indicated in the last line of Table 7.3 for the column $\rho = .30$.

The solid colored line in Figure 7.4 plots the portfolio standard deviation when $\rho = .30$ as a function of the investment proportions. It passes through the two undiversified port-folios of $w_D = 1$ and $w_E = 1$. Note that the **minimum-variance portfolio** has a standard deviation *smaller than that of either of the individual component assets.* This illustrates the effect of diversification.

The other three lines in Figure 7.4 show how portfolio risk varies for other values of the correlation coefficient, holding the variances of each asset constant. These lines plot the values in the other three columns of Table 7.3.

The solid dark straight line connecting the undiversified portfolios of all bonds or all stocks, $w_D = 1$ or $w_E = 1$, shows portfolio standard deviation with perfect positive correlation, $\rho = 1$. In this case there is no advantage from diversification, and the port-folio standard deviation is the simple weighted average of the component asset standard deviations.

The dashed colored curve depicts portfolio risk for the case of uncorrelated assets, $\rho = 0$. With lower correlation between the two assets, diversification is more effective and portfolio risk is lower (at least when both assets are held in positive amounts). The mini-mum portfolio standard deviation when $\rho = 0$ is 10.29% (see Table 7.3), *again lower than the standard deviation of either asset.*

Finally, the triangular broken line illustrates the perfect hedge potential when the two assets are perfectly negatively correlated ($\rho = -1$). In this case the solution for the minimum-variance portfolio is, by Equation 7.12,

$$w_{\text{Min}}(D; \rho = -1) = \frac{\sigma_E}{\sigma_D + \sigma_E} = \frac{20}{12 + 20} = .625$$
$$w_{\text{Min}}(E; \rho = -1) = 1 - .625 = .375$$

and the portfolio variance (and standard deviation) is zero.

We can combine Figures 7.3 and 7.4 to demonstrate the relationship between portfolio risk (standard deviation) and expected return—given the parameters of the available assets.

---

[4]This solution uses the minimization techniques of calculus. Write out the expression for portfolio variance from Equation 7.3, substitute $1 - w_D$ for w_E, differentiate the result with respect to w_D, set the derivative equal to zero, and solve for w_D to obtain

$$w_{\text{Min}}(D) = \frac{\sigma_E^2 - \text{Cov}(r_D, r_E)}{\sigma_D^2 + \sigma_E^2 - 2\,\text{Cov}(r_D, r_E)}$$

Alternatively, with a spreadsheet program such as Excel, you can obtain an accurate solution by using the Solver to minimize the variance. See Appendix A for an example of a portfolio optimization spreadsheet.

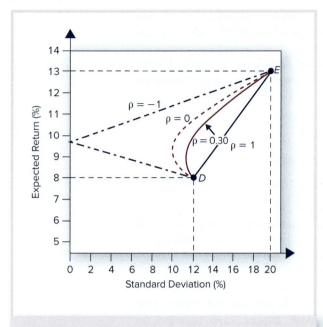

Figure 7.5 Portfolio expected return as a function of standard deviation

This is done in Figure 7.5. For any pair of investment proportions, w_D and w_E, we read the expected return from Figure 7.3 and the standard deviation from Figure 7.4. The resulting pairs of expected return and standard deviation are tabulated in Table 7.3 and plotted in Figure 7.5.

The solid colored curve in Figure 7.5 shows the **portfolio opportunity set** for $\rho = .30$. We call it the portfolio opportunity set because it shows all combinations of portfolio expected return and standard deviation that can be constructed from the two available assets. The other lines show the portfolio opportunity set for other values of the correlation coefficient. The solid black line connecting the two funds shows that there is no benefit from diversification when the correlation between the two is perfectly positive ($\rho = 1$). The opportunity set is not "pushed" to the northwest. The dashed colored line demonstrates the greater benefit from diversification when the correlation coefficient is lower than .30.

Finally, for $\rho = -1$, the portfolio opportunity set is linear, but now it offers a perfect hedging opportunity and the maximum advantage from diversification.

To summarize, although the expected return of any portfolio is simply the weighted average of the asset expected returns, this is not true of the standard deviation. Potential benefits from diversification arise when correlation is less than perfectly positive. The lower the correlation, the greater the potential benefit from diversification. In the extreme case of perfect negative correlation, we have a perfect hedging opportunity and can construct a zero-variance portfolio.

Suppose now an investor wishes to select the optimal portfolio from the opportunity set. The best portfolio will depend on risk aversion. Portfolios to the northeast in Figure 7.5 provide higher rates of return but impose greater risk. The best trade-off among these choices is a matter of personal preference. Investors with greater risk aversion will prefer portfolios to the southwest, with lower expected return but lower risk.[5]

 Concept Check **7.2**

Compute and draw the portfolio opportunity set for the debt and equity funds when the correlation coefficient between them is $\rho = .25$.

[5]Given a level of risk aversion, one can determine the portfolio that provides the highest level of utility. Recall from Chapter 6 that we were able to describe the utility provided by a portfolio as a function of its expected return, $E(r_p)$, and its variance, σ_p^2, according to the relationship $U = E(r_p) - 0.5A\sigma_p^2$. The portfolio mean and variance are determined by the portfolio weights in the two funds, w_E and w_D, according to Equations 7.2 and 7.3. Using those equations and some calculus, we find the optimal investment proportions in the two funds. A warning: To use the following equation (or any equation involving the risk aversion parameter, A), you must express returns in decimal form.

$$w_D = \frac{E(r_D) - E(r_E) + A(\sigma_E^2 - \sigma_D\sigma_E\rho_{DE})}{A(\sigma_D^2 + \sigma_E^2 - 2\sigma_D\sigma_E\rho_{DE})}$$

$$w_E = 1 - w_D$$

Here, too, Excel's Solver or similar software can be used to maximize utility subject to the constraints of Equations 7.2 and 7.3, plus the portfolio constraint that $w_D + w_E = 1$ (i.e., that portfolio weights sum to 1).

7.3   Asset Allocation with Stocks, Bonds, and Bills

When choosing their capital allocation between risky and risk-free portfolios, investors naturally will want to work with the risky portfolio that offers the highest reward-to-volatility or Sharpe ratio. The higher the Sharpe ratio, the greater the expected return corresponding to any level of volatility. Another way to put this is that the best risky portfolio is the one that results in the steepest capital allocation (CAL) line. Steeper CALs provide higher excess returns for any level of risk. Therefore, our next step is the construction of a risky portfolio combining the major asset classes (here a bond and a stock fund) that provides the highest possible Sharpe ratio.

The Sharpe ratio, which we seek to maximize, is defined as the portfolio's risk premium in excess of the risk-free rate, divided by the standard deviation. We often will refer to T-bills as the risk-free asset, but you can think more generally about a money market portfolio playing that role. Before beginning, we point out that restricting ourselves in this example to only stocks, bonds, and bills is actually not as restrictive as it may appear, as this choice includes all three major asset classes.

Asset Allocation with Two Risky Asset Classes

What if our risky assets are still confined to the bond and stock funds, as in the last section, but we can now also invest in risk-free T-bills yielding 5%? We start with a graphical solution. Figure 7.6 shows the opportunity set based on the properties of the bond and stock funds, using the data from Table 7.1 and assuming that $\rho = .3$.

Two possible capital allocation lines (CALs) are drawn from the risk-free rate ($r_f = 5\%$) to two feasible portfolios. The first possible CAL is drawn through the minimum-variance portfolio A, which is invested 82% in bonds and 18% in stocks (Table 7.3, bottom panel, last column). Portfolio A's expected return is 8.90%, and its standard deviation is 11.45%. With a T-bill rate of 5%, its **Sharpe ratio,** which is the slope of the CAL, is

$$S_A = \frac{E(r_A) - r_f}{\sigma_A} = \frac{8.9 - 5}{11.45} = .34$$

Now consider the CAL that uses portfolio B instead of A. Portfolio B invests 70% in bonds and 30% in stocks. Its expected return is 9.5% (a risk premium of 4.5%), and its standard deviation is 11.70%. Thus the Sharpe ratio on the CAL supported by portfolio B is

$$S_B = \frac{9.5 - 5}{11.7} = .38$$

which is higher than the Sharpe ratio of the CAL using the minimum-variance portfolio and T-bills. Hence, portfolio B dominates A: Figure 7.6 shows that CAL$_B$ provides a higher expected return than CAL$_A$ for any level of standard deviation.

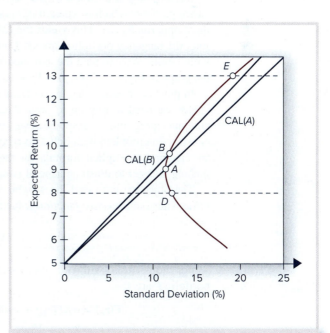

Figure 7.6 The opportunity set of the debt and equity funds and two feasible CALs

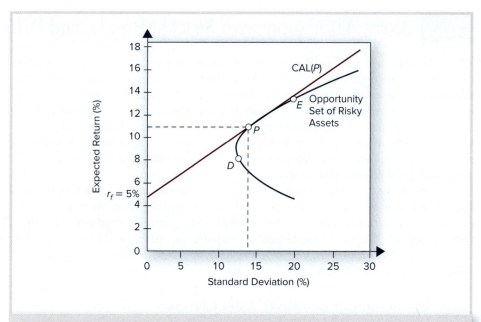

Figure 7.7 The opportunity set of the debt and equity funds with the optimal CAL and the optimal risky portfolio

But why stop at portfolio *B?* We can continue to ratchet the CAL upward to the greatest extent possible, which is where it ultimately reaches the point of tangency with the investment opportunity set. This yields the CAL with the highest feasible Sharpe ratio. Therefore, the tangency portfolio, labeled *P* in Figure 7.7, is the optimal risky portfolio to mix with T-bills. We can read the expected return and standard deviation of portfolio *P* from the graph in Figure 7.7: $E(r_P) = 11\%$ and $\sigma_P = 14.2\%$.

In practice, when we try to construct optimal risky portfolios from more than two risky assets, we need to rely on a spreadsheet (which we present in Appendix A) or another computer program. To start, however, we will demonstrate the solution of the portfolio construction problem with only two risky assets and a risk-free asset. In this simpler case, we can find an explicit formula for the weights of each asset in the optimal portfolio, making it easier to illustrate general issues.

The objective is to find the weights w_D and w_E that result in the highest slope of the CAL. Thus our *objective function* is the Sharpe ratio:

$$S_p = \frac{E(r_p) - r_f}{\sigma_p}$$

For the portfolio with two risky assets, the expected return and standard deviation of portfolio *P* are

$$E(r_p) = w_D E(r_D) + w_E E(r_E)$$
$$= 8w_D + 13w_E$$
$$\sigma_p = [w_D^2 \sigma_D^2 + w_E^2 \sigma_E^2 + 2 w_D w_E \, \text{Cov}(r_D, r_E)]^{1/2}$$
$$= [144w_D^2 + 400w_E^2 + (2 \times 72w_D w_E)]^{1/2}$$

When we maximize the objective function, S_p, we have to satisfy the constraint that the portfolio weights sum to 1.0, that is, $w_D + w_E = 1$. Therefore, we solve an optimization problem formally written as

$$\underset{w_i}{\text{Max}}\, S_p = \frac{E(r_p) - r_f}{\sigma_p}$$

subject to $\sum w_i = 1$. This is a maximization problem that can be solved using standard tools of calculus.

In the case of two risky assets, the solution for the weights of the **optimal risky portfolio**, P, is given by Equation 7.13. Notice that the solution employs *excess* returns (denoted R) rather than total returns (denoted r).[6]

$$w_D = \frac{E(R_D)\sigma_E^2 - E(R_E)\,\text{Cov}(R_D, R_E)}{E(R_D)\sigma_E^2 + E(R_E)\sigma_D^2 - [E(R_D) + E(R_E)]\,\text{Cov}(R_D, R_E)} \qquad \textbf{(7.13)}$$

$$w_E = 1 - w_D$$

Example 7.2   Optimal Risky Portfolio

Using our data, the solution for the optimal risky portfolio is:

$$w_D = \frac{(8 - 5)400 - (13 - 5)72}{(8 - 5)400 + (13 - 5)144 - (8 - 5 + 13 - 5)72} = .40$$

$$w_E = 1 - .40 = .60$$

The expected return and standard deviation of this optimal risky portfolio are

$$E(r_P) = (.4 \times 8) + (.6 \times 13) = 11\%$$

$$\sigma_P = [(.4^2 \times 144) + (.6^2 \times 400) + (2 \times .4 \times .6 \times 72)]^{1/2} = 14.2\%$$

This asset allocation produces an optimal risky portfolio whose CAL has a slope of

$$S_P = \frac{11 - 5}{14.2} = .42$$

which is the Sharpe ratio of portfolio P. Notice that this slope exceeds the slope of any of the other feasible portfolios that we have considered, as it must if it is to be the slope of the best feasible CAL.

In Chapter 6 we found the optimal *complete* portfolio given an optimal *risky* portfolio and the CAL generated by a combination of this portfolio and T-bills. Now that we have constructed the optimal risky portfolio, P, we can use its expected return and volatility along with the individual investor's degree of risk aversion, A, to calculate the optimal proportion of the complete portfolio to invest in the risky component.

---

[6]The solution procedure for two risky assets is as follows. Substitute for $E(r_p)$ from Equation 7.2 and for σ_p from Equation 7.7. Substitute $1 - w_D$ for w_E. Differentiate the resulting expression for S_p with respect to w_D, set the derivative equal to zero, and solve for w_D.

Example 7.3   The Optimal Complete Portfolio

An investor with a coefficient of risk aversion $A = 4$ would take a position in portfolio P of[7]

$$y = \frac{E(r_P) - r_f}{A\sigma_P^2} = \frac{.11 - .05}{4 \times .142^2} = .7439 \qquad \textbf{(7.14)}$$

Thus the investor will invest 74.39% of his or her overall wealth in portfolio P and 25.61% in T-bills. Portfolio P consists of 40% in bonds and 60% in equity (see Example 7.2), so the fraction of total wealth in bonds will be $yw_D = .7439 \times .4 = .2976$, or 29.76%. Similarly, the investment in stocks will be $yw_E = .7439 \times .6 = .4463$, or 44.63%. The graphical solution of this asset allocation problem is presented in Figures 7.8 and 7.9.

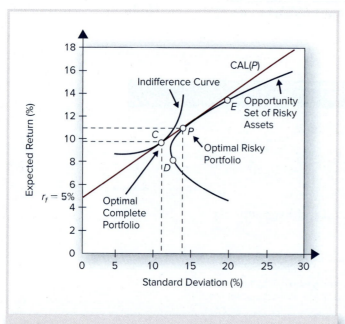

Figure 7.8 Determination of the optimal complete portfolio

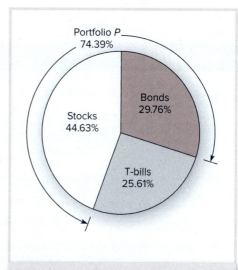

Figure 7.9 The proportions of the optimal complete portfolio

Once we have reached this point, generalizing to the case of many risky assets is straightforward. Before we move on, let us briefly summarize the steps we followed to arrive at the complete portfolio.

1. Specify the return characteristics of all securities (expected returns, variances, covariances).
2. Establish the risky portfolio (asset allocation):
   a. Calculate the optimal risky portfolio, P (Equation 7.13).
   b. Calculate the properties of portfolio P using the weights determined in step (a) and Equations 7.2 and 7.3.

---

[7]Notice that we express returns as decimals in Equation 7.14. This is necessary when using the risk aversion parameter, A, to solve for capital allocation.

The accompanying spreadsheet can be used to analyze the return and risk of a portfolio of two risky assets. The model calculates expected return and volatility for varying weights of each security as well as the optimal risky and minimum-variance portfolios. Graphs are automatically generated for various model inputs. The model allows you to specify a target rate of return and solves for optimal complete portfolios composed of the risk-free asset and the optimal risky portfolio. The spreadsheet is constructed using the two-security return data (expressed as decimals, not percentages) from Table 7.1. This spreadsheet is available in Connect or through your course instructor.

Excel Question

1. Suppose your target expected rate of return is 11%.

    a. What is the lowest-volatility portfolio that provides that expected return?

    b. What is the standard deviation of that portfolio?

    c. What is the composition of that portfolio?

	A	B	C	D	E	F
1	Asset Allocation Analysis: Risk and Return					
2		Expected	Standard	Correlation		
3		Return	Deviation	Coefficient	Covariance	
4	Security 1	0.08	0.12	0.3	0.0072	
5	Security 2	0.13	0.2			
6	T-Bill	0.05	0			
7						
8	Weight	Weight		Expected	Standard	Reward to
9	Security 1	Security 2		Return	Deviation	Volatility
10	1	0		0.08000	0.12000	0.25000
11	0.9	0.1		0.08500	0.11559	0.30281
12	0.8	0.2		0.09000	0.11454	0.34922
13	0.7	0.3		0.09500	0.11696	0.38474
14	0.6	0.4		0.10000	0.12264	0.40771

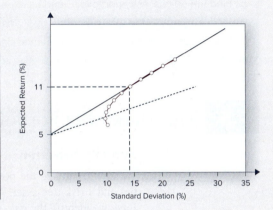

3. Allocate funds between the risky portfolio and the risk-free asset (capital allocation):

    a. Calculate the fraction of the complete portfolio allocated to portfolio *P* (the risky portfolio) and to T-bills (the risk-free asset) (Equation 7.14).

    b. Calculate the share of the complete portfolio invested in each asset and in T-bills.

Recall that our two risky assets, the bond and stock mutual funds, are already diversified portfolios. The diversification *within* each of these portfolios must be credited for a good deal of the risk reduction compared to undiversified single securities. For example, the standard deviation of the rate of return on an average stock is about 50% (see Figure 7.2). In contrast, the standard deviation of our stock-index fund is only 20%, about equal to the historical standard deviation of the S&P 500 portfolio. This is evidence of the importance of diversification within the asset class. Optimizing the asset allocation between bonds and stocks contributed incrementally to the improvement in the Sharpe ratio of the complete portfolio. The CAL using the optimal combination of stocks and bonds (see Figure 7.8) shows that one can achieve an expected return of 13% (matching that of the stock portfolio) with a standard deviation of 18%, which is less than the 20% standard deviation of the stock portfolio.

Concept Check **7.3**

The universe of available securities includes two risky stock funds, A and B, and T-bills. The data for the universe are as follows:

	Expected Return	Standard Deviation
A	10%	20%
B	30	60
T-bills	5	0

The correlation coefficient between funds A and B is −.2.

a. Draw the opportunity set of funds A and B.

b. Find the optimal risky portfolio, P, and its expected return and standard deviation.

c. Find the slope of the CAL supported by T-bills and portfolio P.

d. How much will an investor with A = 5 invest in funds A and B and in T-bills?

7.4   The Markowitz Portfolio Optimization Model

Security Selection

We can generalize the portfolio construction problem to the case of many risky securities and a risk-free asset. As in the two risky assets example, the problem has three parts. First, we identify the risk–return combinations available from the set of risky assets. Next, we identify the optimal portfolio of risky assets by finding the portfolio weights that result in the steepest CAL. Finally, we choose an appropriate complete portfolio by mixing the risk-free asset with the optimal risky portfolio. Before describing the process in detail, let us first present an overview.

The first step is to determine the risk–return opportunities available to the investor. These are summarized by the **minimum-variance frontier** of risky assets. This frontier is a graph of the lowest possible variance that can be attained for a given portfolio expected return. Given the input data for expected returns, variances, and covariances, we can calculate the minimum-variance portfolio consistent with any targeted expected return. The plot of these expected return–standard deviation pairs is presented in Figure 7.10.

Notice that all the individual assets lie to the right inside the frontier, at least when we allow short sales in the construction of risky portfolios.[8] This tells us that risky portfolios comprising only a single asset are inefficient. Diversification allows us to construct portfolios with higher expected returns and lower standard deviations.

All the portfolios that lie on the minimum-variance frontier from the global minimum-variance portfolio and upward provide the best risk–return combinations and thus are candidates for the optimal portfolio. The part of the frontier that lies above the global minimum-variance portfolio, therefore, is called the **efficient frontier of risky assets.**

---

[8]When short sales are prohibited, single securities may lie on the frontier. For example, the security with the highest expected return must lie on the frontier, as that security represents the *only* way that one can obtain a return that high, and so it must also be the minimum-variance way to obtain that return. When short sales are feasible, however, portfolios can be constructed that offer the same expected return and lower variance. These portfolios typically will have short positions in low-expected-return securities.

For any portfolio on the lower portion of the minimum-variance frontier, there is a portfolio with the same standard deviation and a greater expected return positioned directly above it. Hence the bottom part of the minimum-variance frontier is inefficient.

The second part of the optimization plan involves the risk-free asset. As before, we search for the capital allocation line with the highest Sharpe ratio (i.e., the steepest slope) as shown in Figure 7.11.

The CAL generated by the optimal portfolio, P, is the one tangent to the efficient frontier. This CAL dominates all alternative feasible lines (the broken lines that are drawn through the frontier). Portfolio P, therefore, is the optimal risky portfolio.

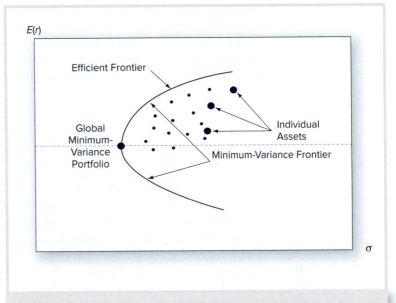

Figure 7.10 The minimum-variance frontier of risky assets

Finally, in the last part of the problem, the individual investor chooses the appropriate mix between the optimal risky portfolio P and T-bills, exactly as in Figure 7.8.

Now let us consider each part of the portfolio construction problem in more detail. In the first part of the problem, risk–return analysis, the portfolio manager needs as inputs a set of estimates for the expected returns of each security and a set of estimates for the covariance matrix. (In Part V, Security Analysis, we will examine the security valuation techniques and methods of financial analysis that analysts use. For now, we will assume that analysts already have spent the time and resources to prepare the inputs.)

The portfolio manager is now armed with the n estimates of $E(r_i)$ and the $n \times n$ estimates of the covariance matrix in which the n diagonal elements are estimates of the variances σ_i^2 and the $n^2 - n = n(n - 1)$ off-diagonal elements are the estimates of the covariances between each pair of asset returns. (You can verify this from Table 7.2 for the case $n = 2$.) We know that each covariance appears twice in this table, so actually we have $n(n - 1)/2$ different covariance estimates. If our portfolio management unit covers 50 securities, our security analysts need to deliver 50 estimates of expected returns, 50 estimates of variances, and $50 \times 49/2 = 1,225$

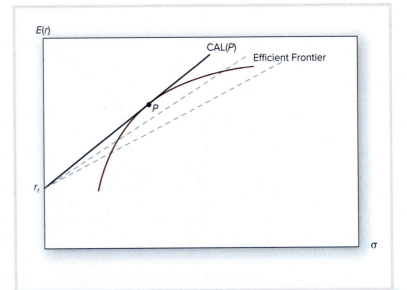

Figure 7.11 The efficient frontier of risky assets with the optimal CAL

different estimates of covariances. This is a daunting task! (We show later how the number of required estimates can be reduced substantially.)

Once these estimates are compiled, the expected return and variance of any risky portfolio with weights in each security, w_i, can be calculated from the bordered covariance matrix or, equivalently, from the following generalizations of Equations 7.2 and 7.3:

$$E(r_p) = \sum_{i=1}^{n} w_i E(r_i) \tag{7.15}$$

$$\sigma_p^2 = \sum_{i=1}^{n} \sum_{j=1}^{n} w_i w_j \, \mathrm{Cov}(r_i, r_j) \tag{7.16}$$

An extended worked example showing how to do this using a spreadsheet is presented in Appendix A of this chapter.

We mentioned earlier that the idea of diversification is age-old. The phrase "don't put all your eggs in one basket" existed long before modern finance theory. It was not until 1952, however, that Harry Markowitz published a formal model of portfolio selection embodying principles of efficient diversification, thereby paving the way for his 1990 Nobel Prize in Economics.[9] His model is precisely step one of portfolio management: the identification of the efficient set of portfolios, or the *efficient frontier of risky assets.*

The principal idea behind the frontier set of risky portfolios is that, for any risk level, we are interested only in that portfolio with the highest expected return. Alternatively, the frontier is the set of portfolios that minimizes the variance for any target expected return.

Indeed, the two methods of computing the efficient set of risky portfolios are equivalent. To see this, consider the graphical representation of these procedures. Figure 7.12 shows the minimum-variance frontier.

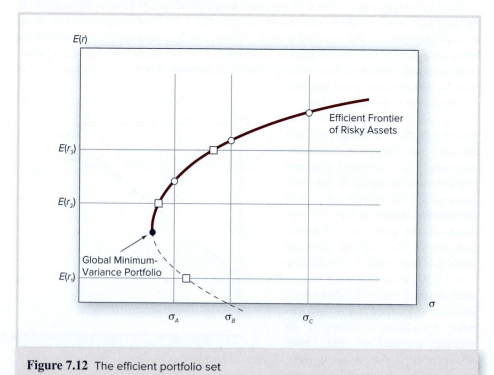

Figure 7.12 The efficient portfolio set

[9]Harry Markowitz, "Portfolio Selection," *Journal of Finance,* March 1952.

The points marked by squares are the result of a variance-minimization program. We first draw the constraints, that is, horizontal lines at the level of required expected returns. We then look for the portfolio with the lowest standard deviation that plots on each horizontal line—in other words, we look for the portfolio that will plot farthest to the left (smallest standard deviation) on that line. When we repeat this for many levels of required expected returns, the shape of the minimum-variance frontier emerges. We then discard the bottom (dashed) half of the frontier, because it is inefficient.

In the alternative approach, we draw a vertical line that represents the standard deviation constraint. We then consider all portfolios that plot on this line (have the same standard deviation) and choose the one with the highest expected return, that is, the portfolio that plots highest on this vertical line. Repeating this procedure for many vertical lines (levels of standard deviation) gives us the points marked by circles that trace the upper portion of the minimum-variance frontier, the efficient frontier.

When this step is completed, we have a list of efficient portfolios because the solution to the optimization program includes the portfolio proportions, w_i, the expected return, $E(r_p)$, and the standard deviation, σ_p.

Let us restate what our portfolio manager has done so far. The estimates generated by the security analysts were transformed into a set of expected rates of return and a covariance matrix. We call this group of estimates the **input list.** This input list is then fed into the optimization program.

Before we proceed to the second step of choosing the optimal risky portfolio from the frontier set, let us consider a practical point. Some clients may be subject to additional constraints. For example, many institutions are prohibited from taking short positions in any asset. For these clients the portfolio manager will add to the optimization program constraints that rule out negative (short) positions in the search for efficient portfolios. In this special case it is possible that single assets may be, in and of themselves, efficient risky portfolios. For example, the asset with the highest expected return will be a frontier portfolio because, without the opportunity of short sales, the only way to obtain that rate of return is to hold the asset as one's entire risky portfolio.

Short-sale restrictions are by no means the only such constraints. For example, some clients may want to ensure a minimal level of expected dividend yield from the optimal portfolio. In this case the input list will be expanded to include a set of expected dividend yields $d_1, \ldots, d_n$ and the optimization program will include an additional constraint that ensures that the expected dividend yield of the portfolio will equal or exceed the desired level, d.

Another type of constraint is aimed at ruling out investments in industries or countries considered ethically or politically undesirable. This is referred to as *socially responsible investing.* Portfolio managers can tailor the efficient set to conform to any desire of the client. Of course, any constraint carries a price tag in the sense that an efficient frontier constructed subject to extra constraints will offer a Sharpe ratio inferior to that of a less constrained one. The client should be made aware of this cost and should carefully consider constraints that are not mandated by law.

Capital Allocation and the Separation Property

Now that we have the efficient frontier, we proceed to step two and introduce the risk-free asset. Figure 7.13 shows the efficient frontier plus three CALs representing various portfolios from the efficient set. As before, we ratchet up the CAL by selecting different portfolios until we reach portfolio P, which is the tangency point of a line from F to the efficient

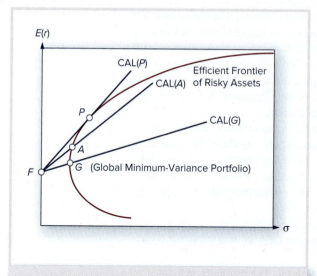

Figure 7.13 Capital allocation lines with various portfolios from the efficient set

frontier. Portfolio *P* maximizes the Sharpe ratio, the slope of the CAL from *F* to portfolios on the efficient frontier. At this point our portfolio manager is done. Portfolio *P* is the optimal risky portfolio for the manager's clients.

There is yet another way to find the best risky portfolio. In this approach, we ask the spreadsheet program to maximize the Sharpe ratio of portfolio *P.* The reason this is worth mentioning is that we can skip the charting of the efficient frontier altogether and proceed directly to find the portfolio that produces the steepest CAL. The program maximizes the Sharpe ratio with no constraint on expected return or variance at all (using just the constraint that portfolio weights must sum to 1.0). Examination of Figure 7.13 shows that the solution strategy is to find the portfolio producing the highest slope of the CAL (Sharpe ratio) regardless of expected return or SD. Expected return and standard deviation are easily computed from the optimal portfolio weights applied to the input list in Equations 7.15 and 7.16. While this last approach does not produce the entire minimum-variance frontier, in many applications, only the optimal risky portfolio is necessary.

This is a good time to ponder our results and their implementation. The most striking conclusion is that a portfolio manager will offer the same risky portfolio, *P,* to all clients regardless of their degree of risk aversion.[10] The client's risk aversion comes into play only in capital allocation, the selection of the desired point *along* the CAL. Thus the only difference between clients' choices is that the more risk-averse client will invest more in the risk-free asset and less in the optimal risky portfolio than will a less risk-averse client. However, both will use portfolio *P* as their optimal risky investment vehicle.

This result is called a **separation property;** it tells us that the portfolio choice problem may be separated into two independent tasks.[11] The first task, determination of the optimal risky portfolio, is purely technical. Given the manager's input list, the best risky portfolio is the same for all clients, regardless of risk aversion. However, the second task, capital allocation, depends on personal preference. Here the client is the decision maker.

The crucial point is that the optimal portfolio *P* that the manager offers is the same for all clients. Put another way, investors with varying degrees of risk aversion would be satisfied with a universe of only two mutual funds: a money market fund for risk-free investments and a mutual fund that holds the optimal risky portfolio, *P,* on the tangency point of the CAL and the efficient frontier. This result makes professional management more efficient and hence less costly. One management firm can serve any number of clients with relatively small incremental administrative costs.

[10]Clients who impose special restrictions (constraints) on the manager, such as dividend yield, will obtain another optimal portfolio. Any constraint that is added to an optimization problem leads, in general, to a different and inferior optimum compared to an unconstrained program.

[11]The separation property was first noted by Nobel Laureate James Tobin, "Liquidity Preference as Behavior toward Risk," *Review of Economic Statistics* 25 (February 1958), pp. 65–86.

A spreadsheet model featuring optimal risky portfolios is available in Connect or through your course instructor. It contains a template similar to the template developed in this section. The model can be used to find optimal mixes of securities for targeted levels of returns for both restricted and unrestricted portfolios. Graphs of the efficient frontier are generated for each set of inputs. The example available at our Web site applies the model to portfolios constructed from equity indexes (called WEBS securities) of several countries.

Excel Questions

1. Find the optimal risky portfolio formed from the eight country index portfolios using the data provided in this box. What is the mean and variance of that portfolio's rate of return?

2. Does the optimal risky portfolio entail a short position in any index? If it does, redo Question 1 but now impose a constraint barring short positions. Explain why this constrained portfolio offers a less attractive risk–return trade-off than the unconstrained portfolio in Question 1.

	A	B	C	D	E	F
1	Efficient Frontier for World Equity Benchmark Securities (WEBS)					
2						
3		Mean	Standard			
4	WEBS	Return	Deviation	Country		
5	EWD	15.5393	26.4868	Sweden		
6	EWH	6.3852	41.1475	Hong Kong		
7	EWI	26.5999	26.0514	Italy		
8	EWJ	1.4133	26.0709	Japan		
9	EWL	18.0745	21.6916	Switzerland		
10	EWP	18.6347	25.0779	Spain		
11	EWW	16.2243	38.7686	Mexico		
12	S&P 500	17.2306	17.1944	U.S.		

In practice, however, different managers will estimate different input lists, thus deriving different efficient frontiers, and offer different "optimal" portfolios to their clients. The source of the disparity lies in the security analysis. It is worth mentioning here that the universal rule of GIGO (garbage in–garbage out) also applies to security analysis. If the quality of the security analysis is poor, a passive portfolio such as a market index fund will result in a higher Sharpe ratio than an active portfolio that uses low-quality security analysis to tilt portfolio weights toward *seemingly* favorable (mispriced) securities.

One particular input list that would lead to a worthless estimate of the efficient frontier is based on recent security average returns. If sample average returns over recent years are used as proxies for the future return on the security, the noise in those estimates will make the resultant efficient frontier virtually useless for portfolio construction.

Consider a stock with an annual standard deviation of 50%. Even if one were to use a 10-year average to estimate its expected return (and 10 years is almost ancient history in the life of a corporation), the standard deviation of that estimate would still be $50/\sqrt{10} = 15.8\%$. Given this level of imprecision, the chances that the sample average represents expected returns for the coming year are negligible.[12]

As we have seen, optimal risky portfolios for different clients also may vary because of portfolio constraints such as dividend-yield requirements, tax considerations, or other

---

[12]Moreover, you cannot avoid this problem by observing the rate of return on the stock more frequently. In Chapter 5 we pointed out that the accuracy of the sample average as an estimate of expected return depends on the length of the sample period; it is not improved by sampling more frequently within a given sample period.

client preferences. Nevertheless, this analysis suggests that a limited number of portfolios may be sufficient to serve the demands of a wide range of investors. This is the theoretical basis of the mutual fund industry.

The (computerized) optimization technique is the easiest part of the portfolio construction problem. The real arena of competition among portfolio managers is in sophisticated security analysis. This analysis, as well as its proper interpretation, is part of the art of portfolio construction.[13]

Concept Check **7.4**

Suppose that two portfolio managers who work for competing investment management houses each employ a group of security analysts to prepare the input list for the Markowitz algorithm. When all is completed, it turns out that the efficient frontier obtained by portfolio manager *A* dominates that of manager *B*. By *dominate,* we mean that *A*'s optimal risky portfolio lies northwest of *B*'s. Hence, given a choice, investors will all prefer the risky portfolio that lies on the CAL of *A*.

a. What should be made of this outcome?

b. Should it be attributed to better security analysis by *A*'s analysts?

c. Could it be that *A*'s computer program is superior?

d. If you were advising clients (and had an advance glimpse at the efficient frontiers of various managers), would you tell them to periodically switch their money to the manager with the most northwesterly portfolio?

The Power of Diversification

Section 7.1 introduced the concept of diversification and the limits to the benefits of diversification resulting from systematic risk. Given the tools we have developed, we can reconsider this intuition more rigorously and at the same time sharpen our insight regarding the power of diversification.

Recall from Equation 7.16, restated here, that the general formula for the variance of a portfolio composed of n risky assets is

$$\sigma_p^2 = \sum_{i=1}^{n} \sum_{j=1}^{n} w_i w_j \, \mathrm{Cov}(r_i, r_j) \tag{7.16}$$

Consider now the naïve diversification strategy in which an *equally weighted* portfolio is constructed, meaning that $w_i = 1/n$ for each security. In this case Equation 7.16 may be rewritten as follows, where we break out the terms for which $i = j$ into a separate sum, noting that $\mathrm{Cov}(r_i, r_i) = \sigma_i^2$:

$$\sigma_p^2 = \frac{1}{n} \sum_{i=1}^{n} \frac{1}{n} \sigma_i^2 + \sum_{\substack{j=1 \\ j \neq i}}^{n} \sum_{i=1}^{n} \frac{1}{n^2} \, \mathrm{Cov}(r_i, r_j) \tag{7.17}$$

Note that there are n variance terms and $n(n-1)$ covariance terms in Equation 7.17.

---

[13]You can find a nice discussion of some practical issues in implementing efficient diversification in a white paper prepared by Wealthcare Capital Management at this address: **www.financeware.com/ruminations/WP_ EfficiencyDeficiency.pdf.** A copy of the report is also available in Connect.

If we define the average variance and average covariance of the securities as

$$\bar{\sigma}^2 = \frac{1}{n} \sum_{i=1}^{n} \sigma_i^2 \qquad (7.18)$$

$$\overline{\text{Cov}} = \frac{1}{n(n-1)} \sum_{\substack{j=1 \\ j \neq i}}^{n} \sum_{i=1}^{n} \text{Cov}(r_i, r_j) \qquad (7.19)$$

we can express portfolio variance as

$$\sigma_p^2 = \frac{1}{n} \bar{\sigma}^2 + \frac{n-1}{n} \overline{\text{Cov}} \qquad (7.20)$$

Now examine the effect of diversification. When the average covariance among security returns is zero, as it would be if all risk were firm-specific, portfolio variance can be driven to zero. We see this from Equation 7.20. The second term on the right-hand side will be zero in this scenario, while the first term approaches zero as n becomes larger. Hence when security returns are uncorrelated, the power of diversification to reduce portfolio risk is unlimited.

However, the more important case is the one in which economywide risk factors impart positive correlation among stock returns. In this case, as the portfolio becomes more highly diversified (n increases), portfolio variance remains positive. Although firm-specific risk, represented by the first term in Equation 7.20, approaches zero as diversification increases (n gets ever larger), the second term simply approaches $\overline{\text{Cov}}$. [Note that $(n - 1)/n = 1 - 1/n$, which approaches 1 for large n.] Thus, the irreducible risk of a diversified portfolio depends on the covariance of the returns of the component securities, which in turn is a function of the importance of systematic factors in the economy.

To see further the fundamental relationship between systematic risk and security correlations, suppose for simplicity that all securities have a common standard deviation, σ, and all security pairs have a common correlation coefficient, ρ. Then the covariance between any pair of securities is $\rho\sigma^2$, and Equation 7.20 becomes

$$\sigma_p^2 = \frac{1}{n} \sigma^2 + \frac{n-1}{n} \rho\sigma^2 \qquad (7.21)$$

The effect of correlation is now explicit. When $\rho = 0$, we again obtain the insurance principle, where portfolio variance approaches zero as n becomes greater. For $\rho > 0$, however, portfolio variance remains positive. In fact, for $\rho = 1$, portfolio variance equals σ^2 regardless of n, demonstrating that diversification is of no benefit: In the case of perfect correlation, all risk is systematic. More generally, as n becomes ever larger, Equation 7.21 shows that variance approaches $\rho\sigma^2$. We can think of this limit as the "systematic variance" of the security market.

Table 7.4 presents portfolio standard deviation as we include ever-greater numbers of securities in the portfolio for two cases, $\rho = 0$ and $\rho = .40$. The table takes σ to be 50%. As one would expect, portfolio risk is greater when $\rho = .40$. More surprising, perhaps, is that portfolio risk diminishes far less rapidly as n increases in the positive correlation case. The correlation among security returns limits the power of diversification.

Note that for a 100-security portfolio, the standard deviation is 5% in the uncorrelated case—still significant compared to the potential of zero standard deviation. For $\rho = .40$, the standard deviation is high, 31.86%, yet it is very close to undiversifiable systematic standard deviation in the infinite-sized security universe, $\sqrt{\rho\sigma^2} = \sqrt{.4 \times 50^2} = 31.62\%$. At this point, further diversification is of little value.

Table 7.4

Risk reduction of equally weighted portfolios in correlated and uncorrelated universes

		$\rho = 0$		$\rho = 0.40$	
Universe Size n	Portfolio Weights $w = 1/n$ (%)	Standard Deviation (%)	Reduction in σ	Standard Deviation (%)	Reduction in σ
1	100	50.00	14.64	50.00	8.17
2	50	35.36		41.83	
5	20	22.36	1.95	36.06	0.70
6	16.67	20.41		35.36	
10	10	15.81	0.73	33.91	0.20
11	9.09	15.08		33.71	
20	5	11.18	0.27	32.79	0.06
21	4.76	10.91		32.73	
100	1	5.00	0.02	31.86	0.00
101	0.99	4.98		31.86	

Perhaps the most important insight from the exercise is this: When we hold diversified portfolios, the contribution to portfolio risk of a particular security will depend on the *covariance* of that security's return with those of other securities, and *not* on the security's variance. As we shall see in Chapter 9, this implies that fair risk premiums also should depend on covariances rather than total variability of returns.

 Concept Check **7.5**

Suppose that the universe of available risky securities consists of a large number of stocks, identically distributed with $E(r) = 15\%$, $\sigma = 60\%$, and a common correlation coefficient of $\rho = .5$.

a. What are the expected return and standard deviation of an equally weighted risky portfolio of 25 stocks?

b. What is the smallest number of stocks necessary to generate an efficient portfolio with a standard deviation equal to or smaller than 43%?

c. What is the systematic risk in this security universe?

d. If T-bills are available and yield 10%, what is the slope of the CML? (Because of the symmetry assumed for all securities in the investment universe, the market index in this economy will be an equally weighted portfolio of all stocks.)

Asset Allocation and Security Selection

As we have seen, the mathematical descriptions of security selection and asset allocation are identical. Both activities call for the construction of an efficient frontier and the choice of a particular portfolio from along that frontier. The determination of the optimal combination of securities proceeds in the same manner as the analysis of the optimal combination of asset classes. Why, then, do we (and the investment community) distinguish between asset allocation and security selection?

Three factors are at work. First, as a result of greater need and ability to save (for college educations, recreation, longer life in retirement, health care needs, etc.), the demand for sophisticated investment management has increased enormously. Second, the widening spectrum of financial markets and financial instruments has put sophisticated investment beyond the capacity of many amateur investors. Finally, there are strong economies of scale in investment analysis. The end result is that the size of a competitive investment company has grown with the industry, and efficiency in organization has become an important issue.

A large investment company is likely to invest both in domestic and international markets and in a broad set of asset classes, each of which requires specialized expertise. Hence the management of each asset-class portfolio needs to be decentralized, and it becomes impossible to simultaneously optimize the entire organization's risky portfolio in one stage, although this would be prescribed as optimal on *theoretical* grounds. In future chapters we will see how optimization of decentralized portfolios can be mindful as well of the entire portfolio of which they are a part.

The practice is, therefore, to optimize the security selection of each asset-class portfolio independently. At the same time, top management continually updates the asset allocation of the organization, adjusting the investment budget allotted to each asset-class portfolio.

Optimal Portfolios and Non-Normal Returns

The portfolio optimization techniques we have used so far assume normal distributions of returns in that standard deviation is taken to be a fully adequate measure of risk. However, potential non-normality of returns requires us to pay attention as well to risk measures that focus on worst-case losses such as value at risk (VaR) or expected shortfall (ES).

In Chapter 6 we suggested that capital allocation to the risky portfolio ideally should account for fat-tailed distributions that can result in extreme values of VaR and ES. Specifically, forecasts of greater than normal VaR and ES should encourage more moderate capital allocations to the risky portfolio. Accounting for the effect of diversification on VaR and ES would be useful as well. Unfortunately, the impact of diversification on tail risk cannot be easily estimated.

A practical way to estimate values of VaR and ES in the presence of fat tails is called *bootstrapping*. We start with a historical sample of returns of each asset in our prospective portfolio. We compute the portfolio return corresponding to a draw of one return from each asset's history. We thus calculate hypothetical (but still empirically based) returns on as many of these random portfolio returns as we wish. Fifty thousand portfolio returns produced in this way can provide a good estimate of VaR and ES values. The forecasted values for VaR and ES of the mean-variance optimal portfolio can then be compared to other candidate portfolios. If these other portfolios yield sufficiently better VaR and ES values, we may prefer one of those to the mean-variance efficient portfolio.

7.5   Risk Pooling, Risk Sharing, and the Risk of Long-Term Investments*

Diversification entails spreading the investment budget across a variety of assets in order to limit overall risk. It is common, as we have done here, to use the analogy between insurance companies spreading risk across policies and investors diversifying their portfolios to illustrate how diversification reduces risk. While that analogy is useful, we actually have to be a bit careful about the source of the risk reduction. We will see here that risk reduction actually requires both *risk pooling* (spreading your exposures across multiple uncorrelated

*The material in this section is more challenging. It may be skipped without impairing the ability to understand later chapters.

risky ventures) as well as *risk sharing* (allowing other investors to share in the risk of a portfolio of assets). The utility of capital markets in a developed economy rests in large part on this distinction.

The confusion between the roles of risk pooling and risk sharing leads to another, related confusion. A widespread, but incorrect, belief is that spreading investments across time, so that average performance reflects returns in several investment periods, offers a sort of "time diversification." Many observers argue that time diversification can make long-term investing less risky. We will see that extending the horizon of a risky investment is analogous to risk pooling. But this application of "the insurance principle" to long-term investments ignores the crucial role of risk sharing in portfolio risk management, and can easily lead to poor investment decisions. Long-term investments are *not* necessarily safer.

In this section, therefore, we try to clarify these issues and explore the appropriate extension of the insurance principle to investment risk over different horizons. We start by reviewing the respective contributions of risk pooling and risk sharing to the benefits of portfolio diversification. With these insights in hand, we can better understand the risk of long-term investments.

Risk Pooling and the Insurance Principle

Risk pooling means adding uncorrelated, risky projects to the investor's portfolio. Applied to the insurance business, risk pooling entails selling many uncorrelated insurance policies. This application of risk pooling as a means to reduce risk has therefore come to be known as the *insurance principle*. Conventional wisdom holds that such pooling is the driving force behind risk management for the insurance industry.

But even brief reflection should convince you that risk pooling cannot be the entire story. How can *adding* new bets (selling additional insurance policies) that are independent of your other bets reduce your total exposure to risk? This would be little different from a gambler in Las Vegas arguing that a few more trips to the roulette table will reduce his total risk by diversifying his overall "portfolio" of wagers. You would immediately realize that the gambler now has more money at stake, and the overall uncertainty in his wealth is clearly greater: While his average gain or loss *per bet* may become more predictable as he repeatedly returns to the table, his total proceeds become less so.

Think about investing $1 in a single risky security, call it *A*, with risky rate of return r_A and total payoff of $1 + r_A$ dollars. The mean of r_A is $E(r)$, the standard deviation is σ, and the variance is σ^2. Now think about risk pooling by taking on another investment of $1 in an *uncorrelated* investment, call it *B*, with return r_B that has the same mean and variance as security *A*. The total payoff to your two-asset portfolio, which we will call portfolio *P*, is $(1 + r_A) + (1 + r_B)$.

The expected *dollar* profit on your $2 investment is $2 \times E(r)$, and, because the covariance between the two investments is zero, the variance of the dollar payoff is $\text{Var}(r_A + r_B) = 2\sigma^2$. It is clear that with double the variance, this position is riskier than one invested only in asset *A*. This is just like the gambler in Las Vegas who goes to the roulette table twice rather than once.

But this greater risk is not readily apparent when we compute only the rate of return statistics of the portfolio. With half the portfolio invested in *A* and half in *B*, the weights on each security are $1/2$, so the expected *rate* of return and the volatility of the rate of return on the two-asset portfolio are:

$$E(r_P) = \tfrac{1}{2} E(r) + \tfrac{1}{2} E(r) = E(r)$$
$$\text{Var}(r_P) = (\tfrac{1}{2})^2 \sigma^2 + (\tfrac{1}{2})^2 \sigma^2 + 2 \times \tfrac{1}{2} \times \tfrac{1}{2} \times \text{Cov}(r_A, r_B) = \tfrac{1}{2} \sigma^2$$
$$\text{SD}(r_P) = \sigma_P = \sqrt{\tfrac{1}{2}} \times \sigma$$

It *looks* like the "diversified" two-asset portfolio is safer; its variance has fallen by a factor of $\frac{1}{2}$. But this apparent safety is an illusion. While its *rate* of return is more predictable, we know the dollar variance of the "risk-pooled portfolio" is double the variance of the one-asset portfolio. Again, this is just like our Las Vegas gambler. With every trip to the roulette table, *percentage* gains (in this case, losses) are more predictable, but *dollar* gains or losses are less so.

Why do we obtain these seemingly conflicting signals of risk? Because we are comparing two portfolios of different sizes. The first investment, in asset *A,* is for only $1. The investment in the two-asset risk-pooled portfolio, *P,* is $2. With twice as much money at risk, it's no wonder that the two-asset portfolio has riskier dollar profits even if its rate of return is more predictable. The standard deviation of the *dollar* profit of portfolio *P* is $2 \times$ $\sigma_P = \$2 \times [\sqrt{1/2} \times \sigma] = \sqrt{2} \times \sigma$, and the variance is $2\sigma^2$, just as we found above.

Risk Sharing

Now think of a variation on our investor's two-asset portfolio. Let him start as before, by putting a dollar into both assets *A* and *B,* but now imagine that he sells off half of his total investment to other investors. In so doing, he augments his risk-pooling strategy with a **risk sharing** strategy. Crucially, this strategy maintains the size of his total investment at $1, even as he adds the second security to his portfolio. Now that the investor's total investment is held fixed, we can compare portfolios using their expected rates of return together with the standard deviation and variance of those rates of return. This is because the rates of return are now applied to the same investment base, and we don't have to worry about scaling up these risk and return measures by the different amounts put at risk.[14]

We've already established that the rate of return on the two-asset portfolio is $\frac{1}{2}(r_A + r_B)$, with expected return $E(r)$ and standard deviation $\sqrt{1/2} \times \sigma$. This reduction in standard deviation on a fixed $1 investment is truly a reduction in risk. Risk pooling, *together with risk sharing,* results in portfolios with a superior risk–return trade-off, in this example, a portfolio with the same expected return but lower volatility.

What does this have to do with the insurance principle? Risk pooling is a large part of what makes the insurance industry tick. But by itself, risk pooling actually increases the volatility of profits as the company writes more and more policies. However, when risk sharing is part of the strategy, allowing more and more investors to share the risk, each investor's personal investment does not have to grow as the insurance company sells more policies. Instead, the many thousands of investors who own shares in the insurance company can determine exactly how much of their investment budget to place in the company independently of how many policies the company has written.

Similarly, capital markets allow investors to gain the benefits of diversification by widely sharing firm-specific risks. When an investor adds more stocks to a risky portfolio but leaves the total size of the portfolio unchanged, she necessarily must own a smaller fraction of each firm included in her portfolio. In other words, she must be sharing progressively more of the risk of that firm with the rest of the capital market. Such sharing reduces her exposure to any particular stock and allows her to be less and less concerned about its firm-specific risk. By enabling investors to combine risk sharing with risk pooling,

[14]There is a good analogy to corporate finance here. You may remember that the IRR rule for evaluating a capital budgeting project expresses profitability on a rate of return basis, whereas the NPV rule evaluates projects in terms of dollar values. While the IRR rule usually will give us the correct accept/reject decision for projects considered in isolation, it does *not* allow you to compare projects of different sizes. In that case, you must use NPV to determine the best choice from a set of mutually exclusive projects. We face a similar problem here. We can't properly compare investments in *A* and *P* using the mean and standard deviation of their rates of return when portfolio *P* is double the size of *A*. But if we compare portfolios of the same size, we *can* compare them using rates of return.

capital markets allow firms to engage in risky projects without imposing undue risk on their shareholders, and in this way facilitate the collective economy's ability to undertake large, possibly risky, ventures.

Diversification and the Sharpe Ratio

While it is clear that risk pooling *by itself* does not reduce risk, we do not mean to suggest that it is unimportant. Risk pooling improves the risk–return trade-off and, therefore, is one crucial part of a diversification strategy. Consider again the one-asset versus two-asset investments above. Security A has a Sharpe ratio of

$$S_A = [E(r) - r_f]/\sigma$$

while the ratio for the two-asset risk-pooled portfolio P is

$$S_P = \frac{\text{Expected dollar risk premium}}{\text{SD(dollar profit)}} = \frac{2\,[E(r) - r_f]}{\sigma\sqrt{2}} = \sqrt{2}S_A$$

The Sharpe ratio for the risk-sharing portfolio (with a fixed \$1 investment) also is $\sqrt{2}$ times that of the one-asset portfolio:

$$\frac{\text{Expected dollar risk premium}}{\text{SD(dollar profit)}} = \frac{E(r) - r_f}{\sigma/\sqrt{2}} = \sqrt{2}S_A$$

Thus, risk pooling improves the Sharpe ratio, regardless of whether risk sharing is part of the strategy.

To summarize, when risk was simply pooled by adding a second, uncorrelated, asset to the initial one-asset portfolio, the expected dollar risk premium doubled, dollar variance doubled, and standard deviation increased by $\sqrt{2}$. Therefore, risk pooling increased the Sharpe ratio by the factor $2/\sqrt{2} = \sqrt{2}$. So while risk increased, the risk–return trade-off was improved. But by adding risk-sharing to the strategy, we reap both the higher Sharpe ratio *as well as* lower total risk. In the risk-sharing strategy, the expected risk premium was unchanged, and standard deviation fell by $\sqrt{2}$. The Sharpe ratio increased by $\sqrt{2}$, just as for the risk-pooling strategy.

These results generalize to diversification beyond two assets. Suppose we consider holding n identical, uncorrelated assets in the portfolio. The expected dollar risk premium scales up in proportion to n in the risk-pooling strategy, but the dollar standard deviation increases by the factor $\sqrt{n}$. Therefore, the Sharpe ratio increases by a factor $n/\sqrt{n} = \sqrt{n}$. Risk sharing combined with risk pooling (thus holding the size of the investment budget fixed) does not affect the expected risk premium, but it does reduce the standard deviation by the factor $\sqrt{n}$ and therefore also increases the Sharpe ratio by $\sqrt{n}$.

Think back to our gambler at the roulette wheel one last time. He would be wrong to argue that diversification means that 100 bets are less risky than 1 bet. His intuition would be correct, however, if he shared those 100 bets with 100 of his friends. A 1/100 share of 100 bets is in fact less risky than one bet. Fixing the amount of his total money at risk as that money is spread across more independent bets is the way for him to reduce risk. True diversification entails spreading a portfolio of *fixed size* across many assets, not merely adding more risky bets to an ever-growing risky portfolio.

Time Diversification and the Investment Horizon

Now we turn to the implications of risk pooling and risk sharing for long-term investing. Think of extending the investment horizon for another period (which means that we now incur the uncertainty of that period's risky return) as analogous to adding another risky asset to our portfolio or adding a new insurance policy to a pool of existing ones. So it is already clear that we should not expect extending the investment horizon while maintaining a fixed asset allocation in each period to reduce risk.

Examining the impact of an extension of the investment horizon requires us to clarify what the alternative is. Suppose you consider an investment in a risky portfolio over the next two years, which we'll call the "long-term investment." How should you compare this decision to a "short-run investment"? We must compare these two strategies over the same period, that is, two years. The short-term investment therefore must be interpreted as an investment in the risky portfolio over the first year and in the risk-free asset over the second year.

Given this comparison, and assuming the risky return in the first year is uncorrelated with that in the second, it becomes clear that the "long-term" strategy is analogous to the multi-asset risk-pooled portfolio. This is because holding on to the risky investment in the second year (rather than withdrawing to the risk-free asset) piles up more risk, just as selling another insurance policy or adding another risky asset to the portfolio would. While extending a risky investment to a longer horizon improves the Sharpe ratio (as does risk pooling), it also increases risk. Thus "time diversification" is not really diversification.

The more accurate analogy to risk sharing for a long-term horizon would be to spread the risky investment budget across each of the investment periods. Compare the following three strategies applied to the whole investment budget over a two-year horizon:

1. Invest the whole budget at risk for one period, and then withdraw the entire proceeds, placing them in a risk-free asset in the other period. Because you are invested in the risky asset for only one year, the risk premium over the whole investment period is $R = E(r) - r_f$, the SD over the two-year period is σ, and the Sharpe ratio is $S = R/\sigma$.

2. Invest the whole budget in the risky asset for *both* periods. The two-year risk premium is $2R$ (assuming continuously compounded rates), the two-year variance is $2\sigma^2$, the two-year SD is $\sqrt{2}\sigma$, and the Sharpe ratio is $\sqrt{2}\,R/\sigma$. This is analogous to risk pooling, taking two "bets" on the risky portfolio instead of just one.

3. Invest *half* the investment budget in the risky position in *each* of two periods, placing the remainder of funds in the risk-free asset. The risk premium in each year is $\frac{1}{2}R$, and the standard deviation in each year is $\frac{1}{2}\sigma$. Therefore, the two-year cumulative risk premium is R, the two-year variance is $2 \times (\frac{1}{2}\sigma)^2 = \frac{1}{2}\sigma^2$, the SD is $\sigma\sqrt{1/2}$, and the Sharpe ratio is $S = \sqrt{2}R/\sigma$. This is analogous to risk sharing, taking a fractional position in each year's investment return.

Strategy 3 is less risky than either alternative. Its expected total return equals Strategy 1's, yet its risk is lower and therefore its Sharpe ratio is higher. It achieves the same Sharpe ratio as Strategy 2 but with standard deviation reduced by a factor of $\sqrt{2}$. In summary, its Sharpe ratio is at least as good as either alternative and, more to the point, its total risk is less than either.

We conclude that risk does not fade in the long run. An investor who contemplates investing in an attractive portfolio, and considers investing a given amount in that portfolio for one period, would find it preferable to put money at risk in that portfolio in as many periods as is feasible; however, to limit cumulative risk, he must also correspondingly decrease the risky budget in each period. If "time diversification" really were a way to limit risk, one would expect it to allow longer-term investors to increase the amount invested in the risky portfolio without increasing the risk of final wealth, but that is unfortunately not the case.

SUMMARY

1. The expected return of a portfolio is the weighted average of the component security expected returns with the investment proportions as weights.

2. The variance of a portfolio is the weighted sum of the elements of the covariance matrix with the product of the investment proportions as weights. Thus the variance of each asset is weighted by the square of its investment proportion. The covariance of each pair of assets appears twice in the covariance matrix; thus the portfolio variance includes twice each covariance weighted by the product of the investment proportions in each of the two assets.

3. Even if the covariances are positive, the portfolio standard deviation is less than the weighted average of the component standard deviations, as long as the assets are not perfectly positively correlated. Thus, portfolio diversification is of value as long as assets are less than perfectly correlated.

4. The greater an asset's covariance with the other assets in the portfolio, the more it contributes to portfolio variance. An asset that is perfectly negatively correlated with a portfolio can serve as a perfect hedge. That perfect hedge asset can reduce the portfolio variance to zero.

5. The efficient frontier is the graphical representation of a set of portfolios that maximize expected return for each level of portfolio risk. Rational investors will choose a portfolio on the efficient frontier.

6. A portfolio manager identifies the efficient frontier by first establishing estimates for asset expected returns and the covariance matrix. This input list is then fed into an optimization program that produces as outputs the investment proportions, expected returns, and standard deviations of the portfolios on the efficient frontier.

7. In general, portfolio managers will arrive at different efficient portfolios because of differences in methods and quality of security analysis. Managers compete on the quality of their security analysis relative to their management fees.

8. If a risk-free asset is available and input lists are identical, all investors will choose the same portfolio on the efficient frontier of risky assets: the portfolio tangent to the CAL. All investors with identical input lists will hold an identical risky portfolio, differing only in how much each allocates to this optimal portfolio and to the risk-free asset. This result is characterized as the separation principle of portfolio construction.

9. Diversification is based on the allocation of a portfolio of fixed size across several assets, limiting the exposure to any one source of risk. Adding additional risky assets to a portfolio, thereby increasing the total amount invested, does not reduce dollar risk, even if it makes the *rate* of return more predictable. This is because that uncertainty is applied to a larger investment base. Nor does investing over longer horizons reduce risk. Increasing the investment horizon is analogous to investing in more assets. It increases total risk. Analogously, the key to the insurance industry is risk sharing—the spreading of many independent sources of risk across many investors, each of whom takes on only a small exposure to any particular source of risk.

KEY TERMS

diversification	nonsystematic risk	minimum-variance frontier
insurance principle	diversifiable risk	efficient frontier of risky
market risk	minimum-variance	assets
systematic risk	portfolio	input list
nondiversifiable risk	portfolio opportunity set	separation property
unique risk	Sharpe ratio	risk pooling
firm-specific risk	optimal risky portfolio	risk sharing

KEY EQUATIONS

The expected rate of return on a portfolio: $E(r_p) = w_D E(r_D) + w_E E(r_E)$

The variance of the return on a portfolio: $\sigma_p^2 = (w_D \sigma_D)^2 + (w_E \sigma_E)^2 + 2(w_D \sigma_D)(w_E \sigma_E)\rho_{DE}$

The Sharpe ratio of a portfolio: $S_p = \dfrac{E(r_p) - r_f}{\sigma_p}$

Sharpe ratio maximizing portfolio weights with two risky assets (D and E) and a risk-free asset:

$$w_D = \frac{\left[E(r_D) - r_f\right]\sigma_E^2 - \left[E(r_E) - r_f\right]\sigma_D \sigma_E \rho_{DE}}{\left[E(r_D) - r_f\right]\sigma_E^2 + \left[E(r_E) - r_f\right]\sigma_D^2 - \left[E(r_D) - r_f + E(r_E) - r_f\right]\sigma_D \sigma_E \rho_{DE}}$$

$$w_E = 1 - w_D$$

Optimal capital allocation to the risky asset, y: $\dfrac{E(r_p) - r_f}{A\sigma_p^2}$

PROBLEM SETS

1. Which of the following factors reflect *pure* market risk for a given corporation?
   a. Increased short-term interest rates.
   b. Fire in the corporate warehouse.
   c. Increased insurance costs.
   d. Death of the CEO.
   e. Increased labor costs.

2. When adding real estate to an asset allocation program that currently includes only stocks, bonds, and cash, which of the properties of real estate returns affect portfolio risk? Explain.
   a. Standard deviation.
   b. Expected return.
   c. Correlation with returns of the other asset classes.

3. Which of the following statements about the minimum-variance portfolio of all risky securities is valid? (Assume short sales are allowed.) Explain.
   a. Its variance must be lower than those of all other securities or portfolios.
   b. Its expected return can be lower than the risk-free rate.
   c. It may be the optimal risky portfolio.
   d. It must include all individual securities.

The following data apply to Problems 4 through 10: A pension fund manager is considering three mutual funds. The first is a stock fund, the second is a long-term government and corporate bond fund, and the third is a T-bill money market fund that yields a rate of 8%. The probability distribution of the risky funds is as follows:

	Expected Return	Standard Deviation
Stock fund (S)	20%	30%
Bond fund (B)	12	15

The correlation between the fund returns is .10.

4. What are the investment proportions in the minimum-variance portfolio of the two risky funds, and what is the expected value and standard deviation of its rate of return?

5. Tabulate and draw the investment opportunity set of the two risky funds. Use investment proportions for the stock fund of 0% to 100% in increments of 20%.

6. Draw a tangent from the risk-free rate to the opportunity set. What does your graph show for the expected return and standard deviation of the optimal portfolio?

7. Solve numerically for the proportions of each asset and for the expected return and standard deviation of the optimal risky portfolio.

8. What is the Sharpe ratio of the best feasible CAL?

9. You require that your portfolio yield an expected return of 14%, and that it be efficient, on the best feasible CAL.

   a. What is the standard deviation of your portfolio?
   b. What is the proportion invested in the T-bill fund and each of the two risky funds?

10. If you were to use only the two risky funds, and still require an expected return of 14%, what would be the investment proportions of your portfolio? Compare its standard deviation to that of the optimized portfolio in Problem 9. What do you conclude?

11. Stocks offer an expected rate of return of 18%, with a standard deviation of 22%. Gold offers an expected return of 10% with a standard deviation of 30%.

   a. In light of the apparent inferiority of gold with respect to both mean return and volatility, would anyone hold gold? If so, demonstrate graphically why one would do so.
   b. Given the data above, reanswer (a) with the additional assumption that the correlation coefficient between gold and stocks equals 1. Draw a graph illustrating why one would or would not hold gold in one's portfolio.
   c. Could the set of assumptions in part (b) for expected returns, standard deviations, and correlation represent an equilibrium for the security market?

12. Suppose that there are many stocks in the security market and that the characteristics of stocks A and B are given as follows:

Stock	Expected Return	Standard Deviation
A	10%	5%
B	15	10

Correlation = −1

Suppose that it is possible to borrow at the risk-free rate, r_f. What must be the value of the risk-free rate? (*Hint:* Think about constructing a risk-free portfolio from stocks A and B.)

13. True or false: Assume that expected returns and standard deviations for all securities (including the risk-free rate for borrowing and lending) are known. In this case, all investors will have the same optimal risky portfolio.

14. True or false: The standard deviation of the portfolio is always equal to the weighted average of the standard deviations of the assets in the portfolio.

15. Suppose you have a project that has a .7 chance of doubling your investment in a year and a .3 chance of halving your investment in a year. What is the standard deviation of the rate of return on this investment?

16. Suppose that you have $1 million and the following two opportunities from which to construct a portfolio:

   a. Risk-free asset earning 12% per year.
   b. Risky asset with expected return of 30% per year and standard deviation of 40%.

   If you construct a portfolio with a standard deviation of 30%, what is its expected rate of return?

The following data are for Problems 17 through 19: The correlation coefficients between several pairs of stocks are as follows: Corr(A, B) = .85; Corr(A, C) = .60; Corr(A, D) = .45. Each stock has an expected return of 8% and a standard deviation of 20%.

17. If your entire portfolio is now composed of stock A and you can add some of only one stock to your portfolio, would you choose (explain your choice):

   a. B
   b. C
   c. D
   d. Need more data

18. Would the answer to Problem 17 change for more risk-averse or risk-tolerant investors? Explain.

19. Suppose that in addition to investing in one more stock you can invest in T-bills as well. Would you change your answers to Problems 17 and 18 if the T-bill rate is 8%?

The following table of compound annual returns by decade applies to Problems 20 and 21.

	1920s*	1930s	1940s	1950s	1960s	1970s	1980s	1990s	2000s
Small-company stocks	−3.72%	7.28%	20.63%	19.01%	13.72%	8.75%	12.46%	13.84%	6.70%
Large-company stocks	18.36	−1.25	9.11	19.41	7.84	5.90	17.60	18.20	−1.00
Long-term gov't bonds	3.98	4.60	3.59	0.25	1.14	6.63	11.50	8.60	5.00
Treasury bills	3.56	0.30	0.37	1.87	3.89	6.29	9.00	5.02	2.70
Inflation	−1.00	−2.04	5.36	2.22	2.52	7.36	5.10	2.93	2.50

*Based on the period 1926–1929.

20. Input the data from the table into a spreadsheet. Compute the serial correlation in decade returns for each asset class and for inflation. Also find the correlation between the returns of various asset classes. What do the data indicate?

21. Convert the asset returns by decade presented in the table into real rates. Repeat the analysis of Problem 20 for the real rates of return.

The following information applies to Problems 22 through 27: Greta, an elderly investor, has a degree of risk aversion of $A = 3$ when applied to return on wealth over a one-year horizon. She is pondering two portfolios, the S&P 500 and a hedge fund, as well as a number of one-year strategies. (All rates are annual and continuously compounded.) The S&P 500 risk premium is estimated at 5% per year, with a SD of 20%. The hedge fund risk premium is estimated at 10% with a SD of 35%. The returns on both of these portfolios in any particular year are uncorrelated with its own returns in other years. They are also uncorrelated with the returns of the other portfolio in other years. The hedge fund claims the correlation coefficient between the annual return on the S&P 500 and the hedge fund return in the same year is zero, but Greta is not fully convinced by this claim.

22. Compute the estimated annual risk premiums, SDs, and Sharpe ratios for the two portfolios.

23. Assuming the correlation between the annual returns on the two portfolios is indeed zero, what would be the optimal asset allocation?

24. What should be Greta's capital allocation?

25. If the correlation coefficient between annual portfolio returns is actually .3, what is the covariance between the returns?

26. Repeat Problem 23 using an annual correlation of .3.

27. Repeat Problem 24 using an annual correlation of .3.

The following data apply to CFA Problems 1 through 3: Hennessy & Associates manages a $30 million equity portfolio for the multimanager Wilstead Pension Fund. Jason Jones, financial vice president of Wilstead, noted that Hennessy had rather consistently achieved the best record among the Wilstead's six equity managers. Performance of the Hennessy portfolio had been clearly superior to that of the S&P 500 in four of the past five years. In the one less-favorable year, the shortfall was trivial.

   Hennessy is a "bottom-up" manager. The firm largely avoids any attempt to "time the market." It also focuses on selection of individual stocks, rather than the weighting of favored industries.

   There is no apparent conformity of style among Wilstead's six equity managers. The five managers, other than Hennessy, manage portfolios aggregating $250 million made up of more than 150 individual issues.

   Jones is convinced that Hennessy is able to apply superior skill to stock selection, but the favorable returns are limited by the high degree of diversification in the portfolio. Over the years, the portfolio generally held 40–50 stocks, with about 2%–3% of total funds committed to each issue.

The reason Hennessy seemed to do well most years was that the firm was able to identify each year 10 or 12 issues that registered particularly large gains.

On the basis of this overview, Jones outlined the following plan to the Wilstead pension committee:

> Let's tell Hennessy to limit the portfolio to no more than 20 stocks. Hennessy will double the commitments to the stocks that it really favors, and eliminate the remainder. Except for this one new restriction, Hennessy should be free to manage the portfolio exactly as before.

All the members of the pension committee generally supported Jones's proposal because all agreed that Hennessy had seemed to demonstrate superior skill in selecting stocks. Yet the proposal was a considerable departure from previous practice, and several committee members raised questions. Respond to each of the following questions.

1. *a.* Will the limitation to 20 stocks likely increase or decrease the risk of the portfolio? Explain.
   b. Is there any way Hennessy could reduce the number of issues from 40 to 20 without significantly affecting risk? Explain.

2. One committee member was particularly enthusiastic concerning Jones's proposal. He suggested that Hennessy's performance might benefit further from reduction in the number of issues to 10. If the reduction to 20 could be expected to be advantageous, explain why reduction to 10 might be less likely to be advantageous. (Assume that Wilstead will evaluate the Hennessy portfolio independently of the other portfolios in the fund.)

3. Another committee member suggested that, rather than evaluate each managed portfolio independently of other portfolios, it might be better to consider the effects of a change in the Hennessy portfolio on the total fund. Explain how this broader point of view could affect the committee decision to limit the holdings in the Hennessy portfolio to either 10 or 20 issues.

4. Which one of the following portfolios cannot lie on the efficient frontier as described by Markowitz?

	Portfolio	Expected Return (%)	Standard Deviation (%)
a.	W	15	36
b.	X	12	15
c.	Z	5	7
d.	Y	9	21

5. Which statement about portfolio diversification is correct?
   a. Proper diversification can reduce or eliminate systematic risk.
   b. Diversification reduces the portfolio's expected return because it reduces a portfolio's total risk.
   c. As more securities are added to a portfolio, total risk typically can be expected to fall at a decreasing rate.
   d. The risk-reducing benefits of diversification do not occur meaningfully until at least 30 individual securities are included in the portfolio.

6. The measure of risk for a security held in a diversified portfolio is:
   a. Specific risk.
   b. Standard deviation of returns.
   c. Reinvestment risk.
   d. Covariance.

7. Portfolio theory as described by Markowitz is most concerned with:
   a. The elimination of systematic risk.
   b. The effect of diversification on portfolio risk.
   c. The identification of unsystematic risk.
   d. Active portfolio management to enhance return.

8. Assume that a risk-averse investor owning stock in Miller Corporation decides to add the stock of either Mac or Green Corporation to her portfolio. All three stocks offer the same expected return and total variability. The correlation of return between Miller and Mac is −.05 and between Miller and Green is +.05. Portfolio risk is expected to:

a. Decline more when the investor buys Mac.
b. Decline more when the investor buys Green.
c. Increase when either Mac or Green is bought.
d. Decline or increase, depending on other factors.

9. Stocks A, B, and C have the same expected return and standard deviation. The following table shows the correlations between the returns on these stocks.

	Stock A	Stock B	Stock C
Stock A	+1.0		
Stock B	+0.9	+1.0	
Stock C	+0.1	−0.4	+1.0

Given these correlations, the portfolio constructed from these stocks having the lowest risk is a portfolio:

a. Equally invested in stocks A and B.
b. Equally invested in stocks A and C.
c. Equally invested in stocks B and C.
d. Totally invested in stock C.

10. Statistics for three stocks, A, B, and C, are shown in the following tables.

Standard Deviations of Returns

Stock:	A	B	C
Standard deviation (%):	40	20	40

Correlations of Returns

Stock	A	B	C
A	1.00	0.90	0.50
B		1.00	0.10
C			1.00

Using *only* the information provided in the tables, and given a choice between a portfolio made up of equal amounts of stocks A and B *or* a portfolio made up of equal amounts of stocks B and C, which portfolio would you recommend? Justify your choice.

11. George Stephenson's current portfolio of $2 million is invested as follows:

Summary of Stephenson's Current Portfolio

	Value	Percent of Total	Expected Annual Return	Annual Standard Deviation
Short-term bonds	$ 200,000	10%	4.6%	1.6%
Domestic large-cap equities	600,000	30	12.4	19.5
Domestic small-cap equities	1,200,000	60	16.0	29.9
Total portfolio	$2,000,000	100%	13.8	23.1

Stephenson soon expects to receive an additional $2 million and plans to invest the entire amount in an index fund that best complements the current portfolio. Stephanie Coppa, CFA, is evaluating the four index funds shown in the following table for their ability to produce a portfolio that will meet two criteria relative to the current portfolio: (1) maintain or enhance expected return and (2) maintain or reduce volatility.

Each fund is invested in an asset class that is not substantially represented in the current portfolio.

Index Fund Characteristics

Index Fund	Expected Annual Return	Expected Annual Standard Deviation	Correlation of Returns with Current Portfolio
Fund *A*	15%	25%	+0.80
Fund *B*	11	22	+0.60
Fund *C*	16	25	+0.90
Fund *D*	14	22	+0.65

Which fund should Coppa recommend to Stephenson? Justify your choice by describing how your chosen fund *best* meets both of Stephenson's criteria. No calculations are required.

12. Abigail Grace has a $900,000 fully diversified portfolio. She subsequently inherits ABC Company common stock worth $100,000. Her financial adviser provided her with the following forecast information:

Risk and Return Characteristics

	Expected Monthly Returns	Standard Deviation of Monthly Returns
Original Portfolio	0.67%	2.37%
ABC Company	1.25	2.95

The correlation coefficient of ABC stock returns with the original portfolio returns is .40.

a. The inheritance changes Grace's overall portfolio, and she is deciding whether to keep the ABC stock. Assuming Grace keeps the ABC stock, calculate the:
   i. Expected return of her new portfolio, which includes the ABC stock.
   ii. Covariance of ABC stock returns with the original portfolio returns.
   iii. Standard deviation of her new portfolio, which includes the ABC stock.
b. If Grace sells the ABC stock, she will invest the proceeds in risk-free government securities yielding .42% monthly. Assuming Grace sells the ABC stock and replaces it with the government securities, calculate the
   i. Expected return of her new portfolio, which includes the government securities.
   ii. Covariance of the government security returns with the original portfolio returns.
   iii. Standard deviation of her new portfolio, which includes the government securities.
c. Determine whether the systematic risk of her new portfolio, which includes the government securities, will be higher or lower than that of her original portfolio.
d. On the basis of conversations with her husband, Grace is considering selling the $100,000 of ABC stock and acquiring $100,000 of XYZ Company common stock instead. XYZ stock has the same expected return and standard deviation as ABC stock. Her husband comments, "It doesn't matter whether you keep all of the ABC stock or replace it with $100,000 of XYZ stock." State whether her husband's comment is correct or incorrect. Justify your response.
e. In a recent discussion with her financial adviser, Grace commented, "If I just don't lose money in my portfolio, I will be satisfied." She went on to say, "I am more afraid of losing money than I am concerned about achieving high returns."
   i. Describe *one* weakness of using standard deviation of returns as a risk measure for Grace.
   ii. Identify an alternate risk measure that is more appropriate under the circumstances.

13. Dudley Trudy, CFA, recently met with one of his clients. Trudy typically invests in a master list of 30 equities drawn from several industries. As the meeting concluded, the client made the following statement: "I trust your stock-picking ability and believe that you should invest my funds in your five best ideas. Why invest in 30 companies when you obviously have stronger opinions

on a few of them?" Trudy plans to respond to his client within the context of modern portfolio theory.

   a. Contrast the concepts of systematic risk and firm-specific risk, and give an example of *each* type of risk.

   b. Critique the client's suggestion. Discuss how both systematic and firm-specific risk change as the number of securities in a portfolio is increased.

E-INVESTMENTS EXERCISES

Go to the **www.investopedia.com/articles/basics/03/050203.asp** Web site to learn more about diversification, the factors that influence investors' risk preferences, and the types of investments that fit into each of the risk categories. Then check out **www.investopedia.com/articles/pf/05/061505.asp** for asset allocation guidelines for various types of portfolios from conservative to very aggressive. What do you conclude about your own risk preferences and the best portfolio type for you? What would you expect to happen to your attitude toward risk as you get older? How might your portfolio composition change?

SOLUTIONS TO CONCEPT CHECKS

1. *a.* The first term will be $w_D \times w_D \times \sigma_D^2$ because this is the element in the top corner of the matrix (σ_D^2) times the term on the column border (w_D) times the term on the row border (w_D). Applying this rule to each term of the covariance matrix results in the sum
   $w_D^2 \sigma_D^2 + w_D w_E \text{Cov}(r_E, r_D) + w_E w_D \text{Cov}(r_D, r_E) + w_E^2 \sigma_E^2$, which is the same as Equation 7.3, because $\text{Cov}(r_E, r_D) = \text{Cov}(r_D, r_E)$.

   b. The bordered covariance matrix is

	w_X	w_Y	w_Z
w_X	σ_X^2	$\text{Cov}(r_X, r_Y)$	$\text{Cov}(r_X, r_Z)$
w_Y	$\text{Cov}(r_Y, r_X)$	σ_Y^2	$\text{Cov}(r_Y, r_Z)$
w_Z	$\text{Cov}(r_Z, r_X)$	$\text{Cov}(r_Z, r_Y)$	σ_Z^2

   There are nine terms in the covariance matrix. Portfolio variance is calculated from these nine terms:

   $$\sigma_P^2 = w_X^2 \sigma_X^2 + w_Y^2 \sigma_Y^2 + w_Z^2 \sigma_Z^2$$
   $$+ w_X w_Y \text{Cov}(r_X, r_Y) + w_Y w_X \text{Cov}(r_Y, r_X)$$
   $$+ w_X w_Z \text{Cov}(r_X, r_Z) + w_Z w_X \text{Cov}(r_Z, r_X)$$
   $$+ w_Y w_Z \text{Cov}(r_Y, r_Z) + w_Z w_Y \text{Cov}(r_Z, r_Y)$$
   $$= w_X^2 \sigma_X^2 + w_Y^2 \sigma_Y^2 + w_Z^2 \sigma_Z^2$$
   $$+ 2 w_X w_Y \text{Cov}(r_X, r_Y) + 2 w_X w_Z \text{Cov}(r_X, r_Z) + 2 w_Y w_Z \text{Cov}(r_Y, r_Z)$$

2. The parameters of the opportunity set are $E(r_D) = 8\%$, $E(r_E) = 13\%$, $\sigma_D = 12\%$, $\sigma_E = 20\%$, and $\rho(D,E) = .25$. From the standard deviations and the correlation coefficient, we generate the covariance matrix:

Fund	D	E
D	144	60
E	60	400

The *global minimum-variance* portfolio is constructed so that

$$w_D = \frac{\sigma_E^2 - \text{Cov}(r_D, r_E)}{\sigma_D^2 + \sigma_E^2 - 2\,\text{Cov}(r_D, r_E)}$$

$$= \frac{400 - 60}{(144 + 400) - (2 \times 60)} = .8019$$

$$w_E = 1 - w_D = .1981$$

Its expected return and standard deviation are

$$E(r_P) = (.8019 \times 8) + (.1981 \times 13) = 8.99\%$$

$$\sigma_P = [w_D^2 \sigma_D^2 + w_E^2 \sigma_E^2 + 2\,w_D w_E\,\text{Cov}(r_D, r_E)]^{1/2}$$

$$= [(.8019^2 \times 144) + (.1981^2 \times 400) + (2 \times .8019 \times .1981 \times 60)]^{1/2}$$

$$= 11.29\%$$

For the other points we simply increase w_D from .10 to .90 in increments of .10; accordingly, w_E ranges from .90 to .10 in the same increments. We substitute these portfolio proportions in the formulas for expected return and standard deviation. Note that when $w_E = 1.0$, the portfolio parameters equal those of the stock fund; when $w_D = 1$, the portfolio parameters equal those of the debt fund.

We thus generate the following table:

w_E	w_D	$E(r)$	σ
0.0	1.0	8.0	12.00
0.1	0.9	8.5	11.46
0.2	0.8	9.0	11.29
0.3	0.7	9.5	11.48
0.4	0.6	10.0	12.03
0.5	0.5	10.5	12.88
0.6	0.4	11.0	13.99
0.7	0.3	11.5	15.30
0.8	0.2	12.0	16.76
0.9	0.1	12.5	18.34
1.0	0.0	13.0	20.00
0.1981	0.8019	8.99	11.29 minimum variance portfolio

You can now draw your graph.

3. *a.* The computations of the opportunity set of the stock and risky bond funds are like those of Question 2 and will not be shown here. You should perform these computations, however, in order to give a graphical solution to part *a*. Note that the covariance between the funds is

$$\text{Cov}(r_A, r_B) = \rho(A, B) \times \sigma_A \times \sigma_B$$

$$= -.2 \times 20 \times 60 = -240$$

b. The proportions in the optimal risky portfolio are given by

$$w_A = \frac{(10 - 5)60^2 - (30 - 5)(-240)}{(10 - 5)60^2 + (30 - 5)20^2 - 30(-240)}$$

$$= .6818$$

$$w_B = 1 - w_A = .3182$$

The expected return and standard deviation of the optimal risky portfolio are

$$E(r_P) = (.6818 \times 10) + (.3182 \times 30) = 16.36\%$$

$$\sigma_P = \{(.6818^2 \times 20^2) + (.3182^2 \times 60^2) + [2 \times .6818 \times .3182(-240)]\}^{1/2}$$

$$= 21.13\%$$

Note that portfolio P is not the global minimum-variance portfolio. The proportions of the latter are given by

$$w_A = \frac{60^2 - (-240)}{60^2 + 20^2 - 2(-240)} = .8571$$

$$w_B = 1 - w_A = .1429$$

With these proportions, the standard deviation of the minimum-variance portfolio is

$$\sigma(\text{min}) = (.8571^2 \times 20^2) + (.1429^2 \times 60^2) + [2 \times .8571 \times .1429 \times (-240)]^{1/2}$$
$$= 17.75\%$$

which is less than that of the optimal risky portfolio.

c. The CAL is the line from the risk-free rate through the optimal risky portfolio. This line represents all efficient portfolios that combine T-bills with the optimal risky portfolio. The slope of the CAL is

$$S = \frac{E(r_P) - r_f}{\sigma_P} = \frac{16.36 - 5}{21.13} = .5376$$

d. Given a degree of risk aversion, A, an investor will choose the following proportion, y, in the optimal risky portfolio (remember to express returns as decimals when using A):

$$y = \frac{E(r_P) - r_f}{A\sigma_P^2} = \frac{.1636 - .05}{5 \times .2113^2} = .5089$$

This means that the optimal risky portfolio, with the given data, is attractive enough for an investor with $A = 5$ to invest 50.89% of his or her wealth in it. Because stock A makes up 68.18% of the risky portfolio and stock B makes up 31.82%, the investment proportions for this investor are

Stock A:	.5089 × 68.18 =	34.70%
Stock B:	.5089 × 31.82 =	16.19%
Total		50.89%

4. Efficient frontiers derived by portfolio managers depend on forecasts of the rates of return on various securities and estimates of risk, that is, the covariance matrix. The forecasts themselves do not control outcomes. Thus preferring managers with rosier forecasts (northwesterly frontiers) is tantamount to rewarding the bearers of good news and punishing the bearers of bad news. What we should do is reward bearers of *accurate* news. Thus, if you get a glimpse of the frontiers (forecasts) of portfolio managers on a regular basis, what you want to do is develop the track record of their forecasting accuracy and steer your advisees toward the more accurate forecaster. Their portfolio choices will, in the long run, outperform the field.

5. The parameters are $E(r) = 15$, $\sigma = 60$, and the correlation between any pair of stocks is $\rho = .5$.

a. The portfolio expected return is invariant to the size of the portfolio because all stocks have identical expected returns. The standard deviation of a portfolio with $n = 25$ stocks is

$$\sigma_P = [\sigma^2/n + \rho \times \sigma^2(n - 1)/n]^{1/2}$$
$$= [60^2/25 + .5 \times 60^2 \times 24/25]^{1/2} = 43.27\%$$

b. Because the stocks are identical, efficient portfolios are equally weighted. To obtain a standard deviation of 43%, we need to solve for n:

$$43^2 = \frac{60^2}{n} + .5 \times \frac{60^2(n - 1)}{n}$$
$$1,849n = 3,600 + 1,800n - 1,800$$
$$n = \frac{1,800}{49} = 36.73$$

Thus we need 37 stocks and will come in with volatility slightly under the target.

c. As n gets very large, the variance of an efficient (equally weighted) portfolio diminishes, leaving only the variance that comes from the covariances among stocks. Therefore,

$$\text{Systematic standard deviation} = \sqrt{\rho \times \sigma^2} = \sqrt{.5 \times 60^2} = 42.43\%$$

Note that with 25 stocks we came within .84% of the systematic risk, that is, the standard deviation of a portfolio of 25 stocks is only .84% higher than 42.43%. With 37 stocks, the standard deviation is 43.01%, which is only .58% greater than 42.43%.

d. If the risk-free is 10%, then the risk premium on any size portfolio is $15 - 10 = 5\%$. The standard deviation of a well-diversified portfolio is (practically) 42.43%; hence the slope of the CAL is

$$S = 5/42.43 = .1178$$

APPENDIX A: A Spreadsheet Model for Efficient Diversification

Several software packages can be used to generate the efficient frontier. We will demonstrate the method using Microsoft Excel. Excel is far from the best program for this purpose and is limited in the number of assets it can handle, but working through a simple portfolio optimizer in Excel can illustrate concretely the nature of the calculations used in more sophisticated "black-box" programs. You will find that even in Excel, the computation of the efficient frontier is not difficult.

We apply the Markowitz portfolio optimization program to the problem of international diversification. We take the perspective of a portfolio manager serving U.S. clients, who wishes to construct for the next year an optimal risky portfolio of large stocks in the U.S. and six developed capital markets (Japan, Germany, the U.K., France, Canada, and Australia). First we describe the input list: forecasts of risk premiums and the covariance matrix. Next, we describe Excel's Solver, and finally we show the solution to the manager's problem.

The Input List

The manager needs to compile an input list of expected returns, variances, and covariances to compute an efficient frontier and the optimal risky portfolio. Spreadsheet 7A.1 shows the calculations.

Panel A lays out the expected excess return for each country index. While these estimates may be guided by historical experience, as we discussed in Chapter 5, using simple historical averages would yield extremely noisy estimates of expected risk premiums because returns are so variable over time. Average returns fluctuate enormously across subperiods, making historical averages highly unreliable estimators. Here, we simply assume the manager has arrived at some reasonable estimates of each country's risk premium through scenario analysis informed by historical experience. These values are presented in column B.

Panel B is the bordered covariance matrix corresponding to Table 7.2 earlier in the chapter. The covariances in this table might reasonably be estimated from a sample of historical returns, as empirically based variance and covariance estimates are far more precise than corresponding estimates of mean returns. It would be common to estimate Panel B using perhaps five years of monthly returns. The Excel function COVARIANCE would compute the covariance between the time series of returns for any pair of countries. We assume the manager has already collected historical returns on each index, plugged each pair of returns into the COVARIANCE function, and obtained the entries that appear in Panel B. The elements on the diagonal of the covariance matrix in Panel B

	A	B	C	D	E	F	G	H	I	J	K	L
1	Efficient Frontier Spreadsheet											
2												
3	Panel A		Expected excess returns (risk premiums) of each country index									
4												
5	U.S.	0.060										
6	U.K.	0.053										
7	France	0.070										
8	Germany	0.080										
9	Australia	0.058										
10	Japan	0.045										
11	Canada	0.059										
12												
13	Panel B		Bordered Covariance Matrix									
14												
15	Portfolio weights ⟶		0.6112	0.8778	−0.2140	−0.5097	0.0695	0.2055	−0.0402			
16	↓		U.S.	U.K.	France	Germany	Australia	Japan	Canada			
17	0.6112	U.S.	0.0224	0.0184	0.0250	0.0288	0.0195	0.0121	0.0205			
18	0.8778	U.K.	0.0184	0.0223	0.0275	0.0299	0.0204	0.0124	0.0206			
19	−0.2140	France	0.0250	0.0275	0.0403	0.0438	0.0259	0.0177	0.0273			
20	−0.5097	Germany	0.0288	0.0299	0.0438	0.0515	0.0301	0.0183	0.0305			
21	0.0695	Australia	0.0195	0.0204	0.0259	0.0301	0.0261	0.0147	0.0234			
22	0.2055	Japan	0.0121	0.0124	0.0177	0.0183	0.0147	0.0353	0.0158			
23	−0.0402	Canada	0.0205	0.0206	0.0273	0.0305	0.0234	0.0158	0.0298			
24	1.0000		0.0078	0.0113	−0.0027	−0.0065	0.0009	0.0026	−0.0005			
25		Risk Prem	0.0383									
26		Std Dev	0.1132									
27		Sharpe	0.3386									
28												
29	Formulas used in key cells											
30	Cell A17 - A23		These are portfolio weights. You can set initial value arbitrarily as long as sum = 1									
31	Cell C15		= A17, and so on. The portfolio weights in column A are copied to row 17.									
32	Cell A24		=SUM(A17:A23)									
33	Cell C24		=C15*SUMPRODUCT($A17:$A23,C17:C23)									
34	Cell D24 through I24		Copied from C24 (note the use of absolute addresses)									
35	Cell C25		=SUMPRODUCT(A17:A23,$B5:$B11)									
36	Cell C26		=SUM(C24:I24)^0.5									
37	Cell C27		=C25/C26									
38												
39	Panel C		Various points along the efficient frontier.									
40				Min var portfolio					Optimal (tangency) portfolio			
41	Risk Prem:	0.0350	0.0383	0.0400	0.0450	0.0500	0.0550	0.0564	0.0575	0.0600	0.0700	0.0800
42	Std Dev:	0.1141	0.1132	0.1135	0.1168	0.1238	0.1340	0.1374	0.1401	0.1466	0.1771	0.2119
43	Sharpe:	0.3066	0.3386	0.3525	0.3853	0.4037	0.4104	0.4107	0.4106	0.4092	0.3953	0.3774
44	U.S.	0.5944	0.6112	0.6195	0.6446	0.6696	0.6947	0.7018	0.7073	0.7198	0.7699	0.8201
45	U.K.	1.0175	0.8778	0.8083	0.5992	0.3900	0.1809	0.1214	0.0758	−0.0283	−0.4465	−0.8648
46	France	−0.2365	−0.2140	−0.2029	−0.1693	−0.1357	−0.1021	−0.0926	−0.0852	−0.0685	−0.0014	0.0658
47	Germany	−0.6077	−0.5097	−0.4610	−0.3144	−0.1679	−0.0213	0.0205	0.0524	0.1253	0.4185	0.7117
48	Australia	0.0588	0.0695	0.0748	0.0907	0.1067	0.1226	0.1271	0.1306	0.1385	0.1704	0.2023
49	Japan	0.2192	0.2055	0.1987	0.1781	0.1575	0.1369	0.1311	0.1266	0.1164	0.0752	0.0341
50	Canada	−0.0459	−0.0402	−0.0374	−0.0288	−0.0203	−0.0118	−0.0093	−0.0075	−0.0032	0.0139	0.0309
51	CAL*	0.0469	0.0465	0.0466	0.0479	0.0508	0.0550	0.0564	0.0575	0.0602	0.0727	0.0870
52	*Risk premium along the CAL = StdDev of portfolio times slope of optimal risky portfolio (Cell I45)											

Spreadsheet 7A.1

Spreadsheet models for international diversification

eXcel

Please visit us at
www.mhhe.com/Bodie11e

are the variances of each country index. You can take square roots to find each country's standard deviation.

The covariance matrix in Panel B is bordered along the top (row 15) and left (column A) by a set of portfolio weights. You can start the procedure off using any arbitrary set of weights as long as they sum to 1. You will be asking Excel to replace these initial weights with the weights that correspond to the portfolios on the efficient frontier.

Cells C25, C26, and C27 calculate some important characteristics of the portfolio defined by the set of portfolio weights. C25 is the expected risk premium on the portfolio, computed by taking a weighted average of country risk premiums (using Excel's SUMPRODUCT function. The formula for cell C25 is presented in cell C35.) Cell C26 computes the standard deviation of any portfolio using the formula developed in Table 7.2. Portfolio variance is given by the sum of cells C24–I24 below the bordered covariance matrix. Cell C26 takes the square root of this sum to produce the standard deviation. Finally C27 is the portfolio's Sharpe ratio, expected excess return divided by standard deviation. This is also the slope of the CAL (capital allocation line) that runs through the portfolio corresponding to the weights in column A. The optimal risky portfolio is the one that maximizes the Sharpe ratio.

Panel C shows the properties of several portfolios along the efficient frontier. The highlighted columns correspond to the minimum-variance and the tangency portfolios. Each column in the panel shows portfolio characteristics and the weighting in each country.

Using the Excel Solver

Excel's Solver is a user-friendly, but quite powerful, optimizer. It has three parts: (1) an objective function, (2) decision variables, and (3) constraints. Figure 7A.1 shows three pictures of the Solver. We will begin by finding the minimum-variance portfolio. The problem is set up in Panel A of the figure.

The top line of the Solver lets you choose a target cell for the "objective function," that is, the variable you are trying to optimize. In Panel A of Figure 7A.1, the target cell is C26, the portfolio standard deviation. Below the target cell, you can choose whether your objective is to maximize, minimize, or set your objective function equal to a value that you specify. Here we choose to minimize the portfolio standard deviation.

The next part of Solver contains the decision variables. These are cells that the Solver can change in order to optimize the objective function in the target cell. Here, we input cells A17–A23, the portfolio weights that we select to minimize portfolio volatility.

The bottom panel of the Solver can include any number of constraints. One constraint that must always appear in portfolio optimization is the "feasibility constraint," namely, that portfolio weights sum to 1.0. When we bring up the dialogue box for constraints, we specify that cell A24 (the sum of weights) must be set equal to 1.0.

When we click "Solve," the Solver finds the weights of the minimum-variance portfolio and places them in column A. The spreadsheet then calculates the risk premium and standard deviation of that portfolio. We save the portfolio weights and its key statistics by copying them to Panel C in Spreadsheet 7A.1. Column C in Panel C shows that the lowest standard deviation (SD) that can be achieved with our input list is 11.32%. This standard deviation is considerably lower than even the lowest SD of the individual indexes.

Now we are ready to find other points along the efficient frontier. We will do this by finding the portfolio that has the lowest possible variance for any targeted risk premium. You can produce the entire efficient frontier in minutes following this procedure.

1. Input to the Solver a constraint that says: Cell C25 (the portfolio risk premium) must equal some desired value, for example .04. The Solver at this point is shown

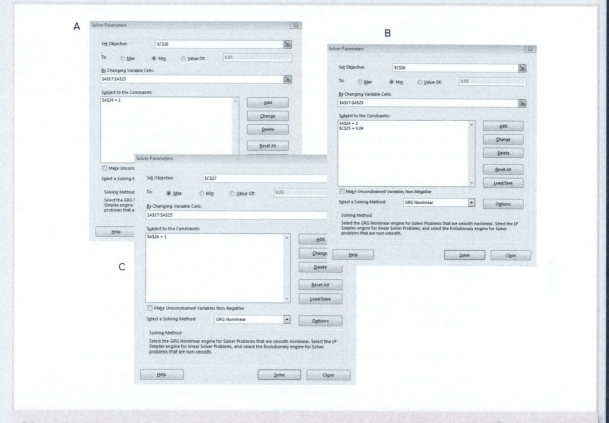

Figure 7A.1 Solver dialog box

in Panel B of Figure 7A.1. There are now two constraints: one for the required risk premium and one for the fact that portfolio weights must sum to 1. Ask Solver to solve, and it will replace the portfolio weights in column A with those corresponding to the portfolio that can achieve the targeted risk premium with the lowest possible standard deviation. This is the portfolio on the efficient frontier with a risk premium of 4%. Again, the spreadsheet calculates the other properties of this portfolio, which you then copy to Panel C.

2. To find another point on the frontier, you input a different desired risk premium, and ask the Solver to solve again.

3. Every time the Solver gives you a solution to the request in (2), copy the results into Panel C, in this way tabulating the collection of points along the efficient frontier.

Finding the Optimal Risky Portfolio on the Efficient Frontier

Now that we have traced out several points along the efficient frontier, our last task is to search for the portfolio with the highest Sharpe ratio. This is the portfolio on the efficient frontier that is tangent to the CAL. To find it, we determine the portfolio weights that maximize the Sharpe ratio. This requires two changes to the Solver. First, change the target cell from cell C26 to cell C27, the Sharpe ratio of the portfolio, and request that the value in this cell be maximized. Next, eliminate the constraint on the risk premium that may be left over from the last time you used the Solver. At this point the Solver looks like Panel C in Figure 7A.1.

The Solver now yields the optimal risky portfolio. Copy the statistics for the optimal portfolio and its weights to Panel C of your spreadsheet. In order to get a clean graph, place the column of the optimal portfolio so that the risk premiums of all portfolios in the spreadsheet are steadily increasing from the risk premium of the minimum-variance portfolio (3.83%) all the way up to 8%.

The resulting efficient frontier is graphed in Figure 7A.2. The data in cells B42 through L42 are used for the horizontal axis (portfolio standard deviation), while B41–L41 are used for the vertical or y-axis and contain the portfolio risk premium.

The Optimal CAL

It is instructive to superimpose on the graph of the efficient frontier in Figure 7A.2 the CAL that identifies the optimal risky portfolio. This CAL has a slope equal to the Sharpe ratio of the optimal risky portfolio. Therefore, at the bottom of Spreadsheet 7A.1, Panel C, we add a row with entries obtained by multiplying the standard deviation of each column's portfolio by the Sharpe ratio of the optimal risky portfolio from cell H43. This results in the risk premium for each portfolio along the CAL. We now add a series to the graph with the standard deviations in B42–L42 as the x-axis and cells B51–L51 as the y-axis. You can see this CAL in Figure 7A.2.

The Optimal Risky Portfolio and the Short-Sales Constraint

With the input list used by the portfolio manager, the optimal risky portfolio calls for short (negative) positions in the stocks of France and Canada (see column H of Spreadsheet 7A.1, Panel C). In many cases, however, the portfolio manager is prohibited from taking short positions. If so, we need to amend the program to preclude short sales.

To accomplish this task, we repeat the exercise, but with one change. We add to the Solver the following constraint: Each element in the column of portfolio weights, A17–A23, must be greater than or equal to zero. You should try to produce the short-sale constrained efficient frontier in your own spreadsheet.

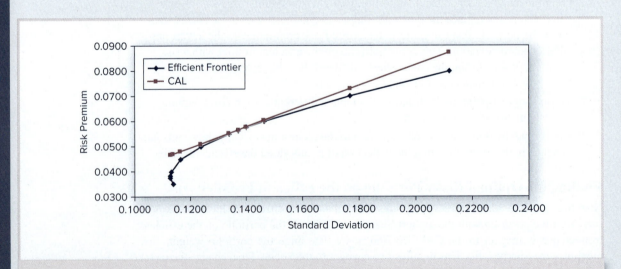

Figure 7A.2 Efficient frontier and CAL for country stock indexes

APPENDIX B: Review of Portfolio Statistics

We base this review of scenario analysis on a two-asset portfolio. We denote the assets D and E (which you may think of as debt and equity), but the risk and return parameters we use in this appendix are not necessarily consistent with those used in Section 7.2.

Expected Returns

We use "expected value" and "mean" interchangeably. For an analysis with n scenarios, where the rate of return in scenario i is $r(i)$ with probability $p(i)$, the expected return is

$$E(r) = \sum_{i=1}^{n} p(i)r(i) \tag{7B.1}$$

If you were to increase the rate of return assumed for each scenario by some amount Δ, then the mean return will increase by Δ. If you multiply the rate in each scenario by a factor w, the new mean will be multiplied by that factor:

$$\sum_{i=1}^{n} p(i) \times [r(i) + \Delta] = \sum_{i=1}^{n} p(i) \times r(i) + \Delta \sum_{i=1}^{n} p(i) = E(r) + \Delta$$

$$\tag{7B.2}$$

$$\sum_{i=1}^{n} p(i) \times [wr(i)] = w \sum_{i=1}^{n} p(i) \times r(i) = wE(r)$$

Example 7B.1   Expected Rates of Return

Column C of Spreadsheet 7B.1 shows scenario rates of return for debt, D. In column D we add 3% to each scenario return and in column E we multiply each rate by .4. The spreadsheet shows how we compute the expected return for columns C, D, and E. It is evident that the mean increases by 3% (from .08 to .11) in column D and is multiplied by .4 (from .08 to 0.032) in column E.

	A	B	C	D	E	F	G
1							
2				Scenario Rates of Return			
3	Scenario	Probability	$r_D(i)$	$r_D(i) + 0.03$	$0.4 \cdot r_D(i)$		
4	1	0.14	−0.10	−0.07	−0.040		
5	2	0.36	0.00	0.03	0.000		
6	3	0.30	0.10	0.13	0.040		
7	4	0.20	0.32	0.35	0.128		
8		Mean	0.080	0.110	0.032		
9		Cell C8	=SUMPRODUCT($B$4:$B$7,C4:C7)				
10							
11							
12							

eXcel

Please visit us at
www.mhhe.com/Bodie11e

Spreadsheet 7B.1

Scenario analysis for bonds

Now let's construct a portfolio that invests a fraction of the investment budget, $w(D)$, in bonds and the fraction $w(E)$ in stocks. The portfolio's rate of return in each scenario and its expected return are given by

$$r_P(i) = w_D r_D(i) + w_E r_E(i)$$

$$E(r_P) = \sum p(i)[w_D r_D(i) + w_E r_E(i)] = \sum p(i) w_D r_D(i) + \sum p(i) w_E r_E(i) \qquad \text{(7B.3)}$$
$$= w_D E(r_D) + w_E E(r_E)$$

The rate of return on the portfolio in each scenario is the weighted average of the component rates. The weights are the fractions invested in these assets, that is, the portfolio weights. The expected return on the portfolio is the weighted average of the asset means.

Example 7B.2   Portfolio Rate of Return

Spreadsheet 7B.2 lays out rates of return for both stocks and bonds. Using assumed weights of .4 for debt and .6 for equity, the portfolio return in each scenario appears in column L. Cell L8 shows the portfolio expected return as .1040, obtained using the SUMPRODUCT function, which multiplies each scenario return (column L) by the scenario probability (column I) and sums the results.

Variance and Standard Deviation

The variance and standard deviation of the rate of return on an asset from a scenario analysis are given by[15]

$$\sigma^2(r) = \sum_{i=1}^{n} p(i)[r(i) - E(r)]^2$$

$$\sigma(r) = \sqrt{\sigma^2(r)}$$
$$\text{(7B.4)}$$

	H	I	J	K	L
1					
2			**Scenario Rates of Return**		**Portfolio Return**
3	**Scenario**	**Probability**	$r_D(i)$	$r_E(i)$	$0.4 \cdot r_D(i) + 0.6 \cdot r_E(i)$
4	1	0.14	−0.10	−0.35	−0.2500
5	2	0.36	0.00	0.20	0.1200
6	3	0.30	0.10	0.45	0.3100
7	4	0.20	0.32	−0.19	0.0140
8		Mean	0.08	0.12	0.1040
9		Cell L4	=0.4*J4+0.6*K4		
10		Cell L8	=SUMPRODUCT($I$4:$I$7,L4:L7)		
11					
12					

Spreadsheet 7B.2

Scenario analysis for bonds and stocks

[15]Variance (here, of an asset rate of return) is not the only possible choice to quantify variability. An alternative would be to use the *absolute* deviation from the mean instead of the *squared* deviation. Thus, the mean absolute deviation (MAD) is sometimes used as a measure of variability. The variance is the preferred measure for several reasons. First, working with absolute deviations is mathematically more difficult. Second, squaring deviations gives more weight to larger deviations. In investments, giving more weight to large deviations (hence, losses) is compatible with risk aversion. Third, when returns are normally distributed, the variance is one of the two parameters that fully characterizes the distribution.

Notice that the unit of variance is percent squared. In contrast, standard deviation, the square root of variance, has the same dimension as the original returns, and therefore is easier to interpret as a measure of return variability.

When you add a fixed incremental return, Δ, to each scenario return, you increase the mean return by that same increment. Therefore, the deviation of the realized return in each scenario from the mean return is unaffected, and both variance and SD are unchanged. In contrast, when you multiply the return in each scenario by a factor w, the variance is multiplied by the square of that factor (and the SD is multiplied by w):

$$\text{Var}(wr) = \sum_{i=1}^{n} p(i) \times [wr(i) - E(wr)]^2 = w^2 \sum_{i=1}^{n} p(i)[r(i) - E(r)]^2 = w^2\sigma^2 \tag{7B.5}$$

$$\text{SD}(wr) = \sqrt{w^2\sigma^2} = w\sigma(r)$$

Excel does not have a direct function to compute variance and standard deviation for a scenario analysis. Its STDEV and VAR functions are designed for time series. We need to calculate the probability-weighted squared deviations directly. To avoid having to first compute columns of squared deviations from the mean, however, we can simplify our problem by expressing the variance as a difference between two easily computable terms:

$$\sigma^2(r) = E[r - E(r)]^2 = E\{r^2 + [E(r)]^2 + 2rE(r)\}$$
$$= E(r)^2 + [E(r)]^2 - 2E(r)E(r) \tag{7B.6}$$
$$= E(r^2) - [E(r)]^2 = \sum_{i=1}^{n} p(i)r(i)^2 - \left[\sum_{i=1}^{n} p(i)r(i)\right]^2$$

Example 7B.3 Calculating the Variance of a Risky Asset in Excel

You can compute the first expression, $E(r^2)$, in Equation 7B.6 using Excel's SUMPRODUCT function. For example, in Spreadsheet 7B.3, $E(r^2)$ is first calculated in cell C21 by using SUMPRODUCT to multiply the scenario probability times the asset return times the asset return again. Then $[E(r)]^2$ is subtracted (notice the subtraction of C20^2 in cell C21), to arrive at variance.

	A	B	C	D	E	F	G
13							
14				Scenario Rates of Return			
15	Scenario	Probability	$r_D(i)$	$r_D(i) + 0.03$	$0.4{*}r_D(i)$		
16	1	0.14	−0.10	−0.07	−0.040		
17	2	0.36	0.00	0.03	0.000		
18	3	0.30	0.10	0.13	0.040		
19	4	0.20	0.32	0.35	0.128		
20		Mean	0.0800	0.1100	0.0240		
21		Variance	0.0185	0.0185	0.0034		
22		SD	0.1359	0.1359	0.0584		
23	Cell C21	=SUMPRODUCT($B$16:$B$19,C16:C19,C16:C19)−C20^2					
24	Cell C22	=C21^0.5					

Spreadsheet 7B.3

Scenario analysis for bonds

eXcel
Please visit us at
www.mhhe.com/Bodie11e

The variance of a *portfolio* return is not as simple to compute as the mean. The portfolio variance is *not* the weighted average of the asset variances. The deviation of the portfolio rate of return in any scenario from its mean return is

$$
\begin{aligned}
r_P - E(r_P) &= w_D r_D(i) + w_E r_E(i) - [w_D E(r_D) + w_E E(r_E)] \\
&= w_D[r_D(i) - E(r_D)] + w_E[r_E(i) - E(r_E)] \\
&= w_D d(i) + w_E e(i)
\end{aligned}
\tag{7B.7}
$$

where the lowercase variables denote deviations from the mean:

$$
\begin{aligned}
d(i) &= r_D(i) - E(r_D) \\
e(i) &= r_E(i) - E(r_E)
\end{aligned}
$$

We express the variance of the portfolio return in terms of these deviations from the mean in Equation 7B.8:

$$
\begin{aligned}
\sigma_P^2 &= \sum_{i=1}^{n} p(i)[r_P - E(r_P)]^2 = \sum_{i=1}^{n} p(i)[w_D d(i) + w_E e(i)]^2 \\
&= \sum_{i=1}^{n} p(i)[w_D^2 d(i)^2 + w_E^2 e(i)^2 + 2 w_D w_E d(i) e(i)] \\
&= w_D^2 \sum_{i=1}^{n} p(i)d(i)^2 + w_E^2 \sum_{i=1}^{n} p(i)e(i)^2 + 2 w_D w_E \sum_{i=1}^{n} p(i)d(i)e(i) \\
&= w_D^2 \sigma_D^2 + w_E^2 \sigma_E^2 + 2 w_D w_E \sum_{i=1}^{n} p(i)d(i)e(i)
\end{aligned}
\tag{7B.8}
$$

The last line in Equation 7B.8 tells us that the variance of a portfolio is the weighted sum of portfolio variances (notice that the weights are the squares of the portfolio weights), plus an additional term that, as we will soon see, makes all the difference.

Notice also that $d(i) \times e(i)$ is the product of the deviations of the scenario returns of the two assets from their respective means. The probability-weighted average of this product is its expected value, which is called *covariance* and is denoted $\mathrm{Cov}(r_D, r_E)$. The covariance between the two assets can have a big impact on the variance of a portfolio.

Covariance

The covariance between two variables equals

$$
\begin{aligned}
\mathrm{Cov}(r_D, r_E) &= E(d \times e) = E\{[r_D - E(r_D)][r_E - E(r_E)]\} \\
&= E(r_D r_E) - E(r_D)E(r_E)
\end{aligned}
\tag{7B.9}
$$

The covariance is an elegant way to quantify the covariation of two variables. This is easiest seen through a numerical example.

Imagine a three-scenario analysis of stocks and bonds such as that given in Spreadsheet 7B.4. In scenario 1, bonds go down (negative deviation) while stocks go up (positive deviation). In scenario 3, bonds are up, but stocks are down. When the rates move in opposite directions, as in this case, the product of the deviations is negative; conversely, if the rates moved in the same direction, the sign of the product would be positive. The magnitude of the product shows the extent of the opposite or common movement in that scenario. The

	A	B	C	D	E	F	G	H
1		Rates of Return			Deviation from Mean			Product of
2	Probability	Bonds	Stocks		Bonds	Stocks		Deviations
3	0.25	−2	30		−8	20		−160
4	0.50	6	10		0	0		0
5	0.25	14	−10		8	−20		−160
6	Mean:	6	10		0	0		−80

Spreadsheet 7B.4

Three-scenario analysis for stocks and bonds

eXcel
Please visit us at
www.mhhe.com/Bodie11e

probability-weighted average of these products therefore summarizes the *average* tendency for the variables to co-vary across scenarios. In the last line of the spreadsheet, we see that the covariance is −80 (cell H6).

Suppose our scenario analysis had envisioned stocks generally moving in the same direction as bonds. To be concrete, let's switch the forecast rates on stocks in the first and third scenarios, that is, let the stock return be −10% in the first scenario and 30% in the third. In this case, the absolute value of both products of these scenarios remains the same, but the signs are positive, and thus the covariance is positive, at +80, reflecting the tendency for both asset returns to vary in tandem. If the levels of the scenario returns change, the intensity of the covariation also may change, as reflected by the magnitude of the product of deviations. The change in the magnitude of the covariance quantifies the change in both direction and intensity of the covariation.

If there is no co-movement at all, because positive and negative products are equally likely, the covariance is zero. Also, if one of the assets is risk-free, its covariance with any risky asset is zero, because its deviations from its mean are identically zero.

The computation of covariance using Excel can be made easy by using the last line in Equation 7B.9. The first term, $E(r_D \times r_E)$, can be computed in one stroke using Excel's SUMPRODUCT function. Specifically, in Spreadsheet 7B.4, SUMPRODUCT(A3:A5, B3:B5, C3:C5) multiplies the probability times the return on debt times the return on equity in each scenario and then sums those three products.

Notice that adding Δ to each rate would not change the covariance because deviations from the mean would remain unchanged. But if you *multiply* either of the variables by a fixed factor, the covariance will increase by that factor. Multiplying both variables results in a covariance multiplied by the products of the factors because

$$\text{Cov}(w_D r_D, w_E r_E) = E\{[w_D r_D - w_D E(r_D)][w_E r_E - w_E E(r_E)]\}$$
$$= w_D w_E \text{Cov}(r_D, r_E) \tag{7B.10}$$

The covariance in Equation 7B.10 is actually the term that we add (twice) in the last line of the equation for portfolio variance, Equation 7B.8. So we find that portfolio variance is the weighted sum (not average) of the individual asset variances, *plus* twice their covariance weighted by the two portfolio weights ($w_D \times w_E$).

Like variance, the dimension (unit) of covariance is percent squared. But here we cannot get to a more easily interpreted dimension by taking the square root, because the average product of deviations can be negative, as it was in Spreadsheet 7B.4. The solution in this case is to scale the covariance by the standard deviations of the two variables, producing the *correlation coefficient.*

Correlation Coefficient

Dividing the covariance by the product of the standard deviations of the variables will generate a pure number called *correlation.* We define correlation as follows:

$$\text{Corr}(r_D, r_E) = \frac{\text{Cov}(r_D, r_E)}{\sigma_D \sigma_E} \tag{7B.11}$$

The correlation coefficient must fall within the range $[-1, 1]$. This can be explained as follows. What two variables should have the highest degree co-movement? Logic says a variable with itself, so let's check it out.

$$\text{Cov}(r_D, r_D) = E\{[r_D - E(r_D)] \times [r_D - E(r_D)]\}$$
$$= E[r_D - E(r_D)]^2 = \sigma_D^2 \tag{7B.12}$$
$$\text{Corr}(r_D, r_D) = \frac{\text{Cov}(r_D, r_D)}{\sigma_D \sigma_D} = \frac{\sigma_D^2}{\sigma_D^2} = 1$$

Similarly, the lowest (most negative) value of the correlation coefficient is -1. (Check this for yourself by finding the correlation of a variable with its own negative.)

An important property of the correlation coefficient is that it is unaffected by both addition and multiplication. Suppose we start with a return on debt, r_D, multiply it by a constant, w_D, and then add a fixed amount Δ. The correlation with equity is unaffected:

$$\text{Corr}(\Delta + w_D r_D, r_E) = \frac{\text{Cov}(\Delta + w_D r_D, r_E)}{\sqrt{\text{Var}(\Delta + w_D r_D)} \times \sigma_E}$$
$$= \frac{w_D \text{Cov}(r_D, r_E)}{\sqrt{w_D^2 \sigma_D^2} \times \sigma_E} = \frac{w_D \text{Cov}(r_D, r_E)}{w_D \sigma_D \times \sigma_E} \tag{7B.13}$$
$$= \text{Corr}(r_D, r_E)$$

Because the correlation coefficient gives more intuition about the relationship between rates of return, we sometimes express the covariance in terms of the correlation coefficient. Rearranging Equation 7B.11, we can write covariance as

$$\text{Cov}(r_D, r_E) = \sigma_D \sigma_E \text{Corr}(r_D, r_E) \tag{7B.14}$$

Example 7B.4   Calculating Covariance and Correlation

Spreadsheet 7B.5 shows the covariance and correlation between stocks and bonds using the same scenario analysis as in the other examples in this appendix. Covariance is calculated using Equation 7B.9. The SUMPRODUCT function used in cell J22 gives us $E(r_D \times r_E)$, from which we subtract $E(r_D) \times E(r_E)$ (i.e., we subtract J20 × K20). Then we calculate correlation in cell J23 by dividing covariance by the product of the asset standard deviations.

eXcel

Please visit us at
www.mhhe.com/Bodie11e

	H	I	J	K	L	M
13						
14			Scenario Rates of Return			
15	Scenario	Probability	$r_D(i)$	$r_E(i)$		
16	1	0.14	−0.10	−0.35		
17	2	0.36	0.00	0.20		
18	3	0.30	0.10	0.45		
19	4	0.20	0.32	−0.19		
20		Mean	0.08	0.12		
21		SD	0.1359	0.2918		
22		Covariance	−0.0034			
23		Correlation	−0.0847			
24	Cell J22	=SUMPRODUCT(I16:I19,J16:J19,K16:K19)−J20*K20				
25	Cell J23	=J22/(J21*K21)				

Spreadsheet 7B.5

Scenario analysis for bonds and stocks

Portfolio Variance

We have seen in Equation 7B.8, with the help of Equation 7B.10, that the variance of a two-asset portfolio is the sum of the individual variances multiplied by the square of the portfolio weights, plus twice the covariance between the rates, multiplied by the product of the portfolio weights:

$$\sigma_P^2 = w_D^2 \sigma_D^2 + w_E^2 \sigma_E^2 + 2 w_D w_E \, \text{Cov}(r_D, r_E)$$
$$= w_D^2 \sigma_D^2 + w_E^2 \sigma_E^2 + 2 w_D w_E \sigma_D \sigma_E \text{Corr}(r_D, r_E) \qquad \text{(7B.15)}$$

Example 7B.5   Calculating Portfolio Variance

We calculate portfolio variance in Spreadsheet 7B.6. Notice there that we calculate the portfolio standard deviation in two ways: once from the scenario portfolio returns (cell E35) and again (in cell E36) using the first line of Equation 7B.15. The two approaches yield the same result. You should try to repeat the second calculation using the correlation coefficient from the second line in Equation 7B.15 instead of covariance in the formula for portfolio variance.

eXcel

Please visit us at
www.mhhe.com/Bodie11e

	A	B	C	D	E	F	G
25							
26							
27							
28			Scenario Rates of Return		Portfolio Return		
29	Scenario	Probability	$r_D(i)$	$r_E(i)$	$0.4*r_D(i)+0.6r_E(i)$		
30	1	0.14	−0.10	−0.35	−0.25		
31	2	0.36	0.00	0.20	0.12		
32	3	0.30	0.10	0.45	0.31		
33	4	0.20	0.32	−0.19	0.014		
34		Mean	0.08	0.12	0.1040		
35		SD	0.1359	0.2918	0.1788		
36		Covariance	−0.0034		SD: 0.1788		
37		Correlation	−0.0847				
38	Cell E35	=SUMPRODUCT(B30:B33,E30:E33,E30:E33)−E34^2)^0.5					
39	Cell E36	=(0.4*C35)^2+(0.6*D35)^2+2*0.4*0.6*C36)^0.5					

Spreadsheet 7B.6

Scenario analysis for bonds and stocks

Suppose that one of the assets, say, E, is replaced with a money market instrument, that is, a risk-free asset. The variance of E is then zero, as is the covariance with D. In that case, as seen from Equation 7B.15, the portfolio standard deviation is just $w_D \sigma_D$. In other words, when we mix a risky portfolio with the risk-free asset, portfolio standard deviation equals the risky asset's standard deviation times the weight invested in that asset. This result was used extensively in Chapter 6.

Index Models

THE MARKOWITZ PROCEDURE introduced in the preceding chapter suffers from two drawbacks. First, the model requires a huge number of estimates to fill the covariance matrix. Second, the model does not provide any guideline to the forecasting of the security risk premiums that are essential to construct the efficient frontier of risky assets. Because past returns are imprecise guides to expected future returns, this drawback can be telling.

In this chapter, we introduce index models that simplify estimation of the covariance matrix and greatly enhance the analysis of security risk premiums. By allowing us to explicitly decompose risk into systematic and firm-specific components, these models also shed considerable light on both the power and the limits of diversification. Further, they allow us to measure these components of risk for particular securities and portfolios.

We begin the chapter by describing a single-factor security market and show how it can justify a single-index model of security returns. Once its properties are analyzed, we proceed to show how the single-index model can be estimated from widely available data. We review the statistical properties of these estimates and show how they relate to the practical issues facing portfolio managers.

Despite the simplification they offer, index models remain true to the concepts of the efficient frontier and portfolio optimization. They can be used to select optimal portfolios nearly as accurately as the much more data-intensive Markowitz algorithm described in the last chapter.

Finally, we examine optimal risky portfolios constructed using the index model. While the principles are the same as those employed in the previous chapter, the properties of the portfolio are easier to derive and interpret in this context. We illustrate how to use the index model by constructing an optimal risky portfolio using a small sample of firms. This portfolio is compared to the corresponding portfolio constructed from the Markowitz model.

8.1   A Single-Factor Security Market

The Input List of the Markowitz Model

The success of a portfolio selection rule depends on the quality of the *input list,* that is, the estimates of expected security returns and the covariance matrix. In the long run, efficient portfolios will beat portfolios with less reliable input lists and consequently inferior reward-to-risk trade-offs.

Suppose your security analysts can thoroughly analyze 50 stocks. This means that your input list will include the following:

$$n = \quad 50 \text{ estimates of expected returns}$$
$$n = \quad 50 \text{ estimates of variances}$$
$$(n^2 - n)/2 = \underline{1{,}225} \text{ estimates of covariances}$$
$$\underline{1{,}325} \text{ total estimates}$$

This is a formidable task, particularly in light of the fact that a 50-security portfolio is relatively small. Doubling n to 100 will nearly quadruple the number of estimates to 5,150. If $n = 3{,}000$, still less than the number of issues included in the Wilshire 5000 index, we need more than 4.5 *million* estimates.

Another difficulty in applying the Markowitz model to portfolio optimization is that errors in the assessment or estimation of correlation coefficients can lead to nonsensical results. This can happen because some sets of correlation coefficients are mutually inconsistent, as the following example demonstrates:[1]

Asset	Standard Deviation (%)	Correlation Matrix		
		A	B	C
A	20	1.00	0.90	0.90
B	20	0.90	1.00	0.00
C	20	0.90	0.00	1.00

Suppose that you construct a portfolio with weights -1.00; 1.00; 1.00, for assets A; B; C, respectively, and calculate the portfolio variance. If you use the standard formulas for portfolio variance, you will find that it appears to be negative (-200)! This of course is not possible: Variances cannot be negative. We conclude that the inputs in the estimated correlation matrix must be mutually inconsistent. Of course, *true* correlation coefficients are always consistent. But we do not know these true correlations and can only estimate them with some imprecision. Unfortunately, as this example illustrates, it is difficult to determine at a quick glance whether a correlation matrix is inconsistent, providing another motivation to seek a model that is easier to implement.

Introducing a model that simplifies the way we describe the sources of security risk allows us to use a smaller, necessarily consistent, and, just as important, more easily

---

[1] We are grateful to Andrew Kaplin and Ravi Jagannathan, Kellogg Graduate School of Management, Northwestern University, for this example.

interpreted set of estimates of risk parameters and risk premiums. The simplification emerges because positive covariances among security returns arise from common economic forces that affect the fortunes of most firms. Some examples of common economic factors are business cycles, interest rates, and the cost of natural resources. "Shocks" (i.e., unexpected changes) to these macroeconomic variables cause, simultaneously, correlated shocks in the rates of return on stocks across the entire market. By decomposing uncertainty into these systemwide versus firm-specific sources, we vastly simplify the problem of estimating covariance and correlation.

Systematic versus Firm-Specific Risk

We focus on risk by separating the actual rate of return on any security, i, into the sum of its previously expected value plus an unanticipated surprise:

$$r_i = E(r_i) + \text{unanticipated surprise} \tag{8.1}$$

The unanticipated component of the stock return can be due either to unexpected developments in issues that are particular to the firm or to unexpected changes in conditions that affect the broad economy. We therefore will decompose the sources of return uncertainty into uncertainty about the economy as a whole, which is captured by a systematic market factor that we will call m, and uncertainty about the firm in particular, which is captured by a *firm-specific* random variable that we will call e_i. The common dependence that virtually all firms have to macroeconomic conditions is the source of the correlation between their security returns.

The market factor, m, measures unanticipated developments in the macroeconomy. For example, it might be the difference between GDP growth and the market's previous expectation of that growth. As such, it has a mean of zero (over time, surprises will average out to zero), with standard deviation of σ_m. In contrast, e_i measures only the firm-specific surprise. As a surprise, it too has zero expected value. Notice that m has no subscript because the same common factor affects all securities. Most important is the fact that m and e_i are assumed to be uncorrelated: Because e_i is firm-specific, it is independent of shocks to the common factor that affect the entire economy. The variance of r_i thus arises from two uncorrelated sources, systematic and firm-specific.

Finally, we recognize that some securities will be more sensitive than others to macroeconomic shocks. For example, auto firms might respond more dramatically to changes in general economic conditions than pharmaceutical firms. We can capture this refinement by assigning each firm a sensitivity coefficient to macro conditions. Therefore, if we denote the sensitivity coefficient for firm i by the Greek letter beta, β_i, we can write the return on each stock in any period as the sum of three terms: the originally expected return, the impact of the common macroeconomic surprise (which depends on the firm's sensitivity to that surprise), and the impact of firm-specific surprises. Equation 8.2 is the algebraic expression of this **single-factor model:**

$$r_i = E(r_i) + \beta_i m + e_i \tag{8.2}$$

There are two uncorrelated random terms on the right-hand side of Equation 8.2, so the total variance of r_i is

$$\sigma_i^2 = \beta_i^2 \sigma_m^2 + \sigma^2(e_i) \tag{8.3}$$

The variance of returns attributable to the marketwide factor is called the systematic risk of the security. This component of variance equals $\beta_i^2 \sigma_m^2$ and is higher when firm i's beta coefficient is higher. "Cyclical" firms have greater sensitivity to the market (higher betas) and therefore have greater systematic risk. The firm-specific component of return variance is $\sigma^2(e_i)$.

Because the index model assumes that firm-specific surprises are mutually uncorrelated, the only source of covariance between any pair of securities is their common dependence on the market return. Therefore, the covariance between two firms' returns depends on the sensitivity of each to the market, as measured by their betas:

$$\text{Cov}(r_i, r_j) = \text{Cov}(\beta_i m + e_i, \beta_j m + e_j) = \beta_i \beta_j \sigma_m^2 \qquad \textbf{(8.4)}$$

The decomposition of return variability into components that depend on a common macroeconomic factor versus firm-specific shocks is compelling but, to be useful, we still need a variable that can proxy for this common factor. This variable must be observable, so we can estimate its volatility as well as the sensitivity of individual securities to variation in its outcome.

8.2   The Single-Index Model

Because the systematic factor affects the rate of return on all stocks, the rate of return on a broad market index can plausibly proxy for that common factor. This approach leads to an equation similar to the single-factor model, which is called a **single-index model** because it uses the market index to stand in for the common factor.

The Regression Equation of the Single-Index Model

The intuition behind the index model can be seen in Figure 8.1. We begin with a historical sample of paired observations of excess returns[2] on the market index and a particular security, let's say shares in Ford. In Figure 8.1, we have 60 pairs of monthly excess returns, one for each month in a five-year sample. Each dot represents the pair of returns in one particular month. For example, in January 2012, Ford's excess return was 15.9% while the market's was 5.4%.

To describe the *typical* relation between the return on Ford and the return on the market index, we fit a straight line through this **scatter diagram.** It is clear from this "line of best fit" that there is a positive relation between Ford's return and the market's. This is evidence for the importance of broad market conditions on the performance of Ford's stock. The slope of the line reflects the sensitivity of Ford's return to market conditions: A steeper line would imply that Ford's rate of return is more responsive to the market return. On the other hand, the scatter diagram also shows that market conditions are not the entire story: If returns *perfectly* tracked those of the market, then all return pairs would lie exactly on the line. The scatter of points *around* the line is evidence that firm-specific events also have a significant impact on Ford's return.

How do we determine the line of best fit in Figure 8.1? We will denote the market index by M, with excess return of $R_M = r_M - r_f$, and standard deviation of σ_M. We estimate the line using a single-variable linear regression. Specifically, we regress Ford's excess return, $R_{\text{Ford}} = r_{\text{Ford}} - r_f$, on the excess return of the index, R_M. More generally, for any stock i,

[2]We use excess returns rather than total returns in this diagram. This is because we treat risk-free T-bills as an alternative parking place for the investor's funds. You will be happy to have moved funds from the risk-free asset to a risky alternative only if its *excess* return turns out to be positive. So the performance of a risky investment is better measured by excess rather than total return.

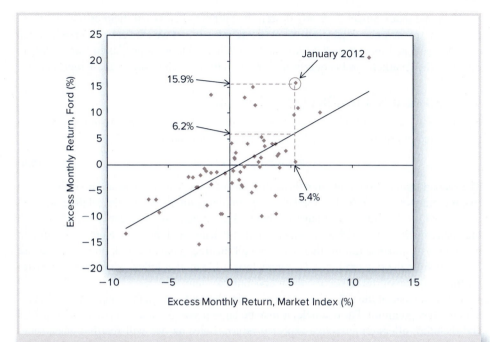

Figure 8.1 Scatter diagram for Ford against the market index and Ford's security characteristic line

denote the pair of excess returns in month t by $R_i(t)$ and $R_M(t)$.[3] Then the index model can be written as the following **regression equation:**

$$R_i(t) = \alpha_i + \beta_i R_M(t) + e_i(t) \qquad \textbf{(8.5)}$$

The intercept of this equation (denoted by the Greek letter alpha, or α) is the security's expected excess return when the market excess return is zero. It is the vertical intercept in Figure 8.1. The slope of the line in the figure is the security's beta coefficient, β_i. Beta is the amount by which the security return tends to increase or decrease for every 1% increase or decrease in the return on the index, and therefore measures the security's sensitivity to the market index. e_i is the zero-mean, firm-specific surprise in the security return in month t, also called the **residual.** The greater the residuals (positive or negative), the wider is the scatter of returns around the straight line in Figure 8.1.

Notice that so far, there is little "theory" in the index model. The model is merely a way to *describe* the typical relation between market returns and returns on particular firms. The average beta of all stocks in the economy is 1; the average response of a stock to changes in a market index composed of all stocks must be 1-for-1. The beta of the market index is, by definition, 1; the index obviously responds 1-for-1 to changes in itself. "Cyclical" or aggressive stocks have higher-than-average sensitivity to the broad economy and therefore have betas greater than 1. Conversely, the betas of "defensive" stocks are less than 1. The returns of these stocks respond less than 1-for-1 to market returns.

---

[3]Practitioners often use a "modified" index model that is similar to Equation 8.5 but that uses total rather than excess returns. This practice is most common when daily data are used. In this case, the rate of return on bills is on the order of only about .01% per day, so total and excess returns are almost indistinguishable.

While the index model is mostly descriptive, it nevertheless will help us address these two important theoretical questions: (1) What relation might we expect to observe between a stock's beta and its expected return? and (2) What value for alpha should we expect to observe when markets are in equilibrium? We will have much to say on these topics below.

The Expected Return–Beta Relationship

Because $E(e_i) = 0$, if we take the expected value of both sides of Equation 8.5, we obtain the expected return–beta relationship of the single-index model:

$$E(R_i) = \alpha_i + \beta_i E(R_M) \tag{8.6}$$

The second term in Equation 8.6 tells us that part of a security's risk premium is due to the risk premium of the index. The market risk premium is multiplied by the relative sensitivity, or beta, of the individual security. This makes intuitive sense because securities with high betas have a magnified sensitivity to market risk and will therefore enjoy a greater risk premium as compensation for this risk. We call this the *systematic* risk premium because it derives from the risk premium that characterizes the market index, which in turn proxies for the condition of the full economy or economic system.

The remainder of the risk premium is given by the first term in the equation, α. Alpha is a *nonmarket* premium. For example, α may be large if you think a security is underpriced and therefore offers an attractive expected return. Later on, we will see that when security prices are in equilibrium, such attractive opportunities ought to be competed away, in which case α will be driven to zero. But for now, let's assume that each security analyst comes up with his or her own estimates of alpha. If managers believe that they can do a superior job of security analysis, then they will be confident in their ability to find stocks with nonzero values of alpha.

We will see shortly that the index model decomposition of an individual security's risk premium to market and nonmarket components greatly clarifies and simplifies the operation of macroeconomic and security analysis within an investment company.

Risk and Covariance in the Single-Index Model

Remember that one of the problems with the Markowitz model is the large number of parameter estimates required to implement it. Now we will see that the index model vastly reduces the number of parameters that must be estimated. In particular, we saw from Equation 8.4 that the covariance between any pair of stocks is determined by their common exposure to market risk; this insight yields great simplification in estimating an otherwise overwhelming set of covariance pairs. Using Equation 8.5, we can derive the following elements of the input list for portfolio optimization from the parameters of the index model:

Total risk = Systematic risk + Firm-specific risk

$$\sigma_i^2 = \beta_i^2 \sigma_M^2 + \sigma^2(e_i)$$

Covariance = Product of betas × Market-index risk

$$\text{Cov}(r_i, r_j) = \beta_i \beta_j \sigma_M^2 \tag{8.7}$$

Correlation = Product of correlations with the market index

$$\text{Corr}(r_i, r_j) = \frac{\beta_i \beta_j \sigma_M^2}{\sigma_i \sigma_j} = \frac{\beta_i \sigma_M^2 \beta_j \sigma_M^2}{\sigma_i \sigma_M \sigma_j \sigma_M} = \text{Corr}(r_i, r_M) \times \text{Corr}(r_j, r_M)$$

Equations 8.6 and 8.7 imply that the set of parameter estimates needed for the single-index model consists of only α_i, β_i, and $\sigma(e_i)$ for each individual security, plus the risk premium and variance of the market index.

Concept Check **8.1**

The data below describe a three-stock financial market that satisfies the single-index model.

Stock	Capitalization	Beta	Mean Excess Return	Standard Deviation
A	$3,000	1.0	10%	40%
B	1,940	0.2	2	30
C	1,360	1.7	17	50

The standard deviation of the market-index portfolio is 25%.

a. What is the mean excess return of the index portfolio?

b. What is the covariance between stock A and stock B?

c. What is the covariance between stock B and the index?

d. Break down the variance of stock B into its systematic and firm-specific components.

The Set of Estimates Needed for the Single-Index Model

We summarize the results for the single-index model in the table below.

	Symbol
1. The stock's expected return if the market is neutral, that is, if the market's excess return, $r_M - r_f$, is zero	α_i
2. The component of return due to movements in the overall market in any period; β_i is the security's responsiveness to market movements	$\beta_i(r_M - r_f)$
3. The unexpected component of return in any period due to unexpected events that are relevant only to this security (firm specific)	e_i
4. The variance attributable to the uncertainty of the common macro-economic factor	$\beta_i^2 \sigma_M^2$
5. The variance attributable to firm-specific uncertainty	$\sigma^2(e_i)$

These calculations show that if we have:

- n estimates of the extra-market expected excess returns, α_i
- n estimates of the sensitivity coefficients, β_i
- n estimates of the firm-specific variances, $\sigma^2(e_i)$
- 1 estimate for the market risk premium, $E(R_M)$
- 1 estimate for the variance of the (common) macroeconomic factor, σ_M^2

then these $(3n + 2)$ estimates will enable us to prepare the entire input list for this single-index-security universe. Thus for a 50-security portfolio, we will need 152 estimates rather than 1,325; for the entire set of approximately 3,400 actively traded stocks in the U.S., we will need 10,202 estimates rather than approximately 5.8 million!

It is easy to see why the index model is such a useful abstraction. For large universes of securities, the number of estimates required for the Markowitz procedure using the index model is only a small fraction of what otherwise would be needed.

Another advantage is less obvious but equally important. The index model abstraction is crucial for specialization of effort in security analysis. If a covariance term had to be calculated directly for each security pair, then security analysts could not specialize by industry. For example, if one group were to specialize in the computer industry and another in the auto industry, who would have the common background to estimate the covariance *between* IBM and GM? Neither group would have the deep understanding of other industries necessary to make an informed judgment of co-movements among industries. In contrast, the index model suggests a simple way to compute covariances. They are due to the common influence of the single macroeconomic factor, represented by the market index return, and can be easily estimated using Equation 8.7.

The simplification derived from the index model assumption is, however, not without cost. The "cost" of the model lies in the restrictions it places on the structure of asset return uncertainty. The classification of uncertainty into a simple dichotomy—macro versus micro risk—oversimplifies sources of real-world uncertainty and misses some important sources of dependence in stock returns. For example, this dichotomy rules out industry events that may affect many firms within an industry without substantially affecting the broad macroeconomy.

This last point is potentially important. Imagine that the single-index model is perfectly accurate, except that the residuals of two stocks, say, British Petroleum (BP) and Royal Dutch Shell, are correlated. The index model will ignore this correlation (it will assume it is zero), while the Markowitz algorithm (which accounts for the full covariance between every pair of stocks) will automatically take the residual correlation into account when minimizing portfolio variance. If the universe of securities from which we construct the optimal portfolio is small, the two models can yield substantively different optimal portfolios. The portfolio resulting from the Markowitz algorithm will place a smaller weight on both BP and Shell because their mutual covariance reduces their diversification value. Conversely, when correlation among residuals is negative, the index model will ignore the potential diversification value of these securities. The resulting "optimal" portfolio will place too little weight on these securities.

The optimal portfolio derived from the single-index model therefore can be significantly inferior to that of the full-covariance (Markowitz) model when stocks with correlated residuals account for a large fraction of the portfolio. If many pairs of the covered stocks exhibit residual correlation, it is possible that a *multi-index* model, which includes additional factors to capture those extra sources of cross-security correlation, would be better suited for portfolio analysis and construction. We will demonstrate the effect of correlated residuals in the spreadsheet example in this chapter, leaving our discussion of multi-index models to later chapters.

✔ Concept Check **8.2**

Suppose that the index model for the excess returns of stocks *A* and *B* is estimated with the following results:

$$R_A = 1.0\% + .9R_M + e_A$$
$$R_B = -2.0\% + 1.1R_M + e_B$$
$$\sigma_M = 20\%$$
$$\sigma(e_A) = 30\%$$
$$\sigma(e_B) = 10\%$$

Find the standard deviation of each stock and the covariance between them.

The Index Model and Diversification

The index model, first suggested by Sharpe,[4] also offers insight into portfolio diversification. Suppose that we choose an equally weighted portfolio of n securities. The excess rate of return on each security is given by

$$R_i = \alpha_i + \beta_i R_M + e_i$$

Similarly, we can write the excess return on the portfolio of stocks as

$$R_P = \alpha_P + \beta_P R_M + e_P \tag{8.8}$$

We now show that, as the number of stocks included in this portfolio increases, the part of the portfolio risk attributable to nonmarket factors becomes ever smaller. This part of the risk is diversified away, and therefore will be of little concern to investors. In contrast, market risk remains, regardless of the number of firms combined into the portfolio.

To understand these results, note that the excess rate of return on this equally weighted portfolio, for which each portfolio weight $w_i = 1/n$, is

$$
\begin{aligned}
R_P &= \sum_{i=1}^{n} w_i R_i = \frac{1}{n} \sum_{i=1}^{n} R_i = \frac{1}{n} \sum_{i=1}^{n} (\alpha_i + \beta_i R_M + e_i) \\
&= \frac{1}{n} \sum_{i=1}^{n} \alpha_i + \left(\frac{1}{n} \sum_{i=1}^{n} \beta_i \right) R_M + \frac{1}{n} \sum_{i=1}^{n} e_i
\end{aligned}
\tag{8.9}
$$

Comparing Equations 8.8 and 8.9, we see that the portfolio has a sensitivity to the market given by

$$\beta_P = \frac{1}{n} \sum_{i=1}^{n} \beta_i \tag{8.10}$$

which is the average of the individual β_is. It has a nonmarket return component of

$$\alpha_P = \frac{1}{n} \sum_{i=1}^{n} \alpha_i \tag{8.11}$$

which is the average of the individual alphas, plus the zero mean variable

$$e_P = \frac{1}{n} \sum_{i=1}^{n} e_i \tag{8.12}$$

which is the average of the firm-specific components. Hence the portfolio's variance is

$$\sigma_P^2 = \beta_P^2 \sigma_M^2 + \sigma^2(e_P) \tag{8.13}$$

The systematic component of the portfolio variance, which we defined as the component that depends on marketwide movements, is $\beta_P^2 \sigma_M^2$ and depends on the average beta coefficient of the individual securities. This part of the risk depends on portfolio beta and σ_M^2 and will persist regardless of the extent of portfolio diversification. No matter how many stocks are held, their common exposure to the market will result in a positive portfolio beta and be reflected in portfolio systematic risk.[5]

In contrast, the nonsystematic component of the portfolio variance is $\sigma^2(e_P)$ and is attributable to the firm-specific components, e_i. Because these e_is are independent, and all have zero expected value, the law of averages can be applied to conclude that as more and more stocks are added to the portfolio, the firm-specific components tend to cancel out,

---

[4]William F. Sharpe, "A Simplified Model of Portfolio Analysis," *Management Science,* January 1963.

[5]In principle, one can construct a portfolio with zero systematic risk by mixing negative β and positive β assets. The point of our discussion is that the vast majority of securities have a positive β, implying that highly diversified portfolios with small holdings in large numbers of assets will indeed have positive systematic risk.

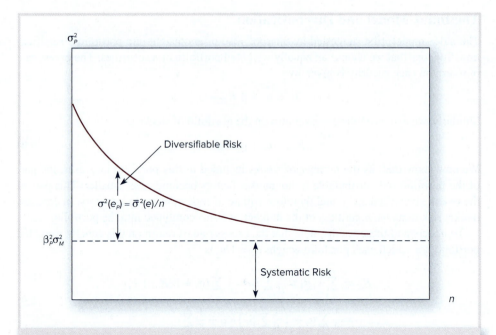

Figure 8.2 The variance of an equally weighted portfolio with risk coefficient β_P in the single-factor economy as a function of the number of firms included in the portfolio

resulting in ever-smaller nonmarket risk. Such risk is thus termed *diversifiable*. To see this more rigorously, examine the formula for the variance of the equally weighted "portfolio" of firm-specific components. Because the e_is are uncorrelated,

$$\sigma^2(e_P) = Var\left(\frac{1}{n}\sum_{i=1}^{n} e_i\right) = \sum_{i=1}^{n}\left(\frac{1}{n}\right)^2 \sigma^2(e_i) = \frac{1}{n}\sum_{i=1}^{n}\frac{\sigma^2(e_i)}{n} = \frac{1}{n}\bar{\sigma}^2(e) \tag{8.14}$$

where $\bar{\sigma}^2(e)$ is the average of the firm-specific variances. Because the average nonsystematic variance is independent of n, when n gets large, $\sigma^2(e_P)$ becomes negligible.

To summarize, as diversification increases, the total variance of a portfolio approaches the systematic variance, defined as the variance of the market index multiplied by the square of the portfolio sensitivity coefficient, β_P^2. This is shown in Figure 8.2.

Figure 8.2 shows that as more and more securities are combined into a portfolio, the portfolio variance decreases because of the diversification of firm-specific risk. However, the power of diversification is limited. Even for very large n, part of the risk remains because of the exposure of virtually all assets to the common, or market, factor. Therefore, systematic risk is said to be nondiversifiable.

This analysis is borne out by empirical evidence. We saw the effect of portfolio diversification on portfolio standard deviations in Figure 7.2. These empirical results are similar to the theoretical graph presented here in Figure 8.2.

 Concept Check **8.3**

Reconsider the two stocks in Concept Check 8.2. Suppose we form an equally weighted portfolio of A and B. What will be the nonsystematic standard deviation of that portfolio?

8.3   Estimating the Single-Index Model

Let's pause here to see how one would actually estimate the parameters of the index model. We work with 60 monthly observations of rates of return for the market index and a particular stock. As in Chapter 5, we will use as the market index a comprehensive value-weighted portfolio of the firms that actively trade on the NYSE, AMEX, and NASDAQ. We will treat T-bills as the risk-free asset, and we will estimate the parameters of the model over the 5-year period ending in December 2015.

The Security Characteristic Line for Ford

Figure 8.3 shows a graph of the excess returns on Ford and the market index over the 60-month period. The graph shows that Ford's returns generally follow those of the index, but with noticeably larger swings. Indeed, the monthly standard deviation of the excess return on the index portfolio over the period was 3.48%, while that of Ford was 7.35%. The larger swings in Ford's excess returns suggest that we should find a greater-than-average sensitivity to the market index, that is, a beta greater than 1.0.

The index model regression Equation 8.5, using Ford as our example firm, is restated as

$$R_{\text{Ford}}(t) = \alpha_{\text{Ford}} + \beta_{\text{Ford}} R_{\text{index}}(t) + e_{\text{Ford}}(t)$$

The equation describes the (linear) dependence of Ford's excess return on the excess return of the market index portfolio. The regression estimates describe a straight line with intercept α_{Ford} and slope β_{Ford}, which we call Ford's **security characteristic line (SCL).**

The vertical distance of each point from the regression line is the value of Ford's residual, $e_{\text{Ford}}(t)$, in that particular month. For example, in January 2012, when the market's excess return was 5.4%, the regression line would have predicted an excess return for Ford of 6.2%. This is the y-axis value on the regression line corresponding to an x-axis value (the market's excess return) of 5.4%. In fact, Ford's excess return in January was 15.9%, implying that the residual return in this month was $15.9 - 6.2 = 9.7\%$. This is evidence of good firm-specific news that contributed 9.7% to Ford's rate of return.

We estimate the parameters of the regression line in Figure 8.1 using Excel's Regression tool (this tool is available as an Add-In under the Data tab). The regression analysis output obtained by using Excel is shown in Table 8.1.

The Explanatory Power of Ford's SCL

Starting with the upper panel of Table 8.1, we see that the correlation of Ford with the market index is fairly high (.628), telling us that returns on Ford generally track those of the market index. The R-square (.394) tells us that variation in the excess returns of the market index explains about 39.4% of the variation in the Ford

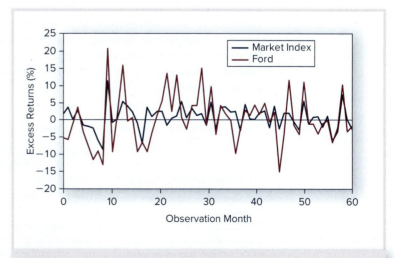

Figure 8.3 Excess returns on Ford and the market index

Table 8.1

Excel output: Regression statistics for Ford's SCL

Regression Statistics				
Multiple R	0.6280			
R-square	0.3943			
Adjusted R-square	0.3839			
Standard error	0.0577			
Observations	60			
	Coefficients	**Standard Error**	**t-Stat**	**p-Value**
Intercept	−0.0098	0.0077	−1.2767	0.2068
Market index	1.3258	0.2157	6.1451	0.0000

series.[6] The adjusted R-square (which is slightly smaller) corrects for an upward bias in R-square that arises because we use the estimated values of two parameters,[7] the slope (beta) and intercept (alpha), rather than their true, but unobservable, values. With 60 observations, this bias is small. The standard error of the regression is the standard deviation of the residual, e. High standard errors imply greater impact (positive and negative) of firm-specific events from one month to the next.

The Estimate of Alpha

We move now to the lower panel of Table 8.1. The intercept ($-.0098 = -.98\%$ per month) is the estimate of Ford's alpha for the sample period. Although this is an economically large value (almost 1% *per month*), it is statistically insignificant. This can be seen from the three statistics next to the estimated coefficient. The first is the standard error of the estimate (.0077). This is a measure of the imprecision of the estimate. If the standard error is large, the range of likely estimation error is correspondingly large. Here, the standard error is nearly as large as the estimated alpha coefficient.

The t-statistic reported in the next column is the ratio of the regression parameter to its standard error. This statistic equals the number of standard errors by which our estimate exceeds zero, and therefore can be used to assess the likelihood that the true but unobserved value might actually be zero rather than the estimate we derived from the data.[8] The intuition is that if the true value were zero, we would be unlikely to observe estimated values far away (i.e., many standard errors) from zero. So large t-statistics imply low probabilities that the true value is zero.

---

[6]The equation for the R-square is the ratio of the systemic variance to total variance:

$$R\text{-square} = \frac{\beta_F^2 \sigma_{\text{index}}^2}{\beta_F^2 \sigma_{\text{index}}^2 + \sigma^2(e_F)}$$

[7]In general, the adjusted R-square (R_A^2) is derived from the unadjusted by $R_A^2 = 1 - (1 - R^2)\dfrac{n-1}{n-k-1}$, where k is the number of independent variables (here, $k = 1$). An additional degree of freedom is lost to the estimate of the intercept.

[8]The t-statistic is based on the assumption that returns are normally distributed. In general, if we standardize the estimate of a normally distributed variable by computing its difference from a hypothesized value and dividing by the standard error of the estimate (to express the difference as a number of standard errors), the resulting variable will have a t-distribution. With a large number of observations, the bell-shaped t-distribution approaches the normal distribution.

Given the t-statistic, we can use a table of the t-distribution (or Excel's TINV function) to find the probability that the true alpha is actually zero despite a regression estimate that differs from zero. This is alternatively called the *level of significance* or, as in Table 8.1, the probability or p-value. The conventional cutoff for statistical significance is a probability of less than 5%, which requires a t-statistic of about 2.0. The regression output shows that the t-statistic for Ford's alpha is only 1.2767, indicating that the estimate is not significantly different from zero. That is, we cannot reject the hypothesis that the true value of alpha equals zero with an acceptable level of confidence. The p-value for the alpha estimate (.2068) indicates that if the true alpha were zero, the probability of obtaining an estimate with an absolute value as large as .0098 would be .2068, or 20.68%, which is not so unlikely. We conclude that the evidence is not strong enough to reject the hypothesis that the true value of alpha is zero.

The Estimate of Beta

The regression output in Table 8.1 shows Ford's beta estimate to be 1.3258, meaning that Ford's share price tended to move 1.3258% for every 1% move in the market index. Such high market sensitivity is not unusual for automobile stocks. The standard error (SE) of the estimate is .2157.

The value of beta and its SE produce a large t-statistic (6.1451), and a p-value of practically zero. We can confidently reject the hypothesis that Ford's true beta is zero. This is hardly surprising in light of Figure 8.3, which showed that Ford's return and that of the market index were clearly related. A more interesting t-statistic might test the hypothesis that Ford's beta is greater than the marketwide average beta of 1. This t-statistic would measure how many standard errors separate the estimated beta from a hypothesized value of 1. Here, despite the large point estimate of Ford's beta, the imprecision of the estimate (reflected in the standard error) results in a t-statistic of only 1.51 and does not allow us to reject the hypothesis that the true beta is 1.

$$\frac{\text{Estimated value} - \text{Hypothesized value}}{\text{Standard error}} = \frac{1.3258 - 1}{.2157} = 1.51$$

In general, precision is not what we would like it to be. For example, if we wanted to construct a confidence interval that includes the true but unobserved value of beta with 95% probability, we would take the estimated value as the center of the interval and then add and subtract about two standard errors. This produces a range between 0.894 and 1.757, which is quite wide.

Firm-Specific Risk

The standard deviation of Ford's residual is 5.77% per month, or 19.99% annually. This is quite large, on top of Ford's already high systematic risk. The standard deviation of systematic risk is $\beta \times \sigma(\text{index}) = 1.3258 \times 3.48\% = 4.61\%$ per month or 15.97% annually. Notice that Ford's firm-specific risk is greater than its systematic risk, a common result for individual stocks. In other words, more of the fluctuation in Ford's monthly return derives from firm-specific factors than from marketwide systematic factors.

Typical Results from Index Model Regressions   Table 8.2 shows index model regressions for a sample of large companies. Notice that the average beta of the firms is .915, not so far from the expected value of 1.0. As one would expect, firms with high

Ticker	Company	Beta	Alpha	R-Square	Residual Std Dev	Standard Error Beta	Standard Error Alpha	Adjusted Beta
MSFT	Microsoft	0.856	0.008	0.224	0.056	0.209	0.007	0.904
KO	Coca-Cola	0.406	0.004	0.129	0.037	0.138	0.005	0.604
XOM	ExxonMobil	0.876	−0.003	0.460	0.033	0.125	0.004	0.917
GE	General Electric	1.093	0.004	0.467	0.041	0.153	0.005	1.062
BA	Boeing	0.944	0.009	0.350	0.045	0.169	0.006	0.963
NEM	Newmont Mining	0.316	−0.016	0.011	0.107	0.400	0.014	0.544
PFE	Pfizer	0.837	0.007	0.432	0.034	0.126	0.004	0.891
F	Ford	1.326	−0.010	0.394	0.058	0.216	0.008	1.217
DIS	Walt Disney	1.352	0.009	0.617	0.037	0.140	0.005	1.235
BP	BP	1.533	−0.012	0.584	0.045	0.170	0.006	1.355
MCD	McDonald's	0.455	0.006	0.186	0.033	0.125	0.004	0.637
WMT	Walmart	0.209	0.003	0.023	0.048	0.179	0.006	0.473
INTC	Intel	0.831	0.006	0.221	0.055	0.205	0.007	0.887
BAC	Bank of America	1.681	−0.005	0.361	0.078	0.294	0.010	1.454
VZ	Verizon	0.237	0.007	0.037	0.042	0.158	0.006	0.492
X	U.S. Steel	1.844	−0.039	0.255	0.111	0.414	0.015	1.563
AMZN	Amazon	0.866	0.018	0.142	0.075	0.279	0.010	0.911
GOOG	Alphabet (Google)	0.799	0.011	0.166	0.063	0.235	0.008	0.866
	AVERAGE	0.915	0.000	0.281	0.055	0.207	0.007	0.943
	STD DEVIATION	0.488	0.013	0.186	0.024	0.088	0.003	0.325

Table 8.2

Index model estimates: Regressions of excess stock returns on the excess return of the broad market index over 60 months, 2011–2015

exposure to the state of the macroeconomy (e.g., U.S. Steel, Ford, and Disney) have betas greater than 1. Firms whose business is less sensitive to the macroeconomy (e.g., Walmart, McDonald's, and Coca-Cola) have betas less than 1.

The average alpha for this sample is almost precisely zero. Because the average non-market risk premium is zero, we conclude that these firms, on average, were neither underpriced nor overpriced. Moreover, there are only two firms in the entire sample for which the estimate of alpha is more than twice its standard error. In other words, the alpha estimates, by and large, are not statistically significant.

The column titled Residual Standard Deviation is the standard deviation of the residual terms, *e,* and is our measure of firm-specific risk. Notice how high that risk is, averaging 5.5% per month. This reminds us again of the importance of diversification. Anyone who concentrates a portfolio in just one or a few securities is bearing an enormous amount of risk that can easily be diversified.

The high levels of firm-specific risk are reflected as well in the *R*-square of these regressions, which average only 28.1%. For this sample of stocks, only 28.1% of return variance is due to market factors, implying that 71.9% is due to firm-specific factors.

8.4   The Industry Version of the Index Model

A portfolio manager who has neither special information about a security nor insight that is unavailable to the general public will take the security's alpha value as zero, and, according to Equation 8.6, will forecast a risk premium for the security equal to $\beta_i R_M$. If we restate this forecast in terms of total returns, one would expect

$$E(r_i) = r_f + \beta_i[E(r_M) - r_f] \tag{8.15}$$

A portfolio manager who has a forecast for the market index, $E(r_M)$, and observes the risk-free T-bill rate, r_f, can use the model to determine the benchmark expected return for any stock. The beta coefficient, the market risk, σ_M^2, and the firm-specific risk, $\sigma^2(e)$, can be estimated from historical SCLs, that is, from regressions of security excess returns on market index excess returns.

There are several proprietary sources for such regression results, sometimes called "beta books." The Web sites listed in Connect for this chapter also provide security betas.

Industry beta services do, however, differ in a few ways from the sort of analysis we presented in Table 8.2. First, they typically use the S&P 500 rather than our broader market index as the proxy for the market factor. Second, they often use total returns, rather than excess returns (deviations from T-bill rates), in the regressions. In this way, they estimate a variant of our index model, which is

$$r = a + br_M + e^* \tag{8.16}$$

instead of

$$r - r_f = \alpha + \beta(r_M - r_f) + e \tag{8.17}$$

To see the effect of this departure, we can rewrite Equation 8.17 as

$$r = r_f + \alpha + \beta r_M - \beta r_f + e = \alpha + r_f(1 - \beta) + \beta r_M + e \tag{8.18}$$

Comparing Equations 8.16 and 8.18, you can see that if r_f is constant over the sample period, both equations have the same independent variable, r_M, and residual, e. Therefore, the slope coefficient will be the same in the two regressions.[9]

However, the intercept that the beta books call ALPHA is really an estimate of $\alpha + r_f(1 - \beta)$. On a monthly basis, $r_f(1 - \beta)$ is small and is likely to be swamped by the volatility of actual stock returns. But it is worth noting that for $\beta \neq 1$, the regression intercept in Equation 8.16 will not equal the index model α as it does when excess returns are used, as in Equation 8.17.

 Concept Check **8.4**

Table 8.2 shows that the estimate of Microsoft's index-model α (per month) regression was .8%. If the monthly T-bill rate during this period was .2%, then what would you predict would be the value of ALPHA reported in a standard industry beta book?

Always remember as well that these alpha estimates are ex post (after the fact) measures. They do not mean that anyone could have forecast these alpha values ex ante (before

---

[9]Actually, r_f does vary over time and so should not be grouped casually with the constant term in the regression. However, variations in r_f are tiny compared with the swings in the market return. The actual volatility in the T-bill rate has only a small impact on the estimated value of β.

the fact). In fact, the name of the game in security analysis is to forecast alpha values ahead of time. A well-constructed portfolio that includes long positions in future positive-alpha stocks and short positions in future negative-alpha stocks will outperform the market index. The key term here is "well constructed," meaning that the portfolio has to balance concentration on high-alpha stocks with the need for risk-reducing diversification. This trade-off is discussed in the next section.

The last column in Table 8.2 is called Adjusted Beta. The motivation for adjusting beta estimates is that, as an empirical matter, beta coefficients seem to move toward 1 over time. One explanation for this phenomenon is intuitive. A business enterprise usually is established to produce a specific product or service, and a new firm may be more unconventional than an older one in many ways, from technology to management style. As it grows, however, a firm often diversifies, first expanding to similar products and later to more diverse operations. As the firm becomes more conventional, it starts to resemble the rest of the economy even more. Thus, its beta coefficient will tend to change in the direction of 1.

Another explanation is statistical. We know that the average beta over all securities is 1. Thus, before estimating the beta of a security, our best forecast would be that it is 1. When we estimate this beta coefficient over a particular sample period, we inevitably sustain some unknown sampling error of the estimated beta. The greater the difference between our beta estimate and 1, the greater is the chance that we have incurred a large estimation error and that beta in a subsequent sample period will be closer to 1.

The estimate of the beta coefficient is the best guess for that particular sample period. Given that beta has a tendency to evolve toward 1, however, a forecast of the future beta coefficient should adjust the sample estimate in that direction.

Table 8.2 adjusts beta estimates in a simple way.[10] It takes the sample estimate of beta and averages it with 1, using weights of two-thirds and one-third:

$$\text{Adjusted beta} = \frac{2}{3} \text{ estimated beta} + \frac{1}{3}(1.0) \tag{8.19}$$

Example 8.1   Adjusted Beta

For the 60 months used in Table 8.2, Ford's beta was estimated at 1.326. Therefore, its adjusted beta is $\frac{2}{3} \times 1.326 + \frac{1}{3} \times 1 = 1.217$, taking it a third of the way toward 1.

In the absence of special information concerning Ford, if our forecast for the return on the market index is 10% and T-bills pay 4%, we infer from the table that the forecast for the rate of return on Ford stock is:

$$E(r_{\text{Ford}}) = r_f + \text{Adjusted beta} \times [E(r_M) - r_f]$$
$$= 4 + 1.217(10 - 4) = 11.3\%$$

Predicting Betas

Adjusted betas are a simple way to recognize that betas estimated from past data may not be the best estimates of future betas: Betas seem to drift toward 1 over time. This suggests that we might want a forecasting model for beta.

One simple approach would be to collect data on beta in different periods and then estimate a regression equation:

$$\text{Current beta} = a + b \text{ (Past beta)} \tag{8.20}$$

---

[10]A more sophisticated method is described in Oldrich A. Vasicek, "A Note on Using Cross-Sectional Information in Bayesian Estimation of Security Betas," *Journal of Finance* 28 (1973), pp. 1233–39.

Given estimates of *a* and *b,* we would then forecast future betas using the rule

$$\text{Forecast beta} = a + b \text{ (Current beta)} \qquad (8.21)$$

There is no reason, however, to limit ourselves to such simple forecasting rules. Why not also investigate the predictive power of other financial variables in forecasting beta? For example, if we believe that firm size and debt ratios are two determinants of beta, we might specify an expanded version of Equation 8.20 and estimate

$$\text{Current beta} = a + b_1 \text{ (Past beta)} + b_2 \text{ (Firm size)} + b_3 \text{ (Debt ratio)}$$

Now we would use estimates of *a* and b_1 through b_3 to forecast future betas.

Such an approach was suggested in an early study by Rosenberg and Guy,[11] who found the following variables to help predict betas:

1. Variance of earnings.
2. Variance of cash flow.
3. Growth in earnings per share.
4. Market capitalization (firm size).
5. Dividend yield.
6. Debt-to-asset ratio.

They also found that even after controlling for a firm's financial characteristics, industry group helps to predict beta. For example, they found that the beta values of gold mining companies are, on average, .827 lower than would be predicted based on financial characteristics alone. This should not be surprising; the −.827 "adjustment factor" for the gold industry reflects the fact that gold values have low or even negative correlation with market returns.

Table 8.3 presents beta estimates and adjustment factors for a subset of firms in the Rosenberg and Guy study.

 Concept Check **8.5**

> Compare the first five and last four industries in Table 8.3. What characteristic seems to determine whether the adjustment factor is positive or negative?

Table 8.3

Industry betas and adjustment factors

Industry	Beta	Adjustment Factor
Agriculture	0.99	−0.140
Drugs and medicine	1.14	−0.099
Telephone	0.75	−0.288
Energy utilities	0.60	−0.237
Gold	0.36	−0.827
Construction	1.27	0.062
Air transport	1.80	0.348
Trucking	1.31	0.098
Consumer durables	1.44	0.132

---

[11]Barr Rosenberg and J. Guy, "Prediction of Beta from Investment Fundamentals, Parts 1 and 2," *Financial Analysts Journal,* May–June and July–August 1976.

8.5   Portfolio Construction Using the Single-Index Model

In this section, we look at the implications of the index model for portfolio construction. These techniques were originally developed by Jack Treynor and Fischer Black and are commonly called the **Treynor-Black model.**[12] Our goal is the same as in the previous chapter, the formation of portfolios with an efficient risk–return trade-off, but given the simplification offered by the index model, our techniques will be different. We will see that the index model offers several advantages, not only in terms of parameter estimation, but also for the analytic simplification and organizational decentralization that it makes possible.

Alpha and Security Analysis

Perhaps the most important advantage of the single-index model is the framework it provides for macroeconomic and security analysis in the preparation of the input list that is so critical to the efficiency of the optimal portfolio. The Markowitz model requires estimates of risk premiums for each security. The estimate of expected return depends on both macroeconomic and individual-firm forecasts. But if many different analysts perform security analysis for a large organization such as a mutual fund company, a likely result is inconsistency in the macroeconomic forecasts that partly underlie expectations of returns across securities.

The single-index model creates a framework that separates these two quite different sources of return variation and makes it easier to ensure consistency across analysts. We can lay down a hierarchy of the preparation of the input list using the framework of the single-index model.

1. Macroeconomic analysis is used to estimate the risk premium and risk of the market index.

2. Statistical analysis is used to estimate the beta coefficients of all securities and their residual variances, $\sigma^2(e_i)$.

3. The portfolio manager uses the estimates for the market-index risk premium and the beta coefficient of a security to establish the expected return of that security *absent* any contribution from security analysis. The purely market-driven expected return is conditional on information common to all securities, not on information gleaned from security analysis of particular firms.

4. Security-specific expected return forecasts (specifically, security alphas) are derived from various security-valuation models (such as those discussed in Part Five). Thus, the alpha value distills the *incremental* risk premium attributable to private information developed from security analysis.

Equation 8.6 tells us that the risk premium on a security not subject to security analysis would be $\beta_i E(R_M)$. The risk premium would derive solely from the security's tendency to follow the market index. Any alpha (i.e., an expected return *beyond* this benchmark risk premium) would be due to some nonmarket factor that would be uncovered through security analysis.

---

[12]Jack Treynor and Fischer Black, "How to Use Security Analysis to Improve Portfolio Selection," *Journal of Business*, January 1973.

The end result of security analysis is the list of alpha values. Statistical methods of estimating beta coefficients are widely known and standardized; hence, we would not expect this portion of the input list to differ greatly across portfolio managers. In contrast, macro and security analysis are far less routine and therefore provide the potential for distinguished performance. Using the index model to disentangle the premiums due to market and nonmarket factors, a portfolio manager can be confident that macro analysts compiling estimates of the market-index risk premium and security analysts compiling alpha values are using consistent estimates for the overall market.

In the context of portfolio construction, alpha is more than just one of the components of expected return. It is the key variable that tells us whether a security is a good or a bad buy. Consider an individual stock for which we have a beta estimate from statistical considerations and an alpha value from security analysis. We easily can find many other securities with identical betas and therefore identical systematic components of their risk premiums. Therefore, what really makes a security attractive or unattractive to a portfolio manager is its alpha value, its premium over and above the premium derived from its tendency to track the market index. A positive-alpha security is a bargain and therefore should be overweighted in the overall portfolio compared to the passive alternative of using the market-index portfolio as the risky vehicle. Conversely, a negative-alpha security is overpriced and, other things equal, its portfolio weight should be reduced. In more extreme cases, the desired portfolio weight might even be negative, that is, a short position (if permitted) would be desirable.

The Index Portfolio as an Investment Asset

The process of charting the efficient frontier using the single-index model can be pursued much like the procedure we used in Chapter 7, where we used the Markowitz model to find the optimal risky portfolio. Here, however, we can benefit from the simplification the index model offers for deriving the input list. Moreover, portfolio optimization highlights another advantage of the single-index model, namely, a simple and intuitively revealing representation of the optimal risky portfolio. Before we get into the mechanics of optimization in this setting, however, we start by considering the role of the index portfolio in the optimal portfolio.

Suppose the prospectus of an investment company limits the universe of assets in which the firm may invest to only stocks included in the S&P 500 index. Suppose that the resources of the company allow coverage of only a relatively small subset of this so-called *investable universe.* If these analyzed firms are the only ones allowed in the portfolio, the portfolio manager may well be worried about limited diversification.

A simple way to avoid inadequate diversification would be to include the S&P 500 portfolio itself as one of the assets of the portfolio. Examination of Equations 8.5 and 8.6 reveals that if we treat the S&P 500 portfolio as the market index, it will have a beta of 1.0 (its sensitivity to itself), no firm-specific risk, and an alpha of zero—there is no non-market component in its expected return. Equation 8.7 shows that the covariance of any security, i, with the index (in this example, the S&P 500) is $\beta_i \sigma_M^2$. To distinguish the S&P 500 from the n securities actively analyzed by the firm, we will designate it as the $(n + 1)$th asset. We can think of the S&P 500 as a *passive portfolio* that the manager would select in the absence of security analysis. It gives broad market exposure without the need for expensive security analysis. However, if the manager is willing to engage in such research, she may be able to devise an *active portfolio* that can be mixed with the index to provide an even better risk–return trade-off.

The Single-Index Model Input List

If the portfolio manager plans to compile a portfolio from a list of n actively researched firms plus a passive market-index portfolio such as the S&P 500, the input list will include the following estimates:

1. Risk premium on the S&P 500 portfolio.
2. Standard deviation of the S&P 500 portfolio.
3. n sets of estimates of (a) beta coefficients, (b) stock residual variances, and (c) alpha values. The alpha values, together with the risk premium of the S&P 500 and the beta of each security, determine the expected return on each security.

The Optimal Risky Portfolio in the Single-Index Model

The single-index model allows us to solve for the optimal risky portfolio directly and to gain insight into the nature of the solution. First, we confirm that we easily can set up the optimization process to chart the efficient frontier in this framework along the lines of the Markowitz model.

With the estimates of the beta and alpha coefficients, plus the risk premium of the index portfolio, we can generate the $n + 1$ expected returns using Equation 8.6. With the estimates of the beta coefficients and residual variances, together with the variance of the index portfolio, we can construct the covariance matrix using Equation 8.7. Given the column of risk premiums and the covariance matrix, we can conduct the optimization program described in Chapter 7.

While the index model allows us to more easily implement the Markowitz model for efficient diversification (the focus of Chapter 7), we can take its description of how diversification works a step further. We showed earlier that the alpha, beta, and residual variance of an equally weighted portfolio are the simple averages of those parameters across component securities. This result is not limited to equally weighted portfolios. It applies to any portfolio, where we need only replace "simple average" with "weighted average," using the portfolio weights. Specifically,

$$\alpha_P = \sum_{i=1}^{n+1} w_i \alpha_i \quad \text{and for the index, } \alpha_{n+1} = \alpha_M = 0$$

$$\beta_P = \sum_{i=1}^{n+1} w_i \beta_i \quad \text{and for the index, } \beta_{n+1} = \beta_M = 1 \qquad \textbf{(8.22)}$$

$$\sigma^2(e_P) = \sum_{i=1}^{n+1} w_i^2 \sigma^2(e_i) \quad \text{and for the index, } \sigma^2(e_{n+1}) = \sigma^2(e_M) = 0$$

The objective is to select portfolio weights, $w_1, \ldots, w_{n+1}$, to maximize the Sharpe ratio of the portfolio. With this set of weights, the expected return, standard deviation, and Sharpe ratio of the portfolio are

$$E(R_P) = \alpha_P + E(R_M)\beta_P = \sum_{i=1}^{n+1} w_i \alpha_i + E(R_M) \sum_{i=1}^{n+1} w_i \beta_i$$

$$\sigma_P = [\beta_P^2 \sigma_M^2 + \sigma^2(e_P)]^{1/2} = \left[\sigma_M^2 \left(\sum_{i=1}^{n+1} w_i \beta_i \right)^2 + \sum_{i=1}^{n+1} w_i^2 \sigma^2(e_i) \right]^{1/2} \qquad \textbf{(8.23)}$$

$$S_P = \frac{E(R_P)}{\sigma_P}$$

At this point, as in the Markowitz procedure, we could use Excel's optimization program to maximize the Sharpe ratio subject to the adding-up constraint that the portfolio weights sum to 1. However, this is not necessary because when returns follow the index model, the optimal portfolio can be derived explicitly, and the solution for the optimal portfolio provides insight into the efficient use of security analysis in portfolio construction. It is instructive to outline the logical thread of the solution. We will not show every algebraic step, but will instead present the major results and interpretation of the procedure.

Before delving into the results, let us first preview the basic trade-off revealed by the model. If we were interested only in diversification, we would just hold the market index. But security analysis gives us the chance to uncover securities with a nonzero alpha and to take a differential position in those securities. The cost of that differential position is a departure from efficient diversification, specifically, the assumption of unnecessary firm-specific risk. The model shows us that the optimal risky portfolio trades off the search for alpha against the departure from efficient diversification.

The optimal risky portfolio turns out to be a combination of two component portfolios: (1) an *active portfolio*, denoted by A, comprised of the n analyzed securities (we call this the *active* portfolio because it follows from active security analysis), and (2) the market-index portfolio, the $(n + 1)$th asset we include to aid in diversification, which we call the *passive portfolio* and denote by M.

Assume first that the active portfolio has a beta of 1. In that case, the optimal weight in the active portfolio would be proportional to the ratio $\alpha_A/\sigma^2(e_A)$. This ratio balances the contribution of the active portfolio (its alpha) against its contribution to the portfolio variance (via residual variance). The analogous ratio for the index portfolio is $E(R_M)/\sigma_M^2$, and hence the initial position in the active portfolio (by "initial position," we mean if its beta were 1) is

$$w_A^0 = \frac{\dfrac{\alpha_A}{\sigma_A^2}}{\dfrac{E(R_M)}{\sigma_M^2}} \tag{8.24}$$

Next, we adjust this position to account for the actual beta of the active portfolio. For any level of σ_A^2, the correlation between the active and passive portfolios is greater when the beta of the active portfolio is higher. This implies less diversification benefit from the passive portfolio and a lower position in it. Correspondingly, the position in the active portfolio increases. The precise modification for the position in the active portfolio is:[13]

$$w_A^* = \frac{w_A^0}{1 + (1 - \beta_A)w_A^0} \tag{8.25}$$

Notice that when $\beta_A = 1, w_A^* = w_A^0$.

The Information Ratio

Equations 8.24 and 8.25 yield the optimal position in the active portfolio once we know its alpha, beta, and residual variance. With w_A^* in the active portfolio and $1 - w_A^*$ invested in the index portfolio, we can compute the expected return, standard deviation, and Sharpe ratio of the optimal risky portfolio. The Sharpe ratio of an optimally constructed risky portfolio

---

[13]The definition of correlation implies that $\rho(R_A, R_M) = \dfrac{\text{Cov}(R_A, R_M)}{\sigma_A\sigma_M} = \beta_A\dfrac{\sigma_M}{\sigma_A}$. Therefore, given the ratio of SD, a higher beta implies higher correlation and smaller benefit from diversification than when $\beta = 1$ in Equation 8.24. This requires the modification given by Equation 8.25.

will exceed that of the index portfolio (the passive strategy). The exact relationship is

$$S_P^2 = S_M^2 + \left[\frac{\alpha_A}{\sigma(e_A)}\right]^2 \tag{8.26}$$

Equation 8.26 shows us that the contribution of the active portfolio (when held in its optimal weight, w_A^*) to the Sharpe ratio of the overall risky portfolio is determined by the ratio of its alpha to its residual standard deviation. This important ratio is widely known as the **information ratio.**[14] It measures the extra return we can obtain from security analysis compared to the firm-specific risk we incur when we over- or underweight securities relative to the passive market index. Equation 8.26 therefore implies that to maximize the overall Sharpe ratio, we must maximize the information ratio of the active portfolio.

It turns out that the information ratio of the active portfolio will be maximized if we invest in each security in proportion to its ratio of $\alpha_i/\sigma^2(e_i)$. This result has a compelling interpretation: It says that the position in each security will be proportional to its ratio of alpha (which investors seek) to diversifiable risk (which they wish to avoid). The higher the ratio, the more of the security they will hold in the active portfolio. Scaling this ratio so that the total position in the active portfolio adds up to w_A^*, the weight in each security is

$$w_i^* = w_A^* \frac{\dfrac{\alpha_i}{\sigma^2(e_i)}}{\displaystyle\sum_{i=1}^{n} \dfrac{\alpha_i}{\sigma^2(e_i)}} \tag{8.27}$$

With this set of weights, the contribution of each security to the information ratio of the active portfolio is the square of its *own* information ratio, that is,

$$\left[\frac{\alpha_A}{\sigma(e_A)}\right]^2 = \sum_{i=1}^{n} \left[\frac{\alpha_i}{\sigma(e_i)}\right]^2 \tag{8.28}$$

The model thus reveals the central role of the information ratio in efficiently taking advantage of security analysis. The positive contribution of a security to the portfolio is made by its addition to the non-market risk premium (its alpha). Its negative impact is to increase the portfolio variance through its firm-specific risk (residual variance).

In contrast to alpha, the market (systematic) component of the risk premium, $\beta_i E(R_M)$, is offset by the security's nondiversifiable (market) risk, $\beta_i^2 \sigma_M^2$, and both are driven by the same beta. This trade-off is not unique to any security, as any security with the same beta makes the same balanced contribution to both risk and return. Put differently, the beta of a security is neither vice nor virtue. It is a property that simultaneously affects the risk *and* risk premium of a security.

We see from Equation 8.27 that if a security's alpha is negative, the security will assume a short position in the optimal risky portfolio. If short positions are prohibited, a negative-alpha security would simply be taken out of the optimization program and assigned a portfolio weight of zero. As the number of securities with nonzero alpha values (or the number with positive alphas if short positions are prohibited) increases, the active portfolio will itself be better diversified and its weight in the overall risky portfolio will increase at the expense of the passive index portfolio.

Finally, we note that the index portfolio is an efficient portfolio only if all alpha values are zero. This makes intuitive sense. Unless security analysis reveals that a security has a nonzero alpha, including it in the active portfolio would make the portfolio less attractive. In

---

[14]Some writers define the information ratio as *excess return* per unit of nonsystematic risk and use *appraisal ratio* to refer to the ratio of *alpha* to nonsystematic risk. We will consistently define the information ratio as the ratio of alpha to the standard deviation of residual returns.

addition to the security's systematic risk, which is compensated for by the market risk premium (through beta), the security would add its firm-specific risk to portfolio variance. With a zero alpha, however, there is no compensation for bearing that firm-specific risk. Hence, if all securities have zero alphas, the optimal weight in the active portfolio will be zero, and the weight in the index portfolio will be 1. However, when security analysis uncovers securities with non-market risk premiums (nonzero alphas), the index portfolio is no longer efficient.

Summary of Optimization Procedure

Once security analysis is complete, the optimal risky portfolio is formed from the index-model estimates of security and market index parameters using these steps:

1. Compute the initial position of each security in the active portfolio as $w_i^0 = \alpha_i / \sigma^2(e_i)$.

2. Scale those initial positions to force portfolio weights to sum to 1 by dividing by their sum, that is, $w_i = \dfrac{w_i^0}{\sum\limits_{i=1}^{n} w_i^0}$.

3. Compute the alpha of the active portfolio: $\alpha_A = \sum\limits_{i=1}^{n} w_i \alpha_i$.

4. Compute the residual variance of the active portfolio: $\sigma^2(e_A) = \sum_{i=1}^{n} w_i^2 \sigma^2(e_i)$.

5. Compute the initial position in the active portfolio: $w_A^0 = \left[\dfrac{\alpha_A / \sigma^2(e_A)}{E(R_M)/\sigma_M^2} \right]$.

6. Compute the beta of the active portfolio: $\beta_A = \sum_{i=1}^{n} w_i \beta_i$.

7. Adjust the initial position in the active portfolio: $w_A^* = \dfrac{w_A^0}{1 + (1 - \beta_A)w_A^0}$.

8. Note: The optimal risky portfolio now has weights: $w_M^* = 1 - w_A^*$; $w_i^* = w_A^* w_i$.

9. Calculate the risk premium of the optimal risky portfolio from the risk premium of the index portfolio and the alpha of the active portfolio:
$E(R_P) = (w_M^* + w_A^* \beta_A)E(R_M) + w_A^* \alpha_A$. Notice that the beta of the risky portfolio is $w_M^* + w_A^* \beta_A$ because the beta of the index portfolio is 1.

10. Compute the variance of the optimal risky portfolio from the variance of the index portfolio and the residual variance of the active portfolio:
$\sigma_P^2 = (w_M^* + w_A^* \beta_A)^2 \sigma_M^2 + [w_A^* \sigma(e_A)]^2$.

An Example

We can illustrate the implementation of the index model by constructing an optimal portfolio using the procedure just outlined. To keep the presentation manageable, we will imagine that the investor is limited to an "investment universe" comprising only the market index and the following six large U.S. corporations: Verizon and AT&T from the telecommunications industry, Target and Walmart from the retailing sector, and Ford and GM from the automobile industry. This example entails only six analyzed stocks, but by virtue of selecting three *pairs* of firms from the same industry with relatively high residual correlations, we put the index model to a severe test. This is because the model ignores the correlation between residuals when producing estimates for the covariance matrix. By ignoring that correlation, the index model will surely underestimate covariances across securities.

Correlation and Covariance Matrix

Panel A in Spreadsheet 8.1 shows estimates of the risk parameters of the market index and the six analyzed securities. These securities have tremendous firm-specific risk (column E). Portfolios concentrated in these (or other) securities would have unnecessarily

	A	B	C	D	E	F	G	H	I	J
1	Panel A: Risk Parameters of the Investable Universe (annualized)									
2										
3		SD of Excess Return	BETA	SD of Systematic Component	SD of Residual	Correlation with the Market Index				
4	Market Index	0.1206	1.0000	0.1206	0.0000	1.0000				
5	WMT (Walmart)	0.1662	0.2095	0.0253	0.1657	0.1520				
6	TGT (Target)	0.1925	0.5265	0.0635	0.1833	0.3298				
7	VZ (Verizon)	0.1481	0.2375	0.0286	0.1466	0.1934				
8	T (AT&T)	0.1358	0.2981	0.0360	0.1321	0.2648				
9	F (Ford)	0.2546	1.3258	0.1599	0.1999	0.6280				
10	GM (General Motors)	0.2973	1.6613	0.2004	0.2215	0.6739				
11										
12	Panel B: Correlation of Residuals									
13										
14		WMT	TGT	VZ	T	F	GM			
15	WMT (Walmart)	1								
16	TGT (Target)	0.405	1							
17	VZ (Verizon)	0.089	−0.071	1						
18	T (AT&T)	0.193	−0.007	0.624	1					
19	F (Ford)	0.095	0.077	−0.230	−0.200	1				
20	GM (General Motors)	0.036	0.175	−0.320	−0.309	0.699	1			
21										
22	Panel C: The Index Model Covariance Matrix									
23										
24			Market Index	WMT	TGT	VZ	T	F	GM	
25		Beta	1.0000	0.2095	0.5265	0.2375	0.2981	1.3258	1.6613	
26	Market Index	1.0000	0.0145	0.0030	0.0077	0.0035	0.0043	0.0193	0.0242	
27	WMT (Walmart)	0.2095	0.0030	0.0276	0.0016	0.0007	0.0009	0.0040	0.0051	
28	TGT (Target)	0.5265	0.0077	0.0016	0.0371	0.0018	0.0023	0.0102	0.0127	
29	VZ (Verizon)	0.2375	0.0035	0.0007	0.0018	0.0219	0.0010	0.0046	0.0057	
30	T (AT&T)	0.2981	0.0043	0.0009	0.0023	0.0010	0.0184	0.0057	0.0072	
31	F (Ford)	1.3258	0.0193	0.0040	0.0102	0.0046	0.0057	0.0648	0.0320	
32	GM (General Motors)	1.6613	0.0242	0.0051	0.0127	0.0057	0.0072	0.0320	0.0884	
33										
34										
35	Panel D: Macro Forecast and Forecasts of Alpha Values									
36										
37	market risk premium =		0.06							
38		Market index	WMT	TGT	VZ	T	F	GM		
39	Alpha	0.0000	0.0150	−0.0100	−0.0050	0.0075	0.0120	0.0025		
40	Beta	1.0000	0.2095	0.5265	0.2375	0.2981	1.3258	1.6613		
41	Risk premium	0.0600	0.0276	0.0216	0.0092	0.0254	0.0915	0.1022		
42										
43	Panel E: Computation of the Optimal Risky Portfolio									
44										
45		Market index	Active Pf A	WMT	TGT	VZ	T	F	GM	Overall Pf
46	$\sigma^2(e)$			0.0275	0.0336	0.0215	0.0174	0.0399	0.0491	
47	$w_i(0) = \alpha_i/\sigma^2(e)$		0.7975	0.5463	−0.2975	−0.2328	0.4301	0.3004	0.0509	
48	w_i		1.0000	0.6850	−0.3730	−0.2918	0.5393	0.3767	0.0639	
49	$[w_i(0)]^2$			0.4693	0.1392	0.0852	0.2908	0.1419	0.0041	
50	α_A		0.0242							
51	$\sigma^2(e_A)$		0.0303							
52	$E(R_M)/\sigma^2(M)$		4.1249							
53	$w_A(0)$		0.1933							
54	β_A		0.6441							
55	w^*(Optimal Risky Port)	0.8191	0.1809	0.1239	−0.0675	−0.0528	0.0975	0.0681	0.0116	
56										
57	Beta	1.0000	0.6441	0.2095	0.5265	0.2375	0.2981	1.3258	1.6613	0.9356
58	Risk premium	0.0600	0.0628	0.0276	0.0216	0.0092	0.0254	0.0915	0.1022	0.0605
59	SD	0.1206	0.1907							0.1172
60	Sharpe Ratio	0.4975	0.3295							0.5165

Spreadsheet 8.1

Implementing the index model

Please visit us at
www.mhhe.com/Bodie11e

high volatility and inferior Sharpe ratios. You can see from these high residual monthly standard deviations the great importance of diversification.

Panel B shows the correlation matrix of the residuals from the regressions of excess returns on the market index. The shaded cells show correlations of pairs of stocks from the same industries, which are as high as .7 for the two auto stocks (GM and Ford). This is in contrast to the assumption of the index model that all residuals are uncorrelated. Of course, these correlations are, to a great extent, high by design, because we intentionally selected pairs of firms from the same industry. Cross-industry correlations are typically far smaller, and the empirical estimates of correlations of residuals for industry indexes (rather than individual stocks in the same industry) would be far more in accord with the index model. In fact, a few of the stocks in this sample actually appear to have negatively correlated residuals. Of course, correlation also is subject to statistical sampling error, and this may be a fluke.

Panel C produces covariances (derived from Equation 8.7) of the single-index model. Variances of the market index and the individual covered stocks appear in the shaded diagonal entries. The variance estimates for the individual stocks equal $\beta_i^2 \sigma_M^2 + \sigma^2(e_i)$. The off-diagonal terms are covariance values and equal $\beta_i \beta_j \sigma_M^2$.

Risk Premium Forecasts   Panel D of Spreadsheet 8.1 contains estimates of alpha and the risk premium for each stock. These alphas would be the most important production of the investment company in a real-life procedure. Statistics plays a small role here; in this arena, macro/security analysis is king. In this example, we simply use illustrative values to demonstrate the portfolio construction process and possible results. You may wonder why we have chosen such small forecast alpha values. The reason is that even when security analysis uncovers a large apparent mispricing, that is, large alpha values, these forecasts must be substantially trimmed to account for the fact that such forecasts are subject to large estimation error. We discuss the important procedure of adjusting actual forecasts in Chapter 27.

The Optimal Risky Portfolio   Panel E of Spreadsheet 8.1 displays calculations for the optimal risky portfolio. They follow the summary outlined above (you should try to replicate these calculations in your own spreadsheet). In this example, we allow short sales. Notice that the weight of each security in the active portfolio (see row 55) has the same sign as the alpha value. Allowing short sales, the positions in the active portfolio are quite large (e.g., the position in Walmart is .6850, see cell D48); this is an aggressive portfolio. As a result, the alpha of the active portfolio (2.42%) is larger than that of any of the individual alpha forecasts. However, this aggressive stance also results in a large residual variance, .0303, which corresponds to a residual standard deviation of 17.4%). Therefore, the position in the active portfolio in the overall risky portfolio is scaled down considerably (see Equation 8.24) and ends up quite modest (.1809; cell C55), reinforcing the notion that diversification considerations are paramount in building the optimal risky portfolio.

The optimal risky portfolio (which combines the active portfolio with the market index) has a risk premium of 6.05%, standard deviation of 11.72%, and a Sharpe ratio of .5165 (cells J58–J60). By comparison, the Sharpe ratio of the index portfolio is .06/.1206 = .4975 (cell B60), which is not far below that of the optimal risky portfolio. The small improvement is a result of the modest alpha forecasts that we used. In Chapter 11 on market efficiency and Chapter 24 on performance evaluation, we demonstrate that such results are common in the mutual fund industry. Of course, a few portfolio managers can and do produce portfolios with better performance.

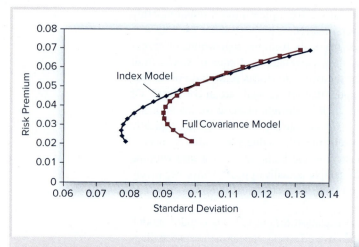

Figure 8.4 Efficient frontier constructed from the index model and the full covariance matrix

The interesting question here is the extent to which the index model produces results that differ from that of the full-covariance (Markowitz) model. Figure 8.4 shows the efficient frontiers from the two models with the example data. (We emphasize again that the difference in these figures reflects different *estimates* of covariances, not differences in investors' actual ability to trade off risk against return.) We find that the efficient frontiers are in fact similar. For conservative portfolios (with lower volatility, toward the left side of the figure), the index model underestimates the volatility and hence overestimates performance. The reverse happens with portfolios that are riskier than the index.

Table 8.4 compares the composition and expected performance of the optimal risky portfolios derived from the two models. The portfolio weights using the full covariance matrix take advantage of the correlation among residuals. For example, Walmart has a positive alpha and Target has a negative alpha, so Walmart is held long and Target is sold short. Because the residuals of the two firms are positively correlated, the full-covariance model dictates a more extreme positive position in Walmart and a more extreme negative position in Target than the index model, relying on the correlation between the two firms to offset the risk from those higher long–short positions. In the end, however, the suggested portfolio weights are not so different, and the optimal risky portfolio from the full-covariance (Markowitz) model has only slightly greater estimated risk premium and slightly greater estimated standard deviation. The Sharpe ratios are nearly identical. Even in this example, where we challenged the index model by applying it to pairs of firms that would be expected to have correlated residuals, it provides results that are remarkably close to the full-covariance model.

Table 8.4

Comparison of optimal risky portfolios derived from the index model and the full-covariance (Markowitz) model

	Index Model	Full-Covariance Model
A. Weights in Optimal Risky Portfolio		
Market index	0.82	0.90
WMT (Walmart)	0.13	0.17
TGT (Target)	−0.07	−0.14
VZ (Verizon)	−0.05	−0.18
T (AT&T)	0.10	0.19
F (Ford)	0.07	0.08
GM (General Motors)	0.01	−0.03
B. Portfolio Characteristics		
Risk premium	0.0605	0.0639
Standard deviation	0.1172	0.1238
Sharpe ratio	0.5165	0.5163

Is the Index Model Inferior to the Full-Covariance Model?   At one level, the index model must be inferior to the full-blown Markowitz model: It imposes additional assumptions that may not be fully accurate. But as our example illustrates, it is far from clear that the index model will be inferior in practical applications.

As an analogy, consider the question of adding additional explanatory variables in a regression equation. In one sense, they should never hurt, since they simply give the equation additional parameters with which to fit a statistical relation. We know that adding explanatory variables will in most cases increase R-square, and in no case will R-square fall. But this does not necessarily imply a better regression equation.[15] A better criterion is whether inclusion of a variable that contributes to in-sample explanatory power is likely to contribute to out-of-sample forecast precision. Adding variables, even ones that may appear significant, sometimes can be hazardous to forecast precision. The predictive value of the explanatory variable depends on two factors, the precision of its coefficient estimate and the precision of the forecast of its value. When we add additional explanatory variables, we introduce errors on both counts. Therefore, a parsimonious model that is "stingy" about inclusion of explanatory variables may be superior.

This problem applies as well to replacing the single-index with the full-blown Markowitz model. The Markowitz model allows far more flexibility in our modeling of asset covariance structure compared to the single-index model. But that advantage may be illusory if we can't estimate those covariances with a sufficient degree of accuracy. Using the full-covariance matrix invokes estimation risk of thousands of terms. Even if the full Markowitz model would be better *in principle,* it is quite possible that the cumulative effect of so many estimation errors will result in a portfolio that is actually inferior to that derived from the single-index model.

Against the potential superiority of the full-covariance model, we have the clear practical advantage of the single-index framework. Its aid in decentralizing macro and security analysis is another decisive advantage.

---

[15]In fact, the adjusted R-square may fall if the additional variable does not contribute enough explanatory power to compensate for the extra degree of freedom it uses.

SUMMARY

1. A single-factor model of the economy classifies sources of uncertainty as systematic (macro-economic) factors or firm-specific (microeconomic) factors. The index model assumes that the macro factor can be represented by a broad index of stock returns.

2. The single-index model drastically reduces the necessary inputs in the Markowitz portfolio selection procedure. It also aids in specialization of labor in security analysis.

3. According to the index model specification, the systematic risk of a portfolio or asset equals $\beta^2 \sigma_M^2$ and the covariance between two assets equals $\beta_i \beta_j \sigma_M^2$.

4. The index model is estimated by applying regression analysis to excess rates of return. The slope of the regression curve is the beta of an asset, whereas the intercept is the asset's alpha during the sample period. The regression line is also called the *security characteristic line.*

5. Practitioners routinely estimate the index model using total rather than excess rates of return. This makes their estimate of alpha equal to $\alpha + r_f (1 - \beta)$.

6. Betas show a tendency to evolve toward 1 over time. Beta forecasting rules attempt to predict this drift. Moreover, other financial variables can be used to help forecast betas.

7. Optimal active portfolios include analyzed securities in direct proportion to their alpha and in inverse proportion to their firm-specific variance. The full risky portfolio is a mixture of the active portfolio and the passive market-index portfolio. The index portfolio is used to enhance the diversification of the overall risky position.

KEY TERMS

single-factor model	regression equation	Treynor-Black model
single-index model	residuals	information ratio
scatter diagram	security characteristic line (SCL)	

KEY EQUATIONS

Single-index model (in excess returns): $R_i(t) = \alpha_i + \beta_i R_M(t) + e_i(t)$

Security risk in index model:

$$\text{Total risk} = \text{Systematic risk} + \text{Firm-specific risk}$$
$$\sigma^2 = \beta^2 \sigma_M^2 + \sigma^2(e)$$

$$\text{Covariance} = \text{Cov}(r_i, r_j) = \text{Product of betas} \times \text{Market-index risk} = \beta_i \beta_j \sigma_M^2$$

Active portfolio management in the index model

Sharpe ratio of optimal risky portfolio: $S_P^2 = S_M^2 + \left[\dfrac{\alpha_A}{\sigma(e_A)}\right]^2$

Asset weight in active portfolio: $w_i^* = w_A^* \dfrac{\dfrac{\alpha_i}{\sigma^2(e_i)}}{\displaystyle\sum_{i=1}^{n} \dfrac{\alpha_i}{\sigma^2(e_i)}}$

Information ratio of active portfolio: $\left[\dfrac{\alpha_A}{\sigma(e_A)}\right]^2 = \displaystyle\sum_{i=1}^{n} \left[\dfrac{\alpha_i}{\sigma(e_i)}\right]^2$

PROBLEM SETS

1. What are the advantages of the index model compared to the Markowitz procedure for obtaining an efficiently diversified portfolio? What are its disadvantages?

2. What is the basic trade-off when departing from pure indexing in favor of an actively managed portfolio?

3. How does the magnitude of firm-specific risk affect the extent to which an active investor will be willing to depart from an indexed portfolio?

4. Why do we call alpha a "nonmarket" return premium? Why are high-alpha stocks desirable investments for active portfolio managers? With all other parameters held fixed, what would happen to a portfolio's Sharpe ratio as the alpha of its component securities increased?

5. A portfolio management organization analyzes 60 stocks and constructs a mean-variance efficient portfolio using only these 60 securities.

   a. How many estimates of expected returns, variances, and covariances are needed to optimize this portfolio?

   b. If one could safely assume that stock market returns closely resemble a single-index structure, how many estimates would be needed?

6. The following are estimates for two stocks.

Stock	Expected Return	Beta	Firm-Specific Standard Deviation
A	13%	0.8	30%
B	18	1.2	40

The market index has a standard deviation of 22% and the risk-free rate is 8%.

   a. What are the standard deviations of stocks A and B?

   b. Suppose that we were to construct a portfolio with proportions:

Stock A:	.30
Stock B:	.45
T-bills:	.25

Compute the expected return, standard deviation, beta, and nonsystematic standard deviation of the portfolio.

7. Consider the following two regression lines for stocks A and B in the following figure.

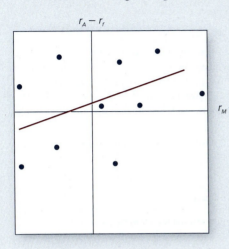
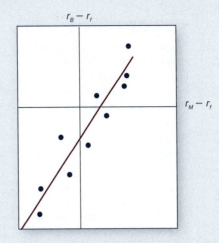

    a. Which stock has higher firm-specific risk?
    b. Which stock has greater systematic (market) risk?
    c. Which stock has higher R^2?
    d. Which stock has higher alpha?
    e. Which stock has higher correlation with the market?

8. Consider the two (excess return) index model regression results for A and B:

$$R_A = 1\% + 1.2 R_M$$

R-square $= .576$

Residual standard deviation $= 10.3\%$

$$R_B = -2\% + .8 R_M$$

R-square $= .436$

Residual standard deviation $= 9.1\%$

    a. Which stock has more firm-specific risk?
    b. Which has greater market risk?
    c. For which stock does market movement explain a greater fraction of return variability?
    d. If r_f were constant at 6% and the regression had been run using total rather than excess returns, what would have been the regression intercept for stock A?

Use the following data for Problems 9 through 14. Suppose that the index model for stocks A and B is estimated from excess returns with the following results:

$$R_A = 3\% + .7 R_M + e_A$$
$$R_B = -2\% + 1.2 R_M + e_B$$
$$\sigma_M = 20\%; \ R\text{-square}_A = .20; \ R\text{-square}_B = .12$$

  9. What is the standard deviation of each stock?

10. Break down the variance of each stock into its systematic and firm-specific components.

11. What are the covariance and the correlation coefficient between the two stocks?

12. What is the covariance between each stock and the market index?

13. For portfolio P with investment proportions of .60 in A and .40 in B, rework Problems 9, 10, and 12.

14. Rework Problem 13 for portfolio Q with investment proportions of .50 in P, .30 in the market index, and .20 in T-bills.

15. A stock recently has been estimated to have a beta of 1.24:
    a. What will a beta book compute as the "adjusted beta" of this stock?
    b. Suppose that you estimate the following regression describing the evolution of beta over time:

$$\beta_t = .3 + .7\beta_{t-1}$$

What would be your predicted beta for next year?

16. Based on current dividend yields and expected growth rates, the expected rates of return on stocks A and B are 11% and 14%, respectively. The beta of stock A is .8, while that of stock B is 1.5. The T-bill rate is currently 6%, while the expected rate of return on the S&P 500 index is 12%. The standard deviation of stock A is 10% annually, while that of stock B is 11%. If you currently hold a passive index portfolio, would you choose to add either of these stocks to your holdings?

17. A portfolio manager summarizes the input from the macro and micro forecasters in the following table:

Micro Forecasts

Asset	Expected Return (%)	Beta	Residual Standard Deviation (%)
Stock A	20	1.3	58
Stock B	18	1.8	71
Stock C	17	0.7	60
Stock D	12	1.0	55

Macro Forecasts

Asset	Expected Return (%)	Standard Deviation (%)
T-bills	8	0
Passive equity portfolio	16	23

a. Calculate expected excess returns, alpha values, and residual variances for these stocks.
b. Construct the optimal risky portfolio.
c. What is the Sharpe ratio for the optimal portfolio?
d. By how much did the position in the active portfolio improve the Sharpe ratio compared to a purely passive index strategy?
e. What should be the exact makeup of the complete portfolio (including the risk-free asset) for an investor with a coefficient of risk aversion of 2.8?

18. Recalculate Problem 17 for a portfolio manager who is not allowed to short sell securities.
    a. What is the cost of the restriction in terms of Sharpe's measure?
    b. What is the utility loss to the investor ($A = 2.8$) given his new complete portfolio?

19. Suppose that on the basis of the analyst's past record, you estimate that the relationship between forecast and actual alpha is:

Actual abnormal return $= .3 \times$ Forecast of alpha

Use the alphas from Problem 17. How much is expected performance affected by recognizing the relation between realized alphas and the original alpha forecasts?

20. Suppose that the alpha forecasts in row 39 of Spreadsheet 8.1 are doubled. All the other data remain the same. Recalculate the optimal risky portfolio. Before you do any calculations, however, use the Summary of Optimization Procedure to estimate a back-of-the-envelope calculation of the information ratio and Sharpe ratio of the newly optimized portfolio. Then recalculate the entire spreadsheet example and verify your back-of-the-envelope calculation.

1. When the annualized monthly percentage rates of return for a stock market index were regressed against the returns for ABC and XYZ stocks over the most recent 5-year period, using an ordinary least squares regression, the following results were obtained:

Statistic	ABC	XYZ
Alpha	−3.20%	7.3%
Beta	0.60	0.97
R^2	0.35	0.17
Residual standard deviation	13.02%	21.45%

Explain what these regression results tell the analyst about risk–return relationships for each stock over the sample period. Comment on their implications for future risk–return relationships, assuming both stocks were included in a diversified common stock portfolio, especially in view of the following additional data obtained from two brokerage houses, which are based on the most recent two years of weekly returns.

Brokerage House	Beta of ABC	Beta of XYZ
A	0.62	1.45
B	0.71	1.25

2. Assume the correlation coefficient between Baker Fund and the market index is .70. What percentage of Baker Fund's total risk is specific (i.e., nonsystematic)?

3. The correlation between the Charlottesville International Fund and the EAFE Market Index of international stocks is 1.0. The expected return on the EAFE Index is 11%, the expected return on Charlottesville International Fund is 9%, and the risk-free return in EAFE countries is 3%. Based on this analysis, what is the implied beta of Charlottesville International?

4. The concept of *beta* is most closely associated with:
   a. Correlation coefficients.
   b. Mean-variance analysis.
   c. Nonsystematic risk.
   d. Systematic risk.

5. Beta and standard deviation differ as risk measures in that beta measures:
   a. Only unsystematic risk, while standard deviation measures total risk.
   b. Only systematic risk, while standard deviation measures total risk.
   c. Both systematic and unsystematic risk, while standard deviation measures only unsystematic risk.
   d. Both systematic and unsystematic risk, while standard deviation measures only systematic risk.

E-INVESTMENTS EXERCISES

Go to **http://finance.yahoo.com** and click on *Stocks* link under the *Investing* tab. Look for the *Stock Screener* link under *Research Tools*. The *Java Yahoo! Finance Screener* lets you create your own screens. In the *Click to Add Criteria* box, find *Trading and Volume* on the menu and choose *Beta*. In the *Conditions* box, choose < = and in the *Values* box, enter *1*. Hit the *Enter* key and then request the top 200 matches in the *Return Top_Matches* box. Click on the *Run Screen* button.

Select the *View Table* tab and sort the results to show the lowest betas at the top of the list by clicking on the *Beta* column header. Which firms have the lowest betas? In which industries do they operate?

Select the *View Histogram* tab and when the histogram appears, look at the bottom of the screen to see the *Show Histogram for* box. Use the menu that comes up when you click on the down arrow to select *Beta*. What pattern(s), if any, do you see in the distributions of betas for firms that have betas less than 1?

✔ SOLUTIONS TO CONCEPT CHECKS

1. *a.* Total market capitalization is $3,000 + 1,940 + 1,360 = 6,300$. Therefore, the mean excess return of the index portfolio is

$$\frac{3,000}{6,300} \times 10 + \frac{1,940}{6,300} \times 2 + \frac{1,360}{6,300} \times 17 = 9.05\% = .0905$$

b. The covariance between stocks A and B equals

$$\text{Cov}(R_A, R_B) = \beta_A \beta_B \sigma_M^2 = 1 \times .2 \times .25^2 = .0125$$

c. The covariance between stock B and the index portfolio equals

$$\text{Cov}(R_B, R_M) = \beta_B \sigma_M^2 = .2 \times .25^2 = .0125$$

d. The total variance of B equals

$$\sigma_B^2 = \text{Var}(\beta_B R_M + e_B) = \beta_B^2 \sigma_M^2 + \sigma^2(e_B)$$

Systematic risk equals $\beta_B^2 \sigma_M^2 = .2^2 \times .25^2 = .0025$.

Thus the firm-specific variance of B equals

$$\sigma^2(e_B) = \sigma_B^2 - \beta_B^2 \sigma_M^2 = .30^2 - .2^2 \times .25^2 = .0875$$

2. The variance of each stock is $\beta^2 \sigma_M^2 + \sigma^2(e)$.

   For stock A, we obtain

$$\sigma_A^2 = .9^2(20)^2 + 30^2 = 1,224$$
$$\sigma_A = 35\%$$

   For stock B,

$$\sigma_B^2 = 1.1^2(20)^2 + 10^2 = 584$$
$$\sigma_B = 24\%$$

   The covariance is

$$\beta_A \beta_B \sigma_M^2 = .9 \times 1.1 \times 20^2 = 396$$

3. $\sigma^2(e_P) = (\frac{1}{2})^2[\sigma^2(e_A) + \sigma^2(e_B)]$
   $= \frac{1}{4}(.30^2 + .10^2)$
   $= .0250$

   Therefore $\sigma(e_P) = .158 = 15.8\%$

4. The industry "beta-book" ALPHA is related to the index-model α by

$$\text{ALPHA} = \alpha_{\text{index model}} + (1 - \beta)r_f$$

   For Microsoft, $\alpha = 0.8\%$, $\beta = .856$, and we are told that r_f was .2% per month. Thus ALPHA = $0.8 + (1 - .856) \times 0.2\% = .8288$.

   The index model and beta-book alpha are quite close in this case because r_f is small and because β is close to 1.

5. The industries with positive adjustment factors are most sensitive to the economy. Their betas would be expected to be higher because the business risk of the firms is higher. In contrast, the industries with negative adjustment factors are in business fields with a lower sensitivity to the economy. Therefore, for any given financial profile, their betas are lower.

The Capital Asset Pricing Model

THE CAPITAL ASSET pricing model, almost always referred to as the CAPM, is one of the centerpieces of modern financial economics. The model gives us a precise prediction of the relationship that we should observe between the risk of an asset and its expected return. This relationship serves two vital functions. First, it provides a benchmark rate of return for evaluating possible investments. For example, if we are analyzing securities, we might be interested in whether the expected return we forecast for a stock is more or less than its "fair" return given its risk. Second, the model helps us to make an educated guess as to the expected return on assets that have not yet been traded in the marketplace. For example, how do we price an initial public offering of stock? How will a major new investment project affect the return investors require on a company's stock?

Although the CAPM does not fully withstand empirical tests, it is widely used because of the insight it offers. All generalizations of the model retain its central conclusion that only systematic risk will be rewarded with a risk premium. While the best way to measure that systematic risk can be subtle, all the more complex cousins of the basic CAPM can be viewed as variations on this fundamental theme.

9.1 The Capital Asset Pricing Model

The capital asset pricing model is a set of predictions concerning equilibrium expected returns on risky assets. Harry Markowitz laid down the foundation of modern portfolio management in 1952. The CAPM was published 12 years later in articles by William Sharpe,[1] John Lintner,[2] and Jan Mossin.[3] The time for this gestation indicates that the leap from Markowitz's portfolio selection model to the CAPM is not trivial.

[1]William Sharpe, "Capital Asset Prices: A Theory of Market Equilibrium," *Journal of Finance,* September 1964.
[2]John Lintner, "The Valuation of Risk Assets and the Selection of Risky Investments in Stock Portfolios and Capital Budgets," *Review of Economics and Statistics,* February 1965.
[3]Jan Mossin, "Equilibrium in a Capital Asset Market," *Econometrica,* October 1966.

The CAPM is based on two sets of assumptions, listed in Table 9.1. The first set pertains to investor behavior and allows us to assume that investors are alike in most important ways, specifically that they are all mean-variance optimizers with a common time horizon and a common set of information reflected in their use of an identical input list. The second set of assumptions pertains to the market setting, asserting that markets are well-functioning with few impediments to trading. Even a cursory consideration of these assumptions reveals that they are fairly strong, and one may justifiably wonder whether a theory derived from them will withstand empirical tests. Therefore, we will devote considerable attention later in the chapter to how the predictions of the model may change when one or more of these restrictive assumptions are relaxed.

Still, the simple version of the CAPM is a good place to start. While the appropriate quantification of risk and the prediction for the exact risk–return trade-off may differ across more sophisticated variants of the model, the central implication of the basic model, that risk premia will be proportional to exposure to systematic risk and independent of firm-specific risk, remains generally valid in its extensions. In part because of this commonality, the simple CAPM remains in wide use despite its empirical shortcomings.

Therefore, we begin by supposing that all investors optimize their portfolios á la Markowitz. That is, each investor uses an input list (expected returns and covariance matrix) to draw an efficient frontier employing all available risky assets and identifies an efficient risky portfolio, *P*, by drawing the tangent CAL (capital allocation line) to the frontier as in Figure 9.1, Panel A. As a result, each investor holds securities in the investable universe with weights arrived at by the Markowitz optimization process. Notice that this framework employs Assumptions 1(a) (investors are all mean-variance optimizers), 2(a) (all assets trade and therefore can be held in investors' portfolios), and 2(b) (investors can borrow or lend at the risk-free rate and therefore can select portfolios from the capital allocation line of the tangency portfolio).

The CAPM asks what would happen if all investors shared an identical investable universe and used the same input list to draw their efficient frontiers. The use of a common input list obviously requires Assumption 1(c), but notice that it also relies on Assumption 1(b), that each investor is optimizing for a common investment horizon. It also implicitly assumes that investor choices will not be affected by differences in tax rates or trading costs that could affect net rates of return (Assumptions 2[c] and 2[d]).

Not surprisingly in light of these assumptions, investors would calculate identical efficient frontiers of risky assets. Facing the same risk-free rate (Assumption 2[b]), they would

Table 9.1

The assumptions of the CAPM

1. Individual behavior
   a. Investors are rational, mean-variance optimizers.
   b. Their common planning horizon is a single period.
   c. Investors all use identical input lists, an assumption often termed **homogeneous expectations.** Homogeneous expectations are consistent with the assumption that all relevant information is publicly available.
2. Market structure
   a. All assets are publicly held and trade on public exchanges.
   b. Investors can borrow or lend at a common risk-free rate, and they can take short positions on traded securities.
   c. No taxes.
   d. No transaction costs.

then draw an identical tangent CAL and naturally all would arrive at the same risky portfolio, *P*. All investors therefore would choose the same set of weights for each risky asset. What must be these weights?

A key insight of the CAPM is this: Because the market portfolio is the aggregation of all of these identical risky portfolios, it too will have the same weights. (Notice that this conclusion relies on Assumption 2[a] because it requires that *all* assets can be traded and included in investors' portfolios.) Therefore, if all investors choose the same risky portfolio, it must be the *market* portfolio, that is, the value-weighted portfolio of all assets in the investable universe. We conclude that the capital allocation line based on each investor's optimal risky portfolio will in fact also be the capital *market* line, as depicted in Figure 9.1, Panel B. This implication will allow us to say much about the risk–return trade-off.

Why Do All Investors Hold the Market Portfolio?

What is the market portfolio? When we sum over, or aggregate, the portfolios of all individual investors, lending and borrowing will cancel out (because each lender has a corresponding borrower), and the value of the aggregate risky portfolio will equal the entire wealth of the economy. This is the **market portfolio, M.** The proportion of each stock in this portfolio equals the market value of the stock (price per share times number of shares outstanding) divided by the sum of the market value of all stocks.[4] This implies that if the weight of GE stock, for example, in each common risky portfolio is 1%, then GE also will constitute 1% of the market portfolio. The same principle applies to the proportion of any stock in each investor's risky portfolio. As a result, the optimal risky portfolio of all investors is simply a share of the market portfolio in Figure 9.1.

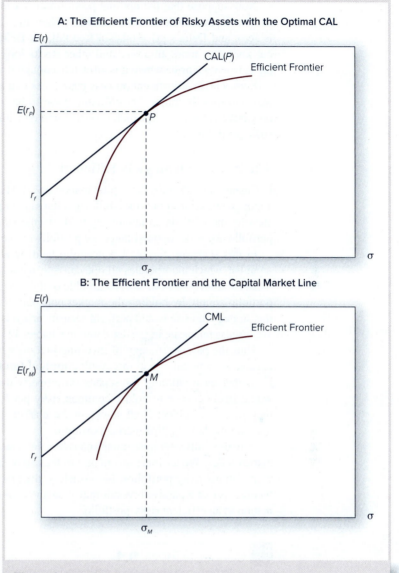

Figure 9.1 Capital allocation line and the capital market line

---

[4]We use the term "stock" for convenience; the market portfolio properly includes all assets in the economy.

Now suppose that the optimal portfolio of our investors does not include the stock of some company, such as Delta Airlines. When all investors avoid Delta stock, the demand is zero, and Delta's price takes a free fall. As Delta stock gets progressively cheaper, it becomes ever more attractive and other stocks look relatively less attractive. Ultimately, Delta reaches a price where it is attractive enough to include in the optimal stock portfolio.

Such a price adjustment process guarantees that all stocks will be included in the optimal portfolio. It shows that *all* assets have to be included in the market portfolio. The only issue is the price at which investors will be willing to include a stock in their optimal risky portfolio.

The Passive Strategy Is Efficient

In Chapter 6 we defined the capital market line (CML) as the CAL that is constructed from a money market account (or T-bills) and the market portfolio. Now you can fully appreciate why the CML is an interesting CAL. In the simple world of the CAPM, the market portfolio, M, is the optimal tangency portfolio on the efficient frontier.

In this scenario, the market portfolio held by all investors is based on the common input list, which incorporates all relevant information about the universe of securities. This means that investors can skip the trouble of doing security analysis and obtain an efficient portfolio simply by holding the market portfolio. (Of course, if everyone were to follow this strategy, no one would perform security analysis and this result would no longer hold. We discuss this issue in greater depth in Chapter 11 on market efficiency.)

Thus the passive strategy of investing in a market-index portfolio is efficient. For this reason, we sometimes call this result a **mutual fund theorem.** The mutual fund theorem is another incarnation of the separation property discussed in Chapter 7. If all investors would freely choose to hold a common risky portfolio identical to the market portfolio, they would not object if all stocks in the market were replaced with shares of a single mutual fund holding that market portfolio.

In reality, different investment managers do create risky portfolios that differ from the market index. We attribute this in part to the use of different input lists in the formation of their optimal risky portfolios. Nevertheless, the practical significance of the mutual fund theorem is that a passive investor may view the market index as a reasonable first approximation to an efficient risky portfolio.

 Concept Check **9.1**

> If there are only a few investors who perform security analysis, and all others hold the market portfolio, M, would the CML still be the efficient CAL for investors who do not engage in security analysis? Why or why not?

The nearby box contains a parable illustrating the argument for indexing. If the passive strategy is efficient, then attempts to beat it simply generate trading and research costs with no offsetting benefit and, ultimately, inferior results.

The Risk Premium of the Market Portfolio

In Chapter 6 we discussed how individual investors go about deciding capital allocation. If all investors choose to invest in portfolio M and the risk-free asset, what can we deduce about the equilibrium risk premium of portfolio M?

The Parable of the Money Managers

Some years ago, in a land called Indicia, revolution led to the overthrow of a socialist regime and the restoration of a system of private property. Former government enterprises were reformed as corporations, which then issued stocks and bonds. These securities were given to a central agency, which offered them for sale to individuals, pension funds, and the like (all armed with newly printed money).

Almost immediately a group of money managers came forth to assist these investors. Recalling the words of a venerated elder, uttered before the previous revolution ("Invest in Corporate Indicia"), they invited clients to give them money, with which they would buy a cross-section of all the newly issued securities. Investors considered this a reasonable idea, and soon everyone held a piece of Corporate Indicia.

Before long the money managers became bored because there was little for them to do. Soon they fell into the habit of gathering at a beachfront casino where they passed the time playing roulette, craps, and similar games, for low stakes, with their own money.

After a while, the owner of the casino suggested a new idea. He would furnish an impressive set of rooms which would be designated the Money Managers' Club. There the members could place bets with one another about the fortunes of various corporations, industries, the level of the Gross Domestic Product, foreign trade, etc. To make the betting more exciting, the casino owner suggested that the managers use their clients' money for this purpose.

The offer was immediately accepted, and soon the money managers were betting eagerly with one another. At the end of each week, some found that they had won money for their clients, while others found that they had lost. But the losses always exceeded the gains, for a certain amount was deducted from each bet to cover the costs of the elegant surroundings in which the gambling took place.

Before long a group of professors from Indicia U. suggested that investors were not well served by the activities being conducted at the Money Managers' Club. "Why pay people to gamble with your money? Why not just hold your own piece of Corporate Indicia?" they said.

This argument seemed sensible to some of the investors, and they raised the issue with their money managers. A few capitulated, announcing that they would henceforth stay away from the casino and use their clients' money only to buy proportionate shares of all the stocks and bonds issued by corporations.

The converts, who became known as managers of Indicia funds, were initially shunned by those who continued to frequent the Money Managers' Club, but in time, grudging acceptance replaced outright hostility. The wave of puritan reform some had predicted failed to materialize, and gambling remained legal. Many managers continued to make their daily pilgrimage to the casino. But they exercised more restraint than before, placed smaller bets, and generally behaved in a manner consonant with their responsibilities. Even the members of the Lawyers' Club found it difficult to object to the small amount of gambling that still went on.

And everyone but the casino owner lived happily ever after.

Source: William F. Sharpe, "The Parable of the Money Managers," *The Financial Analysts' Journal* 32 (July/August 1976), p. 4. Copyright 1976, CFA Institute. Reproduced from *The Financial Analysts' Journal* with permission from the CFA Institute. All rights reserved.

Recall that each individual investor chooses a proportion y, allocated to the optimal portfolio M, such that

$$y = \frac{E(r_M) - r_f}{A\sigma_M^2} \qquad (9.1)$$

where $E(r_M) - r_f = E(R_M)$ is the risk premium (expected excess return) on the market portfolio.

In the simplified CAPM economy, risk-free investments involve borrowing and lending among investors. Any borrowing position must be offset by the lending position of the creditor. This means that net borrowing and lending across all investors must be zero, and therefore, substituting the representative investor's risk aversion, $\overline{A}$, for A, the average position in the risky portfolio is 100%, or $\overline{y} = 1$. Setting $y = 1$ in Equation 9.1 and rearranging, we find that the risk premium on the market portfolio is related to its variance by the average degree of risk aversion:

$$E(R_M) = \overline{A}\sigma_M^2 \qquad (9.2)$$

Concept Check **9.2**

Data from the last nine decades for the S&P 500 index yield the following statistics: average excess return, 8.3%; standard deviation, 20.3%.

a. To the extent that these averages approximated investor expectations for the period, what must have been the average coefficient of risk aversion?

b. If the coefficient of risk aversion were actually 3.5, what risk premium would have been consistent with the market's historical standard deviation?

Expected Returns on Individual Securities

The CAPM is built on the insight that the appropriate risk premium on an asset will be determined by its contribution to the risk of investors' overall portfolios. Portfolio risk is what matters to investors and is what governs the risk premiums they demand.

Remember that in the CAPM, all investors use the same input list, that is, the same estimates of expected returns, variances, and covariances and, therefore, all end up using the market as their optimal risky portfolio. To calculate the variance of the market portfolio, we use the bordered covariance matrix with the market portfolio weights, as discussed in Chapter 7. We highlight GE in this depiction of the n stocks in the market portfolio so that we can measure the contribution of GE to the risk of the market portfolio.

Recall that we calculate the variance of the portfolio by summing over all the elements of the covariance matrix, first multiplying each element by the portfolio weights from the row and the column. The contribution of one stock to portfolio variance therefore can be expressed as the sum of all the covariance terms in the column corresponding to the stock, where each covariance is first multiplied by both the stock's weight from its row and the weight from its column.[5]

Portfolio Weights	w_1	w_2	...	w_{GE}	...	w_n
w_1	$Cov(R_1, R_1)$	$Cov(R_1, R_2)$	...	$Cov(R_1, R_{GE})$	...	$Cov(R_1, R_n)$
w_2	$Cov(R_2, R_1)$	$Cov(R_2, R_2)$	...	$Cov(R_2, R_{GE})$	...	$Cov(R_2, R_n)$
$\vdots$	$\vdots$	$\vdots$		$\vdots$		$\vdots$
w_{GE}	$Cov(R_{GE}, R_1)$	$Cov(R_{GE}, R_2)$	...	$Cov(R_{GE}, R_{GE})$	...	$Cov(R_{GE}, R_n)$
$\vdots$	$\vdots$	$\vdots$		$\vdots$		$\vdots$
w_n	$Cov(R_n, R_1)$	$Cov(R_n, R_2)$	...	$Cov(R_n, R_{GE})$	...	$Cov(R_n, R_n)$

[5]An alternative approach would be to measure GE's contribution to market variance as the sum of the elements in the row *and* the column corresponding to GE. In this case, GE's contribution would be twice the sum in Equation 9.3. The approach that we take allocates contributions to portfolio risk among securities in a convenient manner in that the sum of the contributions of each stock equals the total portfolio variance, whereas the alternative measure of contribution would sum to twice the portfolio variance. This results from a type of double-counting, because adding both the rows and the columns for each stock would result in each entry in the matrix being added twice. Using either approach, GE's contribution to the variance of the market return would be directly proportional to the covariance of its returns with the market.

Thus, the contribution of GE's stock to the variance of the market portfolio is

$$w_{GE}[w_1 \text{Cov}(R_1, R_{GE}) + w_2 \text{Cov}(R_2, R_{GE}) + \cdots + w_{GE} \text{Cov}(R_{GE}, R_{GE}) + \cdots \\ + w_n \text{Cov}(R_n, R_{GE})] \quad \textbf{(9.3)}$$

Notice that every term in the square brackets can be slightly rearranged as follows: $w_i \text{Cov}(R_i, R_{GE}) = \text{Cov}(w_i R_i, R_{GE})$. Moreover, because covariance is additive, the sum of the terms in the square brackets is

$$\sum_{i=1}^{n} w_i \text{Cov}(R_i, R_{GE}) = \sum_{i=1}^{n} \text{Cov}(w_i R_i, R_{GE}) = \text{Cov}\left(\sum_{i=1}^{n} w_i R_i, R_{GE}\right) \quad \textbf{(9.4)}$$

But because $\sum_{i=1}^{n} w_i R_i = R_M$, Equation 9.4 implies that

$$\sum_{i=1}^{n} w_i \text{Cov}(R_i, R_{GE}) = \text{Cov}(R_M, R_{GE})$$

and therefore, GE's contribution to the variance of the market portfolio (Equation 9.3) may be more simply stated as $w_{GE} \text{Cov}(R_M, R_{GE})$.

This should not surprise us. For example, if the covariance between GE and the rest of the market is negative, then GE makes a "negative contribution" to portfolio risk: By providing excess returns that move inversely with the rest of the market, GE stabilizes the return on the overall portfolio. If the covariance is positive, GE makes a positive contribution to overall portfolio risk because its returns reinforce swings in the rest of the portfolio.[6]

We also observe that the contribution of GE to the risk premium of the market portfolio is $w_{GE} E(R_{GE})$. Therefore, the reward-to-risk ratio for investments in GE can be expressed as

$$\frac{\text{GE's contribution to risk premium}}{\text{GE's contribution to variance}} = \frac{w_{GE} E(R_{GE})}{w_{GE} \text{Cov}(R_{GE}, R_M)} = \frac{E(R_{GE})}{\text{Cov}(R_{GE}, R_M)}$$

The market portfolio is the tangency (efficient mean-variance) portfolio. The reward-to-risk ratio for investment in the market portfolio is

$$\frac{\text{Market risk premium}}{\text{Market variance}} = \frac{E(R_M)}{\sigma_M^2} \quad \textbf{(9.5)}$$

The ratio in Equation 9.5 is often called the **market price of risk** because it quantifies the extra return that investors demand to bear portfolio risk. Notice that for *components* of the efficient portfolio, such as shares of GE, we measure risk as the *contribution* to portfolio variance (which depends on its *covariance* with the market). In contrast, for the efficient portfolio itself, variance is the appropriate measure of risk.[7]

---

[6]A positive contribution to variance doesn't imply that diversification isn't beneficial. Excluding GE from the portfolio would require that its weight be assigned to the remaining stocks and that reallocation would increase variance even more. Variance is reduced by including more stocks and reducing the weight of each (i.e., diversifying), despite the fact that each positive-covariance security makes some contribution to variance. Notice in Equation 9.1 that the optimal allocation to the risky portfolio is proportional to the ratio of the risk premium to *variance,* not to standard deviation.

[7]Unfortunately, the market portfolio's Sharpe ratio

$$\frac{E(r_M) - r_f}{\sigma_M}$$

sometimes is referred to as the market price of risk, but it is not. The unit of risk is variance, and the price of risk relates risk premium to variance (or to covariance for incremental risk).

A basic principle of equilibrium is that all investments should offer the same reward-to-risk ratio. If the ratio were better for one investment than another, investors would rearrange their portfolios, tilting toward the alternative with the better trade-off and shying away from the other. Such activity would impart pressure on security prices until the ratios were equalized. Therefore we conclude that the reward-to-risk ratios of GE and the market portfolio should be equal:

$$\frac{E(R_{GE})}{\text{Cov}(R_{GE}, R_M)} = \frac{E(R_M)}{\sigma_M^2} \tag{9.6}$$

To determine the fair risk premium of GE stock, we rearrange Equation 9.6 slightly to obtain

$$E(R_{GE}) = \frac{\text{Cov}(R_{GE}, R_M)}{\sigma_M^2} E(R_M) \tag{9.7}$$

The ratio $\text{Cov}(R_{GE}, R_M)/\sigma_M^2$ measures the contribution of GE stock to the variance of the market portfolio as a fraction of the total variance of the market portfolio. The ratio is called **beta** and is denoted by β. Using this measure, we can restate Equation 9.7 as

$$E(r_{GE}) = r_f + \beta_{GE}[E(r_M) - r_f] \tag{9.8}$$

This **expected return–beta (or mean-beta) relationship** is the most familiar expression of the CAPM to practitioners.

The expected return–beta relationship tells us that the total expected rate of return is the sum of the risk-free rate (compensation for "waiting," i.e., the time value of money) plus a risk premium (compensation for "worrying," specifically about investment returns). Moreover, it makes a very specific prediction about the size of the risk premium: It is the product of a "benchmark risk premium" (that of the broad market portfolio) and the relative risk of the particular asset as measured by its beta (its *contribution* to the risk of the overall risky portfolio).

Notice what the risk premium does *not* depend on: the total volatility of the investment. So, for example, the stock market performance of a firm developing a new drug that may be a great success or a total failure may have extremely high variance, but investors in those shares will not, for that reason, demand a high expected return. They recognize that because the success of the firm is largely independent of macroeconomic risk and the return on the rest of their portfolio, its contribution to overall portfolio risk is low and therefore does not warrant a large risk premium. The CAPM predicts that systematic risk should "be priced," meaning that it commands a risk premium, but firm-specific risk should not be priced by the market.

If the expected return–beta relationship holds for each individual asset, it must hold for any combination or weighted average of assets. Suppose that some portfolio P has weight w_k for stock k, where k takes on values $1, \ldots, n$. Writing out the CAPM Equation 9.8 for each stock, and multiplying each equation by the weight of the stock in the portfolio, we obtain these equations, one for each stock:

$$
\begin{array}{l}
w_1 E(r_1) = w_1 r_f + w_1 \beta_1 [E(r_M) - r_f] \\
+ w_2 E(r_2) = w_2 r_f + w_2 \beta_2 [E(r_M) - r_f] \\
+ \quad \cdots = \cdots \\
\underline{+ w_n E(r_n) = w_n r_f + w_n \beta_n [E(r_M) - r_f]} \\
\quad E(r_P) = r_f + \beta_P [E(r_M) - r_f]
\end{array}
$$

Summing each column shows that the CAPM holds for the overall portfolio because $E(r_P) = \sum_k w_k E(r_k)$ is the expected return on the portfolio and $\beta_P = \sum_k w_k \beta_k$ is the portfolio beta. Incidentally, this result has to be true for the market portfolio itself,

$$E(r_M) = r_f + \beta_M[E(r_M) - r_f]$$

Indeed, this is a tautology because $\beta_M = 1$, as we can verify by noting that

$$\beta_M = \frac{\text{Cov}(R_M, R_M)}{\sigma_M^2} = \frac{\sigma_M^2}{\sigma_M^2}$$

This also establishes 1 as the weighted-average value of beta across all assets. If the market beta is 1, and the market is a portfolio of all assets in the economy, the weighted-average beta of all assets must be 1. Hence betas greater than 1 are considered aggressive in that investment in high-beta stocks entails above-average sensitivity to market swings. Betas below 1 can be described as defensive.

A word of caution: We often hear that well-managed firms will provide high rates of return. We agree this is true if one measures the *firm's* return on its investments in plant and equipment. The CAPM, however, predicts returns on investments in the *securities* of the firm.

Let's say that everyone knows a firm is well run. Its stock price will therefore be bid up, and consequently returns to stockholders who buy at those high prices will not be excessive. Security prices, in other words, already reflect public information about a firm's prospects; therefore only the risk of the company (as measured by beta in the context of the CAPM) should affect expected returns. In a well-functioning market, investors receive high expected returns only if they are willing to bear risk.

Of course, investors do not directly observe expected returns on securities. Rather, they observe security prices and bid those prices up or down. Expected rates of return can at most be inferred from the prices investors pay compared to the cash flows those investments are expected to generate.

 Concept Check **9.3**

Suppose that the risk premium on the market portfolio is estimated at 8% with a standard deviation of 22%. What is the risk premium on a portfolio invested 25% in Toyota and 75% in Ford if they have betas of 1.10 and 1.25, respectively?

The Security Market Line

We can view the expected return–beta relationship as a reward–risk equation. The beta of a security is the appropriate measure of its risk because beta is proportional to the risk the security contributes to the optimal risky portfolio.

Risk-averse mean-variance investors measure the risk of the optimal risky *portfolio* by its variance. Hence, we would expect the risk premium on individual assets to depend on the *contribution* of the asset to the risk of the portfolio. The beta of a stock measures its contribution to the variance of the market portfolio and therefore the required risk premium is a function of beta. The CAPM confirms this intuition, stating further that the security's risk premium is directly proportional to both the beta and the risk premium of the market portfolio; that is, the risk premium equals $\beta[E(r_M) - r_f]$.

The expected return–beta relationship can be portrayed graphically as the **security market line (SML)** in Figure 9.2. Because the market's beta is 1, the slope is the risk premium of the market portfolio. At the point on the horizontal axis where $\beta = 1$, we can

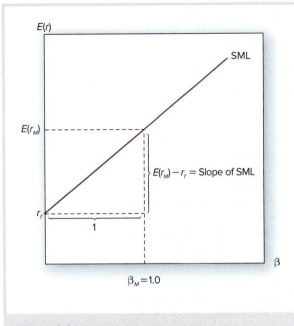

Figure 9.2 The security market line

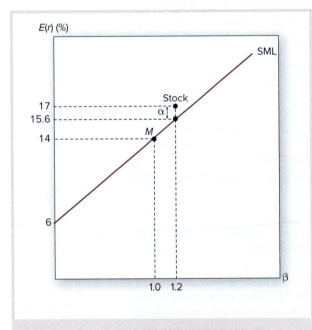

Figure 9.3 The SML and a positive-alpha stock

read off the vertical axis the expected return on the market portfolio.

It is useful to compare the security market line to the capital market line. The CML graphs the risk premiums of *efficient* portfolios (i.e., portfolios composed of the market and the risk-free asset) as a function of portfolio standard deviation. This is appropriate because standard deviation is a valid measure of risk for efficiently diversified portfolios that are candidates for an investor's overall portfolio. The SML, in contrast, graphs *individual asset* risk premiums as a function of asset risk. The relevant measure of risk for individual assets held as parts of well-diversified portfolios is not the asset's standard deviation or variance; it is, instead, the contribution of the asset to the portfolio variance, which we measure by the asset's beta. The SML is valid for both efficient portfolios and individual assets.

The security market line provides a benchmark for the evaluation of investment performance. Given the risk of an investment, as measured by its beta, the SML provides the required rate of return necessary to compensate investors for risk as well as the time value of money.

Because the security market line is the graphic representation of the expected return–beta relationship, "fairly priced" assets plot exactly on the SML; that is, their expected returns are commensurate with their risk. All securities must lie on the SML in market equilibrium. We see here how the CAPM may be of use in the money-management industry. Suppose that the SML relation is used as a benchmark to assess the fair expected return on a risky asset. Then security analysis is performed to calculate the return a money manager actually expects. (Notice that we depart here from the simple CAPM world in that some investors now apply their own unique analysis to derive an "input list" that may differ from that of their competitors.) If a stock is perceived to be a good buy, or underpriced, it will provide an expected return in excess of the fair return stipulated by the SML. Underpriced stocks therefore plot above the SML: Given their betas, their expected returns are greater than dictated by the CAPM. Overpriced stocks plot below the SML.

The difference between the fair and actually expected rate of return on a stock is called the stock's **alpha,** denoted by α. For example, if the market return is expected to be 14%, a stock has a beta of 1.2, and the T-bill rate is 6%, the SML would predict an expected return on the stock of $6 + 1.2(14 - 6) = 15.6\%$. If one believed the stock would provide an expected return of 17%, the implied alpha would be 1.4% (see Figure 9.3).

Concept Check **9.4**

Stock XYZ has an expected return of 12% and risk of $\beta = 1$. Stock ABC has expected return of 13% and $\beta = 1.5$. The market's expected return is 11%, and $r_f = 5\%$.

a. According to the CAPM, which stock is a better buy?

b. What is the alpha of each stock? Plot the SML and each stock's risk–return point on one graph. Show the alphas graphically.

One might say that security analysis (which we treat in Part Five) is about uncovering securities with nonzero alphas. This analysis suggests that the starting point of portfolio management can be a passive market-index portfolio. The portfolio manager will then increase the weights of securities with positive alphas and decrease the weights of securities with negative alphas. We showed one strategy (the Treynor-Black model) for adjusting the portfolio weights in such a manner in Chapter 8.

The CAPM is also useful in capital budgeting decisions. For a firm considering a new project, the CAPM can provide the *required rate of return* that the project needs to yield, based on its beta, to be acceptable to investors. Managers can use the CAPM to obtain this cutoff internal rate of return (IRR), or "hurdle rate," for the project.

Example 9.1   Using the CAPM

Yet another use of the CAPM is in utility rate-making cases. In this case, the issue is the rate of return that a regulated utility should be allowed to earn on its investment in plant and equipment. Suppose that the equityholders have invested $100 million in the firm and that the beta of the equity is .6. If the T-bill rate is 6% and the market risk premium is 8%, then the fair profits to the firm would be assessed as $6 + .6 \times 8 = 10.8\%$ of the $100 million investment, or $10.8 million. The firm would be allowed to set prices at a level expected to generate these profits.

 Concept Check **9.5**

The risk-free rate is 8% and the expected return on the market portfolio is 16%. A firm considers a project that is expected to have a beta of 1.3.

a. What is the required rate of return on the project?

b. If the expected IRR of the project is 19%, should it be accepted?

The CAPM and the Single-Index Market

The index model from the last chapter asserted that security returns could be described by Equation 8.8, which is restated here as Equation 9.9:

$$R_i = \alpha_i + \beta_i R_M + e_i \qquad (9.9)$$

The index model states that the realized excess return on any stock is the sum of the realized excess return due to marketwide factors, $\beta_i R_M$, a nonmarket premium, α_i, and firm-specific outcomes summarized by e_i. Because the expected value of firm-specific surprises is zero, the *expected* excess return, equivalently the risk premium, of stock i would then be given by Equation 9.10:

$$E(R_i) = \alpha_i + \beta_i E(R_M) \tag{9.10}$$

The expected return–beta relationship of the CAPM, which we rearrange very slightly from Equation 9.8, is $E(r_i) - r_f = \beta_i[E(r_M) - r_f]$. Stated in terms of excess returns, this risk–return relation is:

$$E(R_i) = \beta_i E(R_M) \tag{9.11}$$

Comparing Equations 9.10 and 9.11, we see that the prediction of the CAPM is that for every stock, the equilibrium value of α_i is 0. The logic of the CAPM is that the only reason for a stock to provide a premium over the risk-free rate is that the stock imposes systematic risk for which the investor must be compensated. A positive alpha implies reward without risk. Investors will relentlessly pursue positive alpha stocks and bid up their prices; at those higher prices, expected rates of return will be lower. Symmetrically, investors will shun or short sell negative alpha stocks, driving down their prices and driving up their expected returns. This portfolio rebalancing will continue until all alpha values are driven to zero. At this point, investors will be content to fully diversify and eliminate unique risk, that is, to hold the broadest possible market portfolio. When all stocks have zero alphas, the market portfolio is the optimal risky portfolio.[8]

Thus, one implication of the CAPM is that if one estimates the index model regression with a market index that adequately represents the full market portfolio, estimated values of alpha for any group of stocks should cluster around zero. We will turn to some of the empirical evidence on this prediction in Chapter 11.

9.2   Assumptions and Extensions of the CAPM

From the outset, we noted that the CAPM is an elegant model built on a set of uncomfortably restrictive assumptions. This raises the question of what happens to the predicted risk–return relationship when we attempt to generalize the model to accommodate more realistic assumptions. In this section, we will review some variants of the basic model. We organize the discussion by the particular assumption from Table 9.1 that is called into question. We will discover that parts of the model change in important ways, but the fundamental distinction between systematic and diversifiable risk remains.

Identical Input Lists

Assumption 1(c) (investors optimize with the same input list), appears ominously restrictive, but it actually is not all that problematic. When most information is public, it would not be uncommon for investors to be close to agreement on firms' prospects. Moreover, trades of investors who derive different input lists will offset and prices will reflect consensus expectations. We will later allow for the possibility that some investors expend resources to obtain private information and exploit prices that don't reflect the insights derived from this information. But regardless of their success, it is reasonable to conclude that, at least in the absence of private information, investors should assume alpha values are zero.

[8]Recall from Chapter 8 that the weight of a stock in an active portfolio will be zero if its alpha is zero (see Equation 8.24); hence if all alphas are zero, the passive market portfolio will be the optimal risky portfolio.

On the other hand, impediments to selling securities short (which we ruled out in Assumption 2[b]) can upend this conclusion. We start with the fact that short positions are not as easy to take as long ones for three reasons:

1. The liability of investors who hold a short position in an asset is potentially unlimited, since the price may rise without limit. Hence a large short position requires large collateral, and proceeds cannot be used to invest in other risky assets.
2. There is a limited supply of shares of any stock to be borrowed by would-be short sellers. It often happens that investors simply cannot find shares to borrow in order to short.
3. Many investment companies are prohibited from short sales. The U.S. and other countries further restrict short sales by regulation.

Why are short sales important? When prices rise above intrinsic values, rational investors will take short positions, thus holding down the price. But given impediments to short sales, the natural market actions that would normally prevent prices from rising to unsustainable levels are likewise impeded. Such price run-ups are precursors to a correction or even a crash and are a good part of what defines a "bubble."

Taxes also cast doubt on Assumption 1(c) because two investors can realize different after-tax returns from the same stock. Such distortions to the "input list" could, in principle, lead to different after-tax optimal risky portfolios; hence the CAPM required Assumption 2(c) (no taxes). Nevertheless, despite an extension to the CAPM that incorporates personal taxes on dividends and capital gains,[9] there is no decisive evidence that taxes are a major factor in stock returns. A plausible explanation for this negative finding relies on "clientele" and supply effects. If high tax-bracket investors shy away from high-yield (dividend-paying) stocks and thus force down their prices, tax-exempt investors will view the stocks as a bargain and take up the slack in demand. On the other end, if corporations see that high dividend yields reduce stock prices, they simply will substitute stock repurchases for dividends, reinforcing the clientele effect in neutralizing tax effects.

Risk-Free Borrowing and the Zero-Beta Model

Restrictions on borrowing (or significantly higher rates on borrowing than on lending), which violate Assumption 2(b), also can create problems for the CAPM, because borrowers and lenders will arrive at different tangency portfolios and thus different optimal risky portfolios. The market portfolio will no longer be each investor's optimal risky portfolio.

Efficient frontier portfolios have a number of interesting characteristics, independently derived by Merton and Roll.[10] Some of these are:

1. Any portfolio that is a combination of two frontier portfolios is itself on the efficient frontier.
2. Because each investor will still choose his or her optimal risky portfolio from the efficient frontier, the market portfolio will be an aggregation of efficient portfolios and therefore (from the first property) will itself be efficient.
3. Every portfolio on the efficient frontier, except for the global minimum-variance portfolio, has a "companion" portfolio on the bottom (inefficient) half of the

---

[9]Michael J. Brennan, "Taxes, Market Valuation, and Corporate Finance Policy," *National Tax Journal,* December 1973.

[10]Robert C. Merton, "An Analytic Derivation of the Efficient Portfolio Frontier," *Journal of Financial and Quantitative Analysis,* 1972; and Richard Roll, "A Critique of the Asset Pricing Theory's Tests: Part I: On Past and Potential Testability of the Theory," *Journal of Financial Economics* 4 (1977).

frontier with which it is uncorrelated. Because it is uncorrelated, the companion portfolio is referred to as the **zero-beta portfolio** of the efficient portfolio. If we choose the market portfolio M and its zero-beta companion portfolio Z, then we obtain the following CAPM-like equation:

$$E(r_i) - E(r_Z) = [E(r_M) - E(r_Z)]\frac{\text{Cov}(r_i, r_M)}{\sigma_M^2} = \beta_i[E(r_M) - E(r_Z)] \qquad \textbf{(9.12)}$$

Equation 9.12 resembles the SML of the CAPM, except that the risk-free rate is replaced with the expected return on the zero-beta companion of the market-index portfolio. Fischer Black used these properties to show that Equation 9.12 is the CAPM equation that results when investors face restrictions on borrowing.[11]

Risk-tolerant investors are the ones who would like to borrow to leverage up their position in the tangency portfolio. But limits to their ability to borrow or spreads between borrowing and lending impede their ability to do so. Investors who would otherwise wish to borrow and leverage their portfolios but who find it impossible or costly to do so will instead tilt their portfolios toward high-beta (high expected return) stocks and away from low-beta ones. As a result, prices of high-beta stocks will rise, and their risk premiums will fall. In Equation 9.12, the risk premium on the market portfolio is smaller than predicted by the basic CAPM because the expected return on the zero-beta portfolio is greater than the risk-free rate, and therefore the reward to bearing systematic risk is smaller. In other words, the SML will be flatter than in the simple CAPM.

Labor Income and Nontraded Assets

The assertion that all assets are tradable (Assumption 2[a]) is essential for the conclusion that the market portfolio, which is so central to the CAPM, is the common risky portfolio chosen by all investors. In fact, many assets are not tradeable. Private businesses are a large and important part of the economy, but by definition, these businesses do not trade. Neither does human capital, the earning power of individuals. The discounted value of future labor income exceeds the total market value of traded assets. The market value of privately held corporations and businesses is of the same order of magnitude.

These considerations imply that investors may derive very different "optimal risky portfolios." Consider owners of a family business. Their wealth is already highly dependent on the success of the business. Prudence dictates that they avoid further investments in assets that are highly correlated with their businesses. Similarly, investors should avoid stock returns that are positively correlated with their personal income; for example, Boeing employees should avoid investing in the airline and related businesses. Differential investment demands arising from this consideration can lead to violation of the mean-beta equation and derail the mean-variance efficiency of the index portfolio.

Privately held businesses may be the lesser of the two sources of departures from the CAPM. Suppose that privately held businesses have risk characteristics similar to those of traded assets. In this case, individuals can partially offset the diversification problems posed by their nontraded entrepreneurial assets by reducing their portfolio demand for securities of similar, traded assets. Thus, the CAPM expected return–beta equation may not be greatly disrupted by the presence of entrepreneurial income.

However, to the extent that risk characteristics of private enterprises differ from those of traded securities, a portfolio of traded assets that best hedges the risk of typical private business would enjoy elevated demand from the population of private business owners.

---

[11]Fischer Black, "Capital Market Equilibrium with Restricted Borrowing," *Journal of Business,* July 1972.

The price of assets in this portfolio will be bid up relative to the CAPM prediction, and the expected returns on these securities will be lower in relation to their systematic risk. Conversely, securities highly correlated with such risk will require high risk premiums to induce investors to invest in them and may appear to exhibit positive alphas relative to the conventional SML. In fact, Heaton and Lucas show that adding proprietary income to a standard asset-pricing model improves its predictive performance.[12]

The size of labor income and its special nature is of even greater concern for the validity of the CAPM. The possible effect of labor income on equilibrium returns can be appreciated from its important effect on personal portfolio choice. Despite the fact that an individual can reduce some of the uncertainty about future labor income via life insurance, human capital is less "portable" across time and may be more difficult to hedge using traded securities than nontraded business. This may induce hedging demand for stocks of labor-intensive firms with high wage expenses: These firms will do well when wage income is generally depressed, and thus serve as a hedge against wage income uncertainty. The resulting pressure on security prices may reduce the equilibrium expected return on these stocks to levels below those predicted by the CAPM.

Mayers[13] derives the equilibrium expected return–beta equation for an economy in which individuals are endowed with labor income of varying size relative to their nonlabor capital. The resultant SML equation is

$$E(R_i) = E(R_M) \frac{\text{Cov}(R_i, R_M) + \dfrac{P_H}{P_M} \text{Cov}(R_i, R_H)}{\sigma_M^2 + \dfrac{P_H}{P_H} \text{Cov}(R_M, R_H)} \qquad (9.13)$$

where

P_H = Value of aggregate human capital

P_M = Market value of traded assets (market portfolio)

R_H = Excess rate of return on aggregate human capital

The CAPM measure of systematic risk, beta, is replaced in the extended model by an adjusted beta that also accounts for covariance with the portfolio of aggregate human capital. The model thus is consistent with a security market line with a different slope than that of the standard CAPM.

A Multiperiod Model and Hedge Portfolios

Assumption 1(a) states that only the mean and variance of wealth matter to investors. But consider these questions:

1. Would you rather have wealth of $1.1 million and a price of oil of $400 per barrel or $1 million and oil priced at $40 per barrel? If you are a big energy consumer, you may very well be better off with slightly less money and considerably lower energy prices. The lower energy-price scenario leaves you with more to spend on other consumption goods.

---

[12]John Heaton and Deborah Lucas, "Portfolio Choice and Asset Prices: The Importance of Entrepreneurial Risk," *Journal of Finance* 55 (June 2000). This paper offers evidence of the effect of entrepreneurial risk on both portfolio choice and the risk–return relationship.

[13]David Mayers, "Nonmarketable Assets and Capital Market Equilibrium under Uncertainty," in *Studies in the Theory of Capital Markets,* ed. M. C. Jensen (New York: Praeger, 1972).

2. Would you rather have wealth of $1 million and a real interest rate of 10% or $1.1 million and a real rate of 1%? You may be better off with slightly less money but with the ability to invest it to earn higher returns. Your stream of consumption could easily be higher in the lower wealth–higher rate scenario.

3. Would you rather have wealth of $1 million with a market standard deviation of 10% or $1.1 million and a standard derivation of 50%? You may be better off with slightly less money but with the lower volatility. You would then be more comfortable investing a greater share of your wealth in the market index, thereby earning a higher risk premium on your complete portfolio.

These examples show that investors should care about more than the risk and return of their wealth as measured in dollars. They should be more concerned with the stream of consumption that wealth can buy for them. Therefore Assumption 1(a), that investors optimize over the mean and variance of the value of their portfolios, is problematic. The assumption rules out concern with the correlation of asset returns with either inflation or prices of important consumption items such as housing or energy. It also rules out concern with the correlation between asset returns and the parameters of the "investment opportunity set," for example, changes in the volatility of asset returns. The extra demand for assets that can be used to hedge these "extra-market risks" would increase their prices and reduce their risk premiums relative to the prediction of the CAPM.

Similar extra-market risk factors would arise in a multiperiod model, which we ignored when we adopted Assumption 1(b), limiting investors to a common single-period horizon. Consider a possible decline in future interest rates. Investors would be unhappy about this event to the extent that it would reduce the expected income their investments could throw off in the future. Assets whose returns will be higher when interest rates fall (e.g., long-term bonds) would hedge this risk and thus command higher prices and lower risk premiums. Because of such hedging demands, correlation with any parameter describing future investment opportunities can result in violations of the CAPM mean-beta equation.

Robert C. Merton revolutionized financial economics by devising a model of asset pricing that allows us to examine the impacts of these hedging demands.[14] In his basic model, Merton relaxes the "single-period" assumption about investors. He envisions individuals who optimize a lifetime consumption/investment plan and who continually adapt their consumption/investment decisions to changes in wealth, prices, and investment opportunities. In one special case, when uncertainty about portfolio returns is the only source of risk and investment opportunities remain unchanged through time (i.e., there is no change in the risk-free rate or the probability distribution of the return on the market portfolio or individual securities), Merton's so-called intertemporal capital asset pricing model (ICAPM) predicts the same expected return–beta relationship as the simple CAPM.[15]

But the situation changes when we include additional sources of risk. These extra risks are of two general kinds. One concerns changes in the parameters describing investment opportunities, such as future risk-free rates, expected returns, or asset risk. Suppose that the real interest rate may change over time. If it falls in some future period, one's level of wealth will now support a lower stream of real consumption. Future spending plans, for example, for retirement spending, may be put in jeopardy. To the extent that returns on some securities are correlated with changes in the risk-free rate, a portfolio can be formed to hedge such risk, and investors will bid up the price (and bid down the expected return)

---

[14]Merton's classic works are collected in *Continuous-Time Finance* (Oxford, U.K.: Basil Blackwell, 1992).

[15]Eugene F. Fama also made this point in "Multiperiod Consumption-Investment Decisions," *American Economic Review* 60 (1970).

of those hedge assets. Investors will sacrifice some expected return if they can find assets whose returns will be higher when other parameters (in this case, the real risk-free rate) change adversely.

The other additional source of risk concerns the prices of the consumption goods that can be purchased with any amount of wealth. Consider inflation risk. In addition to the expected level and volatility of nominal wealth, investors must be concerned about the cost of living—what those dollars can buy. Therefore, inflation risk is an important extra-market source of risk, and investors may be willing to sacrifice some expected return to purchase securities whose returns will be higher when the cost of living changes adversely. If so, hedging demands for securities that help to protect against inflation risk would affect portfolio choice and thus expected return. One can push this conclusion even further, arguing that empirically significant hedging demands may arise for important subsectors of consumer expenditures; for example, investors may bid up share prices of energy companies that will hedge energy price uncertainty. These sorts of effects may characterize any assets that hedge important extra-market sources of risk.

More generally, suppose we can identify K sources of extra-market risk and find K associated hedge portfolios. Then, Merton's ICAPM expected return–beta equation would generalize the SML to a multi-index version:

$$E(R_i) = \beta_{iM}E(R_M) + \sum_{k=1}^{K} \beta_{ik}E(R_k) \tag{9.14}$$

where β_{iM} is the familiar security beta on the market-index portfolio and β_{ik} is the beta on the kth hedge portfolio. The equation predicts that the risk premium for security i is the sum of the compensation it commands for all of the relevant risk sources to which it is exposed. The first term is the usual risk premium for exposure to market risk. The other terms (in the summation sign) are benchmark risk premiums for each source of extra-market risk times the security beta with respect to that risk source. Thus, this expression generalizes the one-factor SML to a world with multiple sources of systematic risk.

A Consumption-Based CAPM

The logic of the CAPM together with the hedging demands noted in the previous subsection suggest that it might be useful to center the model directly on consumption. Such models were pioneered by Mark Rubinstein, Robert Lucas, and Douglas Breeden.[16]

In a lifetime consumption/investment plan, the investor must in each period balance the allocation of current wealth between today's consumption and the savings and investment that will support future consumption. When optimized, the utility value from an additional dollar of consumption today must be equal to the utility value of the expected future consumption that could be financed by investing that marginal dollar.

Suppose you wish to increase expected consumption growth by allocating some of your savings to a risky portfolio. How would we measure the risk of these assets? As a general rule, investors will value additional income more highly during difficult economic times (when resources are scarce) than in affluent times (when consumption is already abundant). An asset will therefore be viewed as riskier in terms of consumption if it has positive covariance with consumption growth—in other words, if its payoff is higher when consumption is already high but lower when consumption is relatively restricted. Therefore,

---

[16]Mark Rubinstein, "The Valuation of Uncertain Income Streams and the Pricing of Options," *Bell Journal of Economics and Management Science* 7 (1976), pp. 407–25; Robert Lucas, "Asset Prices in an Exchange Economy," *Econometrica* 46 (1978), pp. 1429–45; and Douglas Breeden, "An Intertemporal Asset Pricing Model with Stochastic Consumption and Investment Opportunities," *Journal of Financial Economics* 7 (1979), pp. 265–96.

equilibrium risk premiums will be greater for assets that exhibit higher covariance with consumption growth. Developing this insight, we can write the risk premium on an asset as a function of its "consumption risk" as follows:

$$E(R_i) = \beta_{iC} RP_C \tag{9.15}$$

where portfolio C may be interpreted as a *consumption-tracking portfolio* (also called a *consumption-mimicking portfolio*), that is, the portfolio with the highest correlation with consumption growth; β_{iC} is the slope coefficient in the regression of asset i's excess returns, R_i, on those of the consumption-tracking portfolio; and, finally, RP_C is the risk premium associated with consumption uncertainty, which is measured by the expected excess return on the consumption-tracking portfolio:

$$RP_C = E(R_C) = E(r_C) - r_f \tag{9.16}$$

Notice how similar this conclusion is to the conventional CAPM. The consumption-tracking portfolio in the consumption-based CAPM (often called the CCAPM) plays the role of the market portfolio in the conventional CAPM. This is consistent with its focus on the risk of *consumption* opportunities rather than the risk and return of the *dollar* value of the portfolio. The excess return on the consumption-tracking portfolio plays the role of the excess return on the market portfolio, M. Both approaches result in linear, single-factor models that differ mainly in the identity of the factor they use.

In contrast to the CAPM, the beta of the market portfolio on the market factor of the CCAPM is not necessarily 1. It is perfectly plausible and empirically evident that this beta is substantially greater than 1. This means that in the linear relationship between the market-index risk premium and that of the consumption portfolio,

$$E(R_M) = \alpha_M + \beta_{MC} E(R_C) + \varepsilon_M \tag{9.17}$$

where α_M and ε_M allow for empirical deviation from the exact model in Equation 9.15, and β_{MC} is not necessarily equal to 1.

Because the CCAPM is so similar to the CAPM, one might wonder about its usefulness. Indeed, just as the CAPM is empirically flawed because not all assets are traded, the CCAPM has its own shortcomings. The attractiveness of this model is in that it compactly incorporates hedging demands surrounding consumption uncertainty as well as possible changes in the parameters that characterize investment opportunities. There is a price to pay for this compactness, however. Consumption growth figures are measured with significant error and published infrequently (monthly at the most), compared with financial assets, whose prices are available throughout the day. Nevertheless, some empirical research[17] indicates that this model is more successful in explaining realized returns than the CAPM, which is a reason why students of investments should be familiar with it. We return to this issue, as well as empirical evidence concerning the CCAPM, in Chapter 13.

Liquidity and the CAPM

Finally, transaction costs inhibit trades; this violates Assumption 2(d) (no transaction costs). In fact, the CAPM has little to say about trading activity. In the equilibrium of the CAPM, all investors share all available information and demand identical portfolios of risky assets. The awkward implication of this result is that there is no reason for trade. If all investors hold identical portfolios of risky assets, then when new (unexpected) information arrives, prices will change commensurately, but each investor will continue to hold

---

[17]Ravi Jagannathan and Yong Wang, "Lazy Investors, Discretionary Consumption, and the Cross-Section of Stock Returns," *Journal of Finance* 62 (August 2007), pp. 1633–61.

a piece of the market portfolio, which requires no exchange of assets. How do we square this implication with the observation that on a typical day, trading volume amounts to several billion shares? One obvious answer is heterogeneous expectations, that is, beliefs not shared by the entire market. Diverse beliefs will give rise to trading as investors attempt to profit by rearranging portfolios in accordance with their now-heterogeneous demands. In reality, trading (and trading costs) will be of great importance to investors.

The **liquidity** of an asset is the ease and speed with which it can be sold at fair market value. Part of liquidity is the cost of engaging in a transaction, particularly the bid–ask spread. Another part is price impact—the adverse movement in price one would encounter when attempting to execute a larger trade. Yet another component is immediacy—the ability to sell the asset quickly without reverting to fire-sale prices. Conversely, **illiquidity** can be measured in part by the discount from fair market value a seller must accept if the asset is to be sold quickly. A perfectly liquid asset is one that would entail no illiquidity discount.

Liquidity (or the lack of it) has long been recognized as an important characteristic that affects asset values. In legal cases, courts have routinely applied very steep discounts to the values of businesses that cannot be publicly traded. But liquidity has not always been appreciated as an important factor in security markets, presumably due to the relatively small trading cost per transaction compared with the large costs of trading assets such as real estate. The first breakthrough came in the work of Amihud and Mendelson[18] and today, liquidity is increasingly viewed as an important determinant of prices and expected returns. We supply only a brief synopsis of this important topic here and provide empirical evidence in Chapter 13.

One important component of trading cost is the bid–ask spread. For example, in electronic markets, the limit-order book contains the "inside spread," that is, the difference between the highest price at which some investor will purchase any shares and the lowest price at which another investor is willing to sell. The effective bid–ask spread will also depend on the size of the desired transaction. Larger purchases will require a trader to move deeper into the limit-order book and accept less-attractive prices. While inside spreads on electronic markets often appear extremely low, effective spreads can be much larger, because most limit orders are good for only small numbers of shares.

There is great emphasis today on the component of the spread due to *asymmetric information*. Asymmetric information is the potential for one trader to have private information about the value of the security that is not known to the trading partner. To see why such an asymmetry can affect the market, think about the problems facing someone buying a used car. The seller knows more about the car than the buyer, so the buyer naturally wonders if the seller is trying to get rid of the car because it is a "lemon." At the least, buyers worried about overpaying will shave the prices they are willing to pay for a car of uncertain quality. In extreme cases of asymmetric information, trading may cease altogether.[19] Similarly, traders who post offers to buy or sell at limit prices need to be worried about being picked off by better-informed traders who hit their limit prices only when they are out of line with the intrinsic value of the firm.

Broadly speaking, we may envision investors trading securities for two reasons. Some trades are driven by "noninformational" motives, for example, selling assets to raise cash

---

[18]Yakov Amihud and Haim Mendelson, "Asset Pricing and the Bid–Ask Spread," *Journal of Financial Economics* 17 (1986). A summary of the ensuing large body of literature on liquidity can be found in Yakov Amihud, Haim Mendelson, and Lasse Heje Pedersen, *Market Liquidity: Asset Pricing Risk and Crises* (New York: Cambridge University Press, 2013).

[19]The problem of informational asymmetry in markets was introduced by the 2001 Nobel laureate George A. Akerlof and has since become known as the *lemons problem*. A good introduction to Akerlof's contributions can be found in George A. Akerlof, *An Economic Theorist's Book of Tales* (Cambridge, U.K.: Cambridge University Press, 1984).

for a big purchase, or even just for portfolio rebalancing. These sorts of trades, which are not motivated by private information that bears on the value of the traded security, are called *noise trades*. Security dealers will earn a profit from the bid–ask spread when transacting with noise traders (also called *liquidity traders* because their trades may derive from needs for liquidity, i.e., cash).

Other transactions are initiated by traders who believe they have come across information that a security is mispriced. But if that information gives them an advantage, it must be disadvantageous to the other party in the transaction. In this manner, information traders impose a cost on both dealers and other investors who post limit orders. Although on average dealers make money from the bid–ask spread when transacting with liquidity traders, they will absorb losses from information traders. Similarly, any trader posting a limit order is at risk from information traders. The response is to increase limit-ask prices and decrease limit-bid orders—in other words, the spread must widen. The greater the relative importance of information traders, the greater the required spread to compensate for the potential losses from trading with them. In the end, therefore, liquidity traders absorb most of the cost of the information trades because the bid–ask spread that they must pay on their "innocent" trades widens when informational asymmetry is more severe.

The discount in a security price that results from illiquidity can be surprisingly large, far larger than the bid–ask spread. Consider a security with a bid–ask spread of 1%. If the intrinsic value of the security is midway between the bid and ask price, then the bid is 0.5% below intrinsic value and the ask is 0.5% above. Suppose the stock will change hands once a year for the next three years and then will be held forever by the third buyer. For the last trade, the investor will pay for the security 99.5% or .995 of its fair price; the price is reduced by half the spread that will be incurred when the stock is sold. The second buyer, knowing the security will be sold a year later for .995 of fair value, and having to absorb half the spread upon purchase, will be willing to pay .995 − .005/1.05 = .9902 (i.e., 99.02% of fair value), if the spread from fair value is discounted at a rate of 5%. Finally, the current buyer, knowing the loss next year, when the stock will be sold for .9902 of fair value (a discount of .0098), will pay for the security only .995 − .0098/1.05 = .9857. Thus the discount has ballooned from .5% to 1.43%. In other words, the present values of all three future trading costs (spreads) are discounted into the current price.

To extend this logic, if the security will be traded once a year forever, its current illiquidity cost will equal immediate cost plus the present value of a perpetuity of .5%. At an annual discount rate of 5%, this sum equals .005 + .005/.05 = .105, or 10.5%! Obviously, liquidity is of potentially large value and should not be ignored in deriving the equilibrium value of securities.

When trading costs are higher, the illiquidity discount will be greater. Of course, if someone can buy a share at a lower price, the expected rate of return will be higher. Therefore, we should expect to see less-liquid securities offer higher average rates of return. But this illiquidity premium need not rise in direct proportion to trading cost. If an asset is less liquid, it will be shunned by frequent traders and held instead by longer term traders who are less affected by high trading costs. Hence in equilibrium, investors with long holding periods will, on average, hold more of the illiquid securities, while short-horizon investors will prefer liquid securities. This "clientele effect" mitigates the effect of the bid–ask spread for illiquid securities. The end result is that the liquidity premium should increase with trading costs (measured by the bid–ask spread) at a decreasing rate.

Figure 9.4 confirms this prediction. It shows average monthly returns for stocks stratified by bid–ask spread. The difference in returns between the most liquid stocks (lowest bid–ask spread) and least liquid (highest spread) stocks is about .7% per month. This is

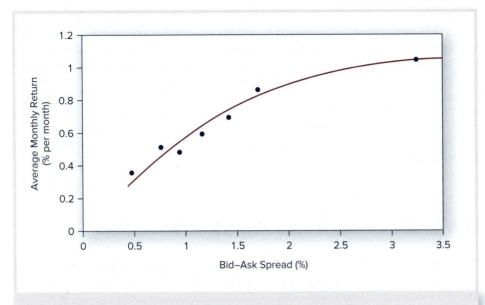

Figure 9.4 The relationship between illiquidity and average returns

Source: Derived from Yakov Amihud and Haim Mendelson, "Asset Pricing and the Bid–Ask Spread," *Journal of Financial Economics* 17 (1986), pp. 223–49.

just about the same magnitude as the monthly market risk premium! Liquidity clearly matters for asset pricing.

So far, we have shown that the expected level of liquidity can affect prices, and therefore expected rates of return. What about unanticipated *changes* in liquidity? In some circumstances, liquidity can unexpectedly dry up. For example, in the financial crisis of 2008, as many investors attempted to reduce leverage and cash out their positions, finding buyers for some assets became difficult. Many mortgage-backed securities stopped trading altogether. Liquidity had evaporated. Nor was this an unheard-of phenomenon. The market crash of 1987, as well as the failure of Long-Term Capital Management in 1998, also saw large declines in liquidity across broad segments of the market.

In fact, several studies have investigated variation in a number of measures of liquidity for large samples of stocks and found that when liquidity in one stock decreases, it tends to decrease in other stocks at the same time; thus liquidity across stocks shows significant correlation.[20] In other words, variation in liquidity has an important systematic component. Not surprisingly, investors demand compensation for exposure to *liquidity risk*. The extra expected return for bearing liquidity risk modifies the CAPM expected return–beta relationship.

Following up on this insight, Amihud demonstrates that firms with greater liquidity uncertainty have higher average returns.[21] Later studies focus on exposure to *marketwide*

[20]See, for example, Tarun Chordia, Richard Roll, and Avanidhar Subrahmanyam, "Commonality in Liquidity," *Journal of Financial Economics* 56 (2000), pp. 3–28, or J. Hasbrouck and D. H. Seppi, "Common Factors in Prices, Order Flows and Liquidity," *Journal of Financial Economics* 59 (2001), pp. 383–411.

[21] Yakov Amihud, "Illiquidity and Stock Returns: Cross-Section and Time-Series Effects," *Journal of Financial Markets* 9 (2002), pp. 31–56.

liquidity risk, as measured by a "liquidity beta." Analogously to a traditional market beta, the liquidity beta measures the sensitivity of a firm's returns to changes in market liquidity (whereas the traditional beta measures return sensitivity to the market return). Firms that provide better returns when market liquidity falls offer some protection against liquidity risk, and thus should be priced higher and offer lower expected returns. In fact, we will see in Chapter 13 that firms with high liquidity betas have offered higher average returns, just as theory predicts.[22] Moreover, the liquidity premium that emerges from these studies appears to be of roughly the same order of magnitude as the market risk premium, suggesting that liquidity should be a first-order consideration when thinking about security pricing.

9.3   The CAPM and the Academic World

Testing the CAPM is surprisingly difficult. We will more systematically look at these tests in Chapter 13. One long-standing thorn in the side of academic researchers is Assumption 1(a) (all assets trade), which leads to the result that the market portfolio must include all risky assets in the economy. In reality, we cannot even observe all the assets that do trade, let alone properly account for those that do not. The theoretical market portfolio, which is central to the CAPM, is impossible to pin down in practice.

Since the theoretical CAPM market portfolio cannot be observed, most tests of the CAPM are directed at the mean-beta relationship as applied to assets with respect to an observed, but perhaps inefficient, stock index portfolio. But if the test rejects the model, is that because the model is faulty or because the index is a faulty proxy for the true market? And if we test one of the more general variants of the CAPM, how can we be sure that we have included a comprehensive set of extra-market hedge portfolios?

Moreover, you may ask, where do we obtain the beta coefficients to use in our statistical tests? We must estimate them for each stock from a time series of stock returns. But we inevitably estimate these parameters with large errors that can lead to an incorrect rejection of the model.[23]

In addition, both alpha and beta, as well as residual variance, are likely time varying. There is nothing in the CAPM that precludes such time variation, but standard regression techniques rule it out and thus may lead to false rejection of the model. There are now well-known techniques to account for time-varying parameters. In fact, Robert Engle won the Nobel Prize for his pioneering work on econometric techniques to deal with time-varying volatility, and a good portion of the applications of these new techniques have been in finance.[24] Nevertheless, these techniques have not salvaged the CAPM.

Finally, betas may vary not purely randomly over time, but in response to changing economic conditions. A "conditional" CAPM allows risk and return to change with a set of

---

[22]See L. Pástor and R. F. Stambaugh, "Liquidity Risk and Expected Stock Returns," *Journal of Political Economy* 111 (2003), pp. 642–685, or V. V. Acharya and L. H. Pedersen, "Asset Pricing with Liquidity Risk," *Journal of Financial Economics* 77 (2005), pp. 375–410.

[23]Merton H. Miller and Myron Scholes, "Rates of Return in Relations to Risk: A Re-Examination of Some Recent Findings," in *Studies in the Theory of Capital Markets,* Michael C. Jensen, ed. (New York: Praeger, 1972).

[24]Engle's work gave rise to the widespread use of so-called ARCH models. ARCH stands for autoregressive conditional heteroskedasticity, which is a fancy way of saying that volatility changes over time, and that recent levels of volatility can be used to form optimal estimates of future volatility.

"conditioning variables" that describe the state of the economy.[25] As importantly, Campbell and Vuolteenaho[26] find that the beta of a security can be decomposed into two components, one that measures sensitivity to changes in corporate profitability and another that measures sensitivity to changes in the market's discount rates. These are found to be quite different in many cases.

A strand of research that has not yet yielded fruit is the search for portfolios that hedge the risk of specific consumption items, as in Merton's Equation 9.14. Portfolios that should hedge presumably important extra-market sources of risk have not yet been found to significantly predict risk premia.

As mentioned in Chapter 5, Fama and French documented the predictive power of size and book-to-market ratios (B/M) for asset returns. They interpret portfolios formed to align with these characteristics as hedging portfolios in the context of Equation 9.14. Following their lead, other papers have now suggested a number of other extra-market risk factors (discussed in the next chapter). But we don't really know what fundamental uncertainties in future investment opportunities are hedged by these factors, leading many to be skeptical of empirically driven identification of extra-market hedging portfolios.

The bottom line is that, in the academic world, the single-index CAPM is considered passé. We don't yet know, however, what shape the successful extension to replace it will take. Stay tuned for future developments.

9.4   The CAPM and the Investment Industry

While academics have been riding multiple-index models in search of a more general version of the CAPM that best explains returns, the industry has by and large stayed with the single-index CAPM.

Interestingly, the CAPM tenet that the market portfolio is efficient cannot be tested because the true market portfolio of all assets cannot be observed in the first place. But as time has passed, it has become ever more evident that consistently beating even a (not very broad) index portfolio such as the S&P 500 is already beyond the power of most investors, even professional ones.

Indirect evidence on the efficiency of the market portfolio can be found in a study by Burton Malkiel,[27] who estimates alpha values for a large sample of equity mutual funds. The results, which appear in Figure 9.5, show that the distribution of alphas is roughly bell shaped, with a mean that is slightly negative but statistically indistinguishable from zero. On average, it does not appear that mutual funds outperform the market index (the S&P 500) on a risk-adjusted basis. A mountain of evidence published since Malkiel's study reconfirms that professional investors on average do not outperform passive market indexes.

This result is important. While we might expect realized alpha values of individual securities to center around zero, professionally managed mutual funds might be

---

[25]There is now a large literature on conditional models of security market equilibrium. Much of it derives from Ravi Jagannathan and Zhenyu Wang, "The Conditional CAPM and the Cross-Section of Expected Returns," *Journal of Finance* 51 (March 1996), pp. 3–53.

[26]John Campbell and Tuomo Vuolteenaho, "Bad Beta, Good Beta," *American Economic Review* 94 (December 2004), pp. 1249–75.

[27]Burton G. Malkiel, "Returns from Investing in Equity Mutual Funds 1971–1991," *Journal of Finance* 50 (June 1995), pp. 549–72.

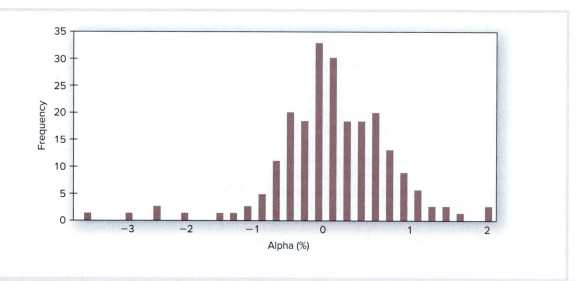

Figure 9.5 Estimates of individual mutual fund alphas, 1972–1991. This is a plot of the frequency distribution of estimated alphas for all-equity mutual funds with 10-year continuous records.

Source: Burton G. Malkiel, "Returns from Investing in Equity Mutual Funds 1971–1991," *Journal of Finance* 50 (June 1995), pp. 549–72.

expected to demonstrate average positive alphas. Funds with superior performance (and we do expect this set to be nonempty) should tilt the sample average to a positive value. The small impact of superior funds on this distribution suggests the difficulty in beating the passive strategy that the CAPM deems to be optimal.

From the standpoint of the industry, an index portfolio that can be beaten by only a tiny fraction of professional managers over a 10-year period may well be taken as ex-ante efficient for all practical purposes, that is, to be used as: (1) a diversification vehicle to mix with an active portfolio from security analysis (discussed in Chapter 8); (2) a benchmark for performance evaluation and compensation (discussed in Chapter 24); (3) a means to adjudicate lawsuits about fair compensation to various risky enterprises; and (4) a means to determine proper prices in regulated industries, allowing shareholders to earn a fair rate of return on their investments, but no more.

SUMMARY

1. The CAPM assumes that investors are single-period planners who agree on a common input list from security analysis and seek mean-variance optimal portfolios.

2. The CAPM assumes that security markets are ideal in the sense that:
   a. Relevant information about securities is widely and publicly available.
   b. There are no taxes or transaction costs.
   c. All risky assets are publicly traded.
   d. Investors can borrow and lend any amount at a fixed risk-free rate.

3. With these assumptions, all investors hold identical risky portfolios. The CAPM holds that in equilibrium the market portfolio is the unique mean-variance efficient tangency portfolio. Thus a passive strategy is efficient.

4. The CAPM market portfolio is a value-weighted portfolio. Each security is held in a proportion equal to its market value divided by the total market value of all securities.

5. If the market portfolio is efficient and the average investor neither borrows nor lends, then the risk premium on the market portfolio is proportional to its variance, σ_M^2, as well as the average coefficient of risk aversion across investors, A:

$$E(r_M) - r_f = \overline{A}\sigma_M^2$$

6. The CAPM implies that the risk premium on any individual asset or portfolio is the product of the risk premium on the market portfolio and the beta coefficient:

$$E(r_i) - r_f = \beta_i[E(r_M) - r_f]$$

where the beta coefficient is the covariance of the asset return with that of the market portfolio as a fraction of the variance of the return on the market portfolio:

$$\beta_i = \frac{\text{Cov}(r_i, r_M)}{\sigma_M^2}$$

7. When risk-free investments are restricted but all other CAPM assumptions hold, then the simple version of the CAPM is replaced by its zero-beta version. Accordingly, the risk-free rate in the expected return–beta relationship is replaced by the zero-beta portfolio's expected rate of return:

$$E(r_i) = E(r_Z) + \beta_i[E(r_M) - E(r_Z)]$$

8. The security market line of the CAPM must be modified to account for labor income and other significant nontraded assets.

9. The simple version of the CAPM assumes that investors have a single-period time horizon. When investors are assumed to be concerned with lifetime consumption and bequest plans, but investors' tastes and security return distributions are stable over time, the market portfolio remains efficient and the simple version of the expected return–beta relationship holds. But if those distributions change unpredictably, or if investors seek to hedge nonmarket sources of risk to their consumption, the simple CAPM will give way to a multifactor version in which the security's exposure to these nonmarket sources of risk command risk premiums.

10. The consumption-based capital asset pricing model (CCAPM) is a single-factor model in which the market portfolio excess return is replaced by that of a consumption-tracking portfolio. By appealing directly to consumption, the model naturally incorporates consumption-hedging considerations and changing investment opportunities within a single-factor framework.

11. Liquidity costs and liquidity risk can be incorporated into the CAPM relationship. Investors demand compensation for expected costs of illiquidity as well as the risk surrounding those costs.

			KEY TERMS
homogeneous expectations	beta	alpha	
market portfolio	expected return–beta (or	zero-beta portfolio	
mutual fund theorem	mean-beta) relationship	liquidity	
market price of risk	security market line (SML)	illiquidity	

KEY EQUATIONS

Market risk premium: $E(R_M) = \bar{A}\sigma_M^2$

Beta: $\beta_i = \dfrac{\text{Cov}(R_i, R_M)}{\sigma_M^2}$

Security market line: $E(r_i) = r_f + \beta_i[E(r_M) - r_f]$

Zero-beta SML: $E(r_i) = E(r_Z) + \beta_i[E(r_M) - E(r_Z)]$

Multifactor SML (in excess returns): $E(R_i) = \beta_{iM}E(R_M) + \sum\limits_{k=1}^{K} \beta_{ik}E(R_k)$

PROBLEM SETS

1. What must be the beta of a portfolio with $E(r_P) = 18\%$, if $r_f = 6\%$ and $E(r_M) = 14\%$?

2. The market price of a security is $50. Its expected rate of return is 14%. The risk-free rate is 6%, and the market risk premium is 8.5%. What will be the market price of the security if its correlation coefficient with the market portfolio doubles (and all other variables remain unchanged)? Assume that the stock is expected to pay a constant dividend in perpetuity.

3. Are the following true or false? Explain.

   a. Stocks with a beta of zero offer an expected rate of return of zero.
   b. The CAPM implies that investors require a higher return to hold highly volatile securities.
   c. You can construct a portfolio with beta of .75 by investing .75 of the investment budget in T-bills and the remainder in the market portfolio.

4. Here are data on two companies. The T-bill rate is 4% and the market risk premium is 6%.

Company	$1 Discount Store	Everything $5
Forecasted return	12%	11%
Standard deviation of returns	8%	10%
Beta	1.5	1.0

What would be the fair return for each company according to the capital asset pricing model (CAPM)?

5. Characterize each company in the previous problem as underpriced, overpriced, or properly priced.

6. What is the expected rate of return for a stock that has a beta of 1.0 if the expected return on the market is 15%?

   a. 15%.
   b. More than 15%.
   c. Cannot be determined without the risk-free rate.

7. Kaskin, Inc., stock has a beta of 1.2 and Quinn, Inc., stock has a beta of .6. Which of the following statements is *most* accurate?

   a. The expected rate of return will be higher for the stock of Kaskin, Inc., than that of Quinn, Inc.
   b. The stock of Kaskin, Inc., has more total risk than the stock of Quinn, Inc.
   c. The stock of Quinn, Inc., has more systematic risk than that of Kaskin, Inc.

8. You are a consultant to a large manufacturing corporation that is considering a project with the following net after-tax cash flows (in millions of dollars):

Years from Now	After-Tax Cash Flow
0	−40
1–10	15

The project's beta is 1.8.

a. Assuming that $r_f = 8\%$ and $E(r_M) = 16\%$, what is the net present value of the project?

b. What is the highest possible beta estimate for the project before its NPV becomes negative?

9. Consider the following table, which gives a security analyst's expected return on two stocks in two particular scenarios for the rate of return on the market:

Market Return	Aggressive Stock	Defensive Stock
5%	−2%	6%
25	38	12

a. What are the betas of the two stocks?

b. What is the expected rate of return on each stock if the two scenarios for the market return are equally likely?

c. If the T-bill rate is 6% and the market return is equally likely to be 5% or 25%, draw the SML for this economy.

d. Plot the two securities on the SML graph. What are the alphas of each?

e. What hurdle rate should be used by the management of the aggressive firm for a project with the risk characteristics of the defensive firm's stock?

For Problems 10 through 16: If the simple CAPM is valid, which of the following situations are possible? Explain. Consider each situation independently.

10.
Portfolio	Expected Return	Beta
A	20%	1.4
B	25%	1.2

11.
Portfolio	Expected Return	Standard Deviation
A	30%	35%
B	40%	25%

12.
Portfolio	Expected Return	Standard Deviation
Risk-free	10%	0%
Market	18%	24%
A	16%	12%

13.
Portfolio	Expected Return	Standard Deviation
Risk-free	10%	0%
Market	18%	24%
A	20%	22%

14.
Portfolio	Expected Return	Beta
Risk-free	10%	0
Market	18%	1.0
A	16%	1.5

15.
Portfolio	Expected Return	Beta
Risk-free	10%	0
Market	18%	1.0
A	16%	0.9

16.

Portfolio	Expected Return	Standard Deviation
Risk-free	10%	0%
Market	18%	24%
A	16%	22%

For Problems 17 through 19: Assume that the risk-free rate of interest is 6% and the expected rate of return on the market is 16%.

17. A share of stock sells for $50 today. It will pay a dividend of $6 per share at the end of the year. Its beta is 1.2. What do investors expect the stock to sell for at the end of the year?

18. I am buying a firm with an expected perpetual cash flow of $1,000 but am unsure of its risk. If I think the beta of the firm is .5, when in fact the beta is really 1, how much *more* will I offer for the firm than it is truly worth?

19. A stock has an expected rate of return of 4%. What is its beta?

20. Two investment advisers are comparing performance. One averaged a 19% rate of return and the other a 16% rate of return. However, the beta of the first investor was 1.5, whereas that of the second investor was 1.

   a. Can you tell which investor was a better selector of individual stocks (aside from the issue of general movements in the market)?
   b. If the T-bill rate was 6% and the market return during the period was 14%, which investor would be considered the superior stock selector?
   c. What if the T-bill rate was 3% and the market return was 15%?

21. Suppose the rate of return on short-term government securities (perceived to be risk-free) is about 5%. Suppose also that the expected rate of return required by the market for a portfolio with a beta of 1 is 12%. According to the capital asset pricing model:

   a. What is the expected rate of return on the market portfolio?
   b. What would be the expected rate of return on a stock with $\beta = 0$?
   c. Suppose you consider buying a share of stock at $40. The stock is expected to pay $3 dividends next year and you expect it to sell then for $41. The stock risk has been evaluated at $\beta = -.5$. Is the stock overpriced or underpriced?

22. Suppose that borrowing is restricted so that the zero-beta version of the CAPM holds. The expected return on the market portfolio is 17%, and on the zero-beta portfolio it is 8%. What is the expected return on a portfolio with a beta of .6?

23. a. A mutual fund with beta of .8 has an expected rate of return of 14%. If $r_f = 5\%$, and you expect the rate of return on the market portfolio to be 15%, should you invest in this fund? What is the fund's alpha?
   b. What passive portfolio comprised of a market-index portfolio and a money market account would have the same beta as the fund? Show that the difference between the expected rate of return on this passive portfolio and that of the fund equals the alpha from part (*a*).

24. Outline how you would incorporate the following into the CCAPM:

   a. Liquidity.
   b. Nontraded assets. (Do you have to worry about labor income?)

CFA® PROBLEMS

1. a. John Wilson is a portfolio manager at Austin & Associates. For all of his clients, Wilson manages portfolios that lie on the Markowitz efficient frontier. Wilson asks Mary Regan, CFA, a managing director at Austin, to review the portfolios of two of his clients, the Eagle Manufacturing Company and the Rainbow Life Insurance Co. The expected returns of the two

portfolios are substantially different. Regan determines that the Rainbow portfolio is virtually identical to the market portfolio and concludes that the Rainbow portfolio must be superior to the Eagle portfolio. Do you agree or disagree with Regan's conclusion that the Rainbow portfolio is superior to the Eagle portfolio? Justify your response with reference to the capital market line.

   b. Wilson remarks that the Rainbow portfolio has a higher expected return because it has greater nonsystematic risk than Eagle's portfolio. Define nonsystematic risk and explain why you agree or disagree with Wilson's remark.

2. Wilson is now evaluating the expected performance of two common stocks, Furhman Labs Inc. and Garten Testing Inc. He has gathered the following information:

   - The risk-free rate is 5%.
   - The expected return on the market portfolio is 11.5%.
   - The beta of Furhman stock is 1.5.
   - The beta of Garten stock is .8.

   Based on his own analysis, Wilson's forecasts of the returns on the two stocks are 13.25% for Furhman stock and 11.25% for Garten stock. Calculate the required rate of return for Furhman Labs stock and for Garten Testing stock. Indicate whether each stock is undervalued, fairly valued, or overvalued.

3. The security market line depicts:

      a. A security's expected return as a function of its systematic risk.
      b. The market portfolio as the optimal portfolio of risky securities.
      c. The relationship between a security's return and the return on an index.
      d. The complete portfolio as a combination of the market portfolio and the risk-free asset.

4. Within the context of the capital asset pricing model (CAPM), assume:

   - Expected return on the market = 15%
   - Risk-free rate = 8%
   - Expected rate of return on XYZ security = 17%
   - Beta of XYZ security = 1.25

   Which one of the following is correct?

      a. XYZ is overpriced.
      b. XYZ is fairly priced.
      c. XYZ's alpha is −.25%.
      d. XYZ's alpha is .25%.

5. What is the expected return of a zero-beta security?

      a. Market rate of return.
      b. Zero rate of return.
      c. Negative rate of return.
      d. Risk-free rate of return.

6. Capital asset pricing theory asserts that portfolio returns are best explained by:

      a. Economic factors.
      b. Specific risk.
      c. Systematic risk.
      d. Diversification.

7. According to CAPM, the expected rate of return of a portfolio with a beta of 1.0 and an alpha of 0 is:

      a. Between r_M and r_f.
      b. The risk-free rate, r_f.
      c. $\beta(r_M - r_f)$.
      d. The expected return on the market, r_M.

For CFA Problems 8 through 9: Refer to the following table, which shows risk and return measures for two portfolios.

Portfolio	Average Annual Rate of Return	Standard Deviation	Beta
R	11%	10%	0.5
S&P 500	14%	12%	1.0

8. When plotting portfolio R on the preceding table relative to the SML, portfolio R lies:
   a. On the SML.
   b. Below the SML.
   c. Above the SML.
   d. Insufficient data given.

9. When plotting portfolio R relative to the capital market line, portfolio R lies:
   a. On the CML.
   b. Below the CML.
   c. Above the CML.
   d. Insufficient data given.

10. Briefly explain whether investors should expect a higher return from holding portfolio A versus portfolio B according to the capital asset pricing model. Assume that both portfolios are well diversified.

	Portfolio A	Portfolio B
Systematic risk (beta)	1.0	1.0
Specific risk for each individual security	High	Low

11. Joan McKay is a portfolio manager for a bank trust department. McKay meets with two clients, Kevin Murray and Lisa York, to review their investment objectives. Each client expresses an interest in changing his or her individual investment objectives. Both clients currently hold well-diversified portfolios of risky assets.
    a. Murray wants to increase the expected return of his portfolio. State what action McKay should take to achieve Murray's objective. Justify your response in the context of the CML.
    b. York wants to reduce the risk exposure of her portfolio but does not want to engage in borrowing or lending activities to do so. State what action McKay should take to achieve York's objective. Justify your response in the context of the SML.

12. Karen Kay, a portfolio manager at Collins Asset Management, is using the capital asset pricing model for making recommendations to her clients. Her research department has developed the information shown in the following exhibit.

Forecast Returns, Standard Deviations, and Betas

	Forecast Return	Standard Deviation	Beta
Stock X	14.0%	36%	0.8
Stock Y	17.0	25	1.5
Market index	14.0	15	1.0
Risk-free rate	5.0		

   a. Calculate expected return and alpha for each stock.
   b. Identify and justify which stock would be more appropriate for an investor who wants to
      i. Add this stock to a well-diversified equity portfolio.
      ii. Hold this stock as a single-stock portfolio.

E-INVESTMENTS EXERCISES

Fidelity provides data on the risk and return of its funds at **www.fidelity.com**. Click on the *Research* link, then choose *Mutual Funds* from the submenu. In the *Search and Compare Funds* section, search over *All Asset Classes*. On the next screen, click on *Risk/Volatility Measures* and set the beta slider to 0.75. Click *Search Funds* to see the results. Select five funds from the resulting list and click *Compare*. Rank the five funds according to their betas and then according to their standard deviations. (You will have to click on *Performance & Risk* to get more detailed information on each fund.) Do both lists rank the funds in the same order? How would you explain any difference in the rankings? Repeat the exercise to compare five funds that have betas greater than or equal to 1.50. Why might the degree of agreement when ranking funds by beta versus standard deviation differ when using high versus low beta funds?

✓ SOLUTIONS TO CONCEPT CHECKS

1. We can characterize the entire population by two representative investors. One is the "uninformed" investor, who does not engage in security analysis and holds the market portfolio, whereas the other optimizes using the Markowitz algorithm with input from security analysis. The uninformed investor does not know what input the informed investor uses to make portfolio purchases. The uninformed investor knows, however, that if the other investor is informed, the market portfolio proportions will be optimal. Therefore, to depart from these proportions would constitute an uninformed bet, which will, on average, reduce the efficiency of diversification with no compensating improvement in expected returns.

2. *a.* Substituting the historical mean and standard deviation in Equation 9.2 yields a coefficient of risk aversion of

$$\overline{A} = \frac{E(r_M) - r_f}{\sigma_M^2} = \frac{.083}{.203^2} = 2.01$$

   b. This relationship also tells us that for the historical standard deviation and a coefficient of risk aversion of 3.5 the risk premium would be

$$E(r_M) - r_f = \overline{A}\sigma_M^2 = 3.5 \times .203^2 = .144 = 14.4\%$$

3. For these investment proportions, w_{Ford}, w_{Toyota}, the portfolio β is

$$\beta_P = w_{Ford}\beta_{Ford} + w_{Toyota}\beta_{Toyota}$$
$$= (.75 \times 1.25) + (.25 \times 1.10) = 1.2125$$

   As the market risk premium, $E(r_M) - r_f$, is 8%, the portfolio risk premium will be

$$E(r_P) - r_f = \beta_P[E(r_M) - r_f]$$
$$= 1.2125 \times 8 = 9.7\%$$

4. The alpha of a stock is its expected return in excess of that required by the CAPM.

$$\alpha = E(r) - \{r_f + \beta[E(r_M) - r_f]\}$$
$$\alpha_{XYZ} = 12 - [5 + 1.0(11 - 5)] = 1\%$$
$$\alpha_{ABC} = 13 - [5 + 1.5(11 - 5)] = -1\%$$

ABC plots below the SML, while *XYZ* plots above.

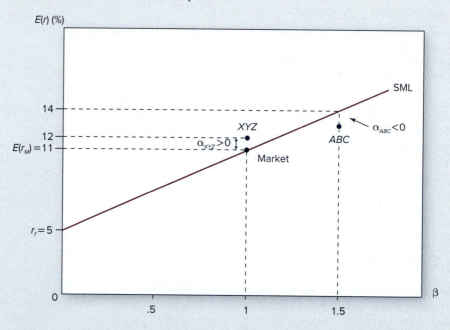

5. The project-specific required return is determined by the project beta together with the market risk premium and the risk-free rate. The CAPM tells us that an acceptable expected rate of return for the project is

$$r_f + \beta[E(r_M) - r_f] = 8 + 1.3(16 - 8) = 18.4\%$$

which becomes the project's hurdle rate. If the IRR of the project is 19%, then it is desirable. Any project with an IRR equal to or less than 18.4% should be rejected.

Arbitrage Pricing Theory and Multifactor Models of Risk and Return

10

THE EXPLOITATION OF security mispricing in such a way that risk-free profits can be earned is called *arbitrage*. It involves the simultaneous purchase and sale of equivalent securities or portfolios in order to profit from discrepancies in their prices. Perhaps the most basic principle of capital market theory is that well-functioning security markets rule out arbitrage opportunities. If actual security prices did allow for arbitrage, the result would be strong pressure on prices that would quickly eliminate the opportunity. Therefore, we can expect security markets to satisfy a "no-arbitrage condition."

In this chapter, we show how no-arbitrage conditions, together with the factor model introduced in Chapter 8, allow us to generalize the security market line of the CAPM to gain richer insight into the risk–return relationship. We begin by showing how the decomposition of risk into market versus firm-specific influences that we introduced in earlier chapters can be extended to deal with the multifaceted nature of systematic risk. Multifactor models of security returns can be used to measure and manage exposure to each

of many economywide factors such as business-cycle risk, interest or inflation rate risk, energy price risk, and so on. These models ultimately lead us to a multifactor version of the security market line in which risk premiums derive from exposure to multiple risk sources, each with their own risk premium.

This approach to the risk–return trade-off is called *arbitrage pricing theory,* or APT. In a single-factor market where there are no extra-market risk factors, the APT leads to a mean return–beta equation identical to that of the CAPM. In a multi-factor market with one or more extra-market risk factors, the APT delivers a mean-beta equation similar to Merton's intertemporal extension of the CAPM (his ICAPM). Finally, we ask how to identify the factors that are likely to be the most important sources of risk. These will be the factors generating substantial hedging demands that brought us to the multifactor CAPM introduced in Chapter 9. Both the APT and the CAPM therefore can lead to multiple-risk versions of the security market line, thereby enriching the insights we can derive about the risk–return relationship.

10.1   Multifactor Models: A Preview

The index model introduced in Chapter 8 gave us a way of decomposing stock variability into market or systematic risk, due largely to macroeconomic events, versus firm-specific or idiosyncratic effects that can be diversified in large portfolios. In the single-index model, the return on a broad market-index portfolio summarized the impact of the macro factor. In Chapter 9 we introduced the possibility that risk premiums may also depend on correlations with extra-market risk factors, such as inflation, or changes in the parameters describing future investment opportunities: interest rates, volatility, market-risk premiums, and betas. For example, returns on an asset whose return increases when inflation increases can be used to hedge uncertainty in the future inflation rate. Its price may rise and its risk premium may fall as a result of investors' extra demand for this asset.

Risk premiums of individual securities should reflect their sensitivities to changes in extra-market risk factors just as their betas on the market index determine their risk premiums in the simple CAPM. When securities can be used to hedge these factors, the resulting hedging demands will turn the SML into a multifactor model, with each significant risk source generating an additional factor. Risk factors can be represented either by returns on these hedge portfolios (just as the index portfolio represents the market factor), or more directly by changes in the risk factors themselves, for example, changes in interest rates or inflation.

Factor Models of Security Returns

We begin with a familiar single-factor model like the one introduced in Chapter 8. Uncertainty in asset returns has two sources: a common or macroeconomic factor and firm-specific events. By construction, the common factor has zero expected value because it measures *new* information concerning the macroeconomy; new information implies a revision to current expectations, and if initial expectations are rational, then such revisions should average out to zero.

If we call F the deviation of the common factor from its expected value, β_i the sensitivity of firm i to that factor, and e_i the firm-specific disturbance, the factor model states that the actual excess return on firm i will equal its initially expected value plus a (zero expected value) random amount attributable to unanticipated economywide events, plus another (zero expected value) random amount attributable to firm-specific events.

Formally, the **single-factor model** of excess returns is described by Equation 10.1:

$$R_i = E(R_i) + \beta_i F + e_i \qquad \qquad \textbf{(10.1)}$$

where $E(R_i)$ is the expected excess return on stock i. Notice that if the macro factor has a value of 0 in any particular period (i.e., no macro surprises), the excess return on the security will equal its previously expected value, $E(R_i)$, plus the effect of firm-specific events only. The nonsystematic components of returns, the e_is, are assumed to be uncorrelated across stocks and with the factor F.

Example 10.1   Factor Models

To illustrate the factor model, suppose that the macro factor, F, represents news about the state of the business cycle, which we will measure by the *unexpected* percentage change in gross domestic product (GDP). The consensus is that GDP will increase by 4% this year. Suppose also that a stock's β value is 1.2. If GDP increases by only 3%, then the value of F would be −1%, representing a 1% disappointment in actual growth versus expected growth. Given the stock's beta value, this disappointment would translate into a return on the stock that is 1.2% lower than previously expected. This macro surprise, together with the firm-specific disturbance, e_i, determines the total departure of the stock's return from its originally expected value.

Concept Check **10.1**

Suppose you currently expect the stock in Example 10.1 to earn a 10% rate of return. Then some macroeconomic news suggests that GDP growth will come in at 5% instead of 4%. How will you revise your estimate of the stock's expected rate of return?

The factor model's decomposition of returns into systematic and firm-specific components is compelling, but confining systematic risk to a single factor is not. Indeed, when we motivated systematic risk as the source of risk premiums in Chapter 9, we noted that extra market sources of risk may arise from a number of sources such as uncertainty about interest rates, inflation, and so on. The market return reflects all of these macro factors as well as the average sensitivity of firms to those factors.

It stands to reason that a more explicit representation of systematic risk, allowing different stocks to exhibit different sensitivities to its various components, would constitute a useful refinement of the single-factor model. It is easy to see that models that allow for several factors—**multifactor models**—can provide better descriptions of security returns.

Apart from their use in building models of equilibrium security pricing, multifactor models are useful in risk management applications. These models give us a simple way to measure investor exposure to various macroeconomic risks and construct portfolios to hedge those risks.

Let's start with a two-factor model. Suppose the two most important macroeconomic sources of risk are uncertainties surrounding the state of the business cycle, news of which we will again measure by unanticipated growth in GDP, and changes in interest rates. We will denote by IR any unexpected change in interest rates. The return on any stock will respond both to sources of macro risk and to its own firm-specific influences. We can write a two-factor model describing the excess return on stock i in some time period as follows:

$$R_i = E(R_i) + \beta_{i\text{GDP}}\,\text{GDP} + \beta_{i\text{IR}}\,\text{IR} + e_i \qquad (10.2)$$

The two macro factors on the right-hand side of the equation comprise the systematic factors in the economy. As in the single-factor model, both of these macro factors have zero expectation: They represent changes in these variables that have not already been anticipated. The coefficients of each factor in Equation 10.2 measure the sensitivity of share returns to that factor. For this reason the coefficients are sometimes called **factor loadings** or, equivalently, **factor betas.** An increase in interest rates is bad news for most firms, so we would expect interest rate betas generally to be negative. As before, e_i reflects firm-specific influences.

To illustrate the advantages of multifactor models, consider two firms, one a regulated electric-power utility in a mostly residential area and the other an airline. Because residential demand for electricity is not very sensitive to the business cycle, the utility has a low beta on GDP. But the utility's stock price may have a relatively high sensitivity to interest rates. Because the cash flow generated by the utility is relatively stable, its present value behaves much like that of a bond, varying inversely with interest rates. Conversely, the performance of the airline is very sensitive to economic activity but is less sensitive to interest rates. It will have a high GDP beta and a lower interest rate beta. Suppose that on a particular day, a news item suggests that the economy will expand. GDP is expected to increase, but so are interest rates. Is the "macro news" on this day good or bad? For the utility, this is bad news: Its dominant sensitivity is to rates. But for the airline, which responds more to GDP, this is good news. Clearly a one-factor or single-index model cannot capture such differential responses to varying sources of macroeconomic uncertainty.

Example 10.2   Risk Assessment Using Multifactor Models

Suppose we estimate the two-factor model in Equation 10.2 for Northeast Airlines and find the following result:

$$R = .133 + 1.2(\text{GDP}) - .3(\text{IR}) + e$$

This tells us that, based on currently available information, the expected excess rate of return for Northeast is 13.3%, but that for every percentage point increase in GDP beyond current expectations, the return on Northeast's shares increases on average by 1.2%, while for every unanticipated percentage point that interest rates increase, Northeast's shares fall on average by .3%.

Factor betas can provide a framework for a hedging strategy. The idea for an investor who wishes to hedge a source of risk is to establish an opposite factor exposure to offset that particular source of risk. Often, futures contracts can be used to hedge particular factor exposures. We explore this application in Chapter 22.

As it stands, however, the multifactor model is no more than a *description* of the factors that affect security returns. There is no "theory" in the equation. The obvious question left unanswered by a factor model like Equation 10.2 is where $E(R)$ comes from, in other words, what determines a security's expected excess rate of return. This is where we need a theoretical model of equilibrium security returns. We therefore now turn to arbitrage pricing theory to help determine the expected value, $E(R)$, in Equations 10.1 and 10.2.

10.2   Arbitrage Pricing Theory

Stephen Ross developed the **arbitrage pricing theory (APT)** in 1976.[1] Like the CAPM, the APT predicts a security market line linking expected returns to risk, but the path it takes to the SML is quite different. Ross's APT relies on three key propositions: (1) Security returns can be described by a factor model; (2) there are sufficient securities to diversify away idiosyncratic risk; and (3) well-functioning security markets do not allow for the persistence of arbitrage opportunities. We begin with a simple version of Ross's model, which assumes that only one systematic factor affects security returns. Once we understand how the model works, it will be much easier to see how it can be generalized to accommodate more than one factor.

[1]Stephen A. Ross, "Return, Risk and Arbitrage," in I. Friend and J. Bicksler, eds., *Risk and Return in Finance* (Cambridge, MA: Ballinger, 1976).

Arbitrage, Risk Arbitrage, and Equilibrium

An **arbitrage** opportunity arises when an investor can earn riskless profits without making a net investment. A trivial example of an arbitrage opportunity would arise if shares of a stock sold for different prices on two different exchanges. For example, suppose IBM sold for $165 on the NYSE but only $163 on NASDAQ. Then you could buy the shares on NASDAQ and simultaneously sell them on the NYSE, clearing a riskless profit of $2 per share without tying up any of your own capital. The **Law of One Price** states that if two assets are equivalent in all economically relevant respects, then they should have the same market price. The Law of One Price is enforced by arbitrageurs: If they observe a violation of the law, they will engage in *arbitrage activity*—simultaneously buying the asset where it is cheap and selling where it is expensive. In the process, they will bid up the price where it is low and force it down where it is high until the arbitrage opportunity is eliminated.

Strategies that exploit violations of the Law of One Price all involve long–short positions. You buy the relatively cheap asset and sell the relatively overpriced one. The *net* investment, therefore, is zero. Moreover, the position is riskless. Therefore, any investor, regardless of risk aversion or wealth, will want to take an infinite position in it. Because those large positions will quickly force prices up or down until the opportunity vanishes, security prices should satisfy a "no-arbitrage condition," that is, a condition that rules out the existence of arbitrage opportunities.

The idea that market prices will move to rule out arbitrage opportunities is perhaps the most fundamental concept in capital market theory. Violation of this restriction would indicate the grossest form of market irrationality.

There is an important difference between arbitrage and risk–return dominance arguments in support of equilibrium price relationships. A dominance argument holds that when an equilibrium price relationship is violated, many investors will make limited portfolio changes, depending on their degree of risk aversion. Aggregation of these limited portfolio changes is required to create a large volume of buying and selling, which in turn restores equilibrium prices. By contrast, when arbitrage opportunities exist, each investor wants to take as large a position as possible; hence it will not take many investors to bring about the price pressures necessary to restore equilibrium. Therefore, implications for prices derived from no-arbitrage arguments are stronger than implications derived from a risk–return dominance argument.

The CAPM is an example of a dominance argument, implying that all investors hold mean-variance efficient portfolios. If a security is mispriced, then investors will tilt their portfolios toward the underpriced and away from the overpriced securities. Pressure on equilibrium prices results from many investors shifting their portfolios, each by a relatively small dollar amount. The assumption that a large number of investors are mean-variance optimizers is critical. In contrast, the implication of a no-arbitrage condition is that a few investors who identify an arbitrage opportunity will mobilize large dollar amounts and quickly restore equilibrium.

Practitioners often use the terms *arbitrage* and *arbitrageurs* more loosely than our strict definition. Arbitrageur often refers to a professional searching for mispriced securities in specific areas such as merger-target stocks, rather than to one who seeks strict (risk-free) arbitrage opportunities. Such activity is sometimes called **risk arbitrage** to distinguish it from pure arbitrage.

Well-Diversified Portfolios

We begin by considering the risk of a portfolio of stocks in a single-factor market. We first show that if a portfolio is well diversified, its firm-specific or nonfactor risk becomes negligible, so that only factor (equivalently, systematic) risk remains. The excess return, R_P, on an n-stock portfolio with weights w_i, $\sum w_i = 1$, is

$$R_P = E(R_P) + \beta_P F + e_P \qquad (10.3)$$

where

$$\beta_P = \sum w_i \beta_i; \quad E(R_P) = \sum w_i E(R_i)$$

are the weighted averages of the β_i and risk premiums of the n securities. The portfolio nonsystematic component (which is uncorrelated with F) is $e_P = \sum w_i e_i$, which similarly is a weighted average of the e_i of the n securities.

There are two random (and uncorrelated) terms on the right-hand side of Equation 10.3, so we can separate the variance of the portfolio into its systematic and nonsystematic sources:

$$\sigma_P^2 = \beta_P^2 \sigma_F^2 + \sigma^2(e_P)$$

where σ_F^2 is the variance of the factor F and $\sigma^2(e_P)$ is the nonsystematic variance of the portfolio, which is given by

$$\sigma^2(e_P) = \text{Variance}\left(\sum w_i e_i\right) = \sum w_i^2 \sigma^2(e_i)$$

In deriving the nonsystematic variance of the portfolio, we depend on the fact that the firm-specific e_is are uncorrelated (so all covariances across assets are zero) and hence, the variance of the "portfolio" of nonsystematic e_is is the weighted sum of the individual nonsystematic variances with the *square* of the investment proportions as weights.

If the portfolio were equally weighted, $w_i = 1/n$, then the nonsystematic variance would be

$$\sigma^2(e_P) = \sum w_i^2 \sigma^2(e_i) = \sum \left(\frac{1}{n}\right)^2 \sigma^2(e_i) = \frac{1}{n}\sum \frac{\sigma^2(e_i)}{n} = \frac{1}{n}\bar{\sigma}^2(e_i)$$

where the last term is the average value of nonsystematic variance across securities. In words, the nonsystematic variance of the portfolio equals the average nonsystematic variance divided by n. Therefore, when n is large, nonsystematic variance approaches zero. This is the effect of diversification.

This property is true of portfolios other than the equally weighted one. Portfolio non-systematic risk will approach zero for *any* portfolio for which each w_i becomes consistently smaller as n gets large (more precisely, for which each w_i^2 approaches zero as n increases). This property motivates us to define a **well-diversified portfolio** as one with each weight, w_i, small enough that for practical purposes the nonsystematic variance, $\sigma^2(e_P)$, is negligible.

 Concept Check **10.2**

a. A portfolio is invested in a very large number of shares (n is large). However, one-half of the portfolio is invested in stock 1, and the rest of the portfolio is equally divided among the other $n - 1$ shares. Is this portfolio well diversified?

b. Another portfolio also is invested in the same n shares, where n is very large. Instead of equally weighting with portfolio weights of $1/n$ in each stock, the weights in half the securities are $1.5/n$ while the weights in the other shares are $.5/n$. Is this portfolio well diversified?

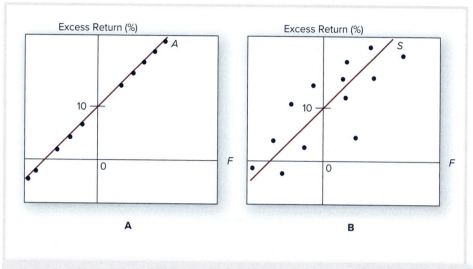

Figure 10.1 Excess returns as a function of the systematic factor: **Panel A,** Well-diversified portfolio A; **Panel B,** Single stock (S).

Because the expected value of e_P for any well-diversified portfolio is zero, and its variance also is effectively zero, any realized value of e_P will be virtually zero. Rewriting Equation 10.1, we conclude that, for a well-diversified portfolio, for all practical purposes

$$R_P = E(R_P) + \beta_P F \qquad (10.4)$$

The solid line in Figure 10.1, Panel A, plots the excess return of a well-diversified portfolio A with $E(R_A) = 10\%$ and $\beta_A = 1$ for various realizations of the systematic factor. The expected return of portfolio A is 10%; this is where the solid line crosses the vertical axis. At this point, the systematic factor is zero, implying no macro surprises. If the macro factor is positive, the portfolio's return exceeds its expected value; if it is negative, the portfolio's return falls short of its mean. The excess return on the portfolio is therefore

$$E(R_A) + \beta_A F = 10\% + 1.0 \times F$$

Compare Panel A in Figure 10.1 with Panel B, which is a similar graph for a single stock (S) with $\beta_S = 1$. The undiversified stock is subject to nonsystematic risk, which is seen in a scatter of points around the line. The well-diversified portfolio's return, in contrast, is determined completely by the systematic factor.

The Security Market Line of the APT

Nonsystematic risk across firms cancels out in well-diversified portfolios, and one would not expect investors to be rewarded for bearing risk that can be eliminated through diversification. Therefore, only the systematic or factor risk of a portfolio of securities should be related to its expected returns. This is the basis of the security market line that we are now ready to derive.

First we show that all well-diversified portfolios with the same beta must have the same expected return. Figure 10.2 plots the returns on two such portfolios, A and B, both with betas of 1, but with differing expected returns: $E(r_A) = 10\%$ and $E(r_B) = 8\%$. Could portfolios A and B coexist with the return pattern depicted? Clearly not: No matter what

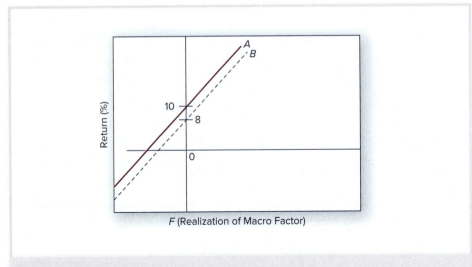

Figure 10.2 Returns as a function of the systematic factor: An arbitrage opportunity

the systematic factor turns out to be, portfolio A outperforms portfolio B, leading to an arbitrage opportunity.

If you sell short \$1 million of B and buy \$1 million of A, a zero-net-investment strategy, you would have a riskless payoff of \$20,000, as follows:

$$
\begin{array}{ll}
(.10 + 1.0 \times F) \times \$1 \text{ million} & \text{from long position in } A \\
-(.08 + 1.0 \times F) \times \$1 \text{ million} & \text{from short position in } B \\
\hline
.02 \times \$1 \text{ million} = \$20,000 & \text{net proceeds}
\end{array}
$$

Your profit is risk-free because the factor risk cancels out across the long and short positions. Moreover, the strategy requires zero-net-investment. You (and others) will pursue it on an infinitely large scale until the resulting pressure on security prices forces the return discrepancy between the two portfolios to disappear. We conclude that such arbitrage activity ensures that well-diversified portfolios with equal betas will have equal expected returns.

What about portfolios with different betas? Their risk premiums must be proportional to beta. To see why, consider Figure 10.3. Suppose that the risk-free rate is 4% and that a well-diversified portfolio, C, with a beta of .5, has an expected return of 6%. Portfolio C plots below the line from the risk-free asset to portfolio A. Consider, therefore, a new portfolio, D, composed of half of portfolio A and half of the risk-free asset. Portfolio D's beta will be $(.5 \times 0 + .5 \times 1.0) = .5$, and its expected return will be $(.5 \times 4 + .5 \times 10) = 7\%$. Now portfolio D has an equal beta but a greater expected return than portfolio C. From our analysis in the previous paragraph we know that this constitutes an arbitrage opportunity. We conclude that, to preclude arbitrage opportunities, the expected return on all well-diversified portfolios must lie on the straight line from the risk-free asset in Figure 10.3.

Notice in Figure 10.3 that risk premiums are indeed proportional to portfolio betas. The risk premium is depicted by the vertical arrow, which measures the distance between the risk-free rate and the expected return on the portfolio. As in the simple CAPM, the risk premium is zero for $\beta = 0$ and rises in direct proportion to β.

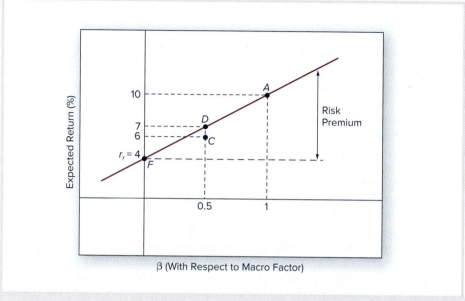

Figure 10.3 An arbitrage opportunity

Figure 10.3 relates the risk premium on well-diversified portfolios to their betas against the macro factor. As a final step, we would like a security market line that relates the portfolio risk premium to its beta against a market index rather than an unspecified macro factor.

Fortunately, this last step is easy to justify. This is because all well-diversified portfolios are perfectly correlated with the macro factor. (Again, look at Figure 10.1, Panel A, which shows that the scatter plot for any well-diversified portfolio lies precisely on the straight line.) Therefore, if a market index portfolio is well diversified, its return will perfectly reflect the value of the macro factor. This means that betas measured against the market index are just as informative about relative levels of systematic risk as are betas measured against the macro factor.

Therefore, we can write the excess return on a well-diversified portfolio P as:[2]

$$R_P = \alpha_P + \beta_P R_M \qquad (10.5)$$

where β_P now denotes the beta against the well-diversified market index.

We know that risk premiums must rise in proportion to beta. Therefore, if a portfolio has (let's say) twice the beta against the macro factor as the market index, its beta with respect to the index will be 2, and it should have twice the risk premium. More generally, for any well-diversified P, the expected excess return must be:

$$E(R_P) = \beta_P E(R_M) \qquad (10.6)$$

In other words, the risk premium (i.e., the expected excess return) on portfolio P is the product of its beta and the risk premium of the market index. Equation 10.6 thus establishes

---

[2]You might have noticed that this transition from a factor model to a market index model is essentially the same argument that we made in Chapter 8, where we started with a factor model (Equation 8.2), and used it to motivate the index model, Equation 8.8.

that the SML of the CAPM must also apply to well-diversified portfolios simply by virtue of the "no-arbitrage" requirement of the APT.

Individual Assets and the APT   We have demonstrated that if arbitrage opportunities are to be ruled out, each well-diversified portfolio's expected excess return must be proportional to its beta. The question is whether this relationship tells us anything about the expected returns on the component stocks. The answer is that if this relationship is to be satisfied by all well-diversified portfolios, it must be satisfied by *almost* all individual securities, although a full proof of this proposition is somewhat difficult. We can illustrate the argument less formally.

Suppose that the expected return–beta relationship is violated for all single assets. Now create a pair of well-diversified portfolios from these assets. What are the chances that in spite of the fact that for any pair of assets the relationship does *not* hold, the relationship *will* hold for both well-diversified portfolios? The chances are small, but it is perhaps possible that the relationships among the single securities are violated in offsetting ways so that somehow it holds for the pair of well-diversified portfolios.

Now construct yet a third well-diversified portfolio. What are the chances that the violations of the relationships for single securities are such that the third portfolio also will fulfill the no-arbitrage expected return–beta relationship? Obviously, the chances are smaller still, but the relationship is possible. Continue with a fourth well-diversified portfolio, and so on. If the no-arbitrage expected return–beta relationship has to hold for each of these different, well-diversified portfolios, it must be virtually certain that the relationship holds for all but a small number of individual securities.

We use the term *virtually certain* advisedly because we must distinguish this conclusion from the statement that all securities surely fulfill this relationship. The reason we cannot make the latter statement has to do with a property of well-diversified portfolios.

Recall that to qualify as well diversified, a portfolio must have very small positions in all securities. If, for example, only one security violates the expected return–beta relationship, then the effect of this violation on a well-diversified portfolio will be too small to be of importance for any practical purpose, and meaningful arbitrage opportunities will not arise. But if many securities violate the expected return–beta relationship, the relationship will no longer hold for well-diversified portfolios, and arbitrage opportunities will be available. Consequently, we conclude that imposing the no-arbitrage condition on a single-factor security market implies maintenance of the expected return–beta relationship for all well-diversified portfolios and for all but possibly a *small* number of individual securities.

Well-Diversified Portfolios in Practice

What is the effect of diversification on portfolio standard deviation *in practice,* where portfolio size is not unlimited? To illustrate, we work out the residual standard deviation (SD) of portfolios of different size under ideal conditions, with equal weights on each component stock. These calculations appear in Table 10.1. The table shows portfolio residual SD as a function of the number of stocks. Equally weighted, 1,000-stock portfolios achieve small but not negligible standard deviations of 1.58% when residual risk is 50% and 3.16% when residual risk is 100%. For 10,000-stock portfolios, the SDs are close to negligible, verifying that diversification can eliminate residual risk, at least in principle, if the investment universe is large enough.

What is a "large" portfolio? Many widely held ETFs or mutual funds hold hundreds of shares, and some funds and indexes such as the Wilshire 5000 contain thousands. Thus, a portfolio of 1,000 stocks is not unheard of, but a portfolio of 10,000 shares is. Therefore, for plausible portfolios, the standard deviations in Table 10.1 make it clear that even broad

Residual SD of each stock = 50%		Residual SD of each stock = 100%	
N	SD(e_P)	N	SD(e_P)
4	25.00	4	50.00
60	6.45	60	12.91
200	3.54	200	7.07
1,000	1.58	1,000	3.16
10,000	0.50	10,000	1.00

Table 10.1

Residual standard deviations as a function of portfolio size

diversification is not likely to achieve the risk reduction of the APT's "well-diversified" ideal. This is a shortcoming in the model. On the other hand, even the levels of residual risk attainable in practice should make the APT's security market line at the very least a good approximation to the risk-return relation. We address the comparative strengths of the APT and the CAPM as models of risk and return in the next section.

10.3   The APT, the CAPM, and the Index Model

Equation 10.6 raises two questions:

1. Is the APT as a model of risk and return superior or inferior to the CAPM? Do we need both models?

2. Suppose a security analyst identifies a positive-alpha portfolio with some remaining residual risk. Don't we already have a prescription for this situation from the Treynor-Black (T-B) procedure applied to the index model (Chapter 8)? Is this framework preferred to the APT?

The APT and the CAPM

The APT serves many of the same functions as the CAPM. It gives us a benchmark for rates of return that can be used in capital budgeting, security valuation, or investment performance evaluation. Moreover, the APT highlights the crucial distinction between nondiversifiable risk (factor risk), which requires a reward in the form of a risk premium, and diversifiable risk, which does not.

In many ways, the APT is an extremely appealing model. It is built on the highly plausible assumption that a rational capital market will preclude arbitrage opportunities. A violation of the APT's pricing relationships will cause extremely strong pressure to restore them even if only a limited number of investors become aware of the disequilibrium. Moreover, the APT provides an expected return–beta relationship using a well-diversified portfolio that can be constructed from a large number of securities. It does not rely on the elusive and impossible-to-observe market portfolio of *all* assets that underpins the CAPM. A well-diversified *index* portfolio can suffice for the APT.

In spite of these apparent advantages, the APT does not fully dominate the CAPM. The CAPM provides an unequivocal statement on the expected return–beta relationship for all securities, whereas the APT implies that this relationship holds for all but perhaps a small number of securities. Because it focuses on the no-arbitrage condition, without the further assumptions of the market or index model, the APT cannot rule out a violation of the expected return–beta relationship for any particular asset. For this, we need the CAPM assumptions and its mean-variance dominance arguments.

Moreover, while the APT is built on the foundation of well-diversified portfolios, we've seen, for example in Table 10.1, that even large portfolios may have non-negligible residual risk. Some indexed portfolios may have hundreds or thousands of stocks, but active portfolios generally cannot, as there is a limit to how many stocks can be actively analyzed in search of alpha.

Despite these shortcomings, the APT is valuable. First, recall that the CAPM requires that almost all investors be mean-variance optimizers. The APT frees us of this assumption. It is sufficient that a small number of sophisticated arbitrageurs scour the market for arbitrage opportunities.

Moreover, when we replace the unobserved market portfolio of the CAPM with an observed, broad index portfolio that may not be efficient, we no longer can be sure that the CAPM predicts risk premiums of all assets with no bias. Therefore, neither model is free of limitations.

In the end, however, it is noteworthy and comforting that despite the very different paths they take to get there, both models arrive at the same security market line. Most important, they both highlight the distinction between firm-specific and systematic risk, which is at the heart of all modern models of risk and return.

The APT and Portfolio Optimization in a Single-Index Market

The APT is couched in a single-factor market[3] and applies with perfect accuracy to *well-diversified* portfolios. It shows arbitrageurs how to generate infinite profits if the risk premium of a well-diversified portfolio deviates from Equation 10.6. The trades executed by these arbitrageurs are the enforcers of the accuracy of this equation.

In effect, the APT shows how to take advantage of security mispricing when diversification opportunities are abundant. When you lock in and scale up an arbitrage opportunity you're sure to be rich as Croesus regardless of the composition of the rest of your portfolio—but only if the arbitrage portfolio is truly risk-free! However, if the arbitrage position is *not* perfectly well diversified, an increase in its scale (borrowing cash, or borrowing shares to go short) will increase the risk of the arbitrage position, potentially without bound. The APT ignores this complication.

Now consider an investor who confronts this single-factor market, and whose security analysis reveals an underpriced asset (or portfolio), that is, one whose risk premium implies a positive alpha. This investor can follow the advice woven throughout Chapters 6, 7, and 8 to construct an optimal risky portfolio. The optimization process will consider both the potential profit from a position in the mispriced asset, as well as the risk of the overall portfolio and efficient diversification. As we saw in Chapter 8, the Treynor-Black (T-B) procedure can be summarized as follows.[4]

   1. Estimate the risk premium and standard deviation of the benchmark (index) portfolio, RP_M and σ_M.

---

[3]The APT is easily extended to a multifactor market, as we show later.

[4]The tediousness of some of the expressions involved in the T-B method should not deter anyone. The calculations are straightforward using a spreadsheet. The estimation of the risk parameters also is a relatively straightforward statistical task. The real difficulty is to uncover security alphas and the macro-factor risk premium, RP_M.

2. Place all the assets that are mispriced into an active portfolio. Call the alpha of the active portfolio α_A, its systematic-risk coefficient β_A, and its residual risk $\sigma(e_A)$. Your optimal risky portfolio will allocate to the active portfolio a weight, w_A^*:

$$w_A^0 = \frac{\alpha_A / \sigma^2(e_A)}{E(R_M) / \sigma_M^2}; \ w_A^* = \frac{w_A^0}{1 + w_A^0(1 - \beta_A)}$$

The allocation to the passive portfolio is then $w_A^* = 1 - w_A^*$. With this allocation, the increase in the Sharpe ratio of the optimal portfolio, S_P, over that of the passive portfolio, S_M, depends on the information ratio of the active portfolio, $IR_A = \alpha_A / \sigma(e_A)$.

3. To maximize the Sharpe ratio of the risky portfolio, you maximize the information ratio of the active portfolio. This is achieved by allocating to each asset in the active portfolio a portfolio weight proportional to: $w_{Ai} = \alpha_i / \sigma^2(e_i)$.

Now see what happens in the T-B model when the residual risk of the active portfolio is zero. This is essentially the assumption of the APT, that a well-diversified portfolio (with zero residual risk) can be formed. When the residual risk of the active portfolio goes to zero, the position in it goes to infinity. This is precisely the same implication as the APT: When portfolios are well-diversified, you will scale up an arbitrage position without bound. Similarly, when the residual risk of an asset in the active T-B portfolio is zero, it will displace all other assets from that portfolio, and thus the residual risk of the active portfolio will be zero and will elicit the same extreme portfolio response.

However, we have seen that, in practice, it is unlikely that residual risk can be driven all the way to zero. When residual risk is not zero, the T-B procedure produces the optimal risky portfolio, which is a compromise between seeking alpha and shunning potentially diversifiable risk. In contrast, by assuming residual risk can be diversified away, the APT ignores it altogether. When residual risk can be made small through diversification, the T-B model prescribes very aggressive (large) positions in mispriced securities that exert great pressure on equilibrium risk premiums to eliminate nonzero alpha values. The T-B model does what the APT is meant to do, but with more flexibility in terms of accommodating the practical limits to diversification. In this sense, Treynor and Black anticipated the development of the APT.

10.4 A Multifactor APT

We have assumed so far that only one systematic factor affects stock returns. This simplifying assumption is in fact too simplistic. We've noted that it is easy to think of several factors driven by the business cycle that might affect stock returns: interest rate fluctuations, inflation rates, and so on. Presumably, exposure to any of these factors will affect a stock's risk and hence its expected return. We can derive a multifactor version of the APT to accommodate these multiple sources of risk.

Suppose that we generalize the single-factor model expressed in Equation 10.1 to a two-factor model:

$$R_i = E(R_i) + \beta_{i1} F_1 + \beta_{i2} F_2 + e_i \tag{10.7}$$

In Example 10.2, factor 1 was the departure of GDP growth from expectations, and factor 2 was the unanticipated change in interest rates. Each factor has zero expected value because each measures the *surprise* in the systematic variable rather than the level of the variable.

Similarly, the firm-specific component of unexpected return, e_i, also has zero expected value. Extending such a two-factor model to any number of factors is straightforward.

The benchmark portfolios in the APT are **factor portfolios,** which are well-diversified portfolios constructed to have a beta of 1 on one of the factors and a beta of zero on any other factor. We can think of each factor portfolio as a *tracking portfolio*. That is, the returns on such a portfolio track the evolution of one particular source of macroeconomic risk but are uncorrelated with other sources of risk. It is possible to form such factor portfolios because we have a large number of securities to choose from, and a relatively small number of factors. The multidimensional SML predicts that the contribution of each source of risk to the security's total risk premium equals the factor beta times the risk premium of the factor portfolio tracking that source of risk. We illustrate with an example.

Example 10.3   Multifactor SML

Suppose that the two factor portfolios, portfolios 1 and 2, have expected returns $E(r_1) = 10\%$ and $E(r_2) = 12\%$ and that the risk-free rate is 4%. The risk premium on the first factor portfolio is $10\% - 4\% = 6\%$, and that on the second factor portfolio is $12\% - 4\% = 8\%$.

Now consider a well-diversified portfolio, portfolio A, with beta on the first factor portfolio, $\beta_{A1} = .5$, and beta on the second factor portfolio, $\beta_{A2} = .75$. The multifactor APT states that the overall risk premium on this portfolio must equal the sum of the risk premiums required as compensation for each source of systematic risk. The risk premium attributable to risk factor 1 is the portfolio's exposure to factor 1, β_{A1}, multiplied by the risk premium earned on the first factor portfolio, $E(r_1) - r_f$. Therefore, the portion of portfolio A's risk premium that is compensation for its exposure to the first factor is $\beta_{A1}[E(r_1) - r_f] = .5(10\% - 4\%) = 3\%$. Similarly, the risk premium attributable to risk factor 2 is $\beta_{A2}[E(r_2) - r_f] = .75(12\% - 4\%) = 6\%$. The total risk premium on the portfolio is $3\% + 6\% = 9\%$ and the total expected return on the portfolio should be $4\% + 9\% = 13\%$.

To generalize Example 10.3, note that the factor exposures of any portfolio, P, are given by its betas, β_{P1} and β_{P2}. A competing portfolio, Q, can be formed by investing in factor portfolios with the following weights: β_{P1} in the first factor portfolio, β_{P2} in the second factor portfolio, and $1 - \beta_{P1} - \beta_{P2}$ in T-bills. By construction, portfolio Q will have betas equal to those of portfolio P and expected return of

$$E(r_Q) = \beta_{P1} E(r_1) + \beta_{P2} E(r_2) + (1 - \beta_{P1} - \beta_{P2})r_f$$
$$= r_f + \beta_{P1}[E(r_1) - r_f] + \beta_{P2}[E(r_2) - r_f] \tag{10.8}$$

This is a two-factor SML, and, as Example 10.4 shows, any well-diversified portfolio with the same betas must have the same expected return as long as capital markets do not allow for easy arbitrage opportunities.

Example 10.4   Mispricing and Arbitrage

Using the numbers in Example 10.3:

$$E(r_Q) = 4 + .5 \times (10 - 4) + .75 \times (12 - 4) = 13\%$$

Suppose the expected return on portfolio A from Example 10.3 were 12% rather than 13%. This return would give rise to an arbitrage opportunity. Form a portfolio from the factor portfolios with the same betas as portfolio A. This requires weights of .5 on the first factor portfolio, .75 on the second factor portfolio, and −.25 on the risk-free asset. This portfolio has exactly the same factor betas as portfolio A: It has a beta of .5 on the first factor because of its .5 weight on the first factor portfolio, and a beta of .75 on the second factor. (The weight of −.25 on risk-free T-bills does not affect the sensitivity to either factor.)

Now invest $1 in portfolio Q and sell (short) $1 in portfolio A. Your net investment is zero, but your expected dollar profit is positive and equal to

$$\$1 \times E(r_Q) - \$1 \times E(r_A) = \$1 \times .13 - \$1 \times .12 = \$.01$$

Moreover, your net position is riskless. Your exposure to each risk factor cancels out because you are long $1 in portfolio Q and short $1 in portfolio A, and both of these well-diversified portfolios have exactly the same factor betas. Thus, if portfolio A's expected return differs from that of portfolio Q's, you can earn positive risk-free profits on a zero-net-investment position. This is an arbitrage opportunity.

Because portfolio Q in Example 10.4 has precisely the same exposures as portfolio A to the two sources of risk, their expected returns also ought to be equal. So portfolio A also ought to have an expected return of 13%. If it does not, then there will be an arbitrage opportunity and great pressure on prices until the opportunity is eliminated.[5] We conclude that any well-diversified portfolio with betas β_{P1} and β_{P2} must have the expected return given in Equation 10.8.

Finally, the extension of the multifactor SML of Equation 10.8 to individual assets is precisely the same as for the one-factor APT. Equation 10.8 cannot be satisfied by every well-diversified portfolio unless it is satisfied approximately by individual securities. Equation 10.8 thus represents the multifactor SML for an economy with multiple sources of risk.

We pointed out earlier that one application of the CAPM is to provide "fair" rates of return for regulated utilities. The multifactor APT can be used to the same ends. The nearby box summarizes a study in which the APT was applied to find the cost of capital for regulated electric companies. Notice that empirical estimates for interest rate and inflation risk premiums in the box are negative, as we argued was reasonable in our discussion of Example 10.2.

 Concept Check **10.3**

Using the factor portfolios of Example 10.3, find the equilibrium rate of return on a portfolio with $\beta_1 = .2$ and $\beta_2 = 1.4$.

[5]The risk premium on portfolio A is 9% (more than the historical risk premium of the S&P 500) despite the fact that its betas, which are both below 1, might *seem* defensive. This highlights another distinction between multifactor and single-factor models. Whereas a beta greater than 1 in a single-factor market is aggressive, we cannot say in advance what would be aggressive or defensive in a multifactor economy where risk premiums depend on the sum of the contributions of several factors.

Using the APT to Find Cost of Capital

Elton, Gruber, and Mei* use the APT to derive the cost of capital for electric utilities. They consider five potential systematic risk factors: unanticipated developments in the term structure of interest rates, the level of interest rates, inflation rates, the business cycle (measured by GDP), foreign exchange rates, and a summary measure they devise to measure other macro factors.

Their first step is to estimate the risk premium associated with exposure to each risk source. They accomplish this in a two-step strategy (which we will describe in considerable detail in Chapter 13):

1. *Estimate "factor loadings" (i.e., betas) of a large sample of firms.* Regress returns of 100 randomly selected stocks against the five systematic factors. They use a time-series regression for each stock (e.g., 60 months of data), therefore estimating 100 regressions, one for each stock.

2. *Estimate the reward earned per unit of exposure to each risk factor.* For each month, regress the return of each stock against the five betas estimated. The coefficient on each beta is the extra average return earned as beta increases (i.e., it is an estimate of the risk premium for that risk factor from that month's data). These estimates are of course subject to sampling error. Therefore, average the risk premium estimates across the 12 months in each year. The *average* response of return to risk is less subject to sampling error.

The risk premiums are in the middle column of the table in the next column.

Notice that some risk premiums are negative. The interpretation of this result is that risk premium should be positive for risk factors you don't want exposure to, but *negative* for factors you *do* want exposure to. For example, you should desire securities that have higher returns when inflation increases and be willing to accept lower expected returns on such securities; this shows up as a negative risk premium.

Factor	Factor Risk Premium	Factor Betas for Niagara Mohawk
Term structure	0.425	1.0615
Interest rates	−0.051	−2.4167
Exchange rates	−0.049	1.3235
Business cycle	0.041	0.1292
Inflation	−0.069	−0.5220
Other macro factors	0.530	0.3046

The study finds that average returns are related to factor betas as follows:

$$r_f + .425\, \beta_{\text{term struc}} - .051\, \beta_{\text{int rate}}$$
$$- .049\, \beta_{\text{ex rate}} + .041\, \beta_{\text{bus cycle}} - .069\, \beta_{\text{inflation}} + .530\, \beta_{\text{other}}$$

Finally, to obtain the cost of capital for a particular firm, the authors estimate the firm's betas against each source of risk, multiply each factor beta by the "cost of factor risk" from the table above, sum over all risk sources to obtain the total risk premium, and add the risk-free rate.

For example, the beta estimates for Niagara Mohawk appear in the last column of the table above. Therefore, its cost of capital is

$$\text{Cost of capital} = r_f + .425 \times 1.0615 - 0.51(-2.4167)$$
$$- .049(1.3235) + .041(.1292)$$
$$- .069(-.5220) + .530(.3046)$$
$$= r_f + .72$$

In other words, the monthly cost of capital for Niagara Mohawk is .72% above the monthly risk-free rate. Its annualized risk premium is therefore .72% × 12 = 8.64%.

*Edwin J. Elton, Martin J. Gruber, and Jianping Mei, "Cost of Capital Using Arbitrage Pricing Theory: A Case Study of Nine New York Utilities," *Financial Markets, Institutions, and Instruments* 3 (August 1994), pp. 46–68.

10.5 The Fama-French (FF) Three-Factor Model

The APT shows us how multiple risk factors can result in a multifactor SML. But how can we identify the most likely sources of systematic risk? One approach comes from Merton's multifactor CAPM, discussed in Chapter 9, in which the extra-market risk factors are due to hedging demands against a range of risks associated with either consumption or investment opportunities. Another approach, which is more pervasive today, uses firm characteristics that seem on empirical grounds to proxy for exposure to systematic risk. The factors chosen are variables that on past evidence have predicted average returns well and therefore may be capturing risk premiums. One example of this approach is the Fama and French three-factor model and its variants, which have come to dominate empirical research in security returns:[6]

$$R_{it} = \alpha_i + \beta_{iM} R_{Mt} + \beta_{iSMB}\, SMB_t + \beta_{iHML}\, HML_t + e_{it} \qquad \textbf{(10.9)}$$

where

SMB = Small Minus Big (i.e., the return of a portfolio of small stocks in excess of the return on a portfolio of large stocks).

HML = High Minus Low (i.e., the return of a portfolio of stocks with a high book-to-market ratio in excess of the return on a portfolio of stocks with a low book-to-market ratio).

Note that in this model the market index does play a role and is expected to capture systematic risk originating from macroeconomic factors.

These two extra-market factors are chosen because of long-standing observations that firm size, measured by market capitalization (the market value of outstanding equity), and the book-to-market ratio (book value per share divided by stock price) predict deviations of average stock returns from levels consistent with the CAPM. Fama and French justify this model on empirical grounds: While SMB and HML are not themselves obvious candidates for relevant risk factors, the argument is that these variables may proxy for hard-to-measure more-fundamental variables. For example, Fama and French point out that firms with high book-to-market ratios are more likely to be in financial distress and that small stocks may be more sensitive to changes in business conditions. Thus, these variables may capture sensitivity to risk factors in the macroeconomy. More evidence on the Fama-French model appears in Chapter 13.

The problem with empirical approaches such as the Fama-French model is that the extra-market factors in these models cannot be clearly identified with a source of risk that is of obvious concern to a significant group of investors. Black[7] points out that when researchers scan and rescan the database of security returns in search of explanatory factors (an activity often called data-snooping), they may eventually uncover past "patterns" that are due purely to chance. However, Fama and French have shown that size and book-to-market ratios have predicted average returns in different time periods and in markets all over the world, thus mitigating potential effects of data-snooping.

The risk premiums associated with Fama-French factors raise the question of whether they reflect a multi-index ICAPM based on extra-market hedging demands or just represent yet-unexplained anomalies, where firm characteristics are correlated with alpha values. This is an important distinction for the debate over the proper interpretation of the model, because the validity of FF-style models may signify either a deviation from rational equilibrium (as there is no rational reason to prefer one or another of these firm characteristics per se) or indicate that firm characteristics identified as empirically associated with average returns are correlated with other (harder to specify) risk factors.

The issue is still unresolved and is revisited in Chapter 13.

---

[6]Eugene F. Fama and Kenneth R. French, "Multifactor Explanations of Asset Pricing Anomalies," *Journal of Finance* 51 (1996), pp. 55–84.

[7]Fischer Black, "Beta and Return," *Journal of Portfolio Management* 20 (1993), pp. 8–18.

SUMMARY

1. Multifactor models seek to improve the explanatory power of single-factor models by explicitly accounting for the various components of systematic risk. These models use indicators intended to capture a wide range of macroeconomic risk factors.

2. Once we allow for multiple risk factors, we conclude that the security market line also ought to be multidimensional, with exposure to each risk factor contributing to the total risk premium of the security.

3. A (risk-free) arbitrage opportunity arises when two or more security prices enable investors to construct a zero-net-investment portfolio that will yield a sure profit. The presence of arbitrage opportunities will generate a large volume of trades that puts pressure on security prices. This pressure will continue until prices reach levels that preclude such arbitrage.

4. When securities are priced so that there are no risk-free arbitrage opportunities, we say that they satisfy the no-arbitrage condition. Price relationships that satisfy the no-arbitrage condition are important because we expect them to hold in real-world markets.

5. Portfolios are called "well diversified" if they include a large number of securities and the investment proportion in each is sufficiently small. The proportion of a security in a well-diversified portfolio is small enough so that for all practical purposes a reasonable change in that security's rate of return will have a negligible effect on the portfolio's rate of return.

6. In a single-factor security market, all well-diversified portfolios have to satisfy the expected return–beta relationship of the CAPM to satisfy the no-arbitrage condition. If all well-diversified portfolios satisfy the expected return–beta relationship, then individual securities also must satisfy this relationship, at least approximately.

7. The APT does not require the restrictive assumptions of the CAPM and its (unobservable) market portfolio. The price of this generality is that the APT does not guarantee this relationship for all securities at all times.

8. A multifactor APT generalizes the single-factor model to accommodate several sources of systematic risk. The multidimensional security market line predicts that exposure to each risk factor contributes to the security's total risk premium by an amount equal to the factor beta times the risk premium of the factor portfolio that tracks that source of risk.

9. The multifactor extension of the single-factor CAPM, the ICAPM, predicts the same multidimensional security market line as the APT. The ICAPM suggests that priced extra-market risk factors will be the ones that lead to significant hedging demand by a substantial fraction of investors. Other approaches to the multifactor APT are more empirically based, where the extra-market factors are selected based on past ability to predict risk premiums.

KEY TERMS

single-factor model	arbitrage pricing theory (APT)	well-diversified portfolio
multifactor model	arbitrage	factor portfolio
factor loading	Law of One Price	
factor beta	risk arbitrage	

KEY EQUATIONS

Single-factor model: $R_i = E(R_i) + \beta_i F + e_i$

Multifactor model (here, 2 factors, F_1 and F_2): $R_i = E(R_i) + \beta_{i1} F_1 + \beta_{i2} F_2 + e_i$

Single-index model: $R_i = \alpha_i + \beta_i R_M + e_i$

Multifactor SML (here, 2 factors, labeled 1 and 2):

$$E(r_i) = r_f + \beta_{i1}[E(r_1) - r_f] + \beta_{i2}[E(r_2) - r_f]$$
$$= r_f + \beta_{i1}E(R_1) + \beta_{i2}E(R_2)$$

where β_{i1} and β_{i2} measure the stock's typical response to returns on each factor portfolio and the risk premiums on the two factor portfolios are $E(R_1)$ and $E(R_2)$.

---

1. Suppose that two factors have been identified for the U.S. economy: the growth rate of industrial production, IP, and the inflation rate, IR. IP is expected to be 3%, and IR 5%. A stock with a beta of 1 on IP and .5 on IR currently is expected to provide a rate of return of 12%. If industrial production actually grows by 5%, while the inflation rate turns out to be 8%, what is your revised estimate of the expected rate of return on the stock?

2. The APT itself does not provide guidance concerning the factors that one might expect to determine risk premiums. How should researchers decide which factors to investigate? Why, for example, is industrial production a reasonable factor to test for a risk premium?

3. If the APT is to be a useful theory, the number of systematic factors in the economy must be small. Why?

4. Suppose that there are two independent economic factors, F_1 and F_2. The risk-free rate is 6%, and all stocks have independent firm-specific components with a standard deviation of 45%. Portfolios A and B are both well-diversified with the following properties:

Portfolio	Beta on F_1	Beta on F_2	Expected Return
A	1.5	2.0	31%
B	2.2	−0.2	27%

What is the expected return–beta relationship in this economy?

5. Consider the following data for a one-factor economy. Both portfolios are well diversified.

Portfolio	E(r)	Beta
A	12%	1.2
F	6%	0.0

Suppose that another portfolio, portfolio E, is well diversified with a beta of .6 and expected return of 8%. Would an arbitrage opportunity exist? If so, what would be the arbitrage strategy?

6. Assume that both portfolios A and B are well diversified, that $E(r_A) = 12\%$, and $E(r_B) = 9\%$. If the economy has only one factor, and $\beta_A = 1.2$, whereas $\beta_B = .8$, what must be the risk-free rate?

7. Assume that stock market returns have the market index as a common factor, and that all stocks in the economy have a beta of 1 on the market index. Firm-specific returns all have a standard deviation of 30%.

   Suppose that an analyst studies 20 stocks and finds that one-half of them have an alpha of +2%, and the other half have an alpha of −2%. Suppose the analyst invests $1 million in an equally weighted portfolio of the positive alpha stocks, and shorts $1 million of an equally weighted portfolio of the negative alpha stocks.

   a. What is the expected profit (in dollars) and standard deviation of the analyst's profit?
   b. How does your answer change if the analyst examines 50 stocks instead of 20 stocks? 100 stocks?

PROBLEM SETS

8. Assume that security returns are generated by the single-index model,

$$R_i = \alpha_i + \beta_i R_M + e_i$$

where R_i is the excess return for security i and R_M is the market's excess return. The risk-free rate is 2%. Suppose also that there are three securities, A, B, and C, characterized by the following data:

Security	β_i	$E(R_i)$	$\sigma(e_i)$
A	0.8	10%	25%
B	1.0	12	10
C	1.2	14	20

a. If $\sigma_M = 20\%$, calculate the variance of returns of securities A, B, and C.
b. Now assume that there are an infinite number of assets with return characteristics identical to those of A, B, and C, respectively. If one forms a well-diversified portfolio of type A securities, what will be the mean and variance of the portfolio's excess returns? What about portfolios composed only of type B or C stocks?
c. Is there an arbitrage opportunity in this market? What is it? Analyze the opportunity graphically.

9. The SML relationship states that the expected risk premium on a security in a one-factor model must be directly proportional to the security's beta. Suppose that this were not the case. For example, suppose that expected return rises more than proportionately with beta as in the figure below.

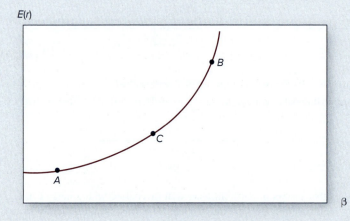

a. How could you construct an arbitrage portfolio? (*Hint:* Consider combinations of portfolios A and B, and compare the resultant portfolio to C.)
b. Some researchers have examined the relationship between average returns on diversified portfolios and the β and β^2 of those portfolios. What should they have discovered about the effect of β^2 on portfolio return?

10. Consider the following multifactor (APT) model of security returns for a particular stock.

Factor	Factor Beta	Factor Risk Premium
Inflation	1.2	6%
Industrial production	0.5	8
Oil prices	0.3	3

a. If T-bills currently offer a 6% yield, find the expected rate of return on this stock if the market views the stock as fairly priced.

b. Suppose that the market expects the values for the three macro factors given in column 1 below, but that the actual values turn out as given in column 2. Calculate the revised expectations for the rate of return on the stock once the "surprises" become known.

Factor	Expected Value	Actual Value
Inflation	5%	4%
Industrial production	3	6
Oil prices	2	0

11. Suppose that the market can be described by the following three sources of systematic risk with associated risk premiums.

Factor	Risk Premium
Industrial production (I)	6%
Interest rates (R)	2
Consumer confidence (C)	4

The return on a particular stock is generated according to the following equation:

$$r = 15\% + 1.0I + .5R + .75C + e$$

Find the equilibrium rate of return on this stock using the APT. The T-bill rate is 6%. Is the stock over- or underpriced? Explain.

12. As a finance intern at Pork Products, Jennifer Wainwright's assignment is to come up with fresh insights concerning the firm's cost of capital. She decides that this would be a good opportunity to try out the new material on the APT that she learned last semester. She decides that three promising factors would be (a) the return on a broad-based index such as the S&P 500; (b) the level of interest rates, as represented by the yield to maturity on 10-year Treasury bonds; and (c) the price of hogs, which is particularly important to her firm. Her plan is to find the beta of Pork Products against each of these factors by using a multiple regression and to estimate the risk premium associated with each exposure factor. Comment on Jennifer's choice of factors. Which are most promising with respect to the likely impact on her firm's cost of capital? Can you suggest improvements to her specification?

Use the following information to answer Problems 13 through 16:

Orb Trust (Orb) has historically leaned toward a passive management style of its portfolios. The only model that Orb's senior management has promoted in the past is the capital asset pricing model (CAPM). Now Orb's management has asked one of its analysts, Kevin McCracken, CFA, to investigate the use of the arbitrage pricing theory (APT) model.

McCracken believes that a two-factor APT model is adequate, where the factors are the sensitivity to changes in real GDP and changes in inflation. McCracken has concluded that the factor risk premium for real GDP is 8% while the factor risk premium for inflation is 2%. He estimates for Orb's High Growth Fund that the sensitivities to these two factors are 1.25 and 1.5, respectively. Using his APT results, he computes the equilibrium expected return of the fund. For comparison purposes, he then uses fundamental analysis to compute the actually expected return of Orb's High Growth Fund. McCracken finds that the two estimates of the Orb High Growth Fund's expected return are equal.

McCracken asks a fellow analyst, Sue Kwon, to provide an estimate of the expected return of Orb's Large Cap Fund based on fundamental analysis. Kwon, who manages the fund, says that the expected return is 8.5% above the risk-free rate. McCracken then applies the APT model to the Large Cap Fund. He finds that the sensitivities to real GDP and inflation are .75 and 1.25, respectively.

McCracken's manager at Orb, Jay Stiles, asks McCracken to construct a portfolio that has a unit sensitivity to real GDP growth but is not affected by inflation. McCracken is confident in his APT estimates for the High Growth Fund and the Large Cap Fund. He then computes the sensitivities for a third fund, Orb's Utility Fund, which has sensitivities equal to 1.0 and 2.0, respectively. McCracken will use his APT results for these three funds to accomplish the task of creating a portfolio with a unit exposure to real GDP and no exposure to inflation. He calls the fund the "GDP Fund." Stiles says such a GDP Fund would be good for clients who are retirees who live off the steady income of their investments. McCracken does not agree with Stiles, but says that the fund would be a good choice if upcoming supply side macroeconomic policies of the government are successful.

13. According to the APT, if the risk-free rate is 4%, what should be McCracken's estimate of the expected return of Orb's High Growth Fund?

14. With respect to McCracken's APT model estimate of Orb's Large Cap Fund and the information Kwon provides, is an arbitrage opportunity available?

15. If the GDP Fund is constructed from the other three funds, which of the following would be its weight in the Utility Fund? (*a*) −2.2; (*b*) −3.2; or (*c*) .3.

16. With respect to the comments of Stiles and McCracken concerning for whom the GDP Fund would be appropriate:

    a. McCracken is correct and Stiles is wrong.
    b. Both are correct.
    c. Stiles is correct and McCracken is wrong.

17. Assume a universe of n (large) securities for which the largest residual variance is not larger than $n\sigma_M^2$. Construct as many different weighting schemes as you can that generate well-diversified portfolios.

18. Derive a more general (than the numerical example in the chapter) demonstration of the APT security market line:

    a. For a single-factor market.
    b. For a multifactor market.

19. Small firms generally have relatively high loadings (high betas) on the SMB (small minus big) factor.

    a. Explain why this is not surprising.
    b. Now suppose two unrelated small firms merge. Each will be operated as an independent unit of the merged company. Would you expect the stock market behavior of the merged firm to differ from that of a portfolio of the two previously independent firms?
    c. How does the merger affect market capitalization?
    d. What is the prediction of the Fama-French model for the risk premium on the merged firm compared to the weighted average of the two component companies?
    e. Do we see here a problem in applying the FF model?

CFA® PROBLEMS

1. Jeffrey Bruner, CFA, uses the capital asset pricing model (CAPM) to help identify mispriced securities. A consultant suggests Bruner use arbitrage pricing theory (APT) instead. In comparing CAPM and APT, the consultant makes the following arguments:

    a. Both the CAPM and APT require a mean-variance efficient market portfolio.
    b. Neither the CAPM nor the APT assumes normally distributed security returns.
    c. The CAPM assumes that one specific factor explains security returns but APT does not.

    State whether each of the consultant's arguments is correct or incorrect. Indicate, for each incorrect argument, why the argument is incorrect.

2. Assume that both X and Y are well-diversified portfolios and the risk-free rate is 8%.

Portfolio	Expected Return	Beta
X	16%	1.00
Y	12	0.25

In this situation you would conclude that portfolios *X* and *Y*:

a. Are in equilibrium.
b. Offer an arbitrage opportunity.
c. Are both underpriced.
d. Are both fairly priced.

3. A zero-investment portfolio with a positive alpha could arise if:

a. The expected return of the portfolio equals zero.
b. The capital market line is tangent to the opportunity set.
c. The Law of One Price remains unviolated.
d. A risk-free arbitrage opportunity exists.

4. According to the theory of arbitrage:

a. High-beta stocks are consistently overpriced.
b. Low-beta stocks are consistently overpriced.
c. Positive alpha investment opportunities will quickly disappear.
d. Rational investors will pursue arbitrage opportunities consistent with their risk tolerance.

5. The general arbitrage pricing theory (APT) differs from the single-factor capital asset pricing model (CAPM) because the APT:

a. Places more emphasis on market risk.
b. Minimizes the importance of diversification.
c. Recognizes multiple unsystematic risk factors.
d. Recognizes multiple systematic risk factors.

6. An investor takes as large a position as possible when an equilibrium price relationship is violated. This is an example of:

a. A dominance argument.
b. The mean-variance efficient frontier.
c. Arbitrage activity.
d. The capital asset pricing model.

7. The feature of the general version of the arbitrage pricing theory (APT) that offers the greatest potential advantage over the *simple* CAPM is the:

a. Identification of anticipated changes in production, inflation, and term structure of interest rates as key factors explaining the risk–return relationship.
b. Superior measurement of the risk-free rate of return over historical time periods.
c. Variability of coefficients of sensitivity to the APT factors for a given asset over time.
d. Use of several factors instead of a single market index to explain the risk–return relationship.

8. In contrast to the capital asset pricing model, arbitrage pricing theory:

a. Requires that markets be in equilibrium.
b. Uses risk premiums based on micro variables.
c. Specifies the number and identifies specific factors that determine expected returns.
d. Does not require the restrictive assumptions concerning the market portfolio.

E-INVESTMENTS EXERCISES

One of the factors in the APT model specified in an influential paper by Chen, Roll, and Ross* is the percent change in unanticipated inflation. Who gains and who loses when inflation changes? Go to **http://hussmanfunds.com/rsi/infsurprises.htm** to see a graph of the Inflation Surprise Index and Economists' Inflation Forecasts.

*See Nai-Fu Chen, Richard Roll, and Stephen Ross, "Economic Forces and the Stock Market," *Journal of Business* 59 (1986).

✔ SOLUTIONS TO CONCEPT CHECKS

1. The GDP beta is 1.2 and GDP growth is 1% better than previously expected. So you will increase your forecast for the stock return by $1.2 \times 1\% = 1.2\%$. The revised forecast is for an 11.2% return.

2. *a.* This portfolio is not well diversified. The weight on the first security does not decline as n increases. Regardless of how much diversification there is in the rest of the portfolio, you will not shed the firm-specific risk of this security.

   b. This portfolio is well diversified. Even though some stocks have three times the weight of other stocks ($1.5/n$ versus $.5/n$), the weight on all stocks approaches zero as n increases. The impact of any individual stock's firm-specific risk will approach zero as n becomes ever larger.

3. The equilibrium return is $E(r) = r_f + \beta_{P1}[E(r_1) - r_f] + \beta_{P2}[E(r_2) - r_f]$. Using the data in Example 10.4:

$$E(r) = 4 + .2 \times (10 - 4) + 1.4 \times (12 - 4) = 16.4\%$$

The Efficient Market Hypothesis

11

ONE OF THE early applications of computers in economics in the 1950s was to analyze economic time series. Business cycle theorists felt that tracing the evolution of several economic variables over time would clarify and predict the progress of the economy through boom and bust periods. A natural candidate for analysis was the behavior of stock market prices over time. Assuming that stock prices reflect the prospects of the firm, recurrent patterns of peaks and troughs in economic performance ought to show up in those prices.

Maurice Kendall examined this proposition in 1953.[1] He found to his great surprise that he could identify no predictable patterns in stock prices. Prices seemed to evolve randomly. They were as likely to go up as they were to go down on any particular day, regardless of past performance. The data provided no way to predict price movements.

At first blush, Kendall's results were disturbing to some financial economists. They seemed to imply that the stock market is dominated by erratic market psychology, or "animal spirits"—that it follows no logical rules. In short, the results appeared to confirm the irrationality of the market. On further reflection, however, economists came to reverse their interpretation of Kendall's study.

It soon became apparent that random price movements indicated a well-functioning or efficient market, not an irrational one. In this chapter we explore the reasoning behind what may seem a surprising conclusion. We show how competition among analysts leads naturally to market efficiency, and we examine the implications of the efficient market hypothesis for investment policy. We also consider empirical evidence that supports and contradicts the notion of market efficiency.

---

[1]Maurice Kendall, "The Analysis of Economic Time Series, Part I: Prices," *Journal of the Royal Statistical Society* 96 (1953).

11.1   Random Walks and the Efficient Market Hypothesis

Suppose Kendall had discovered that stock price changes are predictable. What a gold mine this would have been. If they could use Kendall's equations to predict stock prices, investors would reap unending profits simply by purchasing stocks that the computer model implied were about to increase in price and selling those stocks about to fall in price.

A moment's reflection should be enough to convince yourself that this situation could not persist for long. For example, suppose that the model predicts with great confidence that XYZ stock price, currently at $100 per share, will rise dramatically in three days to $110. What would all investors with access to the model's prediction do today? Obviously, they would place a great wave of immediate buy orders to cash in on the prospective increase in stock price. No one holding XYZ, however, would be willing to sell. The net effect would be an *immediate* jump in the stock price to $110. The forecast of a future price increase will lead instead to an immediate price increase. In other words, the stock price will immediately reflect the "good news" implicit in the model's forecast.

This simple example illustrates why Kendall's attempt to find recurrent patterns in stock price movements was likely to fail. A forecast about favorable *future* performance leads instead to favorable *current* performance, as market participants all try to get in on the action before the price jump.

More generally, one might say that any information that could be used to predict stock performance should already be reflected in stock prices. As soon as there is any information indicating that a stock is underpriced and therefore offers a profit opportunity, investors flock to buy the stock and immediately bid up its price to a fair level, where only ordinary rates of return can be expected. These "ordinary rates" are simply rates of return commensurate with the risk of the stock.

However, if prices are bid immediately to fair levels, given all available information, it must be that they increase or decrease only in response to new information. New information, by definition, must be unpredictable; if it could be predicted, then the prediction would be part of today's information. Thus stock prices that change in response to new (i.e., previously unpredicted) information also must move unpredictably.

This is the essence of the argument that stock prices should follow a **random walk,** that is, that price changes should be random and unpredictable.[2] Far from a proof of market irrationality, randomly evolving stock prices would be the necessary consequence of intelligent investors competing to discover relevant information on which to buy or sell stocks before the rest of the market becomes aware of that information.

Don't confuse randomness in price *changes* with irrationality in the *level* of prices. If prices are determined rationally, then only new information will cause them to change. Therefore, a random walk would be the natural result of prices that always reflect all current knowledge. Indeed, if stock price movements were predictable, that would be damning evidence of stock market inefficiency, because the ability to predict prices would indicate that all available information was not already reflected in stock prices. Therefore, the notion that

---

[2]Actually, we are being a little loose with terminology here. Strictly speaking, we should characterize stock prices as following a submartingale, meaning that the expected change in the price can be positive, presumably as compensation for the time value of money and systematic risk. Moreover, the expected return may change over time as risk factors change. A random walk is more restrictive in that it constrains successive stock returns to be independent *and* identically distributed. Nevertheless, the term "random walk" is commonly used in the looser sense that price changes are essentially unpredictable. We will follow this convention.

stocks already reflect all available information is referred to as the **efficient market hypothesis (EMH)**.[3]

Figure 11.1 illustrates the response of stock prices to new information in an efficient market. The graph plots the price response of a sample of firms that were targets of takeover attempts. In most takeovers, the acquiring firm pays a substantial premium over current market prices. Therefore, announcement of a takeover attempt should cause the stock price to jump. The figure shows that stock prices jump dramatically on the day the news becomes public. However, there is no further drift in prices *after* the announcement date, suggesting that prices reflect the new information, including the likely magnitude of the takeover premium, by the end of the trading day.

Even more dramatic evidence of rapid response to new information may be found in intraday prices. For example, Patell and Wolfson show that most of the stock price response to corporate dividend or earnings announcements occurs within 10 minutes of the announcement.[4] A nice illustration of such rapid adjustment is provided in a study by Busse and Green, who track minute-by-minute stock prices of firms that are featured on CNBC's "Morning" or "Midday Call" segments.[5] Minute 0 in Figure 11.2 is the time at which the stock is mentioned on the midday show. The top line is the average price movement of stocks that receive positive reports, while the bottom line reports returns on stocks with negative reports. Notice that the top line levels off, indicating that the market has fully digested the news within 5 minutes of the report. The bottom line levels off within about 12 minutes.

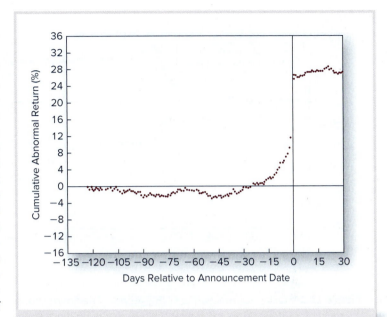

Figure 11.1 Cumulative abnormal returns before takeover attempts: target companies

Source: Arthur Keown and John Pinkerton, "Merger Announcements and Insider Trading Activity," *Journal of Finance* 36 (September 1981). Updates courtesy of Jinghua Yan.

Competition as the Source of Efficiency

Why should we expect stock prices to reflect "all available information"? After all, if you are willing to spend time and money on gathering information, it might seem reasonable that you could turn up something that has been overlooked by the rest of the investment community. When information is costly to uncover and analyze, one would expect investment analysis calling for such expenditures to result in an increased expected return.

---

[3]Market efficiency should not be confused with the idea of efficient portfolios introduced in Chapter 7. An informationally efficient *market* is one in which information is rapidly disseminated and reflected in prices. An efficient *portfolio* is one with the highest expected return for a given level of risk.

[4]J. M. Patell and M. A. Wolfson, "The Intraday Speed of Adjustment of Stock Prices to Earnings and Dividend Announcements," *Journal of Financial Economics* 13 (June 1984), pp. 223–52.

[5]J. A. Busse and T. C. Green, "Market Efficiency in Real Time," *Journal of Financial Economics* 65 (2002), pp. 415–37. You can find an intraday movie version of this figure at **www.bus.emory.edu/cgreen/cnbc.html**.

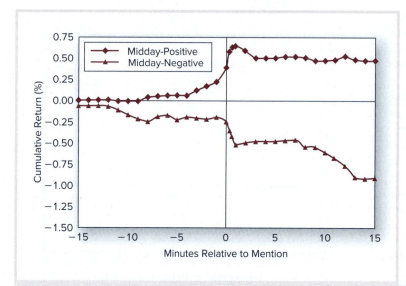

Figure 11.2 Stock price reaction to CNBC reports. The figure shows the reaction of stock prices to on-air stock reports during the "Midday Call" segment on CNBC. The chart plots cumulative returns beginning 15 minutes before the stock report.

Source: J. A. Busse and T. C. Green, "Market Efficiency in Real Time," *Journal of Financial Economics* 65 (2002), p. 422.

This point has been stressed by Grossman and Stiglitz.[6] They argue that investors will have an incentive to spend time and resources to analyze and uncover new information only if such activity is likely to generate higher investment returns. Thus, in market equilibrium, efficient information-gathering activity should be fruitful. Moreover, it would not be surprising to find that the degree of efficiency differs across various markets. For example, emerging markets that are less intensively analyzed than U.S. markets or in which accounting disclosure requirements are less rigorous may be less efficient than U.S. markets. Small stocks that receive relatively little coverage by Wall Street analysts may be less efficiently priced than large ones. Still, while we would not go so far as to say that you absolutely cannot come up with new insights, it makes sense to consider and respect your competition.

Example 11.1   Rewards for Incremental Performance

Consider an investment management fund currently managing a $5 billion portfolio. Suppose that the fund manager can devise a research program that could increase the portfolio rate of return by one-tenth of 1% per year, a seemingly modest amount. This program would increase the dollar return to the portfolio by $5 billion × .001, or $5 million. Therefore, the fund would be willing to spend up to $5 million per year on research to increase stock returns by a mere tenth of 1% per year. With such large rewards for such small increases in investment performance, it should not be surprising that professional portfolio managers are willing to spend large sums on industry analysts, computer support, and research effort, and therefore that price changes are, generally speaking, difficult to predict.

With so many well-backed analysts willing to spend considerable resources on research, easy pickings in the market are rare. Moreover, the incremental rates of return on research activity may be so small that only managers of the largest portfolios will find them worth pursuing.

Although it may not literally be true that "all" relevant information will be uncovered, it is virtually certain that there are many investigators hot on the trail of most leads that seem likely to improve investment performance. Competition among these many well-backed,

[6]Sanford J. Grossman and Joseph E. Stiglitz, "On the Impossibility of Informationally Efficient Markets," *American Economic Review* 70 (June 1980).

Matchmakers for the Information Age

The most precious commodity on Wall Street is information, and informed players can charge handsomely for providing it. An industry of so-called *expert network providers* has emerged for selling access to experts with unique insights about a wide variety of firms and industries to investors who need that information to make decisions. These firms have been dubbed matchmakers for the information age. Experts can range from doctors who help predict the release of blockbuster drugs to meteorologists who forecast weather that can affect commodity prices to business executives who can provide specialized insight about companies and industries.

But some of those experts have peddled prohibited inside information. In 2011, a consultant for Primary Global Research was convicted of selling information to the hedge fund SAC Capital Advisors. Several other employees of Primary Global also were charged with insider trading.

Expert firms are supposed to provide only public information, along with the expert's insights and perspective. But the temptation to hire experts with inside information and charge handsomely for access to them is obvious. The SEC has raised concerns about the boundary between legitimate and illegal services, and several hedge funds in 2011 shut down after raids searched for evidence of such illicit activity.

In the wake of increased scrutiny, compliance efforts of both buyers and sellers of expert information have mushroomed. One of the largest network firms is Gerson Lehrman Group, with a stable of 300,000 experts, which maintains records down to the minute of which of its experts talks to whom and the topics they have discussed.* These records could be turned over to authorities in the event of an insider trading investigation. For their part, some hedge funds have simply ceased working with expert-network firms or have promulgated clearer rules for when their employees may talk with consultants.

Even with these safeguards, however, there remains room for trouble. For example, an investor may meet an expert through a legitimate network and then the two may establish a consulting relationship on their own. This legal matchmaking becomes the precursor to the illegal selling of insider tips. Where there is a will to cheat, there usually will be a way.

*"Expert Networks Are the Matchmakers for the Information Age," *The Economist*, June 16, 2011.

---

highly paid, aggressive analysts ensures that, as a general rule, stock prices ought to reflect available information regarding their proper levels.

Information is often said to be the most precious commodity on Wall Street, and the competition for it is intense. Consider the industry of so-called alternative data firms that has emerged to uncover and sell to large investors information that might shed light on corporate prospects. For example, these firms use satellite imagery to estimate the number of cars parked outside big retailers such as Walmart, thereby getting a sense of daily sales. Other firms use satellite imagery to estimate the height of oil tanks and thus the size of oil stocks. Some firms employ large computer networks and machine learning to keep tabs on social media in the hopes of stumbling on relevant information before it becomes common knowledge.[7]

Sometimes the quest for a competitive advantage can tip over into a search for illegal inside information. For example, in 2011, Raj Rajaratnam, the head of the Galleon Group hedge fund, which once managed $6.5 billion, was convicted for soliciting tips from a network of corporate insiders and traders. In 2014, another successful hedge fund, SAC Capital Advisors, paid $1.8 billion to settle an insider trading probe. While these firms clearly crossed the line separating legitimate and prohibited means to acquire information, that line is often murky. For example, a large industry of *expert network* firms connects (for a fee) investors to industry experts who can provide unique perspective on a company. As the nearby box discusses, this sort of arrangement can easily lead to insider trading and, in fact, was a key component of the case against SAC Capital.

Versions of the Efficient Market Hypothesis

It is common to distinguish among three versions of the EMH: the weak, semistrong, and strong forms of the hypothesis. These versions differ by their notions of what is meant by the term "all available information."

[7]For other interesting examples, see "The Watchers," *The Economist,* August 20, 2016, p. 56.

The **weak-form** hypothesis asserts that stock prices already reflect all information that can be derived by examining market trading data such as the history of past prices, trading volume, or short interest. This version of the hypothesis implies that trend analysis is fruitless. Past stock price data are publicly available and virtually costless to obtain. The weak-form hypothesis holds that if such data ever conveyed reliable signals about future performance, all investors already would have learned to exploit the signals. Ultimately, the signals lose their value as they become widely known because a buy signal, for instance, would result in an immediate price increase.

The **semistrong-form** hypothesis states that all publicly available information regarding the prospects of a firm must be reflected already in the stock price. Such information includes, in addition to past prices, fundamental data on the firm's product line, quality of management, balance sheet composition, patents held, earnings forecasts, and accounting practices. Again, if investors have access to such information from publicly available sources, one would expect it to be reflected in stock prices.

Finally, the **strong-form** version of the efficient market hypothesis states that stock prices reflect all information relevant to the firm, even including information available only to company insiders. This version of the hypothesis is quite extreme. Few would argue with the proposition that corporate officers have access to pertinent information long enough before public release to enable them to profit from trading on that information. Indeed, much of the activity of the Securities and Exchange Commission is directed toward preventing insiders from profiting by exploiting their privileged situation. Rule 10b-5 of the Security Exchange Act of 1934 sets limits on trading by corporate officers, directors, and substantial owners, requiring them to report trades to the SEC. These insiders, their relatives, and any associates who trade on information supplied by insiders are considered in violation of the law.

Defining insider trading is not always easy, however. After all, stock analysts are in the business of uncovering information not already widely known to market participants. As we saw in Chapter 3 as well as in the nearby box, the distinction between private and inside information is sometimes murky.

Notice one thing that all versions of the EMH have in common: They all assert that prices should reflect *available* information. We do not expect traders to be superhuman or market prices to always be right. We will always wish for more information about a company's prospects than will be available. Sometimes market prices will turn out in retrospect to have been outrageously high, at other times absurdly low. The EMH asserts only that at the given time, using current information, we cannot be sure if today's prices will ultimately prove themselves to have been too high or too low. If markets are rational, however, we can expect them to be correct on average.

 Concept Check **11.1**

a. Suppose you observed that high-level managers make superior returns on investments in their company's stock. Would this be a violation of weak-form market efficiency? Would it be a violation of strong-form market efficiency?

b. If the weak-form version of the efficient market hypothesis is valid, must the strong-form version also hold? Conversely, does strong-form efficiency imply weak-form efficiency?

11.2   Implications of the EMH

Technical Analysis

Technical analysis is essentially the search for recurrent and predictable patterns in stock prices. Although technicians recognize the value of information regarding future economic prospects of the firm, they believe that such information is not necessary for a successful trading strategy. This is because whatever the fundamental reason for a change in stock price, if the stock price responds slowly enough, the analyst will be able to identify a trend that can be exploited during the adjustment period. The key to successful technical analysis is a sluggish response of stock prices to fundamental supply-and-demand factors. This prerequisite, of course, is diametrically opposed to the notion of an efficient market.

Technical analysts are sometimes called *chartists* because they study records or charts of past stock prices, hoping to find patterns they can exploit to make a profit. As an example of technical analysis, consider the *relative strength* approach. The chartist compares stock performance over a recent period to performance of the market or other stocks in the same industry. A simple version of relative strength takes the ratio of the stock price to a market indicator such as the S&P 500 index. If the ratio increases over time, the stock is said to exhibit relative strength because its price performance is better than that of the broad market. Such strength presumably may continue for a long enough period of time to offer profit opportunities.

One of the most commonly heard components of technical analysis is the notion of **resistance levels** or **support levels.** These values are said to be price levels above which it is difficult for stock prices to rise, or below which it is unlikely for them to fall, and they are believed to be levels determined by market psychology.

Example 11.2   Resistance Levels

Consider stock XYZ, which traded for several months at a price of $72 and then declined to $65. If the stock eventually begins to increase in price, $72 will be considered a resistance level (according to this theory) because investors who bought originally at $72 will be eager to sell their shares as soon as they can break even on their investment. Therefore, at prices near $72 a wave of selling pressure will exist. Such activity imparts a type of "memory" to the market that allows past price history to influence current stock prospects.

The efficient market hypothesis implies that technical analysis should be fruitless. The past history of prices and trading volume is publicly available at minimal cost. Therefore, any information that was ever available from analyzing past prices has already been reflected in stock prices. As investors compete to exploit their common knowledge of a stock's price history, they necessarily drive stock prices to levels where expected rates of return are exactly commensurate with risk. At those levels one cannot expect abnormal returns.

As an example of how this process works, consider what would happen if the market believed that a level of $72 truly was a resistance level for stock XYZ in Example 11.2. No one would be willing to purchase the stock at a price of $71.50, because it would have almost no room to increase in price, but ample room to fall. However, if no one would buy it at $71.50, then $71.50 would become a resistance level. But then, using a similar analysis, no one would buy it at $71, or $70, and so on. The notion of a resistance level is a logical conundrum. Its simple resolution is the recognition that if the stock is ever to sell at $71.50, investors *must* believe that the price can as easily increase as fall. The fact that investors are willing to purchase (or even hold) the stock at $71.50 is evidence of their belief that they can earn a fair expected rate of return at that price.

An interesting question is whether a technical rule that seems to work will continue to work in the future once it becomes widely recognized. A clever analyst may occasionally uncover a profitable trading rule, but the real test of efficient markets is whether the rule itself becomes reflected in stock prices once its value is discovered. Once a useful technical rule (or price pattern) is discovered, it ought to be invalidated when the mass of traders attempts to exploit it. In this sense, price patterns ought to be *self-destructing*.

Thus the market dynamic is one of a continual search for profitable trading rules, followed by destruction by overuse of those rules found to be successful, followed by more searching for yet-undiscovered rules.

 Concept Check **11.2**

If everyone in the market believes in resistance levels, why is it that these beliefs will not become self-fulfilling prophecies?

Fundamental Analysis

Fundamental analysis uses earnings and dividend prospects of the firm, expectations of future interest rates, and risk evaluation of the firm to determine proper stock prices. Ultimately, it represents an attempt to determine the present discounted value of all the payments a stockholder will receive from each share of stock. If that value exceeds the stock price, the fundamental analyst would recommend purchasing the stock.

Fundamental analysts usually start with a study of past earnings and an examination of company balance sheets. They supplement this analysis with further detailed economic analysis, ordinarily including an evaluation of the quality of the firm's management, the firm's standing within its industry, and the prospects for the industry as a whole. The hope is to attain insight into future performance of the firm that is not yet recognized by the rest of the market. Chapters 17, 18, and 19 provide a detailed discussion of the types of analyses that underlie fundamental analysis.

Once again, the efficient market hypothesis predicts that *most* fundamental analysis also is doomed to failure. If the analyst relies on publicly available earnings and industry information, his or her evaluation of the firm's prospects is not likely to be significantly more accurate than those of rival analysts. Many well-informed, well-financed firms conduct such market research, and in the face of such competition it will be difficult to uncover data not also available to other analysts. Only analysts with a unique insight will be rewarded.

Fundamental analysis is much more difficult than merely identifying well-run firms with good prospects. Discovery of good firms does an investor no good in and of itself if the rest of the market also knows those firms are good. If the knowledge is already public, the investor will be forced to pay a high price for those firms and will not realize a superior rate of return.

The trick is not to identify firms that are good, but to find firms that are *better* than everyone else's estimate. Similarly, troubled firms can be great bargains if their prospects are not quite as bad as their stock prices suggest.

This is why fundamental analysis is difficult. It is not enough to do a good analysis of a firm; you can make money only if your analysis is better than that of your competitors because the market price will already reflect all commonly recognized information.

Active versus Passive Portfolio Management

By now it is apparent that casual efforts to pick stocks are not likely to pay off. Competition among investors ensures that any easily implemented stock evaluation technique will be used widely enough so that any insights derived will be reflected in stock prices. Only serious analysis and uncommon techniques are likely to generate the *differential* insight necessary to yield trading profits.

Moreover, these techniques are economically feasible only for managers of large portfolios. If you have only $100,000 to invest, even a 1% per year improvement in performance generates only $1,000 per year, hardly enough to justify herculean efforts. The billion-dollar manager, however, reaps extra income of $10 million annually from the same 1% increment.

If small investors are at a disadvantage in active portfolio management, what are their choices? The small investor probably is better off investing in mutual funds or exchange-traded funds. By pooling resources in this way, small investors can gain from economies of scale.

More difficult decisions remain, though. Can investors be sure that even large funds have the ability or resources to uncover mispriced stocks? Furthermore, will any mispricing be sufficiently large to repay the costs entailed in active portfolio management?

Proponents of the efficient market hypothesis believe that active management is largely wasted effort and unlikely to justify the expenses incurred. Therefore, they advocate a **passive investment strategy** that makes no attempt to outsmart the market. A passive strategy aims only at establishing a well-diversified portfolio of securities without attempting to find under- or overvalued stocks. Passive management is usually characterized by a buy-and-hold strategy. Because the efficient market theory indicates that stock prices are at fair levels, given all available information, it makes no sense to buy and sell securities frequently, which generates large trading costs without increasing expected performance.

One common strategy for passive management is to create an **index fund,** which is a fund designed to replicate the performance of a broad-based index of stocks. For example, Vanguard's 500 Index Fund holds stocks in direct proportion to their weight in the Standard & Poor's 500 stock price index. The performance of the 500 Index Fund therefore replicates the performance of the S&P 500. Investors in this fund obtain broad diversification with low management fees. The fees can be kept to a minimum because Vanguard does not need to pay analysts to assess stock prospects and does not incur transaction costs from high portfolio turnover. Indeed, while the typical annual charge for an actively managed equity fund is almost 1% of assets, the expense ratio of the 500 Index Fund is only .05%. Vanguard's 500 Index Fund is among the largest equity mutual funds, with over $230 billion of assets in 2016, and between 20% and 25% of assets in equity funds are indexed.

Indexing need not be limited to the S&P 500, however. For example, some of the funds offered by the Vanguard Group track the broader-based CRSP[8] index of the total U.S. equity market, the Barclays U.S. Aggregate Bond Index, the CRSP index of small-capitalization U.S. companies, and the *Financial Times* indexes of the European and Pacific Basin equity markets. Several other mutual fund complexes offer indexed portfolios, but Vanguard dominates the retail market for indexed products.

---

[8]CRSP is the Center for Research in Security Prices at the University of Chicago.

Exchange-traded funds, or ETFs, are a close (and often lower-expense) alternative to indexed mutual funds. As noted in Chapter 4, these are shares in diversified portfolios that can be bought or sold just like shares of individual stock. ETFs matching several broad stock market indexes such as the S&P 500 or CRSP indexes and dozens of international and industry stock indexes are available to investors who want to hold a diversified sector of a market without attempting active security selection.

 Concept Check **11.3**

What would happen to market efficiency if *all* investors attempted to follow a passive strategy?

The Role of Portfolio Management in an Efficient Market

If the market is efficient, why not pick stocks by throwing darts at *The Wall Street Journal* instead of trying rationally to choose a stock portfolio? This is a tempting conclusion to draw from the notion that security prices are fairly set, but it is far too facile. There is a role for rational portfolio management, even in perfectly efficient markets.

You have learned that a basic principle in portfolio selection is diversification. Even if all stocks are priced fairly, each still poses firm-specific risk that can be eliminated through diversification. Therefore, rational security selection, even in an efficient market, calls for the selection of a well-diversified portfolio providing the systematic risk level that the investor wants.

Rational investment policy also requires that tax considerations be reflected in security choice. High-tax-bracket investors generally will not want the same securities that low-tax-bracket investors find favorable. At an obvious level, high-bracket investors find it advantageous to buy tax-exempt municipal bonds despite their relatively low pre-tax yields, whereas those same bonds are unattractive to low-tax-bracket or tax-exempt investors. At a more subtle level, high-bracket investors might want to tilt their portfolios in the direction of capital gains as opposed to interest income, because capital gains are taxed less heavily and because the option to defer the realization of capital gains income is more valuable the higher the current tax bracket. They also will be more attracted to investment opportunities for which returns are sensitive to tax benefits, such as real estate ventures.

A third argument for rational portfolio management relates to the particular risk profile of the investor. For example, a Toyota executive whose annual bonus depends on Toyota's profits generally should not invest additional amounts in auto stocks. To the extent that his or her compensation already depends on Toyota's well-being, the executive is already overinvested in Toyota and should not exacerbate the lack of diversification. This lesson was learned with considerable pain in September 2008 by Lehman Brothers employees who were famously invested in their own firm when the company failed. Roughly 30% of the shares in the firm were owned by its 24,000 employees, and their losses on those shares totaled around $10 billion.

Investors of varying ages also might warrant different portfolio policies with regard to risk bearing. For example, older investors who are essentially living off savings might choose to avoid long-term bonds whose market values fluctuate dramatically with changes in interest rates (discussed in Part Four). Because these investors are living off accumulated savings, they require conservation of principal. In contrast, younger investors might be more inclined toward long-term inflation-indexed bonds. The steady flow of real income over long periods of time that is locked in with these bonds can be more important than preservation of principal to those with long life expectancies.

In conclusion, there is a role for portfolio management even in an efficient market. Investors' optimal positions will vary according to factors such as age, tax bracket, risk aversion, and employment. The role of the portfolio manager in an efficient market is to tailor the portfolio to these needs, rather than to beat the market.

Resource Allocation

We've focused so far on the investment implications of the efficient market hypothesis. Deviations from efficiency may offer profit opportunities to better-informed traders at the expense of less-informed ones.

However, deviations from informational efficiency would also result in a large cost that would be borne by all citizens, namely, inefficient resource allocation. Recall that in a capitalist economy, investments in *real* assets such as plant, equipment, and know-how are guided in large part by the prices of financial assets. For example, if the value of telecommunication capacity reflected in stock market prices exceeds the cost of install-ing such capacity, managers might justifiably conclude that telecom investments seem to have positive net present value. In this manner, capital market prices guide allocation of real resources.

If markets were inefficient and securities commonly mispriced, then resources would be systematically misallocated. Corporations with overpriced securities would be able to obtain capital too cheaply, and corporations with undervalued securities might forgo investment opportunities because the cost of raising capital would be too high. Therefore, inefficient capital markets would diminish one of the most potent benefits of a market economy. As an example of what can go wrong, consider the dot-com bubble of the late 1990s, which sent a strong but, as it turned out, wildly overoptimistic signal about pros-pects for Internet and telecommunication firms and ultimately led to substantial overin-vestment in those industries.

Before writing off markets as a means to guide resource allocation, however, one has to be reasonable about what can be expected from market forecasts. In particular, you shouldn't confuse an efficient market, where all available information is reflected in prices, with a perfect-foresight market. As we said earlier, "all available information" is still far from complete information, and generally rational market forecasts will sometimes be wrong; sometimes, in fact, they will be very wrong.

11.3 Event Studies

The notion of informationally efficient markets leads to a powerful research methodol-ogy. If security prices reflect all currently available information, then price changes must reflect new information. Therefore, it seems that one should be able to measure the impor-tance of an event of interest by examining price changes during the period in which the event occurs.

An **event study** describes a technique of empirical financial research that enables an observer to assess the impact of a particular event on a firm's stock price. A stock market analyst might want to study the impact of dividend changes on stock prices, for example. An event study would quantify the relationship between dividend changes and stock returns.

Analyzing the impact of any particular event is more difficult than it might at first appear. On any day, stock prices respond to a wide range of economic news such as updated forecasts for GDP, inflation rates, interest rates, or corporate profitability. Isolating the part of a stock price movement that is attributable to a specific event is not a trivial exercise.

The general approach starts with a proxy for what the stock's return would have been in the absence of the event. The **abnormal return** due to the event is estimated as the difference between the stock's actual return and this benchmark. Several methodologies for estimating the benchmark return are used in practice. For example, a very simple approach measures the stock's abnormal return as its return minus that of a broad market index. An obvious refinement is to compare the stock's return to those of other stocks matched according to criteria such as firm size, beta, recent performance, or ratio of price to book value per share. Another approach estimates normal returns using an asset pricing model such as the CAPM or one of its multifactor generalizations such as the Fama-French three-factor model.

To illustrate, we use a "market model" to estimate abnormal returns. This approach is based on the index models we introduced in Chapter 9. Recall that a single-index model holds that stock returns are determined by a market factor and a firm-specific factor. The stock return, r_t, during a given period t, would be expressed mathematically as

$$r_t = a + br_{Mt} + e_t \tag{11.1}$$

where r_{Mt} is the market's rate of return during the period and e_t is the part of a security's return resulting from firm-specific events. The parameter b measures sensitivity to the market return, and a is the average rate of return the stock would realize in a period with a zero market return.[9] Equation 11.1 therefore provides a decomposition of r_t into market and firm-specific factors. The firm-specific or abnormal return may be interpreted as the unexpected return that results from the event.

Determination of the abnormal return in a given period requires an estimate of e_t. Therefore, we rewrite Equation 11.1:

$$e_t = r_t - (a + br_{Mt}) \tag{11.2}$$

Equation 11.2 has a simple interpretation: The residual, e_t, that is, the component presumably due to the event in question, is the stock's return over and above what one would predict based on broad market movements in that period, given the stock's sensitivity to the market.

The market model is a highly flexible tool, because it can be generalized to include richer models of benchmark returns, for example, by including industry as well as broad market returns on the right-hand side of Equation 11.1, or returns on indexes constructed to match characteristics such as firm size. However, one must be careful that regression parameters in Equation 11.1 (the intercept a and slope b) are estimated properly. In particular, they must be estimated using data sufficiently separated in time from the event in question that they are not affected by event-period abnormal stock performance. In part because of this vulnerability of the market model, returns on characteristic-matched portfolios have become more widely used benchmarks in recent years.

---

[9]We know from Chapter 9 that the CAPM implies that the intercept a in Equation 11.1 should equal $r_f(1 - \beta)$. Nevertheless, it is customary to estimate the intercept in this equation empirically rather than imposing the CAPM value. One justification for this practice is that empirically fitted security market lines seem flatter than predicted by the CAPM (see Chapter 13), which would make the intercept implied by the CAPM too small.

Example 11.3   Abnormal Returns

Suppose that the analyst has estimated that $a = .05\%$ and $b = .8$. On a day that the market goes up by 1%, you would predict from Equation 11.1 that the stock should rise by an expected value of $.05\% + .8 \times 1\% = .85\%$. If the stock actually rises by 2%, the analyst would infer that firm-specific news that day caused an additional stock return of $2\% - .85\% = 1.15\%$. This is the abnormal return for the day.

We measure the impact of an event by estimating the abnormal return on a stock (or group of stocks) at the moment the information about the event becomes known to the market. For example, in a study of the impact of merger attempts on the stock prices of target firms, the announcement date is the date on which the public is informed that a merger is to be attempted. The abnormal returns of each firm surrounding the announcement date are computed, and the statistical significance and magnitude of the typical abnormal return indicate the impact of the newly released information.

One concern that complicates event studies arises from *leakage* of information. Leakage occurs when information regarding a relevant event is released to a small group of investors before official public release. In this case the stock price might start to increase (in the case of a "good news" announcement) days or weeks before the official announcement date. Any abnormal return on the announcement date is then a poor indicator of the total impact of the information release. A better indicator would be the **cumulative abnormal return (CAR),** which is simply the sum of all abnormal returns over the time period of interest. The cumulative abnormal return thus captures the total firm-specific stock movement for an entire period when the market might be responding to new information.

Figure 11.1 (earlier in the chapter) presents the results from a fairly typical event study. The authors of this study were interested in leakage of information before merger announcements and constructed a sample of firms that were targets of takeover attempts. In most takeovers, stockholders of the acquired firms sell their shares to the acquirer at substantial premiums over market value. Announcement of a takeover attempt is good news for shareholders of the target firm and therefore should cause stock prices to jump.

Figure 11.1 confirms the good-news nature of the announcements. On the announcement day, called day 0, the average cumulative abnormal return (CAR) for the sample of takeover candidates increases substantially, indicating a large and positive abnormal return on the announcement date. Notice that immediately *after* the announcement date the CAR no longer increases or decreases significantly. This is in accord with the efficient market hypothesis. Once the new information became public, the stock prices jumped almost immediately in response to the good news. With prices once again fairly set, reflecting the effect of the new information, further abnormal returns on any particular day are equally likely to be positive or negative. In fact, for a sample of many firms, the average abnormal return should be extremely close to zero, and thus the CAR will show neither upward nor downward drift. This is precisely the pattern shown in Figure 11.1.

The pattern of returns for the days preceding the public announcement date yields some interesting evidence about efficient markets and information leakage. If insider trading rules were perfectly obeyed and perfectly enforced, stock prices should show no abnormal returns on days before the public release of relevant news, because no special firm-specific information would be available to the market before public announcement. Instead, we should observe a clean jump in the stock price only on the announcement day. In fact, Figure 11.1 shows that the prices of the takeover targets clearly start an upward drift 30 days before the public announcement. It appears that information is leaking to some market participants who then purchase the stocks before the public announcement. Such evidence of leakage appears almost universally in event studies, suggesting at least some abuse of insider trading rules.

Nevertheless, the SEC also can take some comfort from patterns such as that in Figure 11.1. If insider trading rules were widely and flagrantly violated, we would expect to see abnormal returns earlier than they appear in these results. For example, in the case of mergers, the CAR would turn positive as soon as acquiring firms decided on their take-over targets, because insiders would start trading immediately. By the time of the public announcement, the insiders would have bid up the stock prices of target firms to levels reflecting the merger attempt, and the abnormal returns on the actual public announce-ment date would be close to zero. The dramatic increase in the CAR that we see on the announcement date indicates that a good deal of these announcements are indeed news to the market and that stock prices do not already reflect complete knowledge about the take-overs. It would appear, therefore, that SEC enforcement does have a substantial effect on restricting insider trading, even if some amount of it still persists.

Event study methodology has become a widely accepted tool to measure the economic impact of a wide range of events. For example, the SEC regularly uses event studies to measure illicit gains captured by traders who may have violated insider trading or other securities laws.[10] Event studies are also used in fraud cases, where the courts must assess damages caused by a fraudulent activity.

Example 11.4   Using Abnormal Returns to Infer Damages

Suppose the stock of a company with market value of $100 million falls by 4% on the day that news of an accounting scandal surfaces. The rest of the market, however, generally does well that day. The market indexes are up sharply and, on the basis of the usual relation-ship between the stock and the market, one would have expected a 2% gain on the stock. We would conclude that the impact of the scandal was a 6% drop in value, the difference between the 2% gain that we would have expected and the 4% drop actually observed. One might then infer that the damages sustained from the scandal were $6 million, because the value of the firm (after adjusting for general market movements) fell by 6% of $100 million when investors became aware of the news and reassessed the value of the stock.

 Concept Check **11.4**

Suppose that we see negative abnormal returns (declining CARs) after an announce-ment date. Is this a violation of efficient markets?

---

[10]For a review of SEC applications of this technique, see Mark Mitchell and Jeffry Netter, "The Role of Financial Economics in Securities Fraud Cases: Applications at the Securities and Exchange Commission," *The Business Lawyer* 49 (February 1994), pp. 545–90.

11.4   Are Markets Efficient?

The Issues

Not surprisingly, the efficient market hypothesis does not exactly arouse enthusiasm in the community of professional portfolio managers. It implies that a great deal of the activity of these managers—the search for undervalued securities—is at best wasted effort, and quite probably harmful to clients because it costs money and leads to imperfectly diversified portfolios. Consequently, the EMH has never been widely accepted on Wall Street, and debate continues today on the degree to which security analysis can improve investment performance. Before discussing empirical tests of the hypothesis, we raise three issues that together imply that the debate probably never will be settled: the *magnitude issue,* the *selection bias issue,* and the *lucky event issue.*

The Magnitude Issue   We noted that an investment manager overseeing a $5 billion portfolio who can improve performance by only .1% per year will increase investment earnings by .001 × $5 billion = $5 million annually. This manager clearly would be worth her salary! Yet can we, as observers, statistically measure her contribution? Probably not: A .1% annual contribution would be swamped by the volatility of the market. Remember, the annual standard deviation of the well-diversified S&P 500 index has been around 20%. Against these fluctuations, a small increase in performance would be hard to detect.

All might agree that stock prices are very close to fair values and that only managers of large portfolios can earn enough trading profits to make the exploitation of minor mispricing worth the effort. According to this view, the actions of intelligent investment managers are the driving force behind the constant evolution of market prices to fair levels. Rather than ask the qualitative question, Are markets efficient? we ought instead to ask a more quantitative question: How efficient are markets?

The Selection Bias Issue   Suppose that you discover an investment scheme that could really make money. You have two choices: either publish your technique in *The Wall Street Journal* to win fleeting fame, or keep your technique secret and use it to earn millions of dollars. Most investors would choose the latter option, which presents us with a conundrum. Only investors who find that an investment scheme cannot generate abnormal returns will be willing to report their findings to the whole world. Hence opponents of the efficient markets' view of the world always can use evidence that various techniques do not provide investment rewards as proof that the techniques that *do* work simply are not being reported to the public. This is a problem in *selection bias;* the outcomes we are able to observe have been preselected in favor of failed attempts. Therefore, we cannot fairly evaluate the true ability of portfolio managers to generate winning stock market strategies.

The Lucky Event Issue   In virtually any month it seems we read an article about some investor or investment company with a fantastic investment performance over the recent past. Surely the superior records of such investors disprove the efficient market hypothesis.

Yet this conclusion is far from obvious. As an analogy to the investment game, consider a contest to flip the most number of heads out of 50 trials using a fair coin. The expected outcome for any person is, of course, 50% heads and 50% tails. If 10,000 people, however, compete in this contest, it would not be surprising if at least one or two contestants flipped more than 75% heads. In fact, elementary statistics tells us that the expected number of

How to Guarantee a Successful Market Newsletter

Suppose you want to make your fortune publishing a market newsletter. You first need to convince potential subscribers that you have talent worth paying for. But what if you have no talent? The solution is simple: Start eight newsletters.

In year 1, let four of your newsletters predict an up-market and four a down-market. In year 2, let half of the originally optimistic group of newsletters continue to predict an up-market and the other half a down-market. Do the same for the originally pessimistic group. Continue in this manner to obtain the pattern of predictions in the table that follows (U = prediction of an up-market, D = prediction of a down-market).

After three years, no matter what has happened to the market, one of the newsletters would have had a perfect prediction record. This is because after three years there are $2^3 = 8$ outcomes for the market, and we have covered all eight possibilities with the eight newsletters. Now, we simply slough off the seven unsuccessful newsletters and market the eighth newsletter based on its perfect track record. If we want to establish a newsletter with a perfect track record over a four-year period, we need $2^4 = 16$ newsletters. A five-year period requires 32 newsletters, and so on.

After the fact, the one newsletter that was always right will attract attention for your uncanny foresight and investors will rush to pay large fees for its advice. Your fortune is made, and you have never even researched the market!

WARNING: This scheme is illegal! The point, however, is that with hundreds of market newsletters, you can find one that has stumbled onto an apparently remarkable string of successful predictions without any real degree of skill. After the fact, someone's prediction history can seem to imply great forecasting skill. This person is the one we will read about in The Wall Street Journal; the others will be forgotten.

Newsletter Predictions								
Year	1	2	3	4	5	6	7	8
1	U	U	U	U	D	D	D	D
2	U	U	D	D	U	U	D	D
3	U	D	U	D	U	D	U	D

contestants flipping 75% or more heads would be two. It would be silly, though, to crown these people the "head-flipping champions of the world." Obviously, they are simply the contestants who happened to get lucky on the day of the event. (See the nearby box.)

The analogy to efficient markets is clear. Under the hypothesis that any stock is fairly priced given all available information, any bet on a stock is simply a coin toss. There is equal likelihood of winning or losing the bet. However, if many investors using a variety of schemes make fair bets, statistically speaking, *some* of those investors will be lucky and win a great majority of the bets. For every big winner, there may be many big losers, but we never hear of these managers. The winners, though, turn up in *The Wall Street Journal* as the latest stock market gurus; then they can make a fortune publishing market newsletters.

Our point is that after the fact there will have been at least one successful investment scheme. A doubter will call the results luck; the successful investor will call it skill. The proper test would be to see whether the successful investors can repeat their performance in another period, yet this approach is rarely taken.

With these caveats in mind, we turn now to some of the empirical tests of the efficient market hypothesis.

✓ Concept Check **11.5**

Legg Mason's Value Trust, managed by Bill Miller, outperformed the S&P 500 in each of the 15 years ending in 2005. Is Miller's performance sufficient to dissuade you from a belief in efficient markets? If not, would *any* performance record be sufficient to dissuade you? Now consider that in the next three years, the fund dramatically underperformed the S&P 500; by the end of 2008, its cumulative 18-year performance was barely different from the index. Does this affect your opinion?

Weak-Form Tests: Patterns in Stock Returns

Returns over Short Horizons   Early tests of efficient markets were tests of the weak form. Could speculators find trends in past prices that would enable them to earn abnormal profits? This is essentially a test of the efficacy of technical analysis.

One way of discerning trends in stock prices is by measuring the *serial correlation* of stock market returns. Serial correlation refers to the tendency for stock returns to be related to past returns. Positive serial correlation means that positive returns tend to follow positive returns (a momentum type of property). Negative serial correlation means that positive returns tend to be followed by negative returns (a reversal or "correction" property). Both Conrad and Kaul[11] and Lo and MacKinlay[12] examine weekly returns of NYSE stocks and find positive serial correlation over short horizons. However, the correlation coefficients of weekly returns tend to be fairly small, at least for large stocks for which price data are the most reliably up-to-date. Thus, while these studies demonstrate weak price trends over short periods,[13] the evidence does not clearly suggest the existence of trading opportunities.

While broad market indexes demonstrate only weak serial correlation, there appears to be stronger momentum in performance across market sectors exhibiting the best and worst recent returns. In an investigation of intermediate-horizon stock price behavior (using 3- to 12-month holding periods), Jegadeesh and Titman[14] found a **momentum effect** in which good or bad recent performance of particular stocks continues over time. They conclude that while the performance of individual stocks is highly unpredictable, *portfolios* of the best-performing stocks in the recent past appear to outperform other stocks with enough reliability to offer profit opportunities. Thus, it appears that there is evidence of short- to intermediate-horizon price momentum in both the aggregate market and cross-sectionally (i.e., across particular stocks).

Returns over Long Horizons   Although studies of short- to intermediate-horizon returns have detected momentum in stock market prices, tests of long-horizon returns (i.e., returns over multiyear periods) have found suggestions of pronounced *negative* long-term serial correlation in the performance of the aggregate market.[15] The latter result has given rise to a "fads hypothesis," which asserts that the stock market might overreact to relevant news. Such overreaction leads to positive serial correlation (momentum) over short time horizons. Subsequent correction of the overreaction leads to poor performance following good performance and vice versa. The corrections mean that a run of positive returns eventually will tend to be followed by negative returns, leading to negative serial correlation over longer horizons. These episodes of apparent overshooting followed by correction give the stock market the appearance of fluctuating around its fair value.

---

[11]Jennifer Conrad and Gautam Kaul, "Time-Variation in Expected Returns," *Journal of Business* 61 (October 1988), pp. 409–25.

[12]Andrew W. Lo and A. Craig MacKinlay, "Stock Market Prices Do Not Follow Random Walks: Evidence from a Simple Specification Test," *Review of Financial Studies* 1 (1988), pp. 41–66.

[13]On the other hand, there is evidence that share prices of individual securities (as opposed to broad market indexes) are more prone to reversals than continuations at very short horizons. See, for example, B. Lehmann, "Fads, Martingales and Market Efficiency," *Quarterly Journal of Economics* 105 (February 1990), pp. 1–28; and N. Jegadeesh, "Evidence of Predictable Behavior of Security Returns," *Journal of Finance* 45 (September 1990), pp. 881–98. However, as Lehmann notes, this is probably best interpreted as due to liquidity problems after big movements in stock prices as market makers adjust their positions in the stock.

[14]Narasimhan Jegadeesh and Sheridan Titman, "Returns to Buying Winners and Selling Losers: Implications for Stock Market Efficiency," *Journal of Finance* 48 (March 1993), pp. 65–91.

[15]Eugene F. Fama and Kenneth R. French, "Permanent and Temporary Components of Stock Prices," *Journal of Political Economy* 96 (April 1988), pp. 24–73; and James Poterba and Lawrence Summers, "Mean Reversion in Stock Prices: Evidence and Implications," *Journal of Financial Economics* 22 (October 1988), pp. 27–59.

These long-horizon results are dramatic but still not conclusive. An alternative inter-pretation of these results holds that they indicate only that the market risk premium varies over time. For example, when the risk premium and the required return on the market rise, stock prices will fall. When the market then rises (on average) at this higher rate of return, the data convey the impression of a stock price recovery. In this view, the apparent overshooting and correction are in fact no more than a rational response of market prices to changes in discount rates.

In addition to studies suggestive of overreaction in overall stock market returns over long horizons, many other studies suggest that over long horizons, extreme performance in particular securities also tends to reverse itself: The stocks that have performed best in the recent past seem to underperform the rest of the market in following periods, while the worst past performers tend to offer above-average future performance. DeBondt and Thaler[16] and Chopra, Lakonishok, and Ritter[17] find strong tendencies for poorly perform-ing stocks in one period to experience sizable reversals over the subsequent period, while the best-performing stocks in a given period tend to follow with poor performance in the following period.

For example, the DeBondt and Thaler study found that if one were to rank the per-formance of stocks over a five-year period and then group stocks into portfolios based on investment performance, the base-period "loser" portfolio (defined as the 35 stocks with the worst investment performance) outperformed the "winner" portfolio (the top 35 stocks) by an average of 25% (cumulative return) in the following three-year period. This **reversal effect,** in which losers rebound and winners fade back, suggests that the stock market overreacts to relevant news. After the overreaction is recognized, extreme investment performance is reversed. This phenomenon would imply that a *contrarian* investment strategy—investing in recent losers and avoiding recent winners—should be profitable. Moreover, these returns seem pronounced enough to be exploited profitably.

Thus it appears that there may be short-run momentum but long-run reversal patterns in price behavior both for the market as a whole and across sectors of the market. One inter-pretation of this pattern is that short-run overreaction (which causes momentum in prices) may lead to long-term reversals (when the market recognizes its past error).

Predictors of Broad Market Returns

Several studies have documented the ability of easily observed variables to predict market returns. For example, Fama and French[18] showed that the return on the aggregate stock mar-ket tends to be higher when the dividend/price ratio, the dividend yield, is high. Campbell and Shiller[19] found that the earnings yield can predict market returns. Keim and Stam-baugh[20] showed that bond market data such as the spread between yields on high- and low-grade corporate bonds also help predict broad market returns.

Again, the interpretation of these results is difficult. On the one hand, they may imply that abnormal stock returns can be predicted, in violation of the efficient market hypothesis.

[16]Werner F. M. DeBondt and Richard Thaler, "Does the Stock Market Overreact?" *Journal of Finance* 40 (1985), pp. 793–805.

[17]Navin Chopra, Josef Lakonishok, and Jay R. Ritter, "Measuring Abnormal Performance: Do Stocks Overre-act?" *Journal of Financial Economics* 31 (1992), pp. 235–68.

[18]Eugene F. Fama and Kenneth R. French, "Dividend Yields and Expected Stock Returns," *Journal of Financial Economics* 22 (October 1988), pp. 3–25.

[19]John Y. Campbell and Robert Shiller, "Stock Prices, Earnings and Expected Dividends," *Journal of Finance* 43 (July 1988), pp. 661–76.

[20]Donald B. Keim and Robert F. Stambaugh, "Predicting Returns in the Stock and Bond Markets," *Journal of Financial Economics* 17 (1986), pp. 357–90.

More probably, however, these variables are proxying for variation in the market risk premium. For example, given a level of dividends or earnings, stock prices will be lower and dividend and earnings yields will be higher when the risk premium (and therefore the expected market return) is higher. Thus a high dividend or earnings yield will be associated with higher market returns. But rather than a violation of market efficiency, the predictability of market returns is due to predictability in the risk premium.

Fama and French[21] showed that the yield spread between high- and low-grade bonds has greater predictive power for returns on low-grade bonds than for returns on high-grade bonds, and greater predictive power for stock returns than for bond returns, suggesting that the predictability in returns is in fact a risk premium rather than evidence of market inefficiency. Similarly, the fact that the dividend yield on stocks helps to predict bond market returns suggests that the yield captures a risk premium common to both markets rather than mispricing in the equity market.

Semistrong Tests: Market Anomalies

Fundamental analysis uses a much wider range of information to create portfolios than does technical analysis. Investigations of the efficacy of fundamental analysis ask whether publicly available information beyond the trading history of a security can be used to improve investment performance; as such, they are tests of semistrong-form market efficiency. Surprisingly, several easily accessible statistics, for example, a stock's price–earnings ratio or its market capitalization, seem to predict abnormal risk-adjusted returns. Findings such as these, which we will review in the following pages, are difficult to reconcile with the efficient market hypothesis and therefore are often referred to as efficient market **anomalies.**

A difficulty in interpreting these tests is that we usually need to adjust for portfolio risk before evaluating the success of an investment strategy. Some tests, for example, have used the CAPM to adjust for risk. However, we know that even if beta is a relevant descriptor of stock risk, the empirically measured quantitative trade-off between risk as measured by beta and expected return differs from the predictions of the CAPM. (We review this evidence in Chapter 13.) If we use the CAPM to adjust portfolio returns for risk, inappropriate adjustments may lead to the conclusion that various portfolio strategies can generate superior returns, when, in fact, the risk adjustment procedure has simply failed.

Another way to put this is to note that tests of risk-adjusted returns are *joint tests* of the efficient market hypothesis *and* the risk adjustment procedure. If it appears that a portfolio strategy can generate superior returns, we must then choose between rejecting the EMH and rejecting the risk adjustment technique. Usually, the risk adjustment technique is based on more-questionable assumptions than is the EMH; by opting to reject the procedure, we are left with no conclusion about market efficiency.

An example of this issue is the discovery by Basu[22] that portfolios of low price–earnings (P/E) ratio stocks have provided higher returns than high P/E portfolios. The **P/E effect** holds up even if returns are adjusted for portfolio beta. Is this a confirmation that the market systematically misprices stocks according to P/E ratio? This would be an extremely surprising and, to us, disturbing conclusion, because analysis of P/E ratios is

[21]Eugene F. Fama and Kenneth R. French, "Business Conditions and Expected Returns on Stocks and Bonds," *Journal of Financial Economics* 25 (November 1989), pp. 3–22.

[22]Sanjoy Basu, "The Investment Performance of Common Stocks in Relation to Their Price-Earnings Ratios: A Test of the Efficient Market Hypothesis," *Journal of Finance* 32 (June 1977), pp. 663–82; and "The Relationship between Earnings Yield, Market Value, and Return for NYSE Common Stocks: Further Evidence," *Journal of Financial Economics* 12 (June 1983).

such a simple procedure. Although it may be possible to earn superior returns through unusual insight, it hardly seems plausible that such a simplistic technique is enough to generate abnormal returns.

Another interpretation of these results is that returns are not properly adjusted for risk. If two firms have the same expected earnings, the riskier stock will sell at a lower price and lower P/E ratio. Because of its higher risk, the low P/E stock also will have higher expected returns. Therefore, unless the CAPM beta fully adjusts for risk, P/E will act as a useful additional descriptor of risk and will be associated with abnormal returns if the CAPM is used to establish benchmark performance.

The Small-Firm Effect   The so-called size or **small-firm effect,** originally documented by Banz,[23] is illustrated in Figure 11.3. It shows the historical performance of portfolios formed by dividing the NYSE stocks into 10 portfolios each year according to firm size (i.e., the total value of outstanding equity). Average annual returns between 1926 and 2015 are consistently higher on the small-firm portfolios. The difference in average annual return between portfolio 10 (with the largest firms) and portfolio 1 (with the smallest firms) is 7.65%. Of course, the smaller-firm portfolios tend to be riskier. But even when returns are adjusted for risk using the CAPM, there is still a consistent premium for the smaller-sized portfolios.

Imagine earning a premium of this size on a billion-dollar portfolio. Yet it is remarkable that following a simple (even simplistic) rule such as "invest in low-capitalization stocks" should enable an investor to earn excess returns. After all, any investor can measure firm size at little cost. One would not expect such minimal effort to yield such large rewards.

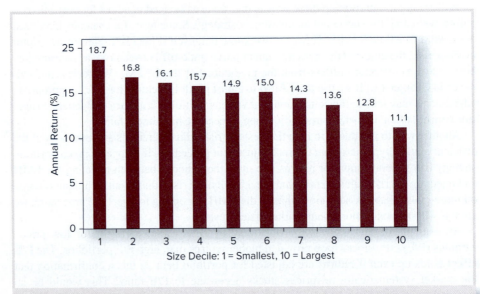

Figure 11.3 Average annual return for 10 size-based portfolios, 1926–2015

Source: Authors' calculations, using data obtained from Professor Ken French's data library at **http://mba.tuck .dartmouth.edu/pages/faculty/ken.french/data_library.html.**

[23]Rolf Banz, "The Relationship between Return and Market Value of Common Stocks," *Journal of Financial Economics* 9 (March 1981).

The Neglected-Firm Effect and Liquidity Effects   Arbel and Strebel[24] gave another interpretation of the small-firm effect. Because small firms tend to be neglected by large institutional traders, information about smaller firms is less available. This information deficiency makes smaller firms riskier investments that command higher returns. "Brand-name" firms, after all, are subject to considerable monitoring from institutional investors, which promises high-quality information, and presumably investors do not purchase "generic" stocks without the prospect of greater returns.

Merton[25] provides a rationale for this **neglected-firm effect.** He shows that neglected firms might be expected to earn higher equilibrium returns as compensation for the risk associated with limited information. In this sense the neglected-firm premium is not strictly a market inefficiency, but is in fact a type of risk premium.

Work by Amihud and Mendelson[26] on the effect of liquidity on stock returns might be related to both the small-firm and neglected-firm effects. As we noted in Chapter 9, investors will demand a rate-of-return premium to invest in less-liquid stocks that entail higher trading costs. In accord with this hypothesis, Amihud and Mendelson showed that these stocks have a strong tendency to exhibit abnormally high risk-adjusted rates of return. Because small and less-analyzed stocks as a rule are less liquid, the liquidity effect might be a partial explanation of their abnormal returns. However, exploiting these effects can be more difficult than it would appear. The high trading costs on small stocks can easily wipe out any apparent abnormal profit opportunity.

Book-to-Market Ratios   Fama and French[27] showed that a powerful predictor of returns across securities is the ratio of the book value of the firm's equity to the market value of equity. Fama and French stratified firms into 10 groups according to book-to-market ratios and examined the average monthly rate of return of each of the 10 groups. Figure 11.4 is an updated version of their results. The decile with the highest book-to-market ratio had an average annual return of 17.2%, while the lowest-ratio decile averaged only 11.1%. The dramatic

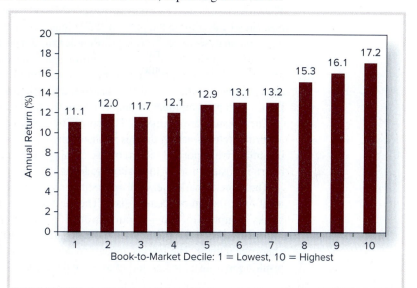

Figure 11.4 Average return as a function of book-to-market ratio, 1926–2015

Source: Authors' calculations, using data obtained from Professor Ken French's data library at **http://mba.tuck.dartmouth.edu/pages/faculty/ken.french/data_library.html.**

[24]Avner Arbel and Paul J. Strebel, "Pay Attention to Neglected Firms," *Journal of Portfolio Management,* Winter 1983.

[25]Robert C. Merton, "A Simple Model of Capital Market Equilibrium with Incomplete Information," *Journal of Finance* 42 (1987), pp. 483–510.

[26]Yakov Amihud and Haim Mendelson, "Asset Pricing and the Bid–Ask Spread," *Journal of Financial Economics* 17 (December 1986), pp. 223–50; and "Liquidity, Asset Prices, and Financial Policy," *Financial Analysts Journal* 47 (November/December 1991), pp. 56–66.

[27]Eugene F. Fama and Kenneth R. French, "The Cross Section of Expected Stock Returns," *Journal of Finance* 47 (1992), pp. 427–65.

dependence of returns on book-to-market ratio is independent of beta, suggesting either that high book-to-market ratio firms are relatively underpriced, or that the book-to-market ratio is serving as a proxy for a risk factor that affects equilibrium expected returns.

In fact, Fama and French found that after controlling for the size and **book-to-market effects,** beta seemed to have no power to explain average security returns.[28] This finding is an important challenge to the notion of rational markets, because it seems to imply that a factor that should affect returns—systematic risk—seems not to matter, while a factor that should not matter—the book-to-market ratio—seems capable of predicting future returns. We will return to the interpretation of this anomaly.

Post–Earnings-Announcement Price Drift   A fundamental principle of efficient markets is that any new information ought to be reflected in stock prices very rapidly. When good news is made public, for example, the stock price should jump immediately. A puzzling anomaly, therefore, is the apparently sluggish response of stock prices to firms' earnings announcements, as uncovered by Ball and Brown.[29] Their results were later confirmed and extended in many other papers.[30]

The "news content" of an earnings announcement can be evaluated by comparing the announcement of actual earnings to the value previously expected by market participants. The difference is the "earnings surprise." (Market expectations of earnings can be roughly measured by averaging the published earnings forecasts of Wall Street analysts or by applying trend analysis to past earnings.) Rendleman, Jones, and Latané[31] provide an influential study of sluggish price response to earnings announcements. They calculate earnings surprises for a large sample of firms, rank the magnitude of the surprise, divide firms into 10 deciles based on the size of the surprise, and calculate abnormal returns for each decile. Figure 11.5 plots cumulative abnormal returns by decile.

Their results are dramatic. The correlation between ranking by earnings surprise and abnormal returns across deciles is unsurprising. There is a large abnormal return (a jump in cumulative abnormal return) on the earnings announcement day (time 0). The abnormal return is positive for positive-surprise firms and negative for negative-surprise firms.

The more remarkable, and interesting, result of the study concerns stock price movement *after* the announcement date. The cumulative abnormal returns of positive-surprise stocks continue to rise—in other words, exhibit momentum—even after the earnings information becomes public, while the negative-surprise firms continue to suffer negative abnormal returns. The market appears to adjust to the earnings information only gradually, resulting in a sustained period of abnormal returns.

[28]However, a study by S. P. Kothari, Jay Shanken, and Richard G. Sloan, "Another Look at the Cross-Section of Expected Stock Returns," *Journal of Finance* 50 (March 1995), pp. 185–224, finds that when betas are estimated using annual rather than monthly returns, securities with high beta values do in fact have higher average returns. Moreover, the authors find a book-to-market effect that is attenuated compared to the results in Fama and French and furthermore is inconsistent across different samples of securities. They conclude that the empirical case for the importance of the book-to-market ratio may be somewhat weaker than the Fama and French study would suggest.

[29]R. Ball and P. Brown, "An Empirical Evaluation of Accounting Income Numbers," *Journal of Accounting Research* 9 (1968), pp. 159–78.

[30]There are volumes of literature on this phenomenon, often referred to as post–earnings-announcement price drift. For example, see V. Bernard and J. Thomas, "Evidence That Stock Prices Do Not Fully Reflect the Implications of Current Earnings for Future Earnings," *Journal of Accounting and Economics* 13 (1990), pp. 305–40; or R. H. Battalio and R. Mendenhall, "Earnings Expectation, Investor Trade Size, and Anomalous Returns Around Earnings Announcements," *Journal of Financial Economics* 77 (2005), pp. 289–319.

[31]Richard J. Rendleman Jr., Charles P. Jones, and Henry A. Latané, "Empirical Anomalies Based on Unexpected Earnings and the Importance of Risk Adjustments," *Journal of Financial Economics* 10 (November 1982), pp. 269–87.

Evidently, one could have earned abnormal profits simply by waiting for earnings announcements and purchasing a stock portfolio of positive-earnings-surprise companies. These are precisely the types of predictable continuing trends that ought to be impossible in an efficient market.

Strong-Form Tests: Inside Information

It would not be surprising if insiders were able to make superior profits trading in their firm's stock. In other words, we do not expect markets to be strong-form efficient; we regulate and limit trades based on inside information. The ability of insiders to trade profitably in their own stock has been documented in studies by Jaffe,[32] Seyhun,[33] Givoly and Palmon,[34] and others. Jaffe's was one of the earlier studies that documented the tendency for stock prices to rise after insiders intensively bought shares and fall after insiders intensively sold shares.

Can other investors benefit by following insiders' trades? The Securities and Exchange Commission requires all insiders to register their trading activity and it publishes these trades in an *Official Summary of Security Transactions and Holdings.* Since 2002, insiders must report large trades to the SEC within two business days. Once the *Official Summary* is published, the trades become public information. At that point, if markets are efficient, fully and immediately processing the information released in the *Official Summary* of trading, an investor should no longer be able to profit from following the pattern of those trades. Several Internet sites contain information on insider trading.

The study by Seyhun, which carefully tracked the public release dates of the *Official Summary,* found that following insider transactions would be to no avail. Although there is some tendency for stock prices to increase even after the *Official Summary* reports insider buying, the abnormal returns are not of sufficient magnitude to overcome transaction costs.

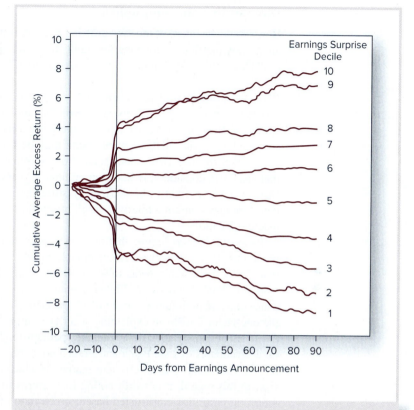

Figure 11.5 Cumulative abnormal returns in response to earnings announcements

Source: R. J. Rendleman Jr., C. P. Jones, and H. A. Latané, "Empirical Anomalies Based on Unexpected Earnings and the Importance of Risk Adjustments," *Journal of Financial Economics* 10 (1982), pp. 269–287.

---

[32]Jeffrey F. Jaffe, "Special Information and Insider Trading," *Journal of Business* 47 (July 1974).

[33]H. Nejat Seyhun, "Insiders' Profits, Costs of Trading and Market Efficiency," *Journal of Financial Economics* 16 (1986).

[34]Dan Givoly and Dan Palmon, "Insider Trading and Exploitation of Inside Information: Some Empirical Evidence," *Journal of Business* 58 (1985).

Interpreting the Anomalies

How should we interpret the ever-growing anomalies literature? Does it imply that markets are grossly inefficient, allowing for simplistic trading rules to offer large profit opportunities? Or are there other, more-subtle interpretations?

Risk Premiums or Inefficiencies?   The small-firm, market-to-book, momentum, and long-term reversal effects are currently among the most puzzling phenomena in empirical finance. There are several interpretations of these effects. First note that to some extent, some of these phenomena may be related. The feature that small firms, low-market-to-book firms, and recent "losers" seem to have in common is a stock price that has fallen considerably in recent months or years. Indeed, a firm can become a small firm or a low-market-to-book firm by suffering a sharp drop in price. These groups therefore may contain a relatively high proportion of distressed firms that have suffered recent difficulties.

Fama and French[35] argue that these effects can be explained as manifestations of risk premiums. Using their three-factor model, introduced in the previous chapter, they show that stocks with higher betas (also known as factor loadings in this context) on size or market-to-book factors have higher average returns; they interpret these returns as evidence of a risk premium associated with the factor. This model does a much better job than the one-factor CAPM in explaining security returns. While size or book-to-market ratios per se are obviously not risk factors, they perhaps might act as proxies for more fundamental determinants of risk. Fama and French argue that these patterns of returns may therefore be consistent with an efficient market in which expected returns are consistent with risk. In this regard, it is worth noting that returns to "style portfolios," for example, the return on portfolios constructed based on the ratio of book-to-market value (specifically, the Fama-French high-minus-low book-to-market portfolio) or firm size (the return on the small-minus-big firm portfolio) do indeed seem to predict business cycles in many countries. Figure 11.6 shows that returns on these portfolios tend to have positive returns in years prior to rapid growth in gross domestic product. We examine the Fama-French paper in more detail in Chapter 13.

The opposite interpretation is offered by Lakonishok, Shleifer, and Vishny,[36] who argue that these phenomena are evidence of inefficient markets, more specifically, of systematic errors in the forecasts of stock analysts. They believe that analysts extrapolate past performance too far into the future, and therefore overprice firms with recent good performance and underprice firms with recent poor performance. Ultimately, when market participants recognize their errors, prices reverse. This explanation is consistent with the reversal effect and also, to a degree, with the small-firm and book-to-market effects because firms with sharp price drops may tend to be small or have high book-to-market ratios.

If Lakonishok, Shleifer, and Vishny are correct, we ought to find that analysts systematically err when forecasting returns of recent "winner" versus "loser" firms. A study by La Porta[37] is consistent with this pattern. He finds that equity of firms for which analysts predict low growth rates of earnings actually perform better than those with high expected earnings growth. Analysts seem overly pessimistic about firms with low growth prospects

---

[35]Eugene F. Fama and Kenneth R. French, "Common Risk Factors in the Returns on Stocks and Bonds," *Journal of Financial Economics* 33 (1993), pp. 3–56.

[36]Josef Lakonishok, Andrei Shleifer, and Robert W. Vishny, "Contrarian Investment, Extrapolation, and Risk," *Journal of Finance* 50 (1995), pp. 541–78.

[37]Raphael La Porta, "Expectations and the Cross Section of Stock Returns," *Journal of Finance* 51 (December 1996), pp. 1715–42.

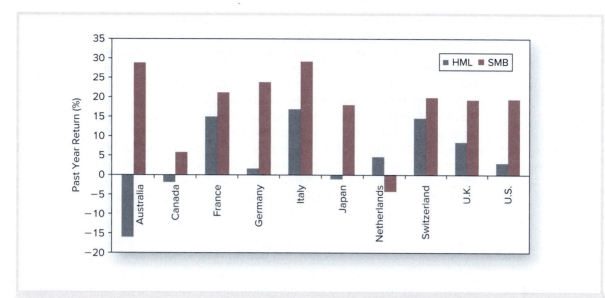

Figure 11.6 Return to style portfolios as predictors of GDP growth. Average difference in the return on the style portfolio in years before good GDP growth versus in years with bad GDP growth. Positive value means the style portfolio does better in years prior to good macroeconomic performance. HML = high-minus-low portfolio, sorted on ratio of book-to-market value. SMB = small-minus-big portfolio, sorted on firm size.

Source: J. Liew and M. Vassalou, "Can Book-to-Market, Size, and Momentum Be Risk Factors That Predict Economic Growth?" *Journal of Financial Economics* 57 (2000), pp. 221–45.

and overly optimistic about firms with high growth prospects. When these too-extreme expectations are "corrected," the low-expected-growth firms outperform high-expected-growth firms.

Anomalies or Data Mining?   We have covered many of the so-called anomalies cited in the literature, but our list could go on and on. Some wonder whether these anomalies are really unexplained puzzles in financial markets, or whether they instead are an artifact of data mining. After all, if one reruns the computer database of past returns over and over and examines stock returns along enough dimensions, simple chance will cause some criteria to *appear* to predict returns.

In this regard, it is noteworthy that some anomalies have not shown much staying power after being reported in the academic literature. For example, after the small-firm effect was published in the early 1980s, it promptly disappeared for much of the rest of the decade.

Still, even acknowledging the potential for data mining, a common thread seems to run through many of the anomalies we have considered, lending support to the notion that there is a real puzzle to explain. Value stocks—defined by low P/E ratio, high book-to-market ratio, or depressed prices relative to historic levels—seem to have provided higher average returns than "glamour" or growth stocks.

One way to address the problem of data mining is to find a dataset that has not already been researched and see whether the relationship in question shows up in the new data. Such studies have revealed size, momentum, and book-to-market effects in security markets around the world. While these phenomena may be a manifestation of a systematic risk premium, the precise nature of that risk is not fully understood.

Anomalies over Time   We pointed out earlier that while no market can be perfectly efficient, in well-functioning markets, anomalies ought to be self-destructing. As market participants learn of profitable trading strategies, their attempts to exploit them should move prices to levels at which abnormal profits are no longer available. Chordia, Subrahmanyam, and Tong[38] look for this dynamic in the pattern of many of the anomalies discussed in this chapter. They focus on abnormal returns associated with several characteristics, including size, book-to-market ratio, momentum, and turnover (which may be inversely related to the neglected firm effect). They break their sample at 1993 and show that the abnormal returns associated with these characteristics in the pre-1993 period largely disappear in the post-1993 period (with the notable exception of the book-to-market effect). Their interpretation is that the market has become more efficient as knowledge about these anomalies has percolated through the investment community. Interestingly, they find that the attenuation of alphas is greatest in the most liquid stocks, where trading activity is least costly.

McLean and Pontiff[39] provide a more comprehensive analysis of the dynamics of market efficiency and a more careful timeline for the likely recognition of anomalies by investors. They identify more than 80 characteristics recognized in the academic literature as associated with abnormal returns. Rather than using a common break point for all characteristics, they carefully track both the publication date of each finding as well as the date the paper was first posted to the Social Science Research Network. This allows them to break the sample for each finding at dates corresponding to when that particular finding became public. They conclude that the post-publication decay in abnormal return is about 35% (e.g., a 5% pre-publication abnormal return to an anomaly-based strategy falls on average to 3.25% after publication).[40] They show that trading volume and variance in stocks identified with anomalies increase, as does short interest in "overpriced" stocks. These patterns are consistent with informed participants attempting to exploit newly recognized mispricing. Moreover, the decay in alpha is most pronounced for stocks that are larger, more liquid, and with low idiosyncratic risk. These are precisely the stocks for which trading activity in pursuit of reliable abnormal returns is most feasible. Thus, while abnormal returns do not fully disappear, these results are consistent with a market groping its way toward greater efficiency over time.

Bubbles and Market Efficiency

Every so often, asset prices seem (at least in retrospect) to lose their grounding in reality. For example, in the tulip mania in 17th-century Holland, tulip prices peaked at several times the annual income of a skilled worker. This episode has become the symbol of a speculative "bubble" in which prices appear to depart from any semblance of intrinsic value. Bubbles seem to arise when a rapid run-up in prices creates a widespread expectation that they will continue to rise. As more and more investors try to get in on the action, they push prices even further. Inevitably, however, the run-up stalls and the bubble ends in a crash.

---

[38]T. Chordia, A. Subrahmanyam, and Q. Tong, "Have Capital Market Anomalies Attenuated in the Recent Era of High Liquidity and Trading Activity?" *Journal of Accounting and Economics* 58 (August 2014), pp. 41–58.

[39]David R. McLean and Jeffrey E. Pontiff, "Does Academic Research Destroy Stock Return Predictability?" *Journal of Finance* 71 (2016), pp. 5–32.

[40]About a third of that decay occurs between the final date of the sample and the publication date, which the authors note may reflect the portion of apparent abnormal returns that actually are due to data mining. The remaining decay would then be attributable to the actions of sophisticated investors whose trades move anomalous prices back toward intrinsic value.

Less than a century after tulip mania, the South Sea Bubble in England became almost as famous. In this episode, the share price of the South Sea Company rose from £128 in January 1720 to £550 in May and peaked at around £1,000 in August—just before the bubble burst and the share price collapsed to £150 in September, leading to widespread bankruptcies among those who had borrowed to buy shares on credit. In fact, the company was a major lender of money to investors willing to buy (and thus bid up) its shares. This sequence may sound familiar to anyone who lived through the dot-com boom and bust of 1995–2002[41] or, more recently, the financial turmoil of 2008, with origins widely attributed to a collapsing housing price bubble.

It is hard to defend the position that security prices in these instances represented rational, unbiased assessments of intrinsic value. And in fact, some economists, most notably Hyman Minsky,[42] have suggested that bubbles arise naturally. During periods of stability and rising prices, investors extrapolate that stability into the future and become more willing to take on risk. Risk premiums shrink, leading to further increases in asset prices, and expectations become even more optimistic in a self-fulfilling cycle. But in the end, pricing and risk taking become excessive and the bubble bursts. Ironically, the initial period of stability fosters behavior that ultimately results in instability.

But beware of jumping to the conclusion that asset prices may generally be thought of as arbitrary and obvious trading opportunities abundant. First, most bubbles become "obvious" only in retrospect. At the time, the price run-up often seems to have a defensible rationale. In the dot-com boom, for example, many contemporary observers rationalized stock price gains as justified by the prospect of a new and more profitable economy, driven by technological advances. Even the irrationality of the tulip mania may have been overblown in its later retelling.[43] In addition, security valuation is intrinsically difficult. Given the considerable imprecision of estimates of intrinsic value, large bets on perceived mispricing may entail hubris.

Moreover, even if you suspect that prices are in fact "wrong," taking advantage of them can be difficult. We explore these issues in more detail in the following chapter, but for now, we simply point out some impediments to making aggressive bets against an asset, among them, the costs of short selling overpriced securities as well as potential problems obtaining the securities to sell short, and the possibility that even if you are ultimately correct, the market may disagree and prices still can move dramatically against you in the short term, thus wiping out your portfolio.

11.5 Mutual Fund and Analyst Performance

We have documented some of the apparent chinks in the armor of efficient market proponents. For investors, the issue of market efficiency boils down to whether skilled investors can make consistent abnormal trading profits. The best test is to look at the performance of market professionals to see if they can generate performance superior to that of a passive

---

[41]The dot-com boom gave rise to the term *irrational exuberance*. In this vein, consider that one company going public in the investment boom of 1720 described itself simply as "a company for carrying out an undertaking of great advantage, but nobody to know what it is."

[42]Hyman P. Minsky, *Stabilizing An Unstable Economy* (New Haven, CT: Yale University Press, 1986).

[43]For interesting discussions of this possibility, see Peter Garber, *Famous First Bubbles: The Fundamentals of Early Manias* (Cambridge, MA: MIT Press, 2000), and Anne Goldgar, *Tulipmania: Money, Honor, and Knowledge in the Dutch Golden Age* (Chicago: University of Chicago Press, 2007).

index fund that buys and holds the market. We will look at two facets of professional performance: that of stock market analysts who recommend investment positions and that of mutual fund managers who actually manage portfolios.

Stock Market Analysts

Stock market analysts historically have worked for brokerage firms, which presents an immediate problem in interpreting the value of their advice: Analysts have tended to be overwhelmingly positive in their assessment of the prospects of firms.[44] For example, on a scale of 1 (strong buy) to 5 (strong sell), the average recommendation for 5,628 covered firms in 1996 was 2.04.[45] As a result, we cannot take positive recommendations (e.g., to buy) at face value. Instead, we must look at either the relative enthusiasm of analyst recommendations, compared to those for other firms, or at the change in consensus recommendations.

Womack[46] focuses on changes in analysts' recommendations and finds that positive changes are associated with increased stock prices of about 5%, and negative changes result in average price decreases of 11%. One might wonder whether these price changes reflect the market's recognition of analysts' superior information or insight about firms or, instead, simply result from new buy or sell pressure brought on by the recommendations themselves. Womack argues that price impact seems to be permanent and therefore consistent with the hypothesis that analysts do in fact reveal new information. Jegadeesh, Kim, Krische, and Lee[47] also find that changes in consensus recommendations are associated with price changes, but that the *level* of consensus recommendations is an inconsistent predictor of future stock performance.

Barber, Lehavy, McNichols, and Trueman[48] focus on the level of consensus recommendations and show that firms with the most-favorable recommendations outperform those with the least-favorable recommendations. While their results seem impressive, the authors note that portfolio strategies based on analyst consensus recommendations would result in extremely heavy trading activity with associated costs that probably would wipe out the potential profits from the strategy.

In sum, the literature suggests that some value is added by analysts, but ambiguity remains. Are superior returns following analyst upgrades due to revelation of new information or due to changes in investor demand in response to the changed outlook? Also, are these results exploitable by investors who necessarily incur trading costs?

Mutual Fund Managers

As we pointed out in Chapter 4, casual evidence does not support the claim that professionally managed portfolios can consistently beat the market. Figure 4.2 in that chapter demonstrated that between 1972 and 2015 the returns of a passive portfolio indexed to the Wilshire 5000 typically would have been better than those of the average equity fund.

---

[44]This problem may be less severe in the future; one recent reform intended to mitigate the conflict of interest in having brokerage firms that sell stocks also provide investment advice is to separate analyst coverage from the other activities of the firm.

[45]B. Barber, R. Lehavy, M. McNichols, and B. Trueman, "Can Investors Profit from the Prophets? Security Analyst Recommendations and Stock Returns," *Journal of Finance* 56 (April 2001), pp. 531–63.

[46]K. L. Womack, "Do Brokerage Analysts' Recommendations Have Investment Value?" *Journal of Finance* 51 (March 1996), pp. 137–67.

[47]N. Jegadeesh, J. Kim, S. D. Krische, and C. M. Lee, "Analyzing the Analysts: When Do Recommendations Add Value?" *Journal of Finance* 59 (June 2004), pp. 1083–124.

[48]Barber et al., op. cit.

On the other hand, there was some (admittedly inconsistent) evidence of persistence in performance, meaning that the better managers in one period tended to be better managers in following periods. Such a pattern would suggest that the better managers can with some consistency outperform their competitors, which is inconsistent with the notion that market prices already reflect all relevant information.

The analyses cited in Chapter 4 were based on total returns; they did not properly adjust returns for exposure to systematic risk factors. In this section we revisit the question of mutual fund performance, paying more attention to the benchmark against which performance ought to be evaluated.

As a first pass, we might examine the risk-adjusted returns (i.e., the alpha) of a large sample of mutual funds. But the market index may not be an adequate benchmark against which to evaluate mutual fund returns. Because mutual funds tend to maintain considerable holdings in equity of small firms, whereas the capitalization-weighted index is dominated by large firms, mutual funds as a whole will tend to outperform the index when small firms outperform large ones and underperform when small firms fare worse. Thus a better benchmark for the performance of funds would be an index that separately incorporates the stock market performance of smaller firms.

The importance of the benchmark can be illustrated by examining the returns on small stocks in various subperiods.[49] In the 20-year period between 1945 and 1964, for example, a small-stock index underperformed the S&P 500 by about 4% per year (i.e., the alpha of the small-stock index after adjusting for systematic risk was −4%). In the following 20-year period between 1965 and 1984, small stocks outperformed the S&P index by 10%. Thus if one were to examine mutual fund returns in the earlier period, they would tend to look poor, not necessarily because fund managers were poor stock pickers, but simply because mutual funds as a group tended to hold more small stocks than were represented in the S&P 500. In the later period, funds would look better on a risk-adjusted basis relative to the S&P 500 because small stocks performed better. The "style choice," that is, the exposure to small stocks (which is an asset allocation decision) would dominate the evaluation of performance even though it has little to do with managers' stock-picking ability.[50]

The conventional performance benchmark today is a four-factor model, which employs the three Fama-French factors (the return on the market index, and returns to portfolios based on size and book-to-market ratio) augmented by a momentum factor (a portfolio constructed based on prior-year stock return). Alphas constructed using an expanded index model using these four factors control for a wide range of mutual fund style choices that may affect average returns, for example, an inclination to growth versus value or small- versus large-capitalization stocks. Figure 11.7 shows a frequency distribution of four-factor alphas for U.S. domestic equity funds.[51] The results show that the distribution of alpha is roughly bell shaped, with a slightly negative mean. On average, it does not appear that these funds outperform their style-adjusted benchmarks.

Consistent with Figure 11.7, Fama and French[52] use the four-factor model to assess the performance of equity mutual funds and show that, while they may exhibit positive alphas

---

[49]This illustration and the statistics cited are based on E. J. Elton, M. J. Gruber, S. Das, and M. Hlavka, "Efficiency with Costly Information: A Reinterpretation of Evidence from Managed Portfolios," *Review of Financial Studies* 6 (1993), pp. 1–22, which is discussed shortly.

[50]Remember that the asset allocation decision is usually in the hands of the individual investor. Investors allocate their investment portfolios to funds in asset classes they desire to hold, and they can reasonably expect only that mutual fund portfolio managers will choose stocks advantageously *within* those asset classes.

[51]We are grateful to Professor Richard Evans for these data.

[52]Eugene F. Fama and Kenneth R. French, "Luck versus Skill in the Cross-Section of Mutual Fund Returns," *Journal of Finance* 65 (2010), pp. 1915–47.

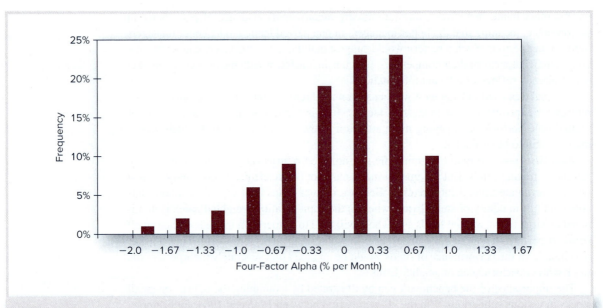

Figure 11.7 Mutual fund alphas computed using a four-factor model of expected return, 1993–2007. (The best and worst 2.5% of observations are excluded from this distribution.)

Source: Professor Richard Evans, University of Virginia, Darden School of Business.

before fees, after the fees charged to their customers, alphas are negative. Likewise, Wermers,[53] who uses both style portfolios as well as the characteristics of the stocks held by mutual funds to control for performance, also finds positive gross alphas but negative net alphas after controlling for fees and risk.

Carhart[54] reexamines the issue of consistency in mutual fund performance and finds that, after controlling for these factors, there is only minor persistence in relative performance across managers. Moreover, much of that persistence seems due to expenses and transactions costs rather than gross investment returns.

However, Bollen and Busse[55] do find evidence of performance persistence, at least over short horizons. They rank mutual fund performance using the four-factor model over a base quarter, assign funds into one of ten deciles according to base-period alpha, and then look at performance in the following quarter. Figure 11.8 illustrates their results. The dark line is the average alpha of funds within each of the deciles in the base period (expressed on a quarterly basis). The steepness of that curve reflects the considerable dispersion in performance in the ranking period. The light line is the average performance of the funds in each decile in the following quarter. The shallowness of this curve indicates that most of the original performance differential disappears. Nevertheless, the plot is still clearly downward sloping, so it appears that, at least over a short horizon such as one quarter, there is some performance consistency. However, that persistence is probably too small a fraction of the original performance differential to justify performance-chasing by mutual fund customers.

[53]R. R. Wermers, "Mutual Fund Performance: An Empirical Decomposition into Stock-Picking Talent, Style, Transaction Costs, and Expenses," *Journal of Finance* 55 (2000), pp. 1655–1703.

[54]Mark M. Carhart, "On Persistence in Mutual Fund Performance," *Journal of Finance* 52 (1997), pp. 57–82.

[55]Nicolas P. B. Bollen and Jeffrey A. Busse, "Short-Term Persistence in Mutual Fund Performance," *Review of Financial Studies* 19 (2004), pp. 569–97.

Figure 11.8 Risk-adjusted performance in ranking quarter and following quarter

This pattern is actually consistent with the prediction of an influential paper by Berk and Green.[56] They argue that skilled mutual fund managers with abnormal performance will attract new funds until the additional costs and complexity of managing those extra funds drive alphas down to zero. Thus, skill will show up not in superior returns, but rather in the amount of funds under management. Therefore, even if managers are skilled, alphas will be short-lived, as they seem to be in Figure 11.8.

Del Guercio and Reuter[57] offer a finer interpretation of mutual fund performance and the Berk-Green hypothesis. They split mutual fund investors into those who buy funds directly for themselves versus those who purchase funds through brokers, reasoning that the direct-sold segment may be more financially literate while the broker-sold segment is less comfortable making financial decisions without professional advice. Consistent with this hypothesis, they show that direct-sold investors direct their assets to funds with positive alphas (consistent with the Berk-Green model), but broker-sold investors generally do not. This provides a greater incentive for direct-sold funds to invest relatively more in alpha-generating inputs such as talented portfolio managers or analysts. Moreover, they show that the after-fee performance of direct-sold funds is as good as that of index funds (again, consistent with Berk-Green), while the performance of broker-sold funds is considerably worse. It thus appears that the average underperformance of actively managed mutual funds is driven largely by broker-sold funds and that this underperformance may be interpreted as an implicit cost that less-informed investors pay for the advice they get from their brokers.

---

[56]J. B. Berk and R. C. Green, "Mutual Fund Flows and Performance in Rational Markets," *Journal of Political Economy* 112 (2004), pp. 1269–95.

[57]Diane Del Guercio and Jonathan Reuter, "Mutual Fund Performance and the Incentive to Generate Alpha," *Journal of Finance* 69 (August 2014), pp. 1673–1704.

In contrast to the extensive studies of equity fund managers, there have been few studies of the performance of bond fund managers. Blake, Elton, and Gruber[58] examined the performance of fixed-income mutual funds. They found that, on average, bond funds underperform passive fixed-income indexes by an amount roughly equal to expenses, and that there is no evidence that past performance can predict future performance. More recently, Chen, Ferson, and Peters (2010)[59] found that, on average, bond mutual funds outperform passive bond indexes in terms of gross returns but underperform once the fees they charge their investors are subtracted, a result similar to those others have found for equity funds.

Thus the evidence on the risk-adjusted performance of professional managers is mixed at best. We conclude that the performance of professional managers is broadly consistent with market efficiency. The amounts by which professional managers as a group beat or are beaten by the market fall within the margin of statistical uncertainty. In any event, it is quite clear that performance superior to passive strategies is far from routine. Studies show either that most managers cannot outperform passive strategies or that if there is a margin of superiority, it is small.

On the other hand, a small number of investment superstars—Peter Lynch (formerly of Fidelity's Magellan Fund), Warren Buffett (of Berkshire Hathaway), John Templeton (of Templeton Funds), and Mario Gabelli (of GAMCO), among them—have compiled career records that show a consistency of superior performance hard to reconcile with absolutely efficient markets. In a careful statistical analysis of mutual fund "stars," Kosowski, Timmerman, Wermers, and White[60] conclude that the stock-picking ability of a minority of managers is sufficient to cover their costs, and that their superior performance tends to persist over time. However, Nobel Prize–winner Paul Samuelson[61] reviewed this investment hall of fame and pointed out that the records of the vast majority of professional money managers offer convincing evidence that there are no easy strategies to guarantee success in the securities markets.

So, Are Markets Efficient?

There is a telling joke about two economists walking down the street. They spot a $20 bill on the sidewalk. One stoops to pick it up, but the other one says, "Don't bother; if the bill were real someone would have picked it up already."

The lesson is clear. An overly doctrinaire belief in efficient markets can paralyze the investor and make it appear that no research effort can be justified. This extreme view is probably unwarranted. There are enough anomalies in the empirical evidence to justify the search for underpriced securities that clearly goes on.

The bulk of the evidence, however, suggests that any supposedly superior investment strategy should be taken with many grains of salt. The market is competitive *enough* that only differentially superior information or insight will earn money; the easy pickings have been picked. In the end it is likely that the margin of superiority that any professional manager can add is so slight that the statistician will not easily be able to detect it.

We conclude that markets are generally very efficient, but that rewards to the especially diligent, intelligent, or creative may in fact be waiting.

[58]Christopher R. Blake, Edwin J. Elton, and Martin J. Gruber, "The Performance of Bond Mutual Funds," *Journal of Business* 66 (July 1993), pp. 371–404.

[59]Y. Chen, W.E. Ferson, and H. Peters, "Measuring the Timing Ability and Performance of Bond Mutual Funds," *Journal of Financial Economics* 98 (2010), pp. 72–89.

[60]R. Kosowski, A. Timmerman, R. Wermers, and H. White, "Can Mutual Fund 'Stars' Really Pick Stocks? New Evidence from a Bootstrap Analysis," *Journal of Finance* 61 (December 2006), pp. 2551–95.

[61]Paul Samuelson, "The Judgment of Economic Science on Rational Portfolio Management," *Journal of Portfolio Management* 16 (Fall 1989), pp. 4–12.

1. Statistical research has shown that to a close approximation stock prices seem to follow a random walk with no discernible predictable patterns that investors can exploit. Such findings are now taken to be evidence of market efficiency, that is, evidence that market prices reflect all currently available information. Only new information will move stock prices, and this information is equally likely to be good news or bad news.

2. Market participants distinguish among three forms of the efficient market hypothesis. The weak form asserts that all information to be derived from past trading data already is reflected in stock prices. The semistrong form claims that all publicly available information is already reflected. The strong form, which generally is acknowledged to be extreme, asserts that all information, including insider information, is reflected in prices.

3. Technical analysis focuses on stock price patterns and on proxies for buy or sell pressure in the market. Fundamental analysis focuses on the determinants of the underlying value of the firm, such as current profitability and growth prospects. Because both types of analysis are based on public information, neither should generate excess profits if markets are operating efficiently.

4. Proponents of the efficient market hypothesis often advocate passive as opposed to active investment strategies. The policy of passive investors is to buy and hold a broad-based market index. They expend resources neither on market research nor on frequent purchase and sale of stocks. Passive strategies may be tailored to meet individual investor requirements.

5. Event studies are used to evaluate the economic impact of events of interest, using abnormal stock returns. Such studies usually show that there is some leakage of inside information to some market participants before the public announcement date. Therefore, insiders do seem to be able to exploit their access to information to at least a limited extent.

6. Empirical studies of technical analysis do not generally support the hypothesis that such analysis can generate superior trading profits. One notable exception to this conclusion is the apparent success of momentum-based strategies over intermediate-term horizons.

7. Several anomalies regarding fundamental analysis have been uncovered. These include the P/E effect, the small-firm effect, the neglected-firm effect, post–earnings-announcement price drift, and the book-to-market effect. Whether these anomalies represent market inefficiency or poorly understood risk premiums is still a matter of debate.

8. By and large, the performance record of professionally managed funds lends little credence to claims that most professionals can consistently beat the market.

SUMMARY

KEY TERMS

random walk	support levels	momentum effect
efficient market hypothesis (EMH)	fundamental analysis	reversal effect
	passive investment strategy	anomalies
weak-form EMH	index fund	P/E effect
semistrong-form EMH	event study	small-firm effect
strong-form EMH	abnormal return	neglected-firm effect
technical analysis	cumulative abnormal return (CAR)	book-to-market effect
resistance levels		

KEY EQUATIONS

Abnormal return = Actual return − Expected return given the return on a market index
$$= r_t - (a + br_{Mt})$$

PROBLEM SETS

1. If markets are efficient, what should be the correlation coefficient between stock returns for two nonoverlapping time periods?

2. A successful firm like Microsoft has consistently generated large profits for years. Is this a violation of the EMH?

3. "If all securities are fairly priced, all must offer equal expected rates of return." Comment.

4. Steady Growth Industries has never missed a dividend payment in its 94-year history. Does this make it more attractive to you as a possible purchase for your stock portfolio?

5. At a cocktail party, your co-worker tells you that he has beaten the market for each of the last three years. Suppose you believe him. Does this shake your belief in efficient markets?

6. "Highly variable stock prices suggest that the market does not know how to price stocks." Comment.

7. Why are the following "effects" considered efficient market anomalies? Are there rational explanations for any of these effects?

    a. P/E effect.
    b. Book-to-market effect.
    c. Momentum effect.
    d. Small-firm effect.

8. If prices are as likely to increase as decrease, why do investors earn positive returns from the market on average?

9. Which of the following (hypothetical) observations would most contradict the proposition that the stock market is *weakly* efficient? Explain.

    a. Over 25% of mutual funds outperform the market on average.
    b. Insiders earn abnormal trading profits.
    c. Every January, the stock market earns abnormal returns.

10. Which of the following sources of market inefficiency would be most easily exploited?

    a. A stock price drops suddenly due to a large sale by an institution.
    b. A stock is overpriced because traders are restricted from short sales.
    c. Stocks are overvalued because investors are exuberant over increased productivity in the economy.

11. Suppose that, after conducting an analysis of past stock prices, you come up with the following observations. Which would appear to *contradict* the *weak form* of the efficient market hypothesis? Explain.

    a. The average rate of return is significantly greater than zero.
    b. The correlation between the return during a given week and the return during the following week is zero.
    c. One could have made superior returns by buying stock after a 10% rise in price and selling after a 10% fall.
    d. One could have made higher-than-average capital gains by holding stocks with low dividend yields.

12. Which of the following statements are true if the efficient market hypothesis holds?

    a. It implies that future events can be forecast with perfect accuracy.
    b. It implies that prices reflect all available information.
    c. It implies that security prices change for no discernible reason.
    d. It implies that prices do not fluctuate.

13. Respond to each of the following comments.

    a. If stock prices follow a random walk, then capital markets are little different from a casino.
    b. A good part of a company's future prospects are predictable. Given this fact, stock prices can't possibly follow a random walk.
    c. If markets are efficient, you might as well select your portfolio by throwing darts at the stock listings in *The Wall Street Journal*.

14. Which of the following would be a viable way to earn abnormally high trading profits if markets are semistrong-form efficient?

    a. Buy shares in companies with low P/E ratios.
    b. Buy shares in companies with recent above-average price changes.
    c. Buy shares in companies with recent below-average price changes.
    d. Buy shares in companies for which you have advance knowledge of an improvement in the management team.

15. Suppose you find that prices of stocks before large dividend increases show on average consistently positive abnormal returns. Is this a violation of the EMH?

16. "If the business cycle is predictable, and a stock has a positive beta, the stock's returns also must be predictable." Respond.

17. Which of the following hypothetical phenomena would be either consistent with or a violation of the efficient market hypothesis? Explain briefly.

    a. Nearly half of all professionally managed mutual funds are able to outperform the S&P 500 in a typical year.
    b. Money managers who outperform the market (on a risk-adjusted basis) in one year are likely to outperform the market in the following year.
    c. Stock prices tend to be predictably more volatile in January than in other months.
    d. Stock prices of companies that announce increased earnings in January tend to outperform the market in February.

18. An index model regression applied to past monthly returns in Ford's stock price produces the following estimates, which are believed to be stable over time:

$$r_F = .10\% + 1.1r_M$$

If the market index subsequently rises by 8% and Ford's stock price rises by 7%, what is the abnormal change in Ford's stock price?

19. The monthly rate of return on T-bills is 1%. The market went up this month by 1.5%. In addition, AmbChaser, Inc., which has an equity beta of 2, surprisingly just won a lawsuit that awards it $1 million immediately.

    a. If the original value of AmbChaser equity were $100 million, what would you guess was the rate of return of its stock this month?
    b. What is your answer to (a) if the market had expected AmbChaser to win $2 million?

20. In a recent closely contested lawsuit, Apex sued Bpex for patent infringement. The jury came back today with its decision. The rate of return on Apex was $r_A = 3.1\%$. The rate of return on Bpex was only $r_B = 2.5\%$. The market today responded to very encouraging news about the unemployment rate, and $r_M = 3\%$. The historical relationship between returns on these stocks and the market portfolio has been estimated from index model regressions as:

$$\text{Apex: } r_A = .2\% + 1.4r_M$$
$$\text{Bpex: } r_B = -.1\% + .6r_M$$

On the basis of these data, which company do you think won the lawsuit?

21. Investors *expect* the market rate of return in the coming year to be 12%. The T-bill rate is 4%. Changing Fortunes Industries' stock has a beta of .5. The market value of its outstanding equity is $100 million.

    a. What is your best guess currently as to the expected rate of return on Changing Fortunes's stock? You believe that the stock is fairly priced.
    b. If the market return in the coming year actually turns out to be 10%, what is your best guess as to the rate of return that will be earned on Changing Fortunes's stock?
    c. Suppose now that Changing Fortunes wins a major lawsuit during the year. The settlement is $5 million. Changing Fortunes' stock return during the year turns out to be 10%. What is your best guess as to the settlement the market previously *expected* Changing Fortunes to receive

from the lawsuit? (Continue to assume that the market return in the year turned out to be 10%.) The magnitude of the settlement is the only unexpected firm-specific event during the year.

22. Dollar-cost averaging means that you buy equal dollar amounts of a stock every period, for example, $500 per month. The strategy is based on the idea that when the stock price is low, your fixed monthly purchase will buy more shares, and when the price is high, fewer shares. Averaging over time, you will end up buying more shares when the stock is cheaper and fewer when it is relatively expensive. Therefore, by design, you will exhibit good market timing. Evaluate this strategy.

23. We know that the market should respond positively to good news and that good-news events such as the coming end of a recession can be predicted with at least some accuracy. Why, then, can we not predict that the market will go up as the economy recovers?

24. You know that firm XYZ is very poorly run. On a scale of 1 (worst) to 10 (best), you would give it a score of 3. The market consensus evaluation is that the management score is only 2. Should you buy or sell the stock?

25. Suppose that during a certain week the Fed announces a new monetary growth policy, Congress surprisingly passes legislation restricting imports of foreign automobiles, and Ford comes out with a new car model that it believes will increase profits substantially. How might you go about measuring the market's assessment of Ford's new model?

26. Good News, Inc., just announced an increase in its annual earnings, yet its stock price fell. Is there a rational explanation for this phenomenon?

27. Shares of small firms with thinly traded stocks tend to show positive CAPM alphas. Is this a violation of the efficient market hypothesis?

28. Examine the accompanying figure, which presents cumulative abnormal returns both before and after dates on which insiders buy or sell shares in their firms. How do you interpret this figure? What are we to make of the pattern of CARs before and after the event date?

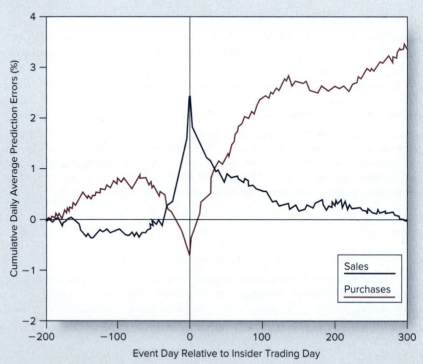

Source: Nejat H. Seyhun, "Insiders, Profits, Costs of Trading and Market Efficiency," *Journal of Financial Economics* 16 (1986).

29. Suppose that as the economy moves through a business cycle, risk premiums also change. For example, in a recession, when people are concerned about their jobs, risk tolerance might be lower and risk premiums might be higher. In a booming economy, tolerance for risk might be higher and premiums lower.

   a. Would a predictably shifting risk premium such as described here be a violation of the efficient market hypothesis?
   b. How might a cycle of increasing and decreasing risk premiums create an appearance that stock prices "overreact," first falling excessively and then seeming to recover?

1. The semistrong form of the efficient market hypothesis asserts that stock prices:

   a. Fully reflect all historical price information.
   b. Fully reflect all publicly available information.
   c. Fully reflect all relevant information, including insider information.
   d. May be predictable.

2. Assume that a company announces an unexpectedly large cash dividend to its shareholders. In an efficient market *without* information leakage, one might expect:

   a. An abnormal price change at the announcement.
   b. An abnormal price increase before the announcement.
   c. An abnormal price decrease after the announcement.
   d. No abnormal price change before or after the announcement.

3. Which one of the following would provide evidence *against* the *semistrong form* of the efficient market theory?

   a. About 50% of pension funds outperform the market in any year.
   b. All investors have learned to exploit management signals about the future performance of the firm.
   c. Trend analysis is worthless in determining stock prices.
   d. Low P/E stocks tend to have positive abnormal returns over the long run.

4. According to the efficient market hypothesis:

   a. High-beta stocks are consistently overpriced.
   b. Low-beta stocks are consistently overpriced.
   c. Positive alphas on stocks will quickly disappear.
   d. Negative alpha stocks consistently yield low returns for arbitrageurs.

5. A "random walk" occurs when:

   a. Stock price changes are random but predictable.
   b. Stock prices respond slowly to both new and old information.
   c. Future price changes are uncorrelated with past price changes.
   d. Past information is useful in predicting future prices.

6. Two basic assumptions of technical analysis are that security prices adjust:

   a. Gradually to new information, and study of the economic environment provides an indication of future market movements.

      b. Rapidly to new information, and study of the economic environment provides an indication of future market movements.

      c. Rapidly to new information, and market prices are determined by the interaction between supply and demand.

      d. Gradually to new information, and prices are determined by the interaction between supply and demand.

7. When technical analysts say a stock has good "relative strength," they mean:

      a. The ratio of the price of the stock to a market or industry index has trended upward.

      b. The recent trading volume in the stock has exceeded the normal trading volume.

      c. The total return on the stock has exceeded the total return on T-bills.

      d. The stock has performed well recently compared to its past performance.

8. Your investment client asks for information concerning the benefits of active portfolio management. She is particularly interested in the question of whether active managers can be expected to consistently exploit inefficiencies in the capital markets to produce above-average returns without assuming higher risk.

    The semistrong form of the efficient market hypothesis asserts that all publicly available information is rapidly and correctly reflected in securities prices. This implies that investors cannot expect to derive above-average profits from purchases made after information has become public because security prices already reflect the information's full effects.

      a. Identify and explain two examples of empirical evidence that tend to support the EMH implication stated above.

      b. Identify and explain two examples of empirical evidence that tend to refute the EMH implication stated above.

      c. Discuss reasons why an investor might choose not to index even if the markets were, in fact, semistrong-form efficient.

9. *a.* Briefly explain the concept of the efficient market hypothesis (EMH) and each of its three forms—weak, semistrong, and strong—and briefly discuss the degree to which existing empirical evidence supports each of the three forms of the EMH.

      b. Briefly discuss the implications of the efficient market hypothesis for investment policy as it applies to:

        i. Technical analysis in the form of charting.

        ii. Fundamental analysis.

      c. Briefly explain the roles or responsibilities of portfolio managers in an efficient market environment.

10. Growth and value can be defined in several ways. "Growth" usually conveys the idea of a portfolio emphasizing or including only issues believed to possess above-average future rates of per-share earnings growth. Low current yield, high price-to-book ratios, and high price-to-earnings ratios are typical characteristics of such portfolios. "Value" usually conveys the idea of portfolios emphasizing or including only issues currently showing low price-to-book ratios, low price-to-earnings ratios, above-average levels of dividend yield, and market prices believed to be below the issues' intrinsic values.

      a. Identify and provide reasons why, over an extended period of time, value-stock investing might outperform growth-stock investing.

      b. Explain why the outcome suggested in (*a*) should not be possible in a market widely regarded as being highly efficient.

E-INVESTMENTS EXERCISE

1. Use data from **finance.yahoo.com** to answer the following questions:

    a. Collect the following data for 25 firms of your choosing.

        i.   Book-to-market ratio.
        ii. Price–earnings ratio.
        iii. Market capitalization (size).
        iv. Price–cash flow ratio (i.e., market capitalization/operating cash flow).
        v.   Another criterion that interests you.

        You can find this information by choosing a company and then clicking on *Key Statistics.* Rank the firms based on each of the criteria separately, and divide the firms into five groups based on their ranking for each criterion. Calculate the average rate of return for each group of firms.

        Do you confirm or reject any of the anomalies cited in this chapter? Can you uncover a new anomaly? Note: For your test to be valid, you must form your portfolios based on criteria observed at the *beginning* of the period. Why?

    b. Under the *Statistics* tab, find the beta of each firm selected in part (a). Use this beta, the T-bill rate, and the return on the S&P 500 to calculate the risk-adjusted abnormal return of each stock group. Does any anomaly uncovered in the previous question persist after controlling for risk?

    c. Now form stock groups that use two criteria simultaneously. For example, form a portfolio of stocks that are both in the lowest quintile of price–earnings ratio and in the highest quintile of book-to-market ratio. Does selecting stocks based on more than one characteristic improve your ability to devise portfolios with abnormal returns? Repeat the analysis by forming groups that meet three criteria simultaneously. Does this yield any further improvement in abnormal returns?

 ## SOLUTIONS TO CONCEPT CHECKS

1. a. A high-level manager might well have private information about the firm. Her ability to trade profitably on that information is not surprising. This ability does not violate weak-form efficiency: The abnormal profits are not derived from an analysis of past price and trading data. If they were, this would indicate that there is valuable information that can be gleaned from such analysis. But this ability does violate strong-form efficiency. Apparently, there is some private information that is not already reflected in stock prices.

    b. The information sets that pertain to the weak, semistrong, and strong form of the EMH can be described by the following illustration:

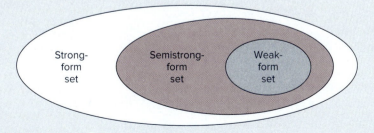

The weak-form information set includes only the history of prices and volumes. The semistrong-form set includes the weak form set *plus* all publicly available information. In turn, the strong-form set includes the semistrong set *plus* insiders' information. It is illegal to act on this incremental information (insiders' private information). The direction of *valid* implication is

Strong-form EMH ⇒ Semistrong-form EMH ⇒ Weak-form EMH

The reverse direction implication is *not* valid. For example, stock prices may reflect all past price data (weak-form efficiency) but may not reflect relevant fundamental data (semistrong-form inefficiency).

2. The point made in the preceding discussion is that the very fact that we observe stock prices near so-called resistance levels belies the assumption that the price can be a resistance level. If a stock is observed to sell *at any price,* then investors must believe that a fair rate of return can be earned if the stock is purchased at that price. It is logically impossible for a stock to have a resistance level *and* offer a fair rate of return at prices just below the resistance level. If we accept that prices are appropriate, we must reject any presumption concerning resistance levels.

3. If *everyone* follows a passive strategy, sooner or later prices will fail to reflect new information. At this point there are profit opportunities for active investors who uncover mispriced securities. As they buy and sell these assets, prices again will be driven to fair levels.

4. Predictably declining CARs do violate the EMH. If one can predict such a phenomenon, a profit opportunity emerges: Sell (or short sell) the affected stocks on an event date just before their prices are predicted to fall.

5. The answer depends on your prior beliefs about market efficiency. Miller's record through 2005 was incredibly strong. On the other hand, with so many funds in existence, it is less surprising that *some* fund would appear to be consistently superior after the fact. Exceptional past performance of a small number of managers is possible by chance even in an efficient market. A better test is provided in "continuation studies." Are better performers in one period more likely to repeat that performance in later periods? Miller's record after 2005 fails the continuation or consistency criterion.

Behavioral Finance and Technical Analysis

THE EFFICIENT MARKET hypothesis makes two important predictions. First, it implies that security prices properly reflect whatever information is available to investors. A second implication follows immediately: Active traders will find it difficult to outperform passive strategies such as holding market indexes. To do so would require differential insight; in a highly competitive market, this is hard to come by.

Unfortunately, it is hard to devise measures of the "true" or intrinsic value of a security and correspondingly difficult to test directly whether prices match those values. Therefore, most tests of market efficiency have focused on the performance of active trading strategies. These tests have been of two kinds. The anomalies literature has examined strategies that apparently *would* have provided superior risk-adjusted returns (e.g., investing in stocks with momentum or in value rather than glamour stocks). Other tests have looked at the results of *actual* investments by asking whether professional managers have been able to beat the market.

Neither class of tests has proven fully conclusive. The anomalies literature suggests that several strategies would have provided superior returns. But there are questions as to whether some of these apparent anomalies reflect risk premiums not captured by simple models of risk and return or even if they merely reflect data mining. Moreover, the apparent inability of the typical money manager to turn these anomalies into superior returns on actual portfolios casts additional doubt on their "reality."

A relatively new school of thought, *behavioral finance,* argues that the sprawling literature on trading strategies has missed a larger and more important point by overlooking the first implication of efficient markets—the *correctness* of security prices. This may be the more important implication, because market economies rely on prices to allocate resources efficiently. The behavioral school argues that even if security prices are wrong, to exploit them still can be difficult and, therefore, the failure to uncover obviously successful trading rules or traders cannot be taken as proof of market efficiency.

Whereas conventional theories presume that investors are rational, behavioral finance starts with the assumption that they are not. We will examine some of the information-processing and behavioral irrationalities uncovered by psychologists in other contexts and show how these tendencies applied to financial markets might result in some of the anomalies discussed in the previous chapter. We then consider the limitations of strategies designed to take advantage of behaviorally induced mispricing. If the limits to

(continued)

(concluded)

such arbitrage activity are severe, mispricing can survive even if some rational investors attempt to exploit it. We turn next to technical analysis and show how behavioral models give some support to techniques that clearly would be useless in efficient markets. We close the chapter with a brief survey of some of these technical strategies.

12.1 The Behavioral Critique

The premise of **behavioral finance** is that conventional financial theory ignores how real people make decisions and that people make a difference.[1] A growing number of economists have come to interpret the anomalies literature as consistent with several "irrationalities" that seem to characterize individuals making complicated decisions. These irrationalities fall into two broad categories: first, that investors do not always process information correctly and therefore infer incorrect probability distributions about future rates of return; and second, that even given a probability distribution of returns, they often make inconsistent or systematically suboptimal decisions.

Of course, the existence of irrational investors would not by itself be sufficient to render capital markets inefficient. If such irrationalities did affect prices, then sharp-eyed arbitrageurs taking advantage of profit opportunities might be expected to push prices back to their proper values. Thus, the second leg of the behavioral critique is that in practice the actions of such arbitrageurs are limited and therefore insufficient to force prices to match intrinsic value.

This leg of the argument is important. Virtually everyone agrees that if prices are right (i.e., price = intrinsic value), then there are no easy profit opportunities. But the reverse is not necessarily true. If behaviorists are correct about limits to arbitrage activity, then the absence of profit opportunities does not necessarily imply that markets are efficient. We've noted that most tests of the efficient market hypothesis have focused on the existence of profit opportunities, often as reflected in the performance of money managers. But their failure to systematically outperform passive investment strategies need not imply that markets are in fact efficient.

We will start our summary of the behavioral critique with the first leg of the argument, surveying a sample of the informational processing errors uncovered by psychologists in other areas. We next examine a few of the behavioral irrationalities that seem to characterize decision makers. Finally, we look at limits to arbitrage activity and conclude with a tentative assessment of the import of the behavioral debate.

Information Processing

Errors in information processing can lead investors to misestimate the true probabilities of possible events or associated rates of return. Several such biases have been uncovered. Here are four of the more important ones.

---

[1]The discussion in this section is largely based on Nicholas Barberis and Richard Thaler, "A Survey of Behavioral Finance," in the *Handbook of the Economics of Finance*, eds. G. M. Constantinides, M. Harris, and R. Stulz (Amsterdam: Elsevier, 2003).

Forecasting Errors   A series of experiments by Kahneman and Tversky[2] indicate that people give too much weight to recent experience compared to prior beliefs when making forecasts (sometimes dubbed a *memory bias*) and tend to make forecasts that are too extreme given the uncertainty inherent in their information. DeBondt and Thaler[3] argue that the P/E effect can be explained by earnings expectations that are too extreme. Specifically, when forecasts of a firm's future earnings are high, perhaps due to favorable recent performance, they tend to be *too* high relative to the objective prospects of the firm. This results in a high initial P/E (due to the excessive optimism built into the stock price) and poor subsequent performance when investors recognize their error. Thus, high P/E firms tend to be poor investments.

Overconfidence   People tend to overestimate the precision of their beliefs or forecasts, and they tend to overestimate their abilities. In one famous survey, 90% of drivers in Sweden ranked themselves as better-than-average drivers. Such overconfidence may be responsible for the prevalence of active versus passive investment management—itself an anomaly to adherents of the efficient market hypothesis. Despite the growing popularity of indexing, a bit less than 25% of the equity in the mutual fund industry is held in indexed accounts. The dominance of active management in the face of the typical underperformance of such strategies (consider the generally disappointing performance of actively managed mutual funds reviewed in Chapter 4 as well as in the previous chapter) is consistent with a tendency to overestimate ability.

An interesting example of overconfidence in financial markets is provided by Barber and Odean,[4] who compare trading activity and average returns in brokerage accounts of men and women. They find that men (in particular, single men) trade far more actively than women, consistent with the generally greater overconfidence among men well documented in the psychology literature. They also find that trading activity is highly predictive of poor investment performance. The top 20% of accounts ranked by portfolio turnover had average returns 7 percentage points lower than the 20% of the accounts with the lowest turnover rates. As they conclude, "trading [and by implication, overconfidence] is hazardous to your wealth."

Overconfidence appears to be a widespread phenomenon, also showing up in many corporate finance contexts. For example, overconfident CEOs are more likely to overpay for target firms when making corporate acquisitions.[5] Just as overconfidence can degrade portfolio investments, it also can lead such firms to make poor investments in real assets.

Conservatism   A **conservatism** bias means that investors are too slow (too conservative) in updating their beliefs in response to new evidence. This means that they might initially underreact to news about a firm, so that prices will fully reflect new information only gradually. Such a bias would give rise to momentum in stock market returns.

[2]D. Kahneman and A. Tversky, "On the Psychology of Prediction," *Psychology Review* 80 (1973), pp. 237–51; and "Subjective Probability: A Judgment of Representativeness," *Cognitive Psychology* 3 (1972), pp. 430–54.

[3]W. F. M. De Bondt and R. H. Thaler, "Do Security Analysts Overreact?" *American Economic Review* 80 (1990), pp. 52–57.

[4]Brad Barber and Terrance Odean, "Boys Will Be Boys: Gender, Overconfidence, and Common Stock Investment," *Quarterly Journal of Economics* 16 (2001), pp. 262–92; and "Trading Is Hazardous to Your Wealth: The Common Stock Investment Performance of Individual Investors," *Journal of Finance* 55 (2000), pp. 773–806.

[5]U. Malmendier and G. Tate, "Who Makes Acquisitions? CEO Overconfidence and the Market's Reaction," *Journal of Financial Economics* 89 (July 2008), pp. 20–43.

Sample Size Neglect and Representativeness   The notion of **representativeness bias** holds that people commonly do not take into account the size of a sample, acting as if a small sample is just as representative of a population as a large one. They may therefore infer a pattern too quickly based on a small sample and extrapolate apparent trends too far into the future. It is easy to see how such a pattern would be consistent with overreaction and correction anomalies. A short-lived run of good earnings reports or high stock returns leads such investors to revise their assessments of likely future performance and thus generate buying pressure that exaggerates the price run-up. Eventually, the gap between price and intrinsic value becomes glaring and the market corrects its initial error. Interestingly, stocks with the best recent performance suffer reversals precisely in the few days surrounding management earnings forecasts or actual earnings announcements, suggesting that the correction occurs just as investors learn that their initial beliefs were too extreme.[6]

 Concept Check **12.1**

We saw in Chapter 11 that stocks seem to exhibit a pattern of short- to middle-term momentum, along with long-term reversals. How might this pattern arise from an interplay between the conservatism and representativeness biases?

Behavioral Biases

Even if information processing were perfect, many studies conclude that individuals would tend to make less-than-fully-rational decisions using that information. These behavioral biases largely affect how investors frame questions of risk versus return and, therefore, make risk–return trade-offs.

Framing   Decisions seem to be affected by how choices are **framed.** For example, an individual may reject a bet when it is posed in terms of the risk surrounding possible gains but may accept that same bet when described in terms of the risk surrounding potential losses. In other words, individuals may act risk averse in terms of gains but risk seeking in terms of losses. But in many cases, the choice of how to frame a risky venture—as involving gains or losses—can be arbitrary.

Example 12.1   Framing

Consider a coin toss with a payoff of $50 for tails. Now consider a gift of $50 that is bundled with a bet that imposes a loss of $50 if that coin toss comes up heads. In both cases, you end up with zero for heads and $50 for tails. But the former description frames the coin toss as posing a risky gain, while the latter frames the coin toss in terms of a risky loss. The difference in framing can lead to different attitudes toward the bet.

Mental Accounting   **Mental accounting** is a specific form of framing in which people segregate certain decisions. For example, an investor may take a lot of risk with one investment account but establish a very conservative position with another account that is dedicated to her child's education. Rationally, it might be better to view both accounts as

[6]N. Chopra, J. Lakonishok, and J. Ritter, "Measuring Abnormal Performance: Do Stocks Overreact?" *Journal of Financial Economics* 31 (1992), pp. 235–68.

part of the investor's overall portfolio with the risk–return profiles of each integrated into a unified framework. Nevertheless, Statman[7] points out that a central distinction between conventional and behavioral finance theory is that the behavioral approach views investors as building their portfolios in "distinct mental account layers in a pyramid of assets," where each layer may be tied to particular goals and elicit different levels of risk aversion.

In another paper, Statman[8] argues that mental accounting is consistent with some investors' irrational preference for stocks with high cash dividends (they feel free to spend dividend income, but would not "dip into capital" by selling a few shares of another stock with the same total rate of return) and with a tendency to ride losing stock positions for too long (because "behavioral investors" are reluctant to realize losses). In fact, as an empirical rule, investors are more likely to sell stocks with gains than those with losses, precisely contrary to a tax-minimization strategy.[9]

Mental accounting also can help explain momentum in stock prices. The *house money effect* refers to gamblers' greater willingness to accept new bets if they currently are ahead. They think of (i.e., frame) the bet as being made with their "winnings account," that is, with the casino's money rather than their own, and thus they are more willing to accept risk. Analogously, after a stock market run-up, individuals may view investments as largely funded out of a "capital gains account," become more tolerant of risk, discount future cash flows at a lower rate, and thus further push up prices.

Regret Avoidance   Psychologists have found that individuals who make decisions that turn out badly have more regret (blame themselves more) when that decision was more unconventional. For example, buying a blue-chip portfolio that turns down is not as painful as experiencing the same losses on an unknown start-up firm. Any losses on the blue-chip stocks can be more easily attributed to bad luck rather than bad decision making and cause less regret. De Bondt and Thaler[10] argue that such **regret avoidance** is consistent with both the size and book-to-market effect. Higher book-to-market firms tend to have depressed stock prices. These firms are "out of favor" and more likely to be in a financially precarious position. Similarly, smaller, less well-known firms are also less conventional investments. Such firms require more "courage" on the part of the investor, which increases the required rate of return. Mental accounting can add to this effect. If investors focus on the gains or losses of individual stocks, rather than on broad portfolios, they can become more risk averse concerning stocks with recent poor performance, discount their cash flows at a higher rate, and thereby create a value-stock risk premium.

 Concept Check **12.2**

> How might the P/E effect (discussed in the previous chapter) also be explained as a consequence of regret avoidance?

---

[7]Meir Statman, "What Is Behavioral Finance?" in *Handbook of Finance,* vol. II, Ch 9, ed. Frank J. Fabozzi (Hoboken, NJ: John Wiley and Sons, 2008), pp. 79–84.

[8]Meir Statman, "Behavioral Finance," *Contemporary Finance Digest* 1 (Winter 1997), pp. 5–22.

[9]H. Shefrin and M. Statman, "The Disposition to Sell Winners Too Early and Ride Losers Too Long: Theory and Evidence," *Journal of Finance* 40 (July 1985), pp. 777–90; and T. Odean, "Are Investors Reluctant to Realize Their Losses?" *Journal of Finance* 53 (1998), pp. 1775–98.

[10]W. F. M. De Bondt and R. H. Thaler, "Further Evidence on Investor Overreaction and Stock Market Seasonality," *Journal of Finance* 42 (1987), pp. 557–81.

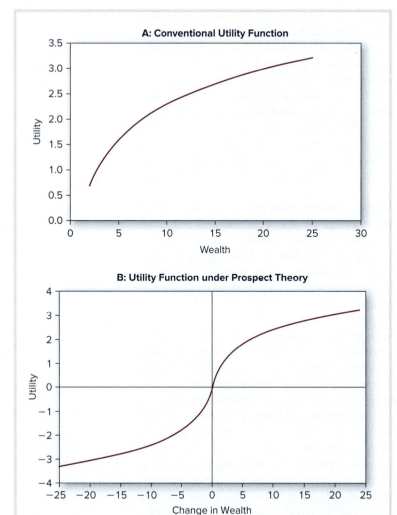

Affect   Conventional models of portfolio choice focus on asset risk and return. But behavioral finance focuses as well on *affect,* which is a feeling of "good" or "bad" that consumers may attach to a potential purchase or investors to a stock. For example, firms with reputations for socially responsible policies or attractive working conditions or those producing popular products may generate higher affect in public perception. If investors favor stocks with good affect, that might drive up prices and drive down average rates of return. Statman, Fisher, and Anginer[11] looked for evidence that affect influences security pricing. They found that stocks ranked high in *Fortune*'s survey of most admired companies (i.e., with high affect) tended to have lower average risk-adjusted returns than the least admired firms, suggesting that their prices have been bid up relative to their underlying profitability, and therefore, that their expected future returns are lower.

Prospect Theory   Prospect theory modifies the analytic description of rational risk-averse investors found in standard financial theory.[12] Figure 12.1, Panel A, illustrates the conventional description of a risk-averse investor. Higher wealth provides higher satisfaction, or "utility," but at a diminishing rate (the curve flattens as the individual becomes wealthier). This gives rise to risk aversion: A gain of $1,000 increases utility by less than a loss of $1,000 reduces it; therefore, investors will reject risky prospects that don't offer a risk premium.

Figure 12.1 Prospect theory. *Panel A:* A conventional utility function is defined in terms of wealth and is concave, resulting in risk aversion. *Panel B:* Under loss aversion, the utility function is defined in terms of losses relative to current wealth. It is also convex to the left of the origin, giving rise to risk-seeking behavior in terms of losses.

Figure 12.1, Panel B, shows a competing description of preferences characterized by "loss aversion." Utility depends not on the *level* of wealth, as in Panel A, but on *changes*

---

[11]Meir Statman, Kenneth L. Fisher, and Deniz Anginer, "Affect in a Behavioral Asset-Pricing Model," *Financial Analysts Journal* 64 (2008), 20–29.

[12]Prospect theory originated with a highly influential paper about decision making under uncertainty by D. Kahneman and A. Tversky, "Prospect Theory: An Analysis of Decision under Risk," *Econometrica* 47 (1979), pp. 263–91.

in wealth from current levels. Moreover, to the left of zero (zero denotes no change from current wealth), the curve is convex rather than concave. This description of investor utility has several implications. Whereas many conventional utility functions imply that investors may become less risk averse as wealth increases, the function in Panel B always re-centers on current wealth, thereby ruling out such decreases in risk aversion and possibly helping to explain high average historical equity risk premiums. Moreover, the convex curvature to the left of the origin in Panel B will induce investors to be risk seeking rather than risk averse when it comes to losses. Consistent with loss aversion, traders in T-bond futures contracts have been observed to assume significantly greater risk in afternoon sessions following morning sessions in which they have lost money.[13]

Limits to Arbitrage

Behavioral biases would not matter for stock pricing if rational arbitrageurs could fully exploit the mistakes of behavioral investors. Trades of profit-seeking investors would correct any misalignment between price and intrinsic value. However, behavioral advocates argue that, in practice, several factors limit the ability to profit from mispricing.[14]

Fundamental Risk   Suppose that a share of Amazon is underpriced. Buying it may present a profit opportunity, but it is hardly risk-free because the presumed market underpricing can get worse. While price eventually should converge to intrinsic value, this may not happen until after the trader's investment horizon. For example, the investor may be a mutual fund manager who may lose clients (not to mention a job!) if short-term performance is poor, or she may be a trader who may run through her capital if the market turns against her, even temporarily. A comment often attributed to the famous economist John Maynard Keynes is that "markets can remain irrational longer than you can remain solvent." The **fundamental risk** incurred in exploiting apparent profit opportunities presumably will limit the activity of traders.

Example 12.2   Fundamental Risk

In much of 2012, the NASDAQ index fluctuated at a level around 3,000. From that perspective, the value the index had reached in 2000, around 5,000, seemed obviously crazy. Surely some investors living through the Internet "bubble" of the late 1990s must have identified the index as grossly overvalued, suggesting a good selling opportunity. But this hardly would have been a riskless arbitrage opportunity. Consider that NASDAQ may also have been overvalued in January 2000 when it crossed above 4,000. An investor in that month who believed that NASDAQ was overvalued at 4,000 and decided to sell it short would have suffered enormous losses as the index increased by another 1,000 points before finally peaking at 5,000. While the investor might have derived considerable satisfaction at eventually being proven right about the overpricing, by entering a few months before the market "corrected," he might also have gone broke.

---

[13]J. D. Coval and T. Shumway, "Do Behavioral Biases Affect Prices?" *Journal of Finance* 60 (February 2005), pp. 1–34.

[14]Some of the more influential references on limits to arbitrage are J. B. DeLong, A. Schleifer, L. Summers, and R. Waldmann, "Noise Trader Risk in Financial Markets," *Journal of Political Economy* 98 (August 1990), pp. 704–38; and A. Schleifer and R. Vishny, "The Limits of Arbitrage," *Journal of Finance* 52 (March 1997), pp. 35–55.

Implementation Costs   Exploiting overpricing can be particularly difficult. Short-selling a security entails costs; short-sellers may have to return the borrowed security on little notice, rendering the horizon of the short sale uncertain. The cost of borrowing shares to initiate a short sale can can fluctuate dramatically; sometimes, there are simply no shares available for borrowing, so it is not even possible to enter into a short sale. Other investors, such as many pension or mutual fund managers, face strict limits on their discretion to short securities. These impediments can limit the ability of arbitrage activity to force prices to fair value.

Model Risk   One always has to worry that an apparent profit opportunity is more apparent than real. Perhaps you are using a faulty model to value the security, and the price actually is right. Mispricing may make a position a good bet, but it is still a risky one, which limits the extent to which it will be pursued.

Limits to Arbitrage and the Law of One Price

While one can debate the implications of much of the anomalies literature, surely the Law of One Price (positing that effectively identical assets should have identical prices) should be satisfied in rational markets. Yet there are several instances where the law seems to have been violated. These instances are good case studies of the limits to arbitrage.

"Siamese Twin" Companies[15]   In 1907, Royal Dutch Petroleum and Shell Transport merged their operations into one firm. The two original companies, which continued to trade separately, agreed to split all profits from the joint company on a 60/40 basis. Shareholders of Royal Dutch receive 60% of the cash flow, and those of Shell receive 40%. One would therefore expect that Royal Dutch should sell for exactly 60/40 = 1.5 times the price of Shell. But this is not the case. Figure 12.2 shows that the relative value of the two firms has departed considerably from this "parity" ratio for extended periods of time.

Doesn't this mispricing give rise to an arbitrage opportunity? If Royal Dutch sells for more than 1.5 times Shell, why not buy relatively underpriced Shell and short sell overpriced Royal? This seems like a reasonable strategy, but if you had followed it in February 1993 when Royal sold for about 10% more than its parity value, Figure 12.2 shows that you would have lost a lot of money as the premium widened to about 17% before finally reversing after 1999. As in Example 12.2, this opportunity posed fundamental risk.

Equity Carve-Outs   Several equity carve-outs also have violated the Law of One Price.[16] To illustrate, consider the case of 3Com, which in 1999 decided to spin off its Palm division. It first sold 5% of its stake in Palm in an IPO, announcing that it would distribute the remaining 95% of its Palm shares to 3Com shareholders six months later in a spinoff. Each 3Com shareholder would receive 1.5 shares of Palm in the spinoff.

Once Palm shares began trading, but prior to the spinoff, the share price of 3Com should have been *at least* 1.5 times that of Palm. After all, each share of 3Com entitled its owner to 1.5 shares of Palm *plus* an ownership stake in a profitable company. Instead, Palm shares at the IPO actually sold for *more* than the 3Com shares. The *stub value* of 3Com (i.e., the value of each 3Com share net of the value of the claim to Palm represented by that share) could be computed as the price of 3Com minus 1.5 times the price of Palm.

---

[15]This discussion is based on K. A. Froot and E. M. Dabora, "How Are Stock Prices Affected by the Location of Trade?" *Journal of Financial Economics* 53 (1999), pp. 189–216.

[16]O. A. Lamont and R. H. Thaler, "Can the Market Add and Subtract? Mispricing in Tech Carve-outs," *Journal of Political Economy* 111 (2003), pp. 227–68.

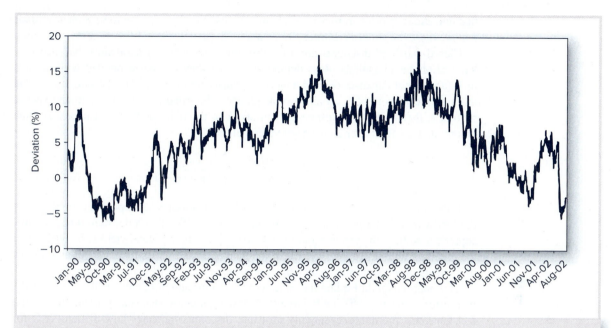

Figure 12.2 Pricing of Royal Dutch relative to Shell *(deviation from parity)*

Source: O. A. Lamont and R. H. Thaler, "Anomalies: The Law of One Price in Financial Markets," *Journal of Economic Perspectives* 17 (Fall 2003), pp. 191–202. Figure 1, p. 196. Used with permission of American Economic Association.

This calculation, however, implies that 3Com's stub value was negative, despite the fact that it was a profitable company with cash assets alone of about $10 per share.

Again, an arbitrage strategy seems obvious. Why not buy 3Com and sell Palm? The limit to arbitrage in this case was the inability of investors to sell Palm short. Virtually all available shares in Palm were already borrowed and sold short, and the negative stub values persisted for more than two months.

Closed-End Funds   We noted in Chapter 4 that closed-end funds often sell for substantial discounts or premiums from net asset value. This is "nearly" a violation of the Law of One Price because one would expect the value of the fund to equal the value of the shares it holds. We say *nearly* because, in practice, there are a few wedges between the value of the closed-end fund and its underlying assets. One is expenses. The fund incurs expenses that ultimately are paid for by investors, and these will reduce share price. On the other hand, if managers can invest fund assets to generate positive risk-adjusted returns, share price might exceed net asset value.

Lee, Shleifer, and Thaler[17] argue that the patterns of discounts and premiums on closed-end funds are driven by changes in investor sentiment. They note that discounts on various funds move together and are correlated with the return on small stocks, suggesting that all are affected by common variation in sentiment. One might consider buying funds selling at a discount from net asset value and selling those trading at a premium, but discounts and premiums can widen, subjecting this strategy to fundamental risk. Pontiff[18] demonstrates

---

[17]C. M. Lee, A. Shleifer, and R. H. Thaler, "Investor Sentiment and the Closed-End Fund Puzzle," *Journal of Finance* 46 (March 1991), pp. 75–109.

[18]Jeffrey Pontiff, "Costly Arbitrage: Evidence from Closed-End Funds," *Quarterly Journal of Economics* 111 (November 1996), pp. 1135–51.

that deviations of price from net asset value in closed-end funds tend to be higher in funds that are more difficult to arbitrage, for example, those with more idiosyncratic volatility.

Closed-end fund discounts are a good example of apparent anomalies that also may have rational explanations. Ross demonstrates that they can be reconciled with rational investors even if expenses or fund abnormal returns are modest.[19] He shows that if a fund has a dividend yield of δ, an alpha (risk-adjusted abnormal return) of α, and an expense ratio of ε, then using the constant-growth dividend discount model (see Chapter 18), the premium of the fund over its net asset value will be

$$\frac{\text{Price} - \text{NAV}}{\text{NAV}} = \frac{\alpha - \varepsilon}{\delta + \varepsilon - \alpha}$$

If the fund manager's performance more than compensates for expenses (i.e., if $\alpha > \varepsilon$), the fund will sell at a premium to NAV; otherwise it will sell at a discount. For example, suppose $\alpha = .015$, the expense ratio is $\varepsilon = .0125$, and the dividend yield is $\delta = .02$. Then the premium will be .14, or 14%. But if the market turns sour on the manager and revises its estimate of α downward to .005, that premium quickly turns into a discount of 27%.

This analysis might explain the pattern of premiums and discounts in closed-end funds; if investors expect a sufficiently large α, they will purchase shares at a premium. But the fact that most premiums eventually turn into discounts indicates how difficult it is for management to fulfill these expectations.[20]

 Concept Check **12.3**

Fundamental risk may be limited by a "deadline" that forces a convergence between price and intrinsic value. What do you think would happen to a closed-end fund's discount if the fund were to announce that it planned to liquidate in six months, at which time it would distribute NAV to its shareholders?

Bubbles and Behavioral Economics

In Example 12.2, we pointed out that the stock market run-up of the late 1990s, and even more spectacularly, the run-up of the technology-heavy NASDAQ market, seems in retrospect to have been an obvious bubble. In a six-year period beginning in 1995, the NASDAQ index increased by a factor of more than 6. Former Fed Chairman Alan Greenspan famously characterized the dot-com boom as an example of "irrational exuberance," and his assessment turned out to be correct: By October 2002, the index fell to less than one-fourth the peak value it had reached only $2\frac{1}{2}$ years earlier. This episode seems to be a case in point for advocates of the behavioral school, exemplifying a market moved by irrational investor sentiment. Moreover, in accord with behavioral patterns, as the dot-com boom developed, it seemed to feed on itself, with investors increasingly confident of their investment prowess (overconfidence bias) and apparently willing to extrapolate short-term patterns into the distant future (representativeness bias).

---

[19]S. A. Ross, "Neoclassical Finance, Alternative Finance and the Closed End Fund Puzzle," *European Financial Management* 8 (2002), pp. 129–37, **http://ssrn.com/abstract=313444.**

[20]We might ask why this logic of discounts and premiums does not apply to open-end mutual funds since they incur similar expense ratios. Because investors in these funds can redeem shares for NAV, the shares cannot sell at a discount to NAV. Expenses in open-end funds reduce returns in each period rather than being capitalized into price and inducing a discount.

Only five years later, another bubble, this time in housing prices, was under way. As in the dot-com bubble, prospects of further price increases fueled speculative demand by purchasers. Shortly thereafter, of course, housing prices stalled and then fell. The bursting bubble set off the worst financial crisis in 75 years.

Bubbles are a lot easier to identify as such once they are over. While they are going on, irrational exuberance is less obvious, and indeed, many financial commentators during the dot-com bubble justified the boom as consistent with glowing forecasts for the "new economy." A simple example shows how hard it can be to tie down the fair value of stock investments.[21]

Example 12.3   A Stock Market Bubble?

In 2000, near the peak of the dot-com boom, the dividends paid by the firms included in the S&P 500 totaled $154.6 million. If the discount rate for the index was 9.2% and the expected dividend growth rate was 8%, the value of these shares according to the constant-growth dividend discount model (see Chapter 18 for more on this model) would be

$$\text{Value} = \frac{\text{Dividend}}{\text{Discount rate} - \text{Growth rate}} = \frac{\$154.6}{.092 - .08} = \$12{,}883 \text{ million}$$

This was quite close to the actual total value of those firms at the time. But the estimate is highly sensitive to the input values, and even a small reassessment of their prospects would result in a big revision of price. Suppose the expected dividend growth rate fell to 7.4%. This would reduce the value of the index to

$$\text{Value} = \frac{\text{Dividend}}{\text{Discount rate} - \text{Growth rate}} = \frac{\$154.6}{.092 - .074} = \$8{,}589 \text{ million}$$

which was about the value to which the S&P 500 firms had fallen by October 2002. In light of this example, the run-up and crash of the 1990s seem easier to reconcile with rational behavior.

Still, other evidence seems to tag the dot-com boom as at least partially irrational. Consider, for example, the results of a study documenting that firms adding ".com" to the end of their names during this period enjoyed a meaningful stock price increase.[22] That doesn't sound like rational valuation.

Evaluating the Behavioral Critique

As investors, we are concerned with the existence of profit opportunities. The behavioral explanations of efficient market anomalies do not give guidance as to how to exploit any irrationality. For investors, the question is still whether there is money to be made from mispricing, and the behavioral literature is largely silent on this point.

However, as we emphasized above, one of the important implications of the efficient market hypothesis is that security prices serve as reliable guides to the allocation of real assets. If prices are distorted, then capital markets will give misleading signals (and incentives) as to where the economy may best allocate resources. In this crucial dimension, the

---

[21]The following example is taken from R. A. Brealey, S. C. Myers, and F. Allen, *Principles of Corporate Finance*, 8th ed. (New York: McGraw-Hill Irwin, 2006).

[22]P. R. Rau, O. Dimitrov, and M. Cooper, "A Rose.com by Any Other Name," *Journal of Finance* 56 (2001), pp. 2371–88.

behavioral critique of the efficient market hypothesis is certainly important irrespective of any implication for investment strategies.

There is considerable debate among financial economists concerning behavioral finance. Many believe that it is too unstructured, in effect allowing virtually any anomaly to be explained by some combination of irrationalities chosen from a laundry list of behavioral biases. While it is easy to "reverse engineer" a behavioral explanation for any particular anomaly, these critics would like to see a consistent or unified behavioral theory that can explain a *range* of behavioral anomalies.

More fundamentally, others are not convinced that the anomalies literature as a whole is a convincing indictment of the efficient market hypothesis. Fama[23] notes that the anomalies are inconsistent in terms of their support for one type of irrationality versus another. For example, some papers document long-term corrections (consistent with overreaction), while others document long-term continuations of abnormal returns (consistent with underreaction). Moreover, the statistical significance of many of these results is hard to assess. Even small errors in choosing a benchmark against which to compare returns can cumulate to large apparent abnormalities in long-term returns.

The behavioral critique of full rationality in investor decision making is well taken, but the extent to which limited rationality affects asset pricing remains controversial. Whether or not investor irrationality affects asset prices, however, behavioral finance already makes important points about portfolio management. Investors who are aware of the potential pitfalls in information processing and decision making that seem to characterize their peers should be better able to avoid such errors. Ironically, the insights of behavioral finance may lead to some of the same policy conclusions embraced by efficient market advocates. For example, an easy way to avoid some of the behavioral minefields is to pursue passive, largely indexed, portfolio strategies. It seems that only rare individuals can consistently beat passive strategies; this conclusion may hold true whether your fellow investors are behavioral or rational.

12.2   Technical Analysis and Behavioral Finance

Technical analysis attempts to exploit recurring and predictable patterns in stock prices to generate superior investment performance. Technicians do not deny the value of fundamental information, but they believe that prices only gradually close in on intrinsic value. As fundamentals shift, astute traders can exploit the adjustment to a new equilibrium.

For example, one of the best-documented behavioral tendencies is the **disposition effect,** which refers to the tendency of investors to hold on to losing investments. Behavioral investors seem reluctant to realize losses. This disposition effect can lead to momentum in stock prices even if fundamental values follow a random walk.[24] The fact that the demand of "disposition investors" for a company's shares depends on the price history of those shares means that prices could close in on fundamental values only over time, consistent with the central motivation of technical analysis.

Behavioral biases may also be consistent with technical analysts' use of volume data. An important behavioral trait noted above is overconfidence, a systematic tendency to

---

[23]E. F. Fama, "Market Efficiency, Long-Term Returns, and Behavioral Finance," *Journal of Financial Economics* 49 (September 1998), pp. 283–306.

[24]Mark Grinblatt and Bing Han, "Prospect Theory, Mental Accounting, and Momentum," *Journal of Financial Economics* 78 (November 2005), pp. 311–39.

overestimate one's abilities. As traders become overconfident, they may trade more, inducing an association between trading volume and market returns.[25] Technical analysis thus uses volume data as well as price history to direct trading strategy.

Finally, technicians believe that market fundamentals can be perturbed by irrational or behavioral factors, sometimes labeled sentiment variables. More or less random price fluctuations will accompany any underlying price trend, creating opportunities to exploit corrections as these fluctuations dissipate.

Trends and Corrections

Much of technical analysis seeks to uncover trends in market prices. This is in effect a search for momentum. Momentum can be absolute, in which case one searches for upward price trends, or relative, in which case the analyst looks to invest in one sector over another (or even take on a long-short position in the two sectors). Relative strength statistics are designed to uncover these potential opportunities.

Momentum and Moving Averages   While we all would like to buy shares in firms whose prices are trending upward, this begs the question of how to identify the underlying direction of prices, if in fact such trends actually exist. A popular tool used for this purpose is the moving average.

The moving average of a stock price is the average price over a given interval, where that interval is updated as time passes. For example, a 50-day moving average traces the average price over the previous 50 days. The average is recomputed each day by dropping the oldest observation and adding the newest. Figure 12.3 is a moving average chart for Intel. Notice that the moving average (the colored curve) is a "smoothed" version of the original data series (the jagged dark curve).

After a period in which prices have been falling, the moving average will be above the current price (because the moving average continues to average in the older and higher

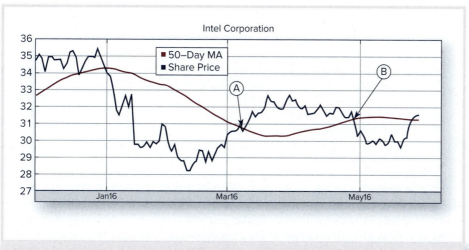

Figure 12.3 Share price and 50-day moving average for Intel (ticker INTC)

Source: Yahoo! Finance, May 28, 2016 **(finance.yahoo.com).**

---

[25]S. Gervais and T. Odean, "Learning to Be Overconfident," *Review of Financial Studies* 14 (2001), pp. 1–27.

prices until they leave the sample period). In contrast, when prices have been rising, the moving average will be below the current price.

Prices breaking through the moving average from below, as at point A in Figure 12.3, are taken as a bullish signal, because this signifies a shift from a falling trend (with prices below the moving average) to a rising trend (with prices above the moving average). Conversely, when prices drop below the moving average, as at point B, analysts might conclude that market momentum has become negative.

Example 12.4   Moving Averages

Consider the following price data. Each observation represents the closing level of the Dow Jones Industrial Average (DJIA) on the last trading day of the week. The 5-week moving average for each week is the average of the DJIA over the previous 5 weeks. For example, the first entry, for week 5, is the average of the index value between weeks 1 and 5: 17,290, 17,380, 17,399, 17,379, and 17,450. The next entry is the average of the index values between weeks 2 and 6, and so on.

Week	DJIA	5-Week Moving Average	Week	DJIA	5-Week Moving Average
1	17,290		11	17,590	17,555
2	17,380		12	17,652	17,586
3	17,399		13	17,625	17,598
4	17,379		14	17,657	17,624
5	17,450	17,380	15	17,699	17,645
6	17,513	17,424	16	17,647	17,656
7	17,500	17,448	17	17,610	17,648
8	17,565	17,481	18	17,595	17,642
9	17,524	17,510	19	17,499	17,610
10	17,597	17,540	20	17,466	17,563

Figure 12.4 plots the level of the index and the 5-week moving average. Notice that while the index itself moves up and down rather abruptly, the moving average is a relatively smooth series, because the impact of each week's price movement is averaged with that of the previous weeks. Week 16 is a bearish point according to the moving average rule. The price series crosses from above the moving average to below it, signifying the beginning of a downward trend in stock prices.

Other techniques also are used to uncover potential momentum in stock prices. Two of the more famous ones are *Elliott wave theory* and *Kondratieff waves.* Both posit the existence of long-term trends in stock market prices that may be disturbed by shorter-term trends as well as daily fluctuations of little importance. Elliott wave theory superimposes long-term and short-term wave cycles in an attempt to describe the complicated pattern of actual price movements. Once the longer-term waves are identified, investors presumably can buy when the long-term direction of the market is positive. While there is considerable noise in the actual evolution of stock prices, by properly interpreting the wave cycles, one can, according to the theory, predict broad movements. Similarly, Kondratieff waves are named after a Russian economist who asserted that the macroeconomy (and therefore

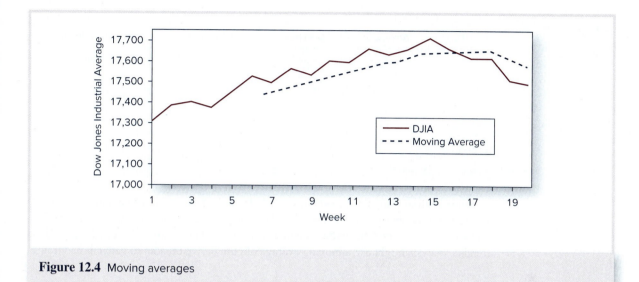

Figure 12.4 Moving averages

the stock market) moves in broad waves lasting between 48 and 60 years. Kondratieff's assertion is hard to evaluate empirically, however, because cycles that last about 50 years provide only two independent data points per century, which is hardly enough data to test the predictive power of the theory.

Relative Strength   **Relative strength** measures the extent to which a security has outperformed or underperformed either the market as a whole or its particular industry. Relative strength is computed by calculating the ratio of the price of the security to a price index for the industry. For example, the relative strength of Toyota versus the auto industry would be measured by movements in the ratio of the price of Toyota divided by the level of an auto industry index. A rising ratio implies Toyota has been outperforming the rest of the industry. If relative strength can be assumed to persist over time, then this would be a signal to buy Toyota.

Similarly, the strength of an industry relative to the whole market can be computed by tracking the ratio of the industry price index to the market price index.

Breadth   The **breadth** of the market is a measure of the extent to which movement in a market index is reflected widely in the price movements of all the stocks in the market. The most common measure of breadth is the spread between the number of stocks that advance and decline in price. If advances outnumber declines by a wide margin, then the market is viewed as being stronger because the rally is widespread. These numbers are reported in *The Wall Street Journal* (see Figure 12.5).

Trading Diary: Volume, Advancers, Decliners

Market Diary

Issues	NYSE	NASDAQ
Advancing	2,070	1,905
Declining	1,003	896
Unchanged	109	180
Total	3,182	2,981

Issues at		
New 52 week high	109	78
New 52 week low	88	22

Share Volume		
Advancing	510,372	1,075,611
Declining	283,331	388,278
Unchanged	10,925	24,067
Total	804,628	1,487,956

Figure 12.5 Market Diary

Source: *The Wall Street Journal Online*, May 28, 2016.

Table 12.1

Breadth

Day	Advances	Declines	Net Advances	Cumulative Breadth
1	1,302	1,248	54	54
2	1,417	1,140	277	331
3	1,203	1,272	−69	262
4	1,012	1,622	−610	−348
5	1,133	1,504	−371	−719

Note: The sum of advances plus declines varies across days because some stock prices are unchanged.

Some analysts cumulate breadth data each day as in Table 12.1. The cumulative breadth for each day is obtained by adding that day's net advances (or declines) to the previous day's total. The direction of the cumulated series is then used to discern broad market trends. Analysts might use a moving average of cumulative breadth to gauge broad trends.

Sentiment Indicators

Behavioral finance devotes considerable attention to market *sentiment,* which may be interpreted as the general level of optimism among investors. Technical analysts have devised several measures of sentiment; we review a few of them.

Trin Statistic   Trading volume is sometimes used to measure the strength of a market rise or fall. Increased investor participation in a market advance or retreat is viewed as a measure of the significance of the movement. Technicians consider market advances to be a more favorable omen of continued price increases when they are associated with increased trading volume. Similarly, market reversals are considered more bearish when associated with higher volume. The **trin statistic** is defined as

$$\text{Trin} = \frac{\text{Volume declining/Number declining}}{\text{Volume advancing/Number advancing}}$$

Therefore, trin is the ratio of average volume in declining issues to average volume in advancing issues. Ratios above 1.0 are considered bearish because the falling stocks would then have higher average volume than the advancing stocks, indicating net selling pressure. *The Wall Street Journal Online* provides the data necessary to compute trin in its Markets Diary section. Using the data in Figure 12.5, trin for the NYSE on this day was:

$$\text{Trin} = \frac{283,331/1,003}{510,372/2,070} = 1.146$$

Remember, however, that for every buyer, there must be a seller of stock. Rising volume in a rising market should not necessarily indicate a larger imbalance of buyers versus sellers. For example, a trin statistic above 1.0, which is considered bearish, could equally well be interpreted as indicating that there is more *buying* activity in declining issues.

Confidence Index   *Barron's* computes a confidence index using data from the bond market. The presumption is that actions of bond traders reveal trends that will emerge soon in the stock market.

The **confidence index** is the ratio of the average yield on 10 top-rated corporate bonds divided by the average yield on 10 intermediate-grade corporate bonds. The ratio will always be below 1 because higher-rated bonds will offer lower promised yields to maturity. When bond traders are optimistic about the economy, however, they might require smaller default premiums on lower-rated debt. Hence, the yield spread will narrow, and the confidence index will approach 1. Therefore, higher values of the confidence index are bullish signals.

 Concept Check **12.4**

> Yields on lower-rated debt will rise after fears of recession have spread through the economy. This will reduce the confidence index. Should the stock market now be expected to fall or will it already have fallen?

Put/Call Ratio   Call options give investors the right to buy a stock at a fixed "exercise" price and therefore are a way of betting on stock price increases. Put options give the right to sell a stock at a fixed price and therefore are a way of betting on stock price decreases.[26] The ratio of outstanding put options to outstanding call options is called the **put/call ratio.** Typically, the put/call ratio hovers around 65%. Because put options do well in falling markets while call options do well in rising markets, deviations of the ratio from historical norms are considered to be a signal of market sentiment and therefore predictive of market movements.

Interestingly, however, a change in the ratio can be given a bullish or a bearish interpretation. Many technicians see an increase in the ratio as bearish, as it indicates growing interest in put options as a hedge against market declines. Thus, a rising ratio is taken as a sign of broad investor pessimism and a coming market decline. Contrarian investors, however, believe that a good time to buy is when the rest of the market is bearish because stock prices are then unduly depressed. Therefore, they would take an increase in the put/call ratio as a signal of a buy opportunity.

A Warning

The search for patterns in stock market prices is nearly irresistible, and the ability of the human eye to discern apparent patterns is remarkable. Unfortunately, it is possible to perceive patterns that really don't exist. Consider Figure 12.6, which presents simulated and actual values of the Dow Jones Industrial Average during 1956 taken from a famous study by Harry Roberts.[27] In Figure 12.6, Panel B, the market appears to present a classic head-and-shoulders pattern where the middle hump (the head) is flanked by two shoulders. When the price index "pierces the right shoulder"—a technical trigger point—it is believed to be heading lower, and it is time to sell your stocks. Figure 12.6, Panel A also looks like a "typical" stock market pattern.

However, one of these panels was generated using "returns" created by a random-number generator and *by construction* were patternless. Can you tell which of the two graphs is constructed from the real value of the Dow and which from the simulated data?[28]

Figure 12.7 shows the weekly price *changes* behind the two panels in Figure 12.6. Here the randomness in both series—the stock price as well as the simulated sequence—is obvious.

A problem related to the tendency to perceive patterns where they don't exist is data mining. After the fact, you can always find patterns and trading rules that would have generated enormous profits. If you test enough rules, some will have worked in the past. Unfortunately, picking a theory that would have worked after the fact carries no guarantee of future success.

---

[26]Puts and calls were defined in Chapter 2, Section 2.5. They are discussed more fully in Chapter 20.

[27]H. Roberts, "Stock Market 'Patterns' and Financial Analysis: Methodological Suggestions," *Journal of Finance* 14 (March 1959), pp. 1–10.

[28]Figure 12.6, Panel A is based on the real data. The graph in Panel B was generated using the randomly generated "returns," but the simulated price path that is plotted appears to follow a pattern much like that of Panel A.

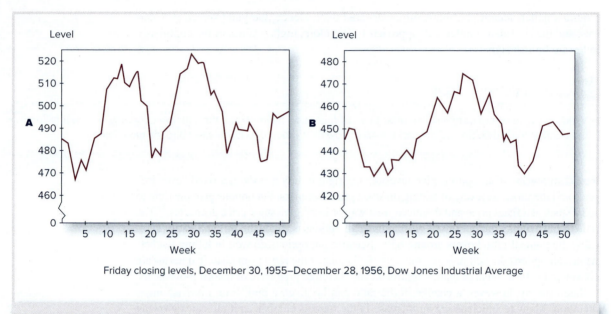

Figure 12.6 Actual and simulated levels for stock market prices of 52 weeks

Source: Harry Roberts, "Stock Market 'Patterns' and Financial Analysis: Methodological Suggestions," *Journal of Finance* 14 (March 1959), pp. 1–10.

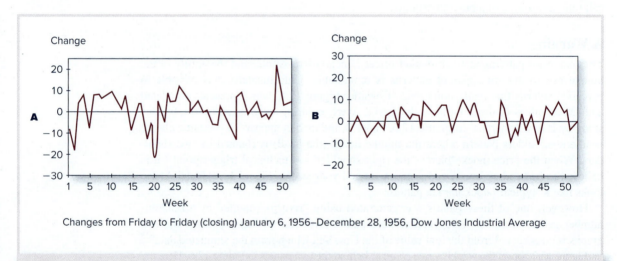

Figure 12.7 Actual and simulated changes in weekly stock prices for 52 weeks

Source: Harry Roberts, "Stock Market 'Patterns' and Financial Analysis: Methodological Suggestions," *Journal of Finance* 14 (March 1959), pp. 1–10.

In evaluating trading rules, you should always ask whether the rule would have seemed reasonable *before* you looked at the data. If not, you might be buying into the one arbitrary rule among many that happened to have worked in the recent past. The hard but crucial question is whether there is reason to believe that what worked in the past should continue to work in the future.

SUMMARY

1. Behavioral finance focuses on systematic irrationalities that characterize investor decision making. These "behavioral shortcomings" may be consistent with several efficient market anomalies.

2. Among the information processing errors uncovered in the psychology literature are memory bias, overconfidence, conservatism, and representativeness. Behavioral tendencies include framing, mental accounting, regret avoidance, and loss aversion.

3. Limits to arbitrage activity impede the ability of rational investors to exploit pricing errors induced by behavioral investors. For example, fundamental risk means that even if a security is mispriced, it still can be risky to attempt to exploit the mispricing. This limits the actions of arbitrageurs who take positions in mispriced securities. Other limits to arbitrage are implementation costs, model risk, and costs to short-selling. Occasional failures of the Law of One Price suggest that limits to arbitrage are sometimes severe.

4. The various limits to arbitrage mean that even if prices do not equal intrinsic value, it still may be difficult to exploit the mispricing. As a result, the failure of traders to beat the market may not be proof that markets are in fact efficient, with prices equal to intrinsic value.

5. Technical analysis is the search for recurring and predictable patterns in stock prices. It is based on the premise that prices only gradually close in on intrinsic value. As fundamentals shift, astute traders can exploit the adjustment to a new equilibrium.

6. Technical analysis also uses volume data and sentiment indicators. These are broadly consistent with several behavioral models of investor activity. Moving averages, relative strength, and breadth are used in other trend-based strategies.

7. Some sentiment indicators are the trin statistic, the confidence index, and the put/call ratio.

KEY TERMS

behavioral finance	regret avoidance	breadth
conservatism	prospect theory	trin statistic
representativeness bias	fundamental risk	confidence index
framing	disposition effect	put/call ratio
mental accounting	relative strength	

PROBLEM SETS

1. Explain how some of the behavioral biases discussed in the chapter might contribute to the success of technical trading rules.

2. Why would an advocate of the efficient market hypothesis believe that even if many investors exhibit the behavioral biases discussed in the chapter, security prices might still be set efficiently?

3. What sorts of factors might limit the ability of rational investors to take advantage of any "pricing errors" that result from the actions of "behavioral investors"?

4. Even if behavioral biases do not affect equilibrium asset prices, why might it still be important for investors to be aware of them?

5. Some advocates of behavioral finance agree with efficient market advocates that indexing is the optimal investment strategy for most investors. But their reasons for this conclusion differ greatly. Compare and contrast the rationale for indexing according to both of these schools of thought.

6. Jill Davis tells her broker that she does not want to sell her stocks that are below the price she paid for them. She believes that if she just holds on to them a little longer they will recover, at which time she will sell them. Which behavioral characteristic is the basis for Davis's decision making?

    a. Loss aversion.
    b. Conservatism.
    c. Representativeness.

7. After Polly Shrum sells a stock, she avoids following it in the media. She is afraid that it may subsequently increase in price. Which behavioral characteristic is the basis for Shrum's decision making?

   a. Fear of regret.
   b. Representativeness.
   c. Mental accounting.

8. All of the following actions are consistent with feelings of regret *except:*

   a. Selling losers quickly.
   b. Hiring a full-service broker.
   c. Holding on to losers too long.

9. Match each example to one of the following behavioral characteristics.

Example	Characteristic
a. Investors are slow to update their beliefs when given new evidence.	i. Disposition effect
b. Investors are reluctant to bear losses caused by their unconventional decisions.	ii. Representativeness bias
c. Investors exhibit less risk tolerance in their retirement accounts versus their other stock accounts.	iii. Regret avoidance
d. Investors are reluctant to sell stocks with "paper" losses.	iv. Conservatism bias
e. Investors disregard sample size when forming views about the future from the past.	v. Mental accounting

10. What do we mean by fundamental risk, and why may such risk allow behavioral biases to persist for long periods of time?

11. What is meant by data mining, and why must technical analysts be careful not to engage in it?

12. Even if prices follow a random walk, they still may not be informationally efficient. Explain why this may be true and why it matters for the efficient allocation of capital in our economy.

13. Use the data from *The Wall Street Journal* in Figure 12.5 to calculate the trin ratio for the NASDAQ. Is the trin ratio bullish or bearish?

14. Calculate breadth for the NYSE using the data in Figure 12.5. Is the signal bullish or bearish?

15. Collect data on the DJIA for a period covering a few months. Try to identify primary trends. Can you tell whether the market currently is in an upward or downward trend?

16. Baa-rated bonds currently yield 6%, while Aa-rated bonds yield 5%. Suppose that due to an increase in the expected inflation rate, the yields on both bonds increase by 1%.

    a. What would happen to the confidence index?
    b. Would this be interpreted as bullish or bearish by a technical analyst?
    c. Does this make sense to you?

17. Table 12A presents price data for Computers, Inc., and a computer industry index. Does Computers, Inc., show relative strength over this period?

18. Using the data in Table 12A, compute a five-day moving average for Computers, Inc. Can you identify any buy or sell signals?

19. Yesterday, the S&P 500 rose by .48%. However, 1,704 issues on the NYSE declined in price while 1,367 advanced. Why might a technical analyst be concerned even though the market index rose on this day?

20. Table 12B contains data on market advances and declines. Calculate cumulative breadth and decide whether this technical signal is bullish or bearish.

21. In Table 12B, if the trading volume in advancing shares on day 1 was 530 million shares, while the volume in declining issues was 440 million shares, what was the trin statistic for that day? Was the trin bullish or bearish?

Trading Day	Computers, Inc.	Industry Index	Trading Day	Computers, Inc.	Industry Index
1	19.63	50.0	21	19.63	54.1
2	20.00	50.1	22	21.50	54.0
3	20.50	50.5	23	22.00	53.9
4	22.00	50.4	24	23.13	53.7
5	21.13	51.0	25	24.00	54.8
6	22.00	50.7	26	25.25	54.5
7	21.88	50.5	27	26.25	54.6
8	22.50	51.1	28	27.00	54.1
9	23.13	51.5	29	27.50	54.2
10	23.88	51.7	30	28.00	54.8
11	24.50	51.4	31	28.50	54.2
12	23.25	51.7	32	28.00	54.8
13	22.13	52.2	33	27.50	54.9
14	22.00	52.0	34	29.00	55.2
15	20.63	53.1	35	29.25	55.7
16	20.25	53.5	36	29.50	56.1
17	19.75	53.9	37	30.00	56.7
18	18.75	53.6	38	28.50	56.7
19	17.50	52.9	39	27.75	56.5
20	19.00	53.4	40	28.00	56.1

Table 12A

Computers, Inc., stock price history

Day	Advances	Declines	Day	Advances	Declines
1	906	704	6	970	702
2	653	986	7	1,002	609
3	721	789	8	903	722
4	503	968	9	850	748
5	497	1,095	10	766	766

Table 12B

Market advances and declines

22. Using the following data, calculate the change in the confidence index from last year to this year. What besides a change in confidence might explain the pattern of yield changes?

	This Year	Last Year
Yield on top-rated corporate bonds	4%	7%
Yield on intermediate-grade corporate bonds	6	9

23. Log in to Connect and link to the material for Chapter 12, where you will find five years of weekly returns for the S&P 500.

    a. Set up a spreadsheet to calculate the 26-week moving average of the index. Set the value of the index at the beginning of the sample period equal to 100. The index value in each week is then updated by multiplying the previous week's level by (1 + Rate of return over previous week).

Please visit us at
www.mhhe.com/Bodie11e

b. Identify every instance in which the index crosses through its moving average from below. In how many of the weeks following a cross-through does the index increase? Decrease?

c. Identify every instance in which the index crosses through its moving average from above. In how many of the weeks following a cross-through does the index increase? Decrease?

d. How well does the moving average rule perform in identifying buy or sell opportunities?

Please visit us at
www.mhhe.com/Bodie11e

24. Log in to Connect and link to the material for Chapter 12, where you will find five years of weekly returns for the S&P 500 and Fidelity's Select Banking Fund (ticker FSRBX).

a. Set up a spreadsheet to calculate the relative strength of the banking sector compared to the broad market. (*Hint:* As in Problem 23, set the initial value of the sector index and the S&P 500 index equal to 100, and use each week's rate of return to update the level of each index.)

b. Identify every instance in which the relative strength ratio increases by at least 5% from its value five weeks earlier. In how many of the weeks following a substantial increase in relative strength does the banking sector outperform the S&P 500? In how many of those weeks does the banking sector underperform the S&P 500?

c. Identify every instance in which the relative strength ratio decreases by at least 5% from its value five weeks earlier. In how many of the weeks following a substantial decrease in relative strength does the banking sector underperform the S&P 500? In how many of those weeks does the banking sector outperform the S&P 500?

d. How well does the relative strength rule perform in identifying buy or sell opportunities?

25. One seeming violation of the Law of One Price is the pervasive discrepancy of closed-end fund prices from their net asset values. Would you expect to observe greater discrepancies on diversified or less-diversified funds? Why?

CFA® PROBLEMS

1. Don Sampson begins a meeting with his financial adviser by outlining his investment philosophy as shown below:

Statement Number	Statement
1	Investments should offer strong return potential but with very limited risk. I prefer to be conservative and to minimize losses, even if I miss out on substantial growth opportunities.
2	All nongovernmental investments should be in industry-leading and financially strong companies.
3	Income needs should be met entirely through interest income and cash dividends. All equity securities held should pay cash dividends.
4	Investment decisions should be based primarily on consensus forecasts of general economic conditions and company-specific growth.
5	If an investment falls below the purchase price, that security should be retained until it returns to its original cost. Conversely, I prefer to take quick profits on successful investments.
6	I will direct the purchase of investments, including derivative securities, periodically. These aggressive investments result from personal research and may not prove consistent with my investment policy. I have not kept records on the performance of similar past investments, but I have had some "big winners."

Select the statement from the table above that best illustrates each of the following behavioral finance concepts. Justify your selection.

a. Mental accounting.

b. Overconfidence (illusion of control).

c. Disposition effect.

2. Monty Frost's tax-deferred retirement account is invested entirely in equity securities. Because the international portion of his portfolio has performed poorly in the past, he has reduced his international equity exposure to 2%. Frost's investment adviser has recommended an increased international equity exposure. Frost responds with the following comments:

a. "On the basis of past poor performance, I want to sell all my remaining international equity securities once their market prices rise to equal their original cost."

b. "Most diversified international portfolios have had disappointing results over the past five years. During that time, however, the market in Country XYZ has outperformed all other markets, even our own. If I do increase my international equity exposure, I would prefer that the entire exposure consist of securities from Country XYZ."

c. "International investments are inherently more risky. Therefore, I prefer to purchase any international equity securities in my 'speculative' account, my best chance at becoming rich. I do not want them in my retirement account, which has to protect me from poverty in my old age."

Frost's adviser is familiar with behavioral finance concepts but prefers a traditional or standard finance approach (modern portfolio theory) to investments.

Indicate the behavioral finance concept that Frost most directly exhibits in each of his three comments. Explain how each of Frost's comments can be countered by using an argument from standard finance.

3. Louise and Christopher Maclin live in the U.K. and currently rent an apartment in London's metropolitan area. During an initial discussion of the Maclins' financial plans, Christopher Maclin makes the following statements to the Maclins' financial adviser, Grant Webb:

a. "I have used the Internet extensively to research the outlook for the housing market over the next five years, and I believe now is the best time to buy a house."

b. "I do not want to sell any bond in my portfolio for a lower price than I paid for the bond."

c. "I will not sell any of my company stock because I know my company and I believe it has excellent prospects for the future."

For each statement (a)–(c) identify the behavioral finance concept most directly exhibited. Explain how each behavioral finance concept is affecting Maclin's investment decision making.

4. During an interview with her investment adviser, a retired investor made the following two statements:

a. "I have been very pleased with the returns I've earned on Petrie stock over the past two years and I am certain that it will be a superior performer in the future."

b. "I am pleased with the returns from the Petrie stock because I have specific uses for that money. For that reason, I certainly want my retirement fund to continue owning the Petrie stock."

Identify which principle of behavioral finance is most consistent with each of the investor's two statements.

5. Claire Pierce comments on her life circumstances and investment outlook:

I must support my parents who live overseas on Pogo Island. The Pogo Island economy has grown rapidly over the past 2 years with minimal inflation, and consensus forecasts call for a continuation of these favorable trends for the foreseeable future. Economic growth has resulted from the export of a natural resource used in an exciting new technology application.

I want to invest 10% of my portfolio in Pogo Island government bonds. I plan to purchase long-term bonds because my parents are likely to live more than 10 years. Experts uniformly do not foresee a resurgence of inflation on Pogo Island, so I am certain that the total returns produced by the bonds will cover my parents' spending needs for many years to come. There should be no exchange rate risk because the bonds are denominated in local currency. I want to buy the Pogo Island bonds, but am not willing to distort my portfolio's long-term asset allocation to do so. The overall mix of stocks, bonds, and other investments should not change. Therefore, I am considering selling one of my U.S. bond funds to raise cash to buy the Pogo Island bonds. One possibility is my High Yield Bond Fund, which has declined 5% in value year to date. I am not excited about this fund's prospects; in fact I think it is likely to decline more, but there is a small probability that it could recover very quickly. So I have decided instead to sell my Core Bond Fund that has appreciated 5% this year. I expect this investment to continue to deliver attractive returns, but there is a small chance this year's gains might disappear quickly.

Once that shift is accomplished, my investments will be in great shape. The sole exception is my Small Company Fund, which has performed poorly. I plan to sell this investment as soon as the price increases to my original cost.

Identify three behavioral finance concepts illustrated in Pierce's comments and describe each of the three concepts. Discuss how an investor practicing standard or traditional finance would challenge each of the three concepts.

E-INVESTMENTS EXERCISES

1. Log on to **finance.yahoo.com** to find the monthly dividend-adjusted closing prices for the most recent 4 years for Abercrombie & Fitch (ANF). Also collect the closing level of the S&P 500 Index over the same period.

   a. Calculate the 4-month moving average of both the stock and the S&P 500 over time. For each series, use Excel to plot the moving average against the actual level of the stock price or index. Examine the instances where the moving average and price series cross. Is the stock more or less likely to increase when the price crosses through the moving average? Does it matter whether the price crosses the moving average from above or below? How reliable would an investment rule based on moving averages be? Perform your analysis for both the stock price and the S&P 500.

   b. Calculate and plot the relative strength of the stock compared to the S&P 500 over the sample period. Find all instances in which relative strength of the stock increases by more than 10 percentage points (e.g., an increase in the relative strength index from .93 to 1.03) and all those instances in which relative strength of the stock decreases by more than 10 percentage points. Is the stock more or less likely to outperform (underperform) the S&P 500 in the following two months when relative strength has increased (decreased)? In other words, does relative strength continue? How reliable would an investment rule based on relative strength be?

2. The Yahoo! Finance charting function allows you to specify comparisons between companies by choosing the *Technical Analysis* tab. Short interest ratios are found in the *Key Statistics* table. Prepare charts of moving averages and obtain short interest ratios for GE and SWY. Prepare a 1-year chart of the 50- and 200-day average price of GE, SWY, and the S&P 500 Index.

   a. Which, if either, of the companies is priced above its 50- and 200-day averages?

   b. Would you consider their charts as bullish or bearish? Why?

   c. What are the short interest ratios for the two companies?

☑ SOLUTIONS TO CONCEPT CHECKS

1. Conservatism implies that investors will at first respond too slowly to new information, leading to trends in prices. Representativeness can lead them to extrapolate trends too far into the future and overshoot intrinsic value. Eventually, when the pricing error is corrected, we observe a reversal.

2. Out-of-favor stocks will exhibit low prices relative to various proxies for intrinsic value such as earnings. Because of regret avoidance, these stocks will need to offer a more attractive rate of return to induce investors to hold them. Thus, low P/E stocks might on average offer higher rates of return.

3. At liquidation, price will equal NAV. This puts a limit on fundamental risk. Investors need only carry the position for a few months to profit from the elimination of the discount. Moreover, as the liquidation date approaches, the discount should dissipate. This greatly limits the risk that the discount can move against the investor. At the announcement of impending liquidation, the discount should immediately disappear, or at least shrink considerably.

4. By the time the news of the recession affects bond yields, it also ought to affect stock prices. The market should fall *before* the confidence index signals that the time is ripe to sell.

Empirical Evidence on Security Returns

WHY DO DIFFERENT securities offer different expected rates of return? According to the CAPM, one thing and only one thing matters: the systematic risk of the security as measured by its beta. Other measures of risk such as firm-specific volatility should be irrelevant, and expected rates of return should rise in direct proportion to beta.

Early tests of the risk-return relationship focused on these stark implications of the model. The results, as we will see shortly, were ambiguous at best. However, further reflection made it clear that it would be almost impossible to conduct a definitive test of the CAPM, in large part because it is so tied to an inherently unobservable market portfolio that encompasses all assets in the economy. Nontraded assets such as human capital could have first-order impacts on the observed risk–return trade-off.

Moreover, variants on the CAPM came swiftly on the heels of the simple one-factor model. These richer models suggested that the risk-return relationship might entail multiple sources of systematic risk. For example, uncertainty about future interest rates or prices of major consumption goods or asset-return volatility could also generate equilibrium risk premia. This implies that we really ought to be testing a multifactor SML.

More recently, researchers have come to realize that non-risk-related considerations such as liquidity costs surrounding security trading also could lead to substantial variation in expected returns. Finally, behavioral-finance issues can potentially lead to security mispricing and dispersion in expected returns.

These many issues present a long agenda for empirical testing of the risk-return relationship. We have space to provide only a brief overview of this vast literature. We begin with tests of the single-factor security market line, the theater where many of the basic methodologies still used today were developed. We proceed to multifactor models, especially the Fama-French three-factor model and its variants, which have become the workhorse models for current empirical research. We also show how liquidity issues can lead to variation in expected returns across securities that are potentially as large as those due to differences in risk. Finally, we examine the empirical implications of consumption-based models such as Merton's intertemporal CAPM and the consumption CAPM.

13.1   The Index Model and the Single-Factor SML

The Expected Return–Beta Relationship

Recall that if the expected return–beta relationship holds with respect to an observable ex ante efficient index, M, the expected rate of return on any security i is

$$E(r_i) = r_f + \beta_i [E(r_M) - r_f] \tag{13.1}$$

where β_i is defined as $\mathrm{Cov}(r_i, r_M)/\sigma_M^2$.

Equation 13.1 tells us that expected return increases along with beta. Therefore, early tests of the CAPM were conducted along the following lines: Collect data on the rates of return on a large sample of stocks as well as the market index and risk-free rate, use that data to estimate the beta of each stock from an index model regression (like the one we employed in Chapter 8), and then test to see whether stocks with high betas have in fact provided higher average returns.

Setting Up the Sample Data   Determine a sample period of, for example, 60 monthly holding periods (five years). For each of the 60 holding periods, collect the rates of return on a large number of stocks, for example, 100, a market portfolio proxy (e.g., the S&P 500), and 1-month (risk-free) T-bills. Your data thus consist of

$r_{it} = 6{,}000$ returns on the 100 stocks over the 60-month sample period; $i = 1, \ldots , 100$, and $t = 1, \ldots , 60$.

$r_{Mt} = 60$ observations of the returns on the S&P 500 index over the sample period (one each month).

$r_{ft} = 60$ observations of the risk-free rate (one each month).

This constitutes a table of $102 \times 60 = 6{,}120$ rates of return.

Estimating the SCL   View Equation 13.1 as a security characteristic line (SCL), as in Chapter 8. You want to estimate how the return on each stock responds to the return on the market index. Therefore, for each stock, i, you estimate the beta coefficient as the slope of a **first-pass regression** equation. (The terminology *first-pass* regression is due to the fact that the estimated coefficients will be used as input into a **second-pass regression.**)

$$r_{it} - r_{ft} = a_i + b_i(r_{Mt} - r_{ft}) + e_{it}$$

You will use the following statistics in later analysis:

$\overline{r_i - r_f}$ = Sample averages (over the 60 observations) of the excess return on each of the 100 stocks.

b_i = Sample estimates of the beta coefficients of each of the 100 stocks.

$\overline{r_M - r_f}$ = Sample average of the excess return of the market index.

$\sigma^2(e_i)$ = Estimates of the variance of the residuals for each of the 100 stocks.

The sample average excess returns on each stock and the market portfolio are taken as estimates of expected excess returns, and the values of b_i are estimates of the true beta coefficients for the 100 stocks during the sample period. $\sigma^2(e_i)$ estimates the nonsystematic risk of each of the 100 stocks. It is understood that all these statistics are subject to estimation error.

a. How many regression estimates of the SCL do we have from the sample?

b. How many observations are there in each of the regressions?

c. According to the CAPM, what should be the intercept in each of these regressions?

Estimating the SML   Now view Equation 13.1 as a security market line (SML) with 100 observations for the stocks in your sample. Given the estimate of beta, we now ask: To what extent does average return increase as beta increases? Therefore, you estimate γ_0 and γ_1 in the following second-pass regression equation with the estimates of beta, b_i, from the first pass as the independent variable:

$$\overline{r_i - r_f} = \gamma_0 + \gamma_1 b_i \qquad i = 1, \ldots, 100 \qquad (13.2)$$

Compare Equations 13.1 and 13.2; you should conclude that if the CAPM is valid, then γ_0 and γ_1 should satisfy

$$\gamma_0 = 0 \text{ and } \gamma_1 = \overline{r_M - r_f}$$

In fact, however, you can go a step further and argue that the key property of the expected return–beta relationship described by the SML is that the expected excess return on securities is determined *only* by systematic risk (as measured by beta) and should be independent of nonsystematic risk, as measured by the variance of the residuals, $\sigma^2(e_i)$, which also were estimated from the first-pass regression. These estimates can be added as a variable in Equation 13.2 of an expanded SML that now looks like this:

$$\overline{r_i - r_f} = \gamma_0 + \gamma_1 b_i + \gamma_2 \sigma^2(e_i) \qquad (13.3)$$

This *second-pass* regression equation is estimated with the hypotheses

$$\gamma_0 = 0; \gamma_1 = \overline{r_M - r_f}; \gamma_2 = 0$$

The hypothesis that $\gamma_2 = 0$ is consistent with the notion that nonsystematic risk should not be "priced," that is, that there is no risk premium earned for bearing nonsystematic risk. More generally, according to the CAPM, the risk premium depends only on beta. Therefore, *any* additional right-hand-side variable in Equation 13.3 beyond beta should have a coefficient that is insignificantly different from zero in the second-pass regression.

Tests of the CAPM

Early tests of the CAPM performed by John Lintner,[1] and later replicated by Merton Miller and Myron Scholes,[2] used annual data on 631 NYSE stocks for 10 years, from 1954 to 1963, and produced the following estimates (with returns expressed as decimals rather than percentages):

Coefficient:	$\gamma_0 = .127$	$\gamma_1 = .042$	$\gamma_2 = .310$
Standard error:	.006	.006	.026
Sample average:		$\overline{r_M - r_f} = .165$	

[1] John Lintner, "Security Prices, Risk and Maximal Gains from Diversification," *Journal of Finance* 20 (December 1965).

[2] Merton H. Miller and Myron Scholes, "Rate of Return in Relation to Risk: A Reexamination of Some Recent Findings," in *Studies in the Theory of Capital Markets,* ed. Michael C. Jensen (New York: Praeger, 1972).

These results are inconsistent with the CAPM. First, the estimated SML is "too flat"; that is, the γ_1 coefficient is too small. The slope should equal $\overline{r_M - r_f} = .165$ (16.5% per year), but it is estimated at only .042. The difference, .122, is about 20 times the standard error of the estimate, .006, which means that the measured slope of the SML is less than it should be by a statistically significant margin. At the same time, the intercept of the estimated SML, γ_0, which is hypothesized to be zero, in fact equals .127, which is more than 20 times its standard error of .006.

Concept Check **13.2**

a. What is the implication of the empirical SML being "too flat"?

b. Do high- or low-beta stocks tend to outperform the predictions of the CAPM?

c. What is the implication of the estimate of γ_2?

The two-stage procedure employed by these researchers (i.e., first estimate security betas using a time-series regression and then use those betas to test the SML relationship between risk and average return) seems straightforward, and the rejection of the CAPM using this approach is disappointing. However, it turns out that there are several difficulties with this approach. First and foremost, stock returns are extremely volatile, which lessens the precision of any tests of average return. For example, the average standard deviation of annual returns of the large stocks in the S&P 500 is about 40%; the average standard deviation of annual returns of the stocks included in these tests is probably even higher.

In addition, there are fundamental concerns about the validity of the tests. First, the market index used in the tests is surely not the "market portfolio" of the CAPM. Second, in light of asset volatility, the security betas from the first-stage regressions are necessarily estimated with substantial sampling error and therefore cannot readily be used as inputs to the second-stage regression. Finally, investors cannot borrow at the risk-free rate, as assumed by the simple version of the CAPM. Let us investigate the implications of these problems in turn.

The Market Index

In what has come to be known as *Roll's critique,* Richard Roll[3] demonstrated that:

1. There is a single testable hypothesis associated with the CAPM: The market portfolio is mean-variance efficient.

2. All the other implications of the model, the best-known being the linear relation between expected return and beta, follow from the market portfolio's efficiency and therefore are not independently testable. There is an "if and only if" relation between the expected return–beta relationship and the efficiency of the market portfolio.

3. In any sample of observations of individual returns there will be an infinite number of ex post (i.e., after the fact) mean-variance efficient portfolios using the sample-period returns and covariances (as opposed to the ex ante *expected* returns and covariances). Sample betas of individual assets estimated against each such ex-post efficient portfolio will be exactly linearly related to the sample average returns of

---

[3]Richard Roll, "A Critique of the Asset Pricing Theory's Tests: Part I: On Past and Potential Testability of the Theory," *Journal of Financial Economics* 4 (1977).

these assets. In other words, if betas are calculated against such portfolios, they will satisfy the SML relation exactly whether or not the *true* market portfolio is mean-variance efficient in an ex ante sense.

4. The CAPM is not testable unless we know the exact composition of the true market portfolio and use it in the tests. This implies that the theory is not testable unless *all* individual assets are included in the sample.

5. Using a proxy such as the S&P 500 for the market portfolio is subject to two difficulties. First, the proxy itself might be mean-variance efficient even when the true market portfolio is not. More likely, the proxy may turn out to be inefficient, but obviously, this alone implies nothing about the true market portfolio's efficiency. Furthermore, most reasonable market proxies will be very highly correlated with each other and with the true market portfolio whether or not they are mean-variance efficient. Such a high degree of correlation will make it seem that the exact composition of the market portfolio is unimportant, but the use of different proxies *can* lead to quite different conclusions. This problem is referred to as **benchmark error,** because it refers to the use of an incorrect benchmark (market proxy) portfolio in the tests of the theory.

Roll and Ross[4] and Kandel and Stambaugh[5] expanded Roll's critique. Essentially, they argued that tests that reject a positive relationship between average return and beta point to inefficiency of the market proxy used in those tests, rather than refuting the theoretical expected return–beta relationship. Importantly, they demonstrate that even if the CAPM is true, even highly diversified portfolios, such as the value- or equally weighted portfolios of all stocks in the sample, may fail to produce a significant average return–beta relationship.

Given the impossibility of testing the CAPM directly, we can retreat to testing the APT, which produces the same expected return–beta equation (the security market line).[6] This model depends only on the index portfolio being well diversified. Choosing a broad market index allows us to test the SML as applied to the chosen index.

Measurement Error in Beta

It is well known in statistics that if the right-hand-side variable of a regression equation is measured with error (in our case, beta is measured with error and is the right-hand-side variable in the second-pass regression), then the slope coefficient of the regression equation will be biased downward and the intercept biased upward. This is consistent with the findings cited above; γ_0 was higher than predicted by the CAPM and γ_1 was lower than predicted.

Indeed, a well-controlled simulation test by Miller and Scholes[7] confirms these arguments. In this test, a random-number generator simulated rates of return with covariances similar to observed ones. The average returns were made to agree exactly with the CAPM. Miller and Scholes then used these randomly generated rates of return in the tests we have

[4]Richard Roll and Stephen A. Ross, "On the Cross-Sectional Relation between Expected Return and Betas," *Journal of Finance* 50 (1995), pp. 185–224.

[5]Schmuel Kandel and Robert F. Stambaugh, "Portfolio Inefficiency and the Cross-Section of Expected Returns," *Journal of Finance* 50 (1995), pp. 185–224; "A Mean-Variance Framework for Tests of Asset Pricing Models," *Review of Financial Studies* 2 (1989), pp. 125–56; and "On Correlations and Inferences about Mean-Variance Efficiency," *Journal of Financial Economics* 18 (1987), pp. 61–90.

[6]Although the APT strictly applies only to well-diversified portfolios, the discussion in Chapter 9 shows that optimization in a single-index market as prescribed by Treynor and Black will generate strong pressure on single securities to satisfy the mean-beta equation as well.

[7]Miller and Scholes, "Rate of Return in Relation to Risk." (See footnote 2.)

described as if they were observed from a sample of stock returns. The results of this "simulated" test were virtually identical to those reached using real data, despite the fact that the simulated returns were *constructed* to obey the SML, that is, the true γ coefficients were $\gamma_0 = 0$, $\gamma_1 = \overline{r_M - r_f}$, and $\gamma_2 = 0$.

This postmortem of the early test gets us back to square one. We can explain away the disappointing test results, but we have no positive results to support the CAPM-APT implications.

The next wave of tests was designed to overcome the measurement error problem that led to biased estimates of the SML. The innovation in these tests, pioneered by Black, Jensen, and Scholes,[8] was to use portfolios rather than individual securities. Combining securities into portfolios diversifies away most of the firm-specific part of returns, thereby enhancing the precision of the estimates of beta and the expected rate of return of the portfolio of securities. This mitigates the statistical problems that arise from measurement error in the beta estimates.

Testing the model with diversified portfolios rather than individual securities completes our retreat from the CAPM to the APT. Additionally, combining stocks into portfolios reduces the number of observations left for the second-pass regression. Suppose we group the 100 stocks into five portfolios of 20 stocks each. The portfolio beta in the first-pass regression will be estimated with far better accuracy. However, with portfolios of 20 stocks each, we are left with only five observations for the second-pass regression.

To get the best of this trade-off, we need to construct portfolios with the largest possible dispersion of beta coefficients. Other things equal, a regression yields more accurate estimates the more widely spaced the observations of the independent variables. We therefore will attempt to maximize the range of the independent variable of the second-pass regression, the portfolio betas. Rather than allocate 20 stocks to each portfolio randomly, we first rank stocks by betas. Portfolio 1 is formed from the 20 highest-beta stocks and portfolio 5 from the 20 lowest-beta stocks. A set of portfolios with small nonsystematic components, e_P, and widely spaced betas will yield reasonably powerful tests of the SML.

Fama and MacBeth (FM)[9] used this methodology to verify that the observed relationship between average excess returns and beta is indeed linear and that nonsystematic risk does not explain average excess returns. Using 20 portfolios constructed according to the Black, Jensen, and Scholes methodology, FM expanded the estimation of the SML equation to include the square of the estimated beta coefficient (to test for linearity of the relationship between returns and betas) and the estimated standard deviation of the residual (to test for the explanatory power of nonsystematic risk). For a sequence of many subperiods, they estimated for each subperiod the equation

$$\overline{r_i - r_f} = \gamma_0 + \gamma_1 b_i + \gamma_2 b_i^2 + \gamma_3 \sigma(e_i) \tag{13.4}$$

The term γ_2 measures potential nonlinearity of return, and γ_3 measures the explanatory power of nonsystematic risk, $\sigma(e_i)$. According to the CAPM, γ_0, γ_2, and γ_3 all should have coefficients of zero in the second-pass regression, and γ_1 should equal the average value of $r_M - r_f$.

FM estimated Equation 13.4 for every month of the period January 1935 through June 1968. The results are summarized in Table 13.1, which shows average values of coefficients

---

[8]Fischer Black, Michael C. Jensen, and Myron Scholes, "The Capital Asset Pricing Model: Some Empirical Tests," in *Studies in the Theory of Capital Markets*, ed. Michael C. Jensen (New York: Praeger, 1972).

[9]Eugene Fama and James MacBeth, "Risk, Return, and Equilibrium: Empirical Tests," *Journal of Political Economy* 81 (March 1973).

Period	1935/6–1968	1935–1945	1946–1955	1956/6–1968
Average γ_0	8	10	8	5
t-statistic (testing $\gamma_0 = 0$)	0.20	0.11	0.20	0.10
Average $r_M - r_f$	130	195	103	95
Average γ_1	114	118	209	34
t-statistic (testing $\gamma_1 = r_M - r_f$)	1.85	0.94	2.39	0.34
Average γ_2	−26	−9	−76	0
t-statistic (testing $\gamma_2 = 0$)	−0.86	−0.14	−2.16	0
Average γ_3	516	817	−378	960
t-statistic (testing $\gamma_3 = 0$)	1.11	0.94	−0.67	1.11
Average R-square	0.31	0.31	0.32	0.29

Table 13.1

Summary of Fama and MacBeth (1973) study (all rates in basis points per month)

and t-statistics for the overall period as well as for three subperiods. FM observed that the coefficients on residual standard deviation (nonsystematic risk), denoted by γ_3, fluctuated greatly from month to month, and its t-statistics were insignificant despite large average values. Thus, the overall test results were reasonably favorable to the security market line of the CAPM (or perhaps more accurately, to the one-factor APT). But time has not been favorable to the CAPM since.

Recent replications of the FM test show that results deteriorate in later periods (since 1968). Worse, even for the FM period, 1935–1968, when the equally weighted NYSE-stock portfolio they used as the market index is replaced with the more appropriate value-weighted index, results turn against the model. In particular, the slope of the SML clearly is too flat.

 Concept Check **13.3**

a. According to Table 13.1, what is the predicted value of the return on a highly diversified zero-beta portfolio for the period 1946–1955? What would the CAPM have predicted for that value? What would the CAPM have predicted for the average values of γ_1 and γ_3 in that period?

b. What would you conclude if you performed the Fama and MacBeth tests and found that the coefficients on β^2 and $\sigma(e)$ were positive?

13.2   Tests of the Multifactor Models

Three types of factors are likely candidates to augment the market risk factor in a multifactor SML: (1) factors that hedge consumption against uncertainty in prices of important consumption categories (e.g., housing or energy) or general inflation, (2) factors that hedge future investment opportunities (e.g., interest rates, market volatility, or the market risk premium), and (3) factors that hedge assets missing from the market index (e.g., labor income or private business).

As we learned from Merton's ICAPM (Chapter 9), these extra-market sources of risk will command a risk premium if there is significant demand to hedge them. We begin with the third source because there is little doubt that nontraded assets in the personal portfolios of investors affect demand for traded risky assets. Hence, a factor representing these assets, that is, one correlated with their returns, should affect risk premiums.

Labor Income

The major factors in the omitted asset category are labor income and private business. Taking on labor income first, Mayers[10] viewed each individual as being endowed with labor income but able to trade only securities and an index portfolio. His model creates a wedge between betas measured against the traded, index portfolio and betas measured against the true market portfolio, which includes aggregate labor income. The result of his model is an SML that is flatter than that of the simple CAPM.

If the value of labor income is not perfectly correlated with the market-index portfolio, then the possibility of negative returns to labor will represent a source of risk not fully captured by the index. But suppose investors can trade a portfolio that is correlated with the return on aggregate human capital. Then their hedging demands against the risk to the value of their human capital might meaningfully influence security prices and risk premia. If so, human capital risk (or some empirical proxy for it) can serve as an additional factor in a multifactor SML. Stocks with a positive beta on the value of labor contribute to exposure to this risk factor; therefore, they will command lower prices, or equivalently, provide a larger-than-CAPM risk premium. Thus, by adding this factor, the SML becomes multidimensional.

Jagannathan and Wang[11] use the rate of change in aggregate labor income as a proxy for changes in the value of human capital. In addition to the standard security betas estimated using the value-weighted stock market index, which we denote β^{vw}, they also estimate the betas of assets with respect to labor income growth, which we denote β^{labor}. Finally, they consider the possibility that business cycles affect asset betas, an issue that has been examined in a number of other studies.[12] These may be viewed as *conditional* betas, as their values are conditional on the state of the economy.

Jagannathan and Wang use the credit spread between the yields on low- versus high-grade corporate bonds as a proxy for the state of the business cycle and estimate asset betas relative to this business cycle variable; we denote this beta as β^{credit}. With the estimates of these three betas for several stock portfolios, they estimate a second-pass regression that includes firm size (market value of equity, denoted ME):

$$E(R_i) = c_0 + c_{size}\log(\text{ME}) + c_{vw}\beta^{vw} + c_{credit}\beta^{credit} + c_{labor}\beta^{labor} \qquad \textbf{(13.5)}$$

They test their model with 100 portfolios that are designed to spread securities on the basis of size and beta. Stocks are sorted into 10 size portfolios, and the stocks within each size decile are further sorted by beta into 10 subportfolios, resulting in 100 portfolios in total. Table 13.2 shows a subset of the various versions of the second-pass estimates. The first two rows in Panel A show the coefficients and *t*-statistics of a test of the CAPM along the lines of the Fama and MacBeth tests introduced in the previous section. The result is a sound rejection of the model, as the coefficient on beta is negative (albeit not statistically significant), implying that average return *falls* with beta. The next two rows show that the

[10]David Mayers, "Nonmarketable Assets and Capital Market Equilibrium under Uncertainty," in *Studies in the Theory of Capital Markets,* ed. Michael C. Jensen (New York: Praeger, 1972), pp. 223–48.

[11]Ravi Jagannathan and Zhenyu Wang, "The Conditional CAPM and the Cross-Section of Expected Returns," *Journal of Finance* 51 (March 1996), pp. 3–54.

[12]For example, Campbell Harvey, "Time-Varying Conditional Covariances in Tests of Asset Pricing Models," *Journal of Financial Economics* 24 (October 1989), pp. 289–317; Wayne Ferson and Campbell Harvey, "The Variation of Economic Risk Premiums," *Journal of Political Economy* 99 (April 1991), pp. 385–415; and Wayne Ferson and Robert Korajczyk, "Do Arbitrage Pricing Models Explain the Predictability of Stock Returns?" *Journal of Business* 68 (July 1995), pp. 309–49.

Coefficient	c_0	c_{vw}	c_{credit}	c_{labor}	c_{size}	R^2
A. The Static CAPM without Human Capital						
Estimate	1.24	−0.10				1.35
t-statistic	5.16	−0.28				
Estimate	2.08	−0.32			−0.11	57.56
t-statistic	5.77	−0.94			−2.30	
B. The Conditional CAPM with Human Capital						
Estimate	1.24	−0.40	0.34	0.22		55.21
t-statistic	4.10	−0.88	1.73	2.31		
Estimate	1.70	−0.40	0.20	0.10	−0.07	64.73
t-statistic	4.14	−1.06	2.72	2.09	−1.30	

Table 13.2

Regression results for various SML specifications

This table gives the estimates for the cross-sectional regression model

$$E(R_{it}) = c_0 + c_{size}\log(ME_i) + c_{vw}\beta_i^{vw} + c_{credit}\beta_i^{credit} + c_{labor}\beta_i^{labor}$$

with either a subset or all of the variables. Here, R_{it} is the excess return on portfolio i ($i = 1, 2, \ldots, 100$) in month t (July 1963–December 1990), R_t^{vw} is the excess return on the value-weighted index of stocks, R_{t-1}^{credit} is the yield spread (i.e., credit spread) between low- and high-grade corporate bonds, and R_t^{labor} is the growth rate in per capita labor income. The β_i^{vw} is the slope coefficient in the OLS regression of R_{it} on a constant and R_t^{vw}. The other betas are estimated in a similar way. The portfolio size, $\log(ME_i)$, is calculated as the equally weighted average of the logarithm of the market value (in millions of dollars) of the stocks in portfolio i. The regression models are estimated by using the Fama-MacBeth procedure. All R^2s are reported as percentages.

CAPM is not helped by the addition of the size factor: The coefficient on beta remains negative. The dramatic increase in R-square (from 1.35% to 57.56%) shows that size explains variations in average returns quite well while beta does not.

In Panel B, the default premium and labor income are included as explanatory variables, but the CAPM expected return–beta relationship is not redeemed: The coefficient on beta is still negative. The default premium is significant, while labor income is borderline significant. When we add size as well, in the last two rows, we find it is no longer significant and only marginally increases explanatory power.

Private (Nontraded) Business

Whereas Jagannathan and Wang focus on labor income, Heaton and Lucas[13] estimate the importance of proprietary business. We expect that private-business owners will reduce demand for traded securities that are positively correlated with their specific entrepreneurial income. If this effect is sufficiently important, aggregate demand for traded securities will be determined in part by the covariance with aggregate noncorporate business income. The risk premium on securities with high covariance with noncorporate business income should be commensurately higher.

Consistent with theory, Heaton and Lucas find that households with higher investments in private business do in fact reduce the fraction of total wealth invested in equity. They also extend Jagannathan and Wang's equation to include the rate of change in proprietary-business wealth. They find that this variable also is significant and improves

[13]John Heaton and Debora Lucas, "Portfolio Choice and Asset Prices: The Importance of Entrepreneurial Risk," *Journal of Finance* 55, no. 3 (June 2000), pp. 1163–98.

the explanatory power of the regression. Again, however, exposure to the market rate of return does not help explain the average rate of return on individual securities and, hence, this implication of the CAPM still finds no support.

Early Tests of the Multifactor CAPM and APT

The multifactor CAPM and APT are elegant theories of how exposure to multiple systematic risk factors should influence expected returns, but they provide little guidance concerning which factors (sources of risk) ought to result in risk premiums. A test of this hypothesis would require three stages:

1. Specification of risk factors.
2. Identification of portfolios that hedge these fundamental risk factors.
3. Test of the explanatory power and risk premiums of the hedge portfolios.

A Macro Factor Model

Chen, Roll, and Ross[14] identify several possible variables that might proxy for systematic factors:

IP = Growth rate in industrial production.
EI = Changes in expected inflation measured by changes in short-term (T-bill) interest rates.
UI = Unexpected inflation defined as the difference between actual and expected inflation.
CG = Unexpected changes in risk premiums measured by the difference between the returns on corporate Baa-rated bonds and long-term government bonds.
GB = Unexpected changes in the term premium measured by the difference between the returns on long- and short-term government bonds.

With the identification of these potential economic factors, Chen, Roll, and Ross skip the procedure of identifying factor portfolios (the portfolios that have the highest correlation with the factors). Instead, by using the factors themselves, they implicitly assume that factor portfolios exist that can proxy for the factors. They use these factors in a test similar to that of Fama and MacBeth.

A critical part of the methodology is the grouping of stocks into portfolios. Recall that in the single-factor tests, portfolios were constructed to span a wide range of betas to enhance the power of the test. In a multifactor framework the efficient criterion for grouping is less obvious. Chen, Roll, and Ross choose to group the sample stocks into 20 portfolios by size (market value of outstanding equity), a variable that is known to be associated with average stock returns.

They first use five years of monthly data to estimate the factor betas of the 20 portfolios in 20 first-pass regressions.

$$r = a + \beta_M r_M + \beta_{IP} IP + \beta_{EI} EI + \beta_{UI} UI + \beta_{CG} CG + \beta_{GB} GB + e \qquad \textbf{(13.6a)}$$

where M stands for the stock market index. Chen, Roll, and Ross use as the market index both the value-weighted NYSE index (VWNY) and the equally weighted NYSE index (EWNY).

Using the 20 sets of first-pass estimates of factor betas as the independent variables, they next estimate the second-pass regression (with 20 observations):

$$r = \gamma_0 + \gamma_M \beta_M + \gamma_{IP} \beta_{IP} + \gamma_{EI} \beta_{EI} + \gamma_{UI} \beta_{UI} + \gamma_{CG} \beta_{CG} + \gamma_{GB} \beta_{GB} + e \qquad \textbf{(13.6b)}$$

where the gammas become estimates of the risk premiums on the various factors.

[14]Nai-Fu Chen, Richard Roll, and Stephen Ross, "Economic Forces and the Stock Market," *Journal of Business* 59 (1986).

Table 13.3

Economic variables and pricing (percent per month × 10), multi-variate approach

A	EWNY	IP	EI	UI	CG	GB	Constant
	5.021	14.009	−0.128	−0.848	0.130	−5.017	6.409
	(1.218)	(3.774)	(−1.666)	(−2.541)	(2.855)	(−1.576)	(1.848)
B	**VWNY**	**IP**	**EI**	**UI**	**CG**	**GB**	**Constant**
	−2.403	11.756	−0.123	−0.795	8.274	−5.905	10.713
	(−0.633)	(3.054)	(−1.600)	(−2.376)	(2.972)	(−1.879)	(2.755)

VWNY = Return on the value-weighted NYSE index; EWNY = Return on the equally weighted NYSE index; IP = Monthly growth rate in industrial production; EI = Change in expected inflation; UI = Unanticipated inflation; CG = Unanticipated change in the risk premium (Baa and under return − Long-term government bond return); GB = Unanticipated change in the term structure (long-term government bond return − Treasury-bill rate); t-statistics are in parentheses.

Source: Modified from Nai-Fu Chen, Richard Roll, and Stephen Ross, "Economic Forces and the Stock Market," *Journal of Business* 59 (1986).

Chen, Roll, and Ross estimate this second-pass regression for every month of their sample period, reestimating the first-pass factor betas once every 12 months. The estimated risk premiums (the values for the parameters, γ) are averaged over all the second-pass regressions.

Note in Table 13.3 that the two market indexes EWNY and VWNY are not statistically significant (their t-statistics of 1.218 and −.633 are less than 2). Note also that the VWNY factor has the "wrong" sign in that it seems to imply a negative market-risk premium. Industrial production (IP), the risk premium on corporate bonds (CG), and unanticipated inflation (UI) are the factors that appear to have significant explanatory power.

13.3   Fama-French-Type Factor Models

The multifactor models that currently occupy center stage are the three-factor model introduced by Fama and French (FF) and its several variants.[15] The systematic factors in the FF model are firm size and book-to-market ratio (B/M) as well as the market index. These additional factors are empirically motivated by the observations, discussed in Chapter 11, that historical-average returns on stocks of small firms and on stocks with high ratios of book equity to market equity (B/M) are higher than predicted by the security market line of the CAPM.

However, Fama and French did more than document the empirical role of size and B/M in explaining rates of return. They also introduced a general method to generate factor portfolios and applied their method to these firm characteristics. Exploring this innovation is a useful way to understand the empirical building blocks of a multifactor asset pricing model.

Suppose you find, as Fama and French did, that stock market capitalization (or "market cap") seems to predict alpha values in a CAPM equation. On average, the smaller the market cap, the greater the alpha of a stock. This finding would add size to the list of anomalies that refute the CAPM.

But suppose you believe that size is related to a stock's sensitivity to changes in future investment opportunities. Then, what appears as alpha in a single-factor CAPM is really an extra-market source of risk in a multifactor CAPM. If this sounds far-fetched, here's a story: When investors anticipate a market downturn, they adjust their portfolios to minimize their exposure to losses. Suppose that small stocks generally are harder hit in down markets, akin

[15]Eugene F. Fama and Kenneth R. French, "Common Risk Factors in the Returns on Stocks and Bonds," *Journal of Financial Economics* 33 (1993), pp. 3–56.

to a larger beta in bad times. Then investors will avoid such stocks in favor of the less-sensitive stocks of larger firms. This would explain a risk premium to small size *beyond* the beta on contemporaneous market returns. An "alpha" for size may be instead an ICAPM risk premium for assets with greater sensitivity to deterioration in future investment opportunities.

FF propose a method to quantify the size risk premium. Recall that the distribution of corporate size is asymmetric: a few big and many small corporations. Since the NYSE is the exchange where bigger stocks trade, Fama and French first determine the median size of NYSE stocks. They use this median to classify all traded U.S. stocks (NYSE + AMEX + NASDAQ) as big or small and create one portfolio of big stocks and another of small stocks. Finally, each of these portfolios is value-weighted for efficient diversification.

As in the APT, Fama and French construct a zero-net-investment size-factor portfolio by going long the small- and going short the big-stock portfolio. The return of this portfolio, called SMB (small minus big), is simply the return on the small-stock portfolio minus the return on the big-stock portfolio. If size is priced, then this portfolio will exhibit a risk premium. Because the SMB portfolio is highly diversified, it joins the market-index portfolio in a two-factor APT model with size as the extra-market source of risk. In the two-factor SML, the risk premium on any asset should be determined by its loadings (betas) on the two-factor portfolios. This is a testable hypothesis.

Fama and French use this approach to form both size and book-to-market ratio (B/M) factors. To create these two extra-market risk factors, they double-sort stocks by both size and B/M. They break the U.S. stock population into three groups based on B/M ratio: the bottom 30% (low), the middle 40% (medium), and the top 30% (high). Now six portfolios are created based on the intersections of the size and B/M sorts: Small/Low; Small/Medium; Small/High; Big/Low; Big/Medium; Big/High. Each of these six portfolios is value weighted.

The returns on the Big and Small portfolios are:

$$R_S = \frac{1}{3}(R_{S/L} + R_{S/M} + R_{S/H}); \ R_B = \frac{1}{3}(R_{B/L} + R_{B/M} + R_{B/H})$$

Similarly, the returns on the high and low (Value and Growth[16]) portfolios are:

$$R_H = \frac{1}{2}(R_{S/H} + R_{B/H}); \ R_L = \frac{1}{2}(R_{S/L} + R_{B/L})$$

The returns of the zero-net-investment factors SMB (Small minus Big, i.e., Long Small and Short Big), and HML (High minus Low, i.e., Long High B/M and Short Low B/M) are created from these portfolios:

$$R_{SMB} = R_S - R_B; \ R_{HML} = R_H - R_L$$

We measure the sensitivity of individual stocks to the factors by estimating the factor betas from first-pass regressions of stock excess returns on the excess return of the market index as well as on R_{SMB} and R_{HML}. These factor betas should, as a group, predict the total risk premium. Therefore, the Fama-French three-factor asset-pricing model is[17]

$$E(r_i) - r_f = a_i + b_i[E(r_M) - r_f] + s_i E[R_{SMB}] + h_i E[R_{HML}] \qquad \textbf{(13.7)}$$

---

[16]High B/M stocks are called *value* assets because, for the large part, their market values derive from assets already in place. Low B/M are called *growth* stocks because their market values derive from expected growth in future cash flows. One needs to assume high growth to justify the prices at which the assets trade. At the same time, however, a firm that falls into hard times will see its market price fall and its B/M ratio rise. So some of the so-called value firms may actually be distressed firms. This subgroup of the value-firm portfolio may well account for the value premium of the B/M factor.

[17]We subtract the risk-free rate from the return on the market portfolio, but do not subtract r_f from SMB or HML. These are already return premiums (or differences in returns on two portfolios): small versus big or high versus low. By subtracting the risk-free rate from the market portfolio, the first factor also becomes an excess return. So each factor has the interpretation of a risk premium: The first is the premium for systematic risk, the second is a risk premium associated with size, and the third is a risk premium associated with value versus growth characteristics.

The coefficients b_i, s_i, and h_i are the betas (also called *loadings* in this context) of the stock on the three factors. If these are the only risk factors, excess returns on all assets should be fully explained by risk premiums due to these factor loadings. In other words, if these factors fully explain asset returns, the intercept of the equation should be zero.

In a survey of asset pricing tests, Goyal[18] applies Equation 13.7 to the returns of 25 portfolios of all U.S. stocks sorted by size and B/M ratio. Figure 13.1 shows the average actual return of each portfolio over the period 1946–2010 against returns predicted by the CAPM (Panel A) and by the FF three-factor model (Panel B). In this test, the FF model provides a clear improvement over the CAPM.

Size and B/M as Risk Factors

Liew and Vassalou[19] show that returns on style portfolios (HML or SMB) seem to predict GDP growth, and thus may in fact capture some aspects of business cycle risk. Each bar in Figure 13.2 is the average difference in the return on the HML or SMB portfolio in years before good GDP growth versus in years with poor GDP growth. Positive values mean the portfolio does better in years prior to good macroeconomic performance. The predominance of positive values leads them to conclude that the returns on the HML and SMB portfolios are positively related to future

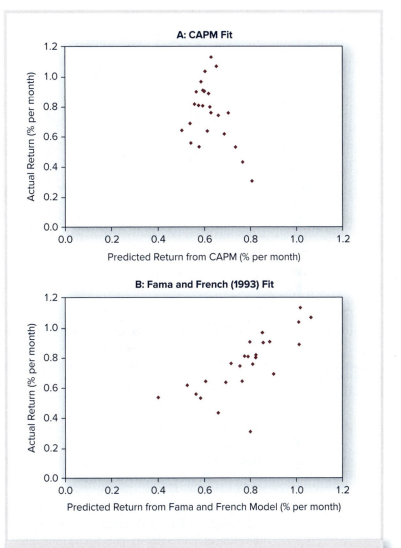

Figure 13.1 CAPM versus the Fama and French model. The figure plots the average actual returns versus returns predicted by CAPM and the FF model for 25 size and book-to-market double-sorted portfolios.

Source: Amit Goyal, "Empirical Cross Sectional Asset Pricing: A Survey," *Financial Markets and Portfolio Management* 26 (2012), pp. 3–38.

growth in the macroeconomy, and so may be proxies for business cycle risk. Thus, at least part of the size and value premiums may reflect rational rewards for greater risk exposure.

Petkova and Zhang[20] also try to tie the average return premium on value (high B/M) portfolios to risk premiums. Their approach uses a conditional CAPM. In the conventional CAPM, we treat both the market risk premium and firm betas as given parameters.

[18]Amit Goyal, "Empirical Cross Sectional Asset Pricing: A Survey," *Financial Markets and Portfolio Management* 26 (2012), pp. 3–38.

[19]J. Liew and M. Vassalou, "Can Book-to-Market, Size and Momentum Be Risk Factors That Predict Economic Growth?" *Journal of Financial Economics* 57 (2000), pp. 221–45.

[20]Ralitsa Petkova and Lu Zhang, "Is Value Riskier than Growth?" *Journal of Financial Economics* 78 (2005), pp. 187–202.

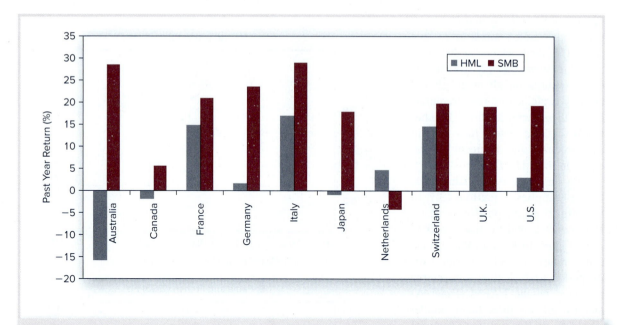

Figure 13.2 Difference in return to factor portfolios in year prior to above-average versus below-average GDP growth. Both SMB and HML portfolio returns tend to be higher in years preceding better GDP growth.

Source: J. Liew and M. Vassalou, "Can Book-to-Market, Size and Momentum Be Risk Factors That Predict Economic Growth?" *Journal of Financial Economics* 57 (2000), pp. 221–45.

In contrast, as we noted earlier in the chapter, the conditional CAPM allows both of these terms to vary over time, and possibly to co-vary. If a stock's beta is higher when the market risk premium is high, this positive association leads to a "synergy" in its risk premium, which is the product of its incremental beta and market risk premium.

What might lead to such an association between beta and the market risk premium? Zhang[21] focuses on irreversible investments. He notes that firms classified as value firms (with high book-to-market ratios) on average will have greater amounts of tangible capital. Investment irreversibility puts such firms more at risk for economic downturns because in a severe recession, they will suffer from excess capacity from assets already in place. In contrast, growth firms are better able to deal with a downturn by deferring investment plans. The greater exposure of high book-to-market firms to recessions will result in higher down-market betas. Moreover, some evidence suggests that the market risk premium also is higher in down markets, when investors are feeling more economic pressure and anxiety. The combination of these two factors might impart a positive correlation between the beta of high B/M firms and the market risk premium.

To quantify these notions, Petkova and Zhang attempt to fit both beta and the market risk premium to a set of "state variables," that is, variables that summarize the state of the economy. These are:

DIV = Market dividend yield
DEFLT = Default spread on corporate bonds (Baa – Aaa rates)
TERM = Term structure spread (10-year –1-year Treasury rates)
TB = 1-month T-bill rate

[21]Lu Zhang, "The Value Premium," *Journal of Finance* 60 (2005), pp. 67–103.

They estimate a first-pass regression, but first substitute these state variables for beta as follows:

$$R_{HML} = \alpha + \beta R_{Mt} + e_i$$

$$= \alpha + \underbrace{[b_0 + b_1\,DIV_t + b_2\,DEFLT_t + b_3\,TERM_t + b_4\,TB_t]}R_{Mt} + e_i$$

$$= \beta_t \leftarrow a\ \textit{time-varying}\ \text{beta}$$

The strategy is to estimate parameters b_0 through b_4 and then fit beta using the values of the four state variables at each date. In this way, they can estimate beta in each period.

Similarly, one can directly estimate the determinants of a time-varying market risk premium, using the same set of state variables:

$$r_{Mt} - r_{ft} = c_0 + c_1\,DIV_t + c_2\,DEFLT_t + c_3\,TERM_t + c_4\,TB_t + e_t$$

The fitted value from this regression is the estimate of the market risk premium.

Finally, Petkova and Zhang examine the relationship between beta and the market risk premium. They define the state of economy by the size of the premium. A peak is defined as the periods with the 10% lowest risk premiums; a trough has the 10% highest risk premiums. The results, presented in Figure 13.3, support the notion of a countercyclical value beta: The beta of the HML portfolio is negative in good economies, meaning that the beta of value stocks (high book-to-market) is less than that of growth stocks (low B/M), but the reverse is true in recessions. While the covariance between the HML beta and the market risk premium is not sufficient to explain by itself the average return premium on value portfolios, it does suggest that at least part of the explanation may be a rational risk premium.

Behavioral Explanations

On the other side of the debate, several authors make the case that the value premium is a manifestation of market irrationality. The essence of the argument is that analysts tend to extrapolate recent performance too far out into the future, and thus tend to overestimate

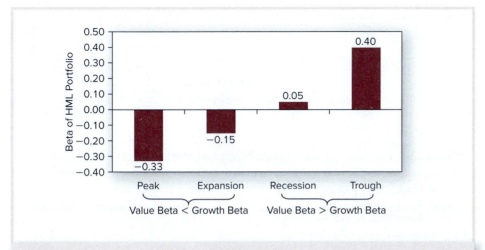

Figure 13.3 HML beta in different economic states. The beta of the HML portfolio is higher when the market risk premium is higher.

Source: Ralitsa Petkova and Lu Zhang, "Is Value Riskier than Growth?" *Journal of Financial Economics* 78 (2005), pp. 187–202.

the value of firms with good recent performance. When the market realizes its mistake, the prices of these firms fall. Thus, on average, "glamour firms," which are characterized by recent good performance, high prices, and lower book-to-market ratios, tend to underperform "value firms" because their high prices reflect excessive optimism relative to those lower book-to-market firms.

Figure 13.4, from a study by Chan, Karceski, and Lakonishok,[22] makes the case for overreaction. Firms are sorted into deciles based on income growth in the past five years. By construction, the growth rates uniformly increase from the first through the tenth decile (see the solid dark line in the figure). The book-to-market ratio for each decile at the *end* of the five-year period (the dashed colored line) tracks recent growth very well: B/M falls steadily with growth over the past five years. This is evidence that *past* growth is extrapolated and then impounded in price. High past growth leads to higher prices and lower B/M ratios.

But B/M at the *beginning* of a five-year period shows little or even a positive association with subsequent growth (the solid colored line), implying that market capitalization today is *inversely* related to growth prospects. In other words, the firms with lower B/M (glamour firms) experience no better or even worse average future income growth than other firms. The implication is that the market ignores evidence that past growth cannot be extrapolated far into the future. The book-to-market ratio may reflect past growth better than future growth, consistent with extrapolation error.

More direct evidence supporting extrapolation error is provided by La Porta, Lakonishok, Shleifer, and Vishny,[23] who examine stock price performance when actual earnings

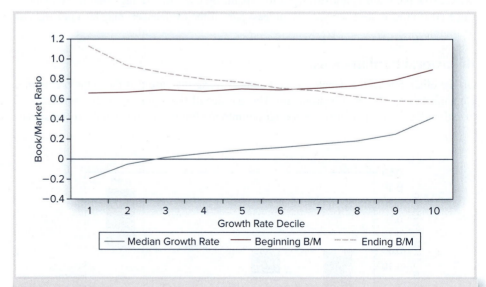

Figure 13.4 The book-to-market ratio reflects past growth, but not future growth prospects. B/M tends to fall with income growth experienced at the *end* of a five-year period, but actually increases slightly with future income growth rates.

Source: L. K. C. Chan, J. Karceski, and J. Lakonishok, "The Level and Persistence of Growth Rates," *Journal of Finance* 58 (April 2003), pp. 643–84.

[22]L. K. C. Chan, J. Karceski, and J. Lakonishok, "The Level and Persistence of Growth Rates," *Journal of Finance* 58 (April 2003), pp. 643–84.

[23] R. La Porta, J. Lakonishok, A. Shleifer, and R. W. Vishny, "Good News for Value Stocks," *Journal of Finance* 52 (1997), pp. 859–874.

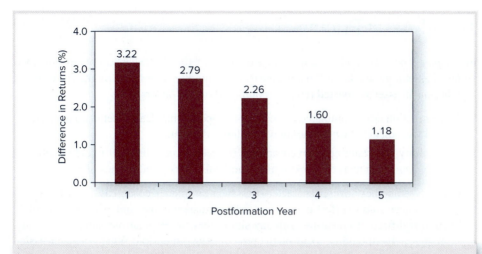

Figure 13.5 Value minus growth returns surrounding earnings announcements, 1971–1992. Announcement effects are measured for each of four years following classification as a value versus a growth firm.

Source: R. La Porta, J. Lakonishok, A. Shleifer, and R. W. Vishny, "Good News for Value Stocks," *Journal of Finance* 52 (1997), pp. 859–874.

are released to the public. Firms are classified as growth versus value stocks, and the difference in their stock price performance at earnings announcements for four years following the classification date is then examined. Figure 13.5 demonstrates that growth stocks underperform value stocks surrounding these announcements. We conclude that when news of actual earnings is released to the public, the market is relatively disappointed in stocks it has been treating as growth firms.

Momentum: A Fourth Factor

Since the seminal Fama-French three-factor model was introduced, a fourth factor has come to be added to the standard controls for stock return behavior. This is a momentum factor. As we first saw in Chapter 11, Jegadeesh and Titman uncovered a tendency for good or bad performance of stocks to persist over several months, a sort of momentum property.[24] Carhart added this momentum effect to the three-factor model as a tool to evaluate mutual fund performance.[25] The factor is constructed in the same way and is denoted by WML (winners minus losers). Versions of this factor take winners/losers based on 1–12 months of past returns. Carhart found that much of what appeared to be the alpha of many mutual funds could in fact be explained as due to their loadings or sensitivities to market momentum. The original Fama-French model augmented with a momentum factor has become a common four-factor model used to evaluate abnormal performance of a stock portfolio.

Of course, this additional factor presents further conundrums of interpretation. To characterize the original Fama-French factors as reflecting obvious sources of risk is already a bit of a challenge. A momentum factor seems even harder to position as reflecting a risk–return trade-off.

---

[24]Narasimhan Jegadeesh and Sheridan Titman, "Returns to Buying Winners and Selling Losers: Implications for Stock Market Efficiency," *Journal of Finance* 48 (March 1993), pp. 65–91.

[25]Mark M. Carhart, "On Persistence in Mutual Fund Performance," *Journal of Finance* 52 (March 1997), pp. 57–82.

13.4   Liquidity and Asset Pricing

In Chapter 9 we saw that an important extension of the CAPM incorporates considerations of asset liquidity. Unfortunately, measuring liquidity is far from trivial. The effect of liquidity on an asset's expected return is composed of two factors:

1. Transaction costs dominated by the bid–ask spread that dealers set to compensate for losses incurred when trading with informed traders.

2. Liquidity *risk* resulting from covariance between *changes* in asset liquidity with both *changes* in market-index liquidity and with market-index rates of return.

Liquidity embodies several characteristics such as trading costs, ease of sale, necessary price concessions to effect a quick transaction, market depth, and price predictability. As such, it is difficult to measure with any single statistic. Popular measures of liquidity, or, more precisely, illiquidity, focus on the price impact dimension: What price concession might a seller have to offer in order to accomplish a large sale of an asset or, conversely, what premium must a buyer offer to make a large purchase?

One measure of illiquidity is employed by Pástor and Stambaugh, who look for evidence of price reversals, especially following large trades.[26] Their idea is that if stock price movements tend to be partially reversed on the following day, then we can conclude that part of the original price change was not due to perceived changes in intrinsic value (these price changes would not tend to be reversed) but was, instead, a symptom of price impact associated with the original trade. Reversals suggest that part of the original price change was a concession on the part of trade initiators who needed to offer higher purchase prices or accept lower selling prices to complete their trades in a timely manner. Pástor and Stambaugh use regression analysis to show that reversals do in fact tend to be larger when associated with higher trading volume—exactly the pattern that one would expect if part of the price move is a liquidity phenomenon. They run a first-stage regression of returns on lagged returns and trading volume. The coefficient on the latter term measures the tendency of high-volume trades to be accompanied by larger reversals.

Another measure of illiquidity, proposed by Amihud, also focuses on the association between large trades and price movements.[27] His measure is:

$$\text{ILLIQ} = \text{Monthly average of daily} \left[\frac{\text{Absolute value(Stock return)}}{\text{Dollar volume}} \right]$$

This measure of illiquidity is based on the price impact per dollar of transactions in the stock and can be used to estimate both liquidity cost and liquidity risk.

Finally, Sadka uses trade-by-trade data to devise a third measure of liquidity.[28] He begins with the observation that part of price impact, a major component of illiquidity cost, is due to asymmetric information. (For a review, see our discussion of liquidity in Chapter 9 for a review of asymmetric information and the bid–ask spread.) He then uses

[26]L. Pástor and R. F. Stambaugh, "Liquidity Risk and Expected Stock Returns," *Journal of Political Economy* 111 (2003), pp. 642–85.

[27]Yakov Amihud, "Illiquidity and Stock Returns: Cross-Section and Time-Series Effects," *Journal of Financial Markets* 5 (2002), pp. 31–56.

[28]Ronnie Sadka, "Momentum and Post-earnings Announcement Drift Anomalies: The Role of Liquidity Risk," *Journal of Financial Economics* 80 (2006), pp. 309–49.

regression analysis to break out the component of price impact that is due to information issues. The liquidity of firms can wax or wane as the prevalence of informationally motivated trades varies, giving rise to liquidity risk.

Any of these liquidity measures can be averaged over stocks to devise measures of marketwide illiquidity. Given market illiquidity, we can then measure the "liquidity beta" of any individual stock (the sensitivity of returns to changes in market liquidity) and estimate the impact of liquidity risk on expected return. If stocks with high liquidity betas have higher average returns, we conclude that liquidity is a "priced factor," meaning that exposure to it offers higher expected return as compensation for the risk.

Pástor and Stambaugh conclude that liquidity risk is in fact a priced factor and that the risk premium associated with it is quantitatively significant. They sort portfolios into deciles based on liquidity beta and then compute the average alphas of the stocks in each decile using two models that *ignore* liquidity: the CAPM and the Fama-French three-factor model. Figure 13.6 shows that the alpha computed under either model rises substantially across liquidity-beta deciles, clear evidence that when controlling for other factors, average return rises along with liquidity risk. Not surprisingly, the relationship between liquidity risk and alpha across deciles is more regular for the Fama-French model, as it controls for a wider range of other influences on average return.

Pástor and Stambaugh also test the impact of the liquidity beta on alpha computed from a four-factor model (that also controls for momentum) and obtain similar results. In fact, they suggest that the liquidity risk factor may account for a good part of the apparent profitability of the momentum strategy.

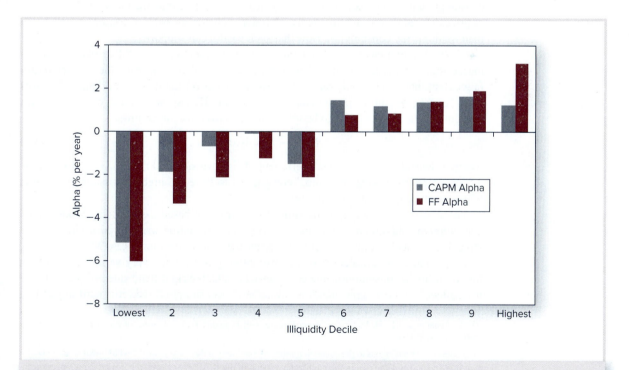

Figure 13.6 Alphas of value-weighted portfolios sorted on liquidity betas

Source: L. Pástor and R. F. Stambaugh, "Liquidity Risk and Expected Stock Returns," *Journal of Political Economy* 111 (2003), pp. 642–85, Table 4.

Acharya and Pedersen use Amihud's measure to test for price effects associated with the average *level* of illiquidity as well as a liquidity risk premium.[29] They demonstrate that expected stock returns depend on the average level of illiquidity. (Figure 9.4 in Chapter 9 shows a similar result.) But Acharya and Pedersen demonstrate that stock returns depend on several liquidity betas as well: the sensitivity of individual stock illiquidity to market illiquidity, the sensitivity of stock returns to market illiquidity, and the sensitivity of stock illiquidity to market return. They conclude that adding these liquidity effects to the conventional CAPM increases our ability to explain expected asset returns.

13.5 Consumption-Based Asset Pricing and the Equity Premium Puzzle

In the last chapter, we provided a brief introduction to Merton's multifactor or intertemporal CAPM (commonly called the ICAPM), and its close cousin, the consumption CAPM (the CCAPM). Both of these models envision investors attempting to devise an investment plan that will maximize the utility they derive from a lifetime flow of consumption. In each period, the investor must choose how much to consume versus how much to invest to provide for future consumption, as well as how to allocate the portfolio of funds invested for the future.

The consumption model implies that what matters to investors is not their wealth per se, but their lifetime flow of consumption. There can be slippage between wealth and consumption due to variation in factors such as the risk-free rate, the market risk premium, or prices of major consumption items. Therefore, a better measure of consumer well-being than wealth is the consumption flow that such wealth can support.

Given this framework, the generalization of the standard CAPM is that instead of measuring systematic risk based on the covariance of returns with the market return (a measure that focuses only on wealth), we are better off using the covariance of returns with "aggregate" or economywide consumption. Hence, we would expect the risk premium of the market index to be related to that covariance as follows:

$$E(r_M) - r_f = A\text{Cov}(r_M, r_C) \tag{13.8}$$

where A depends on the average coefficient of risk aversion and r_C is the rate of return on a "consumption-tracking portfolio," constructed to have the highest possible correlation with growth in aggregate consumption.

The first wave of attempts to estimate consumption-based asset pricing models used consumption data directly rather than returns on consumption-tracking portfolios. By and large, these tests found the CCAPM no better than the conventional CAPM in explaining risk premiums. The problem is that consumption growth is not very variable. With such low volatility in consumption, the covariance term on the right-hand side of Equation 13.8 is also low.[30] In turn, with such low "systematic" consumption risk, it is hard to justify a

---

[29]V. V. Acharya and L. H. Pedersen, "Asset Pricing with Liquidity Risk," *Journal of Financial Economics* 77 (2005), pp. 375–410.

[30]Equation 13.8 is analogous to the equation for the risk premium in the conventional CAPM—that is, that $E(r_M) - r_f = A\text{Cov}(r_M, r_M) = A\text{Var}(r_M)$. In the multifactor version of the ICAPM, however, the market is no longer mean-variance efficient, so the risk premium of the market index will not be proportional to its variance. The APT also implies a linear relationship between risk premium and covariance with relevant factors, but it is silent about the slope of the relationship because it avoids assumptions about utility.

market risk premium as large as the one we have observed historically unless we assume implausibly high levels of risk aversion. This empirical problem is called the *equity premium puzzle*.[31]

More recent research improves the quality of estimation in several ways. First, rather than using consumption growth directly, it uses consumption-tracking portfolios. The available (infrequent) data on aggregate consumption are used only to construct the consumption-tracking portfolio. The frequent and accurate data on the return on these portfolios may then be used to test the asset pricing model. (On the other hand, any inaccuracy in the construction of the consumption-mimicking portfolios will muddy the relationship between asset returns and consumption risk.)

For example, a study by Jagannathan and Wang focuses on year-over-year fourth-quarter consumption and employs a consumption-tracking portfolio.[32] Table 13.4, excerpted from their study, shows that the Fama-French factors are in fact associated with consumption betas as well as excess returns. The top panel contains familiar results: Moving across each row, we see that higher book-to-market ratios are associated with higher average returns. Similarly, moving down each column, we see that larger size generally implies lower average returns. The novel results are in the lower panel: A high book-to-market ratio is associated with higher consumption beta, and larger firm size is associated with lower consumption beta. The suggestion is that the explanatory power of the Fama-French factors for average returns may in fact reflect differences in consumption risk of those portfolios.

Size	Book-to-Market			
	Low	Medium	High	
Average annual excess returns* (%)				
Small	6.19	12.24	17.19	
Medium	6.93	10.43	13.94	
Big	7.08	8.52	9.5	
Consumption beta*				
Small	3.46	4.26	5.94	
Medium	2.88	4.35	5.71	
Big	3.39	2.83	4.41	

Table 13.4

Annual excess returns and consumption betas

*Average annual excess returns on the 25 Fama-French portfolios from 1954 to 2003. Consumption betas estimated by the time series regression

$$R_{i,t} = \alpha_i + \beta_{i,c} g_{ct} + e_{i,t},$$

where $R_{i,t}$ is the excess return over the risk-free rate, and g_{ct} is annual consumption growth calculated using fourth-quarter consumption data.

Source: Ravi Jagannathan and Yong Wang, "Lazy Investors, Discretionary Consumption, and the Cross-Section of Stock Returns," *Journal of Finance* 62 (August 2006), pp. 1623–61.

[31]Notice that the conventional CAPM does not pose such problems. In the CAPM, $E(r_M) - r_f = A\mathrm{Var}(r_M)$. A risk premium of .085 (8.5%) and a standard deviation of .20 (20%, or variance of .04) imply a coefficient of risk aversion of .085/.04 = 2.125, which is quite plausible.

[32]Ravi Jagannathan and Yong Wang, "Lazy Investors, Discretionary Consumption, and the Cross-Section of Stock Returns," *Journal of Finance* 62 (August 2006), pp. 1623–61.

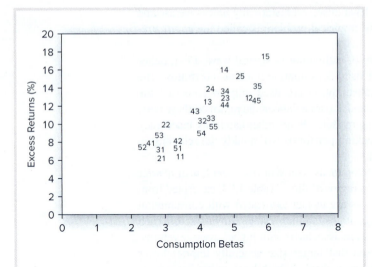

Figure 13.7 Cross section of stock returns: Fama-French 25 portfolios, 1954–2003

Annual excess returns and consumption betas. This figure plots the average annual excess returns on the 25 Fama-French portfolios and their consumption betas. Each two-digit number represents one portfolio. The first digit refers to the size quintile (1 = smallest, 5 = largest), and the second digit refers to the book-to-market quintile (1 = lowest, 5 = highest).

Figure 13.7 shows that the average returns of the 25 Fama-French portfolios are strongly associated with their consumption betas.

Moreover, the standard CCAPM focuses on a representative consumer/investor, thereby ignoring information about heterogeneous investors with different levels of wealth and consumption habits. For example, the covariance between market returns and consumption is far higher when we focus on the consumption risk of households that actually hold financial securities.[33] This observation mitigates the equity risk premium puzzle.

Expected versus Realized Returns

Fama and French offer another interpretation of the equity premium puzzle.[34] Using stock index returns from 1872 to 1999, they report the average risk-free rate, average stock market return (represented by the S&P 500 index), and resultant risk premium for the overall period and subperiods:

Period	Risk-Free Rate	S&P 500 Return	Equity Premium
1872–1999	4.87	10.97	6.10
1872–1949	4.05	8.67	4.62
1950–1999	6.15	14.56	8.41

The big increase in the average excess return on equity after 1949 suggests that the equity premium puzzle is largely a creature of modern times.

Fama and French suspect that estimating the risk premium from average realized returns may be the problem. They use the constant-growth dividend-discount model (for a review, see an introductory finance text or Chapter 18) to estimate expected returns and find that for the period 1872–1949, the dividend discount model (DDM) yields similar estimates of the *expected* risk premium as the average *realized* excess return. But for the period 1950–1999, the DDM yields a much smaller risk premium, which suggests that the high average excess return in this period may have exceeded the returns investors actually expected to earn at the time.

In the constant-growth DDM, the expected capital gains rate on the stock will equal the growth rate of dividends. As a result, the expected total return on the firm's stock will be the sum of dividend yield (dividend/price) plus the expected dividend growth rate, g:

$$E(r) = \frac{D_1}{P_0} + g \qquad (13.9)$$

[33]C. J. Malloy, T. Moskowitz, and A. Vissing-Jørgensen, "Long-Run Stockholder Consumption Risk and Asset Returns," *Journal of Finance* 64 (December 2009), pp. 2427–80.

[34] Eugene Fama and Kenneth French, "The Equity Premium," *Journal of Finance* 57, no. 2 (2002).

where D_1 is end-of-year dividends and P_0 is the current price of the stock. Fama and French treat the S&P 500 as representative of the average firm and use Equation 13.9 to produce estimates of $E(r)$.

For each year, $t = 1, \ldots, T$, Fama and French estimate expected return from the sum of the dividend yield (D_t/P_{t-1}) plus the dividend growth rate $(g_t = D_t/D_{t-1} - 1)$. In contrast, the *realized* return is the dividend yield plus the rate of capital gains $(P_t/P_{t-1} - 1)$. Because the dividend yield is common to both estimates, the difference between the expected and realized return equals the difference between the dividend growth and capital gains rates. While dividend growth and capital gains were similar in the earlier period, capital gains significantly exceeded the dividend growth rate in modern times. Hence, Fama and French conclude that the equity premium puzzle may be due at least in part to unanticipated capital gains in the latter period.

Fama and French argue that dividend growth rates produce more reliable estimates of the capital gains investors actually expected to earn than the average of their realized capital gains. They point to three reasons:

1. Average realized returns over 1950–1999 exceeded the internal rate of return on corporate investments. If those average returns were representative of expectations, we would have to conclude that firms were willingly engaging in negative-NPV investments.

2. The statistical precision of estimates from the DDM are far higher than those using average historical returns. The standard error of the estimates of the risk premium from realized returns greatly exceeds the standard error from the dividend discount model (see the following table).

3. The reward-to-volatility (Sharpe) ratio derived from the DDM is far more stable than that derived from realized returns. If risk aversion remains the same over time, we would expect the Sharpe ratio to be stable.

The evidence for the second and third points is shown in the following table, where estimates from the dividend discount model (DDM) and from realized returns (Realized) are shown side by side.

Period	Mean Return		Standard Error		t-Statistic		Sharpe Ratio	
	DDM	Realized	DDM	Realized	DDM	Realized	DDM	Realized
1872–1999	4.03	6.10	1.14	1.65	3.52	3.70	0.22	0.34
1872–1949	4.35	4.62	1.76	2.20	2.47	2.10	0.23	0.24
1950–1999	3.54	8.41	1.03	2.45	3.42	3.43	0.21	0.51

Fama and French's study provides a simple explanation for the equity premium puzzle, namely, that observed rates of return in the recent half-century were unexpectedly high. It also implies that forecasts of future excess returns will be lower than past averages.

Survivorship Bias

The equity premium puzzle emerged from long-term averages of U.S. stock returns. There are reasons to suspect that these estimates of the risk premium are subject to survivorship bias, as the United States had one of the most successful economies in the world, an outcome that would not have seemed inevitable much before the second World War. Jurion and Goetzmann assembled a database of capital appreciation indexes for the stock markets of 39 countries over the period 1921–1996.[35] Figure 13.8 shows that U.S. equities

[35]Philippe Jurion and William N. Goetzmann, "Global Stock Markets in the Twentieth Century," *Journal of Finance* 54, no. 3 (June 1999).

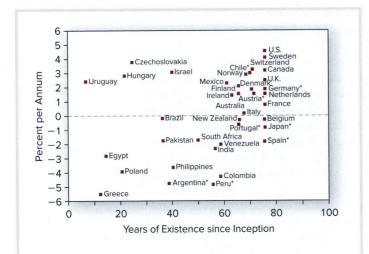

Figure 13.8 Real returns on global stock markets. The figure displays average real returns for 39 markets over the period 1921 to 1996. Markets are sorted by years of existence. An asterisk indicates that the market suffered a long-term break.

Source: Philippe Jurion and William N. Goetzmann, "Global Stock Markets in the Twentieth Century," *Journal of Finance* 54, no. 3 (June 1999).

had the highest real return of all countries, at 4.3% annually, versus a median of .8% for other countries. Moreover, unlike the United States, many other countries have had equity markets that actually closed, either permanently or for extended periods of time, following economic disruptions caused by war or revolution.

The implication of these results is that using average U.S. data may impart a form of survivorship bias to our estimate of expected returns, because unlike many other countries, the United States has never been a victim of such extreme problems. Estimating risk premiums from the experience of the country with the highest average return and ignoring the evidence from stock markets that did not survive for the full sample period will impart an upward bias in estimates of expected returns. The high realized equity premium obtained for the United States may not be indicative of required returns.

As an analogy, think of the effect of survivorship bias in the mutual fund industry. We know that some companies regularly close down their worst-performing mutual funds. If performance studies include only mutual funds for which returns are available during an entire sample period, the average returns of the funds that make it into the sample will be reflective of the performance of long-term survivors only. With the failed funds excluded from the sample, the average measured performance of mutual fund managers will be better than one could reasonably expect from the full sample of managers. Think back to the box in Chapter 11, "How to Guarantee a Successful Market Newsletter." If one starts many newsletters with a range of forecasts, and continues only the newsletters that turned out to have successful advice, then it will *appear* from the sample of survivors that the average newsletter had forecasting skill.

Extensions to the CAPM May Resolve the Equity Premium Puzzle

Constantinides argues that the standard CAPM can be extended to account for observed excess returns by relaxing some of its assumptions, in particular, by recognizing that consumers face uninsurable and idiosyncratic income shocks, for example, the loss of employment.[36] The prospect of such events is higher in economic downturns and bad outcomes such as job loss are not shared evenly across all members of the economy. This observation can take us a long way toward understanding the risk–return trade-off as well as its variation across the business cycle.

In addition, life-cycle considerations are important and often overlooked. Borrowing constraints become important when placed in the context of the life cycle. The imaginary

[36]George M. Constantinides, "Understanding the Equity Risk Premium Puzzle," in *Handbooks in Finance: Handbook of the Equity Risk Premium,* ed. Rajnish Mehra (Amsterdam: Elsevier, 2008), pp. 331–59.

"representative consumer" who holds all stock and bond market wealth does not face borrowing constraints. Young consumers, however, do face meaningful borrowing constraints. Constantinides traces their impact on the equity premium, the demand for bonds, and on the limited participation of many consumers in the capital markets. Finally, he shows that adding habit formation[37] to the conventional utility function helps justify higher risk premiums than those that would be predicted by the covariance of stock returns with aggregate consumption growth. He argues that integrating the notions of habit formation, incomplete risk sharing, the life cycle, borrowing constraints, and other sources of limited stock market participation is a promising vantage point from which to study the prices of assets and their returns, both theoretically and empirically.

Finally, another attempt[38] to resolve the equity premium puzzle appeals to the idea of "long-run risk." Suppose that an increase in consumption growth this year signals to the market that growth likely will be higher for several years to come. In that event, while the covariance between asset returns and *contemporaneous* consumption growth may be low, the covariance of returns with the present value of the entire consumption stream will be much larger. This long-run forward-looking view generates much higher values for systematic (consumption-based) risk and makes the historical equity premium far easier to justify.

Liquidity and the Equity Premium Puzzle

We've seen that liquidity risk is potentially important in explaining the cross section of stock returns. The illiquidity premium may be on the same order of magnitude as the market risk premium. Therefore, the common practice of treating the average excess return on a market index as an estimate of a risk premium per se is too simplistic. Part of that average excess return is almost certainly compensation for *liquidity* risk rather than just the (systematic) *volatility* of returns. If this is recognized, the equity premium puzzle may be less of a puzzle than it first appears.

Behavioral Explanations of the Equity Premium Puzzle

Barberis and Huang explain the puzzle as an outcome of irrational investor behavior.[39] The key elements of their approach are loss aversion and narrow framing, two well-known features of decision making under risk in experimental settings. Narrow framing is the idea that investors evaluate every risk they face in isolation. Thus, investors will focus on total volatility rather than the low correlation of a stock portfolio with other components of wealth, and therefore they will require a higher risk premium than rational models would predict. Combined with loss aversion, investor behavior will generate large risk premiums despite the fact that traditionally measured risk aversion is low. (See Chapter 12 for more discussion of loss aversion and other behavioral biases.)

Models that incorporate these effects can generate a large equilibrium equity risk premium and a low and stable risk-free rate, even when consumption growth is smooth and

---

[37]*Habit formation* refers to the observation that investors may become acclimated to a given level of consumption that they have experienced or observed over extended periods of time. It becomes hard to cut back from a consumption level you view as "normal," even if it might appear luxuriant to someone else. Habit formation can make investors act as if they are more risk averse, as they can become highly sensitive to losses even if it appears that they have a comfortable cushion to absorb poor returns.

[38]Ravi Bansal and Amir Yaron, "Risks for the Long Run: A Potential Resolution of Asset Pricing Puzzles," *Journal of Finance* 59, 2004, pp. 1639–72.

[39]Nicholas Barberis and Ming Huang, "The Loss Aversion/Narrow Framing Approach to the Equity Premium Puzzle," in *Handbooks in Finance: Handbook of the Equity Risk Premium*, ed. Rajnish Mehra (Amsterdam: Elsevier, 2008), pp. 199–229.

only weakly correlated with the stock market. Moreover, they can do so for parameter values that correspond to plausible predictions about attitudes to independent monetary gambles.

The behavioral analysis of the equity premium also has implications for a closely related puzzle, the stock market participation puzzle. Narrow framing can explain why a segment of the population that one would expect to participate in the stock market still avoids it. The assessment of stock market volatility in isolation ignores its limited impact on consumption. Loss aversion that exaggerates disutility of losses relative to a reference point magnifies this effect.

SUMMARY

1. Early tests of the single-factor CAPM rejected the SML, finding that nonsystematic risk was related to average security returns. Later tests controlling for the measurement error in beta found that nonsystematic risk does not explain portfolio returns but also that the estimated SML is too flat compared with what the CAPM would predict.

2. Roll's critique implies that the usual CAPM test is a test only of the mean-variance efficiency of a prespecified market *proxy* and therefore that tests of the linearity of the expected return–beta relationship do not bear on the validity of the model.

3. Tests of the single-index model that account for human capital and cyclical variations in asset betas are more supportive of the single-index CAPM and APT. Moreover, anomalies such as the size and book-to-market effects are mitigated once these variables are accounted for.

4. The dominant multifactor models today are variants of the Fama-French model, incorporating market, size, value, momentum, and, sometimes, liquidity factors. Debate continues on whether returns associated with these extra-market factors reflect rational risk premia or behaviorally induced mispricing.

5. Early research on consumption-based capital asset pricing models was disappointing, but more recent work is more encouraging. In some studies, consumption betas help to explain average portfolio returns and are associated with the Fama-French factors. These results support Fama and French's conjecture that their factors proxy for more fundamental sources of risk.

6. The equity premium puzzle originates from the observation that equity returns exceeded the risk-free rate to an extent that is inconsistent with the covariance of returns with consumption risk and reasonable levels of risk aversion—at least when average rates of return are taken to represent expectations. Some explanations for this puzzle focus on incomplete risk sharing or on habit formation. Other explanations are empirically based. For example, the puzzle emerges primarily from excess returns in the post–World War II period. It is plausible that the extent of the economic success of the United States in the post-war period was unexpected, making historical averages unrepresentative of prior expected values. Alternative estimates of expected returns using the dividend growth model instead of average returns suggest that excess returns on stocks were high largely because of unexpectedly large capital gains.

KEY TERMS

first-pass regression   second-pass regression   benchmark error

KEY EQUATIONS

First-pass regression equation: $r_{it} - r_{ft} = a_i + b_i(r_{Mt} - r_{ft}) + e_{it}$

Second-pass regression equation: $\overline{r_i - r_f} = \gamma_0 + \gamma_1 b_i$

Fama-French three-factor model: $E(r_i) - r_f = a_i + b_i[E(r_M) - r_f] + s_i E[R_{SMB}] + h_i E[R_{HML}]$

The following annual excess rates of return were obtained for nine individual stocks (A–I) and a market index. Use this information to complete Problems 1–7.

Stock Excess Returns (%)

Year	Market Index	A	B	C	D	E	F	G	H	I
1	29.65	33.88	−25.20	36.48	42.89	−39.89	39.67	74.57	40.22	90.19
2	−11.91	−49.87	24.70	−25.11	−54.39	44.92	−54.33	−79.76	−71.58	−26.64
3	14.73	65.14	−25.04	18.91	−39.86	−3.91	−5.69	26.73	14.49	18.14
4	27.68	14.46	−38.64	−23.31	−0.72	−3.21	92.39	−3.82	13.74	0.09
5	5.18	15.67	61.93	63.95	−32.82	44.26	−42.96	101.67	24.24	8.98
6	25.97	−32.17	44.94	−19.56	69.42	90.43	76.72	1.72	77.22	72.38
7	10.64	−31.55	−74.65	50.18	74.52	15.38	21.95	−43.95	−13.40	28.95
8	1.02	−23.79	47.02	−42.28	28.61	−17.64	28.83	98.01	28.12	39.41
9	18.82	−4.59	28.69	−0.54	2.32	42.36	18.93	−2.45	37.65	94.67
10	23.92	−8.03	48.61	23.65	26.26	−3.65	23.31	15.36	80.59	52.51
11	−41.61	78.22	−85.02	−0.79	−68.70	−85.71	−45.64	2.27	−72.47	−80.26
12	−6.64	4.75	42.95	−48.60	26.27	13.24	−34.34	−54.47	−1.50	−24.46

1. Perform the first-pass regressions and tabulate the summary statistics.

2. Specify the hypotheses for a test of the second-pass regression for the SML.

3. Perform the second-pass SML regression by regressing the average excess return of each portfolio on its beta.

4. Summarize your test results and compare them to the results reported in the text.

5. Group the nine stocks into three portfolios, maximizing the dispersion of the betas of the three resultant portfolios. Repeat the test and explain any changes in the results.

6. Explain Roll's critique as it applies to the tests performed in Problems 1–5.

7. Plot the capital market line (CML), the nine stocks, and the three portfolios on a graph of average returns versus standard deviation. Compare the mean-variance efficiency of the three portfolios and the market index. Does the comparison support the CAPM?

Suppose that, in addition to the market factor that has been considered in Problems 1–7, a second factor is considered. The values of this factor for years 1 to 12 were as follows:

Year	% Change in Factor Value	Year	% Change in Factor Value
1	−9.84	7	−3.52
2	6.46	8	8.43
3	16.12	9	8.23
4	−16.51	10	7.06
5	17.82	11	−15.74
6	−13.31	12	2.03

8. Perform the first-pass regressions as did Chen, Roll, and Ross and tabulate the relevant summary statistics. (*Hint:* Use a multiple regression as in a standard spreadsheet package. Estimate the betas of the 12 stocks on the two factors.)

9. Specify the hypothesis for a test of a second-pass regression for the two-factor SML.

10. Do the data suggest a two-factor economy?

11. Can you identify a factor portfolio for the second factor?

12. Suppose you own your own business, which now makes up about half your net worth. On the basis of what you have learned in this chapter, how would you structure your portfolio of financial assets?

1. Identify and briefly discuss three criticisms of beta as used in the capital asset pricing model.

2. Richard Roll, in an article on using the capital asset pricing model (CAPM) to evaluate portfolio performance, indicated that it may not be possible to evaluate portfolio management ability if there is an error in the benchmark used.

   a. In evaluating portfolio performance, describe the general procedure, with emphasis on the benchmark employed.

   b. Explain what Roll meant by *benchmark error* and identify the specific problem with this benchmark.

   c. Draw a graph that shows how a portfolio that has been judged as superior relative to a "measured" security market line (SML) can be inferior relative to the "true" SML.

   d. Assume that you are informed that a given portfolio manager has been evaluated as superior when compared to the Dow Jones Industrial Average, the S&P 500, and the NYSE Composite Index. Explain whether this consensus would make you feel more comfortable regarding the portfolio manager's true ability.

   e. Although conceding the possible problem with benchmark errors as set forth by Roll, some contend this does not mean the CAPM is incorrect, but only that there is a measurement problem when implementing the theory. Others contend that because of benchmark errors the whole technique should be scrapped. Take and defend one of these positions.

3. Bart Campbell, CFA, is a portfolio manager who has recently met with a prospective client, Jane Black. After conducting a survey market line (SML) performance analysis using the Dow Jones Industrial Average as her market proxy, Black claims that her portfolio has experienced superior performance. Campbell uses the capital asset pricing model as an investment performance measure and finds that Black's portfolio plots below the SML. Campbell concludes that Black's apparent superior performance is a function of an incorrectly specified market proxy, not superior investment management. Justify Campbell's conclusion by addressing the likely effects of an incorrectly specified market proxy on both beta and the slope of the SML.

SOLUTIONS TO CONCEPT CHECKS

1. The SCL is estimated for each stock; hence we need to estimate 100 equations. Our sample consists of 60 monthly rates of return for each of the 100 stocks and for the market index. Thus each regression is estimated with 60 observations. Equation 13.1 in the text shows that when stated in excess return form, the SCL should pass through the origin, that is, have a zero intercept.

2. When the SML has a positive intercept and its slope is less than the mean excess return on the market portfolio, it is flatter than predicted by the CAPM. Low-beta stocks therefore have yielded returns that, on average, were higher than they should have been on the basis of their beta. Conversely, high-beta stocks were found to have yielded, on average, lower returns than they should have on the basis of their betas. The positive coefficient on γ_2 implies that stocks with higher values of firm-specific risk had on average higher returns. This pattern, of course, violates the predictions of the CAPM.

3. a. According to Equation 13.4, γ_0 is the average excess return earned on a stock with zero beta and zero firm-specific risk. The CAPM predicts this should have been zero. In fact, for the 1946–1955 period, the value was 8 basis points or .08% per month (see Table 13.1). But this estimate was not statistically significantly different from zero. According to the CAPM, γ_1 should equal the average market risk premium, which for the 1946–1955 period was 103 basis points, or 1.03% per month. The estimated value was 2.09% per month. Finally, the CAPM predicts that γ_3, the coefficient on firm-specific risk, should have been zero. While the actual estimate is not zero, the difference from zero is not statistically significant.

   b. A positive coefficient on β^2 would indicate that the relationship between risk and return is nonlinear. High-beta securities would provide expected returns more than proportional to risk. A positive coefficient on $\sigma(e)$ would indicate that firm-specific risk affects expected return, a direct contradiction of the CAPM and APT.

Bond Prices and Yields

14

IN THE PREVIOUS chapters on risk and return relationships, we treated securities at a high level of abstraction. We assumed implicitly that a prior, detailed analysis of each security already had been performed and that its risk and return features had been assessed.

We now turn to specific analyses of particular security markets. We examine valuation principles, determinants of risk and return, and portfolio strategies commonly used within and across the various markets.

We begin by analyzing **debt securities.** A debt security is a claim on a specified periodic stream of income. Debt securities are often called *fixed-income securities* because they promise either a fixed stream of income or one that is determined according to a specified formula. These securities have the advantage of being relatively easy to understand because the payment formulas are specified in advance. Uncertainty about their cash flows is minimal as long as the issuer of the security is sufficiently creditworthy. That makes these securities a convenient starting point for

our analysis of the universe of potential investment vehicles.

The bond is the basic debt security, and this chapter starts with an overview of the universe of bond markets, including Treasury, corporate, and international bonds. We turn next to bond pricing, showing how bond prices are set in accordance with market interest rates and why bond prices change with those rates. Given this background, we can compare the myriad measures of bond returns such as yield to maturity, yield to call, holding-period return, and realized compound rate of return. We show how bond prices evolve over time, discuss certain tax rules that apply to debt securities, and show how to calculate after-tax returns.

Finally, we consider the impact of default or credit risk on bond pricing and look at the determinants of credit risk and the default premium built into bond yields. Credit risk is central to fixed-income derivatives such as collateralized debt obligations and credit default swaps, so we examine these instruments as well.

14.1 Bond Characteristics

A **bond** is a security that is issued in connection with a borrowing arrangement. The borrower issues (i.e., sells) a bond to the lender for some amount of cash; the bond is the "IOU" of the borrower. The arrangement obligates the issuer to make specified payments to the bondholder on specified dates. A typical coupon bond obligates the issuer to make semiannual payments of interest to the bondholder for the life of the bond. These are called *coupon payments* because in precomputer days, most bonds had coupons that investors would clip off and present to claim the interest payment. When the bond matures, the issuer repays the debt by paying the bond's **par value** (equivalently, its **face value**). The **coupon rate** of the bond determines the interest payment: The annual payment is the coupon rate times the bond's par value. The coupon rate, maturity date, and par value of the bond are part of the **bond indenture,** which is the contract between the issuer and the bondholder.

To illustrate, a bond with par value of $1,000 and coupon rate of 8% might be sold to a buyer for $1,000. The bondholder is then entitled to a payment of 8% of $1,000, or $80 per year, for the stated life of the bond, say, 30 years. The $80 payment typically comes in two semiannual installments of $40 each. At the end of the 30-year life of the bond, the issuer also pays the $1,000 par value to the bondholder.

Bonds usually are issued with coupon rates set just high enough to induce investors to pay par value to buy the bond. Sometimes, however, **zero-coupon bonds** are issued that make no coupon payments. In this case, investors receive par value at the maturity date but receive no interest payments until then: The bond has a coupon rate of zero. These bonds are issued at prices considerably below par value, and the investor's return comes solely from the difference between the issue price and the payment of par value at maturity. We will return to these bonds later.

Treasury Bonds and Notes

Figure 14.1 is an excerpt from the listing of Treasury issues. Treasury notes are issued with original maturities ranging between 1 and 10 years, while Treasury bonds are issued with maturities ranging from 10 to 30 years. Both bonds and notes may be purchased directly from the Treasury in denominations of only $100, but denominations of $1,000 are far more common. Both make semiannual coupon payments.

The highlighted bond in Figure 14.1 matures on May 15, 2046. Its coupon rate is 2.5%. Par value typically is $1,000; thus the bond pays interest of $25 per year in two semiannual payments of $12.50. Payments are made in May and November of each year. Although bonds usually are sold in denominations of $1,000, the bid and ask prices are quoted as a percentage of par value.[1] Therefore, the ask price is

U.S. Treasury Quotes

MATURITY	COUPON	BID	ASKED	CHANGE	ASKED YIELD (%)
May 15 18	1.000	100.3984	100.4141	−0.0859	0.791
May 15 19	0.875	99.8125	99.8281	−0.0859	0.933
Feb 15 21	7.875	130.5781	130.5938	−0.2656	1.225
Aug 15 25	6.875	144.4141	144.4297	−0.5391	1.670
Aug 15 25	2.000	102.2813	102.2969	−0.3438	1.730
May 15 30	6.250	152.3984	152.4609	−0.7969	1.950
Nov 15 41	3.125	111.7891	111.8203	−0.8750	2.496
May 15 46	2.500	97.9922	98.0234	−0.9063	2.595

Figure 14.1 Prices and yields of U.S. Treasury bonds

Source: *The Wall Street Journal Online,* May 16, 2016.

---

[1] Recall that the bid price is the price at which you can sell the bond to a dealer. The ask price, which is slightly higher, is the price at which you can buy the bond from a dealer.

98.0234% of par, or $980.234. The minimum price increment, or tick size, in *The Wall Street Journal* listing is $^1/_{128}$, so this bond may also be viewed as selling for $98\ ^3/_{128}$ percent of par value.[2]

The last column, labeled "Asked Yield to Maturity," is the yield to maturity on the bond based on the ask price. The yield to maturity is a measure of the average rate of return to an investor who purchases the bond for the ask price and holds it until its maturity date. We will have much to say about yield to maturity below.

Accrued Interest and Quoted Bond Prices   The bond prices that you see quoted in the financial pages are not actually the prices that investors pay for the bond. This is because the quoted price does not include the interest that accrues between coupon payment dates.

If a bond is purchased between coupon payments, the buyer must pay the seller for accrued interest, the prorated share of the upcoming semiannual coupon. For example, if 30 days have passed since the last coupon payment, and there are 182 days in the semiannual coupon period, the seller is entitled to a payment of accrued interest of 30/182 of the semiannual coupon. The sale, or *invoice,* price of the bond would equal the stated price (sometimes called the *flat price*) plus the accrued interest.

In general, the formula for the amount of accrued interest between two dates is

$$\text{Accrued interest} = \frac{\text{Annual coupon payment}}{2} \times \frac{\text{Days since last coupon payment}}{\text{Days separating coupon payments}}$$

Example 14.1   Accrued Interest

Suppose that the coupon rate is 8%. Then the annual coupon is $80 and the semiannual coupon payment is $40. Because 30 days have passed since the last coupon payment, the accrued interest on the bond is $40 × (30/182) = $6.59. If the quoted price of the bond is $990, then the invoice price will be $990 + $6.59 = $996.59.

The practice of quoting bond prices net of accrued interest explains why the price of a maturing bond is listed at $1,000 rather than $1,000 plus one coupon payment. A purchaser of an 8% coupon bond one day before the bond's maturity would receive $1,040 (par value plus semiannual interest) on the following day and so should be willing to pay a total price of $1,040 for the bond. The bond price is quoted net of accrued interest in the financial pages and thus appears as $1,000.[3]

Corporate Bonds

Like the government, corporations borrow money by issuing bonds. Figure 14.2 is a sample of listings for a few actively traded corporate bonds. Although some bonds trade electronically on the NYSE Bonds platform, most bonds are traded over-the-counter in

---

[2]Bonds traded on formal exchanges are subject to minimum tick sizes set by the exchange. For example, the minimum price increment on the 2-year Treasury bond futures contract (traded on the Chicago Board of Trade) is 1/128, although longer-term T-bonds have larger tick sizes. Private traders can negotiate their own tick size. For example, one can find price quotes on Bloomberg screens with tick sizes as low as 1/256.

[3]In contrast to bonds, stocks do not trade at flat prices with adjustments for "accrued dividends." Whoever owns the stock when it goes "ex-dividend" receives the entire dividend payment, and the stock price reflects the value of the upcoming dividend. The price therefore typically falls by about the amount of the dividend on the "ex-day." There is no need to differentiate between reported and invoice prices for stocks.

ISSUER NAME	SYMBOL	COUPON	MATURITY	MOODY'S/S&P/ FITCH	HIGH	LOW	LAST	CHANGE	YIELD %
COMMONWEALTH BK AUSTRALIA MEDIUM TERM NT	CBAU3828562	2.250%	Mar 16 17	Aaa//AAA	100.892	100.892	100.892	0.0020	1.1102
WALGREENS BOOTS ALLIANCE INC	WAG4182650	4.800%	Nov 18 44	Baa2 /BBB /BBB	103.367	100.560	100.560	−2.0100	4.7634
ANHEUSER BUSCH INBEV FIN INC	BUD4327481	3.650%	Feb 01 26	A3 //	104.593	104.096	104.249	−0.0130	3.1254
HSBC HLDGS PLC	HBC3699239	6.100%	Jan 14 42	A1 //AA−	129.300	128.850	128.850	1.4860	4.2419
SOUTHERN CO	SO4365686	1.850%	Jul 01 19	Baa2 //A−	100.438	100.324	100.324	−0.0310	1.7411
WESTPAC BKG CORP	WBK4248362	1.550%	May 25 18	Aa2 //AA−	100.246	100.148	100.148	−0.1900	1.4738
GOLDMAN SACHS GROUP INC	GS4302031	4.750%	Oct 21 45	A3 /BBB+ /A	107.139	106.419	106.727	0.0500	4.3389
HSBC HLDGS PLC	HBC4365146	3.900%	May 25 26	A1 //	101.564	100.889	101.564	0.1580	3.7109
NEWELL BRANDS INC	NWL4346211	2.600%	Mar 29 19	Baa3 //BBB−	103.118	101.774	101.774	0.2360	1.9510
LLOYDS TSB BK PLC	LYG3833921	4.200%	Mar 28 17	A1 //A+	102.462	102.389	102.389	−0.0770	1.2682

Figure 14.2 Listing of corporate bonds

Source: FINRA (Financial Industry Regulatory Authority), May 31, 2016.

a network of bond dealers linked by a computer quotation system. In practice, the bond market can be quite "thin," with few investors interested in trading a particular issue at any particular time.

The bond listings in Figure 14.2 include the coupon, maturity, price, and yield to maturity of each bond. The "rating" column is the estimation of bond safety given by the three major bond-rating agencies—Moody's, Standard & Poor's, and Fitch. Bonds with gradations of A ratings are safer than those with B ratings or below. As a general rule, safer bonds with higher ratings promise lower yields to maturity than other bonds with similar maturities. We will return to this topic toward the end of the chapter.

Call Provisions on Corporate Bonds   Some corporate bonds are issued with call provisions allowing the issuer to repurchase the bond at a specified *call price* before the maturity date. For example, if a company issues a bond with a high coupon rate when market interest rates are high and interest rates later fall, the firm might like to retire the high-coupon debt and issue new bonds at a lower coupon rate to reduce interest payments. This is called *refunding*. **Callable bonds** typically come with a period of call protection, an initial time during which the bonds are not callable. Such bonds are referred to as *deferred* callable bonds.

The option to call the bond is valuable to the firm, allowing it to buy back the bonds and refinance at lower interest rates when market rates fall. Of course, the firm's benefit is the bondholder's burden. Holders of called bonds must forfeit their bonds for the call price, thereby giving up the attractive coupon rate on their original investment. To compensate investors for this risk, callable bonds are issued with higher coupons and promised yields to maturity than noncallable bonds.

✔ Concept Check **14.1**

Suppose that Verizon issues two bonds with identical coupon rates and maturity dates. One bond is callable, however, whereas the other is not. Which bond will sell at a lower price?

Convertible Bonds   **Convertible bonds** give bondholders an option to exchange each bond for a specified number of shares of common stock of the firm. The *conversion ratio* is the number of shares for which each bond may be exchanged. Suppose a convertible bond is issued at par value of $1,000 and is convertible into 40 shares of a firm's stock. The current stock price is $20 per share, so the option to convert is not profitable now. Should the stock price later rise to $30, however, each bond may be converted profitably into $1,200 worth of stock. The *market conversion value* is the current value of the shares for which the bonds may be exchanged. At the $20 stock price, for example, the bond's conversion value is $800. The *conversion premium* is the excess of the bond's value over its conversion value. If the bond were selling currently for $950, its premium would be $150.

Convertible bondholders benefit from price appreciation of the company's stock. Again, this benefit comes at a price: Convertible bonds offer lower coupon rates and stated or promised yields to maturity than do nonconvertible bonds. However, the actual return on the convertible bond may exceed the stated yield to maturity if the option to convert becomes profitable.

We discuss convertible and callable bonds further in Chapter 20.

Puttable Bonds   While the callable bond gives the issuer the option to extend or retire the bond at the call date, the *extendable* or **put bond** gives this option to the bondholder. If the bond's coupon rate exceeds current market yields, for instance, the bondholder will choose to extend the bond's life. If the bond's coupon rate is too low, it will be optimal not to extend; in this case, the bondholder will instead reclaim principal, which can be invested at current yields.

Floating-Rate Bonds   **Floating-rate bonds** make interest payments that are tied to some measure of current market rates. For example, the rate might be adjusted annually to the current T-bill rate plus 2%. If the 1-year T-bill rate at the adjustment date is 4%, the bond's coupon rate over the next year would then be 6%. This arrangement means that the bond always pays approximately current market rates.

The major risk involved in floaters has to do with changes in the firm's financial strength. The yield spread is fixed over the life of the security, which may be many years. If the financial health of the firm deteriorates, then investors will demand a greater yield premium than is offered by the security. In this case, the price of the bond will fall. Although the coupon rate on floaters adjusts to changes in the general level of market interest rates, it does not adjust to changes in the financial condition of the firm.

Preferred Stock

Although preferred stock strictly speaking is considered to be equity, it often is included in the fixed-income universe. This is because, like bonds, preferred stock promises to pay a specified stream of dividends. However, unlike bonds, the failure to pay the promised dividend does not result in corporate bankruptcy. Instead, the dividends owed simply cumulate, and the common stockholders may not receive any dividends until the preferred stockholders have been paid in full. In the event of bankruptcy, preferred stockholders' claims to the firm's assets have lower priority than those of bondholders but higher priority than those of common stockholders.

Preferred stock commonly pays a fixed dividend. Therefore, it is in effect a perpetuity, providing a level cash flow indefinitely. In contrast, floating-rate preferred stock is much like floating-rate bonds. The dividend rate is linked to a measure of current market interest rates and is adjusted at regular intervals.

Unlike interest payments on bonds, dividends on preferred stock are not considered tax-deductible expenses to the firm. This reduces their attractiveness as a source of capital to issuing firms. On the other hand, there is an offsetting tax advantage to preferred stock. When one corporation buys the preferred stock of another corporation, it pays taxes on only 30% of the dividends received. For example, if the firm's tax bracket is 35%, and it receives $10,000 in preferred-dividend payments, it will pay taxes on only $3,000 of that income: Total taxes owed on the income will be .35 × $3,000 = $1,050. The firm's effective tax rate on preferred dividends is therefore only .30 × 35% = 10.5%. Given this tax rule, it is not surprising that most preferred stock is held by corporations.

Preferred stock rarely gives its holders full voting privileges in the firm. However, if the preferred dividend is skipped, the preferred stockholders may then be provided some voting power.

Other Domestic Issuers

There are, of course, several issuers of bonds in addition to the Treasury and private corporations. For example, state and local governments issue municipal bonds. The outstanding feature of these is that interest payments are tax-free. We examined municipal bonds, the value of the tax exemption, and the equivalent taxable yield of these bonds in Chapter 2.

Government agencies such as the Federal Home Loan Bank Board, the Farm Credit agencies, and the mortgage pass-through agencies Ginnie Mae, Fannie Mae, and Freddie Mac also issue considerable amounts of bonds. These too were reviewed in Chapter 2.

International Bonds

International bonds are commonly divided into two categories, *foreign bonds* and *Eurobonds*. Foreign bonds are issued by a borrower from a country other than the one in which the bond is sold. The bond is denominated in the currency of the country in which it is marketed. For example, if a German firm sells a dollar-denominated bond in the United States, the bond is considered a foreign bond. These bonds are given colorful names based on the countries in which they are marketed. For example, foreign bonds sold in the United States are called *Yankee bonds*. Like other bonds sold in the United States, they are registered with the Securities and Exchange Commission. Yen-denominated bonds sold in Japan by non-Japanese issuers are called *Samurai bonds*. British pound-denominated foreign bonds sold in the United Kingdom are called *bulldog bonds*.

In contrast to foreign bonds, Eurobonds are denominated in one currency, usually that of the issuer, but sold in other national markets. For example, the Eurodollar market refers to dollar-denominated bonds sold outside the United States (not just in Europe), although London is the largest market for Eurodollar bonds. Because the Eurodollar market falls outside U.S. jurisdiction, these bonds are not regulated by U.S. federal agencies. Similarly, Euroyen bonds are yen-denominated bonds selling outside Japan, Eurosterling bonds are pound-denominated bonds selling outside the United Kingdom, and so on.

Innovation in the Bond Market

Issuers constantly develop innovative bonds with unusual features; these issues illustrate that bond design can be extremely flexible. The novel bonds discussed next will give you a sense of the potential variety in security design.

Inverse Floaters   These are similar to the floating-rate bonds we described earlier, except that the coupon rate on these bonds *falls* when the general level of interest rates rises. Investors in these bonds suffer doubly when rates rise. Not only does the present value of each dollar of cash flow from the bond fall as the discount rate rises, but the level of those cash flows falls as well. Of course, investors in these bonds benefit doubly when rates fall.

Asset-Backed Bonds   Miramax has issued bonds with coupon rates tied to the financial performance of *Pulp Fiction* and other films. Domino's Pizza has issued bonds with payments backed by revenues from its pizza franchises. These are examples of asset-backed securities. The income from a specified group of assets is used to service the debt. More conventional asset-backed securities are mortgage-backed securities or securities backed by auto or credit card loans, as we discussed in Chapter 2.

Catastrophe Bonds   Oriental Land Company, which manages Tokyo Disneyland, issued a bond in 1999 with a final payment that depended on the occurrence of an earthquake near the park. More recently, FIFA (the Fédération Internationale de Football Association) issued catastrophe bonds with payments that would have been halted if terrorism had forced the cancellation of the 2006 World Cup. These bonds are a way to transfer "catastrophe risk" from the firm to the capital markets. Investors in these bonds receive compensation for taking on the risk in the form of higher coupon rates. But in the event of a catastrophe, the bondholders will give up all or part of their investments. "Disaster" can be defined by total insured losses or by criteria such as wind speed in a hurricane or Richter level in an earthquake. Issuance of catastrophe bonds has grown in recent years as insurers have sought ways to spread their risks across a wider spectrum of the capital market.

Indexed Bonds   Indexed bonds make payments that are tied to a general price index or the price of a particular commodity. For example, Mexico has issued bonds with payments that depend on the price of oil. Some bonds are indexed to the general price level. The United States Treasury started issuing such inflation-indexed bonds in January 1997. They are called Treasury Inflation Protected Securities (TIPS). By tying the par value of the bond to the general level of prices, coupon payments as well as the final repayment of par value on these bonds increase in direct proportion to the Consumer Price Index. Therefore, the interest rate on these bonds is a risk-free real rate.

To illustrate how TIPS work, consider a newly issued bond with a 3-year maturity, par value of $1,000, and a coupon rate of 4%. For simplicity, we will assume the bond makes annual coupon payments. Assume that inflation turns out to be 2%, 3%, and 1% in the next three years. Table 14.1 shows how the bond's cash flows will be calculated. The first payment comes at the end of the first year, at $t = 1$. Because inflation over the year was 2%, the par value of the bond increases from $1,000 to $1,020; because the coupon rate is 4%, the coupon payment is 4% of this amount, or $40.80. Notice that par value increases by the inflation rate, and because the coupon payments are 4% of par, they too increase in proportion to the general price level. Therefore, the cash flows paid by the bond are fixed in *real*

Table 14.1

Principal and interest payments for a Treasury Inflation Protected Security

Time	Inflation in Year Just Ended	Par Value	Coupon Payment	+	Principal Repayment	=	Total Payment
0		$1,000.00					
1	2%	1,020.00	$40.80		$ 0		$ 40.80
2	3	1,050.60	42.02		0		42.02
3	1	1,061.11	42.44		1,061.11		1,103.55

terms. When the bond matures, the investor receives a final coupon payment of $42.44 plus the (price-level-indexed) repayment of principal, $1,061.11.[4]

The *nominal* rate of return on the bond in the first year is

$$\text{Nominal return} = \frac{\text{Interest} + \text{Price appreciation}}{\text{Initial price}} = \frac{40.80 + 20}{1,000} = 6.80\%$$

The real rate of return is precisely the 4% real yield on the bond:

$$\text{Real return} = \frac{1 + \text{Nominal return}}{1 + \text{Inflation}} - 1 = \frac{1.0608}{1.02} - 1 = .04, \text{ or } 4\%$$

One can show in a similar manner (see Problem 18 in the end-of-chapter problems) that the rate of return in each of the three years is 4% as long as the real yield on the bond remains constant. If real yields do change, then there will be capital gains or losses on the bond. In mid-2016, the real yield on long-term TIPS bonds was about 0.9%.

14.2   Bond Pricing

Because a bond's coupon and principal repayments all occur months or years in the future, the price an investor would be willing to pay for a claim to those payments depends on the value of dollars to be received in the future compared to dollars in hand today. This "present value" calculation depends in turn on market interest rates. As we saw in Chapter 5, the nominal risk-free interest rate equals the sum of (1) a real risk-free rate of return and (2) a premium above the real rate to compensate for expected inflation. In addition, because most bonds are not riskless, the discount rate will embody an additional premium that reflects bond-specific characteristics such as default risk, liquidity, tax attributes, call risk, and so on.

We simplify for now by assuming there is one interest rate that is appropriate for discounting cash flows of any maturity, but we can relax this assumption easily. In practice, there may be different discount rates for cash flows accruing in different periods. For the time being, however, we ignore this refinement.

To value a security, we discount its expected cash flows by the appropriate discount rate. The cash flows from a bond consist of coupon payments until the maturity date plus the final payment of par value. Therefore,

Bond value = Present value of coupons + Present value of par value

---

[4]By the way, total nominal income (i.e., coupon plus that year's increase in principal) is treated as taxable income in each year.

If we call the maturity date T and call the interest rate r, the bond value can be written as

$$\text{Bond value} = \sum_{t=1}^{T} \frac{\text{Coupon}}{(1+r)^t} + \frac{\text{Par value}}{(1+r)^T} \qquad (14.1)$$

The summation sign in Equation 14.1 directs us to add the present value of each coupon payment; each coupon is discounted based on the time until it will be paid. The first term on the right-hand side of Equation 14.1 is the present value of an annuity. The second term is the present value of a single amount, the final payment of the bond's par value.

You may recall from an introductory finance class that the present value of a $1 annuity that lasts for T periods when the interest rate equals r is $\frac{1}{r}\left[1 - \frac{1}{(1+r)^T}\right]$. We call this expression the T-period *annuity factor* for an interest rate of r.[5] Similarly, we call $\frac{1}{(1+r)^T}$ the *PV factor*, that is, the present value of a single payment of $1 to be received in T periods. Therefore, we can write the price of the bond as

$$\text{Price} = \text{Coupon} \times \frac{1}{r}\left[1 - \frac{1}{(1+r)^T}\right] + \text{Par value} \times \frac{1}{(1+r)^T} \qquad (14.2)$$

$$= \text{Coupon} \times \text{Annuity factor}(r, T) + \text{Par value} \times \text{PV factor}(r, T)$$

Example 14.2   Bond Pricing

We discussed earlier an 8% coupon, 30-year maturity bond with par value of $1,000 paying 60 semiannual coupon payments of $40 each. Suppose that the interest rate is 8% annually, or $r = 4\%$ per six-month period. Then the value of the bond can be written as

$$\text{Price} = \sum_{t=1}^{60} \frac{\$40}{(1.04)^t} + \frac{\$1,000}{(1.04)^{60}} \qquad (14.3)$$

$$= \$40 \times \text{Annuity factor}(4\%, 60) + \$1,000 \times \text{PV factor}(4\%, 60)$$

It is easy to confirm that the present value of the bond's 60 semiannual coupon payments of $40 each is $904.94 and that the $1,000 final payment of par value has a present value of $95.06, for a total bond value of $1,000. You can calculate this value directly from Equation 14.2, perform these calculations on any financial calculator (see Example 14.3 below), use a spreadsheet program (see column F of Spreadsheet 14.1), or use a set of present value tables.

In this example, the coupon rate equals the market interest rate, and the bond price equals par value. If the interest rate were not equal to the bond's coupon rate, the bond

---

[5]Here is a quick derivation of the formula for the present value of an annuity. An annuity lasting T periods can be viewed as equivalent to a perpetuity whose first payment comes at the end of the current period *less* another perpetuity whose first payment comes at the end of the $(T+1)^{st}$ period. The immediate perpetuity net of the delayed perpetuity provides exactly T payments. We know that the value of a $1 per period perpetuity is $1/r$. Therefore, the present value of the delayed perpetuity is $1/r$ discounted for T additional periods, or $\frac{1}{r} \times \frac{1}{(1+r)^T}$.

The present value of the annuity is the present value of the first perpetuity minus the present value of the delayed perpetuity, or $\frac{1}{r}\left[1 - \frac{1}{(1+r)^T}\right]$.

would not sell at par value. For example, if the interest rate were to rise to 10% (5% per six months), the bond's price would fall by $189.29 to $810.71, as follows:

$$\$40 \times \text{Annuity factor}(5\%, 60) + \$1{,}000 \times \text{PV factor}(5\%, 60)$$
$$= \$757.17 + \$53.54 = \$810.71$$

At a higher interest rate, the present value of the payments to be received by the bondholder is lower. Therefore, bond prices fall as market interest rates rise. This illustrates a crucial general rule in bond valuation.[6]

Bond prices are tedious to calculate without a spreadsheet or a financial calculator, but they are easy to calculate with either. Financial calculators designed with present and future value formulas already programmed can greatly simplify calculations of the sort we just encountered in Example 14.2. The basic financial calculator uses five keys that correspond to the inputs for time-value-of-money problems such as bond pricing:

1. n is the number of time periods. In the case of a bond, n equals the number of periods until the bond matures. If the bond makes semiannual payments, n is the number of half-year periods or, equivalently, the number of semiannual coupon payments. For example, if the bond has 10 years until maturity, you would enter 20 for n, since each payment period is one-half year.

2. i is the interest rate per period, expressed as a percentage (not as a decimal). For example, if the interest rate is 6%, you would enter 6, not .06.

3. PV is the present value. Many calculators require that PV be entered as a negative number, in recognition of the fact that purchase of the bond is a cash *outflow,* while the receipt of coupon payments and face value are cash *inflows.*

4. FV is the future value or face value of the bond. In general, FV is interpreted as a one-time future payment of a cash flow, which, for bonds, is the face (i.e., par) value.

5. PMT is the amount of any recurring payment. For coupon bonds, PMT is the coupon payment; for zero-coupon bonds, PMT will be zero.

Given any four of these inputs, the calculator will solve for the fifth. We can illustrate with the bond presented in Example 14.2.

Example 14.3   Bond Pricing on a Financial Calculator

To find the bond's price when the annual market interest rate is 8%, you would enter these inputs (in any order):

n	60	The bond has a maturity of 30 years, so it makes 60 semiannual payments.
i	4	The *semiannual* market interest rate is 4%.
FV	1,000	The bond will provide a one-time cash flow of $1,000 when it matures.
PMT	40	Each semiannual coupon payment is $40.

[6]Here is a trap to avoid. You should not confuse the bond's *coupon* rate, which determines the interest paid to the bondholder, with the market interest rate. Once a bond is issued, its coupon rate is fixed. When the *market* interest rate increases, investors discount any fixed payments at a higher discount rate, which implies that present values and bond prices fall.

On most calculators, you now punch the "compute" key (labeled *COMP* or *CPT*) and then enter PV to obtain the bond price, that is, the present value today of the bond's cash flows. If you do this, you should find a value of −1,000. The negative sign signifies that while the investor receives cash flows from the bond, the price paid to *buy* the bond is a cash *out*flow, or a negative cash flow.

If you want to find the value of the bond when the interest rate is 10% (the second part of Example 14.2), just enter 5% for the semiannual interest rate (type "5" and then "/"), and when you compute PV, you will find that it is −810.71.

Figure 14.3 shows the price of the 30-year, 8% coupon bond for a range of interest rates, including 8%, at which the bond sells at par, and 10%, at which it sells for $810.71. The negative slope illustrates the inverse relationship between prices and yields. The shape of the curve in Figure 14.3 implies that an increase in the interest rate results in a price decline that is smaller than the price gain resulting from a decrease of equal magnitude in the interest rate. This property of bond prices is called *convexity* because of the convex shape of the bond price curve. This curvature reflects the fact that progressive increases in the interest rate result in progressively smaller reductions in the bond price.[7] Therefore, the price curve becomes flatter at higher interest rates. We return to convexity in Chapter 16.

 Concept Check **14.2**

Calculate the price of the 30-year, 8% coupon bond for a market interest rate of 3% per half-year. Compare the capital gain for the interest rate decline to the loss incurred when the rate increases from 4% to 5%.

Corporate bonds typically are issued at par value. This means that the underwriters of the bond issue (the firms that market the bonds to the public for the issuing corporation) must choose a coupon rate that very closely approximates market yields. In a primary issue, the underwriters attempt to sell the newly issued bonds directly to their customers. If the coupon rate is inadequate, investors will not pay par value for the bonds.

After the bonds are issued, bondholders may buy or sell bonds in secondary markets. In these markets, bond prices fluctuate inversely with the market interest rate.

The inverse relationship between price and yield is a central feature of fixed-income securities. Interest rate fluctuations represent the main source of risk in the fixed-income market, and we devote

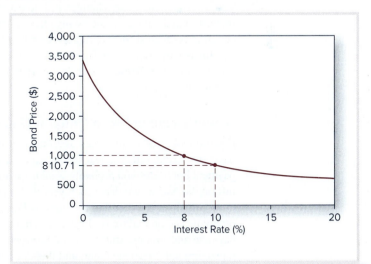

Figure 14.3 The inverse relationship between bond prices and yields. Price of an 8% coupon bond with 30-year maturity making semiannual payments

[7]The progressively smaller impact of interest rate increases results largely from the fact that at higher rates the bond is worth less. Therefore, an additional increase in rates operates on a smaller initial base, resulting in a smaller price decline.

Table 14.2

Bond prices at different interest rates (8% coupon bond, coupons paid semiannually)

Time to Maturity	Bond Price at Given Market Interest Rate				
	2%	4%	6%	8%	10%
1 year	1,059.11	1,038.83	1,019.13	1,000.00	981.41
10 years	1,541.37	1,327.03	1,148.77	1,000.00	875.35
20 years	1,985.04	1,547.11	1,231.15	1,000.00	828.41
30 years	2,348.65	1,695.22	1,276.76	1,000.00	810.71

considerable attention in Chapter 16 to assessing the sensitivity of bond prices to market yields. For now, however, we simply highlight one key factor that determines that sensitivity, namely, the maturity of the bond.

As a general rule, keeping all other factors the same, the longer the maturity of the bond, the greater the sensitivity of price to fluctuations in the interest rate. For example, consider Table 14.2, which presents the price of an 8% coupon bond at different market yields and times to maturity. For any departure of the interest rate from 8% (the rate at which the bond sells at par value), the change in the bond price is greater for longer times to maturity.

This makes sense. If you buy the bond at par with an 8% coupon rate, and market rates subsequently rise, then you suffer a loss: You have tied up your money earning 8% when alternative investments offer higher returns. This is reflected in a capital loss on the bond—a fall in its market price. The longer the period for which your money is tied up, the greater the loss, and correspondingly the greater the drop in the bond price. In Table 14.2, the row for 1-year maturity bonds shows little price sensitivity—that is, with only one year's earnings at stake, changes in interest rates are not too threatening. But for 30-year maturity bonds, interest rate swings have a large impact on bond prices. The force of discounting is greatest for the longest-term bonds.

This is why short-term Treasury securities such as T-bills are considered to be the safest. In addition to being free of default risk, they are also largely free of price risk attributable to interest rate volatility.

Bond Pricing between Coupon Dates

Equation 14.2 for bond prices assumes that the next coupon payment is in precisely one payment period, either a year for an annual payment bond or six months for a semiannual payment bond. But you probably want to be able to price bonds all 365 days of the year, not just on the one or two dates each year that it makes a coupon payment!

In principle, the fact that the bond is between coupon dates does not affect the pricing problem. The procedure is always the same: Compute the present value of each remaining payment and sum up. But if you are between coupon dates, there will be fractional periods remaining until each payment, and this does complicate the arithmetic computations.

Fortunately, bond pricing functions are included in most spreadsheet programs such as Excel. The spreadsheet allows you to enter today's date as well as the maturity date of the bond and so can provide prices for bonds at any date. The nearby box shows you how.

As we pointed out earlier, bond prices are typically quoted net of accrued interest. These prices, which appear in the financial press, are called *flat prices*. The actual *invoice price* that a buyer pays for the bond includes accrued interest. Thus,

$$\text{Invoice price} = \text{Flat price} + \text{Accrued interest}$$

eXcel APPLICATIONS: Bond Pricing

Excel and most other spreadsheet programs provide built-in functions to compute bond prices and yields. They typically ask you to input both the date you buy the bond (called the *settlement date*) and the maturity date of the bond. The Excel function for bond price is

= PRICE(settlement date, maturity date, annual coupon rate, yield to maturity, redemption value as percent of par value, number of coupon payments per year)

For the 2.5% coupon May 2046 maturity bond highlighted in Figure 14.1, we would enter the values in Spreadsheet 14.1. (Notice that in spreadsheets, we must enter interest rates as decimals, not percentages). Alternatively, we could simply enter the following function in Excel:

= PRICE(DATE(2016,5,15), DATE(2046,5,15), .025, .02595, 100, 2)

The DATE function in Excel, which we use for both the settlement and maturity date, uses the format DATE(year,month,day). The first date is May 15, 2016, when the bond is purchased, and the second is May 15, 2046, when it matures. Most bonds pay coupons either on the 15th or the last business day of the month.

Notice that the coupon rate and yield to maturity are expressed as decimals, not percentages. In most cases, redemption value is 100 (i.e., 100% of par value), and the resulting price similarly is expressed as a percent of par value. Occasionally, however, you may encounter bonds that pay off at a premium or discount to par value. One example would be callable bonds, discussed shortly.

The value of the bond returned by the pricing function is 98.0282 (cell B12), which nearly matches the price reported in

Table 14.1. (The yield to maturity is reported to only three decimal places, which results in a little rounding error.) This bond has just paid a coupon. In other words, the settlement date is precisely at the beginning of the coupon period, so no adjustment for accrued interest is necessary.

To illustrate the procedure for bonds between coupon payments, consider the 2% coupon August 2025 bond, also appearing in Figure 14.1. Using the entries in column D of the spreadsheet, we find in cell D12 that the (flat) price of the bond is 102.2977, which matches the price given in the figure except for a few cents' rounding error.

What about the bond's invoice price? Rows 13 through 16 make the necessary adjustments. The function described in cell C13 counts the days since the last coupon. This day count is based on the bond's settlement date, maturity date, coupon period (1 = annual; 2 = semiannual), and day count convention (choice 1 uses actual days). The function described in cell C14 counts the total days in each coupon payment period. Therefore, the entries for accrued interest in row 15 are the semiannual coupon multiplied by the fraction of a coupon period that has elapsed since the last payment. Finally, the invoice price in row 16 is the sum of the flat price plus accrued interest.

As a final example, suppose you wish to find the price of the bond in Example 14.2. It is a 30-year maturity bond with a coupon rate of 8% (paid semiannually). The market interest rate given in the latter part of the example is 10%. However, you are not given a specific settlement or maturity date. You can still use the PRICE function to value the bond. Simply choose an *arbitrary* settlement date (January 1, 2000, is convenient) and let the maturity date be 30 years hence. The appropriate inputs appear in column F of the spreadsheet, with the resulting price, 81.0707% of face value, appearing in cell F16.

	A	B	C	D	E	F	G
1		2.5% coupon bond,		2% coupon bond,		8% coupon bond,	
2		maturing May 15, 2046	Formula in column B	maturing August 2025		30-year maturity	
3							
4	Settlement date	5/15/2016	= DATE (2016, 5, 15)	5/15/2016		1/1/2000	
5	Maturity date	5/15/2046	= DATE (2046, 5, 15)	8/15/2025		1/1/2030	
6	Annual coupon rate	0.025		0.02		0.08	
7	Yield to maturity	0.02595		0.0173		0.1	
8	Redemption value (% of face value)	100		100		100	
9	Coupon payments per year	2		2		2	
10							
11							
12	Flat price (% of par)	98.0282	=PRICE(B4,B5,B6,B7,B8,B9)	102.2977		81.0707	
13	Days since last coupon	0	=COUPDAYBS(B4,B5,2,1)	90		0	
14	Days in coupon period	184	=COUPDAYS(B4,B5,2,1)	182		182	
15	Accrued interest	0	=(B13/B14)*B6*100/2	0.495		0	
16	Invoice price	98.0282	=B12+B15	102.7922		81.0707	

Spreadsheet 14.1

Bond Pricing in Excel

When a bond pays its coupon, flat price equals invoice price, because at that moment, accrued interest reverts to zero. However, this will be the exceptional case, not the rule.

Excel pricing functions provide the flat price of the bond. To find the invoice price, we need to add accrued interest. Fortunately, Excel also provides functions that count the days since the last coupon payment date and thus can be used to compute accrued interest. The nearby box also illustrates how to use these functions. The box provides examples using a bond that has just paid a coupon, and so has zero accrued interest, as well as a bond that is between coupon dates.

14.3   Bond Yields

Most bonds do not sell for par value. But ultimately, barring default, they will mature to par value. Therefore, we would like a measure of rate of return that accounts for both current income and the price increase or decrease over the bond's life. The yield to maturity is the standard measure of the total rate of return. However, it is far from perfect, and we will explore several variations of this measure.

Yield to Maturity

In practice, an investor considering the purchase of a bond is not quoted a promised rate of return. Instead, the investor must use the bond price, maturity date, and coupon payments to infer the return offered by the bond over its life. The **yield to maturity (YTM)** is defined as the interest rate that makes the present value of a bond's payments equal to its price. This interest rate is often interpreted as a measure of the average rate of return that will be earned on a bond if it is bought now and held until maturity. To calculate the yield to maturity, we solve the bond price equation for the interest rate given the bond's price.

Example 14.4   Yield to Maturity

Suppose an 8% coupon, 30-year bond is selling at $1,276.76. What average rate of return would be earned by an investor purchasing the bond at this price? We find the interest rate at which the present value of the remaining 60 semiannual payments equals the bond price. This is the rate consistent with the observed price of the bond. Therefore, we solve for r in the following equation:

$$\$1{,}276.76 = \sum_{t=1}^{60}\frac{\$40}{(1+r)^t} + \frac{\$1{,}000}{(1+r)^{60}}$$

or, equivalently,

$$1{,}276.76 = 40 \times \text{Annuity factor}(r, 60) + 1{,}000 \times \text{PV factor}(r, 60)$$

These equations have only one unknown variable, the interest rate, r. As we will see in a moment, you can use a financial calculator or spreadsheet to confirm that the solution is $r = .03$, or 3%, per half-year. This is the bond's yield to maturity.

The financial press reports yields on an annualized basis, and annualizes the bond's semiannual yield using simple interest techniques, resulting in an annual percentage rate, or APR. Yields annualized using simple interest are also called "bond equivalent yields." Therefore, the semiannual yield would be doubled and reported in the newspaper as a bond equivalent yield of 6%. The *effective* annual yield of the bond, however, accounts for compound interest. If one earns 3% interest every six months, then after one year, each dollar invested grows with interest to $\$1 \times (1.03)^2 = \$1.0609$, and the effective annual interest rate on the bond is 6.09%.

In Example 14.4, we asserted that a financial calculator or spreadsheet can be used to find the yield to maturity on the coupon bond. Here are two examples demonstrating how you can use these tools. Example 14.5 illustrates the use of financial calculators while Example 14.6 uses Excel.

Example 14.5   Finding the Yield to Maturity Using a Financial Calculator

n	60	The bond has a maturity of 30 years, so it makes 60 semiannual payments.
PMT	40	Each semiannual coupon payment is $40.
PV	(−)1,276.76	The bond can be purchased for $1,276.76, which on some calculators must be entered as a negative number as it is a cash outflow.
FV	1,000	The bond will provide a one-time cash flow of $1,000 when it matures.

Given these inputs, you now use the calculator to find the interest rate at which $1,276.76 actually equals the present value of the 60 payments of $40 each plus the one-time payment of $1,000 at maturity. On some calculators, you first punch the "compute" key (labeled *COMP* or *CPT*) and then enter i to have the interest rate computed. If you do so, you will find that $i = 3$, or 3% semiannually, as we claimed. Notice that just as the cash flows are paid semiannually, the computed interest rate is a rate per semiannual time period. The bond equivalent yield will be reported in the financial press as 6%.

Excel also contains built-in functions that you can use to find yield to maturity. Example 14.6, along with Spreadsheet 14.2, illustrates these functions.

Example 14.6   Finding Yield to Maturity Using Excel

Excel's function for yield to maturity is:

= YIELD(settlement date, maturity date, annual coupon rate, bond price, redemption value as percent of par value, number of coupon payments per year)

The bond price used in the function should be the reported, or "flat," price, without accrued interest. For example, to find the yield to maturity of the semiannual payment bond in Example 14.4, we would use column B of Spreadsheet 14.2. If the coupons were paid only annually, we would change the entry for payments per year to 1 (see cell D8), and the yield would fall slightly to 5.99%.

	A	B	C	D	E
1		Semiannual coupons		Annual coupons	
2					
3	Settlement date	1/1/2000		1/1/2000	
4	Maturity date	1/1/2030		1/1/2030	
5	Annual coupon rate	0.08		0.08	
6	Bond price (flat)	127.676		127.676	
7	Redemption value (% of face value)	100		100	
8	Coupon payments per year	2		1	
9					
10	Yield to maturity (decimal)	0.0600		0.0599	
11					
12	The formula entered here is: =YIELD(B3,B4,B5,B6,B7,B8)				

Spreadsheet 14.2

Finding yield to maturity in Excel

The bond's yield to maturity is the internal rate of return on an investment in the bond. The yield to maturity can be interpreted as the compound rate of return over the life of the bond under the assumption that all bond coupons can be reinvested at that yield.[8] Yield to maturity is widely accepted as a proxy for average return.

Yield to maturity differs from the **current yield** of a bond, which is the bond's annual coupon payment divided by the bond price. For example, for the 8%, 30-year bond currently selling at $1,276.76, the current yield would be $80/$1,276.76 = .0627, or 6.27%, per year. In contrast, recall that the effective annual yield to maturity is 6.09%. For this bond, which is selling at a premium over par value ($1,276 rather than $1,000), the coupon rate (8%) exceeds the current yield (6.27%), which exceeds the yield to maturity (6.09%). The coupon rate exceeds current yield because the coupon rate divides the coupon payments by par value ($1,000), which is less than the bond price ($1,276). In turn, the current yield exceeds yield to maturity because the yield to maturity accounts for the built-in capital loss on the bond; the bond bought today for $1,276 will eventually fall in value to $1,000 at maturity.

Examples 14.4, 14.5, and 14.6 illustrate a general rule: For **premium bonds** (bonds selling above par value), coupon rate is greater than current yield, which in turn is greater than yield to maturity. For **discount bonds** (bonds selling below par value), these relationships are reversed (see Concept Check 14.3).

It is common to hear people talking loosely about the yield on a bond. In these cases, they almost always are referring to the yield to maturity.

 Concept Check **14.3**

What will be the relationship among coupon rate, current yield, and yield to maturity for bonds selling at discounts from par? Illustrate using the 30-year maturity, 8% (semiannual payment) coupon bond, assuming it is selling at a yield to maturity of 10%.

Yield to Call

Yield to maturity is calculated on the assumption that the bond will be held until maturity. What if the bond is callable, however, and may be retired prior to the maturity date? How should we measure average rate of return for bonds subject to a call provision?

Figure 14.4 illustrates the risk of call to the bondholder. The top curve is the value of a "straight" (i.e., noncallable) bond with par value $1,000, an 8% coupon rate, and a 30-year time to maturity as a function of the market interest rate. If interest rates fall, the bond price, which equals the present value of the promised payments, can rise substantially.

Now consider a bond that has the same coupon rate and maturity date but is callable at 110% of par value, or $1,100. When interest rates fall, the present value of the bond's *scheduled* payments rises, but the call provision allows the issuer to repurchase the bond at the call price. If the call price is less than the present value of the scheduled payments, the issuer may call the bond back from the bondholder.

The lower curve in Figure 14.4 is the value of the callable bond. At high interest rates, the risk of call is negligible because the present value of scheduled payments is less than

---

[8]If the reinvestment rate does not equal the bond's yield to maturity, the compound rate of return will differ from YTM. This is demonstrated below in Examples 14.8 and 14.9.

the call price; therefore the values of the straight and callable bonds converge. At lower rates, however, the values of the bonds begin to diverge, with the difference reflecting the value of the firm's option to reclaim the callable bond at the call price. At very low rates, the present value of scheduled payments exceeds the call price, so the bond is called. Its value at this point is simply the call price, $1,100.

This analysis suggests that bond market analysts might be more interested in a bond's yield to call rather than yield to maturity, especially if the bond is likely to be called. The yield to call is calculated just like the yield to maturity except that the time until call replaces time until maturity, and the call price replaces the par value. This computation is sometimes called "yield to first call," as it assumes the issuer will call the bond as soon as it may do so.

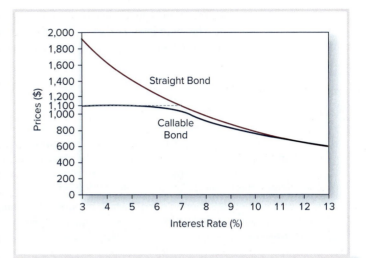

Figure 14.4 Bond prices: Callable and straight debt (coupon = 8%; maturity = 30 years; semiannual payments)

Example 14.7   Yield to Call

Suppose the 8% coupon, 30-year maturity bond sells for $1,150 and is callable in 10 years at a call price of $1,100. Its yield to maturity and yield to call would be calculated using the following inputs:

	Yield to Call	Yield to Maturity
Coupon payment	$40	$40
Number of semiannual periods	20 periods	60 periods
Final payment	$1,100	$1,000
Price	$1,150	$1,150

Yield to call is then 6.64%. [To confirm this on a calculator, input $n = 20$; PV = (−)1150; FV = 1100; PMT = 40; compute i as 3.32%, or 6.64% bond equivalent yield.] Yield to maturity is 6.82%. [To confirm, input $n = 60$; PV = (−)1150; FV = 1000; PMT = 40; compute i as 3.41% or 6.82% bond equivalent yield.] In Excel, you can calculate yield to call as = YIELD(DATE(2000,1,1), DATE(2010,1,1), .08, 115, 110, 2). Notice that redemption value is input as 110, that is, 110% of par value.

While most callable bonds are issued with an initial period of explicit call protection, an additional implicit form of call protection operates for bonds selling at deep discounts from their call prices. Even if interest rates fall a bit, deep-discount bonds still will sell below the call price and thus will not be subject to a call.

Premium bonds that might be selling near their call prices, however, are especially apt to be called if rates fall further. If interest rates fall, a callable premium bond is likely to provide a lower return than could be earned on a discount bond whose potential price appreciation is not limited by the likelihood of a call. Investors in premium bonds therefore may be more interested in the bond's yield to call than its yield to maturity because it may appear to them that the bond will be retired at the call date.

Concept Check **14.4**

a. The yield to maturity on two 10-year maturity bonds currently is 7%. Each bond has a call price of $1,100. One bond has a coupon rate of 6%, the other 8%. Assume for simplicity that bonds are called as soon as the present value of their remaining payments exceeds their call price. What will be the capital gain on each bond if the market interest rate suddenly falls to 6%?

b. A 20-year maturity 9% coupon bond paying coupons semiannually is callable in five years at a call price of $1,050. The bond currently sells at a yield to maturity of 8%. What is the yield to call?

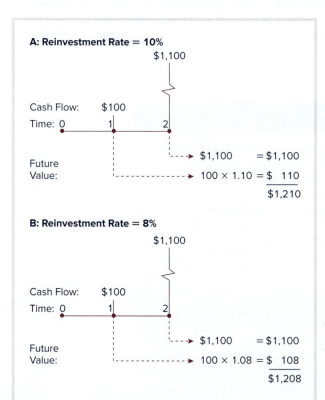

Figure 14.5 Growth of invested funds

Realized Compound Return versus Yield to Maturity

Yield to maturity will equal the rate of return realized over the life of the bond if all coupons are reinvested at an interest rate equal to the bond's yield to maturity. Consider, for example, a 2-year bond selling at par value paying a 10% coupon once a year. The yield to maturity is 10%. If the $100 coupon payment is reinvested at an interest rate of 10%, the $1,000 investment in the bond will grow after two years to $1,210, as illustrated in Figure 14.5, Panel A. The coupon paid in the first year is reinvested and grows with interest to a second-year value of $110, which together with the second coupon payment and payment of par value in the second year results in a total value of $1,210.

To summarize, the initial value of the investment is $V_0 = \$1,000$. The final value in two years is $V_2 = \$1,210$. The compound rate of return, therefore, is calculated as follows:

$$V_0(1 + r)^2 = V_2$$
$$\$1,000(1 + r)^2 = \$1,210$$
$$r = .10 = 10\%$$

With a reinvestment rate equal to the 10% yield to maturity, the **realized compound return** equals yield to maturity.

But what if the reinvestment rate is not 10%? If the coupon can be invested at more than 10%, funds will grow to more than $1,210, and the realized compound return will exceed 10%. If the reinvestment rate is less than 10%, so will be the realized compound return. Consider the following example.

Example 14.8   Realized Compound Return

If the interest rate earned on the first coupon is less than 10%, the final value of the investment will be less than $1,210, and the realized compound return will be less than 10%. To
illustrate, suppose the interest rate at which the coupon can be invested is only 8%. The following calculations are illustrated in Figure 14.5, Panel B.

Future value of first coupon payment with interest earnings = $100 × 1.08 =	$ 108
+ Cash payment in second year (final coupon plus par value)	$1,100
= Total value of investment with reinvested coupons	$1,208

The realized compound return is the compound rate of growth of invested funds, assuming
that all coupon payments are reinvested. The investor purchased the bond for par at $1,000,
and this investment grew to $1,208.

$$V_0(1 + r)^2 = V_2$$
$$\$1,000(1 + r)^2 = \$1,208$$
$$r = .0991 = 9.91\%$$

Example 14.8 highlights the problem with conventional yield to maturity when reinvestment rates can change over time. Conventional yield to maturity will not equal realized
compound return. However, in an economy with future interest rate uncertainty, the rates at
which interim coupons will be reinvested are not yet known. Therefore, although realized
compound return can be computed *after* the investment period ends, it cannot be computed
in advance without a forecast of future reinvestment rates. This reduces much of the attraction of the realized return measure.

Forecasting the realized compound yield over various holding periods or investment
horizons is called **horizon analysis.** The forecast of total return depends on your forecasts
of *both* the price of the bond when you sell it at the end of your horizon *and* the rate at
which you are able to reinvest coupon income. The sales price depends in turn on the yield
to maturity at the horizon date. With a longer investment horizon, however, reinvested
coupons will be a larger component of your final proceeds.

Example 14.9   Horizon Analysis

Suppose you buy a 30-year, 7.5% (annual payment) coupon bond for $980 (when its yield
to maturity is 7.67%) and plan to hold it for 20 years. Your forecast is that the bond's yield
to maturity will be 8% when it is sold and that the reinvestment rate on the coupons will
be 6%. At the end of your investment horizon, the bond will have 10 years remaining until
expiration, so the forecast sales price (using a yield to maturity of 8%) will be $966.45. The
20 coupon payments will grow with compound interest to $2,758.92. (This is the future value
of a 20-year $75 annuity with an interest rate of 6%.)

On the basis of these forecasts, your $980 investment will grow in 20 years to $966.45 +
$2,758.92 = $3,725.37. This corresponds to an annualized compound return of 6.90%:

$$V_0(1 + r)^{20} = V_{20}$$
$$\$980(1 + r)^{20} = \$3,725.37$$
$$r = .0690 = 6.90\%$$

Examples 14.8 and 14.9 demonstrate that as interest rates change, bond investors are actually subject to two sources of offsetting risk. On the one hand, when rates rise, bond prices fall, which reduces the value of the portfolio. On the other hand, reinvested coupon income will compound more rapidly at those higher rates. This **reinvestment rate risk** will offset the impact of price risk. In Chapter 16, we will explore this trade-off in more detail and will discover that by carefully tailoring their bond portfolios, investors can precisely balance these two effects for any given investment horizon.

14.4   Bond Prices over Time

A bond will sell at par value when its coupon rate equals the market interest rate. In these circumstances, the investor receives fair compensation for the time value of money in the form of the recurring coupon payments. No further capital gain is necessary to provide fair compensation.

When the coupon rate is lower than the market interest rate, the coupon payments alone will not provide investors as high a return as they could earn elsewhere in the market. To receive a competitive return on such an investment, investors also need some price appreciation on their bonds. The bonds, therefore, must sell below par value to provide a "built-in" capital gain on the investment.

Example 14.10   Fair Holding-Period Return

To illustrate built-in capital gains or losses, suppose a bond was issued several years ago when the interest rate was 7%. The bond's annual coupon rate was thus set at 7%. (We will suppose for simplicity that the bond pays its coupon annually.) Now, with three years left in the bond's life, the interest rate is 8% per year. The bond's market price is the present value of the remaining annual coupons plus payment of par value. That present value is[9]

$$\$70 \times \text{Annuity factor}(8\%, 3) + \$1,000 \times \text{PV factor}(8\%, 3) = \$974.23$$

which is less than par value.

In another year, after the next coupon is paid and remaining maturity falls to two years, the bond would sell at

$$\$70 \times \text{Annuity factor}(8\%, 2) + \$1,000 \times \text{PV factor}(8\%, 2) = \$982.17$$

thereby yielding a capital gain over the year of $7.94. If an investor had purchased the bond at $974.23, the total return over the year would equal the coupon payment plus capital gain, or $70 + $7.94 = $77.94. This represents a rate of return of $77.94/$974.23, or 8%, exactly the rate of return currently available elsewhere in the market.

✓ Concept Check **14.5**

At what price will the bond in Example 14.10 sell in yet another year, when only one year remains until maturity? What is the rate of return to an investor who purchases the bond when its price is $982.17 and sells it one year hence?

---

[9]Using a calculator, enter $n = 3$, $i = 8$, PMT = 70, FV = 1000, and compute PV.

When bond prices are set according to the present value formula, any discount from par value provides an anticipated capital gain that will augment a below-market coupon rate by just enough to provide a fair total rate of return. Conversely, if the coupon rate exceeds the market interest rate, the interest income by itself is greater than that available elsewhere in the market. Investors will bid up the price of these bonds above their par values. As the bonds approach maturity, they will fall in value because fewer of these above-market coupon payments remain. The resulting capital losses offset the large coupon payments so that the bondholder again receives only a competitive rate of return.

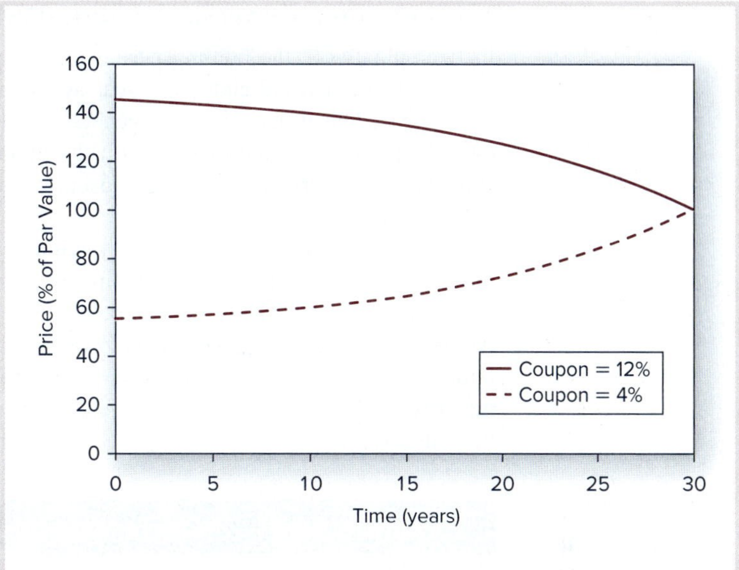

Problem 14 at the end of the chapter asks you to work through the case of the high-coupon bond. Figure 14.6 traces out the price paths (net of accrued interest) of two bonds, each selling at a yield to maturity of 8%. One bond has a coupon rate above 8%, while the other has a coupon rate below 8%. The low-coupon bond enjoys capital gains as price steadily approaches par value, whereas the high-coupon bond suffers capital losses.[10]

Figure 14.6 Price path of two 30-year maturity bonds, each selling at a yield to maturity of 8%. Bond price approaches par value as maturity date approaches.

We use these examples to show that each bond offers investors the same total rate of return. Although the capital gains versus income components differ, the price of each bond is set to provide competitive rates, as we should expect in well-functioning capital markets. Security returns all should be comparable on an after-tax risk-adjusted basis. If they are not, investors will try to sell low-return securities, thereby driving down their prices until the total return at the now-lower price is competitive with other securities. Prices should continue to adjust until all securities are fairly priced in that expected returns are comparable, given appropriate risk and tax adjustments.

We see evidence of this price adjustment in Figure 14.1. Compare the two bonds maturing in August 2025. One has a coupon rate of 6.875%, while the other's coupon rate is only 2%. But the higher coupon rate on the first bond does not mean that it offers a higher return; instead, it sells at a higher price. The yields to maturity on the two bonds are nearly equal, both just about 1.7%. This makes sense, since investors should care about their total return, including both coupon income as well as price change. In the end, prices of similar-maturity bonds adjust until yields are pretty much equalized.

Of course, the yields across bonds in Figure 14.1 are not all precisely equal. Clearly, longer term bonds at this time offered higher promised yields, a common pattern and one that reflects the relative risks of the bonds. We will explore the relationship between yield and time to maturity in the next chapter.

---

[10]If the market interest rate is volatile, the price path will be "jumpy," vibrating around the price path in Figure 14.6 and reflecting capital gains or losses as interest rates fluctuate. Ultimately, however, the price must reach par value at the maturity date, so the price of the premium bond will fall over time while that of the discount bond will rise.

Yield to Maturity versus Holding-Period Return

In Example 14.10, the holding-period return and the yield to maturity were equal. The bond yield started and ended the year at 8%, and the bond's holding-period return also equaled 8%. This turns out to be a general result. When the yield to maturity is unchanged over the period, the rate of return on the bond will equal that yield. As we noted, this should not be surprising: The bond must offer a rate of return competitive with those available on other securities.

However, when yields fluctuate, so will a bond's rate of return. Unanticipated changes in market rates will result in unanticipated changes in bond returns and, after the fact, a bond's holding-period return can be better or worse than the yield at which it initially sells. An increase in the bond's yield acts to reduce its price, which reduces the holding-period return. In this event, the holding-period return is likely to be less than the initial yield to maturity.[11] Conversely, a decline in yield will result in a holding-period return greater than the initial yield.

Example 14.11   Yield to Maturity versus Holding-Period Return

Consider a 30-year bond paying an annual coupon of $80 and selling at par value of $1,000. The bond's initial yield to maturity is 8%. If the yield remains at 8% over the year, the bond price will remain at par, so the holding-period return also will be 8%. But if the yield falls below 8%, the bond price will increase. Suppose the yield falls and the price increases to $1,050. Then the holding-period return is greater than 8%:

$$\text{Holding-period return} = \frac{\$80 + (\$1,050 - \$1,000)}{\$1,000} = .13, \text{ or } 13\%$$

 Concept Check **14.6**

Show that if yield to maturity increases, then holding-period return is *less* than initial yield. For example, suppose in Example 14.11 that by the end of the first year, the bond's yield to maturity is 8.5%. Find the one-year holding-period return and compare it to the bond's initial 8% yield to maturity.

Here is another way to think about the difference between yield to maturity and holding-period return. Yield to maturity depends only on the bond's coupon, *current* price, and par value at maturity. All of these values are observable today, so yield to maturity can be easily calculated. Yield to maturity is commonly interpreted as a measure of the *average* rate of return if the investment in the bond is held until the bond matures. In contrast, holding-period return is the rate of return over a particular investment period and depends on the market price of the bond at the end of that holding period; of course this price is *not* known today. Because bond prices over the holding period will respond to unanticipated changes in interest rates, holding-period return can at most be forecast.

---

[11]We have to be a bit careful here. When yields increase, coupon income can be reinvested at higher rates, which offsets the impact of the initial price decline. If your holding period is sufficiently long, the positive impact of the higher reinvestment rate can more than offset the initial price decline. But common performance evaluation periods for portfolio managers are no more than one year, and over these shorter horizons the price impact will almost always dominate the impact of the reinvestment rate. We discuss the trade-off between price risk and reinvestment rate risk more fully in Chapter 16.

Zero-Coupon Bonds and Treasury Strips

Original-issue discount bonds are less common than coupon bonds issued at par. These are bonds that are issued intentionally with low coupon rates that cause the bond to sell at a discount from par value. The most common example of this type of bond is the *zero-coupon bond,* which carries no coupons and provides all of its return in the form of price appreciation. Zeros provide only one cash flow to their owners, on the maturity date of the bond.

U.S. Treasury bills are examples of short-term zero-coupon instruments. If the bill has face value of $10,000, the Treasury issues or sells it for some amount less than $10,000, agreeing to repay $10,000 at maturity. All of the investor's return comes in the form of price appreciation.

Longer-term zero-coupon bonds are commonly created from coupon-bearing notes and bonds. A bond dealer who purchases a Treasury coupon bond may ask the Treasury to break down the cash flows to be paid by the bond into a series of independent securities, where each security is a claim to one of the payments of the original bond. For example, a 10-year coupon bond would be "stripped" of its 20 semiannual coupons, and each coupon payment would be treated as a stand-alone zero-coupon bond. The maturities of these bonds would thus range from six months to 10 years. The final payment of principal would be treated as another stand-alone zero-coupon security. Each of the payments is now treated as an independent security and is assigned its own CUSIP number (by the Committee on Uniform Securities Identification Procedures). The CUSIP number is the security identifier that allows for electronic trading over the Fedwire system, a network that connects all Federal Reserve banks and their branches. The payments are still considered obligations of the U.S. Treasury. The Treasury program under which coupon stripping is performed is called STRIPS (Separate Trading of Registered Interest and Principal of Securities), and these zero-coupon securities are called Treasury *strips.*

What should happen to prices of zeros as time passes? On their maturity dates, zeros must sell for par value. Before maturity, however, they should sell at discounts from par, because of the time value of money. As time passes, price should approach par value. In fact, if the interest rate is constant, a zero's price will increase at exactly the rate of interest.

To illustrate, consider a zero with 30 years until maturity, and suppose the market interest rate is 10% per year. The price of the bond today is $1,000/$(1.10)^{30} = \$57.31$. Next year, with only 29 years until maturity, if the yield is still 10%, the price will be $1,000/(1.10)^{29} = \$63.04$, a 10% increase over its previous-year value. Because the par value of the bond is now discounted for one less year, its price has increased by the 1-year discount factor.

Figure 14.7 presents the price path of a 30-year zero-coupon bond for an annual market interest rate of 10%. The bond's price rises exponentially, not linearly, until its maturity.

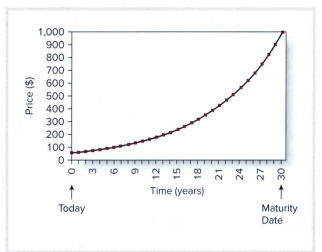

Figure 14.7 The price of a 30-year zero-coupon bond over time at a yield to maturity of 10%. Price equals $1,000/(1.10)^{T}$, where T is time until maturity.

After-Tax Returns

The tax authorities recognize that the "built-in" price appreciation on original-issue discount (OID) bonds such as zero-coupon bonds represents an implicit interest payment to the holder of the security. The IRS, therefore, calculates a price appreciation schedule to impute taxable interest income for the built-in appreciation during a tax year, even if the asset is not sold or does not mature until a future year. Any additional gains or losses that arise from changes in market interest rates are treated as capital gains or losses if the OID bond is sold during the tax year.

Example 14.12   Taxation of Original-Issue Discount Bonds

Continuing with the example in the text, if the interest rate originally is 10%, the 30-year zero will be issued at a price of $1,000/1.10^{30} = $57.31. The following year, the IRS will calculate what the bond price would be if the yield were still 10%. This is $1,000/1.10^{29} = $63.04. Therefore, the IRS imputes interest income of $63.04 − $57.31 = $5.73. This amount is subject to tax. Notice that the *imputed* interest income is based on a "constant yield method" that ignores any changes in market interest rates.

If interest rates actually fall, let's say to 9.9%, the bond price will be $1,000/1.099^{29} = $64.72. If the bond is sold, then the difference between $64.72 and $63.04 will be treated as capital gains income and taxed at the capital gains tax rate. If the bond is not sold, then the price difference is an unrealized capital gain and will not result in taxes in that year. In either case, the investor must pay taxes on the $5.73 of imputed interest at the rate on ordinary income.

The procedure illustrated in Example 14.12 applies as well to the taxation of other original-issue discount bonds, even if they are not zero-coupon bonds. Consider, as an example, a 30-year maturity bond that is issued with a coupon rate of 4% and a yield to maturity of 8%. For simplicity, we will assume that the bond pays coupons once annually. Because of the low coupon rate, the bond will be issued at a price far below par value, specifically at $549.69. If the bond's yield to maturity is still 8%, then its price in one year will rise to $553.66. (Confirm this for yourself.) This would provide a pretax holding-period return (HPR) of exactly 8%:

$$HPR = \frac{\$40 + (\$553.66 - \$549.69)}{\$549.69} = .08$$

The increase in the bond price based on a constant yield, however, is treated as interest income, so the investor is required to pay taxes on the explicit coupon income, $40, as well as the imputed interest income of $553.66 − $549.69 = $3.97. If the bond's yield actually changes during the year, the difference between the bond's price and the constant-yield value of $553.66 will be treated as capital gains income if the bond is sold.

 Concept Check **14.7**

Suppose that the yield to maturity of the 4% coupon, 30-year maturity bond falls to 7% by the end of the first year and that the investor sells the bond after the first year. If the investor's federal plus state tax rate on interest income is 38% and the combined tax rate on capital gains is 20%, what is the investor's after-tax rate of return?

14.5   Default Risk and Bond Pricing

Although bonds generally *promise* a fixed flow of income, that income stream is not risk-less unless the investor can be sure the issuer will not default on the obligation. While U.S. government bonds may be treated as free of default risk, this is not true of corporate bonds. Therefore, the actual payments on these bonds are uncertain, for they depend to some degree on the ultimate financial status of the firm.

Bond default risk, usually called **credit risk,** is measured by Moody's Investor Services, Standard & Poor's Corporation, and Fitch Investors Service, all of which provide financial information on firms as well as quality ratings of large corporate and municipal bond issues. International sovereign bonds, which also entail default risk, especially in emerging markets, also are commonly rated for default risk. Each rating firm assigns letter grades to the bonds of corporations and municipalities to reflect their assessment of the safety of the bond issue. The top rating is AAA or Aaa, a designation awarded to only about a dozen firms. Moody's modifies each rating class with a 1, 2, or 3 suffix (e.g., Aaa1, Aaa2, Aaa3) to provide a finer gradation of ratings. The other agencies use a + or − modification.

Those rated BBB or above (S&P, Fitch) or Baa and above (Moody's) are considered **investment-grade bonds,** whereas lower-rated bonds are classified as **speculative-grade** or **junk bonds.** Defaults on low-grade issues are not uncommon. For example, almost half of the bonds rated CCC by Standard & Poor's at issue have defaulted within 10 years. Highly rated bonds rarely default, but even these bonds are not free of credit risk. For example, in 2001 WorldCom sold $11.8 billion of bonds with an investment-grade rating. Only a year later, the firm filed for bankruptcy and its bondholders lost more than 80% of their investment. Certain regulated institutional investors such as insurance companies have not always been allowed to invest in speculative-grade bonds.

Figure 14.8 provides the definitions of each bond rating classification.

Junk Bonds

Junk bonds, also known as *high-yield bonds,* are nothing more than speculative-grade (low-rated or unrated) bonds. Before 1977, almost all junk bonds were "fallen angels," that is, bonds issued by firms that originally had investment-grade ratings but that had since been downgraded. In 1977, however, firms began to issue "original-issue junk."

Much of the credit for this innovation is given to Drexel Burnham Lambert, and especially its trader Michael Milken. Drexel had long enjoyed a niche as a junk bond trader and had established a network of potential investors in junk bonds. Firms not able to muster an investment-grade rating were happy to have Drexel (and other investment bankers) market their bonds directly to the public, as this opened up a new source of financing. Junk issues were a lower-cost financing alternative than borrowing from banks.

High-yield bonds gained considerable notoriety in the 1980s when they were used as financing vehicles in leveraged buyouts and hostile takeover attempts. Shortly thereafter, however, the junk bond market suffered. The legal difficulties of Drexel and Michael Milken in connection with Wall Street's insider trading scandals of the late 1980s tainted the junk bond market.

At the height of Drexel's difficulties, the high-yield bond market nearly dried up. Since then, the market has rebounded dramatically. However, the average credit quality of newly issued high-yield debt issued today is higher than the average quality in the boom years of the 1980s. Of course, junk bonds are still more vulnerable to economic distress than

Bond Ratings				
	Very High Quality	**High Quality**	**Speculative**	**Very Poor**
Standard & Poor's	AAA AA	A BBB	BB B	CCC D
Moody's	Aaa Aa	A Baa	Ba B	Caa C
	At times both Moody's and Standard & Poor's have used adjustments to these ratings: S&P uses plus and minus signs: A+ is the strongest A rating and A− the weakest. Moody's uses a 1, 2, or 3 designation, with 1 indicating the strongest.			

Moody's	S&P	
Aaa	AAA	Debt rated Aaa and AAA has the highest rating. Capacity to pay interest and principal is extremely strong.
Aa	AA	Debt rated Aa and AA has a very strong capacity to pay interest and repay principal. Together with the highest rating, this group comprises the high-grade bond class.
A	A	Debt rated A has a strong capacity to pay interest and repay principal, although it is somewhat more susceptible to the adverse effects of changes in circumstances and economic conditions than debt in higher-rated categories.
Baa	BBB	Debt rated Baa and BBB is regarded as having an adequate capacity to pay interest and repay principal. Whereas it normally exhibits adequate protection parameters, adverse economic conditions or changing circumstances are more likely to lead to a weakened capacity to pay interest and repay principal for debt in this category than in higher-rated categories. These bonds are medium-grade obligations.
Ba B Caa Ca	BB B CCC CC	Debt rated in these categories is regarded, on balance, as predominantly speculative with respect to capacity to pay interest and repay principal in accordance with the terms of the obligation. BB and Ba indicate the lowest degree of speculation, and CC and Ca the highest degree of speculation. Although such debt will likely have some quality and protective characteristics, these are outweighed by large uncertainties or major risk exposures to adverse conditions. Some issues may be in default.
C	C	This rating is reserved for income bonds on which no interest is being paid.
D	D	Debt rated D is in default, and payment of interest and/or repayment of principal is in arrears.

Figure 14.8 Definitions of each bond rating class

Source: Stephen A. Ross and Randolph W. Westerfield, *Corporate Finance,* Copyright 1988 (St. Louis: Times Mirror/Mosby College Publishing, reproduced with permission from the McGraw-Hill Companies, Inc.). Data from various editions of *Standard & Poor's Bond Guide* and *Moody's Bond Guide.*

investment-grade bonds. During the financial crisis of 2008–2009, prices on these bonds fell dramatically, and their yields to maturity rose equally dramatically. The spread between yields on B-rated bonds and Treasuries widened from around 3% in early 2007 to an astonishing 19% by the beginning of 2009.

Determinants of Bond Safety

Bond rating agencies base their quality ratings largely on an analysis of the level and trend of some of the issuer's financial ratios. The key ratios used to evaluate safety are:

1. *Coverage ratios*—Ratios of company earnings to fixed costs. For example, the *times-interest-earned ratio* is the ratio of earnings before interest payments and taxes to interest obligations. The *fixed-charge coverage ratio* includes lease payments and sinking fund payments with interest obligations to arrive at the ratio of earnings to all fixed cash obligations (sinking funds are described below). Low or falling coverage ratios signal possible cash flow difficulties.

2. *Leverage (e.g., debt-to-equity) ratios*—A too-high leverage ratio indicates excessive indebtedness, signaling the possibility the firm will be unable to earn enough to satisfy the obligations on its bonds.

3. *Liquidity ratios*—The two most common liquidity ratios are the *current ratio* (current assets/current liabilities) and the *quick ratio* (current assets excluding inventories/current liabilities). These ratios measure the firm's ability to pay bills coming due with its most liquid assets.

4. *Profitability ratios*—Measures of rates of return on assets or equity. Profitability ratios are indicators of a firm's overall financial health. The *return on assets* (earnings before interest and taxes divided by total assets) or *return on equity* (net income/ equity) are the most popular of these measures. Firms with higher returns on assets or equity should be better able to raise money in security markets because they offer prospects for better returns on the firm's investments.

5. *Cash flow-to-debt ratio*—This is the ratio of total cash flow to outstanding debt.

Moody's periodically computes median values of selected ratios for firms in several rating classes, which we present in Table 14.3. Of course, ratios must be evaluated in the context of industry standards, and analysts differ in the weights they place on particular ratios. Nevertheless, Table 14.3 demonstrates the tendency of ratios to improve along with the firm's rating class.

Many studies have tested whether financial ratios can in fact be used to predict default risk. One of the best-known series of tests was conducted by Edward Altman, who used

	Aaa	Aa	A	Baa	Ba	B	C
EBITA/Assets (%)	20.9%	15.6%	13.8%	10.9%	9.1%	7.1%	4.0%
Operating profit margin (%)	22.0%	17.1%	17.6%	14.1%	11.2%	8.9%	4.1%
EBITA to interest coverage (multiple)	28.9	15.1	9.7	5.9	3.5	1.7	0.6
Debt/EBITDA (multiple)	0.58	2.03	1.83	2.58	3.41	5.26	8.35
Debt/(Debt + Equity)	19.3%	50.2%	38.6%	46.2%	51.7%	72.0%	98.0%
Funds from operations/Total debt (multiple)	1.335	0.385	0.425	0.296	0.206	0.120	0.031
Retained cash flow/Net debt (multiple)	1.3	0.3	0.4	0.3	0.2	0.1	0.0

Table 14.3

Financial ratios by rating class

Note: EBITA is earnings before interest, taxes, and amortization. EBITDA is earnings before interest, taxes, depreciation, and amortization.
Source: Moody's Financial Metrics, *Key Ratios by Rating and Industry for Global Non-Financial Corporations,* December 2013.

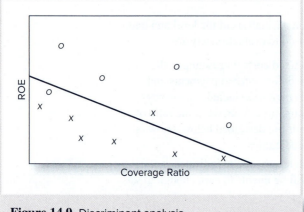

Figure 14.9 Discriminant analysis

discriminant analysis to predict bankruptcy. With this technique a firm is assigned a score based on its financial characteristics. If its score exceeds a cut-off value, the firm is deemed creditworthy. A score below the cut-off value indicates significant bankruptcy risk in the near future.

To illustrate the technique, suppose that we were to collect data on the return on equity (ROE) and coverage ratios of a sample of firms, and then keep records of any corporate bankruptcies. In Figure 14.9 we plot the ROE and coverage ratios for each firm, using X for firms that eventually went bankrupt and O for those that remained solvent. Clearly, the X and O firms show different patterns of data, with the solvent firms typically showing higher values for the two ratios.

The discriminant analysis determines the equation of the line that best separates the X and O observations. Suppose that the equation of the line is $.75 = .9 \times \text{ROE} + .4 \times \text{Cov-}$erage. Then, based on its own financial ratios, each firm is assigned a "Z-score" equal to $.9 \times \text{ROE} + .4 \times \text{Coverage}$. If its Z-score exceeds .75, the firm plots above the line and is considered a safe bet; Z-scores below .75 foretell financial difficulty.

Altman found the following equation to best separate failing and nonfailing firms:

$$Z = 3.1\frac{\text{EBIT}}{\text{Total assets}} + 1.0\frac{\text{Sales}}{\text{Assets}} + .42\frac{\text{Shareholders' equity}}{\text{Total liabilities}}$$

$$+.85\frac{\text{Retained earnings}}{\text{Total assets}} + .72\frac{\text{Working capital}}{\text{Total assets}}$$

where EBIT = earnings before interest and taxes.[12] Z-scores below 1.23 indicate vulnerability to bankruptcy, scores between 1.23 and 2.90 are a gray area, and scores above 2.90 are considered safe.

 Concept Check **14.8**

> Suppose we add a new variable equal to current liabilities/current assets to Altman's equation. Would you expect this variable to receive a positive or negative coefficient?

Bond Indentures

A bond is issued with an *indenture,* which is the contract between the issuer and the bondholder. Part of the indenture is a set of restrictions that protect the rights of the bondholders. Such restrictions include provisions relating to collateral, sinking funds, dividend

---

[12]Altman's original work was published in Edward I. Altman, "Financial Ratios, Discriminant Analysis, and the Prediction of Corporate Bankruptcy," *Journal of Finance* 23 (September 1968). This equation is from his updated study, *Corporate Financial Distress and Bankruptcy,* 2nd ed. (New York: Wiley, 1993), p. 29. Altman's analysis is updated and extended in W. H. Beaver, M. F. McNichols, and J-W. Rhie, "Have Financial Statements Become Less Informative? Evidence from the Ability of Financial Ratios to Predict Bankruptcy," *Review of Accounting Studies* 10 (2005), pp. 93–122.

policy, and further borrowing. The issuing firm agrees to these *protective covenants* in order to market its bonds to investors concerned about the safety of the bond issue.

Sinking Funds   Bonds call for the payment of par value at the end of the bond's life. This payment constitutes a large cash commitment for the issuer. To help ensure the commitment does not create a cash flow crisis, the firm agrees to establish a **sinking fund** to spread the payment burden over several years. The fund may operate in one of two ways:

1. The firm may repurchase a fraction of the outstanding bonds in the open market each year.
2. The firm may purchase a fraction of the outstanding bonds at a special call price associated with the sinking fund provision. The firm has an option to purchase the bonds at either the market price or the sinking fund price, whichever is lower. To allocate the burden of the sinking fund call fairly among bondholders, the bonds chosen for the call are selected at random based on serial number.[13]

The sinking fund call differs from a conventional bond call in two important ways. First, the firm can repurchase only a limited fraction of the bond issue at the sinking fund call price. At most, some indentures allow firms to use a *doubling option,* which allows repurchase of double the required number of bonds at the sinking fund call price. Second, while callable bonds generally have call prices above par value, the sinking fund call price usually is set at the bond's par value.

Although sinking funds ostensibly protect bondholders by making principal repayment more likely, they can hurt the investor. The firm will choose to buy back discount bonds (selling below par) at market price, while exercising its option to buy back premium bonds (selling above par) at par. Therefore, if interest rates fall and bond prices rise, firms will benefit from the sinking fund provision that enables them to repurchase their bonds at below-market prices. In these circumstances, the firm's gain is the bondholder's loss.

One bond issue that does not require a sinking fund is a *serial bond* issue, in which the firm sells bonds with staggered maturity dates. As bonds mature sequentially, the principal repayment burden for the firm is spread over time, just as it is with a sinking fund. One advantage of serial bonds over sinking fund issues is that there is no uncertainty introduced by the possibility that a particular bond will be called for the sinking fund. The disadvantage, however, is that bonds of different maturity dates are not interchangeable, which reduces the liquidity of the issue.

Subordination of Further Debt   One of the factors determining bond safety is total outstanding debt of the issuer. If you bought a bond today, you would be understandably distressed to see the firm tripling its outstanding debt tomorrow. Your bond would be riskier than it appeared when you bought it. To prevent firms from harming bondholders in this manner, **subordination clauses** restrict the amount of additional borrowing. Additional debt might be required to be subordinated in priority to existing debt; that is, in the event of bankruptcy, *subordinated* or *junior* debtholders will not be paid unless and until the prior senior debt is fully paid off.

---

[13]Although it is less common, the sinking fund provision also may call for periodic payments to a trustee, with the payments invested so that the accumulated sum can be used for retirement of the entire issue at maturity.

Dividend Restrictions   Covenants also limit the dividends firms may pay. These limitations protect the bondholders because they force the firm to retain assets rather than paying them out to stockholders. A typical restriction disallows payments of dividends if cumulative dividends paid since the firm's inception exceed cumulative retained earnings plus proceeds from sales of stock.

Collateral   Some bonds are issued with specific collateral behind them. **Collateral** is a particular asset that the bondholders receive if the firm defaults on the bond. If the collateral is property, the bond is called a *mortgage bond.* If the collateral takes the form of other securities held by the firm, the bond is a *collateral trust bond.* In the case of equipment, the bond is known as an *equipment obligation bond.* This last form of collateral is used most commonly by firms such as railroads, where the equipment is fairly standard and can be easily sold to another firm should the firm default.

Collateralized bonds generally are considered safer than general **debenture bonds,** which are *unsecured,* meaning they do not provide for specific collateral. Credit risk of unsecured bonds depends on the general earning power of the firm. If the firm defaults, debenture owners become general creditors of the firm. Because they are safer, collateralized bonds generally offer lower yields than general debentures.

Figure 14.10 shows the terms of a huge $6.5 billion bond issue by Apple in 2015. We have added some explanatory notes alongside the terms of the issue.

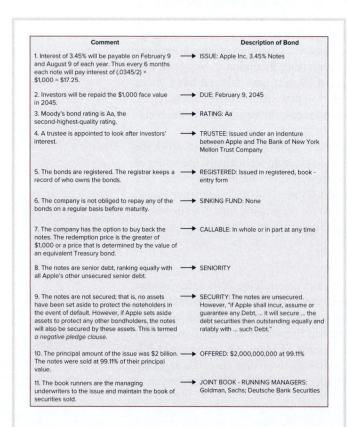

Figure 14.10 Apple's 2015 bond issue.

Yield to Maturity and Default Risk

Because corporate bonds are subject to default risk, we must distinguish between the bond's promised yield to maturity and its expected yield. The promised or stated yield will be realized only if the firm meets the obligations of the bond issue. Therefore, the stated yield is the *maximum possible* yield to maturity of the bond. The expected yield to maturity must take into account the possibility of a default.

For example, at the height of the financial crisis in October 2008, as Ford Motor Company struggled, its bonds due in 2028 were rated CCC and were selling at about 33% of par value, resulting in a yield to maturity of about 20%. Investors did not really believe the expected rate of return on these bonds was 20%. They recognized that there was a decent chance that bondholders would not receive all the payments promised in the bond contract and that the yield based on *expected* cash flows was far less than the yield based on *promised* cash flows. As it turned out, of course, Ford weathered the storm, and investors who purchased its bonds made a very nice profit: The bonds were selling in mid-2016 for about 117% of par value, about 3.5 times their value in 2008.

Example 14.13   Expected versus Promised Yield to Maturity

Suppose a firm issued a 9% coupon bond 20 years ago. The bond now has 10 years left until its maturity date, but the firm is having financial difficulties. Investors believe that the firm will be able to make good on the remaining interest payments, but at the maturity date, the firm will be forced into bankruptcy, and bondholders will receive only 70% of par value. The bond is selling at $750.

Yield to maturity (YTM) would then be calculated using the following inputs:

	Expected YTM	Stated YTM
Coupon payment	$45	$45
Number of semiannual periods	20 periods	20 periods
Final payment	$700	$1,000
Price	$750	$750

The stated yield to maturity, which is based on promised payments, is 13.7%. Based on the expected payment of $700 at maturity, however, the yield to maturity is only 11.6%. The stated yield to maturity is greater than the yield investors actually expect to earn.

Example 14.13 suggests that when a bond becomes more subject to default risk, its price will fall, and therefore its promised yield to maturity will rise. Similarly, the default premium, the spread between the stated yield to maturity and that on otherwise-comparable Treasury bonds, will rise. However, its expected yield to maturity, which ultimately is tied to the systematic risk of the bond, will be far less affected. Let's continue Example 14.13.

Example 14.14   Default Risk and the Default Premium

Suppose that the condition of the firm in Example 14.13 deteriorates further, and investors now believe that the bond will pay off only 55% of face value at maturity. Because of the higher risk, investors now demand an expected yield to maturity of 12% (i.e., 6% semiannually), which is .4% higher than in Example 14.13. But the price of the bond will fall from $750 to $688 [$n = 20$; $i = 6$; FV = 550; PMT = $45]. At this price, the stated yield to maturity based on promised cash flows is 15.2%. While the expected yield to maturity has increased by .4%, the drop in price has caused the promised yield to maturity to rise by 1.5%.

 Concept Check **14.9**

What is the expected yield to maturity in Example 14.14 if the firm is in even worse condition? Investors expect a final payment of only $500, and the bond price has fallen to $650.

To compensate for the possibility of default, corporate bonds must offer a **default premium.** The default premium is the difference between the promised yield on a

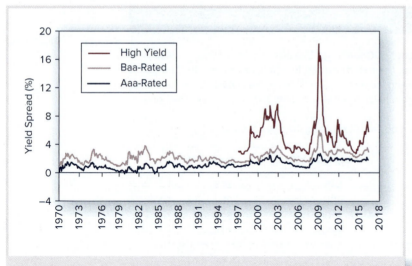

Figure 14.11 Yield spreads between corporate and 10-year Treasury bonds

Source: Federal Reserve Bank of St. Louis.

corporate bond and the yield of an otherwise-identical government bond that is riskless in terms of default. If the firm remains solvent and actually pays the investor all of the promised cash flows, the investor will realize a higher yield to maturity than would be realized from the government bond. If, however, the firm goes bankrupt, the corporate bond is likely to provide a lower return than the government bond. The corporate bond has the potential for both better and worse performance than the default-free Treasury bond. In other words, it is riskier.

The pattern of default premiums offered on risky bonds is sometimes called the *risk structure of interest rates.* The greater the default risk, the higher the default premium. Figure 14.11 shows spreads between yields to maturity of bonds of different risk classes. You can see here clear evidence of credit-risk premiums on promised yields. Note, for example, the incredible run-up of credit spreads during the financial crisis of 2008–2009.

Credit Default Swaps

A **credit default swap (CDS)** is, in effect, an insurance policy on the default risk of a bond or loan. The CDS seller collects annual payments for the term of the contract but must compensate the buyer for loss of bond value in the event of a default.[14] To illustrate, as the Greek government struggled to deal with its debt burden, the annual premium on a 5-year Greek government CDS in 2010 was about 3%, meaning that the CDS buyer would pay the seller an annual "insurance premium" of $3.00 for each $100 of bond principal. In contrast, CDS prices on 5-year bonds of the financially strong German government were less than .5%.

As originally envisioned, credit default swaps were designed to allow lenders to buy protection against default risk. The natural buyers of CDSs would then be large bondholders or banks that wished to enhance the creditworthiness of their outstanding loans. Even if the borrower had a shaky credit standing, the "insured" debt would be as safe as the issuer of the CDS. An investor holding a bond with a BB rating could, in principle, raise the effective quality of the debt to AAA by buying a CDS on the issuer.

This insight suggests how CDS contracts should be priced. If a BB-rated corporate bond bundled with insurance via a CDS is effectively equivalent to an AAA-rated bond, then the premium on the swap ought to approximate the yield spread between AAA-rated

[14]Actually, credit default swaps may pay off even short of an actual default. The contract specifies the particular "credit events" that will trigger a payment. For example, restructuring (rewriting the terms of a firm's outstanding debt as an alternative to formal bankruptcy proceedings) may be defined as a triggering credit event.

and BB-rated bonds.[15] The risk structure of interest rates and CDS prices ought to be tightly aligned.

Figure 14.12 shows the prices of 5-year CDS contracts on Greek government debt between 2009 and 2010 as well as the spread between yields on Greek and German government bonds. As the strongest economy in the euro zone, German bonds are the natural candidate to play the role of the "risk-free benchmark." As expected, the credit spread and CDS prices move almost in lockstep.

You can see that both the credit spread and the CDS price started to increase dramatically toward the end of 2009. As perceptions of Greece's credit risk increased, so did the price of insuring its debt. Ultimately, in what amounted to the largest ever sovereign default, lenders agreed in 2012 to reduce Greece's debt by around $130 billion.

CDS contracts trade on corporate as well as sovereign debt. While CDSs were conceived as a form of bond insurance, it wasn't long before investors realized that they could be used to speculate on the financial health of particular issuers. For example, an investor in early 2008 who predicted the imminent financial crisis might have purchased CDS contracts on mortgage bonds as well as the debt of financial firms and would have profited as their CDS prices spiked in September. In fact, hedge fund manager John Paulson famously did just this. His bearish bets in 2007–2008 on commercial banks and Wall Street firms as well as on some riskier mortgage-backed securities made his funds more than $15 billion, bringing him a personal payoff of more than $3.7 billion.

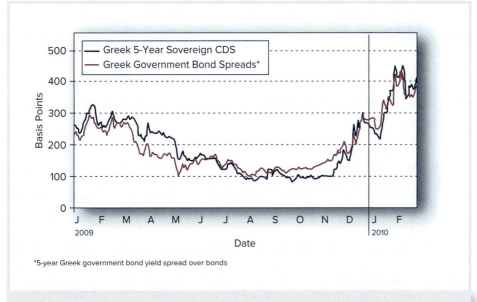

*5-year Greek government bond yield spread over bonds

Figure 14.12 Prices of 5-year Greek government credit default swaps

Source: Bloomberg, August 1, 2012, http://www.bloomberg.com/quote/CDBR1U5:IND/chart.

[15]We say "approximate" because there are some differences between highly rated bonds and bonds synthetically enhanced with credit default swaps. For example, the term of the swap may not match the maturity of the bond. Tax treatment of coupon payments versus swap payments may differ, as may the liquidity of the bonds. Finally, some CDSs may entail one-time up-front payments as well as annual premiums.

Credit Default Swaps, Systemic Risk, and the Financial Crisis of 2008–2009

The credit crisis of 2008–2009, when lending among banks and other financial institutions effectively seized up, was in large measure a crisis of transparency. The biggest problem was a widespread lack of confidence in the financial standing of counterparties to a trade. If one institution could not be confident that another would remain solvent, it would understandably be reluctant to offer it a loan. When doubt about the credit exposure of customers and trading partners spiked to levels not seen since the Great Depression, the market for loans dried up.

Credit default swaps in particular were cited for fostering doubts about counterparty reliability. By August 2008, $63 trillion of such swaps were reportedly outstanding. (By comparison, U.S. gross domestic product in 2008 was about $14 trillion.) As the subprime mortgage market collapsed and the economy entered a deep recession, the potential obligations on these contracts ballooned to levels previously considered unimaginable and the ability of CDS sellers to honor their commitments appeared in doubt. For example, the huge insurance firm AIG alone had sold more than $400 billion of CDS contracts on subprime mortgages and other loans and was days from insolvency. But AIG's insolvency could have triggered the insolvency of other firms that had relied on its promise of protection against loan defaults. These in turn might have triggered further defaults. In the end, the government felt compelled to rescue AIG to prevent a chain reaction of insolvencies.

Counterparty risk and lax reporting requirements made it effectively impossible to tease out firms' exposures to credit risk. One problem was that CDS positions did not have to be accounted for on balance sheets. And the possibility of one default setting off a sequence of further defaults meant that lenders were exposed to the default of an institution with which they did not even directly trade. Such knock-on effects create *systemic risk,* in which the entire financial system can freeze up. With the ripple effects of bad debt extending in ever-widening circles, lending to anyone can seem imprudent.

In the aftermath of the credit crisis, the Dodd-Frank Act called for new regulation and reforms. One reform is a central clearinghouse for credit derivatives such as CDS contracts. Such a system fosters transparency of positions and allows the clearinghouse to replace traders' offsetting long and short positions with a single net position. It also requires daily recognition of gains or losses on positions through a margin or collateral account. If losses mount, positions have to be unwound before growing to unsustainable levels. Allowing traders to accurately assess counterparty risk, and limiting such risk through margin accounts and the extra back-up of the clearinghouse, can go a long way in limiting systemic risk.

Credit Risk and Collateralized Debt Obligations

Collateralized debt obligations (CDOs) emerged in the last decade as a major mechanism to reallocate credit risk in the fixed-income markets. To create a CDO, a financial institution, commonly a bank, first would establish a legally distinct entity to buy and later resell a portfolio of bonds or other loans. A common vehicle for this purpose was the so-called Structured Investment Vehicle (SIV).[16] An SIV raises funds, often by issuing short-term commercial paper, and uses the proceeds to buy corporate bonds or other forms of debt such as mortgage loans or credit card debt. These loans are first pooled together and then split into a series of classes known as *tranches.* (*Tranche* is the French word for "slice.")

Each tranche is given a different level of seniority in terms of its claims on the underlying loan pool, and each can be sold as a stand-alone security. As the loans in the underlying pool make their interest payments, the proceeds are distributed to pay interest to each tranche in order of seniority. This priority structure implies that each tranche has a different exposure to credit risk.

Figure 14.13 illustrates a typical setup. The senior tranche is on top. Its investors may account for perhaps 80% of the principal of the entire pool. But it has first claim on *all* the debt service. Using our numbers, even if 20% of the debt pool defaults, enough principal is repaid to fully pay off the senior tranche. Once the highest seniority tranche is paid off, the next-lower class (e.g., the mezzanine 1 tranche in Figure 14.13) receives the proceeds

---

[16]The legal separation of the bank from the SIV allowed the ownership of the loans to be conducted off the bank's balance sheet, and thus avoided capital requirements the bank would otherwise have encountered.

		Senior-Subordinated Tranche Structure	Typical Terms
		Senior tranche	70–90% of notional principal, coupon similar to Aa-Aaa rated bonds
		Mezzanine 1	5–15% of principal, investment-grade rating
Bank	Structured investment vehicle, SIV		
		Mezzanine 2	5–15% of principal, higher-quality junk rating
		Equity/first loss/ residual tranche	<2%, unrated, coupon rate with 20% credit spread

Figure 14.13 Collateralized debt obligations

from the pool of loans until its claims also are satisfied. Using junior tranches to insulate senior tranches from credit risk in this manner, one can create Aaa-rated bonds even from a junk-bond portfolio.

Of course, shielding senior tranches from default risk means that the risk is concentrated on the lower tranches. The bottom tranche—called alternatively the equity, first-loss, or residual tranche—has last call on payments from the pool of loans, or, put differently, is at the head of the line in terms of absorbing default or delinquency risk.

Not surprisingly, investors in tranches with the greatest exposure to credit risk demand the highest coupon rates. Therefore, while the lower mezzanine and equity tranches bear the most risk, they will provide the highest returns if credit experience turns out favorably.

Mortgage-backed CDOs were an investment disaster in 2007–2009. These were CDOs formed by pooling subprime mortgage loans made to individuals whose credit standing did not allow them to qualify for conventional mortgages. When home prices stalled in 2007 and interest rates on these typically adjustable-rate loans reset to market levels, mortgage delinquencies and home foreclosures soared, and investors in these securities lost billions of dollars. Even investors in highly rated tranches experienced large losses.

Not surprisingly, the rating agencies that had certified these tranches as investment-grade came under considerable fire. Questions were raised concerning conflicts of interest: Because the rating agencies are paid by bond issuers, the agencies were accused of responding to pressure to ease their standards.

While CDO issuance fell dramatically in the wake of the financial crisis, they have more recently enjoyed a comeback. However, newer CDOs generally appear to be safer than their pre-crisis cousins. The Dodd-Frank Act requires CDOs' issuers to retain a material portion of the credit risk of the underlying portfolio. This requirement provides an incentive for issuers to limit credit risk rather than simply off-load it onto another investor. Moreover, banks under the Basel III accord are obligated to hold more capital against the risk of losses. Finally, CDOs today are less likely to hold subprime residential mortgages and more likely to hold higher-rated securities with less leverage.

SUMMARY

1. Fixed-income securities are distinguished by their promise to pay a fixed or specified stream of income to their holders. The coupon bond is a typical fixed-income security.

2. Treasury notes and bonds have original maturities greater than one year. They are issued at or near par value, with their prices quoted net of accrued interest.

3. Callable bonds should offer higher promised yields to maturity to compensate investors for the fact that they will not realize full capital gains should the interest rate fall and the bonds be called away from them at the stipulated call price. Bonds often are issued with a period of call protection. In addition, discount bonds selling significantly below their call price offer implicit call protection.

4. Put bonds give the bondholder rather than the issuer the option to terminate or extend the life of the bond.

5. Convertible bonds may be exchanged, at the bondholder's discretion, for a specified number of shares of stock. Convertible bondholders "pay" for this option by accepting a lower coupon rate on the security.

6. Floating-rate bonds pay a coupon rate at a fixed premium over a reference short-term interest rate. Risk is limited because the rate is tied to current market conditions.

7. The yield to maturity is the single interest rate that equates the present value of a security's cash flows to its price. Bond prices and yields are inversely related. For premium bonds, the coupon rate is greater than the current yield, which is greater than the yield to maturity. The order of these inequalities is reversed for discount bonds.

8. The yield to maturity is often interpreted as an estimate of the average rate of return to an investor who purchases a bond and holds it until maturity. However, when future rates are uncertain, actual returns including reinvested coupons may diverge from yield to maturity. Related measures are yield to call, realized compound yield, and expected (versus promised) yield to maturity.

9. Prices of zero-coupon bonds rise exponentially over time, providing a rate of appreciation equal to the interest rate. The IRS treats this built-in price appreciation as imputed taxable interest income to the investor.

10. When bonds are subject to potential default, the stated yield to maturity is the maximum possible yield to maturity that can be realized by the bondholder. In the event of default, however, that promised yield will not be realized. To compensate bond investors for default risk, bonds must offer default premiums, that is, promised yields in excess of those offered by default-free government securities. If the firm remains healthy, its bonds will provide higher returns than government bonds. Otherwise the returns may be lower.

11. Bond safety is often measured using financial ratio analysis. Bond indentures are safeguards to protect the claims of bondholders. Common indentures specify sinking fund requirements, collateralization of the loan, dividend restrictions, and subordination of future debt.

12. Credit default swaps provide insurance against the default of a bond or loan. The swap buyer pays an annual premium to the swap seller but collects a payment equal to lost value if the loan later goes into default.

13. Collateralized debt obligations are used to reallocate the credit risk of a pool of loans. The pool is sliced into tranches, with each tranche assigned a different level of seniority in terms of its claims on the cash flows from the underlying loans. High seniority tranches are usually quite safe, with credit risk concentrated on the lower level tranches. Each tranche can be sold as a stand-alone security.

KEY TERMS

debt securities	zero-coupon bonds	current yield
bond	callable bond	premium bonds
par value	convertible bond	discount bond
face value	put bond	realized compound return
coupon rate	floating-rate bonds	horizon analysis
bond indenture	yield to maturity (YTM)	reinvestment rate risk

credit risk
investment-grade bond
speculative-grade bond
junk bond

sinking fund
subordination clauses
collateral
debenture bond

default premium
credit default swap (CDS)
collateralized debt obligation
   (CDO)

KEY EQUATIONS

Price of a coupon bond:

$$\text{Price} = \text{Coupon} \times \frac{1}{r}\left[1 - \frac{1}{(1+r)^T}\right] + \text{Par value} \times \frac{1}{(1+r)^T}$$

$$= \text{Coupon} \times \text{Annuity factor}(r, T) + \text{Par value} \times \text{PV factor}(r, T)$$

PROBLEM SETS

1. Define the following types of bonds:
   a. Catastrophe bond
   b. Eurobond
   c. Zero-coupon bond
   d. Samurai bond
   e. Junk bond
   f. Convertible bond
   g. Serial bond
   h. Equipment obligation bond
   i. Original-issue discount bond
   j. Indexed bond
   k. Callable bond
   l. Puttable bond

2. Two bonds have identical times to maturity and coupon rates. One is callable at 105, the other at 110. Which should have the higher yield to maturity? Why?

3. The stated yield to maturity and realized compound yield to maturity of a (default-free) zero-coupon bond will always be equal. Why?

4. Why do bond prices go down when interest rates go up? Don't bond lenders like to receive high interest rates?

5. A bond with an annual coupon rate of 4.8% sells for $970. What is the bond's current yield?

6. Which security has a higher *effective* annual interest rate?
   a. A 3-month T-bill selling at $97,645 with par value $100,000.
   b. A coupon bond selling at par and paying a 10% coupon semiannually.

7. Treasury bonds paying an 8% coupon rate with *semiannual* payments currently sell at par value. What coupon rate would they have to pay in order to sell at par if they paid their coupons *annually*? (*Hint:* What is the effective annual yield on the bond?)

8. Consider a bond with a 10% coupon and yield to maturity = 8%. If the bond's yield to maturity remains constant, then in one year, will the bond price be higher, lower, or unchanged? Why?

9. Consider an 8% coupon bond selling for $953.10 with three years until maturity making *annual* coupon payments. The interest rates in the next three years will be, with certainty, $r_1 = 8\%$, $r_2 = 10\%$, and $r_3 = 12\%$. Calculate the bond's (*a*) yield to maturity and (*b*) realized compound yield.

10. Assume you have a 1-year investment horizon and are trying to choose among three bonds. All have the same degree of default risk and mature in 10 years. The first is a zero-coupon bond that pays $1,000 at maturity. The second has an 8% coupon rate and pays the $80 coupon once per year. The third has a 10% coupon rate and pays the $100 coupon once per year.
   a. If all three bonds are now priced to yield 8% to maturity, what are the prices of: (i) the zero-coupon bond; (ii) the 8% coupon bond; (iii) the 10% coupon bond?
   b. If you expect their yields to maturity to be 8% at the beginning of next year, what will be the price of each bond?
   c. What is your before-tax holding-period return on each bond?

d. If your tax bracket is 30% on ordinary income and 20% on capital gains income, what will be the after-tax rate of return on each bond?

e. Recalculate your answers to parts (b)–(d) under the assumption that you expect the yields to maturity on each bond to be 7% at the beginning of next year.

11. A 20-year maturity bond with par value of $1,000 makes semiannual coupon payments at a coupon rate of 8%. Find the bond equivalent and effective annual yield to maturity of the bond if the bond price is:

   a. $950
   b. $1,000
   c. $1,050

12. Repeat Problem 11 using the same data, but now assume that the bond makes its coupon payments annually. Why are the yields you compute lower in this case?

13. Fill in the table below for the following zero-coupon bonds, all of which have par values of $1,000.

Price	Maturity (years)	Bond-Equivalent Yield to Maturity
a. $400	20	____
b. $500	20	____
c. $500	10	____
d. —	10	10%
e. —	10	8%
f. $400	—	8%

14. Consider a bond paying a coupon rate of 10% per year semiannually when the market interest rate is only 4% per half-year. The bond has three years until maturity.

   a. Find the bond's price today and six months from now after the next coupon is paid.
   b. What is the total (6-month) rate of return on the bond?

15. A bond with a coupon rate of 7% makes semiannual coupon payments on January 15 and July 15 of each year. *The Wall Street Journal* reports the ask price for the bond on January 30 at 100.125. What is the invoice price of the bond? The coupon period has 182 days.

16. A bond has a current yield of 9% and a yield to maturity of 10%. Is the bond selling above or below par value? Explain.

17. Is the coupon rate of the bond in Problem 16 more or less than 9%?

18. Return to Table 14.1, showing the cash flows for TIPS bonds.

   a. What is the nominal rate of return on the bond in year 2?
   b. What is the real rate of return in year 2?
   c. What is the nominal rate of return on the bond in year 3?
   d. What is the real rate of return in year 3?

19. A newly issued 20-year maturity, zero-coupon bond is issued with a yield to maturity of 8% and face value $1,000. Find the imputed interest income in: (a) the first year; (b) the second year; and (c) the last year of the bond's life.

20. A newly issued 10-year maturity, 4% coupon bond making *annual* coupon payments is sold to the public at a price of $800. What will be an investor's taxable income from the bond over the coming year? The bond will not be sold at the end of the year. The bond is treated as an original-issue discount bond.

21. A 30-year maturity, 8% coupon bond paying coupons semiannually is callable in five years at a call price of $1,100. The bond currently sells at a yield to maturity of 7% (3.5% per half-year).

   a. What is the yield to call?
   b. What is the yield to call if the call price is only $1,050?
   c. What is the yield to call if the call price is $1,100 but the bond can be called in two years instead of five years?

22. A 10-year bond of a firm in severe financial distress has a coupon rate of 14% and sells for $900. The firm is currently renegotiating the debt, and it appears that the lenders will allow the firm to reduce coupon payments on the bond to one-half the originally contracted amount. The firm can handle these lower payments. What is (*a*) the stated and (*b*) the expected yield to maturity of the bonds? The bond makes its coupon payments annually.

23. A 2-year bond with par value $1,000 making annual coupon payments of $100 is priced at $1,000. What is the yield to maturity of the bond? What will be the realized compound yield to maturity if the 1-year interest rate next year turns out to be (*a*) 8%, (*b*) 10%, (*c*) 12%?

24. Suppose that today's date is April 15. A bond with a 10% coupon paid semiannually every January 15 and July 15 is quoted as selling at an ask price of 101.25. If you buy the bond from a dealer today, what price will you pay for it?

25. Assume that two firms issue bonds with the following characteristics. Both bonds are issued at par.

	ABC Bonds	XYZ Bonds
Issue size	$1.2 billion	$150 million
Maturity	10 years*	20 years
Coupon	6%	7%
Collateral	First mortgage	General debenture
Callable	Not callable	In 10 years
Call price	None	110
Sinking fund	None	Starting in 5 years

*Bond is extendible at the discretion of the bondholder for an additional 10 years.

Ignoring credit quality, identify four features of these issues that might account for the lower coupon on the ABC debt. Explain.

26. An investor believes that a bond may temporarily increase in credit risk. Which of the following would be the most liquid method of exploiting this?

   a. The purchase of a credit default swap.
   b. The sale of a credit default swap.
   c. The short sale of the bond.

27. Which of the following *most accurately* describes the behavior of credit default swaps?

   a. When credit risk increases, swap premiums increase.
   b. When credit and interest rate risk increase, swap premiums increase.
   c. When credit risk increases, swap premiums increase, but when interest rate risk increases, swap premiums decrease.

28. Describe the likely effect on the yield to maturity of a bond resulting from:

   a. An increase in the issuing firm's times-interest-earned ratio.
   b. An increase in the issuing firm's debt-to-equity ratio.
   c. An increase in the issuing firm's quick ratio.

29. A large corporation issued both fixed- and floating-rate notes five years ago, with terms given in the following table:

	6% Coupon Note	Floating-Rate Note
Issue size	$250 million	$280 million
Original maturity	20 years	10 years
Current price (% of par)	93	98
Current coupon	6%	4%
Coupon adjusts	Fixed coupon	Every year
Coupon reset rule	—	1-year T-bill rate + 2%
Callable	10 years after issue	10 years after issue
Call price	106	102.50
Sinking fund	None	None
Yield to maturity	6.9%	—
Price range since issued	$85–$112	$97–$102

a. Why is the price range greater for the 6% coupon bond than the floating-rate note?

b. What factors could explain why the floating-rate note is not always sold at par value?

c. Why is the call price for the floating-rate note not of great importance to investors?

d. Is the probability of a call for the fixed-rate note high or low?

e. If the firm were to issue a fixed-rate note with a 15-year maturity, what coupon rate would it need to offer to issue the bond at par value?

f. Why is an entry for yield to maturity for the floating-rate note not appropriate?

30. Masters Corp. issued two bonds with 20-year maturities. Both bonds are callable at $1,050. The first bond was issued at a deep discount with a coupon rate of 4% and a price of $580 to yield 8.4%. The second bond was issued at par value with a coupon rate of 8.75%.

a. What is the yield to maturity of the par bond? Why is it higher than the yield of the discount bond?

b. If you expect rates to fall substantially in the next two years, which bond has the higher expected rate of return?

c. In what sense does the discount bond offer "implicit call protection"?

31. A newly issued bond pays its coupons once annually. Its coupon rate is 5%, its maturity is 20 years, and its yield to maturity is 8%.

a. Find the holding-period return for a 1-year investment period if the bond is selling at a yield to maturity of 7% by the end of the year.

b. If you sell the bond after one year, what taxes will you owe if the tax rate on interest income is 40% and the tax rate on capital gains income is 30%? The bond is subject to original-issue discount tax treatment.

c. What is the after-tax holding-period return on the bond?

d. Find the realized compound yield *before taxes* for a 2-year holding period, assuming that (i) you sell the bond after two years, (ii) the bond yield is 7% at the end of the second year, and (iii) the coupon can be reinvested for one year at a 3% interest rate.

e. Use the tax rates in part (*b*) to compute the *after-tax* 2-year realized compound yield. Remember to take account of OID tax rules.

1. Leaf Products may issue a 10-year maturity fixed-income security, which might include a sinking fund provision and either refunding or call protection.

a. Describe a sinking fund provision.

b. Explain the impact of a sinking fund provision on:

i. The expected average life of the proposed security.

ii. Total principal and interest payments over the life of the proposed security.

c. From the investor's point of view, explain the rationale for demanding a sinking fund provision.

2. Bonds of Zello Corporation with a par value of $1,000 sell for $960, mature in five years, and have a 7% annual coupon rate paid semiannually.

a. Calculate the:

i. Current yield.

ii. Yield to maturity to the nearest whole percent (i.e., 3%, 4%, 5%, etc.).

iii. Realized compound yield for an investor with a 3-year holding period and a reinvestment rate of 6% over the period. At the end of three years the 7% coupon bonds with two years remaining will sell to yield 7%.

b. Cite one major shortcoming for each of the following fixed-income yield measures:

i. Current yield.

ii. Yield to maturity.

iii. Realized compound yield.

3. On May 30, 2016, Janice Kerr is considering one of the newly issued 10-year AAA corporate bonds shown in the following exhibit.

Description	Coupon	Price	Callable	Call Price
Sentinal, due May 30, 2026	4.00%	100	Noncallable	NA
Colina, due May 30, 2026	4.20%	100	Currently callable	102

a. Suppose that market interest rates decline by 100 basis points (i.e., 1%). Contrast the effect of this decline on the price of each bond.

b. Should Kerr prefer the Colina or the Sentinal bond when rates are expected to rise? Which should she prefer when rates are expected to fall?

c. What would be the effect, if any, of an increase in the *volatility* of interest rates on the prices of each bond?

4. A convertible bond has the following features:

Coupon	5.25%
Maturity	June 15, 2030
Market price of bond	$77.50
Market price of underlying common stock	$28.00
Annual dividend	$1.20
Conversion ratio	20.83 shares

Calculate the conversion premium for this bond.

5. *a.* Explain the impact on the offering yield of adding a call feature to a proposed bond issue.

b. Explain the impact on the bond's expected life of adding a call feature to a proposed bond issue.

c. Describe one advantage and one disadvantage of including callable bonds in a portfolio.

6. *a.* An investment in a coupon bond will provide the investor with a return equal to the bond's yield to maturity at the time of purchase if:

   i. The bond is not called for redemption at a price that exceeds its par value.

   ii. All sinking fund payments are made in a prompt and timely fashion over the life of the issue.

   iii. The reinvestment rate is the same as the bond's yield to maturity and the bond is held until maturity.

   iv. All of the above.

b. A bond with a call feature:

   i. Is attractive because the immediate receipt of principal plus premium produces a high return.

   ii. Is more apt to be called when interest rates are high because the interest savings will be greater.

   iii. Will usually have a higher yield to maturity than a similar noncallable bond.

   iv. None of the above.

c. In which *one* of the following cases is the bond selling at a discount?

   i. Coupon rate is greater than current yield, which is greater than yield to maturity.

   ii. Coupon rate, current yield, and yield to maturity are all the same.

   iii. Coupon rate is less than current yield, which is less than yield to maturity.

   iv. Coupon rate is less than current yield, which is greater than yield to maturity.

d. Consider a 5-year bond with a 10% coupon that has a present yield to maturity of 8%. If interest rates remain constant, one year from now the price of this bond will be:

   i. Higher

   ii. Lower

   iii. The same

   iv. Par

E-INVESTMENTS EXERCISE

Go to **www.finra-markets.morningstar.com/bondcenter,** click on the *Bonds* tab on the left side of the Web page, click on the *Search* tab, and enter a company ticker symbol (e.g., AAPL for Apple). When you submit your request, you will be given a list of all bonds issued by Apple. Using this procedure, find the ratings on bonds of at least 10 companies. Try to choose a sample with a wide range of ratings. Then go to a Web site such as **money.msn.com** or **finance.yahoo.com** and obtain for each firm as many of the financial ratios tabulated in Table 14.3 as you can find. Which ratios seem to best explain credit ratings?

SOLUTIONS TO CONCEPT CHECKS

1. The callable bond will sell at the *lower* price. Investors will not be willing to pay as much if they know that the firm retains a valuable option to reclaim the bond for the call price if interest rates fall.

2. At a semiannual interest rate of 3%, the bond is worth $40 × Annuity factor (3%, 60) + $1,000 × PV factor(3%, 60) = $1,276.76, which results in a capital gain of $276.76. This exceeds the capital loss of $189.29 (i.e., $1,000 − $810.71) when the semiannual interest rate increased to 5%.

3. Yield to maturity exceeds current yield, which exceeds coupon rate. Take as an example the 8% coupon bond with a yield to maturity of 10% per year (5% per half-year). Its price is $810.71, and therefore its current yield is 80/810.71 = .0987, or 9.87%, which is higher than the coupon rate but lower than the yield to maturity.

4. *a.* The bond with the 6% coupon rate currently sells for 30 × Annuity factor(3.5%, 20) + 1,000 × PV factor(3.5%, 20) = $928.94. If the interest rate immediately drops to 6% (3% per half-year), the bond price will rise to $1,000, for a capital gain of $71.06, or 7.65%. The 8% coupon bond currently sells for $1,071.06. If the interest rate falls to 6%, the present value of the *scheduled* payments increases to $1,148.77. However, the bond will be called at $1,100, for a capital gain of only $28.94, or 2.70%.

   b. The current price of the bond can be derived from its yield to maturity. Using your calculator, set: $n = 40$ (semiannual periods); payment = $45 per period; future value = $1,000; interest rate = 4% per semiannual period. Calculate present value as $1,098.96. Now we can calculate yield to call. The time to call is 5 years, or 10 semiannual periods. The price at which the bond will be called is $1,050. To find yield to call, we set: $n = 10$ (semiannual periods); payment = $45 per period; future value = $1,050; present value = $1,098.96. Calculate yield to call as 3.72%, or 7.44% bond equivalent yield.

5. Price = $70 × Annuity factor(8%, 1) + $1,000 × PV factor(8%, 1) = $990.74

$$\text{Rate of return to investor} = \frac{\$70 + (\$990.74 - \$982.17)}{\$982.17} = .080 = 8\%$$

6. By year-end, remaining maturity is 29 years. If the yield to maturity were still 8%, the bond would still sell at par and the holding-period return would be 8%. At a higher yield, price and return will be lower. Suppose, for example, that the yield to maturity rises to 8.5%. With annual payments of $80 and a face value of $1,000, the price of the bond will be $946.70 [$n = 29$; $i = 8.5\%$; PMT = $80; FV = $1,000]. The bond initially sold at $1,000 when issued at the start of the year. The holding-period return is

$$\text{HPR} = \frac{80 + (946.70 - 1,000)}{1,000} = .0267 = 2.67\%$$

which is less than the initial yield to maturity of 8%.

7. At the lower yield, the bond price will be $631.67 [$n = 29$, $i = 7\%$, FV = $1,000, PMT = $40]. Therefore, total after-tax income is

Coupon	$40 × (1 − .38)	= $24.80
Imputed interest	($553.66 − $549.69) × (1 − .38)	= 2.46
Capital gains	($631.67 − $553.66) × (1 − .20)	= 62.41
Total income after taxes		$89.67

Rate of return = 89.67/549.69 = .163 = 16.3%.

8. It should receive a negative coefficient. A high ratio of liabilities to assets is a bad omen for a firm, and that should lower its credit rating.

9. The coupon payment is $45. There are 20 semiannual periods. The final payment is assumed to be $500. The present value of expected cash flows is $650. The expected yield to maturity is 6.317% semiannual or annualized, 12.63%, bond equivalent yield.

The Term Structure of Interest Rates

IN CHAPTER 14 we assumed for the sake of simplicity that the same constant interest rate is used to discount cash flows of any maturity. In the real world, this is rarely the case. We have seen, for example, that in 2016 short-term Treasury bonds and notes carried yields to maturity less than 1%, while the longest-term bonds offered yields of about 2.5%. At the time that these bond prices were quoted, anyway, the longer-term securities had higher yields. This, in fact, is a typical pattern, but as we shall see below, the relationship between time to maturity and yield to maturity can vary dramatically from one period to another. In this chapter we explore the pattern of interest rates for different-term assets. We attempt to identify the factors that account for that pattern

and determine what information may be gleaned from an analysis of the so-called **term structure of interest rates,** the structure of interest rates for discounting cash flows of different maturities.

We demonstrate how the prices of Treasury bonds may be derived from prices and yields of stripped zero-coupon Treasury securities. We also examine the extent to which the term structure reveals market-consensus forecasts of future interest rates and how the presence of interest rate risk may affect those inferences. Finally, we show how traders can use the term structure to compute forward rates that represent interest rates on "forward," or deferred, loans, and consider the relationship between forward rates and future interest rates.

15.1   The Yield Curve

In the last chapter, Figure 14.1 demonstrated that while yields to maturity on bonds of similar maturities are reasonably close, they do differ. When these bond prices and yields were compiled, long-term bonds sold at higher yields than short-term bonds. Practitioners commonly summarize the relationship between yield and maturity graphically in a **yield curve,** which is a plot of yield to maturity as a function of time to maturity. The yield curve is one of the key concerns of fixed-income investors. It is central to bond valuation and, as well, allows investors to gauge their expectations for future interest rates against those of the market. Such a comparison is often the starting point in the formulation of a fixed-income portfolio strategy.

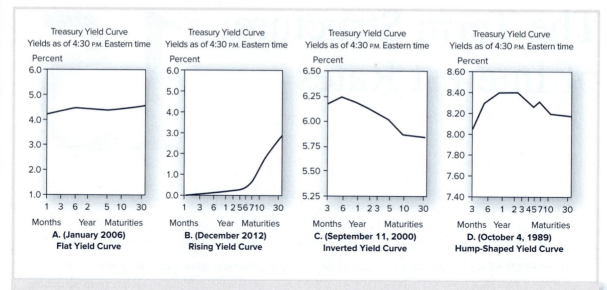

Figure 15.1 Treasury yield curves

Source: Various editions of *The Wall Street Journal.*

In 2016, the yield curve was rising, with long-term bonds offering yields higher than those of short-term bonds. But the relationship between yield and maturity can vary widely. Figure 15.1 illustrates yield curves of several different shapes. Panel A is the almost-flat curve of early 2006. Panel B is a more typical upward-sloping curve from 2012. Panel C is a downward-sloping or "inverted" curve, and Panel D is hump-shaped, first rising and then falling.

Bond Pricing

If yields on different-maturity bonds are not all equal, how should we value coupon bonds that make payments at many different times? For example, suppose that yields on zero-coupon Treasury bonds of different maturities are as given in Table 15.1. The table tells us that zero-coupon bonds with 1-year maturity sell at a yield to maturity of $y_1 = 5\%$, 2-year zeros sell at yields of $y_2 = 6\%$, and 3-year zeros sell at yields of $y_3 = 7\%$. Which of these rates should we use to discount bond cash flows? The answer: all of them. The trick is to consider each bond cash flow—either coupon or principal payment—as at least potentially sold off separately as a stand-alone zero-coupon bond.

Recall the Treasury STRIPS program we introduced in the last chapter (Section 14.4). Stripped Treasuries are zero-coupon bonds created by selling each coupon or principal

Table 15.1	Maturity (years)	Yield to Maturity (%)	Price
Prices and yields to maturity on zero-coupon bonds ($1,000 face value)	1	5%	$952.38 = $1,000/1.05
	2	6	$890.00 = $1,000/1.06^2$
	3	7	$816.30 = $1,000/1.07^3$
	4	8	$735.03 = $1,000/1.08^4$

payment from a whole Treasury bond as a separate cash flow. For example, a 1-year maturity T-bond paying semiannual coupons can be split into a 6-month maturity zero (by selling the first coupon payment as a stand-alone security) and a 12-month zero (corresponding to payment of final coupon and principal). Treasury stripping suggests exactly how to value a coupon bond. If each cash flow can be (and in practice often is) sold off as a separate security, then the value of the whole bond should equal the total value of its cash flows bought piece by piece in the STRIPS market.

What if it weren't? Then there would be easy profits to be made. For example, if investment bankers ever noticed a bond selling for less than the amount at which the sum of its parts could be sold, they would buy the bond, strip it into stand-alone zero-coupon securities, sell off the stripped cash flows, and profit by the price difference. If the bond were selling for *more* than the sum of the values of its individual cash flows, they would run the process in reverse: buy the individual zero-coupon securities in the STRIPS market, *reconstitute* (i.e., reassemble) the cash flows into a coupon bond, and sell the whole bond for more than the cost of the pieces. Both **bond stripping** and **bond reconstitution** offer opportunities for *arbitrage*—the exploitation of mispricing among two or more securities to clear a riskless economic profit. Any violation of the Law of One Price, that identical cash flow bundles must sell for identical prices, gives rise to arbitrage opportunities.

To value each stripped cash flow, we simply look up its appropriate discount rate in *The Wall Street Journal.* Because each coupon payment matures at a different time, we discount by using the yield appropriate to its particular maturity—this is the yield on a Treasury strip maturing at the time of that cash flow. We can illustrate with an example.

Example 15.1   Valuing Coupon Bonds

Suppose the yields on stripped Treasuries are as given in Table 15.1, and we wish to value a 10% coupon bond with a maturity of three years. For simplicity, assume the bond makes its payments annually. Then the first cash flow, the $100 coupon paid at the end of the first year, is discounted at 5%; the second cash flow, the $100 coupon at the end of the second year, is discounted for two years at 6%; and the final cash flow consisting of the final coupon plus par value, or $1,100, is discounted for three years at 7%. The value of the coupon bond is therefore

$$\frac{100}{1.05} + \frac{100}{1.06^2} + \frac{1,100}{1.07^3} = 95.238 + 89.000 + 897.928 = \$1,082.17$$

Calculate the yield to maturity of the coupon bond in Example 15.1, and you may be surprised. Its yield to maturity is 6.88%; so while its maturity matches that of the 3-year zero in Table 15.1, its yield is a bit lower.[1] This reflects the fact that the 3-year coupon bond may usefully be thought of as a *portfolio* of three implicit zero-coupon bonds, one corresponding to each cash flow. The yield on the coupon bond is then an amalgam of the yields on each of the three components of the "portfolio." Think about what this means: If their coupon rates differ, bonds of the same maturity generally will not have the same yield to maturity.

What then do we mean by "the" yield curve? In fact, in practice, traders refer to several yield curves. The **pure yield curve** refers to the curve for stripped, or zero-coupon,

---

[1]Remember that the yield to maturity of a coupon bond is the *single* interest rate at which the present value of cash flows equals market price. To calculate the coupon bond's yield to maturity on your calculator or spreadsheet, set $n = 3$; price $= -1,082.17$; future value $= 1,000$; payment $= 100$. Then compute the interest rate.

Treasuries. In contrast, the **on-the-run yield curve** refers to the plot of yield as a function of maturity for recently issued coupon bonds selling at or near par value. As we've just seen, there may be significant differences in these two curves. The yield curves published in the financial press, for example, in Figure 15.1, are typically on-the-run curves. On-the-run Treasuries have the greatest liquidity, so traders have keen interest in their yield curve.

 Concept Check **15.1**

Using the data in Table 15.1, calculate the price and yield to maturity of a 3-year bond with a coupon rate of 4% making annual coupon payments. Does its yield match that of either the 3-year zero or the 10% coupon bond considered in Example 15.1? Why is the yield spread between the 4% bond and the zero smaller than the yield spread between the 10% bond and the zero?

15.2 The Yield Curve and Future Interest Rates

We've told you what the yield curve is, but we haven't yet had much to say about where it comes from. For example, why is the curve sometimes upward-sloping and other times downward-sloping? How do expectations for the evolution of interest rates affect the shape of today's yield curve?

These questions do not have simple answers, so we will begin with an admittedly idealized framework, and then extend the discussion to more realistic settings. To start, consider a world with no uncertainty, specifically, one in which all investors already know the path of future interest rates.

The Yield Curve under Certainty

If interest rates are certain, what should we make of the fact that the yield on the 2-year zero coupon bond in Table 15.1 is greater than that on the 1-year zero? It can't be that one bond is expected to provide a higher rate of return than the other. This would not be possible in a certain world—with no risk, all bonds (in fact, all securities!) must offer identical returns, or investors will bid up the price of the high-return bond until its rate of return is no longer superior to that of other bonds.

Instead, the upward-sloping yield curve is evidence that short-term rates are going to be higher next year than they are now. To see why, consider two 2-year bond strategies. The first strategy entails buying the 2-year zero offering a 2-year yield to maturity of $y_2 = 6\%$, and holding it until maturity. The zero has face value $1,000, so it is purchased today for $1,000/1.06^2 = \$890$ and matures in two years to $1,000. The total 2-year growth factor for the investment is therefore $1,000/\$890 = 1.06^2 = 1.1236$.

Now consider an alternative 2-year strategy. Invest the same $890 in a 1-year zero-coupon bond with a yield to maturity of 5%. When that bond matures, reinvest the proceeds in another 1-year bond. Figure 15.2 illustrates these two strategies. The interest rate that 1-year bonds will offer next year is denoted as r_2.

Remember, both strategies must provide equal returns—neither entails any risk. Therefore, the proceeds after two years to either strategy must be equal:

$$\text{Buy and hold 2-year zero} = \text{Roll over 1-year bonds}$$
$$\$890 \times 1.06^2 = \$890 \times 1.05 \times (1 + r_2)$$

We find next year's interest rate by solving $1 + r_2 = 1.06^2/1.05 = 1.0701$, or $r_2 = 7.01\%$. So while the 1-year bond offers a lower yield to maturity than the 2-year bond (5% versus

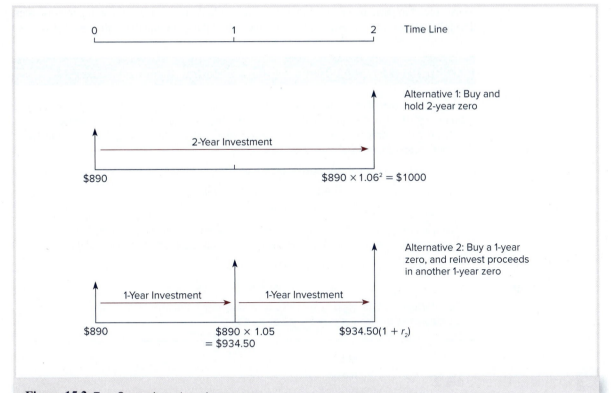

Figure 15.2 Two 2-year investment programs

6%), we see that it has a compensating advantage: It allows you to roll over your funds into another short-term bond next year when rates will be higher. Next year's interest rate is higher than today's by just enough to make rolling over 1-year bonds equally attractive as investing in the 2-year bond.

To distinguish between yields on long-term bonds versus short-term rates that will be available in the future, practitioners use the following terminology. They call the yield to maturity on zero-coupon bonds the **spot rate,** meaning the rate that prevails *today* for a time period corresponding to the zero's maturity. In contrast, the **short rate** for a given time interval (e.g., one year) refers to the interest rate for that interval available at different points in time. In our example, the short rate today is 5%, and the short rate next year will be 7.01%.

Not surprisingly, the 2-year spot rate is an average of today's short rate and next year's short rate. But because of compounding, that average is a geometric one.[2] We see this by again equating the total return on the two competing 2-year strategies:

$$(1 + y_2)^2 = (1 + r_1) \times (1 + r_2)$$
$$1 + y_2 = [(1 + r_1) \times (1 + r_2)]^{1/2}$$

(15.1)

Equation 15.1 begins to tell us why the yield curve might take on different shapes at different times. When next year's short rate, r_2, is greater than this year's short rate, r_1, the average of the two rates is higher than today's rate, so $y_2 > r_1$ and the yield curve slopes upward. If next year's short rate were less than r_1, the yield curve would slope downward.

---

[2]In an arithmetic average, we add *n* numbers and divide by *n*. In a geometric average, we multiply *n* numbers and take the *n*th root.

Thus, at least in part, the yield curve reflects the market's assessments of coming interest rates. The following example uses a similar analysis to find the short rate that will prevail in year 3.

Example 15.2   Finding a Future Short Rate

Now we compare two 3-year strategies. One is to buy a 3-year zero, with a yield to maturity from Table 15.1 of 7%, and hold it until maturity. The other is to buy a 2-year zero yielding 6% and roll the proceeds into a 1-year bond in year 3, at the short rate r_3. The growth factor for the invested funds under each policy will be:

Buy and hold 3-year zero = Buy 2-year zero; roll proceeds into 1-year bond

$$(1 + y_3)^3 = (1 + y_2)^2 \times (1 + r_3)$$
$$1.07^3 = 1.06^2 \times (1 + r_3)$$

which implies that $r_3 = 1.07^3/1.06^2 - 1 = .09025 = 9.025\%$. Again, notice that the yield on the 3-year bond reflects a geometric average of the discount factors for the next three years:

$$1 + y_3 = [(1 + r_1) \times (1 + r_2) \times (1 + r_3)]^{1/3}$$
$$1.07 = [1.05 \times 1.0701 \times 1.09025]^{1/3}$$

We conclude that the yield or spot rate on a long-term bond reflects the path of short rates anticipated by the market over the life of the bond.

 Concept Check **15.2**

Use Table 15.1 to find the short rate that will prevail in the fourth year. Confirm that the discount factor on the 4-year zero is a geometric average of 1 + the short rates in the next four years.

Figure 15.3 summarizes the results of our analysis and emphasizes the difference between short rates and spot rates. The top line presents the short rates for each year. The lower lines present spot rates—or, equivalently, yields to maturity on zero-coupon bonds for different holding periods—extending from the present to each relevant maturity date.

Holding-Period Returns

We've argued that the multiyear cumulative returns on all of our competing bonds ought to be equal. What about holding-period returns over shorter periods such as a year? You might think that bonds selling at higher yields to maturity will offer higher 1-year returns, but this is not the case. In fact, once you stop to think about it, it's clear that this *cannot* be true. In a world of certainty, all bonds must offer identical returns, or investors will flock to the higher-return securities, bidding up their prices, and reducing their returns. We can illustrate by using the bonds in Table 15.1.

Example 15.3   Holding-Period Returns on Zero-Coupon Bonds

The 1-year bond in Table 15.1 can be bought today for $1,000/1.05 = $952.38 and will mature to its par value in one year. It pays no coupons, so total investment income is just its price appreciation, and its rate of return is ($1,000 − $952.38)/$952.38 = .05. The 2-year bond can be bought for $1,000/1.06^2 = 890.00. Next year, the bond will have a remaining maturity of one year and the 1-year interest rate will be 7.01%. Therefore, its price next year will be $1,000/1.0701 = 934.49, and its 1-year holding-period rate of return will be ($934.49 − $890.00)/$890.00 = .05, for an identical 5% rate of return.

 Concept Check **15.3**

Show that the rate of return on the 3-year zero in Table 15.1 also will be 5%. (*Hint:* Next year, the bond will have a maturity of two years.) Use the short rates derived in Figure 15.3 to compute the 2-year spot rate that will prevail a year from now.

Forward Rates

The following equation generalizes our approach to inferring a future short rate from the yield curve of zero-coupon bonds. It equates the total return on two *n*-year investment strategies: buying and holding an *n*-year zero-coupon bond versus buying an $(n − 1)$-year zero and rolling over the proceeds into a 1-year bond.

$$(1 + y_n)^n = (1 + y_{n-1})^{n-1} \times (1 + r_n) \tag{15.2}$$

where n denotes the period in question, and y_n is the yield to maturity of a zero-coupon bond with an n-period maturity. Given the observed yield curve, we can solve Equation 15.2 for the short rate in the last period:

$$(1 + r_n) = \frac{(1 + y_n)^n}{(1 + y_{n-1})^{n-1}} \tag{15.3}$$

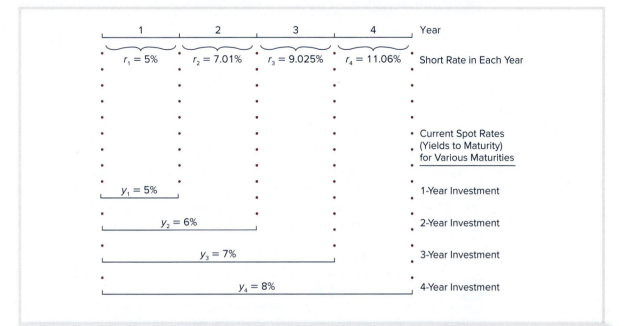

Figure 15.3 Short rates versus spot rates

Equation 15.3 has a simple interpretation. The numerator on the right-hand side is the total growth factor of an investment in an n-year zero held until maturity. Similarly, the denominator is the growth factor of an investment in an $(n - 1)$-year zero. Because the former investment lasts for one more year than the latter, the difference in these growth factors must be the gross rate of return available in year n when the $(n - 1)$-year zero can be rolled over into a 1-year investment.

Of course, when future interest rates are uncertain, as they are in reality, there is no meaning to inferring "the" future short rate. No one knows today what the future interest rate will be. At best, we can speculate as to its expected value and associated uncertainty. Nevertheless, it still is common to use Equation 15.3 to investigate the implications of the yield curve for future interest rates. Recognizing that future interest rates are uncertain, we call the interest rate that we infer in this matter the **forward interest rate** rather than the *future short rate* because it need not be the interest rate that actually will prevail at the future date.

If the forward rate for period n is denoted f_n, we then define f_n by the equation

$$(1 + f_n) = \frac{(1 + y_n)^n}{(1 + y_{n-1})^{n-1}}$$ (15.4)

Equivalently, we may rewrite Equation 15.4 as

$$(1 + y_n)^n = (1 + y_{n-1})^{n-1}(1 + f_n)$$ (15.5)

In this formulation, the forward rate is *defined* as the "break-even" interest rate that equates the return on an n-period zero-coupon bond to that of an $(n - 1)$-period zero-coupon bond rolled over into a 1-year bond in year n. The actual total returns on the two n-year strategies will be equal if the short interest rate in year n turns out to equal f_n.

Example 15.4   Forward Rates

Suppose a bond trader uses the data presented in Table 15.1. The forward rate for year 4 would be computed as

$$1 + f_4 = \frac{(1 + y_4)^4}{(1 + y_3)^3} = \frac{1.08^4}{1.07^3} = 1.1106$$

Therefore, the forward rate is $f_4 = .1106$, or 11.06%.

We emphasize again that the interest rate that actually will prevail in the future need not equal the forward rate, which is calculated from today's data. Indeed, the forward rate may not even equal the expected value of the future short interest rate. We address this issue in the next section. For now, however, we note that forward rates equal future short rates in the *special case* of interest rate certainty.

 Concept Check **15.4**

You've been exposed to many "rates" in the last few pages. Explain the difference among spot rates, short rates, and forward rates.

The spreadsheet below (available in Connect or through your course instructor) can be used to estimate prices and yields of coupon bonds and to calculate the forward rates for both single-year and multiyear periods. Spot yields are derived for the yield curve of bonds that are selling at their par value, also referred to as the current coupon or "on-the-run" bond yield curve.

The spot rates for each maturity date are used to calculate the present value of each period's cash flow. The sum of these cash flows is the price of the bond. Given its price, the bond's yield to maturity can then be computed. If you were to err and use the yield to maturity of the on-the-run bond to discount each of the bond's coupon payments, you would find a significantly different price. That difference is calculated in the worksheet.

Excel Questions

1. Change the spot rate in the spreadsheet to 8% for all maturities. The forward rates will all be 8%. Why is this not surprising?

2. The spot rates in column B decrease for longer maturities, and the forward rates decrease even more rapidly with maturity. What happens to the pattern of forward rates if you input spot rates that increase with maturity? Why?

	A	B	C	D	E	F	G	H
56		Forward Rate Calculations						
57								
58		Spot Rate	1-yr for.	2-yr for.	3-yr for.	4-yr for.	5-yr for.	6-yr for.
59	Period							
60	1	8.0000%	7.9792%	7.6770%	7.2723%	6.9709%	6.8849%	6.7441%
61	2	7.9896%	7.3757%	6.9205%	6.6369%	6.6131%	6.4988%	6.5520%
62	3	7.7846%	6.4673%	6.2695%	6.3600%	6.2807%	6.3880%	6.1505%
63	4	7.4537%	6.0720%	6.3065%	6.2186%	6.3682%	6.0872%	6.0442%
64	5	7.1760%	6.5414%	6.2920%	6.4671%	6.0910%	6.0387%	5.8579%
65	6	7.0699%	6.0432%	6.4299%	5.9413%	5.9134%	5.7217%	5.6224%
66	7	6.9227%	6.8181%	5.8904%	5.8701%	5.6414%	5.5384%	5.3969%
67	8	6.9096%	4.9707%	5.3993%	5.2521%	5.2209%	5.1149%	5.1988%

15.3 Interest Rate Uncertainty and Forward Rates

The term structure is harder to interpret when future interest rates are uncertain. In a certain world, different investment strategies with common terminal dates must provide equal rates of return. For example, two consecutive 1-year investments in zeros would need to offer the same total return as an equal-sized investment in a 2-year zero. Therefore, under certainty,

$$(1 + r_1)(1 + r_2) = (1 + y_2)^2 \qquad\qquad \textbf{(15.6)}$$

What can we say when r_2 is not known today?

For example, suppose that today's rate is $r_1 = 5\%$ and that the *expected* short rate for the following year is $E(r_2) = 6\%$. If investors cared only about the expected value of the interest rate, then the yield to maturity on a 2-year zero would be determined by using the expected short rate in Equation 15.6:

$$(1 + y_2)^2 = (1 + r_1) \times [1 + E(r_2)] = 1.05 \times 1.06$$

The price of a 2-year zero would be $\$1,000/(1 + y_2)^2 = \$1,000/(1.05 \times 1.06) = \$898.47$.

But now consider a short-term investor who wishes to invest only for one year. She can purchase the 1-year zero for $\$1,000/1.05 = \$952.38$ and lock in a riskless 5% return because she knows that at the end of the year, the bond will be worth its maturity value of

$1,000. She also can purchase the 2-year zero. Its *expected* rate of return also is 5%: Next year, the bond will have one year to maturity, and we expect that the 1-year interest rate will be 6%, implying a price of $943.40 and a holding-period return of 5%.

But the rate of return on the 2-year bond is risky. If next year's interest rate turns out to be above expectations, that is, greater than 6%, the bond price will be below $943.40; conversely if r_2 turns out to be less than 6%, the bond price will exceed $943.40. Why should this short-term investor buy the *risky* 2-year bond when its expected return is 5%, no better than that of the *risk-free* 1-year bond? Clearly, she would not hold the 2-year bond unless it offered a higher expected rate of return. This requires that the 2-year bond sell at a lower price than the $898.47 value we derived when we ignored risk.

Example 15.5   Bond Prices and Forward Rates with Interest Rate Risk

Suppose that most investors have short-term horizons and therefore are willing to hold the 2-year bond only if its price falls to $881.83. At this price, the expected holding-period return on the 2-year bond is 7% (because 943.40/881.83 = 1.07). The risk premium of the 2-year bond, therefore, is 2%; it offers an expected rate of return of 7% versus the 5% risk-free return on the 1-year bond. At this risk premium, investors are willing to bear the price risk associated with interest rate uncertainty.

When bond prices reflect a risk premium, however, the forward rate, f_2, no longer equals the expected short rate, $E(r_2)$. Although we have assumed that $E(r_2) = 6\%$, it is easy to confirm that $f_2 = 8\%$. The yield to maturity on a 2-year zero selling at $881.83 is 6.49%, and

$$1 + f_2 = \frac{(1 + y_2)^2}{1 + y_1} = \frac{1.0649^2}{1.05} = 1.08$$

The result in Example 15.5—that the forward rate exceeds the expected short rate—should not surprise us. We defined the forward rate as the interest rate that would need to prevail in the second year to make the long- and short-term investments equally attractive, *ignoring risk*. But when we account for risk, short-term investors will shy away from the long-term bond unless its expected return exceeds that of the 1-year bond. Therefore, the risk-averse investor would be willing to hold the long-term bond only if the expected value of the short rate is less than the break-even value, f_2, because the lower the expectation of r_2, the greater the anticipated return on the long-term bond.

Therefore, if most individuals are short-term investors, bonds must have prices that make f_2 greater than $E(r_2)$. The forward rate will embody a premium compared with the expected future short-interest rate. This **liquidity premium** compensates short-term investors for the uncertainty about the price at which they will be able to sell their long-term bonds at the end of the year.[3]

 Concept Check **15.5**

Suppose that the required liquidity premium for the short-term investor is 1%. What must $E(r_2)$ be if f_2 is 7%?

---

[3]*Liquidity* refers to the ability to sell an asset easily at a predictable price. Because long-term bonds have greater price risk, they are considered less liquid in this context and thus must offer a premium.

Perhaps surprisingly, we also can imagine scenarios in which long-term bonds can be perceived by investors to be *safer* than short-term bonds. To see how, we now consider a "long-term" investor, who wishes to invest for a full 2-year period. Suppose she can purchase a $1,000 par value 2-year zero-coupon bond for $890 and lock in a guaranteed yield to maturity of $y_2 = 6\%$. Alternatively, she can roll over two 1-year investments. In this case an investment of $890 would grow in two years to $890 \times 1.05 \times (1 + r_2)$, which is an uncertain amount today because r_2 is not yet known. The break-even year 2 interest rate is, once again, the forward rate, 7.01%, because the forward rate is *defined* as the rate that equates the terminal value of the two investment strategies.

The expected value of the payoff of the rollover strategy is $890 \times 1.05 \times [1 + E(r_2)]$. If $E(r_2)$ equals the forward rate, f_2, then the expected value of the payoff from the rollover strategy will equal the *known* payoff from the 2-year-maturity-bond strategy.

Is this a reasonable presumption? Once again, it is reasonable only if the investor does not care about the uncertainty surrounding the final value of the rollover strategy. Whenever that risk is important, however, the long-term investor will not be willing to engage in the rollover strategy unless its expected return exceeds that of the 2-year bond. In this case the investor would require that

$$(1.05)\,[1 + E(r_2)] > (1.06)^2 = (1.05)(1 + f_2)$$

which implies that $E(r_2)$ *exceeds* f_2.

Therefore, if all investors were long-term investors, no one would be willing to hold short-term bonds unless rolling over those bonds offered a reward for bearing interest rate risk. This would cause the forward rate to be less than the expected future spot rate.

For example, suppose that in fact $E(r_2) = 8\%$. The liquidity premium therefore is negative: $f_2 - E(r_2) = 7.01\% - 8\% = -.99\%$. This is exactly opposite from the conclusion that we drew in the first case of the short-term investor. Clearly, whether forward rates will equal expected future short rates depends on investors' readiness to bear interest rate risk, as well as their willingness to hold bonds that do not correspond to their investment horizons.

15.4   Theories of the Term Structure

The Expectations Hypothesis

The simplest theory of the term structure is the **expectations hypothesis.** A common version states that the forward rate equals the market consensus expectation of the future short interest rate; that is, $f_2 = E(r_2)$, and liquidity premiums are zero. If $f_2 = E(r_2)$, yields on long-term bonds depend only on expectations of future short rates. Therefore, we can use the forward rates derived from the yield curve to infer market expectations of future short rates. For example, with $(1 + y_2)^2 = (1 + r_1) \times (1 + f_2)$ from Equation 15.5, according to the expectations hypothesis, we may also conclude that $(1 + y_2)^2 = (1 + r_1) \times [1 + E(r_2)]$. The yield to maturity would thus be determined solely by current and expected future one-period interest rates. An upward-sloping yield curve would be clear evidence that investors anticipate increases in interest rates.

 Concept Check **15.6**

If the expectations hypothesis is valid, what can we conclude about the premiums necessary to induce investors to hold bonds of different maturities from their investment horizons?

The Expectations Hypothesis and Forward Inflation Rates

Forward rates derived from conventional bonds are nominal interest rates. But by using price-level-indexed bonds such as TIPS, we can also calculate forward *real* interest rates. Recall that the difference between the real rate and the nominal rate is approximately the expected inflation rate. Therefore, comparing real and nominal forward rates might give us a glimpse of the market's expectation of future inflation rates. The real versus nominal spread is a sort of forward inflation rate.

As part of its monetary policy, the Federal Reserve Board periodically reduces its target federal funds rate in an attempt to stimulate the economy. The following page capture from a Bloomberg screen shows the minute-by-minute spread between the 5-year forward nominal interest rate and forward real rate on one day the Fed announced such a policy change. The spread immediately widened at the announcement, signifying that the market expected the more expansionary monetary policy to eventually result in a higher inflation rate. The increase in the inflation rate implied by the graph is fairly mild, about .05%, from about 2.53% to 2.58%, but the impact of the announcement is very clear, and the speed of adjustment to the announcement was impressive.

By the way, nothing limits us to nominal bonds when using the expectations hypothesis. The nearby box points out that we can apply the theory to the term structure of real interest rates as well, and thereby learn something about market expectations of coming inflation rates.

Liquidity Preference Theory

We've seen that short-term investors will be unwilling to hold long-term bonds unless the forward rate exceeds the expected short interest rate, $f_2 > E(r_2)$, whereas long-term investors will be unwilling to hold short bonds unless $E(r_2) > f_2$. In other words, both groups of investors require a premium to hold bonds with maturities different from their investment horizons. Advocates of the **liquidity preference theory** of the term structure believe that short-term investors dominate the market so that the forward rate will generally exceed the expected short rate. The excess of f_2 over $E(r_2)$, the *liquidity premium,* is predicted to be positive.

 Concept Check **15.7**

The liquidity premium hypothesis also holds that *issuers* of bonds prefer to issue long-term bonds to lock in borrowing costs. How would this preference contribute to a positive liquidity premium?

To illustrate the differing implications of these theories for the term structure of interest rates, suppose the short interest rate is expected to be constant indefinitely. Specifically, suppose that $r_1 = 5\%$ and that $E(r_2) = 5\%$, $E(r_3) = 5\%$, and so on. Under the expectations hypothesis, the 2-year yield to maturity could be derived from the following:

$$(1 + y_2)^2 = (1 + r_1)\left[1 + E(r_2)\right]$$
$$= (1.05)(1.05)$$

so that y_2 equals 5%. Similarly, yields on bonds of all maturities would equal 5%.

In contrast, under the liquidity preference theory, f_2 would exceed $E(r_2)$. To illustrate, suppose the liquidity premium is 1%, so f_2 is 6%. Then, for 2-year bonds:

$$(1 + y_2)^2 = (1 + r_1)(1 + f_2)$$
$$= 1.05 \times 1.06 = 1.113$$

implying that $1 + y_2 = 1.055$. Similarly, if f_3 also equals 6%, then the yield on 3-year bonds would be determined by

$$(1 + y_3)^3 = (1 + r_1)(1 + f_2)(1 + f_3)$$
$$= 1.05 \times 1.06 \times 1.06 = 1.17978$$

implying that $1 + y_3 = 1.0567$. The plot of the yield curve in this situation would be given as in Figure 15.4, Panel A. Such an upward-sloping yield curve is commonly observed in practice.

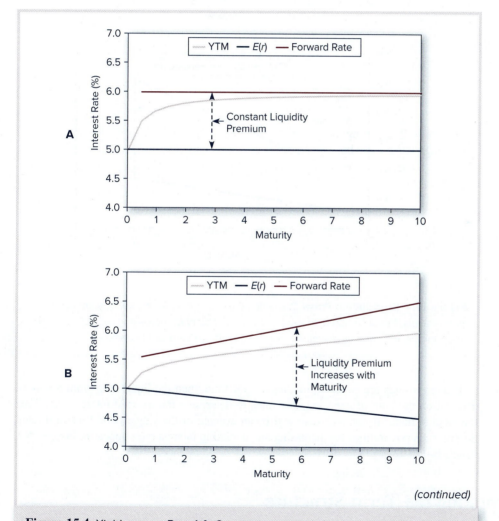

(continued)

Figure 15.4 Yield curves. ***Panel A:*** Constant expected short rate. Liquidity premium of 1%. Result: a rising yield curve. ***Panel B:*** Declining expected short rates. Increasing liquidity premiums. Result: a rising yield curve despite falling expected interest rates.

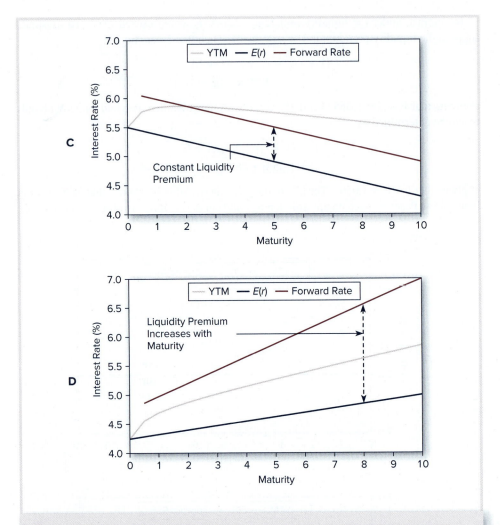

Figure 15.4 (Concluded) *Panel C:* Declining expected short rates. Constant liquidity premiums. Result: a hump-shaped yield curve. *Panel D:* Increasing expected short rates. Increasing liquidity premiums. Result: a sharply rising yield curve.

If interest rates are expected to change over time, then the liquidity premium may be overlaid on the path of expected spot rates to determine the forward interest rate. Then the yield to maturity for each date will be an average of the single-period forward rates. Several such possibilities for increasing and declining interest rates appear in Figure 15.4, Panels B–D.

15.5 Interpreting the Term Structure

If the yield curve reflects expectations of future short rates, then it offers a potentially powerful tool for fixed-income investors. If we can use the term structure to infer the expectations of other investors in the economy, we can use those expectations as benchmarks for our own analysis. For example, if we are relatively more optimistic than other investors that interest rates will fall, we will be more willing to extend our portfolios into longer-term bonds. Therefore, in this section, we will take a careful look at what information can be gleaned from a careful analysis of the term structure. Unfortunately, while the yield curve does reflect expectations of future interest rates, it also reflects other factors such as liquidity premiums. Moreover, forecasts of interest rate changes may have different investment implications depending on whether those changes are driven by changes in the expected inflation rate or the real rate, and this adds another layer of complexity to the interpretation of the term structure.

We have seen that under certainty, 1 plus the yield to maturity on a zero-coupon bond is simply the geometric average of 1 plus the future short rates that will prevail over the life of the bond. This is the meaning of Equation 15.1, which we give in general form here:

$$1 + y_n = [(1 + r_1)(1 + r_2) \cdots (1 + r_n)]^{1/n}$$

When future rates are uncertain, we modify Equation 15.1 by replacing future short rates with forward rates:

$$1 + y_n = [(1 + r_1)(1 + f_2)(1 + f_3) \cdots (1 + f_n)]^{1/n} \tag{15.7}$$

Thus there is a direct relationship between yields on various maturity bonds and forward interest rates.

First, we ask what factors can account for a rising yield curve. Mathematically, if the yield curve is rising, f_{n+1} must exceed y_n. In words, the yield curve is upward-sloping at any maturity date, n, for which the forward rate for the coming period is greater than the yield at that maturity. This rule follows from the notion of the yield to maturity as an average (albeit a geometric average) of forward rates.

If the yield curve rises as one moves to longer maturities, the extension to a longer maturity must result in the inclusion of a "new" forward rate higher than the average of the previously observed rates. This is analogous to the observation that if a new student's test score increases the class average, her score must exceed the class's average without her score. Similarly, to increase the yield to maturity, an above-average forward rate must be added to the other rates used in the averaging computation.

Example 15.6   Forward Rates and the Slopes of the Yield Curve

If the yield to maturity on 3-year zero-coupon bonds is 7%, then the yield on 4-year bonds will satisfy the following equation:

$$(1 + y_4)^4 = (1.07)^3 (1 + f_4)$$

If $f_4 = .07$, then y_4 also will equal .07. (Confirm this!) If f_4 is greater than 7%, y_4 will exceed 7%, and the yield curve will slope upward. For example, if $f_4 = .08$, then $(1 + y_4)^4 = (1.07)^3(1.08) = 1.3230$, and $y_4 = .0725$.

 Concept Check **15.8**

Look back at Table 15.1. Show that y_4 will exceed y_3 if and only if the forward interest rate for period 4 is greater than 7%, which is the yield to maturity on the 3-year bond, y_3.

Given that an upward-sloping yield curve implies a forward rate higher than the spot, or current, yield to maturity, we ask next what can account for that higher forward rate. The challenge is that there always are two possible answers to this question. Recall that the forward rate can be related to the expected future short rate according to:

$$f_n = E(r_n) + \text{Liquidity premium} \qquad (15.8)$$

where the liquidity premium might be necessary to induce investors to hold bonds of maturities that do not correspond to their preferred investment horizons.

By the way, the liquidity premium need not be positive, although that is the position generally taken by advocates of the liquidity premium hypothesis. We showed previously that if most investors have long-term horizons, the liquidity premium in principle could be negative.

In any case, Equation 15.8 shows that there are two reasons that the forward rate could be high. Either investors expect rising interest rates, meaning that $E(r_n)$ is high, or they require a large premium for holding longer-term bonds. Although it is tempting to infer from a rising yield curve that investors believe that interest rates will eventually increase, this does not necessarily follow. Indeed, Panel A in Figure 15.4 provides a simple counterexample. There, the short rate is expected to stay at 5% forever. Yet there is a constant 1% liquidity premium so that all forward rates are 6%. The result is that the yield curve continually rises, starting at a level of 5% for 1-year bonds, but eventually approaching 6% for long-term bonds as more and more forward rates at 6% are averaged into the yields to maturity.

Therefore, while expectations of increases in future interest rates can result in a rising yield curve, the converse is not true: A rising yield curve does not in and of itself imply expectations of higher future interest rates. Potential liquidity premiums confound any simple attempt to extract expectations from the term structure. But estimating the market's expectations is crucial because only by comparing your own expectations to those reflected in market prices can you determine whether you are relatively bullish or bearish on interest rates.

One very rough approach to deriving expected future spot rates is to assume that liquidity premiums are constant. An estimate of that premium can be subtracted from the forward rate to obtain the market's expected interest rate. For example, again making use of the example plotted in Panel A of Figure 15.4, the researcher would estimate from historical data that a typical liquidity premium in this economy is 1%. After calculating the forward rate from the yield curve to be 6%, the expectation of the future spot rate would be determined to be 5%.

This approach has little to recommend it for two reasons. First, it is next to impossible to obtain precise estimates of a liquidity premium. The general approach to doing so would be to compare forward rates and eventually realized future short rates and to calculate the average difference between the two. However, the deviations between the two values can be quite large and unpredictable because of unanticipated economic events that affect the realized short rate. The data are too noisy to calculate a reliable estimate of the expected premium. Second, there is no reason to believe that the liquidity premium should be constant. Figure 15.5 shows the rate of return variability of prices of long-term Treasury bonds since 1971. Interest rate risk fluctuated dramatically during the period. So we should expect risk premiums on various maturity bonds to fluctuate, and empirical evidence suggests that liquidity premiums do in fact fluctuate over time.

Still, very steep yield curves are interpreted by many market professionals as warning signs of impending rate increases. In fact, the yield curve is a good predictor of the business cycle as a whole, because long-term rates tend to rise in anticipation of an expansion in economic activity.

The usually observed upward slope of the yield curve, especially for short maturities, is the empirical basis for the liquidity premium doctrine that long-term bonds offer a positive liquidity premium. Because the yield curve normally has an upward slope due to risk premiums, a downward-sloping yield curve is taken as a strong indication that yields are more likely than not to fall. The prediction of declining interest rates is in turn often interpreted as a signal of a coming recession. For this reason, it is

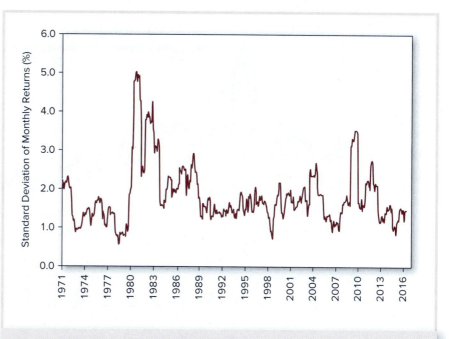

Figure 15.5 Price volatility of long-term Treasury bonds

not surprising that the slope of the yield curve is one of the key components of the index of leading economic indicators.

Figure 15.6 presents a history of yields on 90-day Treasury bills and 10-year Treasury bonds. Yields on the longer-term bonds *generally* exceed those on the bills, meaning that the yield curve generally slopes upward. Moreover, the exceptions to this rule do seem to precede episodes of falling short rates, which, if anticipated, would induce a downward-sloping yield curve. For example, the figure shows that 1980–1981 were years in which 90-day yields exceeded long-term yields. These years preceded both a drastic drop in the general level of rates and a steep recession.

Why might interest rates fall? There are two factors to consider: the real rate and the inflation premium. Recall that the nominal interest rate is composed of the real rate plus a factor to compensate for the effect of inflation:

$$1 + \text{Nominal rate} = (1 + \text{Real rate})(1 + \text{Inflation rate})$$

or, approximately,

$$\text{Nominal rate} \approx \text{Real rate} + \text{Inflation rate}$$

Therefore, an expected change in interest rates can be due to changes in either expected real rates or expected inflation rates. Usually, it is important to distinguish between these two possibilities because the economic environments associated with them may vary substantially. High real rates may indicate a rapidly expanding economy, high government budget deficits, and tight monetary policy. Although high inflation rates can arise out of a rapidly expanding economy, inflation also may be caused by rapid expansion of the money supply or supply-side shocks to the economy such as interruptions in oil supplies. These

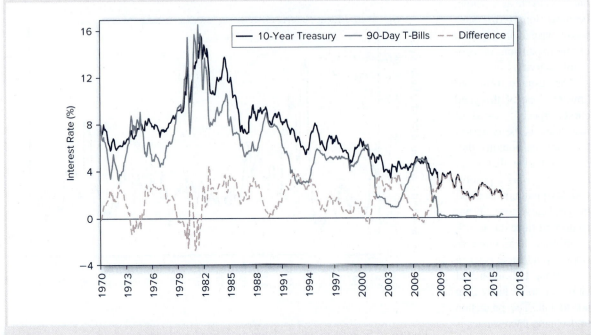

Figure 15.6 Term spread: Yields on 10-year versus 90-day Treasury securities

factors have very different implications for investments. Even if we conclude from an analysis of the yield curve that rates will fall, we need to analyze the macroeconomic factors that might cause such a decline.

15.6 Forward Rates as Forward Contracts

We have seen that forward rates may be derived from the yield curve, using Equation 15.5. In general, forward rates will not equal the eventually realized short rate, or even today's expectation of what that short rate will be. But there is still an important sense in which the forward rate is a market interest rate. Suppose that you wanted to arrange *now* to make a loan at some future date. You would agree today on the interest rate that will be charged, but the loan would not commence until some time in the future. How would the interest rate on such a "forward loan" be determined? Perhaps not surprisingly, it would be the forward rate of interest for the period of the loan. Let's use an example to see how this might work.

Example 15.7   Forward Interest Rate Contract

Suppose the price of 1-year maturity zero-coupon bonds with face value $1,000 is $952.38 and the price of 2-year zeros with $1,000 face value is $890. The yield to maturity on the 1-year bond is therefore 5%, while that on the 2-year bond is 6%. The forward rate for the second year is thus

$$f_2 = \frac{(1 + y_2)^2}{(1 + y_1)} - 1 = \frac{1.06^2}{1.05} - 1 = .0701, \text{ or } 7.01\%$$

Now consider the strategy laid out in the following table. In the first column we present data for this example, and in the last column we generalize. We denote by $B_0(T)$ today's price of a zero-coupon bond with face value $1,000 maturing at time T.

	Initial Cash Flow	In General
Buy a 1-year zero-coupon bond	−952.38	$-B_0(1)$
Sell 1.0701 2-year zeros	+890 × 1.0701 = 952.38	$+B_0(2) \times (1 + f_2)$
	0	0

The initial cash flow (at time 0) is zero. You pay $952.38, or in general $B_0(1)$, for a zero maturing in one year, and you receive $890, or in general $B_0(2)$, for each zero you sell maturing in two years. By selling 1.0701 of these bonds, you set your initial cash flow to zero.[4]

At time 1, the 1-year bond matures and you receive $1,000. At time 2, the 2-year maturity zero-coupon bonds that you sold mature, and you have to pay 1.0701 × $1,000 = $1,070.10. Your cash flow stream is shown in Figure 15.7, Panel A. Notice that you have created a "synthetic" forward loan: You effectively *will* borrow $1,000 a year from now and repay $1,070.10 a year later. The rate on this forward loan is therefore 7.01%, precisely equal to the forward rate for the second year.

A: Forward Rate = 7.01%

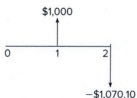

B: For a General Forward Rate. The short rates in the two periods are r_1 (which is observable today) and r_2 (which is not). The rate that can be locked in for a one-period-ahead loan is f_2.

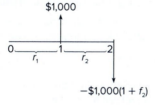

Figure 15.7 Engineering a synthetic forward loan

[4]Of course, one cannot sell a fraction of a bond, but you can think of this part of the transaction as follows. If you sold one of these bonds, you would effectively be borrowing $890 for a 2-year period. Selling 1.0701 of these bonds simply means that you are borrowing $890 × 1.0701 = $952.38.

In general, to construct the synthetic forward loan, you sell $(1 + f_2)$ 2-year zeros for every 1-year zero that you buy. This makes your initial cash flow zero because the prices of the 1- and 2-year zeros differ by the factor $(1 + f_2)$; notice that

$$B_0(1) = \frac{\$1,000}{(1 + y_1)} \text{ while } B_0(2) = \frac{\$1,000}{(1 + y_2)^2} = \frac{\$1,000}{(1 + y_1)(1 + f_2)}$$

Therefore, when you sell $(1 + f_2)$ 2-year zeros you generate just enough cash to buy one 1-year zero. Both zeros mature to a face value of $1,000, so the difference between the cash inflow at time 1 and the cash outflow at time 2 is the same factor, $1 + f_2$, as illustrated in Figure 15.7, Panel B. As a result, f_2 is the rate on the forward loan.

Obviously, you can construct a synthetic forward loan for periods beyond the second year, and you can construct such loans for multiple periods. For example, if you want to obtain a forward loan that begins in year 3 and ends in year 5, you would issue a 5-year zero-coupon bond (thus borrowing for five years) and buy a 3-year zero (thus lending for three years). Your borrowing and lending positions cancel out for the first three years, effectively leaving you with a borrowing position that starts after year 3 and continues until the end of year 5. Problems 18 and 19 at the end of the chapter lead you through the details of some of these variants.

 Concept Check **15.9**

Suppose that the price of 3-year zero-coupon bonds is $816.30. What is the forward rate for the third year? How would you construct a synthetic 1-year forward loan that commences at $t = 2$ and matures at $t = 3$?

SUMMARY

1. The term structure of interest rates refers to the interest rates for various terms to maturity embodied in the prices of default-free zero-coupon bonds.

2. In a world of certainty, all investments must provide equal total returns for any investment period. Short-term holding-period returns on all bonds would be equal in a risk-free economy; all returns would be equal to the rate available on short-term bonds. Similarly, total returns from rolling over short-term bonds over longer periods would equal the total return available from long-maturity bonds.

3. The forward rate of interest is the break-even future interest rate that would equate the total return from a rollover strategy to that of a longer-term zero-coupon bond. It is defined by the equation

$$(1 + y_{n-1})^{n-1}(1 + f_n) = (1 + y_n)^n$$

where n is a given number of periods from today. This equation can be used to show that yields to maturity and forward rates are related by the equation

$$(1 + y_n)^n = (1 + r_1)(1 + f_2)(1 + f_3) \cdots (1 + f_n)$$

4. A common version of the expectations hypothesis holds that forward interest rates are unbiased estimates of expected future interest rates. However, there are good reasons to believe that forward rates differ from expected short rates because of a risk premium known as a *liquidity premium*. A positive liquidity premium can cause the yield curve to slope upward even if no increase in short rates is anticipated.

5. The existence of liquidity premiums makes it extremely difficult to infer expected future interest rates from the yield curve. Such an inference would be made easier if we could assume the

liquidity premium remained reasonably stable over time. However, both empirical and theoretical considerations cast doubt on the constancy of that premium.

6. Forward rates are market interest rates in the important sense that commitments to forward (i.e., deferred) borrowing or lending arrangements can be made at these rates.

KEY TERMS

term structure of interest rates	pure yield curve	forward interest rate
yield curve	on-the-run yield curve	liquidity premium
bond stripping	spot rate	expectations hypothesis
bond reconstitution	short rate	liquidity preference theory

KEY EQUATIONS

Forward rate of interest: $1 + f_n = \dfrac{(1 + y_n)^n}{(1 + y_{n-1})^{n-1}}$

Yield to maturity given sequence of forward rates: $1 + y_n = [(1 + r_1)(1 + f_2)(1 + f_3) \cdots (1 + f_n)]^{1/n}$

Liquidity premium = Forward rate − Expected short rate

PROBLEM SETS

1. What is the relationship between forward rates and the market's expectation of future short rates? Explain in the context of both the expectations hypothesis and the liquidity preference theory of the term structure of interest rates.

2. Under the expectations hypothesis, if the yield curve is upward-sloping, the market must expect an increase in short-term interest rates. True/false/uncertain? Why?

3. Under the liquidity preference theory, if inflation is expected to be falling over the next few years, long-term interest rates will be higher than short-term rates. True/false/uncertain? Why?

4. If the liquidity preference hypothesis is true, what shape should the term structure curve have in a period where interest rates are expected to be constant?

   a. Upward sloping.
   b. Downward sloping.
   c. Flat.

5. Which of the following is true according to the pure expectations theory? Forward rates:

   a. Exclusively represent expected future short rates.
   b. Are biased estimates of market expectations.
   c. Always overestimate future short rates.

6. Assuming the pure expectations theory is correct, an upward-sloping yield curve implies:

   a. Interest rates are expected to increase in the future.
   b. Longer-term bonds are riskier than short-term bonds.
   c. Interest rates are expected to decline in the future.

7. The following is a list of prices for zero-coupon bonds of various maturities.

   a. Calculate the yield to maturity for a bond with a maturity of (i) one year; (ii) two years; (iii) three years; (iv) four years.
   b. Calculate the forward rate for (i) the second year; (ii) the third year; (iii) the fourth year.

Maturity (years)	Price of Bond
1	$943.40
2	898.47
3	847.62
4	792.16

8. *a.* Assuming that the expectations hypothesis is valid, compute the expected price of the 4-year
    bond in Problem 7 at the end of (i) the first year; (ii) the second year; (iii) the third year;
    (iv) the fourth year.

    b. What is the rate of return of the bond in years 1, 2, 3, and 4? Conclude that the expected
    return equals the forward rate for each year.

9. Consider the following $1,000 par value zero-coupon bonds:

Bond	Years to Maturity	YTM(%)
A	1	5%
B	2	6
C	3	6.5
D	4	7

According to the expectations hypothesis, what is the market's expectation of the yield curve
one year from now? Specifically, what are the expected values of next year's yields on bonds
with maturities of (*a*) one year? (*b*) two years? (*c*) three years?

10. The term structure for zero-coupon bonds is currently:

Maturity (years)	YTM (%)
1	4%
2	5
3	6

Next year at this time, *you* expect it to be:

Maturity (years)	YTM (%)
1	5%
2	6
3	7

a. What do *you* expect the rate of return to be over the coming year on a 3-year zero-coupon
bond?

b. Under the expectations theory, what yields to maturity does *the market* expect to observe on
1- and 2-year zeros at the end of the year?

c. Is the market's expectation of the return on the 3-year bond greater or less than yours?

11. The yield to maturity on 1-year zero-coupon bonds is currently 7%; the YTM on 2-year zeros is
8%. The Treasury plans to issue a 2-year maturity *coupon* bond, paying coupons once per year
with a coupon rate of 9%. The face value of the bond is $100.

a. At what price will the bond sell?

b. What will the yield to maturity on the bond be?

c. If the expectations theory of the yield curve is correct, what is the market expectation of the
price for which the bond will sell next year?

d. Recalculate your answer to part (*c*) if you believe in the liquidity preference theory and you
believe that the liquidity premium is 1%.

12. Below is a list of prices for zero-coupon bonds of various maturities.

Maturity (years)	Price of $1,000 Par Bond (zero-coupon)
1	$943.40
2	873.52
3	816.37

a. An 8.5% coupon $1,000 par bond pays an annual coupon and will mature in three years.
What should the yield to maturity on the bond be?

b. If at the end of the first year the yield curve flattens out at 8%, what will be the 1-year
holding-period return on the coupon bond?

13. Prices of zero-coupon bonds reveal the following pattern of forward rates:

Year	Forward Rate
1	5%
2	7
3	8

In addition to the zero-coupon bond, investors also may purchase a 3-year bond making annual payments of $60 with par value $1,000.

a. What is the price of the coupon bond?
b. What is the yield to maturity of the coupon bond?
c. Under the expectations hypothesis, what is the expected realized compound yield of the coupon bond?
d. If you forecast that the yield curve in one year will be flat at 7%, what is your forecast for the expected rate of return on the coupon bond for the 1-year holding period?

14. You observe the following term structure:

	Effective Annual YTM
1-year zero-coupon bond	6.1%
2-year zero-coupon bond	6.2
3-year zero-coupon bond	6.3
4-year zero-coupon bond	6.4

a. If you believe that the term structure next year will be the same as today's, calculate the return on (i) the 1-year zero and (ii) the 4-year zero.
b. Which bond provides a greater expected 1-year return?
c. Redo your answers to parts (a) and (b) if you believe in the expectations hypothesis.

15. The yield to maturity (YTM) on 1-year zero-coupon bonds is 5%, and the YTM on 2-year zeros is 6%. The YTM on 2-year-maturity coupon bonds with coupon rates of 12% (paid annually) is 5.8%.

a. What arbitrage opportunity is available for an investment banking firm?
b. What is the profit on the activity?

16. Suppose that a 1-year zero-coupon bond with face value $100 currently sells at $94.34, while a 2-year zero sells at $84.99. You are considering the purchase of a 2-year-maturity bond making *annual* coupon payments. The face value of the bond is $100, and the coupon rate is 12% per year.

a. What is the yield to maturity of the 2-year zero?
b. What is the yield to maturity of the 2-year coupon bond?
c. What is the forward rate for the second year?
d. According to the expectations hypothesis, what are (i) the expected price of the coupon bond at the end of the first year and (ii) the expected holding-period return on the coupon bond over the first year?
e. Will the expected rate of return be higher or lower if you accept the liquidity preference hypothesis?

17. The current yield curve for default-free zero-coupon bonds is as follows:

Maturity (years)	YTM (%)
1	10%
2	11
3	12

a. What are the implied 1-year forward rates?
b. Assume that the pure expectations hypothesis of the term structure is correct. If market expectations are accurate, what will be the yield to maturity on 1-year zero-coupon bonds next year?

    c. What about the yield on 2-year zeros?

    d. If you purchase a 2-year zero-coupon bond now, what is the expected total rate of return over the next year? (*Hint:* Compute the current and expected future prices.) Ignore taxes.

    e. What is the expected total rate of return over the next year on a 3-year zero-coupon bond?

    f. What should be the current price of a 3-year maturity bond with a 12% coupon rate paid annually?

    g. If you purchased the coupon bond at the price you computed in part (*f*), what would your total expected rate of return be over the next year (coupon plus price change)? Ignore taxes.

18. Suppose that the prices of zero-coupon bonds with various maturities are given in the following table. The face value of each bond is $1,000.

Maturity (years)	Price
1	$925.93
2	853.39
3	782.92
4	715.00
5	650.00

    a. Calculate the forward rate of interest for each year.

    b. How could you construct a 1-year forward loan beginning in year 3? Confirm that the rate on that loan equals the forward rate.

    c. Repeat part (*b*) for a 1-year forward loan beginning in year 4.

19. Use the data from Problem 18. Suppose that you want to construct a *2-year* maturity forward loan commencing in 3 years.

    a. Suppose that you buy *today* one 3-year maturity zero-coupon bond. How many 5-year maturity zeros would you have to sell to make your initial cash flow equal to zero?

    b. What are the cash flows on this strategy in each year?

    c. What is the effective 2-year interest rate on the effective 3-year-ahead forward loan?

    d. Confirm that the effective 2-year forward interest rate equals $(1 + f_4) \times (1 + f_5) - 1$. You therefore can interpret the 2-year loan rate as a 2-year forward rate for the last two years. Alternatively, show that the effective 2-year forward rate equals

$$\frac{(1 + y_5)^5}{(1 + y_3)^3} - 1$$

CFA®
PROBLEMS

1. Briefly explain why bonds of different maturities have different yields in terms of the expectations and liquidity preference hypotheses. Briefly describe the implications of each hypothesis when the yield curve is (1) upward-sloping and (2) downward-sloping.

2. Which one of the following statements about the term structure of interest rates is true?

    a. The expectations hypothesis indicates a flat yield curve if anticipated future short-term rates exceed current short-term rates.

    b. The expectations hypothesis contends that the long-term rate is equal to the anticipated short-term rate.

    c. The liquidity premium theory indicates that, all else being equal, longer maturities will have lower yields.

    d. The liquidity preference theory contends that lenders prefer to buy securities at the short end of the yield curve.

3. The following table shows yields to maturity of zero-coupon Treasury securities.

Term to Maturity (years)	Yield to Maturity (%)
1	3.50%
2	4.50
3	5.00
4	5.50
5	6.00
10	6.60

  a. Calculate the forward 1-year rate of interest for year 3.
  b. Describe the conditions under which the calculated forward rate would be an unbiased estimate of the 1-year spot rate of interest for that year.
  c. Assume that a few months earlier, the forward 1-year rate of interest for that year had been significantly higher than it is now. What factors could account for the decline in the forward rate?

4. The 6-month Treasury bill spot rate is 4%, and the 1-year Treasury bill spot rate is 5%. What is the implied 6-month forward rate for six months from now?

5. The tables below show, respectively, the characteristics of two annual-pay bonds from the same issuer with the same priority in the event of default, and spot interest rates. Neither bond's price is consistent with the spot rates. Using the information in these tables, recommend either bond A or bond B for purchase.

Bond Characteristics

	Bond A	Bond B
Coupons	Annual	Annual
Maturity	3 years	3 years
Coupon rate	10%	6%
Yield to maturity	10.65%	10.75%
Price	98.40	88.34

Spot Interest Rates

Term (years)	Spot Rates (zero-coupon)
1	5%
2	8
3	11

6. Sandra Kapple is a fixed-income portfolio manager who works with large institutional clients. Kapple is meeting with Maria VanHusen, consultant to the Star Hospital Pension Plan, to discuss management of the fund's approximately $100 million Treasury bond portfolio. The current U.S. Treasury yield curve is given in the following table. VanHusen states, "Given the large differential between 2- and 10-year yields, the portfolio would be expected to experience a higher return over a 10-year horizon by buying 10-year Treasuries, rather than buying 2-year Treasuries and reinvesting the proceeds into 2-year T-bonds at each maturity date."

Maturity	Yield	Maturity	Yield
1 year	2.00%	6 years	4.15%
2	2.90	7	4.30
3	3.50	8	4.45
4	3.80	9	4.60
5	4.00	10	4.70

a. Indicate whether VanHusen's conclusion is correct, based on the pure expectations hypothesis.

b. VanHusen discusses with Kapple alternative theories of the term structure of interest rates and gives her the following information about the U.S. Treasury market:

Maturity (years)	2	3	4	5	6	7	8	9	10
Liquidity premium (%)	0.55	0.55	0.65	0.75	0.90	1.10	1.20	1.50	1.60

Use this additional information and the liquidity preference theory to determine what the slope of the yield curve implies about the direction of future expected short-term interest rates.

7. A portfolio manager at Superior Trust Company is structuring a fixed-income portfolio to meet the objectives of a client. The portfolio manager compares coupon U.S. Treasuries with zero-coupon stripped U.S. Treasuries and observes a significant yield advantage for the stripped bonds:

Term	Coupon U.S. Treasuries	Zero-Coupon Stripped U.S. Treasuries
3 years	5.50%	5.80%
7	6.75	7.25
10	7.25	7.60
30	7.75	8.20

Briefly discuss why zero-coupon stripped U.S. Treasuries could have higher yields to maturity than coupon U.S. Treasuries with the same final maturity.

8. The shape of the U.S. Treasury yield curve appears to reflect two expected Federal Reserve reductions in the federal funds rate. The current short-term interest rate is 5%. The first reduction of approximately 50 basis points (bp) is expected six months from now and the second reduction of approximately 50 bp is expected one year from now. The current U.S. Treasury term premiums are 10 bp per year for each of the next three years (out through the 3-year benchmark).

However, the market also believes that the Federal Reserve reductions will be reversed in a single 100-bp increase in the federal funds rate 2½ years from now. You expect liquidity premiums to remain 10 bp per year for each of the next three years (out through the 3-year benchmark).

Describe or draw the shape of the Treasury yield curve out through the 3-year benchmark. Which term structure theory supports the shape of the U.S. Treasury yield curve you've described?

9. U.S. Treasuries represent a significant holding in many pension portfolios. You decide to analyze the yield curve for U.S. Treasury notes.

a. Using the data in the table below, calculate the 5-year spot and forward rates assuming annual compounding. Show your calculations.

U.S. Treasury Note Yield Curve Data

Years to Maturity	Par Coupon Yield to Maturity	Calculated Spot Rates	Calculated Forward Rates
1	5.00	5.00	5.00
2	5.20	5.21	5.42
3	6.00	6.05	7.75
4	7.00	7.16	10.56
5	7.00	?	?

b. Define and describe each of the following three concepts:

   i. Short rate

   ii. Spot rate

   iii. Forward rate

   Explain how these concepts are related.

c. You are considering the purchase of a zero-coupon U.S. Treasury note with four years to maturity. On the basis of the above yield-curve analysis, calculate both the expected yield to maturity and the price for the security. Show your calculations.

10. The spot rates of interest for five U.S. Treasury securities are shown in the following exhibit. Assume all securities pay interest annually.

Spot Rates of Interest

Term to Maturity	Spot Rate of Interest
1 year	13.00%
2	12.00
3	11.00
4	10.00
5	9.00

a. Compute the 2-year implied forward rate for a deferred loan beginning in three years.

b. Compute the price of a 5-year annual-pay Treasury security with a coupon rate of 9% by using the information in the exhibit.

E-INVESTMENTS EXERCISES

Go to **stockcharts.com/freecharts/yieldcurve.php** where you will find a dynamic or "living" yield curve, a moving picture of the yield curve over time. Hit the *Animate* button to start the demonstration. Is the yield curve usually upward- or downward-sloping? What about today's yield curve? How much does the slope of the curve vary? Which varies more: short-term or long-term rates? Can you explain why this might be the case?

✔ SOLUTIONS TO CONCEPT CHECKS

1. The price of the 3-year bond paying a $40 coupon is

$$\frac{40}{1.05} + \frac{40}{1.06^2} + \frac{1040}{1.07^3} = 38.095 + 35.600 + 848.950 = \$922.65$$

At this price, the yield to maturity is 6.945% [$n = 3$; PV = (−)922.65; FV = 1,000; PMT = 40]. This bond's yield to maturity is closer to that of the 3-year zero-coupon bond than is the yield to maturity of the 10% coupon bond in Example 15.1. This makes sense: This bond's coupon rate is lower than that of the bond in Example 15.1. A greater fraction of its value is tied up in the final payment in the third year, and so it is not surprising that its yield is closer to that of a pure 3-year zero-coupon security.

2. We compare two investment strategies in a manner similar to Example 15.2:

Buy and hold 4-year zero = Buy 3-year zero; roll proceeds into 1-year bond

$$(1 + y_4)^4 = (1 + y_3)^3 \times (1 + r_4)$$
$$1.08^4 = 1.07^3 \times (1 + r_4)$$

which implies that $r_4 = 1.08^4/1.07^3 - 1 = .11056 = 11.056\%$. Now we confirm that the yield on the 4-year zero reflects the geometric average of the discount factors for the next 3 years:

$$1 + y_4 = [(1 + r_1) \times (1 + r_2) \times (1 + r_3) \times (1 + r_4)]^{1/4}$$
$$1.08 = [1.05 \times 1.0701 \times 1.09025 \times 1.11056]^{1/4}$$

3. The 3-year bond can be bought today for $1,000/1.07^3 = \$816.30$. Next year, it will have a remaining maturity of two years. The short rate in year 2 will be 7.01% and the short rate in year 3

will be 9.025%. Therefore, the bond's yield to maturity next year will be related to these short rates according to

$$(1 + y_2)^2 = 1.0701 \times 1.09025 = 1.1667$$

and its price next year will be $1,000/(1 + y_2)^2 = \$1,000/1.1667 = \$857.12$. The 1-year holding-period rate of return is therefore $(\$857.12 - \$816.30)/\$816.30 = .05$, or 5%.

4. The n-period *spot* rate is the yield to maturity on a zero-coupon bond with a maturity of n periods. The *short* rate for period n is the *one-period* interest rate that will prevail in period n. Finally, the *forward* rate for period n is the short rate that would satisfy a "break-even condition" equating the total returns on two n-period investment strategies. The first strategy is an investment in an n-period zero-coupon bond; the second is an investment in an $n - 1$ period zero-coupon bond "rolled over" into an investment in a one-period zero. Spot rates and forward rates are observable today, but because interest rates evolve with uncertainty, future short rates are not. *In the special case* in which there is no uncertainty in future interest rates, the forward rate calculated from the yield curve would equal the short rate that will prevail in that period.

5. $7\% - 1\% = 6\%$.

6. The risk premium will be zero.

7. If issuers prefer to issue long-term bonds, they will be willing to accept higher expected interest costs on long bonds over short bonds. This willingness combines with investors' demands for higher rates on long-term bonds to reinforce the tendency toward a positive liquidity premium.

8. In general, from Equation 15.5, $(1 + y_n)^n = (1 + y_{n-1})^{n-1} \times (1 + f_n)$. In this case, $(1 + y_4)^4 = (1.07)^3 \times (1 + f_4)$. If $f_4 = .07$, then $(1 + y_4)^4 = (1.07)^4$ and $y_4 = .07$. If f_4 is greater than .07, then y_4 also will be greater, and conversely if f_4 is less than .07, then y_4 will be as well.

9. The 3-year yield to maturity is $\left(\dfrac{1,000}{816.30} \right)^{1/3} - 1 = .07 = 7.0\%$

The forward rate for the third year is therefore

$$f_3 = \frac{(1 + y_3)^3}{(1 + y_2)^2} - 1 = \frac{1.07^3}{1.06^2} - 1 = .0903 = 9.03\%$$

(Alternatively, note that the ratio of the price of the 2-year zero to the price of the 3-year zero is $1 + f_3 = 1.0903$.) To construct the synthetic loan, buy one 2-year maturity zero, and sell 1.0903 3-year maturity zeros. Your initial cash flow is zero, your cash flow at time 2 is +$1,000, and your cash flow at time 3 is −$1,090.30, which corresponds to the cash flows on a 1-year forward loan commencing at time 2 with an interest rate of 9.03%.

Managing Bond Portfolios

IN THIS CHAPTER we turn to various fixed-income portfolio strategies, making a distinction between passive and active approaches. A *passive investment strategy* takes market prices of securities as set fairly. Rather than attempting to beat the market by exploiting superior information or insight, passive managers act to maintain an appropriate risk-return balance given market opportunities. One special case of passive management is an immunization strategy that attempts to insulate or immunize the portfolio from interest rate risk. In contrast, an *active investment strategy* attempts to achieve returns greater than those commensurate with the risk borne. In the context of bond management, this style of management can take two forms. Active managers use either interest rate forecasts to predict movements in the entire bond market or some form of intramarket analysis to identify particular sectors of the market or particular bonds that are relatively mispriced.

Because interest rate risk is crucial to formulating both active and passive strategies, we begin our discussion with an analysis of the sensitivity of bond prices to interest rate fluctuations. This sensitivity is measured by the duration of the bond, and we devote considerable attention to what determines bond duration. We discuss several passive investment strategies and show how duration-matching techniques can be used to immunize the holding-period return of a portfolio from interest rate risk. After examining the broad range of applications of the duration measure, we consider refinements in the way that interest rate sensitivity is measured, focusing on the concept of bond convexity. Duration is important in formulating active investment strategies as well, and we conclude the chapter with a discussion of active fixed-income strategies. These include policies based on interest rate forecasting as well as intramarket analysis that seeks to identify relatively attractive sectors or securities within the fixed-income market.

16.1 Interest Rate Risk

We have seen already that bond prices and yields are inversely related, and we know that interest rates can fluctuate substantially. As interest rates rise and fall, bondholders experience capital losses and gains. These gains or losses make fixed-income investments risky, even if the coupon and principal payments are guaranteed, as in the case of Treasury obligations.

Why do bond prices respond to interest rate fluctuations? Remember that in a competitive market all securities must offer investors fair expected rates of return. If a bond is issued with an 8% coupon when competitive yields are 8%, then it will sell at par value. If the market rate rises to 9%, however, who would be willing to pay par value for an 8% coupon bond? The bond price must fall until its expected return increases to the competitive level of 9%. Conversely, if the market rate falls to 7%, the 8% coupon on the bond will be attractive compared to yields on alternative investments. In response, investors eager for that return will bid up the bond price until the total rate of return for someone purchasing at that higher price is no better than the market rate.

Interest Rate Sensitivity

The sensitivity of bond prices to changes in market interest rates is obviously of great concern to investors. To gain some insight into the determinants of interest rate risk, turn to Figure 16.1, which presents the percentage change in price corresponding to changes in yield to maturity for four bonds that differ according to coupon rate, initial yield to

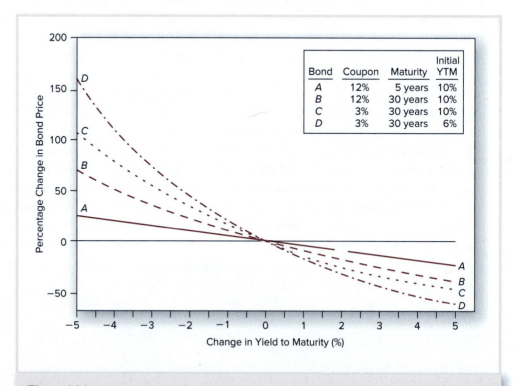

Figure 16.1 Change in bond price as a function of change in yield to maturity

maturity, and time to maturity. All four bonds illustrate that bond prices decrease when yields rise and that the price curve is convex, meaning that decreases in yields have bigger impacts on price than increases in yields of equal magnitude. We summarize these observations in the following two propositions:

1. *Bond prices and yields are inversely related: As yields increase, bond prices fall; as yields fall, bond prices rise.*
2. *An increase in a bond's yield to maturity results in a smaller price change than a decrease in yield of equal magnitude.*

Now compare the interest rate sensitivity of bonds *A* and *B*, which are identical except for maturity. Figure 16.1 shows that bond *B*, which has a longer maturity than bond *A*, exhibits greater sensitivity to interest rate changes. This illustrates another general property:

3. *Prices of long-term bonds tend to be more sensitive to interest rate changes than prices of short-term bonds.*

This is not surprising. If rates increase, for example, the bond is less valuable as its cash flows are discounted at a now-higher rate. The impact of the higher discount rate will be greater as that rate is applied to more-distant cash flows.

Notice that while bond *B* has six times the maturity of bond *A*, it has less than six times the interest rate sensitivity. Although interest rate sensitivity generally increases with maturity, it does so less than proportionally as bond maturity increases. Therefore, our fourth property is that:

4. *The sensitivity of bond prices to changes in yields increases at a decreasing rate as maturity increases. In other words, interest rate risk is less than proportional to bond maturity.*

Bonds *B* and *C*, which are alike in all respects except for coupon rate, illustrate another point. The lower-coupon bond exhibits greater sensitivity to changes in interest rates. This turns out to be a general property of bond prices:

5. *Interest rate risk is inversely related to the bond's coupon rate. Prices of low-coupon bonds are more sensitive to changes in interest rates than prices of high-coupon bonds.*

Finally, bonds *C* and *D* are identical except for the yield to maturity at which the bonds currently sell. Yet bond *C*, with a higher yield to maturity, is less sensitive to changes in yields. This illustrates our final property:

6. *The sensitivity of a bond's price to a change in its yield is inversely related to the yield to maturity at which the bond currently is selling.*

The first five of these general properties were described by Malkiel[1] and are sometimes known as Malkiel's bond-pricing relationships. The last property was demonstrated by Homer and Liebowitz.[2]

Maturity is a major determinant of interest rate risk. However, maturity alone is not sufficient to measure interest rate sensitivity. For example, bonds *B* and *C* in Figure 16.1 have the same maturity, but the higher-coupon bond has less price sensitivity to interest rate changes. Obviously, we need to know more than a bond's maturity to quantify its interest rate risk.

---

[1]Burton G. Malkiel, "Expectations, Bond Prices, and the Term Structure of Interest Rates," *Quarterly Journal of Economics* 76 (May 1962), pp. 197–218.

[2]Sidney Homer and Martin L. Liebowitz, *Inside the Yield Book: New Tools for Bond Market Strategy* (Englewood Cliffs, NJ: Prentice Hall, 1972).

Table 16.1

Prices of 8% coupon bond (coupons paid semiannually)

Yield to Maturity (APR)	T = 1 Year	T = 10 Years	T = 20 Years
8%	1,000.00	1,000.00	1,000.00
9%	990.64	934.96	907.99
Fall in price (%)*	0.94%	6.50%	9.20%

*Equals value of bond at a 9% yield to maturity divided by value of bond at (the original) 8% yield, minus 1.

To see why bond characteristics such as coupon rate or yield to maturity affect interest rate sensitivity, let's start with a simple numerical example. Table 16.1 gives bond prices for 8% semiannual coupon bonds at different yields to maturity and times to maturity, T. [The interest rates are expressed as annual percentage rates (APRs), meaning that the true six-month yield is doubled to obtain the stated annual yield.] The shortest-term bond falls in value by less than 1% when the interest rate increases from 8% to 9%. The 10-year bond falls by 6.5%, and the 20-year bond by over 9%.

Now look at a similar computation using a zero-coupon bond rather than the 8% coupon bond. The results are shown in Table 16.2. Notice that for each maturity, the price of the zero-coupon bond falls by a greater proportional amount than the price of the 8% coupon bond. Because we know that long-term bonds are more sensitive to interest rate movements than are short-term bonds, this observation suggests that in some sense a zero-coupon bond must represent a longer-term bond than an equal-time-to-maturity coupon bond.

In fact, this insight about the effective maturity of a bond is a useful one that we can make mathematically precise. To start, note that the times to maturity of the two bonds in this example are not perfect measures of the long- or short-term nature of the bonds. The 20-year 8% bond makes many coupon payments, most of which come years before the bond's maturity date. Each of these payments may be considered to have its own "maturity." In the previous chapter, we pointed out that it can be useful to view a coupon bond as a "portfolio" of coupon payments. The effective maturity of the bond is therefore some sort of average of the maturities of *all* the cash flows. The zero-coupon bond, by contrast, makes only one payment at maturity. Its time to maturity is, therefore, a well-defined concept.

Higher-coupon-rate bonds have a higher fraction of value tied to coupons rather than final payment of par value, and so the "portfolio of coupons" is more heavily weighted toward the earlier, short-maturity payments, which gives it lower "effective maturity." This explains Malkiel's fifth rule, that price sensitivity falls with coupon rate.

Similar logic explains our sixth rule, that price sensitivity falls with yield to maturity. A higher yield reduces the present value of all of the bond's payments, but more so for more-distant payments. Therefore, at a higher yield, a higher proportion of the bond's value is due to its earlier payments, which have lower effective maturity and interest rate sensitivity. The overall sensitivity of the bond price to changes in yields is thus lower.

Table 16.2

Prices of zero-coupon bond (semiannual compounding)

Yield to Maturity (APR)	T = 1 Year	T = 10 Years	T = 20 Years
8%	924.56	456.39	208.29
9%	915.73	414.64	171.93
Fall in price (%)*	0.96%	9.15%	17.46%

*Equals value of bond at a 9% yield to maturity divided by value of bond at (the original) 8% yield, minus 1.

Duration

To deal with the ambiguity of the "maturity" of a bond making many payments, we need a measure of the average maturity of the bond's promised cash flows. We would also like to use such an effective maturity measure as a guide to the sensitivity of a bond to interest rate changes, because we have noted that price sensitivity tends to increase with time to maturity.

Frederick Macaulay[3] termed the effective maturity concept the *duration* of the bond. **Macaulay's duration** equals the weighted average of the times to each coupon or principal payment. The weight associated with each payment time clearly should be related to the "importance" of that payment to the value of the bond. In fact, the weight applied to each payment time is the proportion of the total value of the bond accounted for by that payment, that is, the present value of the payment divided by the bond price.

We define the weight, w_t, associated with the cash flow made at time t (denoted CF_t) as:

$$w_t = \frac{CF_t/(1 + y)^t}{\text{Bond price}}$$

where y is the bond's yield to maturity. The numerator on the right-hand side of this equation is the present value of the cash flow occurring at time t while the denominator is the value of all the bond's payments. These weights sum to 1.0 because the sum of the cash flows discounted at the yield to maturity equals the bond price.

Using these values to calculate the weighted average of the times until the receipt of each of the bond's payments, we obtain Macaulay's duration formula:

$$D = \sum_{t=1}^{T} t \times w_t \tag{16.1}$$

As an example of the application of Equation 16.1, we derive in Spreadsheet 16.1 the durations of an 8% coupon and zero-coupon bond, each with two years to maturity. We

	A	B	C	D	E	F	G
1			Time until		PV of CF		Column (C)
2			Payment		(Discount rate =		times
3		Period	(Years)	Cash Flow	5% per period)	Weight*	Column (F)
4	A. 8% coupon bond	1	0.5	40	38.095	0.0395	0.0197
5		2	1.0	40	36.281	0.0376	0.0376
6		3	1.5	40	34.554	0.0358	0.0537
7		4	2.0	1040	855.611	0.8871	1.7741
8	Sum:				964.540	1.0000	1.8852
9							
10	B. Zero-coupon	1	0.5	0	0.000	0.0000	0.0000
11		2	1.0	0	0.000	0.0000	0.0000
12		3	1.5	0	0.000	0.0000	0.0000
13		4	2.0	1000	822.702	1.0000	2.0000
14	Sum:				822.702	1.0000	2.0000
15							
16	Semiannual int rate:	0.05					
17							
18	*Weight = Present value of each payment (column E) divided by the bond price.						

Spreadsheet 16.1

Calculating the duration of two bonds

Column sums subject to rounding error.

[3]Frederick Macaulay, *Some Theoretical Problems Suggested by the Movements of Interest Rates, Bond Yields, and Stock Prices in the United States since 1856* (New York: National Bureau of Economic Research, 1938).

	A	B	C	D	E	F	G
1			Time until		PV of CF		Column (C)
2			Payment		(Discount rate =		times
3		Period	(Years)	Cash Flow	5% per period)	Weight	Column (F)
4	A. 8% coupon bond	1	0.5	40	=D4/(1+$B$16)^B4	=E4/E$8	=F4*C4
5		2	1	40	=D5/(1+$B$16)^B5	=E5/E$8	=F5*C5
6		3	1.5	40	=D6/(1+$B$16)^B6	=E6/E$8	=F6*C6
7		4	2	1040	=D7/(1+$B$16)^B7	=E7/E$8	=F7*C7
8	Sum:				=SUM(E4:E7)	=SUM(F4:F7)	=SUM(G4:G7)
9							
10	B. Zero-coupon	1	0.5	0	=D10/(1+$B$16)^B10	=E10/E$14	=F10*C10
11		2	1	0	=D11/(1+$B$16)^B11	=E11/E$14	=F11*C11
12		3	1.5	0	=D12/(1+$B$16)^B12	=E12/E$14	=F12*C12
13		4	2	1000	=D13/(1+$B$16)^B13	=E13/E$14	=F13*C13
14	Sum:				=SUM(E10:E13)	=SUM(F10:F13)	=SUM(G10:G13)
15							
16	Semiannual int rate:	0.05					

Spreadsheet 16.2

Spreadsheet formulas for calculating duration

assume that the yield to maturity on each bond is 10%, or 5% per half-year. The present value of each payment is discounted at 5% per period for the number of (semiannual) periods shown in column B. The weight associated with each payment time (column F) is the present value of the payment for that period (column E) divided by the bond price (the sum of the present values in column E).

The numbers in column G are the products of time to payment and payment weight. Each of these products corresponds to one of the terms in Equation 16.1. According to that equation, we can calculate the duration of each bond by adding the numbers in column G.

The duration of the zero-coupon bond is exactly equal to its time to maturity, two years. This makes sense, because with only one payment, the average time until payment must be the bond's maturity. In contrast, the 2-year coupon bond has a shorter duration of 1.8852 years.

Spreadsheet 16.2 shows the spreadsheet formulas used to produce the entries in Spreadsheet 16.1. The inputs in the spreadsheet—specifying the cash flows the bond will pay—are given in columns B–D. In column E we calculate the present value of each cash flow using the assumed yield to maturity, in column F we calculate the weights for Equation 16.1, and in column G we compute the product of time to payment and payment weight. Each of these terms corresponds to one of the values that is summed in Equation 16.1. The sums computed in cells G8 and G14 are therefore the durations of each bond. Using the spreadsheet, you can easily answer several "what if" questions such as the one in Concept Check 16.1.

 Concept Check **16.1**

Suppose the interest rate decreases to 9% as an annual percentage rate. What will happen to the prices and durations of the two bonds in Spreadsheet 16.1?

Duration is a key concept in fixed-income portfolio management for at least three reasons. First, as we have noted, it is a simple summary statistic of the effective average maturity of the portfolio. Second, it turns out to be an essential tool in immunizing portfolios from interest rate risk. We explore this application in Section 16.3. Third, duration is a measure of the interest rate sensitivity of a portfolio, which we explore here.

We have seen that a bond's price sensitivity to interest rate changes generally increases with maturity. Duration enables us to quantify this relationship. Specifically, it can be shown that when interest rates change, the proportional change in a bond's price can be related to the change in its yield to maturity, y, according to the rule

$$\frac{\Delta P}{P} = -D \times \left[\frac{\Delta(1 + y)}{1 + y} \right] \tag{16.2}$$

The proportional price change equals the proportional change in 1 plus the bond's yield times the bond's duration.

Practitioners commonly use Equation 16.2 in a slightly different form. They define **modified duration** as $D^* = D/(1 + y)$, note that $\Delta(1 + y) = \Delta y$, and rewrite Equation 16.2 as

$$\frac{\Delta P}{P} = -D^* \Delta y \tag{16.3}$$

The percentage change in bond price is just the product of modified duration and the change in the bond's yield to maturity. Because the percentage change in the bond price is proportional to modified duration, modified duration is a natural measure of the bond's exposure to changes in interest rates. Actually, as we will see below, Equation 16.2, or equivalently, Equation 16.3, is only approximately valid for large changes in the bond's yield. The approximation becomes exact as one considers smaller, or localized, changes in yields.[4]

Example 16.1   Duration and Interest Rate Risk

Consider the 2-year maturity, 8% coupon bond in Spreadsheet 16.1 making semiannual coupon payments and selling at a price of $964.540, for a yield to maturity of 10%. The duration of this bond is 1.8852 years. For comparison, we will also consider a zero-coupon bond with maturity *and duration* of 1.8852 years. As we found in Spreadsheet 16.1, because the coupon bond makes payments semiannually, it is best to treat one "period" as a half-year. So the duration of each bond is 1.8852 × 2 = 3.7704 (semiannual) periods, with a per-period interest rate of 5%. The modified duration of each bond is therefore 3.7704/1.05 = 3.591 semiannual periods.

Suppose the semiannual interest rate increases from 5% to 5.01%. According to Equation 16.3, the bond prices should fall by

$$\Delta P/P = -D^* \Delta y = -3.591 \times .01\% = -.03591\%$$

---

[4]Students of calculus will recognize that modified duration is proportional to the derivative of the bond's price with respect to changes in the bond's yield. For small changes in yield, Equation 16.3 can be restated as

$$D^* = -\frac{1}{P}\frac{dP}{dy}$$

As such, it gives a measure of the slope of the bond price curve only in the neighborhood of the current price. In fact, Equation 16.3 can be derived by differentiating the following bond pricing equation with respect to y:

$$P = \sum_{t=1}^{T} \frac{CF_t}{(1 + y)^t}$$

where CF_t is the cash flow paid to the bondholder at date t; CF_t represents either a coupon payment before maturity or final coupon plus par value at the maturity date.

Now compute the price change of each bond directly. The coupon bond, which initially sells at $964.540, falls to $964.1942 when its yield increases to 5.01%, which is a percentage decline of .0359%. The zero-coupon bond initially sells for $1,000/1.05$^{3.7704}$ = 831.9704. At the higher yield, it sells for $1,000/1.0501$^{3.7704}$ = 831.6717. This price also falls by .0359%.

We conclude that bonds with equal durations do in fact have equal interest rate sensitivity and that (at least for small changes in yields) the percentage price change is the modified duration times the change in yield.[5]

 Concept Check **16.2**

a. In Concept Check 16.1, you calculated the price and duration of a 2-year maturity, 8% coupon bond making semiannual coupon payments when the market interest rate is 9%. Now suppose the interest rate increases to 9.05%. Calculate the new value of the bond and the percentage change in the bond's price.

b. Calculate the percentage change in the bond's price predicted by the duration formula in Equation 16.2 or 16.3. Compare this value to your answer for part (a).

What Determines Duration?

Malkiel's bond price relations, which we laid out in the previous section, characterize the determinants of interest rate sensitivity. Duration allows us to quantify that sensitivity. For example, if we wish to speculate on interest rates, duration tells us how strong a bet we are making. Conversely, if we wish to remain "neutral" on rates, and simply match the interest rate sensitivity of a chosen bond-market index, duration allows us to measure that sensitivity and mimic it in our own portfolio. For these reasons, it is crucial to understand the determinants of duration. Therefore, in this section, we present several "rules" that summarize most of its important properties. These rules are also illustrated in Figure 16.2, where durations of bonds of various coupon rates, yields to maturity, and times to maturity are plotted.

We have already established:

Rule 1 for Duration   The duration of a zero-coupon bond equals its time to maturity.

We have also seen that a coupon bond has a lower duration than a zero with equal maturity because coupons early in the bond's life lower the bond's weighted average time until payments. This illustrates another general property:

Rule 2 for Duration   Holding maturity constant, a bond's duration is lower when the coupon rate is higher.

This property corresponds to Malkiel's fifth relationship and is due to the impact of early coupon payments on the weighted-average maturity of a bond's payments. The higher these coupons, the higher the weights on the early payments and the lower the weighted average maturity of the payments. In other words, a higher fraction of the total value of the bond is tied up in the (earlier) coupon payments, whose values are relatively insensitive to yields, rather than the (later and more yield-sensitive) repayment of par value.

---

[5]Notice another implication of Example 16.1: We see from the example that when the bond makes payments semiannually, it is best to treat each payment period as a half-year. This implies that when we calculate modified duration, we divide Macaulay's duration by (1 + Semiannual yield to maturity). It is more common to write this divisor as (1 + Bond equivalent yield/2). In general, if a bond were to make n payments a year, modified duration would be related to Macaulay's duration by $D^* = D/(1 + y_{BEY}/n)$.

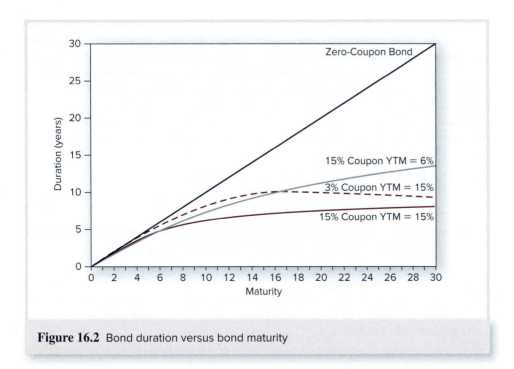

Figure 16.2 Bond duration versus bond maturity

Compare the plots in Figure 16.2 of the durations of the 3% and 15% coupon bonds with identical yields of 15%. The plot of the duration of the 15% coupon bond lies below the corresponding plot for the 3% coupon bond.

Rule 3 for Duration   Holding the coupon rate constant, a bond's duration generally increases with its time to maturity. Duration always increases with maturity for bonds selling at par or at a premium to par.

This property of duration corresponds to Malkiel's third relationship, and it is fairly intuitive. What is surprising is that duration need not always increase with time to maturity. It turns out that for some deep-discount bonds (such as the 3% coupon bond in Figure 16.2), duration may eventually fall with increases in maturity. However, for virtually all traded bonds, it is safe to assume that duration increases with maturity.

Notice in Figure 16.2 that the maturity and duration of the zero-coupon bond are equal. However, for coupon bonds, duration increases by less than a year with a year's increase in maturity.

Although long-maturity bonds generally will be high-duration bonds, duration is a better measure of the long-term nature of the bond because it also accounts for coupon payments. Time to maturity is an adequate statistic only when the bond pays no coupons; then, maturity and duration are equal.

Notice also in Figure 16.2 that the two 15% coupon bonds have different durations when they sell at different yields to maturity. The lower-yield bond has longer duration. This makes sense, because at lower yields the more distant payments made by the bond have relatively greater present values and account for a greater share of the bond's total value. Thus in the weighted-average calculation of duration the distant payments receive greater weights, which results in a higher duration measure. This establishes rule 4:

Rule 4 for Duration   Holding other factors constant, the duration of a coupon bond is higher when the bond's yield to maturity is lower.

As we noted above, the intuition for this property is that while a higher yield reduces the present value of all of the bond's payments, it reduces the value of more-distant payments by a greater proportional amount. Therefore, at higher yields a higher fraction of the total value of the bond lies in its earlier payments, thereby reducing effective maturity. Rule 4, which is the sixth bond-pricing relationship above, applies to coupon bonds. For zeros, of course, duration equals time to maturity, regardless of the yield to maturity.

Finally, we present a formula for the duration of a perpetuity. This rule is derived from and consistent with the formula for duration given in Equation 16.1 but may be easier to use for infinitely lived bonds.

Rule 5 for Duration   The duration of a level perpetuity is

$$\text{Duration of perpetuity} = \frac{1+y}{y} \tag{16.4}$$

For example, at a 10% yield, the duration of a perpetuity that pays $100 once a year forever is $1.10/.10 = 11$ years, but at an 8% yield it is $1.08/.08 = 13.5$ years.

 Concept Check **16.3**

> Show that the duration of the perpetuity increases as the interest rate decreases in accordance with rule 4.

Equation 16.4 makes it obvious that maturity and duration can differ substantially. The maturity of the perpetuity is infinite, whereas the duration of the instrument at a 10% yield is only 11 years. The present-value-weighted cash flows early on in the life of the perpetuity dominate the computation of duration.

Notice from Figure 16.2 that as their maturities become ever longer, the durations of the two coupon bonds with yields of 15% both converge to the duration of the perpetuity with the same yield, 7.67 years.

The equations for the durations of coupon bonds are somewhat tedious and spreadsheets like Spreadsheet 16.1 are cumbersome to modify for different maturities and coupon rates. Moreover, they assume that the bond is at the beginning of a coupon payment period. Fortunately, spreadsheet programs such as Excel come with generalizations of these equations that can accommodate bonds between coupon payment dates. Spreadsheet 16.3 illustrates how to use Excel to compute duration. The spreadsheet uses many of the same conventions as the bond-pricing spreadsheets described in Chapter 14.

Spreadsheet 16.3

Using Excel functions to compute duration

	A	B	C
1	**Inputs**		**Formula in column B**
2	Settlement date	1/1/2000	=DATE(2000,1,1)
3	Maturity date	1/1/2002	=DATE(2002,1,1)
4	Coupon rate	0.08	0.08
5	Yield to maturity	0.10	0.10
6	Coupons per year	2	2
7			
8	**Outputs**		
9	Macaulay duration	1.8852	=DURATION(B2,B3,B4,B5,B6)
10	Modified duration	1.7955	=MDURATION(B2,B3,B4,B5,B6)

Maturity (years)	Coupon Rates (per Year)				
	2%	4%	6%	8%	10%
1	0.995	0.990	0.985	0.981	0.976
5	4.742	4.533	4.361	4.218	4.095
10	8.762	7.986	7.454	7.067	6.772
20	14.026	11.966	10.922	10.292	9.870
Infinite (perpetuity)	13.000	13.000	13.000	13.000	13.000

Table 16.3

Bond durations (yield to maturity = 8% bond equivalent yield; semiannual coupons)

The settlement date (i.e., today's date) and maturity date are entered in cells B2 and B3 using Excel's date function, DATE(year, month, day). The coupon and maturity rates are entered as decimals in cells B4 and B5, and the payment periods per year are entered in cell B6. Macaulay and modified duration appear in cells B9 and B10. The spreadsheet confirms that the duration of the bond we looked at in Spreadsheet 16.1 is indeed 1.8852 years. For this 2-year maturity bond, we don't have a specific settlement date. We arbitrarily set the settlement date to January 1, 2000, and use a maturity date precisely two years later.

 Concept Check **16.4**

Use Spreadsheet 16.3 to test some of the rules for duration presented a few pages ago. What happens to duration when you change the coupon rate of the bond? The yield to maturity? The maturity? What happens to duration if the bond pays its coupons annually rather than semiannually? Why intuitively is duration shorter with semiannual coupons?

Durations can vary widely among traded bonds. Table 16.3 presents durations computed from Spreadsheet 16.3 for several bonds all paying semiannual coupons and yielding 4% per half-year. Notice that duration decreases as coupon rates increase, and increases with time to maturity. According to Table 16.3 and Equation 16.2, if the interest rate increases from 8% to 8.1%, the 6% coupon 20-year bond falls in value by about 10.922 × .1%/1.04 = 1.05%, whereas the 10% coupon 1-year bond falls by only .976 × .1%/1.04 = .094%.[6] Notice also from Table 16.3 that duration is independent of coupon rate only for perpetuities.

16.2 Convexity

As a measure of interest rate sensitivity, duration clearly is a key tool in fixed-income portfolio management. Yet the duration rule for the impact of interest rates on bond prices is only an approximation. Equation 16.2, or its equivalent, Equation 16.3, which we repeat here, states that the percentage change in the value of a bond approximately equals the product of modified duration times the change in the bond's yield:

$$\frac{\Delta P}{P} = -D^* \, \Delta y$$

---

[6]Notice that because the bonds pay their coupons semiannually, we calculate modified duration using the semiannual yield to maturity, 4%, in the denominator.

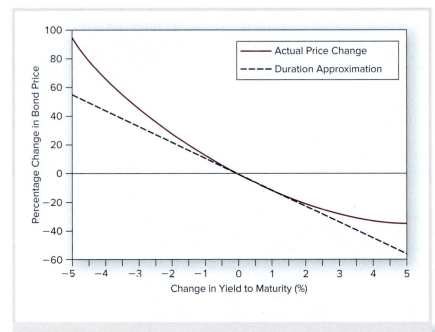

Figure 16.3 Bond price convexity: 30-year maturity, 8% coupon bond; initial yield to maturity = 8%

In other words, the percentage price change is directly proportional to the change in the bond's yield. If this were *exactly* so, however, a graph of the percentage change in bond price as a function of the change in its yield would plot as a straight line, with slope equal to $-D^*$. Yet Figure 16.1 makes it clear that the relationship between bond prices and yields is *not* linear. The duration rule is a good approximation for small changes in bond yield, but it is less accurate for larger changes.

Figure 16.3 illustrates this point. Like Figure 16.1, the figure presents the percentage change in bond price in response to a change in the bond's yield to maturity. The curved line is the percentage price change for a 30-year maturity, 8% annual payment coupon bond, selling at an initial yield to maturity of 8%. The straight line is the percentage price change predicted by the duration rule. The slope of the straight line is the modified duration of the bond at its initial yield to maturity. The modified duration of the bond at this yield is 11.26 years, so the straight line is a plot of $-D^*\Delta y = -11.26 \times \Delta y$. Notice that the two plots are tangent at the initial yield. Thus for small changes in the bond's yield to maturity, the duration rule is quite accurate. However, for larger changes, there is progressively more "daylight" between the two plots, demonstrating that the duration rule becomes progressively less accurate.

Notice from Figure 16.3 that the duration approximation (the straight line) always understates the value of the bond; it underestimates the increase in bond price when the yield falls, and it overestimates the decline in price when the yield rises. This is due to the curvature of the true price-yield relationship. Curves with shapes like that of the price-yield relationship are said to be *convex*, and the curvature of the price-yield curve is called the **convexity** of the bond.

We can measure convexity as the rate of change of the slope of the price-yield curve, expressed as a fraction of the bond price.[7] As a practical rule, you can view bonds with

---

[7]We pointed out in footnote 4 that Equation 16.3 for modified duration can be written as $dP/P = -D^*dy$. Thus $D^* = 1/P \times dP/dy$ is the slope of the price-yield curve expressed as a fraction of the bond price. Similarly, the convexity of a bond equals the *second* derivative (the rate of change of the slope) of the price-yield curve divided by bond price: Convexity $= 1/P \times d^2P/dy^2$. The formula for the convexity of a bond with a maturity of T years making annual coupon payments is

$$\text{Convexity} = \frac{1}{P \times (1 + y)^2}\sum_{t=1}^{T}\left[\frac{\text{CF}_t}{(1 + y)^t}(t^2 + t)\right]$$

where CF_t is the cash flow paid to the bondholder at date t; CF_t represents either a coupon payment before maturity or final coupon plus par value at the maturity date.

higher convexity as exhibiting higher curvature in the price-yield relationship. The convexity of noncallable bonds such as that in Figure 16.3 is positive: The slope increases (i.e., becomes less negative) at higher yields.

Convexity allows us to improve the duration approximation for bond price changes. Accounting for convexity, Equation 16.3 can be modified as follows:[8]

$$\frac{\Delta P}{P} = -D^* \Delta y + \tfrac{1}{2} \times \text{Convexity} \times (\Delta y)^2 \qquad \textbf{(16.5)}$$

The first term on the right-hand side is the same as the duration rule, Equation 16.3. The second term is the modification for convexity. Notice that for a bond with positive convexity, the second term is positive, regardless of whether the yield rises or falls. This insight corresponds to our observation that the duration rule always underestimates the new value of a bond following a change in its yield. The more accurate Equation 16.5, which accounts for convexity, always predicts a higher bond price than Equation 16.2. Of course, if the change in yield is small, the convexity term, which is multiplied by $(\Delta y)^2$ in Equation 16.5, will be extremely small and will add little to the approximation. Thus convexity is more important as a practical matter when potential interest rate changes are large.

Example 16.2   Convexity

The bond in Figure 16.3 has a 30-year maturity, an 8% coupon, and sells at an initial yield to maturity of 8%. Because the coupon rate equals yield to maturity, the bond sells at par value, or $1,000. The modified duration of the bond at its initial yield is 11.26 years, and its convexity is 212.4, which can be verified using the formula in footnote 7. (You can find a spreadsheet to calculate the convexity of a 30-year bond in Connect or through your course instructor.) If the bond's yield increases from 8% to 10%, the bond price will fall to $811.46, a decline of 18.85%. The duration rule, Equation 16.2, would predict a price decline of

$$\frac{\Delta P}{P} = -D^* \Delta y = -11.26 \times .02 = -.2252, \text{ or } -22.52\%$$

which is considerably more than the bond price actually falls. The duration-with-convexity rule, Equation 16.4, is far more accurate:

$$\frac{\Delta P}{P} = -D^* \Delta y + \tfrac{1}{2} \times \text{Convexity} \times (\Delta y)^2$$

$$= -11.26 \times .02 + \tfrac{1}{2} \times 212.4 \times (.02)^2 = -.1827, \text{ or } -18.27\%$$

which is far closer to the exact change in bond price. (Notice that when we use Equation 16.5, we must express interest rates as decimals rather than percentages. The change in rates from 8% to 10% is represented as $\Delta y = .02$.)

If the change in yield were smaller, say, .1%, convexity would matter less. The price of the bond actually would fall to $988.85, a decline of 1.115%. Without accounting for convexity, we would predict a price decline of

$$\frac{\Delta P}{P} = -D^* \Delta y = -11.26 \times .001 = -.01126, \text{ or } -1.126\%$$

Accounting for convexity, we get almost the precisely correct answer:

$$\frac{\Delta P}{P} = -11.26 \times .001 + \tfrac{1}{2} \times 212.4 \times (.001)^2 = -.01115, \text{ or } -1.115\%$$

Nevertheless, the duration rule is quite accurate in this case, even without accounting for convexity.

---

[8]To use the convexity rule, you must express interest rates as decimals rather than percentages.

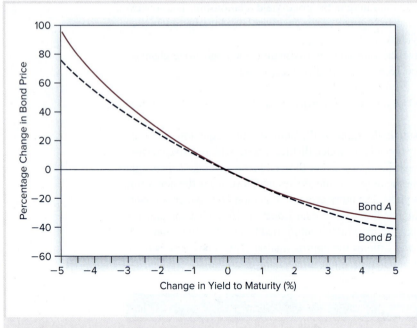

Figure 16.4 Convexity of two bonds

Why Do Investors Like Convexity?

Convexity is generally considered a desirable trait. Bonds with greater curvature gain more in price when yields fall than they lose when yields rise. For example, in Figure 16.4 bonds *A* and *B* have the same duration at the initial yield. The plots of their proportional price changes as a function of interest rate changes are tangent, meaning that their sensitivities to changes in yields at that point are equal. However, bond *A* is more convex than bond *B*. It enjoys greater price increases and smaller price decreases when interest rates fluctuate by larger amounts. If interest rates are volatile, this is an attractive asymmetry that increases the expected return on the bond, because bond *A* will benefit more from rate decreases and suffer less from rate increases. Of course, if convexity is desirable, it will not be available for free: Investors will have to pay higher prices and accept lower yields to maturity on bonds with greater convexity.

Duration and Convexity of Callable Bonds

Look at Figure 16.5, which depicts the price-yield curve for a callable bond. When interest rates are high, the curve is convex, as it would be for a straight bond. For example, at an interest rate of 10%, the price-yield curve lies above its tangency line. But as rates fall, there is a ceiling on the possible price: The bond cannot be worth more than its call price. So as rates fall, we sometimes say that the bond is subject to price compression—its value is "compressed" to the call price. In this region, for example at an interest rate of 5%, the price-yield curve lies *below* its tangency line, and the curve is said to have *negative convexity*.[9]

In the region of negative convexity, the price-yield curve exhibits an *unattractive* asymmetry. Interest rate increases result in a larger price decline than the price gain corresponding to an interest rate decrease of equal magnitude. The asymmetry arises from the fact that the bond issuer has retained an option to call back the bond. If rates rise, the bondholder loses, as would be the case for a straight bond. But if rates fall, rather than reaping a large capital gain, the investor may have the bond called back from her. The bondholder is thus in a "heads I lose, tails I don't win" position. Of course, she was compensated for this unattractive situation when she purchased the bond. Callable bonds sell at lower initial prices (higher initial yields) than otherwise comparable straight bonds.

The effect of negative convexity is highlighted in Equation 16.5. When convexity is negative, the second term on the right-hand side is necessarily negative, meaning that bond

---

[9]If you've taken a calculus course, you will recognize that the curve is *concave* in this region. However, rather than saying that these bonds exhibit concavity, bond traders prefer the terminology "negative convexity."

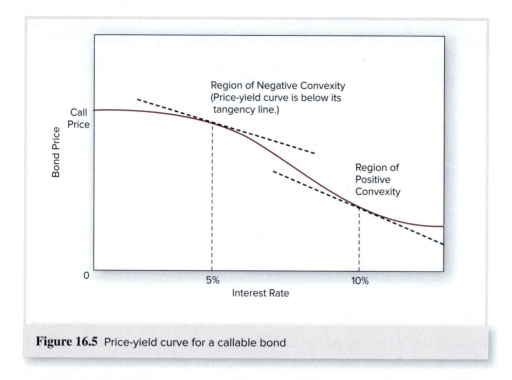

Figure 16.5 Price-yield curve for a callable bond

price performance will be worse than would be predicted by the duration approximation. However, callable bonds or, more generally, bonds with "embedded options," are difficult to analyze in terms of Macaulay's duration. This is because in the presence of such options, the future cash flows provided by the bonds are no longer known. If the bond may be called, for example, its cash flow stream may be terminated and its principal repaid earlier than was initially anticipated. Because cash flows are random (they depend on the realization of interest rates), we can hardly take a weighted average of times until each future cash flow, as would be necessary to compute Macaulay's duration.

The convention on Wall Street is to compute the **effective duration** of bonds with embedded options. Effective duration cannot be computed with a simple formula involving known cash flows such as Equation 16.1. Instead, more complex bond valuation approaches that account for the embedded options are used, and effective duration is *defined* as the proportional change in the bond price per unit change in market interest rates:

$$\text{Effective duration} = -\frac{\Delta P/P}{\Delta r} \qquad \textbf{(16.6)}$$

This equation *seems* merely like a slight manipulation of the modified duration formula in Equation 16.3. However, there are important differences. First, note that we do not compute effective duration relative to a change in the bond's own yield to maturity. (The denominator is Δr, not Δy.) This is because for bonds with embedded options, which may be called early, maturity is no longer fixed, and so the yield to maturity becomes a less relevant statistic. Instead, we calculate price change relative to a shift in the level of the term structure of interest rates. Second, the effective duration formula relies on a pricing methodology that accounts for embedded options. This means that the effective duration will be a function of variables that would not matter to conventional duration, for example, the volatility of interest rates. In contrast, modified or Macaulay duration can be computed directly from the promised bond cash flows and yield to maturity.

Example 16.3   Effective Duration

Suppose that a callable bond with a call price of $1,050 is selling today for $980. If the yield curve shifts up by .5%, the bond price will fall to $930. If it shifts down by .5%, the bond price will rise to $1,010. To compute effective duration, we compute:

$$\Delta r = \text{Assumed increase in rates} - \text{Assumed decrease in rates}$$
$$= .5\% - (-.5\%) = 1\% = .01$$
$$\Delta P = \text{Price at .5\% increase in rates} - \text{Price at .5\% decrease in rates}$$
$$= \$930 - \$1,010 = -\$80$$

Then the effective duration of the bond is

$$\text{Effective duration} = -\frac{\Delta P/P}{\Delta r} = -\frac{-\$80/\$980}{.01} = 8.16 \text{ years}$$

In other words, the bond price changes by 8.16% for a 1 percentage point swing in rates around current values.

 Concept Check **16.5**

What are the differences among Macaulay duration, modified duration, and effective duration?

Duration and Convexity of Mortgage-Backed Securities

In practice, the biggest market for which call provisions are important is the market for mortgage-backed securities. As described in Chapter 1, lenders that originate mortgage loans commonly sell them to federal agencies such as the Federal National Mortgage Association (FNMA, or Fannie Mae) or the Federal Home Loan Mortgage Corporation (FHLMC, or Freddie Mac). The original borrowers (the homeowners) continue to make their monthly payments to their lenders, but the lenders pass these payments along to the agency that has purchased the loan. In turn, the agencies may combine many mortgages into a pool called a mortgage-backed security, and then sell that security in the fixed-income market. These securities are called *pass-throughs* because the cash flows from the borrowers are first passed through to the agency (Fannie Mae or Freddie Mac) and then passed through again to the ultimate purchaser of the mortgage-backed security.

As an example, suppose that ten 30-year mortgages, each with principal value of $100,000, are grouped together into a million-dollar pool. If the mortgage rate is 8%, then the monthly payment on each loan would be $733.76. (The interest component of the first payment is $.08 \times 1/12 \times \$100,000 = \$666.67$; the remaining $67.09 is "amortization," or scheduled repayment of principal. In later periods, with a lower principal balance, less of the monthly payment goes to interest and more goes to amortization.) The owner of the mortgage-backed security would receive $7,337.60, the total payment from the 10 mortgages in the pool.[10]

But the homeowner has the right to prepay the loan at any time. For example, if mortgage rates go down, he may decide to take a new loan at a lower rate, using the proceeds to

---

[10]Actually, the financial institution that continues to service the loan and the pass-through agency that guarantees the loan each retain a portion of the monthly payment as a charge for their services. Thus, the monthly payment received by the investor is a bit less than the amount paid by the borrower.

pay off the original loan. The right to prepay the loan is, of course, precisely analogous to the right to refund a callable bond. The call price for the mortgage is simply the remaining principal balance on the loan. Therefore, the mortgage-backed security is best viewed as a pool of *callable* amortizing loans.

Mortgage-backs are subject to the same negative convexity as other callable bonds. When rates fall and homeowners prepay their mortgages, the repayment of principal is passed through to the investors. Rather than enjoying capital gains on their investment, they simply receive the outstanding principal balance on the loan. Therefore, the value of the mortgage-backed security as a function of interest rates, presented in Figure 16.6, looks much like the plot for a callable bond.

There are some differences between the mortgage-backs and callable corporate bonds, however. For example, you will commonly find mortgage-backs selling for more than their principal balance. This is because homeowners do not refinance their loans as soon as interest rates drop. Some homeowners do not want to incur the costs or hassles of refinancing unless the benefit is great enough, others may decide not to refinance if they are planning to move shortly, and others may simply be unsophisticated in making the refinancing decision. Therefore, while the mortgage-backed security exhibits negative convexity at low rates, its implicit call price (the principal balance on the loan) is not a firm ceiling on its value.

Simple mortgage-backs have also given rise to a rich set of mortgage-backed derivatives. For example, a CMO (collateralized mortgage obligation) further redirects the cash flow stream of the mortgage-backed security to several classes of derivative securities called "tranches." These tranches may be designed to allocate interest rate risk to investors most willing to bear that risk.[11]

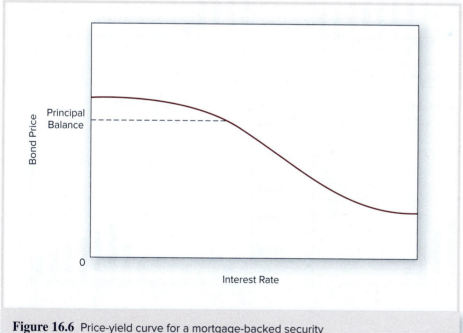

Figure 16.6 Price-yield curve for a mortgage-backed security

---

[11]In Chapter 14, we examined how collateralized debt obligations or CDOs use tranche structures to reallocate *credit risk* among different classes. Credit risk in agency-sponsored mortgage-backed securities is not really an issue because the mortgage payments are guaranteed by the agency and the federal government; in the CMO market, tranche structure is used to allocate *interest rate risk* rather than credit risk across classes.

The following table is an example of a very simple CMO structure. The underlying mortgage pool is divided into three tranches, each with a different effective maturity and therefore interest rate risk exposure. Suppose the original pool has $10 million of 15-year-maturity mortgages, each with an interest rate of 10.5%, and is subdivided into three tranches as follows:

Tranche A = $4 million principal	"Short-pay" tranche
Tranche B = $3 million principal	"Intermediate-pay" tranche
Tranche C = $3 million principal	"Long-pay" tranche

Suppose further that in each year, 8% of outstanding loans in the pool prepay. Then total cash flows in each year to the whole mortgage pool are given in Panel A of Figure 16.7.

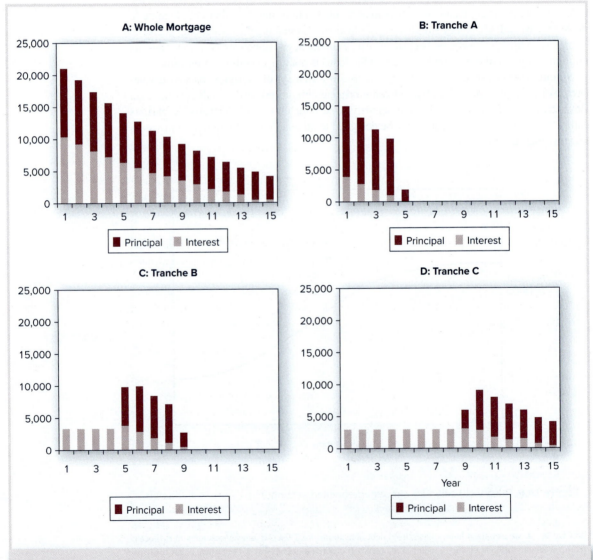

Figure 16.7 *Panel A:* Cash flows to whole mortgage pool; *Panels B–D:* Cash flows to three tranches

Total payments shrink by 8% each year, as that percentage of the loans in the original pool is paid off. The light portions of each bar represent interest payments, while the dark portions are principal payments, including both loan amortization and prepayments.

In each period, each tranche receives the interest owed it based on the promised coupon rate and outstanding principal balance. But initially, *all* principal payments, both prepayments and amortization, go to tranche A (Figure 16.7, Panel B). Notice from Panels C and D that tranches B and C receive only interest payments until tranche A is retired. Once tranche A is fully paid off, all principal payments go to tranche B. Finally, when B is retired, all principal payments go to C. This makes tranche A a "short-pay" class, with the lowest effective duration, while tranche C is the longest-pay tranche. This is therefore a relatively simple way to allocate interest rate risk among tranches.

Many variations on the theme are possible and employed in practice. Different tranches may receive different coupon rates. Some tranches may be given preferential treatment in terms of uncertainty over mortgage prepayment speeds. Complex formulas may be used to dictate the cash flows allocated to each tranche. In essence, the mortgage pool is treated as a source of cash flows that can be reallocated to different investors in accordance with their different tastes.

16.3   Passive Bond Management

Passive managers take bond prices as fairly set and seek to control only the risk of their fixed-income portfolio. Two broad classes of passive management are pursued in the fixed-income market. The first is an indexing strategy that attempts to replicate the performance of a given bond index. The second broad class of passive strategies is known as immunization techniques; they are used widely by financial institutions such as insurance companies and pension funds and are designed to shield the overall financial status of the institution from exposure to interest rate fluctuations.

Although indexing and immunization strategies are alike in that they accept market prices as correctly set, they are very different in terms of risk exposure. A bond-index portfolio will have the same risk–reward profile as the bond market index to which it is tied. In contrast, immunization strategies seek to establish a virtually zero-risk profile, in which interest rate movements have no impact on the value of the firm. We discuss both types of strategies in this section.

Bond-Index Funds

In principle, bond market indexing is similar to stock market indexing. The idea is to create a portfolio that mirrors the composition of an index that measures the broad market. In the U.S. equity market, for example, the S&P 500 is the most commonly used index for stock-index funds, and these funds simply buy shares of each firm in the S&P 500 in proportion to the market value of outstanding equity. A similar strategy is used for bond-index funds, but as we shall see shortly, several modifications are required because of difficulties unique to the bond market and its indexes.

Three major indexes of the U.S. bond market are the Barclays Capital U.S. Aggregate Bond Index, the Citigroup U.S. Broad Investment Grade (USBIG) Index, and the Bank of America/Merrill Lynch Domestic Master index. All are market-value-weighted indexes of total returns. All three include government, corporate, mortgage-backed, and Yankee bonds in their universes. (Yankee bonds are dollar-denominated, SEC-registered bonds of foreign issuers sold in the United States.)

One challenge in constructing an indexed bond portfolio arises from the fact that these indexes include thousands of securities, making it quite difficult to purchase each security in the index in proportion to its market value. Moreover, many bonds are very thinly traded, meaning that identifying their owners and purchasing the securities at a fair market price can be difficult.

Bond-index funds also face more difficult rebalancing problems than do stock-index funds. Bonds are continually dropped from the index as they approach maturity. Moreover, as new bonds are issued, they are added to the index. Therefore, in contrast to equity indexes, the securities used to compute bond indexes constantly change. As they do, the manager must update or rebalance the portfolio to maintain a close match between the composition of the portfolio and the bonds included in the index. The fact that bonds generate considerable interest income that must be reinvested further complicates the job of the index fund manager.

In practice, it is infeasible to precisely replicate the broad bond indexes. Instead, a stratified sampling or *cellular* approach is often pursued. Figure 16.8 illustrates the idea behind the cellular approach. First, the bond market is stratified into several subclasses. Figure 16.8 shows a simple two-way breakdown by maturity and issuer; in practice, however, criteria such as the bond's coupon rate or the credit risk of the issuer also would be used to form cells. Bonds falling within each cell are then considered reasonably homogeneous. Next, the percentages of the entire universe (i.e., the bonds included in the index that is to be matched) falling within each cell are computed and reported, as we have done for a few of the cells in Figure 16.8. Finally, the portfolio manager establishes a bond portfolio with representation for each cell that matches the weight of that cell in the bond universe. In this way, the characteristics of the portfolio in terms of maturity, coupon rate, credit risk, industrial representation, and so on will match the characteristics of the index, and the performance of the portfolio likewise should closely match the index.

Both mutual funds and exchange-traded funds that track the broad bond market are available to retail investors. For example, Vanguard's Total Bond Market Index Fund (ticker VBMFX) and Barclays Aggregate Bond Fund iShare (ticker AGG) both track the broad U.S. bond market.

Sector Term to Maturity	Treasury	Agency	Mortgage-backed	Industrial	Finance	Utility	Yankee
<1 year	12.1%						
1–3 years	5.4%						
3–5 years			4.1%				
5–7 years							
7–10 years		0.1%					
10–15 years							
15–30 years			9.2%			3.4%	
30+ years							

Figure 16.8 Stratification of bonds into cells

Pension Funds Lost Ground Despite Broad Market Gains

With the S&P 500 providing a 16% rate of return, 2012 was a good year for the stock market, and this performance helped boost the balance sheets of U.S. pension funds. Yet despite the increase in the value of their assets, the total estimated pension deficit of 400 large U.S. companies *rose* by nearly $80 billion, and many of these firms entered 2013 needing to shore up their pension funds with billions of dollars of additional cash. Ford Motor Co. alone predicted that it would contribute $5 billion to its fund.*

How could this happen? Blame the decline in interest rates during the year that were in part the force behind the stock market gains. As rates fell, the present value of pension obligations to retirees rose even faster than the value of the assets backing those promises. It turns out that the value of pension liabilities is more sensitive to interest rate changes than the value of the typical assets held in those funds. So even

though falling rates tend to pump up asset returns, they pump up liabilities even more. In other words, the duration of fund investments is shorter than the duration of fund obligations. This duration mismatch makes funds vulnerable to interest rate declines.

Why don't funds better match asset and liability durations? One reason is that fund managers are often evaluated based on their performance relative to standard bond market indexes. Those indexes tend to have far shorter durations than pension fund liabilities. So to some extent, managers may be keeping their eyes on the wrong ball, one with the wrong interest rate sensitivity.

*These estimates appear in Mike Ramsey and Vipal Monga, "Low Rates Force Companies to Pour Cash into Pensions," *The Wall Street Journal*, February 3, 2013.

Immunization

In contrast to indexing strategies, many institutions try to insulate their portfolios from interest rate risk altogether. Generally, there are two ways of viewing this risk. Some institutions, such as banks, are concerned with protecting current net worth or net market value against interest rate fluctuations. Other investors, such as pension funds, may face an obligation to make payments after a given number of years. These investors are more concerned with protecting the future values of their portfolios.

What is common to all investors, however, is interest rate risk. The net worth of the firm or the ability to meet future obligations fluctuates with interest rates. **Immunization** techniques refer to strategies used by such investors to shield their overall financial status from interest rate risk.

Many banks and thrift institutions have a natural mismatch between asset and liability maturity structures. Bank liabilities are primarily the deposits owed to customers, most of which are short-term and, consequently, have low duration. Bank assets by contrast are composed largely of outstanding commercial and consumer loans or mortgages. These assets have longer duration, and their values are correspondingly more sensitive to interest rate fluctuations. When interest rates increase unexpectedly, banks can suffer serious decreases in net worth—their assets fall in value by more than their liabilities.

Similarly, a pension fund may have a mismatch between the interest rate sensitivity of the assets held in the fund and the present value of its liabilities—the promise to make payments to retirees. The nearby box illustrates the dangers that pension funds face when they neglect to consider the interest rate exposure of *both* assets and liabilities. For example, in some recent years pension funds lost ground despite the fact that they enjoyed excellent investment returns. As interest rates fell, the value of their liabilities grew even faster than the value of their assets. The lesson is that funds should match the interest rate exposure of assets and liabilities so that the value of assets will track the value of liabilities whether rates rise or fall. In other words, the financial manager might want to *immunize* the fund against interest rate volatility.

Pension funds are not alone in this concern. Any institution with a future fixed obligation might consider immunization a reasonable risk management policy. Insurance companies, for example, also pursue immunization strategies. In fact, the tactic of immunization was introduced by F. M. Redington,[12] an actuary for a life insurance company. The idea is that duration-matched assets and liabilities let the asset portfolio meet the firm's obligations despite interest rate movements.

Consider, for example, an insurance company that issues a guaranteed investment contract, or GIC, for $10,000. (Essentially, GICs are zero-coupon bonds issued by the insurance company to its customers. They are popular products for individuals' retirement-savings accounts.) If the GIC has a 5-year maturity and a guaranteed interest rate of 8%, the insurance company promises to pay $10,000 \times 1.08^5 = $14,693.28 in five years.

Suppose that the insurance company chooses to fund its obligation with $10,000 of 8% *annual* coupon bonds, selling at par value, with six years to maturity. As long as the market interest rate stays at 8%, the company has fully funded the obligation, as the present value of the obligation exactly equals the value of the bonds.

Table 16.4, Panel A, shows that if interest rates remain at 8%, the accumulated funds from the bond will grow to exactly the $14,693.28 obligation. Over the 5-year period,

Payment Number	Years Remaining until Obligation	Accumulated Value of Invested Payment		
A. Rates Remain at 8%				
1	4	$800 \times (1.08)^4$	=	$ 1,088.39
2	3	$800 \times (1.08)^3$	=	1,007.77
3	2	$800 \times (1.08)^2$	=	933.12
4	1	$800 \times (1.08)^1$	=	864.00
5	0	$800 \times (1.08)^0$	=	800.00
Sale of bond	0	10,800/1.08	=	10,000.00
				$14,693.28
B. Rates Fall to 7%				
1	4	$800 \times (1.07)^4$	=	$ 1,048.64
2	3	$800 \times (1.07)^3$	=	980.03
3	2	$800 \times (1.07)^2$	=	915.92
4	1	$800 \times (1.07)^1$	=	856.00
5	0	$800 \times (1.07)^0$	=	800.00
Sale of bond	0	10,800/1.07	=	$10,093.46
				$14,694.05
C. Rates Increase to 9%				
1	4	$800 \times (1.09)^4$	=	$ 1,129.27
2	3	$800 \times (1.09)^3$	=	1,036.02
3	2	$800 \times (1.09)^2$	=	950.48
4	1	$800 \times (1.09)^1$	=	872.00
5	0	$800 \times (1.09)^0$	=	800.00
Sale of bond	0	10,800/1.09	=	9,908.26
				$14,696.02

Table 16.4

Terminal value of a bond portfolio after five years (all proceeds reinvested)

Note: The sale price of the bond portfolio equals the portfolio's final payment ($10,800) divided by $1 + r$, because the time to maturity of the bonds will be 1 year at the time of sale.

---

[12]F. M. Redington, "Review of the Principle of Life-Office Valuations," *Journal of the Institute of Actuaries* 78 (1952).

year-end coupon income of $800 is reinvested at the prevailing 8% market interest rate. At the end of the period, the bonds can be sold for $10,000; they still will sell at par value because the coupon rate still equals the market interest rate. Total income after five years from reinvested coupons and the sale of the bond is precisely $14,693.28.

If interest rates change, however, two offsetting influences will affect the ability of the fund to grow to the targeted value of $14,693.28. If interest rates rise, the fund will suffer a capital loss, impairing its ability to satisfy the obligation. The bonds will be worth less in five years than if interest rates had remained at 8%. However, at a higher interest rate, reinvested coupons will grow at a faster rate, offsetting the capital loss. In other words, fixed-income investors face two offsetting types of interest rate risk: *price risk* and *reinvestment rate risk*. Increases in interest rates cause capital losses but at the same time increase the rate at which reinvested income will grow. If the portfolio duration is chosen appropriately, these two effects will cancel out exactly. When the portfolio duration is set equal to the investor's horizon date, the accumulated value of the investment fund at the horizon date will be unaffected by interest rate fluctuations. *For a horizon equal to the portfolio's duration, price risk and reinvestment risk are precisely offsetting.*

In our example, the duration of the 6-year maturity bonds used to fund the GIC is just about five years. Because the fully funded plan has equal duration for its assets and liabilities, the insurance company should be immunized against interest rate fluctuations. To confirm this, let's check that the bond can generate enough income to pay off the obligation in five years regardless of interest rate movements.

In Table 16.4, Panels B and C illustrate two possible interest rate scenarios: Rates either fall to 7% (Panel B) or increase to 9% (Panel C). In both cases, the annual coupon payments are reinvested at the new interest rate, which is assumed to change before the first coupon payment, and the bond is sold in year 5 to help satisfy the obligation of the GIC.

Panel B shows that if interest rates fall to 7%, the total funds will accumulate to $14,694.05, providing a small surplus of $.77. If rates increase to 9% as in Panel C, the fund accumulates to $14,696.02, providing a small surplus of $2.74.

Several points are worth highlighting. First, duration matching balances the difference between the accumulated value of the coupon payments (reinvestment rate risk) and the sale value of the bond (price risk). That is, when interest rates fall, the coupons grow less than in the base case, but the higher value of the bond offsets this. When interest rates rise, the value of the bond falls, but the coupons more than make up for this loss because they are reinvested at the higher rate. Figure 16.9 illustrates this case. The solid curve traces the

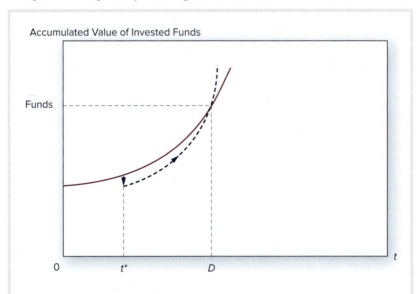

Figure 16.9 Growth of invested funds. The solid colored curve represents the growth of portfolio value at the original interest rate. If interest rates increase at time *t**, the portfolio value initially falls but increases thereafter at the faster rate represented by the broken curve. At time *D* (duration), the curves cross.

Connect contains a spreadsheet that is useful in understanding the concept of holding-period immunization. The spreadsheet calculates duration and holding-period returns on bonds of any maturity. The spreadsheet shows how price risk and reinvestment risk offset if a bond is sold at its duration.

Excel Questions

1. When rates increase by 100 basis points (bp), what is the change in the future sales price of the bond? The value of reinvested coupons?
2. What if rates increase by 200 bp?
3. What is the relation between price risk and reinvestment rate risk as we consider larger changes in bond yields?

	A	B	C	D	E	F	G	H
1								
2								
3	Yield to maturity	11.580%						
4	Coupon rate	14.000%						
5	Years to maturity	7.0						
6	Par value	$1,000.00						
7	Holding period	5.0						
8	Duration	5.000251		5.000251				
9	Market price	$1,111.929		$1,111.929				
10								
11	If YTM increases 200 basis points:			2.00%		If YTM increases 200 basis points:		
12	Yield to maturity	13.580%				Yield to maturity	12.580%	
13	Future value of coupons	$917.739		$917.739		Future value of coupons	$899.705	
14	Sale of bond	$1,006.954		1,006.954		Sale of bond	$1,023.817	
15	Accumulated value	$1,924.693				Accumulated value	$1,923.522	
16	Internal rate of return	11.5981%				Internal rate of return	11.5845%	
17								

accumulated value of the bonds if interest rates remain at 8%. The dashed curve shows that value if interest rates happen to increase. The initial impact is a capital loss, but this loss eventually is offset by the now-faster growth rate of reinvested funds. At the 5-year horizon date, equal to the bond's duration, the two effects just cancel, leaving the company able to satisfy its obligation with the accumulated proceeds from the bond.

We can also analyze immunization in terms of present as opposed to future values. Panel A in Table 16.5 shows the initial balance sheet for the insurance company's GIC.

Table 16.5

Market value balance sheet

Assets		Liabilities	
A. Interest Rate = 8%			
Bonds	$10,000	Obligation	$10,000
B. Interest Rate = 7%			
Bonds	$10,476.65	Obligation	$10,476.11
C. Interest Rate = 9%			
Bonds	$ 9,551.41	Obligation	$ 9,549.62

Notes:

Value of bonds = 800 × Annuity factor (r, 6) + 10,000 × PV factor (r, 6)

Value of obligation = $\dfrac{14,693.28}{(1 + r)^5}$ = 14,693.28 × PV factor (r, 5)

Both assets and the obligation have market values of $10,000, so the plan is just fully funded. Panels B and C in the table show that whether the interest rate increases or decreases, the value of the bonds funding the GIC and the present value of the company's obligation change by virtually identical amounts. Regardless of the interest rate change, the plan remains fully funded, with the surplus in Panels B and C in Table 16.5 just about zero. The duration-matching strategy has ensured that both assets and liabilities react equally to interest rate fluctuations.

Figure 16.10 is a graph of the present values of the bond and the single-payment obligation as a function of the interest rate. At the current rate of 8%, the values are equal, and the obligation is fully funded by the bond. Moreover, the two present value curves are tangent at $y = 8\%$. As interest rates change, the change in value of both the asset and the obligation is equal, so the obligation remains fully funded. For greater changes in the interest rate, however, the present value curves diverge. This reflects the fact that the fund actually shows a small surplus in Table 16.4 at market interest rates other than 8%.

If the obligation was immunized, why is there *any* surplus in the fund? The answer is convexity. Figure 16.10 shows that the coupon bond has greater convexity than the obligation it funds. Hence, when rates move substantially, the bond value exceeds the present value of the obligation by a noticeable amount.

This example highlights the importance of **rebalancing** immunized portfolios. As interest rates and asset durations change, a manager must rebalance the portfolio to realign its duration with the duration of the obligation. Moreover, even if interest rates do not change, asset durations *will* change solely because of the passage of time. Recall from Figure 16.2 that duration generally decreases less rapidly than does maturity. Thus, even if

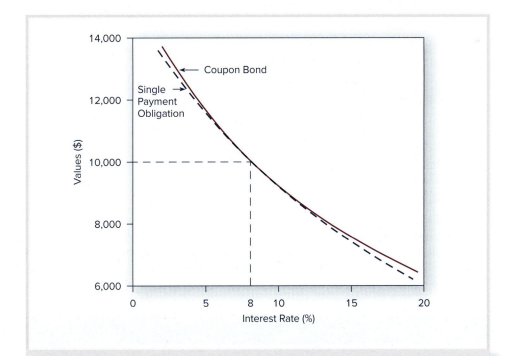

Figure 16.10 Immunization. The coupon bond fully funds the obligation at an interest rate of 8%. Moreover, the present value curves are tangent at 8%, so the obligation will remain fully funded even if rates change by a small amount.

an obligation is immunized at the outset, as time passes the durations of the asset and liability will fall at different rates. Without rebalancing, durations will become unmatched. Obviously, immunization is a passive strategy only in the sense that it does not involve attempts to identify undervalued securities. Immunization managers still proactively update and monitor their positions.

Example 16.4   Constructing an Immunized Portfolio

An insurance company must make a payment of $19,487 in seven years. The market interest rate is 10%, so the present value of the obligation is $10,000. The company's portfolio manager wishes to fund the obligation using 3-year zero-coupon bonds and perpetuities paying annual coupons. (We focus on zeros and perpetuities to keep the algebra simple.) How can the manager immunize the obligation?

Immunization requires that the duration of the portfolio of assets equal the duration of the liability. We can proceed in four steps:

1. *Calculate the duration of the liability.* In this case, the liability duration is simple to compute. It is a single-payment obligation with duration of seven years.

2. *Calculate the duration of the asset portfolio.* The portfolio duration is the weighted average of duration of each component asset, with weights proportional to the funds placed in each asset. The duration of the zero-coupon bond is simply its maturity, three years. The duration of the perpetuity is $1.10/.10 = 11$ years. Therefore, if the fraction of the portfolio invested in the zero is called w and the fraction invested in the perpetuity is $(1 - w)$, the portfolio duration will be

$$\text{Asset duration} = w \times 3 \text{ years} + (1 - w) \times 11 \text{ years}$$

3. *Find the asset mix that sets the duration of assets equal to the 7-year duration of liabilities.* This requires us to solve for w in the following equation:

$$w \times 3 \text{ years} + (1 - w) \times 11 \text{ years} = 7 \text{ years}$$

   This implies that $w = \frac{1}{2}$. The manager should invest half the portfolio in the zero and half in the perpetuity. This will result in an asset duration of seven years.

4. *Fully fund the obligation.* Because the obligation has a present value of $10,000, and the fund will be invested equally in the zero and the perpetuity, the manager must purchase $5,000 of the zero-coupon bond and $5,000 of the perpetuity. (The *face value* of the zero will be $5,000 \times 1.10^3 = $6,655$.)

Even if a position is immunized, however, the portfolio manager still cannot rest. This is because of the need for rebalancing in response to changes in interest rates. Moreover, even if rates do not change, the passage of time also will affect duration and require rebalancing. Let us continue Example 16.4 and see how the portfolio manager can maintain an immunized position.

Example 16.5   Rebalancing

Suppose that one year has passed, and the interest rate remains at 10%. The portfolio manager of Example 16.4 needs to reexamine her position. Is the position still fully funded? Is it still immunized? If not, what actions are required?

First, examine funding. The present value of the obligation will have grown to $11,000, as it is one year closer to maturity. The manager's funds also have grown to $11,000: The zero-coupon bonds have increased in value from $5,000 to $5,500 with the passage of time, while the perpetuity has paid its annual $500 coupon and remains worth $5,000. Therefore, the obligation is still fully funded.

The portfolio weights must be changed, however. The zero-coupon bond now has a duration of two years, while the perpetuity's duration remains at 11 years. The obligation is now due in six years. The weights must now satisfy the equation

$$w \times 2 + (1 - w) \times 11 = 6$$

which implies that $w = \frac{5}{9}$. To rebalance the portfolio and maintain the duration match, the manager now must invest a total of $11,000 \times \frac{5}{9} = $6,111.11$ in the zero-coupon bond. This requires that the entire $500 coupon payment be invested in the zero, with an additional $111.11 of the perpetuity sold and invested in the zero-coupon bond.

Of course, rebalancing of the portfolio entails transaction costs as assets are bought or sold, so one cannot rebalance continuously. In practice, an appropriate compromise must be established between the desire for perfect immunization, which requires continual rebalancing, and the need to control trading costs, which dictates less frequent rebalancing.

 Concept Check **16.6**

> Look again at Example 16.5. What would be the immunizing weights in the second year if the interest rate had fallen to 8%?

Cash Flow Matching and Dedication

The problems associated with immunization appear to have a simple solution. Why not simply buy a zero-coupon bond with face value equal to the projected cash outlay? If we follow the principle of **cash flow matching** we automatically immunize the portfolio from interest rate risk because the cash flow from the bond and the obligation exactly offset each other.

Cash flow matching on a multiperiod basis is referred to as a **dedication strategy.** In this case, the manager selects either zero-coupon or coupon bonds with total cash flows in each period that match a series of obligations. The advantage of dedication is that it is a once-and-for-all approach to eliminating interest rate risk. Once the cash flows are matched, there is no need for rebalancing.

Cash flow matching is not more widely pursued probably because of the constraints that it imposes on bond selection. Immunization or dedication strategies are appealing to firms that do not wish to bet on general movements in interest rates, but these firms may want to immunize using bonds that they perceive are undervalued. Cash flow matching, however, places so many more constraints on the bond selection process that it can be impossible to pursue a dedication strategy using only "underpriced" bonds. Firms looking for underpriced bonds give up exact and easy dedication for the possibility of achieving superior returns from the bond portfolio.

Sometimes, cash flow matching is simply not possible. To cash flow match for a pension fund that is obligated to pay out a perpetual flow of income to current and future retirees, the pension fund would need to purchase fixed-income securities with maturities ranging up to hundreds of years. Such securities do not exist, making exact dedication infeasible.

 Concept Check **16.7**

How would an increase in trading costs affect the attractiveness of dedication versus immunization?

Other Problems with Conventional Immunization

If you look back at the definition of duration in Equation 16.1, you note that it uses the bond's yield to maturity to calculate the weight applied to the time until each coupon payment. Given this definition and limitations on the proper use of yield to maturity, it is perhaps not surprising that this notion of duration is strictly valid only for a flat yield curve for which all payments are discounted at a common interest rate.

If the yield curve is not flat, then the definition of duration must be modified and $CF_t/(1 + y)^t$ replaced with the present value of CF_t, where the present value of each cash flow is calculated by discounting with the appropriate spot interest rate from the zero-coupon yield curve corresponding to the date of the *particular* cash flow, instead of by discounting with the *bond's* yield to maturity. Moreover, even with this modification, duration matching will immunize portfolios only for parallel shifts in the yield curve. Clearly, this sort of restriction is unrealistic. As a result, much work has been devoted to generalizing the notion of duration. Multifactor duration models have been developed to allow for tilts and other distortions in the shape of the yield curve, in addition to shifts in its level. However, the added complexity of such models does not appear to pay off in terms of substantially greater effectiveness.[13]

Finally, immunization can be an inappropriate goal in an inflationary environment. Immunization is essentially a nominal notion and makes sense only for nominal liabilities. It makes no sense to immunize a projected obligation that will grow with the price level using nominal assets such as bonds. For example, if your child will attend college in 15 years and if the annual cost of tuition is expected to be $50,000 at that time, immunizing your portfolio at a locked-in terminal value of $50,000 is not necessarily a risk-reducing strategy. The tuition obligation will vary with the realized inflation rate, whereas the asset portfolio's final value will not. As a result, the tuition obligation will not be matched by the value of the portfolio.

16.4   Active Bond Management

Sources of Potential Profit

Broadly speaking, there are two sources of potential value in active bond management. The first is interest rate forecasting, which tries to anticipate movements across the entire spectrum of the fixed-income market. If interest rate declines are anticipated, managers will increase portfolio duration (and vice versa). The second source of potential profit is identification of relative mispricing within the fixed-income market. An analyst, for example,

---

[13]G. O. Bierwag, G. C. Kaufman, and A. Toevs, eds., *Innovations in Bond Portfolio Management: Duration Analysis and Immunization* (Greenwich, CT: JAI Press, 1983).

might believe that the default premium on one particular bond is unnecessarily large and therefore that the bond is underpriced.

These techniques will generate abnormal returns only if the analyst's information or insight is superior to that of the market. You cannot profit from knowledge that rates are about to fall if prices already reflect this information. You know this from our discussion of market efficiency. Valuable information is differential information. In this context it is worth noting that interest rate forecasters have a notoriously poor track record. If you consider this record, you will approach attempts to time the bond market with caution.

Homer and Liebowitz (see footnote 2) coined a popular taxonomy of active bond portfolio strategies. They characterize portfolio rebalancing activities as one of four types of *bond swaps*. In the first two swaps, the investor typically believes that the yield relationship between particular bonds or sectors is only temporarily out of alignment. When the aberration is eliminated, gains can be realized on the underpriced bond. The period of realignment is called the *workout period*.

1. The **substitution swap** is an exchange of one bond for a nearly identical substitute. The substituted bonds should be of essentially equal coupon, maturity, quality, call features, sinking fund provisions, and so on. This swap would be motivated by a belief that the market has temporarily mispriced the two bonds, and that the discrepancy between the prices of the bonds represents a profit opportunity.

    An example of a substitution swap would be a sale of a 20-year maturity, 6% coupon Toyota bond that is priced to provide a yield to maturity of 6.05%, coupled with a purchase of a 6% coupon Honda bond with the same time to maturity that yields 6.15%. If the bonds have about the same credit rating, there is no apparent reason for the Honda bonds to provide a higher yield. Therefore, the higher yield actually available in the market makes the Honda bond seem relatively attractive. Of course, the equality of credit risk is an important condition. If the Honda bond is in fact riskier, then its higher yield does not represent a bargain.

2. The **intermarket spread swap** is pursued when an investor believes that the yield spread between two sectors of the bond market is temporarily out of line. For example, if the current spread between corporate and government bonds is expected to narrow, the investor will shift from government bonds into corporate bonds. If the yield spread does in fact narrow, corporates will outperform governments. For example, if the yield spread between 10-year Treasury bonds and 10-year Baa-rated corporate bonds is now 3%, and the historical spread has been only 2%, you might consider selling holdings of Treasury bonds and replacing them with corporates.

    Of course, you need to consider carefully whether there is a good reason that the yield spread seems out of alignment. Perhaps the default premium on corporate bonds increased because the market expects a severe recession. In this case, the wider spread would not represent attractive pricing of corporates relative to Treasuries, but would simply be an adjustment for a perceived increase in credit risk.

3. The **rate anticipation swap** is pegged to interest rate forecasting. If investors believe that rates will fall, they will swap into bonds of longer duration. For example, the investor might sell a 5-year maturity Treasury bond, replacing it with a 25-year maturity Treasury bond. The new bond has the same lack of credit risk as the old one, but it has longer duration. Conversely, when rates are expected to rise, investors will swap into shorter duration bonds.

4. The **pure yield pickup swap** is pursued not in response to perceived mispricing, but as a means of increasing return by holding higher-yield bonds. When the yield curve is upward-sloping, the yield pickup swap entails moving into longer-term

bonds. This strategy must be viewed as an attempt to earn an expected term premium in higher-yield bonds and comes at the price of increased interest rate risk. The investor who swaps the shorter-term bond for the longer one will earn a higher rate of return as long as the yield curve does not shift up during the holding period. Of course if it does, the longer-duration bond will suffer a greater capital loss.

We can add a fifth swap, called a **tax swap,** to this list. This simply refers to a swap to exploit some tax advantage. For example, an investor may swap from one bond that has decreased in price to another if realization of capital losses is advantageous for tax purposes.

Horizon Analysis

One form of interest rate forecasting, which we encountered in Chapter 14, is called **horizon analysis.** The analyst using this approach selects a particular holding period and predicts the yield curve at the end of that period. Given a bond's time to maturity at the end of the holding period, its yield can be read from the predicted yield curve and its end-of-period price calculated. Then the analyst adds the coupon income and prospective capital gain of the bond to find the total return on the bond over the holding period.

Example 16.6   Horizon Analysis

A 20-year maturity bond with a 10% coupon rate (paid annually) currently sells at a yield to maturity of 9%. A portfolio manager with a 2-year horizon needs to forecast the total return on the bond over the coming two years. In two years, the bond will have an 18-year maturity. The analyst forecasts that two years from now, 18-year bonds will sell at yields to maturity of 8%, and that coupon payments can be reinvested in short-term securities over the coming two years at a rate of 7%.

To calculate the 2-year return on the bond, the analyst would perform the following calculations:

1. Current price = $100 × Annuity factor (9%, 20 years)
   + $1,000 × PV factor (9%, 20 years)
   = $1,091.29

2. Forecast price = $100 × Annuity factor (8%, 18 years)
   + $1,000 × PV factor (8%, 18 years)
   = $1,187.44

3. The future value of reinvested coupons will be ($100 × 1.07) + $100 = $207

4. The 2-year return is $\dfrac{\$207 + (\$1,187.44 - \$1,091.29)}{\$1,091.29} = 0.278$, or 27.8%

The annualized rate of return over the 2-year period would then be $1.278^{1/2} - 1 = 0.13$, or 13%.

 Concept Check **16.8**

What will be the rate of return in Example 16.6 if the manager forecasts that in two years the yield on 18-year bonds will be 10% and the reinvestment rate for coupons will be 8%?

1. Even default-free bonds such as Treasury issues are subject to interest rate risk. Longer-term bonds generally are more sensitive to interest rate shifts than are short-term bonds. A measure of the average life of a bond is Macaulay's duration, defined as the weighted average of the times until each payment made by the security, with weights proportional to the present value of the payment.

2. Duration is a direct measure of the sensitivity of a bond's price to a change in its yield. The proportional change in a bond's price equals the negative of duration multiplied by the proportional change in $1 + y$.

3. Convexity refers to the curvature of a bond's price-yield relationship. Accounting for convexity can substantially improve the accuracy of the duration approximation for the response of bond prices to changes in yields.

4. Immunization is a passive fixed-income portfolio management strategy. It attempts to render the individual or firm immune from movements in interest rates. This may take the form of immunizing net worth or, instead, immunizing the future accumulated value of a fixed-income portfolio.

5. Immunization of a fully funded plan is accomplished by matching the durations of assets and liabilities. To maintain an immunized position as time passes and interest rates change, the portfolio must be periodically rebalanced. Classic immunization also depends on parallel shifts in a flat yield curve. Given that this assumption is unrealistic, immunization generally will be less than complete. To mitigate the problem, multifactor duration models can be used to allow for variation in the shape of the yield curve.

6. A more direct form of immunization is dedication, or cash-flow matching. If portfolio cash flows are perfectly matched to those of projected liabilities, rebalancing will be unnecessary.

7. Active bond management consists of interest rate forecasting techniques and intermarket spread analysis. One popular taxonomy classifies active strategies as substitution swaps, intermarket spread swaps, rate anticipation swaps, and pure yield pickup swaps.

8. Horizon analysis is a type of interest rate forecasting. In this procedure the analyst forecasts the position of the yield curve at the end of some holding period and from that yield curve predicts corresponding bond prices. Bonds then can be ranked according to expected total rates of return over the holding period.

SUMMARY

KEY TERMS

Macaulay's duration	rebalancing	rate anticipation swap
modified duration	cash flow matching	pure yield pickup swap
convexity	dedication strategy	tax swap
effective duration	substitution swap	horizon analysis
immunization	intermarket spread swap	

KEY EQUATIONS

Macaulay's duration: $D = \sum_{t=1}^{T} t \times w_t$

Modified duration: $D^* = D/(1 + y)$

Bond price risk: $\dfrac{\Delta P}{P} = -D \times \left[\dfrac{\Delta(1 + y)}{1 + y} \right] = -D^* \times \Delta y$

Duration of perpetuity $= \dfrac{1 + y}{y}$

Bond price risk including convexity:

$\dfrac{\Delta P}{P} = -D^* \Delta y + \frac{1}{2} \times \text{Convexity} \times (\Delta y)^2$

Effective duration $= -\dfrac{\Delta P/P}{\Delta r}$

PROBLEM SETS

1. Prices of long-term bonds are more volatile than prices of short-term bonds. However, yields to maturity of short-term bonds fluctuate more than yields of long-term bonds. How do you reconcile these two empirical observations?

2. How can a perpetuity, which has an infinite maturity, have a duration as short as 10 or 20 years?

3. A 9-year bond has a yield of 10% and a duration of 7.194 years. If the market yield changes by 50 basis points, what is the percentage change in the bond's price?

4. *a.* Find the duration of a 6% coupon bond making *annual* coupon payments if it has three years until maturity and has a yield to maturity of 6%.
   b. What is the duration if the yield to maturity is 10%?

5. Repeat Problem 4, but now assume the coupons are paid semiannually.

6. *a.* The historical yield spread between AAA bonds and Treasury bonds widened dramatically during the financial crisis in 2008. If you believed that the spread would soon return to more typical historical levels, what should you have done?
   b. This would be an example of what sort of bond swap?

7. You predict that interest rates are about to fall. Which bond will give you the highest capital gain?
   a. Low coupon, long maturity.
   b. High coupon, short maturity.
   c. High coupon, long maturity.
   d. Zero coupon, long maturity.

8. Rank the durations or effective durations of the following pairs of bonds:
   a. Bond A is a 6% coupon bond, with a 20-year time to maturity selling at par value. Bond B is a 6% coupon bond, with a 20-year time to maturity selling below par value.
   b. Bond A is a 20-year noncallable coupon bond with a coupon rate of 6%, selling at par. Bond B is a 20-year callable bond with a coupon rate of 7%, also selling at par.

9. An insurance company must make payments to a customer of $10 million in one year and $4 million in five years. The yield curve is flat at 10%.
   a. If it wants to fully fund and immunize its obligation to this customer with a *single* issue of a zero-coupon bond, what maturity bond must it purchase?
   b. What must be the face value and market value of that zero-coupon bond?

10. Long-term Treasury bonds currently are selling at yields to maturity of nearly 6%. You expect interest rates to fall. The rest of the market thinks that they will remain unchanged over the coming year. In each question, choose the bond that will provide the higher holding-period return over the next year if you are correct. Briefly explain your answer.
    a. i. A Baa-rated bond with coupon rate 6% and time to maturity 20 years.
        ii. An Aaa-rated bond with coupon rate of 6% and time to maturity 20 years.
    b. i. An A-rated bond with coupon rate 3% and maturity 20 years, callable at 105.
        ii. An A-rated bond with coupon rate 6% and maturity 20 years, callable at 105.
    c. i. A 4% coupon noncallable T-bond with maturity 20 years and YTM = 6%.
        ii. A 7% coupon noncallable T-bond with maturity 20 years and YTM = 6%.

11. Currently, the term structure is as follows: 1-year zero-coupon bonds yield 7%; 2-year zero-coupon bonds yield 8%; 3-year and longer-maturity zero-coupon bonds all yield 9%. You are choosing between 1-, 2-, and 3-year maturity bonds all paying annual coupons of 8%.
    a. What is the price of each bond today?
    b. What will be the price of each bond in one year if the yield curve is flat at 9% at that time?
    c. What will be the rate of return on each bond?

12. You will be paying $10,000 a year in tuition expenses at the end of the next two years. Bonds currently yield 8%.
    a. What is the present value and duration of your obligation?
    b. What maturity zero-coupon bond would immunize your obligation?

   c. Suppose you buy a zero-coupon bond with value and duration equal to your obligation. Now suppose that rates immediately increase to 9%. What happens to your net position, that is, to the difference between the value of the bond and that of your tuition obligation?

   d. What if rates fall immediately to 7%?

13. Pension funds pay lifetime annuities to recipients. If a firm will remain in business indefinitely, the pension obligation will resemble a perpetuity. Suppose, therefore, that you are managing a pension fund with obligations to make perpetual payments of $2 million per year to beneficiaries. The yield to maturity on all bonds is 16%.

   a. If the duration of 5-year maturity bonds with coupon rates of 12% (paid annually) is four years and the duration of 20-year maturity bonds with coupon rates of 6% (paid annually) is 11 years, how much of each of these coupon bonds (in market value) will you want to hold to both fully fund and immunize your obligation?

   b. What will be the par value of your holdings in the 20-year coupon bond?

14. You are managing a portfolio of $1 million. Your target duration is 10 years, and you can invest in two bonds, a zero-coupon bond with maturity of five years and a perpetuity, each currently yielding 5%.

   a. How much of (i) the zero-coupon bond and (ii) the perpetuity will you hold in your portfolio?

   b. How will these fractions change *next year* if target duration is now nine years?

15. My pension plan will pay me $10,000 once a year for a 10-year period. The first payment will come in exactly five years. The pension fund wants to immunize its position.

   a. What is the duration of its obligation to me? The current interest rate is 10% per year.

   b. If the plan uses 5-year and 20-year zero-coupon bonds to construct the immunized position, how much money ought to be placed in each bond?

   c. What will be the *face value* of the holdings in each zero?

16. A 30-year maturity bond making annual coupon payments with a coupon rate of 12% has duration of 11.54 years and convexity of 192.4. The bond currently sells at a yield to maturity of 8%.

   a. Use a financial calculator or spreadsheet to find the price of the bond if its yield to maturity falls to 7%.

   b. What price would be predicted by the duration rule?

   c. What price would be predicted by the duration-with-convexity rule?

   d. What is the percent error for each rule? What do you conclude about the accuracy of the two rules?

   e. Repeat your analysis if the bond's yield to maturity increases to 9%. Are your conclusions about the accuracy of the two rules consistent with parts (*a*) – (*d*)?

17. Frank Meyers, CFA, is a fixed-income portfolio manager for a large pension fund. A member of the Investment Committee, Fred Spice, is very interested in learning about the management of fixed-income portfolios. Spice has approached Meyers with several questions.

   Meyers decides to illustrate fixed-income trading strategies to Spice using a fixed-rate bond and note. Both bonds have semiannual coupon periods. Unless otherwise stated, all interest rate changes are parallel. The characteristics of these securities are shown in the following table. He also considers a 9-year floating-rate bond (floater) that pays a floating rate semiannually and is currently yielding 5%.

Characteristics of Fixed-Rate Bond and Fixed-Rate Note

	Fixed-Rate Bond	Fixed-Rate Note
Price	107.18	100.00
Yield to maturity	5.00%	5.00%
Time to maturity (years)	9	4
Modified duration (years)	6.9848	3.5851

Spice asks Meyers about how a fixed-income manager would position his portfolio to capitalize on expectations of increasing interest rates. Which of the following would be the most appropriate strategy?

a. Shorten his portfolio duration.
b. Buy fixed-rate bonds.
c. Lengthen his portfolio duration.

18. Spice asks Meyers (see Problem 17) to quantify price changes from changes in interest rates. To illustrate, Meyers computes the value change for the fixed-rate note in the table. Specifically, he assumes an increase in the level of interest rate of 100 basis points. Using the information in the table, what is the predicted change in the price of the fixed-rate note?

Please visit us at
www.mhhe.com/Bodie11e

19. Find the duration of a bond with a settlement date of May 27, 2020, and maturity date November 15, 2031. The coupon rate of the bond is 7%, and the bond pays coupons semiannually. The bond is selling at a bond-equivalent yield to maturity of 8%. You can use Spreadsheet 16.2, available in Connect or through your course instructor.

20. A 30-year maturity bond has a 7% coupon rate, paid annually. It sells today for $867.42. A 20-year maturity bond has a 6.5% coupon rate, also paid annually. It sells today for $879.50. A bond market analyst forecasts that in five years, 25-year maturity bonds will sell at yields to maturity of 8% and 15-year maturity bonds will sell at yields of 7.5%. Because the yield curve is upward sloping, the analyst believes that coupons will be invested in short-term securities at a rate of 6%.

a. Calculate the (annualized) expected rate of return of the 30-year bond over the 5-year period.
b. What is the (annualized) expected return of the 20-year bond?

Please visit us at
www.mhhe.com/Bodie11e

21. a. Use a spreadsheet to calculate the durations of the two bonds in Spreadsheet 16.1 if the annual interest rate increases to 12%. Why does the duration of the coupon bond fall while that of the zero remains unchanged? (*Hint:* Examine what happens to the weights computed in column F.)

b. Use the same spreadsheet to calculate the duration of the coupon bond if the coupon is 12% instead of 8% and the semiannual interest rate is again 5%. Explain why duration is lower than in Spreadsheet 16.1. (Again, start by looking at column F.)

22. a. Footnote 7 presents the formula for the convexity of a bond. Build a spreadsheet to calculate the convexity of a 5-year, 8% coupon bond making annual payments at the initial yield to maturity of 10%.

b. What is the convexity of a 5-year zero-coupon bond?

23. A 12.75-year maturity zero-coupon bond selling at a yield to maturity of 8% (effective annual yield) has convexity of 150.3 and modified duration of 11.81 years. A 30-year maturity 6% coupon bond making annual coupon payments also selling at a yield to maturity of 8% has nearly identical duration—11.79 years—but considerably higher convexity of 231.2.

a. Suppose the yield to maturity on both bonds increases to 9%. (i) What will be the actual percentage capital loss on each bond? (ii) What percentage capital loss would be predicted by the duration-with-convexity rule?

b. Repeat part (*a*), but this time assume the yield to maturity decreases to 7%.

c. Compare the performance of the two bonds in the two scenarios, one involving an increase in rates, the other a decrease. Based on the comparative investment performance, explain the attraction of convexity.

d. In view of your answer to part (*c*), do you think it would be possible for two bonds with equal duration but different convexity to be priced initially at the same yield to maturity if the yields on both bonds always increased or decreased by equal amounts, as in this example? (*Hint:* Would anyone be willing to buy the bond with lower convexity under these circumstances?)

24. A newly issued bond has a maturity of 10 years and pays a 7% coupon rate (with coupon payments coming once annually). The bond sells at par value.

   a. What are the convexity and the duration of the bond? Use the formula for convexity in footnote 7.
   b. Find the actual price of the bond assuming that its yield to maturity immediately increases from 7% to 8% (with maturity still 10 years).
   c. What price would be predicted by the modified duration rule (Equation 16.3)? What is the percentage error of that rule?
   d. What price would be predicted by the modified duration-with-convexity rule (Equation 16.5)? What is the percentage error of that rule?

25. a. Use a spreadsheet to answer this question and assume the yield curve is flat at a level of 4%. Calculate the convexity of a "bullet" fixed-income portfolio, that is, a portfolio with a single cash flow. Suppose a single $1,000 cash flow is paid in year 5.
   b. Now calculate the convexity of a "ladder" fixed-income portfolio, that is, a portfolio with equal cash flows over time. Suppose the security makes $100 cash flows in each of years 1–9, so that its duration is close to the bullet in part (a).
   c. Do ladders or bullets have greater convexity?

Please visit us at
www.mhhe.com/Bodie11e

1. a. Explain the impact on the offering yield of adding a call feature to a proposed bond issue.
   b. Explain the impact on *both* effective bond duration and convexity of adding a call feature to a proposed bond issue.

2. a. A 6% coupon bond paying interest annually has a modified duration of 10 years, sells for $800, and is priced at a yield to maturity of 8%. If the YTM increases to 9%, what is the predicted change in price based on the bond's duration?
   b. A 6% coupon bond with semiannual coupons has a convexity (in years) of 120, sells for 80% of par, and is priced at a yield to maturity of 8%. If the YTM increases to 9.5%, what is the predicted contribution of convexity to the percentage change in price due to convexity?
   c. A bond with annual coupon payments has a coupon rate of 8%, yield to maturity of 10%, and Macaulay duration of 9 years. What is the bond's modified duration?
   d. When interest rates decline, the duration of a 30-year bond selling at a premium:

      i. Increases.
      ii. Decreases.
      iii. Remains the same.
      iv. Increases at first, then declines.

   e. If a bond manager swaps a bond for one that is identical in terms of coupon rate, maturity, and credit quality but offers a higher yield to maturity, the swap is:

      i. A substitution swap.
      ii. An interest rate anticipation swap.
      iii. A tax swap.
      iv. An intermarket spread swap.

   f. Which bond has the longest duration?

      i. 8-year maturity, 6% coupon.
      ii. 8-year maturity, 11% coupon.
      iii. 15-year maturity, 6% coupon.
      iv. 15-year maturity, 11% coupon.

3. A newly issued bond has the following characteristics:

Coupon	Yield to Maturity	Maturity	Macaulay's Duration
8%	8%	15 years	10 years

a. Calculate modified duration using the information above.

b. Explain why modified duration is a better measure than maturity when calculating the bond's sensitivity to changes in interest rates.

c. Identify the direction of change in modified duration if:

   i. The coupon of the bond were 4%, not 8%.

   ii. The maturity of the bond were 7 years, not 15 years.

d. Define convexity and explain how modified duration and convexity are used to approximate the bond's percentage change in price, given a change in interest rates.

4. Bonds of Zello Corporation with a par value of $1,000 sell for $960, mature in five years, and have a 7% annual coupon rate paid semiannually.

a. Calculate each of the following yields:

   i. Current yield.

   ii. Yield to maturity to the nearest whole percent (i.e., 3%, 4%, 5%, etc.).

   iii. Horizon yield (also called total compound return) for an investor with a 3-year holding period and a reinvestment rate of 6% over the period. At the end of three years, the 7% coupon bonds with two years remaining will sell to yield 7%.

b. Cite a major shortcoming for each of the following fixed-income yield measures:

   i. Current yield.

   ii. Yield to maturity.

   iii. Horizon yield (also called total compound return).

5. Sandra Kapple presents Maria VanHusen with a description, given in the following table, of the bond portfolio held by the Star Hospital Pension Plan. All securities in the bond portfolio are noncallable U.S. Treasury securities.

Par Value (U.S. $)	Treasury Security	Market Value (U.S. $)	Current Price	Price if Yields Change		Effective Duration
				Up 100 Basis Points	Down 100 Basis Points	
$48,000,000	2.375% due 2015	$48,667,680	101.391	99.245	103.595	2.15
50,000,000	4.75% due 2040	50,000,000	100.000	86.372	116.887	—
98,000,000	Total bond portfolio	98,667,680	—	—	—	—

a. Calculate the effective duration of each of the following:

   i. The 4.75% Treasury security due 2040.

   ii. The total bond portfolio.

b. VanHusen remarks to Kapple, "If you changed the maturity structure of the bond portfolio to result in a portfolio duration of 5.25 years, the price sensitivity of the portfolio would be identical to that of a single, noncallable Treasury security that also has a duration of 5.25 years." In what circumstance would VanHusen's remark be correct?

6. One common goal among fixed-income portfolio managers is to earn high incremental returns on corporate bonds versus government bonds of comparable durations. The approach of some corporate-bond portfolio managers is to find and purchase those corporate bonds having the largest initial spreads over comparable-duration government bonds. John Ames, HFS's fixed-income manager, believes that a more rigorous approach is required if incremental returns are to be maximized.

The following table presents data relating to one set of corporate/government spread relationships present in the market at a given date:

Bond Rating	Initial Spread over Governments	Expected Horizon Spread	Initial Duration	Expected Duration 1 Year from Now
Aaa	31 b.p.	31 b.p.	4 years	3.1 years
Aa	40 b.p.	50 b.p.	4 years	3.1 years

Note: 1 b.p. = 1 basis point, or .01%.

a. Recommend purchase of either Aaa or Aa bonds for a 1-year investment horizon given a goal of maximizing expected returns.

b. Ames chooses not to rely *solely* on initial spread relationships. His analytical framework considers a full range of other key variables likely to impact realized incremental returns, including call provisions and potential changes in interest rates. Describe variables, in addition to those identified above, that Ames should include in his analysis and explain how each of these could cause realized incremental returns to differ from those indicated by initial spread relationships.

7. Patrick Wall is considering the purchase of one of the two bonds described in the following table. Wall realizes his decision will depend primarily on effective duration, and he believes that interest rates will decline by 50 basis points at all maturities over the next six months.

Characteristic	CIC	PTR
Market price	101.75	101.75
Maturity date	June 1, 2025	June 1, 2025
Call date	Noncallable	June 1, 2020
Annual coupon	5.25%	6.35%
Interest payment	Semiannual	Semiannual
Effective duration	7.35	5.40
Yield to maturity	5.02%	6.10%
Credit rating	A	A

a. Calculate the percentage price change forecasted by effective duration for both the CIC and PTR bonds if interest rates decline by 50 basis points over the next six months.

b. Calculate the 6-month horizon return (in percent) for each bond if the actual CIC bond price equals 105.55 and the actual PTR bond price equals 104.15 at the end of six months.

c. Wall is surprised by the fact that although interest rates fell by 50 basis points, the actual price change for the CIC bond was greater than the price change forecasted by effective duration, whereas the actual price change for the PTR bond was less than the price change forecasted by effective duration. Explain why the actual price change would be greater for the CIC bond and less for the PTR bond.

8. You are the manager for the bond portfolio of a pension fund. The policies of the fund allow for the use of active strategies in managing the bond portfolio.

It appears that the economic cycle is beginning to mature, inflation is expected to accelerate, and in an effort to contain the economic expansion, the central bank is moving toward tighter monetary policy. For each of the situations below, state which one of the two bonds you would prefer. Briefly justify your answer in each case.

a. Government of Canada (Canadian pay) 3% coupon due in 2020 and priced at 98.75 to yield 3.50% to maturity.

or

Government of Canada (Canadian pay) 3% coupon due in 2030 and priced at 91.75 to yield 4.19% to maturity.

    b. Texas Power and Light Co. 4.50% coupon due in 2025, rated AAA, and priced at 90 to yield 5.02% to maturity.

or

    Arizona Public Service Co. 4.45% coupon due in 2025, rated A–, and priced at 92 to yield 5.85% to maturity.

    c. Commonwealth Edison 2.75% due in 2024, rated Baa, and priced at 91 to yield 6.2% to maturity.

or

    Commonwealth Edison 7.375% due in 2024, rated Baa, and priced at 114.40 to yield 6.2% to maturity.

    d. Shell Oil Co. 5.50% sinking fund debentures due in 2030, rated AAA (sinking fund begins September 2018 at par), and priced at 89 to yield 6.1% to maturity.

or

    Warner-Lambert 5.75% sinking fund debentures due in 2030, rated AAA (sinking fund begins April 2023 at par), and priced at 89 to yield 6.1% to maturity.

    e. Bank of Montreal (Canadian pay) 3% certificates of deposit due in 2019, rated AAA, and priced at 100 to yield 3% to maturity.

or

    Bank of Montreal (Canadian pay) floating-rate note due in 2021, rated AAA. Coupon currently set at 1.8% and priced at 100 (coupon adjusted semiannually to .5% above the 3-month Government of Canada Treasury-bill rate).

9. A member of a firm's investment committee is very interested in learning about the management of fixed-income portfolios. He would like to know how fixed-income managers position portfolios to capitalize on their expectations concerning three factors which influence interest rates:

    a. Changes in the level of interest rates.
    b. Changes in yield spreads across/between sectors.
    c. Changes in yield spreads as to a particular instrument.

    Formulate and describe a fixed-income portfolio management strategy for each of these factors that could be used to exploit a portfolio manager's expectations about that factor. (*Note:* Three strategies are required, one for each of the listed factors.)

10. Carol Harrod is the investment officer for a $100 million U.S. pension fund. The fixed-income portion of the portfolio is actively managed, and a substantial portion of the fund's large capitalization U.S. equity portfolio is indexed and managed by Webb Street Advisors.

    Harrod has been impressed with the investment results of Webb Street's equity index strategy and is considering asking Webb Street to index a portion of the actively managed fixed-income portfolio.

    a. Describe the advantages and disadvantages of bond indexing relative to active bond management.
    b. Webb Street manages indexed bond portfolios. Discuss how an indexed bond portfolio is constructed under stratified sampling (cellular) methods.
    c. Describe the main source of tracking error for the cellular method.

11. Janet Meer is a fixed-income portfolio manager. Noting that the current shape of the yield curve is flat, she considers the purchase of a newly issued, 7% coupon, 10-year maturity, option-free corporate bond priced at par. The bond has the following features:

	Change in Yields	
	Up 10 Basis Points	Down 10 Basis Points
Price	99.29	100.71
Convexity measure	35.00	
Convexity adjustment	0.0035	

a. Calculate the modified duration of the bond.

b. Meer is also considering the purchase of a newly issued, 7.25% coupon, 12-year maturity option-free corporate bond. She wants to evaluate this second bond's price sensitivity to an instantaneous, downward parallel shift in the yield curve of 200 basis points. Based on the following data, what will be its price change in this yield-curve scenario?

Original issue price	Par value, to yield 7.25%
Modified duration (at original price)	7.90
Convexity measure	41.55
Convexity adjustment (yield change of 200 basis points)	1.66

c. Meer asks her assistant to analyze several callable bonds, given the expected downward parallel shift in the yield curve. Meer's assistant argues that if interest rates fall enough, convexity for a callable bond will become negative. Is the assistant's argument correct?

12. Noah Kramer, a fixed-income portfolio manager based in the country of Sevista, is considering the purchase of a Sevista government bond. Kramer decides to evaluate two strategies for implementing his investment in Sevista bonds. Table 16A gives the details of the two strategies, and Table 16B contains the assumptions that apply to both strategies.

Strategy	5-Year Maturity (Modified Duration = 4.83)	15-Year Maturity (Modified Duration = 14.35)	25-Year Maturity (Modified Duration = 23.81)
I	$5 million	0	$5 million
II	0	$10 million	0

Table 16A

Investment strategies (amounts are market-value invested)

Market value of bonds	$10 million
Bond maturities	5 and 25 years or 15 years
Bond coupon rates	0.00% (zero coupon)
Target modified duration	15 years

Table 16B

Investment strategy assumptions

Before choosing one of the two bond-investment strategies, Kramer wants to analyze how the market value of the bonds will change if an instantaneous interest rate shift occurs immediately after his investment. The details of the interest rate shift are shown in Table 16C. Calculate, for the instantaneous interest rate shift shown in Table 16C, the percent change in the market value of the bonds that will occur under each strategy.

Maturity	Interest Rate Change
5 year	Down 75 basis points (bps)
15 year	Up 25 bps
25 year	Up 50 bps

Table 16C

Instantaneous interest rate shift immediately after investment

13. As part of your analysis of debt issued by Monticello Corporation, you are asked to evaluate two of its bond issues, shown in the following table.

	Bond A (Callable)	Bond B (Noncallable)
Maturity	2027	2027
Coupon	11.50%	7.25%
Current price	125.75	100.00
Yield to maturity	7.70%	7.25%
Modified duration to maturity	6.20	6.80
Call date	2021	—
Call price	105	—
Yield to call	5.10%	—
Modified duration to call	3.10	—

a. Using the duration and yield information in the table above, compare the price and yield behavior of the two bonds under each of the following two scenarios:

  i. Strong economic recovery with rising inflation expectations.
  ii. Economic recession with reduced inflation expectations.

b. Using the information in the table, calculate the projected price change for bond B if its yield to maturity falls by 75 basis points.

c. Describe the shortcoming of analyzing bond A strictly to call or to maturity.

E-INVESTMENTS EXERCISES

Go to **http://www.tipsinc.com/ficalc/calc.tips**. Choose the link for the general-purpose bond calculator. The calculator provides yield to maturity, modified duration, and bond convexity as the bond's price changes. Experiment by trying different inputs. What happens to duration and convexity as coupon increases? As maturity increases? As price increases (holding coupon fixed)?

 # SOLUTIONS TO CONCEPT CHECKS

1. Use Spreadsheet 16.1 with a semiannual discount rate of 4.5%.

	Period	Time until Payment (Years)	Cash Flow	PV of CF (Discount rate = 4.5% per period)	Weight	Weight × Time
A. 8% Coupon Bond	1	0.5	40	38.278	0.0390	0.0195
	2	1.0	40	36.629	0.0373	0.0373
	3	1.5	40	35.052	0.0357	0.0535
	4	2.0	1,040	872.104	0.8880	1.7761
Sum:				982.062	1.0000	1.8864
B. Zero-Coupon	1	0.5	0	0.000	0.0000	0.0000
	2	1.0	0	0.000	0.0000	0.0000
	3	1.5	0	0.000	0.0000	0.0000
	4	2.0	1,000	838.561	1.0000	2.0000
Sum:				838.561	1.0000	2.0000

The duration of the 8% coupon bond increases to 1.8864 years. Price increases to $982.062. The duration of the zero-coupon bond is unchanged at two years, although its price also increases (to $838.561) when the interest rate falls.

2. *a.* If the interest rate increases from 9% to 9.05%, the bond price falls from $982.062 to $981.177. The percentage change in price is −0.0901%.

   b. Using the initial semiannual rate of 4.5%, duration is 1.8864 years (see Concept Check 16.1), so the duration formula would predict a price change of

$$-\frac{1.8864}{1.045} \times .0005 = -.000903 = -.0903\%$$

   which is almost the same answer that we obtained from direct computation in part (*a*).

3. The duration of a level perpetuity is $(1 + y)/y$ or $1 + 1/y$, which clearly falls as y increases. Tabulating duration as a function of y we get

y	D
0.01	101 years
0.02	51
0.05	21
0.10	11
0.20	6

4. In agreement with the duration rules presented in the chapter, you should find that duration is shorter when the coupon rate or yield to maturity is higher. Duration increases with maturity for most bonds. Duration is shorter when coupons are paid semiannually rather than annually because on average, payments come earlier. Instead of waiting until year-end to receive the annual coupon, investors receive half the coupon midyear.

5. Macaulay's duration is defined as the weighted average of the time until receipt of each bond payment. Modified duration is defined as Macaulay's duration divided by $1 + y$ (where y is yield per payment period, e.g., a semiannual yield if the bond pays semiannual coupons). One can demonstrate that for a straight bond, modified duration approximately equals the percentage change in bond price per change in yield. Effective duration captures this last property of modified duration. It is *defined* as percentage change in bond price per change in market interest rates. Effective duration for a bond with embedded options requires a valuation method that allows for such options in computing price changes. Effective duration cannot be related to a weighted average of times until payments, because those payments are themselves uncertain.

6. The perpetuity's duration now would be $1.08/.08 = 13.5$. We need to solve the following equation for *w:*

$$w \times 2 + (1 - w) + 13.5 = 6$$

Therefore $w = .6522$.

7. Dedication would be more attractive. Cash flow matching eliminates the need for rebalancing and thus saves transaction costs.

8. Current price = $1,091.29

   Forecasted price = $100 × Annuity factor(10%, 18 years) + $1,000 × PV factor (10%, 18 years)

             = $1,000

The future value of reinvested coupons will be $(\$100 \times 1.08) + \$100 = \$208$

The 2-year return is $\dfrac{\$208 + (\$1,000 - \$1,091.29)}{\$1,091.29} = 0.107$, or 10.7%

The annualized rate of return over the 2-year period would then be $(1.107)^{1/2} - 1 = .052$, or 5.2%.

Macroeconomic and Industry Analysis

THE INTRINSIC VALUE OF A stock depends on the dividend and earnings that can be expected from the firm. This is the heart of **fundamental analysis**—that is, the analysis of the determinants of value such as earnings prospects. Ultimately, the business success of the firm determines the dividends it can pay to shareholders and the price it will command in the stock market. Because the prospects of the firm are tied to those of the broader economy, however, fundamental analysis must consider the business environment in which the firm operates. For some firms, macroeconomic and industry circumstances might have a greater influence on profits than the firm's relative performance within its industry. In other words, investors need to keep the big economic picture in mind.

Therefore, in analyzing a firm's prospects, it often makes sense to start with the broad economic environment, examining the state of the aggregate economy and even the international economy. From there, one considers the implications of the outside environment on the industry in which the firm operates. Finally, the firm's position within the industry is examined.

This chapter treats the broad-based aspects of fundamental analysis—macroeconomic and industry analysis. The two chapters that follow cover firm-specific analysis. We begin with a discussion of international factors relevant to firm performance and move on to an overview of the significance of the key variables usually used to summarize the state of the macroeconomy. We then discuss government macroeconomic policy. We conclude the analysis of the macroenvironment with a discussion of business cycles. Finally, we move to industry analysis, treating issues concerning the sensitivity of the firm to the business cycle, the typical life cycle of an industry, and strategic issues that affect industry performance.

17.1 The Global Economy

A top-down analysis of a firm's prospects must start with the global economy. The international economy might affect a firm's export prospects, the price competition it faces from competitors, or the profits it makes on investments abroad. Table 17.1 shows the

Table 17.1

Economic
performance

	Stock Market Return, 2015 (%)		
	In Local Currency	**In U.S. Dollars**	**Forecasted Growth in GDP, 2016 (%)**
Brazil	−12.7	−40.0	−1.9
Britain	−3.8	−8.8	2.2
Canada	−9.5	−24.3	1.9
China	10.1	5.3	6.4
France	10.0	−0.8	1.3
Germany	10.8	−0.2	1.7
Greece	−25.3	−32.6	2.2
Hong Kong	−6.8	−6.7	2.1
India	−5.2	−9.9	7.6
Italy	13.0	2.7	1.3
Japan	8.8	8.2	1.2
Mexico	0.6	−13.9	2.8
Russia	17.0	−2.7	−0.3
Singapore	−14.2	−19.6	3.0
South Korea	2.6	−3.5	2.7
Spain	−6.2	−15.4	2.7
Thailand	−14.3	−21.9	4.0
U.S.	−0.6	−0.6	2.5

Source: *The Economist*, January 2, 2016.

importance of the global or broad regional macroeconomy to firms' prospects. For example, stock markets in southeast Asia, such as those in Thailand and Singapore, had very poor years as regional growth rates slowed.

Despite the importance of regional macroeconomic conditions, there can be considerable variation in economic performance across countries even within regions. In Europe, for example, the German economy was forecast to expand at a rate of 1.7% while the Russian economy was expected to shrink, with forecast growth of −.3%.

Perhaps surprisingly, stock market returns did not always align with macroeconomic expectations. This reflects the impact of near market efficiency, where stock returns are driven by performance relative to previous expectations. For example, despite the fact that its economic growth rate was pretty much in the middle of the pack, the Greek stock market suffered extremely poor performance in 2015. The recovery of its economy was not as strong as previously anticipated, and its stock market took a steep dive.

These data illustrate that the national economic environment can be a crucial determinant of industry performance. It is far harder for businesses to succeed in a contracting economy than in an expanding one. This observation highlights the role of a big-picture macroeconomic analysis as a fundamental part of the investment process.

In addition, political uncertainty can pose considerable economic risks. The sovereign debt crises of the last decade offer a compelling illustration of the interplay between politics and economics. The prospects of a bailout for Greece and possibly for other troubled countries in the European Union were in large part political issues but with enormous consequences for the world economy. Similarly, the rivalry within OPEC between Iran and Saudi Arabia has been in large part a pitched political battle, but one with huge economic consequences as it affects the global price of oil. The exit of the U.K. from the EU was another political battle with big economic implications. Stock markets around the world plummeted on the day the U.K. voted for "Brexit," and the British pound declined by more than 10% against the U.S. dollar. At this level of analysis, it is clear that politics and economics are intimately entwined.

Other political issues that are less sensational but still extremely important to economic growth and investment returns include issues of protectionism and trade policy, the free flow of capital, and the status of a nation's workforce.

One obvious factor that affects the international competitiveness of a country's industries is the exchange rate between that country's currency and other currencies. The **exchange rate** is the rate at which domestic currency can be converted into foreign currency. For example, in mid-2016, it took about 104 Japanese yen to purchase 1 U.S. dollar. We would say that the exchange rate is ¥104 per dollar or, equivalently, $.0096 per yen.

As exchange rates fluctuate, the dollar value of goods priced in foreign currency similarly fluctuates. In 1980, the dollar–yen exchange rate was about $.0045 per yen. Because the exchange rate in 2016 was $.0096 per yen, a U.S. citizen would need more than twice as many dollars in 2016 to buy a product selling for ¥10,000 as would have been required in 1980. If the Japanese producer were to maintain a fixed yen price for its product, the price expressed in U.S. dollars would more than double. This would make Japanese products more expensive to U.S. consumers, however, and result in lost sales. Obviously, appreciation of the yen creates a problem for Japanese producers that must compete with U.S. producers.

Figure 17.1 shows the change in the purchasing power of the U.S. dollar relative to the purchasing power of the currencies of several major industrial countries from 2003 through 2015. The ratio of purchasing powers is called the "real," or inflation-adjusted, exchange rate. The change in the real exchange rate measures how much more or less expensive foreign goods have become to U.S. citizens, accounting for both exchange rate fluctuations and inflation differentials across countries. A positive value in Figure 17.1 means that the

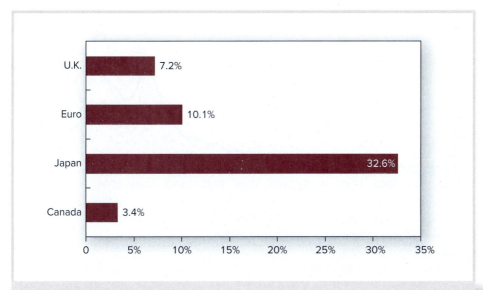

Figure 17.1 Change in real exchange rate: U.S. dollar versus major currencies, 2003–2015

Source: Authors' calculations using data from OECD.

dollar has gained purchasing power relative to another currency; a negative number would indicate a depreciating dollar. Therefore, we see that the U.S. dollar has appreciated in real terms relative to each currency in Figure 17.1. Goods priced in foreign currencies have become less expensive to U.S. consumers; conversely, goods priced in U.S. dollars have become less affordable to consumers abroad.

17.2   The Domestic Macroeconomy

The macroeconomy is the environment in which all firms operate. The importance of the macroeconomy in determining investment performance is illustrated in Figure 17.2, which compares the level of the S&P 500 stock price index to forecasts of earnings per share of the S&P 500 companies. The graph shows that stock prices tend to rise along with earnings. While the exact ratio of stock price to earnings varies with factors such as interest rates, risk, inflation rates, and other variables, the graph does illustrate that as a general rule the ratio has tended to be in the range of 12 to 25. Given "normal" price–earnings ratios, we would expect the S&P 500 index to fall within these boundaries. While the earnings-multiplier rule clearly is not perfect—note the dramatic increase in the price–earnings multiple during the dot-com boom of the late 1990s—it also seems clear that the level of the broad market and aggregate earnings do trend together.[1] Thus, the first step in forecasting the performance of the broad market is to assess the status of the economy as a whole.

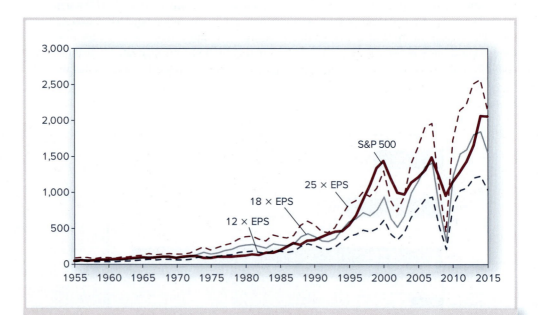

Figure 17.2 S&P 500 index versus earnings per share

Source: Authors' calculations using data from *The Economic Report of the President.*

[1]Figure 17.2 shows that 2009 was another year in which the P/E multiple was much higher than even 25 times earnings. This reflects the fact that earnings in that year, at the height of the deep recession, were dramatically below trend projections. Market prices reflect earnings prospects well into the future and therefore fell by less than earnings in that particular year. As we will see in Chapter 18, P/E ratios are best interpreted relative to future, not past, earnings: Stock prices are forward-looking measures of firm value.

The ability to forecast the macroeconomy can translate into spectacular investment performance. But it is not enough to forecast the macroeconomy well. You must forecast it *better* than your competitors to earn abnormal profits. In this section, we will review some of the key economic statistics used to describe the state of the macroeconomy.

Key Economic Indicators

Gross Domestic Product   **Gross domestic product,** or **GDP,** is the measure of the economy's total production of goods and services. Rapidly growing GDP indicates an expanding economy with ample opportunity for a firm to increase sales. Another popular measure of the economy's output is *industrial production.* This statistic provides a measure of economic activity more narrowly focused on the manufacturing side of the economy.

Employment   The **unemployment rate** is the percentage of the total labor force (i.e., those who are either working or actively seeking employment) yet to find work. The unemployment rate measures the extent to which the economy is operating at full capacity. The unemployment rate is a factor related to workers only, but further insight into the strength of the economy can be gleaned from the unemployment rate for other factors of production. Analysts also look at the factory *capacity utilization rate,* which is the ratio of actual output from factories to potential output.

Inflation   The rate at which the general level of prices rise is called **inflation.** High rates of inflation often are associated with "overheated" economies, that is, economies where the demand for goods and services is outstripping productive capacity, which leads to upward pressure on prices. Most governments walk a fine line in their economic policies. They hope to stimulate their economies enough to maintain nearly full employment, but not so much as to bring on inflationary pressures. The perceived trade-off between inflation and unemployment is at the heart of many macroeconomic policy disputes. There is considerable room for disagreement as to the relative costs of these policies as well as the economy's relative vulnerability to these pressures at any particular time.

Interest Rates   High interest rates reduce the present value of future cash flows, thereby reducing the attractiveness of investment opportunities. For this reason, real interest rates are key determinants of business investment expenditures. Demand for housing and high-priced consumer durables such as automobiles, which are commonly financed, also is highly sensitive to interest rates because interest rates affect interest payments. (In Chapter 5, Section 5.1, we examined the determinants of interest rates.)

Budget Deficit   The **budget deficit** of the federal government is the difference between government spending and revenues. Any budgetary shortfall must be offset by government borrowing. Large amounts of government borrowing can force up interest rates by increasing the total demand for credit in the economy. Economists generally believe excessive government borrowing will "crowd out" private borrowing and investing by forcing up interest rates and choking off business investment.

Sentiment   Consumers' and producers' optimism or pessimism concerning the economy is an important determinant of economic performance. If consumers have confidence in their future income levels, for example, they will be more willing to spend on big-ticket items. Similarly, businesses will increase production and inventory levels if they anticipate higher demand for their products. In this way, beliefs influence how much consumption and investment will be pursued and affect the aggregate demand for goods and services.

Concept Check **17.1**

Consider an economy where the dominant industry is automobile production for domestic consumption as well as export. Now suppose the auto market is hurt by an increase in the length of time people use their cars before replacing them. Describe the probable effects of this change on (*a*) GDP, (*b*) unemployment, (*c*) the government budget deficit, and (*d*) interest rates.

17.3   Demand and Supply Shocks

A useful way to organize your analysis of the factors that might influence the macro-economy is to classify any impact as a supply or demand shock. A **demand shock** is an event that affects the demand for goods and services in the economy. Examples of positive demand shocks are reductions in tax rates, increases in the money supply, increases in government spending, or increases in foreign export demand. A **supply shock** is an event that influences production capacity and costs. Examples of supply shocks are changes in the price of imported oil; freezes, floods, or droughts that might destroy large quantities of agricultural crops; changes in the educational level of an economy's workforce; or changes in the wage rates at which the labor force is willing to work.

Demand shocks are usually characterized by aggregate output moving in the same direction as interest rates and inflation. For example, a big increase in government spending will tend to stimulate the economy and increase GDP. It also might increase interest rates by increasing the demand for borrowed funds by the government as well as by businesses that might desire to borrow to finance new ventures. Finally, it could increase the inflation rate if the demand for goods and services is raised to a level at or beyond the total productive capacity of the economy.

Supply shocks are usually characterized by aggregate output moving in the opposite direction of inflation and interest rates. For example, a big increase in the price of imported oil will be inflationary because costs of production will rise, which eventually will lead to increases in prices of finished goods. The increase in inflation rates over the near term can lead to higher nominal interest rates. Against this background, aggregate output will be falling. With raw materials more expensive, the productive capacity of the economy is reduced, as is the ability of individuals to purchase goods at now-higher prices. GDP, therefore, tends to fall.

How can we relate this framework to investment analysis? You want to identify the industries that will be most helped or hurt in any macroeconomic scenario you envision. For example, if you forecast a tightening of the money supply, you might want to avoid industries such as automobile producers that might be hurt by the likely increase in interest rates. We caution you again that these forecasts are no easy task. Macroeconomic predictions are notoriously unreliable. And again, you must be aware that in all likelihood your forecast will be made using only publicly available information. Any investment advantage you have will be a result only of better analysis—not better information.

17.4   Federal Government Policy

As the previous section would suggest, the government has two broad classes of macroeconomic tools—those that affect the demand for goods and services and those that affect the supply. For much of postwar history, demand-side policy was of primary interest. The focus was on government spending, tax levels, and monetary policy. Since the 1980s, however, increasing attention has been focused on supply-side economics. Broadly interpreted, supply-side concerns have to do with enhancing the productive capacity of the economy, rather than increasing the demand for the goods and services the economy can produce. In practice, supply-side economists have focused on the appropriateness of the incentives to work, innovate, and take risks that result from our system of taxation. However, issues such as national policies on education, infrastructure (such as communication and transportation systems), and research and development also are properly regarded as part of supply-side macroeconomic policy.

Fiscal Policy

Fiscal policy refers to the government's spending and tax actions and is part of "demand-side management." Fiscal policy is probably the most direct way either to stimulate or to slow the economy. Decreases in government spending directly deflate the demand for goods and services. Similarly, increases in tax rates immediately siphon income from consumers and result in fairly rapid decreases in consumption.

Ironically, although fiscal policy has the most immediate impact on the economy, the formulation and implementation of such policy is usually painfully slow and involved. This is because fiscal policy requires enormous amounts of compromise between the executive and legislative branches. Tax and spending policy must be initiated and voted on by Congress, which requires considerable political negotiations, and any legislation passed must be signed by the president, requiring more negotiation. Thus, although the impact of fiscal policy is relatively immediate, its formulation is so cumbersome that fiscal policy cannot in practice be used to fine-tune the economy.

Moreover, much of government spending, such as that for Medicare or Social Security, is nondiscretionary, meaning that it is determined by formula rather than policy and cannot be changed in response to economic conditions. This places even more rigidity into the formulation of fiscal policy.

A common way to summarize the net impact of government fiscal policy is to look at the government's budget deficit or surplus, which is simply the difference between revenues and expenditures. A large deficit means the government is spending considerably more than it is taking in by way of taxes. The net effect is to increase the demand for goods (via spending) by more than it reduces the demand for goods (via taxes), thereby stimulating the economy.

Monetary Policy

Monetary policy refers to the manipulation of the money supply to affect the macroeconomy and is the other main leg of demand-side policy. Monetary policy works largely through its impact on interest rates. Increases in the money supply lower short-term interest rates, ultimately encouraging investment and consumption demand. Over longer periods, however, most economists believe a higher money supply leads only to a higher price level and does not have a permanent effect on economic activity. Thus the monetary authorities face a difficult balancing act. Expansionary monetary policy probably will lower interest rates and thereby stimulate investment and some consumption demand in the short run, but these circumstances ultimately will lead only to higher prices. The stimulation/inflation trade-off is implicit in all debate over proper monetary policy.

Fiscal policy is cumbersome to implement but has a fairly direct impact on the economy, whereas monetary policy is easily formulated and implemented but has a less immediate impact. Monetary policy is determined by the Board of Governors of the Federal Reserve System. Board members are appointed by the president for 14-year terms and are reasonably insulated from political pressure. The board is small enough, and often sufficiently dominated by its chairperson, that policy can be formulated and modulated relatively easily.

Implementation of monetary policy also is quite direct. The most widely used tool is the open market operation, in which the Fed buys or sells bonds for its own account.

When the Fed buys securities, it simply "writes a check," thereby increasing the money supply. (Unlike us, the Fed can pay for the securities without drawing down funds at a bank account.) Conversely, when the Fed sells a security, the money paid for it leaves the money supply. Open market operations occur daily, allowing the Fed to fine-tune its monetary policy.

Other tools at the Fed's disposal are the discount rate, which is the interest rate it charges banks on short-term loans, and the reserve requirement, which is the fraction of deposits that banks must hold as cash on hand or as deposits with the Fed. Reductions in the discount rate signal a more expansionary monetary policy. Lowering reserve requirements allows banks to make more loans with each dollar of deposits and stimulates the economy by increasing the effective money supply.

While the discount rate is under the direct control of the Fed, it is changed relatively infrequently. The *federal funds rate* is by far the better guide to Federal Reserve policy. The federal funds rate is the interest rate at which banks make short-term, usually overnight, loans to each other. These loans occur because some banks need to borrow funds to meet reserve requirements, while other banks have excess funds. Unlike the discount rate, the fed funds rate is a market rate, meaning that it is determined by supply and demand rather than being set administratively. Nevertheless, the Federal Reserve Board targets the fed funds rate, expanding or contracting the money supply through open market operations as it nudges the fed funds rate to its targeted value. This is the benchmark short-term U.S. interest rate, and as such it has considerable influence on other interest rates in the United States and the rest of the world.

Monetary policy affects the economy in a more roundabout way than fiscal policy. Whereas fiscal policy directly stimulates or dampens the economy, monetary policy works largely through its impact on interest rates. Increases in the money supply lower interest rates, which stimulates investment demand. As the quantity of money in the economy increases, investors will find that their portfolios of assets include too much money. They will rebalance their portfolios by buying securities such as bonds, forcing bond prices up and interest rates down. In the longer run, individuals may increase their holdings of stocks as well and ultimately buy real assets, which stimulates consumption demand directly. The ultimate effect of monetary policy on investment and consumption demand, however, is less immediate than that of fiscal policy.

 Concept Check **17.2**

> Suppose the government wants to stimulate the economy without increasing interest rates. What combination of fiscal and monetary policy might accomplish this goal?

Supply-Side Policies

Fiscal policy and monetary policy are demand-oriented tools that affect the economy by stimulating the total demand for goods and services. The implicit belief is that the economy will not by itself arrive at a full employment equilibrium and that macroeconomic policy can push the economy toward this goal. In contrast, supply-side policies treat the issue of the productive capacity of the economy. The goal is to create an environment in which workers and owners of capital have the maximum incentive and ability to produce and develop goods.

Supply-side economists also pay considerable attention to tax policy. Whereas demand-siders look at the effect of taxes on consumption demand, supply-siders focus on incentives and marginal tax rates. They argue that lowering tax rates will elicit more investment and improve incentives to work, thereby enhancing economic growth. Some go so far as to claim that reductions in tax rates can lead to increases in tax revenues because the lower tax rates will cause the economy and the revenue tax base to grow by more than the tax rate is reduced.

Concept Check **17.3**

> Large tax cuts in 2001 were followed by relatively rapid growth in GDP. How would demand-side and supply-side economists differ in their interpretations of this phenomenon?

17.5   Business Cycles

We've looked at the tools the government uses to fine-tune the economy, attempting to maintain low unemployment and low inflation. Despite these efforts, economies repeatedly seem to pass through good and bad times. One determinant of the broad asset allocation decision of many analysts is a forecast of whether the macroeconomy is improving or deteriorating. A forecast that differs from the market consensus can have a major impact on investment strategy.

The Business Cycle

The economy recurrently experiences periods of expansion and contraction, although the length and depth of those cycles can be irregular. This recurring pattern of recession and recovery is called the **business cycle.** Transition points across cycles are called peaks and troughs. A **peak** is the transition from the end of an expansion to the start of a contraction. A **trough** occurs at the bottom of a recession just as the economy enters a recovery.

As the economy passes through different stages of the business cycle, the relative performance of different industry groups might be expected to vary. For example, at a trough, just as the economy begins to recover from a recession, one would expect that **cyclical industries,** those with above-average sensitivity to the state of the economy, would tend to outperform other industries. Examples of cyclical industries are producers of durable goods such as automobiles. Because purchases of these goods can be deferred during a recession, sales are particularly sensitive to macroeconomic conditions. Other cyclical industries are producers of capital goods, that is, goods used by other firms to produce their own products. When demand is slack, few companies will be expanding and purchasing capital goods. Therefore, the capital goods industry bears the brunt of a slowdown but does well in an expansion.

In contrast to cyclical firms, **defensive industries** have little sensitivity to the business cycle. These are industries that produce goods for which sales and profits are least sensitive to the state of the economy. Defensive industries include food producers and processors, pharmaceutical firms, and public utilities. These industries will outperform others when the economy enters a recession.

The cyclical/defensive classification corresponds well to the notion of systematic or market risk introduced in our discussion of portfolio theory. When perceptions about the health of the economy become more optimistic, for example, the prices of most stocks will increase as forecasts of profitability rise. Because the cyclical firms are most sensitive to such developments, their stock prices will rise the most. Thus firms in cyclical industries will tend to have high-beta stocks. In general, then, stocks of cyclical firms will show the best results when economic news is positive but the worst results when that news is bad. Conversely, defensive firms will have low betas and performance that is relatively unaffected by overall market conditions.

If your assessments of the state of the business cycle were reliably more accurate than those of other investors, you would simply choose cyclical industries when you are relatively more optimistic about the economy and defensive firms when you are relatively more pessimistic. Unfortunately, it is not so easy to determine when the economy is passing through a peak or a trough. If it were, choosing between cyclical and defensive industries would be easy. As we know from our discussion of efficient markets, however, attractive investment choices will rarely be obvious. It usually is not apparent that a recession or expansion has started or ended until several months after the fact. With hindsight, the transitions from expansion to recession and back might be apparent, but it is often quite difficult to say whether the economy is heating up or slowing down at any moment.

Economic Indicators

Given the cyclical nature of the business cycle, it is not surprising that to some extent the cycle can be predicted. A set of cyclical indicators computed by the Conference Board helps forecast, measure, and interpret short-term fluctuations in economic activity. **Leading economic indicators** are those economic series that tend to rise or fall in advance of the rest of the economy. *Coincident* and *lagging* indicators, as their names suggest, move in tandem with or somewhat after the broad economy, respectively.

Ten series are grouped into a widely followed composite index of leading economic indicators. Similarly, four coincident and seven lagging indicators form separate indexes. The composition of these indexes appears in Table 17.2.

Figure 17.3 graphs these three series. The shaded areas in the figure all represent periods of recession. The dates at the top of the chart (with format Year: Month) correspond to peaks and troughs (i.e., the turning points between expansions and contractions). While the index of leading indicators consistently turns before the rest of the economy, its lead time is somewhat erratic. Moreover, the lead time for peaks is consistently longer than that for troughs.

Table 17.2		
Indexes of economic indicators	**A.**	**Leading Indicators**
	1.	Average weekly hours of production workers (manufacturing)
	2.	Initial claims for unemployment insurance
	3.	Manufacturers' new orders (consumer goods and materials industries)
	4.	Institute of Supply Management's "Index of New Orders"
	5.	New orders for nondefense capital goods
	6.	New private housing units authorized by local building permits
	7.	Yield curve slope: 10-year Treasury minus federal funds rate
	8.	Stock prices, 500 common stocks
	9.	Leading index of credit market conditions
	10.	Index of consumer expectations for business conditions
	B.	**Coincident Indicators**
	1.	Employees on nonagricultural payrolls
	2.	Personal income less transfer payments
	3.	Industrial production
	4.	Manufacturing and trade sales
	C.	**Lagging Indicators**
	1.	Average duration of unemployment
	2.	Ratio of trade inventories to sales
	3.	Change in index of labor cost per unit of output
	4.	Average prime rate charged by banks
	5.	Commercial and industrial loans outstanding
	6.	Ratio of consumer installment credit outstanding to personal income
	7.	Change in consumer price index for services

Source: The Conference Board, *Business Cycle Indicators,* June 2016.

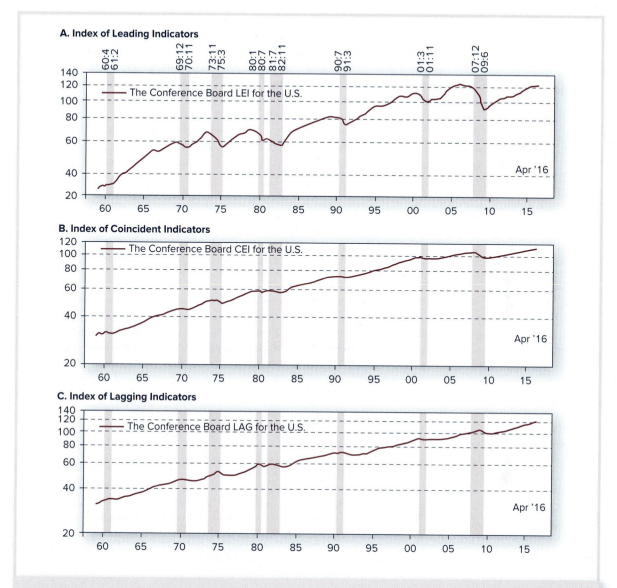

Figure 17.3 Indexes of leading, coincident, and lagging indicators (Panel A: leading indicators; Panel B: coincident indicators; Panel C: lagging indicators)

Note: Shaded areas represent recessions.

Source: The Conference Board, *Business Cycle Indicators*, June 2016.

The stock market price index is a leading indicator. This is as it should be, as stock prices are forward-looking predictors of future profitability. Unfortunately, this makes the series of leading indicators much less useful for investment policy—by the time the series predicts an upturn, the market has already made its move. Although the business cycle may be somewhat predictable, the stock market may not be. This is just one more manifestation of the efficient markets hypothesis.

Other leading indicators focus directly on decisions made today that will affect production in the near future. For example, manufacturers' new orders for goods, contracts, and orders for plant and equipment and housing starts all signal a coming expansion in the economy.

A wide range of economic indicators is released to the public on a regular "economic calendar." Table 17.3 is an economic calendar listing the public announcement dates and sources for about 20 statistics of interest. These announcements are reported in the financial press, for example, *The Wall Street Journal*, as they are released. They also are available at many sites on the Web, for example, at the Yahoo! Finance Web site. Figure 17.4 is a brief excerpt from the Economic Calendar page at Yahoo! The page gives a list of the announcements released the week of June 14, 2016. Notice that recent forecasts of each variable are provided along with the actual value of each statistic. This is useful because, in an efficient market, security prices already will reflect market expectations. The *new* information in the announcement will determine the market response.

Statistic	Release Date*	Source	Web Site
Auto and truck sales	2nd of month	Commerce Department	**commerce.gov**
Business inventories	15th of month	Commerce Department	**commerce.gov**
Construction spending	1st business day of month	Commerce Department	**commerce.gov**
Consumer confidence	Last Tuesday of month	Conference Board	**conference-board.org**
Consumer credit	5th business day of month	Federal Reserve Board	**federalreserve.gov**
Consumer price index (CPI)	13th of month	Bureau of Labor Statistics	**bls.gov**
Durable goods orders	26th of month	Commerce Department	**commerce.gov**
Employment cost index	End of first month of quarter	Bureau of Labor Statistics	**bls.gov**
Employment record (unemployment, average workweek, nonfarm payrolls)	1st Friday of month	Bureau of Labor Statistics	**bls.gov**
Existing home sales	25th of month	National Association of Realtors	**realtor.org**
Factory orders	1st business day of month	Commerce Department	**commerce.gov**
Gross domestic product	3rd–4th week of month	Commerce Department	**commerce.gov**
Housing starts	16th of month	Commerce Department	**commerce.gov**
Industrial production	15th of month	Federal Reserve Board	**federalreserve.gov**
Initial claims for jobless benefits	Thursdays	Department of Labor	**dol.gov**
International trade balance	20th of month	Commerce Department	**commerce.gov**
Index of leading economic indicators	Beginning of month	Conference Board	**conference-board.org**
Money supply	Thursdays	Federal Reserve Board	**federalreserve.gov**
New home sales	Last business day of month	Commerce Department	**commerce.gov**
Producer price index	11th of month	Bureau of Labor Statistics	**bls.gov**
Productivity and costs	2nd month in quarter (approx. 7th day of month)	Bureau of Labor Statistics	**bls.gov**
Retail sales	13th of month	Commerce Department	**commerce.gov**
Survey of purchasing managers	1st business day of month	Institute for Supply Management	**ism.ws**

Table 17.3

Economic calendar

*Many of these release dates are approximate.

Date	Time (ET)	Statistic	For	Actual	Briefing Forecast	Market Expects	Prior	Revised From
June 14	8:30 AM	Export prices	May	1.0%	NA	NA	0.4%	0.5%
June 14	8:30 AM	Retail sales	May	0.5%	0.4%	0.3%	1.3%	—
June 14	10:00 AM	Business inventories	Apr	0.1%	0.3%	0.2%	0.3%	0.4%
June 15	8:30 AM	PPI	May	0.4%	0.4%	0.3%	0.2%	—
June 15	8:30 AM	Empire manufacturing	June	6.0	−4.0	−1.6	−9.0	—
June 15	9:15 AM	Industrial production	May	−0.4%	−0.4%	−0.1%	0.6%	0.7%
June 15	9:15 AM	Capacity utilization	May	74.9%	75.1%	75.2%	75.3%	75.4%
June 16	8:30 AM	CPI	May	0.2%	0.3%	0.3%	0.4%	—
June 16	8:30 AM	Continuing claims	06/04	2157K	NA	NA	2112K	2095K
June 16	8:30 AM	Current account balance	Q1	−$124.8B	−$124.8B	−$125.4B	−$113.4B	−$125.3B
June 17	8:30 AM	Housing starts	May	1164K	1150K	1150K	1167K	1172K
June 17	8:30 AM	Building permits	May	1138K	1144K	1150K	1130K	1116K

Figure 17.4 Economic calendar at Yahoo!, week of June 14, 2016

Source: Yahoo! Finance, Earnings Calendar, biz.yahoo.com, June 20, 2016.

Other Indicators

You can find lots of important information about the state of the economy from sources other than the official components of the economic calendar or the components of business cycle indicators. Table 17.4, which is derived from some suggestions in *Inc.* magazine,[2] contains a few.

CEO polls	The Business Roundtable surveys CEOs about planned capital spending, a good measure of their optimism about the economy.
www.businessroundtable.org	
Temp jobs	A useful leading indicator. Businesses often hire temporary workers as the economy first picks up, until it is clear that an upturn is going to be sustained. This series is available at the Bureau of Labor Statistics Web site.
(search for "Temporary Help Services")	
www.bls.gov	
Walmart sales	Walmart sales are a good indicator of the retail sector. It publishes its same-store sales weekly.
stock.walmart.com/investors/financial-information/comparable-store-sales/default.aspx	
Commercial and industrial loans	These loans are used by small and medium-sized firms. Information is published weekly by the Federal Reserve.
www.federalreserve.gov	
Semiconductors	The book-to-bill ratio (i.e., new sales versus actual shipments) indicates whether demand in the technology sector is increasing (ratio > 1) or falling. This ratio is published by Semiconductor Equipment and Materials International.
www.semi.org/en/MarketInfo/Book-to-Bill	
Commercial structures	Investment in structures is an indicator of businesses' forecasts of demand for their products in the near future. This series is compiled by the Bureau of Economic Analysis as part of its GDP series.
http://bea.doc.gov	

Table 17.4

Useful economic indicators

[2]Gene Sperling, "The Insider's Guide to Economic Forecasting," *Inc.*, August 2003, p. 96.

17.6   Industry Analysis

Industry analysis is important for the same reason that macroeconomic analysis is. Just as it is difficult for an industry to perform well when the macroeconomy is ailing, it is unusual for a firm in a troubled industry to perform well. Similarly, just as we have seen that economic performance can vary widely across countries, performance also can vary widely across industries. Figure 17.5 illustrates the dispersion of industry performance. It shows return on equity based on 2015–2016 profitability for several major industry groups. ROE ranged from 6.4% for oil and gas companies to 37.3% in the airline industry.

Given the wide variation in profitability, it is not surprising that industry groups exhibit considerable dispersion in their stock market performance. Figure 17.6 presents the stock market performance of the same industries included in Figure 17.5. The spread in performance is remarkable, ranging from a 47.9% gain in the water utility industry to an 18.5% loss in the asset management industry. This range of performance was very much available to virtually all investors. Industry-focused exchange traded funds such as iShares trade like stocks and thus allow even small investors to take a position in each traded industry. Alternatively, one can invest in mutual funds with an industry focus. For example, Fidelity offers over 40 sector funds, each with a particular industry focus.

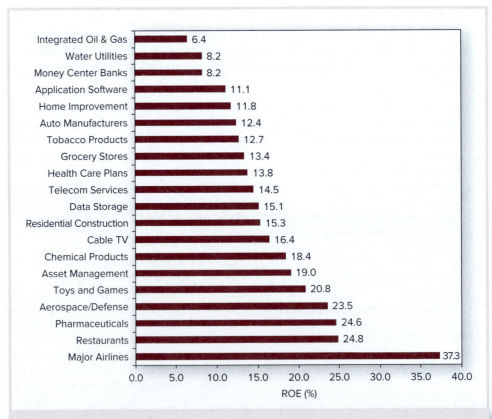

Figure 17.5 Return on equity by industry, 2015–2016

Source: Yahoo! Finance, **finance.yahoo.com,** June 15, 2016.

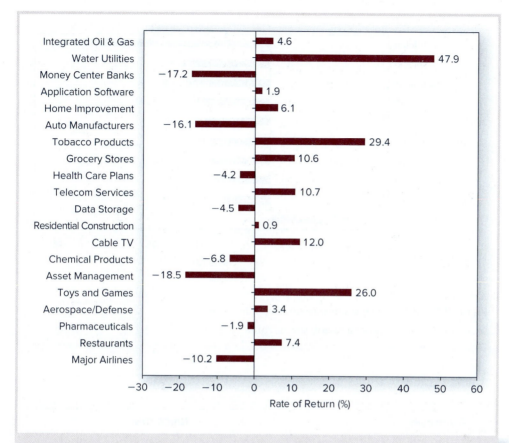

Figure 17.6 Industry stock price performance, 12 months ending June 2016

Defining an Industry

Although the concept of an "industry" seems clear-cut, deciding where to draw the line between one industry and another can be difficult in practice. Consider, for example, one of the industries depicted in Figure 17.5, application software firms. Industry ROE in 2015–2016 was 11.1%. But there is substantial variation of focus within this group, and one might well be justified in further dividing these firms into distinct subindustries. Their differences may result in considerable dispersion in financial performance. Figure 17.7 shows ROE for a sample of the firms included in this industry, confirming that performance did indeed vary widely: from −17.1% for Symantec to 41.7% for Intuit.

A useful way to define industry groups in practice is given by the North American Industry Classification System, or **NAICS codes.**[3] These are codes assigned to group firms for statistical analysis. The first two digits of the NAICS codes denote very broad industry classifications. For example, Table 17.5 shows that the codes for all construction firms start with 23. The next digits define the industry grouping more narrowly. For example, codes starting with 236 denote *building* construction, 2361 denotes *residential* construction, and

---

[3]These codes are used for firms operating inside the NAFTA (North American Free Trade Agreement) region, which includes the U.S., Mexico, and Canada. NAICS codes replaced the Standard Industry Classification or SIC codes previously used in the U.S.

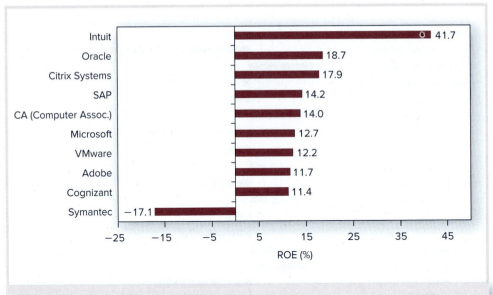

Figure 17.7 ROE of major software development firms

Source: Yahoo! Finance, **finance.yahoo.com,** June 15, 2016.

Table 17.5

Examples of NAICS industry codes

NAICS Code	NAICS Title
23	Construction
236	Construction of Buildings
2361	Residential Building Construction
23611	Residential Building Construction
236115	New Single-Family Housing Construction
236116	New Multifamily Housing Construction
236118	Residential Remodelers
2362	Nonresidential Building Construction
23621	Industrial Building Construction
23622	Commercial and Institutional Building Construction

236115 denotes *single-family* construction. The first five digits of the NAICS codes are common across all three NAFTA countries. The sixth digit is country-specific and allows for a finer partition of industries. Firms with the same four-digit NAICS codes are commonly taken to be in the same industry.

NAICS industry classifications are not perfect. For example, both Kohl's and Neiman Marcus might be classified as "Department Stores." Yet the former is a high-volume "value" store, whereas the latter is a high-margin elite retailer. Are they really in the same industry? Still, these classifications are a tremendous aid in conducting industry analysis because they provide a means of focusing on very broad or fairly narrowly defined groups of firms.

Several other industry classifications are provided by other analysts; for example, Standard & Poor's reports on the performance of about 100 industry groups. S&P computes stock price indexes for each group, which is useful in assessing past investment performance. The *Value Line Investment Survey* reports on the conditions and prospects of about 1,700 firms, grouped into about 90 industries. Value Line's analysts prepare forecasts of the performance of industry groups as well as of each firm.

Sensitivity to the Business Cycle

Once the analyst forecasts the state of the macroeconomy, it is necessary to determine the implication of that forecast for specific industries. Not all industries are equally sensitive to the business cycle.

For example, Figure 17.8 plots changes in retail sales (year over year) in two industries: jewelry and grocery stores. Clearly, sales of jewelry, which is a luxury good, fluctuate more widely than those of groceries. Jewelry sales jumped in 1999 at the height of the dot-com boom but fell steeply in the recessions of 2001 and 2008–2009. In contrast, sales growth in the grocery industry is relatively stable, with no years in which sales meaningfully decline. These patterns reflect the fact that jewelry is a discretionary good, whereas most grocery products are staples for which demand will not fall significantly even in hard times.

Three factors will determine the sensitivity of a firm's earnings to the business cycle. First is the sensitivity of sales. Necessities will show little sensitivity to business conditions. Examples of industries in this group are food, drugs, and medical services. Other industries with low sensitivity are those for which income is not a crucial determinant of demand. Tobacco products are an example of this type of industry. Another industry in this group is movies, because consumers tend to substitute movies for more expensive sources of entertainment when income levels are low. In contrast, firms in industries such as machine tools, steel, autos, and transportation are highly sensitive to the state of the economy.

The second factor determining business cycle sensitivity is operating leverage, which refers to the division between fixed and variable costs. (Fixed costs are those the firm

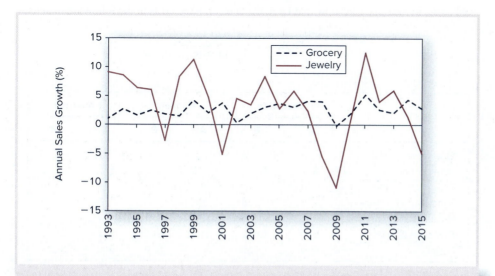

Figure 17.8 Industry cyclicality: Growth of sales, year over year, in two industries; sales of jewelry show much greater variation than sales of groceries

incurs regardless of its production levels. Variable costs are those that rise or fall as the firm produces more or less product.) Firms with greater amounts of variable as opposed to fixed costs will be less sensitive to business conditions. This is because in economic down-turns, these firms can reduce costs as output falls in response to falling sales. Profits for firms with high fixed costs will swing more widely with sales because costs do not move to offset revenue variability. Firms with high fixed costs are said to have high operating lever-age, because small swings in business conditions can have large impacts on profitability.

Example 17.1   Operating Leverage

Consider two firms operating in the same industry with identical revenues in all phases of the business cycle: recession, normal, and expansion. Firm A has short-term leases on most of its equipment and can reduce its lease expenditures when production slackens. It has fixed costs of $5 million and variable costs of $1 per unit of output. Firm B has long-term leases on most of its equipment and must make lease payments regardless of economic conditions. Its fixed costs are higher, $8 million, but its variable costs are only $.50 per unit. Table 17.6 shows that Firm A will do better in recessions than Firm B, but not as well in expansions. A's costs move in conjunction with its revenues to help performance in downturns and impede performance in upturns.

We can quantify operating leverage by measuring how sensitive profits are to changes in sales. The **degree of operating leverage (DOL)** is defined as

$$DOL = \frac{\text{Percentage change in profits}}{\text{Percentage change in sales}}$$

DOL greater than 1 indicates some operating leverage. For example, if DOL = 2, then for every 1% change in sales, profits will change by 2% in the same direction, either up or down.

We have seen that the degree of operating leverage increases with a firm's exposure to fixed costs. In fact, one can show that DOL depends on fixed costs in the following manner:[4]

$$DOL = 1 + \frac{\text{Fixed costs}}{\text{Profits}}$$

Table 17.6

Operating leverage of firms A and B throughout business cycle

	Recession		Normal		Expansion	
	A	B	A	B	A	B
Sales (million units)	5	5	6	6	7	7
Price per unit	$ 2	$ 2	$ 2	$ 2	$ 2	$ 2
Revenue ($ million)	10	10	12	12	14	14
Fixed costs ($ million)	5	8	5	8	5	8
Variable costs ($ million)	5	2.5	6	3	7	3.5
Total costs ($ million)	$10	$10.5	$11	$11	$12	$11.5
Profits	$ 0	$ (0.5)	$ 1	$ 1	$ 2	$ 2.5

[4]Operating leverage and DOL are treated in more detail in most corporate finance texts.

Example 17.2   Degree of Operating Leverage

Return to the two firms illustrated in Table 17.6 and compare profits and sales in the normal scenario for the economy with those in a recession. Profits of Firm A fall by 100% (from $1 million to zero) when sales fall by 16.7% (from $6 million to $5 million):

$$\text{DOL(Firm A)} = \frac{\text{Percentage change in profits}}{\text{Percentage change in sales}} = \frac{-100\%}{-16.7\%} = 6$$

We can confirm the relationship between DOL and fixed costs as follows:

$$\text{DOL(Firm A)} = 1 + \frac{\text{Fixed costs}}{\text{Profits}} = 1 + \frac{\$5 \text{ million}}{\$1 \text{ million}} = 6$$

Firm B has higher fixed costs, and its operating leverage is higher. Again, compare data for a normal scenario to a recession. Profits for Firm B fall by 150%, from $1 million to −$.5 million. Operating leverage for Firm B is therefore

$$\text{DOL(Firm B)} = \frac{\text{Percentage change in profits}}{\text{Percentage change in sales}} = \frac{-150\%}{-16.7\%} = 9$$

which reflects its higher level of fixed costs:

$$\text{DOL(Firm B)} = 1 + \frac{\text{Fixed costs}}{\text{Profits}} = 1 + \frac{\$8 \text{ million}}{\$1 \text{ million}} = 9$$

The third factor influencing business cycle sensitivity is financial leverage, which is the use of borrowing. Interest payments on debt must be paid regardless of sales. They are fixed costs that also increase the sensitivity of profits to business conditions. (We will have more to say about financial leverage in Chapter 19.)

Investors should not always prefer industries with lower sensitivity to the business cycle. Firms in sensitive industries will have high-beta stocks and are riskier. But while they swing lower in downturns, they also swing higher in upturns. As always, the issue you need to address is whether the expected return on the investment is fair compensation for the risks borne.

 Concept Check **17.4**

Determine the profits of Firm C in the three scenarios, assuming fixed costs of $2 million and variable costs of $1.50 per unit. What are your conclusions regarding operating leverage and business risk?

Sector Rotation

One way that many analysts think about the relationship between industry analysis and the business cycle is the notion of **sector rotation.** The idea is to shift the portfolio more heavily into industry or sector groups that are expected to outperform others based on one's assessment of the state of the business cycle.

Figure 17.9 is a stylized depiction of the business cycle. Near the peak of the business cycle, the economy might be overheated, with high inflation and interest rates and price pressures on basic commodities. This might be a good time to invest in firms engaged in natural resource extraction and processing such as minerals or petroleum.

Following a peak, when the economy enters a contraction or recession, one would expect defensive industries that are less sensitive to economic conditions, for example,

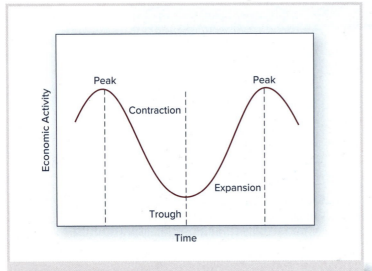

Figure 17.9 A stylized depiction of the business cycle

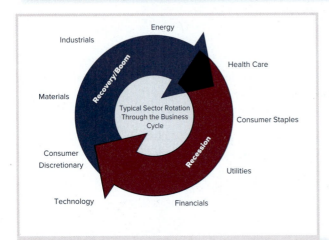

Figure 17.10 Sector rotation

Source: Sam Stovall, *BusinessWeek Online,* "A Cyclical Take on Performance."

pharmaceuticals, food, and other necessities, to be the best performers. At the height of the contraction, financial firms will be hurt by shrinking loan volume and higher default rates. Toward the end of the recession, however, contractions induce lower inflation and interest rates, which favor financial firms.

At the trough of a recession, the economy is poised for recovery and subsequent expansion. Firms might thus be spending on purchases of new equipment to meet anticipated increases in demand. This, then, would be a good time to invest in capital goods industries, such as equipment, transportation, or construction.

Finally, in an expansion, the economy is growing rapidly. Cyclical industries such as consumer durables and luxury items will be most profitable in this stage of the cycle. Banks might also do well in expansions, since loan volume will be high and default exposure low when the economy is growing rapidly.

Figure 17.10 illustrates sector rotation. When investors are relatively pessimistic about the economy, they will shift into noncyclical industries such as consumer staples or health care. When anticipating an expansion, they will prefer more cyclical industries such as materials and technology.

Don't forget that sector rotation, like any other form of market timing, will be successful only if one anticipates the next stage of the business cycle better than other investors. The business cycle depicted in Figure 17.10 is highly stylized. In real life, it is never as clear how long each phase of the cycle will last, nor how extreme it will be. These forecasts are where analysts need to earn their keep.

✓ Concept Check **17.5**

In which phase of the business cycle would you expect the following industries to enjoy their best performance?

a. Newspapers

b. Machine tools

c. Beverages

d. Timber

Industry Life Cycles

Examine the biotechnology industry and you will find many firms with high rates of investment, high rates of return on investment, and low dividend payout rates. Do the same for the public utility industry and you will find lower rates of return, lower investment rates, and higher dividend payout rates. Why should this be?

The biotech industry is still new. Recently, available technologies have created opportunities for highly profitable investment of resources. New products are protected by patents, and profit margins are high. With such lucrative investment opportunities, firms find it advantageous to put all profits back into the firm. The companies grow rapidly on average.

Eventually, however, growth must slow. The high profit rates will induce new firms to enter the industry. Increasing competition will hold down prices and profit margins. New technologies become proven and more predictable, risk levels fall, and entry becomes even easier. As internal investment opportunities become less attractive, a lower fraction of profits is reinvested in the firm. Cash dividends increase.

Ultimately, in a mature industry, we observe "cash cows," firms with stable dividends and cash flows and little risk. Growth rates might be similar to that of the overall economy. Industries in early states of their life cycles offer high-risk/high-potential-return investments. Mature industries offer lower-risk, lower-return profiles.

This analysis suggests that a typical **industry life cycle** might be described by four stages: a start-up stage, characterized by extremely rapid growth; a consolidation stage, characterized by growth that is less rapid but still faster than that of the general economy; a maturity stage, characterized by growth no faster than the general economy; and a stage of relative decline, in which the industry grows less rapidly than the rest of the economy, or actually shrinks. This industry life cycle is illustrated in Figure 17.11. Let us turn to an elaboration of each of these stages.

Start-Up Stage   The early stages of an industry are often characterized by a new technology or product such as desktop personal computers in the 1980s, cell phones in the 1990s, or the smartphones introduced in 2007. At this stage, it is difficult to predict which firms will emerge as industry leaders. Some firms will turn out to be wildly successful, and others will fail altogether. Therefore, there is considerable risk in selecting one particular firm within the industry. For example, in the smartphone industry, there was and continues to be a battle among competing technologies, such as Android versus iPhone.

At the industry level, however, it is clear that sales and earnings will grow at an extremely rapid rate because the new product has not yet saturated its market. For example, in 2010, relatively few households had smartphones. The potential market for the product therefore was huge. In contrast to this situation, consider the market for a mature product like refrigerators. Almost all households in the United States already have refrigerators, so the market for this good is primarily composed of households replacing old ones, which obviously limits the potential growth rate.

Consolidation Stage   After a product becomes established, industry leaders begin to emerge. For example, by 2015, Apple and Samsung had a combined market share of 35%. The survivors from the

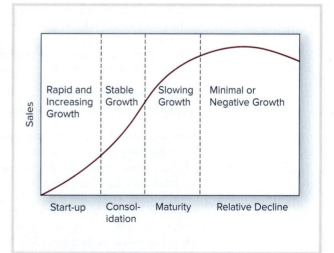

Figure 17.11 The industry life cycle

start-up stage are more stable, and market share is easier to predict. Therefore, the performance of the surviving firms will more closely track the performance of the overall industry. The industry still grows faster than the rest of the economy as the product penetrates the marketplace and becomes more commonly used.

Maturity Stage   At this point, the product has reached its full potential for use by consumers. Further growth might merely track growth in the general economy. The product has become far more standardized, and producers are forced to compete to a greater extent on the basis of price. This leads to narrower profit margins and further pressure on profits. Firms at this stage sometimes are characterized as cash cows, having reasonably stable cash flow but offering little opportunity for profitable expansion. The cash flow is best "milked from" rather than reinvested in the company.

We pointed to desktop PCs as a start-up industry in the 1980s. By the mid-1990s it was a mature industry, with high market penetration, considerable price competition, low profit margins, and slowing sales. By the 1990s, desktops were progressively giving way to laptops, which were in their own start-up stage. Within a dozen years, laptops had in turn entered a maturity stage, with standardization, low profit margins, and new competition from tablets.

Relative Decline   In this stage, the industry might grow at less than the rate of the overall economy, or it might even shrink. This could be due to obsolescence of the product, competition from new low-cost suppliers, or competition from new products; consider for example, the steady displacement of desktops, first by laptops and now by tablets.

At which stage in the life cycle are investments in an industry most attractive? Conventional wisdom is that investors should seek firms in high-growth industries. This recipe for success is simplistic, however. If the security prices already reflect the likelihood for high growth, then it is too late to make money from that knowledge. Moreover, high growth and fat profits encourage competition from other producers. The exploitation of profit opportunities brings about new sources of supply that eventually reduce prices, profits, investment returns, and finally growth. This is the dynamic behind the progression from one stage of the industry life cycle to another. The famous portfolio manager Peter Lynch makes this point in *One Up on Wall Street:*

> Many people prefer to invest in a high-growth industry, where there's a lot of sound and fury. Not me. I prefer to invest in a low-growth industry. . . . In a low-growth industry, especially one that's boring and upsets people [such as funeral homes or the oil-drum retrieval business], there's no problem with competition. You don't have to protect your flanks from potential rivals . . . and this gives you the leeway to continue to grow.[5]

In fact, Lynch uses an industry classification system in a very similar spirit to the life-cycle approach we have described. He places firms in the following six groups:

Slow Growers   Large and aging companies that will grow only slightly faster than the broad economy. These firms have matured from their earlier fast-growth phase. They usually have steady cash flow and pay a generous dividend, indicating that the firm is generating more cash than can be profitably reinvested in the firm.

Stalwarts   Large, well-known firms like Coca-Cola, Hershey's, or Colgate-Palmolive. They grow faster than the slow growers, but are not in the very rapid growth start-up stage. They also tend to be in noncyclical industries that are relatively unaffected by recessions.

---

[5]Peter Lynch with John Rothchild, *One Up on Wall Street* (New York: Penguin, 1990), p. 131.

Fast Growers   Small and aggressive new firms with annual growth rates in the neighborhood of 20% to 25%. Company growth can be due to broad industry growth or to an increase in market share in a more mature industry.

Cyclicals   These are firms with sales and profits that regularly expand and contract along with the business cycle. Examples are auto companies, steel companies, or the construction industry.

Turnarounds   These are firms that are in bankruptcy or soon might be. If they can recover from what might appear to be imminent disaster, they can offer tremendous investment returns. A good example of this type of firm would be Chrysler in 1982, when it required a government guarantee on its debt to avoid bankruptcy. The stock price rose 15-fold in the next five years.

Asset Plays   These are firms that have valuable assets not currently reflected in the stock price. For example, a company may own or be located on valuable real estate that is worth as much as or more than the company's business enterprises. Sometimes the hidden asset can be tax-loss carryforwards. Other times the assets may be intangible. For example, a cable company might have a valuable list of cable subscribers. These assets do not immediately generate cash flow and so may be more easily overlooked by other analysts attempting to value the firm.

Industry Structure and Performance

The maturation of an industry involves regular changes in the firm's competitive environment. As a final topic, we examine the relationship among industry structure, competitive strategy, and profitability. Michael Porter has highlighted these five determinants of competition: threat of entry from new competitors, rivalry between existing competitors, price pressure from substitute products, bargaining power of buyers, and bargaining power of suppliers.[6]

Threat of Entry   New entrants to an industry put pressure on price and profits. Even if a firm has not yet entered an industry, the potential for it to do so places pressure on prices, because high prices and profit margins will encourage entry by new competitors. Therefore, barriers to entry can be a key determinant of industry profitability. Barriers can take many forms. For example, existing firms may already have secure distribution channels for their products based on long-standing relationships with customers or suppliers that would be costly for a new entrant to duplicate. Brand loyalty also makes it difficult for new entrants to penetrate a market and gives firms more pricing discretion. Proprietary knowledge or patent protection also may give firms advantages in serving a market. Finally, an existing firm's experience in a market may give it cost advantages due to the learning that takes place over time.

Rivalry between Existing Competitors   When there are several competitors in an industry, there will generally be more price competition and lower profit margins as competitors seek to expand their share of the market. Slow industry growth contributes to this competition, because expansion must come at the expense of a rival's market share. High fixed costs also create pressure to reduce prices, because fixed costs put greater pressure on firms to operate near full capacity. Industries producing relatively homogeneous goods are also subject to considerable price pressure, because firms cannot compete on the basis of product differentiation.

[6]Michael Porter, *Competitive Advantage: Creating and Sustaining Superior Performance* (New York: Free Press, 1985).

Pressure from Substitute Products   Substitute products means that the industry faces competition from firms in related industries. For example, sugar producers compete with corn syrup producers. Wool producers compete with synthetic fiber producers. The availability of substitutes limits the prices that can be charged to customers.

Bargaining Power of Buyers   If a buyer purchases a large fraction of an industry's output, it will have considerable bargaining power and can demand price concessions. For example, auto producers can put pressure on suppliers of auto parts. This reduces the profitability of the auto parts industry.

Bargaining Power of Suppliers   If a supplier of a key input has monopolistic control over the product, it can demand higher prices for the good and squeeze profits out of the industry. One special case of this issue pertains to organized labor as a supplier of a key input to the production process. Labor unions engage in collective bargaining to increase the wages paid to workers. When the labor market is highly unionized, a significant share of the potential profits in the industry can be captured by the workforce.

The key factor determining the bargaining power of suppliers is the availability of substitute products. If substitutes are available, the supplier has little clout and cannot extract higher prices.

SUMMARY

1. Macroeconomic policy aims to maintain the economy near full employment without aggravating inflationary pressures. The proper trade-off between these two goals is a source of ongoing debate.

2. The traditional tools of macroeconomic policy are government spending and tax collection, which constitute fiscal policy, and manipulation of the money supply via monetary policy. Expansionary fiscal policy can stimulate the economy and increase GDP but tends to increase interest rates. Expansionary monetary policy works by lowering interest rates.

3. The business cycle is the economy's recurring pattern of expansions and recessions. Leading economic indicators can be used to anticipate the evolution of the business cycle because their values tend to change before those of other key economic variables.

4. Industries differ in their sensitivity to the business cycle. More sensitive industries tend to be those producing high-priced durable goods for which the consumer has considerable discretion as to the timing of purchase. Examples are jewelry, automobiles, or consumer durables. Other sensitive industries are those that produce capital equipment for other firms. Operating leverage and financial leverage increase sensitivity to the business cycle.

5. Industries generally pass through a predictable life cycle. In the start-up stage, growth is rapid as a new product begins to permeate the economy, but it is difficult at this point to predict which firms will emerge as industry leaders. As the product becomes established, the industry enters a consolidation stage and industry leaders begin to emerge. In the maturity stage, the product has largely saturated the market, and further growth merely tracks that of the general economy. Finally, the industry enters a stage of relative decline as it faces competition from new products.

KEY TERMS

fundamental analysis	supply shock	defensive industries
exchange rate	fiscal policy	leading economic indicators
gross domestic product (GDP)	monetary policy	NAICS codes
unemployment rate	business cycle	degree of operating leverage
inflation	peak	(DOL)
budget deficit	trough	sector rotation
demand shock	cyclical industries	industry life cycle

1. What monetary and fiscal policies might be prescribed for an economy in a deep recession?

2. If you believe the U.S. dollar will depreciate more dramatically than other investors anticipate, what will be your stance on investments in U.S. auto producers?

3. Choose an industry and identify the factors that will determine its performance in the next three years. What is your forecast for performance in that time period?

4. What are the differences between bottom-up and top-down approaches to security valuation? What are the advantages of a top-down approach?

5. What characteristics will give firms greater sensitivity to business cycles?

6. Unlike other investors, you believe the Fed is going to loosen monetary policy. What would be your recommendations about investments in the following industries?

   a. Gold mining
   b. Construction

7. According to supply-side economists, what will be the long-run impact on prices of a reduction in income tax rates?

8. Which of the following is consistent with a steeply upwardly sloping yield curve?

   a. Monetary policy is expansive and fiscal policy is expansive.
   b. Monetary policy is expansive while fiscal policy is restrictive.
   c. Monetary policy is restrictive and fiscal policy is restrictive.

9. Which of the following is *not* a governmental structural policy that supply-side economists believe would promote long-term growth in an economy?

   a. A redistributive tax system.
   b. A promotion of competition.
   c. Minimal government interference in the economy.

10. Consider two firms producing smartphones. One uses a highly automated robotics process, whereas the other uses workers on an assembly line and pays overtime when there is heavy production demand.

    a. Which firm will have higher profits in a recession?
    b. In a boom?
    c. Which firm's stock will have a higher beta?

11. Here are four industries and four forecasts for the macroeconomy. Match the industry to the scenario in which it is likely to be the best performer.

Industry	Economic Forecast
a. Housing construction	i. *Deep recession:* falling inflation, interest rates, and GDP
b. Health care	ii. *Superheated economy:* rapidly rising GDP, increasing inflation and interest rates
c. Gold mining	iii. *Healthy expansion:* rising GDP, mild inflation, low unemployment
d. Steel production	iv. *Stagflation:* falling GDP, high inflation

12. In which stage of the industry life cycle would you place the following industries? (*Note:* There is considerable room for disagreement concerning the "correct" answers to this question.)

    a. Oil well equipment.
    b. Computer hardware.
    c. Computer software.
    d. Genetic engineering.
    e. Railroads.

13. For each pair of firms, choose the one that you think would be more sensitive to the business cycle.

    a. General Autos or General Pharmaceuticals.
    b. Friendly Airlines or Happy Cinemas.

14. Why do you think the index of consumer expectations for business conditions is a useful leading indicator of the macroeconomy? (See Table 17.2.)

15. Why do you think the change in the index of labor cost per unit of output is a useful lagging indicator of the macroeconomy? (See Table 17.2.)

16. General Weedkillers dominates the chemical weed control market with its patented product Weed-ex. The patent is about to expire, however. What are your forecasts for changes in the industry? Specifically, what will happen to industry prices, sales, the profit prospects of General Weedkillers, and the profit prospects of its competitors? What stage of the industry life cycle do you think is relevant for the analysis of this market?

17. Your business plan for your proposed start-up firm envisions first-year revenues of $120,000, fixed costs of $30,000, and variable costs equal to one-third of revenue.

    a. What are expected profits based on these expectations?
    b. What is the degree of operating leverage based on the estimate of fixed costs and expected profits?
    c. If sales are 10% below expectation, what will be the decrease in profits?
    d. Show that the percentage decrease in profits equals DOL times the 10% drop in sales.
    e. Based on the DOL, what is the largest percentage shortfall in sales relative to original expectations that the firm can sustain before profits turn negative?
    f. What are break-even sales at this point?
    g. Confirm that your answer to (f) is correct by calculating profits at the break-even level of sales.

Use the following case in answering Problems 18 through 21: Institutional Advisors for All Inc., or IAAI, is a consulting firm that primarily advises all types of institutions such as foundations, endowments, pension plans, and insurance companies. IAAI also provides advice to a select group of individual investors with large portfolios. One of the claims the firm makes in its advertising is that IAAI devotes considerable resources to forecasting and determining long-term trends; then it uses commonly accepted investment models to determine how these trends should affect the performance of various investments. The members of the research department of IAAI recently reached some conclusions concerning some important macroeconomic trends. For instance, they have seen an upward trend in job creation and consumer confidence and predict that this should continue for the next few years. Other domestic leading indicators that the research department at IAAI wishes to consider are industrial production, average weekly hours in manufacturing, the S&P 500 stock index, the money supply, and the index of consumer expectations.

In light of the predictions for job creation and consumer confidence, the investment advisers at IAAI want to make recommendations for their clients. They use established theories that relate job creation and consumer confidence to inflation and interest rates and then incorporate the forecast movements in inflation and interest rates into established models for explaining asset prices. Their primary concern is to forecast how the trends in job creation and consumer confidence should affect bond prices and how those trends should affect stock prices.

The members of the research department at IAAI also note that stocks have been trending up in the past year, and this information is factored into the forecasts of the overall economy that they deliver. The researchers consider an upward-trending stock market a positive economic indicator in itself; however, they disagree as to the reason this should be the case.

18. The researchers at IAAI have forecast positive trends for both job creation and consumer confidence. Which, if either, of these trends should have a positive effect on stock prices?

19. Stock prices are useful as a leading indicator. To explain this phenomenon, which of the following is *most* accurate? Stock prices:

    a. Predict future interest rates as well as trends in other indicators.
    b. Do not predict future interest rates, nor are they correlated with other leading indicators; the usefulness of stock prices as a leading indicator is a mystery.
    c. Reflect the trends in other leading indicators only and do not have predictive power of their own.

20. Which of the domestic series that the IAAI research department listed for use as leading indicators is *least* appropriate?

   a. Industrial production.

   b. Average weekly hours in manufacturing.

   c. The S&P 500 index.

21. IAAI uses primarily historical data in its calculations and forecasts. Which of the following regarding the actions of IAAI is *most* accurate?

   a. Credit risk premiums may be useful to IAAI because they are based on actual market expectations.

   b. IAAI should use a moving average of recent stock returns when times are bad because it will result in a high expected equity risk premium.

   c. Long time spans should be used so that regime changes can be factored into the forecasts.

Use the following case in answering Problems 22 through 25: Mary Smith, a Level II CFA candidate, was recently hired for an analyst position at the Bank of Ireland. Her first assignment is to examine the competitive strategies employed by various French wineries.

Smith's report identifies four wineries that are the major players in the French wine industry. Key characteristics of each are cited in Table 17A. In the body of Smith's report, she includes a discussion of the competitive structure of the French wine industry. She notes that over the past five years, the French wine industry has not responded to changing consumer tastes. Profit margins have declined steadily and the number of firms representing the industry has decreased from 10 to 4. It appears that participants in the French wine industry must consolidate in order to survive.

Smith's report notes that French consumers have strong bargaining power over the industry. She supports this conclusion with five key points, which she labels "Bargaining Power of Buyers":

- Many consumers are drinking more beer than wine with meals and at social occasions.
- Increasing sales over the Internet have allowed consumers to better research the wines, read opinions from other customers, and identify which producers have the best prices.
- The French wine industry is consolidating and consists of only 4 wineries today compared to 10 wineries five years ago.
- More than 65% of the business for the French wine industry consists of purchases from restaurants. Restaurants typically make purchases in bulk, buying four to five cases of wine at a time.
- Land where the soil is fertile enough to grow grapes necessary for the wine production process is scarce in France.

After completing the first draft of her report, Smith takes it to her boss, Ron VanDriesen, to review. VanDriesen tells her that he is a wine connoisseur himself and often makes purchases from the South Winery. Smith tells VanDriesen, "In my report I have classified the South Winery as a stuck-in-the-middle firm. It tries to be a cost leader by selling its wine at a price that is slightly below the other firms, but it also tries to differentiate itself from its competitors by producing wine in bottles with curved necks, which increases its cost structure. The end result is that the South Winery's profit margin gets squeezed from both sides." VanDriesen replies, "I have met members of the management team from the South Winery at a couple of the wine conventions I have attended. I believe that the South Winery could succeed at following both a cost leadership and a differentiation strategy if its

	South Winery	North Winery	East Winery	West Winery
Founding date	1750	1903	1812	1947
Generic competitive strategy	?	Cost leadership	Cost leadership	Cost leadership
Major customer market (more than 80% concentration)	France	France	England	U.S.
Production site	France	France	France	France

Table 17A

Characteristics of Four Major French Wineries

operations were separated into distinct operating units, with each unit pursuing a different competitive strategy." Smith makes a note to do more research on generic competitive strategies to verify VanDriesen's assertions before publishing the final draft of her report.

22. If the French home currency were to greatly appreciate in value compared to the English currency, what is the likely impact on the competitive position of the East Winery?

    a. Make the firm less competitive in the English market.
    b. No impact, since the major market for East Winery is England, not France.
    c. Make the firm more competitive in the English market.

23. Which of Smith's points effectively support the conclusion that consumers have strong bargaining power over the industry?

24. Smith notes in her report that the West Winery might differentiate its wine product on attributes that buyers perceive to be important. Which of the following attributes would be the *most likely* area of focus for the West Winery to create a differentiated product?

    a. The method of delivery for the product.
    b. The price of the product.
    c. A focus on customers aged 30 to 45.

25. Smith knows that a firm's generic strategy should be the centerpiece of a firm's strategic plan. On the basis of a compilation of research and documents, Smith makes three observations about the North Winery and its strategic planning process:

    i. North Winery's price and cost forecasts account for future changes in the structure of the French wine industry.
    ii. North Winery places each of its business units into one of three categories: build, hold, or harvest.
    iii. North Winery uses market share as the key measure of its competitive position.

    Which observation(s) *least* support(s) the conclusion that the North Winery's strategic planning process is guided and informed by its generic competitive strategy?

26. Atech has fixed costs of $7 million and profits of $4 million. Its competitor, ZTech, is roughly the same size and this year earned the same profits, $4 million. However, ZTech operates with fixed costs of $5 million and lower variable costs.

    a. Which firm has higher operating leverage?
    b. Which firm will likely have higher profits if the economy strengthens?

27. OceanGate sells external hard drives for $200 each. Its total fixed costs are $30 million, and its variable costs per unit are $140. The corporate tax rate is 30%. If the economy is strong, the firm will sell 2 million drives, but if there is a recession, it will sell only half as many.

    a. What will be the percentage decline in sales if the economy enters a recession?
    b. What will be the percentage decline in profits if the economy enters a recession?
    c. Comparing your answers to (a) and (b), how would you measure the operating leverage of this firm?

1. Briefly discuss what actions the U.S. Federal Reserve would likely take in pursuing an *expansionary* monetary policy using each of the following three monetary tools:

    a. Reserve requirements.
    b. Open market operations.
    c. Discount rate.

2. An unanticipated expansionary monetary policy has been implemented. Indicate the impact of this policy on each of the following four variables:

    a. Inflation rate.
    b. Real output and employment.
    c. Real interest rate.
    d. Nominal interest rate.

3. Universal Auto is a large multinational corporation headquartered in the United States. For segment reporting purposes, the company is engaged in two businesses: production of motor vehicles and information processing services.

The motor vehicle business is by far the larger of Universal's two segments. It consists mainly of domestic U.S. passenger car production, but it also includes small truck manufacturing operations in the United States and passenger car production in other countries. This segment of Universal has had weak operating results for the past several years, including a large loss in 2017. Although the company does not reveal the operating results of its domestic passenger car segments, that part of Universal's business is generally believed to be primarily responsible for the weak performance of its motor vehicle segment.

Idata, the information processing services segment of Universal, was started by Universal about 15 years ago. This business has shown strong, steady growth that has been entirely internal; no acquisitions have been made.

An excerpt from a research report on Universal prepared by Paul Adams, a CFA candidate, states: "Based on our assumption that Universal will be able to increase prices significantly on U.S. passenger cars in 2018, we project a multibillion dollar profit improvement."

a. Discuss the concept of an industrial life cycle by describing each of its four phases.
b. Identify where each of Universal's two primary businesses—passenger cars and information processing—is in such a cycle.
c. Discuss how product pricing should differ between Universal's two businesses, based on the location of each in the industrial life cycle.

4. Adams's research report (see CFA Problem 3) continued as follows: "With a business recovery already under way, the expected profit surge should lead to a much higher price for Universal Auto stock. We strongly recommend purchase."

a. Discuss the business cycle approach to investment timing. (Your answer should describe actions to be taken on both stocks and bonds at different points over a typical business cycle.)
b. Assuming Adams's assertion is correct (that a business recovery is already under way), evaluate the timeliness of his recommendation to purchase Universal Auto, a cyclical stock, based on the business cycle approach to investment timing.

5. Janet Ludlow is preparing a report on U.S.-based manufacturers in the electric toothbrush industry and has gathered the information shown in Tables 17B and 17C. Ludlow's report concludes that the electric toothbrush industry is in the maturity (i.e., late) phase of its industry life cycle.

a. Select and justify three factors from Table 17B that *support* Ludlow's conclusion.
b. Select and justify three factors from Table 17C that *refute* Ludlow's conclusion.

	2011	2012	2013	2014	2015	2016
Return on equity						
Electric toothbrush industry index	12.5%	12.0%	15.4%	19.6%	21.6%	21.6%
Market index	10.2	12.4	14.6	19.9	20.4	21.2
Average P/E						
Electric toothbrush industry index	28.5×	23.2×	19.6×	18.7×	18.5×	16.2×
Market index	10.4	11.4	14.6	18.9	18.1	19.1
Dividend payout ratio						
Electric toothbrush industry index	8.8%	8.0%	12.1%	12.1%	14.3%	17.1%
Market index	39.2	40.1	38.6	43.7	41.8	39.1
Average dividend yield						
Electric toothbrush industry index	0.3%	0.3%	0.6%	0.7%	0.8%	1.0%
Market index	3.8	3.2	2.6	2.2	2.3	2.1

Table 17B

Ratios for electric toothbrush industry index and broad stock market index

- **Industry Sales Growth**—Industry sales have grown at 15–20% per year in recent years and are expected to grow at 10–15% per year over the next 3 years.
- **Non-U.S. Markets**—Some U.S. manufacturers are attempting to enter fast-growing non-U.S. markets, which remain largely unexploited.
- **Mail Order Sales**—Some manufacturers have created a new niche in the industry by selling electric toothbrushes directly to customers through mail order. Sales for this industry segment are growing at 40% per year.
- **U.S. Market Penetration**—The current penetration rate in the United States is 60% of households and will be difficult to increase.
- **Price Competition**—Manufacturers compete fiercely on the basis of price, and price wars within the industry are common.
- **Niche Markets**—Some manufacturers are able to develop new, unexploited niche markets in the United States based on company reputation, quality, and service.
- **Industry Consolidation**—Several manufacturers have recently merged, and it is expected that consolidation in the industry will increase.
- **New Entrants**—New manufacturers continue to enter the market.

Table 17C

Characteristics of the electric toothbrush manufacturing industry

6. As a securities analyst, you have been asked to review a valuation of a closely held business, Wigwam Autoparts Heaven, Inc. (WAH), prepared by the Red Rocks Group (RRG). You are to give an opinion on the valuation and to support your opinion by analyzing each part of the valuation. WAH's sole business is automotive parts retailing. The RRG valuation includes a section called "Analysis of the Retail Autoparts Industry," based completely on the data in Table 17D and the following additional information:

   - WAH and its principal competitors each operated more than 150 stores at year-end 2016.
   - The average number of stores operated per company engaged in the retail autoparts industry is 5.3.
   - The major customer base for autoparts sold in retail stores consists of young owners of old vehicles. These owners do their own automotive maintenance out of economic necessity.

   a. One of RRG's conclusions is that the retail autoparts industry as a whole is in the maturity stage of the industry life cycle. Discuss three relevant items of data from Table 17D that support this conclusion.
   b. Another RRG conclusion is that WAH and its principal competitors are in the consolidation stage of their life cycle.

      i. Cite three relevant items of data from Table 17D that support this conclusion.
      ii. Explain how WAH and its principal competitors can be in a consolidation stage while their industry as a whole is in the maturity stage.

7. a. If the exchange rate for the British pound goes from U.S.$1.55 to U.S.$1.35, then the pound has:
      i. Appreciated and the British will find U.S. goods cheaper.
      ii. Appreciated and the British will find U.S. goods more expensive.
      iii. Depreciated and the British will find U.S. goods more expensive.
      iv. Depreciated and the British will find U.S. goods cheaper.
   b. Changes in which of the following are likely to affect interest rates?
      i. Inflation expectations.
      ii. Size of the federal deficit.
      iii. Money supply.
   c. According to the supply-side view of fiscal policy, if the impact on total tax revenues is the same, does it make any difference whether the government cuts taxes by either reducing marginal tax rates or increasing the personal exemption allowance?
      i. No, both methods of cutting taxes will exert the same impact on aggregate supply.
      ii. No, people in both cases will increase their saving, expecting higher future taxes, and thereby offset the stimulus effect of lower current taxes.

	2017	2016	2015	2014	2013	2012	2011	2010	2009	2008
Population 18–29 years old (percentage change)	−1.8%	−2.0%	−2.1%	−1.4%	−0.8%	−0.9%	−1.1%	−0.9%	−0.7%	−0.3%
Number of households with income more than $35,000 (percentage change)	6.0%	4.0%	8.0%	4.5%	2.7%	3.1%	1.6%	3.6%	4.2%	2.2%
Number of households with income less than $35,000 (percentage change)	3.0%	−1.0%	4.9%	2.3%	−1.4%	2.5%	1.4%	−1.3%	0.6%	0.1%
Number of cars 5–15 years old (percentage change)	0.9%	−1.3%	−6.0%	1.9%	3.3%	2.4%	−2.3%	−2.2%	−8.0%	1.6%
Automotive aftermarket industry retail sales (percentage change)	5.7%	1.9%	3.1%	3.7%	4.3%	2.6%	1.3%	0.2%	3.7%	2.4%
Consumer expenditures on automotive parts and accessories (percentage change)	2.4%	1.8%	2.1%	6.5%	3.6%	9.2%	1.3%	6.2%	6.7%	6.5%
Sales growth of retail autoparts companies with 100 or more stores	17.0%	16.0%	16.5%	14.0%	15.5%	16.8%	12.0%	15.7%	19.0%	16.0%
Market share of retail autoparts companies with 100 or more stores	19.0%	18.5%	18.3%	18.1%	17.0%	17.2%	17.0%	16.9%	15.0%	14.0%
Average operating margin of retail autoparts companies with 100 or more stores	12.0%	11.8%	11.2%	11.5%	10.6%	10.6%	10.0%	10.4%	9.8%	9.0%
Average operating margin of all retail autoparts companies	5.5%	5.7%	5.6%	5.8%	6.0%	6.5%	7.0%	7.2%	7.1%	7.2%

Table 17D

Selected retail autoparts industry data

iii. Yes, the lower marginal tax rates alone will increase the incentive to earn marginal income and thereby stimulate aggregate supply.

iv. Yes, interest rates will increase if marginal tax rates are lowered, whereas they will tend to decrease if the personal exemption allowance is raised.

E-INVESTMENTS EXERCISES

1. Is the U.S. economy in a recession or not? Check the "official" opinion at the National Bureau of Economic Research (NBER) at **www.nber.org/data.** Link to the Official Business Cycle Dates. How does the NBER select the beginning or end of a recession (follow the available link for a discussion of this topic)? What period in U.S. economic history was the longest expansion? Contraction? Look at the *Announcement Dates* section toward the bottom of the page. How much of a time lag is there between when a peak or a trough occurs and when it is announced? What implication does this have for investors?

2. Use data from **finance.yahoo.com/industries** to answer the following questions.

    a. Click on the link for *Complete Industry List.* Find the Price/Book ratios for the Biotech and the Electric Utilities industries. Do the differences make sense in light of their different stages in the industry life cycle?

    b. Now look at each industry's Price/Earnings ratio and Dividend Yield. Again, do the differences make sense in light of their different stages in the industry life cycle?

SOLUTIONS TO CONCEPT CHECKS

1. The downturn in the auto industry will reduce the demand for the product of this economy. The economy will, at least in the short term, enter a recession. This would suggest that:

   a. GDP will fall.

   b. The unemployment rate will rise.

   c. The government deficit will increase. Income tax receipts will fall, and government expenditures on social welfare programs probably will increase.

   d. Interest rates should fall. The contraction in the economy will reduce the demand for credit. Moreover, the lower inflation rate will reduce nominal interest rates.

2. Expansionary fiscal policy coupled with expansionary monetary policy will stimulate the economy, with the loose monetary policy keeping down interest rates.

3. A traditional demand-side interpretation of the tax cuts is that the resulting increase in after-tax income increased consumption demand and stimulated the economy. A supply-side interpretation is that the reduction in marginal tax rates made it more attractive for businesses to invest and for individuals to work, thereby increasing economic output.

4. Firm C has the lowest fixed cost and highest variable costs. It should be least sensitive to the business cycle. In fact, it is. Its profits are highest of the three firms in recessions but lowest in expansions.

	Recession	Normal	Expansion
Revenue	$10	$12	$14
Fixed cost	2	2	2
Variable cost	7.5	9	10.5
Profits	$ 0.5	$ 1	$ 1.5

5. a. Newspapers will do best in an expansion when advertising volume is increasing.

   b. Machine tools are a good investment at the trough of a recession, just as the economy is about to enter an expansion and firms may need to increase capacity.

   c. Beverages are defensive investments, with demand that is relatively insensitive to the business cycle. Therefore, they are relatively attractive investments if a recession is forecast.

   d. Timber is a good investment at a peak period, when natural resource prices are high and the economy is operating at full capacity.

Equity Valuation Models

18

AS OUR DISCUSSION of market efficiency indicated, finding undervalued securities will never be easy. Still, there are enough chinks in the armor of the efficient market hypothesis that the search for such securities should not be dismissed out of hand. Moreover, it is the ongoing search for mispriced securities that maintains a nearly efficient market. Even minor mispricing would allow a stock market analyst to earn his salary.

This chapter describes the valuation models that stock market analysts use to uncover mispriced securities. The models presented are those used by *fundamental analysts,* those analysts who use information concerning the current and prospective profitability of a company to assess its fair market value. We start with a discussion of alternative measures of the value of a company. From there, we progress to quantitative tools called *dividend discount models,* which security analysts commonly use to measure the value of a firm as an ongoing concern. Next we turn to price–earnings, or P/E, ratios, explaining why they are of such interest to analysts but also highlighting some of their shortcomings. We explain how P/E ratios are tied to dividend valuation models and, more generally, to the growth prospects of the firm.

We close the chapter with a discussion and extended example of free cash flow models used by analysts to value firms based on forecasts of the cash flows that will be generated from the firms' business endeavors. Finally, we apply the several valuation tools covered in the chapter to a real firm and find some disparity in their conclusions—a conundrum that will confront any security analyst—and consider reasons for these discrepancies.

18.1 Valuation by Comparables

The purpose of fundamental analysis is to identify stocks that are mispriced relative to some measure of "true" value that can be derived from observable financial data. There are many convenient sources of relevant data. For U.S. companies, the Securities and Exchange Commission provides information at its EDGAR Web site, **www.sec.gov/edgar .shtml.** The SEC requires all public companies (except foreign companies and companies with less than $10 million in assets and 500 shareholders) to file registration statements, periodic reports, and other forms electronically through EDGAR. Anyone can access and download this information. Many Web sites such as **finance.yahoo.com, money.msn.com,** or **finance.google.com** also provide analysis and data derived from the EDGAR reports.

Table 18.1 shows some financial highlights for Microsoft as well as some comparable data for other firms in the software applications industry. The price per share of Microsoft's common stock is $49.71, and the total market value or capitalization of those shares (called *market cap* for short) is $391 billion. Under the heading "Valuation," Table 18.1 shows the ratio of Microsoft's stock price to several benchmarks. Its share price is 17.2 times its (per share) earnings in the most recent 12 months, 5.3 times its recent book value, and 4.5 times its sales. The last valuation ratio, PEG, is the P/E ratio divided by the growth rate of earnings. We would expect more rapidly growing firms to sell at higher multiples of *current* earnings (more on this below), so PEG normalizes the P/E ratio by the growth rate.

These valuation ratios are commonly used to assess the valuation of one firm compared to others in the same industry, and we will consider all of them. The column to the right gives comparable ratios for other firms in the software applications industry. For example, an analyst might note that Microsoft's price/earnings ratio is below the industry average. Microsoft's ratio of market value to **book value,** the net worth of the company as reported on the balance sheet, is also below industry norms, 5.3 versus 8.7. These ratios might indicate that its stock is underpriced. However, Microsoft is a more mature firm than many in the industry, and perhaps this discrepancy reflects a lower expected future growth rate. In fact, its PEG ratio is actually above the industry average. Clearly, rigorous valuation models will be necessary to sort through these sometimes conflicting signals of value.

Limitations of Book Value

Shareholders in a firm are sometimes called "residual claimants," which means that the value of their stake is what is left over when the liabilities of the firm are subtracted from its assets. Shareholders' equity is this net worth. However, the values of both assets and

Table 18.1

Financial highlights for Microsoft Corporation, June 14, 2016

	Microsoft	Industry Average
Price per share	$ 49.71	
Common shares outstanding (billion)	7.86	
Market capitalization ($ billion)	$391	
Latest 12 months		
Sales ($ billion)	$ 86.90	
EBITDA ($ billion)	$ 29.20	
Net income ($ billion)	$ 10.50	
Earnings per share	$ 1.33	
Valuation	**Microsoft**	**Industry Average**
Price/Earnings	17.2	29.1
Price/Book	5.3	8.7
Price/Sales	4.5	
PEG	2.3	1.5
Profitability		
ROE (%)	12.7	16.1
ROA (%)	8.2	
Operating profit margin (%)	27.0	23.5
Net profit margin (%)	12.1	13.8

Source: Compiled from data available at **finance.yahoo.com,** June 14, 2016.

liabilities recognized in financial statements are based on historical—not current—values. For example, the book value of an asset equals the *original* cost of acquisition less some adjustment for depreciation, even if the market price of that asset has changed over time. Moreover, depreciation allowances are used to allocate the original cost of the asset over several years, but do not reflect loss of actual value.

Whereas book values are based on original cost, market values measure the *current* values of assets and liabilities. The market value of the shareholders' equity investment equals the difference between the current values of all assets and liabilities. We've emphasized that current values generally will not match historical ones. Equally or even more important, many assets, such as the value of a good brand name or specialized expertise developed over many years, may not even be included on the financial statements. Market prices therefore reflect the value of the firm as a going concern. It would be unusual if the market price of a stock were exactly equal to its book value.

Can book value represent a "floor" for the stock's price, below which level the market price can never fall? Although Microsoft's book value per share in 2016 was less than its market price, other evidence disproves this notion. While it is not common, there are always some firms selling at a market price below book value. In 2016, for example, such unfortunate firms included Honda, Bank of America, Mitsubishi, and Citigroup.

A better measure of a floor for the stock price is the firm's **liquidation value** per share. This represents the amount of money that could be realized by breaking up the firm, selling its assets, repaying its debt, and distributing the remainder to the shareholders. If the market price of equity drops below liquidation value, the firm becomes attractive as a takeover target. A corporate raider would find it profitable to buy enough shares to gain control and then actually to liquidate.

Another measure of firm value is the **replacement cost** of assets less liabilities. Some analysts believe the market value of the firm cannot remain for long too far above its replacement cost (sometimes called *reproduction cost*) because if it did, competitors would enter the market. The resulting competitive pressure would drive down the market value of all firms until they fell to replacement cost.

This idea is popular among economists, and the ratio of market price to replacement cost is known as **Tobin's q,** after the Nobel Prize–winning economist James Tobin. In the long run, according to this view, the ratio of market price to replacement cost will tend toward 1, but the evidence is that this ratio can differ significantly from 1 for very long periods.

Although focusing on the balance sheet can give some useful information about a firm's liquidation value or its replacement cost, the analyst must usually turn to expected future cash flows for a better estimate of the firm's value as a going concern. We therefore turn to the quantitative models that analysts use to value common stock based on forecasts of future earnings and dividends.

18.2   Intrinsic Value versus Market Price

The most popular model for assessing the value of a firm as a going concern starts from the observation that an investor in stock expects a return consisting of cash dividends and capital gains or losses. We begin by assuming a 1-year holding period and supposing that ABC stock has an expected dividend per share, $E(D_1)$, of $4; the current price of a share, P_0, is $48; and the expected price at the end of a year, $E(P_1)$, is $52. For now, don't worry about how you derive your forecast of next year's price. At this point we ask only whether the stock seems attractively priced *today* given your forecast of *next year's* price.

The *expected* holding-period return is $E(D_1)$ plus the expected price appreciation, $E(P_1) - P_0$, all divided by the current price, P_0:

$$\text{Expected HPR} = E(r) = \frac{E(D_1) + [E(P_1) - P_0]}{P_0}$$

$$= \frac{4 + (52 - 48)}{48} = .167, \text{ or } 16.7\%$$

Thus, the stock's expected holding-period return is the sum of the expected dividend yield, $E(D_1)/P_0$, and the expected rate of price appreciation, the capital gains yield, $[E(P_1) - P_0]/P_0$.

But what is the required rate of return for ABC stock? The CAPM states that when stock market prices are at equilibrium levels, the rate of return that investors can expect to earn on a security is $r_f + \beta[E(r_M) - r_f]$. Thus, the CAPM may be viewed as providing an estimate of the rate of return an investor can reasonably expect to earn on a security given its risk as measured by beta. This is the return that investors will require of any other investment with equivalent risk. We will denote this required rate of return as k. If a stock is priced "correctly," it will offer investors a "fair" return, that is, its *expected* return will equal its *required* return. Of course, the goal of a security analyst is to find stocks that are mispriced. An underpriced stock will provide an expected return greater than the required return.

Suppose that $r_f = 6\%$, $E(r_M) - r_f = 5\%$, and the beta of ABC is 1.2. Then according to the CAPM, the value of k is

$$k = 6\% + 1.2 \times 5\% = 12\%$$

The expected holding-period return, 16.7%, therefore exceeds the required rate of return based on ABC's risk by a margin of 4.7%. Naturally, the investor will want to include more of ABC stock in the portfolio than a passive strategy would indicate.

Another way to see this is to compare the intrinsic value of a share of stock to its market price. The **intrinsic value,** denoted V_0, is defined as the present value of all cash payments (on a per share basis) to the stockholder, including dividends as well as the proceeds from the ultimate sale of the stock, discounted at the appropriate risk-adjusted interest rate, k. If the intrinsic value, or the investor's own estimate of what the stock is really worth, exceeds the market price, the stock is considered undervalued and a good investment. For ABC, using a 1-year investment horizon and a forecast that the stock can be sold at the end of the year at price $P_1 = \$52$, the intrinsic value is

$$V_0 = \frac{E(D_1) + E(P_1)}{1 + k} = \frac{\$4 + \$52}{1.12} = \$50$$

Equivalently, at a price of $50, the investor would derive a 12% rate of return—just equal to the required rate of return—on an investment in the stock. However, at the current price of $48, the stock is underpriced compared to intrinsic value. At this price, it provides better than a fair rate of return relative to its risk. Using the terminology of the CAPM, it is a positive-alpha stock, and investors will want to buy more of it than they would following a passive strategy.

If the intrinsic value turns out to be lower than the current market price, investors should buy less of it than under the passive strategy. It might even pay to go short on ABC stock, as we discussed in Chapter 3.

In market equilibrium, the current market price will reflect the intrinsic value estimates of all market participants. This means the individual investor whose V_0 estimate differs from the market price, P_0, in effect must disagree with some or all of the market consensus estimates of $E(D_1)$, $E(P_1)$, or k. A common term for the market consensus value of the required rate of return, k, is the **market capitalization rate,** which we use often throughout this chapter.

 Concept Check **18.1**

You expect the price of IBX stock to be $59.77 per share a year from now. Its current market price is $50, and you expect it to pay a dividend one year from now of $2.15 per share.

a. What are the stock's expected dividend yield, its rate of price appreciation (the capital gains yield), and the total holding-period return?

b. If the stock has a beta of 1.15, the risk-free rate is 6% per year, and the expected rate of return on the market portfolio is 14% per year, what is the required rate of return on IBX stock?

c. What is the intrinsic value of IBX stock, and how does it compare to the current market price?

18.3   Dividend Discount Models

Consider an investor who buys a share of Steady State Electronics stock, planning to hold it for one year. The intrinsic value of the share is the present value of the dividend to be received at the end of the first year, D_1, and the expected sales price, P_1. We will henceforth use the simpler notation P_1 instead of $E(P_1)$ to avoid clutter. Keep in mind, though, that future prices and dividends are unknown, and we are dealing with expected values, not certain values. We've already established

$$V_0 = \frac{D_1 + P_1}{1 + k} \qquad\qquad (18.1)$$

Although this year's dividends are fairly predictable given a company's history, you might ask how we can estimate P_1, the year-end price. According to Equation 18.1, V_1 (the year-end intrinsic value) will be

$$V_1 = \frac{D_2 + P_2}{1 + k}$$

If we assume the stock will be selling for its intrinsic value next year, then $V_1 = P_1$, and we can substitute this value for P_1 into Equation 18.1 to find

$$V_0 = \frac{D_1}{1 + k} + \frac{D_2 + P_2}{(1 + k)^2}$$

This equation may be interpreted as the present value of dividends plus sales price for a 2-year holding period. Of course, now we need to come up with a forecast of P_2. Continuing in the same way, we can replace P_2 by $(D_3 + P_3)/(1 + k)$, which relates P_0 to the value of dividends plus the expected sales price for a 3-year holding period.

More generally, for a holding period of H years, we can write the stock value as the present value of dividends over the H years, plus the ultimate sale price, P_H:

$$V_0 = \frac{D_1}{1+k} + \frac{D_2}{(1+k)^2} + \cdots + \frac{D_H + P_H}{(1+k)^H} \qquad (18.2)$$

Note the similarity between this formula and the bond valuation formula developed in Chapter 14. Each relates price to the present value of a stream of payments (coupons in the case of bonds, dividends in the case of stocks) and a final payment (the face value of the bond, or the sales price of the stock). The key differences in the case of stocks are the uncertainty of dividends, the lack of a fixed maturity date, and the unknown sales price at the horizon date. Indeed, one can continue to substitute for price indefinitely, to conclude

$$V_0 = \frac{D_1}{1+k} + \frac{D_2}{(1+k)^2} + \frac{D_3}{(1+k)^3} + \cdots \qquad (18.3)$$

Equation 18.3 states that the stock price should equal the present value of all expected future dividends into perpetuity. This formula is called the **dividend discount model (DDM)** of stock prices.

It is tempting, but incorrect, to conclude from Equation 18.3 that the DDM focuses exclusively on dividends and ignores capital gains as a motive for investing in stock. Indeed, we assume explicitly in Equation 18.1 that capital gains (as reflected in the expected sales price, P_1) are part of the stock's value. Don't forget that the price at which you can sell a stock in the future depends on dividend forecasts at that time.

The reason only dividends appear in Equation 18.3 is not that investors ignore capital gains. It is instead that those capital gains will reflect dividend forecasts at the time the stock is sold. That is why in Equation 18.2 we can write the stock price as the present value of dividends plus sales price for *any* horizon date. P_H is the present value at time H of all dividends expected to be paid after the horizon date. That value is then discounted back to today, time 0. The DDM asserts that stock prices are determined ultimately by the cash flows accruing to stockholders, and those are dividends.[1]

The Constant-Growth DDM

Equation 18.3 as it stands is still not very useful in valuing a stock because it requires dividend forecasts for every year into the indefinite future. To make the DDM practical, we need to introduce some simplifying assumptions. A useful and common first pass is to assume that dividends are trending upward at a stable growth rate that we will call g. For example, if $g = .05$, and the most recently paid dividend was $D_0 = 3.81$, expected future dividends are

$$
\begin{aligned}
D_1 &= D_0(1+g) &&= 3.81 \times 1.05 &&= 4.00 \\
D_2 &= D_0(1+g)^2 &&= 3.81 \times (1.05)^2 &&= 4.20 \\
D_3 &= D_0(1+g)^3 &&= 3.81 \times (1.05)^3 &&= 4.41
\end{aligned}
$$

and so on. Using these dividend forecasts in Equation 18.3, we solve for intrinsic value as

$$V_0 = \frac{D_0(1+g)}{1+k} + \frac{D_0(1+g)^2}{(1+k)^2} + \frac{D_0(1+g)^3}{(1+k)^3} + \cdots$$

---

[1] If investors never expected a dividend to be paid, then this model implies that the stock would have no value. To reconcile the DDM with the fact that non-dividend-paying stocks do have a market value, one must assume that investors expect that some day it may pay out some cash, even if only a liquidating dividend.

This equation can be simplified to[2]

$$V_0 = \frac{D_0(1 + g)}{k - g} = \frac{D_1}{k - g} \qquad (18.4)$$

Notice in Equation 18.4 that we calculate intrinsic value by dividing D_1 (not D_0) by $k - g$. If the market capitalization rate for Steady State is 12%, this equation implies that the intrinsic value of a share of Steady State stock is

$$\frac{\$3.81(1 + .05)}{.12 - .05} = \frac{\$4.00}{.12 - .05} = \$57.14$$

Equation 18.4 is called the **constant-growth DDM,** or the Gordon model, after Myron J. Gordon, who popularized the model. It should remind you of the formula for the present value of a perpetuity. If dividends were expected not to grow, then the dividend stream would be a simple perpetuity, and the valuation formula would be[3] $V_0 = D_1/k$. Equation 18.4 generalizes the perpetuity formula for the case of a *growing* perpetuity. As g increases (for a given value of D_1), the stock price also rises.

Example 18.1   Preferred Stock and the DDM

Preferred stock that pays a fixed dividend can be valued using the constant-growth dividend discount model. The constant-growth rate of dividends is simply zero. For example, to value a preferred stock paying a fixed dividend of $2 per share when the discount rate is 8%, we compute

$$V_0 = \frac{\$2}{.08 - 0} = \$25$$

---

[2]Here is a proof. By definition,

$$V_0 = \frac{D_1}{1 + k} + \frac{D_1(1 + g)}{(1 + k)^2} + \frac{D_1(1 + g)^2}{(1 + k)^3} + \cdots \qquad (a)$$

Multiplying through by $(1 + k)/(1 + g)$, we obtain

$$\frac{(1 + k)}{(1 + g)} V_0 = \frac{D_1}{(1 + g)} + \frac{D_1}{(1 + k)} + \frac{D_1(1 + g)}{(1 + k)^2} + \cdots \qquad (b)$$

Subtracting equation (a) from equation (b), we find that

$$\frac{1 + k}{1 + g} V_0 - V_0 = \frac{D_1}{(1 + g)}$$

which implies

$$\frac{(k - g)V_0}{(1 + g)} = \frac{D_1}{(1 + g)}$$

$$V_0 = \frac{D_1}{k - g}$$

[3]Recall from introductory finance that the present value of a $1 per year perpetuity is $1/k$. For example, if $k = 10\%$, the value of the perpetuity is $\$1/.10 = \$10$. Notice that if $g = 0$ in Equation 18.4, the constant-growth DDM formula is the same as the perpetuity formula.

Example 18.2   The Constant-Growth DDM

High Flyer Industries has just paid its annual dividend of $3 per share. The dividend is expected to grow at a constant rate of 8% indefinitely. The beta of High Flyer stock is 1.0, the risk-free rate is 6%, and the market risk premium is 8%. What is the intrinsic value of the stock? What would be your estimate of intrinsic value if you believed that the stock was riskier, with a beta of 1.25?

Because a $3 dividend has just been paid and the growth rate of dividends is 8%, the forecast for the year-end dividend is $3 × 1.08 = $3.24. The market capitalization rate (using the CAPM) is 6% + 1.0 × 8% = 14%. Therefore, the value of the stock is

$$V_0 = \frac{D_1}{k-g} = \frac{\$3.24}{.14 - .08} = \$54$$

If the stock is perceived to be riskier, its value must be lower. At the higher beta, the market capitalization rate is 6% + 1.25 × 8% = 16%, and the stock is worth only

$$\frac{\$3.24}{.16 - .08} = \$40.50$$

The constant-growth DDM is valid only when g is less than k. If dividends were expected to grow forever at a rate faster than k, the value of the stock would be infinite. If an analyst derives an estimate of g greater than k, that growth rate must be unsustainable in the long run. The appropriate valuation model to use in this case is a multistage DDM such as those discussed below.

The constant-growth DDM is so widely used by stock market analysts that it is worth exploring some of its implications and limitations. The constant-growth rate DDM implies that a stock's value will be greater:

1. The larger its expected dividend per share.
2. The lower the market capitalization rate, k.
3. The higher the expected growth rate of dividends.

Another implication of the constant-growth model is that the stock price is expected to grow at the same rate as dividends. To see this, suppose Steady State stock is selling at its intrinsic value of $57.14, so that $V_0 = P_0$. Then

$$P_0 = \frac{D_1}{k-g}$$

Notice that price is proportional to dividends. Therefore, next year, when the dividends paid to Steady State stockholders are expected to be higher by $g = 5\%$, price also should increase by 5%. To confirm this, we can write

$$D_2 = \$4(1.05) = \$4.20$$

$$P_1 = \frac{D_2}{k-g} = \frac{\$4.20}{.12 - .05} = \$60.00$$

which is 5% higher than the current price of $57.14. To generalize,

$$P_1 = \frac{D_2}{k-g} = \frac{D_1(1+g)}{k-g} = \frac{D_1}{k-g}(1+g) = P_0(1+g)$$

Therefore, the DDM implies that when dividends grow at a constant rate, the rate of price appreciation in any year will equal that growth rate, g. For a stock whose market price equals its intrinsic value ($V_0 = P_0$), the expected holding-period return will be

$$E(r) = \text{Dividend yield} + \text{Capital gains yield}$$

$$= \frac{D_1}{P_0} + \frac{P_1 - P_0}{P_0} = \frac{D_1}{P_0} + g \qquad (18.5)$$

This formula offers a means to infer the market capitalization rate of a stock, for if the stock is selling at its intrinsic value, then $E(r) = k$, implying that $k = D_1/P_0 + g$. By observing the dividend yield, D_1/P_0, and estimating the growth rate of dividends, we can compute k. This equation is also known as the *discounted cash flow (DCF) formula*.

This approach is often used in rate hearings for regulated public utilities. The regulatory agency responsible for approving utility pricing decisions is mandated to allow the firms to charge just enough to cover costs plus a "fair" profit, that is, one that allows a competitive return on the investment the firm has made in its productive capacity. In turn, that return is taken to be the expected return investors require on the stock of the firm. The $D_1/P_0 + g$ formula provides a means to infer that required return.

Example 18.3   The Constant-Growth Model

Suppose that Steady State Electronics wins a major contract for its new computer chip. The very profitable contract will enable it to increase the growth rate of dividends from 5% to 6% without reducing the current dividend from the projected value of $4.00 per share. What will happen to the stock price? What will happen to future expected rates of return on the stock?

The stock price ought to increase in response to the good news about the contract, and indeed it does. The stock price jumps from its original value of $57.14 to a post-announcement price of

$$\frac{D_1}{k - g} = \frac{\$4.00}{.12 - .06} = \$66.67$$

Investors who are holding the stock when the good news about the contract is announced will receive a substantial windfall.

On the other hand, at the new price the expected rate of return on the stock is 12%, just as it was before the new contract was announced:

$$E(r) = \frac{D_1}{P_0} + g = \frac{\$4.00}{\$66.67} + .06 = .12, \text{ or } 12\%$$

This makes sense. Once the news about the contract is reflected in the stock price, the expected rate of return will be consistent with the risk of the stock. Because that risk has not changed, neither should the expected rate of return.

 Concept Check **18.2**

a. IBX's stock dividend at the end of this year is expected to be $2.15, and it is expected to grow at 11.2% per year forever. If the required rate of return on IBX stock is 15.2% per year, what is its intrinsic value?

b. If IBX's current market price is equal to this intrinsic value, what is next year's expected price?

c. If an investor were to buy IBX stock now and sell it after receiving the $2.15 dividend a year from now, what is the expected capital gain (i.e., price appreciation) in percentage terms? What are the dividend yield and the holding-period return?

Convergence of Price to Intrinsic Value

Now suppose that the current market price of ABC stock is only $48 per share and, therefore, that the stock is undervalued by $2 per share. In this case the expected rate of price appreciation depends on an additional assumption about whether the discrepancy between the intrinsic value and the market price will disappear, and if so, when.

One fairly common assumption is that the discrepancy will never disappear and that the market price will trend upward at rate g forever. This implies that the discrepancy between intrinsic value and market price also will grow at the same rate. In our example:

Now	Next Year
$V_0 = \$50$	$V_1 = \$50 \times 1.04 = \$52$
$P_0 = \$48$	$P_1 = \$48 \times 1.04 = \$49.92$
$V_0 - P_0 = \$2$	$V_1 - P_1 = \$2 \times 1.04 = \$2.08$

Under this assumption the expected HPR will exceed the required rate, because the dividend yield is higher than it would be if P_0 were equal to V_0. In our example the dividend yield would be 8.33% instead of 8%, so that the expected HPR would be 12.33% rather than 12%:

$$E(r) = \frac{D_1}{P_0} + g = \frac{\$4}{\$48} + .04 = .0833 + .04 = .1233$$

An investor who identifies this undervalued stock can get an expected dividend that exceeds the required yield by 33 basis points. This excess return is earned *each year,* and the market price never catches up to intrinsic value.

An alternative assumption is that the gap between market price and intrinsic value will disappear by the end of the year. In that case we would have $P_1 = V_1 = \$52$, and

$$E(r) = \frac{D_1}{P_0} + \frac{P_1 - P_0}{P_0} = \frac{4}{48} + \frac{52 - 48}{48} = .0833 + .0833 = .1667$$

The assumption of complete catch-up to intrinsic value produces a much larger 1-year HPR. In future years, however, the stock is expected to generate only fair rates of return.

Many stock analysts assume that a stock's price will approach its intrinsic value gradually over time—for example, over a 5-year period. This puts their expected 1-year HPR somewhere between the bounds of 12.33% and 16.67%.

Stock Prices and Investment Opportunities

Consider two companies, Cash Cow, Inc., and Growth Prospects, each with expected earnings in the coming year of $5 per share. Both companies could in principle pay out all of these earnings as dividends, maintaining a perpetual dividend flow of $5 per share. If the market capitalization rate were $k = 12.5\%$, both companies would then be valued at $D_1/k = \$5/.125 = \$40$ per share. Neither firm would grow in value, because with all earnings paid out as dividends, and no earnings reinvested in the firm, both companies' capital stock and earnings capacity would remain unchanged over time; earnings[4] and dividends would not grow.

[4]Actually, we are referring here to earnings net of the funds necessary to maintain the productivity of the firm's capital, that is, earnings net of "economic depreciation." In other words, the earnings figure should be interpreted as the maximum amount of money the firm could pay out each year in perpetuity without depleting its productive capacity. For this reason, the net earnings number may be quite different from the accounting earnings figure that the firm reports in its financial statements. We explore this further in Chapter 19.

Now suppose one of the firms, Growth Prospects, engages in projects that generate a return on investment of 15%, which is greater than the required rate of return, $k = 12.5\%$. It would be foolish for such a company to pay out all of its earnings as dividends. If Growth Prospects retains or plows back some of its earnings into its profitable projects, it can earn a 15% rate of return for its shareholders, whereas if it pays out all earnings as dividends, it forgoes the projects, leaving shareholders to invest the dividends in other opportunities at a fair market rate of only 12.5%. Suppose, therefore, that Growth Prospects chooses a lower **dividend payout ratio** (the fraction of earnings paid out as dividends), reducing payout from 100% to 40%, maintaining a **plowback ratio** (the fraction of earnings reinvested in the firm) at 60%. The plowback ratio is also referred to as the **earnings retention ratio.**

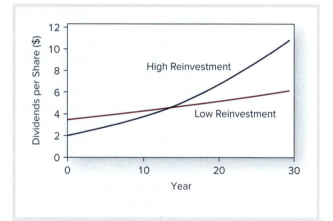

Figure 18.1 Dividend growth for two earnings reinvestment policies

The dividend of the company, therefore, will be $2 (40% of $5 earnings) instead of $5. Will share price fall? No—it will rise! Although dividends initially fall under the earnings reinvestment policy, subsequent growth in the assets of the firm because of reinvested profits will generate growth in future dividends, which will be reflected in today's share price.

Figure 18.1 illustrates the dividend streams generated by Growth Prospects under two dividend policies. A low-reinvestment-rate plan allows the firm to pay higher initial dividends, but results in a lower dividend growth rate. Eventually, a high-reinvestment-rate plan will provide higher dividends. If the dividend growth generated by the reinvested earnings is high enough, the stock will be worth more under the high-reinvestment strategy.

How much growth will be generated? Suppose Growth Prospects starts with plant and equipment of $100 million and is all equity financed. With a return on investment or equity (ROE) of 15%, total earnings are ROE × $100 million = .15 × $100 million = $15 million. There are 3 million shares of stock outstanding, so earnings per share are $5, as posited above. If 60% of the $15 million in this year's earnings is reinvested, then the value of the firm's assets will increase by .60 × $15 million = $9 million, or by 9%. The percentage increase in assets is the rate at which income was generated (ROE) times the plowback ratio (the fraction of earnings reinvested in the firm), which we will denote as b.

Now endowed with 9% more assets, the company earns 9% more income and pays out 9% higher dividends. The growth rate of the dividends, therefore, is[5]

$$g = \text{ROE} \times b = .15 \times .60 = .09$$

If the stock price equals its intrinsic value, it should sell at

$$P_0 = \frac{D_1}{k - g} = \frac{\$2}{.125 - .09} = \$57.14$$

---

[5]We can derive this relationship more generally by noting that with a fixed ROE, earnings (which equal ROE × book value) will grow at the same rate as the book value of the firm. Abstracting from issuance of new shares of stock, the growth rate of book value equals reinvested earnings/book value. Therefore,

$$g = \frac{\text{Reinvested earnings}}{\text{Book value}} = \frac{\text{Reinvested earnings}}{\text{Total earnings}} \times \frac{\text{Total earnings}}{\text{Book value}} = b \times \text{ROE}$$

When Growth Prospects pursued a no-growth policy and paid out all earnings as dividends, the stock price was only $40. Therefore, you can think of $40 as the value per share of the assets the company already has in place.

When Growth Prospects decided to reduce current dividends and reinvest some of its earnings in new investments, its stock price increased. The increase in the stock price reflects the fact that the planned investments provide an expected rate of return greater than the required rate. In other words, the investment opportunities have positive net present value. The value of the firm rises by the NPV of these investment opportunities. This net present value is also called the **present value of growth opportunities,** or **PVGO.**

Therefore, we can think of the value of the firm as the sum of the value of assets already in place, or the no-growth value of the firm, plus the net present value of the future investments the firm will make, which is the PVGO. For Growth Prospects, PVGO = $17.14 per share:

$$\text{Price} = \text{No-growth value per share} + \text{PVGO}$$

$$P_0 = \frac{E_1}{k} + \text{PVGO} \tag{18.6}$$

$$57.14 = 40 + 17.14$$

We know that in reality, dividend cuts almost always are accompanied by steep drops in stock prices. Does this contradict our analysis? Not necessarily: Dividend cuts are usually taken as bad news about the future prospects of the firm, and it is the *new information* about the firm—not the reduced dividend yield per se—that is responsible for the stock price decline.

For example, when J.P. Morgan cut its quarterly dividend from 38 cents to 5 cents a share in 2009, its stock price actually increased by about 5%. The company was able to convince investors that the cut would conserve cash and prepare the firm to weather a severe recession. When investors were convinced that the dividend cut made sense, the stock price actually increased. Similarly, when BP announced in the wake of the massive 2010 Gulf oil spill that it would suspend dividends for the rest of the year, its stock price did not budge. The cut already had been widely anticipated, so it was not new information. These examples show that stock price declines in response to dividend cuts are really a response to the information conveyed by the cut.

It is important to recognize that growth per se is not what investors desire. Growth enhances company value only if it is achieved by investment in projects with attractive profit opportunities (i.e., with ROE > k). To see why, let's now consider Growth Prospects's unfortunate sister company, Cash Cow, Inc. Cash Cow's ROE is only 12.5%, just equal to the required rate of return, k. Therefore, the net present value of its investment opportunities is zero. We've seen that following a zero-growth strategy with b = 0 and g = 0, the value of Cash Cow will be $E_1/k = \$5/.125 = \$40$ per share. Now suppose Cash Cow chooses a plowback ratio of b = .60, the same as Growth Prospects's plowback. Then g would increase to

$$g = \text{ROE} \times b = .125 \times .60 = .075$$

but the stock price is still $40:

$$P_0 = \frac{D_1}{k - g} = \frac{\$2}{.125 - .075} = \$40$$

which is no different from the no-growth strategy.

When Cash Cow reduced dividends to free funds for reinvestment in the firm, it generated only enough growth to maintain the stock price at its current level. This makes sense: If the firm's projects yield only what investors can earn on their own, shareholders cannot be made better off by a high-reinvestment-rate policy. This demonstrates that "growth" is not the same as growth opportunities. To justify reinvestment, the firm must engage in projects with better prospective returns than those shareholders can find elsewhere. Notice also that the PVGO of Cash Cow is zero: $PVGO = P_0 - E_1/k = 40 - 40 = 0$. With $ROE = k$, there is no advantage to plowing funds back into the firm; this shows up as PVGO of zero. In fact, this is why firms with considerable cash flow but limited investment prospects are called "cash cows." The cash these firms generate is best taken out of, or "milked from," the firm.

Example 18.4   Growth Opportunities

Takeover Target is run by entrenched management that insists on reinvesting 60% of its earnings in projects that provide an ROE of 10%, despite the fact that the firm's capitalization rate is $k = 15\%$. The firm's year-end dividend will be $2 per share, paid out of earnings of $5 per share. At what price will the stock sell? What is the present value of growth opportunities? Why would such a firm be a takeover target for another firm?

Given current management's investment policy, the dividend growth rate will be

$$g = ROE \times b = 10\% \times .60 = 6\%$$

and the stock price should be

$$P_0 = \frac{\$2}{.15 - .06} = \$22.22$$

The present value of growth opportunities is

$$PVGO = \text{Price per share} - \text{No-growth value per share}$$
$$= \$22.22 - E_1/k = \$22.22 - 5/.15 = -\$11.11$$

PVGO is *negative*. This is because the net present value of the firm's projects is negative: The rate of return on those assets is less than the opportunity cost of capital.

Such a firm would be subject to takeover, because another firm could buy the firm for the market price of $22.22 per share and increase the value of the firm by changing its investment policy. For example, if the new management simply paid out all earnings as dividends, the value of the firm would increase to its no-growth value, $E_1/k = \$5/.15 = \$33.33$.

 Concept Check **18.3**

a. Calculate the price of a firm with a plowback ratio of .60 if its ROE is 20%. Current earnings, E_1, will be $5 per share, and $k = 12.5\%$.

b. What if ROE is 10%, which is less than the market capitalization rate? Compare the firm's price in this instance to that of a firm with the same ROE and E_1, but a plowback ratio of $b = 0$.

Life Cycles and Multistage Growth Models

As useful as the constant-growth DDM formula is, you need to remember that it is based on a simplifying assumption, namely, that the dividend growth rate will be constant forever. In fact, firms typically pass through life cycles with very different dividend profiles in different phases. In early years, there are ample opportunities for profitable reinvestment in the company. Payout ratios are low, and growth is correspondingly rapid. In later years, the firm matures, production capacity is sufficient to meet market demand, competitors enter the market, and attractive opportunities for reinvestment may become harder to find. In this mature phase, the firm may choose to increase the dividend payout ratio, rather than retain earnings. Dividend growth slows because the company has fewer investment opportunities.

Table 18.2 illustrates this pattern. It gives Value Line's forecasts of return on capital, dividend payout ratio, and 3-year projected growth rate in earnings per share for a sample of the firms included in the computer software industry versus those of East Coast electric utilities. (We compare return on capital rather than return on equity because the latter is affected by leverage, which tends to be far greater in the electric utility industry than in the software industry. Return on capital measures operating income per dollar of total long-term financing, regardless of whether the source of the capital supplied is debt or equity. We will return to this issue in Chapter 19.)

By and large, the software firms have attractive investment opportunities. The median return on capital of these firms is forecast to be 14.8%, and the firms have responded with high plowback ratios. Most of these firms pay no dividends at all. The high return on capital and high plowback result in rapid growth. The median projected growth rate of earnings per share in this group is 12.0%.

In contrast, the electric utilities are more representative of mature firms. Their median return on capital is lower, 6.3%; dividend payout is higher, 67.5%; and median growth is lower, 4.6%. We conclude that the higher payouts of the electric utilities reflect their more limited opportunities to reinvest earnings at attractive rates of return.

Table 18.2

Financial ratios in two industries

	Ticker	Return on Capital (%)	Payout Ratio (%)	Growth Rate 2017–2020
Computer software				
Adobe Systems	ADBE	14.5%	0.0%	20.4%
Citrix	CTXS	20.0	0.0	7.2
Cognizant	CTSH	18.5	0.0	22.2
Computer Associates	CA	13.0	38.0	12.4
Intuit	INTU	30.5	24.0	14.3
Microsoft	MSFT	23.0	52.0	11.5
Oracle	ORCL	15.0	20.0	8.4
Red Hat	RHT	14.5	0.0	15.3
Symantec	SYMC	13.5	25.0	9.0
SAP	SAP	13.5	36.0	7.3
Median		14.8%	22.0%	12.0%
Electric utilities (East Coast)				
Dominion Resources	D	8.5%	73.0%	10.1%
Consolidated Edison	ED	5.5	69.0	1.6
Duke Energy	DUK	5.0	75.0	3.8
Eversource	ES	6.0	58.0	6.0
FirstEnergy	FE	5.5	48.0	4.5
Nextera Energy	NEE	7.5	69.0	6.3
Public Service Enterprise	PEG	7.0	56.0	6.3
South Carolina E & G	SCG	6.0	60.0	4.7
Southern Company	SO	6.5	75.0	4.6
Tampa Electric	TE	6.5	66.0	3.9
Median		6.3%	67.5%	4.6%

To value companies with temporarily high growth, analysts use a multistage version of the dividend discount model. For example, a **two-stage dividend discount model** allows for an initial high-growth period before the firm settles down to a sustainable growth trajectory. The combined present value of dividends in the initial high-growth period is calculated first. Then, once the firm is projected to settle down to a steady-growth phase, the constant-growth DDM is applied to value the remaining stream of dividends.

Let's try this approach with an actual firm. Figure 18.2 is a Value Line Investment Survey report on General Electric. Some of the relevant information in 2016 is highlighted.

GE's beta appears at the circled A, its recent stock price at the B, the per-share dividend payments at the C, the ROE (referred to as *return on shareholder equity*) at the D, and the dividend payout ratio (referred to as *all dividends to net profits*) at the E. The rows ending at C, D, and E are historical time series. The boldfaced, italicized entries under 2017 are estimates for that year. Similarly, the entries in the far right column (labeled 15–17) are forecasts for some time between 2019–2021, which we will take to be 2020.

Value Line projects fairly rapid growth in the near term, with dividends rising from $1.04 in 2017 to $1.60 in 2020. This growth rate cannot be sustained indefinitely. We can obtain dividend inputs for this initial period by using the explicit forecasts for 2017 and 2020 and linear interpolation for the years between:

| 2017 | $1.04 | 2019 | $1.41 |
| 2018 | $1.22 | 2020 | $1.60 |

Now let us assume the dividend growth rate levels off in 2020. What is a good guess for that steady-state growth rate? Value Line forecasts a dividend payout ratio of .53 and an ROE of 19.5%, implying long-term growth will be

$$g = \text{ROE} \times b = 19.5\% \times (1 - .53) = 9.17\%$$

Value Line rounds this estimate off to 9% (see the entry for "Retained [Earnings] to Common Equity" near the circled D), so we too will set $g = 9\%$.

Our estimate of GE's intrinsic value using an investment horizon of 2020 is therefore obtained from Equation 18.2, which we restate here:

$$V_{2016} = \frac{D_{2017}}{1+k} + \frac{D_{2018}}{(1+k)^2} + \frac{D_{2019}}{(1+k)^3} + \frac{D_{2020} + P_{2020}}{(1+k)^4}$$

$$= \frac{1.04}{1+k} + \frac{1.22}{(1+k)^2} + \frac{1.41}{(1+k)^3} + \frac{1.60 + P_{2020}}{(1+k)^4}$$

Here, P_{2020} represents the forecast price at which we can sell our shares at the end of 2020, when dividends are assumed to enter their constant-growth phase. That price, according to the constant-growth DDM, should be

$$P_{2020} = \frac{D_{2021}}{k-g} = \frac{D_{2020}(1+g)}{k-g} = \frac{1.60 \times 1.09}{k - .09}$$

The only variable remaining to be determined to calculate intrinsic value is the market capitalization rate, k.

One way to obtain k is from the CAPM. Observe from the Value Line report that GE's beta is 1.10. The risk-free rate on long-term Treasury bonds in 2016 was about 2.5%.[6]

[6]When valuing long-term assets such as stocks, it is common to treat the long-term Treasury bond, rather than short-term T-bills, as the risk-free asset.

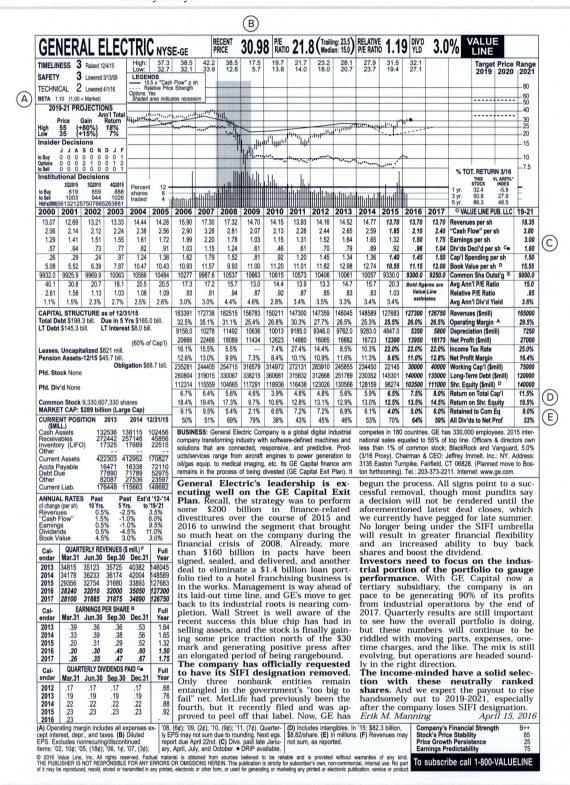

Figure 18.2 Value Line Investment Survey report on General Electric

Source: *Value Line Investment Survey,* April 15, 2016. Reprinted with permission of Value Line Investment Survey © 2016 Value Line Publishing, Inc. All rights reserved.

Suppose that the market risk premium was forecast at 8%, roughly in line with its historical average. This would imply that the forecast for the market return was

$$\text{Risk-free rate} + \text{Market risk premium} = 2.5\% + 8\% = 10.5\%$$

Therefore, we can solve for the market capitalization rate as

$$k = r_f + \beta[E(r_M) - r_f] = 2.5\% + 1.10(10.5\% - 2.5\%) = 11.3\%$$

Our forecast for the stock price in 2020 is thus

$$P_{2020} = \frac{\$1.60 \times 1.09}{.113 - .09} = \$75.83$$

and today's estimate of intrinsic value is

$$V_{2016} = \frac{1.04}{1.113} + \frac{1.22}{(1.113)^2} + \frac{1.41}{(1.113)^3} + \frac{1.60 + 75.83}{(1.113)^4} = \$53.40$$

We know from the Value Line report that GE's actual price was $30.98 (at the circled B). Our intrinsic value analysis indicates that the stock was considerably underpriced. Should we increase our holdings?

Perhaps. But before betting the farm, stop to consider how much confidence you should place in this estimate. We've had to guess at dividends in the near future, the appropriate discount rate, and the ultimate growth rate of those dividends. Moreover, we've assumed GE will follow a relatively simple two-stage growth process. In practice, the growth of dividends can follow more complicated patterns. Even small errors in these approximations could upset a conclusion.

In particular, it is clear that an overwhelming portion of GE's intrinsic value derives from the forecasted 2020 sales price of $75.83. If that sales price is overstated, so will be our estimate of intrinsic value. And we have good reason to be suspicious. We have calculated the sales price assuming GE's growth rate in 2020 and beyond will be 9%, which seems implausibly optimistic as a sustainable value. More likely, GE will still be enjoying rapid growth in 2020 and will not yet have settled down to a sustainable long-run growth phase. Notice that the 9% "sustainable growth rate" was itself derived using Value Line's assumption that ROE in 2020 will be 19.5%, also an implausibly high estimate for a sustainable long-run value. We clearly want to revisit this assumption and will return to it in a moment using a multi-stage growth model that generalizes the two-stage approach we are using here.

For now, however, let's just suppose we have overestimated GE's sustainable growth prospects and that the actual growth rate in the post-2020 period will be 7% rather than 9%. Using this lower estimate in the two-stage dividend discount model implies an intrinsic value in 2016 of only $29.93, which is *less* than the stock price. Our conclusion regarding intrinsic value versus price is reversed.

The exercise highlights the importance of performing sensitivity analysis when you attempt to value stocks. Your estimates of stock values are no better than your assumptions. Sensitivity analysis will highlight the inputs that need to be most carefully examined. For example, even modest changes in the estimated growth rate for the post-2020 period result in big changes in intrinsic value. Similarly, small changes in the assumed capitalization rate would change intrinsic value substantially. On the other hand, reasonable changes in the dividends forecast between 2017 and 2020 would have a small impact on intrinsic value.

 Concept Check **18.4**

Confirm that the intrinsic value of GE using $g = 7\%$ is $29.93. (*Hint:* First calculate the stock price in 2020. Then calculate the present value of all interim dividends plus the present value of the 2020 sales price.)

Multistage Growth Models

The two-stage growth model that we just considered for GE is a good start toward realism, but clearly we can do even better by allowing our valuation model to accomodate more flexible patterns of growth. Multistage growth models allow dividends per share to grow at several different rates as the firm matures. Many analysts use three-stage growth models. They may assume an initial period of high dividend growth (or instead make year-by-year forecasts of dividends for the short term), a final period of sustainable growth, and a transition period between, during which dividend growth rates taper off from the initial rapid rate to the ultimate sustainable rate. These models are conceptually no harder to work with than a two-stage model, but they require many more calculations and can be tedious to do by hand. It is easy, however, to build an Excel spreadsheet for such a model.

Spreadsheet 18.1 is an example of such a model. Column B contains the inputs we have used so far for GE. Column E contains dividend forecasts. In cells E2 through E5 we present the Value Line estimates for the next 4 years. Dividend growth in this period is about 15.4% annually. Rather than assume a sudden transition to constant dividend growth rate starting in 2020, we assume instead that the dividend growth rate will remain at 15.4% in the coming year, but will decline steadily through 2031, finally reaching a constant terminal growth rate of 6% (see column F). This is far more realistic as a sustainable growth rate than the 9% value we used in the two-stage model.

Each dividend in the transition period is the previous year's dividend times that year's growth rate. Terminal value once the firm finally enters a constant-growth stage (cell G17) is computed from the constant-growth DDM. Investor cash flow in each period (column H) equals dividends in each year plus the terminal value in 2032. The present value of these cash flows is computed in cell H19 as $35.70.

	A	B	C	D	E	F	G	H	I
1	Inputs for GE			Year	Dividend	Div growth	Term value	Investor CF	
2	beta	1.1		2017	1.04			1.04	
3	mkt_prem	0.08		2018	1.23			1.23	
4	rf	0.025		2019	1.41			1.41	
5	k_equity	0.1130		2020	1.60			1.60	
6	term_gwth	0.060		2021	1.85	0.1544		1.85	
7				2022	2.11	0.1450		2.11	
8				2023	2.40	0.1355		2.40	
9				2024	2.70	0.1261		2.70	
10				2025	3.02	0.1166		3.02	
11				2026	3.34	0.1072		3.34	
12	Value line			2027	3.67	0.0978		3.67	
13	forecasts of			2028	3.99	0.0883		3.99	
14	annual dividends			2029	4.31	0.0789		4.31	
15				2030	4.61	0.0694		4.61	
16				2031	4.89	0.0600		4.89	
17	Transitional period			2032	5.18	0.0600	103.57	108.75	
18	with slowing dividend								
19	growth							35.70	= PV of CF
20		Beginning of constant			E17* (1+F17)/(B5−F17)				
21		growth period						NPV(B5, H2:H17)	

Spreadsheet 18.1

A three-stage growth model for General Electric

eXcel

Please visit us at

www.mhhe.com/Bodie11e

18.4   The Price–Earnings Ratio

The Price–Earnings Ratio and Growth Opportunities

Much of the real-world discussion of stock market valuation concentrates on the firm's **price–earnings multiple,** the ratio of price per share to earnings per share, commonly called the P/E ratio. Our discussion of growth opportunities shows why stock market analysts focus on the P/E ratio. Both companies considered, Cash Cow and Growth Prospects, had earnings per share (EPS) of $5, but Growth Prospects reinvested 60% of earnings in prospects with an ROE of 15%, whereas Cash Cow paid out all earnings as dividends. Cash Cow had a price of $40, giving it a P/E multiple of 40/5 = 8.0, whereas Growth Prospects sold for $57.14, giving it a multiple of 57.14/5 = 11.4. This observation suggests the P/E ratio might serve as a useful indicator of expectations of growth opportunities.

We can see how growth opportunities are reflected in P/E ratios by rearranging Equation 18.6 to

$$\frac{P_0}{E_1} = \frac{1}{k}\left(\frac{1 + \text{PVGO}}{E/k}\right) \tag{18.7}$$

When PVGO = 0, Equation 18.7 shows that $P_0 = E_1/k$. The stock is valued like a non-growing perpetuity of E_1, and the P/E ratio is just $1/k$. However, as PVGO becomes an increasingly dominant contributor to price, the P/E ratio can rise dramatically.

The ratio of PVGO to E/k has a straightforward interpretation. It is the ratio of the component of firm value due to growth opportunities to the component of value due to assets already in place (i.e., the no-growth value of the firm, E/k). When future growth opportunities dominate the estimate of total value, the firm will command a high price relative to current earnings. Thus a high P/E multiple indicates that a firm enjoys ample growth opportunities.

P/E multiples do vary with growth prospects. Between 1996 and 2015, for example, FedEx's P/E ratio averaged about 17.4 while Consolidated Edison's (an electric utility) average P/E was only 14.0. These numbers do not necessarily imply that FedEx was over-priced compared to Con Ed. If investors believed FedEx would grow faster than Con Ed, the higher price per dollar of earnings would be justified. That is, an investor might well pay a higher price per dollar of *current* earnings if he or she expects that earnings stream to grow more rapidly. In fact, FedEx's growth rate has been consistent with its higher P/E multiple. Over this period, its earnings per share grew at 10.5% per year while Con Ed's earnings growth rate was only 1.7%. (Later in the chapter, where we turn to practical issues in interpreting P/E ratios, Figure 18.4 presents the EPS history of the two companies.)

We conclude that the P/E ratio reflects the market's optimism concerning a firm's growth prospects. Analysts must decide whether they are more or less optimistic than the belief implied by the market multiple. If they are more optimistic, they will recommend buying the stock.

There is a way to make these insights more precise. Look again at the constant-growth DDM formula, $P_0 = D_1/(k - g)$. Now recall that dividends equal the earnings that are *not* reinvested in the firm: $D_1 = E_1(1 - b)$. Recall also that $g = \text{ROE} \times b$. Hence, substituting for D_1 and g, we find that

$$P_0 = \frac{E_1(1 - b)}{k - \text{ROE} \times b}$$

implying the P/E ratio is

$$\frac{P_0}{E_1} = \frac{1-b}{k - \text{ROE} \times b} \tag{18.8}$$

It is easy to verify that the P/E ratio increases with ROE. This makes sense, because high-ROE projects give the firm good opportunities for growth.[7] We also can verify that the P/E ratio increases for higher plowback, b, as long as ROE exceeds k. This too makes sense. When a firm has good investment opportunities, the market will reward it with a higher P/E multiple if it exploits those opportunities more aggressively by plowing back more earnings into those opportunities.

However, growth is not desirable for its own sake. Examine Table 18.3 where we use Equation 18.8 to compute both growth rates and P/E ratios for different combinations of ROE and b. Although growth always increases with the plowback ratio (move across the rows in Panel A), the P/E ratio does not (move across the rows in Panel B). In the top row of Panel B, the P/E falls as the plowback ratio increases. In the middle row, it is unaffected by plowback. In the third row, it increases.

This pattern has a simple interpretation. When the expected ROE is less than the required return, k, investors prefer that the firm pay out earnings as dividends rather than reinvest earnings in the firm at an inadequate rate of return. That is, for ROE lower than k, the value of the firm falls as plowback increases. Conversely, when ROE exceeds k, the firm offers attractive investment opportunities, so the value of the firm is enhanced as those opportunities are more fully exploited by increasing the plowback ratio.

Finally, where ROE just equals k, the firm offers "break-even" investment opportunities with a fair rate of return. In this case, investors are indifferent between reinvestment of earnings in the firm or elsewhere at the market capitalization rate, because the rate of return in either case is 12%. Therefore, the stock price is unaffected by the plowback ratio.

We conclude that the higher the plowback ratio, the higher the growth rate, but a higher plowback ratio does not necessarily mean a higher P/E ratio. Higher plowback increases P/E only if investments undertaken by the firm offer an expected rate of return greater than the market capitalization rate. Otherwise, increasing plowback hurts investors because more money is sunk into projects with inadequate rates of return.

Table 18.3		Plowback Ratio (b)			
Effect of ROE and plowback on growth and the P/E ratio		0	0.25	0.50	0.75
	ROE	A. Growth Rate (g)			
	10%	0	2.5%	5.0%	7.5%
	12	0	3.0	6.0	9.0
	14	0	3.5	7.0	10.5
	ROE	B. P/E Ratio			
	10%	8.33	7.89	7.14	5.56
	12	8.33	8.33	8.33	8.33
	14	8.33	8.82	10.00	16.67

Assumption: $k = 12\%$ per year.

[7]Equation 18.8 is a simple rearrangement of the DDM formula, with ROE $\times b = g$. Because that formula requires that $g < k$, Equation 18.8 is valid only when ROE $\times b < k$.

Notwithstanding these fine points, P/E ratios frequently are taken as proxies for the expected growth in dividends or earnings. In fact, a Wall Street rule of thumb is that the growth rate ought to be roughly equal to the P/E ratio. In other words, the ratio of P/E to g, often called the *PEG ratio,* should be about 1.0. Peter Lynch, the famous portfolio manager, puts it this way in his book *One Up on Wall Street:*

> The P/E ratio of any company that's fairly priced will equal its growth rate. I'm talking here about growth rate of earnings here. . . . . If the P/E ratio of Coca Cola is 15, you'd expect the company to be growing at about 15% per year, etc. But if the P/E ratio is less than the growth rate, you may have found yourself a bargain.

Example 18.5   P/E Ratio versus Growth Rate

Let's try Lynch's rule of thumb. Assume that

$r_f = 8\%$	(roughly the value when Peter Lynch was writing)
$r_M - r_f = 8\%$	(about the historical average market risk premium)
$b = .4$	(a typical value for the plowback ratio in the United States)

Therefore, $r_M = r_f +$ market risk premium $= 8\% + 8\% = 16\%$, and $k = 16\%$ for an average ($\beta = 1$) company. If we also accept as reasonable that ROE $= 16\%$ (the same value as the expected return on the stock), we conclude that

$$g = \text{ROE} \times b = 16\% \times .4 = 6.4\%$$

and

$$\frac{P}{E} = \frac{1 - .4}{.16 - .064} = 6.26$$

Thus, the P/E ratio and g are about equal using these assumptions, consistent with the rule of thumb.

However, note that this rule of thumb, like almost all others, will not work in all circumstances. For example, the yield on long-term Treasury bonds today is more like 2.5%, so a comparable forecast of r_M today would be

$$r_f + \text{Market risk premium} = 2.5\% + 8\% = 10.5\%$$

If we continue to focus on a firm with $\beta = 1$, and if ROE still is about the same as k, then

$$g = 10.5\% \times .4 = 4.2\%$$

while

$$\frac{P}{E} = \frac{1 - .4}{.105 - .042} = 9.5$$

The P/E ratio and g now diverge and the PEG ratio is now 2.3. Nevertheless, lower-than-average PEG ratios are still widely seen as signaling potential underpricing.

The importance of growth opportunities is most evident in the valuation of start-up firms. For example, in the dot-com boom of the late 1990s, many companies that had yet to turn a profit were valued by the market at billions of dollars. The perceived value of these companies was *exclusively* as growth opportunities. For example, the online auction firm eBay had 1998 profits of $2.4 million, far less than the $45 million profit earned by the traditional auctioneer Sotheby's; yet eBay's market value was more than 10 times greater: $22 billion versus $1.9 billion. As it turns out, the market was quite right to value eBay so much more aggressively than Sotheby's. eBay's net income in 2015 was $1.7 billion, more than 10 times that of Sotheby's.

Of course, when company valuation is determined primarily by growth opportunities, those values can be very sensitive to reassessments of such prospects. When the market became more skeptical of the business prospects of most Internet retailers at the close of the 1990s, that is, as it revised the estimates of growth opportunities downward, their stock prices plummeted.

As perceptions of future prospects wax and wane, share price can swing wildly. Growth prospects are intrinsically difficult to tie down; ultimately, however, those prospects drive the value of the most dynamic firms in the economy.

The nearby box contains a simple valuation analysis. Facebook's 2012 IPO was among the most highly anticipated in decades, and there was widespread speculation about the price at which it would eventually trade in the stock market. There was considerable dispersion among analysts about what the stock would be worth. The points of contention in their analysis turned on two key questions. First, what was a reasonable projection for the growth rate of Facebook's profits? Second, what multiple of earnings was appropriate to translate an earnings forecast into a price forecast? These are precisely the questions addressed by our stock valuation models.

 Concept Check **18.5**

ABC stock has an expected ROE of 12% per year, expected earnings per share of $2, and expected dividends of $1.50 per share. Its market capitalization rate is 10% per year.

a. What are its expected growth rate, its price, and its P/E ratio?

b. If the plowback ratio were .4, what would be the expected dividend per share, the growth rate, price, and the P/E ratio?

P/E Ratios and Stock Risk

One important implication of any stock-valuation model is that (holding all else equal) riskier stocks will have lower P/E multiples. We can see this quite easily in the context of the constant-growth model by examining the formula for the P/E ratio (Equation 18.8):

$$\frac{P}{E} = \frac{1-b}{k-g}$$

Riskier firms will have higher required rates of return, that is, higher values of k. Therefore, the P/E multiple will be lower. This is true even outside the context of the constant-growth model. For *any* expected earnings and dividend stream, the present value of those cash flows will be lower when the stream is perceived to be riskier. Hence the stock price and the ratio of price to earnings will be lower.

Of course, you can find many small, risky, start-up companies with very high P/E multiples. This does not contradict our claim that P/E multiples should fall with risk; instead it is evidence of the market's expectations of high growth rates for those companies. This is why we said that high-risk firms will have lower P/E ratios *holding all else equal.* Given a growth projection, the P/E multiple will be lower when risk is perceived to be higher.

Pitfalls in P/E Analysis

No description of P/E analysis is complete without mentioning some of its pitfalls. First, consider that the denominator in the P/E ratio is accounting earnings, which are influenced by somewhat arbitrary accounting rules such as the use of historical cost in depreciation

Facebook's IPO

As Facebook's IPO drew near, valuation estimates by professional analysts were surprisingly disparate, ranging from as little as $50 billion to as much as $125 billion.

Disputes over fair value turned on a few key questions: Just how fast would the company be able to grow? How much profit would it be able to derive from advertising? And what earnings multiple would the market be willing to pay for that profit stream?

Everyone believed that Facebook had many years of rapid growth before it, but even so, its recent growth rate was lower than in its early years. While revenue grew 88% in 2011, and net income grew 65%, that increase was nevertheless considerably below the 154% increase in revenue from 2009 to 2010.

Francis Gaskins, president of **IPOdesktop.com,** which analyzes IPOs for investors, estimated Facebook's value at no more than $50 billion.* Even that value, at the low end of the range of most analysts, seemed generous in some respects: It would have been 50 times Facebook's 2011 profits of $1 billion, and a P/E multiple of 50 was more than triple the market's average price-to-earnings ratio at the time.

However, much higher estimates also were offered. For example, an analyst at Wedge Partners believed the value could top $100 billion. If Facebook traded at 15 to 18 times next year's EBITDA (expected earnings before interest, taxes and certain noncash charges), it would result in a stock valuation of around $89 billion. But he argued that if Facebook could generate faster growth in ad spending, that could justify a multiple as high as 20 times earnings, implying a $110 billion valuation. By comparison, more mature companies such as Microsoft or Google traded at 7 to 10 times EBITDA. Gaskins was unconvinced, pointing out that at a $100 billion valuation Facebook would be worth about half as much as Google, even though Google's sales and profits were 10 times that of Facebook.

In the end, based on its IPO price, the market valued Facebook at about $90 billion.

*The valuation estimates cited in this box appeared in Randall Smith, "Facebook's $100 Billion Question," *The Wall Street Journal,* February 3, 2012.

and inventory valuation. In times of high inflation, historic cost depreciation and inventory costs will tend to underrepresent true economic values, because the replacement cost of both goods and capital equipment will rise with the general level of prices. As Figure 18.3 demonstrates, P/E ratios generally have been inversely related to the inflation rate. In part, this reflects the market's assessment that earnings in high inflation periods are of "lower quality," artificially distorted by inflation, and warranting lower P/E ratios.

Earnings management is the practice of using flexibility in accounting rules to improve the apparent profitability of the firm. We will have much to say on this topic in the next chapter on interpreting financial statements. A version of earnings management that became common in the 1990s was the reporting of "pro forma earnings" measures.

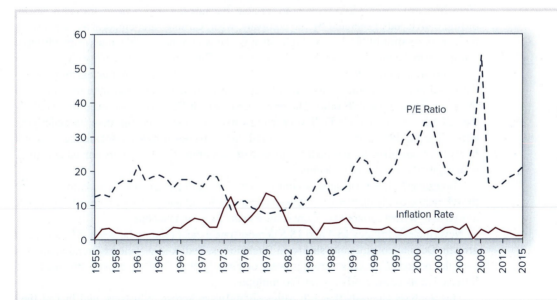

Figure 18.3 P/E ratios of the S&P 500 index and inflation

Pro forma earnings are calculated ignoring certain expenses, for example, restructuring charges, stock-option expenses, or write-downs of assets from continuing operations. Firms argue that ignoring these expenses gives a clearer picture of the underlying profitability of the firm. Comparisons with earlier periods probably would make more sense if those costs were excluded.

But when there is too much leeway for choosing what to exclude, it becomes hard for investors or analysts to interpret the numbers or to compare them across firms. The lack of standards gives firms considerable leeway to manage earnings.

Even generally accepted accounting principles (GAAP) allow firms considerable discretion to manage earnings. For example, in the late 1990s, Kellogg took restructuring charges, which are supposed to be one-time events, nine quarters in a row. Were these really one-time events, or were they more appropriately treated as ordinary expenses? Given the available leeway in managing earnings, the justified P/E multiple becomes difficult to gauge.

Another confounding factor in the use of P/E ratios is related to the business cycle. We were careful in deriving the DDM to define earnings as being net of *economic* depreciation, that is, the maximum flow of income that the firm could pay out without depleting its productive capacity. But reported earnings are computed in accordance with GAAP and need not correspond to economic earnings. Beyond this, however, notions of a normal or justified P/E ratio, as in Equation 18.7 or 18.8, assume implicitly that earnings rise at a constant rate, or, put another way, on a smooth trend line. In contrast, reported earnings can fluctuate dramatically around a trend line over the course of the business cycle.

Another way to make this point is to note that the "normal" P/E ratio predicted by Equation 18.8 is the ratio of today's price to the *trend value* of future earnings, E_1. The P/E ratio reported in the financial pages of the newspaper, by contrast, is the ratio of price to the most recent *past* accounting earnings. Current accounting earnings can differ considerably from future economic earnings. Because ownership of stock conveys the right to future as well as current earnings, the ratio of price to most recent earnings can vary substantially over the business cycle, as accounting earnings and the trend value of economic earnings diverge by greater and lesser amounts.

As an example, Figure 18.4 graphs the earnings per share of FedEx and Con Ed since 1996. Note that FedEx's EPS is far more variable. Because the market values the entire stream of future dividends generated by the company, when earnings are temporarily depressed, the P/E ratio should tend to be high—that is, the denominator of the ratio responds more sensitively to the business cycle than the numerator. This pattern is borne out well.

Figure 18.5 graphs the P/E ratios of the two firms. FedEx has greater earnings volatility and more variability in its P/E ratio. Its clearly higher average growth rate shows up in its generally higher P/E ratio. The only year in which Con Ed's ratio exceeded FedEx's was 2012, during which FedEx's earnings rose at a far faster rate than its underlying trend. The market seems to have decided that this earnings performance was not likely to be sustainable, and FedEx's price rose less dramatically than its annual earnings. Consequently, its P/E ratio declined.

This example shows why analysts must be careful in using P/E ratios. There is no way to say the P/E ratio is overly high or low without referring to the company's long-run growth prospects, as well as to current earnings per share relative to the long-run trend line.

Nevertheless, Figures 18.4 and 18.5 demonstrate a clear relation between P/E ratios and growth. Despite considerable short-run fluctuations, FedEx's EPS clearly trended upward over the period. Con Ed's earnings were essentially flat. FedEx's growth prospects are reflected in its consistently higher P/E multiple.

This analysis suggests that P/E ratios should vary across industries, and in fact they do. Figure 18.6 shows P/E ratios in 2016 for a sample of industries. Notice that the industries with the highest multiples—such as application software or cable TV—have attractive investment opportunities and relatively high growth rates, whereas the industries with the lowest ratios—for example, auto manufacturers and airlines—are in more mature or less profitable industries with limited growth opportunities. The relationship between P/E and growth is not perfect, which is not surprising in light of the pitfalls discussed in this section, but as a general rule, the P/E multiple does appear to track growth opportunities.

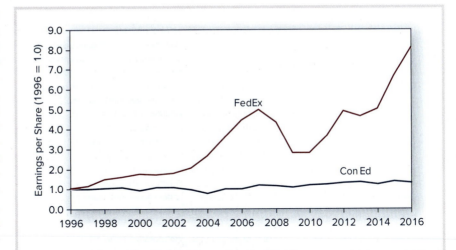

Figure 18.4 Earnings growth for two companies

Combining P/E Analysis and the DDM

Some analysts use P/E ratios in conjunction with earnings forecasts to estimate the price of a stock at an investor's horizon date. The GE analysis in Figure 18.2 shows that Value Line forecast a P/E ratio for 2020 of 15. EPS for 2020 was forecast at $3, implying a price in 2020 of 15 × $3 = $45. Given an estimate of $45 for the 2020

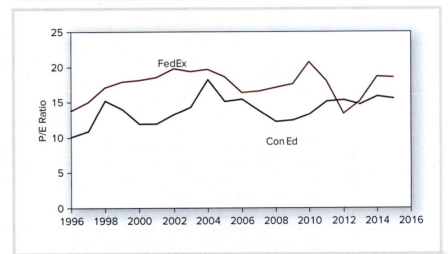

Figure 18.5 Price–earnings ratios

sales price, we would compute intrinsic value in 2016 as

$$V_{2016} = \frac{1.04}{1.113} + \frac{1.22}{(1.113)^2} + \frac{1.41}{(1.113)^3} + \frac{1.60 + 45}{(1.113)^4} = \$33.31$$

Other Comparative Valuation Ratios

The price–earnings ratio is an example of a comparative valuation ratio. Such ratios are used to assess the valuation of one firm versus another based on a fundamental indicator such as earnings. For example, an analyst might compare the P/E ratios of two firms in the same industry to test whether the market is valuing one firm "more aggressively" than the other. Other comparative ratios that are commonly used include the price-to-book ratio, the price-to-cash-flow ratio, and the price-to-sales ratio.

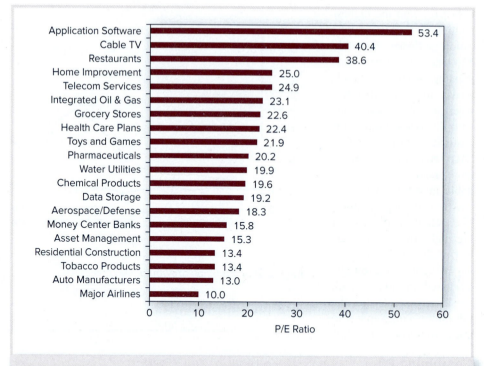

Figure 18.6 P/E ratios for different industries

Source: Yahoo! Finance, **finance.yahoo.com**, June 4, 2016.

Price-to-Book Ratio   This is the ratio of price per share divided by book value per share. As we noted earlier in this chapter, some analysts view book value as a useful measure of value and therefore treat the ratio of price to book value as an indicator of how aggressively the market values the firm.

Price-to-Cash-Flow Ratio   Earnings as reported on the income statement can be affected by the company's choice of accounting practices and thus are commonly viewed as subject to some imprecision and even manipulation. In contrast, cash flow—which tracks cash actually flowing into or out of the firm—is less affected by accounting decisions. As a result, some analysts prefer to use the ratio of price to cash flow per share rather than price to earnings per share. Some analysts use operating cash flow when calculating this ratio; others prefer "free cash flow," that is, operating cash flow net of new investment.

Price-to-Sales Ratio   Many start-up firms have no earnings. As a result, the price–earnings ratio for these firms is meaningless. The price-to-sales ratio (the ratio of stock price to the annual sales per share) may be used as an alternative valuation benchmark for these firms. Of course, price-to-sales ratios can vary markedly across industries, because profit margins vary widely.

Be creative: Sometimes a standard valuation ratio simply will not be available, and you will have to devise your own. In the 1990s, some analysts valued retail Internet firms based on the number of hits their Web sites received. As it turns out, they valued these firms using too-generous "price-to-hits" ratios. Nevertheless, in a new investment environment, these analysts used the information available to them to devise the best valuation tools they could.

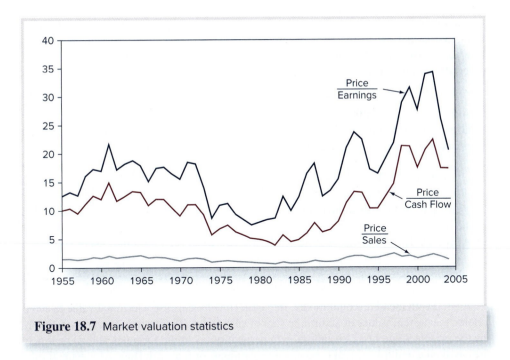

Figure 18.7 Market valuation statistics

Figure 18.7 presents the behavior of several valuation measures. While the levels of these ratios differ considerably, for the most part, they track each other fairly closely, with upturns and downturns at the same times.

18.5   Free Cash Flow Valuation Approaches

An alternative approach to the dividend discount model values the firm using free cash flow, that is, cash flow available to the firm or its equityholders net of capital expenditures. This approach is particularly useful for firms that pay no dividends, for which the dividend discount model would be difficult to implement. But free cash flow models may be applied to any firm and can provide useful insights about firm value beyond the DDM.

One approach is to discount the *free cash flow* for the *firm* (FCFF) at the weighted-average cost of capital to obtain the value of the firm, and subtract the then-existing value of debt to find the value of equity. Another is to focus from the start on the free cash flow to *equityholders* (FCFE), discounting those directly at the cost of equity to obtain the market value of equity.

The free cash flow to the firm is the after-tax cash flow generated by the firm's operations, net of investments in capital, and net working capital. It includes cash flows available to both debt- and equityholders.[8] It equals:

$$\text{FCFF} = \text{EBIT}(1 - t_c) + \text{Depreciation} - \text{Capital expenditures} - \text{Increase in NWC} \quad \textbf{(18.9)}$$

where

EBIT = earnings before interest and taxes

t_c = the corporate tax rate

NWC = net working capital

[8]This is firm cash flow assuming all-equity financing. Any tax advantage to debt financing is recognized by using an after-tax cost of debt in the computation of weighted-average cost of capital. This issue is discussed in any introductory corporate finance text.

Alternatively, we can focus on cash flow available to equityholders. This will differ from free cash flow to the firm by after-tax interest expenditures, as well as by cash flow associated with net issuance or repurchase of debt (i.e., principal repayments minus proceeds from issuance of new debt).

$$\text{FCFE} = \text{FCFF} - \text{Interest expense} \times (1 - t_c) + \text{Increases in net debt} \qquad \textbf{(18.10)}$$

A free cash flow to the firm valuation model discounts year-by-year cash flows plus some estimate of terminal value, V_T. In Equation 18.11, we use the constant-growth model to estimate terminal value and discount at the weighted-average cost of capital.

$$\text{Firm value} = \sum_{t=1}^{T} \frac{\text{FCFF}_t}{(1 + \text{WACC})^t} + \frac{V_T}{(1 + \text{WACC})^T} \text{ where } V_T = \frac{\text{FCFF}_{T+1}}{\text{WACC} - g} \qquad \textbf{(18.11)}$$

To find equity value, we subtract the existing market value of debt from the derived value of the firm.

Alternatively, we can discount free cash flows to *equity* (FCFE) at the cost of *equity, k_E*.

$$\text{Intrinsic value of equity} = \sum_{t=1}^{T} \frac{\text{FCFE}_t}{(1 + k_E)^t} + \frac{E_T}{(1 + k_E)^T} \text{ where } E_T = \frac{\text{FCFE}_{T+1}}{k_E - g} \qquad \textbf{(18.12)}$$

As in the dividend discount model, free cash flow models use a terminal value to avoid adding the present values of an infinite sum of cash flows. That terminal value may simply be the present value of a constant-growth perpetuity (as in the formulas above) or it may be based on a multiple of EBIT, book value, earnings, or free cash flow. As a general rule, estimates of intrinsic value depend critically on terminal value.

Spreadsheet 18.2 presents a free cash flow valuation of GE using the data supplied by Value Line in Figure 18.2. We start with the free cash flow to the firm approach given in Equation 18.9. Panel A of the spreadsheet lays out values supplied by Value Line for 2016, 2017, and 2020. Entries for middle years are interpolated from beginning and final values. Panel B calculates free cash flow. The sum of after-tax profits in row 11 (from Value Line) plus after-tax interest payments in row 12 [i.e., interest expense $\times (1 - t_c)$] equals EBIT$(1 - t_c)$. In row 13 we subtract the change in net working capital, in row 14 we add back depreciation, and in row 15 we subtract capital expenditures. The result in row 17 is the free cash flow to the firm, FCFF, for each year between 2017 and 2020.

To find the present value of these cash flows, we will discount at WACC, which is calculated in Panel C. WACC is the weighted average of the after-tax cost of debt and the cost of equity in each year. When computing WACC, we must account for the change in leverage forecast by Value Line. To compute the cost of equity, we will use the CAPM as in our earlier (dividend discount model) valuation exercise, but accounting for the fact that equity beta will decline each year as the firm reduces leverage.[9]

To find GE's cost of debt, we note that its long-term bonds were rated A1 by Moody's in 2016 and that yields to maturity on this quality debt at the time were about 3.8%. GE's

---

[9]Call β_L the firm's equity beta at the initial level of leverage as provided by Value Line. Equity betas reflect both business risk and financial risk. When a firm changes its capital structure (debt/equity mix), it changes financial risk, and therefore equity beta changes. How should we recognize the change in financial risk? As you may remember from an introductory corporate finance class, you must first unleverage beta. This leaves us with business risk. We use the following formula to find unleveraged beta, β_U (where D/E is the firm's current debt-equity ratio):

$$\beta_U = \frac{\beta_L}{1 + (D/E)(1 - t_c)}$$

Then, we re-leverage beta in any particular year using the forecast capital structure for that year (which reintroduces the financial risk associated with that year's capital structure):

$$\beta_L = \beta_U [1 + (D/E)(1 - t_c)]$$

	A	B	C	D	E	F	G	H	I	J	K	L	M
1			2016	2017	2018	2019	2020						
2	**A. Input Data**												
3	P/E		20.30	18.98	17.65	16.33	15.00						
4	Cap spending/shr		1.45	1.50	1.50	1.50	1.50						
5	LT Debt ($M)		140,000	135,000	130,000	125,000	120,000						
6	Shares (million)		9,300	9,250	9,167	9,083	9,000						
7	EPS		1.50	1.75	2.17	2.58	3.00						
8	Working capital		30,000	40,000	51,667	63,333	75,000						
9													
10	**B. Cash Flow Calculations**												
11	Profits ($M, after tax)		13,950	16,175	19,783	23,392	27,000						
12	Interest ($M, after tax)		3,458	3,335	3,211	3,088	2,964			= (1-tax_rate) × r_debt × LT debt			
13	Chg working cap ($M)			10,000	11,667	11,667	11,667						
14	Depreciation ($M)		5,350	5,800	6,283	6,767	7,250						
15	Cap Spending ($M)			13,875	13,750	13,625	13,500						
16								Terminal value					
17	FCFF ($M)			1,435	3,861	7,954	12,047	487,368					
18	FCFE ($M)			−6,900	−4,350	−133	4,083	395,683		assumes fixed debt ratio after 2020			
19													
20	**C. Discount Rate Calculations**												
21	Current beta	1.1								from Value Line			
22	Unlevered beta	0.832								current beta/[1 + (1-tax)*debt/equity]			
23	Terminal growth	0.06											
24	tax_rate	0.35											
25	r_debt	0.038								YTM in 2016 on A1 rated LT debt			
26	Risk-free rate	0.025											
27	Market risk prem	0.08											
28	MV equity		283,185				405,000			Row 3 × Row 11			
29	Debt/Value		0.33	0.31	0.28	0.25	0.23			linear trend from initial to final value			
30	Levered beta		1.100	1.070	1.043	1.017	0.993			unlevered beta × [1 + (1-tax)*debt/equity]			
31	k_equity		0.113	0.111	0.108	0.106	0.104	0.104	from CAPM and levered beta				
32	WACC		0.084	0.084	0.085	0.086	0.086	0.086	(1-t)*r_debt*D/V + k_equity*(1-D/V)				
33	PV factor for FCFF		1.000	0.922	0.850	0.783	0.721	0.721	Discount each year at WACC				
34	PV factor for FCFE		1.000	0.900	0.812	0.734	0.665	0.665	Discount each year at k_equity				
35													
36	**D. Present Values**									Intrinsic val	Equity val	Intrin/share	
37	PV(FCFF)			1,323	3,282	6,227	8,684	351,287		370,803	230,803	24.82	
38	PV(FCFE)			−6,213	−3,534	−98	2,715	263,060		255,930	255,930	27.52	

Spreadsheet 18.2

Free cash flow valuation of General Electric

debt-to-value ratio (assuming its debt is selling near par value) is computed in row 29. In 2016, the ratio was .33. Based on Value Line forecasts, it will fall to .23 by 2020. We interpolate the debt-to-value ratio for the intermediate years. WACC is computed in row 32. WACC increases slightly over time as leverage declines between 2016 and 2020. The present value factor for cash flows accruing in each year is the previous year's factor divided by (1 + WACC) for that year. The present value of each cash flow (row 37) is the free cash flow times the cumulative discount factor.

The terminal value of the firm (cell H17) is computed from the constant-growth model as $FCFF_{2020} \times (1 + g)/(WACC_{2020} - g)$, where g (cell B23) is the assumed value for the steady growth rate. We assume in the spreadsheet that $g = .06$, in line with the long-run growth rate used in Spreadsheet 18.1. Terminal value is also discounted back to 2016 (cell H37), and the intrinsic value of the firm is thus found as the sum of discounted free cash flows between 2017 and 2020 plus the discounted terminal value. Finally, the value of debt in 2016 is subtracted from firm value to arrive at the intrinsic value of equity in 2016 (cell K37), and value per share is calculated in cell L37 as equity value divided by number of shares.

The free cash flow to equity approach yields a similar intrinsic value for the stock.[10] Free cash flow to equity (row 18) is obtained from FCFF by subtracting after-tax interest expense and net debt repurchases. FCFE in the early years is negative because the firm is devoting $5 billion a year to reducing debt, which more than absorbs the profits the firm is expected to earn. However, profits are expected to increase rapidly, and FCFE turns positive after 2019. FCFE is discounted at the equity rate. Like WACC, the cost of equity changes each period as leverage changes. The present value factor for equity cash flows is presented in row 34. Equity value is reported in cell J38, which is put on a per share basis in cell L38.

Spreadsheet 18.2 is available in Connect or through your course instructor.

Comparing the Valuation Models

In principle, the free cash flow approach is fully consistent with the dividend discount model and should provide the same estimate of intrinsic value if one can extrapolate to a period in which the firm begins to pay dividends growing at a constant rate. This was demonstrated in two famous papers by Modigliani and Miller.[11] However, in practice, you will find that values from these models may differ, sometimes substantially. This is due to the fact that in practice, analysts are always forced to make simplifying assumptions. For example, how long will it take the firm to enter a constant-growth stage? How should depreciation best be treated? What is the best estimate of ROE? Answers to questions like these can have a big impact on value, and it is not always easy to maintain consistent assumptions across the models.

We have now valued GE using several approaches, with estimates of intrinsic value as follows:

Model	Intrinsic Value
Two-stage dividend discount model	$53.40
DDM with earnings multiple terminal value	33.31
Three-stage DDM	35.70
Free cash flow to the firm	24.82
Free cash flow to equity	27.52
Market price (from Value Line)	30.98

What should we make of these differences? Aside from the two-stage DDM, which clearly assumes GE will enter a sustainable growth period earlier and with a higher growth rate than is realistic, the estimates of intrinsic value cluster pretty much symmetrically around the actual market price. The dividend discount models tend to give estimates that exceed price, while the estimates from the free cash flow models are less than price. But by and large, there is no clear signal that GE is substantially mispriced.

On balance, therefore, this valuation exercise suggests that finding bargains is not generally going to be easy. Although applying these models is straightforward, establishing

---

[10]Over the 2016–2020 period, Value Line predicts that GE will retire a considerable fraction of its outstanding debt. The implied debt repurchases are a use of cash and reduce the cash flow available to equity. Such repurchases cannot be sustained indefinitely, however, for debt outstanding would soon be run down to zero. Therefore, in our estimate of the terminal value of equity, we compute the final cash flow assuming that, starting in 2020, GE will begin *issuing* enough debt to maintain its debt-to-value ratio. This approach is consistent with the assumption of constant growth and constant discount rates after 2020.

[11]Franco Modigliani and M. Miller, "The Cost of Capital, Corporation Finance, and the Theory of Investment," *American Economic Review,* June 1958; and "Dividend Policy, Growth, and the Valuation of Shares," *Journal of Business,* October 1961.

proper inputs is not. This should not be surprising. In even a moderately efficient market, finding profit opportunities will be more involved than analyzing Value Line data for a few hours. These models are extremely useful to analysts, however, because they provide ballpark estimates of intrinsic value. More than that, they force rigorous thought about underlying assumptions and highlight the variables with the greatest impact on value and the greatest payoff to further analysis.

The Problem with DCF Models

Our estimates of GE's intrinsic value are all based on discounted cash flow (DCF) models, in which we calculate the present value of forecasted cash flows and a terminal sales price at some future date. It is clear from our calculations that most of the action in these models is in the terminal value and that this value can be highly sensitive to even small changes in some input values (see, e.g., Concept Check 18.4). Therefore, you must recognize that DCF valuation estimates are almost always going to be imprecise. Growth opportunities and future growth rates are especially hard to pin down.

For this reason, many value investors employ a hierarchy of valuation. They view the most reliable components of value as the items on the balance sheet that, in principle, can be sold and for which estimates of market value are readily available. Real estate, plant, and equipment would fall in this category.

A somewhat less reliable component of value is the economic profit on assets already in place. For example, a company like Intel earns a far higher ROE on its investments in chip-making facilities than its cost of capital. The present value of these "economic profits," or economic value added,[12] is a major component of Intel's market value. This component of value is less certain than its balance sheet assets, however, because there is always a concern that new competitors will enter the market, force down prices and profit margins, and reduce the return on Intel's investments. Thus, one needs to carefully assess the barriers to entry that protect Intel's pricing and profit margins. We noted some of these barriers in the last chapter, where we discussed the role of industry analysis, market structure, and competitive position (see Section 17.6).

Finally, the least reliable components of value are growth opportunities, the purported ability of firms like Intel to invest in positive-NPV ventures that contribute to high market valuations today. Value investors don't deny that such opportunities exist, but they are skeptical that precise values can be attached to them and, therefore, tend to be less willing to make investment decisions that depend on the value of those opportunities.

18.6   The Aggregate Stock Market

The most popular approach to valuing the overall stock market is the earnings multiplier approach applied at the aggregate level. The first step is to forecast corporate profits for the coming period. Then we derive an estimate of the earnings multiplier, the aggregate P/E ratio, based on a forecast of long-term interest rates. The product of the two forecasts is the estimate of the end-of-period level of the market.

The forecast of the P/E ratio of the market is sometimes derived from a graph similar to that in Figure 18.8, which plots the *earnings yield* (earnings per share divided by price per share, the reciprocal of the P/E ratio) of the S&P 500 and the yield to maturity on 10-year Treasury bonds. The two series clearly move together over time and suggest that this

---

[12]We discuss economic value added in greater detail in Chapter 19.

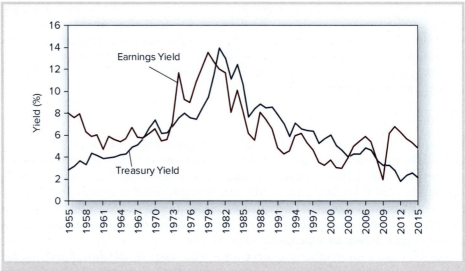

Figure 18.8 Earnings yield of S&P 500 versus 10-year Treasury-bond yield

relationship and the current yield on 10-year Treasury bonds could help in forecasting the earnings yield on the S&P 500. Given the earnings yield, a forecast of earnings could be used to predict the level of the S&P in some future period. Let's illustrate with a simple example.

Example 18.6   Forecasting the Aggregate Stock Market

In mid-2016, the forecast for 12-month earnings per share for the S&P 500 portfolio was about $118. The 10-year Treasury bond yield was about 2.5%. As a first approach, we might posit that the spread between the earnings yield and the Treasury yield, which was around 2.6%, will remain at that level by the end of the year. Given a Treasury yield of 2.5%, this would imply an earnings yield for the S&P of 5.1%, and a P/E ratio of 1/.051 = 19.61. Our forecast for the level of the S&P index would then be 19.61 × 118 = 2,314. Given a current value for the S&P 500 of 2,093, this would imply a 1-year capital gain on the index of 221/2,093 = 10.5%.

Of course, there is uncertainty regarding all three inputs into this analysis: the actual earnings on the S&P 500 stocks, the level of Treasury yields at year-end, and the spread between the Treasury yield and the earnings yield. One would wish to perform sensitivity or scenario analysis to examine the impact of changes in all of these variables. To illustrate, consider Table 18.4, which shows a simple scenario analysis treating possible effects of variation in the Treasury bond yield. The scenario analysis shows that forecast level of the stock market varies inversely and with dramatic sensitivity to interest rate changes.

Some analysts use an aggregate version of the dividend discount model rather than an earnings multiplier approach. All of these models, however, rely heavily on forecasts of such macroeconomic variables as GDP, interest rates, and the rate of inflation, which are difficult to predict accurately.

Because stock prices reflect expectations of future dividends, which are tied to the economic fortunes of firms, it is not surprising that the performance of a broad-based stock index like the S&P 500 is taken as a leading economic indicator, that is, a predictor of the

Table 18.4

S&P 500 index forecasts under various interest-rate scenarios

	Pessimistic Scenario	Most Likely Scenario	Optimistic Scenario
Treasury bond yield	3.0%	2.5%	2.0%
Earnings yield	5.6%	5.1%	4.6%
Resulting P/E ratio	17.86	19.61	21.74
EPS forecast	118	118	118
Forecast for S&P 500	2,107	2,314	2,565

Forecast for the earnings yield on the S&P 500 equals Treasury bond yield plus 2.6%. The P/E ratio is the reciprocal of the forecast earnings yield.

performance of the aggregate economy. Stock prices are viewed as embodying consensus forecasts of economic activity and are assumed to move up or down in anticipation of movements in the economy. The government's index of leading economic indicators, which is taken to predict the progress of the business cycle, is made up in part of recent stock market performance. However, the predictive value of the market is far from perfect. A well-known joke, often attributed to Paul Samuelson, is that the market has forecast eight of the last five recessions.

SUMMARY

1. One approach to firm valuation is to focus on the firm's book value, either as it appears on the balance sheet or as adjusted to reflect current replacement cost of assets or liquidation value. Another approach is to focus on the present value of expected future dividends.

2. The dividend discount model holds that the price of a share of stock should equal the present value of all future dividends per share, discounted at an interest rate commensurate with the risk of the stock.

3. Dividend discount models give estimates of the intrinsic value of a stock. If price does not equal intrinsic value, the rate of return will differ from the equilibrium return based on the stock's risk. The actual return will depend on the rate at which the stock price is predicted to revert to its intrinsic value.

4. The constant-growth version of the DDM asserts that if dividends are expected to grow at a constant rate forever, the intrinsic value of the stock is determined by the formula

$$V_0 = \frac{D_1}{k - g}$$

This version of the DDM is simplistic in its assumption of a constant value of g. There are more-sophisticated multistage versions of the model for more-complex environments. When the constant-growth assumption is reasonably satisfied and the stock is selling for its intrinsic value, the formula can be inverted to infer the market capitalization rate for the stock:

$$k = \frac{D_1}{P_0} + g$$

5. The constant-growth dividend discount model is best suited for firms that are expected to exhibit stable growth rates over the foreseeable future. In reality, however, firms progress through life cycles. In early years, attractive investment opportunities are ample and the firm responds with high plowback ratios and rapid dividend growth. Eventually, however, growth rates level off to more sustainable values. Three-stage growth models are well suited to such a pattern. These models allow for an initial period of rapid growth, a final period of steady dividend growth, and

a middle, or transition, period in which the dividend growth rate declines from its initial high rate to the lower sustainable rate.

6. Stock market analysts devote considerable attention to a company's price-to-earnings ratio. The P/E ratio is a useful measure of the market's assessment of the firm's growth opportunities. Firms with no growth opportunities should have a P/E ratio that is just the reciprocal of the capitalization rate, k. As growth opportunities become a progressively more important component of the total value of the firm, the P/E ratio will increase.

7. The expected growth rate of earnings is related both to the firm's expected profitability and to its dividend policy. The relationship can be expressed as

$$g = (\text{ROE on new investment}) \times (1 - \text{Dividend payout ratio})$$

8. You can relate any DDM to a simple capitalized earnings model by comparing the expected ROE on future investments to the market capitalization rate, k. If the two rates are equal, then the stock's intrinsic value reduces to expected earnings per share (EPS) divided by k.

9. Many analysts form their estimates of a stock's value by multiplying their forecast of next year's EPS by a predicted P/E multiple. Some analysts mix the P/E approach with the dividend discount model. They use an earnings multiplier to forecast the terminal value of shares at a future date, and add the present value of that terminal value with the present value of all interim dividend payments.

10. The free cash flow approach is the one used most often in corporate finance. The analyst first estimates the value of the firm as the present value of expected future free cash flows to the entire firm and then subtracts the value of all claims other than equity. Alternatively, free cash flows to equity can be discounted at a discount rate appropriate to the risk of the stock.

11. The models presented in this chapter can be used to explain and forecast the behavior of the aggregate stock market. The key macroeconomic variables that determine the level of stock prices in the aggregate are interest rates and corporate profits.

KEY TERMS		
book value	dividend discount model	present value of growth
liquidation value	(DDM)	opportunities (PVGO)
replacement cost	constant-growth DDM	two-stage dividend discount
Tobin's q	dividend payout ratio	model
intrinsic value (of a share)	plowback ratio	price–earnings multiple
market capitalization rate	earnings retention ratio	earnings management

KEY EQUATIONS

Intrinsic value: $V_0 = \dfrac{D_1}{1 + k} + \dfrac{D_2}{(1 + k)^2} + \cdots + \dfrac{D_H + P_H}{(1 + k)^H}$

Constant-growth DDM: $V_0 = \dfrac{D_1}{k - g}$

Growth opportunities: $\text{Price} = \dfrac{E_1}{k} + \text{PVGO}$

Determinant of *P/E* ratio: $\dfrac{P_0}{E_1} = \dfrac{1}{k}\left(1 + \dfrac{\text{PVGO}}{E_1/k}\right)$

Free cash flow to the firm:

$$\text{FCFF} = \text{EBIT}(1 - t_c) + \text{Depreciation} - \text{Capital expenditures} - \text{Increases in NWC}$$

Free cash flow to equity: $\text{FCFE} = \text{FCFF} - \text{Interest expense} \times (1 - t_c) + \text{Increases in net debt}$

1. In what circumstances would you choose to use a dividend discount model rather than a free cash flow model to value a firm?

2. In what circumstances is it most important to use multistage dividend discount models rather than constant-growth models?

3. If a security is underpriced (i.e., intrinsic value > price), then what is the relationship between its market capitalization rate and its expected rate of return?

4. Deployment Specialists pays a current (annual) dividend of $1.00 and is expected to grow at 20% for 2 years and then at 4% thereafter. If the required return for Deployment Specialists is 8.5%, what is the intrinsic value of its stock?

5. Jand, Inc., currently pays a dividend of $1.22, which is expected to grow indefinitely at 5%. If the current value of Jand's shares based on the constant-growth dividend discount model is $32.03, what is the required rate of return?

6. A firm pays a current dividend of $1.00 which is expected to grow at a rate of 5% indefinitely. If current value of the firm's shares is $35.00, what is the required return based on the constant-growth dividend discount model (DDM)?

7. Tri-coat Paints has a current market value of $41 per share with earnings of $3.64. What is the present value of its growth opportunities (PVGO) if the required return is 9%?

8. *a.* Computer stocks currently provide an expected rate of return of 16%. MBI, a large computer company, will pay a year-end dividend of $2 per share. If the stock is selling at $50 per share, what must be the market's expectation of the dividend growth rate?

   b. If dividend growth forecasts for MBI are revised downward to 5% per year, what will happen to the price of MBI stock?

   c. What (qualitatively) will happen to the company's price–earnings ratio?

9. *a.* MF Corp. has an ROE of 16% and a plowback ratio of 50%. If the coming year's earnings are expected to be $2 per share, at what price will the stock sell? The market capitalization rate is 12%.

   b. What price do you expect MF shares to sell for in three years?

10. The market consensus is that Analog Electronic Corporation has an ROE = 9%, a beta of 1.25, and plans to maintain indefinitely its traditional plowback ratio of 2/3. This year's earnings were $3 per share. The annual dividend was just paid. The consensus estimate of the coming year's market return is 14%, and T-bills currently offer a 6% return.

    a. Find the price at which Analog stock should sell.

    b. Calculate the P/E ratio.

    c. Calculate the present value of growth opportunities.

    d. Suppose your research convinces you Analog will announce momentarily that it will immediately reduce its plowback ratio to 1/3. Find the intrinsic value of the stock.

    e. The market is still unaware of this decision. Explain why V_0 no longer equals P_0 and why V_0 is greater or less than P_0.

11. The FI Corporation's dividends per share are expected to grow indefinitely by 5% per year.

    a. If this year's year-end dividend is $8 and the market capitalization rate is 10% per year, what must the current stock price be according to the DDM?

    b. If the expected earnings per share are $12, what is the implied value of the ROE on future investment opportunities?

    c. How much is the market paying per share for growth opportunities (i.e., for an ROE on future investments that exceeds the market capitalization rate)?

12. The stock of Nogro Corporation is currently selling for $10 per share. Earnings per share in the coming year are expected to be $2. The company has a policy of paying out 50% of its earnings each year in dividends. The rest is retained and invested in projects that earn a 20% rate of return per year. This situation is expected to continue indefinitely.

a. Assuming the current market price of the stock reflects its intrinsic value as computed using the constant-growth DDM, what rate of return do Nogro's investors require?

b. By how much does its value exceed what it would be if all earnings were paid as dividends and nothing were reinvested?

c. If Nogro were to cut its dividend payout ratio to 25%, what would happen to its stock price?

d. What if Nogro eliminated the dividend?

13. The risk-free rate of return is 8%, the expected rate of return on the market portfolio is 15%, and the stock of Xyrong Corporation has a beta coefficient of 1.2. Xyrong pays out 40% of its earnings in dividends, and the latest earnings announced were $10 per share. Dividends were just paid and are expected to be paid annually. You expect that Xyrong will earn an ROE of 20% per year on all reinvested earnings forever.

a. What is the intrinsic value of a share of Xyrong stock?

b. If the market price of a share is currently $100, and you expect the market price to be equal to the intrinsic value one year from now, what is your expected 1-year holding-period return on Xyrong stock?

14. The Digital Electronic Quotation System (DEQS) Corporation pays no cash dividends currently and is not expected to for the next five years. Its latest EPS was $10, all of which was reinvested in the company. The firm's expected ROE for the next five years is 20% per year, and during this time it is expected to continue to reinvest all of its earnings. Starting in year 6, the firm's ROE on new investments is expected to fall to 15%, and the company is expected to start paying out 40% of its earnings in cash dividends, which it will continue to do forever after. DEQS's market capitalization rate is 15% per year.

a. What is your estimate of DEQS's intrinsic value per share?

b. Assuming its current market price is equal to its intrinsic value, what do you expect to happen to its price over the next year?

c. What do you expect to happen to price in the following year?

d. What effect would it have on your estimate of DEQS's intrinsic value if you expected DEQS to pay out only 20% of earnings starting in year 6?

excel

Please visit us at
www.mhhe.com/Bodie11e

15. Recalculate the intrinsic value of GE in each of the following scenarios by using the three-stage growth model of Spreadsheet 18.1 (available in Connect; link to Chapter 18 material). Treat each scenario independently.

a. The terminal growth rate will be 7%.

b. GE's actual beta is 1.0.

c. The market risk premium is 7.5%.

excel

Please visit us at
www.mhhe.com/Bodie11e

16. Recalculate the intrinsic value of GE shares using the free cash flow model of Spreadsheet 18.2 (available in Connect; link to Chapter 18 material) under each of the following assumptions. Treat each scenario independently.

a. GE's P/E ratio starting in 2020 (cell G3) will be 16.

b. GE's unlevered beta (cell B22) is 0.8.

c. The market risk premium (cell B27) is 7.5%.

17. The Duo Growth Company just paid a dividend of $1 per share. The dividend is expected to grow at a rate of 25% per year for the next three years and then to level off to 5% per year forever. You think the appropriate market capitalization rate is 20% per year.

a. What is your estimate of the intrinsic value of a share of the stock?

b. If the market price of a share is equal to this intrinsic value, what is the expected dividend yield?

c. What do you expect its price to be one year from now?

d. Is the implied capital gain consistent with your estimate of the dividend yield and the market capitalization rate?

18. The Generic Genetic (GG) Corporation pays no cash dividends currently and is not expected to for the next four years. Its latest EPS was $5, all of which was reinvested in the company. The firm's expected ROE for the next four years is 20% per year, during which time it is

expected to continue to reinvest all of its earnings. Starting in year 5, the firm's ROE on new investments is expected to fall to 15% per year. GG's market capitalization rate is 15% per year.

a. What is your estimate of GG's intrinsic value per share?

b. Assuming its current market price is equal to its intrinsic value, what do you expect to happen to its price over the next year?

19. The MoMi Corporation's cash flow from operations before interest and taxes was $2 million in the year just ended, and it expects that this will grow by 5% per year forever. To make this happen, the firm will have to invest an amount equal to 20% of pretax cash flow each year. The tax rate is 35%. Depreciation was $200,000 in the year just ended and is expected to grow at the same rate as the operating cash flow. The appropriate market capitalization rate for the unleveraged cash flow is 12% per year, and the firm currently has debt of $4 million outstanding. Use the free cash flow approach to value the firm's equity.

20. Chiptech, Inc., is an established computer chip firm with several profitable existing products as well as some promising new products in development. The company earned $1 a share last year, and just paid out a dividend of $.50 per share. Investors believe the company plans to maintain its dividend payout ratio at 50%. ROE equals 20%. Everyone in the market expects this situation to persist indefinitely.

a. What is the market price of Chiptech stock? The required return for the computer chip industry is 15%, and the company has just gone ex-dividend (i.e., the next dividend will be paid a year from now, at $t = 1$).

b. Suppose you discover that Chiptech's competitor has developed a new chip that will eliminate Chiptech's current technological advantage in this market. This new product, which will be ready to come to the market in two years, will force Chiptech to reduce the prices of its chips to remain competitive. This will decrease ROE to 15%, and, because of falling demand for its product, Chiptech will decrease the plowback ratio to .40. The plowback ratio will be decreased at the end of the second year, at $t = 2$: The annual year-end dividend for the second year (paid at $t = 2$) will be 60% of that year's earnings. What is your estimate of Chiptech's intrinsic value per share? (*Hint:* Carefully prepare a table of Chiptech's earnings and dividends for each of the next three years. Pay close attention to the change in the payout ratio in $t = 2$.)

c. No one else in the market perceives the threat to Chiptech's market. In fact, you are confident that no one else will become aware of the change in Chiptech's competitive status until the competitor firm publicly announces its discovery near the end of year 2. What will be the rate of return on Chiptech stock in the coming year (i.e., between $t = 0$ and $t = 1$)? (*Hint for parts c through e:* Pay attention to when the *market* catches on to the new situation. A table of dividends and market prices over time might help.)

d. What will be the rate of return on Chiptech stock in the second year (between $t = 1$ and $t = 2$)?

e. What will be the rate of return on Chiptech stock in the third year (between $t = 2$ and $t = 3$)?

1. At Litchfield Chemical Corp. (LCC), a director of the company said that the use of dividend discount models by investors is "proof" that the higher the dividend, the higher the stock price.

a. Using a constant-growth dividend discount model as a basis of reference, evaluate the director's statement.

b. Explain how an increase in dividend payout would affect each of the following (holding all other factors constant):
   i. Sustainable growth rate.
   ii. Growth in book value.

2. Helen Morgan, CFA, has been asked to use the DDM to determine the value of Sundanci, Inc. Morgan anticipates that Sundanci's earnings and dividends will grow at 32% for two years and 13% thereafter. Calculate the current value of a share of Sundanci stock by using a two-stage dividend discount model and the data from Tables 18A and 18B.

Table 18A

Sundanci actual 2015 and 2016 financial statements for fiscal years ending May 31 ($ million, except per-share data)

Income Statement	2015	2016
Revenue	$ 474	$ 598
Depreciation	20	23
Other operating costs	368	460
Income before taxes	86	115
Taxes	26	35
Net income	60	80
Dividends	18	24
Earnings per share	$0.714	$0.952
Dividend per share	$0.214	$0.286
Common shares outstanding (millions)	84.0	84.0
Balance Sheet	**2015**	**2016**
Current assets	$ 201	$ 326
Net property, plant, and equipment	474	489
Total assets	$ 675	$ 815
Current liabilities	57	141
Long-term debt	0	0
Total liabilities	$ 57	$ 141
Shareholders' equity	618	674
Total liabilities and equity	675	815
Capital expenditures	34	38

Table 18B

Selected financial information

Required rate of return on equity	14%
Growth rate of industry	13%
Industry P/E ratio	26

3. Abbey Naylor, CFA, has been directed to determine the value of Sundanci's stock using the Free Cash Flow to Equity (FCFE) model. Naylor believes that Sundanci's FCFE will grow at 27% for two years and 13% thereafter. Capital expenditures, depreciation, and working capital are all expected to increase proportionately with FCFE.

   a. Calculate the amount of FCFE per share for the year 2016, using the data from Table 18A.
   b. Calculate the current value of a share of Sundanci stock based on the two-stage FCFE model.
   c. i. Describe one limitation of the two-stage DDM model that is addressed by using the two-stage FCFE model.
      ii. Describe one limitation of the two-stage DDM model that is *not* addressed by using the two-stage FCFE model.

4. Christie Johnson, CFA, has been assigned to analyze Sundanci using the constant dividend growth price/earnings (P/E) ratio model. Johnson assumes that Sundanci's earnings and dividends will grow at a constant rate of 13%.

   a. Calculate the P/E ratio based on information in Tables 18A and 18B and on Johnson's assumptions for Sundanci.
   b. Identify, within the context of the constant dividend growth model, how each of the following factors would affect the P/E ratio:

   - Risk (beta) of Sundanci.
   - Estimated growth rate of earnings and dividends.
   - Market risk premium.

5. Dynamic Communication is a U.S. industrial company with several electronics divisions. The company has just released its 2018 annual report. Tables 18C and 18D present a summary of Dynamic's financial statements for the years 2017 and 2018. Selected data from the financial statements for the years 2014 to 2016 are presented in Table 18E.

 a. A group of Dynamic shareholders has expressed concern about the zero growth rate of dividends in the last four years and has asked for information about the growth of the company. Calculate Dynamic's sustainable growth rates in 2015 and 2018. Your calculations should use beginning-of-year balance sheet data.

 b. Determine how the change in Dynamic's sustainable growth rate (2018 compared to 2015) was affected by changes in its retention ratio and its financial leverage. (*Note:* Your calculations should use beginning-of-year balance sheet data.)

Table 18C

Dynamic Communication balance sheets

	$ Million	
	2018	2017
Cash and equivalents	$ 149	$ 83
Accounts receivable	295	265
Inventory	275	285
Total current assets	$ 719	$ 633
Gross fixed assets	9,350	8,900
Accumulated depreciation	(6,160)	(5,677)
Net fixed assets	$3,190	$3,223
Total assets	$3,909	$3,856
Accounts payable	$ 228	$ 220
Notes payable	0	0
Accrued taxes and expenses	0	0
Total current liabilities	$ 228	$ 220
Long-term debt	$1,650	$1,800
Common stock	50	50
Additional paid-in capital	0	0
Retained earnings	1,981	1,786
Total shareholders' equity	$2,031	$1,836
Total liabilities and shareholders' equity	$3,909	$3,856

Table 18D

Dynamic Communication statements of income (U.S. $ millions except for share data)

	2018	2017
Total revenues	$3,425	$3,300
Operating costs and expenses	2,379	2,319
Earnings before interest, taxes, depreciation, and amortization (EBITDA)	$1,046	$ 981
Depreciation and amortization	483	454
Operating income (EBIT)	$ 563	$ 527
Interest expense	104	107
Income before taxes	$ 459	$ 420
Taxes (40%)	184	168
Net income	$ 275	$ 252
Dividends	$ 80	$ 80
Change in retained earnings	$ 195	$ 172
Earnings per share	$ 2.75	$ 2.52
Dividends per share	$ 0.80	$ 0.80
Number of shares outstanding (millions)	100	100

Table 18E

Dynamic Communica-
tion selected data from
financial statements
(U.S. $ millions except
for share data)

	2016	2015	2014
Total revenues	$3,175	$3,075	$3,000
Operating income (EBIT)	495	448	433
Interest expense	104	101	99
Net income	$ 235	$ 208	$ 200
Dividends per share	$ 0.80	$ 0.80	$ 0.80
Total assets	$3,625	$3,414	$3,230
Long-term debt	$1,750	$1,700	$1,650
Total shareholders' equity	$1,664	$1,509	$1,380
Number of shares outstanding (millions)	100	100	100

6. Mike Brandreth, an analyst who specializes in the electronics industry, is preparing a research report on Dynamic Communication. A colleague suggests to Brandreth that he may be able to determine Dynamic's implied dividend growth rate from Dynamic's current common stock price, using the Gordon growth model. Brandreth believes that the appropriate required rate of return for Dynamic's equity is 8%.

   a. Assume that the firm's current stock price of $58.49 equals intrinsic value. What sustained rate of dividend growth as of December 2018 is implied by this value? Use the constant-growth dividend discount model (i.e., the Gordon growth model).

   b. The management of Dynamic has indicated to Brandreth and other analysts that the company's current dividend policy will be continued. Is the use of the Gordon growth model to value Dynamic's common stock appropriate or inappropriate? Justify your response based on the assumptions of the Gordon growth model.

7. Peninsular Research is initiating coverage of a mature manufacturing industry. John Jones, CFA, head of the research department, gathered the following fundamental industry and market data to help in his analysis:

Forecast industry earnings retention rate	40%
Forecast industry return on equity	25%
Industry beta	1.2
Government bond yield	6%
Equity risk premium	5%

   a. Compute the price-to-earnings (P_0/E_1) ratio for the industry based on this fundamental data.

   b. Jones wants to analyze how fundamental P/E ratios might differ among countries. He gathered the following economic and market data:

Fundamental Factors	Country A	Country B
Forecast growth in real GDP	5%	2%
Government bond yield	10%	6%
Equity risk premium	5%	4%

   Determine whether each of these fundamental factors would cause P/E ratios to be generally higher for Country A or Country B.

8. Janet Ludlow's firm requires all its analysts to use a two-stage dividend discount model (DDM) and the capital asset pricing model (CAPM) to value stocks. Using the CAPM and DDM, Ludlow has valued QuickBrush Company at $63 per share. She now must value SmileWhite Corporation.

a. Calculate the required rate of return for SmileWhite by using the information in the following table:

	QuickBrush	SmileWhite
Beta	1.35	1.15
Market price	$45.00	$30.00
Intrinsic value	$63.00	?
Notes:		
Risk-free rate	4.50%	
Expected market return	14.50%	

b. Ludlow estimates the following EPS and dividend growth rates for SmileWhite:

First 3 years	12% per year
Years thereafter	9% per year

Estimate the intrinsic value of SmileWhite by using the table above and the two-stage DDM. Dividends per share in the most recent year were $1.72.

c. Recommend QuickBrush or SmileWhite stock for purchase by comparing each company's intrinsic value with its current market price.

d. Describe one strength of the two-stage DDM in comparison with the constant-growth DDM. Describe one weakness inherent in all DDMs.

9. Rio National Corp. is a U.S.-based company and the largest competitor in its industry. Tables 18F through 18I present financial statements and related information for the company. Table 18J presents relevant industry and market data.

The portfolio manager of a large mutual fund comments to one of the fund's analysts, Katrina Shaar: "We have been considering the purchase of Rio National Corp. equity shares, so I would like you to analyze the value of the company. To begin, based on Rio National's past performance, you can assume that the company will grow at the same rate as the industry."

a. Calculate the intrinsic value of a share of Rio National equity on December 31, 2017, using the Gordon constant-growth model and the capital asset pricing model.

b. Calculate the sustainable growth rate of Rio National on December 31, 2017. Use 2017 beginning-of-year balance sheet values.

	2017	2016
Cash	$ 13.00	$ 5.87
Accounts receivable	30.00	27.00
Inventory	209.06	189.06
Current assets	$252.06	$221.93
Gross fixed assets	474.47	409.47
Accumulated depreciation	(154.17)	(90.00)
Net fixed assets	$320.30	$319.47
Total assets	$572.36	$541.40
Accounts payable	$ 25.05	$ 26.05
Notes payable	0.00	0.00
Current portion of long-term debt	0.00	0.00
Current liabilities	$ 25.05	$ 26.05
Long-term debt	240.00	245.00
Total liabilities	$265.05	$271.05
Common stock	160.00	150.00
Retained earnings	147.31	120.35
Total shareholders' equity	$307.31	$270.35
Total liabilities and shareholders' equity	$572.36	$541.40

Table 18F

Rio National Corp. summary year-end balance sheets (U.S. $ millions)

Table 18G

Rio National Corp. summary income statement for the year ended December 31, 2017 (U.S. $ millions)

Revenue	$300.80
Total operating expenses	(173.74)
Operating profit	$127.06
Gain on sale	4.00
Earnings before interest, taxes, depreciation, & amortization (EBITDA)	$131.06
Depreciation and amortization	(71.17)
Earnings before interest & taxes (EBIT)	$ 59.89
Interest	(16.80)
Income tax expense	(12.93)
Net income	$ 30.16

Table 18H

Rio National Corp. supplemental notes for 2017

Note 1:	Rio National had $75 million in capital expenditures during the year.	
Note 2:	A piece of equipment that was originally purchased for $10 million was sold for $7 million at year-end, when it had a net book value of $3 million. Equipment sales are unusual for Rio National.	
Note 3:	The decrease in long-term debt represents an unscheduled principal repayment; there was no new borrowing during the year.	
Note 4:	On January 1, 2017, the company received cash from issuing 400,000 shares of common equity at a price of $25.00 per share.	
Note 5:	A new appraisal during the year increased the estimated market value of land held for investment by $2 million, which was not recognized in 2017 income.	

Table 18I

Rio National Corp. common equity data for 2017

Dividends paid (U.S. $ millions)	$3.20
Weighted-average shares outstanding	16,000,000
Dividend per share	$0.20
Earnings per share	$1.89
Beta	1.80

Note: The dividend payout ratio is expected to be constant.

Table 18J

Industry and market data December 31, 2017

Risk-free rate of return	4.00%
Expected rate of return on market index	9.00%
Median industry price/earnings (P/E) ratio	19.90
Expected industry earnings growth rate	12.00%

10. While valuing the equity of Rio National Corp. (see CFA Problem 9), Katrina Shaar is considering the use of either cash flow from operations (CFO) or free cash flow to equity (FCFE) in her valuation process.

    a. State two adjustments that Shaar should make to cash flow from operations to obtain free cash flow to equity.

    b. Shaar decides to calculate Rio National's FCFE for the year 2017, starting with net income. Determine for each of the five supplemental notes given in Table 18H whether an adjustment should be made to net income to calculate Rio National's free cash flow to equity for the year 2017, and the dollar amount of any adjustment.

    c. Calculate Rio National's free cash flow to equity for the year 2017.

11. Shaar (see CFA Problem 10) has revised slightly her estimated earnings growth rate for Rio National and, using normalized (underlying trend) EPS, which is adjusted for temporary impacts on earnings, now wants to compare the current value of Rio National's equity to that of the industry, on a growth-adjusted basis. Selected information about Rio National and the industry is given in Table 18K.

Compared to the industry, is Rio National's equity overvalued or undervalued on a P/E-to-growth (PEG) basis, using normalized (underlying trend) earnings per share? Assume that the risk of Rio National is similar to the risk of the industry.

Rio National	
Estimated earnings growth rate	11.00%
Current share price	$25.00
Normalized (underlying trend) EPS for 2017	$ 1.71
Weighted-average shares outstanding during 2017	16,000,000
Industry	
Estimated earnings growth rate	12.00%
Median price/Earnings (P/E) ratio	19.90

Table 18K

Rio National
Corp. vs. industry

E-INVESTMENTS EXERCISES

1. Choose 10 firms that interest you and download their financial statements from any of these Web sites: **finance.yahoo.com, finance.google.com,** or **money.msn.com.**

   a. For each firm, find the return on equity (ROE), the number of shares outstanding, the dividends per share, and the net income. Record them in a spreadsheet.

   b. Calculate the total amount of dividends paid (Dividends per share × Number of shares outstanding), the dividend payout ratio (Total dividends paid/Net income), and the plowback ratio (1 − Dividend payout ratio).

   c. Compute the sustainable growth rate, $g = b \times$ ROE, where b equals the plowback ratio.

   d. Compare the growth rates (g) with the P/E ratios of the firms by plotting the P/Es against the growth rates in a scatter diagram. Is there a relationship between the two?

   e. Find the price-to-book, price-to-sales, and price-to-operating-cash-flow ratios for your sample of firms. Use a line chart to plot these three ratios on the same set of axes. What relationships do you see among the three series?

   f. For each firm, compare the 3-year growth rate of earnings per share with the growth rate you calculated above. Is the actual rate of earnings growth correlated with the sustainable growth rate you calculated?

2. Now calculate the intrinsic value of three of the firms you selected in the previous question. Make reasonable judgments about the market risk premium and the risk-free rate, or find estimates from the Internet.

   a. What is the required return on each firm based on the CAPM?

   b. Try using a two-stage growth model, making reasonable assumptions about how future growth rates will differ from current growth rates. Compare the intrinsic values derived from the two-stage model to the intrinsic values you find assuming a constant-growth rate. Which estimate seems more reasonable for each firm?

3. Now choose one of your firms and look up the other firms in the same industry. Perform a "Valuation by Comparables" analysis by looking at the price/earnings, price/book value, price/sales, and price/cash flow ratios of the firms relative to each other and to the industry average. Which of the firms seem to be overvalued? Which seem to be undervalued? Can you think of reasons for any apparent mispricing?

4. The actually expected return on a stock based on estimates of future dividends and future price can be compared to the "required" or equilibrium return given its risk. If the expected return is greater than the required return, the stock may be an attractive investment.

   First calculate the expected holding-period return (HPR) on Target Corporation's stock based on its current price, its expected price, and its expected dividend.

   a. Go to MSN's money central at **www.msn.com/en-us/money.** Get information for Target (enter TGT under quote search). Find the range of forecasted year-ahead prices. Find the range for estimated target price for the next fiscal year.

   b. Collect information about today's price and the dividend rate. What is the company's expected dividend in dollars for the next fiscal year?

   c. Use these inputs to calculate the range of Target's HPRs for the next year.

SOLUTIONS TO CONCEPT CHECKS

1. *a.* Dividend yield = $2.15/$50 = 4.3%.
    Capital gains yield = (59.77 − 50)/50 = 19.54%.

    Total return = 4.3% + 19.54% = 23.84%.

    b. $k = 6\% + 1.15(14\% − 6\%) = 15.2\%$.

    c. $V_0 = (\$2.15 + \$59.77)/1.152 = \$53.75$, which exceeds the market price. This would indicate a "buy" opportunity.

2. *a.* $D_1/(k − g) = \$2.15/(.152 − .112) = \$53.75$.

    b. $P_1 = P_0(1 + g) = \$53.75(1.112) = \$59.77$.

    c. The expected capital gain equals $59.77 − $53.75 = $6.02, for a percentage gain of 11.2%. The dividend yield is $D_1/P_0 = 2.15/53.75 = 4\%$, for a holding-period return of 4% + 11.2% = 15.2%.

3. *a.* $g = \text{ROE} \times b = 20\% \times .60 = 12\%$.
    $D_1 = .4 \times E_1 = .4 \times \$5 = \$2$.

    $P_0 = \$2/(.125 − .12) = \$400$.

    b. When the firm invests in projects with ROE less than k, its stock price falls. If $b = .60$, then $g = 10\% \times .60 = 6\%$ and $P_0 = \$2/(.125 − .06) = \$30.77$. In contrast, if $b = 0$, then $P_0 = \$5/.125 = \$40$.

4. $V_{2016} = \dfrac{1.04}{(1.113)} + \dfrac{1.22}{(1.113)^2} + \dfrac{1.41}{(1.113)^3} + \dfrac{1.60 + P_{2020}}{(1.113)^4}$

    To estimate P_{2020} in this equation, use the constant-growth dividend discount model, but assuming the sustainable growth rate will be $g = 7\%$.

    $$P_{2020} = \frac{1.60 \times (1 + g)}{k − g} = \frac{\$1.712}{.113 − .07} = \$39.81$$

    Therefore, $V_{2016} = \$29.93$.

5. *a.* ROE = 12%.
    $b = \$.50/\$2.00 = .25$.

    $g = \text{ROE} \times b = 12\% \times .25 = 3\%$.

    $P_0 = D_1/(k − g) = \$1.50/(.10 − .03) = \$21.43$.

    $P_0/E_1 = \$21.43/\$2.00 = 10.71$.

    b. If $b = .4$, then $.4 \times \$2 = \$.80$ would be reinvested and the remainder of earnings, or $1.20, would be paid as dividends.

    $g = 12\% \times .4 = 4.8\%$.

    $P_0 = D_1/(k − g) = \$1.20/(.10 − .048) = \$23.08$.

    $P_0/E_1 = \$23.08/\$2.00 = 11.54$.

Financial Statement Analysis

IN THE PREVIOUS chapter, we explored equity valuation techniques. These techniques take the firm's dividends and earnings prospects as inputs. Although the valuation analyst is interested in economic earnings streams, only financial accounting data are readily available. What can we learn from a company's accounting data that can help us estimate the intrinsic value of its common stock? In this chapter, we show how investors can use financial data as inputs into stock valuation analysis.

We start by reviewing the basic sources of such data—the income statement, the balance sheet, and the statement of cash flows. We note the difference between economic and accounting earnings. Although economic earnings are

more important for issues of valuation, they can at best be estimated, so, in practice, analysts always begin their evaluation of the firm using accounting data. We show how analysts use financial ratios to explore the sources of a firm's profitability and evaluate the "quality" of its earnings in a systematic fashion. We also examine the impact of debt policy on various financial ratios.

Finally, we conclude with a discussion of the challenges you will encounter when using financial statement analysis as a tool in uncovering mispriced securities. Some of these issues arise from differences in firms' accounting procedures. Others are due to inflation-induced distortions in accounting numbers.

19.1 The Major Financial Statements

The Income Statement

The **income statement** is a summary of the profitability of the firm over a period of time, such as a year. It presents revenues generated during the operating period, the expenses incurred during that same period, and the company's net earnings or profits, which are simply the difference between revenues and expenses.

It is useful to distinguish among four broad classes of expenses: cost of goods sold, which is the direct cost attributable to producing the product sold by the firm; general and administrative expenses, which correspond to overhead expenses, salaries, advertising, and other costs of operating the firm that are not directly attributable to production; interest expense on the firm's debt; and taxes on earnings owed to federal and local governments.

Table 19.1 presents an income statement for Home Depot (HD). At the top are the company's revenues from operations. Next come operating expenses (i.e., the costs incurred in the course of generating those revenues, including a depreciation allowance). The difference between operating revenues and operating costs is called *operating income.* Income or expenses from other, primarily nonrecurring, sources are then added or subtracted to obtain earnings before interest and taxes (EBIT), which is what the firm would have earned if not for obligations to its creditors and the tax authorities. EBIT is a measure of the profitability of the firm's operations, ignoring any interest burden attributable to debt financing. The income statement then goes on to subtract net interest expense from EBIT to arrive at taxable income. Finally, the income tax due the government is subtracted to arrive at net income, the "bottom line" of the income statement.

Analysts also commonly prepare a *common-size income statement,* in which all items on the income statement are expressed as a fraction of total revenue. This makes it easier to compare firms of different sizes. The right-hand column of Table 19.1 is Home Depot's common-size income statement.

In the previous chapter, we saw that stock valuation models require a measure of **economic earnings**—the sustainable cash flow that can be paid out to stockholders without impairing the productive capacity of the firm. In contrast, **accounting earnings** are affected by several conventions regarding the valuation of assets such as inventories (e.g., LIFO versus FIFO treatment) and by the way some expenditures such as capital investments are recognized over time (as depreciation expenses). We discuss problems with some of these accounting conventions in greater detail later in the chapter. In addition to these accounting issues, as the firm makes its way through the business cycle, its earnings will rise above or fall below the trend line that might more accurately reflect sustainable economic earnings.

Table 19.1

Consolidated statement of income for Home Depot

	$ Million	Percent of Revenue
Operating revenues		
Net sales	$88,519	100.0%
Operating expenses		
Cost of goods sold	$58,254	65.8%
Selling, general, and administrative expenses	14,938	16.9
Other	1,690	1.9
Depreciation	1,863	2.1
Total operating expenses	$76,745	86.7%
Earnings before interest and income taxes	$11,774	13.3%
Interest expense	752	0.8
Taxable income	$11,022	12.5%
Taxes	4,012	4.5
Net income	$ 7,010	7.9%
Allocation of net income		
Dividends	$ 3,031	3.4%
Addition to retained earnings	$ 3,979	4.5%

Note: Sums subject to rounding error.
Source: Home Depot *Annual Report,* year ending January 2016.

This introduces an added complication in interpreting net income figures. One might wonder how closely accounting earnings approximate economic earnings and, correspondingly, how useful accounting data might be to investors attempting to value the firm.

In fact, the net income figure on the firm's income statement does convey considerable information concerning a firm's prospects: Stock prices respond vigorously when firms announce earnings greater than market analysts or investors had anticipated.

The Balance Sheet

While the income statement provides a measure of profitability over a period of time, the **balance sheet** provides a "snapshot" of the financial condition of the firm at a particular moment. The balance sheet is a list of the firm's assets and liabilities at that moment. The difference in assets and liabilities is the net worth of the firm, also called *shareholders'* or *stockholders' equity.* Like income statements, balance sheets are reasonably standardized in presentation. Table 19.2 is HD's balance sheet.

The first section of the balance sheet gives a listing of the assets of the firm. Current assets are presented first. These are cash and other items such as accounts receivable or inventories that will be converted into cash within one year. Next comes a listing of long-term or "fixed" assets. *Tangible fixed assets* are items such as buildings, equipment, or vehicles. HD also has several intangible assets such as a respected brand name and expertise. But accountants generally are reluctant to include these assets on the balance sheet, as they are so hard to value. However, when one firm purchases another for a premium over its book value, that difference, called "goodwill," is listed on the balance sheet as an *intangible fixed asset.* HD lists goodwill at $2,102 million.[1] The sum of current and fixed assets is total assets, the last line of the assets section of the balance sheet.

The liability and shareholders' equity (also called stockholders' equity) section is arranged similarly. First come short-term, or "current," liabilities such as accounts payable, accrued taxes, and debts due within one year. Following this is long-term debt and other liabilities due in more than one year. The difference between total assets and total liabilities is stockholders' equity. This is the net worth, or book value, of the firm.

Stockholders' equity is divided into par value of stock, additional paid-in capital, and retained earnings, although this division is usually unimportant. Briefly, par value plus additional paid-in capital represent the proceeds realized from the sale of stock to the public. Conversely, when the firm repurchases stock from the public, this is treated as a "negative share issuance," and shareholders' equity falls. These repurchased shares are held in the company's treasury and are, therefore, known as **treasury stock.** The shares held by investors are said to be **issued** and **outstanding.** Home Depot's par value plus paid-in capital is negative, −$24,657 million, signifying that the firm has spent more repurchasing previously issued stock than it originally raised by selling that stock. Of course, considerable profits have been reinvested in the business on the shareholders' behalf, and this shows up as retained earnings in Table 19.2. The entry for retained earnings shows the cumulative buildup of equity from profits plowed back into the firm.

The entries in the left-hand columns of the balance sheet in Table 19.2 present the dollar value of each asset. Just as they compute common-size income statements, however, analysts also find it convenient to use *common-size balance sheets* when comparing firms

---

[1]Firms are required to test their goodwill assets for "impairment" each year. If the value of the acquired firm is clearly less than its purchase price, that amount must be charged off as an expense. For example, in 2012 Hewlett-Packard wrote off $8.8 billion on its earlier purchase of the software company Autonomy Corp. amid charges that Autonomy had overstated its profitability prior to the purchase. AOL Time Warner set a record when it recognized an impairment of $99 billion in 2002 following the January 2001 merger of Time Warner with AOL.

Assets	$ Million	Percent of Total Assets	Liabilities and Shareholders' Equity	$ Million	Percent of Total Assets
Current assets			Current liabilities		
Cash and marketable securities	$ 2,216	5.2%	Debt due for repayment	427	1.0%
Receivables	1,890	4.4	Accounts payable	10,533	24.8
Inventories	11,809	27.8	Other current liabilities	1,566	3.7
Other current assets	1,078	2.5	Total current liabilities	$12,526	29.4%
Total current assets	$16,993	39.9%			
Fixed assets			Long-term debt	$20,888	49.1%
Tangible fixed assets			Other long-term liabilities	1,965	4.6
Property, plant, and equipment	$22,191	52.2%	Deferred long-term liability charges	854	0
Other long-term assets	1,263	3.0	Total liabilities	$36,233	85.2%
Total tangible fixed assets	$23,454	55.1%	Shareholders' equity		
			Common stock and other paid-in capital	−$24,657	−57.9%
Intangible fixed assets			Retained earnings	30,973	72.8%
Goodwill	$ 2,102	4.9%	Total shareholders' equity	$ 6,316	14.8%
Total fixed assets	$25,556	60.1%	Total liabilities and shareholders' equity	$42,549	100.0%
Total assets	$42,549	100.0%			

Table 19.2

Consolidated balance sheet for Home Depot

Note: Column sums subject to rounding error.

Source: Home Depot Annual Report, year ending January 2016.

of different sizes. Therefore, each item is also expressed as a percentage of total assets. These entries appear in the right-hand columns of Table 19.2.

The Statement of Cash Flows

The income statement and balance sheets are based on accrual methods of accounting, which means that revenues and expenses are recognized at the time of a sale even if no cash has yet been exchanged. In contrast, the **statement of cash flows** tracks the cash implications of transactions. For example, if goods are sold now, with payment due in 60 days, the income statement will treat the revenue as generated when the sale occurs, and the balance sheet will be immediately augmented by accounts receivable, but the statement of cash flows will not show an increase in available cash until the bill is paid.

Table 19.3 is the statement of cash flows for HD. The first entry listed under "cash provided by operations" is net income. The next entries modify that figure for components of income that have been recognized but for which cash has not yet changed hands. For example, HD's accounts receivable increased by $181 million. This portion of sales was claimed on the income statement, but the cash had not yet been collected. Increases in accounts receivable are in effect an investment in working capital and, therefore, reduce the cash flows realized from operations. Similarly, increases in accounts payable mean that expenses have been recognized, but cash has not yet left the firm. Any payment delay increases the company's net cash flows in this period.

Another major difference between the income statement and the statement of cash flows involves depreciation, which is a major addition to income in the adjustment section

	$ Million
Cash provided by operations	
Net income	$ 7,009
Adjustments to net income	
Depreciation	1,863
Changes in working capital	
Decrease (increase) in receivables	(181)
Decrease (increase) in inventories	(546)
Increase (decrease) in other current liabilities	1,151
Changes due to other operating activities	77
Total adjustments	$ 2,364
Cash provided by operations	$ 9,373
Cash flows from investments	
Gross investment in tangible fixed assets	$(3,126)
Investments in other assets	44
Cash provided by (used for) investments	$(2,982)
Cash provided by (used for) financing activities	
Additions to (reductions in) long-term debt	$ 4,012
Net issues (repurchases of) shares	(6,772)
Dividends	(3,031)
Other	4
Cash provided by (used for) financing activities	$(5,787)
Net increase in cash	$ 604

Table 19.3

Statement of cash flows for Home Depot

Source: Home Depot *Annual Report,* year ending January 2016.

of the statement of cash flows. The income statement attempts to "smooth" large capital expenditures over time. The depreciation expense on the income statement does this by recognizing such expenditures over a period of many years rather than at the specific time of purchase. In contrast, the statement of cash flows recognizes the cash implication of a capital expenditure when it occurs. Therefore, it adds back the depreciation "expense" that was used to compute net income; instead, it acknowledges a capital expenditure when it is paid. It does so by reporting cash flows separately for operations, investing, and financing activities. This way, any large cash flows, such as those for big investments, can be recognized without affecting the measure of cash provided by operations.

The second section of the statement of cash flows is the accounting of cash flows from investing activities. For example, HD used $3,126 million of cash investing in tangible fixed assets. These entries are investments in the assets necessary for the firm to maintain or enhance its productive capacity.

Finally, the last section of the statement lists the cash flows realized from financing activities. Issuance of securities will contribute positive cash flows, while repurchase or redemption of outstanding securities uses up cash. For example, HD expended $6,772 million to repurchase shares of its stock, which was a major use of cash. Its dividend payments, $3,031 million, also used cash. In total, HD's financing activities absorbed $5,787 million.

To summarize, HD's operations generated a cash flow of $9,373 million. Some of that cash, $2,982 million, went to pay for new investments. Another part, $5,787 million, went to pay dividends and retire outstanding securities. HD's cash holdings therefore increased by $9,373 - 2,982 - 5,787 = $604 million. This is reported on the last line of Table 19.3.

The statement of cash flows provides important evidence on the well-being of a firm. If a company cannot pay its dividends and maintain the productivity of its capital stock out of cash flow from operations, for example, and must resort to borrowing to meet these demands, this is a serious warning that the firm cannot maintain the dividend payout at its current level in the long run. The statement of cash flows will reveal this developing problem when it shows that cash flow from operations is inadequate and that borrowing is being used to maintain dividend payments at unsustainable levels.

19.2   Measuring Firm Performance

In Chapter 1, we pointed out that a natural goal of the firm is to maximize value, but that various agency problems, or conflicts of interest, may impede that goal. How can we measure how well the firm is actually performing? Financial analysts have come up with a mind-numbing list of financial ratios that measure many aspects of firm performance. Therefore, before getting lost in the trees, let's first pause to consider what sorts of ratios may be related to the ultimate objective of added value.

Two broad activities are the responsibility of a firm's financial managers: investment decisions and financing decisions. Investment, or capital budgeting, decisions pertain to the firm's *use* of capital: the business activities in which it is engaged. Here, the questions we will wish to answer pertain to the profitability of those projects. How should profitability be measured? How does the acceptable level of profitability depend on risk and the opportunity cost of the funds used to pay for the firm's many projects? In contrast, financial decisions pertain to the firm's *sources* of capital. Is there a sufficient supply of financing to meet projected needs for growth? Does the financing plan rely too heavily on borrowed funds? Is there sufficient liquidity to deal with unexpected cash needs?

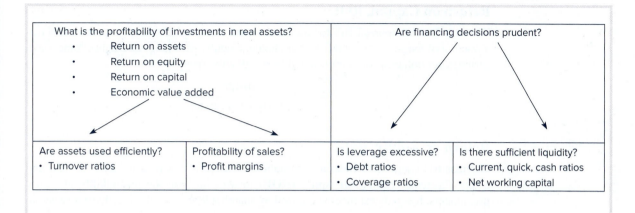

Figure 19.1 Important financial questions and some ratios that help answer them

These questions suggest that we organize the ratios we choose to examine along the lines given in Figure 19.1. The figure shows that when evaluating the firm's investment activities, we will ask two questions: How efficiently does the firm deploy its assets, and how profitable are its sales? In turn, aspects of both efficiency and profitability can be measured with several ratios. Efficiency is typically assessed using several turnover ratios, while the profitability of sales is commonly measured with various profit margins. Similarly, when evaluating financing decisions, we look at both leverage and liquidity, and we will see that aspects of each of these two concepts also can be measured with an array of statistics.

The next section explains how to calculate and interpret some of these key financial ratios and shows how many of them are related.

19.3 Profitability Measures

Big firms naturally earn greater profits than smaller ones. Therefore, most profitability measures focus on earnings per dollar employed. The most common measures are return on assets, return on capital, and return on equity.

Return on Assets, ROA

Return on assets (ROA) equals earnings before interest and taxes (EBIT) as a fraction of the firm's total assets.[2]

$$\text{ROA} = \frac{\text{EBIT}}{\text{Total assets}}$$

The numerator of this ratio may be viewed as total operating income of the firm. Therefore, ROA tells us the income earned per dollar deployed in the firm.

---

[2]ROA sometimes is computed using EBIT × (1 − Tax rate) in the numerator. Sometimes it is computed using after-tax operating income (i.e., Net income + Interest × [1 − Tax rate]). Sometimes, it even is calculated using just net income in the numerator, although this definition ignores altogether the income the firm has generated for debt investors. Unfortunately, definitions of many key financial ratios are not fully standardized.

Return on Capital, ROC

Whereas ROA compares EBIT to total assets, **return on capital (ROC)** expresses EBIT as a fraction of long-term capital (i.e., shareholders' equity plus long-term debt). It measures earnings per dollar of long-term capital invested in the firm.

$$ROC = \frac{EBIT}{\text{Long-term capital}}$$

Return on Equity, ROE

Whereas ROA and ROC measure profitability relative to funds raised by both debt and equity financing, **return on equity (ROE)** focuses only on the profitability of equity investments. It equals net income realized by shareholders per dollar they have invested in the firm.

$$ROE = \frac{\text{Net income}}{\text{Shareholders' equity}}$$

We noted in Chapter 18 that ROE is one of the two basic factors in determining a firm's growth rate of earnings. Sometimes it is reasonable to assume that future ROE will approximate its past value, but a high ROE in the past does not necessarily imply a firm's future ROE will be high. It can be dangerous to accept historical values as indicators of future values. While data from the recent past may provide information regarding expected performance, keep your focus on the future. Expectations of *future* dividends and earnings determine the intrinsic value of the company's stock.

Not surprisingly, ROA and ROE are linked, but as we will see next, their relationship is affected by the firm's financial policies.

Financial Leverage and ROE

ROE is affected by the firm's debt-equity mix as well as the interest rate on its debt. An example will show why. Suppose Nodett is a firm that is all-equity financed and has total assets of $100 million. Assume it pays corporate taxes at the rate of 40% of taxable earnings.

Table 19.4 shows Nodett's sales, earnings before interest and taxes, and net profits under three scenarios representing phases of the business cycle. It also shows two of the most commonly used profitability measures: operating ROA, which equals EBIT/Assets, and ROE, which equals net profits/equity.

Somdett is an otherwise identical firm to Nodett, but it has financed $40 million of its $100 million of assets with debt bearing an interest rate of 8%. It pays annual interest expenses of $3.2 million. Table 19.5 shows how Somdett's ROE differs from Nodett's.

Annual sales, EBIT, and therefore ROA for both firms are the same in each of the three scenarios; in other words, business risk for the two companies is identical. But their

Table 19.4	Scenario	Sales ($ millions)	EBIT ($ millions)	ROA (% per year)	Net Profit ($ millions)	ROE (% per year)
Nodett's profitability over the business cycle	Bad year	80	5	5	3	3
	Normal year	100	10	10	6	6
	Good year	120	15	15	9	9

Table 19.5

Impact of financial leverage on ROE

		Nodett		Somdett	
Scenario	EBIT ($ millions)	Net Profits ($ millions)	ROE (%)	Net Profits* ($ millions)	ROE† (%)
Bad year	5	3	3	1.08	1.8
Normal year	10	6	6	4.08	6.8
Good year	15	9	9	7.08	11.8

*Somdett's after-tax profits are given by .6(EBIT − $3.2 million).
†ROE = net profit/equity. Somdett's equity is only $60 million.

financial risk differs. Although Nodett and Somdett have the same ROA in each scenario, Somdett's ROE exceeds that of Nodett in normal and good years and is lower in bad years.

We can summarize the exact relationship among ROE, ROA, and leverage in the following equation:[3]

$$\text{ROE} = (1 - \text{Tax rate})\left[\text{ROA} + (\text{ROA} - \text{Interest rate})\frac{\text{Debt}}{\text{Equity}}\right] \quad (19.1)$$

This result makes sense: If ROA exceeds the borrowing rate, the firm earns more on its money than it pays out to creditors. The surplus earnings are available to the firm's owners, the equityholders, which increases ROE. If, on the other hand, ROA is less than the interest rate paid on debt, then ROE will decline by an amount that depends on the debt-to-equity ratio.

Example 19.1   Leverage and ROE

To illustrate the application of Equation 19.1, look at Table 19.5. In a normal year, Nodett has an ROE of 6%, which is .6 (i.e., 1 minus the tax rate) times its ROA of 10%. However, Somdett, which borrows at an interest rate of 8% and maintains a debt-to-equity ratio of ⅔, has an ROE of 6.8%. The calculation using Equation 19.1 is

$$\text{ROE} = .6[10\% + (10\% - 8\%)\tfrac{2}{3}]$$
$$= .6[10\% + \tfrac{4}{3}\%] = 6.8\%$$

Somdett's debt makes a positive contribution to ROE in this scenario because the firm's ROA exceeds the interest rate on its debt.

[3]The derivation of Equation 19.1 is as follows:

$$\text{ROE} = \frac{\text{Net profit}}{\text{Equity}} = \frac{\text{EBIT} - \text{Interest} - \text{Taxes}}{\text{Equity}} = \frac{(1 - \text{Tax rate})(\text{EBIT} - \text{Interest})}{\text{Equity}}$$
$$= (1 - \text{Tax rate})\left[\frac{(\text{ROA} \times \text{Assets}) - (\text{Interest rate} \times \text{Debt})}{\text{Equity}}\right]$$
$$= (1 - \text{Tax rate})\left[\text{ROA} \times \frac{\text{Equity} + \text{Debt}}{\text{Equity}} - \text{Interest rate} \times \frac{\text{Debt}}{\text{Equity}}\right]$$
$$= (1 - \text{Tax rate})\left[\text{ROA} + (\text{ROA} - \text{Interest rate})\frac{\text{Debt}}{\text{Equity}}\right]$$

Table 19.5 shows that financial leverage increases the risk of the equityholder returns. Somdett's ROE is worse than Nodett's in bad years, but it is better in good years. The presence of debt makes Somdett's ROE more sensitive to the business cycle. Even though the two companies have equal business risk (reflected in their identical EBITs in all three scenarios), Somdett's stockholders bear greater financial risk than Nodett's because all of the firm's business risk is absorbed by a smaller base of equity investors.

Even if financial leverage increases the expected ROE of Somdett relative to Nodett (as it seems to in Table 19.5), this does not imply that Somdett's share price will be higher. Financial leverage increases the risk of the firm's equity as surely as it raises the expected ROE, and the higher discount rate will offset the higher expected earnings.

 Concept Check **19.1**

Mordett is a company with the same assets as Nodett and Somdett but it has a debt-to-equity ratio of 1.0 and an interest rate of 9%. What would its net profit and ROE be in a bad year, a normal year, and a good year?

Economic Value Added

While profitability measures such as ROA, ROC, and ROE are commonly used to measure performance, profitability is really not enough. A firm should be viewed as successful only if the return on its projects is better than the rate investors could expect to earn for themselves (on a risk-adjusted basis) in the capital market. Plowing back funds into the firm increases stock price *only* if the firm earns a higher rate of return on the reinvested funds than the opportunity cost of capital, that is, the market capitalization rate. To account for this opportunity cost, we might measure the success of the firm using the *difference* between the return on capital, ROC, and the opportunity cost of capital, k. **Economic value added (EVA)** is the spread between ROC and k multiplied by the capital invested in the firm. It therefore measures the dollar value of the firm's return in excess of its opportunity cost. Another term for EVA (the term coined by Stern Stewart, a consulting firm that has promoted its use) is **residual income.**

Example 19.2   Economic Value Added

In 2015, HD had a weighted-average cost of capital of 7.7% (based on its cost of debt, its capital structure, its equity beta, and estimates derived from the CAPM for the cost of equity). Its return on capital was 17.5%, fully 9.8% greater than the opportunity cost of capital on its investments in plant, equipment, and know-how. In other words, each dollar invested by HD earned about 9.8 cents more than the return that investors could have anticipated by investing in equivalent-risk stocks. HD earned this superior rate of return on a capital base of $27.15 billion. Its economic value added, that is, its return in excess of opportunity cost, was therefore $(.175 - .077) \times \$27.15 = \$2.66$ billion.

Table 19.6 shows EVA for a small sample of firms. The EVA leader in this sample was Apple. Notice that Walmart's EVA was greater than HD's, despite a smaller margin between its ROC and the cost of capital. This is because Walmart applied its margin to a much larger capital base. At the other extreme, Honda and Pfizer earned less than their opportunity costs of capital, which resulted in negative EVAs.

Table 19.6

Economic value added, 2015

	Ticker	EVA ($ billion)	Capital ($ billion)	ROC (%)	Cost of Capital (%)
Apple	AAPL	11.18	210.41	14.76	9.45
Walmart	WMT	3.28	126.08	7.42	4.82
Home Depot	HD	2.66	27.15	17.50	7.69
Intel	INTC	1.21	86.81	9.25	7.85
Walt Disney	DIS	0.51	63.58	10.18	9.37
Microsoft	MSFT	0.21	121.00	8.19	8.01
AT&T	T	0.20	257.30	4.82	4.74
Pfizer	PFE	−1.83	102.92	5.56	7.34
Honda	HMC	−4.47	123.07	1.72	5.36

Source: Authors' calculations using data from **finance.yahoo.com**. Actual EVA estimates reported by Stern Stewart differ from the values in Table 19.6 because of adjustments to the accounting data involving issues such as treatment of research and development expenses, taxes, advertising expenses, and depreciation. The estimates in Table 19.6 are designed to show the logic behind EVA but must be taken as imprecise.

Notice that even the EVA "losers" in Table 19.6 reported positive accounting profits. For example, by conventional standards, Honda was solidly profitable in 2015, with a positive ROC of 1.72%. But its cost of capital was higher, at 5.36%. By this standard, it did not cover its opportunity cost of capital and, therefore, returned a negative EVA. EVA treats the opportunity cost of capital as a real cost that, like other costs, should be deducted from revenues to arrive at a more meaningful "bottom line." A firm that is earning accounting profits but not covering its opportunity cost might be able to redeploy its capital to better uses. Therefore, a growing number of firms now calculate EVA and tie managers' compensation to it.

19.4 Ratio Analysis

Decomposition of ROE

To understand the factors affecting a firm's ROE, particularly its trend over time and its performance relative to competitors, analysts often "decompose" ROE into the product of a series of ratios. Each component ratio is in itself meaningful, and the process serves to focus the analyst's attention on the separate factors influencing performance. This kind of decomposition of ROE is often called the **DuPont system.**

One useful decomposition of ROE is

$$\text{ROE} = \frac{\text{Net profit}}{\text{Equity}} = \underset{(1)}{\frac{\text{Net profits}}{\text{Pretax profits}}} \times \underset{(2)}{\frac{\text{Pretax profits}}{\text{EBIT}}} \times \underset{(3)}{\frac{\text{EBIT}}{\text{Sales}}} \times \underset{(4)}{\frac{\text{Sales}}{\text{Assets}}} \times \underset{(5)}{\frac{\text{Assets}}{\text{Equity}}} \quad \textbf{(19.2)}$$

Table 19.7 shows all these ratios for Nodett and Somdett under the three different economic scenarios. Let us first focus on factors 3 and 4. Notice that their product equals EBIT/Assets, which is the firm's ROA.

Factor 3 is known as the firm's operating **profit margin** or **return on sales (ROS),** which equals operating profit per dollar of sales. In a normal year, profit margin is .10, or 10%; in a bad year, it is .0625, or 6.25%; and in a good year, it is .125, or 12.5%.

		(1)	(2)	(3)	(4)	(5)	(6)
	ROE	Net Profits/ Pretax Profits	Pretax Profits/EBIT	EBIT/Sales (Margin)	Sales/Assets (Turnover)	Assets/ Equity	Compound Leverage Factor (2) × (5)
Bad year							
Nodett	0.030	0.6	1.000	0.0625	0.800	1.000	1.000
Somdett	0.018	0.6	0.360	0.0625	0.800	1.667	0.600
Normal year							
Nodett	0.060	0.6	1.000	0.1000	1.000	1.000	1.000
Somdett	0.068	0.6	0.680	0.1000	1.000	1.667	1.134
Good year							
Nodett	0.090	0.6	1.000	0.1250	1.200	1.000	1.000
Somdett	0.118	0.6	0.787	0.1250	1.200	1.667	1.311

Table 19.7

Ratio decomposition analysis for Nodett and Somdett

Factor 4, the ratio of sales to total assets, is known as **total asset turnover (ATO).** It indicates the efficiency of the firm's use of assets in the sense that it measures the annual sales generated by each dollar of assets. In a normal year, ATO for both firms is 1.0 per year, meaning that sales of $1 per year were generated per dollar of assets. In a bad year, this ratio declines to .8 per year, and in a good year, it rises to 1.2 per year.

Comparing Nodett and Somdett, we see that factors 3 and 4 do not depend on a firm's financial leverage. The firms' ratios are equal to each other in all three scenarios. Similarly, factor 1, the ratio of net income after taxes to pretax profit, is the same for both firms. We call this the *tax-burden ratio.* Its value reflects both the government's tax code and the policies pursued by the firm in trying to minimize its tax burden. In our example it does not change over the business cycle, remaining a constant .6.

Although factors 1, 3, and 4 are not affected by a firm's capital structure, factors 2 and 5 are. Factor 2 is the ratio of pretax profits to EBIT. The firm's pretax profits will be greatest when there are no interest payments to be made to debtholders. In fact, another way to express this ratio is

$$\frac{\text{Pretax profits}}{\text{EBIT}} = \frac{\text{EBIT} - \text{Interest expense}}{\text{EBIT}}$$

We will call this factor the *interest-burden ratio.* It takes on its highest possible value, 1, for Nodett, which has no financial leverage. The higher the degree of financial leverage, the lower the interest-burden ratio. Nodett's ratio does not vary over the business cycle. It is fixed at 1.0, reflecting the total absence of interest payments. For Somdett, however, because interest expense is fixed in a dollar amount while EBIT varies, the interest burden ratio varies from a low of .36 in a bad year to a high of .787 in a good year.

A closely related statistic to the interest-burden ratio is the **interest coverage ratio,** or **times interest earned.** The ratio is defined as

$$\text{Interest coverage} = \text{EBIT/Interest expense}$$

A high coverage ratio indicates that the likelihood of bankruptcy is low because annual earnings are significantly greater than annual interest obligations. It is widely used by both lenders and borrowers in determining the firm's debt capacity and is a major determinant of the firm's bond rating.

Factor 5, the ratio of assets to equity, is a measure of the firm's degree of financial leverage. It is called the **leverage ratio** and is equal to 1 plus the total debt-to-equity ratio.[4] As shown in Table 19.7, Nodett has a leverage ratio of 1, while Somdett's leverage ratio is 1.667.

From our discussion in Section 19.2, we know that financial leverage helps boost ROE only if ROA is greater than the interest rate on the firm's debt. How is this fact reflected in the ratios of Table 19.7?

The answer is that the full impact of leverage in this framework equals the product of the interest burden and leverage ratios (i.e., factors 2 and 5 in Table 19.7). This product is called the *compound leverage factor* and is shown in Column 6. Nodett's compound leverage factor equals 1.0 in all three scenarios. In contrast, Somdett's compound leverage factor is greater than 1.0 in normal years (1.134) and in good years (1.311), indicating a positive contribution of financial leverage to ROE. It is less than 1 in bad years, reflecting the fact that when ROA falls below the interest rate, ROE falls with increased use of debt.

We can summarize all of these relationships as follows. From Equation 19.2,

$$ROE = Tax\ burden \times Interest\ burden \times Margin \times Turnover \times Leverage$$

Because

$$ROA = Margin \times Turnover \qquad\qquad \textbf{(19.3)}$$

and

$$Compound\ leverage\ factor = Interest\ burden \times Leverage$$

we can decompose ROE equivalently as follows:

$$ROE = Tax\ burden \times ROA \times Compound\ leverage\ factor \qquad\qquad \textbf{(19.4)}$$

Equation 19.3 shows that ROA is the *product* of margin and turnover. High values of one of these ratios are often accompanied by low values of the other. For example, Walmart has low profit margins but high turnover, while Tiffany has high margins but low turnover. Firms would love to have high values for both margin and turnover, but this generally will not be possible: Retailers with high markups will sacrifice sales volume, and conversely, those with low turnover need high margins just to remain viable. Therefore, comparing these ratios in isolation usually is meaningful only in evaluating firms following similar strategies in the same industry. Cross-industry comparisons can be misleading.

Figure 19.2 shows evidence of the turnover-profit margin trade-off. Each point in the figure corresponds to the profit margin-turnover pair for one particular industry. Industries with high turnover, such as food stores, tend to have low profit margins, while industries with high margins, such as computer peripherals, tend to have low turnover. The two curved lines in the figure trace out turnover-margin combinations that result in an ROA of either 3% or 10%. You can see that most industries lie inside of this range, so ROA across industries demonstrates far less variation than either turnover or margin taken in isolation.

---

[4] $\dfrac{Assets}{Equity} = \dfrac{Equity + Debt}{Equity} = 1 + \dfrac{Debt}{Equity}$

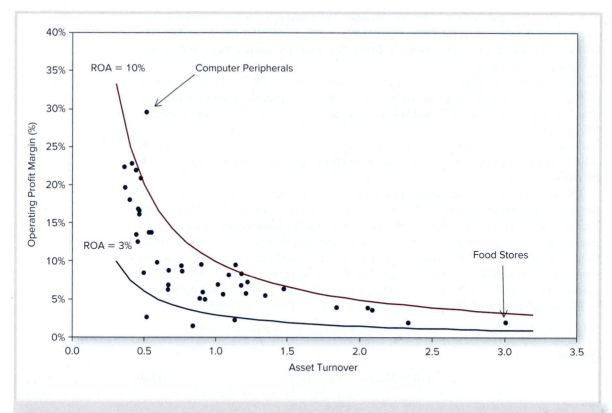

Figure 19.2 Operating profit margin, and asset turnover for 45 industries, 2015

Source: U.S. Census Bureau, *Quarterly Report for Manufacturing and Trade Corporations, Second Quarter 2015* (**www.census.gov/econ/qfr**). This is an updated version of a figure that first appeared in Thomas I. Selling and Clyde P. Stickney, "The Effects of Business Environments and Strategy on a Firm's Rate of Return on Assets," *Financial Analysts Journal,* January–February 1989, pp. 43–52.

Example 19.3   Margin versus Turnover

Consider two firms with the same ROA of 10% per year. The first is a discount chain, the second is a gas and electric utility.

As Table 19.8 shows, the discount chain has a "low" profit margin of 2% and achieves a 10% ROA by "turning over" its assets five times per year. The capital-intensive utility, on the other hand, has a "low" asset turnover ratio of only .5 times per year and achieves its 10% ROA through its higher profit margin of 20%. The point here is that a "low" margin or asset turnover ratio need not indicate a troubled firm. Each ratio must be interpreted in light of industry norms.

Table 19.8

Differences between profit margin and asset turnover across industries

	Margin × ATO = ROA		
Discount chain	2%	5.0	10%
Utility	20%	0.5	10%

Concept Check **19.2**

> Prepare a ratio decomposition analysis for the Mordett firm in Concept Check 19.1, creating a table similar to Table 19.7.

Turnover and Other Asset Utilization Ratios

To understand a firm's ratio of sales to assets, it is often helpful to compute comparable efficiency-of-utilization, or turnover, ratios for subcategories of assets. For example, we can think about turnover relative to fixed rather than total assets:

$$\text{Fixed-asset turnover} = \frac{\text{Sales}}{\text{Fixed assets}}$$

This ratio measures sales per dollar of the firm's money tied up in fixed assets.

To illustrate how you can compute this and other ratios from a firm's financial statements, consider Growth Industries, Inc. (GI). GI's historical income statement and opening and closing balance sheets for the years 2014–2017 appear in Table 19.9.

	2014	2015	2016	2017
Income statements				
Sales revenue		$100,000	$120,000	$144,000
Cost of goods sold (including depreciation)		55,000	66,000	79,200
Depreciation		15,000	18,000	21,600
Selling and administrative expenses		15,000	18,000	21,600
Operating income		30,000	36,000	43,200
Interest expense		10,500	19,095	34,391
Taxable income		19,500	16,905	8,809
Income tax (40% rate)		7,800	6,762	3,524
Net income		$ 11,700	$ 10,143	$ 5,285
Balance sheets (end of year)				
Cash and marketable securities	$ 50,000	$ 60,000	$ 72,000	$ 86,400
Accounts receivable	25,000	30,000	36,000	43,200
Inventories	75,000	90,000	108,000	129,600
Net plant and equipment	150,000	180,000	216,000	259,200
Total assets	$300,000	$360,000	$432,000	$518,400
Accounts payable	$ 30,000	$ 36,000	$ 43,200	$ 51,840
Short-term debt	45,000	87,300	141,957	214,432
Long-term debt (8% bonds maturing in 2029)	75,000	75,000	75,000	75,000
Total liabilities	$150,000	$198,300	$260,157	$341,272
Shareholders' equity (1 million shares outstanding)	$150,000	$161,700	$171,843	$177,128
Other data				
Market price per common share at year-end		$ 93.60	$ 61.00	$ 21.00

Table 19.9

Growth Industries, Inc., financial statements ($ thousand)

GI's total asset turnover in 2017 was .303, which was below the industry average of .4. To understand better why GI underperformed, we can compute asset utilization ratios separately for fixed assets, inventories, and accounts receivable.

GI's sales in 2017 were $144 million. Its only fixed assets were plant and equipment, which were $216 million at the beginning of the year and $259.2 million at year's end. Average fixed assets for the year were, therefore, $237.6 million [($216 million + $259.2 million)/2]. GI's fixed-asset turnover for 2017 therefore was $144 million per year/ $237.6 million = .606 per year. In other words, for every dollar of fixed assets, there were $.606 in sales.

Comparable figures for the fixed-asset turnover ratio for 2015 and 2016 and the 2017 industry average are:

2015	2016	2017	2017 Industry Average
0.606	0.606	0.606	0.700

GI's fixed asset turnover has been stable over time and below the industry average.

Notice that when a financial ratio includes one item from the income statement, which covers a period of time, and another from a balance sheet, which is a "snapshot" at a particular time, common practice is to take the average of the beginning and end-of-year balance sheet figures. Thus in computing the fixed-asset turnover ratio we divide sales (from the income statement) by average fixed assets (from the balance sheet).

Another widely followed turnover ratio is the **inventory turnover ratio,** which is the ratio of cost of goods sold per dollar of average inventory. (We use the cost of goods sold instead of sales revenue in the numerator to maintain consistency with inventory, which is valued at cost.) This ratio measures the speed with which inventory is turned over.

In 2015, GI's cost of goods sold (excluding depreciation) was $40 million, and its average inventory was $82.5 million [($75 million + $90 million)/2]. Its inventory turnover was, therefore, .485 per year ($40 million/$82.5 million). In 2016 and 2017, inventory turnover remained the same, which was below the industry average of .5 per year. In other words, GI was burdened with a higher level of inventories per dollar of sales than its competitors. This higher investment in working capital in turn resulted in a higher level of assets per dollar of sales or profits and a lower ROA than its competitors.

Another aspect of efficiency surrounds management of accounts receivable, which is often measured by *days sales in receivables,* that is, the average level of accounts receivable expressed as a multiple of daily sales. It is computed as average accounts receivable/ sales × 365 and may be interpreted as the number of days' worth of sales tied up in accounts receivable. You can also think of it as the average lag between the date of sale and the date payment is received; therefore, it is also called the **average collection period.**

For GI in 2017 the average collection period was 100.4 days:

$$\frac{(\$36 \text{ million} + \$43.2 \text{ million})/2}{\$144 \text{ million}} \times 365 = 100.4 \text{ days}$$

The industry average was only 60 days. This statistic tells us that GI's average receivables per dollar of sales exceeds that of its competitors. Again, this implies a higher required investment in working capital and, ultimately, a lower ROA.

In summary, these ratios show us that GI's poor total asset turnover relative to the industry is in part caused by lower-than-average fixed-asset turnover and inventory turnover and higher-than-average days receivables. This suggests GI may be having problems with excess plant capacity along with poor inventory and receivables management practices.

Liquidity Ratios

Leverage is one measure of the safety of a firm's debt. Debt ratios compare the firm's indebtedness to broad measures of its assets, and coverage ratios compare various measures of earning power against the cash flow needed to satisfy debt obligations. But leverage is not the only determinant of financial prudence. You also want to know that a firm can lay its hands on cash either to pay its scheduled obligations or to meet unforeseen obligations. **Liquidity** is the ability to convert assets into cash at short notice. Liquidity is commonly measured using the current ratio, quick ratio, and cash ratio.

1. **Current ratio:** Current assets/Current liabilities. This ratio measures the ability of the firm to pay off its current liabilities by liquidating its current assets (i.e., turning them into cash). It indicates the firm's ability to avoid insolvency in the short run. GI's current ratio in 2015, for example, was $(60 + 30 + 90)/(36 + 87.3) = 1.46$. In other years, it was

2015	2016	2017	2017 Industry Average
1.46	1.17	0.97	2.0

   This represents an unfavorable time trend and poor standing relative to the industry. This troublesome pattern is not surprising given the working capital burden resulting from GI's subpar performance with respect to receivables and inventory management.

2. **Quick ratio:** (Cash + Marketable securities + Receivables)/Current liabilities. This ratio is also called the **acid test ratio.** It has the same denominator as the current ratio, but its numerator includes only cash, cash equivalents, and receivables. The quick ratio is a better measure of liquidity than the current ratio for firms whose inventory is not readily convertible into cash. GI's quick ratio shows the same disturbing trends as its current ratio:

2015	2016	2017	2017 Industry Average
0.73	0.58	0.49	1.0

3. **Cash ratio.** A company's receivables are less liquid than its holdings of cash and marketable securities. Therefore, in addition to the quick ratio, analysts also compute a firm's cash ratio, defined as

$$\text{Cash ratio} = \frac{\text{Cash} + \text{Marketable securities}}{\text{Current liabilities}}$$

GI's cash ratios are

2015	2016	2017	2017 Industry Average
0.487	0.389	0.324	0.70

GI's liquidity ratios have fallen dramatically over this 3-year period, and by 2017, its liquidity measures are far below industry averages. The decline in the liquidity ratios combined with the decline in the coverage ratio (you can confirm that times interest earned has also fallen over this period) suggest that its credit rating has been declining as well, and, no doubt, GI is considered a relatively poor credit risk in 2017.

Market Price Ratios: Growth versus Value

The **market–book-value (P/B) ratio** equals the market price of a share of the firm's common stock divided by its *book value,* that is, shareholders' equity per share. Some analysts consider the stock of a firm with a low market–book value to be a "safer" investment, seeing the book value as a "floor" supporting the market price. These analysts presumably view book value as the level below which market price will not fall because the firm always has the option to liquidate, or sell, its assets for their book values. However, this view is questionable. In fact, some firms do sell below book value. For example, we've already seen (Section 18.1) that in mid-2016, shares in Bank of America, Citigroup, Honda, and Mitsubishi sold for less than book value. Nevertheless, a low market–book-value ratio is seen by some as providing a "margin of safety," and some analysts will screen out or reject high-P/B firms in their stock selection process.

A better interpretation of the market-price-to-book-value ratio is as a measure of growth opportunities. Recall from the previous chapter that we may view the two components of firm value as assets in place and growth opportunities. As Example 19.4 illustrates, firms with greater growth opportunities will tend to exhibit higher multiples of market price to book value.

Example 19.4   Market-Price-to-Book-Value Ratio and Growth Options

Consider two firms, both with book value per share of $10, both with a market capitalization rate of 15%, and both with plowback ratios of .60.

Bright Prospects has an ROE of 20%, which is well in excess of the market capitalization rate; this ROE implies that the firm is endowed with ample growth opportunities. With ROE = .20, Bright Prospects will earn $2 per share this year. With its plowback ratio of .60, it pays out a dividend of $D_1 = (1 - .6) \times \$2 = \$.80$, has a growth rate of $g = b \times$ ROE $= .60 \times .20 = .12$, and has a stock price of $D_1/(k - g) = \$.80/(.15 - .12) = \$26.67$. Its price–book ratio is $26.67/10 = 2.667$.

In contrast, Past Glory has an ROE of only 15%, just equal to the market capitalization rate. It therefore will earn $1.50 per share this year and will pay a dividend of $D_1 = .4 \times \$1.50 = \$.60$. Its growth rate is $g = b \times$ ROE $= .60 \times .15 = .09$, and its stock price is $D_1/(k - g) = \$.60/(.15 - .09) = \$10$. Its price–book ratio is $\$10/\$10 = 1.0$. Not surprisingly, a firm that earns just the required rate of return on its investments will sell for book value, and no more.

We conclude that the market-price-to-book-value ratio is determined in large part by growth prospects.

Another measure used to place firms along a growth versus value spectrum is the **price–earnings (P/E) ratio.** In fact, we saw in the last chapter that the ratio of the present value of growth options to the value of assets in place largely determines the P/E multiple. While low-P/E stocks allow you to pay less per dollar of *current* earnings, the high-P/E stock may still be a better bargain if its earnings are expected to grow quickly enough.[5]

Many analysts nevertheless believe that low-P/E stocks are more attractive than high-P/E stocks. And in fact, low-P/E stocks have generally been positive-alpha investments using the CAPM as a return benchmark. But an efficient market adherent would discount this track record, arguing that such a simplistic rule could not really generate abnormal returns, and that the CAPM may not be a good benchmark for returns in this case.

[5]Remember, though, P/E ratios reported in the financial press are based on *past* earnings, while price is determined by the firm's prospects of *future* earnings. Therefore, reported P/E ratios may reflect variation in current earnings around a trend line.

In any event, the important points to remember are that ownership of the stock conveys the right to future as well as current earnings and, therefore, that a high P/E ratio may best be interpreted as a signal that the market views the firm as enjoying attractive growth opportunities.

Before leaving the P/B and P/E ratios, it is worth pointing out an important relationship between them:

$$\text{ROE} = \frac{\text{Earnings}}{\text{Book value}} = \frac{\text{Market price}}{\text{Book value}} \div \frac{\text{Market price}}{\text{Earnings}} \tag{19.5}$$
$$= \text{P/B ratio} \div \text{P/E ratio}$$

Rearranging these terms, we find that a firm's P/E ratio equals its price-to-book ratio divided by ROE:

$$\frac{P}{E} = \frac{P/B}{\text{ROE}}$$

Thus a company with a high P/B ratio can still have a relatively low P/E ratio if its ROE is sufficiently high.

Wall Street often distinguishes between "good firms" and "good investments." A good firm may be highly profitable, with a correspondingly high ROE. But if its stock price is bid up to a level commensurate with this ROE, its P/B ratio will also be high, and the stock price may be a relatively large multiple of earnings, thus reducing its attractiveness as an investment. The high ROE of the firm does not by itself imply that the *stock* is a good investment. Conversely, troubled firms with low ROEs can be good investments if their prices are low enough.

Table 19.10 summarizes the ratios reviewed in this section.

 Concept Check **19.3**

What were GI's ROE, P/E, and P/B ratios in the year 2017? How do they compare to the industry average ratios, which were: ROE = 8.64%; P/E = 8; P/B = .69? How does GI's earnings yield in 2017 compare to the industry average?

Choosing a Benchmark

We have discussed how to calculate the principal financial ratios. To evaluate the performance of a given firm, however, you need a benchmark to which you can compare its ratios. One obvious benchmark is the ratio for the same company in earlier years. For example, Figure 19.3 shows HD's return on assets, profit margin, and asset turnover ratio for the last few years. You can see that a good part of the decline in ROA between 2005 and 2009 was due to HD's falling profit margin. In 2008, margin improved but turnover fell, resulting in a further drop in ROA. But in the last few years, ROA improved dramatically, propelled by simultaneous increases in both margin and turnover.

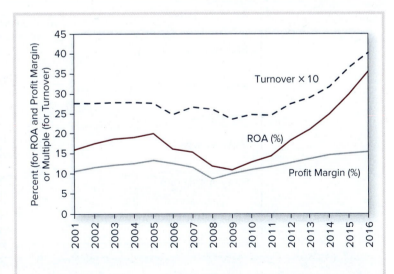

Figure 19.3 DuPont decomposition for Home Depot

Table 19.10

Summary of key financial ratios

Leverage	
Interest burden	$\dfrac{\text{EBIT} - \text{Interest expense}}{\text{EBIT}}$
Interest coverage (times interest earned)	$\dfrac{\text{EBIT}}{\text{Interest expense}}$
Leverage	$\dfrac{\text{Assets}}{\text{Equity}} = 1 + \dfrac{\text{Debt}}{\text{Equity}}$
Compound leverage factor	Interest burden $\times$ Leverage
Asset utilization	
Total asset turnover	$\dfrac{\text{Sales}}{\text{Average total assets}}$
Fixed asset turnover	$\dfrac{\text{Sales}}{\text{Average fixed assets}}$
Inventory turnover	$\dfrac{\text{Cost of goods sold}}{\text{Average inventories}}$
Days sales in receivables	$\dfrac{\text{Average accounts receivable}}{\text{Annual sales}} \times 365$
Liquidity	
Current ratio	$\dfrac{\text{Current assets}}{\text{Current liabilities}}$
Quick ratio	$\dfrac{\text{Cash} + \text{Marketable securities} + \text{Receivables}}{\text{Current liabilities}}$
Cash ratio	$\dfrac{\text{Cash} + \text{Marketable securities}}{\text{Current liabilities}}$
Profitability	
Return on assets	$\dfrac{\text{EBIT}}{\text{Average total assets}}$
Return on equity	$\dfrac{\text{Net income}}{\text{Average stockholders' equity}}$
Return on sales (profit margin)	$\dfrac{\text{EBIT}}{\text{Sales}}$
Market price	
Market-to-book	$\dfrac{\text{Price per share}}{\text{Book value per share}}$
Price–earnings ratio	$\dfrac{\text{Price per share}}{\text{Earnings per share}}$
Earnings yield	$\dfrac{\text{Earnings per share}}{\text{Price per share}}$

	LT Debt Assets	Interest Coverage	Current Ratio	Quick Ratio	Asset Turnover	Profit Margin (%)	Return on Assets (%)	Return on Equity (%)	Payout Ratio
All manufacturing	0.25	3.85	1.32	0.88	0.62	8.06	4.99	11.85	0.59
Food products	0.27	5.74	1.65	1.06	0.86	8.18	7.03	12.71	0.40
Clothing	0.22	8.00	2.11	1.11	1.12	8.72	9.74	21.43	0.46
Aerospace	0.21	7.59	1.19	0.44	0.69	10.45	7.24	25.61	0.40
Chemicals	0.31	3.79	1.11	0.80	0.40	14.79	5.87	15.96	0.48
Drugs	0.32	3.42	0.98	0.73	0.31	16.93	5.21	16.76	0.43
Machinery	0.22	2.56	1.46	0.94	0.66	4.83	3.19	4.32	1.11
Electrical	0.21	3.93	1.21	0.80	0.58	7.41	4.29	5.09	1.87
Motor vehicles	0.14	6.82	1.08	0.77	1.24	5.39	6.66	15.98	0.49
Computer and electronic	0.25	3.68	1.37	1.12	0.39	10.34	4.05	13.94	0.45

Table 19.11

Financial ratios for major industry groups

Source: U.S. Department of Commerce, *Quarterly Financial Report for Manufacturing, Mining and Trade Corporations*, first quarter 2016. Available at **http://www2.census.gov/econ/qfr/current/qfr_pub.pdf**.

It is also helpful to compare financial ratios to those of other firms in the same industry. Financial ratios for industries are published by the U.S. Department of Commerce (see Table 19.11), Dun & Bradstreet (*Industry Norms and Key Business Ratios*), and the Risk Management Association, or RMA (*Annual Statement Studies*). A broad range of financial ratios is also easily accessible on the Web.

Table 19.11 presents ratios for a sample of major industry groups to give you a feel for some of the differences across industries. You should note that while some ratios, such as asset turnover or the total debt ratio, reflect stable firm and industry characteristics and therefore tend to be correspondingly stable over time, others, such as return on assets or equity, are more sensitive to current business conditions.

19.5   An Illustration of Financial Statement Analysis

In her 2019 annual report to the shareholders of Growth Industries, Inc., the president wrote: "2019 was another successful year for Growth Industries. As in 2018, sales, assets, and operating income all continued to grow at a rate of 20%."

Is she right?

We can evaluate her statement by conducting a ratio analysis of Growth Industries. Our purpose is to assess GI's performance in the recent past, evaluate its future prospects, and determine whether its market price reflects its intrinsic value.

Table 19.12 shows some key financial ratios we can compute from GI's financial statements. The president is certainly right about the growth rate in sales, assets, and operating income. Inspection of GI's key financial ratios, however, contradicts her first sentence: 2019 was not another successful year for GI—it appears to have been another miserable one.

Year	ROE	(1) Net Profits/ Pretax Profits	(2) Pretax Profits/ EBIT	(3) EBIT/ Sales (Margin)	(4) Sales/ Assets (Turnover)	(5) Assets/ Equity	(6) Compound Leverage Factor (2) × (5)	(7) ROA (3) × (4)	P/E	P/B
2017	7.51%	0.6	0.650	30%	0.303	2.117	1.376	9.09%	8	0.58
2018	6.08	0.6	0.470	30	0.303	2.375	1.116	9.09	6	0.35
2019	3.03	0.6	0.204	30	0.303	2.723	0.556	9.09	4	0.12
Industry average	8.64	0.6	0.800	30	0.400	1.500	1.200	12.00	8	0.69

Table 19.12

Key financial ratios of Growth Industries, Inc.

ROE has been declining steadily, from 7.51% in 2017 to 3.03% in 2019. A comparison of GI's 2019 ROE to the 2019 industry average of 8.64% makes the deteriorating time trend appear especially alarming. The low and falling market-to-book-value ratio and the falling price–earnings ratio indicate investors are less and less optimistic about the firm's future profitability.

The fact that ROA has not been declining, however, tells us that the source of the declining time trend in GI's ROE must be related to financial leverage. And we see that as GI's leverage ratio climbed from 2.117 in 2017 to 2.723 in 2019, its interest-burden ratio (column 2) worsened, from .650 to .204, with the net result that the compound leverage factor fell from 1.376 to .556.

The rapid increase in short-term debt from year to year and the concurrent increase in interest expense (see Table 19.9) make it clear that to finance its 20% growth rate in sales, GI has incurred sizable amounts of short-term debt at high interest rates. The firm is paying rates of interest greater than the ROA it is earning on the investment financed with the new borrowing. As the firm has expanded, its situation has become ever more precarious.

In 2019, for example, the average interest rate on GI's short-term debt was 20% versus an ROA of 9.09%. (You can calculate the interest rate on GI's short-term debt using the data in Table 19.9 as follows. The balance sheet shows us that the coupon rate on its long-term debt was 8%, and its par value was $75 million. Therefore the interest paid on the long-term debt was .08 × $75 million = $6 million. Total interest paid in 2019 was $34,391,000, so the interest paid on the short-term debt must have been $34,391,000 − $6,000,000 = $28,391,000. This is 20% of GI's short-term debt at the start of the year.)

GI's problems become clear when we examine its statement of cash flows in Table 19.13. The statement is derived from the income statement and balance sheet data in Table 19.9. GI's cash flow from operations is falling steadily, from $12,700,000 in 2017 to $6,725,000 in 2019. The firm's investment in plant and equipment, by contrast, has increased greatly. Net plant and equipment (i.e., net of depreciation) rose from $150,000,000 in 2016 to $259,200,000 in 2019 (see Table 19.9). This near doubling of capital assets makes the decrease in cash flow from operations all the more troubling.

The source of the difficulty is GI's enormous amount of short-term borrowing. In a sense, the company is being run as a pyramid scheme. It borrows more and more each year to maintain its 20% growth rate in assets and income. However, the new assets are not

	2017	2018	2019
Cash flow from operating activities			
Net income	$ 11,700	$ 10,143	$ 5,285
+ Depreciation	15,000	18,000	21,600
+ Decrease (increase) in accounts receivable	(5,000)	(6,000)	(7,200)
+ Decrease (increase) in inventories	(15,000)	(18,000)	(21,600)
+ Increase in accounts payable	6,000	7,200	8,640
Cash provided by operations	$ 12,700	$ 11,343	$ 6,725
Cash flow from investing activities			
Investment in plant and equipment*	$(45,000)	$(54,000)	$(64,800)
Cash flow from financing activities			
Dividends paid†	$ 0	$ 0	$ 0
Short-term debt issued	42,300	54,657	72,475
Change in cash and marketable securities‡	$ 10,000	$ 12,000	$ 14,400

Table 19.13

Growth Industries, Inc., statement of cash flows ($ thousand)

*Gross investment equals increase in net plant and equipment plus depreciation.
†We can conclude that no dividends are paid because stockholders' equity increases each year by the full amount of net income, implying a plowback ratio of 1.0.
‡Equals cash flow from operations plus cash flow from investment activities plus cash flow from financing activities. Note that this equals the yearly change in cash and marketable securities on the balance sheet.

generating enough cash flow to support the extra interest burden of the debt, as the falling cash flow from operations indicates. Eventually, when the firm loses its ability to borrow further, its growth will be at an end.

At this point GI stock might be an attractive investment. Its market price is only 12% of its book value, and with a P/E ratio of 4, its earnings yield is 25% per year. GI is a likely candidate for a takeover by another firm that might replace GI's management and build shareholder value through a radical change in policy.

 Concept Check **19.4**

You have the following information for IBX Corporation for the years 2016 and 2018 (all figures are in $ million):

	2016	2018
Net income	$ 253.7	$ 239.0
Pretax income	411.9	375.6
EBIT	517.6	403.1
Average assets	4,857.9	3,459.7
Sales	6,679.3	4,537.0
Shareholders' equity	2,233.3	2,347.3

What is the trend in IBX's ROE? How can you account for this trend in terms of tax burden, margin, turnover, and financial leverage?

19.6   Comparability Problems

Financial statement analysis gives us a good amount of ammunition for evaluating a company's performance and future prospects. But comparing financial results of different companies is not so simple. There is more than one acceptable way to represent various items of revenue and expense according to generally accepted accounting principles (GAAP). This means two firms may have exactly the same economic income yet very different accounting incomes.

Interpreting a single firm's performance over time is even more complicated when inflation distorts the dollar measuring rod. Comparability problems are especially acute in this case because the impact of inflation on reported results often depends on the particular method the firm adopts to account for inventories and depreciation. Earnings and financial ratios must be adjusted to a uniform standard before comparing financial results across firms and over time. Other important potential sources of noncomparability include the capitalization of leases and other expenses, the treatment of pension costs, and allowances for reserves.

Inventory Valuation

There are two commonly used ways to value inventories: **LIFO** (last-in first-out) and **FIFO** (first-in first-out). We can explain the difference using a numerical example.

Suppose Generic Products, Inc. (GPI), has a constant inventory of 1 million units of generic goods. The inventory turns over once per year, meaning the ratio of cost of goods sold to inventory is 1.

The LIFO system calls for valuing the million units used up during the year at the current cost of production, so that the last goods produced are considered the first ones to be sold. They are valued at today's cost.

The FIFO system assumes that the units used up or sold are the ones that were added to inventory first, and goods sold are therefore valued at original cost.

If the price of generic goods has been constant, say at the level of $1, the book value of inventory and the cost of goods sold will be the same, $1 million under both systems. But suppose the price of generic goods rises by 10 cents per unit during the year as a result of general inflation.

LIFO accounting would result in a cost of goods sold of $1.1 million, whereas the end-of-year balance sheet value of the 1 million units in inventory remains $1 million. The balance sheet value of inventories is calculated as the cost of the goods still in inventory. Under LIFO the last goods produced are assumed to be sold at the current cost of $1.10; the goods remaining are the previously produced goods, at a cost of only $1. You can see that although LIFO accounting accurately measures the cost of goods sold today, it understates the current value of the remaining inventory in an inflationary environment.

In contrast, under FIFO accounting, the cost of goods sold would be $1 million, and the end-of-year balance sheet value of the inventory would be $1.1 million. The result is that the LIFO firm has both a lower reported profit and a lower balance sheet value of inventories than the FIFO firm.

LIFO results in a more realistic estimate of economic earnings (i.e., real sustainable cash flow) because it uses up-to-date prices to evaluate the cost of goods sold. However, it induces balance sheet distortions when it values investment in inventories at original cost. This practice results in an upward bias in ROE because the investment base on which return is earned is undervalued.

Depreciation

Another source of problems is the measurement of depreciation, which is a key factor in computing true earnings. The accounting and economic measures of depreciation can differ markedly. According to the *economic* definition, depreciation is the amount the firm must reinvest to sustain its real productive capacity at the current level. The *accounting* measurement is quite different. Accounting depreciation is the portion of the original acquisition cost of an asset allocated in each accounting period over an arbitrarily specified life of the asset. This is the figure reported in financial statements.

Assume, for example, that a firm buys machines with a useful economic life of 20 years at $100,000 apiece. In its financial statements, however, the firm can depreciate the machines over 10 years using the straight-line method, for $10,000 per year in depreciation. Thus after 10 years a machine will be fully depreciated on the books, even though it remains a productive asset that will not need replacement for another 10 years.

In computing accounting earnings, this firm will overestimate depreciation in the first 10 years of the machine's economic life and underestimate it in the last 10 years. This will cause reported earnings to be understated compared with economic earnings in the first 10 years and overstated in the last 10 years.

Depreciation comparability problems add one more wrinkle. A firm can use different depreciation methods for tax purposes than for other reporting purposes. Most firms use accelerated depreciation methods for tax purposes and straight-line depreciation in published financial statements. There also are differences across firms in their estimates of the depreciable life of plant, equipment, and other depreciable assets.

Another complication arises from inflation. Because conventional depreciation is based on historical costs rather than on the current replacement cost of assets, measured depreciation in periods of inflation is understated relative to replacement cost, and *real* economic income (sustainable cash flow) is correspondingly overstated.

For example, suppose Generic Products, Inc., has a machine with a 3-year useful life that originally cost $3 million. Annual straight-line depreciation is $1 million, regardless of what happens to the replacement cost of the machine. Suppose inflation in the first year turns out to be 10%. Then the true annual depreciation expense is $1.1 million in current terms, whereas conventionally measured depreciation remains fixed at $1 million per year. Accounting income overstates *real* economic income by $.1 million.

Inflation and Interest Expense

Although inflation can cause distortions in the measurement of a firm's inventory and depreciation costs, it has perhaps an even greater effect on the calculation of *real* interest expense. Nominal interest rates include an inflation premium that compensates the lender for inflation-induced erosion in the real value of principal. From the perspective of both lender and borrower, therefore, part of what is conventionally measured as interest expense should be treated more properly as repayment of principal.

Example 19.5   Inflation and Real Income

Suppose Generic Products has debt outstanding with a face value of $10 million at an interest rate of 10% per year. Interest expense as conventionally measured is $1 million per year. However, suppose inflation during the year is 6%, so that the real interest rate is 4%. Then $.6 million of what appears as interest expense on the income statement is really an inflation premium, or compensation for the anticipated reduction in the real value of the $10 million principal; only $.4 million is *real* interest expense. The $.6 million reduction in the purchasing power of the outstanding principal may be thought of as repayment of principal, rather than as an interest expense. Real income of the firm is, therefore, understated by $.6 million.

Mismeasurement of real interest means inflation deflates the computation of real income. The effects of inflation on the reported values of inventories and depreciation that we have discussed work in the opposite direction.

 Concept Check **19.5**

In a period of rapid inflation, companies ABC and XYZ have the same *reported* earnings. ABC uses LIFO inventory accounting, has relatively fewer depreciable assets, and has more debt than XYZ. XYZ uses FIFO inventory accounting. Which company has the higher *real* income, and why?

Fair Value Accounting

Many major assets and liabilities are not traded in financial markets and do not have easily observable values. For example, we cannot simply look up the values of employee stock options, health care benefits for retired employees, or buildings and other real estate. While the true financial status of a firm may depend critically on these values, which can swing widely over time, common practice has been to simply value them at historic cost. Proponents of **fair value accounting,** also known as **mark-to-market accounting,** argue that financial statements would give a truer picture of the firm if they better reflected the current market values of all assets and liabilities.

The Financial Accounting Standards Board's Statement No. 157 on fair value accounting places assets in one of three "buckets." Level 1 assets are traded in active markets and therefore should be valued at their market price. Level 2 assets are not actively traded, but their values still may be estimated using observable market data on similar assets. They can be "marked to a matrix" of comparable securities. Level 3 assets are hardest to value. Here it is difficult even to identify other assets that are similar enough to serve as benchmarks for their market values; one has to resort to pricing models to estimate their intrinsic values. Rather than mark to market, these values are often called "mark to model," although they are also disparagingly known as mark-to-make-believe, as the estimates are so prone to manipulation by creative use of model inputs. Since 2012, firms have been required to disclose more about the methods and assumptions used in their valuation models and to describe the sensitivity of their valuation estimates to changes in their methodology.

Critics of fair value accounting argue that it relies too heavily on estimates. Such estimates potentially introduce considerable noise in firms' accounts and can induce great profit volatility as fluctuations in asset valuations are recognized. Even worse, subjective valuations may offer management a tempting tool to manipulate earnings or the apparent financial condition of the firm at opportune times. As just one example, Bergstresser, Desai, and Rauh[6] find that firms make more aggressive assumptions about returns on

---

[6]D. Bergstresser, M. Desai, and J. Rauh, "Earnings Manipulation, Pension Assumptions, and Managerial Investment Decisions," *Quarterly Journal of Economics* 121 (2006), pp. 157–95.

Mark-to-Market Accounting: Cure or Disease?

As banks and other institutions holding mortgage-backed securities revalued their portfolios throughout 2008, their net worth fell along with the value of those securities. The losses on these securities were painful enough, but their further implications only increased the banks' woes. For example, banks are required to maintain adequate levels of capital relative to assets. If capital reserves decline, a bank may be forced to shrink until its remaining capital is once again adequate compared to its asset base. But such shrinkage may require the bank to cut back on its lending, which restricts its customers' access to credit. It may also require asset sales, and if many banks attempt to shrink their portfolios at once, waves of forced sales may put further pressure on prices, resulting in additional write-downs and reductions to capital in a self-feeding cycle. Critics of mark-to-market accounting therefore contend that it exacerbated the problems of an already reeling economy.

Advocates, however, argue that the critics confuse the message with the messenger. Mark-to-market accounting makes transparent losses that have already been incurred, but it does not cause those losses. Critics retort that when markets are faltering, market prices may be unreliable. If trading activity has largely broken down, and assets can be sold only at fire-sale prices, then those prices may no longer be indicative of fundamental value. Markets cannot be efficient if they are not even functioning. In the turmoil surrounding the defaulted mortgages weighing down bank portfolios, one of the early proposals of then–Treasury secretary Henry Paulson was for the government to buy bad assets at "hold to maturity" prices based on estimates of intrinsic value in a normally functioning market. In that spirit, FASB approved new guidelines in 2009 allowing valuation based on an estimate of the price that would prevail in an orderly market rather than the one that could be received in a forced liquidation.

Waiving write-down requirements may best be viewed as thinly veiled regulatory forbearance. Regulators know that losses have been incurred and that capital has been impaired. But by allowing firms to carry assets on their books at model rather than market prices, the unpleasant implications of that fact for capital adequacy may be politely ignored for a time. Even so, if the goal is to avoid forced sales in a distressed market, transparency may nevertheless be the best policy. Better to acknowledge losses and explicitly modify capital regulations to help institutions recover their footing in a difficult economy than to deal with losses by ignoring them. After all, why bother preparing financial statements if they are allowed to obscure the true condition of the firm?

Before abandoning fair value accounting, it would be prudent to consider the alternative. Traditional historic-cost accounting, which would allow firms to carry assets on the books at their original purchase price, has even less to recommend it. It would leave investors without an accurate sense of the condition of shaky institutions, and by the same token lessen the pressure on those firms to get their houses in order. Dealing with losses must surely require acknowledging them.

defined benefit pension plans (which lowers the computed present value of pension obligations) during periods in which executives are actively exercising their stock options.

A contentious debate over the application of fair value accounting to troubled financial institutions erupted in 2008 when even values of financial securities such as subprime mortgage pools and derivative contracts backed by these pools came into question as trading in these instruments dried up. Without well-functioning markets, estimating (much less observing) market values was, at best, a precarious exercise. For example, employees at Credit Suisse were convicted of intentionally overstating the value of thinly traded mortgage bonds during the financial crisis to improve the apparent profitability of their trading activities.

Many observers feel that mark-to-market accounting exacerbated the financial meltdown by forcing banks to excessively write down asset values; others feel that a failure to mark would have been tantamount to willfully ignoring reality and abdicating the responsibility to redress problems at nearly or already insolvent banks. The nearby box discusses the debate.

Quality of Earnings and Accounting Practices

Many firms make accounting choices that will present their financial statements in the best possible light. The different choices available to firms give rise to the comparability problems we have discussed. As a result, earnings statements for different companies may be more or less rosy presentations of true economic earnings—sustainable cash flow that can be paid to shareholders without impairing the firm's productive capacity. Analysts commonly evaluate the **quality of earnings** reported by a firm. This concept refers to the realism and conservatism of the earnings number, in other words, the extent to which we might expect the reported level of earnings to be sustained.

Examples of the types of factors that influence quality of earnings are:

- *Allowance for bad debt.* Most firms sell goods using trade credit and must make an allowance for bad debt. An unrealistically low allowance overestimates the payments the firm is likely to receive and therefore reduces the quality of reported earnings.

- *Nonrecurring items.* Some items that affect earnings should not be expected to recur regularly. These include asset sales, effects of accounting changes, effects of exchange rate movements, or unusual investment income. For example, in years with large stock market returns, some firms enjoy large capital gains on securities held. These contribute to that year's earnings, but should not be expected to repeat regularly. Such gains would be considered a "low-quality" component of earnings. Similarly, investment gains in corporate pension plans generate large but one-off contributions to reported earnings.

- *Earnings smoothing.* In 2003, Freddie Mac was the subject of an accounting scandal when it was revealed that it had improperly reclassified mortgages held in its portfolio in an attempt to *reduce* its current earnings. Why would it take such actions? Because later, if earnings turned down, Freddie could "release" earnings by reversing these transactions, and thereby create the appearance of steady earnings growth. Indeed, almost until its sudden collapse in 2008, Freddie Mac's nickname on Wall Street was "Steady Freddie." Similarly, in the four quarters ending in October 2012, the four largest U.S. banks released $18.2 billion in reserves, which accounted for nearly one-quarter of their pretax income.[7] Such "earnings" are clearly not sustainable over the long-term and therefore must be considered low quality.

- *Revenue recognition.* Under GAAP accounting, a firm is allowed to recognize a sale before it is paid. This is why firms have accounts receivable. But sometimes it can be hard to know when to recognize sales. For example, suppose a computer firm signs a contract to provide products and services over a 5-year period. Should the projected revenue be booked immediately or spread out over five years? A more extreme version of this problem is called "channel stuffing," in which firms "sell" large quantities of goods to customers, but give them the right to later either refuse delivery or return the product. The revenue from the "sale" is booked now, but the likely returns are not recognized until they occur (in a future accounting period). Hewlett-Packard argued in 2012 that it was led to overpay for its acquisition of Autonomy Corp. when Autonomy artificially enhanced its financial performance using channel stuffing. For example, Autonomy apparently sold software valued at over £4 billion to Tikit Group; it booked the entire deal as revenue but would not be paid until Tikit actually sold software to its clients.[8] Thus, several years' worth of only tentative future sales was recognized in 2010. HP paid about $11.1 billion for Autonomy, and only one year later wrote down its investment by $8.8 billion.

---

[7]Michael Rapoport, "Bank Profit Spigot to Draw Scrutiny," *The Wall Street Journal,* October 11, 2012.
[8]Ben Worthen, Paul Sonne, and Justin Scheck, "Long Before H-P Deal, Autonomy's Red Flags," *The Wall Street Journal,* November 26, 2012.

If you see accounts receivable increasing far faster than sales, or becoming a larger percentage of total assets, beware of these practices. Given the wide latitude firms have in how they recognize revenue, many analysts choose instead to concentrate on cash flow, which is far harder for a company to manipulate.

• *Off-balance-sheet assets and liabilities.* Suppose that one firm guarantees the outstanding debt of another firm, perhaps a firm in which it has an ownership stake. That obligation ought to be disclosed as a *contingent liability,* because it may require payments down the road. But these obligations may not be reported as part of the firm's outstanding debt. Before its bankruptcy in 2001, Enron became notorious for this practice. Although it had guaranteed the debts of other companies, it failed to recognize these potential liabilities on its balance sheet. To the contrary, it obscured its exposure behind the veil of paper firms—its so-called special-purpose entities (SPEs).

  You need to keep your eye on other off-balance sheet items as well. A primary example is leasing. Airlines, for example, may show no aircraft on their balance sheets but have long-term leases that are virtually equivalent to debt-financed ownership. However, if the leases are treated as operating rather than capital leases, they may appear only as footnotes to the financial statements.

International Accounting Conventions

The examples cited above illustrate some of the problems that analysts can encounter when attempting to interpret financial data. Even greater problems arise in the interpretation of the financial statements of foreign firms. This is because these firms do not follow GAAP guidelines. Accounting practices in various countries differ to greater or lesser extents from U.S. standards. Here are some of the major issues that you should be aware of when using the financial statements of foreign firms:

• *Reserving practices.* Many countries allow firms considerably more discretion in setting aside reserves for future contingencies than is typical in the United States. Because additions to reserves result in a charge against income, reported earnings are subject to managerial discretion.

• *Depreciation.* In the United States, firms typically maintain separate sets of accounts for tax and reporting purposes. For example, accelerated depreciation is typically used for tax purposes, whereas straight-line depreciation is used for reporting purposes. In contrast, most other countries do not allow dual sets of accounts, and most firms in foreign countries use accelerated depreciation to minimize taxes despite the fact that it results in lower reported earnings. This makes reported earnings of foreign firms lower than they would be if the firms were allowed to use the U.S. practice.

• *Intangibles.* Treatment of intangibles such as goodwill can vary widely. Are they amortized or expensed? If amortized, over what period? Such issues can have a large impact on reported profits.

The effect of different accounting practices can be substantial. Figure 19.4 compares P/E ratios in different countries as reported and restated on a common basis. While P/E multiples have changed considerably since this study was published, these results illustrate how different accounting rules can have a big impact on these ratios.

Some of the differences between U.S. and European accounting standards arise from different philosophies regarding regulating accounting practice. GAAP accounting in the U.S. is rules-based, with detailed, explicit, and lengthy rules governing almost any

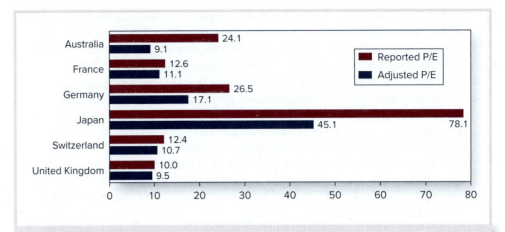

Figure 19.4 Adjusted versus reported price–earnings ratios

Source: "Figure J: Adjusted versus Reported Price/Earnings Ratio" from Lawrence S. Speidell and Vinod Bavishi, "GAAP Arbitrage: Valuation Opportunities in International Accounting Standards," *Financial Analysts Journal,* November–December 1992, pp. 58–66. Copyright 1992, CFA Institute. Reproduced from the *Financial Analysts Journal* with permission from the CFA Institute.

circumstance that can be anticipated. In contrast, the **international financial reporting standards (IFRS)** used in the European Union as well as in about 100 other countries such as Australia, Canada, Brazil, India, and China, are principles-based, setting out general approaches for the preparation of financial statements. While IFRS rules are more flexible, firms must be prepared to demonstrate that their accounting choices are consistent with its underlying principles.

For some years, the SEC worked to bring U.S. accounting standards more in line with international rules. In 2007, the SEC began allowing foreign firms to issue securities in the U.S. if their financial statements were prepared using IFRS. Subsequently, it went even further when it proposed allowing large U.S. multinational firms to report earnings using IFRS rather than GAAP and announced that it hoped to eventually adopt IFRS more broadly. But after many years of protracted negotiations, it become clear by 2014 that the SEC's plan to move to IFRS had stalled. While the SEC and IASB (International Accounting Standards Board) continue to collaborate on accounting rules, there is little immediate prospect for a single global accounting standard that will include the United States.

19.7   Value Investing: The Graham Technique

No presentation of fundamental security analysis would be complete without a discussion of the ideas of Benjamin Graham, the greatest of the investment "gurus." Until the evolution of modern portfolio theory in the latter half of the 20th century, Graham was the single most important thinker, writer, and teacher in the field of investment analysis. His influence on investment professionals, among them his now equally famous student Warren Buffet, remains very strong.

Graham's magnum opus is *Security Analysis,* written with Columbia Professor David Dodd in 1934. Its message is similar to the ideas presented in this chapter. Graham believed careful analysis of a firm's financial statements could turn up bargain stocks. Over the years, he developed many different rules for determining the most important financial ratios and the critical values for judging a stock to be undervalued. Through many editions, his book has been so influential and successful that widespread adoption of Graham's techniques has led to the elimination of the very bargains they are designed to identify.

In a 1976 seminar, Graham said:

> I am no longer an advocate of elaborate techniques of security analysis in order to find superior value opportunities. This was a rewarding activity, say, forty years ago, when our textbook "Graham and Dodd" was first published; but the situation has changed a good deal since then. In the old days any well-trained security analyst could do a good professional job of selecting undervalued issues through detailed studies; but in the light of the enormous amount of research now being carried on, I doubt whether in most cases such extensive efforts will generate sufficiently superior selections to justify their cost. To that very limited extent I'm on the side of the "efficient market" school of thought now generally accepted by the professors.[9]

Nonetheless, in that same seminar, Graham suggested a simplified approach to identifying bargain stocks:

> My first, more limited, technique confines itself to the purchase of common stocks at less than their working-capital value, or net current-asset value, giving no weight to the plant and other fixed assets, and deducting all liabilities in full from the current assets. We used this approach extensively in managing investment funds, and over a 30-odd-year period we must have earned an average of some 20 percent per year from this source. I consider it a foolproof method of systematic investment—once again, not on the basis of individual results but in terms of the expectable group income.

There are two convenient sources of information for those interested in trying out the Graham technique: Both Standard & Poor's *Outlook* and *The Value Line Investment Survey* carry lists of stocks selling below net working capital value.

[9]As cited by John Train in *Money Masters* (New York: Harper & Row, 1987).

SUMMARY

1. The primary focus of the security analyst should be the firm's real economic earnings rather than its reported earnings. Accounting earnings as reported in financial statements can be a biased estimate of real economic earnings, although empirical studies reveal that reported earnings convey considerable information concerning a firm's prospects.

2. Firm profitability depends on both the efficiency with which it uses its assets (commonly measured by turnover ratios) as well as the profitability of sales (commonly measured by profit margins). Financing decisions also should be prudent, so analysts also take great interest in leverage ratios and liquidity ratios.

3. A firm's ROE is a key determinant of the growth rate of its earnings. ROE is affected profoundly by the firm's degree of financial leverage. An increase in a firm's debt-to-equity ratio will raise its ROE and hence its growth rate only if the interest rate on the debt is less than the firm's return on assets.

4. It is often helpful to the analyst to decompose a firm's ROE ratio into the product of several accounting ratios and to analyze their separate behavior over time and across companies within an industry. A useful breakdown is

$$ROE = \frac{\text{Net profits}}{\text{Pretax profits}} \times \frac{\text{Pretax profits}}{\text{EBIT}} \times \frac{\text{EBIT}}{\text{Sales}} \times \frac{\text{Sales}}{\text{Assets}} \times \frac{\text{Assets}}{\text{Equity}}$$

5. Other accounting ratios that have a bearing on a firm's profitability and/or risk are fixed-asset turnover, inventory turnover, days sales in receivables, and the current, quick, and interest coverage ratios.

6. Two ratios that make use of the market price of the firm's common stock in addition to its financial statements are the ratios of market-to-book value and price to earnings. Analysts sometimes take low values for these ratios as a margin of safety or a sign that the stock is a bargain. However, both ratios may be better interpreted as signals of growth prospects.

7. Good firms are not necessarily good investments. Stock market prices of successful firms may be bid up to levels that reflect that success. If so, the price of these firms relative to their earnings prospects may not constitute a bargain.

8. A major problem in the use of data obtained from a firm's financial statements is comparability. Firms have a great deal of latitude in how they choose to compute various items of revenue and expense. It is, therefore, necessary for the security analyst to adjust accounting earnings and financial ratios to a uniform standard before attempting to compare financial results across firms.

9. Comparability problems can be acute in a period of inflation. Inflation can create distortions in accounting for inventories, depreciation, and interest expense.

10. Fair value or mark-to-market accounting requires that most assets be valued at current market value rather than historical cost. This policy has proved to be controversial because ascertaining true market value in many instances is difficult, and critics contend that financial statements are therefore unduly volatile. Advocates argue that financial statements should reflect the best estimate of current asset values.

11. International financial reporting standards have become progressively accepted throughout the world, even to some extent in the United States. They differ from traditional U.S. GAAP procedures in that they are principles-based rather than rules-based.

KEY TERMS

income statement	residual income	quick ratio
economic earnings	DuPont system	acid test ratio
accounting earnings	profit margin	cash ratio
balance sheet	return on sales (ROS)	market–book-value (P/B) ratio
treasury stock	total asset turnover (ATO)	price–earnings (P/E) ratio
issued shares	interest coverage ratio	LIFO
outstanding shares	times interest earned	FIFO
statement of cash flows	leverage ratio	fair value accounting
return on assets (ROA)	inventory turnover ratio	mark-to-market accounting
return on capital (ROC)	average collection period	quality of earnings
return on equity (ROE)	liquidity	international financial
economic value added (EVA)	current ratio	reporting standards (IFRS)

KEY EQUATIONS

ROE and leverage: $\text{ROE} = (1 - \text{Tax rate})\left(\text{ROA} + (\text{ROA} - \text{Interest rate})\dfrac{\text{Debt}}{\text{Equity}}\right)$

DuPont formula: $\text{ROE} = \dfrac{\text{Net profits}}{\text{Pretax profits}} \times \dfrac{\text{Pretax profits}}{\text{EBIT}} \times \dfrac{\text{EBIT}}{\text{Sales}} \times \dfrac{\text{Sales}}{\text{Assets}} \times \dfrac{\text{Assets}}{\text{Equity}}$

Another DuPont formula: $\text{ROA} = \text{Margin} \times \text{Turnover}$

PROBLEM SETS

1. Use the financial statements of Heifer Sports Inc. in Table 19A to find the following information for Heifer's:

   a. Inventory turnover ratio in 2017.
   b. Debt/equity ratio in 2017.

Income Statement	2017	
Sales	$5,500,000	
Cost of goods sold	2,850,000	
Depreciation	280,000	
Selling and administrative expenses	1,500,000	
EBIT	$ 870,000	
Interest expense	130,000	
Taxable income	$ 740,000	
Taxes	330,000	
Net income	$ 410,000	
Balance Sheet, Year-End	**2017**	**2016**
Assets		
Cash	$ 50,000	$ 40,000
Accounts receivable	660,000	690,000
Inventory	490,000	480,000
Total current assets	$1,200,000	$1,210,000
Fixed assets	3,100,000	2,800,000
Total assets	$4,300,000	$4,010,000
Liabilities and shareholders' equity		
Accounts payable	$ 340,000	$ 450,000
Short-term debt	480,000	550,000
Total current liabilities	$ 820,000	$1,000,000
Long-term bonds	2,520,000	2,200,000
Total liabilities	$3,340,000	$3,200,000
Common stock	$ 310,000	$ 310,000
Retained earnings	650,000	500,000
Total shareholders' equity	$ 960,000	$ 810,000
Total liabilities and shareholders' equity	$4,300,000	$4,010,000

Table 19A

Heifer Sports Inc. financial statements

    c. Cash flow from operating activities in 2017.
    d. Average collection period.
    e. Asset turnover ratio.
    f. Interest coverage ratio.
    g. Operating profit margin.
    h. Return on equity.
    i. P/E ratio.
    j. Compound leverage ratio.
    k. Net cash provided by operating activities.

2. What is the major difference between the approach of international financial reporting standards versus U.S. GAAP accounting? What are the advantages and disadvantages of each?

3. If markets are truly efficient, does it matter whether firms engage in earnings management? On the other hand, if firms manage earnings, what does that say about management's view on efficient markets?

4. What financial ratios would a credit rating agency such as Moody's or Standard & Poor's be most interested in? Which ratios would be of most interest to a stock market analyst deciding whether to buy a stock for a diversified portfolio?

5. The Crusty Pie Co., which specializes in apple turnovers, has a return on sales higher than the industry average, yet its ROA is the same as the industry average. How can you explain this?

6. The ABC Corporation has a profit margin on sales below the industry average, yet its ROA is above the industry average. What does this imply about its asset turnover?

7. Firm A and Firm B have the same ROA, yet Firm A's ROE is higher. How can you explain this?

8. Use the DuPont system and the following data to find return on equity.

Leverage ratio (assets/equity)	2.2
Total asset turnover	2.0
Net profit margin	5.5%
Dividend payout ratio	31.8%

9. Recently, Galaxy Corporation lowered its allowance for doubtful accounts by reducing bad debt expense from 2% of sales to 1% of sales. Ignoring taxes, what are the immediate effects on (*a*) operating income and (*b*) operating cash flow?

Use the following case in answering Problems 10 through 12: Hatfield Industries is a large manufacturing conglomerate based in the United States with annual sales in excess of $300 million. Hatfield is currently under investigation by the Securities and Exchange Commission (SEC) for accounting irregularities and possible legal violations in the presentation of the company's financial statements. A due diligence team from the SEC has been sent to Hatfield's corporate headquarters in Philadelphia for a complete audit in order to further assess the situation.

Several unique circumstances at Hatfield are discovered by the SEC due diligence team during the course of the investigation:

- Management has been involved in ongoing negotiations with the local labor union, of which approximately 40% of its full-time labor force are members. Labor officials are seeking increased wages and pension benefits, which Hatfield's management states is not possible at this time due to decreased profitability and a tight cash flow situation. Labor officials have accused Hatfield's management of manipulating the company's financial statements to justify not granting any concessions during the course of negotiations.
- All new equipment obtained over the past several years has been established on Hatfield's books as operating leases, although past acquisitions of similar equipment were nearly always classified as capital leases. Financial statements of industry peers indicate that capital leases for this type of equipment are the norm. The SEC wants Hatfield's management to provide justification for this apparent deviation from "normal" accounting practices.
- Inventory on Hatfield's books has been steadily increasing for the past few years in comparison to sales growth. Management credits the boost in overall production to improved operating efficiencies in its production methods. The SEC is seeking evidence that Hatfield somehow may have manipulated its inventory accounts.

The SEC due diligence team is not necessarily searching for evidence of fraud but of possible manipulation of accounting standards for the purpose of misleading shareholders and other interested parties. Initial review of Hatfield's financial statements indicates that, at a minimum, certain practices have resulted in low-quality earnings.

10. Labor officials believe that the management of Hatfield is attempting to understate its net income to avoid making any concessions in the labor negotiations. Which of the following actions by management will *most likely* result in low-quality earnings?

a. Lengthening the life of a depreciable asset in order to lower the depreciation expense.
b. Lowering the discount rate used in the valuation of the company's pension obligations.
c. The recognition of revenue at the time of delivery rather than when payment is received.

11. Hatfield has begun recording all new equipment leases on its books as operating leases, a change from its consistent past use of capital leases, in which the present value of lease payments is recognized as a debt obligation. What is the *most likely* motivation behind Hatfield's change in accounting methodology? Hatfield is attempting to:

a. Improve its leverage ratios and reduce its perceived leverage.

    b. Reduce its cost of goods sold and increase its profitability.

    c. Increase its operating margins relative to industry peers.

12. The SEC due diligence team is searching for the reason behind Hatfield's inventory build-up relative to its sales growth. One way to identify a deliberate manipulation of financial results by Hatfield is to search for:

    a. A decline in inventory turnover.

    b. Receivables that are growing faster than sales.

    c. A delay in the recognition of expenses.

13. A firm has an ROE of 3%, a debt-to-equity ratio of .5, and a tax rate of 35% and pays an interest rate of 6% on its debt. What is its operating ROA?

14. A firm has a tax burden ratio of .75, a leverage ratio of 1.25, an interest burden of .6, and a return on sales of 10%. The firm generates $2.40 in sales per dollar of assets. What is the firm's ROE?

15. Use the following cash flow data for Rocket Transport to find Rocket's

    a. Net cash provided by or used in investing activities.

    b. Net cash provided by or used in financing activities.

    c. Net increase or decrease in cash for the year.

Cash dividend	$ 80,000
Purchase of bus	$ 33,000
Interest paid on debt	$ 25,000
Sales of old equipment	$ 72,000
Repurchase of stock	$ 55,000
Cash payments to suppliers	$ 95,000
Cash collections from customers	$300,000

16. Consider the following data for the firms Acme and Apex:

	Equity ($ million)	Debt ($ million)	ROC (%)	Cost of Capital (%)
Acme	100	50	17	9
Apex	450	150	15	10

    a. Which firm has the higher economic value added?

    b. Which firm has the higher economic value added per dollar of invested capital?

---

1. The information in the following exhibit comes from the notes to the financial statements of QuickBrush Company and SmileWhite Corporation:

CFA® PROBLEMS

	QuickBrush	SmileWhite
Goodwill	The company amortizes goodwill over 20 years.	The company amortizes goodwill over 5 years.
Property, plant, and equipment	The company uses a straight-line depreciation method over the economic lives of the assets, which range from 5 to 20 years for buildings.	The company uses an accelerated depreciation method over the economic lives of the assets, which range from 5 to 20 years for buildings.
Accounts receivable	The company uses a bad debt allowance of 2% of accounts receivable.	The company uses a bad debt allowance of 5% of accounts receivable.

Determine which company has the higher quality of earnings by discussing each of the three notes.

2. Scott Kelly is reviewing MasterToy's financial statements in order to estimate its sustainable growth rate. Consider the information presented in the following exhibit.

MasterToy Inc.: Actual 2017 and estimated 2018 financial statements for fiscal year ending December 31 ($ million, except per-share data)

	2017	2018	Change (%)
Income Statement			
Revenue	$4,750	$5,140	7.6%
Cost of goods sold	2,400	2,540	
Selling, general, and administrative	1,400	1,550	
Depreciation	180	210	
Goodwill amortization	10	10	
Operating income	$ 760	$ 830	8.4
Interest expense	20	25	
Income before taxes	$ 740	$ 805	
Income taxes	265	295	
Net income	$ 475	$ 510	
Earnings per share	$ 1.79	$ 1.96	8.6
Average shares outstanding (millions)	265	260	
Balance Sheet			
Cash	$ 400	$ 400	
Accounts receivable	680	700	
Inventories	570	600	
Net property, plant, and equipment	800	870	
Intangibles	500	530	
Total assets	$2,950	$3,100	
Current liabilities	550	600	
Long-term debt	300	300	
Total liabilities	$ 850	$ 900	
Stockholders' equity	2,100	2,200	
Total liabilities and equity	$2,950	$3,100	
Book value per share	$ 7.92	$ 8.46	
Annual dividend per share	$ 0.55	$ 0.60	

a. Identify and calculate the components of the DuPont formula.
b. Calculate the ROE for 2018 using the components of the DuPont formula.
c. Calculate the sustainable growth rate for 2018 from the firm's ROE and plowback ratios.

3. Use the following data to solve this problem.

Cash payments for interest	$(12)
Retirement of common stock	(32)
Cash payments to merchandise suppliers	(85)
Purchase of land	(8)
Sale of equipment	30
Payments of dividends	(37)
Cash payment for salaries	(35)
Cash collection from customers	260
Purchase of equipment	(40)

a. What are cash flows from operating activities?
b. What are cash flows from investing activities?
c. What are cash flows from financing activities?

4. Janet Ludlow is a recently hired analyst. After describing the electric toothbrush industry, her first report focuses on two companies, QuickBrush Company and SmileWhite Corporation, and concludes:

> QuickBrush is a more profitable company than SmileWhite, as indicated by the 40% sales growth and substantially higher margins it has produced over the last few years. SmileWhite's sales and earnings are growing at a 10% rate and produce much lower margins. We do not think SmileWhite is capable of growing faster than its recent growth rate of 10%, whereas QuickBrush can sustain a 30% long-term growth rate.

a. Criticize Ludlow's analysis and conclusion that QuickBrush is more profitable, as defined by return on equity (ROE), than SmileWhite and that it has a higher sustainable growth rate. Use only the information provided in Tables 19B and 19C. Support your criticism by calculating and analyzing:

- The five components that determine ROE.
- The two ratios that determine sustainable growth: ROE and plowback.

Income Statement	December 2015	December 2016	December 2017	
Revenue	$3,480	$5,400	$7,760	
Cost of goods sold	2,700	4,270	6,050	
Selling, general, and administrative expense	500	690	1,000	
Depreciation and amortization	30	40	50	
Operating income (EBIT)	$ 250	$ 400	$ 660	
Interest expense	0	0	0	
Income before taxes	$ 250	$ 400	$ 660	
Income taxes	60	110	215	
Income after taxes	$ 190	$ 290	$ 445	
Diluted EPS	$ 0.60	$ 0.84	$ 1.18	
Average shares outstanding (000)	317	346	376	
Financial Statistics	**December 2015**	**December 2016**	**December 2017**	**3-Year Average**
COGS as % of sales	77.59%	79.07%	77.96%	78.24%
General and administrative as % of sales	14.37	12.78	12.89	13.16
Operating margin	7.18	7.41	8.51	
Pretax income/EBIT	100.00	100.00	100.00	
Tax rate	24.00	27.50	32.58	
Balance Sheet	**December 2015**	**December 2016**	**December 2017**	
Cash and cash equivalents	$ 460	$ 50	$ 480	
Accounts receivable	540	720	950	
Inventories	300	430	590	
Net property, plant, and equipment	760	1,830	3,450	
Total assets	$2,060	$3,030	$5,470	
Current liabilities	$ 860	$1,110	$1,750	
Total liabilities	$ 860	$1,110	$1,750	
Stockholders' equity	1,200	1,920	3,720	
Total liabilities and equity	$2,060	$3,030	$5,470	
Market price per share	$21.00	$30.00	$45.00	
Book value per share	$ 3.79	$ 5.55	$ 9.89	
Annual dividend per share	$ 0.00	$ 0.00	$ 0.00	

Table 19B

QuickBrush Company financial statements: yearly data ($000 except per-share data)

Income Statement	December 2015	December 2016	December 2017	
Revenue	$104,000	$110,400	$119,200	
Cost of goods sold	72,800	75,100	79,300	
Selling, general, and administrative expense	20,300	22,800	23,900	
Depreciation and amortization	4,200	5,600	8,300	
Operating income	$ 6,700	$ 6,900	$ 7,700	
Interest expense	600	350	350	
Income before taxes	$ 6,100	$ 6,550	$ 7,350	
Income taxes	2,100	2,200	2,500	
Income after taxes	$ 4,000	$ 4,350	$ 4,850	
Diluted EPS	$ 2.16	$ 2.35	$ 2.62	
Average shares outstanding (000)	1,850	1,850	1,850	

Financial Statistics	December 2015	December 2016	December 2017	3-Year Average
COGS as % of sales	70.00%	68.00%	66.53%	68.10%
General and administrative as % of sales	19.52	20.64	20.05	20.08
Operating margin	6.44	6.25	6.46	
Pretax income/EBIT	91.04	94.93	95.45	
Tax rate	34.43	33.59	34.01	

Balance Sheet	December 2015	December 2016	December 2017
Cash and cash equivalents	$ 7,900	$ 3,300	$ 1,700
Accounts receivable	7,500	8,000	9,000
Inventories	6,300	6,300	5,900
Net property, plant, and equipment	12,000	14,500	17,000
Total assets	$ 33,700	$ 32,100	$ 33,600
Current liabilities	$ 6,200	$ 7,800	$ 6,600
Long-term debt	9,000	4,300	4,300
Total liabilities	$ 15,200	$ 12,100	$ 10,900
Stockholders' equity	18,500	20,000	22,700
Total liabilities and equity	$ 33,700	$ 32,100	$ 33,600
Market price per share	$ 23.00	$ 26.00	$ 30.00
Book value per share	$ 10.00	$ 10.81	$ 12.27
Annual dividend per share	$ 1.42	$ 1.53	$ 1.72

Table 19C

SmileWhite Corporation financial statements: yearly data ($000 except per-share data)

b. Explain how QuickBrush has produced an average annual earnings per share (EPS) growth rate of 40% over the last two years with an ROE that has been declining. Use only the information provided in Table 19B.

Use the following case in answering CFA Problems 5 through 8: Eastover Company (EO) is a large, diversified forest products company. Approximately 75% of its sales are from paper and forest products, with the remainder from financial services and real estate. The company owns 5.6 million acres of timberland, which is carried at very low historical cost on the balance sheet.

Peggy Mulroney, CFA, is an analyst at the investment counseling firm of Centurion Investments. She is assigned the task of assessing the outlook for Eastover, which is being considered for purchase, and comparing it to another forest products company in Centurion's portfolios, Southampton Corporation (SHC). SHC is a major producer of lumber products in the United States. Building products, primarily lumber and plywood, account for 89% of SHC's sales, with pulp accounting for the remainder. SHC owns 1.4 million acres of timberland, which is also carried at historical cost on the balance sheet. In SHC's case, however, that cost is not as far below current market as Eastover's.

Mulroney began her examination of Eastover and Southampton by looking at the five components of return on equity (ROE) for each company. For her analysis, Mulroney elected to define equity as total shareholders' equity, including preferred stock. She also elected to use year-end data rather than averages for the balance sheet items.

5. *a.* On the basis of the data shown in Tables 19D and 19E, calculate each of the five ROE components for Eastover and Southampton in 2017. Using the five components, calculate ROE for both companies in 2017.

   b. Referring to the components calculated in part (*a*), explain the difference in ROE for Eastover and Southampton in 2017.

   c. Using 2017 data, calculate the sustainable growth rate for both Eastover and Southampton. Discuss the appropriateness of using these calculations as a basis for estimating future growth.

Income Statement Summary	2013	2014	2015	2016	2017
Sales	$5,652	$6,990	$7,863	$8,281	$7,406
Earnings before interest and taxes (EBIT)	$ 568	$ 901	$1,037	$ 708	$ 795
Interest expense (net)	(147)	(188)	(186)	(194)	(195)
Income before taxes	$ 421	$ 713	$ 851	$ 514	$ 600
Income taxes	(144)	(266)	(286)	(173)	(206)
Tax rate	34%	37%	33%	34%	34%
Net income	$ 277	$ 447	$ 565	$ 341	$ 394
Preferred dividends	(28)	(17)	(17)	(17)	(0)
Net income to common	$ 249	$ 430	$ 548	$ 324	$ 394
Common shares outstanding (millions)	196	204	204	205	201
Balance Sheet Summary	**2013**	**2014**	**2015**	**2016**	**2017**
Current assets	$1,235	$1,491	$1,702	$1,585	$1,367
Timberland assets	649	625	621	612	615
Property, plant, and equipment	4,370	4,571	5,056	5,430	5,854
Other assets	360	555	473	472	429
Total assets	$6,614	$7,242	$7,852	$8,099	$8,265
Current liabilities	$1,226	$1,186	$1,206	$1,606	$1,816
Long-term debt	1,120	1,340	1,585	1,346	1,585
Deferred taxes	1,000	1,000	1,016	1,000	1,000
Equity–preferred	364	350	350	400	0
Equity–common	2,904	3,366	3,695	3,747	3,864
Total liabilities and equity	$6,614	$7,242	$7,852	$8,099	$8,265

Table 19D

Eastover Company ($ million, except shares outstanding)

Income Statement Summary	2013	2014	2015	2016	2017
Sales	$1,306	$1,654	$1,799	$2,010	$1,793
Earnings before interest and taxes (EBIT)	$ 120	$ 230	$ 221	$ 304	$ 145
Interest expense (net)	(13)	(36)	(7)	(12)	(8)
Income before taxes	$ 107	$ 194	$ 214	$ 292	$ 137
Income taxes	(44)	(75)	(79)	(99)	(46)
Tax rate	41%	39%	37%	34%	34%
Net income	$ 63	$ 119	$ 135	$ 193	$ 91
Common shares outstanding (millions)	38	38	38	38	38
Balance Sheet Summary	2013	2014	2015	2016	2017
Current assets	$ 487	$ 504	$ 536	$ 654	$ 509
Timberland assets	512	513	508	513	518
Property, plant, and equipment	648	681	718	827	1,037
Other assets	141	151	34	38	40
Total assets	$1,788	$1,849	$1,796	$2,032	$2,104
Current liabilities	$ 185	$ 176	$ 162	$ 180	$ 195
Long-term debt	536	493	370	530	589
Deferred taxes	123	136	127	146	153
Equity	944	1,044	1,137	1,176	1,167
Total liabilities and equity	$1,788	$1,849	$1,796	$2,032	$2,104

Table 19E

Southampton Corporation ($ million, except shares outstanding)

6. *a.* Mulroney recalled from her CFA studies that the constant-growth discounted dividend model was one way to arrive at a valuation for a company's common stock. She collected current dividend and stock price data for Eastover and Southampton, shown in Table 19F. Using 11% as the required rate of return (i.e., discount rate) and a projected growth rate of 8%, compute a constant-growth DDM value for Eastover's stock and compare the computed value for Eastover to its stock price indicated in Table 19G.

   b. Mulroney's supervisor commented that a two-stage DDM may be more appropriate for companies such as Eastover and Southampton. Mulroney believes that Eastover and Southampton could grow more rapidly over the next three years (i.e., 2019–2021) and then settle in at a lower but sustainable rate of growth beyond 2021. Her estimates are indicated in Table 19H. Using 11% as the required rate of return, compute the two-stage DDM value of Eastover's stock and compare that value to its stock price indicated in Table 19G.

   c. Discuss advantages and disadvantages of using a constant-growth DDM. Briefly discuss how the two-stage DDM improves upon the constant-growth DDM.

7. In addition to the discounted dividend model approach, Mulroney decided to look at the price–earnings ratio and price–book ratio, relative to the S&P 500, for both Eastover and Southampton. Mulroney elected to perform this analysis using 2014–2018 and current data.

   a. Using the data in Tables 19F and 19G, compute both the current and the 5-year (2014–2018) average relative price–earnings ratios and relative price–book ratios for Eastover and Southampton (i.e., ratios relative to those for the S&P 500). Discuss each company's current (2018) relative price–earnings ratio compared to its 5-year average relative price–earnings ratio and each company's current relative price–book ratio as compared to its 5-year average relative price–book ratio.

   b. Briefly discuss one disadvantage for each of the relative price–earnings and relative price–book approaches to valuation.

	2013	2014	2015	2016	2017	2018	5-Year Average (2014–2018)
Eastover Company							
Earnings per share	$ 1.27	$ 2.12	$ 2.68	$ 1.56	$ 1.87	$ 0.90	
Dividends per share	0.87	0.90	1.15	1.20	1.20	1.20	
Book value per share	14.82	16.54	18.14	18.55	19.21	17.21	
Stock price							
High	28	40	30	33	28	30	
Low	20	20	23	25	18	20	
Close	25	26	25	28	22	27	
Average P/E	18.9	14.2	9.9	18.6	12.3	27.8	
Average P/B	1.6	1.8	1.5	1.6	1.2	1.5	
Southampton Corporation							
Earnings per share	$ 1.66	$ 3.13	$ 3.55	$ 5.08	$ 2.46	$ 1.75	
Dividends per share	0.77	0.79	0.89	0.98	1.04	1.08	
Book value per share	24.84	27.47	29.92	30.95	31.54	32.21	
Stock price							
High	34	40	38	43	45	46	
Low	21	22	26	28	20	26	
Close	31	27	28	39	27	44	
Average P/E	16.6	9.9	9.0	7.0	13.2	20.6	
Average P/B	1.1	1.1	1.1	1.2	1.0	1.1	
S&P 500							
Average P/E	15.8	16.0	11.1	13.9	15.6	19.2	15.2
Average P/B	1.8	2.1	1.9	2.2	2.1	2.3	2.1

Table 19F

Valuation of Eastover Company and Southampton Corporation compared to S&P 500

	Current Share Price	Current Dividends per Share	2019 EPS Estimate	Current Book Value per Share
Eastover	$ 28	$ 1.20	$ 1.60	$ 17.32
Southampton	48	1.08	3.00	32.21
S&P 500	1660	48.00	82.16	639.32

Table 19G

Current information

	Next 3 Years (2019, 2020, 2021)	Growth Beyond 2021
Eastover	12%	8%
Southampton	13%	7%

Table 19H

Projected growth rates as of year-end 2018

8. Mulroney previously calculated a valuation for Southampton for both the constant-growth and two-stage DDM as shown below:

Constant-Growth Approach	Two-Stage Approach
$29	$35.50

Using only the information provided and your answers to CFA Problems 5 through 7, select the stock (EO or SHC) that Mulroney should recommend as the better value, and justify your selection.

9. In reviewing the financial statements of the Graceland Rock Company, you note that net income increased while cash flow from operations decreased from 2017 to 2018.

   a. Explain how net income could increase for Graceland Rock Company while cash flow from operations decreased. Give some illustrative examples.
   b. Explain why cash flow from operations may be a good indicator of a firm's "quality of earnings."

10. A firm has net sales of $3,000, cash expenses (including taxes) of $1,400, and depreciation of $500. If accounts receivable increase over the period by $400, what would be cash flow from operations?

11. A company's current ratio is 2.0. Suppose the company uses cash to retire notes payable due within one year. What would be the effect on the current ratio and asset turnover ratio?

12. Jones Group has been generating stable after-tax return on equity (ROE) despite declining operating income. Explain how it might be able to maintain its stable after-tax ROE.

13. The DuPont formula defines the net return on shareholders' equity as a function of the following components:

   - Operating margin
   - Asset turnover
   - Interest burden
   - Financial leverage
   - Income tax rate

   Using only the data in Table 19I:

   a. Calculate each of the five components listed above for 2014 and 2018, and calculate the return on equity (ROE) for 2014 and 2018, using all of the five components.
   b. Briefly discuss the impact of the changes in asset turnover and financial leverage on the change in ROE from 2014 to 2018.

	2014	2018
Income Statement Data		
Revenues	$542	$979
Operating income	38	76
Depreciation and amortization	3	9
Interest expense	3	0
Pretax income	32	67
Income taxes	13	37
Net income after tax	$ 19	$ 30
Balance Sheet Data		
Fixed assets	$ 41	$ 70
Total assets	245	291
Working capital	123	157
Total debt	$ 16	$ 0
Total shareholders' equity	$159	$220

Table 19I

Income statements and balance sheets

E-INVESTMENTS EXERCISES

1. Go to **finance.yahoo.com** to find information about Vulcan Materials Company (VMC), Southwest Airlines (LUV), Honda Motor Company (HMC), Nordstrom, Inc. (JWN), and Abbott Laboratories (ABT). Download the most recent income statement and balance sheet for each company.

   a. Calculate the operating profit margin (Operating profit/Sales) and the asset turnover (Sales/Assets) for each firm.

   b. Calculate the return on assets directly (ROA = Operating profit/Total assets), and then confirm it by calculating ROA = Operating margin × Asset turnover.

   c. In what industries do these firms operate? Do the ratios make sense when you consider the industry types?

   d. For the firms that have relatively low ROAs, does the source of the problem seem to be the operating profit margin, the asset turnover, or both?

   e. Calculate the return on equity (ROE = Net income/Equity) for each firm. For the two firms with the lowest ROEs, perform a DuPont analysis to isolate the source(s) of the problem.

2. From Yahoo's Industry Center (**biz.yahoo.com/ie/**) select *Complete Industry List* and then the Toys & Games industry. Pick two companies from the list and do the following for each firm:

   a. Retrieve the latest annual balance sheet for each company. Calculate the common-size percentages for the balance sheet in the new column.

   b. Compare the firms' investments in accounts receivable, inventory, and net plant, property, and equipment. Which firm has more invested in these items on a percentage basis?

   c. Compare the firms' investments in current liabilities and long-term liabilities. Does one firm have a significantly higher burden in either of these areas?

   d. Analyze the firms' capital structures by examining the debt ratios and the percentages of preferred and common equity. How much do the firms' capital structures differ from each other?

3. Select a company of interest to you and link to its annual cash flow statement under the company's *Financials* tab. Answer the following questions about the firm's cash flow activities.

   a. Did the firm have positive or negative cash flow from operations?

   b. Did the firm invest in or sell off long-term investments?

   c. What were the major sources of financing for the firm?

   d. What was the net change in cash?

   e. Did exchange rates have any effect on the firm's cash flows?

   Now answer these questions:

   f. How liquid is the firm?

   g. How well is the firm using its assets?

   h. How effectively is the firm using leverage?

   i. How profitable is the firm?

✓ SOLUTIONS TO CONCEPT CHECKS

1. A debt-to-equity ratio of 1 implies that Mordett will have $50 million of debt and $50 million of equity. Interest expense will be .09 × $50 million, or $4.5 million per year. Mordett's net profits and ROE over the business cycle will therefore be

Scenario	EBIT	Nodett		Mordett	
		Net Profits	ROE	Net Profits*	ROE†
Bad year	$ 5 million	$3 million	3%	$0.3 million	.6%
Normal year	10	6	6	3.3	6.6
Good year	15	9	9	6.3	12.6

*Mordett's after-tax profits are given by .6 (EBIT − $4.5 million).
†Mordett's equity is only $50 million.

2.

Ratio Decomposition Analysis for Mordett

	ROE	(1) Net Profits/ Pretax Profits	(2) Pretax Profits/EBIT	(3) EBIT/Sales (Margin)	(4) Sales/Assets (Turnover)	(5) Assets/ Equity	(6) Compound Leverage Factor (2) × (5)
Bad year							
Nodett	0.030	0.6	1.000	0.0625	0.800	1.000	1.000
Somdett	0.018	0.6	0.360	0.0625	0.800	1.667	0.600
Mordett	0.006	0.6	0.100	0.0625	0.800	2.000	0.200
Normal year							
Nodett	0.060	0.6	1.000	0.100	1.000	1.000	1.000
Somdett	0.068	0.6	0.680	0.100	1.000	1.667	1.134
Mordett	0.066	0.6	0.550	0.100	1.000	2.000	1.100
Good year							
Nodett	0.090	0.6	1.000	0.125	1.200	1.000	1.000
Somdett	0.118	0.6	0.787	0.125	1.200	1.667	1.311
Mordett	0.126	0.6	0.700	0.125	1.200	2.000	1.400

3. GI's ROE in 2017 was 3.03%, computed as follows:

$$ROE = \frac{\$5,285}{.5(\$171,843 + \$177,128)} = .0303, \text{ or } 3.03\%$$

Its P/E ratio was 4 = $21/$5.285 and its P/B ratio was .12 = $21/$177. Its earnings yield was 25% compared with an industry average of 12.5%.

Note that in our calculations P/E does not equal (P/B)/ROE because (following common practice) we have computed ROE with *average* shareholders' equity in the denominator and P/B with *end*-of-year shareholders' equity in the denominator.

4.

IBX Ratio Analysis

Year	ROE	(1) Net Profits/ Pretax Profits	(2) Pretax Profits/ EBIT	(3) EBIT/Sales (Margin)	(4) Sales/ Assets (Turnover)	(5) Assets/ Equity	(6) Compound Leverage Factor (2) × (5)	(7) ROA (3) × (4)
2018	11.4%	0.616	0.796	7.75%	1.375	2.175	1.731	10.65%
2016	10.2	0.636	0.932	8.88	1.311	1.474	1.374	11.65

ROE increased despite a decline in operating margin and a decline in the tax-burden ratio because of increased leverage and turnover. Note that ROA declined from 11.65% in 2016 to 10.65% in 2018.

5. LIFO accounting results in lower reported earnings than does FIFO. Fewer assets to depreciate result in lower reported earnings because there is less bias associated with the use of historic cost. More debt results in lower reported earnings because the inflation premium in the interest rate is treated as part of interest expense and not as repayment of principal. If ABC has the same reported earnings as XYZ despite these three sources of downward bias, its real earnings must be greater.

Options Markets: Introduction

DERIVATIVE SECURITIES, OR more simply *derivatives,* play a large and increasingly important role in financial markets. These are securities whose prices are determined by, or "derive from," the prices of other securities.

Options and futures contracts are both derivative securities. Their payoffs depend on the value of other securities. Swaps, which we will discuss in Chapter 23, also are derivatives. Because the values of derivatives depend on the values of other securities, they can be powerful tools for both hedging and speculation. We will investigate these applications in the next four chapters, starting in this chapter with options.

Trading of standardized options contracts on a national exchange started in 1973 when the Chicago Board Options Exchange (CBOE) began listing call options. These contracts were almost immediately a great success, crowding out the previously existing over-the-counter options market.

Option contracts are traded now on several exchanges. They are written on common stock, stock indexes, foreign exchange, agricultural commodities, precious metals, and interest rate futures. In addition, the over-the-counter market has enjoyed a tremendous resurgence in recent years as trading in custom-tailored options has exploded. Popular and potent tools in modifying portfolio characteristics, options have become essential tools a portfolio manager must understand.

This chapter is an introduction to options markets. It explains how puts and calls work and examines their investment characteristics. Popular option strategies are considered next. Finally, we examine a range of securities with embedded options such as callable or convertible bonds, and we take a quick look at some so-called exotic options.

20.1 The Option Contract

A **call option** gives its holder the right to purchase an asset for a specified price, called the **exercise** or **strike price,** on or before some specified expiration date. For example, a February call option on shares of IBM with exercise price $150 entitles its owner to purchase IBM for a price of $150 at any time up to and including the expiration date in

February. The holder of the call is not required to exercise it. She will exercise her option to buy only if IBM's share price exceeds the strike price. If the share price remains below the strike price, the option will be left unexercised. If not exercised before the expiration date, a call option simply expires and becomes valueless. Therefore, on the expiration date, if the stock price is greater than the exercise price, the call value equals the difference between the stock price and the exercise price; but if the stock price is less than the exercise price, the call expires worthless. The *net profit* on the call is the value of the option minus the price originally paid to purchase it.

The purchase price of the option is called the **premium.** It represents the compensation the call buyer pays for the right to exercise only when exercise is desirable.

Sellers of call options, who are said to *write* calls, receive premium income now as payment against the possibility they will be required at some later date to deliver the asset in return for an exercise price less than the market value of the asset. If the option is left to expire worthless, the call writer clears a profit equal to the premium collected when the option was initially sold. But if the call is exercised, the option writer's profit is the premium income *minus* the difference between the value of the stock that must be delivered and the exercise price that is paid for those shares. If that difference is larger than the initial premium, the writer will incur a loss.

Example 20.1   Profits and Losses on a Call Option

Consider the August 2016 expiration call option on a share of IBM with an exercise price of $150 selling on June 30, 2016, for $4.10. Until the expiration date, the call holder may exercise the option to buy shares of IBM for $150. Because the stock price on June 30 is only $149.60, it clearly would not make sense at the moment to exercise the option to buy at $150. Indeed, if IBM remains below $150 by the expiration date, the call will be left to expire worthless. On the other hand, if IRM is selling above $150 at expiration, the call holder will find it optimal to exercise. For example, if IBM sells for $152 on August 19, the option will be exercised, as it will give its holder the right to pay $150 for a stock worth $152. The value of each option on the expiration date would then be

$$\text{Value at expiration} = \text{Stock price} - \text{Exercise price} = \$152 - \$150 = \$2$$

Despite the $2 payoff at expiration, the call holder still realizes a loss of $2.10 on the investment because the initial purchase price was $4.10:

$$\text{Profit} = \text{Final value} - \text{Original investment} = \$2.00 - \$4.10 = -\$2.10$$

Nevertheless, exercise of the call is optimal at expiration if the stock price exceeds the exercise price because the exercise proceeds will offset at least part of the purchase price. The call buyer will clear a profit if IBM is selling above $154.10 at the expiration date. At that stock price, the net proceeds from exercise will just cover the original cost of the call.

A **put option** gives its holder the right to *sell* an asset for a specified exercise or strike price on or before some expiration date. An August expiration put on IBM with an exercise price of $150 entitles its owner to sell IBM stock to the put writer for $150 even if the market price of IBM is less than that value. Whereas profits on call options increase when the asset price rises, profits on put options increase when the asset price *falls*. A put will be exercised only if the price of the underlying asset is less than the exercise price, that is, only if its holder can deliver for the exercise price an asset with a lesser market value. (One doesn't need to own the shares of IBM to exercise the put option. Upon exercise, the investor's broker purchases the necessary shares of IBM at the market price and immediately delivers, or "puts them," to an option writer for the exercise price.) The owner of the put profits by the difference between the exercise price and market price.

Example 20.2   Profits and Losses on a Put Option

Now consider the August 2016 expiration put option on IBM with an exercise price of $150, selling on June 30 for $5.91. It entitled its owner to sell a share of IBM for $150 at any time until August 19. If the holder of the put buys a share of IBM and immediately exercises the right to sell it at $150, net proceeds will be $150 − $149.60 = $.40. Obviously, an investor who pays $5.91 for the put has no intention of exercising it immediately. If, on the other hand, IBM is selling for $141 at expiration, the put will turn out to be a profitable investment. Its value at expiration would be

$$\text{Value at expiration} = \text{Exercise price} - \text{Stock price} = \$150 - \$141 = \$9$$

and the investor's profit would be $9 − $5.91 = $3.09. This is a holding period return of $3.09/$5.91 = .52, or 52%—over only 50 days! Obviously, put option sellers on June 30 (who are on the other side of the transaction) would not consider this outcome to be very likely.

An option is described as **in the money** when its exercise would produce a positive cash flow. Therefore, a call option is in the money when the asset price is greater than the exercise price, and a put option is in the money when the asset price is less than the exercise price. Conversely, a call is **out of the money** when the asset price is less than the exercise price; no one would exercise the right to purchase for the strike price an asset worth less than that amount. A put option is out of the money when the exercise price is less than the asset price. Options are **at the money** when the exercise price and asset price are equal.

Options Trading

Some options trade on over-the-counter (OTC) markets. The OTC market offers the advantage that the terms of the option contract—the exercise price, expiration date, and number of shares committed—can be tailored to the needs of the traders. The costs of establishing an OTC option contract, however, are higher than for exchange-traded options.

Options contracts traded on exchanges are standardized by allowable expiration dates and exercise prices for each listed option. Each stock option contract provides for the right to buy or sell 100 shares of stock (except when stock splits occur after the contract is listed and the contract is adjusted for the terms of the split).

Standardization of the terms of listed option contracts means all market participants trade in a limited and uniform set of securities. This increases the depth of trading in any particular option, which lowers trading costs and increases market liquidity.

Most options trading in the United States initially took place on the Chicago Board Options Exchange (CBOE). However, by 2003 the electronic International Securities Exchange displaced the CBOE as the largest options market, and virtually all trading today is electronic.

PRICES AT CLOSE JUNE 30, 2016

I B M (IBM) Underlying Stock Price: 149.60

Expiration	Strike	Call Last	Call Volume	Call Open Interest	Put Last	Put Volume	Put Open Interest
July 15, 2016	145	5.18	37	6319	0.48	79	5659
August 19, 2016	145	6.98	137	1943	3.60	512	2476
October 21, 2016	145	8.42	12	1310	6.35	80	1086
July 15, 2016	150	1.85	478	6521	1.81	1649	5763
August 19, 2016	150	4.10	472	2373	5.91	81	2911
October 21, 2016	150	5.43	23	2604	8.42	77	3101
July 15, 2016	155	0.79	337	13492	5.95	77	3847
August 19, 2016	155	1.90	113	5215	8.45	9	1748
October 21, 2016	155	3.60	8	1681	11.70	12	728

Figure 20.1 Prices of stock options on IBM on June 30, 2016

Source: Google Finance, **www.google.com/finance.**

Figure 20.1 is a small sample of listed stock option quotations for IBM on June 30, 2016. The most recent recorded price for IBM shares was $149.60 per share,[1] so the exercise (or strike) prices in the figure bracket the current stock price. If the stock price moves outside the range of exercise prices of the existing set of options, new options with appropriate exercise prices may be offered. Therefore, at any time, both in-the-money and out-of-the-money options will be listed, as in this figure.

Figure 20.1 shows both call and put options listed for each expiration date and exercise price. The three sets of columns for each option report closing price, trading volume in contracts, and open interest (number of outstanding contracts). When we compare prices of call options with the same expiration date but different exercise prices in Figure 20.1, we see that the value of a call is lower when the exercise price is higher. This makes sense, because the right to purchase a share at a lower exercise price is more valuable than the right to purchase at a higher price. Thus, the August expiration IBM call option with strike price $150 sells for $4.10, whereas the $155 exercise price August call sells for only $1.90. Conversely, put options are worth *more* when the exercise price is higher: You would rather have the right to sell shares for $155 than for $150 and this is reflected in the prices of the puts. Thus, the August expiration put option with strike price $155 sells for $8.45, whereas the $150 exercise price August put sells for only $5.91.

Because trading in any particular option can be sporadic, it is not unusual to find option prices that appear out of line with other prices. You might see, for example, two calls with different exercise prices that seem to sell for the same price. This discrepancy arises because the last trades for these options may have occurred at different times during the day. At any moment, the call with the lower exercise price must be worth more than an otherwise-identical call with a higher exercise price.

Expirations of most exchange-traded options tend to be fairly short, ranging up to only several months. For larger firms and several stock indexes, however, longer-term options are traded with expirations ranging up to several years. These options are called LEAPS (for *Long-Term Equity AnticiPation Securities*).

Concept Check **20.1**

a. What will be the proceeds and net profits to an investor who purchases the August expiration IBM calls with exercise price $150 if the stock price at expiration is $160? What if the stock price at expiration is $140?

b. Now answer part (*a*) for an investor who purchases the August expiration IBM put option with exercise price $150.

[1]Occasionally, this price may not match the closing price listed for the stock on the stock market page. This is because some NYSE stocks also trade on exchanges that close after the NYSE, and the stock pages may reflect the more recent closing price. The options exchanges, however, close with the NYSE, so the closing NYSE stock price is appropriate for comparison with the closing option price.

American and European Options

An **American option** allows its holder to exercise the right to purchase (if a call) or sell (if a put) the underlying asset on *or before* the expiration date. **European options** allow for exercise of the option only on the expiration date. American options, because they allow more leeway than their European counterparts, generally will be more valuable. Most traded options in the United States are American style. Foreign currency options and stock index options are notable exceptions to this rule, however.

Adjustments in Option Contract Terms

Because options convey the right to buy or sell shares at a stated price, stock splits would radically alter their value if the terms of the options contract were not adjusted to account for the stock split. For example, reconsider the IBM call options in Figure 20.1. If IBM were to announce a 2-for-1 split, its share price would fall from about $150 to about $75. A call option with exercise price $150 would be just about worthless, with virtually no possibility that the stock would sell at more than $150 before the options expired.

To account for a stock split, the exercise price is reduced by a factor of the split, and the number of options held is increased by that factor. For example, each original call option with exercise price of $150 would be altered after a 2-for-1 split to two new options, with each new option carrying an exercise price of $75. A similar adjustment is made for stock dividends of more than 10%; the number of shares covered by each option is increased in proportion to the stock dividend, and the exercise price is reduced by that proportion.

In contrast to stock dividends, cash dividends do not affect the terms of an option contract. Because payment of a cash dividend reduces the selling price of the stock without inducing offsetting adjustments in the option contract, the value of the option is affected by dividend policy. Other things being equal, call option values are lower for high-dividend payout policies, because such policies slow the rate of increase of stock prices; conversely, put values are higher for high-dividend payouts. (Of course, the option values do not necessarily rise or fall on the dividend payment or ex-dividend dates. Dividend payments are anticipated, so the effect of the payment already is built into the original option price.)

 Concept Check **20.2**

> Suppose that IBM's stock price at the exercise date is $160, and the exercise price of the call is $150. What is the payoff on one option contract? After a 2-for-1 split, the stock price is $80, the exercise price is $75, and the option holder now can purchase 200 shares. Show that the split leaves the payoff from the option unaffected.

The Options Clearing Corporation

The Options Clearing Corporation (OCC), the clearinghouse for options trading, is jointly owned by the exchanges on which stock options are traded. Buyers and sellers of options who agree on a price will strike a deal. At this point, the OCC steps in. The OCC places itself between the two traders, becoming the effective buyer of the option from the writer and the effective writer of the option to the buyer. All individuals, therefore, deal only with the OCC, which effectively guarantees contract performance.

When an option holder exercises an option, the OCC arranges for a member firm with clients who have written that option to make good on the option obligation. The member firm selects from its clients who have written that option to fulfill the contract. The selected client must deliver 100 shares of stock for each call option contract written or must purchase 100 shares at the exercise price for each put option contract written.

Because the OCC guarantees contract performance, it requires option writers to post margin to guarantee that they can fulfill their obligations. The margin required is determined in part by the amount by which the option is in the money, because that value is an indicator of the potential obligation of the option writer. When the required margin exceeds the posted margin, the writer will receive a margin call. In contrast, the holder of the option need not post margin because the holder will exercise the option only if it is advantageous to do so. After purchase of the option, no further money is at risk.

Margin requirements are determined in part by the other securities held in the investor's portfolio. For example, a call option writer owning the stock against which the option is written can satisfy the margin requirement simply by allowing a broker to hold that stock in the brokerage account. The stock is then guaranteed to be available for delivery should the call option be exercised. If the underlying security is not owned, however, the margin requirement is determined by the value of the underlying security as well as by the amount by which the option is in or out of the money. Out-of-the-money options require less margin from the writer, for expected payouts are lower.

Other Listed Options

Options on assets other than stocks are also widely traded. These include options on market indexes and industry indexes, on foreign currency, and even on the futures prices of agricultural products, gold, silver, fixed-income securities, and stock indexes. We will discuss some of these products.

Index Options   An index option is a call or put based on a stock market index such as the S&P 500 or the NASDAQ 100. Index options are traded on several broad-based indexes as well as on several industry-specific indexes and even commodity price indexes. We discussed many of these indexes in Chapter 2.

The construction of the indexes can vary across contracts or exchanges. For example, the S&P 100 index is a value-weighted average of the 100 stocks in the Standard & Poor's 100 stock group. The weights are proportional to the market value of outstanding equity for each stock. The Dow Jones Industrial Index, by contrast, is a price-weighted average of 30 stocks.

Option contracts on many foreign stock indexes also trade. For example, options on the (Japanese) Nikkei Stock Index trade on the Singapore as well as the Chicago Mercantile Exchange. Options on European indexes such as the Financial Times Share Exchange (FTSE 100) trade on the NYSE-Euronext Exchange. The Chicago Board Options Exchange also lists options on industry indexes such as the oil or high-tech industries.

In contrast to stock options, index options do not require that the call writer actually "deliver the index" upon exercise or that the put writer "purchase the index." Instead, a cash settlement procedure is used. The payoff that would accrue upon exercise of the option is calculated, and the option writer simply pays that amount to the option holder. The payoff is equal to the difference between the exercise price of the option and the value of the index. For example, if the S&P index is at 2100 when a call option on the index with exercise price 2090 is exercised, the holder of the call receives a cash payment of the difference, 2100 − 2090, times the contract multiplier of $100, or $1,000 per contract.

Options on the major indexes, that is, the S&P 100 (often called the OEX after its ticker symbol), the S&P 500 (the SPX), the NASDAQ 100 (the NDX), and the Dow Jones Industrials (the DJX), are the most actively traded contracts on the CBOE. Together, these contracts dominate CBOE volume.

Futures Options   Futures options give their holders the right to buy or sell a specified futures contract, using as a futures price the exercise price of the option. Although the delivery process is slightly complicated, the terms of futures options contracts are designed in effect to allow the option to be written on the futures price itself. The option holder receives upon exercise a net payoff equal to the difference between the current futures price on the specified asset and the exercise price of the option. Thus if the futures price is, say, $37, and the call has an exercise price of $35, the holder who exercises the call option on the futures gets a payoff of $2.

Foreign Currency Options   A currency option offers the right to buy or sell a specified quantity of foreign currency for a specified number of U.S. dollars. Currency option contracts call for purchase or sale of the currency in exchange for a specified number of U.S. dollars. Contracts are quoted in cents or fractions of a cent per unit of foreign currency.

There is an important difference between currency options and currency *futures* options. The former provide payoffs that depend on the difference between the exercise price and the exchange rate at expiration. The latter are foreign exchange futures options that provide payoffs that depend on the difference between the exercise price and the exchange rate *futures price* at expiration. Because exchange rates and exchange rate futures prices generally are not equal, the options and futures-options contracts will have different values, even with identical expiration dates and exercise prices. Trading volume in currency futures options dominates trading in currency options.

Interest Rate Options   Options are traded on Treasury notes and bonds, Treasury bills, and government bonds of other major economies such as the U.K. or Japan. Options on several interest rates also trade. Among these are contracts on Treasury bond, Treasury note, federal funds, LIBOR, Euribor,[2] and Eurodollar futures.

20.2 | Values of Options at Expiration

Call Options

Recall that a call option gives the right to purchase a security at the exercise price. Suppose you hold a call option on FinCorp stock with an exercise price of $100, and FinCorp is now selling at $110. You can exercise your option to purchase the stock at $100 and simultaneously sell the shares at the market price of $110, clearing $10 per share. Yet if the shares fall below $100, you can sit on the option and do nothing, realizing no further gain or loss. The value of the call option at expiration equals

$$\text{Payoff to call holder} = \begin{cases} S_T - X & \text{if } S_T > X \\ 0 & \text{if } S_T \leq X \end{cases}$$

where S_T is the value of the stock at expiration and X is the exercise price. This formula emphasizes the option property because the payoff cannot be negative. The option is exercised only if S_T exceeds X. If S_T is less than X, the option expires with zero value. The loss to the option holder in this case equals the price originally paid for the option. More generally, the *profit* to the option holder is the option payoff at expiration minus the original purchase price.

---

[2]The Euribor market is similar to the LIBOR market (see Chapter 2), but the interest rate charged in the Euribor market is the interbank rate for euro-denominated deposits.

The value at expiration of the call with exercise price $100 is given by the schedule:

Stock price	$90	$100	$110	$120	$130
Option value	0	0	10	20	30

For stock prices at or below $100, the option is worthless. Above $100, the option is worth the excess of the stock price over $100. The option's value increases by $1 for each dollar increase in the stock price. This relationship is depicted in Figure 20.2.

The solid line is the value of the call at expiration. The net *profit* equals the gross payoff less the initial price of the call. Suppose the call cost $14. Then the profit to the call holder would be given by the dashed (bottom) line of Figure 20.2. At option expiration, the investor suffers a loss of $14 if the stock price is less than or equal to $100.

Profits do not become positive until the stock price at expiration exceeds $114. At that price, the payoff to the call, $S_T - X = \$114 - \$100 = \$14$, equals the initial cost of the call.

Conversely, the writer of the call incurs losses if the stock price is high. In that scenario, the writer will receive a call and will be obligated to deliver a stock worth S_T for only X dollars:

$$\text{Payoff to call writer} = \begin{cases} -(S_T - X) & \text{if } S_T > X \\ 0 & \text{if } S_T \leq X \end{cases}$$

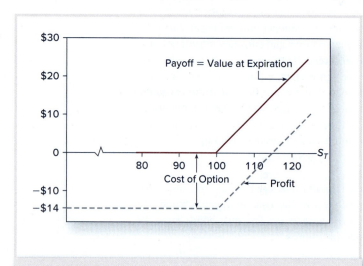

Figure 20.2 Payoff and profit to call option at expiration

The call writer, who is exposed to losses if the stock price increases, is willing to bear this risk in return for the option premium.

Figure 20.3 shows the payoff and profit diagrams for the call writer. These are the mirror images of the corresponding diagrams for the call holder. The break-even point for the option writer also is $114. The (negative) payoff at that point just offsets the premium originally received when the option was written.

Put Options

A put option is the right to sell an asset at the exercise price. In this case, the holder will not exercise the option unless the asset is worth *less* than the exercise price. For example, if FinCorp shares were to fall to $90, a put option with exercise price $100 could be exercised to clear $10 for its holder. The holder would purchase a share for $90 and simultaneously deliver it to the put option writer for the exercise price of $100.

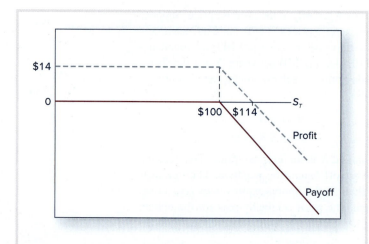

Figure 20.3 Payoff and profit to call writer at expiration

The value of a put option at expiration is

$$\text{Payoff to put holder} = \begin{cases} 0 & \text{if } S_T \geq X \\ X - S_T & \text{if } S_T < X \end{cases}$$

The solid line in Figure 20.4 plots the payoff at expiration to the holder of a put option on FinCorp stock with an exercise price of $100. If the stock price at expiration is above $100, the put has no value, as the right to sell the shares at $100 would not be exercised. Below a price of $100, the put value at expiration increases by $1 for each dollar the stock price falls. The dashed line in Figure 20.4 plots the put option owner's profit at expiration, net of the initial cost of the put.

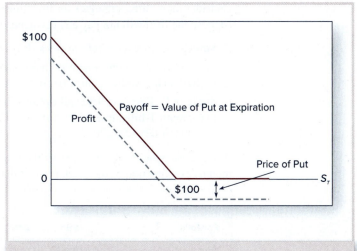

Figure 20.4 Payoff and profit to put option at expiration

Writing puts *naked* (i.e., writing a put without an offsetting short position in the stock for hedging purposes) exposes the writer to losses if the market falls. Writing naked, deep-out-of-the-money puts was once considered an attractive way to generate income, as it was believed that as long as the market did not fall sharply before the option expiration, the option premium could be collected without the put holder ever exercising the option against the writer. Because only sharp drops in the market could result in losses to the put writer, the strategy was not viewed as overly risky. However, in the wake of the market crash of October 1987, such put writers suffered huge losses. Participants now perceive much greater risk to this strategy.

 Concept Check **20.3**

Consider these four option strategies: (i) buy a call; (ii) write a call; (iii) buy a put; (iv) write a put.

a. For each strategy, plot both the payoff and profit diagrams as a function of the final stock price.

b. Why might one characterize both buying calls and writing puts as "bullish" strategies? What is the difference between them?

c. Why might one characterize both buying puts and writing calls as "bearish" strategies? What is the difference between them?

Option versus Stock Investments

Purchasing call options is a bullish strategy; that is, the calls provide profits when stock prices increase. Purchasing puts, in contrast, is a bearish strategy. Symmetrically, writing calls is bearish, whereas writing puts is bullish. Because option values depend on the price of the underlying stock, purchase of options may be viewed as a substitute for direct purchase or sale of a stock. Why might an option strategy be preferable to direct stock transactions?

For example, why would you purchase a call option rather than buy shares of stock directly? Maybe you believe the stock will increase in value from its current level, which in our examples we will take to be $100. You know your analysis could be incorrect, however, and the shares could fall in price. Suppose a 6-month maturity call option with exercise price $100 currently sells for $10, and the interest rate for the period is 3%.

Consider these three strategies for investing a sum of money, say, $10,000. For simplicity, suppose the firm will not pay any dividends until after the 6-month period.

Strategy A: Invest entirely in stock. Buy 100 shares, each selling for $100.

Strategy B: Invest entirely in at-the-money call options. Buy 1,000 calls, each selling for $10. (This would require 10 contracts, each for 100 shares.)

Strategy C: Purchase 100 call options for $1,000. Invest your remaining $9,000 in 6-month T-bills, to earn 3% interest. The bills will grow in value from $9,000 to $9,000 × 1.03 = $9,270.

Let's trace the possible values of these three portfolios when the options expire in six months as a function of the stock price at that time:

	Stock Price					
Portfolio	$95	$100	$105	$110	$115	$120
Portfolio A: All stock	$9,500	$10,000	$10,500	$11,000	$11,500	$12,000
Portfolio B: All options	0	0	5,000	10,000	15,000	20,000
Portfolio C: Call plus T-bills	9,270	9,270	9,770	10,270	10,770	11,270

Portfolio A will be worth 100 times the share price. Portfolio B is worthless unless shares sell for more than the exercise price of the call. Once that point is reached, the portfolio is worth 1,000 times the excess of the stock price over the exercise price. Finally, portfolio C is worth $9,270 from the investment in T-bills plus any profits from the 100 call options. Remember that each of these portfolios involves the same $10,000 initial investment. The rates of return on these three portfolios are as follows:

	Stock Price					
Portfolio	$95	$100	$105	$110	$115	$120
Portfolio A: All stock	−5.0%	0.0%	5.0%	10.0%	15.0%	20.0%
Portfolio B: All options	−100.0	−100.0	−50.0	0.0	50.0	100.0
Portfolio C: Call plus T-bills	−7.3	−7.3	−2.3	2.7	7.7	12.7

These rates of return are graphed in Figure 20.5.

Comparing the returns of portfolios B and C to those of the simple investment in stock represented by portfolio A, we see that options offer two interesting features. First, an option offers leverage. Compare the returns of portfolios B and A. Unless the stock increases from its initial value of $100, the value of portfolio B falls precipitously to zero— a rate of return of negative 100%. Conversely, modest increases in the rate of return on the stock result in disproportionate increases in the option rate of return. For example, a 4.3% increase in the stock price from $115 to $120 would increase the rate of return on the call from 50% to 100%. In this sense, calls are a levered investment on the stock. Their values respond more than proportionately to changes in the stock value.

Figure 20.5 vividly illustrates this point. The slope of the all-option portfolio is far steeper than that of the all-stock portfolio, reflecting its greater proportional sensitivity to the value of the underlying security. The leverage factor is the reason investors (illegally) exploiting inside information commonly choose options as their investment vehicle.

The potential insurance value of options is the second interesting feature, as portfolio C shows. The T-bill-plus-option portfolio cannot be worth less than $9,270 after 6 months, as the option can always be left to expire worthless. The worst possible rate of return on portfolio C is −7.3%, compared to a (theoretically) worst possible rate of return on the stock of −100% if the company were to go bankrupt. Of course, this insurance comes at a price: When the share price increases, portfolio C, the option-plus-bills portfolio, does not perform as well as portfolio A, the all-stock portfolio.

This simple example makes an important point. Although options can be used by speculators as effectively leveraged stock positions, as in portfolio B, they also can be used by investors who desire to tailor their risk exposures in creative ways, as in portfolio C. For example, the call-plus-bills strategy of portfolio C provides a rate of return profile quite unlike that of the stock alone. The absolute limitation on downside risk is a novel and attractive feature of this strategy. We next discuss several option strategies that provide other novel risk profiles that might be attractive to hedgers and other investors.

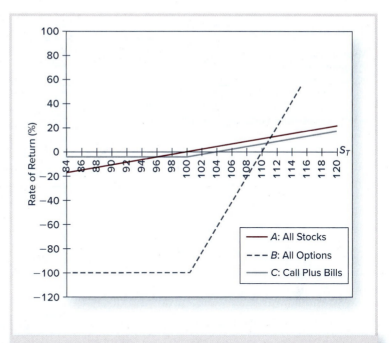

Figure 20.5 Rate of return to three strategies

20.3 Option Strategies

An unlimited variety of payoff patterns can be achieved by combining puts and calls with various exercise prices. We explain in this section the motivation and structure of some of the more popular strategies.

Protective Put

Imagine you would like to invest in a stock, but you are unwilling to bear potential losses beyond some given level. Investing in the stock alone seems risky to you because in principle you could lose all the money you invest. You might consider instead investing in stock and purchasing a put option on the stock. Table 20.1 shows the total value of your portfolio at option expiration: Whatever happens to the stock price, you are guaranteed a payoff at least equal to the put option's exercise price because the put gives you the right to sell your shares for that price.

Example 20.3   Protective Put

Suppose the strike price is $X = \$100$ and the stock is selling at $97 at option expiration. Then the value of your total portfolio is $100. The stock is worth $97 and the value of the expiring put option is

$$X - S_T = \$100 - \$97 = \$3$$

Another way to look at it is that you are holding the stock and a put contract giving you the right to sell the stock for $100. The right to sell locks in a minimum portfolio value of $100. On the other hand, if the stock price is above $100, say, $104, then the right to sell a share at $100 is worthless. You allow the put to expire unexercised, ending up with a share of stock worth $S_T = \$104$.

Table 20.1

Value of a protective put portfolio at option expiration

	$S_T \leq X$	$S_T > X$
Stock	S_T	S_T
+ Put	$X - S_T$	0
Total	X	S_T

Figure 20.6 illustrates the payoff and profit to this **protective put** strategy. The solid line in Figure 20.6, Panel C, is the total payoff. The dashed line is displaced downward by the cost of establishing the position, $S_0 + P$. Notice that potential losses are limited.

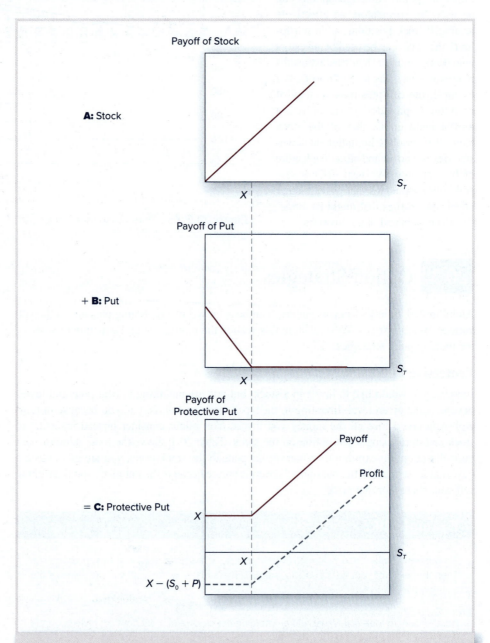

Figure 20.6 Value of a protective put position at option expiration

It is instructive to compare the profit on the protective put strategy with that of the stock investment. For simplicity, consider an at-the-money protective put, so that $X = S_0$. Figure 20.7 compares the profits for the two strategies. The profit on the stock is zero if the stock price remains unchanged and $S_T = S_0$. It rises or falls by $1 for every dollar swing in the ultimate stock price. The profit on the protective put is negative and equal to the cost of the put if S_T is below S_0. The profit on the protective put increases one for one with increases in the stock price once S_T exceeds S_0.

Figure 20.7 makes it clear that the protective put offers some insurance against stock price declines in that it limits losses. Therefore, protective put strategies provide a form of *portfolio insurance*. The cost of the protection is that if the stock price increases, your profit is reduced by the amount you expended on the put, which turned out to be unneeded.

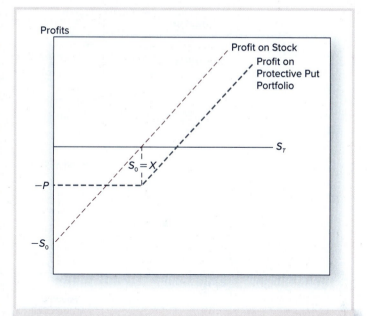

Figure 20.7 Protective put versus stock investment (at-the-money option)

This example also shows that despite the common perception that derivatives mean risk, derivative securities can be used effectively for *risk management*. In fact, such risk management is becoming accepted as part of the fiduciary responsibility of financial managers. Indeed, in one often-cited court case, *Brane v. Roth,* a company's board of directors was successfully sued for failing to use derivatives to hedge the price risk of grain held in storage. Such hedging might have been accomplished using protective puts.

The claim that derivatives are best viewed as risk management tools may seem surprising in light of the credit crisis of the last few years. The crisis was immediately precipitated when the highly risky positions that many financial institutions had established in credit derivatives blew up 2007–2008, resulting in large losses and government bailouts. Still, the same characteristics that make derivatives potent tools to increase risk also make them highly effective in managing risk, at least when used properly. Derivatives have aptly been compared to power tools: very useful in skilled hands, but also very dangerous when not handled with care.

Covered Calls

A **covered call** position is the purchase of a share of stock with a simultaneous sale of a call option on that stock. The call is "covered" because the potential obligation to deliver the stock can be satisfied using the stock held in the portfolio. Writing an option without an offsetting stock position is called by contrast *naked option writing*. The value of a covered call position at expiration, presented in Table 20.2, equals the stock value minus the value of the call. The call value is *subtracted* because the covered call position involves writing a call to another investor who may exercise it at your expense.

The solid line in Figure 20.8, Panel C, is the payoff. You see that the total position is worth S_T when the stock price at time T is below X and rises to a maximum of X when S_T exceeds X. In essence, the sale of the call options means the call writer has sold the claim

Table 20.2

Value of a covered call position at option expiration

	$S_T \leq X$	$S_T > X$
Payoff of stock	S_T	S_T
+ Payoff of written call	-0	$-(S_T - X)$
Total	S_T	X

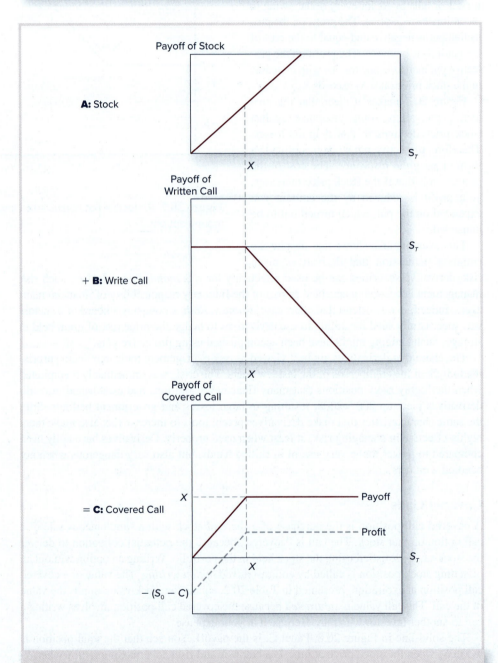

Figure 20.8 Value of a covered call position at expiration

to any stock value above X in return for the initial premium (the call price). Therefore, at expiration, the position is worth at most X. The dashed line in Figure 20.8, Panel C, is the net profit to the covered call.

Writing covered call options has been a popular investment strategy among institutional investors. Consider the managers of a fund invested largely in stocks. They might find it appealing to write calls on some or all of the stock in order to boost income by the premiums collected. Although they thereby forfeit potential capital gains should the stock price rise above the exercise price, if they view X as the price at which they plan to sell the stock anyway, then the call may be viewed as a kind of "sell discipline." The written call guarantees the stock sale will occur as planned.

Example 20.4   Covered Call

Assume a pension fund holds 1,000 shares of stock, with a current price of $100 per share. Suppose the portfolio manager intends to sell all 1,000 shares if the share price hits $110, and a call expiring in 60 days with an exercise price of $110 currently sells for $5. By writing 10 call contracts (for 100 shares each) the fund can pick up $5,000 in extra income. The fund would lose its share of profits from any movement of the stock price above $110 per share, but given that it would have sold its shares at $110, it would not have realized those profits anyway.

Straddle

A long **straddle** is established by buying both a call and a put on a stock, each with the same exercise price, X, and the same expiration date, T. Straddles are useful strategies for investors who believe a stock will move a lot in price but are uncertain about the direction of the move. For example, suppose you believe an important court case that will make or break a company is about to be settled, and the market is not yet aware of the situation. The stock will either double in value if the case is settled favorably or will drop by half if the settlement goes against the company. The straddle position will do well regardless of the outcome because its value rises when the stock price makes extreme upward or downward moves from X.

The worst-case scenario for a straddle is no movement in the stock price. If S_T equals X, both the call and the put expire worthless, and the investor's outlay for the purchase of both options is lost. Straddle positions, therefore, are bets on volatility. An investor who establishes a straddle must view the stock as more volatile than the market does. Conversely, investors who *write* straddles—selling both a call and a put—must believe the stock is less volatile. They collect the option premiums now, hoping the stock price will not change much before option expiration.

The payoff to a straddle is presented in Table 20.3. The solid line in Figure 20.9, Panel C, illustrates this payoff. Notice the portfolio payoff is always positive, except at the one point where the portfolio has zero value, $S_T = X$. You might wonder why all investors don't pursue such a seemingly "no-lose" strategy. The reason is that the straddle requires that both the put and call be purchased. The value of the portfolio at expiration, while never negative, still must exceed the initial cash outlay for a straddle investor to clear a profit.

The dashed line in Figure 20.9, Panel C, is the profit diagram. The profit line lies below the payoff line by the cost of purchasing the straddle, $P + C$. It is clear from the diagram

Table 20.3

Value of a straddle position at option expiration

	$S_T < X$	$S_T \geq X$
Payoff of call	0	$S_T - X$
+ Payoff of put	$X - S_T$	0
Total	$X - S_T$	$S_T - X$

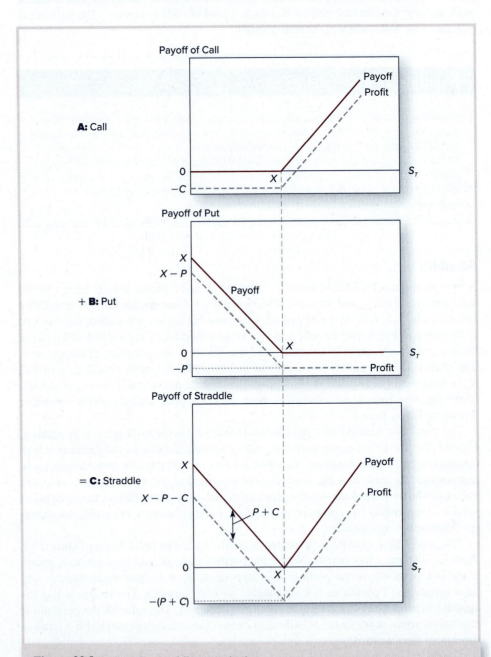

Figure 20.9 Value of a straddle at expiration

that the straddle generates a loss unless the stock price deviates substantially from X. The stock price must depart from X by the total amount expended to purchase the call and the put for the straddle to clear a profit.

Strips and *straps* are variations of straddles. A strip is two puts and one call on a security with the same exercise price and expiration date. A strap is two calls and one put.

 Concept Check **20.4**

> Graph the profit and payoff diagrams for strips and straps.

Spreads

A **spread** is a combination of two or more call options (or two or more puts) on the same stock with differing exercise prices or times to maturity. Some options are bought, whereas others are sold, or written. A *money spread* involves the purchase of one option and the simultaneous sale of another with a different exercise price. A *time spread* refers to the sale and purchase of options with differing expiration dates.

Consider a money spread in which one call option is bought at an exercise price X_1, whereas another call with an identical expiration date, but higher exercise price, X_2, is written. The payoff will be the difference in the value of the call held and the value of the call written, as in Table 20.4.

There are now three instead of two outcomes to distinguish: the lowest-price region where S_T is below both exercise prices, a middle region where S_T is between the two exercise prices, and a high-price region where S_T exceeds both exercise prices. Figure 20.10 illustrates the payoff and profit to this strategy, which is called a *bullish spread* because the payoff either increases or is unaffected by stock price increases.

One motivation for a bullish spread might be that the investor thinks one option is overpriced relative to another. For example, an investor who believes an $X = \$100$ call is cheap compared to an $X = \$110$ call might establish the spread, even without a strong desire to take a bullish position in the stock.

Collars

A **collar** is an options strategy that brackets the value of a portfolio between two bounds. Suppose that an investor currently is holding a large position in FinCorp stock, which is currently selling at $100 per share. A lower bound of $90 can be placed on the value of the portfolio by buying a protective put with exercise price $90. This protection, however, requires that the investor pay the put premium. To raise the money to pay for the put, the investor might write a call option, say, with exercise price $110. The call might sell for roughly the same price as the put, meaning that the net outlay for the two options positions is approximately zero. Writing the call limits the portfolio's upside potential. Even if the stock price moves above $110, the investor will do no better than $110, because at a higher price the stock will be called away. Thus the investor obtains the downside protection represented by the exercise price of the put by selling her claim to any upside potential beyond the exercise price of the call.

Table 20.4

Value of a bullish spread position at expiration

	$S_T \leq X_1$	$X_1 < S_T \leq X_2$	$S_T \geq X_2$
Payoff of purchased call, exercise price = X_1	0	$S_T - X_1$	$S_T - X_1$
+ Payoff of written call, exercise price = X_2	−0	−0	$-(S_T - X_2)$
Total	0	$S_T - X_1$	$X_2 - X_1$

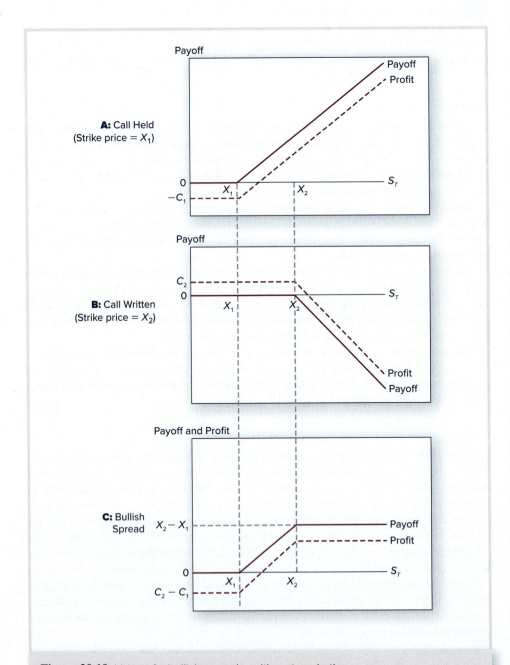

Figure 20.10 Value of a bullish spread position at expiration

eXcel APPLICATIONS: Spreads and Straddles

Using spreadsheets to analyze combinations of options is very helpful. Once the basic models are built, it is easy to extend the analysis to different bundles of options. The Excel model "Spreads and Straddles" shown below can be used to evaluate the profitability of different strategies. You can access this spreadsheet in Connect or through your course instructor.

Excel Question

1. Use the data in this spreadsheet to plot the profit on a bullish spread (see Figure 20.10) with $X_1 = 120$ and $X_2 = 130$.

	A	B	C	D	E	F	G	H	I	J	K	L
1						Spreads and Straddles						
2												
3	Stock Prices											
4	Beginning Market Price	116.5										
5	Ending Market Price	130						X 110 Straddle			X 120 Straddle	
6							Ending	Profit		Ending	Profit	
7	Buying Options:						Stock Price	−15.40		Stock Price	−24.00	
8	Call Options Strike	Price	Payoff	Profit	Return %		50	24.60		50	36.00	
9	110	22.80	20.00	−2.80	−12.28%		60	14.60		60	26.00	
10	120	16.80	10.00	−6.80	−40.48%		70	4.60		70	16.00	
11	130	13.60	0.00	−13.60	−100.00%		80	−5.40		80	6.00	
12	140	10.30	0.00	−10.30	−100.00%		90	−15.40		90	−4.00	
13							100	−25.40		100	−14.00	
14	Put Options Strike	Price	Payoff	Profit	Return %		110	−35.40		110	−24.00	
15	110	12.60	0.00	−12.60	−100.00%		120	−25.40		120	−34.00	
16	120	17.20	0.00	−17.20	−100.00%		130	−15.40		130	−24.00	
17	130	23.60	0.00	−23.60	−100.00%		140	−5.40		140	−14.00	
18	140	30.50	10.00	−20.50	−67.21%		150	4.60		150	−4.00	
19							160	14.60		160	6.00	
20	Straddle	Price	Payoff	Profit	Return %		170	24.60		170	16.00	
21	110	35.40	20.00	−15.40	−43.50%		180	34.60		180	26.00	
22	120	34.00	10.00	−24.00	−70.59%		190	44.60		190	36.00	
23	130	37.20	0.00	−37.20	−100.00%		200	54.60		200	46.00	
24	140	40.80	10.00	−30.80	−75.49%		210	64.60		210	56.00	
25												

Example 20.5   Collars

A collar would be appropriate for an investor who has a target wealth goal in mind but is unwilling to risk losses beyond a certain level. If you are contemplating buying a house for $220,000, for example, you might set this figure as your goal. Your current wealth may be $200,000, and you are unwilling to risk losing more than $20,000. A collar established by (1) purchasing 2,000 shares of stock currently selling at $100 per share, (2) purchasing 2,000 put options (20 options contracts) with exercise price $90, and (3) writing 2,000 calls with exercise price $110 would give you a good chance to realize the $20,000 capital gain without risking a loss of more than $20,000.

 Concept Check **20.5**

Graph the payoff diagram for the collar described in Example 20.5.

20.4   The Put-Call Parity Relationship

We saw in the previous section that a protective put portfolio, comprising a stock position and a put option on that position, provides a payoff with a guaranteed minimum value, but with unlimited upside potential. This is not the only way to achieve such protection, however. A call-plus-bills portfolio also can provide limited downside risk with unlimited upside potential.

Consider the strategy of buying a call option and, in addition, buying Treasury bills with face value equal to the exercise price of the call, and with maturity date equal to the expiration date of the option. For example, if the exercise price of the call option is $100, then each option contract (which is written on 100 shares) would require payment of $10,000 upon exercise. Therefore, you would purchase a T-bill with a maturity value of $10,000. More generally, for each option that you hold with exercise price X, you would purchase a risk-free zero-coupon bond with face value X.

Examine the value of this position at time T, when the options expire and the zero-coupon bond matures:

	$S_T \leq X$	$S_T > X$
Value of call option	0	$S_T - X$
Value of zero-coupon bond	$\underline{X}$	$\underline{X}$
Total	X	S_T

If the stock price is below the exercise price, the call is worthless, but the bond matures to its face value, X. It therefore provides a floor value to the portfolio. If the stock price exceeds X, then the payoff to the call, $S_T - X$, is added to the face value of the bond to provide a total payoff of S_T. The payoff to this portfolio is precisely identical to the payoff of the protective put that we derived in Table 20.1.

If two portfolios always provide equal values, then they must cost the same amount to establish. Therefore, the call-plus-bond portfolio must cost the same as the stock-plus-put portfolio. Each call costs C. The riskless zero-coupon bond costs $X/(1 + r_f)^T$. Therefore, the call-plus-bond portfolio costs $C + X/(1 + r_f)^T$. The stock costs S_0 to purchase now (at time zero), while the put costs P. Therefore, we conclude that

$$C + \frac{X}{(1 + r_f)^T} = S_0 + P \qquad (20.1)$$

Equation 20.1 is called the **put-call parity theorem** because it represents the proper relationship between put and call prices. If the parity relation is ever violated, an arbitrage opportunity arises. For example, suppose you collect these data for a certain stock:

Stock price	$110
Call price (1-year expiration, $X = \$105$)	$ 17
Put price (1-year expiration, $X = \$105$)	$ 5
Risk-free interest rate	5% per year

We can use these data in Equation 20.1 to see if parity is violated:

$$C + \frac{X}{(1 + r_f)^T} \stackrel{?}{=} S_0 + P$$

$$17 + \frac{105}{1.05} \stackrel{?}{=} 110 + 5$$

$$117 \neq 115$$

This result, a violation of parity—117 does not equal 115—indicates mispricing. To exploit the mispricing, you buy the relatively cheap portfolio (the stock-plus-put position represented on the right-hand side of the equation) and sell the relatively expensive portfolio (the call-plus-bond position corresponding to the left-hand side). Therefore, if

| | Immediate | Cash Flow in 1 Year | | Table 20.5 |
Position	Cash Flow	$S_T < 105$	$S_T \geq 105$	Arbitrage strategy
Buy stock	−110	S_T	S_T	
Borrow $105/1.05 = $100	+100	−105	−105	
Sell call	+17	0	$-(S_T - 105)$	
Buy put	−5	$105 - S_T$	0	
Total	2	0	0	

you *buy* the stock, *buy* the put, *write* the call, and *borrow* $100 for one year (because borrowing money is the opposite of buying a bond), you should earn arbitrage profits.

Let's examine the payoff to this strategy. In one year, the stock will be worth S_T. The $100 borrowed will be paid back with interest, resulting in a cash outflow of $105. The written call will result in a cash outflow of $S_T - $105 if S_T exceeds $105. The purchased put pays off $105 - S_T$ if the stock price is below $105.

Table 20.5 summarizes the outcome. The immediate cash inflow is $2. In one year, the various positions provide exactly offsetting cash flows: The $2 inflow is realized without any offsetting outflows. This is an arbitrage opportunity that investors will pursue on a large scale until buying and selling pressure restores the parity condition expressed in Equation 20.1.

Equation 20.1 actually applies only to options on stocks that pay no dividends before the expiration date of the option. The extension of the parity condition for European call options on dividend-paying stocks is, however, straightforward. Problem 12 at the end of the chapter leads you through the demonstration. The more general formulation of the put-call parity condition is

$$P = C - S_0 + PV(X) + PV(\text{dividends}) \tag{20.2}$$

where PV(dividends) is the present value of the dividends that will be paid by the stock during the life of the option. If the stock does not pay dividends, Equation 20.2 becomes identical to Equation 20.1.

Notice that this generalization would apply as well to European options on assets other than stocks. Instead of using dividend income in Equation 20.2, we would let any income paid out by the underlying asset play the role of the stock dividends. For example, European put and call options on bonds would satisfy the same parity relationship, except that the bond's coupon income would replace the stock's dividend payments in the parity formula.

Even this generalization, however, applies only to European options, as the cash flow streams from the two portfolios represented by the two sides of Equation 20.2 will match only if each position is held until expiration. If a call and a put may be optimally exercised at different times before their common expiration date, then the equality of payoffs cannot be assured, or even expected, and the portfolios will have different values.

Example 20.6   Put-Call Parity

Let's see how well parity works using the data in Figure 20.1 on the IBM options. The August expiration call with exercise price $150 and time to expiration of 50 days cost $4.10 while the corresponding put option cost $5.91. IBM was selling for $149.60, and the annualized short-term interest rate on this date was 0.2%. IBM was expected to pay a dividend of $1.40 with an ex-dividend date of August 6, 37 days hence. According to parity, we should find that

$$P = C + PV(X) - S_0 + PV(\text{dividends})$$

$$5.91 = 4.10 + \frac{150}{(1.002)^{50/365}} - 149.60 + \frac{1.40}{(1.002)^{37/365}}$$

$$5.91 = 4.10 + 149.959 - 149.60 + 1.40$$

$$5.91 = 5.859$$

So parity is violated by about $.051 per share. Is this a big enough difference to exploit? Almost certainly not. You have to weigh the potential profit against the trading costs of the call, put, and stock. More important, given the fact that options trade relatively infrequently, this deviation from parity might not be "real," but may instead be attributable to "stale" (i.e., out-of-date) price quotes at which you cannot actually trade.

20.5 Option-Like Securities

Even if you never traded an option directly, you would still need to appreciate their properties. This is because many financial instruments and agreements have features that convey implicit or explicit options to one or more parties. To value and use these securities correctly, you must understand their embedded option attributes.

Callable Bonds

You know from Chapter 14 that many corporate bonds are issued with call provisions entitling the issuer to buy bonds back from bondholders at some time in the future at a specified call price. The bond issuer holds a call option with exercise price equal to the price at which the bond can be repurchased. A callable bond arrangement therefore is essentially a sale of a *straight bond* (a bond with no option features such as callability or convertibility) to the investor and the concurrent issuance of a call option by the investor to the bond-issuing firm.

There must be some compensation for the firm's implicit call option. If the callable bond were issued with the same coupon rate as a straight bond, it would sell at a lower price: the price difference would equal the value of the call. To sell callable bonds at par, firms must issue them with coupon rates higher than the coupons on straight debt. The higher coupons are the investor's compensation for the call option retained by the issuer.

Figure 20.11 illustrates this optionlike property. The horizontal

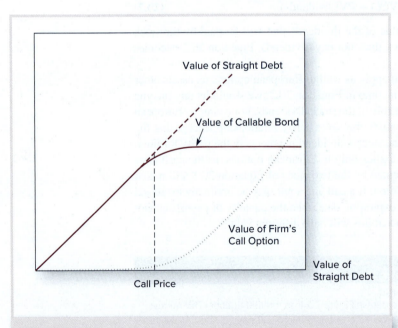

Figure 20.11 Values of callable bonds compared with straight bonds

axis is the value of a straight bond with otherwise identical terms to the callable bond. The dashed 45-degree line represents the value of straight debt. The solid line is the value of the callable bond, and the dotted line is the value of the call option retained by the firm. A callable bond's potential for capital gains is limited by the firm's option to repurchase at the call price.

Concept Check **20.6**

How is a callable bond similar to a covered call strategy on a straight bond?

The option inherent in callable bonds actually is more complex than an ordinary call option, because usually it may be exercised only after some initial period of *call protection*. The price at which the bond is callable may change over time also. Unlike exchange-listed options, these features are defined in the initial bond covenant and will depend on the needs of the issuing firm and its perception of the market's tastes.

Concept Check **20.7**

Suppose the period of call protection is extended. How will the coupon rate the company needs to offer on its bonds change to enable the issuer to sell the bonds at par value?

Convertible Securities

Convertible bonds and convertible preferred stock convey options to the holder of the security rather than to the issuing firm. A convertible security typically gives its holder the right to exchange each bond or share of preferred stock for a fixed number of shares of common stock, regardless of the market prices of the securities at the time.

For example, a bond with a *conversion ratio* of 10 allows its holder to convert one bond of par value $1,000 into 10 shares of common stock. Alternatively, we say the *conversion price* in this case is $100: To receive 10 shares of stock, the investor sacrifices bonds with face value $1,000 or, put another way, $100 of face value per share. If the present value of the bond's scheduled payments is less than 10 times the value of one share of stock, it may pay to convert; that is, the conversion option is in the money. A bond worth $950 with a conversion ratio of 10 could be converted profitably if the stock were selling above $95, as the value of the 10 shares received for each bond surrendered would exceed $950. Most convertible bonds are issued "deep out of the money." That is, the issuer sets the conversion ratio so that conversion will not be profitable unless there is a substantial increase in stock prices and/or decrease in bond prices from the time of issue.

A bond's *conversion value* equals the value it would have if you converted it into stock immediately. Clearly, a bond must sell for at least its conversion value. If it did not, you could purchase the bond, convert it, and clear an immediate profit. This condition could never persist, for all investors would pursue such a strategy and ultimately would bid up the price of the bond.

The straight bond value, or "bond floor," is the value the bond would have if it were not convertible into stock. The bond must sell for more than its straight bond value because a convertible bond has more value; it is in fact a straight bond plus a valuable call option. Therefore, the convertible bond has two lower bounds on its market price: the conversion value and the straight bond value.

 Concept Check **20.8**

Should a convertible bond issued at par value have a higher or lower coupon rate than a nonconvertible bond issued at par?

Figure 20.12 illustrates the optionlike properties of the convertible bond. Figure 20.12, Panel A, shows the value of the straight debt as a function of the stock price of the issuing firm. For healthy firms, the straight debt value is almost independent of the value of

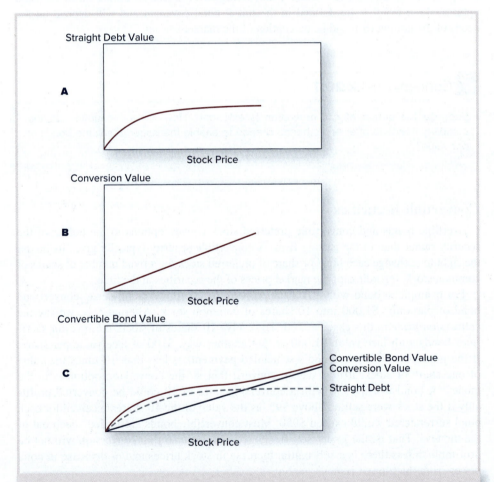

Figure 20.12 Value of a convertible bond as a function of stock price. *Panel A,* Straight debt value, or bond floor. *Panel B,* Conversion value of the bond. *Panel C,* Total value of convertible bond.

the stock because default risk is small. However, if the firm is close to bankruptcy (stock prices are low), default risk increases, and the straight bond value falls. Panel B shows the conversion value of the bond. Panel C compares the value of the convertible bond to these two lower bounds.

When stock prices are low, the straight bond value is the effective lower bound, and the conversion option is nearly irrelevant. The convertible will trade like straight debt. When stock prices are high, the bond's price is determined by its conversion value. With conversion all but guaranteed, the bond is essentially equity in disguise. We can illustrate with two examples.

	Bond *A*	Bond *B*
Annual coupon	$80	$80
Maturity date	10 years	10 years
Quality rating	Baa	Baa
Conversion ratio	20	25
Stock price	$30	$50
Conversion value	$600	$1,250
Market yield on 10-year Baa-rated bonds	8.5%	8.5%
Value as straight debt	$967	$967
Actual bond price	$972	$1,255
Reported yield to maturity	8.42%	4.76%

Bond *A* has a conversion value of only $600. Its value as straight debt, in contrast, is $967. This is the present value of the coupon and principal payments at a market rate for straight debt of 8.5%. The bond's price is $972, so the premium over straight bond value is only $5, reflecting the low probability of conversion. Its reported yield to maturity based on scheduled coupon payments and the market price of $972 is 8.42%, close to that of straight debt.

The conversion option on bond *B* is in the money. Conversion value is $1,250, and the bond's price, $1,255, reflects its value as equity (plus $5 for the protection the bond offers against stock price declines). The bond's reported yield is 4.76%, far below the comparable yield on straight debt. The big yield sacrifice is attributable to the far greater value of the conversion option.

In theory, we could value convertible bonds by treating them as straight debt plus call options. In practice, however, this approach is often impractical for several reasons:

1. The conversion price frequently increases over time, which means the exercise price of the option changes.

2. Stocks may pay several dividends over the life of the bond, further complicating the option-valuation analysis.

3. Most convertibles also are callable at the discretion of the firm. In essence, both the investor and the issuer hold options on each other. If the issuer exercises its call option to repurchase the bond, the bondholders typically have a month during which they still can convert. When issuers use a call option, knowing bondholders will choose to convert, the issuer is said to have *forced a conversion*. These conditions together mean the actual maturity of the bond is indeterminate.

Warrants

Warrants are essentially call options issued by a firm. One important difference between calls and warrants is that exercise of a warrant requires the firm to issue a new share of stock—the total number of shares outstanding increases. Exercise of a call option requires only that the writer of the call deliver an already-issued share of stock to discharge the obligation. In that case, the number of shares outstanding remains fixed. Also unlike call options, warrants result in a cash flow to the firm when the warrant holder pays the exercise price. These differences mean that warrant values will differ somewhat from the values of call options with identical terms.

Like convertible debt, warrant terms may be tailored to meet the needs of the firm. Also like convertible debt, warrants generally are protected against stock splits and dividends in that the exercise price and the number of warrants held are adjusted to offset the effects of the split.

Warrants are often issued in conjunction with another security. Bonds, for example, may be packaged together with a warrant "sweetener," frequently a warrant that may be sold separately. This is called a *detachable warrant.*

Issue of warrants and convertible securities creates the potential for an increase in outstanding shares of stock if exercise occurs. Exercise obviously would affect financial statistics that are computed on a per-share basis, so annual reports must provide earnings per share figures under the assumption that all convertible securities and warrants are exercised. These figures are called *fully diluted earnings per share.*[3]

Collateralized Loans

Many loan arrangements require that the borrower put up collateral to guarantee the loan will be paid back. In the event of default, the lender takes possession of the collateral. A *nonrecourse loan* gives the lender no recourse beyond the right to the collateral. That is, the lender may not sue the borrower for further payment if the collateral turns out not to be valuable enough to repay the loan.

This arrangement gives an implicit call option to the borrower. Assume the borrower is obligated to pay back L dollars at the maturity of the loan. The collateral will be worth S_T dollars at maturity. (Its value today is S_0.) The borrower has the option to wait until loan maturity and repay the loan only if the collateral is worth more than the L dollars necessary to satisfy the loan. If the collateral is worth less than L, the borrower can default on the loan, discharging the obligation by forfeiting the collateral, which is worth only S_T.[4]

Another way of describing such a loan is to view the borrower as turning over the collateral to the lender but retaining the right to reclaim it by paying off the loan. The transfer of the collateral with the right to reclaim it is equivalent to a payment of S_0 dollars, less a simultaneous recovery of a sum that resembles a call option with exercise price L. In effect, the borrower turns over collateral but keeps an option to "repurchase" it for L dollars at the maturity of the loan if L turns out to be less than S_T. This is a call option.

---

[3]We should note that the exercise of a convertible bond need not reduce EPS. Diluted EPS will be less than undiluted EPS only if interest saved (per share) on the convertible bonds is less than the prior EPS.

[4]In reality, of course, defaulting on a loan is not so simple. There are losses of reputation involved as well as considerations of ethical behavior. This is a description of a pure nonrecourse loan where both parties agree from the outset that only the collateral backs the loan and that default is not to be taken as a sign of bad faith if the collateral is insufficient to repay the loan.

A third way to look at a collateralized loan is to assume that the borrower will repay the L dollars with certainty but also retain the option to sell the collateral to the lender for L dollars, even if S_T is less than L. In this case, the sale of the collateral would generate the cash necessary to satisfy the loan. The ability to "sell" the collateral for a price of L dollars represents a put option, which guarantees the borrower can raise enough money to satisfy the loan simply by turning over the collateral.

It is perhaps surprising to realize that we can describe the same loan as involving either a put option or a call option, as the payoffs to calls and puts are so different. Yet the equivalence of the two approaches is nothing more than a reflection of the put-call parity relationship. In our call-option description of the loan, the value of the borrower's liability is $S_0 - C$: The borrower turns over the asset, which is a transfer of S_0 dollars, but retains a call worth C dollars. In the put-option description, the borrower is obligated to pay L dollars but retains the put, which is worth P: The present value of this net obligation is $L/(1 + r_f)^T - P$. Because these alternative descriptions are equivalent ways of viewing the same loan, the value of the obligations must be equal:

$$S_0 - C = \frac{L}{(1 + r_f)^T} - P \tag{20.3}$$

Treating L as the exercise price of the option, Equation 20.3 is simply the put-call parity relationship.

Figure 20.13 illustrates these different ways to view the loan. Figure 20.13, Panel A, is the value of the payment to be received by the lender, which equals the minimum of S_T or L. Panel B shows that this amount can be expressed as S_T minus the payoff of the call implicitly written by the lender and held by the borrower. Panel C shows it also can be viewed as a receipt of L dollars minus the proceeds of a put option.

Levered Equity and Risky Debt

Investors holding stock in incorporated firms are protected by limited liability, which means that if the firm cannot pay its debts, the firm's creditors may attach only the firm's assets, not sue the corporation's equityholders for further payment. In effect, any time the corporation borrows money, the maximum possible collateral for the loan is the total of the firm's assets. If the firm declares bankruptcy, we can interpret this as an admission that the assets of the firm are insufficient to satisfy the claims against it. The corporation may discharge its obligations by transferring ownership of the firm's assets to the creditors.

Just as is true for nonrecourse collateralized loans, the required payment to the creditors represents the exercise price of the implicit option, while the value of the firm is the underlying asset. The equityholders have a put option to transfer their ownership claims on the firm to the creditors in return for the face value of the firm's debt.

Alternatively, we may view the equityholders as retaining a call option. They have, in effect, already transferred their ownership claim to the firm to the creditors but have retained the right to reacquire that claim by paying off the loan. Hence the equityholders have the option to "buy back" the firm for a specified price: They have a call option.

The significance of this observation is that analysts can value corporate bonds using option-pricing techniques. The default premium required of risky debt in principle can be estimated by using option-valuation models. We consider some of these models in Chapter 21.

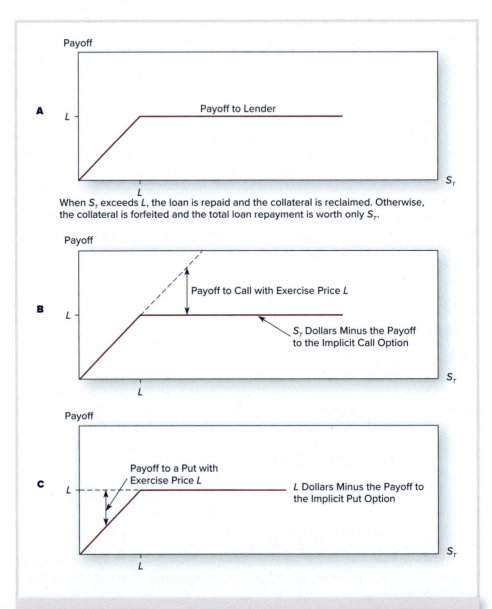

Figure 20.13 Collateralized loan. *Panel A,* Payoff to collateralized loan. *Panel B,* Lender can be viewed as collecting the collateral from the borrower, but issuing an option to the borrower to call back the collateral for the face value of the loan. *Panel C,* Lender can be viewed as collecting a risk-free loan from the borrower, but issuing a put to the borrower to sell the collateral for the face value of the loan.

20.6 Financial Engineering

One of the attractions of options is the ability they provide to create investment positions with payoffs that depend in a variety of ways on the values of other securities. We have seen evidence of this capability in the various options strategies examined in Section 20.4.

Options also can be used to custom-design new securities or portfolios with desired patterns of exposure to the price of an underlying security. In this sense, options (and futures contracts, to be discussed in Chapters 22 and 23) provide the ability to engage in *financial engineering,* the creation of portfolios with specified payoff patterns.

A simple example of a product engineered with options is the index-linked certificate of deposit. Index-linked CDs enable retail investors to take small positions in index options. Unlike conventional CDs, which pay a fixed rate of interest, these CDs pay depositors a specified fraction of the rate of return on a market index such as the S&P 500, while guaranteeing a mini-

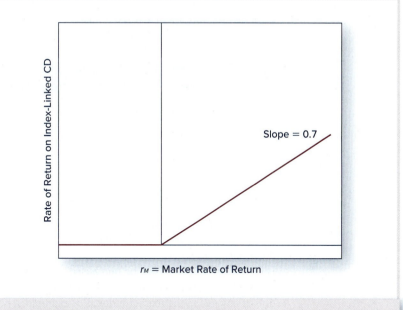

Figure 20.14 Return on index-linked CD

mum rate of return should the market fall. For example, the index-linked CD may offer 70% of any market increase but protect its holder from any market decrease by guaranteeing at least no loss.

The index-linked CD is clearly a type of call option. If the market rises, the depositor profits according to the *participation rate* or *multiplier,* in this case 70%; if the market falls, the investor is insured against loss. Just as clearly, the bank offering these CDs is in effect writing call options and can hedge its position by buying index calls in the options market. Figure 20.14 shows the nature of the bank's obligation to its depositors.

How might the bank set the appropriate multiplier? To answer this, note various features of the option:

1. The price the depositor is paying for the options is the forgone interest on the conventional CD that could be purchased. Because interest is received at the end of the period, the present value of the interest payment on each dollar invested is $r_f/(1 + r_f)$. Therefore, the depositor trades a sure payment with present value per dollar invested of $r_f/(1 + r_f)$ for a return that depends on the market's performance. Conversely, the bank can fund its obligation using the interest that it would have paid on a conventional CD.

2. The option we have described is an at-the-money option, meaning that the exercise price equals the current value of the stock index. The option goes into the money as soon as the market index increases from its level at the inception of the contract.

3. We can analyze the option on a per-dollar-invested basis. For example, the option costs the depositor $r_f/(1 + r_f)$ dollars per dollar placed in the index-linked CD. The market price of the option per dollar invested is C/S_0: The at-the-money option costs C dollars and is written on one unit of the market index, currently at S_0.

Now it is easy to determine the multiplier that the bank can offer on the CDs. It receives from its depositors a "payment" of $r_f/(1 + r_f)$ per dollar invested. It costs the bank C/S_0 to purchase the call option on a $1 investment in the market index. Therefore, if $r_f/(1 + r_f)$

is, for example, 70% of C/S_0, the bank can purchase at most .7 call option on the $1 investment and the multiplier will be .7. More generally, the break-even multiplier on an index-linked CD is $r_f/(1 + r_f)$ divided by C/S_0.

Example 20.7   Indexed-Linked CDs

Suppose that $r_f = 6\%$ per year, and that 6-month maturity at-the-money calls on the market index currently cost $50. The index is at 1,000. Then the option costs $50/1,000 = \$.05$ per dollar of market value. The CD rate is 3% per 6 months, meaning that $r_f/(1 + r_f) = .03/1.03 = .0291$. Therefore, the multiplier would be $.0291/.05 = .5825$.

The index-linked CD has several variants. Investors can purchase similar CDs that guarantee a positive minimum return if they are willing to settle for a smaller multiplier. In this case, the option is "purchased" by the depositor for $(r_f - r_{min})/(1 + r_f)$ dollars per dollar invested, where r_{min} is the guaranteed minimum return. Because the purchase price is lower, fewer options can be purchased, which results in a lower multiplier. Another variant of the "bullish" CD we have described is the *bear CD,* which pays depositors a fraction of any *fall* in the market index. For example, a bear CD might offer a rate of return of .6 times any percentage decline in the S&P 500.

 Concept Check **20.9**

Continue to assume that $r_f = 3\%$ per half-year, that at-the-money calls sell for $50, and that the market index is at 1,000. What would be the multiplier for 6-month bullish equity-linked CDs offering a guaranteed minimum return of .5% over the term of the CD?

20.7   Exotic Options

Options markets have been tremendously successful. Investors clearly value the portfolio strategies made possible by trading options; this is reflected in the heavy trading volume in these markets. Success breeds imitation, and in recent years we have witnessed considerable innovation in the range of option instruments available to investors. Part of this innovation has occurred in the market for customized options, which now trade in active over-the-counter markets. Many of these options have terms that would have been highly unusual even a few years ago; they are therefore called *exotic options.* In this section, we survey a few of the more interesting variants of these new instruments.

Asian Options

You already have been introduced to American- and European-style options. Asian-style options are options with payoffs that depend on the *average* price of the underlying asset during at least some portion of the life of the option. For example, an Asian call option may have a payoff equal to the average stock price over the last three months minus the strike price if that difference is positive, and zero otherwise. These options may be of interest, for example, to firms that wish to hedge a profit stream that depends on the average price of a commodity over some period of time.

Barrier Options

Barrier options have payoffs that depend not only on some asset price at option expiration, but also on whether the underlying asset price has crossed through some "barrier." For example, a down-and-out option is one type of barrier option that automatically expires worthless if and when the stock price falls below some barrier price. Similarly, down-and-in options will not provide a payoff unless the stock price *does* fall below some barrier at least once during the life of the option. These options also are referred to as knock-out and knock-in options.

Lookback Options

Lookback options have payoffs that depend in part on the minimum or maximum price of the underlying asset during the life of the option. For example, a lookback call option might provide a payoff equal to the *maximum* stock price during the life of the option minus the exercise price, instead of the *final* stock price minus the exercise price. Such an option provides (for a price, of course) a form of perfect market timing, providing the call holder with a payoff equal to the one that would accrue if the asset were purchased for X dollars and later sold at what turns out to be its high price.

Currency-Translated Options

Currency-translated options have either asset or exercise prices denominated in a foreign currency. For example, the *quanto* allows an investor to fix in advance the exchange rate at which an investment in a foreign currency can be converted back into dollars. The right to translate a fixed amount of foreign currency into dollars at a given exchange rate is a simple foreign exchange option. Quantos are more interesting because the amount of currency that will be translated into dollars depends on the investment performance of the foreign security. Therefore, a quanto in effect provides a *random number* of options.

Digital Options

Digital options, also called binary or "bet" options, have fixed payoffs that depend on whether a condition is satisfied by the price of the underlying asset. For example, a digital call option might pay off a fixed amount of $100 if the stock price at maturity exceeds the exercise price.

SUMMARY

1. A call option is the right to buy an asset at an agreed-upon exercise price. A put option is the right to sell an asset at a given exercise price.

2. American-style options allow exercise on or before the expiration date. European options allow exercise only on the expiration date. Most traded options are American style.

3. Options are traded on stocks, stock indexes, foreign currencies, fixed-income securities, and several futures contracts.

4. Options can be used either to lever up an investor's exposure to an asset price or to provide insurance against volatility of asset prices. Popular option strategies include covered calls, protective puts, straddles, spreads, and collars.

5. The put-call parity theorem relates the prices of put and call options. If the relationship is violated, arbitrage opportunities will result. Specifically, the relationship that must be satisfied is

$$P = C - S_0 + PV(X) + PV(\text{dividends})$$

where X is the exercise price of both the call and the put options, PV(X) is the present value of a claim to X dollars to be paid at the expiration date of the options, and PV(dividends) is the present value of dividends to be paid before option expiration.

6. Many commonly traded securities embody option characteristics. Examples of these securities are callable bonds, convertible bonds, and warrants. Other arrangements such as collateralized loans and limited-liability borrowing can be analyzed as conveying implicit options to one or more parties.

7. Trading in so-called exotic options now takes place in an active over-the-counter market.

KEY TERMS	call option	at the money	spread
	exercise (or strike) price	American option	collar
	premium	European option	put-call parity theorem
	put option	protective put	warrant
	in the money	covered call	
	out of the money	straddle	

KEY EQUATIONS

Payoff to call investor $= \begin{cases} S_T - X & \text{if } S_T > X \\ 0 & \text{if } S_T \le X \end{cases}$

Payoff to put investor $= \begin{cases} 0 & \text{if } S_T > X \\ X - S_T & \text{if } S_T \le X \end{cases}$

Put-call parity: $P = C - S_0 + \text{PV}(X) + \text{PV(dividends)}$

PROBLEM SETS

1. We said that options can be used either to scale up or reduce overall portfolio risk. What are some examples of risk-increasing and risk-reducing options strategies? Explain each.

2. What are the trade-offs facing an investor who is considering buying a put option on an existing portfolio?

3. What are the trade-offs facing an investor who is considering writing a call option on an existing portfolio?

4. Why do you think the most actively traded options tend to be the ones that are near the money?

5. Turn back to Figure 20.1, which lists prices of various IBM options. Use the data in the figure to calculate the payoff and the profits for investments in each of the following July expiration options, assuming that the stock price on the expiration date is $150.

   a. Call option, $X = \$145$.
   b. Put option, $X = \$145$.
   c. Call option, $X = \$150$.
   d. Put option, $X = \$150$.
   e. Call option, $X = \$155$.
   f. Put option, $X = \$155$.

6. Suppose you think Apple stock is going to appreciate substantially in value in the next year. Say the stock's current price, S_0, is $100, and a call option expiring in one year has an exercise price, X, of $100 and is selling at a price, C, of $10. With $10,000 to invest, you are considering three alternatives.

   a. Invest all $10,000 in the stock, buying 100 shares.
   b. Invest all $10,000 in 1,000 options (10 contracts).
   c. Buy 100 options (one contract) for $1,000, and invest the remaining $9,000 in a money market fund paying 4% annual interest.

What is your rate of return for each alternative for the following four stock prices in one year? Summarize your results in the table and diagram below.

	Price of Stock One Year from Now			
	$80	$100	$110	$120
a. All stocks (100 shares)				
b. All options (1,000 shares)				
c. Bills + 100 options				

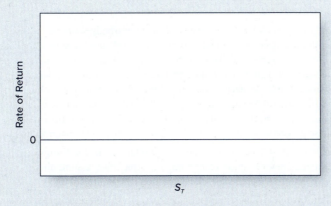

7. The common stock of the P.U.T.T. Corporation has been trading in a narrow price range for the past month, and you are convinced it is going to break far out of that range in the next three months. You do not know whether it will go up or down, however. The current price of the stock is $100 per share, and the price of a 3-month call option at an exercise price of $100 is $10.

    a. If the risk-free interest rate is 10% per year, what must be the price of a 3-month put option on P.U.T.T. stock at an exercise price of $100? (The stock pays no dividends.)

    b. What would be a simple options strategy to exploit your conviction about the stock price's future movements? How far would it have to move in either direction for you to make a profit on your initial investment?

8. The common stock of the C.A.L.L. Corporation has been trading in a narrow range around $50 per share for months, and you believe it is going to stay in that range for the next three months. The price of a 3-month put option with an exercise price of $50 is $4.

    a. If the risk-free interest rate is 10% per year, what must be the price of a 3-month call option on C.A.L.L. stock at an exercise price of $50 if it is at the money? (The stock pays no dividends.)

    b. What would be a simple options strategy using a put and a call to exploit your conviction about the stock price's future movement? What is the most money you can make on this position? How far can the stock price move in either direction before you lose money?

    c. How can you create a position involving a put, a call, and riskless lending that would have the same payoff structure as the stock at expiration? What is the net cost of establishing that position now?

9. You are a portfolio manager who uses options positions to customize the risk profile of your clients. In each case, what strategy is best given your client's objective?

    a. • Performance to date: Up 16%.
       • Client objective: Earn at least 15%.
       • Your scenario: Good chance of large gains or large losses between now and end of year.

        i. Long straddle.
        ii. Long bullish spread.
        iii. Short straddle.

b. • Performance to date: Up 16%.
   • Client objective: Earn at least 15%.
   • Your scenario: Good chance of large losses between now and end of year.
      i. Long put options.
      ii. Short call options.
      iii. Long call options.

10. An investor purchases a stock for $38 and a put for $.50 with a strike price of $35. The inves-
    tor sells a call for $.50 with a strike price of $40. What is the maximum profit and loss for this
    position? Draw the profit and loss diagram for this strategy as a function of the stock price at
    expiration.

11. Imagine that you are holding 5,000 shares of stock, currently selling at $40 per share. You are
    ready to sell the shares but would prefer to put off the sale until next year for tax reasons. If you
    continue to hold the shares until January, however, you face the risk that the stock will drop in
    value before year-end. You decide to use a collar to limit downside risk without laying out a good
    deal of additional funds. January call options with a strike of $45 are selling at $2, and January
    puts with a strike price of $35 are selling at $3. What will be the value of your portfolio in January
    (net of the proceeds from the options) if the stock price ends up at: (a) $30, (b) $40, or (c) $50?
    Compare these proceeds to what you would realize if you simply continued to hold the shares.

12. In this problem, we derive the put-call parity relationship for European options on stocks
    that pay dividends before option expiration. For simplicity, assume that the stock makes one
    dividend payment of D per share at the expiration date of the option.

    a. What is the value of a stock-plus-put position on the expiration date of the option?
    b. Now consider a portfolio comprising a call option and a zero-coupon bond with the same
       maturity date as the option and with face value $(X + D)$. What is the value of this portfolio
       on the option expiration date? You should find that its value equals that of the stock-plus-put
       portfolio regardless of the stock price.
    c. What is the cost of establishing the two portfolios in parts (a) and (b)? Equate the costs of
       these portfolios, and you will derive the put-call parity relationship, Equation 20.2.

13. a. A butterfly spread is the purchase of one call at exercise price X_1, the sale of two calls at
       exercise price X_2, and the purchase of one call at exercise price X_3. X_1 is less than X_2, and
       X_2 is less than X_3 by equal amounts, and all calls have the same expiration date. Graph the
       payoff diagram to this strategy.
    b. A vertical combination is the purchase of a call with exercise price X_2 and a put with exercise
       price X_1, with X_2 greater than X_1. Graph the payoff to this strategy.

14. A bearish spread is the purchase of a call with exercise price X_2 and the sale of a call with
    exercise price X_1, with X_2 greater than X_1. Graph the payoff to this strategy and compare it to
    Figure 20.10.

15. Joseph Jones, a manager at Computer Science, Inc. (CSI), received 10,000 shares of company
    stock as part of his compensation package. The stock currently sells at $40 a share. Joseph
    would like to defer selling the stock until the next tax year. In January, however, he will need to
    sell all his holdings to provide for a down payment on his new house. Joseph is worried about
    the price risk involved in keeping his shares. At current prices, he would receive $400,000 for
    the stock. If the value of his stock holdings falls below $350,000, his ability to come up with the
    necessary down payment would be jeopardized. On the other hand, if the stock value rises
    to $450,000, he would be able to maintain a small cash reserve even after making the down
    payment. Joseph considers three investment strategies:

    a. Strategy A is to write January call options on the CSI shares with strike price $45. These
       calls are currently selling for $3 each.
    b. Strategy B is to buy January put options on CSI with strike price $35. These options also sell
       for $3 each.
    c. Strategy C is to establish a zero-cost collar by writing the January calls and buying the
       January puts.

Evaluate each of these strategies with respect to Joseph's investment goals. What are the advantages and disadvantages of each? Which would you recommend?

16. Use the spreadsheet from the Excel Application box on spreads and straddles (available in Connect or through your course instructor; link to Chapter 20 material) to answer these questions.

e**Xcel**
Please visit us at
www.mhhe.com/Bodie11e

   a. Plot the payoff and profit diagrams to a straddle position with an exercise (strike) price of $130. Assume the options are priced as they are in the Excel Application.
   b. Plot the payoff and profit diagrams to a bullish spread position with exercise (strike) prices of $120 and $130. Assume the options are priced as they are in the Excel Application.

17. Some agricultural price support systems have guaranteed farmers a minimum price for their output. Describe the program provisions as an option. What is the asset? The exercise price?

18. In what ways is owning a corporate bond similar to writing a put option? A call option?

19. An executive compensation scheme might provide a manager a bonus of $1,000 for every dollar by which the company's stock price exceeds some cutoff level. In what way is this arrangement equivalent to issuing the manager call options on the firm's stock?

20. Consider the following options portfolio. You write an August expiration call option on IBM with exercise price $150. You write an August IBM put option with exercise price $145.

   a. Graph the payoff of this portfolio at option expiration as a function of IBM's stock price at that time.
   b. What will be the profit/loss on this position if IBM is selling at $153 on the option expiration date? What if IBM is selling at $160? Use the data in Figure 20.1 to answer this question.
   c. At what two stock prices will you just break even on your investment?
   d. What kind of "bet" is this investor making; that is, what must this investor believe about IBM's stock price to justify this position?

21. Consider the following portfolio. You write a put option with exercise price 90 and buy a put option on the same stock with the same expiration date with exercise price 95.

   a. Plot the value of the portfolio at the expiration date of the options.
   b. On the same graph, plot the profit of the portfolio. Which option must cost more?

22. A FinCorp put option with strike price 60 trading on the Acme options exchange sells for $2. To your amazement, a FinCorp put with the same maturity selling on the Apex options exchange but with strike price 62 also sells for $2. If you plan to hold the options positions to expiration, devise a zero-net-investment arbitrage strategy to exploit the pricing anomaly. Draw the profit diagram at expiration for your position.

23. Assume a stock has a value of $100. The stock is expected to pay a dividend of $2 per share at year-end. An at-the-money European-style put option with one-year maturity sells for $7. If the annual interest rate is 5%, what must be the price of a 1-year at-the-money European call option on the stock?

24. You buy a share of stock, write a 1-year call option with $X = \$10$, and buy a 1-year put option with $X = \$10$. Your net outlay to establish the entire portfolio is $9.50. (a) What is the payoff of your portfolio? (b) What must be the risk-free interest rate? The stock pays no dividends.

25. You write a put option with $X = 100$ and buy a put with $X = 110$. The puts are on the same stock and have the same expiration date.

   a. Draw the payoff graph for this strategy.
   b. Draw the profit graph for this strategy.
   c. If the underlying stock has positive beta, does this portfolio have positive or negative beta?

26. Joe Finance has just purchased a stock index fund, currently selling at $2,400 per share. To protect against losses, Joe also purchased an at-the-money European put option on the fund for $120, with exercise price $2,400, and 3-month time to expiration. Sally Calm, Joe's financial adviser, points out that Joe is spending a lot of money on the put. She notes that 3-month puts with strike prices of $2,340 cost only $90, and suggests that Joe use the cheaper put.

   a. Analyze Joe's and Sally's strategies by drawing the *profit* diagrams for the stock-plus-put positions for various values of the stock fund in three months.

   b. When does Sally's strategy do better? When does it do worse?
   c. Which strategy entails greater systematic risk?

27. You write a call option with $X = 50$ and buy a call with $X = 60$. The options are on the same stock and have the same expiration date. One of the calls sells for $3; the other sells for $9.

   a. Draw the payoff graph for this strategy at the option expiration date.
   b. Draw the profit graph for this strategy.
   c. What is the break-even point for this strategy? Is the investor bullish or bearish on the stock?

28. Devise a portfolio using only call options and shares of stock with the following value (payoff) at the option expiration date. If the stock price is currently $53, what kind of bet is the investor making?

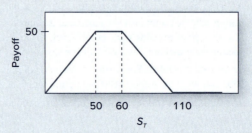

29. You are attempting to formulate an investment strategy. On the one hand, you think there is great upward potential in the stock market and would like to participate in the upward move if it materializes. However, you are not able to afford substantial stock market losses and so cannot run the risk of a stock market collapse, which you think is also a possibility. Your investment adviser suggests a protective put position: Buy both shares in a market index stock fund and put options on those shares with 3-month expiration and exercise price of $1,170. The stock index fund is currently selling for $1,350. However, your uncle suggests you instead buy a 3-month call option on the index fund with exercise price $1,260 and buy 3-month T-bills with face value $1,260.

   a. On the same graph, draw the *payoffs* to each of these strategies as a function of the stock fund value in three months. (*Hint:* Think of the options as being on one "share" of the stock index fund, with the current price of each share of the fund equal to $1,350.)
   b. Which portfolio must require a greater initial outlay to establish? (*Hint:* Does either portfolio provide a final payout that is always at least as great as the payoff of the other portfolio?)
   c. Suppose the market prices of the securities are as follows:

Stock fund	$1,350
T-bill (face value $1,260)	$1,215
Call (exercise price $1,260)	$ 180
Put (exercise price $1,170)	$ 9

   Make a table of the profits realized for each portfolio for the following values of the stock price in three months: $S_T = \$1,000, \$1,260, \$1,350, \$1,440$.

   Graph the profits to each portfolio as a function of S_T on a single graph.

   d. Which strategy is riskier? Which should have a higher beta?
   e. Explain why the data for the securities given in part (c) do *not* violate the put-call parity relationship.

30. Netflix is selling for $100 a share. A Netflix call option with one month until expiration and an exercise price of $105 sells for $2 while a put with the same strike and expiration sells for $6.94. What is the market price of a zero-coupon bond with face value $105 and 1-month maturity? What is the risk-free interest rate expressed as an effective annual yield?

31. Demonstrate that an at-the-money call option on a given stock must cost more than an at-the-money put option on that stock with the same expiration. The stock will pay no dividends until after the expiration date. (*Hint:* Use put-call parity.)

1. Donna Donie, CFA, has a client who believes the common stock price of TRT Materials (currently $58 per share) could move substantially in either direction in reaction to an expected court decision involving the company. The client currently owns no TRT shares, but asks Donie for advice about implementing a strangle strategy to capitalize on the possible stock price movement. A strangle is a portfolio of a put and a call with a higher exercise price but the same expiration date. Donie gathers the TRT option-pricing data:

Characteristic	Call Option	Put Option
Price	$ 5	$ 4
Strike price	$60	$55
Time to expiration	90 days from now	90 days from now

   a. Recommend whether Donie should choose a long strangle strategy or a short strangle strategy to achieve the client's objective.
   b. Calculate, at expiration for the appropriate strangle strategy in part (a), the:

      i. Maximum possible loss per share.
      ii. Maximum possible gain per share.
      iii. Break-even stock price(s).

2. Martin Bowman is preparing a report distinguishing traditional debt securities from structured note securities. Discuss how the following structured note securities differ from a traditional debt security with respect to coupon and principal payments:

   a. Equity index-linked notes.
   b. Commodity-linked bear bond.

3. Suresh Singh, CFA, is analyzing a convertible bond. The characteristics of the bond and the underlying common stock are given in the following exhibit:

Convertible Bond Characteristics	
Par value	$1,000
Annual coupon rate (annual pay)	6.5%
Conversion ratio	22
Market price	105% of par value
Straight value	99% of par value
Underlying Stock Characteristics	
Current market price	$40 per share
Annual cash dividend	$1.20 per share

   Compute the bond's:

   a. Conversion value.
   b. Market conversion price.

4. Rich McDonald, CFA, is evaluating his investment alternatives in Ytel Incorporated by analyzing a Ytel convertible bond and Ytel common equity. Characteristics of the two securities are given in the following exhibit:

Characteristics	Convertible Bond	Common Equity
Par value	$1,000	—
Coupon (annual payment)	4%	—
Current market price	$980	$35 per share
Straight bond value	$925	—
Conversion ratio	25	—
Conversion option	At any time	—
Dividend	—	$0
Expected market price in 1 year	$1,125	$45 per share

a. Calculate, based on the exhibit, the:

    i. Current market conversion price for the Ytel convertible bond.
    ii. Expected 1-year rate of return for the Ytel convertible bond.
    iii. Expected 1-year rate of return for the Ytel common equity.

One year has passed and Ytel's common equity price has increased to $51 per share. Also, over the year, the interest rate on Ytel's nonconvertible bonds of the same maturity increased, while credit spreads remained unchanged.

b. Name the two components of the convertible bond's value. Indicate whether the value of each component should decrease, stay the same, or increase in response to the:

    i. Increase in Ytel's common equity price.
    ii. Increase in interest rates.

5. a. Consider a bullish spread option strategy using a call option with a $25 exercise price priced at $4 and a call option with a $40 exercise price priced at $2.50. If the price of the stock increases to $50 at expiration and each option is exercised on the expiration date, the net profit per share at expiration (ignoring transaction costs) is:

    i. $8.50
    ii. $13.50
    iii. $16.50
    iv. $23.50

b. A put on XYZ stock with a strike price of $40 is priced at $2.00 per share, while a call with a strike price of $40 is priced at $3.50. What is the maximum per-share loss to the writer of the uncovered put and the maximum per-share gain to the writer of the uncovered call?

	Maximum Loss to Put Writer	Maximum Gain to Call Writer
i.	$38.00	$ 3.50
ii.	$38.00	$36.50
iii.	$40.00	$ 3.50
iv.	$40.00	$40.00

E-INVESTMENTS EXERCISES

1. Go to **www.nasdaq.com** and select *IBM* in the quote section. Once you have the information quote, request the information on options (look for the Tab for the *Option Chain*). Access prices for calls and puts that are closest to the money. For example, if the price of IBM is $151, use options with an exercise price of $150. Use options with time to expiration of about one month and two months.

    a. What are the prices for the put and call with one month time to expiration?

    b. What would be the cost of a straddle using these options?

    c. At expiration, what would be the break-even stock prices for the straddle?

    d. What would be the percentage increase or decrease in the stock price required to break even?

    e. What are the prices of the put and call with two-months time until expiration?

    f. What would be the cost of a straddle using the two-month expiration? At expiration, what would be the break-even stock prices for the straddle?

    g. What would be the percentage increase or decrease in the stock price required to break even?

✅ SOLUTIONS TO CONCEPT CHECKS

1. *a.* Denote the stock price at call option expiration by S_T, and the exercise price by X. Value at expiration = $S_T - X = S_T - \$150$ if this value is positive; otherwise the call expires worthless.

   Profit = Final value − Price of call option = Proceeds − \$4.10.

	$S_T = \$140$	$S_T = \$160$
Proceeds	\$0	\$10
Profits	−\$4.10	\$5.90

   b. Value at expiration = $X - S_T = \$150 - S_T$ if this value is positive; otherwise the put expires worthless.

   Profit = Final value − Price of put option = Proceeds − \$5.91.

	$S_T = \$140$	$S_T = \$160$
Proceeds	\$10	\$0
Profits	+\$4.09	−\$5.91

2. Before the split, the final payoff would have been $100 \times (\$160 - \$150) = \$1{,}000$. After the split, the payoff is $200 \times (\$80 - \$75) = \$1{,}000$. The payoff is unaffected.

3. *a*

Buy Call

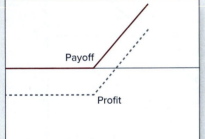

Write Put

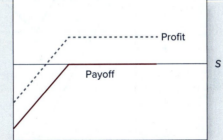

Write Call

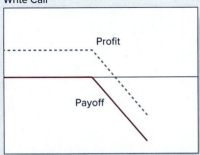

Buy Put

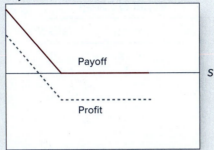

b. The payoffs and profits to both buying calls and writing puts generally are higher when the stock price is higher. In this sense, both positions are bullish. Both involve potentially taking delivery of the stock. However, the call holder will *choose* to take delivery when the stock price is high, while the put writer *is obligated* to take delivery when the stock price is low.

c. The payoffs and profits to both writing calls and buying puts generally are higher when the stock price is lower. In this sense, both positions are bearish. Both involve potentially making delivery of the stock. However, the put holder will *choose* to make delivery when the stock price is low, while the call writer *is obligated* to make delivery when the stock price is high.

4.

Payoff to a Strip

	$S_T \leq X$	$S_T > X$
2 Puts	$2(X - S_T)$	0
1 Call	0	$S_T - X$

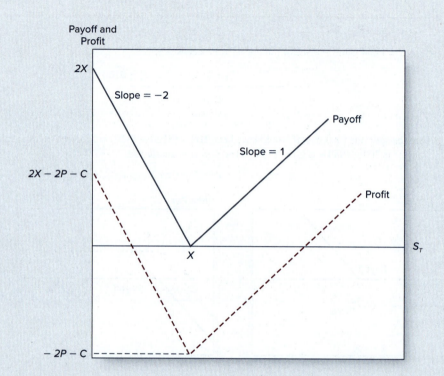

Payoff to a Strap

	$S_T \leq X$	$S_T > X$
1 Put	$X - S_T$	0
2 Calls	0	$2(S_T - X)$

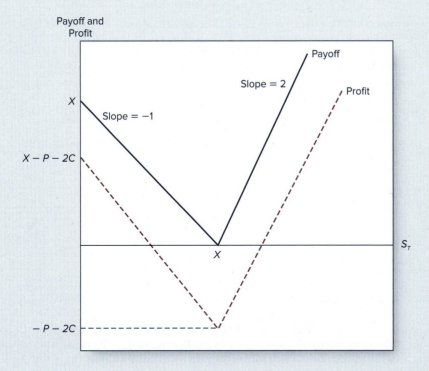

5. The payoff table on a per-share basis is as follows:

	$S_T \leq 90$	$90 \leq S_T \leq 110$	$S_T > 110$
Buy put ($X = 90$)	$90 - S_T$	0	0
Share	S_T	S_T	S_T
Write call ($X = 110$)	0	0	$-(S_T - 110)$
TOTAL	90	S_T	110

The graph of the payoff (on a per share basis) is as follows. If you multiply the per-share values by 2,000, you will see that the collar provides a minimum payoff of $180,000 (representing a maximum loss of $20,000) and a maximum payoff of $220,000 (which is the cost of the house).

6. The covered call strategy would consist of a straight bond with a call written on the bond. The value of the strategy at option expiration as a function of the value of the straight bond is given by the solid colored payoff line in the following figure, which is virtually identical to Figure 20.11.

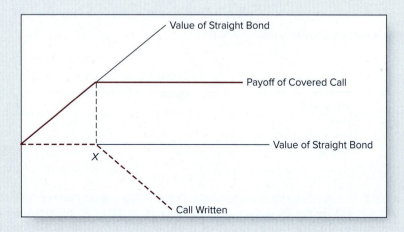

7. The call option is worth less as call protection is expanded. Therefore, the coupon rate need not be as high.

8. Lower. Investors will accept a lower coupon rate in return for the conversion option.

9. The depositor's implicit cost per dollar invested is now only ($.03 − $.005)/1.03 = $.02427 per 6-month period. Calls cost 50/1,000 = $.05 per dollar invested in the index. The multiplier falls to .02427/.05 = .4854.

Option Valuation

21

IN THE PREVIOUS chapter, we examined option markets and strategies. We noted that many securities contain embedded options that affect both their values and their risk–return characteristics. In this chapter, we turn our attention to option-valuation issues. Most option-valuation models require a considerable background in statistics. Still, many of the ideas and insights of these models can be demonstrated in simple examples, and we will concentrate on these.

We start with a discussion of the factors that ought to affect option prices. After this discussion, we present several bounds within which option prices must lie. Next we turn to quantitative models, starting with a simple "two-state" option-valuation model and then showing how this approach can be generalized into a useful and accurate pricing tool. We then move on to one particular valuation formula, the famous Black-Scholes model, one of the most significant breakthroughs in finance theory in several decades. Finally, we look at some of the more important applications of option-pricing theory in portfolio management and control.

Option-pricing models allow us to "back out" market estimates of stock-price volatility, and we will examine these measures of implied volatility. Next we turn to some of the more important applications of option-pricing theory in risk management. Finally, we take a brief look at some of the empirical evidence on option pricing and the implications of that evidence concerning the limitations of the Black-Scholes model.

21.1 Option Valuation: Introduction

Intrinsic and Time Values

Consider a call option that is out of the money at the moment, with the stock price below the exercise price. This does not mean the option is valueless. Even though immediate exercise would be unprofitable, the call still has value because there is always a chance the stock price will rise above the exercise price by the expiration date. If not, the worst that can happen is that the option will expire with zero value.

The value $S_0 - X$ is sometimes called the **intrinsic value** of in-the-money call options because it gives the payoff that could be obtained by immediate exercise. Intrinsic value is set equal to zero for out-of-the-money or at-the-money options. The difference between the actual call price and the intrinsic value is commonly called the **time value** of the option.

"Time value" is unfortunate terminology because it may confuse the option's time value with the time value of money. Time value in the options context refers simply to the difference between the option's price and the value it would have if it were expiring immediately. It is the part of the option's value that may be attributed to the fact that it still has positive time to expiration.

Most of an option's time value typically is a type of "volatility value." Because the option holder can choose not to exercise, the payoff cannot be worse than zero. Even if a call option is out of the money now, it still will sell for a positive price because it offers the potential for a profit if the stock price increases, while imposing no risk of additional loss should the stock price fall. The volatility value lies in the value of the right *not* to exercise if that action would be unprofitable. The option to exercise, as opposed to the obligation to exercise, provides insurance against poor stock price performance.

As the stock price increases substantially, it becomes likely that the call option will be exercised by expiration. Ultimately, with exercise all but assured, the volatility value becomes minimal. As the stock price gets ever larger, the option value approaches the "adjusted" intrinsic value, the stock price minus the present value of the exercise price, $S_0 - \text{PV}(X)$.

Why should this be? If you are virtually certain the option will be exercised and the stock purchased for X dollars, it is as though you own the stock already. The stock certificate, with a value today of S_0, might as well be sitting in your safe-deposit box now, as it will be there shortly. You just haven't paid for it yet. The present value of your obligation is the present value of X, so the net value of the call option is $S_0 - \text{PV}(X)$.[1]

Figure 21.1 illustrates the call option valuation function. The value curve shows that when the stock price is very low, the option is nearly worthless, because there is almost no chance that it will be exercised. When the stock price is very high, the option value approaches adjusted intrinsic value. In the midrange case, where the option is approximately at the money, the option curve diverges from the straight lines corresponding to adjusted intrinsic value. This is because although exercise today would have a negligible (or negative) payoff, the volatility value of the option is quite high in this region.

The call always increases in value with the stock price. The slope is greatest, however, when the option is deep in the money. In this case, exercise is all but assured, and the option increases in price one-for-one with the stock price.

Determinants of Option Values

We can identify at least six factors that should affect the value of a call option: the stock price, the exercise price, the volatility of the stock price, the time to expiration, the interest rate, and the dividend rate of the stock. The call option should increase in value with the stock price and decrease in value with the exercise price because the payoff to a call, if exercised, equals $S_T - X$. The expected payoff increases with the difference $S_0 - X$.

---

[1]This discussion presumes that the stock pays no dividends until after option expiration. If the stock does pay dividends before expiration, then there *is* a reason you would care about getting the stock now rather than at expiration—getting it now entitles you to the interim dividend payments. In this case, the adjusted intrinsic value of the option must subtract the value of the dividends the stock will pay out before the call is exercised. Adjusted intrinsic value would more generally be defined as $S_0 - \text{PV}(X) - \text{PV}(D)$, where D is the dividend to be paid before option expiration.

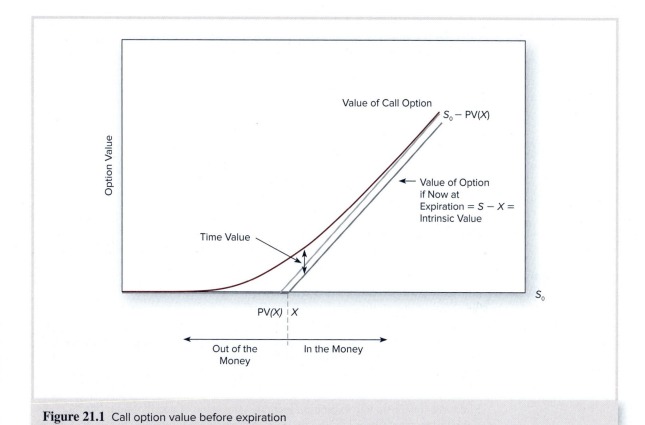

Figure 21.1 Call option value before expiration

Call option values also increase with the volatility of the underlying stock price. To see why, compare a scenario where possible stock prices at expiration may range from $10 to $50 to one where they range only from $20 to $40. In both cases, the expected, or average, stock price will be $30. Suppose the exercise price on a call option is also $30. What are the option payoffs?

High-Volatility Scenario					
Stock price	$10	$20	$30	$40	$50
Option payoff	0	0	0	10	20
Low-Volatility Scenario					
Stock price	$20	$25	$30	$35	$40
Option payoff	0	0	0	5	10

If each outcome is equally likely, with probability .2, the expected payoff to the option under high-volatility conditions will be $6, but under low-volatility conditions the expected payoff is half as much, only $3.

Although the expected stock price in both scenarios is $30, the average option payoff is greater in the high-volatility scenario. The source of this extra value is the limited loss an option holder can suffer, or the volatility value of the call. No matter how far below $30 the stock price drops, the option holder will get zero. We see that extremely poor stock price performance is no worse for the call option holder than moderately poor performance.

Table 21.1

Determinants of call option values

If This Variable Increases . . .	The Value of a Call Option
Stock price, S	Increases
Exercise price, X	Decreases
Volatility, σ	Increases
Time to expiration, T	Increases
Interest rate, r_f	Increases
Dividend payouts	Decreases

In the case of good stock performance, however, the call will expire in the money, and it will be more profitable the higher the stock price. Thus extremely good stock outcomes can improve the option payoff without limit, but extremely poor outcomes cannot worsen the payoff below zero. This asymmetry means that volatility in the underlying stock price increases the expected payoff to the option, thereby enhancing its value.[2]

 Concept Check **21.1**

Use the high and low volatility scenarios that we used for the call option to show that put options also are worth more when volatility is higher.

Similarly, longer time to expiration increases the value of a call option. For more distant expiration dates, there is more time for unpredictable future events to affect prices, and the range of likely stock prices increases. This has an effect similar to that of increased volatility. Moreover, as time to expiration lengthens, the present value of the exercise price falls, thereby benefiting the call option holder and increasing the option value. As a corollary to this issue, call option values are higher when interest rates rise (holding the stock price constant) because higher interest rates also reduce the present value of the exercise price.

Finally, the dividend payout policy of the firm affects option values. A high-dividend payout policy puts a drag on the rate of growth of the stock price. For any expected total rate of return on the stock, a higher dividend yield must imply a lower expected rate of capital gain. This drag decreases the potential payoff from the call option, thereby lowering its value. Table 21.1 summarizes these relationships.

 Concept Check **21.2**

Prepare a table like Table 21.1 for the determinants of put option values. How should American put values respond to increases in S, X, σ, T, r_f, and dividend payouts?

[2]You should be careful interpreting the relationship between volatility and option value. Neither the focus of this analysis on total (as opposed to systematic) volatility nor the conclusion that options buyers seem to like volatility contradicts modern portfolio theory. In conventional discounted cash flow analysis, we find the discount rate appropriate for a *given* distribution of future cash flows. Greater risk implies a higher discount rate and lower present value. Here, however, the cash flow from the *option* depends on the volatility of the *stock*. The option value increases not because traders like risk but because the expected cash flow to the option holder increases along with the volatility of the underlying asset.

21.2   Restrictions on Option Values

Several quantitative models of option pricing have been devised, and we will examine some of them later in this chapter. All models, however, rely on simplifying assumptions. You might wonder which properties of option values are truly general and which depend on the particular simplifications. To start with, we will consider some of the more important general properties of option prices. Some of these properties have important implications for the effect of stock dividends on option values and the possible profitability of early exercise of an American option.

Restrictions on the Value of a Call Option

The most obvious restriction on the value of a call option is that its value cannot be negative. Because the option need not be exercised, it cannot impose any liability on its holder; moreover, as long as there is any possibility that at some point the option can be exercised profitably, it will command a positive price. Its payoff is zero at worst, and possibly positive, so it has some positive value.

We can place another lower bound on the value of a call option. Suppose that the stock will pay a dividend of D dollars just before the option expiration date, denoted by T (where today is time 0). Now compare two portfolios, one consisting of a call option on one share of stock and the other a leveraged equity position consisting of that share and borrowing of $(X + D)/(1 + r_f)^T$ dollars. The loan repayment is $X + D$ dollars, due on the expiration date of the option. For example, for a one-year maturity option with exercise price $70, dividends to be paid of $5, and an effective annual interest of 5%, you would purchase one share of stock and borrow $75/1.05 = $71.43. In one year, when the loan matures, the payment due is $75. At that time, the payoff to the leveraged equity position is given by the following table (where S_T denotes the stock price at the option expiration date).

	In General	Our Numbers
Stock value	$S_T + D$	$S_T + 5$
− Payback of loan	$-(X + D)$	-75
Total	$S_T - X$	$S_T - 70$

Notice that the payoff to the stock is the ex-dividend stock value plus dividends received. Whether the total payoff to the stock-plus-borrowing position is positive or negative depends on whether S_T exceeds X. The net cash outlay required to establish this leveraged equity position is $S_0 - 71.43, or, more generally, $S_0 - (X + D)/(1 + r_f)^T$, that is, the current price of the stock, S_0, less the initial cash inflow from the borrowing position.

The payoff to the call option will be $S_T - X$ if the option expires in the money and zero otherwise. Thus the option payoff is equal to the leveraged equity payoff when that payoff is positive and greater when the leveraged equity position has a negative payoff. Because the option's payoff is always greater than or equal to that of the leveraged equity position, its price must exceed the cost of establishing that position.

Therefore, the value of the call must be greater than $S_0 - (X + D)/(1 + r_f)^T$, or, more generally,

$$C \geq S_0 - \text{PV}(X) - \text{PV}(D)$$

where $\text{PV}(X)$ denotes the present value of the exercise price and $\text{PV}(D)$ is the present value of the dividends the stock will pay at the option's expiration. More generally, we can interpret $\text{PV}(D)$ as the present value of any and all dividends to be paid prior to the option expiration date. Because we know already that the value of a call option must be nonnegative, we may conclude that C is greater than the *maximum* of either 0 or $S_0 - \text{PV}(X) - \text{PV}(D)$.

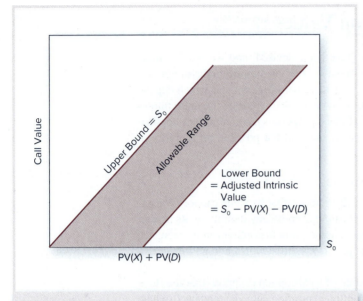

Figure 21.2 Range of possible call option values

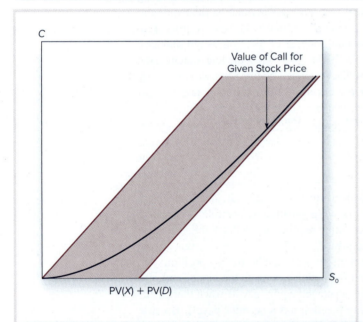

Figure 21.3 Call option value as a function of the current stock price

We also can place an upper bound on the possible value of the call; this bound is simply the stock price. No one would pay more than S_0 dollars for the right to purchase a stock currently worth S_0 dollars. Thus $C \leq S_0$.

Figure 21.2 demonstrates graphically the range of prices that is ruled out by these upper and lower bounds for the value of a call option. Any option value outside the shaded area is not possible according to the restrictions we have derived. Before expiration, the call option value normally will be *within* the allowable range, touching neither the upper nor lower bound, as in Figure 21.3.

Early Exercise and Dividends

A call option holder who wants to close out that position has two choices: exercise the call or sell it. If the holder exercises at time t, the call will provide a payoff of $S_t - X$, assuming, of course, that the option is in the money. We have just seen that the option can be sold for at least $S_t - PV(X) - PV(D)$. Therefore, if the stock does not pay a dividend, the call must be worth at least $S_t - PV(X)$. Because the present value of X is less than X itself, it follows that

$$C \geq S_t - PV(X) > S_t - X$$

The implication here is that the proceeds from a sale of the option (at price C) must exceed the proceeds from an exercise $(S_t - X)$. It is economically more attractive to sell the call, which keeps it alive, than to exercise and thereby end the option. In other words, calls on non-dividend-paying stocks are "worth more alive than dead."

If it never pays to exercise a call option before expiration, the right to exercise early actually must be valueless. We conclude that the values of otherwise identical American and European call options on stocks paying no dividends are equal. This simplifies matters, because any valuation formula that applies to the European call, for which only one exercise date need be considered, also must apply to an American call.

As most stocks do pay dividends, you may wonder whether this result is just a theoretical curiosity. It is not: Reconsider our argument and you will see that all that we really require is that the stock pay no dividends *until the option expires*. This condition will be true for many real-world options.

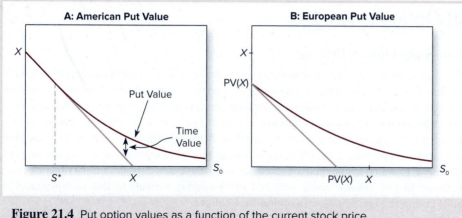

Figure 21.4 Put option values as a function of the current stock price

Early Exercise of American Puts

Early exercise of American *put options* sometimes will be rational regardless of dividends. To see why, start with an extreme example. Suppose that you purchase a put option, and almost immediately the firm goes bankrupt and its stock price falls to zero. Of course you want to exercise now, because the stock price can fall no lower. Immediate exercise gives you immediate receipt of the exercise price, which can be invested to start generating income. Delay in exercise means a time-value-of-money cost. The right to exercise a put option before expiration must have value.

Now suppose instead that the firm is only *nearly* bankrupt, with the stock selling at just a few cents. Immediate exercise may still be optimal. After all, the stock price can fall by only a very small amount, meaning that the proceeds from future exercise cannot be more than a few cents greater than the proceeds from immediate exercise. Against this possibility of a tiny increase in proceeds must be weighed the time-value-of-money cost of deferring exercise. Clearly, there is some stock price below which early exercise is optimal.

This argument also proves that the American put must be worth more than its European counterpart. The American put allows you to exercise anytime before expiration. Because the right to exercise early may be useful in some circumstances, it will command a premium. The American put therefore will sell for a higher price than a European put with otherwise identical terms.

Figure 21.4, Panel A, illustrates the value of an American put option as a function of the current stock price, S_0. Once the stock price drops below a critical value, denoted S^* in the figure, exercise becomes optimal. At that point the option-pricing curve is tangent to the straight line depicting the intrinsic value of the option. If and when the stock price reaches S^*, the put option is exercised and its payoff equals its intrinsic value.

In contrast, the value of the European put, which is graphed in Figure 21.4, Panel B, is not asymptotic to the intrinsic value line. Because early exercise is prohibited, the maximum value of the European put is PV(X), which occurs at the point $S_0 = 0$. Obviously, for a long enough horizon, PV(X) can be made arbitrarily small.

 Concept Check **21.3**

In light of this discussion, explain why the put-call parity relationship is valid only for European options on non-dividend-paying stocks. If the stock pays no dividends, what *inequality* for American options would correspond to the parity theorem?

21.3   Binomial Option Pricing

Two-State Option Pricing

A complete understanding of commonly used option-valuation formulas is difficult without a substantial mathematics background. Nevertheless, we can develop valuable insight into option valuation by considering a simple special case. Assume that a stock price can take only two possible values at option expiration: The stock will either increase to a given higher price or decrease to a given lower price. Although this may seem an extreme simplification, it provides a useful introduction to more complicated and realistic models. Moreover, it can be extended to describe far more reasonable specifications of stock price behavior. In fact, several major financial firms employ variants of this simple model to value options and securities with option-like features.

Suppose the stock now sells at $S_0 = \$100$, and the price will either increase by a factor of $u = 1.20$ to $120 ($u$ stands for "up") or fall by a factor of $d = .9$ to $90 ($d$ stands for "down") by year-end. A call option might specify an exercise price of $110 and a time to expiration of 1 year. The interest rate is 10%. At year-end, the payoff to the call will be either $0, if the stock price falls, or $10, if the stock price increases to $120.

These possibilities are illustrated by the following value "trees":

Stock price   Call option value

Now compare the payoff of the call to that of a portfolio consisting of one share of the stock and borrowing of $81.82 at the interest rate of 10%. The payoff of this portfolio also depends on the stock price at year-end:

	$90	$120
Value of stock at year-end	$90	$120
− Repayment of loan with interest	−90	−90
Total	$ 0	$ 30

We know the cash outlay to establish the portfolio is $18.18: $100 for the stock, less the $81.82 proceeds from borrowing. Therefore the portfolio's value tree is

The payoff of this portfolio is exactly three times that of the call option for either value of the stock price. Because the portfolio replicates the payoff of the three calls, we call it a *replicating portfolio*. Moreover, because their payoffs are the same, the three calls and the replicating portfolio must have the same value. Therefore,

$$3C = \$18.18$$

or each call should sell at $C = \$6.06$. Thus, given the stock price, exercise price, interest rate, and volatility of the stock price (as represented by the spread between the up or down movements), we can derive the fair value for the call option.

This valuation approach relies heavily on the notion of replication. With only two possible end-of-year values of the stock, the payoffs to the levered stock portfolio replicate the payoffs to three call options and, therefore, command the same market price. Replication is behind most option-pricing formulas. For more complex price distributions for stocks, the replication technique is correspondingly more complex, but the principles remain the same.

One way to view the role of replication is to note that, using the numbers assumed for this example, a portfolio made up of one share of stock and three call options written is perfectly hedged. Its year-end value is independent of the ultimate stock price:

Stock value	$90	$120
− Obligations from 3 calls written	−0	−30
Net payoff	$90	$ 90

The investor has formed a riskless portfolio, with a payout of $90. Its value must be the present value of $90, or $90/1.10 = $81.82. The value of the portfolio, which equals $100 from the stock held long, minus $3C$ from the three calls written, should equal $81.82. Hence $100 − 3C = 81.82, or $C = 6.06.

The ability to create a perfect hedge is the key to this argument. The hedge locks in the end-of-year payout, which therefore can be discounted using the *risk-free* interest rate. To find the value of the option in terms of the value of the stock, we do not need to know either the option's or the stock's beta or expected rate of return. When a perfect hedge can be established, the final stock price does not affect the investor's payoff, so the stock's risk and return parameters have no bearing.

The hedge ratio of this example is one share of stock to three calls, or one-third. This ratio has an easy interpretation in this context: It is the ratio of the range of the values of the option to those of the stock across the two possible outcomes. The stock, which originally sells for $S_0 = 100$, will be worth either $d \times $100 = 90 or $u \times $100 = 120, for a range of $30. If the stock price increases, the call will be worth $C_u = 10, whereas if the stock price decreases, the call will be worth $C_d = 0$, for a range of $10. The ratio of ranges, 10/30, is one-third, which is the hedge ratio we have established.

The hedge ratio equals the ratio of ranges because the option and stock are perfectly correlated in this two-state example. Because they are perfectly correlated, a perfect hedge requires that they be held in a fraction determined only by relative volatility.

We can generalize the hedge ratio for other two-state option problems as

$$H = \frac{C_u - C_d}{u S_0 - d S_0}$$

where C_u or C_d refers to the call option's value when the stock goes up or down, respectively, and $u S_0$ and $d S_0$ are the stock prices in the two states. The hedge ratio, H, is the ratio of the swings in the possible end-of-period values of the option and the stock. If the investor writes one option and holds H shares of stock, the value of the portfolio will be unaffected by the stock price. In this case, option pricing is easy: Simply set the value of the hedged portfolio equal to the present value of the known payoff.

Using our example, the option-pricing technique would proceed as follows:

1. Given the possible end-of-year stock prices, $u S_0 = 120$ and $d S_0 = 90$, and the exercise price of 110, calculate that $C_u = 10$ and $C_d = 0$. The stock price range is 30, while the option price range is 10.

2. Find that the hedge ratio of $10/30 = \frac{1}{3}$.

3. Find that a portfolio made up of $\frac{1}{3}$ share with one written option would have an end-of-year value of $30 with certainty.

4. Show that the present value of $30 with a 1-year interest rate of 10% is $27.27.

5. Set the value of the hedged position to the present value of the certain payoff:

$$\frac{1}{3}S_0 - C_0 = \$27.27$$

$$\$33.33 - C_0 = \$27.27$$

6. Solve for the call's value, $C_0 = \$6.06$.

What if the option is overpriced, perhaps selling for $6.50? Then you can make arbitrage profits. Here is how:

		Cash Flow in 1 Year for Each Possible Stock Price	
	Initial Cash Flow	$S_1 = 90$	$S_1 = 120$
1. Write 3 options	$ 19.50	$ 0	$-30
2. Purchase 1 share	-100	90	120
3. Borrow $80.50 at 10% interest; repay in 1 year	80.50	-88.55	-88.55
Total	$ 0	$ 1.45	$ 1.45

Although the net initial investment is zero, the payoff in one year is positive and riskless. If the option were underpriced, one would simply reverse this arbitrage strategy: Buy the option, and sell the stock short to eliminate price risk. Note, by the way, that the present value of the profit to the arbitrage strategy above exactly equals three times the amount by which the option is overpriced. The present value of the risk-free profit of $1.45 at a 10% interest rate is $1.318. With three options written in the strategy above, this translates to a profit of $.44 per option, exactly the amount by which the option was overpriced: $6.50 versus the "fair value" of $6.06.

 Concept Check **21.4**

Suppose the call option had been underpriced, selling at $5.50. Formulate the arbitrage strategy to exploit the mispricing, and show that it provides a riskless cash flow in one year of $.6167 per option purchased. Compare the present value of this cash flow to the option mispricing.

Generalizing the Two-State Approach

Although the two-state stock price model seems simplistic, we can generalize it to incorporate more realistic assumptions. To start, suppose we were to break up the year into two 6-month segments, and then assert that over each half-year segment the stock price could take on two values. In this example, we will say it can increase 10% (i.e., $u = 1.10$) or decrease 5% (i.e., $d = .95$). A stock initially selling at 100 could follow these possible paths over the course of the year:

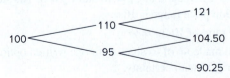

The midrange value of 104.50 can be attained by two paths: an increase of 10% followed by a decrease of 5%, or a decrease of 5% followed by a 10% increase.

There are now three possible end-of-year values for the stock and three for the option:

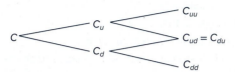

Using methods similar to those we followed above, we could value C_u from knowledge of C_{uu} and C_{ud}, then value C_d from knowledge of C_{du} and C_{dd}, and finally value C from knowledge of C_u and C_d. And there is no reason to stop at 6-month intervals. We could next break the year into four 3-month units, or twelve 1-month units, or 365 1-day units, each of which would be posited to have a two-state process. Although the calculations become quite numerous and correspondingly tedious, they are easy to program into a computer, and such computer programs are used widely by participants in the options market.

Example 21.1   Binomial Option Pricing

Suppose that the risk-free interest rate is 5% per 6-month period and we wish to value a call option with exercise price $110 on the stock described in the two-period price tree just above. We start by finding the value of C_u. From this point, the call can rise to an expiration-date value of $C_{uu} = \$11$ (because at this point the stock price is $u \times u \times S_0 = \$121$) or fall to a final value of $C_{ud} = 0$ (because at this point, the stock price is $u \times d \times S_0 = \$104.50$, which is less than the $110 exercise price). Therefore the hedge ratio at this point is

$$H = \frac{C_{uu} - C_{ud}}{uuS_0 - udS_0} = \frac{\$11 - 0}{\$121 - 104.50} = \frac{2}{3}$$

Thus, the following portfolio will be worth $209 at option expiration regardless of the ultimate stock price:

	$udS_0 = \$104.50$	$uuS_0 = \$121$
Buy 2 shares at price $uS_0 = \$110$	$209	$242
Write 3 calls at price C_u	0	−33
Total	$209	$209

The portfolio must have a current market value equal to the present value of $209:

$$2 \times 110 - 3C_u = \$209/1.05 = \$199.047$$

Solve to find that $C_u = \$6.984$.

Next we find the value of C_d. It is easy to see that this value must be zero. If we reach this point (corresponding to a stock price of $95), the stock price at option expiration will be either $104.50 or $90.25; in either case, the option will expire out of the money. (More formally, we could note that with $C_{ud} = C_{dd} = 0$, the hedge ratio is zero, and a portfolio of zero shares will replicate the payoff of the call!)

Finally, we solve for C using the values of C_u and C_d. Concept Check 21.5 leads you through the calculations that show the option value to be $4.434.

Concept Check **21.5**

Show that the initial value of the call option in Example 21.1 is $4.434.

a. Confirm that the spread in option values is $C_u - C_d = \$6.984$.
b. Confirm that the spread in stock values is $uS_0 - dS_0 = \$15$.
c. Confirm that the hedge ratio is .4656 shares purchased for each call written.
d. Demonstrate that the value in one period of a portfolio comprised of .4656 shares and one call written is riskless.
e. Calculate the present value of this payoff.
f. Solve for the option value.

Making the Valuation Model Practical

As we break the year into progressively finer subintervals, the range of possible year-end stock prices expands. For example, when we increase the number of subperiods to three, the number of possible stock prices increases to four, as demonstrated in the following stock price tree:

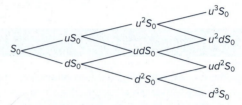

Thus, by allowing for an ever-greater number of subperiods, we can overcome one of the apparent limitations of the valuation model: that the number of possible end-of-period stock prices is small.

Notice that extreme events such as $u^3 S_0$ or $d^3 S_0$ are relatively rare, as they require either three consecutive increases or decreases in the three subintervals. More moderate, or mid-range, results such as $u^2 d S_0$ can be arrived at by more than one path—any combination of two price increases and one decrease will result in stock price $u^2 d S_0$. There are three of these paths: *uud, udu, duu.* In contrast, only one path, *uuu,* results in a stock price of $u^3 S_0$. Thus midrange values are more likely. As we make the model more realistic and break up the option maturity into more and more subperiods, the probability distribution for the final stock price begins to resemble the familiar bell-shaped curve, with highly unlikely extreme outcomes and far more likely midrange outcomes. The exact probability of each outcome is given by the binomial probability distribution, and this multiperiod approach to option pricing is therefore called the **binomial model.**

But we still need to answer an important practical question. Before the binomial model can be used to value actual options, we need a way to choose reasonable values for *u* and *d.* The spread between up and down movements in the price of the stock reflects the volatility of its rate of return, so the choice for *u* and *d* should depend on that volatility. Call σ your estimate of the standard deviation of the stock's continuously compounded annualized rate of return, and Δt the length of each subperiod. To make the standard deviation of the stock in the binomial model match your estimate of σ, it turns out that you can set $u = \exp(\sigma \sqrt{\Delta t})$ and $d = \exp(-\sigma \sqrt{\Delta t})$.[3] You can see that the proportional difference between *u* and *d* increases with both annualized volatility as well as the length of the subperiod. This makes sense, as both higher σ and longer holding periods make future stock prices more uncertain. The following example illustrates how to use this calibration.

[3]Notice that $d = 1/u$. This is the most common, but not the only, way to calibrate the model to empirical volatility. For alternative methods, see Robert L. McDonald, *Derivatives Markets,* 3rd ed. (Boston: Pearson/Addison-Wesley, 2013), Ch. 10.

Example 21.2 Calibrating u and d to Stock Volatility

Suppose you are using a 3-period model to value a 1-year option on a stock with volatility (i.e., annualized standard deviation) of $\sigma = .30$. With a time to expiration of $T = 1$ year, and three subperiods, you would calculate $\Delta t = T/n = 1/3$, $u = \exp(\sigma\sqrt{\Delta t}) = \exp(.30\sqrt{1/3}) = 1.189$ and $d = \exp(-\sigma\sqrt{\Delta t}) = \exp(-.30\sqrt{1/3}) = .841$. Given the probability of an up movement, you could then work out the probability of any final stock price. For example, suppose the probability that the stock price increases is .554 and the probability that it decreases is .446.[4] Then the probability of stock prices at the end of the year would be as follows:

Event	Possible Paths	Probability	Final Stock Price
3 down movements	ddd	$0.446^3 = 0.089$	$59.48 = 100 \times 0.841^3$
2 down and 1 up	ddu, dud, udd	$3 \times 0.446^2 \times 0.554 = 0.330$	$84.10 = 100 \times 1.189 \times 0.841^2$
1 down and 2 up	uud, udu, duu	$3 \times 0.446 \times 0.554^2 = 0.411$	$118.89 = 100 \times 1.189^2 \times 0.841$
3 up movements	uuu	$0.554^3 = 0.170$	$168.09 = 100 \times 1.189^3$

We plot this probability distribution in Figure 21.5, Panel A. Notice that the two middle end-of-period stock prices are, in fact, more likely than either extreme.

Now we can extend Example 21.2 by breaking up the option maturity into ever-shorter subintervals. As we do, the stock price distribution becomes increasingly plausible, as we demonstrate in Example 21.3.

Example 21.3 Increasing the Number of Subperiods

In Example 21.2, we broke up the year into three subperiods. Let's now look at the cases of 6 and 20 subperiods.

Subperiods, n	$\Delta t = T/n$	$u = \exp(\sigma\sqrt{\Delta t})$	$d = \exp(-\sigma\sqrt{\Delta t})$
3	0.333	$\exp(0.173) = 1.189$	$\exp(-0.173) = 0.841$
6	0.167	$\exp(0.122) = 1.130$	$\exp(-0.122) = 0.885$
20	0.050	$\exp(0.067) = 1.069$	$\exp(-0.067) = 0.935$

We plot the resulting probability distributions in Panels B and C of Figure 21.5.[5]

[4]Using this probability, the continuously compounded expected rate of return on the stock is .10. In general, the formula relating the probability of an upward movement to the annual expected rate of return, r, is
$$p = \frac{\exp(r\Delta t) - d}{u - d}.$$
[5]We adjust the probabilities of up versus down movements using the formula in footnote 4 to make the distributions in Figure 21.5 comparable. In each panel, p is chosen so that the stock's expected annualized, continuously compounded rate of return is 10%.

Notice that the right tail of the distribution in Panel C is noticeably longer than the left tail. In fact, as the number of intervals increases, the distribution progressively approaches the skewed log-normal (rather than the symmetric normal) distribution. Even if the stock price were to decline in *each* subinterval, it can never drop below zero. But there is no corresponding upper bound on its potential performance. This asymmetry gives rise to the skewness of the distribution.

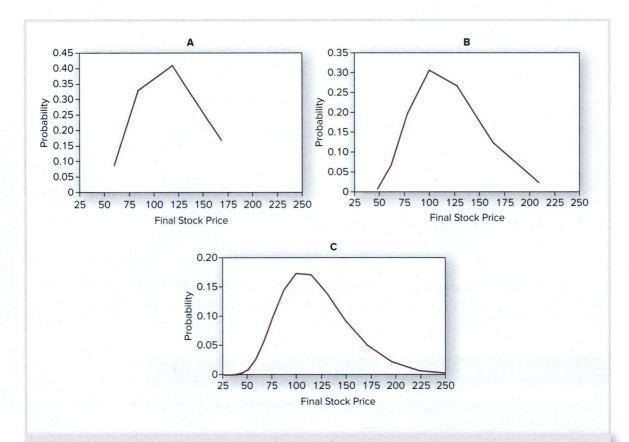

Figure 21.5 Probability distributions for final stock price. Possible outcomes and associated probabilities. In each panel, the stock's annualized, continuously compounded expected rate of return is 10% and its standard deviation is 30%. *Panel A.* Three subintervals. In each subinterval, the stock can increase by 18.9% or fall by 15.9%. *Panel B.* Six subintervals. In each subinterval, the stock can increase by 13.0% or fall by 11.5%. *Panel C.* Twenty subintervals. In each subinterval, the stock can increase by 6.9% or fall by 6.5%.

Eventually, as we divide the option maturity into an ever-greater number of subintervals, each node of the event tree corresponds to a smaller and smaller time interval. The possible stock price movement within each time interval is correspondingly small. As those many intervals pass, the end-of-period stock price more and more closely

A Risk-Neutral Shortcut

We pointed out earlier in the chapter that the binomial model valuation approach is arbitrage-based. We can value the option by replicating it with shares of stock plus borrowing. The ability to replicate the option means that its price relative to the stock and the interest rate must be based only on the technology of replication and *not* on risk preferences. It cannot depend on risk aversion or the capital asset pricing model or any other model of equilibrium risk-return relationships.

This insight—that the pricing model must be independent of risk aversion—leads to a very useful shortcut to valuing options. Imagine a *risk-neutral economy,* that is, an economy in which all investors are risk-neutral. This hypothetical economy must value options the same as our real one because risk aversion cannot affect the valuation formula.

In a risk-neutral economy, investors would not demand risk premiums and would therefore value all assets by discounting expected payoffs at the risk-free rate of interest. Therefore, a security such as a call option would be valued by discounting its expected cash flow at the risk-free rate: $C = \frac{\text{"}E\text{"}(CF)}{1 + r_f}$. We put the expectation operator E in quotation marks to signify that this is not the true expectation, but the expectation that would prevail in the hypothetical risk-neutral economy. To be consistent, we must calculate this expected cash flow using the rate of return the stock *would* have in the risk-neutral economy, *not* using its true rate of return. But if we successfully maintain consistency, the value derived for the hypothetical economy should match the one in our own.

How do we compute the expected cash flow from the option in the risk-neutral economy? Because there are no risk premiums, the stock's expected rate of return must equal the risk-free rate. Call p the probability that the stock price increases. Then p must be chosen to equate the expected rate of increase of the stock price to the risk-free rate (we ignore dividends here):

$$\text{"}E\text{"}(S_1) = p(uS) + (1 - p)dS = (1 + r_f)S$$

This implies that $p = \frac{1 + r_f - d}{u - d}$. We call p a *risk-neutral probability* to distinguish it from the true, or "objective," probability. To illustrate, in our two-state example at the beginning of Section 21.3, we had $u = 1.2$, $d = .9$, and $r_f = .10$. Given these values, $p = \frac{1 + .10 - .9}{1.2 - .9} = \frac{2}{3}$.

Now let's see what happens if we use the discounted cash flow formula to value the option in the risk-neutral economy. We continue to use the two-state example from Section 21.3. We find the present value of the option payoff using the risk-neutral probability and discount at the risk-free interest rate:

$$C = \frac{\text{"}E\text{"}(CF)}{1 + r_f} = \frac{pC_u + (1 - p)C_d}{1 + r_f} = \frac{2/3 \times 10 + 1/3 \times 0}{1.10} = 6.06$$

This answer exactly matches the value we found using our no-arbitrage approach!

We repeat: This is not truly an expected discounted value.

- The *numerator* is not the true expected cash flow from the option because we use the risk-neutral probability, p, rather than the true probability.

- The *denominator* is not the proper discount rate for option cash flows because we do not account for the risk.

- In a sense, these two "errors" cancel out. But this is not just luck: We are *assured* to get the correct result because the no-arbitrage approach implies that risk preferences cannot affect the option value. Therefore, the value computed for the risk-neutral economy *must* equal the value that we obtain in our economy.

When we move to the more realistic multiperiod model, the calculations are more cumbersome, but the idea is the same. Footnote 4 shows how to relate p to any expected rate of return and volatility estimate. Simply set the expected rate of return on the stock equal to the risk-free rate, use the resulting probability to work out the expected payoff from the option, discount at the risk-free rate, and you will find the option value. These calculations are actually fairly easy to program in Excel.

---

resembles a lognormal distribution.[6] Thus the apparent oversimplification of the two-state model can be overcome by progressively subdividing any period into many subperiods.

At any node, one still can set up a portfolio that is perfectly hedged over the next tiny time interval. Then, at the end of that interval, on reaching the next node, a new hedge ratio can be computed and the portfolio composition could be revised to remain hedged

---

[6]Actually, more complex considerations enter here. The limit of this process is lognormal only if we assume also that stock prices move continuously, by which we mean that over small time intervals only small price movements can occur. This rules out rare events such as sudden, extreme price moves in response to dramatic information (like a takeover attempt). For a treatment of this type of "jump process," see John C. Cox and Stephen A. Ross, "The Valuation of Options for Alternative Stochastic Processes," *Journal of Financial Economics* 3 (January–March 1976), pp. 145–66; or Robert C. Merton, "Option Pricing When Underlying Stock Returns Are Discontinuous," *Journal of Financial Economics* 3 (January–March 1976), pp. 125–44.

over the coming small interval. By continuously revising the hedge position, the portfolio remains hedged and earns a riskless rate of return over each interval. This is called *dynamic hedging,* the continued updating of the hedge ratio as time passes. As the dynamic hedge becomes ever finer, the resulting option-valuation procedure becomes more precise. The nearby box offers further refinements on the use of the binomial model.

 Concept Check **21.6**

In the table in Example 21.3, *u* and *d* both get closer to 1 (*u* is smaller and *d* is larger) as the time interval Δ*t* shrinks. Why does this make sense? Does the fact that *u* and *d* are each closer to 1 mean that the total volatility of the stock over the remaining life of the option is lower?

21.4 Black-Scholes Option Valuation

While the binomial model is extremely flexible, a computer is needed for it to be useful in actual trading. An option-pricing *formula* would be far easier to use than the tedious algorithm involved in the binomial model. It turns out that such a formula can be derived if one is willing to make just two more assumptions: that both the risk-free interest rate and stock price volatility are constant over the life of the option. In this case, as the time to expiration is divided into ever-more subperiods, the distribution of the stock price at expiration progressively approaches the lognormal distribution, as suggested by Figure 21.5. When the stock price distribution is actually lognormal, we can derive an exact option-pricing formula.

The Black-Scholes Formula

Financial economists searched for years for a workable option-pricing model before Black and Scholes[7] and Merton[8] derived a formula for the value of a call option. Scholes and Merton shared the 1997 Nobel Prize in Economics for their accomplishment.[9] Now widely used by options market participants, the **Black-Scholes pricing formula** for a call option is

$$C_0 = S_0 N(d_1) - Xe^{-rT} N(d_2) \qquad (21.1)$$

where

$$d_1 = \frac{\ln(S_0/X) + (r + \sigma^2/2)T}{\sigma\sqrt{T}}$$

$$d_2 = d_1 - \sigma\sqrt{T}$$

---

[7]Fischer Black and Myron Scholes, "The Pricing of Options and Corporate Liabilities," *Journal of Political Economy* 81 (May–June 1973).

[8]Robert C. Merton, "Theory of Rational Option Pricing," *Bell Journal of Economics and Management Science* 4 (Spring 1973).

[9]Fischer Black passed away in 1995.

and

C_0 = Current call option value.

S_0 = Current stock price.

$N(d)$ = The probability that a random draw from a standard normal distribution will be less than d. This equals the area under the normal curve up to d, as in the shaded area of Figure 21.6. In Excel, this function is called NORMSDIST(d) or NORM.S.DIST(d, TRUE).

X = Exercise price.

e = The base of the natural log function, approximately 2.71828. In Excel, e^x can be evaluated using the function EXP(x).

r = Risk-free interest rate (the annualized continuously compounded rate on a safe asset with the same maturity as the expiration date of the option, which is to be distinguished from r_f, the discrete period interest rate).

T = Time to expiration of option, in years.

ln = Natural logarithm function. In Excel, ln(x) can be calculated using the built-in function LN(x).

σ = Standard deviation of the annualized continuously compounded rate of return of the stock.

Notice a surprising feature of Equation 21.1: The option value does *not* depend on the expected rate of return on the stock. In a sense, this information is already built into the formula with the inclusion of the stock price, which itself reflects the stock's risk and return characteristics. This version of the Black-Scholes formula is predicated on the assumption that the stock pays no dividends.

Although you may find the Black-Scholes formula intimidating, we can explain it at a somewhat intuitive level. The trick is to view the $N(d)$ terms (loosely) as risk-adjusted probabilities that the call option will expire in the money. First, look at Equation 21.1 assuming both $N(d)$ terms are close to 1.0, that is, when there is a very high probability the option will be exercised. Then the call option value is equal to $S_0 - Xe^{-rT}$, which is what we called earlier the adjusted intrinsic value, $S_0 - PV(X)$. This makes sense; if exercise is certain, we have a claim on a stock with current value S_0, and an obligation with present value $PV(X)$, or, with continuous compounding, Xe^{-rT}.

Now look at Equation 21.1 assuming the $N(d)$ terms are close to zero, meaning the option almost certainly will not be exercised. Then the equation confirms that the call is worth nothing. For middle-range values of $N(d)$ between 0 and 1, Equation 21.1 tells us that the call value can be viewed as the present value of the call's potential payoff adjusting for the probability of in-the-money expiration.

How do the $N(d)$ terms serve as risk-adjusted probabilities? This question quickly

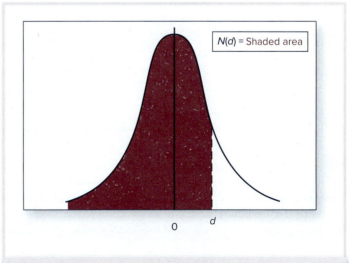

Figure 21.6 A standard normal curve

leads us into advanced statistics. Notice, however, that $\ln(S_0/X)$, which appears in the numerator of d_1 and d_2, is approximately the percentage amount by which the option is currently in or out of the money. For example, if $S_0 = 105$ and $X = 100$, the option is 5% in the money, and $\ln(105/100) = .049$. Similarly, if $S_0 = 95$, the option is 5% out of the money, and $\ln(95/100) = -.051$. The denominator, $\sigma\sqrt{T}$, adjusts the amount by which the option is in or out of the money for the volatility of the stock price over the remaining life of the option. An option in the money by a given percent is more likely to stay in the money if both stock price volatility and time to expiration are low. Therefore, $N(d_1)$ and $N(d_2)$ increase with the probability that the option will expire in the money.

Example 21.4   Black-Scholes Valuation

You can use the Black-Scholes formula fairly easily. Suppose you want to value a call option under the following circumstances:

Stock price:	$S_0 = 100$
Exercise price:	$X = 95$
Interest rate:	$r = .10$ (10% per year)
Time to expiration:	$T = .25$ (3 months or one-quarter of a year)
Standard deviation:	$\sigma = .50$ (50% per year)

First calculate

$$d_1 = \frac{\ln(100/95) + (.10 + .5^2/2).25}{.5\sqrt{.25}} = .43$$

$$d_2 = .43 - .5\sqrt{.25} = .18$$

Next find $N(d_1)$ and $N(d_2)$. The values of the normal distribution are tabulated and may be found in many statistics textbooks. A table of $N(d)$ is provided here as Table 21.2. The normal distribution function, $N(d)$, is also provided in any spreadsheet program. In Microsoft Excel, for example, the function name is NORMSDIST or NORM.S.DIST. Using either Excel or Table 21.2 we find that

$$N(.43) = .6664$$

$$N(.18) = .5714$$

Thus the value of the call option is

$$C = 100 \times .6664 - 95e^{-.10 \times .25} \times .5714$$

$$= 66.64 - 52.94 = \$13.70$$

 Concept Check **21.7**

Recalculate the value of the call option in Example 21.4 using a standard deviation of .6 instead of .5. Confirm that the option is worth more using the higher stock-return volatility.

What if the option price in Example 21.4 were $15 rather than $13.70? Is the option mispriced? Maybe, but before betting your fortune on that, you may want to reconsider the valuation analysis. First, like all models, the Black-Scholes formula is based on some simplifying abstractions that make the formula only approximately valid.

d	N(d)	d	N(d)	d	N(d)	d	N(d)	d	N(d)	d	N(d)
−3.00	0.0013	−1.58	0.0571	−0.76	0.2236	0.06	0.5239	0.86	0.8051	1.66	0.9515
−2.95	0.0016	−1.56	0.0594	−0.74	0.2297	0.08	0.5319	0.88	0.8106	1.68	0.9535
−2.90	0.0019	−1.54	0.0618	−0.72	0.2358	0.10	0.5398	0.90	0.8159	1.70	0.9554
−2.85	0.0022	−1.52	0.0643	−0.70	0.2420	0.12	0.5478	0.92	0.8212	1.72	0.9573
−2.80	0.0026	−1.50	0.0668	−0.68	0.2483	0.14	0.5557	0.94	0.8264	1.74	0.9591
−2.75	0.0030	−1.48	0.0694	−0.66	0.2546	0.16	0.5636	0.96	0.8315	1.76	0.9608
−2.70	0.0035	−1.46	0.0721	−0.64	0.2611	0.18	0.5714	0.98	0.8365	1.78	0.9625
−2.65	0.0040	−1.44	0.0749	−0.62	0.2676	0.20	0.5793	1.00	0.8414	1.80	0.9641
−2.60	0.0047	−1.42	0.0778	−0.60	0.2743	0.22	0.5871	1.02	0.8461	1.82	0.9656
−2.55	0.0054	−1.40	0.0808	−0.58	0.2810	0.24	0.5948	1.04	0.8508	1.84	0.9671
−2.50	0.0062	−1.38	0.0838	−0.56	0.2877	0.26	0.6026	1.06	0.8554	1.86	0.9686
−2.45	0.0071	−1.36	0.0869	−0.54	0.2946	0.28	0.6103	1.08	0.8599	1.88	0.9699
−2.40	0.0082	−1.34	0.0901	−0.52	0.3015	0.30	0.6179	1.10	0.8643	1.90	0.9713
−2.35	0.0094	−1.32	0.0934	−0.50	0.3085	0.32	0.6255	1.12	0.8686	1.92	0.9726
−2.30	0.0107	−1.30	0.0968	−0.48	0.3156	0.34	0.6331	1.14	0.8729	1.94	0.9738
−2.25	0.0122	−1.28	0.1003	−0.46	0.3228	0.36	0.6406	1.16	0.8770	1.96	0.9750
−2.20	0.0139	−1.26	0.1038	−0.44	0.3300	0.38	0.6480	1.18	0.8810	1.98	0.9761
−2.15	0.0158	−1.24	0.1075	−0.42	0.3373	0.40	0.6554	1.20	0.8849	2.00	0.9772
−2.10	0.0179	−1.22	0.1112	−0.40	0.3446	0.42	0.6628	1.22	0.8888	2.05	0.9798
−2.05	0.0202	−1.20	0.1151	−0.38	0.3520	0.44	0.6700	1.24	0.8925	2.10	0.9821
−2.00	0.0228	−1.18	0.1190	−0.36	0.3594	0.46	0.6773	1.26	0.8962	2.15	0.9842
−1.98	0.0239	−1.16	0.1230	−0.34	0.3669	0.48	0.6844	1.28	0.8997	2.20	0.9861
−1.96	0.0250	−1.14	0.1271	−0.32	0.3745	0.50	0.6915	1.30	0.9032	2.25	0.9878
−1.94	0.0262	−1.12	0.1314	−0.30	0.3821	0.52	0.6985	1.32	0.9066	2.30	0.9893
−1.92	0.0274	−1.10	0.1357	−0.28	0.3897	0.54	0.7054	1.34	0.9099	2.35	0.9906
−1.90	0.0287	−1.08	0.1401	−0.26	0.3974	0.56	0.7123	1.36	0.9131	2.40	0.9918
−1.88	0.0301	−1.06	0.1446	−0.24	0.4052	0.58	0.7191	1.38	0.9162	2.45	0.9929
−1.86	0.0314	−1.04	0.1492	−0.22	0.4129	0.60	0.7258	1.40	0.9192	2.50	0.9938
−1.84	0.0329	−1.02	0.1539	−0.20	0.4207	0.62	0.7324	1.42	0.9222	2.55	0.9946
−1.82	0.0344	−1.00	0.1587	−0.18	0.4286	0.64	0.7389	1.44	0.9251	2.60	0.9953
−1.80	0.0359	−0.98	0.1635	−0.16	0.4365	0.66	0.7454	1.46	0.9279	2.65	0.9960
−1.78	0.0375	−0.96	0.1685	−0.14	0.4443	0.68	0.7518	1.48	0.9306	2.70	0.9965
−1.76	0.0392	−0.94	0.1736	−0.12	0.4523	0.70	0.7580	1.50	0.9332	2.75	0.9970
−1.74	0.0409	−0.92	0.1788	−0.10	0.4602	0.72	0.7642	1.52	0.9357	2.80	0.9974
−1.72	0.0427	−0.90	0.1841	−0.08	0.4681	0.74	0.7704	1.54	0.9382	2.85	0.9978
−1.70	0.0446	−0.88	0.1894	−0.06	0.4761	0.76	0.7764	1.56	0.9406	2.90	0.9981
−1.68	0.0465	−0.86	0.1949	−0.04	0.4841	0.78	0.7823	1.58	0.9429	2.95	0.9984
−1.66	0.0485	−0.84	0.2005	−0.02	0.4920	0.80	0.7882	1.60	0.9452	3.00	0.9986
−1.64	0.0505	−0.82	0.2061	0.00	0.5000	0.82	0.7939	1.62	0.9474	3.05	0.9989
−1.62	0.0526	−0.80	0.2119	0.02	0.5080	0.84	0.7996	1.64	0.9495		
−1.60	0.0548	−0.78	0.2177	0.04	0.5160						

Table 21.2

Cumulative normal distribution

Some of the important assumptions underlying the formula are the following:

1. The stock will pay no dividends until after the option expiration date.
2. Both the interest rate, r, and variance rate, σ^2, of the stock are constant (or in slightly more general versions of the formula, both are *known* functions of time—any changes are perfectly predictable).
3. Stock prices are continuous, meaning that sudden extreme jumps such as those in the aftermath of an announcement of a takeover attempt are ruled out.

Variants of the Black-Scholes formula have been developed to deal with many of these limitations.

Second, even within the context of the Black-Scholes model, you must be sure of the accuracy of the parameters used in the formula. Four of these—S_0, X, T, and r—are straightforward. The stock price, exercise price, and time to expiration are readily determined. The interest rate used is the money market rate for a maturity equal to that of the option, and the dividend payout is reasonably predictable, at least over short horizons.

The last input, though, the standard deviation of the stock return, is not directly observable. It must be estimated from historical data, from scenario analysis, or from the prices of other options, as we will describe momentarily.

We saw in Chapter 5 that the historical variance of stock market returns can be calculated from n observations as follows:

$$\sigma^2 = \frac{n}{n-1} \sum_{t=1}^{n} \frac{(r_t - \bar{r})^2}{n}$$

where $\bar{r}$ is the average return over the sample period. The rate of return on day t is defined to be consistent with continuous compounding as $r_t = \ln(S_t/S_{t-1})$. [We note again that the natural logarithm of a ratio is approximately the percentage difference between the numerator and denominator so that $\ln(S_t/S_{t-1})$ is a measure of the rate of return of the stock from time $t - 1$ to time t.] Historical variance commonly is computed using daily returns over periods of several months. Because the volatility of stock returns must be estimated, however, it is always possible that discrepancies between an option price and its Black-Scholes value are simply artifacts of error in the estimation of the stock's volatility.

In fact, market participants often give the option-valuation problem a different twist. Rather than calculating a Black-Scholes option value for a given stock's standard deviation, they ask instead: What standard deviation would be necessary for the option price that I observe to be consistent with the Black-Scholes formula? This is called the **implied volatility** of the option, the volatility level for the stock implied by the option price. Investors can then judge whether they think the actual stock standard deviation exceeds the implied volatility. If it does, the option is considered a good buy; if actual volatility seems greater than the implied volatility, its fair price would exceed the observed price.

Another variation is to compare two options on the same stock with equal expiration dates but different exercise prices. The option with the higher implied volatility would be considered relatively expensive, because a higher standard deviation is required to justify its price. The analyst might consider buying the option with the lower implied volatility and writing the option with the higher implied volatility.

The Black-Scholes valuation formula, as well as the implied volatility, is easily calculated using an Excel spreadsheet like Spreadsheet 21.1. The model inputs are provided in column B, and the outputs are given in column E. The formulas for d_1 and d_2 are provided in the spreadsheet, and the Excel formula NORMSDIST(d_1) or NORM.S.DIST(d_1, TRUE) is used to calculate $N(d_1)$. Cell E6 contains the Black-Scholes formula. (The formula in the spreadsheet actually includes an adjustment for dividends, as described in the next section.)

	A	B	C	D	E	F	G	H	I	J
1	**INPUTS**			**OUTPUTS**			**FORMULA FOR OUTPUT IN COLUMN E**			
2	Standard deviation (annual)	0.2783		d1	0.0029		(LN(B5/B6)+(B4−B7+.5*B2^2)*B3)/(B2*SQRT(B3))			
3	Maturity (in years)	0.5		d2	−0.1939		E2−B2*SQRT(B3)			
4	Risk-free rate (annual)	0.06		N(d1)	0.5012		NORMSDIST(E2)			
5	Stock price	100		N(d2)	0.4231		NORMSDIST(E3)			
6	Exercise price	105		B/S call value	7.0000		B5*EXP(−B7*B3)*E4−B6*EXP(−B4*B3)*E5			
7	Dividend yield (annual)	0		B/S put value	8.8968		B6*EXP(−B4*B3)*(1−E5)−B5*EXP(−B7*B3)*(1−E4)			

Spreadsheet 21.1

Spreadsheet to calculate Black-Scholes call option values

eXcel
Please visit us at
www.mhhe.com/Bodie11e

To compute an implied volatility, we can use the Goal Seek command from the What-If Analysis menu (which can be found under the Data tab) in Excel. See Figure 21.7 for an illustration. Goal Seek asks us to change the value of one cell to make the value of another cell (called the *target cell*) equal to a specific value. For example, if we observe a call option selling for $7 with other inputs as given in the spreadsheet, we can use Goal Seek to change the value in cell B2 (the standard deviation of the stock) to set the option value in cell E6 equal to $7. The target cell, E6, is the call price, and the spreadsheet manipulates cell B2. When you click *OK,* the spreadsheet finds that a standard deviation equal to .2783 is consistent with a call price of $7; this would be the option's implied volatility if it were selling at $7.

	A	B	C	D	E	F	G	H	I	J
1	INPUTS			OUTPUTS			FORMULA FOR OUTPUT IN COLUMN E			
2	Standard deviation (annual)	0.2783		d1	0.0029		(LN(B5/B6)+(B4−B7+.5*B2^2)*B3)/(B2*SQRT(B3))			
3	Maturity (in years)	0.5		d2	−0.1939		E2−B2*SQRT(B3)			
4	Risk-free rate (annual)	0.06		N(d1)	0.5012		NORMSDIST(E2)			
5	Stock price	100		N(d2)	0.4231		NORMSDIST(E3)			
6	Exercise price	105		B/S call value	7.0000		B5*EXP(−B7*B3)*E4−B6*EXP(−B4*B3)*E5			
7	Dividend yield (annual)	0		B/S put value	8.8968		B6*EXP(−B4*B3)*(1−E5) − B5*EXP(−B7*B3)*(1−E4)			

Goal Seek
Set cell: $E$6
To value: 7
By changing cell: $B$2
OK Cancel

Figure 21.7 Using Goal Seek to find implied volatility

eXcel
Please visit us at
www.mhhe.com/Bodie11e

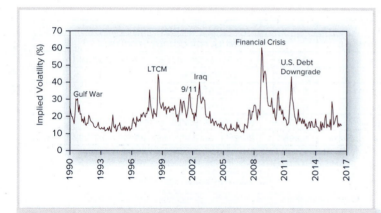

Figure 21.8 Implied volatility of the S&P 500 (VIX index)

Source: Chicago Board Options Exchange, **www.cboe.com**.

The Chicago Board Options Exchange regularly computes the implied volatility of major stock indexes. Figure 21.8 is a graph of the implied (30-day) volatility of the S&P 500 since 1990. During periods of turmoil, implied volatility can spike quickly. Notice the peaks in January 1991 (Gulf War), August 1998 (collapse of Long-Term Capital Management), September 11, 2001 (terrorist attacks in the U.S.), 2002 (build-up to invasion of Iraq), and, most dramatically, during 2008 (the financial crisis). Because implied volatility correlates with crisis, it is sometimes called an "investor fear gauge."

A futures contract on the 30-day implied volatility of the S&P 500 has traded on the CBOE Futures Exchange since 2004. The payoff of the contract depends on market implied volatility at the expiration of the contract. The ticker symbol of the contract is VIX.

Figure 21.8 reveals an awkward empirical fact. While the Black-Scholes formula is derived assuming that stock volatility is constant, the time series of implied volatilities derived from that formula is in fact far from constant. This contradiction reminds us that the Black-Scholes model (like all models) is a simplification that does not capture all aspects of real markets. In this particular context, extensions of the pricing model that allow stock volatility to evolve randomly over time would be desirable, and, in fact, many extensions of the model along these lines have been developed.[10]

The fact that volatility changes unpredictably means that it can be difficult to choose the proper volatility input to use in any option-pricing model. A considerable amount of recent research has been devoted to techniques to predict changes in volatility. These techniques, known as *ARCH* and *stochastic volatility* models, posit that changes in volatility are partially predictable and that by analyzing recent levels and trends in volatility, one can improve predictions of future volatility.[11]

 Concept Check **21.8**

Suppose the call option in Spreadsheet 21.1 actually is selling for $8. Is its implied volatility more or less than 27.83%? Use the spreadsheet (available in Connect) and Goal Seek to find its implied volatility at this price.

---

[10]Influential articles on this topic are J. Hull and A. White, "The Pricing of Options on Assets with Stochastic Volatilities," *Journal of Finance* (June 1987), pp. 281–300; J. Wiggins, "Option Values under Stochastic Volatility," *Journal of Financial Economics* (December 1987), pp. 351–72; and S. Heston, "A Closed-Form Solution for Options with Stochastic Volatility with Applications to Bonds and Currency Options," *Review of Financial Studies* 6 (1993), pp. 327–43. For a review, see E. Ghysels, A. Harvey, and E. Renault, "Stochastic Volatility," in *Handbook of Statistics, Vol. 14: Statistical Methods in Finance,* ed. G. S. Maddala (Amsterdam: North Holland, 1996).

[11]For an introduction to these models see Carol Alexander, *Market Risk Analysis*, Vol. 4 (England: Wiley, 2009).

Dividends and Call Option Valuation

We noted earlier that the Black-Scholes call option formula applies to stocks that do not pay dividends. When dividends are to be paid before the option expires, we need to adjust the formula. The payment of dividends raises the possibility of early exercise, and for most realistic dividend payout schemes the valuation formula becomes significantly more complex than the Black-Scholes equation.

When stocks pay quarterly dividends, their share prices decline by a discrete amount, roughly equal to the amount of the dividend. In some cases, it will be rational for the call holder to exercise just before the stock goes ex dividend. This introduces uncertainty into "maturity" of the call. Will it be exercised at the ex-dividend date or held until the expiration date?[12] Variations on the Black-Scholes formula have been developed that can accommodate dividends, but the resulting valuation formulas are more complex and become rapidly more difficult as the number of possible dividend payments increase.[13]

In one special case, the dividend adjustment takes a simple form and allows us to use a slight variant of the Black-Scholes formula. Suppose the underlying asset pays a continuous flow of income. This might be a reasonable assumption for options on a stock index, where different stocks in the index pay dividends on different days, so that dividend income arrives in a more or less continuous flow. If the dividend yield, denoted δ, is constant, one can show that the present value of that dividend flow accruing until the option expiration date is $S_0 (1 - e^{-\delta T})$.[14] In this case, $S_0 - \text{PV(Div)} = S_0 e^{-\delta T}$, and we can use the Black-Scholes call option formula on the dividend-paying asset simply by substituting $S_0 e^{-\delta T}$ for S_0 in the original formula. This approach is used in Spreadsheet 21.1.

One warning about this practice, however. Even with continuous dividends, it may be rational to exercise the call option early, so strictly speaking, the modified Black-Scholes formula would apply only to European options. As a general rule, American calls on dividend paying stocks will be worth more than European ones even if dividends are continuous.

Put Option Valuation

We have concentrated so far on call option valuation. We can derive Black-Scholes European put option values from call option values using the put-call parity theorem. To value the put option, we simply calculate the value of the corresponding call option in Equation 21.1 from the Black-Scholes formula, and solve for the put option value (on a non-dividend paying stock) as

$$P = C + \text{PV}(X) - S_0$$
$$= C + Xe^{-rT} - S_0$$

(21.2)

We calculate the present value of the exercise price using continuous compounding to be consistent with the Black-Scholes formula.

---

[12]While the stock price falls by a discrete amount on the ex-dividend date, the option price does not. The dividend is announced in advance and is anticipated by the market. The option price will adjust smoothly over time to reflect the approaching dividend payment.

[13]An exact formula for American call valuation on dividend-paying stocks has been developed in Richard Roll, "An Analytic Valuation Formula for Unprotected American Call Options on Stocks with Known Dividends," *Journal of Financial Economics* 5 (November 1977). The technique has been discussed and revised in Robert Geske, "A Note on an Analytical Formula for Unprotected American Call Options on Stocks with Known Dividends," *Journal of Financial Economics* 7 (December 1979); and Robert E. Whaley, "On the Valuation of American Call Options on Stocks with Known Dividends," *Journal of Financial Economics* 9 (June 1981).

[14]For intuition about this formula, notice that $e^{-\delta T}$ approximately equals $1 - \delta T$, so the value of the dividend is approximately $\delta T S_0$.

Sometimes, it is easier to work with a put option valuation formula directly. If we substitute the Black-Scholes formula for a call in Equation 21.2, we obtain the value of a European put option as

$$P = Xe^{-rT}[1 - N(d_2)] - S_0[1 - N(d_1)] \tag{21.3}$$

Example 21.5   Black-Scholes Put Valuation

Using data from Example 21.4 ($C = \$13.70$, $X = \$95$, $S_0 = \$100$, $r = .10$, $\sigma = .50$, and $T = .25$), Equation 21.3 implies that a European put option on that stock with identical exercise price and time to expiration is worth

$$\$95e^{-.10 \times .25}(1 - .5714) - \$100(1 - .6664) = \$6.35$$

Notice that this value is consistent with put-call parity:

$$P = C + PV(X) - S_0 = 13.70 + 95e^{-.10 \times .25} - 100 = 6.35$$

As we noted traders can do, we might then compare this formula value to the actual put price as one step in formulating a trading strategy.

Dividends and Put Option Valuation

Equation 21.2 and Equation 21.3 are valid for European puts on non-dividend-paying stocks. As we did for call options, if the underlying asset pays a dividend, we can find European put values by substituting $S_0 - PV(\text{Div})$ for S_0. Cell E7 in Spreadsheet 21.1 allows for a continuous dividend flow with a dividend yield of δ. In that case $S_0 - PV(\text{Div}) = S_0 e^{-\delta T}$.

However, listed put options on stocks are American options that offer the opportunity of early exercise, and we have seen that the right to exercise puts early can turn out to be valuable. This means that an American put option must be worth more than the corresponding European option. Therefore, Equation 21.2 and Equation 21.3 describe only the lower bound on the true value of the American put. However, in many applications the approximation is very accurate.

21.5   Using the Black-Scholes Formula

Hedge Ratios and the Black-Scholes Formula

In Chapter 20, we considered two investments in FinCorp stock: 100 shares or 1,000 call options. We saw that the call option position was more sensitive to swings in the stock price than was the all-stock position. To analyze the overall exposure to a stock price more precisely, however, it is necessary to quantify these relative sensitivities. We can summarize the overall exposure of portfolios of options with various exercise prices and times to expiration using the **hedge ratio,** the change in option price for a $1 increase in the stock price. A call option, therefore, has a positive hedge ratio and a put option a negative hedge ratio. The hedge ratio is commonly called the option's **delta.**

If you were to graph the option value as a function of the stock value, as we have done for a call option in Figure 21.9, the hedge ratio is simply the slope of the curve evaluated at the current stock price. For example, suppose the slope of the curve at $S_0 = \$120$ equals .60. As the stock increases in value by $1, the option increases by approximately $.60, as the figure shows.

For every call option written, .60 share of stock would be needed to hedge the investor's portfolio. If one writes 10 options and holds six shares of stock, according to the hedge ratio of .6, a $1 increase in stock price will result in a gain of $6 on the stock holdings, whereas the loss on the 10 options written will be $10 \times \$.60$, an equivalent $6. The stock price movement leaves total wealth unaltered, which is what a hedged position is intended to do.

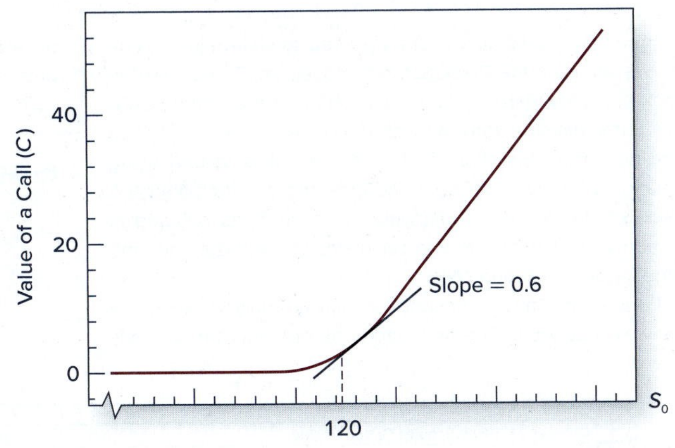

Figure 21.9 Call option value and hedge ratio

Black-Scholes hedge ratios are particularly easy to compute. The hedge ratio for a call is $N(d_1)$, whereas the hedge ratio for a put is $N(d_1) - 1$. We defined $N(d_1)$ as part of the Black-Scholes formula in Equation 21.1. Recall that $N(d)$ stands for the area under the standard normal curve up to d. Therefore, the call option hedge ratio must be positive and less than 1.0, whereas the put option hedge ratio is negative and of smaller absolute value than 1.0.

Figure 21.9 verifies that the slope of the call option valuation function is less than 1.0, approaching 1.0 only as the stock price becomes much greater than the exercise price. This tells us that option values change less than one-for-one with changes in stock prices. Why should this be? Suppose an option is so far in the money that you are absolutely certain it will be exercised. In that case, every dollar increase in the stock price would increase the option value by $1. But if there is a reasonable chance the call option will expire out of the money, even after a moderate stock price gain, a $1 increase in the stock price will not necessarily increase the ultimate payoff to the call; therefore, the call price will not respond by a full dollar.

The fact that hedge ratios are less than 1.0 does not contradict our earlier observation that options offer leverage and disproportionate sensitivity to stock price movements. Although *dollar* movements in option prices are less than dollar movements in the stock price, the *rate of return* volatility of options remains greater than stock return volatility because options sell at lower prices. In our example, with the stock selling at $120, and a hedge ratio of .6, an option with exercise price $120 may sell for $5. If the stock price increases to $121, the call price would be expected to increase by only $.60, to $5.60. The percentage increase in the option value is $\$.60/\$5.00 = 12\%$, however, whereas the stock price increase is only $\$1/\$120 = .83\%$. The ratio of the percentage changes is $12\%/.83\% = 14.4$. For every 1% increase in the stock price, the option price increases by 14.4%. This ratio, the percentage change in option price per percentage change in stock price, is called the **option elasticity.**

The hedge ratio is an essential tool in portfolio management and control. An example will show why.

The spreadsheet below can be used to determine option values using the Black-Scholes model. The inputs are the stock price, standard deviation, expiration of the option, exercise price, risk-free rate, and dividend yield. The call option is valued using Equation 21.1, and the put is valued using Equation 21.3. For both calls and puts, the dividend-adjusted Black-Scholes formula substitutes $Se^{-\delta T}$ for S, as outlined in Section 21.4. The model also calculates the intrinsic and time value for both puts and calls.

Further, the model presents sensitivity analysis using the one-way data table. The first workbook presents the analysis of calls while the second workbook presents similar analysis for puts. You can find these spreadsheets in Connect or through your course instructor.

Excel Questions

1. Find the value of the call and put options using the parameters given in this box but changing the standard deviation to .25. What happens to the value of each option?

2. What is implied volatility if the call option is selling for $9?

	A	B	C	D	E	F	G	H	I	J	K	L	M	N
1	Chapter 21- Black-Scholes Option Pricing						LEGEND:							
2	Call Valuation & Call Time Premiums						Enter data							
3							Value calculated							
4							See comment							
5	Standard deviation (σ)	0.27830												
6	Variance (annual, σ^2)	0.07745			Call			Call			Call			Call
7	Time to expiration (years, T)	0.50		Standard	Option		Standard	Time		Stock	Option		Stock	Time
8	Risk-free rate (annual, r)	6.00%		Deviation	Value		Deviation	Value		Price	Value		Price	Value
9	Current stock price (S_0)	$100.00			7.000			7.000			7.000			7.000
10	Exercise price (X)	$105.00		0.15	3.388		0.150	3.388		$60	0.017		$60	0.017
11	Dividend yield (annual, δ)	0.00%		0.18	4.089		0.175	4.089		$65	0.061		$65	0.061
12				0.20	4.792		0.200	4.792		$70	0.179		$70	0.179
13	d_1	0.0029095		0.23	5.497		0.225	5.497		$75	0.440		$75	0.440
14	d_2	−0.193878		0.25	6.202		0.250	6.202		$80	0.935		$80	0.935
15	$N(d_1)$	0.50116		0.28	6.907		0.275	6.907		$85	1.763		$85	1.763
16	$N(d_2)$	0.42314		0.30	7.612		0.300	7.612		$90	3.014		$90	3.014
17	Black-Scholes call value	$6.99992		0.33	8.317		0.325	8.317		$95	4.750		$95	4.750
18	Black-Scholes put value	$8.89670		0.35	9.022		0.350	9.022		$100	7.000		$100	7.000
19				0.38	9.726		0.375	9.726		$105	9.754		$105	9.754
20				0.40	10.429		0.400	10.429		$110	12.974		$110	7.974
21	Intrinsic value of call	$0.00000		0.43	11.132		0.425	11.132		$115	16.602		$115	6.602
22	Time value of call	6.99992		0.45	11.834		0.450	11.834		$120	20.572		$120	5.572
23				0.48	12.536		0.475	12.536		$125	24.817		$125	4.817
24	Intrinsic value of put	$5.00000		0.50	13.236		0.500	13.236		$130	29.275		$130	4.275
25	Time value of put	3.89670								$135	33.893		$135	3.893

Example 21.6 Hedge Ratios

Consider two portfolios, one holding 750 FinCorp calls and 200 shares of FinCorp and the other holding 800 shares of FinCorp. Which portfolio has greater dollar exposure to FinCorp price movements? You can answer this question easily by using the hedge ratio.

Each option changes in value by H dollars for each dollar change in stock price, where H stands for the hedge ratio. Thus, if H equals .6, the 750 options are equivalent to $.6 \times 750 = 450$ shares in terms of the response of their market value to FinCorp stock price movements. The first portfolio has less dollar sensitivity to stock price change because the 450 share-equivalents of the options plus the 200 shares actually held are less than the 800 shares held in the second portfolio.

This is not to say, however, that the first portfolio is less sensitive to the stock's rate of return. As we noted in discussing option elasticities, the first portfolio may have lower total value than the second, so despite its lower sensitivity in terms of dollar value, it might have greater rate of return sensitivity.

Concept Check **21.9**

What is the elasticity of a put option currently selling for $4 with exercise price $120 and hedge ratio −.4 if the stock price is currently $122?

Portfolio Insurance

In Chapter 20, we showed that protective put strategies offer a sort of insurance policy on an asset. The protective put has proven to be extremely popular with investors. Even if the asset price falls, the put conveys the right to sell the asset for the exercise price, which is a way to lock in a minimum portfolio value. With an at-the-money put ($X = S_0$), the maximum possible loss is the cost of the put. The asset can be sold for X, which equals its original value, so even if the asset price falls, the investor's net loss over the period is just the cost of the put. If the asset value increases, however, upside potential is unlimited. Figure 21.10 graphs the profit or loss on a protective put position as a function of the change in the value of the underlying asset, P.

While the protective put is a simple and convenient way to achieve **portfolio insurance,** that is, to limit the worst-case portfolio rate of return, there are practical difficulties in trying to insure a portfolio of stocks. First, unless the investor's portfolio corresponds to a standard market index for which puts are traded, a put option on the portfolio will not be available for purchase. And if index puts are used to protect a non-indexed portfolio, tracking error can result. For example, if the portfolio falls in value while the market index rises, the put will fail to provide the intended protection. Moreover, the maturities of traded options may not match the investor's horizon. Therefore, rather than using option strategies, investors may use trading strategies that mimic the payoff to a protective put option.

Here is the general idea. Even if a put option on the desired portfolio does not exist, a theoretical option-pricing model (such as the Black-Scholes model) can be used to determine how that option's price would respond to the portfolio's value if it did trade.

For example, if stock prices were to fall, the put option would increase in value. The option model could quantify this relationship. The net exposure of the (hypothetical) protective put portfolio to swings in stock prices is the sum of the exposures of the two components of the portfolio, the stock and the put.

We can create "synthetic" protective put positions by holding a quantity of stocks with the same net exposure to market swings as the hypothetical protective put position. The key to this strategy is the option delta, that is, the change in the price of the protective put option per change in the value of the underlying stock portfolio.

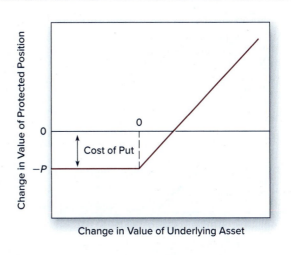

Figure 21.10 Profit on a protective put strategy

Example 21.7   Synthetic Protective Put Options

Suppose a portfolio is currently valued at $100 million. An at-the-money put option on the portfolio might have a hedge ratio or delta of −.6, meaning the option's value swings $.60 for every dollar change in portfolio value, but in an opposite direction. Suppose the stock portfolio falls in value by 2%. The profit on a hypothetical protective put position (if the put existed) would be as follows (in millions of dollars):

Loss on stocks	2% of $100 =	$2.00
Gain on put	$0.6 \times \$2.00 =$	1.20
Net loss		= $0.80

We create the synthetic option position by selling a proportion of shares equal to the put option's delta (i.e., selling 60% of the shares) and placing the proceeds in risk-free T-bills. The rationale is that the hypothetical put option would have offset 60% of any change in the stock portfolio's value, so one must reduce portfolio risk directly by selling 60% of the equity and putting the proceeds into a risk-free asset. Total return on a synthetic protective put position with $60 million in risk-free investments such as T-bills and $40 million in equity is

Loss on stocks	2% of $40 =	$0.80
Loss on bills		= 0
Net loss		= $0.80

The synthetic and actual protective put positions have equal returns. We conclude that if you sell a proportion of shares equal to the put option's delta and place the proceeds in cash equivalents, your exposure to the stock market will equal that of the desired protective put position.

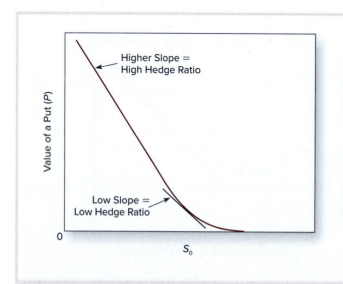

Figure 21.11 Hedge ratios change as the stock price fluctuates

The challenge with this procedure is that deltas constantly change. Figure 21.11 shows that as the stock price falls, the magnitude of the appropriate hedge ratio increases. Therefore, market declines require extra hedging, that is, additional conversion of equity into cash. This constant updating of the hedge ratio is called **dynamic hedging** (alternatively, delta hedging).

Dynamic hedging is one reason portfolio insurance has been said to contribute to market volatility. Market declines trigger additional sales of stock as portfolio insurers strive to increase their hedging. These additional sales are seen as reinforcing or exaggerating market downturns.

In practice, portfolio insurers often do not actually buy or sell stocks directly when they update their hedge positions. Instead, they minimize trading costs by buying or selling stock index futures as a substitute for sale of the stocks themselves. As you will see in Chapter 22, stock prices and index futures prices usually are very tightly linked by cross-market arbitrageurs so that futures transactions can be used as reliable proxies for stock transactions. Instead of selling equities based on the put option's delta, insurers will sell an equivalent number of futures contracts.[15]

Several portfolio insurers suffered great setbacks during the market crash of October 19, 1987, when the market suffered an unprecedented 1-day loss of about 20%. A description of what happened then should let you appreciate the complexities of applying a seemingly straightforward hedging concept.

1. Market volatility at the crash was much greater than ever encountered before. Put option deltas based on historical experience were too low; insurers under-hedged, held too much equity, and suffered excessive losses.

2. Prices moved so fast that insurers could not keep up with the necessary rebalancing. They were "chasing deltas" that kept getting away from them. The futures market also saw a "gap" opening, where the opening price was nearly 10% below the previous day's close. The price dropped before insurers could update their hedge ratios.

3. Execution problems were severe. First, current market prices were unavailable, with trade execution and the price quotation system hours behind, which made computation of correct hedge ratios impossible. Moreover, trading in stocks and stock futures ceased during some periods. The continuous rebalancing capability that is essential for a viable insurance program vanished during the precipitous market collapse.

4. Futures prices traded at steep discounts to their proper levels compared to reported stock prices, thereby making the sale of futures (as a proxy for equity sales) seem expensive. Although you will see in Chapter 22 that stock index futures prices should have exceeded the value of the stock index on October 19, Figure 21.12 shows that futures sold far below the stock index level on that day. When some

Figure 21.12 S&P 500 cash-to-futures spread in points

Source: *Report of the Presidential Task Force on Market Mechanisms*, Nicholas Brady, Chairman. January, 1988, p. 33.

---

[15]Notice, however, that the use of index futures reintroduces the problem of tracking error between the portfolio and the market index.

insurers gambled that the futures price would recover to its expected premium over the stock index and chose to defer sales, they remained underhedged. As the market fell farther, their portfolios experienced substantial losses.

Although most observers at the time believed that the portfolio insurance industry would never recover from the market crash, delta hedging is still alive and well on Wall Street. Dynamic hedges are widely used by large firms to hedge potential losses from options positions. For example, when Microsoft ended its employee stock option program in 2003, its investment banker J.P. Morgan purchased many already-issued options of Microsoft employees, and it was widely expected that Morgan would protect its options position by selling shares in Microsoft using a delta hedging strategy.[16]

Option Pricing and the Crisis of 2008–2009

Merton[17] shows how option pricing models can provide insight into the financial crisis of 2008–2009. The key to understanding his argument is to remember that when banks lend to or buy the debt of firms with limited liability, they implicitly write a put option to the borrower (see Chapter 20, Section 20.5). If the borrower has sufficient assets to pay off the loan when it comes due, it will do so, and the lender will be fully repaid. But if the borrower has insufficient assets, it can declare bankruptcy and discharge its obligations by transferring ownership of the firm to its creditors. The borrower's ability to satisfy the loan by transferring ownership is equivalent to the right to "sell" itself to the creditor for the face value of the loan. This arrangement is therefore just like a put option on the firm with exercise price equal to the stipulated loan repayment.

Consider the payoff to the lender at loan maturity (time T) as a function of the value of the borrowing firm, V_T, when the loan, with face value L, comes due. If $V_T \geq L$, the lender is paid off in full. But if $V_T < L$, the lender gets the firm, which is worth less than the promised payment L.

We can write the payoff in a way that emphasizes the implicit put option:

$$\text{payoff} = \begin{cases} L \\ V_T \end{cases} = L - \begin{cases} 0 & \text{if } V_T \geq L \\ L - V_T & \text{if } V_T < L \end{cases} \qquad \textbf{(21.4)}$$

Equation 21.4 shows that the payoff on the loan equals L (when the firm has sufficient assets to pay off the debt), *minus* the payoff of a put option on the value of the firm (V_T) with an exercise price of L. Therefore, we may view risky lending as a combination of safe lending, with a guaranteed payoff of L, combined with a short position in a put option on the borrower.

When firms sell credit default swaps (see Chapter 14, Section 14.5), the implicit put option is even clearer. Here, the CDS seller agrees to make up any losses due to the insolvency of a bond issuer. If the issuer goes bankrupt, leaving assets of only V_T for the creditors, the CDS seller is obligated to make up the difference, $L - V_T$. This is in essence a pure put option.

Now think about the exposure of these implicit put writers to changes in the financial health of the underlying firm. The value of a put option on V_T appears in Figure 21.13. When the firm is financially strong (i.e., V is far greater than L), the slope of the curve

---

[16]To read more about this episode, see Jathon Sapsford and Ken Brown, "J.P. Morgan Rolls Dice on Microsoft Options," *The Wall Street Journal*, July 9, 2003.

[17]This material is based on a lecture given by Robert Merton at MIT in March 2009. You can find the lecture online at http://video.mit.edu/watch/observations-on-the-science-of-finance-in-the-practice-of-finance-9449/.

is nearly zero, implying that there is little exposure of the implicit put writer (either the bank or the CDS writer) to the value of the borrowing firm. For example, when firm value is 1.75 times the value of the debt, the light line drawn tangent to the put value curve has a slope of only −.040. But if there is a big shock to the economy, and firm value falls, not only does the value of the implicit put rise, but its slope is now steeper (see the steep, dark tangent line), implying that exposure to further shocks is now far greater. When firm value is only 75% of the value of the loan, the slope of the line tangent to the put value valuation curve is far steeper, −.644. You can see how as you get closer to the edge of the cliff, it gets easier and easier to slide right off.

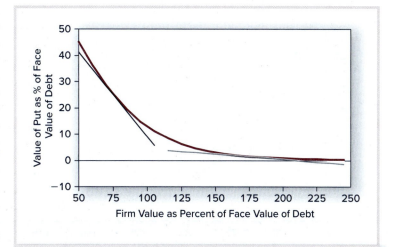

Figure 21.13 Value of the implicit put option in a loan guarantee as a percentage of the face value of debt (Debt maturity = 1 year; Standard deviation of value of firm = 40%; Risk free rate = 6%)

We often hear people say that a shock to asset values of the magnitude of the financial crisis was a 10-sigma event, by which they mean that such an event was so extreme that it would be 10 standard deviations away from an expected outcome, making it virtually inconceivable. But Figure 21.13 shows that standard deviation may be a moving target, increasing dramatically as the firm weakens. As the economy falters and put options go further into the money, their sensitivity to further shocks increases, increasing the risk that even worse losses may be around the corner. The built-in instability of risk exposures makes a scenario like the crisis more plausible and should give us pause when we discount an extreme scenario as "almost impossible."

Option Pricing and Portfolio Theory

We've just seen that the option pricing model predicts that security risk characteristics can be unstable. For example, as the firm weakens, the risk of its debt can quickly accelerate. So, too, can equity risk change dramatically as the firm's financial condition deteriorates. We know from the last chapter (Section 20.5) that equity in a levered firm is like a call option on the value of the firm. If firm value exceeds the value of the firm's maturing debt, the firm can choose to pay off the debt, retaining the difference between firm value and the face value of its debt. If not, the firm can default on the loan, turning the firm over to its creditors, and the equityholders get nothing. In this sense, equity is a call option, and the firm's total value is the underlying asset.

Earlier in this section, we saw that the *elasticity* of an option measures the sensitivity of its rate of return to the rate of return on the underlying asset. For example, if a call option's elasticity is 5, its rate of return will swing five times as widely as the rate of return on the underlying asset. This would imply that both the option's beta and its standard deviation are five times the beta and standard deviation of the underlying asset.

Therefore, when compiling the "input list" for creating an efficient portfolio, we may wish to think of equity as an implicit call option and compute its elasticity with respect to the total value of the firm. For example, if the covariance of the firm's *assets* with other securities is stable, then we can use elasticity to find the covariance of the firm's *equity*

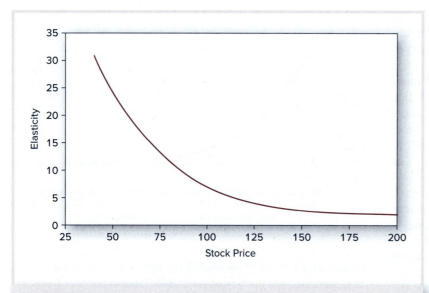

Figure 21.14 Call option elasticity as a function of stock price
(Parameters: σ = .25; *T* = .5, *r* = .06; *X* = 100)

with those securities. This will allow us to calculate beta and standard deviation.

Unfortunately, elasticity can itself be a moving target. As the firm gets weaker, its elasticity will increase, potentially very quickly. Figure 21.14 uses the Black-Scholes model to plot call option elasticity as a function of the value of the underlying stock. Notice that as the firm gets closer to insolvency (the value of firm assets falls below the face value of debt), equity elasticity shoots up, and even small changes in financial condition can lead to major changes in risk. Elasticity is far more stable (and closer to 1) when the firm is healthy (i.e., the implicit call option is deep in the money). Therefore, equity risk characteristics will be far more stable for healthy firms than for precarious ones.

Hedging Bets on Mispriced Options

Suppose you believe that the standard deviation of FinCorp stock returns will be 35% over the next few weeks, but FinCorp put options are selling at a price consistent with a volatility of 33%. Because the put's implied volatility is less than your forecast of the stock volatility, you believe the option is underpriced. Using your assessment of volatility in an option-pricing model like the Black-Scholes formula, you would estimate that the fair price for the puts exceeds the actual price.

Does this mean that you ought to buy put options? Perhaps, but by doing so, you risk losses if FinCorp stock performs well, *even if* you are correct about the volatility. You would like to separate your bet on volatility from the "attached" bet inherent in purchasing a put that FinCorp's stock price will fall. In other words, you would like to speculate on the option mispricing by purchasing the put option, but hedge the resulting exposure to the performance of FinCorp stock.

The option *delta* can be interpreted as a hedge ratio that can be used for this purpose. The delta was defined as

$$\text{Delta} = \frac{\text{Change in value of option}}{\text{Change in value of stock}} \tag{21.5}$$

Therefore, delta is the slope of the option-pricing curve.

This ratio tells us precisely how many shares of stock we must hold to offset our exposure to FinCorp. For example, if the put's delta is −.6, then it will fall by $.60 for every one-dollar increase in the stock price, and we need to hold .6 share of stock to hedge each put. If we purchase 10 option contracts, each for 100 shares, we would need to buy 600 shares of stock. If the stock price rises by $1, each put option will decrease in value by

$.60, resulting in a loss of $600. However, the loss on the puts will be offset by a gain on the stock holdings of $1 per share × 600 shares.

To see how the profits on this strategy might develop, let's use the following example.

Example 21.8   Speculating on Mispriced Options

Suppose option expiration T is 60 days; put price P is $4.495; exercise price X is $90; stock price S is $90; and the risk-free rate r is 4%. We assume that the stock will not pay a dividend in the next 60 days. Given these data, the implied volatility on the option is 33%, as we posited. However, you believe the true volatility is 35%, implying that the fair put price is $4.785. Therefore, if the market assessment of volatility is revised to the value you believe is correct, your profit will be $.29 per put purchased.

Recall that the hedge ratio, or delta, of a put option equals $N(d_1) - 1$, where $N(\cdot)$ is the cumulative normal distribution function and

$$d_1 = \frac{\ln(S/X) + (r + \sigma^2/2)T}{\sigma\sqrt{T}}$$

Using your estimate of $\sigma = .35$, you find that the hedge ratio $N(d_1) - 1 = -.453$.

Suppose, therefore, that you purchase 10 option contracts (1,000 puts) and purchase 453 shares of stock. Once the market "catches up" to your presumably better volatility estimate, the put options purchased will increase in value. If the market assessment of volatility changes as soon as you purchase the options, your profits should equal $1,000 \times \$.29 = \$290$. The option price will be affected as well by any change in the stock price, but this part of your exposure will be eliminated if the hedge ratio is chosen properly. Your profit should be based solely on the effect of the change in the implied volatility of the put, with the impact of the stock price hedged away.

Table 21.3 illustrates your profits as a function of the stock price assuming that the put price changes to reflect *your* estimate of volatility. Panel B shows that the put option alone can provide profits or losses depending on whether the stock price falls or rises. We see in Panel C, however, that each *hedged* put option provides profits nearly equal to the original mispricing, regardless of the change in the stock price.

Table 21.3

Profit on hedged put portfolio

A. Cost to Establish Hedged Position

1,000 put options @ $4.495/option	$ 4,495
453 shares @ $90/share	40,770
Total outlay	$45,265

B. Value of Put Option as a Function of the Stock Price at Implied Volatility of 35%

Stock price:	89	90	91
Put price	$ 5.254	$ 4.785	$ 4.347
Profit (loss) on each put	0.759	0.290	(0.148)

C. Value of and Profit on Hedged Put Portfolio

Stock price:	89	90	91
Value of 1,000 put options	$ 5,254	$ 4,785	$ 4,347
Value of 453 shares	40,317	40,770	41,223
Total	$45,571	$45,555	$45,570
Profit (= Value − Cost from Panel A)	306	290	305

✔ Concept Check **21.10**

Suppose you bet on volatility by purchasing calls instead of puts. How would you hedge your exposure to stock-price fluctuations? What is the hedge ratio?

Notice in Example 21.8 that the profit is not exactly independent of the stock price. This is because as the stock price changes, so do the deltas used to calculate the hedge ratio. The hedge ratio in principle would need to be continually adjusted as deltas evolve. The sensitivity of the delta to the stock price is called the **gamma** of the option. Option gammas are analogous to bond convexity. In both cases, the curvature of the value function means that hedge ratios or durations change with market conditions, making rebalancing a necessary part of hedging strategies.

A variant of the strategy in Example 21.8 involves cross-option speculation. Suppose you observe a 45-day expiration call option on FinCorp with strike price 95 selling at a price consistent with a volatility of $\sigma = 33\%$ while another 45-day call with strike price 90 has an implied volatility of only 27%. Because the underlying asset and expiration date are identical, you conclude that the call with the higher implied volatility is relatively over-priced. To exploit the mispricing, you might buy the cheap calls (with strike price 90 and implied volatility of 27%) and write the expensive calls (with strike price 95 and implied volatility 33%). If the risk-free rate is 4% and FinCorp is selling at $90 per share, the calls purchased will be priced at $3.6202 and the calls written will be priced at $2.3735.

Despite the fact that you are long one call and short another, your exposure to FinCorp stock-price uncertainty will not be hedged using this strategy. This is because calls with different strike prices have different sensitivities to the price of the underlying asset. The lower-strike-price call has a higher delta and therefore greater exposure to the price of Fin-Corp. If you take an equal number of positions in these two options, you will inadvertently establish a bullish position in FinCorp, as the calls you purchase have higher deltas than the calls you write. In fact, you may recall from Chapter 20 that this portfolio (long call with low exercise price and short call with high exercise price) is called a *bullish spread*.

To establish a hedged position, we can use the hedge ratio approach as follows. Consider the 95-strike-price options you write as the asset that hedges your exposure to the 90-strike-price options you purchase. Then the hedge ratio is

$$H = \frac{\text{Change in value of 90-strike-price call for \$1 change in FinCorp}}{\text{Change in value of 95-strike-price call for \$1 change in FinCorp}}$$

$$= \frac{\text{Delta of 90-strike-price call}}{\text{Delta of 95-strike-price call}} > 1$$

You need to write *more* than one call with the higher strike price to hedge the purchase of each call with the lower strike price. Because the prices of higher-strike-price calls are less sensitive to FinCorp prices, more of them are required to offset the exposure.

Suppose the true annual volatility of the stock is midway between the two implied vola-tilities, so $\sigma = 30\%$. We know that the delta of a call option is $N(d_1)$. Therefore, the deltas of the two options and the hedge ratio are computed as follows:

Option with strike price 90:

$$d_1 = \frac{\ln(90/90) + (.04 + .30^2/2) \times 45/365}{.30\sqrt{45/365}} = .0995$$

$$N(d_1) = .5396$$

Option with strike price 95:

$$d_1 = \frac{\ln(90/95) + (.04 + .30^2/2) \times 45/365}{.30\sqrt{45/365}} = -.4138$$

$$N(d_1) = .3395$$

Hedge ratio:

$$\frac{.5396}{.3395} = 1.589$$

Therefore, for every 1,000 call options purchased with strike price 90, we need to write 1,589 call options with strike price 95. Following this strategy enables us to bet on the relative mispricing of the two options without taking a position on FinCorp. Panel A of Table 21.4 shows that the position will result in a cash inflow of $151.30. The premium income on the calls written exceeds the cost of the calls purchased.

When you establish a position in stocks and options that is hedged with respect to fluctuations in the price of the underlying asset, your portfolio is said to be **delta neutral,** meaning that the portfolio has no tendency to either increase or decrease in value when the stock price fluctuates.

Let's check that our options position is in fact delta neutral. Suppose that the implied volatilities of the two options come back into alignment just after you establish your position, so that both options are priced at implied volatilities of 30%. You expect to profit from the increase in the value of the call purchased as well as from the decrease in the value of the call written. The option prices at 30% volatility are given in Panel B of Table 21.4 and the values of your position for various stock prices are presented in Panel C. Although the profit or loss on each option is affected by the stock price, the value of the delta-neutral option portfolio is positive and essentially independent of the stock price. Moreover, we saw in Panel A that the portfolio would have been established without ever requiring a cash outlay. You would have cash inflows both when you establish the portfolio *and* when you liquidate it after the implied volatilities converge to 30%.

Table 21.4

Profits on delta-neutral options portfolio

A. Cost Flow When Portfolio Is Established

Purchase 1,000 calls ($X = 90$) @ $3.6202
(option priced at implied volatility of 27%) $3,620.20 cash outflow
Write 1,589 calls ($X = 95$) @ $2.3735
(option priced at implied volatility of 33%)   3,771.50 cash inflow
Total $ 151.30 net cash inflow

B. Option Prices at Implied Volatility of 30%

Stock price:	89	90	91
90-strike-price calls	$3.478	$3.997	$4.557
95-strike-price calls	1.703	2.023	2.382

C. Value of Portfolio after Implied Volatilities Converge to 30%

Stock price:	89	90	91
Value of 1,000 calls held	$3,478	$3,997	$4,557
−Value of 1,589 calls written	2,705	3,214	3,785
Total	$ 773	$ 782	$ 772

This unusual profit opportunity arises because you have identified option prices out of alignment. By exploiting the pricing discrepancy using a delta-neutral strategy, you should earn profits regardless of the price movement in FinCorp stock.

Delta-neutral hedging strategies are also subject to practical problems, the most important of which is the difficulty in assessing the proper volatility for the coming period. If the volatility estimate is incorrect, so will be the deltas, and the overall position will not be perfectly hedged. Moreover, option or option-plus-stock positions generally will not be neutral with respect to changes in volatility. For example, a put option hedged by a stock might be delta neutral, but it is not volatility neutral. Changes in the market assessments of volatility will affect the option price even if the stock price is unchanged.

These problems can be serious because volatility estimates are never fully reliable. First, volatility cannot be observed directly and must be estimated from past data. Second, we've seen that both historical and implied volatilities fluctuate over time. Therefore, we are always shooting at a moving target. Although delta-neutral positions are hedged against changes in the price of the underlying asset, they still are subject to *volatility risk,* the risk incurred from unpredictable changes in volatility. The sensitivity of an option price to changes in volatility is called the option's **vega.** While delta-neutral option hedges might eliminate exposure fluctuations in the value of the underlying asset, they do not eliminate volatility risk.

21.6   Empirical Evidence on Option Pricing

The Black-Scholes option-pricing model has been subject to an enormous number of empirical tests. For the most part, the results of the studies have been positive in that the Black-Scholes model generates option values fairly close to the actual prices at which options trade. At the same time, some regular empirical failures of the model have been noted.

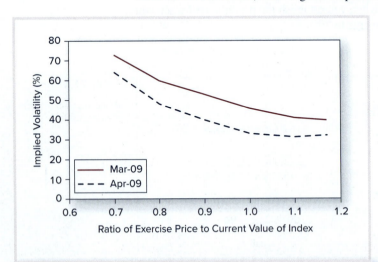

Figure 21.15 Implied volatility as a function of option "moneyness," i.e., ratio of exercise price to asset price, on two dates

Source: *The CBOE Skew Index,* Chicago Board Options Exchange, 2010.

The biggest problem concerns volatility. If the model were accurate, the implied volatility of all options on a particular stock with the same expiration date would be equal—after all, the underlying asset and expiration date are the same for each option, so the volatility inferred from each also ought to be the same. But in fact, when one actually plots implied volatility as a function of exercise price, the typical results appear as in Figure 21.15, which treats S&P 500 index options as the underlying asset. Implied volatility steadily falls as the exercise price rises. Clearly, the Black-Scholes model is missing something.

Rubinstein[18] was one of the first to suggest that the problem with the model has to do with fears of a market crash like that of October 1987. The idea is that deep

---

[18]Mark Rubinstein, "Implied Binomial Trees," *Journal of Finance* 49 (July 1994), pp. 771–818.

out-of-the-money puts would be nearly worthless if stock prices evolve smoothly, because the probability of the stock falling by a large amount (and the put option thereby moving into the money) in a short time would be very small. But a possibility of a sudden large downward jump that could move the puts into the money, as in a market crash, would impart greater value to these options. Thus, the market might price these options as though there is a bigger chance of a large drop in the stock price than would be suggested by the Black-Scholes assumptions. The result of the higher option price is a greater implied volatility.

Interestingly, Rubinstein points out that prior to the 1987 market crash, plots of implied volatility like the one in Figure 21.15 were relatively flat, consistent with the notion that the market was then less attuned to fears of a crash. However, postcrash plots have been consistently downward sloping, exhibiting a shape often called the *option smirk*. When we use option-pricing models that allow for more general stock price distributions, including crash risk and random changes in volatility, they generate downward-sloping implied volatility curves similar to those shown in Figure 21.15.[19]

[19]For an extensive discussion of these more general models, see R. L. McDonald, *Derivatives Markets,* 3rd ed. (Boston: Pearson Education [Addison-Wesley], 2013).

SUMMARY

1. Option values may be viewed as the sum of intrinsic value plus time or "volatility" value. The volatility value is the right to choose not to exercise if the stock price moves against the holder. Thus the option holder cannot lose more than the cost of the option regardless of stock price performance.

2. Call options are more valuable when the exercise price is lower, when the stock price is higher, when the interest rate is higher, when the time to expiration is greater, when the stock's volatility is greater, and when dividends are lower.

3. Call options must sell for at least the stock price less the present value of the exercise price and dividends to be paid before expiration. This implies that a call option on a non-dividend-paying stock may be sold for more than the proceeds from immediate exercise. Thus European calls are worth as much as American calls on stocks that pay no dividends, because the right to exercise the American call early has no value.

4. Options may be valued using a binomial pricing model that assumes the stock price can take on only two values by the end of any short time period. As the number of such periods increases, the binomial model can approximate more realistic stock price distributions. The Black-Scholes formula may be seen as a limiting case of the binomial option model as the holding period is divided into progressively smaller subperiods when the interest rate and stock volatility are constant.

5. The Black-Scholes formula applies to options on stocks that pay no dividends. Dividend adjustments may be adequate to price European calls on dividend-paying stocks, but the proper treatment of American calls on dividend-paying stocks requires more complex formulas.

6. It may be optimal to exercise put options early, whether or not the stock pays dividends. Therefore, American puts generally are worth more than European puts.

7. European put values can be derived from the call value and the put-call parity relationship. This technique cannot be applied to American puts for which optimal early exercise is a possibility.

8. The implied volatility of an option is the standard deviation of stock returns consistent with the option's market price. It can be backed out of an option-pricing model by finding the stock volatility that makes the option's value equal to its observed price.

9. The hedge ratio (or option delta) is the number of shares of stock required to hedge the price risk involved in writing one option. Hedge ratios are near zero for deep out-of-the-money call options and approach 1.0 for deep in-the-money calls.

10. Although call option deltas are less than 1.0, their elasticities are greater than 1.0. The rate of return on a call (as opposed to the dollar return) responds more than one-for-one with stock returns.

11. Portfolio insurance can be obtained by purchasing a protective put option on an equity position. When the appropriate put is not traded, portfolio insurance entails a dynamic hedge strategy where a fraction of the equity portfolio equal to the desired put option's delta is sold and placed in risk-free securities.

12. The option delta is used to determine the hedge ratio for options positions. Delta-neutral portfolios are independent of price changes in the underlying asset. Even delta-neutral option portfolios are subject to volatility risk, however.

13. Empirically, implied volatilities derived from the Black-Scholes formula tend to be higher on options with lower exercise prices. This may be evidence that the option prices reflect the possibility of a sudden dramatic decline in stock prices. Such "crashes" are inconsistent with the Black-Scholes assumptions.

KEY TERMS			
intrinsic value	hedge ratio	gamma
time value	delta	delta neutral
binomial model	option elasticity	vega
Black-Scholes pricing formula	portfolio insurance	
implied volatility	dynamic hedging	

KEY EQUATIONS

Binomial model: $u = \exp(\sigma \sqrt{\Delta t})$; $d = \exp(-\sigma \sqrt{\Delta t})$; $p = \dfrac{\exp(r\Delta t) - d}{u - d}$

Put-call parity: $P = C + PV(X) - S_0 + PV(\text{dividends})$

Black-Scholes formula (no dividend case): $SN(d_1) - Xe^{-rT}N(d_2)$

where $d_1 = \dfrac{\ln(S/X) + (r + \frac{1}{2}\sigma^2)T}{\sigma\sqrt{T}}$; $d_2 = d_1 - \sigma\sqrt{T}$

Delta (or hedge ratio): $H = \dfrac{\text{Change in option value}}{\text{Change in stock value}}$

PROBLEM SETS

1. We showed in the text that the value of a call option increases with the volatility of the stock. Is this also true of put option values? Use the put-call parity theorem as well as a numerical example to prove your answer.

2. Would you expect a $1 increase in a call option's exercise price to lead to a decrease in the option's value of more or less than $1?

3. Is a put option on a high-beta stock worth more than one on a low-beta stock? The stocks have identical firm-specific risk.

4. All else equal, is a call option on a stock with a lot of firm-specific risk worth more than one on a stock with little firm-specific risk? The betas of the two stocks are equal.

5. All else equal, will a call option with a high exercise price have a higher or lower hedge ratio than one with a low exercise price?

6. In each of the following questions, you are asked to compare two options with parameters as given. The risk-free interest rate for *all* cases should be assumed to be 4%. Assume the stocks on which these options are written pay no dividends.

   a.
Put	T	X	σ	Price of Option
A	0.5	50	0.20	$10
B	0.5	50	0.25	$10

Which put option is written on the stock with the lower price?

    i. A.

    ii. B.

    iii. Not enough information.

b.

Put	T	X	σ	Price of Option
A	0.5	50	0.2	$10
B	0.5	50	0.2	$12

Which put option must be written on the stock with the lower price?

    i. A.

    ii. B.

    iii. Not enough information.

c.

Call	S	X	σ	Price of Option
A	50	50	0.20	$12
B	55	50	0.20	$10

Which call option must have the lower time to expiration?

    i. A.

    ii. B.

    iii. Not enough information.

d.

Call	T	X	S	Price of Option
A	0.5	50	55	$10
B	0.5	50	55	$12

Which call option is written on the stock with higher volatility?

    i. A.

    ii. B.

    iii. Not enough information.

e.

Call	T	X	S	Price of Option
A	0.5	50	55	$10
B	0.5	50	55	$7

Which call option is written on the stock with higher volatility?

    i. A.

    ii. B.

    iii. Not enough information.

7. Reconsider the determination of the hedge ratio in the two-state model (see Section 21.2), where we showed that one-third share of stock would hedge one option. What would be the hedge ratio for the following exercise prices: (*a*) 120, (*b*) 110, (*c*) 100, (*d*) 90? (*e*) What do you conclude about the hedge ratio as the option becomes progressively more in the money?

8. Show that Black-Scholes call option hedge ratios also increase as the stock price increases. Consider a 1-year option with exercise price $50, on a stock with annual standard deviation 20%. The T-bill rate is 3% per year. Find $N(d_1)$ for stock prices (*a*) $45, (*b*) $50, and (*c*) $55.

9. We will derive a two-state put option value in this problem. Data: $S_0 = 100$; $X = 110$; $1 + r = 1.10$. The two possibilities for S_T are 130 and 80.

    a. Show that the range of S is 50, whereas that of P is 30 across the two states. What is the hedge ratio of the put?

    b. Form a portfolio of three shares of stock and five puts. What is the (nonrandom) payoff to this portfolio?

    c. What is the present value of the portfolio?

    d. Given that the stock currently is selling at 100, solve for the value of the put.

10. *a.* Calculate the value of a call option on the stock in Problem 9 with an exercise price of 110.

    b. Verify that the put-call parity theorem is satisfied by your answers to Problem 9 and part (*a*). (Do not use continuous compounding to calculate the present value of *X* in this example because we are using a two-state model here with discrete periods, not a continuous-time Black-Scholes model.)

11. Use the Black-Scholes formula to find the value of a call option on the following stock:

Time to expiration	6 months
Standard deviation	50% per year
Exercise price	$50
Stock price	$50
Annual interest rate	3%
Dividend	0

12. Find the Black-Scholes value of a put option on the stock in Problem 11 with the same exercise price and expiration as the call option.

13. Recalculate the value of the call option in Problem 11, successively substituting one of the changes below while keeping the other parameters as in Problem 11:

    a. Time to expiration = 3 months.

    b. Standard deviation = 25% per year.

    c. Exercise price = $55.

    d. Stock price = $55.

    e. Interest rate = 5%.

Consider each scenario independently. Confirm that the option value changes in accordance with the prediction of Table 21.1.

14. A call option with *X* = $50 on a stock currently priced at *S* = $55 is selling for $10. Using a volatility estimate of $\sigma = .30$, you find that $N(d_1) = .6$ and $N(d_2) = .5$. The risk-free interest rate is zero. Is the implied volatility based on the option price more or less than .30? Explain.

15. What would be the Excel formula in Spreadsheet 21.1 for the Black-Scholes value of a straddle position?

Use the following case in answering Problems 16 through 21: Mark Washington, CFA, is an analyst with BIC. One year ago, BIC analysts predicted that the U.S. equity market would most likely experience a slight downturn and suggested delta-hedging the BIC portfolio. As predicted, the U.S. equity markets did indeed experience a downturn of approximately 4% over a 12-month period. However, portfolio performance for BIC was disappointing, lagging its peer group by nearly 10%. Washington has been told to review the options strategy to determine why the hedged portfolio did not perform as expected.

16. Which of the following *best* explains a delta-neutral portfolio? A delta-neutral portfolio is perfectly hedged against:

    a. Small price changes in the underlying asset.

    b. Small price decreases in the underlying asset.

    c. All price changes in the underlying asset.

17. After discussing the concept of a delta-neutral portfolio, Washington determines that he needs to further explain the concept of delta. Washington draws the value of an option as a function of the underlying stock price. Using this diagram, indicate how delta is interpreted. Delta is the:

    a. Slope in the option price diagram.

    b. Curvature of the option price graph.

    c. Level in the option price diagram.

18. Washington considers a put option that has a delta of $-.65$. If the price of the underlying asset decreases by $6, then what is the best estimate of the change in option price?

19. BIC owns 51,750 shares of Smith & Oates. The shares are currently priced at $69. A call option on Smith & Oates with a strike price of $70 is selling at $3.50 and has a delta of .69. What is the number of call options necessary to create a delta-neutral hedge?

20. Return to Problem 19. Will the number of call options written for a delta-neutral hedge increase or decrease if the stock price falls?

21. Which of the following statements regarding the goal of a delta-neutral portfolio is *most* accurate? One example of a delta-neutral portfolio is to combine a:

    a. Long position in a stock with a short position in call options so that the value of the portfolio does not change with changes in the value of the stock.

    b. Long position in a stock with a short position in a call option so that the value of the portfolio changes with changes in the value of the stock.

    c. Long position in a stock with a long position in call options so that the value of the portfolio does not change with changes in the value of the stock.

22. Should the rate of return of a call option on a long-term Treasury bond be more or less sensitive to changes in interest rates than is the rate of return of the underlying bond?

23. If the stock price falls and the call price rises, then what has happened to the call option's implied volatility?

24. If the time to expiration falls and the put price rises, then what has happened to the put option's implied volatility?

25. According to the Black-Scholes formula, what will be the hedge ratio (delta) of a call option as the stock price becomes infinitely large? Explain briefly.

26. According to the Black-Scholes formula, what will be the hedge ratio (delta) of a put option for a very small exercise price?

27. The hedge ratio of an at-the-money call option on IBM is .4. The hedge ratio of an at-the-money put option is −.6. What is the hedge ratio of an at-the-money straddle position on IBM?

28. Consider a 6-month expiration European call option with exercise price $105. The underlying stock sells for $100 a share and pays no dividends. The risk-free rate is 5%. What is the implied volatility of the option if the option currently sells for $8? Use Spreadsheet 21.1 (available in Connect; link to Chapter 21 material) to answer this question.

eXcel
Please visit us at
www.mhhe.com/Bodie11e

    a. Go to the Data tab of the spreadsheet and select Goal Seek from the What-If menu. The dialog box will ask you for three pieces of information. In that dialog box, you should *set cell E6 to value 8 by changing cell* B2. In other words, you ask the spreadsheet to find the value of standard deviation (which appears in cell B2) that forces the value of the option (in cell E6) equal to $8. Then click OK, and you should find that the call is now worth $8, and the entry for standard deviation has been changed to a level consistent with this value. This is the call's implied standard deviation at a price of $8.

    b. What happens to implied volatility if the option is selling at $9?

    c. Why has implied volatility increased?

    d. What happens to implied volatility if the option price is unchanged at $8, but the time until option expiration is lower, say, only 4 months? Why?

    e. What happens to implied volatility if the option price is unchanged at $8, but the exercise price is lower, say, only $100? Why?

    f. What happens to implied volatility if the option price is unchanged at $8, but the stock price is lower, say, only $98? Why?

29. A collar is established by buying a share of stock for $50, buying a 6-month put option with exercise price $45, and writing a 6-month call option with exercise price $55. On the basis of the volatility of the stock, you calculate that for a strike price of $45 and expiration of 6 months, $N(d_1) = .60$, whereas for the exercise price of $55, $N(d_1) = .35$.

    a. What will be the gain or loss on the collar if the stock price increases by $1?

    b. What happens to the delta of the portfolio if the stock price becomes very large?

    c. What happens to the delta of the portfolio if the stock price becomes very small?

30. These three put options are all written on the same stock. One has a delta of −.9, one a delta of −.5, and one a delta of −.1. Assign deltas to the three puts by filling in this table.

Put	X	Delta
A	10	(a)
B	20	(b)
C	30	(c)

31. You are *very* bullish (optimistic) on stock EFG, much more so than the rest of the market. In each question, choose the portfolio strategy that will give you the biggest dollar profit if your bullish forecast turns out to be correct. Explain your answer.

    a. *Choice A:* $10,000 invested in calls with X = 50.
       Choice B: $10,000 invested in EFG stock.
    b. *Choice A:* 10 call option contracts (for 100 shares each), with X = 50.
       Choice B: 1,000 shares of EFG stock.

32. You would like to be holding a protective put position on the stock of XYZ Co. to lock in a guaranteed minimum value of $100 at year-end. XYZ currently sells for $100. Over the next year the stock price will increase by 10% or decrease by 10%. The T-bill rate is 5%. Unfortunately, no put options are traded on XYZ Co.

    a. Suppose the desired put option were traded. How much would it cost to purchase?
    b. What would have been the cost of the protective put portfolio?
    c. What portfolio position in stock and T-bills will ensure you a payoff equal to the payoff that would be provided by a protective put with X = 100? Show that the payoff to this portfolio and the cost of establishing the portfolio match those of the desired protective put.

33. Return to Example 21.1. Use the binomial model to value a 1-year European put option with exercise price $110 on the stock in that example. Confirm that your solution for the put price satisfies put-call parity.

34. Suppose that the risk-free interest rate is zero. Would an American put option ever be exercised early? Explain.

35. Let $p(S, T, X)$ denote the value of a European put on a stock selling at S dollars, with time to maturity T, and with exercise price X, and let $P(S, T, X)$ be the value of an American put.

    a. Evaluate $p(0, T, X)$.
    b. Evaluate $P(0, T, X)$.
    c. Evaluate $p(S, T, 0)$.
    d. Evaluate $P(S, T, 0)$.
    e. What does your answer to part (b) tell you about the possibility that American puts may be exercised early?

36. You are attempting to value a call option with an exercise price of $100 and one year to expiration. The underlying stock pays no dividends, its current price is $100, and you believe it has a 50% chance of increasing to $120 and a 50% chance of decreasing to $80. The risk-free rate of interest is 10%. Calculate the call option's value using the two-state stock price model.

37. Consider an increase in the volatility of the stock in the previous problem. Suppose that if the stock increases in price, it will increase to $130, and that if it falls, it will fall to $70. Show that the value of the call option is now higher than the value derived in the previous problem.

38. Calculate the value of a put option with exercise price $100 using the data in Problem 36. Show that put-call parity is satisfied by your solution.

39. XYZ Corp. will pay a $2 per share dividend in two months. Its stock price currently is $60 per share. A call option on XYZ has an exercise price of $55 and 3-month time to expiration. The risk-free interest rate is .5% per month, and the stock's volatility (standard deviation) = 7%

per month. Find the Black-Scholes value of the option. (*Hint*: Try defining one "period" as a month, rather than as a year, and think about the net-of-dividend value of each share.)

40. "The beta of a call option on General Electric is greater than the beta of a share of General Electric." True or false?

41. "The beta of a call option on the S&P 500 index with an exercise price of 1,930 is greater than the beta of a call on the index with an exercise price of 1,940." True or false?

42. What will happen to the hedge ratio of a convertible bond as the stock price becomes very large?

43. Goldman Sachs believes that market volatility will be 20% annually for the next three years. Three-year at-the-money call and put options on the market index sell at an implied volatility of 22%. What options portfolio can Goldman establish to speculate on its volatility belief without taking a bullish or bearish position on the market? Using Goldman's estimate of volatility, 3-year at-the-money options have $N(d_1) = .6$.

44. You are holding call options on a stock. The stock's beta is .75, and you are concerned that the stock market is about to fall. The stock is currently selling for $5 and you hold 1 million options on the stock (i.e., you hold 10,000 contracts for 100 shares each). The option delta is .8. How much of the market-index portfolio must you buy or sell to hedge your market exposure?

45. Imagine you are a provider of portfolio insurance. You are establishing a 4-year program. The portfolio you manage is currently worth $100 million, and you hope to provide a minimum return of 0%. The equity portfolio has a standard deviation of 25% per year, and T-bills pay 5% per year. Assume for simplicity that the portfolio pays no dividends (or that all dividends are reinvested).

    a. How much should be placed in bills? How much in equity?
    b. What should the manager do if the stock portfolio falls by 3% on the first day of trading?

46. Suppose that call options on ExxonMobil stock with time to expiration 3 months and strike price $90 are selling at an implied volatility of 30%. ExxonMobil stock currently is $90 per share, and the risk-free rate is 4%.

    a. If you believe the true volatility of the stock is 32%, would you want to buy or sell call options?
    b. Now you need to hedge your option position against changes in the stock price. How many shares of stock will you hold for each option contract purchased or sold?

47. Using the data in Problem 46, suppose that 3-month put options with a strike price of $90 are selling at an implied volatility of 34%. Construct a delta-neutral portfolio comprising positions in calls and puts that will profit when the option prices come back into alignment.

48. Suppose that JPMorgan Chase sells call options on $1.25 million worth of a stock portfolio with beta = 1.5. The option delta is .8. It wishes to hedge its resultant exposure to a market advance by buying a market-index portfolio.

    a. How many dollars' worth of the market-index portfolio should it purchase to hedge its position?
    b. Now it decides to use market index puts to hedge its exposure. Should it buy or sell puts? How many? The index at current prices represents $1,000 worth of stock.

49. Suppose you are attempting to value a 1-year expiration option on a stock with volatility (i.e., annualized standard deviation) of $\sigma = .40$. What would be the appropriate values for u and d if your binomial model is set up using:

    a. 1 period of 1 year.
    b. 4 subperiods, each 3 months.
    c. 12 subperiods, each 1 month.

50. You build a binomial model with one period and assert that over the course of a year, the stock price will either rise by a factor of 1.5 or fall by a factor of 2/3. What is your implicit assumption about the volatility of the stock's rate of return over the next year?

51. Use the put-call parity relationship to demonstrate that an at-the-money call option on a nondividend-paying stock must cost more than an at-the-money put option. Show that the prices of the put and call will be equal if $S_0 = (1 + r)^T$.

52. Return to Problem 36. Value the call option using the risk-neutral shortcut described in the box in Section 21.3. Confirm that your answer matches the value you get using the two-state approach.

53. Return to Problem 38.
    a. What will be the payoff to the put, P_u, if the stock goes up?
    b. What will be the payoff, P_d, if the stock price falls?
    c. Value the put option using the risk-neutral shortcut described in the box in Section 21.3.
    d. Confirm that your answer matches the value you get using the two-state approach.

CFA PROBLEMS

1. The board of directors of Abco Company is concerned about the downside risk of a $100 million equity portfolio in its pension plan. The board's consultant has proposed temporarily (for 1 month) hedging the portfolio with either futures or options. Referring to the following table, the consultant states:
    a. "The $100 million equity portfolio can be fully protected on the downside by selling (shorting) 4,000 futures contracts."
    b. "The cost of this protection is that the portfolio's expected rate of return will be zero percent."

Market, Portfolio, and Contract Data	
Equity index level	99.00
Equity futures price	100.00
Futures contract multiplier	$250
Portfolio beta	1.20
Contract expiration (months)	3

   Critique the accuracy of each of the consultant's two statements.

2. Michael Weber, CFA, is analyzing several aspects of option valuation, including the determinants of the value of an option, the characteristics of various models used to value options, and the potential for divergence of calculated option values from observed market prices.
    a. What is the expected effect on the value of a call option on common stock if the volatility of the underlying stock price decreases? If the time to expiration of the option increases?
    b. Using the Black-Scholes option-pricing model and an estimate of stock return volatility, Weber calculates the price of a 3-month call option and notices the option's calculated value is different from its market price. With respect to Weber's use of the Black-Scholes option-pricing model,
       i. Discuss why the calculated value of an out-of-the-money European option may differ from its market price.
       ii. Discuss why the calculated value of an American option may differ from its market price.

3. Joel Franklin is a portfolio manager responsible for derivatives. Franklin observes an American-style option and a European-style option with the same strike price, expiration, and underlying stock. Franklin believes that the European-style option will have a higher premium than the American-style option.
    a. Critique Franklin's belief that the European-style option will have a higher premium. Franklin is asked to value a 1-year European-style call option for Abaco Ltd. common stock, which last traded at $43.00. He has collected the information in the following table.

Closing stock price	$43.00
Call and put option exercise price	45.00
1-year put option price	4.00
1-year Treasury bill rate	5.50%
Time to expiration	One year

b. Calculate, using put-call parity and the information provided in the table, the European-style call option value.

c. State the effect, if any, of each of the following three variables on the value of a call option. (No calculations required.)

   i. An increase in short-term interest rate.

   ii. An increase in stock price volatility.

   iii. A decrease in time to option expiration.

4. A stock index is currently trading at 50. Paul Tripp, CFA, wants to value 2-year index options using the binomial model. The stock will either increase in value by 20% or fall in value by 20%. The annual risk-free interest rate is 6%. No dividends are paid on any of the underlying securities in the index.

a. Construct a two-period binomial tree for the value of the stock index.

b. Calculate the value of a European call option on the index with an exercise price of 60.

c. Calculate the value of a European put option on the index with an exercise price of 60.

d. Confirm that your solutions for the values of the call and the put satisfy put-call parity.

5. Ken Webster manages a $400 million equity portfolio benchmarked to the S&P 500 index. Webster believes the market is overvalued when measured by several traditional fundamental/economic indicators. He is concerned about potential losses but recognizes that the S&P 500 index could nevertheless move above its current 1,766 level.

Webster is considering the following *option collar* strategy:

- Protection for the portfolio can be attained by purchasing an S&P 500 index put with a strike price of 1,760.

- The put can be approximately financed by selling one 1,800 strike-price call for every put purchased.

- Because the combined delta of the call and put positions (see following table) is greater than -1 (i.e., $-.44 - 30 = -.77$), the options will not lose more than the underlying portfolio will gain if the market advances.

The information in the following table describes the two options used to create the collar.

Characteristics	1,800 Call	1,760 Put
Option price	$34.10	$32.20
Option implied volatility	22%	24%
Option's delta	0.30	−0.44

Notes:
- Ignore transaction costs.
- S&P 500 historical 30-day volatility = 23%.
- Time to option expiration = 30 days.

a. Describe the potential returns of the combined portfolio (the underlying portfolio plus the option collar) if after 30 days the S&P 500 index has:

   i. Risen approximately 5% to 1,854.

   ii. Remained at 1,766 (no change).

   iii. Declined by approximately 5% to 1,682.

   (No calculations are necessary.)

   b. Discuss the effect on the hedge ratio (delta) of *each* option as the S&P 500 approaches the level of *each* of the potential outcomes listed in part (*a*).
   c. Evaluate the pricing of *each* of the following in relation to the volatility data provided:
      i. The put.
      ii. The call.

E-INVESTMENTS EXERCISES

1. Use information from **finance.yahoo.com** to answer the following questions.

   a. What is Coke's current price?

   b. Now enter the ticker "KO" (for Coca-Cola) and find the *AnalystOpinion* tab. What is the mean 12-month target price for Coke? Based on this forecast, would at-the-money calls or puts have the higher expected profit?

   c. What is the spread between the high and low target stock prices, expressed as a percentage of Coke's current stock price? How (qualitatively) should the spread be related to the price at which Coke options trade?

   d. Calculate the implied volatility of the call option closest to the money with time to expiration of about three months. You can use Spreadsheet 21.1 (available in Connect) to calculate implied volatility using the Goal Seek command.

   e. Now repeat the exercise for Pepsi (ticker: PEP). What would you expect to be the relationship between the high versus low target price spread and the implied volatility of the two companies? Are your expectations consistent with actual option prices?

   f. Suppose you believe that the volatility of KO is going to increase from currently anticipated levels. Would its call options be overpriced or underpriced? What about its put options?

   g. Could you take positions in both puts and calls on KO in such a manner as to speculate on your volatility beliefs without taking a stance on whether the stock price is going to increase or decrease? Would you buy or write each type of option?

   h. How would your relative positions in puts and calls be related to the delta of each option?

2. Calculating implied volatility can be difficult if you don't have a spreadsheet handy. Fortunately, many tools are available on the Web to perform the calculation; for example, **www.numa.com** contains option calculators that also compute implied volatility.

   Using daily price data (available from **finance.yahoo.com**), calculate the annualized standard deviation of the daily percentage change in a stock price. Try calculating standard deviation using historical data covering (a) 60 days, (b) 120 days, and (c) 180 days. For the same stock, use the numa Web site to find the implied volatility. The input for the risk-free rate may be found at **www.bloomberg.com/markets/rates/index.html**.Option price data can be retrieved from **www.cboe.com**.

   Which sample period for calculating historical standard deviation seems most correlated with implied volatility?

 ## SOLUTIONS TO CONCEPT CHECKS

1. To understand the impact of higher volatility, consider the same scenarios as for the call. The low-volatility scenario yields a lower expected payoff.

High volatility	Stock price	$10	$20	$30	$40	$50
	Put payoff	$20	$10	$ 0	$ 0	$ 0
Low volatility	Stock price	$20	$25	$30	$35	$40
	Put payoff	$10	$ 5	$ 0	$ 0	$ 0

2. If This Variable Increases . . .   The Value of a Put Option

S	Decreases
X	Increases
σ	Increases
T	Increases*
r_f	Decreases
Dividend payouts	Increases

*For American puts, increase in time to expiration must increase value. One can always choose to exercise early if this is optimal; the longer expiration date simply expands the range of alternatives open to the option holder which must make the option more valuable. For a European put, where early exercise is not allowed, longer time to expiration can have an indeterminate effect. Longer expiration increases volatility value because the final stock price is more uncertain, but it reduces the present value of the exercise price that will be received if the put is exercised. The net effect on put value can be positive or negative.

3. The parity relationship assumes that all options are held until expiration and that there are no cash flows until expiration. These assumptions are valid only in the special case of European options on non-dividend-paying stocks. If the stock pays no dividends, the American and European calls are equally valuable, whereas the American put is worth more than the European put. Therefore, although the parity theorem for European options states that

$$P = C - S_0 + \text{PV}(X)$$

in fact, P will be *greater* than this value if the put is American.

4. Because the option now is underpriced, we want to reverse our previous strategy.

		Cash Flow in 1 Year for Each Possible Stock Price	
	Initial Cash Flow	$S = 90$	$S = 120$
Buy 3 options	−16.50	0	30
Short-sell 1 share; repay in 1 year	100	−90	−120
Lend $83.50 at 10% interest rate	−83.50	91.85	91.85
TOTAL	0	1.85	1.85

The riskless cash flow in 1 year per option is $1.85/3 = $.6167, and the present value is $.6167/1.10 = $.56, precisely the amount by which the option is underpriced.

5. a. $C_u - C_d = \$6.984 - 0$
   b. $uS_0 - dS_0 = \$110 - \$95 = \$15$
   c. $6.984/15 = .4656$
   d.

	Value in Next Period as Function of Stock Price	
Action Today (time 0)	$dS_0 = \$95$	$uS_0 = \$110$
Buy 0.4656 shares at price $S_0 = \$100$	$44.232	$51.216
Write 1 call at price C_0	0	−6.984
TOTAL	$44.232	$44.232

The portfolio must have a market value equal to the present value of $44.232.

   e. $44.232/1.05 = $42.126
   f. $.4656 \times \$100 - C_0 = \$42.126$
      $C_0 = \$46.56 - \$42.126 = \$4.434$

6. When Δt shrinks, there should be lower possible dispersion in the stock price by the end of the subperiod because each shorter subperiod offers less time in which new information can move stock prices. However, as the time interval shrinks, there will be a correspondingly greater number of these subperiods until option expiration. Thus, *total* volatility over the remaining life

of the option will be unaffected. In fact, take another look at Figure 21.5. There, despite the fact that u and d each get closer to 1 as the number of subintervals increases and the length of each subinterval falls, the total volatility of the stock return until option expiration is unaffected.

7. Because $\sigma = .6$, $\sigma^2 = .36$.

$$d_1 = \frac{\ln(100/95) + (.10 + .36/2).25}{.6\sqrt{.25}} = .4043$$

$$d_2 = d_1 - .6\sqrt{.25} = .1043$$

Using Table 21.2 and interpolation, or from a spreadsheet function:

$$N(d_1) = .6570$$
$$N(d_2) = .5415$$
$$C = 100 \times .6570 - 95e^{-.10 \times .25} \times .5415 = 15.53$$

8. Implied volatility exceeds .2783. Given a standard deviation of .2783, the option value is $7. A higher volatility is needed to justify an $8 price. Using Spreadsheet 21.1 and Goal Seek, you can confirm that implied volatility at an option price of $8 is .3138.

9. A $1 increase in stock price is a percentage increase of $1/122 = .82\%$. The put option price will *fall* by $(.4 \times \$1) = \$.40$, a percentage decrease of $\$.40/\$4 = 10\%$. Elasticity is $-10/.82 = -12.2$.

10. The delta for a call option is $N(d_1)$, which is positive, and in this case is .547. Therefore, for every 10 option contracts purchased, you would need to *short* 547 shares of stock.

Futures Markets

FUTURES AND FORWARD contracts are like options in that they specify purchase or sale of some underlying security at some future date. The key difference is that the holder of an option is not compelled to buy or sell and will not do so unless the trade is advantageous. A futures or forward contract, however, carries the obligation to go through with the agreed-upon transaction.

A forward contract is not an investment in the strict sense that funds are paid for an asset. It is only a commitment today to transact in the future. Forward arrangements are part of our study of investments, however, because they offer powerful means to hedge other investments and generally modify portfolio characteristics.

Forward markets for future delivery of various commodities go back at least to ancient Greece. Organized *futures markets,* though, are a relatively modern development, dating only to the 19th century. Futures markets replace informal forward contracts with highly standardized, exchange-traded securities.

While futures markets have their roots in agricultural products and commodities, the markets today are dominated by trading in financial futures such as those on stock indexes, interest-rate-dependent securities such as government bonds, and foreign exchange. The markets themselves also have changed, with trading today largely taking place in electronic markets.

This chapter describes the workings of futures markets and the mechanics of trading in these markets. We show how futures contracts are useful investment vehicles for both hedgers and speculators and how the futures price relates to the spot price of an asset. We also show how futures can be used in several risk-management applications. This chapter deals with general principles of future markets. Chapter 23 describes specific futures markets in greater detail.

22.1 The Futures Contract

To see how futures and forwards work and how they might be useful, consider the portfolio diversification problem facing a farmer growing a single crop, let's say wheat. The entire planting season's revenue depends critically on the highly volatile crop price. The farmer can't easily diversify his position because virtually his entire wealth is tied up in the crop.

The miller who must purchase wheat for processing faces a risk management problem that is the mirror image of the farmer's. He is subject to profit uncertainty because of the unpredictable cost of the wheat.

Both parties can hedge their risk by entering into a **forward contract** calling for the farmer to deliver the wheat when harvested at a price agreed upon now, regardless of the market price at harvest time. No money need change hands at this time. A forward contract is simply a deferred-delivery sale of some asset with the sales price agreed on now. All that is required is that each party must be willing to lock in the ultimate delivery price. The contract protects each party from future price fluctuations.

Futures markets formalize and standardize forward contracting. Buyers and sellers trade in a centralized futures exchange. The exchange standardizes the types of contracts that may be traded: It establishes contract size, the acceptable grade of commodity, contract delivery dates, and so forth. Although standardization eliminates much of the flexibility available in forward contracting, it offers the offsetting advantage of liquidity because many traders will concentrate on the same small set of contracts. Futures contracts also differ from forward contracts in that they call for a daily settling up of any gains or losses on the contract. By contrast, no money changes hands in forward contracts until the delivery date.

The centralized market, standardization of contracts, and depth of trading in each contract allows futures positions to be liquidated easily rather than renegotiated with the other party to the contract. Because the exchange guarantees the performance of each party, costly credit checks on other traders are not necessary. Instead, each trader simply posts a good-faith deposit, called the *margin,* to guarantee contract performance.

The Basics of Futures Contracts

The futures contract calls for delivery of a commodity at a specified delivery or maturity date, for an agreed-upon price, called the **futures price,** to be paid at contract maturity. The contract specifies precise requirements for the commodity. For agricultural commodities, the exchange sets allowable grades (e.g., No. 2 hard winter wheat or No. 1 soft red wheat). The place and means of delivery of the commodity are specified as well. Delivery of agricultural commodities is made by transfer of warehouse receipts issued by approved warehouses. For financial futures, delivery may be made by wire transfer; for index futures, delivery may be accomplished by a cash settlement procedure such as those for index options. Although the futures contract technically calls for delivery of an asset, delivery rarely occurs. Instead, parties to the contract much more commonly close out their positions before contract maturity, taking gains or losses in cash.

Because the futures exchange specifies all the terms of the contract, the traders need bargain only over the futures price. The trader taking the **long position** commits to purchasing the commodity on the delivery date. The trader who takes the **short position** commits to delivering the commodity at contract maturity. The trader in the long position is said to "buy" a contract; the short-side trader "sells" a contract. The words *buy* and *sell* are figurative only, because a contract is not really bought or sold like a stock or bond; it is entered into by mutual agreement. At the time the contract is entered into, no money changes hands.

Figure 22.1 shows prices for several futures contracts as they appear in *The Wall Street Journal.* The boldface heading lists in each case the commodity, the exchange where the futures contract is traded, the contract size, and the pricing unit. The first agricultural contract listed is for corn, traded on the Chicago Board of Trade (CBT). (The CBT merged with the Chicago Mercantile Exchange in 2007 but still maintains a separate identity.) Each contract calls for delivery of 5,000 bushels, and prices in the entry are quoted in cents per bushel.

The next two rows detail price data for contracts expiring on various dates. The July 2016 maturity corn contract, for example, opened during the day at a futures price of

Futures Contracts | WSJ.com/commodities

Metal & Petroleum Futures

	Open	High hi lo	low	Settle	Chg	Open interest
Copper-High (CMX)-25,000 lbs.; $ per lb.						
July	2.2290	2.2455	2.1615	**2.1815**	−0.0335	3,552
Sept	2.2300	2.2480	2.1620	**2.1835**	−0.0335	108,854
Gold (CMX)-100 troy oz.; $ per troy oz.						
July	1342.20	1356.80	1339.70	**1356.40**	19.70	2,070
Aug	1345.00	1360.30	1338.50	**1358.70**	19.70	440,422
Oct	1345.00	1363.50	1345.00	**1362.20**	19.70	37,171
Dec	1352.10	1366.90	1345.70	**1365.80**	19.80	106,265
Feb'17	1353.30	1369.10 ▲	1353.30	**1368.90**	19.90	15,796
June	1365.00	1373.80	1357.30	**1374.30**	20.00	12,523
Palladium (NYM)-50 troy oz.; $ per troy oz.						
Aug	609.00	609.00 ▲	609.00	**609.85**	−3.00	3
Sept	605.65	617.40	590.60	**602.65**	−3.00	21,127
Dec	609.65	612.80	598.05	**603.35**	−2.90	492
Platinum (NYM)-50 troy oz.; $ per troy oz..						
July	1064.60	1073.20	1052.00	**1072.00**	17.70	635
Oct	1062.00	1079.30	1050.20	**1076.90**	19.80	58,916
Silver (CMX)-5,000 troy oz.; $ per troy oz.						
July	19.755	21.095 ▲	19.625	**19.866**	0.322	1,089
Sept	19.840	21.225 ▲	19.610	**19.907**	0.319	159,362
Crude Oil, Light Sweet (NYM)-1,000 bbls.; $ per bbl.						
Aug	49.11	49.35	46.33	**46.60**	−2.39	418,068
Sept	49.90	50.03	47.29	**47.29**	−2.36	282,684
Oct	50.45	50.62	47.61	**47.91**	−2.34	106,633
Nov	50.92	51.20	48.51	**48.51**	−2.31	108,604
Dec	51.59	51.75	49.07	**49.07**	−2.27	244,771
Dec'17	54.24	54.40	51.94	**52.27**	−1.82	140,180
NY Harbor ULSD (NYM)-42,000 gal.; $ per gal.						
Aug	1.5174	1.5258	1.4333	**1.4456**	−.0659	93,236
March	1.5343	1.5444	1.4548	**1.4673**	−.0637	66,430
Gasoline-NY RBOB (NYM)-42,000 gal.; $ per gal.						
Aug	1.5176	1.5249	1.4157	**1.4287**	−.0848	118,778
Sept	1.5223	1.5317	1.4274	**1.4413**	−.0787	78,861
Natural Gas (NYM)-10,000 MMBtu.; $ per MMBtu.						
Aug	2.915	2.945	2.752	**2.764**	−.223	212,803
Sept	2.915	2.944	2.752	**2.758**	−.223	216,642
Oct	2.960	2.931	2.798	**2.802**	−.211	111,498
Nov	3.065	3.115	2.946	**2.955**	−.187	65,908
Jan'17	3.410	3.472	3.327	**3.341**	−.151	108,006
March	3.335	3.395	3.268	**3.284**	−.131	62,935

Agriculture Futures

	Open	High hi lo	low	Settle	Chg	Open interest
Corn (CBT)-5,000 bu.; cents per bu.						
July	348.00	350.00 ▼	333.75	**344.00**	−9.00	7,872
Sept	356.25	356.50 ▼	341.00	**350.75**	−9.25	563,370
Oats (CBT)-5,000 bu.; cents per bu.						
July	208.00	208.50	205.25	**216.00**	10.50	108
Dec	192.00	193.75 ▼	188.25	**191.50**	−1.25	5,695
Soybeans (CBT)-5,000 bu.; cents per bu.						
July	1150.25	1150.25	1110.00	**1117.00**	−51.75	5,672
May	1120.00	1120.00	1073.50	**1077.25**	−60.25	428,587
Soybean Meal (CBT)-100 tons.; $ per ton.						
July	399.20	399.20	383.00	**385.40**	−19.40	3,886
Dec	391.50	391.70	378.00	**378.00**	−20.00	162,712
Soybean Oil (CBT)-60,000 lbs.; cents per lb.						
July	31.03	31.37	30.52	**30.82**	−.21	2,732
Dec	31.85	31.99	31.01	**31.32**	−.32	172,625
Rough Rice (CBT)-2,000 cwt.; cents per cwt.						
July	1032.00	1036.00	1020.00	**1028.50**	−8.00	70
Sept	1042.00	1054.00	1024.00	**1031.00**	−14.00	7,702
Wheat (CBT)-5,000 bu.; cents per bu.						
July	416.25	418.25 ▼	405.00	**419.50**	3.25	776
Sept	430.25	434.50 ▼	415.75	**433.50**	3.25	249,335
Wheat (KC)-5,000 bu.; cents per bu.						
July	391.00	398.75 ▼	385.00	**402.00**	7.75	799
Sept	500.00	509.25 ▼	493.75	**508.25**	8.25	27,512
Cattle-Feeder (CME)-50,000 lbs.; cents per lb.						
Aug	142.575	144.475	139.750	**144.075**	1.625	24,745
Sept	141.675	143.650	139.150	**143.350**	1.650	5,964
Cattle-Live (CME)-40,000 lbs.; cents per lb.						
Aug	113.050	114.225	111.075	**113.650**	.675	115,581
Oct	113.375	114.475	111.150	**114.000**	.725	64,211
Hogs-Lean (CME)-40,000 lbs.; cents per lb.						
July	82.750	83.650	81.950	**82.050**	−.625	17,601
Aug	83.950	84.825	82.175	**83.250**	−.700	93,143
Lumber (CME)-110,000 bd.ft; $ per1,000 bd. ft.						
July	308.50	317.50	306.30	**317.50**	8.20	554
Sept	315.10	325.00	311.60	**322.80**	7.80	3,152
Milk (CME)-200,000 lbs.; cents per lb.						
July	15.05	15.08	14.89	**14.97**	−.10	5,449
Aug	15.98	15.98	15.59	**15.70**	−.19	4,689
Cocoa (ICE-US)-10 metric tons; $ per ton.						
July	3,104	3,104	3,104	**3,104**	70	24
Sept	3,010	3,069	2,984	**3,065**	70	91,001

	Open	High hi lo	low	Settle	Chg	Open interest
Coffee (ICE-US)-37,500 lbs.; cents per lb.						
July	145.60	145.60	143.00	**144.20**	−.65	137
Sept	146.20	147.20	144.10	**145.55**	−.85	99,385
Sugar-World (ICE-US)-112,000 lbs.; cents per lb.						
Oct	20.56	21.10	20.46	**20.87**	.09	475,726
March'17	20.56	21.13	20.55	**20.94**	.10	210,447
Sugar-Domestic (ICE-US)-112,000 lbs.; cents per lb.						
Sept	28.25	28.25	28.05	**28.05**	−.16	1,480
Jan'17	27.00	27.00 ▲	27.00	**26.65**	−.38	1,416
Cotton (ICE-US)-50,000 lbs.; cents per lb.						
July	62.92	62.92	62.92	**63.75**	.13	49
Dec	65.50	66.14	64.25	**65.21**	.22	150,428
Orange Juice (ICE-US)-15,000 lbs.; cents per lb.						
July	185.00	187.65 ▲	185.00	**186.65**	5.80	579
Sept	177.20	185.00 ▲	174.60	**183.60**	5.35	14,113

Interest Rate Futures

	Open	High hi lo	low	Settle	Chg	Open interest
Treasury Bonds (CBT)-$100,000; pts 32nds of 100%						
Sept	174-130	176-130	173-240	**176-080**	2-18.0	559,142
June	172-280	174-270	172-140	**174-120**	2-19.0	82
Treasury Notes (CBT)-$100,000; pts 32nds of 100%						
Sept	133-095	133-315	133-000	**133-285**	26.0	2,777,302
Dec	132-200	133-020	132-200	**133-000**	27.0	2,637
5 Yr. Treasury Notes (CBT)-$100,000; pts 32nds of 100%						
Sept	1222-075	122-185	122-027	**122-155**	−11.0	2,644,19
2 Yr. Treasury Notes (CBT)-$200,000; pts 32nds of 100%						
Sept	109-210	109-235	109-197	**109-227**	2.5	1,081,786
30 Day Federal Funds (CBT)-$5,000,000; 100-daily avg.						
July	99.615	99.618	99.615	**99.618**	−.002	193,832
Aug	99.625	99.625	99.620	**99.625**	−.005	167,407
10 Yr. Del. Int. Rate Swaps (CBT)-$100,000; pts 32nds of 100%						
Sept	108.750	108.875 ▲	108.469	**108.781**	.781	25,579
1 Month Libor (CME)-$3,000,000; pts of 100%						
July	99.5450	99.5450	99.5425	**99.5375**	.0025	1,602
Aug	99.5300	99.5300	99.5300	**99.5375**	.0025	870
Eurodollar (CME)-$1,000,000; pts of 100%						
July	99.3600	99.3600	99.3500	**99.3500**	−.0100	189,055
Sept	99.3500	99.3550	99.3350	**99.3450**	−.0050	1,198,322
Dec	99.3100	99.3200	99.2950	**99.3200**	.0100	1,347,476
Dec'17	99.1600	99.2150	99.1350	**99.2050**	−.0550	1,178,481

Currency Futures

	Open	High hi lo	low	Settle	Chg	Open interest
Japanese Yen (CME)-¥12,500,000; $ per 100¥						
Sept	.9769	.9881	.9750	**.9871**	.0092	146,909
Dec	.9800	.9913	.9786	**.9905**	.0093	620
Canadian Dollar (CME)-CAD 100,000; $ per CAD						
Sept	.7746	.7795	.7682	**.7701**	−.0043	111,561
Dec	.7746	.7793	.7686	**.7702**	−.0042	3,681
British Pound (CME)-£62,500; $ per £						
Sept	1.3285	1.3351 ▼	1.3010	**1.3037**	−.0256	216,881
Dec	1.3330	1.3366 ▼	1.3029	**1.3054**	−.0254	1,575
Swiss Franc (CME)-CHF 125,000; $ per CHF						
Sept	1.0307	1.0368	1.0271	**1.0273**	−.0038	34,888
Australian Dollar (CME)-AUD 100,000; $ per AUD						
Sept	.7441	.7527	.7433	**.7440**	−.0023	71,326
Dec	.7469	.7500	.7413	**.7417**	−.0023	1,053
Mexican Peso (CME)-MXN 500,000; $ per MXN						
Dec	.05333	.05422	.05330	**.05226**	−.00118	242
Euro (CME)-€125,000; $ per €						
Sept	1.1165	1.1216	1.1092	**1.1101**	−.0065	343,690
Dec	1.1198	1.1254	1.1131	**1.1140**	−.0064	4,523

Index Futures

	Open	High hi lo	low	Settle	Chg	Open interest
Mini DJ Industrial Average (CBT)-$5 × index						
Sept	17880	17924	17689	**17762**	−104	103,682
Dec	17780	17807	17601	**17668**	−104	290
Mini S&P 500 (CME)-$50 × index						
Sept	2099.75	2104.75	2072.50	**2082.70**	−13.55	2,964,059
Dec	2089.50	2095.75	2064.00	**2074.10**	−13.65	12,960
Mini S&P Midcap 400 (CME)-$100 × index						
Sept	1499.50	1503.70	1469.80	**1478.20**	−18.50	79,923
Dec	1486.00	1486.00	1486.00	**1472.00**	−18.50	11
Mini Nasdaq 100 (CME)-$20 × index						
Sept	4438.8	4451.5	4377.5	**4404.0**	−29.3	197,945
Dec	4429.8	4442.0	4371.3	**4396.5**	−28.3	322
Mini Russell 2000 (ICE-US)-$100 × index						
Sept	1155.10	1155.10	1128.90	**1135.40**	−18.80	329,992
Dec	1153.30	1153.30	1149.90	**1130.40**	−18.80	933
Mini Russell 1000 (ICE-US)-$100 × index						
Sept	1152.10	1154.40	1146.80	**1151.90**	−8.70	5,307
U.S. Doller Index (ICE-US)-$1,000 × index						
Sept	95.63	96.34	95.38	**96.26**	.55	45,977
Dec	95.75	96.34	95.47	**96.30**	.55	2,405

Figure 22.1 Futures listings

Source: *The Wall Street Journal*, July 6, 2016.

348 cents per bushel. The highest futures price during the day was 350.00, the lowest was 333.75, and the settlement price (a representative trading price during the last few minutes of trading) was 344. The settlement price decreased by 9 cents from the previous trading day. Finally, open interest, or the number of outstanding contracts, was 7,872. Similar information is given for each maturity date.

The trader holding the long position, that is, the person who will purchase the good, profits from price increases. Suppose that when the contract matures in July, the price of corn turns out to be 349 cents per bushel. The long-position trader who entered the contract at the futures price of 344 cents therefore earns a profit of 5 cents per bushel. As each contract calls for delivery of 5,000 bushels, the profit to the long position equals $5,000 \times \$.05 = \$250$ per contract. Conversely, the short position loses 5 cents per bushel. The short position's loss equals the long position's gain.

To summarize, at maturity:

$$\text{Profit to long} = \text{Spot price at maturity} - \text{Original futures price}$$

$$\text{Profit to short} = \text{Original futures price} - \text{Spot price at maturity}$$

where the spot price is the actual market price of the commodity at the time of the delivery.

The futures contract, therefore, is a *zero-sum game,* with losses and gains netting out to zero. Every long position is offset by a short position. The aggregate profits to futures trading, summing over all investors, also must be zero, as is the net exposure to changes in the commodity price. For this reason, the establishment of a futures market in a commodity should not have a major impact on prices in the spot market for that commodity.

Figure 22.2, Panel A, is a plot of the profits realized by an investor who enters the long side of a futures contract as a function of the price of the asset on the maturity date. Notice that profit is zero when the ultimate spot price, P_T, equals the initial futures price, F_0. Profit per unit of the underlying asset rises or falls one-for-one with changes in the final spot price. Unlike the payoff of a call option, the payoff of the long futures position can be negative: This will be the case if the spot price falls below the original futures price. Unlike the holder of a call, who has an *option* to buy, the long futures position trader cannot simply walk away from the contract. Also unlike options, in the case of futures there is no need to distinguish gross payoffs from net profits. This is because the futures contract is not purchased; it is simply a contract that is agreed to by two parties. The futures price adjusts to make the present value of entering into a new contract equal to zero.

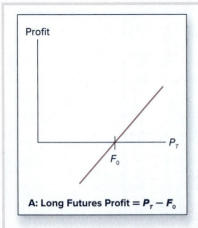

A: Long Futures Profit = $P_T - F_0$

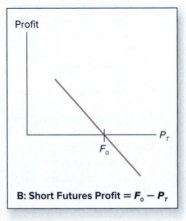

B: Short Futures Profit = $F_0 - P_T$

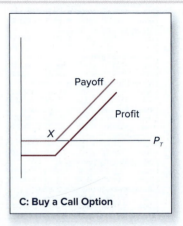

C: Buy a Call Option

Figure 22.2 Profits to buyers and sellers of futures and options contracts

The distinction between futures and options is highlighted by comparing Panel A of Figure 22.2 to the payoff and profit diagrams for an investor in a call option with exercise price, X, chosen equal to the futures price F_0 (see Panel C). The futures investor is exposed to considerable losses if the asset price falls. In contrast, the investor in the call cannot lose more than the cost of the option.

Figure 22.2, Panel B, is a plot of the profits realized by an investor who enters the short side of a futures contract. It is the mirror image of the profit diagram for the long position.

 Concept Check **22.1**

a. Compare the profit diagram in Figure 22.2, Panel B, to the payoff diagram for a long position in a put option. Assume the exercise price of the option equals the initial futures price.

b. Compare the profit diagram in Figure 22.2, Panel B, to the payoff diagram for an investor who writes a call option.

Existing Contracts

Futures and forward contracts are traded on a wide variety of goods in four broad categories: agricultural commodities, metals and minerals (including energy commodities), foreign currencies, and financial futures (fixed-income securities and stock market indexes). In addition to indexes on broad stock indexes, one can trade **single-stock futures** on several actively traded individual stocks and narrowly based stock indexes on the OneChicago electronic market.

Table 22.1 offers a sample of the various contracts trading in 2016. While the table includes many contracts, the large and ever-changing array of markets makes this list

Foreign Currencies	Agricultural	Metals and Energy	Interest Rate Futures	Equity Indexes
British pound	Corn	Copper	Eurodollar	S&P 500 index
Canadian dollar	Oats	Aluminum	Euroyen	Dow Jones Industrials
Japanese yen	Soybeans	Gold	Euro-denominated bond	S&P Midcap 400
Euro	Soybean meal	Platinum	Euroswiss	NASDAQ 100
Swiss franc	Soybean oil	Palladium	Sterling	NYSE index
Australian dollar	Wheat	Silver	British government bond	Russell 2000 index
Mexican peso	Barley	Crude oil	German government bond	Nikkei 225 (Japanese)
Brazilian real	Flaxseed	Heating oil	Italian government bond	FTSE index (British)
	Palm oil	Gas oil	Canadian government bond	CAC-40 (French)
	Rye	Natural gas	Treasury bonds	DAX-30 (German)
	Cattle	Gasoline	Treasury notes	All ordinary (Australian)
	Hogs	Propane	Treasury bills	Toronto 35 (Canadian)
	Pork bellies	Kerosene	LIBOR	Dow Jones Euro STOXX 50
	Cocoa	Fuel oil	EURIBOR	Industry indexes:
	Coffee	Iron ore	Interest rate swaps	• Banking
	Cotton	Electricity	Federal funds rate	• Telecom
	Milk	Weather	Bankers' acceptance	• Utilities
	Orange juice			• Health care
	Sugar			• Technology
	Lumber			
	Rice			

Table 22.1

Sample of futures contracts

Prediction Markets

If you find S&P 500 or T-bond contracts a bit dry, perhaps you'd be interested in futures contracts with payoffs that depend on the winner of the next presidential election, or the severity of the next influenza season, or the host city of the 2028 Olympics. You can now find "futures markets" in these events and many others.

For example, both Iowa Electronic Markets (**www.biz.uiowa .edu/iem**) and the *Politics* page of BetFair (**www.betfair.com**) maintain presidential futures markets. In September 2016, you could have purchased a contract that would pay off $1 in November if Hillary Clinton won the presidential race but nothing if she lost. The contract price (expressed as a percentage of face value) therefore may be viewed as the probability of a Clinton victory, at least according to the consensus view of market participants at the time. If you believed in September that the probability of a Clinton victory was 55%, you would have been prepared to pay up to $.55 for the contract. Alternatively, if you had wished to bet against Clinton, you could have *sold* the contract. Similarly, you could have bet on (or against) a Donald Trump victory using his contract. (When there are only two relevant parties, betting on one is equivalent to betting against the other, but in other elections, such as primaries where there are several viable candidates, selling one candidate's contract is not the same as buying another's.)

The accompanying figure shows the price of Democratic and Republican contracts from November 2014 through Election Day. The price clearly tracks each party's perceived prospects. You can see Clinton's price rise to above $.90 in the week just before the election as the polls increasingly suggested she would win. Her price then declined substantially when the FBI announced it was reopening its investigation into her e-mail server. By the day before the election, with the investigation again apparently closed, her price had rebounded to $.80: Her victory seemed nearly inevitable, at least until the votes were counted.

Interpreting prediction market prices as probabilities actually requires a caveat. Because the contract payoff is risky, the price of the contract may reflect a risk premium. Therefore, to be precise, these probabilities are actually risk-neutral probabilities (see Chapter 21). In practice, however, it seems unlikely that the risk premium associated with these contracts is substantial.

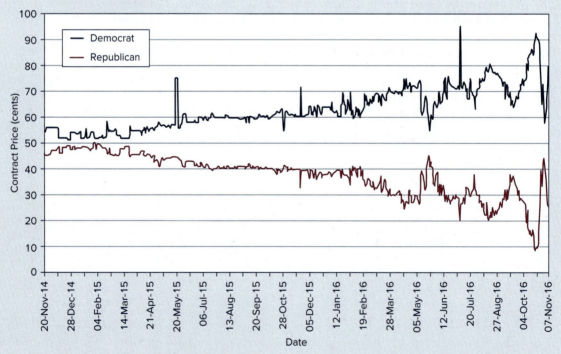

Prediction markets for the 2016 presidential election. Contract on each party pays $1 if the party wins the election. Price is in cents.

Source: Iowa Electronic Markets, downloaded November 16, 2016.

necessarily incomplete. The nearby box discusses some comparatively fanciful futures markets, sometimes called *prediction markets,* in which payoffs may be tied to the winner of presidential elections, the box office receipts of a particular movie, or anything else in which participants are willing to take positions.

Outside the futures markets, a well-developed network of banks and brokers has established a forward market in foreign exchange. This forward market is not a formal exchange in the sense that the exchange specifies the terms of the traded contract. Instead, participants in a forward contract may negotiate for delivery of any quantity of goods at any date, whereas in the formal futures markets contract size and delivery dates are set by the exchange. In forward arrangements, banks and brokers simply negotiate contracts for clients (or themselves) as needed. This market is huge. In London alone, the largest currency market, around $2 trillion of currency trades each day.

22.2   Trading Mechanics

The Clearinghouse and Open Interest

Until about 15 years ago, most futures trades in the United States occurred among floor traders in the "trading pit" for each contract. Today, however, trading is overwhelmingly conducted through electronic networks, particularly for financial futures.

Once a trade is agreed to, the **clearinghouse** enters the picture. Rather than having the long and short traders hold contracts with each other, the clearinghouse becomes the seller of the contract for the long position and the buyer of the contract for the short position. The clearinghouse is obligated to deliver the commodity to the long position and to pay for delivery from the short; consequently, the clearinghouse's position nets to zero. This arrangement makes the clearinghouse the trading partner of each trader, both long and short. The clearinghouse, bound to perform on its side of each contract, is the only party that can be hurt by the failure of any trader to satisfy the obligations of the futures contract. This arrangement is necessary because a futures contract calls for future performance, which cannot be as easily guaranteed as an immediate stock transaction.

Figure 22.3, Panel A, shows what would happen in the absence of the clearinghouse. The trader in the long position would be obligated to pay the futures price to the short position, and the trader in the short position would be obligated to deliver the commodity. Panel B shows how the clearinghouse becomes an intermediary, acting as the trading partner for each side of the contract. The clearinghouse's position is neutral, as it takes a long and a short position for each transaction.

The clearinghouse makes it possible for traders to liquidate positions easily. If you are currently long and want to undo your position, you simply instruct your broker to enter the short side of a contract. This is called a *reversing trade*. The exchange nets out your long and short positions, reducing your net position to zero. Your zero net position eliminates the need to fulfill at maturity either the original long or reversing short position.

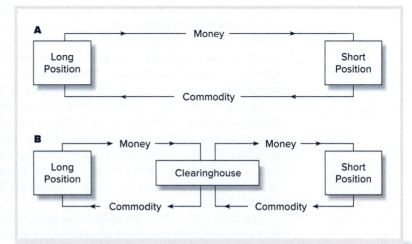

Figure 22.3 *Panel A,* Trading without a clearinghouse. *Panel B,* Trading with a clearinghouse.

The **open interest** on the contract is the number of contracts outstanding. (Long and short positions are not counted separately, meaning that open interest can be defined either as the number of long or short contracts outstanding. The clearinghouse's position nets out to zero, and so is not counted in the computation of open interest.) When contracts begin trading, open interest is zero. As time passes, open interest increases as progressively more contracts are entered.

There are many apocryphal stories about futures traders who wake up to discover a small mountain of wheat or corn on their front lawn. But the truth is that futures contracts rarely result in actual delivery of the underlying asset. Traders establish long or short positions in contracts that will benefit from a rise or fall in the futures price and almost always close out, or reverse, those positions before the contract expires. The fraction of contracts that result in actual delivery is estimated to range from less than 1% to 3%, depending on the commodity and activity in the contract. In the unusual case of actual deliveries of commodities, they occur via regular channels of supply, most often ware-house receipts.

You can see the typical pattern of open interest in Figure 22.1. In the gold contract, for example, the July contract is approaching maturity, and open interest is small; most contracts have been reversed already. The greatest open interest is in the August contract. For other contracts, for example, crude oil, for which the nearest maturity date isn't until August, open interest is highest in the nearest contract.

The Margin Account and Marking to Market

The total profit or loss realized by the long trader who buys a contract at time 0 and closes, or reverses, it at time t is just the change in the futures price over the period, $F_t - F_0$. Symmetrically, the short trader earns $F_0 - F_t$.

The process by which profits or losses accrue to traders is called *marking to market*. At initial execution of a trade, each trader establishes a margin account. The margin is a security account consisting of cash or near-cash securities, such as Treasury bills, that ensures the trader is able to satisfy the obligations of the futures contract. Because both parties to a contract are exposed to losses, both must post margin. To illustrate, return to the first corn contract listed in Figure 22.1. If the initial required margin on corn, for example, is 10%, then each trader must put up $1,720 per contract. This is 10% of the value of the contract, $3.44 per bushel × 5,000 bushels per contract.

Because the initial margin may be satisfied by posting interest-earning securities, the requirement does not impose a significant opportunity cost of funds on the trader. The initial margin is usually set between 5% and 15% of the total value of the contract. Contracts written on assets with more volatile prices require higher margins.

On any day that futures contracts trade, futures prices may rise or may fall. Instead of waiting until the maturity date for traders to realize all gains and losses, the clearinghouse requires all positions to recognize profits as they accrue daily. If the futures price of corn rises from 344 to 346 cents per bushel, the clearinghouse credits the margin account of the long position for 5,000 bushels times 2 cents per bushel, or $100 per contract. Conversely, the clearinghouse takes this amount from the margin account of the short position for each contract held.

This daily settling is called **marking to market.** It means the maturity date of the contract does not govern realization of profit or loss. Instead, as futures prices change, the proceeds accrue to the trader's margin account immediately. We will provide a more detailed example of this process shortly.

✔ Concept Check **22.2**

What must be the net inflow or outlay from marking to market for the clearinghouse?

Marking to market is the major way in which futures and forward contracts differ, besides contract standardization. Futures follow this pay-(or receive-)as-you-go method. Forward contracts are simply held until maturity, and no funds are transferred until that date.

If a trader accrues sustained losses from daily marking to market, the margin account may fall below a critical value called the **maintenance margin.** If the value of the account falls below this value, the trader receives a margin call, requiring that the margin account be replenished or the position be reduced to a size commensurate with the remaining funds. Margins and margin calls safeguard the position of the clearinghouse. Positions are closed out before the margin account is exhausted—the trader's losses are covered, and the clearinghouse is not put at risk.

Example 22.1   Maintenance Margin

Suppose the maintenance margin is 5% while the initial margin was 10% of the value of the corn, or $1,720. Then a margin call will go out when the original margin account has fallen in half, by about $860. Each 1-cent decline in the corn price results in a $50 loss to the long position. Therefore, the futures price need only fall by 18 cents (or 5% of its current value) to trigger a margin call.

On the contract maturity date, the futures price will equal the spot price of the commodity. As a maturing contract calls for immediate delivery, the futures price on that day must equal the spot price—the cost of the commodity from the two competing sources is equalized in a competitive market.[1] You may obtain delivery of the commodity either by purchasing it directly in the spot market or by entering the long side of a futures contract.

A commodity available from two sources (spot or futures market) must be priced identically, or else investors will rush to purchase it from the cheap source in order to sell it in the high-priced market. Such arbitrage activity could not persist without prices adjusting to eliminate the arbitrage opportunity. Therefore, the futures price and the spot price must converge at maturity. This is called the **convergence property.**

For an investor who establishes a long position in a contract now (time 0) and holds that position until maturity (time T), the sum of all daily settlements will equal $F_T - F_0$, where F_T stands for the futures price at contract maturity. Because of convergence, however, the futures price at maturity, F_T, equals the spot price, P_T, so total futures profits also may be expressed as $P_T - F_0$. Thus we see that profits on a futures contract held to maturity perfectly track changes in the value of the underlying asset. Moreover, the total profit on a *futures* contract held until maturity is the same as that on a *forward* contract calling for the long trader to pay F_0 for an asset that ultimately will be worth P_T. For this reason, futures and forwards are often treated as nearly interchangeable.

---

[1]Small differences between the spot and futures price at maturity may persist because of transportation costs, but this is a minor factor.

Example 22.2   Marking to Market

Assume the 5-day maturity futures price for silver is currently $20.10 per ounce. Suppose that over the next 5 days, the futures price evolves as follows:

Day	Futures Price
0 (today)	$20.10
1	20.20
2	20.25
3	20.18
4	20.18
5 (maturity)	20.21

The daily mark-to-market settlements for each contract held by the long position will be as follows:

Day	Profit (Loss) per Ounce × 5,000 Ounces/Contract = Daily Proceeds	
1	20.20 − 20.10 = 0.10	$500
2	20.25 − 20.20 = 0.05	250
3	20.18 − 20.25 = −0.07	−350
4	20.18 − 20.18 = 0	0
5	20.21 − 20.18 = 0.03	150
		Sum = $550

The profit on Day 1 is the increase in the futures price from the previous day, or ($20.20 − $20.10) per ounce. Because each silver contract on the Commodity Exchange (CMX) calls for purchase and delivery of 5,000 ounces, the total profit per contract is 5,000 times $.10, or $500. On Day 3, when the futures price falls, the long position's margin account will be debited by $350. By Day 5, the sum of all daily proceeds is $550. This is exactly equal to 5,000 times the difference between the final futures price of $20.21 and the original futures price of $20.10. Because the final futures price equals the spot price on that date, the sum of all the daily proceeds (per ounce of silver held long) also equals $P_T - F_0$.

Cash versus Actual Delivery

Most futures contracts call for delivery of an actual commodity such as a particular grade of wheat or a specified amount of foreign currency if the contract is not reversed before maturity. For agricultural commodities, where quality of the delivered good may vary, the exchange sets quality standards as part of the futures contract. In some cases, contracts may be settled with higher- or lower-grade commodities. In these cases, a premium or discount is applied to the delivered commodity to adjust for the quality difference.

Some futures contracts call for **cash settlement.** An example is a stock index futures contract where the underlying asset is an index such as the Standard & Poor's 500. Delivery of every stock in the index clearly would be impractical. Hence the contract calls for "delivery" of a cash amount equal to the value that the index attains on the maturity date of the contract. The sum of all the daily settlements from marking to market results in the long position realizing total profits or losses of $S_T - F_0$, where S_T is the value of the stock index on the maturity date T and F_0 is the original futures price. Cash settlement closely mimics actual delivery, except the cash value of the asset rather than the asset itself is delivered.

More concretely, the widely traded E-mini S&P 500 index contract calls for delivery of $50 times the value of the index.[2] Suppose that at maturity, the S&P 500 is at a level of 2,000. Instead of delivering shares of all 500 stocks included in the index, cash settlement would require the short trader to deliver $50 × 2,000, or $100,000. This provides the trader exactly the same profit as would result from directly purchasing 50 units of the index for $100,000 and then delivering it for $50 times the original futures price.

Regulations

Futures markets are regulated by the federal Commodities Futures Trading Commission. The CFTC sets capital requirements for member firms of the futures exchanges, authorizes trading in new contracts, and oversees maintenance of daily trading records.

The futures exchange may set limits on the amount by which futures prices may change from one day to the next. For example, if the price limit on silver contracts were set at $1 and silver futures close today at $22.10 per ounce, then trades in silver tomorrow may vary only between $21.10 and $23.10 per ounce. The exchanges may increase or reduce price limits in response to perceived changes in the price volatility of the underlying asset. Price limits are often eliminated as contracts approach maturity, usually in the last month of trading.

Price limits traditionally are viewed as a means to limit violent price fluctuations. This reasoning seems dubious. Suppose an international monetary crisis overnight drives up the spot price of silver to $30. No one would sell silver futures at prices for future delivery as low as $22.10. Instead, the futures price would rise each day by the $1 limit, although the quoted price would represent only an unfilled bid order—no contracts would trade at the low quoted price. After several days of limit moves of $1 per day, the futures price would finally reach its equilibrium level, and trading would occur again. This process means no one could unload a position until the price reached its equilibrium level. We conclude that price limits offer no real protection against fluctuations in equilibrium prices.

Taxation

Because of the mark-to-market procedure, investors do not have control over the tax year in which they realize gains or losses. Instead, price changes are realized gradually, with each daily settlement. Therefore, taxes are paid at year-end on cumulated profits or losses, regardless of whether the position has been closed out. As a general rule, 60% of futures gains or losses are treated as long term, and 40% are treated as short term.

22.3   Futures Markets Strategies

Hedging and Speculation

Hedging and speculating are two polar uses of futures markets. A speculator uses a futures contract to profit from movements in futures prices, a hedger to protect against price movement.

If speculators believe prices will increase, they will take a long position for expected profits. Conversely, they exploit expected price declines by taking a short position.

[2]The original S&P 500 contract had a multiplier of $500, later reduced to $250. However, the all-electronically traded version of the contract, usually referred to as the E-mini, has a multiplier of $50. The great majority of futures trading on the S&P 500 is now conducted on the E-mini rather than the original "big" contract.

Example 22.3   Speculating with Oil Futures

Suppose you believe that crude oil prices are going to increase and therefore decide to purchase crude oil futures. Each contract calls for delivery of 1,000 barrels of oil, so for every $1 increase in the futures price of crude, the long position gains $1,000 and the short position loses that amount.

Conversely, suppose you think that prices are heading lower and therefore sell a contract. If crude oil prices do in fact fall, then you will gain $1,000 per contract for every $1 that prices decline.

If the futures price for delivery in February is $52 and crude oil is selling at the contract maturity date for $53, the long side will profit by $1,000 per contract purchased. The short side will lose an identical amount on each contract sold. On the other hand, if oil has fallen to $51, the long side will lose, and the short side will gain, $1,000 per contract.

Why does a speculator buy a futures contract? Why not buy the underlying asset directly? One reason lies in transaction costs, which are far smaller in futures markets.

Another important reason is the leverage that futures trading provides. Recall that futures contracts require traders to post margin considerably less than the value of the asset underlying the contract. Therefore, they allow speculators to achieve much greater leverage than is available from direct trading in a commodity.

Example 22.4   Futures and Leverage

Suppose the initial margin requirement for the oil contract is 10%. At a current futures price of $52, and contract size of 1,000 barrels, this would require margin of $.10 \times 52 \times 1,000 = \$5,200$. A $1 increase in oil prices represents an increase of 1.92%, and results in a $1,000 gain on the contract for the long position. This is a percentage gain of 19.2% on the $5,200 posted as margin, precisely 10 times the percentage increase in the oil price. The 10-to-1 ratio of percentage changes reflects the leverage inherent in the futures position, because the contract was established with an initial margin of one-tenth the value of the underlying asset.

Hedgers, by contrast, use futures to insulate themselves against price movements. A firm planning to sell oil, for example, might anticipate a period of market volatility and wish to protect its revenue against price fluctuations. To hedge the total revenue derived from the sale, the firm enters a short position in oil futures. As the following example illustrates, this locks in its total proceeds (i.e., revenue from the sale of the oil plus proceeds from its futures position).

Example 22.5   Hedging with Oil Futures

Consider an oil distributor planning to sell 100,000 barrels of oil in February that wishes to hedge against a possible decline in oil prices. Because each contract calls for delivery of 1,000 barrels, it would sell 100 contracts that mature in February. Any decrease in prices would then generate a profit on the contracts that would offset the lower sales revenue from the oil.

To illustrate, suppose that the only three possible prices for oil in February are $51, $52, and $53 per barrel. The revenue from the oil sale will be 100,000 times the price per barrel.

The profit on each contract sold will be 1,000 times any decline in the futures price. At maturity, the convergence property ensures that the final futures price will equal the spot price of oil. Therefore, the profit on the 100 contracts sold will equal $100{,}000 \times (F_0 - P_T)$, where P_T is the oil price on the delivery date, and F_0 is the original futures price, $52.

Now consider the firm's overall position. The total revenue in February can be computed as follows:

	Oil Price in February, P_T		
	$51	**$52**	**$53**
Revenue from oil sale: $100{,}000 \times P_T$	$5,100,000	$5,200,000	$5,300,000
+ Profit on futures: $100{,}000 \times (F_0 - P_T)$	100,000	0	−100,000
Total proceeds	$5,200,000	$5,200,000	$5,200,000

The revenue from the oil sale plus the proceeds from the contracts equals the current futures price, $52 per barrel. The variation in the price of the oil is precisely offset by the profits or losses on the futures position. For example, if oil falls to $51 a barrel, the short futures position generates $100,000 profit, just enough to bring total revenues to $5,200,000. The total is the same as if one were to arrange today to sell the oil in February at the futures price.

Figure 22.4 illustrates the nature of the hedge in Example 22.5. The upward-sloping line is the revenue from the sale of oil. The downward-sloping line is the profit on the futures contract. The horizontal line is the sum of sales revenue plus futures profits. This line is flat, as the hedged position is independent of oil prices.

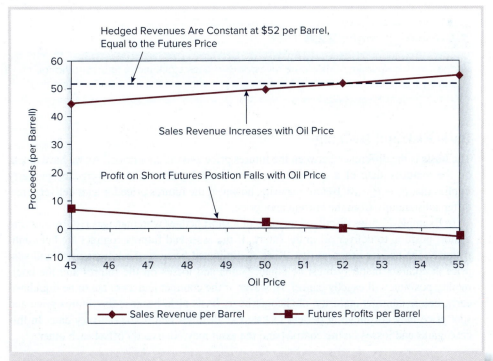

Figure 22.4 Hedging revenues using futures, Example 22.5 (Futures price = $52 per barrel)

To generalize Example 22.5, note that oil will sell for P_T per barrel at the maturity of the contract. The profit per barrel on the futures will be $F_0 - P_T$. Therefore, total revenue is $P_T + (F_0 - P_T) = F_0$, which is independent of the eventual oil price.

The oil distributor in Example 22.5 engaged in a *short hedge,* entering a short futures position to offset risk in the sales price of a particular asset. A *long hedge* is the analogous hedge for someone who wishes to eliminate the risk of an uncertain purchase price. For example, a power supplier planning to purchase oil may be afraid that prices might rise by the time of the purchase. As Concept Check 22.3 illustrates, the supplier might *buy* oil futures to lock in the net purchase price at the time of the transaction.

 Concept Check **22.3**

As in Example 22.5, suppose that oil will be selling in February for $51, $52, or $53 per barrel. Consider a firm that plans to buy 100,000 barrels of oil in February. Show that if the firm buys 100 oil contracts today, its net expenditures in February will be hedged and equal to $5,200,000.

Exact futures hedging may be impossible for some goods because the necessary futures contract is not traded. For example, a portfolio manager might want to hedge the value of a diversified, actively managed portfolio for a period of time. However, futures contracts are listed only on indexed portfolios. Nevertheless, because returns on the manager's diversified portfolio will have a high correlation with returns on broad-based indexed portfolios, an effective hedge may be established by selling index futures contracts. Hedging a position using futures on another asset is called *cross-hedging.*

 Concept Check **22.4**

What are the sources of risk to an investor who uses stock index futures to hedge an actively managed stock portfolio? How might you estimate the magnitude of that risk?

Basis Risk and Hedging

The **basis** is the difference between the futures price and the spot price.[3] As we have noted, on the maturity date of a contract, the basis must be zero: The convergence property implies that $F_T - P_T = 0$. Before maturity, however, the futures price for later delivery may differ substantially from the current spot price.

In Example 22.5 we discussed the case of a short hedger who manages risk by entering a short position to deliver oil in the future. If the asset and futures contract are held until maturity, the hedger bears no risk. Risk is eliminated because the futures price and spot price at contract maturity must be equal: Gains and losses on the futures and the commodity position will exactly cancel. However, if the contract and asset are to be liquidated early, before contract maturity, the hedger bears **basis risk,** because the futures price and spot price may not move in perfect lockstep at all times before the delivery date. In this case, gains and losses on the contract and the asset may not exactly offset each other.

---

[3]Usage of the word *basis* is somewhat loose. It sometimes is used to refer to the futures-spot difference $F - P$, and sometimes to the spot-futures difference $P - F$. We will consistently call the basis $F - P$.

Some speculators try to profit from movements in the basis. Rather than betting on the direction of the futures or spot prices per se, they bet on the changes in the difference between the two. A long spot–short futures position will profit when the basis narrows.

Example 22.6   Speculating on the Basis

Consider an investor holding 100 ounces of gold, who is short one gold-futures contract. Suppose that gold today sells for $1,391 an ounce, and the futures price for June delivery is $1,396 an ounce. Therefore, the basis is currently $5. Tomorrow, the spot price might increase to $1,395, while the futures price increases to $1,399, so the basis narrows to $4.
   The investor's gains and losses are as follows:

Gain on holdings of gold (per ounce): $1,395 − $1,391 = $4

Loss on gold futures position (per ounce): $1,399 − $1,396 = $3

The net gain is the decrease in the basis, or $1 per ounce.

A related strategy is a **calendar spread** position, where the investor takes a long position in a futures contract of one maturity and a short position in a contract on the same commodity, but with a different maturity.[4] Profits accrue if the difference in futures prices between the two contracts changes in the hoped-for direction, that is, if the futures price on the contract held long increases by more (or decreases by less) than the futures price on the contract held short.

Example 22.7   Speculating on the Spread

Consider an investor who holds a September maturity contract long and a June contract short. If the September futures price increases by 5 cents while the June futures price increases by 4 cents, the net gain will be 5 cents − 4 cents, or 1 cent. Like basis strategies, spread positions aim to exploit movements in relative price structures rather than profit from movements in the general level of prices.

22.4   Futures Prices

The Spot-Futures Parity Theorem

We have seen that a futures contract can be used to hedge changes in the value of the underlying asset. If the hedge is perfect, meaning that the asset-plus-futures portfolio has no risk, then the hedged position must provide a rate of return equal to the rate on other risk-free investments. Otherwise, there will be arbitrage opportunities that investors will exploit until prices are brought back into line. This insight can be used to derive the theoretical relationship between a futures price and the price of its underlying asset.

Suppose for simplicity that a stock market index such as the S&P 500 currently is at 1,000 and an investor who holds $1,000 in an indexed mutual fund wishes to temporarily hedge her exposure to market risk. Assume that the indexed portfolio pays year-end dividends of $20. Finally, assume that the futures price for year-end delivery of the

---

[4]Yet another strategy is an *intercommodity spread,* in which the investor buys a contract on one commodity and sells a contract on a different commodity.

contract is $1,010.^5$ Let's examine the end-of-year proceeds for various values of the stock index if the investor hedges her portfolio by entering the short side of the futures contract.

Final value of stock portfolio, S_T	$ 970	$ 990	$1,010	$1,030	$1,050	$1,070
Payoff from short futures position (equals $F_0 - F_T = \$1,010 - S_T$)	40	20	0	−20	−40	−60
Dividend income	20	20	20	20	20	20
Total	$1,030	$1,030	$1,030	$1,030	$1,030	$1,030

The payoff from the short futures position equals the difference between the original futures price, $1,010, and the year-end stock price. This is because of convergence: The futures price at contract maturity will equal the stock price at that time.

Notice that the overall position is perfectly hedged. Any increase in the value of the indexed stock portfolio is offset by an equal decrease in the payoff of the short futures position, resulting in a final value independent of the stock price. The $1,030 total payoff is the sum of the current futures price, $F_0 = \$1,010$, and the $20 dividend. It is as though the investor arranged to sell the stock at year-end for the current futures price, thereby eliminating price risk and locking in total proceeds equal to the futures price plus dividends paid before the sale.

What rate of return is earned on this riskless position? The stock investment requires an initial outlay of $1,000, whereas the futures position is established without an initial cash outflow. Therefore, the $1,000 portfolio grows to a year-end value of $1,030, providing a rate of return of 3%. More generally, a total investment of S_0, the current stock price, grows to a final value of $F_0 + D$, where D is the dividend payout on the portfolio. The rate of return is therefore

$$\text{Rate of return on hedged stock portfolio} = \frac{(F_0 + D) - S_0}{S_0}$$

This return is essentially riskless. We observe F_0 at the beginning of the period when we enter the futures contract. While dividend payouts are not perfectly riskless, they are highly predictable over short periods, especially for diversified portfolios. Any uncertainty is *extremely* small compared to the uncertainty in stock prices.

Presumably, 3% must be the rate of return available on other riskless investments. If not, then investors would face two competing risk-free strategies with different rates of return, a situation that could not last. Therefore, we conclude that

$$\frac{(F_0 + D) - S_0}{S_0} = r_f$$

Rearranging, we find that the futures price must be

$$F_0 = S_0(1 + r_f) - D = S_0(1 + r_f - d) \tag{22.1}$$

where d is the dividend yield on the indexed stock portfolio, defined as D/S_0. This result is called the **spot-futures parity theorem.** It gives the normal or theoretically correct relationship between spot and futures prices. Any deviation from parity would give rise to risk-free arbitrage opportunities.

---

[5]Actually, the E-mini futures contract on the S&P 500 calls for delivery of $50 times the value of the index, so that each contract would be settled for $50 times the index. With the index at the assumed value of 1,000, each contract would hedge about $50 × 1,000 = $50,000 worth of stock. Of course, institutional investors would consider a stock portfolio of this size to be quite small. We will simplify by assuming that you can buy a contract for one unit rather than 50 units of the index.

Example 22.8   Futures Market Arbitrage

Suppose that parity were violated. For example, suppose the risk-free interest rate were only 1% so that according to Equation 22.1, the futures price should be $1,000(1.01) − $20 = $990. The actual futures price, $F_0 = $1,010$, is $20 higher than its "appropriate" value. This implies that an investor can make arbitrage profits by shorting the relatively overpriced futures contract and buying the relatively underpriced stock portfolio using money borrowed at the 1% market interest rate. The proceeds from this strategy would be as follows:

Action	Initial Cash Flow	Cash Flow in 1 Year
Borrow $1,000, repay with interest in 1 year	+1,000	$-1,000(1.01) = -$1,010$
Buy stock index for $1,000	−1,000	$S_T + 20 dividend
Enter short futures position ($F_0 = $1,010$)	0	$$1,010 - S_T$
Total	0	$20

The net initial investment of the strategy is zero. But its cash flow in one year is $20 regardless of the stock price. In other words, it is riskless. This payoff is precisely equal to the mispricing of the futures contract relative to its parity value, 1,010 − 990.

When parity is violated, the strategy to exploit the mispricing produces an arbitrage profit—a riskless profit requiring no initial net investment. If such an opportunity existed, market participants would rush to take advantage of it. The results? The stock price would be bid up, and/or the futures price offered down until Equation 22.1 were satisfied. A similar analysis applies to the possibility that F_0 is less than $990. In this case, you simply reverse the strategy above to earn riskless profits. We conclude, therefore, that in a well-functioning market in which arbitrage opportunities are competed away, $F_0 = S_0(1 + r_f) - D$.

 Concept Check **22.5**

Return to the arbitrage strategy laid out in Example 22.8. What would be the three steps of the strategy if F_0 were too low, say, $980? Work out the cash flows of the strategy now and in one year in a table like the one in the example. Confirm that your profits equal the mispricing of the contract.

The arbitrage strategy of Example 22.8 can be represented more generally as follows:

Action	Initial Cash Flow	Cash Flow in 1 Year
1. Borrow S_0 dollars	S_0	$-S_0(1 + r_f)$
2. Buy stock for S_0	$-S_0$	$S_T + D$
3. Enter short futures position	0	$F_0 - S_T$
Total	0	$F_0 - S_0(1 + r_f) + D$

The initial cash flow is zero by construction: The money necessary to purchase the stock in step 2 is borrowed in step 1, and the futures position in step 3, which is used to hedge the value of the stock position, does not require an initial outlay. Moreover, the total cash flow at year-end is riskless because it involves only terms that are already known when the contract is entered into. If the final cash flow were not zero, all investors would try to cash in on the arbitrage opportunity. Ultimately prices would change until the year-end cash flow is reduced to zero, at which point F_0 would equal $S_0(1 + r_f) - D$.

The parity relationship also is called the **cost-of-carry relationship** because it asserts that the futures price is determined by the relative costs of buying a stock with deferred delivery in the futures market versus buying it in the spot market with immediate delivery and "carrying" it in inventory. If you buy stock now, you tie up your funds and incur a time-value-of-money cost of r_f per period. On the other hand, you receive dividend payments with a current yield of d. The net carrying cost advantage of deferring delivery of the stock is therefore $r_f - d$ per period. This advantage must be offset by a differential between the futures price and the spot price. The price differential just offsets the cost-of-carry advantage when $F_0 = S_0(1 + r_f - d)$.

The parity relationship is easily generalized to multiperiod applications. We simply recognize that the difference between the futures and spot price will be larger as the maturity of the contract is longer. This reflects the longer period to which we apply the net cost of carry. For contract maturity of T periods, the parity relationship is

$$F_0 = S_0(1 + r_f - d)^T \tag{22.2}$$

Notice that when the dividend yield is less than the risk-free rate, Equation 22.2 implies that futures prices will exceed spot prices, and by greater amounts for longer times to contract maturity. But when $d > r_f$, as is the case today, the income yield on the stock exceeds the forgone (risk-free) interest that could be earned on the money invested; in this event, the futures price will be less than the current stock price, again by greater amounts for longer maturities. You can confirm that this is so by examining the S&P 500 contract listings in Figure 22.1.

Although dividends of individual securities may fluctuate unpredictably, the annualized dividend yield of a broad-based index such as the S&P 500 is fairly stable, recently in the neighborhood of a bit more than 2% per year. The yield is seasonal, however, with regular peaks and troughs, so the dividend yield for the relevant months must be the one used. Figure 22.5 illustrates the yield pattern for the S&P 500. Some months, such as January or April, have consistently low yields, while others, such as May, have consistently high ones.[6]

We have described parity in terms of stocks and stock index futures, but it should be clear that the logic applies as well to any financial futures contract. For gold futures, for example, we would simply set the dividend yield to zero. For bond contracts, we would let the coupon income on the bond play the role of dividend payments. In both cases, the parity relationship would be essentially the same as Equation 22.2.

The arbitrage strategy described above should convince you that these parity relationships are more than just theoretical results. Any violations of the parity relationship give rise to arbitrage opportunities that can provide large profits to traders. We will see in Chapter 23 that index arbitrage in the stock market is a tool to exploit violations of the parity relationship for stock index futures contracts.

Spreads

Just as we can predict the relationship between spot and futures prices, there are similar ways to determine the proper relationships among futures prices for contracts of different maturity dates. Equation 22.2 shows that the futures price is in part determined by time to maturity. If the risk-free rate is greater than the dividend yield (i.e., $r_f > d$), then the

---

[6]The high value for the dividend yield in 2009 reflects the financial crisis. You learned in your corporate finance class that firms are reluctant to reduce dividends. When the economy entered the crisis and stock prices fell dramatically, dividend payouts did not fall as precipitously. Therefore, the ratio of dividends to stock prices increased.

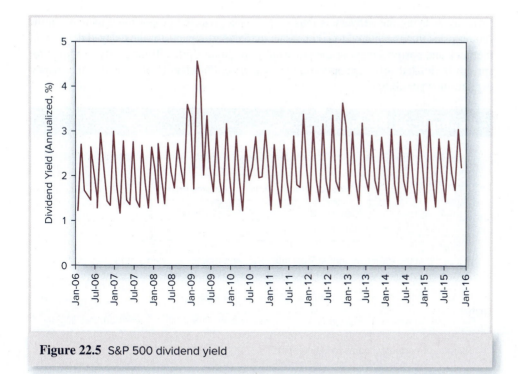

Figure 22.5 S&P 500 dividend yield

futures price will be higher on longer-maturity contracts and if $r_f < d$, longer-maturity futures prices will be lower. You can confirm from Figure 22.1 that in 2016, when the risk-free rate was below the dividend yield, the longer-maturity S&P 500 contract did have a lower futures price than the shorter term contract. For futures on assets like gold, which pay no "dividend yield," we can set $d = 0$ and conclude that F *must* increase as time to maturity increases.

To be more precise about spread pricing, call $F(T_1)$ the current futures price for delivery at date T_1, and $F(T_2)$ the futures price for delivery at date T_2. Let d be the dividend yield of the stock. We know from the parity Equation 22.2 that

$$F(T_1) = S_0(1 + r_f - d)^{T_1}$$
$$F(T_2) = S_0(1 + r_f - d)^{T_2}$$

As a result,

$$F(T_2)/F(T_1) = (1 + r_f - d)^{(T_2 - T_1)}$$

Therefore, the basic parity relationship for spreads is

$$F(T_2) = F(T_1)(1 + r_f - d)^{(T_2 - T_1)} \tag{22.3}$$

Equation 22.3 should remind you of the spot-futures parity relationship. The major difference is in the substitution of $F(T_1)$ for the current spot price. The intuition is also similar. Delaying delivery from T_1 to T_2 assures the long position that the stock will be purchased for $F(T_2)$ dollars at T_2 but does not require that money be tied up in the stock until T_2. The savings realized are the net cost of carry between T_1 and T_2. Delaying delivery from T_1 until T_2 frees up $F(T_1)$ dollars, which earn risk-free interest at r_f. The delayed delivery of the stock also results in the lost dividend yield between T_1 and T_2. The net cost of carry saved by delaying the delivery is thus $r_f - d$. This gives the proportional increase in the futures price that is required to compensate market participants for the delayed delivery of the stock and postponement of the payment of the futures price. If the parity condition for spreads is violated, arbitrage opportunities will arise. (Problem 19 at the end of the chapter explores this possibility.)

Example 22.9   Spread Pricing

To see how to use Equation 22.3, consider the following data for a hypothetical contract:

Contract Maturity Data	Futures Price
January 15	$105.00
March 15	104.75

Suppose that the effective annual T-bill rate is 1% and that the dividend yield is 2% per year. The "correct" March futures price given the January price is, according to Equation 22.3,

$$105(1 + .01 - .02)^{2/12} = 104.82$$

The actual March futures price is 104.75, meaning that the March futures price is slightly underpriced compared to the January futures price and that, aside from transaction costs, an arbitrage opportunity seems to be present.

Equation 22.3 shows that futures prices with different maturities should all move together. This is not surprising because all are linked to the same spot price through the parity relationship. Figure 22.6 plots futures prices on gold for three maturity dates. It is apparent that the prices move in virtual lockstep and that the more distant delivery dates command higher futures prices, as Equation 22.3 predicts.

Forward versus Futures Pricing

Until now we have paid little attention to the differing time profile of returns of futures and forward contracts. Instead, we have taken the sum of daily mark-to-market proceeds to the

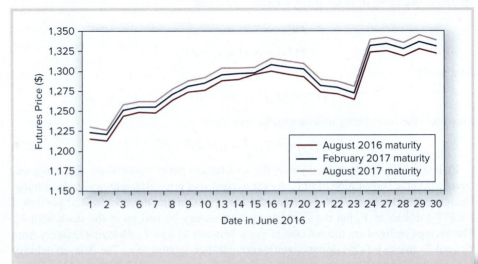

Figure 22.6 Gold futures prices for three contracts with different maturity dates

The parity spreadsheet allows you to calculate futures prices corresponding to a spot price for different maturities, interest rates, and income yields. You can use the spreadsheet to see how prices of more distant contracts will fluctuate with spot prices and the cost of carry. You can learn more about this spreadsheet by using the version available in Connect or through your course instructor.

(the difference in futures prices for the long versus short maturity contracts) if the interest rate increases by 2%?

2. What happens to the time spread if the income yield increases by 2%?

3. What happens to the spread if the income yield equals the interest rate?

Excel Questions

1. Experiment with different values for both income yield and interest rate. What happens to the size of the time spread

	A	B	C	D	E
1		**Spot Futures Parity and Time Spreads**			
2					
3	Spot price	100			
4	Income yield (%)	2		Futures prices versus maturity	
5	Interest rate (%)	1.5			
6	Today's date	5/10/2017		Spot price	100.00
7	Maturity date 1	11/10/2017		Futures 1	99.75
8	Maturity date 2	7/10/2018		Futures 2	99.42
9	Maturity date 3	9/10/2018		Futures 3	99.33
10					
11	Time to maturity 1	0.50			
12	Time to maturity 2	1.17			
13	Time to maturity 3	1.33			

long position as $P_T - F_0$ and assumed for convenience that the entire profit accrues on the delivery date. Strictly speaking, our parity theorems apply only to forward pricing because they assume that contract proceeds are in fact realized only on delivery. In contrast, the actual timing of cash flows conceivably might affect the futures price.

Futures prices will deviate from parity when marking to market gives a systematic advantage to either the long or short position. If marking to market tends to favor the long position, for example, the futures price should exceed the forward price, because the long position will be willing to pay a premium for the advantage of marking to market.

When will marking to market favor either a long or short trader? A trader will benefit if daily settlements are received (and can be invested) when the interest rate is high; symmetrically, a trader will benefit when daily settlements are paid (and can be financed) when the interest rate is low. Because long positions will benefit if futures prices tend to rise when interest rates are high, they will be willing to accept a higher futures price if there is a positive correlation between interest rates and changes in futures prices. In this situation, the "fair" futures price will exceed the forward price. Conversely, a negative correlation means that marking to market favors the short position and implies that the equilibrium futures price should be below the forward price.

For most contracts, the covariance between futures prices and interest rates is so low that the difference between futures and forward prices will be negligible. However, contracts on long-term fixed-income securities are an important exception to this rule. In this case, because prices have a high correlation with interest rates, the covariance can be large enough to generate a meaningful spread between forward and futures prices.

Futures Prices versus Expected Spot Prices

So far we have considered the relationship between futures prices and the *current* spot price. What about the relationship between the futures price and the *expected value* of the spot price? In other words, how well does the futures price forecast the ultimate spot price? Three traditional theories have been put forth: the expectations hypothesis, normal backwardation, and contango. Today's consensus is that all of these traditional hypotheses are subsumed by modern portfolio theory. Figure 22.7 shows the expected path of futures under the three traditional hypotheses.

Expectations Hypothesis

The *expectations hypothesis* is the simplest theory of futures pricing. It states that the futures price equals the expected value of the future spot price: $F_0 = E(P_T)$. Under this theory the expected profit to either position of a futures contract would equal zero: The short position's expected profit is $F_0 - E(P_T)$, whereas the long's is $E(P_T) - F_0$. With $F_0 = E(P_T)$, the expected profit to either side is zero. This hypothesis relies on a notion of risk neutrality. If all market participants are risk neutral, they should agree on a futures price that provides an expected profit of zero to all parties.

The expectations hypothesis resembles market equilibrium in a world with no uncertainty; that is, if prices of goods at all future dates were currently known, then the futures price for delivery at any particular date would equal the currently known future spot price for that date. It is a tempting but incorrect leap to then assert that under uncertainty the futures price should equal the currently *expected* spot price. This view ignores the risk premiums that must be built into futures prices when ultimate spot prices are uncertain.

Normal Backwardation

This theory is associated with the famous British economists John Maynard Keynes and John Hicks. They argued that for most commodities there are natural hedgers who wish to shed risk. For example, wheat farmers desire to shed the risk of uncertain wheat prices. These farmers will take short positions to deliver wheat at a guaranteed price; they will short hedge. To induce speculators to take the corresponding long positions, the farmers need to offer them an expectation of profit. They will enter the long side of the contract only if the futures price is below the expected spot price of wheat, for an expected profit of $E(P_T) - F_0$. The speculators' expected profit is the farmers' expected loss, but farmers are willing to bear this expected loss to avoid the risk of uncertain wheat prices. The theory of *normal backwardation* thus suggests that the futures price will be bid down to a

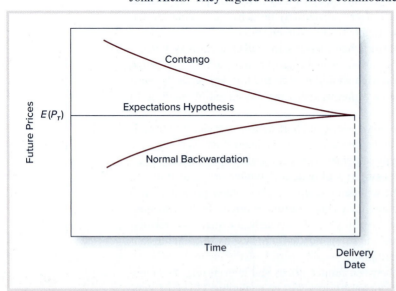

Figure 22.7 Futures price over time, in the special case that the expected spot price remains unchanged

level below the expected spot price and will rise over the life of the contract until the maturity date, at which point $F_T = P_T$.

Although this theory recognizes the important role of risk premiums in futures markets, it is based on total variability rather than on systematic risk. (This is not surprising, as Keynes wrote almost 40 years before the development of modern portfolio theory.) The modern view refines the measure of risk used to determine appropriate risk premiums.

Contango

The polar hypothesis to backwardation holds that the natural hedgers are the purchasers of a commodity, rather than the suppliers. In the case of wheat, for example, we would view grain processors as willing to pay a premium to lock in the price that they must pay for wheat. These processors hedge by taking a long position in the futures market; therefore, they are called long hedgers, whereas farmers are short hedgers. Because long hedgers will agree to pay high futures prices to shed risk, and because speculators must be paid a premium to enter the short position, the *contango* theory holds that F_0 must exceed $E(P_T)$.

It is clear that any commodity will have both natural long hedgers and short hedgers. The compromise traditional view, called the "net hedging hypothesis," is that F_0 will be less than $E(P_T)$ when short hedgers outnumber long hedgers and vice versa. The strong side of the market will be the side (short or long) that has more natural hedgers. The strong side must pay a premium to induce speculators to enter into enough contracts to balance the "natural" supply of long and short hedgers.

Modern Portfolio Theory

The three traditional hypotheses all envision a mass of speculators willing to enter either side of the futures market if they are sufficiently compensated for the risk they incur. Modern portfolio theory fine-tunes this approach by refining the notion of risk used in the determination of risk premiums. Simply put, if commodity prices pose positive systematic risk, futures prices must be lower than expected spot prices.

To illustrate this approach, consider once again a stock paying no dividends. If $E(P_T)$ denotes the expected time-T stock price and k denotes the required rate of return on the stock, then the price of the stock today must equal the present value of its expected future payoff as follows:

$$P_0 = \frac{E(P_T)}{(1+k)^T} \tag{22.4}$$

We also know from the spot-futures parity relationship that

$$P_0 = \frac{F_0}{(1+r_f)^T} \tag{22.5}$$

Therefore, the right-hand sides of Equations 22.4 and 22.5 must be equal. Equating these terms allows us to solve for F_0 in terms of the expected spot price:

$$F_0 = E(P_T)\left(\frac{1+r_f}{1+k}\right)^T \tag{22.6}$$

You can see immediately from Equation 22.6 that F_0 will be less than the expectation of P_T whenever k is greater than r_f, which will be the case for any positive-beta asset. This means that the long side of the contract will make an expected profit [F_0 will be lower than $E(P_T)$] when the commodity exhibits positive systematic risk (k is greater than r_f).

Why should this be? A long futures position will provide a profit (or loss) of $P_T - F_0$. If the ultimate value of P_T entails positive systematic risk, so will the profit to the long position. Speculators with well-diversified portfolios will be willing to enter long futures positions only if they receive compensation for bearing that risk in the form of positive expected profits. Their expected profits will be positive only if $E(P_T)$ is greater than F_0. Conversely, the short position's profit is the negative of the long position's and will have negative systematic risk. Diversified investors in the short position will be willing to suffer that expected loss to lower portfolio risk and will be willing to enter the contract even when F_0 is less than $E(P_T)$. We conclude that if P_T has positive beta, F_0 must be less than the expectation of P_T while the analysis is reversed for negative-beta assets.

 Concept Check **22.6**

> What must be true of the risk of the spot price of an asset if the futures price is an unbiased estimate of the ultimate spot price?

SUMMARY

1. Forward contracts call for future delivery of an asset at a currently agreed-on price. The long trader purchases the good, and the short trader delivers it. If the price of the asset at the maturity of the contract exceeds the forward price, the long side benefits by virtue of acquiring the good at the contract price.

2. A futures contract is similar to a forward contract, differing most importantly in the aspects of standardization and marking to market, which is the process by which gains and losses on futures contract positions are settled daily. In contrast, forward contracts call for no cash transfers until contract maturity.

3. Futures contracts are traded on organized exchanges that standardize the size of the contract, the grade of the deliverable asset, the delivery date, and the delivery location. Traders negotiate only over the contract price. This standardization increases liquidity and means that buyers and sellers can easily find many traders for a desired purchase or sale.

4. The clearinghouse steps in between each pair of traders, acting as the short position for each long and as the long position for each short. In this way traders need not be concerned about the performance of the trader on the opposite side of the contract. In turn, traders post margins to guarantee their own performance.

5. The long position's gain or loss between time 0 and time t is $F_t - F_0$. Because at the maturity date, T, $F_T = P_T$, the long's profit if the contract is held until maturity is $P_T - F_0$, where P_T is the spot price at time T and F_0 is the original futures price. The short position's profit is $F_0 - P_T$.

6. Futures contracts may be used for hedging or speculating. Speculators use the contracts to take a stand on the ultimate price of an asset. Short hedgers take short positions in contracts to offset any gains or losses on the value of an asset already held in inventory. Long hedgers take long positions to offset gains or losses in the purchase price of a good.

7. The spot-futures parity relationship states that the equilibrium futures price on an asset providing no service or payments (such as dividends) is $F_0 = P_0(1 + r_f)^T$. If the futures price deviates from this value, then market participants can earn arbitrage profits.

8. If the asset provides services or payments with yield d, the parity relationship becomes $F_0 = P_0(1 + r_f - d)^T$. This model is also called the cost-of-carry model, because it states that the futures price must exceed the spot price by the net cost of carrying the asset until maturity date T.

9. The equilibrium futures price will be less than the currently expected time T spot price if the spot price exhibits systematic risk. This provides an expected profit for the long position who bears the risk and imposes an expected loss on the short position who is willing to accept that expected loss as a means to shed systematic risk.

KEY EQUATIONS

Spot-futures parity: $F_0(T) = S_0 (1 + r - d)^T$

Futures spread parity: $F_0(T_2) = F_0(T_1) (1 + r - d)^{(T_2 - T_1)}$

Futures vs. expected spot prices: $F_0 = E(P_T)\left(\dfrac{1 + r_f}{1 + k}\right)^T$

PROBLEM SETS

1. Why is there no futures market in cement?
2. Why might individuals purchase futures contracts rather than the underlying asset?
3. What is the difference in cash flow between short-selling an asset and entering a short futures position?
4. Are the following statements true or false? Why?
   a. All else equal, the futures price on a stock index with a high dividend yield should be higher than the futures price on an index with a low dividend yield.
   b. All else equal, the futures price on a high-beta stock should be higher than the futures price on a low-beta stock.
   c. The beta of a short position in the S&P 500 futures contract is negative.
5. What is the difference between the futures price and the value of the futures contract?
6. Evaluate the criticism that futures markets siphon off capital from more productive uses.
7. a. Turn to the Mini-S&P 500 contract in Figure 22.1. If the margin requirement is 10% of the futures price times the contract multiplier of $50, how much must you deposit with your broker to trade the September maturity contract?
   b. If the September futures price were to increase to 2,090, what percentage return would you earn on your net investment if you entered the long side of the contract at the price shown in the figure?
   c. If the September futures price falls by 1%, what is your percentage return?
8. a. A single-stock futures contract on a non-dividend-paying stock with current price $150 has a maturity of 1 year. If the T-bill rate is 3%, what should the futures price be?
   b. What should the futures price be if the maturity of the contract is 3 years?
   c. What if the interest rate is 6% and the maturity of the contract is 3 years?
9. Determine how a portfolio manager might use financial futures to hedge risk in each of the following circumstances:
   a. You own a large position in a relatively illiquid bond that you want to sell.
   b. You have a large gain on one of your Treasuries and want to sell it, but you would like to defer the gain until the next tax year.
   c. You will receive your annual bonus next month that you hope to invest in long-term corporate bonds. You believe that bonds today are selling at quite attractive yields, and you are concerned that bond prices will rise over the next few weeks.
10. Suppose the value of the S&P 500 stock index is currently 2,000.
    a. If the 1-year T-bill rate is 3% and the expected dividend yield on the S&P 500 is 2%, what should the 1-year maturity futures price be?
    b. What if the T-bill rate is less than the dividend yield, for example, 1%?
11. Consider a stock that pays no dividends on which a futures contract, a call option, and a put option trade. The maturity date for all three contracts is T, the exercise price of both the put and the call is X, and the futures price is F. Show that if $X = F$, then the call price equals the put price. Use parity conditions to guide your demonstration.
12. It is now January. The current interest rate is 2%. The June futures price for gold is $1,500, whereas the December futures price is $1,510. Is there an arbitrage opportunity here? If so, how would you exploit it?

13. OneChicago has just introduced a single-stock futures contract on Brandex stock, a company that currently pays no dividends. Each contract calls for delivery of 1,000 shares of stock in 1 year. The T-bill rate is 6% per year.

    a. If Brandex stock now sells at $120 per share, what should the futures price be?

    b. If the Brandex price drops by 3%, what will be the change in the futures price and the change in the investor's margin account?

    c. If the margin on the contract is $12,000, what is the percentage return on the investor's position?

14. The multiplier for a futures contract on a stock market index is $50. The maturity of the contract is 1 year, the current level of the index is 1,800, and the risk-free interest rate is .5% per month. The dividend yield on the index is .2% per month. Suppose that after 1 month, the stock index is at 1,820.

    a. Find the cash flow from the mark-to-market proceeds on the contract. Assume that the parity condition always holds exactly.

    b. Find the holding-period return if the initial margin on the contract is $5,000.

15. You are a corporate treasurer who will purchase $1 million of bonds for the sinking fund in 3 months. You believe rates will soon fall, and you would like to repurchase the company's sinking fund bonds (which currently are selling below par) in advance of requirements. Unfortunately, you must obtain approval from the board of directors for such a purchase, and this can take up to 2 months. What action can you take in the futures market to hedge any adverse movements in bond yields and prices until you can actually buy the bonds? Will you be long or short? Why? A qualitative answer is fine.

16. The S&P portfolio pays a dividend yield of 1% annually. Its current value is 2,000. The T-bill rate is 4%. Suppose the S&P futures price for delivery in 1 year is 2,050. Construct an arbitrage strategy to exploit the mispricing and show that your profits 1 year hence will equal the mispricing in the futures market.

17. The Excel Application box in the chapter (available in Connect; link to Chapter 22 material) shows how to use the spot-futures parity relationship to find a "term structure of futures prices," that is, futures prices for various maturity dates.

    a. Suppose that today is January 1, 2016. Assume the interest rate is 3% per year and a stock index currently at 2,000 pays a dividend yield of 2.0%. Find the futures price for contract maturity dates of: (i) February 14, 2016, (ii) May 21, 2016, and (iii) November 18, 2016.

    b. What happens to the term structure of futures prices if the dividend yield is higher than the risk-free rate? For example, what if the dividend yield is 4%?

18. *a.* How should the parity condition (Equation 22.2) for stocks be modified for futures contracts on Treasury bonds? What should play the role of the dividend yield in that equation?

    b. In an environment with an upward-sloping yield curve, should T-bond futures prices on more-distant contracts be higher or lower than those on near-term contracts?

    c. Confirm your intuition by examining Figure 22.1.

19. Consider this arbitrage strategy to derive the parity relationship for spreads: (1) enter a long futures position with maturity date T_1 and futures price $F(T_1)$; (2) enter a short position with maturity T_2 and futures price $F(T_2)$; (3) at T_1, when the first contract expires, buy the asset and borrow $F(T_1)$ dollars at rate r_f; (4) pay back the loan with interest at time T_2.

    a. What are the total cash flows to this strategy at times 0, T_1, and T_2?

    b. Why must profits at time T_2 be zero if no arbitrage opportunities are present?

    c. What must the relationship between $F(T_1)$ and $F(T_2)$ be for the profits at T_2 to be equal to zero? This relationship is the parity relationship for spreads.

1. Joan Tam, CFA, believes she has identified an arbitrage opportunity for a commodity as indicated by the following information:

Spot price for commodity	$120
Futures price for commodity expiring in 1 year	$125
Interest rate for 1 year	8%

 a. Describe the transactions necessary to take advantage of this specific arbitrage opportunity.

 b. Calculate the arbitrage profit.

2. Michelle Industries issued a Swiss franc–denominated 5-year discount note for SFr200 million. The proceeds were converted to U.S. dollars to purchase capital equipment in the United States. The company wants to hedge this currency exposure and is considering the following alternatives:

   - At-the-money Swiss franc call options.
   - Swiss franc forwards.
   - Swiss franc futures.

 a. Contrast the essential characteristics of each of these three derivative instruments.

 b. Evaluate the suitability of each in relation to Michelle's hedging objective, including both advantages and disadvantages.

3. Identify the fundamental distinction between a futures contract and an option contract, and briefly explain the difference in the manner that futures and options modify portfolio risk.

4. Maria VanHusen, CFA, suggests that using forward contracts on fixed-income securities can be used to protect the value of the Star Hospital Pension Plan's bond portfolio against the possibility of rising interest rates. VanHusen prepares the following example to illustrate how such protection would work:

   - A 10-year bond with a face value of $1,000 is issued today at par value. The bond pays an annual coupon.
   - An investor intends to buy this bond today and sell it in 6 months.
   - The 6-month risk-free interest rate today is 5% (annualized).
   - A 6-month forward contract on this bond is available, with a forward price of $1,024.70.
   - In 6 months, the price of the bond, including accrued interest, is forecast to fall to $978.40 as a result of a rise in interest rates.

 a. Should the investor buy or sell the forward contract to protect the value of the bond against rising interest rates during the holding period?

 b. Calculate the value of the forward contract for the investor at the maturity of the forward contract if VanHusen's bond-price forecast turns out to be accurate.

 c. Calculate the change in value of the combined portfolio (the underlying bond and the appropriate forward contract position) 6 months after contract initiation.

5. Sandra Kapple asks Maria VanHusen about using futures contracts to protect the value of the Star Hospital Pension Plan's bond portfolio if interest rates rise. VanHusen states:

 a. "Selling a bond futures contract will generate positive cash flow in a rising interest rate environment prior to the maturity of the futures contract."

 b. "The cost of carry causes bond futures contracts to trade for a higher price than the spot price of the underlying bond prior to the maturity of the futures contract."

 Comment on the accuracy of each of VanHusen's two statements.

E-INVESTMENTS EXERCISES

Go to the Chicago Mercantile Exchange site at **www.cme.com.** From the *Trading* tab, select the link to *Equity Index,* and then link to the NASDAQ-100 E-mini contract. Now find the tab for *Contract Specifications.*

1. What is the contract size for the futures contract?

2. What is the settlement method for the futures contract?

3. For what months are the futures contracts available?

4. Click the link to view *Price Limits* and then *U.S. Equity Price Limits.* What is the current value of the 7% down limit for the S&P 500 contract?

5. Click on *Calendar.* What is the settlement date of the shortest-maturity outstanding contract? The longest-maturity contract?

SOLUTIONS TO CONCEPT CHECKS

1.

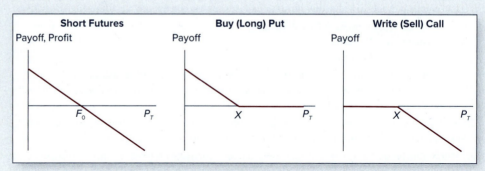

2. The clearinghouse has a zero net position in all contracts. Its long and short positions are offsetting, so that net cash flow from marking to market must be zero.

3.

	Oil Price in February, P_T		
	$51	$52	$53
Cash flow to purchase oil: $-100{,}000 \times P_T$	−$5,100,000	−$5,200,000	−$5,300,000
+ Profit on long futures: $100{,}000 \times (P_T - F_0)$	−100,000	0	+100,000
Total cash flow	−$5,200,000	−$5,200,000	−$5,200,000

4. The risk would be that the index and the portfolio do not move perfectly together. Thus basis risk involving the spread between the futures price and the portfolio value could persist even if the index futures price were set perfectly relative to the index itself. You can measure this risk using the index model introduced in Chapter 8. If you regress the return of the active portfolio on the return of the index portfolio, the regression R-square will equal the proportion of the variance of the active portfolio's return that could have been hedged using the index futures contract. You can also measure the risk of the imperfectly hedged position using the standard error of the regression, which tells you the standard deviation of the residuals in the index model. Because these are the components of the risky returns that are independent of the market index, this standard deviation measures the variability of the portion of the active portfolio's return that *cannot* be hedged using the index futures contract.

5. The futures price, $980, is $10 below the parity value of $990. The cash flow to the following strategy is riskless and equal to this mispricing.

Action	Initial Cash Flow	Cash Flow in 1 Year
Lend S_0 dollars	−1,000	$1{,}000(1.01) = 1{,}010$
Sell stock short	+1,000	$-S_T - 20$
Long futures	0	$S_T - 980$
Total	0	$10 risklessly

6. It must have zero beta. If the futures price is an unbiased estimator, then we infer that it has a zero risk premium, which means that beta must be zero.

Futures, Swaps, and Risk Management

CHAPTER 22 provided an introduction to the operation of futures markets and the principles of futures pricing. This chapter explores both pricing and risk management in selected futures markets in more depth. Most of the growth has been in financial futures, which dominate trading, so we emphasize these contracts.

Hedging refers to techniques that offset *particular* sources of risk. Hedging activities therefore are more limited and more focused than more ambitious strategies seeking an optimal risk–return profile for an entire portfolio. Because futures contracts are written on specific quantities such as stock index values, foreign exchange rates, commodity prices, and so on, they are ideally suited for these applications. In this chapter we consider several hedging applications, illustrating

general principles using a variety of contracts. We also show how hedging strategies can be used to isolate bets on perceived profit opportunities.

We begin with foreign exchange futures, showing how forward exchange rates are determined by interest rate differentials across countries and examining how firms can use futures to manage exchange rate risk. We then move on to stock-index futures, where we focus on program trading and index arbitrage. Next we turn to futures contracts written on fixed-income securities, as well as contracts written directly on interest rates. We also examine commodity futures pricing. Finally, we turn to swaps markets in foreign exchange and fixed-income securities. We will see that swaps can be interpreted as portfolios of forward contracts and valued accordingly.

23.1 Foreign Exchange Futures

The Markets

Exchange rates between currencies vary continually and often substantially. This variability can be a source of concern for anyone involved in international business. A U.S. exporter who sells goods in England, for example, will be paid in British pounds, and the dollar value of those pounds depends on the exchange rate at the time payment is made. Until that date, the U.S. exporter is exposed to foreign exchange rate risk. This risk can be hedged through currency futures or forward markets. For example, if you know you will receive £100,000 in 90 days, you can sell those pounds forward today in the forward market and lock in an exchange rate equal to today's forward price.

The forward market in foreign exchange is fairly informal. It is simply a network of banks and brokers that allows customers to enter forward contracts to purchase or sell currency in the future at a currently agreed-upon rate of exchange. The bank market in currencies is among the largest in the world, and most large traders with sufficient credit-worthiness execute their trades here rather than in futures markets. Unlike those in futures markets, contracts in forward markets are not standardized in a formal market setting. Moreover, there is no marking to market, as would occur in futures markets. Currency forward contracts call for execution only at the maturity date. Participants need to consider *counterparty risk,* the possibility that a trading partner may not be able to make good on its obligations under the contract if prices move against it. For this reason, traders who participate in forward markets must have solid creditworthiness.

Currency *futures,* however, trade in formal exchanges such as the Chicago Mercantile Exchange (in its International Monetary Market) or the London International Financial Futures Exchange (LIFFE). Here contracts are standardized by size, and daily marking to market is observed. Moreover, standard clearing arrangements allow traders to enter or reverse positions easily. Margin positions are used to ensure contract performance, which is in turn guaranteed by the exchange's clearinghouse, so the identity and creditworthiness of the counterparty to a trade are less of a concern.

Figure 23.1 reproduces *The Wall Street Journal* listing of foreign exchange rates. The listing gives the number of U.S. dollars required to purchase some unit of foreign currency, so-called *direct quotes,* and then the amount of foreign currency needed to purchase $1, *indirect quotes.* By custom, some exchange rates (the British pound or the euro) are typically quoted using indirect rates, for example, $1.3269/£, but most currencies are quoted using indirect rates, for example, ¥102.71/$. The quotes in Figure 23.1 are spot rates (i.e., exchange rates for immediate delivery).

Figure 23.2 presents listings for currency futures contracts. The futures markets employ exclusively direct quotes (the number of dollars needed to purchase a given unit of foreign currency). The futures contracts specify the size of each contract and the maturity date (there are only four maturity dates in each calendar year). There are also very active forward markets in foreign currency. In forward markets, traders can negotiate to deliver any quantity of currency on any delivery date that is mutually agreeable to both sides of the contract.

Figure 23.2 reproduces futures listings, which show the number of dollars needed to purchase a given unit of foreign currency. In Figure 23.1, both spot and forward exchange rates are listed for various delivery dates.

Interest Rate Parity

As is true of stocks and stock futures, there is a spot-futures exchange rate relationship that will prevail in well-functioning markets. Should this so-called **interest rate parity relationship** be violated, arbitrageurs will be able to make risk-free profits in foreign exchange markets with zero net investment. Their actions will force futures and spot exchange rates back into alignment. Another term for interest rate parity is the **covered interest arbitrage relationship.**

We can illustrate the interest rate parity theorem by using two currencies, the U.S. dollar and the British (U.K.) pound. Call E_0 the current exchange rate between the two currencies, that is, E_0 dollars are required to purchase one pound. F_0, the forward price, is the

Currencies U.S.-dollar foreign-exchange rates in late New York trading

Country/currency	Fri in US$	per US$	US$ vs. YTD chg (%)	Country/currency	Fri in US$	per US$	US$ vs. YTD chg (%)
Americas				**Thailand** baht	0.2873	34.810	−3.4
Argentina peso	0.0663	15.0920	**16.6**	**Vietnam** dong	0.00004486	22293	**0.6**
Brazil real	0.3055	3.2735	**−17.4**	**Europe**			
Canada dollar	0.7664	1.3049	**−5.7**	**Czech Rep.** koruna	0.04157	24.055	**−3.3**
Chile peso	0.001487	672.40	**−5.1**	**Denmark** krone	0.1509	6.6262	**−3.6**
Colombia peso	0.0003424	2920.55	**−8.0**	**Euro area** euro	1.1234	0.8902	**−3.3**
Ecuador US dollar	1	1	**unch**	**Hungary** Forint	0.003630	275.48	**−5.2**
Mexico peso	0.529	18.9093	**9.9**	**Iceland** krona	0.008734	114.50	**−12.0**
Peru new sol	0.2946	3.395	**−0.6**	**Norway** krone	0.1212	8.2524	**−6.7**
Uruguay peso	0.3415	29.2800	**−2.1**	**Poland** zloty	0.2588	3.8643	**−1.5**
Venezuela b. fuerte	0.100100	9.9901	**58.4**	**Russia** ruble	0.1544	64.762	**−9.9**
Asia-Pacific				**Sweden** krona	0.1177	8.4950	**0.6**
Australian dollar	0.7541	1.3261	**−3.4**	**Switzerland** franc	1.0252	0.9754	**−2.7**
China yuan	0.1495	6.6876	**3.0**	**Turkey** lira	0.3368	2.9695	**1.8**
Hong Kong dollar	0.1289	7.7571	**0.1**	**Ukraine** hryvnia	0.0375	26.6860	**11.2**
India rupee	0.01494	66.919	**1.1**	**UK** pound	1.3269	0.7536	**11.1**
Indonesia rupiah	0.0000758	13184	**−4.7**	**Middle East/Africa**			
Japan yen	0.009737	102.71	**−14.6**	**Bahrain** dinar	2.6524	0.3770	**−0.02**
Kazakhstan tenge	0.002953	338.66	**−0.03**	**Egypt** pound	0.1128	8.8643	**13.2**
Macau pataca	0.1247	8.0201	**0.2**	**Israel** shekel	0.2660	3.7594	**−3.4**
Malaysia ringgit	.2437	4.1039	**−4.6**	**Kuwait** dinar	3.3167	0.3015	**−0.7**
New Zealand dollar	.7325	1.3652	**−6.7**	**Oman** sul rial	2.5976	0.3850	**...**
Pakistan rupee	0.00959	104.310	**−0.6**	**Qatar** rial	0.2751	3.635	**−0.2**
Philippines peso	0.211	47.416	**1.2**	**Saudi Arabia** riyal	0.2666	3.7510	**−0.1**
Singapore dollar	.7360	1.3587	**−4.2**	**Saudi Africa** rand	0.0694	14.4196	**−6.8**
South Korea won	0.0009019	1108.73	**−5.7**				
Sri Lanka rupee	0.0068927	145.08	**0.6**		Close	Net Chg	%Chg	YTD%Chg
Taiwan dollar	0.3160	31.643	**−3.9**	**WSJ Dollar Index**	86.51	0.42	0.49	−4.06

Figure 23.1 Spot exchange rates for September 9, 2016.

Source: *The Wall Street Journal online,* September 10, 2016.

	Open	Contract High hi lo	low	Settle	Chg	Open interest
Japanese Yen(CME) -¥12,500,000; $ per 100¥						
Sept	0.9766	0.9809	0.9705	**0.9739**	−0.021	133,123
Dec	0.9805	0.9848	0.9744	**0.9779**	−0.021	28,550
Canadian Dollar (CME) - CAD 100,000; $ per CAD						
Sept	0.7734	0.7753	0.7661	**0.7676**	−.0065	110,859
Dec	0.7741	0.7765	0.7666	**0.7681**	−.0064	13,007
British Pound (CME) -£62,500; $ per £						
Sept	1.3301	1.3337	1.3239	**1.3273**	−.0029	222,007
Dec	1.3321	1.3358	1.3262	**1.3295**	−.0029	34,890
Swiss Franc (CME) -CHF125,000; $ per CHF						
Sept	1.0288	1.0301	1.0223	**1.0257**	−.0026	38,439
Dec	1.0345	1.0352	1.0274	**1.0308**	−.0027	4,146

Figure 23.2 Foreign exchange futures, September 9, 2016.

Source: *The Wall Street Journal,* September 10, 2016.

number of dollars agreed to today for purchase of one pound at time T. Call the risk-free rates in the United States and United Kingdom r_{US} and r_{UK}, respectively.

The interest rate parity theorem then states that the proper relationship between E_0 and F_0 is

$$F_0 = E_0 \left(\frac{1 + r_{US}}{1 + r_{UK}} \right)^T \qquad (23.1)$$

For example, if $r_{US} = .04$ and $r_{UK} = .05$ annually, while $E_0 = \$2$ per pound, then the proper futures price for a 1-year contract would be

$$\$2.00 \left(\frac{1.04}{1.05} \right) = \$1.981 \text{ per pound}$$

Consider the intuition behind Equation 23.1. If r_{US} is less than r_{UK}, money invested in the United States will grow at a slower rate than money invested in the United Kingdom. Why then don't all investors choose to invest their money in the United Kingdom? One important reason is that the dollar may be appreciating relative to the pound. Although dollar investments in the United States grow slower than pound investments in the United Kingdom, each dollar may be worth more pounds in the forward market than in the spot market. Such a forward premium can exactly offset the advantage of the higher U.K. interest rate.

To complete the argument, we ask how an appreciating dollar would show up in Equation 23.1. If the dollar is appreciating, fewer dollars are required to purchase each pound, and the forward exchange rate F_0 (in dollars per pound) will be less than E_0, the current exchange rate. This is exactly what Equation 23.1 tells us: When r_{US} is less than r_{UK}, F_0 must be less than E_0. The forward premium of the dollar embodied in the ratio of F_0 to E_0 exactly compensates for the difference in interest rates available in the two countries. Of course, the argument also works in reverse: If r_{US} is greater than r_{UK}, then F_0 is greater than E_0.

Example 23.1   Covered Interest Arbitrage

What if the interest rate parity relationship were violated? For example, suppose the futures price is $\$1.97/\pounds$ instead of $\$1.981/\pounds$. You could adopt the following strategy. Let E_1 denote the exchange rate ($/\pounds) that will prevail in one year. E_1 is, of course, a random variable from the perspective of today's investors.

Action	Initial Cash Flow ($)	CF in 1 Year ($)
1. Borrow 1 U.K. pound in London. Convert to dollars. Repay £1.05 at year-end.	2.00	$-E_1(\pounds 1.05)$
2. Lend $2.00 in the United States at the U.S. interest rate.	−2.00	$\$2.00(1.04)$
3. Enter a contract to purchase £1.05 at a (futures) price of $F_0 = \$1.97/\pounds$.	0	$\pounds 1.05(E_1 - \$1.97/\pounds)$
Total	0	$\$0.0115$

In step 1, you exchange the one pound borrowed in the United Kingdom for $2 at the current exchange rate. After one year you must repay the pound borrowed with interest. Because the loan is made in the United Kingdom at the U.K. interest rate, you would repay £1.05, which would be worth $E_1(1.05)$ dollars. The U.S. loan in step 2 is made at the U.S.

interest rate of 4%. The futures position in step 3 results in receipt of £1.05, for which you would pay $1.97 each, and then convert into dollars at exchange rate E_1.

Note that the exchange rate risk here is exactly offset between the pound obligation in step 1 and the futures position in step 3. The profit from the strategy is therefore risk-free and requires no net investment.

To generalize the strategy in Example 23.1:

Action	Initial CF ($)	CF in 1 Year ($)
1. Borrow 1 U.K. pound in London. Convert to dollars.	E_0	$-\$E_1(1 + r_{UK})$
2. Use proceeds of borrowing in London to lend in the U.S.	$-\$E_0$	$\$E_0(1 + r_{US})$
3. Enter $(1 + r_{UK})$ futures positions to purchase 1 pound for F_0 dollars.	0	$(1 + r_{UK})(E_1 - F_0)$
Total	0	$E_0(1 + r_{US}) - F_0(1 + r_{UK})$

The first step requires borrowing one pound in the United Kingdom. With a current exchange rate of E_0, the one pound is converted into E_0 dollars, which is a cash inflow. In one year the British loan must be paid off with interest, requiring a payment in pounds of $(1 + r_{UK})$, or in dollars of $E_1(1 + r_{UK})$. In the second step, the proceeds of the British loan are invested in the United States. This involves an initial cash outflow of $\$E_0$, and a cash inflow of $\$E_0(1 + r_{US})$ in one year. Finally, the exchange risk involved in the British borrowing is hedged in step 3. Here, the $(1 + r_{UK})$ pounds necessary to satisfy the British loan are purchased ahead in the futures contract.

The net proceeds to the arbitrage portfolio are risk-free and given by $E_0(1 + r_{US}) - F_0(1 + r_{UK})$. If this value is positive, borrow in the United Kingdom, lend in the United States, and enter a long futures position to eliminate foreign exchange risk. If the value is negative, borrow in the United States, lend in the United Kingdom, and take a short position in pound futures. When prices preclude arbitrage opportunities, the expression must equal zero. This no-arbitrage condition implies that

$$F_0 = \frac{1 + r_{US}}{1 + r_{UK}} E_0 \qquad (23.2)$$

which is the interest rate parity theorem for a 1-year horizon.

 Concept Check **23.1**

What would be the arbitrage strategy and associated profits in Example 23.1 if the initial futures price were $F_0 = \$2.01/\text{pound}$?

Example 23.2   Covered Interest Arbitrage

Ample evidence bears out the interest rate parity relationship. For example, on September 9, 2016, the dollar-denominated LIBOR interest rate with maturity of 3 months was .85% while the comparable U.K. pound-denominated rate was lower, at .38%. Therefore, we should have expected the forward exchange rate (in $/£) to be higher than the spot rate. This is exactly what we observe: While the spot rate was $1.3269/£ (see Figure 23.1), the forward rate was $1.3295/£ (Figure 23.2). More specifically, interest rate parity would imply that the forward rate should have been $1.3269 \times (1.0085/1.0038)^{1/4} = 1.3285$, just about equal to the actual rate.

Direct versus Indirect Quotes

The exchange rate in Examples 23.1 and 23.2 is expressed as dollars per pound. This is an example of a *direct* exchange rate quote. The euro-dollar exchange rate is also typically expressed as a direct quote. In contrast, exchange rates for other currencies such as the Japanese yen or Swiss franc are typically expressed as *indirect* quotes, that is, as units of foreign currency per dollar, for example, 92 yen per dollar. For currencies expressed as indirect quotes, depreciation of the dollar would result in a *decrease* in the quoted exchange rate ($1 buys fewer yen); in contrast, dollar depreciation versus the pound would show up as a *higher* exchange rate (more dollars are required to buy £1). When the exchange rate is quoted as foreign currency per dollar, the domestic and foreign exchange rates in Equation 23.2 must be switched: In this case the equation becomes

$$F_0 \text{ (foreign currency/\$)} = \frac{1 + r_{\text{foreign}}}{1 + r_{\text{US}}} \times E_0 \text{ (foreign currency/\$)}$$

If the interest rate in the U.S. is higher than in Japan, the dollar will sell in the forward market at a lower price (will buy fewer yen) than in the spot market.

Using Futures to Manage Exchange Rate Risk

Consider a U.S. firm that exports most of its product to Great Britain. The firm is vulnerable to fluctuations in the dollar/pound exchange rate for several reasons. First, the dollar value of the pound-denominated revenue derived from its customers will fluctuate with the exchange rate. Second, the pound price that the firm can charge its customers in the United Kingdom will itself be affected by the exchange rate. For example, if the pound depreciates by 10% relative to the dollar, the firm would need to increase the pound price of its goods by 10% in order to maintain the dollar-equivalent price. However, the firm might not be able to raise the price by 10% if it faces competition from British producers or if it believes the higher pound-denominated price would reduce demand for its product.

To offset its foreign exchange exposure, the firm might engage in transactions that bring it profits when the pound depreciates. The lost profits from business operations resulting from a depreciation will then be offset by gains on its financial transactions. For example, if the firm enters a futures contract to deliver pounds for dollars at an exchange rate agreed to today, then if the pound depreciates, the futures position will yield a profit.

For example, suppose the futures price is currently $1.40 per pound for delivery in three months. If the firm enters a futures contract with a futures price of $1.40 per pound, and the exchange rate in three months is $1.30 per pound, then the profit to the short position is $F_0 - F_T = \$1.40 - \$1.30 = \$.10$ per pound.

How many pounds should be sold in the futures market to most fully offset the exposure to exchange rate fluctuations? Suppose the dollar value of profits in the next quarter will fall by $200,000 for every $.10 depreciation of the pound. To hedge, we need a futures position that provides $200,000 extra profit for every $.10 that the pound depreciates. Therefore, we need a futures position to deliver £2,000,000. As we have just seen, the profit per pound on the futures contract equals the difference in the current futures price and the ultimate exchange rate; therefore, the foreign exchange profits resulting from a $.10 depreciation[1] will equal $.10 × 2,000,000 = $200,000.

The proper hedge position in pound futures is independent of the actual depreciation in the pound as long as the relationship between profits and exchange rates is approximately linear. For example, if the pound depreciates by only half as much, $.05, the firm would lose only $100,000 in operating profits. The futures position would also return half the profits: $.05 × 2,000,000 = $100,000, again just offsetting the operating exposure. If the pound *appreciates,* the hedge position still (unfortunately in this case) offsets the operating exposure. If the pound appreciates by $.05, the firm might gain $100,000 from the enhanced value of the pound; however, it will lose that amount on its obligation to deliver the pounds for the original futures price.

The hedge ratio is the number of futures positions necessary to hedge the risk of the unprotected portfolio, in this case the firm's export business. In general, we can think of the **hedge ratio** as the number of hedging vehicles (e.g., futures contracts) one would establish to offset the risk of a particular unprotected position. The hedge ratio, H, in this case is

$$H = \frac{\text{Change in value of unprotected position for a given change in exchange rate}}{\text{Profit derived from one futures position for the same change in exchange rate}}$$

$$= \frac{\text{\$200,000 per \$.10 change in \$/£ exchange rate}}{\text{\$.10 profit per pound delivered per \$.10 change in \$/£ exchange rate}}$$

$$= £2,000,000 \text{ to be delivered}$$

Because each pound-futures contract on the Chicago Mercantile Exchange calls for delivery of 62,500 pounds, you would sell 2,000,000/62,500 per contract = 32 contracts.

One interpretation of the hedge ratio is as a ratio of sensitivities to the underlying source of uncertainty. The sensitivity of operating profits is $200,000 per swing of $.10 in the exchange rate. The sensitivity of futures profits is $.10 per pound to be delivered per swing of $.10 in the exchange rate. Therefore, the hedge ratio is 200,000/.10 = 2,000,000 pounds.

We could just as easily have defined the hedge ratio in terms of futures contracts. Because each contract calls for delivery of 62,500 pounds, the profit on each contract per swing of $.10 in the exchange rate is $6,250. Therefore, the hedge ratio defined in units of futures contracts is $200,000/$6,250 = 32 contracts, as we found above.

 Concept Check **23.2**

> Suppose a U.S. importer is harmed when the *dollar* depreciates. Specifically, suppose that its profits decrease by $200,000 for every $.05 rise in the dollar/pound exchange rate. How many contracts should the firm enter? Should it take the long side or the short side of the contracts?

Given the sensitivity of the unhedged position to changes in the exchange rate, calculating the risk-minimizing hedge position is easy. Estimating that sensitivity is much harder. For an exporting firm, for example, a naïve view might focus only on the expected pound-denominated revenue, and then contract to deliver that number of pounds in the futures or

---

[1]Actually, the profit on the contract depends on the changes in the futures price, not the spot exchange rate. For simplicity, we call the decline in the futures price the depreciation in the pound.

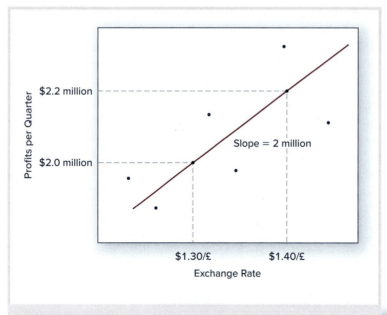

Figure 23.3 Profits as a function of the exchange rate

forward market. This approach, however, fails to recognize that pound revenue is itself a function of the exchange rate because the U.S. firm's competitive position in the U.K. is determined in part by the exchange rate.

One approach relies, in part, on historical relationships. Suppose, for example, that the firm prepares a scatter diagram as in Figure 23.3 that relates its business profits (measured in dollars) in each of the last 40 quarters to the dollar/pound exchange rate in that quarter. Profits generally are lower when the exchange rate is lower, that is, when the pound depreciates. To quantify that sensitivity, we might estimate the following regression equation:

$$\text{Profits} = a + b(\$/£ \text{ exchange rate})$$

The slope of the regression, the estimate of b, is the sensitivity of quarterly profits to the exchange rate. For example, if the estimate of b turns out to be 2,000,000, as in Figure 23.3, then on average, a $1 *increase* in the value of the pound results in a $2,000,000 *increase* in quarterly profits. This, of course, is the sensitivity we posited when we asserted that a $.10 drop in the dollar/pound exchange rate would decrease profits by $200,000.

Of course, one must interpret regression output with care. For example, one would not want to extrapolate the historical relationship between profitability and exchange rates exhibited in a period when the exchange rate hovered between $1.20 and $1.50 per pound to scenarios in which the exchange rate might be forecast at below $1.00 per pound or above $2.00 per pound.

In addition, extrapolating past relationships into the future can be dangerous. We saw in Chapter 8 that regression betas from the index model tend to vary over time; such problems are not unique to the index model. Moreover, regression estimates are just that—estimates. Parameters of a regression equation are sometimes measured with considerable imprecision.

Still, historical relationships are often a good place to start when looking for the average sensitivity of one variable to another. These slope coefficients are not perfect, but they are still useful indicators of hedge ratios.

✓ Concept Check **23.3**

United Millers purchases corn to make cornflakes. When the price of corn increases, the cost of making cereal increases, resulting in lower profits. Historically, profits per quarter have been related to the price of corn according to the equation: Profits = $8 million − 1 million × Price per bushel. How many bushels of corn should United Millers purchase in the corn futures market to hedge its corn-price risk?

23.2 Stock-Index Futures

The Contracts

In contrast to most futures contracts, which call for delivery of a specified commodity, stock-index contracts are settled by a cash amount equal to the value of the index on the contract maturity date times a multiplier that scales the size of the contract. The total profit to the long position is $S_T - F_0$, where S_T is the value of the stock index on the maturity date. Cash settlement avoids the costs that would be incurred if the short trader had to purchase the stocks in the index and deliver them to the long position, and if the long position then had to sell the stocks for cash. Instead, the long trader receives $S_T - F_0$ dollars, and the short trader $F_0 - S_T$ dollars. These profits duplicate those that would arise with actual delivery.

There are several stock-index futures contracts currently traded. Table 23.1 lists some of the major ones, showing under contract size the multiplier used to calculate contract settlements. An E-mini S&P 500 contract, for example, with a futures price of 2,000 and a final index value of 2,005 would result in a profit for the long side of $\$50 \times (2,005 - 2,000) = \$250$. The S&P 500 contract by far dominates the market in U.S. stock index futures.[2]

The broad-based U.S. stock market indexes are all highly correlated. Table 23.2 is a correlation matrix for four well-known indexes: the S&P 500, the Dow Jones Industrial Average, the Russell 2000 index of small capitalization stocks, and the NASDAQ 100. The highest correlation, .979, is between the two large-cap indexes, the S&P 500 and the DJIA. The NASDAQ 100, which is dominated by technology firms, and the Russell 2000

Contract	Underlying Market Index	Contract Size	Exchange
S&P 500 (E-mini)	Standard & Poor's 500 Index, a value-weighted arithmetic average of 500 stocks.	$50 times S&P 500 index	Chicago Mercantile Exchange
Mini-Dow Jones Industrial Average (DJIA)	Dow Jones Industrial Average, price-weighted average of 30 firms	$5 times index	Chicago Board of Trade
Mini-Russell 2000	Index of 2,000 smaller firms	$50 times index	Intercontinental Exchange (ICE)
NASDAQ 100	Value-weighted arithmetic average of 100 of the largest over-the-counter stocks	$100 times index	Chicago Mercantile Exchange
Nikkei 225	Nikkei 225 stock average	$5 times Nikkei Index	Chicago Mercantile Exchange
FTSE 100	Financial Times Stock Exchange Index of 100 U.K. firms	£10 times FTSE Index	London International Financial Futures Exchange
DAX-30	Index of 30 German stocks	25 euros times index	Eurex
CAC-40	Index of 40 French stocks	10 euros times index	Euronext Paris
Hang Seng	Value-weighted index of largest firms in Hong Kong	50 Hong Kong dollars times index	Hong Kong Exchange

Table 23.1

Sample of stock-index futures

[2]As we pointed out in Chapter 22, the "big" S&P contract has a multiplier of $250. But the E-mini dominates trading in S&P 500 futures.

Table 23.2

Correlation coeffi-
cients using monthly
returns, 2008–2012

	S&P	DJIA	Russell	NASDAQ
S&P 500	1	0.979	0.948	0.928
DJIA		1	0.908	0.876
Russell 2000			1	0.898
NASDAQ 100				1

index of small-cap firms have smaller correlations with the large-cap indexes and with each other, but even these are above .85.

Creating Synthetic Stock Positions: An Asset Allocation Tool

One reason stock-index futures are so popular is that they can substitute for holdings in the underlying stocks themselves. Index futures let investors participate in broad market movements without actually buying or selling large amounts of stock.

Because of this, we say futures represent "synthetic" holdings of the market portfolio. Instead of holding the market directly, the investor takes a long futures position in the index. The transaction costs involved in establishing and liquidating futures positions are much lower than taking actual spot positions. "Market timers," who speculate on broad market moves rather than on individual securities, are large players in stock-index futures for this reason.

One means to market time, for example, is to shift between Treasury bills and broad-based stock market holdings. Timers attempt to shift from bills into the market before market upturns, and to shift back into bills to avoid market downturns, thereby profiting from broad market movements. Market timing of this sort, however, can result in huge trading costs. An attractive alternative is to invest in Treasury bills and hold varying amounts of market-index futures contracts, which are far cheaper to trade.

The strategy works like this. When timers are bullish, they will establish many long futures positions that they can liquidate quickly and cheaply when expectations turn bearish. Rather than shifting back and forth between T-bills and stocks, they buy and hold T-bills and adjust only the futures position.

You can construct a T-bill plus index futures position that duplicates the payoff to holding the stock index itself. Here is how:

1. Purchase as many market-index futures contracts as you need to establish your desired stock position. A desired holding of $1,000 multiplied by the S&P 500 index, for example, would require the purchase of 20 contracts because each contract calls for delivery of $50 multiplied by the index.

2. Invest enough money in T-bills to cover the payment of the futures price at the contract's maturity date. The necessary investment is simply the present value of the futures price.

Example 23.3   Synthetic Positions Using Stock-Index Futures

Suppose that an institutional investor wants to invest $100 million in the market for one month and, to minimize trading costs, chooses to buy the S&P 500 E-mini futures contracts as a substitute for actual stock holdings. If the index is now at 2,000, the 1-month delivery futures price is 2,020, and the T-bill rate is 1% per month, it would buy 1,000 contracts. (Each contract controls $50 \times 2,000 = \$100,000$ worth of stock, and $100 million/$100,000 = 1,000.) The institution thus has a long position on $50,000 times the S&P 500 index (1,000 contracts times the contract multiplier of $50). To cover payment of the futures price, it must buy bills with 50,000 times the present value of the futures price. This equals $50,000 \times (2,020/1.01) = \$100$ million market value of bills. Notice that the $100 million outlay in bills is precisely equal to the amount that would have been needed to buy the stock directly. (The face value of the bills will be $50,000 \times 2,020 = \$101$ million.)

This is an artificial, or synthetic, stock position. What is the value of this portfolio at the maturity date? Call S_T the value of the stock index on the maturity date T and, as usual, let F_0 be the original futures price:

	In General (Per Unit of the Index)	Our Numbers
1. Profits from contract	$S_T - F_0$	$50,000(S_T - 2,020)$
2. Face value of T-bills	F_0	$101,000,000$
Total	S_T	$50,000 S_T$

The total payoff on the contract maturity date is exactly proportional to the value of the stock index. In other words, adopting this portfolio strategy is equivalent to holding the stock index itself, aside from the issue of interim dividend distributions and tax treatment.

The bills-plus-futures contracts strategy in Example 23.3 may be viewed as a 100% stock strategy. At the other extreme, investing in zero futures results in a 100% bills position. Moreover, a short futures position will result in a portfolio equivalent to that obtained by short-selling the stock market index, because in both cases the investor gains from decreases in the stock price. Bills-plus-futures mixtures clearly allow for a flexible and low-transaction-cost approach to market timing. The futures positions may be established or reversed quickly and cheaply. Also, because the short futures position allows the investor to earn interest on T-bills, it is superior to a conventional short sale of the stock, where the investor may earn little or no interest on the proceeds of the short sale.

 Concept Check **23.4**

The market timing strategy of Example 23.3 also can be achieved by an investor who holds an indexed stock portfolio and "synthetically exits" the position using futures if and when he turns pessimistic concerning the market. Suppose the investor holds $100 million of stock (which is 50,000 times the current value of the index). What futures position added to the stock holdings would create a synthetic T-bill exposure when he is bearish on the market? Confirm that the profits are effectively risk-free using a table like that in Example 23.3.

Index Arbitrage

Whenever the actual futures price differs from its parity value, there is an opportunity for profit. This is why the parity relationships are so important. Far from being theoretical academic constructs, they are in fact a guide to trading rules that can generate large profits. **Index arbitrage** is an investment strategy that exploits divergences between the actual futures price and its theoretically correct parity value.

In principle, index arbitrage is simple. If the futures price is too high, short the futures contract and buy the stocks in the index. If it is too low, go long in futures and short the stocks. You can perfectly hedge your position and should earn arbitrage profits equal to the mispricing of the contract.

Although it is simple in theory, index arbitrage can be difficult to implement. The problem lies in buying "the stocks in the index." Selling or purchasing shares in all 500 stocks in the S&P 500 is impractical for two reasons. The first is transaction costs, which may outweigh any profits to be made from the arbitrage. Second, index arbitrage calls for the purchase or sale of shares of 500 different firms simultaneously, and any lags in the execution of such a strategy can destroy the effectiveness of a plan to exploit temporary price discrepancies. Don't forget that others also will be trying to exploit any deviations from parity, and if they trade first, they may move prices before your trade is executed.

Arbitrageurs need to trade an entire portfolio of stocks quickly and simultaneously if they hope to exploit disparities between the futures price and its corresponding stock index. For this they need a coordinated trading program; hence the term **program trading,** which refers to purchases or sales of entire portfolios of stocks. Electronic trading enables traders to submit coordinated buy or sell programs to the stock market at once.[3]

The success of these arbitrage positions and associated program trades depends on only two things: the relative levels of spot and futures prices and synchronized trading in the two markets. Because arbitrageurs exploit disparities in futures and spot prices, absolute price levels are unimportant.

Using Index Futures to Hedge Market Risk

Futures contracts also may be used to hedge market exposure. Suppose, for example, that you manage a $30 million portfolio with a beta of .8. You are bullish on the market over the long term, but you are afraid that over the next two months, the market is vulnerable to a sharp downturn. If trading were costless, you could sell your portfolio, place the proceeds in T-bills for two months, and then reestablish your position after you perceive that the risk of the downturn has passed. In practice, however, this strategy would result in unacceptable trading costs, not to mention tax problems resulting from the realization of capital gains or losses on the portfolio. An alternative approach would be to use stock index futures to hedge your market exposure.

Example 23.4   Hedging Market Risk

Suppose that the S&P 500 index currently is at 2,000. A decrease in the index to 1,950 would represent a drop of 2.5%. With a portfolio beta of .8, you would expect a loss of .8 × 2.5% = 2%, or in dollar terms, .02 × $30 million = $600,000. Therefore, the sensitivity of your portfolio value to market movements is $600,000 per 50-point movement in the S&P 500 index.

To hedge this risk, you could sell stock index futures. When your portfolio falls in value along with declines in the broad market, the futures contract will provide an offsetting profit.

The sensitivity of a futures contract to market movements is easy to determine. With its contract multiplier of $50, the profit on the S&P 500 futures contract varies by $2,500

---

[3]One might also attempt to exploit violations of parity using ETFs linked to the market index, but ETFs may trade in less liquid markets where it can be difficult to trade large quantities without moving prices.

for every 50-point swing in the index. Therefore, to hedge your market exposure for two months, you could calculate the hedge ratio as follows:

$$H = \frac{\text{Change in portfolio value}}{\text{Profit on one futures contract}} = \frac{\$600,000}{\$2,500} = 240 \text{ contracts (short)}$$

You would enter the short side of the contracts, because you want profits from the contract to offset the exposure of your portfolio to the market. Because your portfolio does poorly when the market falls, you need a position that will do well when the market falls.

We also could approach the hedging problem in Example 23.4 using a similar regression procedure as that illustrated in Figure 23.3 for foreign exchange risk. The predicted value of the portfolio is graphed in Figure 23.4 as a function of the value of the S&P 500 index. With a beta of .8, the slope of the relationship is 12,000: A 2.5% increase in the index, from 2,000 to 2,050, results in a capital gain of 2% of $30 million, or $600,000. Therefore, your portfolio will increase in value by $12,000 for each increase of one point in the index. As a result, you should enter a short position on 12,000 units of the S&P 500 index to fully offset your exposure to marketwide movements. Because the contract multiplier is $50 times the index, you need to sell 12,000/50 = 240 contracts.

Notice that when the slope of the regression line relating your unprotected position to the value of an asset is positive, your hedge strategy calls for a *short* position in that asset. The hedge ratio is the negative of the regression slope. This is because the hedge position should offset your initial exposure. If you do poorly when the asset value falls, you need a short position that will do well when the asset value falls.

Active managers sometimes believe that a particular asset is underpriced, but that the market as a whole is about to fall. Even if the asset is a good buy relative to other stocks in

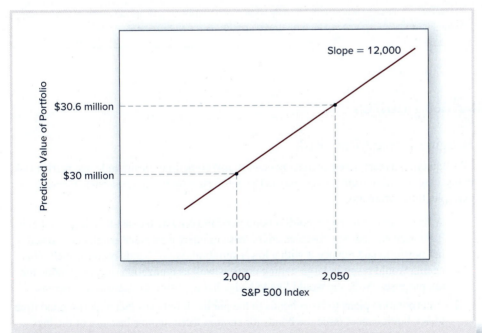

Figure 23.4 Predicted value of the portfolio as a function of the market index

the market, it still might perform poorly in a broad market downturn. To solve this problem, the manager would like to separate the bet on the firm from the bet on the market: The bet on the company must be offset with a hedge against the market exposure that normally would accompany a purchase of the stock. In other words, the manager seeks a **market-neutral bet** on the stock, by which we mean that a position on the stock is taken to capture its alpha (its abnormal risk-adjusted expected return), but that market exposure is fully hedged, resulting in a position beta of zero.

By allowing investors to hedge market performance, the futures contract allows the portfolio manager to make stock picks without concern for the market exposure of those stocks. After the stocks are chosen, the resulting market risk of the portfolio can be modulated to any degree using the stock futures contracts. Here again, the stock's beta is the key to the hedging strategy. We discuss market-neutral strategies in more detail in Chapter 26.

Example 23.5   Market-Neutral Active Stock Selection

Suppose the beta of the stock is $\frac{2}{3}$, and the manager purchases \$750,000 worth of the stock. For every 3% drop in the broad market, the stock would be expected to respond with a drop of $\frac{2}{3} \times 3\% = 2\%$, or \$15,000. The S&P 500 contract will fall by 60 points from a current value of 2,000 if the market drops 3%. With the contract multiplier of \$50, this would entail a profit to a short futures position of $60 \times \$50 = \$3,000$ per contract. Therefore, the market risk of the stock can be offset by shorting five S&P contracts. More formally, we can calculate the hedge ratio as

$$H = \frac{\text{Expected change in stock value per 3\% market drop}}{\text{Profit on one short contract per 3\% market drop}}$$

$$= \frac{\$15,000 \text{ swing in unprotected position}}{\$3,000 \text{ profit per contract}}$$

$$= 5 \text{ contracts}$$

Now that market risk is hedged, the only source of variability in the performance of the stock-plus-futures portfolio will be the firm-specific performance of the stock.

23.3 Interest Rate Futures

Hedging Interest Rate Risk

Like equity managers, fixed-income managers also sometimes desire to hedge market risk, in this case resulting from movements in the entire structure of interest rates. Consider, for example, these problems:

1. A fixed-income manager holds a bond portfolio on which considerable capital gains have been earned. She foresees an increase in interest rates but is reluctant to sell her portfolio and replace it with a lower-duration mix of bonds because such rebalancing would result in large trading costs as well as realization of capital gains for tax purposes. Still, she would like to hedge her exposure to interest rate increases.

2. A corporation plans to issue bonds to the public. It believes that now is a good time to act, but it cannot issue the bonds for another three months because of the lags inherent in SEC registration. It would like to hedge the uncertainty surrounding the yield at which it eventually will be able to sell the bonds.

3. A pension fund will receive a large cash inflow next month that it plans to invest in long-term bonds. It is concerned that interest rates may fall by the time it can make the investment and would like to lock in the yield currently available on long-term issues.

In each of these cases, the investment manager wishes to hedge interest rate uncertainty. To illustrate the procedures that might be followed, we will focus on the first example, and suppose that the portfolio manager has a $10 million bond portfolio with a modified duration of 9 years.[4] If, as feared, market interest rates increase and the bond portfolio's yield also rises, say, by 10 basis points (.10%), the fund will suffer a capital loss. Recall from Chapter 16 that the capital loss in percentage terms will be the product of modified duration, D^*, and the increase in the portfolio yield. Therefore, the loss will be

$$D^* \times \Delta y = 9 \times .10\% = .90\%$$

or $90,000. This establishes that the sensitivity of the value of the unprotected portfolio to changes in market yields is $9,000 per 1 basis point change in the yield. Market practitioners call this ratio the **price value of a basis point,** or PVBP. The PVBP represents the sensitivity of the dollar value of the portfolio to changes in interest rates. Here, we've shown that

$$\text{PVBP} = \frac{\text{Change in portfolio value}}{\text{Predicted change in yield}} = \frac{\$90,000}{10 \text{ basis points}} = \$9,000 \text{ per basis point}$$

One way to hedge this risk is to take an offsetting position in an interest rate futures contract, for example, the Treasury bond contract. The bond nominally calls for delivery of $100,000 par value T-bonds with 6% coupons and 20-year maturity. In practice, the contract delivery terms are fairly complicated because many bonds with different coupon rates and maturities may be substituted to settle the contract. To simplify, we will assume that the bond to be delivered already is known and has a modified duration of 10 years. Finally, suppose that the futures price currently is $90 per $100 par value. Because the contract actually requires delivery of $100,000 par value of bonds, the contract multiplier is $1,000.

Given these data, we can calculate the PVBP for the futures contract. If the yield on the delivery bond increases by 10 basis points, the bond value will fall by $D^* \times .1\% = 10 \times .1\% = 1\%$. The futures price also will decline 1%, from 90 to 89.10.[5] Because the contract multiplier is $1,000, the gain on each short contract will be $1,000 \times .90 = \$900$. Therefore, the PVBP for one futures contract is $900/10-basis-point change, or $90 for a change in yield of 1 basis point.

Now we can easily calculate the hedge ratio as follows:

$$H = \frac{\text{PVBP of portfolio}}{\text{PVBP of hedge vehicle}} = \frac{\$9,000}{\$90 \text{ per contract}} = 100 \text{ contracts}$$

Therefore, 100 T-bond futures contracts will offset the portfolio's exposure to interest rate fluctuations.

Notice that this is another example of a market-neutral strategy. In Example 23.5, which illustrated an equity-hedging strategy, stock-index futures were used to drive a portfolio beta to zero. In this application, we used a T-bond contract to drive the interest rate exposure of a bond position to zero. The hedged fixed-income position has a duration (or a PVBP) of zero. The source of risk differs, but the hedging strategy is essentially the same.

---

[4]Recall that modified duration, D^*, is related to duration, D, by the formula $D^* = D/(1 + y)$, where y is the bond's yield to maturity. If the bond pays coupons semiannually, then y should be measured as a semiannual yield. For simplicity, we will assume annual coupon payments and treat y as the effective annual yield to maturity.

[5]This assumes the futures price will be exactly proportional to the bond price, which ought to be nearly true.

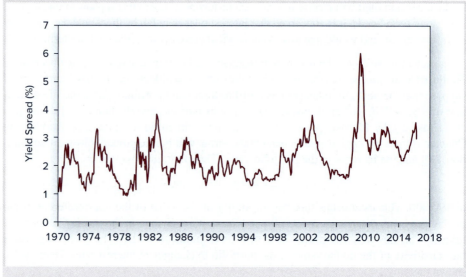

Figure 23.5 Yield spread between 10-year Treasury and Baa-rated corporate bonds

Concept Check 23.5

Suppose the bond portfolio is twice as large, $20 million, but that its modified duration is only 4.5 years. Show that the proper hedge position in T-bond futures is the same as the value just calculated, 100 contracts.

Although the hedge ratio is easy to compute, the hedging problem in practice is more difficult. We assumed in our example that the yields on the T-bond contract and the bond portfolio would move perfectly in unison. Although interest rates on various fixed-income instruments do tend to vary in tandem, there is considerable slippage across sectors of the fixed-income market. For example, Figure 23.5 shows that the spread between long-term corporate and 10-year Treasury bond yields has fluctuated considerably over time. Our hedging strategy would be fully effective only if the yield spread across the two sectors of the fixed-income market were constant (or at least perfectly predictable) so that yield changes in both sectors were equal.

This problem highlights the fact that most hedging activity is in fact **cross-hedging,** meaning that the hedge vehicle is a different asset than the one to be hedged. To the extent that there is slippage between prices or yields of the two assets, the hedge will not be perfect. Cross-hedges can eliminate a large fraction of the total risk of the unprotected portfolio, but you should be aware that they typically are far from risk-free positions.

23.4   Swaps

Swaps are multiperiod extensions of forward contracts. For example, rather than agreeing to exchange British pounds for U.S. dollars at an agreed-upon forward price at one single date, a **foreign exchange swap** would call for an exchange of currencies on several future dates. The parties might exchange $1.6 million for £1 million in each of the next five years.

Similarly, **interest rate swaps** call for the exchange of a series of cash flows proportional to a given interest rate for a corresponding series of cash flows proportional to a floating interest rate.[6] One party might exchange a variable cash flow equal to $1 million times a short-term interest rate for $1 million times a fixed interest rate of 5% for each of the next seven years.

The swap market is a huge component of the derivatives market, with around $400 trillion in interest rate and exchange rate swap agreements outstanding. We will illustrate how these contracts work by using a simple interest rate swap as an example.

Example 23.6   Interest Rate Swap

Consider the manager of a large portfolio that currently includes $100 million par value of long-term bonds paying an average coupon rate of 7%. The manager believes interest rates are about to rise. As a result, he would like to sell the bonds and replace them with either short-term or floating-rate issues. However, it would be exceedingly expensive in terms of transaction costs to replace the portfolio every time the forecast for interest rates is updated. A cheaper and more flexible approach is to "swap" the $7 million a year in interest income the portfolio currently generates for an amount of money tied to the short-term interest rate. That way, if rates do rise, so will the portfolio's interest income.

A swap dealer might advertise its willingness to exchange, or "swap," a cash flow based on the LIBOR rate for one based on a fixed rate of 7%. (The LIBOR, or London Interbank Offered Rate, is the interest rate at which banks borrow from each other in the Eurodollar market. It is the most commonly used short-term interest rate in the swap market.) The portfolio manager would then enter into a swap agreement with the dealer to pay 7% on **notional principal** of $100 million and receive payment of the LIBOR rate on that amount of notional principal.[7] In other words, the manager swaps a payment of .07 × $100 million for a payment of LIBOR × $100 million. The manager's *net* cash flow from the swap agreement is therefore (LIBOR − .07) × $100 million. Note that the swap arrangement does not mean that a loan has been made. The participants have agreed only to exchange a fixed cash flow for a variable one.

Now consider the net cash flow to the manager's portfolio in three interest rate scenarios:

	LIBOR Rate		
	6.5%	7.0%	7.5%
Interest income from bond portfolio (= 7% of $100 million bond portfolio)	$7,000,000	$7,000,000	$7,000,000
Cash flow from swap [= (LIBOR − 7%) × notional principal of $100 million]	(500,000)	0	500,000
Total (= LIBOR × $100 million)	$6,500,000	$7,000,000	$7,500,000

Notice that the total income on the overall position—bonds plus swap agreement—equals the LIBOR rate in each scenario times $100 million. The manager has, in effect, converted a fixed-rate bond portfolio into a synthetic floating-rate portfolio.

---

[6]Interest rate swaps have nothing to do with the Homer-Liebowitz bond swap taxonomy described in Chapter 16.

[7]The participants to the swap do not loan each other money. They agree only to exchange a fixed cash flow for a variable cash flow that depends on the short-term interest rate. This is why the principal is described as *notional*. The notional principal is simply a way to describe the size of the swap agreement. In this example, a 7% fixed rate is exchanged for the LIBOR rate; the difference between LIBOR and 7% is multiplied by notional principal to determine the net cash flow.

Swaps and Balance Sheet Restructuring

Example 23.6 illustrates why swaps have tremendous appeal to fixed-income managers. These contracts provide a means to quickly, cheaply, and anonymously restructure the balance sheet. Suppose a corporation that has issued fixed-rate debt believes that interest rates are likely to fall; it might prefer to have issued floating-rate debt. In principle, it could issue floating-rate debt and use the proceeds to buy back the outstanding fixed-rate debt. But it is faster and easier to convert the outstanding fixed-rate debt into synthetic floating-rate debt by entering a swap to receive a fixed interest rate (offsetting its fixed-rate coupon obligation) and paying a floating rate.

Conversely, a bank that pays current market interest rates to its depositors, and thus is exposed to increases in rates, could enter a swap to receive a floating rate and pay a fixed rate on some amount of notional principal. This swap position, added to its floating-rate deposit liability, would result in a net liability of a fixed stream of cash. The bank might then be able to invest in long-term fixed-rate loans without encountering interest rate risk.

For another example, consider a fixed-income portfolio manager. Swaps enable the manager to switch back and forth between a fixed- or floating-rate profile quickly and cheaply as the forecast for the interest rate changes. A manager who holds a fixed-rate portfolio can transform it into a synthetic floating-rate portfolio by entering a pay fixed–receive floating swap and can later transform it back by entering the opposite side of a similar swap.

Foreign exchange swaps also enable the firm to quickly and cheaply restructure its balance sheet. Suppose, for example, that a firm issues $10 million in debt at an 8% coupon rate but actually prefers that its interest obligations be denominated in British pounds. For example, the issuing firm might be a British corporation that perceives advantageous financing opportunities in the United States but prefers pound-denominated liabilities. Then the firm, whose debt currently obliges it to make dollar-denominated payments of $800,000, can agree to swap a given number of pounds each year for $800,000. By so doing, it effectively covers its dollar obligation and replaces it with a new pound-denominated obligation.

 Concept Check **23.6**

Show how a firm that has issued a floating-rate bond with a coupon equal to the LIBOR rate can use swaps to convert that bond into synthetic fixed-rate debt. Assume the terms of the swap allow an exchange of LIBOR for a fixed rate of 8%.

The Swap Dealer

What about the swap dealer? Why is the dealer, which is typically a financial intermediary such as a bank, willing to take on the opposite side of the swaps desired by these participants in these hypothetical swaps?

Consider a dealer who takes on one side of a swap, let's say paying LIBOR and receiving a fixed rate. The dealer will search for another trader in the swap market who wishes to receive a fixed rate and pay LIBOR. For example, Company A may have issued a 7% coupon fixed-rate bond that it wishes to convert into synthetic floating-rate debt, while Company B may have issued a floating-rate bond tied to LIBOR that it wishes to convert into synthetic fixed-rate debt. The dealer will enter a swap with Company A in which it pays a fixed rate and receives LIBOR, and will enter another swap with Company B in which it pays LIBOR and receives a fixed rate. When the two swaps are combined, the dealer's position is effectively neutral on interest rates, paying LIBOR on one swap and receiving it on another. Similarly, the dealer pays a fixed rate on one swap and receives it on another. The dealer becomes little more than an intermediary, funneling payments from one party to the other.[8] The dealer finds this activity profitable because it will charge a bid-ask spread on the transaction.

This rearrangement is illustrated in Figure 23.6. Company A has issued 7% fixed-rate debt (the leftmost arrow in the figure) but enters a swap to pay the dealer LIBOR and receive a 6.95% fixed rate. Therefore, the company's net payment is 7% + (LIBOR − 6.95%) = LIBOR + .05%. It has thus transformed its fixed-rate debt into synthetic floating-rate debt. Conversely, Company B has issued floating-rate debt paying LIBOR (the rightmost arrow), but enters a swap to pay a 7.05% fixed rate in return for LIBOR. Therefore, its net payment is LIBOR + (7.05% − LIBOR) = 7.05%. It has thus transformed its floating-rate debt into synthetic fixed-rate debt. The bid-ask spread, the source of the dealer's profit, in the example illustrated in Figure 23.6 is .10% of notional principal each year.

 Concept Check **23.7**

> A pension fund holds a portfolio of money market securities that the manager believes are paying excellent yields compared to other comparable-risk short-term securities. However, the manager believes that interest rates are about to fall. What type of swap will allow the fund to continue to hold its portfolio of short-term securities while at the same time benefiting from a decline in rates?

Other Interest Rate Contracts

Swaps are multiperiod forward contracts that trade over the counter. There are also exchange-listed contracts that trade on interest rates. The biggest of these in terms of trading activity is the Eurodollar contract, the listing for which we show in Figure 23.7. The

Figure 23.6 Interest rate swap. Company B pays a fixed rate of 7.05% to the swap dealer in return for LIBOR. Company A receives 6.95% from the dealer in return for LIBOR. The swap dealer realizes a cash flow each period equal to .10% of notional principal.

[8]Actually, things are a bit more complicated. The dealer is more than just an intermediary because it bears the credit risk that one or the other of the parties to the swap might default on the obligation. Referring to Figure 23.6, if firm A defaults on its obligation, for example, the swap dealer still must maintain its commitment to firm B. In this sense, the dealer does more than simply pass through cash flows to the other swap participants.

		Contract				Open
	Open	High hi lo	Low	Settle	Chg	interest
Eurodollar (CME) - $1,000,000; pts of 100%						
Sept	99.1200	99.1275 ▲	99.1075	**99.1175**	−0.0025	1,046,998
Dec	99.0450	99.0550	99.0250	**99.0350**	−0.0100	1,488,878
March'17	99.0150	99.0200	98.9800	**98.9950**	−0.0150	1,117,165
Dec	98.9050	98.9150	98.8600	**98.8750**	−0.0300	1,367,955

Figure 23.7 Eurodollar futures, September 9, 2016

Source: *The Wall Street Journal,* September 10, 2016.

profit on this contract is proportional to the difference between the LIBOR rate at contract maturity and the contract rate entered into at contract inception. There are analogous rates on interbank loans in other currencies. For example, one close cousin of LIBOR is EURIBOR, which is the rate at which euro-denominated interbank loans within the euro zone are offered by one prime bank to another.

The listing conventions for the Eurodollar contract are a bit peculiar. Consider, for example, the first contract listed, which matures in September 2016. The settlement price is presented as $F_0 = 99.1175$, or approximately 99.12. However, this value is not really a price. In effect, participants in the contract negotiate over the contract interest rate, and the so-called futures price is actually set equal to 100 − contract rate. Because the futures price is 99.12, the contract rate is 100 − 99.12, or .88%. Similarly, the final futures price on contract maturity date will be marked to $F_T = 100 - \text{LIBOR}_T$. Thus, profits to the buyer of the contract will be proportional to

$$F_T - F_0 = (100 - \text{LIBOR}_T) - (100 - \text{Contract rate}) = \text{Contract rate} - \text{LIBOR}_T$$

Thus, the contract design allows participants to trade directly on the LIBOR rate. The contract multiplier is $1 million, but the LIBOR rate on which the contract is written is a 3-month (quarterly) rate; for each basis point that the (annualized) LIBOR increases, the quarterly interest rate increases by only ¼ of a basis point, and the profit to the buyer decreases by

$$.0001 \times \tfrac{1}{4} \times \$1,000,000 = \$25$$

Examine the payoff on the contract and you will see that, in effect, the Eurodollar contract allows traders to "swap" a fixed interest rate (the contract rate) for a floating rate (LIBOR). Thus, this is in effect a one-period interest rate swap. Notice in Figure 23.7 that the total open interest on this contract is enormous—almost 3 million contracts just for maturities extending to 1 year. Moreover, while not presented in *The Wall Street Journal,* significant trading in Eurodollars takes place for contract maturities extending out to 10 years. Contracts with such long-term maturities are quite unusual. They reflect the fact that the Eurodollar contract is used by dealers in long-term interest rate swaps as a hedging tool.

Swap Pricing

How can the fair swap rate be determined? For example, how would we know what fixed interest rate is a fair exchange for LIBOR? Or, what is the fair swap rate between dollars and pounds for a foreign exchange swap? To answer these questions we can exploit the analogy between a swap agreement and forward or futures contracts.

Consider a swap agreement to exchange dollars for pounds for one period only. Next year, for example, one might exchange $1 million for £.5 million. This is no more than a simple forward contract in foreign exchange. The dollar-paying party is contracting to buy British pounds in one year for a number of dollars agreed to today. The forward exchange rate for 1-year delivery is $F_1 = \$2.00$/pound. We know from the interest rate parity relationship that this forward price should be related to the spot exchange rate, E_0, by the formula $F_1 = E_0(1 + r_{US})/(1 + r_{UK})$. Because a one-period swap is in fact a forward contract, the fair swap rate is also given by the parity relationship.

Now consider an agreement to trade foreign exchange for two periods. This agreement could be structured as a portfolio of two separate forward contracts. If so, the forward price for the exchange of currencies in 1 year would be $F_1 = E_0(1 + r_{US})/(1 + r_{UK})$, while the forward price for the exchange in the second year would be $F_2 = E_0[(1 + r_{US})/(1 + r_{UK})]^2$. As an example, suppose that $E_0 = \$2.03$/pound, $r_{US} = 5\%$, and $r_{UK} = 7\%$. Then, using the parity relationship, prices for forward delivery would be $F_1 = \$2.03/£ \times (1.05/1.07) = \$1.992/£$ and $F_2 = \$2.03/£ \times (1.05/1.07)^2 = \$1.955/£$. Figure 23.8, Panel A, illustrates this sequence of cash exchanges assuming that the swap calls for delivery of one pound in each year. Although the dollars to be paid in each of the two years are known today, they differ from year to year.

In contrast, a swap agreement to exchange currency for two years would call for a fixed exchange rate to be used for the entire duration of the swap. This means that the same number of dollars would be paid per pound in each year, as illustrated in Figure 23.8, Panel B. Because the forward prices for delivery in each of the next two years are $\$1.992/£$ and $\$1.955/£$, the fixed exchange rate that makes the two-period swap a fair deal must be between these two values. Therefore, the dollar payer underpays for the pound in the first year (compared to the forward exchange rate) and overpays in the second year. Thus, the swap can be viewed as a portfolio of forward transactions, but instead of each exchange being priced independently, one forward price is applied to all of the transactions.

Figure 23.8 Forward contracts versus swaps

Given this insight, it is easy to determine the fair swap price. If we were to purchase one pound per year for two years using two independent forward agreements, we would pay F_1 dollars in one year and F_2 dollars in two years. If instead we enter a swap, we pay a constant rate of F^* dollars per pound. Because both strategies buy the same "package of cash flows" (i.e., £1 for each of the next two years), they must be equally costly. We conclude that

$$\frac{F_1}{1 + y_1} + \frac{F_2}{(1 + y_2)^2} = \frac{F^*}{1 + y_1} + \frac{F^*}{(1 + y_2)^2}$$

where y_1 and y_2 are the appropriate yields from the yield curve for discounting dollar cash flows of 1- and 2-year maturities, respectively. In our example, where we have assumed a flat U.S. yield curve at 5%, we would solve

$$\frac{1.992}{1.05} + \frac{1.955}{1.05^2} = \frac{F^*}{1.05} + \frac{F^*}{1.05^2}$$

which implies that $F^* = 1.974$. The same principle would apply to a foreign exchange swap of any other maturity. In essence, we need to find the level annuity, F^*, with the same present value as the stream of annual cash flows that would be incurred in a sequence of forward agreements.

Interest rate swaps can be priced using precisely the same analysis. Here, the forward contract is on an interest rate. For example, if you swap LIBOR for a 7% fixed rate with notional principal of $100, then you have entered a forward contract for delivery of $100 times LIBOR for a fixed "forward" price of $7. If the swap agreement is for many periods, the fair spread will be determined by the entire sequence of interest rate forward prices over the life of the swap.

Credit Risk in the Swap Market

The rapid growth of the swap market has given rise to increasing concern about credit risk in these markets and the possibility of a default by a major swap trader. Actually, although credit risk in the swap market certainly is not trivial, it is not nearly as large as the magnitude of notional principal in these markets would suggest. To see why, think about the losses one trader would incur if its counterparty defaulted.

At the time the transaction is initiated, it has zero net present value to both parties for the same reason that a futures contract has zero value at inception: Both are simply contracts to exchange cash in the future at terms established today, and those terms make both parties willing to enter the deal. In other words, at contract inception, the net present value of the contract must be zero. Even if one party were to back out of the deal at this moment, it would not cost the counterparty anything, because another trader could be found to take its place.

Once interest or exchange rates change, however, the situation is not as simple. Suppose, for example, that interest rates increase shortly after an interest-rate swap agreement has begun. The floating-rate payer therefore suffers a loss, while the fixed-rate payer enjoys a gain. If the floating-rate payer reneges on its commitment at this point, the fixed-rate payer suffers a loss. However, that loss is not as large as the notional principal of the swap, for the default of the floating-rate payer relieves the fixed-rate payer from its obligation as well. The loss is only the *difference* between the values of the fixed-rate and floating-rate obligations, not the *total* value of the payments that the floating-rate payer was originally obligated to make.

Example 23.7   Credit Risk in Swaps

Consider a swap written on $1 million of notional principal that calls for exchange of LIBOR for a fixed rate of 4% for five years. Suppose, for simplicity, that the yield curve is currently flat at 4%. With LIBOR thus equal to 4%, no cash flows will be exchanged unless interest rates change. But now suppose that the yield curve immediately shifts up to 5%. The floating-rate payer now is obligated to pay a cash flow of $(.05 - .04) \times \$1$ million $= \$10,000$ each year to the fixed-rate payer (as long as rates remain at 5%). If the floating-rate payer defaults on the swap, the fixed-rate payer loses the prospect of that 5-year annuity. The present value of that annuity is $10,000 × Annuity factor (5%, 5 years) = $43,295, which is only a bit more than 4% of notional principal. We conclude that the credit risk of the swap is far less than notional principal.

Credit Default Swaps

Despite the similarity in names, a **credit default swap (CDS)** is wholly different from an interest rate or currency swap. As we saw in Chapter 14, payment on a CDS is tied to the financial status of one or more reference firms; the CDS therefore allows two counterparties to take positions on the credit risk of those firms. When a particular "credit event" is triggered, say, default on an outstanding bond or failure to pay interest, the swap seller is expected to cover the loss in the market value of the bond. He may be obligated to pay par value to take delivery of the defaulted bond (in which case the swap is said to entail *physical settlement*) or may instead pay the swap buyer the difference between the par value and market value of the bond (termed *cash settlement*). The swap purchaser pays a periodic fee to the seller for this protection against credit events.

Unlike interest rate swaps, credit default swaps do not entail periodic netting of one reference rate against another. They are in fact more like insurance policies written on particular credit events. Bondholders may buy these swaps to transfer their credit risk exposure to the swap seller, effectively enhancing the credit quality of their portfolios. Unlike conventional insurance policies, however, swaps allow you to buy "insurance" on bonds that you don't actually own. Therefore, credit default swaps can be used purely to speculate on changes in the credit standing of the reference firms.

23.5   Commodity Futures Pricing

Commodity futures prices are governed by the same general considerations as stock futures. One difference, however, is that the cost of "carrying" commodities, especially those subject to spoilage, is greater than the cost of carrying financial assets. The underlying asset for some contracts, such as electricity futures, simply cannot be "carried" or held in a portfolio. Finally, spot prices for some commodities demonstrate marked seasonal patterns that can affect futures pricing.

Pricing with Storage Costs

In addition to interest costs, carrying commodities also entails storage costs, insurance costs, and an allowance for spoilage of goods in storage. To price commodity futures, we use the familiar arbitrage strategy that calls for holding the asset and hedging its value with a short position in a futures contract. We will denote the price of the commodity at contract maturity (time T) as P_T, and to simplify, we will assume that all noninterest carrying costs (C) are paid in one lump sum at maturity.

Action	Initial Cash Flow	CF at Time T
Buy asset; pay carrying costs at T	$-P_0$	$P_T - C$
Borrow P_0; repay with interest at time T	P_0	$-P_0(1 + r_f)$
Short futures position	0	$F_0 - P_T$
Total	0	$F_0 - P_0(1 + r_f) - C$

Because market prices should not allow for arbitrage opportunities, the terminal cash flow of this zero-net-investment, risk-free strategy should be zero.

If the cash flow were positive, this strategy would yield guaranteed profits for no investment. If the cash flow were negative, the reverse of this strategy also would yield risk-free profits. In practice, the reverse strategy would involve a short sale of the commodity. This is unusual but may be done as long as the short sale contract appropriately accounts for storage costs.[9] Thus, we conclude that

$$F_0 = P_0(1 + r_f) + C$$

Finally, if we define $c = C/P_0$, and interpret c as the percentage "rate" of carrying costs, we may write

$$F_0 = P_0(1 + r_f + c) \tag{23.3}$$

which is a (1-year) parity relationship for futures involving storage costs.

Compare Equation 23.3 to the parity relation for stocks, Equation 22.1 from the previous chapter, and you will see that they are extremely similar. In fact, if we think of carrying costs as a "negative dividend," the equations are identical. This result makes intuitive sense because, instead of receiving a dividend yield of d, the storer of the commodity must pay a storage cost of c. Obviously, this parity relationship is simply an extension of those we have seen already.

Although we have called c the carrying cost of the commodity, it is better to interpret it more generally as the *net* carrying cost, that is, the carrying cost net of the benefits derived from holding the commodity in inventory. For example, part of the "convenience yield" of goods held in inventory is the protection against stocking out, which may result in lost production or sales.

It is vital to note that we derive Equation 23.3 assuming that the asset can and will be bought and stored if the parity relation is violated; it therefore applies only to goods that *are* stored. Two kinds of commodities cannot be expected to be stored. The first kind is commodities for which storage is technologically not feasible, such as electricity. The second includes goods that are not stored for economic reasons. For example, it would be foolish to buy an agricultural commodity now, planning to store it for ultimate use in three years. Because agricultural prices fall as each crop is harvested, it usually makes no sense to store the commodity across crop cycles. Someone who anticipates need for the crop in three years would be wise to delay the purchase until after the harvest of the third year and avoid paying storage costs. Moreover, if the crop in the third year is comparable to this year's, you could obtain it at roughly the same price as you would pay this year. By waiting to purchase, you avoid both interest and storage costs.

[9]Robert A. Jarrow and George S. Oldfield, "Forward Contracts and Futures Contracts," *Journal of Financial Economics* 9 (1981).

Because storage across harvests generally will be avoided, Equation 23.3 should not be expected to apply for holding periods that span harvest times, nor should it apply to perishable goods that are available only "in season." Whereas the futures price for gold, which is a stored commodity, increases steadily with the maturity of the contract, the futures price for wheat is seasonal; its futures price typically falls across harvests between March and July as new supplies become available.

Figure 23.9 is a stylized version of the seasonal price pattern for an agricultural product. Clearly this pattern differs from financial assets such as stocks or gold for which there is no seasonal price movement. Financial assets are priced so that holding them in a portfolio produces a fair expected return. Agricultural prices, in contrast, are subject to steep periodic drops as each crop is harvested, which makes storage across harvests generally unprofitable and therefore upends arbitrage strategies like those that led to Equation 23.3.

Futures pricing across seasons therefore requires a different approach that is not based on storage. In place of general no-arbitrage restrictions we rely instead on discounted cash flow (DCF) analysis.

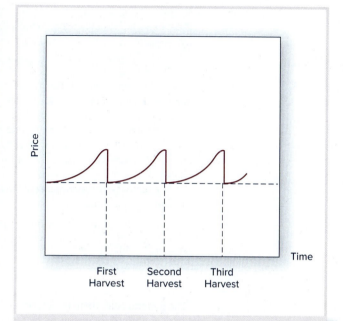

Figure 23.9 Typical agricultural price pattern over the season; prices adjusted for inflation

 Concept Check **23.8**

People are willing to buy and "store" shares of stock despite the fact that their purchase ties up capital. Most people, however, are not willing to buy and store soybeans. What is the difference in the properties of the expected evolution of stock prices versus soybean prices that accounts for this result?

Discounted Cash Flow Analysis for Commodity Futures

Given the current expectation of the spot price of the commodity at some future date and a measure of the risk characteristics of that price, we can measure the present value of a claim to receive the commodity at that future date. We obtain the appropriate risk premium from a model such as the CAPM or APT and discount the expected spot price at the appropriate risk-adjusted interest rate, as illustrated in the following example.

Example 23.8   Commodity Futures Pricing

Table 23.3, which presents betas on a variety of commodities, shows that the beta of orange juice was estimated to be .117. If the T-bill rate is currently 5% and the historical market risk premium is about 8%, the appropriate discount rate for orange juice would be given by the CAPM as

$$5\% + .117 \times 8\% = 5.94\%$$

If the expected spot price for orange juice six months from now is $1.45 per pound, the present value of a 6-month deferred claim to a pound of orange juice is

$$\$1.45/(1.0594)^{\frac{1}{2}} = \$1.409$$

What would be the proper futures price for orange juice? The contract calls for the ultimate exchange of orange juice for the futures price. We have just shown that the present value of the juice is $1.409. This should equal the present value of the futures price that will be paid for the juice. A commitment to a payment of F_0 dollars in six months has a present value of $F_0/(1.05)^{1/2} = .976 \times F_0$. Notice that the discount rate applied to the futures price is the risk-free rate of 5%, because the promised payment is fixed and therefore independent of market conditions.

To equate the present values of the promised payment of F_0 and the promised receipt of orange juice, we would set

$$.976F_0 = \$1.409$$

or $F_0 = \$1.444$.

The general rule, then, to determine the appropriate futures price is to equate the present value of the future payment of F_0 and the present value of the commodity to be received. This implies

$$\frac{F_0}{(1 + r_f)^T} = \frac{E(P_T)}{(1 + k)^T}$$

or

$$F_0 = E(P_T)\left(\frac{1 + r_f}{1 + k}\right)^T \tag{23.4}$$

where k is the required rate of return on the commodity, which may be obtained from a risk-return model such as the CAPM.

Table 23.3

Commodity betas

Commodity	Beta	Commodity	Beta
Wheat	−0.370	Orange juice	0.117
Corn	−0.429	Propane	−3.851
Oats	0.000	Cocoa	−0.291
Soybeans	−0.266	Silver	−0.272
Soybean oil	−0.650	Copper	0.005
Soybean meal	0.239	Cattle	0.365
Broilers	−1.692	Hogs	−0.148
Plywood	0.660	Pork bellies	−0.062
Potatoes	−0.610	Eggs	−0.293
Platinum	0.221	Lumber	−0.131
Wool	0.307	Sugar	−2.403
Cotton	−0.015		

Source: Zvi Bodie and Victor Rosansky, "Risk and Return in Commodity Futures," *Financial Analysts Journal* 36 (May–June 1980). Copyright 1980, CFA Institute. Reproduced from the *Financial Analysts Journal* with permission from the CFA Institute. All rights reserved.

Equation 23.4 is perfectly consistent with the spot-futures parity relationship. For example, apply Equation 23.4 to the futures price for a stock paying no dividends. Because the entire return on the stock is in the form of capital gains, the expected rate of capital gains must equal k, the required rate of return on the stock. Thus, the expected price of the stock is its current price times $(1 + k)^T$, or $E(P_T) = P_0(1 + k)^T$. Substituting this expression into Equation 23.4 results in $F_0 = P_0(1 + r_f)^T$, which is exactly the parity relationship.

 Concept Check **23.9**

Suppose that the systematic risk of orange juice were to increase, holding the expected time T price of juice constant. If the expected spot price is unchanged, would the futures price change? In what direction? What is the intuition behind your answer?

1. Foreign exchange futures trade on several foreign currencies, as well as on a European currency index. The interest rate parity relationship for foreign exchange futures is

$$F_0 = E_0 \left(\frac{1 + r_{\text{US}}}{1 + r_{\text{foreign}}} \right)^T$$

with exchange rates quoted as dollars per foreign currency. Deviations of the futures price from this value imply an arbitrage opportunity. Empirical evidence, however, suggests that generally the parity relationship is satisfied.

2. Futures contracts calling for cash settlement are traded on various stock market indexes. The contracts may be mixed with Treasury bills to construct artificial equity positions, which makes them potentially valuable tools for market timers. Market index contracts are used also by arbitrageurs who attempt to profit from violations of the stock-futures parity relationship.

3. Hedging requires investors to purchase assets that will offset the sensitivity of their portfolios to particular sources of risk. A hedged position requires that the hedging vehicle provide profits that vary inversely with the value of the position to be protected.

4. The hedge ratio is the number of hedging vehicles such as futures contracts required to offset the risk of the unprotected position. The hedge ratio for systematic market risk is proportional to the size and beta of the underlying stock portfolio. The hedge ratio for fixed-income portfolios is proportional to the price value of a basis point, which in turn is proportional to modified duration and the size of the portfolio.

5. Many investors such as hedge funds use hedging strategies to create market-neutral bets on perceived instances of relative mispricing between two or more securities. These are not arbitrage strategies, but pure plays on a particular perceived profit opportunity.

6. Interest rate futures contracts may be written on the *prices* of debt securities (as in the case of Treasury-bond futures contracts) or on interest rates directly (as in the case of Eurodollar contracts).

7. Swaps, which call for the exchange of a series of cash flows, may be viewed as portfolios of forward contracts. Each transaction may be viewed as a separate forward agreement. However, instead of pricing each exchange independently, the swap sets one "forward price" that applies to all of the transactions. Therefore, the swap price will be an average of the forward prices that would prevail if each exchange were priced separately.

8. Commodity futures pricing is complicated by costs for storage of the underlying commodity. When the asset is willingly stored by investors, the storage costs net of convenience yield enter the futures pricing equation as follows:

$$F_0 = P_0(1 + r_f + c)^T$$

The non–interest net carrying costs, c, play the role of a "negative dividend" in this context.

9. When commodities are not stored for investment purposes, the equilibrium futures price can be derived from general risk–return principles. In this case,

$$F_0 = E(P_T)\left(\frac{1 + r_f}{1 + k}\right)^T$$

The equilibrium (risk–return) and the no-arbitrage predictions of the proper futures price are consistent with one another for stored commodities.

KEY TERMS

hedging	index arbitrage	foreign exchange swap
interest rate parity relationship	program trading	interest rate swap
covered interest arbitrage	market-neutral bet	notional principal
relationship	price value of a basis point	credit default swap (CDS)
hedge ratio	cross-hedging	

KEY EQUATIONS

Interest rate parity (covered interest arbitrage) for direct exchange rate quote: $F_0 = E_0\left(\dfrac{1 + r_{US}}{1 + r_{foreign}}\right)^T$

Hedging with futures: Hedge ratio $= \dfrac{\text{Change in portfolio value}}{\text{Profit on one futures contract}}$

Parity for stored commodities: $F_0 = P_0(1 + r_f + c)^T$

Futures price versus expected spot price: $F_0 = E(P_T)\left(\dfrac{1 + r_f}{1 + k}\right)^T$

PROBLEM SETS

1. A stock's beta is a key input to hedging in the equity market. A bond's duration is key in fixed-income hedging. How are they used similarly? Are there any differences in the calculations necessary to formulate a hedge position in each market?

2. A U.S. exporting firm may use foreign exchange futures to hedge its exposure to exchange rate risk. Its position in futures will depend in part on anticipated payments from its customers denominated in foreign currency.

   a. In general, however, should its position in futures be more or less than the number of contracts necessary to hedge these anticipated cash flows? (*Hint*: Think about the firm's stream of cash flows extending out over many years.)

   b. What other considerations might enter into the hedging strategy?

3. Both gold-mining firms and oil-producing firms might choose to use futures to hedge uncertainty in future revenues due to price fluctuations. But trading activity sharply tails off for maturities beyond one year. Suppose a firm wishes to use available (short maturity) contracts to hedge commodity prices at a more distant horizon, say, four years from now. Do you think the hedge will be more effective for the oil- or the gold-producing firm?

4. You believe that the spread between municipal bond yields and U.S. Treasury bond yields is going to narrow in the coming month. How can you profit from such a change using the municipal bond and T-bond futures contracts?

5. Consider the futures contract written on the S&P 500 index and maturing in one year. The interest rate is 3%, and the future value of dividends expected to be paid over the next year is $35. The current index level is 2,000. Assume that you can short sell the S&P index.

    a. Suppose the expected rate of return on the market is 8%. What is the expected level of the index in one year?

    b. What is the theoretical no-arbitrage price for a 1-year futures contract on the S&P 500 stock index?

    c. Suppose the actual futures price is 2,012. Is there an arbitrage opportunity here? If so, how would you exploit it?

6. Suppose that the value of the S&P 500 stock index is 2,000.

    a. If each E-mini futures contract (with a contract multiplier of $50) costs $25 to trade with a discount broker, how much is the transaction cost per dollar of stock controlled by the futures contract?

    b. If the average price of a share on the NYSE is about $40, how much is the transaction cost per "typical share" controlled by one futures contract?

    c. For small investors, a typical transaction cost per share in stocks directly is about 10 cents per share. How many times the transactions costs in futures markets is this?

7. You manage a $19.5 million portfolio, currently all invested in equities, and believe that the market is on the verge of a big but short-lived downturn. You would move your portfolio temporarily into T-bills, but you do not want to incur the transaction costs of liquidating and reestablishing your equity position. Instead, you decide to temporarily hedge your equity holdings with E-mini S&P 500 index futures contracts.

    a. Should you be long or short the contracts? Why?

    b. If your equity holdings are invested in a market-index fund, into how many contracts should you enter? The S&P 500 index is now at 1,950 and the contract multiplier is $50.

    c. How does your answer to part (b) change if the beta of your portfolio is .6?

8. A manager is holding a $1 million stock portfolio with a beta of 1.25. She would like to hedge the risk of the portfolio using the S&P 500 stock index futures contract. How many dollars' worth of the index should she sell in the futures market to minimize the volatility of her position?

9. Suppose that the relationship between the rate of return on IBM stock, the market index, and a computer industry index can be described by the following regression equation: $r_{IBM} = .5r_M + .75r_{Industry}$. If a futures contract on the computer industry is traded, how would you hedge the exposure to the systematic and industry factors affecting the performance of IBM stock? Specifically, how many dollars' worth of the market and industry index contracts would you buy or sell for each dollar held in IBM?

10. Suppose that the spot price of the euro is currently $1.10. The 1-year futures price is $1.15. Is the interest rate higher in the United States or the euro zone?

11. a. The spot price of the British pound is currently $1.50. If the risk-free interest rate on 1-year government bonds is 1% in the United States and 2% in the United Kingdom, what must be the forward price of the pound for delivery one year from now?

    b. How could an investor make risk-free arbitrage profits if the forward price were higher than the price you gave in answer to part (a)? Give a numerical example.

12. Consider the following information:

$$r_{US} = 4\%; r_{UK} = 7\%$$
$$E_0 = 2.00 \text{ dollars per pound}$$
$$F_0 = 1.98 \text{ (1-year delivery)}$$

where the interest rates are annual yields on U.S. or U.K. bills. Given this information:

    a. Where would you lend?

    b. Where would you borrow?

    c. How could you arbitrage?

13. Farmer Brown grows Number 1 red corn and would like to hedge the value of the coming harvest. However, the futures contract is traded on the Number 2 yellow grade of corn. Suppose that yellow corn typically sells for 90% of the price of red corn. If he grows 100,000 bushels, and each futures contract calls for delivery of 5,000 bushels, how many contracts should Farmer Brown buy or sell to hedge his position?

14. Return to Figure 23.7. Suppose the LIBOR rate when the first listed Eurodollar contract matures in September is .60%. What will be the profit or loss to each side of the Eurodollar contract?

15. Yields on short-term bonds tend to be more volatile than yields on long-term bonds. Suppose that you have estimated that the yield on 20-year bonds changes by 10 basis points for every 15-basis-point move in the yield on 5-year bonds. You hold a $1 million portfolio of 5-year maturity bonds with modified duration 4 years and desire to hedge your interest rate exposure with T-bond futures, which currently have modified duration 9 years and sell at $F_0 = \$95$. How many futures contracts should you sell?

16. A manager is holding a $1 million bond portfolio with a modified duration of 8 years. She would like to hedge the risk of the portfolio by short-selling Treasury bonds. The modified duration of T-bonds is 10 years. How many dollars' worth of T-bonds should she sell to minimize the variance of her position?

17. A corporation plans to issue $10 million of 10-year bonds in three months. At current yields the bonds would have modified duration of 8 years. The T-note futures contract is selling at $F_0 = 100$ and has modified duration of 6 years. How can the firm use this futures contract to hedge the risk surrounding the yield at which it will be able to sell its bonds? Both the bond and the contract are at par value.

18. *a.* If the spot price of gold is $1,500 per troy ounce, the risk-free interest rate is 2%, and storage and insurance costs are zero, what should be the forward price of gold for delivery in one year? Use an arbitrage argument to prove your answer.
    b. Show how you could make risk-free arbitrage profits if the forward price is $1,550.

19. If the corn harvest today is poor, would you expect this fact to have any effect on today's futures prices for corn to be delivered (post-harvest) two years from today? Under what circumstances will there be no effect?

20. Suppose that the price of corn is risky, with a beta of .5. The monthly storage cost is $.03 per bushel, and the current spot price is $5.50, with an expected spot price in three months of $5.88. If the expected rate of return on the market is 0.9% per month, with a risk-free rate of 0.5% per month, would you store corn for three months?

21. Suppose the U.S. yield curve is flat at 4% and the euro yield curve is flat at 3%. The current exchange rate is $1.20 per euro. What will be the swap rate on an agreement to exchange currency over a 3-year period? The swap will call for the exchange of 1 million euros for a given number of dollars in each year.

22. Desert Trading Company has issued $100 million worth of long-term bonds at a fixed rate of 7%. The firm then enters into an interest rate swap where it pays LIBOR and receives a fixed 6% on notional principal of $100 million. What is the firm's effective interest rate on its borrowing?

23. Firm ABC enters a 5-year swap with firm XYZ to pay LIBOR in return for a fixed 6% rate on notional principal of $10 million. Two years from now, the market rate on 3-year swaps is LIBOR for 5%; at this time, firm XYZ goes bankrupt and defaults on its swap obligation.
    a. Why is firm ABC harmed by the default?
    b. What is the market value of the loss incurred by ABC as a result of the default?
    c. Suppose instead that ABC had gone bankrupt. How do you think the swap would be treated in the reorganization of the firm?

24. Suppose that at the present time, one can enter 5-year swaps that exchange LIBOR for 5%. An *off-market swap* would then be defined as a swap of LIBOR for a fixed rate other than 5%. For example, a firm with 7% coupon debt outstanding might like to convert to synthetic

floating-rate debt by entering a swap in which it pays LIBOR and receives a fixed rate of 7%. What up-front payment will be required to induce a counterparty to take the other side of this swap? Assume notional principal is $10 million.

25. Suppose the 1-year futures price on a stock-index portfolio is 1,914, the stock index currently is 1,900, the 1-year risk-free interest rate is 3%, and the year-end dividend that will be paid on a $1,900 investment in the market index portfolio is $40.

   a. By how much is the contract mispriced?
   b. Formulate a zero-net-investment arbitrage portfolio and show that you can lock in riskless profits equal to the futures mispricing.
   c. Now assume (as is true for small investors) that if you short sell the stocks in the market index, the proceeds of the short sale are kept with the broker, and you do not receive any interest income on the funds. Is there still an arbitrage opportunity (assuming that you don't already own the shares in the index)? Explain.
   d. Given the short-sale rules, what is the no-arbitrage *band* for the stock-futures price relationship? That is, given a stock index of 1,900, how high and how low can the futures price be without giving rise to arbitrage opportunities?

26. Consider these futures market data for the June delivery S&P 500 contract, exactly one year from today. The S&P 500 index is at 1,950, and the June maturity contract is at $F_0 = 1,951$.

   a. If the current interest rate is 2.5%, and the average dividend rate of the stocks in the index is 1.9%, what fraction of the proceeds of stock short sales would need to be available to you to earn arbitrage profits?
   b. Suppose now that you in fact have access to 90% of the proceeds from a short sale. What is the lower bound on the futures price that rules out arbitrage opportunities?
   c. By how much does the actual futures price fall below the no-arbitrage bound?
   d. Formulate the appropriate arbitrage strategy, and calculate the profits to that strategy.

---

1. Donna Doni, CFA, wants to explore potential inefficiencies in the futures market. The TOBEC stock index has a spot value of 185. TOBEC futures contracts are settled in cash and underlying contract values are determined by multiplying $100 times the index value. The current annual risk-free interest rate is 6.0%.

   a. Calculate the theoretical price of the futures contract expiring six months from now, using the cost-of-carry model. The index pays no dividends.
   The total (round-trip) transaction cost for trading a futures contract is $15.
   b. Calculate the lower bound for the price of the futures contract expiring six months from now.

2. Suppose your client says, "I am invested in Japanese stocks but want to eliminate my exposure to this market for a period of time. Can I accomplish this without the cost and inconvenience of selling out and buying back in again if my expectations change?"

   a. Briefly describe a strategy to hedge both the local market risk and the currency risk of investing in Japanese stocks.
   b. Briefly explain why the hedge strategy you described in part (a) might not be fully effective.

3. René Michaels, CFA, plans to invest $1 million in U.S. government cash equivalents for the next 90 days. Michaels's client has authorized her to use non–U.S. government cash equivalents, but only if the currency risk is hedged to U.S. dollars by using forward currency contracts.

   a. Calculate the U.S. dollar value of the hedged investment at the end of 90 days for each of the two cash equivalents in the table below. Show all calculations.
   b. Briefly explain the theory that best accounts for your results.
   c. On the basis of this theory, estimate the implied interest rate for a 90-day U.S. government cash equivalent.

Interest Rates
90-Day Cash Equivalents

Japanese government	7.6%
Swiss government	8.6%

Exchange Rates
Currency Units per U.S. Dollar

	Spot	90-Day Forward
Japanese yen	133.05	133.47
Swiss franc	1.5260	1.5348

4. After studying Iris Hamson's credit analysis, George Davies is considering whether he can increase the holding-period return on Yucatan Resort's excess cash holdings (which are held in pesos) by investing those cash holdings in the Mexican bond market. Although Davies would be investing in a peso-denominated bond, the investment goal is to achieve the highest holding-period return, measured in U.S. dollars, on the investment.

Davies finds the higher yield on the Mexican 1-year bond, which is considered to be free of credit risk, to be attractive, but he is concerned that depreciation of the peso will reduce the holding-period return, measured in U.S. dollars. Hamson has prepared the following selected financial data to help Davies make the decision:

Selected Economic and Financial Data

U.S. 1-year Treasury bond yield	2.5%
Mexican 1-year bond yield	6.5%

Nominal Exchange Rates

Spot	9.5000 Pesos = U.S. $1.00
1-year forward	9.8707 Pesos = U.S. $1.00

Hamson recommends buying the Mexican 1-year bond and hedging the foreign currency exposure using the 1-year forward exchange rate. Calculate the U.S. dollar holding-period return that would result from the transaction recommended by Hamson. Is the U.S. dollar holding-period return resulting from the transaction more or less than that available in the U.S.?

5. *a.* Pamela Itsuji, a currency trader for a Japanese bank, is evaluating the price of a 6-month Japanese yen/U.S. dollar currency futures contract. She gathers the following currency and interest rate data:

Japanese yen/U.S. dollar spot currency exchange rate	¥124.30/$1.00
6-month Japanese interest rate	0.10%
6-month U.S. interest rate	3.80%

Calculate the theoretical price for a 6-month Japanese yen/U.S. dollar currency futures contract, using the data above.

b. Itsuji is also reviewing the price of a 3-month Japanese yen/U.S. dollar currency futures contract, using the currency and interest rate data shown below. Because the 3-month Japanese interest rate has just increased to .50%, Itsuji recognizes that an arbitrage opportunity exists and decides to borrow $1 million U.S. dollars to purchase Japanese yen. Calculate the yen arbitrage profit from Itsuji's strategy, using the following data:

Japanese yen/U.S. dollar spot currency exchange rate	¥124.30/$1.00
New 3-month Japanese interest rate	0.50%
3-month U.S. interest rate	3.50%
3-month currency futures contract value	¥123.2605/$1.00

6. Janice Delsing, a U.S.-based portfolio manager, manages an $800 million portfolio ($600 million in stocks and $200 million in bonds). In reaction to anticipated short-term market events, Delsing wishes to adjust the allocation to 50% stock and 50% bonds through the use of futures. Her position will be held only until "the time is right to restore the original asset allocation." Delsing determines a financial futures–based asset allocation strategy is appropriate. The stock futures index multiplier is $250 and the denomination of the bond futures contract is $100,000. Other information relevant to a futures-based strategy is as follows:

Bond portfolio modified duration	5 years
Bond portfolio yield to maturity	7%
Price value of a basis point of bond futures	$97.85
Stock-index futures price	1378
Stock portfolio beta	1.0

   a. Describe the financial futures–based strategy needed and explain how the strategy allows Delsing to implement her allocation adjustment. No calculations are necessary.

   b. Compute the number of *each* of the following needed to implement Delsing's asset allocation strategy:

     i.   Bond futures contracts.

     ii. Stock-index futures contracts.

7. You are provided the information outlined as follows to be used in solving this problem.

Issue	Price	Yield to Maturity	Modified Duration*
U.S. Treasury bond 11¾% maturing Nov. 15, 2032	100	11.75%	7.6 years
U.S. Treasury long bond futures contract (contract expiration in 6 months)	63.33	11.85%	8.0 years
XYZ Corporation bond 12½% maturing June 1, 2023 (sinking fund debenture, rated AAA)	93	13.50%	7.2 years

Volatility of AAA corporate bond yields relative to U.S. Treasury bond yields = 1.25 to 1.0 (1.25 times)

Assume no commission and no margin requirements on U.S. Treasury long bond futures contracts. Assume no taxes.

One U.S. Treasury bond futures contract is a claim on $100,000 par value long-term U.S. Treasury bonds.

*Modified duration = Duration/(1 + y).

   Situation A A fixed-income manager holding a $20 million market value position of U.S. Treasury 11¾% bonds maturing November 15, 2032, expects the economic growth rate and the inflation rate to be above market expectations in the near future. Institutional rigidities prevent any existing bonds in the portfolio from being sold in the cash market.

Situation B The treasurer of XYZ Corporation has recently become convinced that interest rates will decline in the near future. He believes it is an opportune time to purchase his company's sinking fund bonds in advance of requirements because these bonds are trading at a discount from par value. He is preparing to purchase in the open market $20 million par value XYZ Corporation 12½% bonds maturing June 1, 2023. A $20 million par value position of these bonds is currently offered in the open market at 93. Unfortunately, the treasurer must obtain approval from the board of directors for such a purchase, and this approval process can take up to two months. The board of directors' approval in this instance is only a formality.

For each of these two situations, demonstrate how interest rate risk can be hedged using the Treasury bond futures contract. Show all calculations, including the number of futures contracts used.

8. You ran a regression of the yield of KC Company's 10-year bond on the 10-year U.S. Treasury benchmark's yield using month-end data for the past year. You found the following result:

$$\text{Yield}_{KC} = 0.54 + 1.22 \text{ Yield}_{\text{Treasury}}$$

where Yield_{KC} is the yield on the KC bond and $\text{Yield}_{\text{Treasury}}$ is the yield on the U.S. Treasury bond. The modified duration on the 10-year U.S. Treasury is 7.0 years, and modified duration on the KC bond is 6.93 years.

a. Calculate the percentage change in the price of the 10-year U.S. Treasury, assuming a 50-basis-point change in the yield on the 10-year U.S. Treasury.

b. Calculate the percentage change in the price of the KC bond, using the regression equation above, assuming a 50-basis-point change in the yield on the 10-year U.S. Treasury.

E-INVESTMENTS EXERCISES

Go to the Chicago Mercantile Exchange Web site (**www.cme.com**) and link to the tab for *CME Products,* then *Foreign Exchange (FX).* Link to the *Canadian Dollar* contracts and answer the following questions about the futures contract (see *Contract Specifications*):

What is the size (units of $CD) of each contract?

What is the tick size (minimum price increment) for the contract?

What time period during the day is the contract traded?

If the delivery option is exercised, when and where does delivery take place?

 ## SOLUTIONS TO CONCEPT CHECKS

1. According to interest rate parity, F_0 should be $1.981. Because the futures price is too high, we should reverse the arbitrage strategy just considered.

	CF Now ($)	CF in 1 Year
1. Borrow $2.00 in the U.S. Convert to 1 U.K. pound.	+2.00	−2.00(1.04)
2. Lend the 1 pound in the U.K.	−2.00	$1.05E_1$
3. Enter a contract to sell 1.05 pounds at a futures price of $2.01/£.	0	£1.05($2.01/£ − E_1)
Total	0	$.0305

2. Because the firm does poorly when the dollar depreciates, it hedges with a futures contract that will provide profits when the dollar declines. It needs to enter a *long* position in pound futures, which means that it will earn profits on the contract when the futures price increases, that is, when more dollars are required to purchase one pound. The specific hedge ratio is determined by noting that if the number of dollars required to buy one pound rises by $.05, profits decrease by $200,000 at the same time that the profit on a long future contract would increase by $.05 × 62,500 = $3,125. The hedge ratio is

$$\frac{\$200{,}000 \text{ per } \$.05 \text{ depreciation in the dollar}}{\$3{,}125 \text{ per contract per } \$.05 \text{ depreciation}} = 64 \text{ contracts long}$$

3. Each $1 increase in the price of corn reduces profits by $1 million. Therefore, the firm needs to enter futures contracts to purchase 1 million bushels at a price stipulated today. The futures position will profit by $1 million for each increase of $1 in the price of corn. The profit on the contract will offset the lost profits on operations.

4.

	In General (per unit of index)	Our Numbers
Hold 50,000 units of indexed stock portfolio with $S_0 = 2{,}000$.	S_T	$50{,}000\, S_T$
Sell 1,000 contracts.	$F_0 - S_T$	$1{,}000 \times \$50 \times (2{,}020 - S_T)$
Total	F_0	$\$101{,}000{,}000$

The net cash flow is riskless, and provides a 1% monthly rate of return, equal to the risk-free rate.

5. The price value of a basis point is still $9,000, as a 1-basis-point change in the interest rate reduces the value of the $20 million portfolio by .01% × 4.5 = .045%. Therefore, the number of futures needed to hedge the interest rate risk is the same as for a portfolio half the size with double the modified duration.

6.

	LIBOR		
Cash flow to the firm	7%	8%	9%
As bond issuer, firm pays (LIBOR × $10 million)	−700,000	−800,000	−900,000
As fixed payer on the swap, firm receives $10 million × (LIBOR −.08)	−100,000	0	+100,000
Net cash flow	−800,000	−800,000	−800,000

Regardless of the LIBOR rate, the firm's net cash outflow equals .08 × principal, just as if it had issued a fixed-rate bond with a coupon of 8%.

7. The manager would like to hold on to the money market securities because of their attractive relative pricing compared to other short-term assets. However, there is an expectation that rates will fall. The manager can hold this *particular* portfolio of short-term assets and still benefit from the drop in interest rates by entering a swap to pay a short-term interest rate and receive a fixed interest rate. The resulting synthetic fixed-rate portfolio will increase in value if rates do fall.

8. Stocks offer a total return (capital gain plus dividends) large enough to compensate investors for the time value of the money tied up in the stock. Agricultural prices do not necessarily increase

over time. In fact, across a harvest, crop prices will fall. The returns necessary to make storage economically attractive are lacking.

9. If systematic risk were higher, the appropriate discount rate, k, would increase. Referring to Equation 23.4, we conclude that F_0 would fall. Intuitively, the claim to 1 pound of orange juice is worth less today if its expected price is unchanged, while the risk associated with the value of that claim increases. Therefore, the amount investors are willing to pay today for future delivery is lower.

Portfolio Performance Evaluation

MOST FINANCIAL ASSETS are managed by professional investors, who thus at least indirectly allocate the lion's share of capital across firms. Efficient allocation therefore depends on the quality of these professionals and the ability of financial markets to identify and direct capital to the best stewards. Therefore, if capital markets are to be reasonably efficient, investors must be able to measure the performance of their asset managers.

How can we evaluate the performance of a portfolio manager? It turns out that even an average portfolio return is not as straightforward to measure as it might seem. In addition, adjusting average returns for risk presents a host of other problems. In the end, performance evaluation is far from trivial.

We begin this chapter with the measurement of portfolio returns. From there we move on to conventional approaches to risk adjustment. We consider the situations in which each of the standard risk-adjusted performance measures will be of most interest to investors and show how style analysis may be viewed as a generalization of the index model and the alpha statistic that it generates.

Performance measurement becomes far more difficult when managers change portfolio composition during the measurement period, so we also examine the complications posed by changes in the risk characteristics of the portfolio. One particular way in which this may occur is when managers attempt to time the broad market and adjust portfolio beta in anticipation of market movements. Market timing raises a wide range of issues in performance evaluation.

We close the chapter with a look at performance attribution techniques. These are tools used to decompose managers' performance into results that can be attributed to security selection, sector selection, and asset allocation decisions.

24.1 The Conventional Theory of Performance Evaluation

Average Rates of Return

We defined the holding-period return (HPR) in Section 5.1 of Chapter 5 and explained the difference between the arithmetic and geometric average. Suppose we evaluate the performance of a portfolio over a period of 20 years. The *arithmetic average* return is the sum of the 20 annual returns divided by 20. In contrast, the *geometric average* is the constant annual return over the 20 years that would provide the same total cumulative return over the entire investment period. Therefore, the geometric average, r_G, is defined by

$$(1 + r_G)^{20} = (1 + r_1)(1 + r_2) \cdots (1 + r_{20})$$

The right-hand side of this equation is the compounded final value of a $1 investment earning the 20 annual rates of return. The left-hand side is the compounded value of a $1 investment earning r_G *each* year. We solve for $1 + r_G$ as

$$1 + r_G = [(1 + r_1)(1 + r_2) \cdots (1 + r_{20})]^{1/20}$$

Each return has an equal weight in the geometric average. For this reason, the geometric average is referred to as a **time-weighted average.**

Time-Weighted Returns versus Dollar-Weighted Returns

To set the stage for the more subtle issues that follow, let's start with a trivial example. Consider a stock paying a dividend of $2 annually that currently sells for $50. You purchase the stock today, collect the $2 dividend, and then sell the stock for $53 at year-end. Your rate of return is

$$\frac{\text{Total proceeds}}{\text{Initial investment}} = \frac{\text{Income} + \text{Capital gain}}{50} = \frac{2 + 3}{50} = .10, \text{ or } 10\%$$

Another way to derive the rate of return that is useful in the more difficult multiperiod case is to set up the investment as a discounted cash flow problem. Call r the rate of return that equates the present value of all cash flows from the investment with the initial outlay. In our example, the stock is purchased for $50 and generates cash flows at year-end of $2 (dividend) plus $53 (sale of stock). Therefore, we solve $50 = (2 + 53)/(1 + r)$ to find again that $r = .10$, or 10%.

When we consider investments over a period during which cash was added to or withdrawn from the portfolio, measuring the rate of return becomes more difficult. To continue our example, suppose that you purchase a second share of the same stock at the end of the first year, and hold both shares until the end of year 2, at which point you sell each share for $54. Total cash outlays are shown below.

Time	Outlay
0	$50 to purchase first share
1	$53 to purchase second share a year later
	Proceeds
1	$2 dividend from initially purchased share
2	$4 dividend from the 2 shares held in the second year, plus $108 received from selling both shares at $54 each

Using the discounted cash flow (DCF) approach, we can solve for the average return over the two years by equating the present values of the cash inflows and outflows:

$$50 + \frac{53}{1 + r} = \frac{2}{1 + r} + \frac{112}{(1 + r)^2}$$

resulting in $r = 7.117\%$. This is the internal rate of return on the investment.[1]

---

[1] Excel's function XIRR calculates IRR. The function provides the IRR between any two dates given a starting value, cash flows at various dates in between (with additions given as negative numbers, and withdrawals as positive values), and a final value on the closing date.

The internal rate of return is called the **dollar-weighted rate of return.** It is "dollar weighted" because the stock's performance in the second year, when two shares of stock are held, has a greater influence on the average overall return than the first-year return, when only one share is held.

The time-weighted (geometric average) return is 7.81%:

$$r_1 = \frac{53 + 2 - 50}{50} = .10 = 10\% \qquad r_2 = \frac{54 + 2 - 53}{53} = 0.566 = 5.66\%$$

$$r_G = (1.10 \times 1.0566)^{1/2} - 1 = .0781 = 7.81\%$$

The dollar-weighted average is less than the time-weighted average in this example because the return in the second year, when more money was invested, is lower.

 Concept Check **24.1**

Shares of XYZ Corp. pay a $2 dividend at the end of every year on December 31. An investor buys two shares of the stock on January 1 at a price of $20 each, sells one of those shares for $22 a year later on the next January 1, and sells the second share an additional year later for $19. Find the dollar- and time-weighted rates of return on the 2-year investment.

Adjusting Returns for Risk

Evaluating performance based on average return alone is not very useful because returns must be adjusted for risk before they can be compared meaningfully. The simplest and most popular way to make the adjustment is to compare rates of return with those of other investment funds with similar risk characteristics. For example, high-yield bond portfolios are grouped into one **comparison universe,** growth stock equity funds are grouped into another, and so on. Then the (usually time-weighted) average returns of each fund within the universe are ordered, and each portfolio manager receives a percentile ranking of relative performance within the comparison group. For example, the manager with the ninth-best performance in a universe of 100 funds would be the 90th percentile manager: Her performance was better than 90% of all competing funds over the evaluation period.

These relative rankings are usually displayed in a chart such as that in Figure 24.1. The chart summarizes performance rankings over four periods: 1 quarter, 1 year, 3 years, and 5 years. The top and bottom lines of each box are drawn at the rate of return of the 95th and 5th percentile managers. The three dashed lines correspond to the rates of return of the 75th, 50th (median), and 25th percentile managers. The diamond is drawn at the average return of a particular fund and the square is drawn at the return of a benchmark index, such as the S&P 500. The placement of the diamond

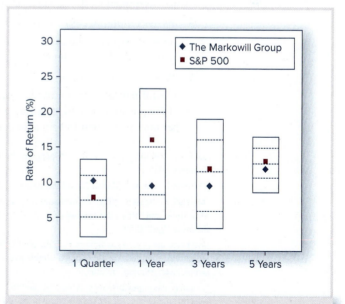

Figure 24.1 Universe comparison, periods ending December 31, 2022

within the box is an easy-to-read representation of the performance of the fund relative to the comparison universe.

This comparison of performance with other managers of similar investment style is a useful first step in evaluating performance. However, such rankings can be misleading. Within a particular universe, some managers may concentrate on particular subgroups, so that portfolio characteristics are not truly comparable. For example, within the equity universe, one manager may concentrate on high-beta or aggressive growth stocks. Similarly, within fixed-income universes, durations can vary across managers. These considerations suggest that a more precise means for risk adjustment is desirable.

Methods of risk-adjusted performance evaluation using mean-variance criteria came on stage simultaneously with the capital asset pricing model. Jack Treynor,[2] William Sharpe,[3] and Michael Jensen[4] recognized immediately the implications of the CAPM for rating the performance of managers. Within a short time, academicians were in command of a battery of performance measures, and a bounty of scholarly investigation of mutual fund performance was pouring from ivory towers. Shortly thereafter, agents emerged who were willing to supply rating services to portfolio managers and their clients.

But while widely used, risk-adjusted performance measures each have their own limitations. Moreover, their reliability requires quite a long history of consistent management with a steady level of performance and a representative sample of investment environments: bull as well as bear markets.

We start by cataloging some possible risk-adjusted performance measures for a portfolio, P, and examine the circumstances in which each might be most relevant.

1. *Sharpe ratio:* $(\bar{r}_P - \bar{r}_f)/\sigma_P$

   Sharpe's ratio divides average portfolio excess return over the sample period by the standard deviation of returns over that period. It measures the reward to (total) volatility trade-off.[5]

2. *Treynor measure:* $(\bar{r}_P - \bar{r}_f)/\beta_P$

   Like the Sharpe ratio, **Treynor's measure** gives excess return per unit of risk, but it uses systematic risk instead of total risk.

3. *Jensen's alpha:* $\alpha_P = \bar{r}_P - [\bar{r}_f + \beta_P(\bar{r}_M - \bar{r}_f)]$

   Jensen's alpha is the average return on the portfolio over and above that predicted by the CAPM, given the portfolio's beta and the average market return.[6]

4. *Information ratio:* $\alpha_P/\sigma(e_P)$

   The **information ratio** divides the alpha of the portfolio by the nonsystematic risk of the portfolio, called "tracking error" in the industry. It measures abnormal return per unit of risk that in principle could be diversified away by holding a market

---

[2]Jack L. Treynor, "How to Rate Management Investment Funds," *Harvard Business Review* 43 (January–February 1966).

[3]William F. Sharpe, "Mutual Fund Performance," *Journal of Business* 39 (January 1966).

[4]Michael C. Jensen, "The Performance of Mutual Funds in the Period 1945–1964," *Journal of Finance,* May 1968; and "Risk, the Pricing of Capital Assets, and the Evaluation of Investment Portfolios," *Journal of Business,* April 1969.

[5]We place bars over r_f as well as r_P to denote the fact that because the risk-free rate may not be constant over the measurement period, we are taking a sample average, just as we do for r_P. Equivalently, we may simply compute sample average *excess* returns.

[6]In many cases performance evaluation assumes a multifactor market. For example, when the Fama-French 3-factor model is used, Jensen's alpha will be: $\alpha_P = \overline{r_P - r_f} - \beta_{PM}(\overline{r_M - r_f}) - s_P \bar{r}_{SMB} - h_P \bar{r}_{HML}$ where s_P is the loading on the SMB portfolio and h_P is the loading on the HML portfolio. A multifactor version of the Treynor measure also exists. See footnote 13.

index portfolio. (We should note that industry jargon tends to be a little loose concerning this topic. Some define the information ratio as excess return—rather than alpha—per unit of nonsystematic risk, using *appraisal ratio* to refer to the ratio of alpha to nonsystematic risk. But terminology in the profession is not fully uniform, and you may well encounter both of these definitions of the information ratio. We will consistently define it as we have done here, specifically as the ratio of alpha to the standard deviation of residual returns.)

Each performance measure has some appeal. But as Concept Check 24.2 shows, these competing measures do not necessarily provide consistent assessments of performance, because the risk measures used to adjust returns differ substantially. Therefore, we need to consider the circumstances in which each of these measures is appropriate.

 Concept Check **24.2**

Consider the following data for a particular sample period:

	Portfolio P	Market M
Average return	35%	28%
Beta	1.20	1.00
Standard deviation	42%	30%
Tracking error (nonsystematic risk), $\sigma(e)$	18%	0

Calculate the following performance measures for portfolio P and the market: Sharpe, Jensen (alpha), Treynor, information ratio. The T-bill rate during the period was 6%. By which measures did portfolio P outperform the market?

The Sharpe Ratio for Overall Portfolios

Earlier chapters of this text help to determine the criteria for the investor's optimal risky portfolio. If investor preferences can be summarized by a mean-variance utility function such as that introduced in Chapter 6, we can arrive at a relatively simple criterion. The particular utility function that we used is

$$U = E(r_P) - \tfrac{1}{2}A\sigma_P^2$$

where A is the coefficient of risk aversion. With mean-variance preferences, the investor wants to maximize the Sharpe ratio $[E(r_P) - r_f]/\sigma_P$. Recall that this criterion led to the selection of the tangency portfolio in Chapter 7. The problem reduces to the search for the portfolio with the highest possible Sharpe ratio.

Thus, when we are selecting or evaluating an investor's entire risky portfolio, the appropriate criterion is the Sharpe ratio, the "reward-to-risk" ratio of excess expected return to portfolio standard deviation. We focus on total volatility rather than systematic risk because we are looking at the full portfolio rather than a small component of it. The benchmark for acceptable performance is the Sharpe ratio of the market index, since the investor can easily opt for a passive strategy by investing in an indexed equity mutual fund. The actively managed portfolio must offer a higher Sharpe ratio than the market index if it is to be an acceptable candidate for the investor's optimal risky portfolio.

The M^2 Measure and the Sharpe Ratio   While the Sharpe ratio can be used to rank portfolio performance, its numerical value is not easy to interpret. Comparing the ratios for portfolios M and P in Concept Check 24.2, you should have found that $S_P = .69$ and $S_M = .73$. This suggests that portfolio P underperformed the market index. But is a difference of .04 in the Sharpe ratio economically meaningful? We often compare rates of return, but these values are difficult to interpret.

An equivalent representation of Sharpe's ratio was proposed by Graham and Harvey, and later popularized by Leah Modigliani of Morgan Stanley and her grandfather Franco Modigliani, past winner of the Nobel Prize in Economics.[7] Their approach has been dubbed the M^2 measure (for Modigliani-squared). Like the Sharpe ratio, M^2 focuses on total volatility as a measure of risk, but its risk adjustment leads to an easy-to-interpret differential return relative to the benchmark index.

To compute M^2, we imagine that an active portfolio, P, is mixed with a position in T-bills so that the resulting "adjusted" portfolio matches the volatility of a passive market index such as the S&P 500. For example, if the active portfolio has 1.5 times the standard deviation of the index, you would mix it with T-bills using proportions of 1/3 in bills and 2/3 in the active portfolio. The resulting adjusted portfolio, which we call P^*, would then have the same standard deviation as the index. (If the active portfolio had *lower* standard deviation than the index, it would be leveraged by borrowing money and investing the proceeds in the portfolio.) Because the market index and portfolio P^* have the same standard deviation, we may compare their performance simply by comparing returns. This is the M^2 measure for portfolio P:

$$M_P^2 = r_{P*} - r_M \tag{24.1}$$

Example 24.1 M^2 Measure

Using the data in Concept Check 24.2, P has a standard deviation of 42% versus a market standard deviation of 30%. Therefore, the adjusted portfolio P^* would be formed by mixing bills and portfolio P with weights $30/42 = .714$ in P and $1 - .714 = .286$ in bills. The return on this portfolio would be $(.286 \times 6\%) + (.714 \times 35\%) = 26.7\%$, which is 1.3% less than the market return. Thus portfolio P has an M_P^2 measure of -1.3%.

A graphical representation of M^2 appears in Figure 24.2. We move down the capital allocation line corresponding to portfolio P (by mixing P with T-bills) until we reduce the standard deviation of the adjusted portfolio to match that of the market index. M_P^2 is then the vertical distance (the difference in expected returns) between portfolios P^* and M. You can see from Figure 24.2 that P will have a negative M^2 when its capital allocation line is less steep than the capital market line, that is, when its Sharpe ratio is less than that of the market index.[8]

---

[7] John R. Graham and Campbell R. Harvey, "Grading the Performance of Market Timing Newsletters," *Financial Analysts Journal* 53 (November/December 1997), pp. 54–66; and Franco Modigliani and Leah Modigliani, "Risk-Adjusted Performance," *Journal of Portfolio Management*, Winter 1997, pp. 45–54.

[8] M^2 is positive when the portfolio's Sharpe ratio exceeds the market's. Letting R denote excess returns and S denote Sharpe measures, the geometry of Figure 24.2 implies that $R_{P*} = S_P \sigma_M$, and therefore that

$$M^2 = r_{P*} - r_M = R_{P*} - R_M = S_P \sigma_M - S_M \sigma_M = (S_P - S_M)\sigma_M$$

M^2 and the Sharpe ratio therefore always rank order portfolios identically.

The Treynor Ratio

In many circumstances, you may have to select funds or portfolios that will be mixed together to form the investor's overall risky portfolio. For example, the manager in charge of a large pension plan might parcel out the total assets to several portfolio managers. Consider CalPERS (the California Public Employee Retirement System), which had a portfolio of about $300 billion in 2016. Like many large plans, it uses a *funds of funds* approach, allocating the endowment among a number of professional managers (funds). How should you compare performance across candidate managers in this context?

When employing a number of managers, nonsystematic risk will be largely diversified away, so systematic risk becomes the relevant measure of risk. The appropriate performance metric when evaluating potential *components* of the full risky portfolio is now the Treynor measure: this reward-to-risk ratio divides expected excess return by *systematic* risk (i.e., by beta).

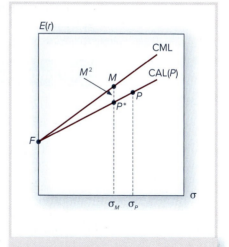

Figure 24.2 M^2 of portfolio P

The properties of portfolios P and Q are laid out in Table 24.1 and plotted in Figure 24.3. We plot P and Q in the expected return–beta (rather than the expected return–standard deviation) plane, because we assume that P and Q are two of many subportfolios in the fund, and thus that nonsystematic risk will be largely diversified away. The security market line (SML) shows the value of α_P and α_Q as the distance of P and Q above the SML.

If we invest w_Q in Q and $w_F = 1 - w_Q$ in T-bills, the resulting portfolio, Q^*, will have alpha and beta values proportional to Q's alpha and beta scaled down by w_Q:

$$\alpha_{Q^*} = w_Q \alpha_Q$$
$$\beta_{Q^*} = w_Q \beta_Q$$

Thus, all portfolios such as Q^*, generated by mixing Q with T-bills, plot on a straight line from the origin through Q. We call it the T-line for the Treynor measure, which is the slope of this line.

Figure 24.3 shows the T-line for portfolio P as well. P has a steeper T-line; despite its lower

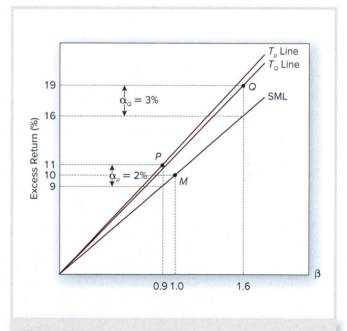

Figure 24.3 Treynor's measure

	Portfolio P	Portfolio Q	Market
Beta	0.90	1.60	1.0
Excess return ($\bar{r} - \bar{r}_f$)	11%	19%	10%
Alpha*	2%	3%	0

Table 24.1

Portfolio performance

*Alpha = Excess return − (Beta × Market excess return)
= $(\bar{r} - r_f) - \beta(\bar{r}_M - \bar{r}_f) = \bar{r} - [\bar{r}_f + \beta(\bar{r}_M - \bar{r}_f)]$

alpha, P is a better portfolio after all. For any *given* beta, a mixture of P with T-bills will give a better alpha than a mixture of Q with T-bills.

Example 24.2   Equalizing Beta

Suppose we choose to mix Q with T-bills to create a portfolio Q^* with a beta equal to that of P. We find the necessary proportion by solving for w_Q:

$$\beta_{Q^*} = w_Q \beta_Q = 1.6 w_Q = \beta_P = .9$$
$$w_Q = \text{\textfrac{9}{16}}$$

Portfolio Q^* therefore has an alpha of

$$\alpha_{Q^*} = \text{\textfrac{9}{16}} \times 3\% = 1.69\%$$

which is less than that of P.

The slope of the T-line, giving the trade-off between excess return and beta, is the appropriate performance criterion in this case. The slope for P, denoted by T_P, is given by

$$T_P = \frac{\bar{r}_P - \bar{r}_f}{\beta_P}$$

Like M^2, Treynor's measure is a percentage. If you subtract the market's excess return from Treynor's measure, you will obtain the difference between the return on the T_P line in Figure 24.3 and the SML, at the point where $\beta = 1$. Analogous to M^2, we might dub this difference T^2. Keep in mind though that M^2 and T^2 are as different as Sharpe's measure is from Treynor's. They may well rank portfolios differently.

The Information Ratio

Here is another situation that calls for yet another performance criterion. Consider a pension fund with a largely passive and well-diversified position—for example, a portfolio that resembles an indexed equity fund. Now the fund decides to add a position in an active portfolio to its current position. For example, a university might employ a hedge fund as a possible addition to its core positions in more traditional portfolios that were established primarily with concerns of diversification in mind.

As we saw in Chapter 8, when the hedge fund (or another active position) is optimally combined with the baseline indexed portfolio, the improvement in the Sharpe measure will be determined by its information ratio $\alpha_H / \sigma(e_H)$, according to

$$S_P^2 = S_M^2 + \left[\frac{\alpha_H}{\sigma(e_H)} \right]^2 \tag{24.2}$$

Equation 24.2 tells us that the appropriate performance measure for the hedge fund, H, is its information ratio (IR). If you are looking for active managers to add to a currently indexed position, you will want to select potential candidates with the best information ratios.

The information ratio is yet another version of a reward-to-risk ratio. In this context, the reward is the alpha of the active position. It is the expected return on that incremental portfolio over and above the risk premium that would normally correspond to its systematic risk. On the other hand, the incremental position tilts the total risky portfolio away from the passive index, and therefore entails risk that could in principle be diversified. The information ratio quantifies the trade-off between alpha and diversifiable risk.

We can summarize the preceding discussion with the following table, which shows the definition of the various performance measures and the situations in which each is the relevant performance measure.

Performance Measure	Definition	Application
Sharpe	$\dfrac{\text{Excess return}}{\text{Standard deviation}}$	When choosing among portfolios competing for the overall risky portfolio
Treynor	$\dfrac{\text{Excess return}}{\text{Beta}}$	When ranking many portfolios that will be mixed to form the overall risky portfolio
Information ratio	$\dfrac{\text{Alpha}}{\text{Residual standard deviation}}$	When evaluating a portfolio to be mixed with the benchmark portfolio

The Role of Alpha in Performance Measures

Given the central role of alpha in the index model, the CAPM, and other models of risk versus return, you may be surprised that we have not encountered a situation in which alpha is the criterion used to choose one fund over another. But don't conclude from this that alpha does not matter! With some algebra, we can derive the relationship between the performance measures discussed so far and the alpha of the portfolio. The following table shows these relationships. In all cases, you can see that it is impossible to outperform the passive market index unless the fund is expected to generate a positive alpha. Because superior performance requires positive alpha, it is the most widely used performance measure.

	Treynor (T_p)	Sharpe* (S_p)	Information Ratio
Relation to alpha	$\dfrac{E(r_p) - r_f}{\beta_p} = \dfrac{\alpha_p}{\beta_p} + T_M$	$\dfrac{E(r_p) - r_f}{\sigma_p} = \dfrac{\alpha_p}{\sigma_p} + \rho S_M$	$\dfrac{\alpha_p}{\sigma(e_p)}$
Improvement compared to market index	$T_p - T_M = \dfrac{\alpha_p}{\beta_p}$	$S_p - S_M = \dfrac{\alpha_p}{\sigma_p} - (1 - \rho)S_M$	$\dfrac{\alpha_p}{\sigma(e_p)}$

*ρ denotes the correlation coefficient between portfolio P and the market, and is less than 1.

However, while positive alpha is *necessary,* it is not sufficient to guarantee that a portfolio will outperform the index: Taking advantage of mispricing means departing from full diversification, which entails a cost in terms of nonsystematic risk. A mutual fund can achieve a positive alpha, yet, at the same time, increase its volatility enough that its Sharpe ratio will actually fall.

Implementing Performance Measurement: An Example

To illustrate some of the calculations underlying portfolio evaluation, let's look at the performance of portfolio P over the last 12 months. Table 24.2 shows its excess return in each month as well as those of an alternative portfolio Q, and the market index portfolio M. The bottom two rows in Table 24.2 provide the sample average and standard deviation of each portfolio. From these, and regressions of P and Q on M, we can compute the necessary performance statistics. These appear in Table 24.3.

The performance statistics in Table 24.3 show that portfolio Q is more aggressive than P, in the sense that its beta is significantly higher (1.40 versus .70). At the same time, its lower residual standard deviation shows that P is better diversified than Q (2.02%

The following performance measurement spreadsheet computes all the performance measures discussed in this section. You can see how relative ranking differs according to the criterion selected. This Excel model is available in Connect or through your course instructor.

Excel Questions

1. Examine the performance measures of the funds included in the spreadsheet. Rank performance and determine whether the rankings are consistent using each measure. What explains these results?

2. Which fund would you choose if you were considering investing the entire risky portion of your portfolio? What if you were considering adding a small position in one of these funds to a portfolio currently invested in the market index?

	A	B	C	D	E	F	G	H	I	J	K
1	Performance Measurement							LEGEND			
2								Enter data			
3								Value calculated			
4								See comment			
5											
6					Non-						
7		Average	Standard	Beta	systematic	Sharpe's	Treynor's	Jensen's	M2	T2	Information
8	Fund	Return	Deviation	Coefficient	Risk	Measure	Measure	Measure	Measure	Measure	Ratio
9	Alpha	28.00%	27.00%	1.7000	5.00%	0.8148	0.1294	−0.0180	−0.0015	−0.0106	−0.3600
10	Omega	31.00%	26.00%	1.6200	6.00%	0.9615	0.1543	0.0232	0.0235	0.0143	0.3867
11	Omicron	22.00%	21.00%	0.8500	2.00%	0.7619	0.1882	0.0410	−0.0105	0.0482	2.0500
12	Millennium	40.00%	33.00%	2.5000	27.00%	1.0303	0.1360	−0.0100	0.0352	−0.0040	−0.0370
13	Big Value	15.00%	13.00%	0.9000	3.00%	0.6923	0.1000	−0.0360	−0.0223	−0.0400	−1.2000
14	Momentum Watcher	29.00%	24.00%	1.4000	16.00%	0.9583	0.1643	0.0340	0.0229	0.0243	0.2125
15	Big Potential	15.00%	11.00%	0.5500	1.50%	0.8182	0.1636	0.0130	−0.0009	0.0236	0.8667
16	S & P Index Return	20.00%	17.00%	1.0000	0.00%	0.8235	0.1400	0.0000	0.0000	0.0000	0.0000
17	T-Bill Return	6.00%		0.0000							
18											
19	Ranking By Sharpe's Measure				Non-						
20		Average	Standard	Beta	systematic	Sharpe's	Treynor's	Jensen's	M2	T2	Information
21	Fund	Return	Deviation	Coefficient	Risk	Measure	Measure	Measure	Measure	Measure	Ratio

Table 24.2

Excess returns for portfolios P and Q and the market index M over 12 months

Month	Portfolio P	Alternative Q	Index M
1	3.58%	2.81%	2.20%
2	−4.91	−1.15	−8.41
3	6.51	2.53	3.27
4	11.13	37.09	14.41
5	8.78	12.88	7.71
6	9.38	39.08	14.36
7	−3.66	−8.84	−6.15
8	5.56	0.83	2.74
9	−7.72	0.85	−15.27
10	7.76	12.09	6.49
11	−4.01	−5.68	−3.13
12	0.78	−1.77	1.41
Average	2.77	7.56	1.64
Standard deviation	6.45	15.55	8.84

Table 24.3

Performance statistics

	Portfolio P	Portfolio Q	Portfolio M
Sharpe ratio	0.43	0.49	0.19
M^2	2.16	2.66	0.00
SCL regression statistics			
Alpha	1.63	5.26	0.00
Beta	0.70	1.40	1.00
Treynor	3.97	5.38	1.64
T^2	2.34	3.74	0.00
$\sigma(e)$	2.02	9.81	0.00
Information ratio	0.81	0.54	0.00
R-square	0.91	0.64	1.00

Table 24.3

Performance statistics

versus 9.81%). Both portfolios outperformed the benchmark market index, as is evident from their higher Sharpe ratios (and thus positive M^2) and their positive alphas.

Which portfolio is more attractive based on reported performance? If P or Q represents the entire investment fund, Q would be preferable on the basis of its higher Sharpe measure (.49 vs. .43) and better M^2 (2.66% vs. 2.16%). For the second scenario, where P and Q are competing for a role as one of a number of subportfolios, Q also dominates because its Treynor measure is higher (5.38 vs. 3.97). However, as an active portfolio to be mixed with the index portfolio, P is preferred because its information ratio [IR $= \alpha/\sigma(e)$] is higher (.81 vs. .54). Thus, the example illustrates that the right way to evaluate a portfolio depends in large part on how the portfolio fits into the investor's overall investment plan.

This analysis is based on 12 months of data only, a period too short to lend statistical significance to the conclusions. Nevertheless, the analysis illustrates what one might wish to do with more extensive data. A model that calculates these performance measures is available in Connect.

Realized Returns versus Expected Returns

When evaluating a portfolio, the evaluator knows neither the portfolio manager's original expectations nor whether those expectations made sense. One can only observe performance after the fact and hope that the inherent "noise" in investment outcomes does not obscure true underlying ability. To avoid mistaken inferences, we have to determine the "significance level" of a performance measure to know whether it reliably indicates ability.

To illustrate, consider the portfolio manager Joe Dart. Suppose that his portfolio has provided an alpha of 20 basis points per month, an impressive 2.4% per year before compounding. Let us assume that the return distribution of Joe's portfolio has constant mean, beta, and alpha, a heroic assumption, but one that is in line with the usual treatment of performance measurement. Suppose that for the measurement period, Joe's portfolio beta is 1.2 and the monthly standard deviation of the residual (nonsystematic risk) is $\sigma(e) = .02$ (i.e., 2% per month). With a market index standard deviation of 6.5% per month (22.5% per year), Joe's portfolio systematic variance is

$$\beta^2 \sigma_M^2 = 1.2^2 \times 6.5^2 = 60.84$$

and hence the correlation coefficient between his portfolio and the market index is

$$\rho = \left[\frac{\beta^2 \sigma_M^2}{\beta^2 \sigma_M^2 + \sigma^2(e)} \right]^{1/2} = \left[\frac{60.84}{60.84 + 4} \right]^{1/2} = .97$$

which shows that his portfolio is quite well diversified.

To estimate Joe's portfolio alpha from the security characteristic line (SCL), we regress portfolio excess returns on the market index. Suppose that we are in luck and (despite the underlying noise in investment returns) our regression estimates yield precisely the true parameters. That means that our SCL estimates for the N months are

$$\hat{\alpha} = .2\%, \quad \hat{\beta} = 1.2, \quad \hat{\sigma}(e) = 2\%$$

As outside evaluators who run such a regression, however, we do not know the true values. To assess whether the alpha estimate reflects true skill and not just luck due to statistical chance, we compute the t-statistic of the alpha estimate to determine whether we are justified in rejecting the hypothesis that Joe's true alpha is zero, that is, that he has no superior ability.

The standard error of the alpha estimate in the SCL regression is approximately

$$\hat{\sigma}(\alpha) = \frac{\hat{\sigma}(e)}{\sqrt{N}}$$

where N is the number of observations and $\hat{\sigma}(e)$ is the sample estimate of nonsystematic risk. The t-statistic for the estimate of alpha is then

$$t(\hat{\alpha}) = \frac{\hat{\alpha}}{\hat{\sigma}(\alpha)} = \frac{\hat{\alpha}\sqrt{N}}{\hat{\sigma}(e)} \tag{24.3}$$

Suppose that we require a significance level of 5% to reject the null hypothesis. With a large number of observations, this requires a $t(\hat{\alpha})$ value of at least 1.96. With $\hat{\alpha} = .2$ and $\hat{\sigma}(e) = 2$ we solve Equation 24.3 for N and find that

$$1.96 = \frac{.2\sqrt{N}}{2}$$

$$N = 384 \text{ months}$$

or 32 years!

What have we shown? Here is an analyst who has very substantial ability. The example is biased in his favor in the sense that we have assumed away statistical complications. Nothing changes in the parameters over a long period of time. Furthermore, the sample period "behaves" perfectly. Regression estimates are all perfect. Still, it will take Joe's entire working career to get to the point where statistics will confirm his true ability. We have to conclude that even moderate levels of statistical noise make performance evaluation extremely difficult in practice.

Now add to the imprecision of performance estimates the fact that the typical tenure of a fund manager is generally less than 5 years. By the time you are lucky enough to find a fund whose historic superior performance you are confident of, its manager is likely ready to move, or has already moved elsewhere. The nearby box explores this topic further.

✔ Concept Check **24.3**

Suppose an analyst has a measured alpha of .2% with a standard error of 2%, as in our example. What is the probability that the positive alpha is due to luck of the draw and that true ability is zero?

Should You Follow Your Fund Manager?

The whole idea of investing in a mutual fund is to leave the stock and bond picking to the professionals. But frequently, events don't turn out quite as expected—the manager resigns, gets transferred, or dies. A big part of the investor's decision to buy a managed fund is based on the manager's record, so changes like these can come as an unsettling surprise.

There are no rules about what happens in the wake of a manager's departure. It turns out, however, that there is strong evidence to suggest that a manager's real contribution to fund performance is highly overrated. For example, research company Morningstar compared funds that experienced management changes between 1990 and 1995 with those that kept the same managers. In the five years ending in June 2000, the top-performing funds of the previous five years tended to keep beating their peers—despite losing any fund managers. Those funds that performed badly in the first half of the 1990s continued to do badly, regardless of management changes. While mutual fund management companies will undoubtedly continue to create star managers and tout their past records, investors should stay focused on fund performance.

Funds are promoted on their managers' track records, which normally span a three- to five-year period. But performance data that goes back only a few years is hardly a valid measure of talent. To be statistically sound, evidence of a manager's track record needs to span, at a minimum, 10 years or more.

The mutual fund industry may look like a merry-go-round of managers, but that shouldn't worry most investors. Many mutual funds are designed to go through little or no change when a manager leaves. That is because, according to a strategy designed to reduce volatility and succession worries, mutual funds are managed by teams of stock pickers, who each run a portion of the assets, rather than by a solo manager with co-captains. Meanwhile, even so-called star managers are nearly always surrounded by researchers and analysts, who can play as much of a role in performance as the manager who gets the headlines.

Don't underestimate the breadth and depth of a fund company's "managerial bench." The larger, established investment companies generally have a large pool of talent to draw on. They are also well aware that investors are prone to depart from a fund when a managerial change occurs.

Lastly, for investors who worry about management changes, there is a solution: index funds. These mutual funds buy stocks and bonds that track a benchmark index like the S&P 500 rather than relying on star managers to actively pick securities. In this case, it doesn't really matter if the manager leaves. Most importantly, index fund investors are not charged the steep fees that are needed to pay star management salaries.

Source: Shauna Carther, "Should You Follow Your Fund Manager?" *Investopedia.com,* March 3, 2010. Provided by Forbes.

24.2 Style Analysis

The index model regression can be viewed as a way to measure and describe facets of a portfolio manager's investment style. Portfolios with high betas are called highly cyclical or aggressive because they are very responsive to economywide developments. Low beta portfolios are described as defensive. Multifactor models generalize this idea, describing the portfolio's exposure to several risk factors or segments of the market. Each of these exposures can be viewed as an implicit sort of asset allocation decision.

Style analysis was introduced by Nobel laureate William Sharpe as a tool to systematically measure the exposures of managed portfolios.[9] The popularity of the concept was aided by a well-known study[10] concluding that 91.5% of the variation in returns of 82 mutual funds could be explained by the funds' asset allocation to bills, bonds, and stocks. While later studies have taken issue with the exact interpretation of these results, there is widespread agreement that asset allocation is responsible for a high proportion of the variation across funds in investment performance.

Sharpe's idea was to regress fund returns on indexes representing a range of asset classes. The regression coefficient on each index would then measure the fund's

[9]William F. Sharpe, "Asset Allocation: Management Style and Performance Evaluation," *Journal of Portfolio Management,* Winter 1992, pp. 7–19.

[10]Gary Brinson, Brian Singer, and Gilbert Beebower, "Determinants of Portfolio Performance," *Financial Analysts Journal,* May/June 1991.

Table 24.4

Style analysis for Fidelity's
Magellan Fund

Style Portfolio	Regression Coefficient
T-bill	0
Small cap	0
Medium cap	35
Large cap	61
High P/E (growth)	5
Medium P/E	0
Low P/E (value)	0
Total	100
R-square	97.5

Source: Authors' calculations. Return data for Magellan obtained from **finance.yahoo.com/funds** and return data for style portfolios obtained from the Web page of Professor Kenneth French: **mba.tuck .dartmouth.edu/pages/faculty/ken.french/data_library.html.**

implicit allocation to that "style." Because funds are barred from short positions, the regression coefficients are constrained to be either zero or positive and to sum to 100%, so as to represent a complete asset allocation. The *R*-square of the regression would then measure the percentage of return variability attributable to style choice rather than security selection. The intercept measures the average return from security selection of the fund portfolio. It therefore tracks the average success of security selection over the sample period.

To illustrate Sharpe's approach, we use monthly returns on Fidelity Magellan's Fund during the famous manager Peter Lynch's tenure between October 1986 and September 1991, with results shown in Table 24.4. While seven asset classes are included in this analysis (of which six are represented by stock indexes and one is the T-bill alternative), the regression coefficients are positive for only three, namely, large capitalization stocks, medium cap stocks, and high P/E (growth) stocks. These portfolios alone explain 97.5% of the variance of Magellan's returns. In other words, a tracking portfolio made up of the three style portfolios, with weights as given in Table 24.4, would explain the vast majority of Magellan's variation in monthly performance. We conclude that the fund returns are well represented by three style portfolios.

The proportion of return variability *not* explained by asset allocation can be attributed to security selection within asset classes, as well as timing that shows up as periodic changes in allocation. For Magellan, residual variability was $100 - 97.5 = 2.5\%$. This sort of result is commonly interpreted as evidence against the importance of security selection, but such a conclusion misses the important role of the intercept in this regression. (The *R*-square of the regression can be 100%, and yet the intercept can be positive due to consistently superior stock selection.) For Magellan, the intercept was 32 basis points per month, providing a cumulative abnormal return over the 5-year period of 19.19%. The superior performance of Magellan in this period is displayed in Figure 24.4, which plots the combined impact of the intercept plus monthly residuals relative to the tracking portfolio composed of the individual style portfolios. Except for the period surrounding the crash of October 1987, Magellan's return consistently increased relative to the benchmark portfolio.

Style analysis provides an alternative to performance evaluation based on the security market line (SML) of the CAPM. The SML uses only one comparison portfolio, the broad

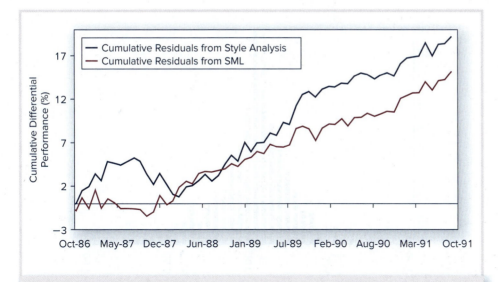

Figure 24.4 Fidelity Magellan Fund cumulative return difference: Fund versus style benchmark and fund versus SML benchmark

Source: Authors' calculations.

market index, whereas style analysis more freely constructs a tracking portfolio from a number of specialized indexes. To compare the two approaches, the security characteristic line (SCL) of Magellan was estimated by regressing its excess return on the excess return of the broad market index composed of all NYSE, AMEX, and NASDAQ stocks. The beta estimate for Magellan was 1.11 and the R-square of the regression was .99. The alpha value (intercept) of this regression was an impressive 25 basis points per month, reflected in a cumulative abnormal return of 15.19% for the period.

How can we explain the higher R-square of the regression with only one factor (the market index) relative to the style regression, which deploys six stock indexes? The answer is that style analysis imposes extra constraints on the regression coefficients: It forces them to be positive and to sum to 1.0. This "neat" representation may not be consistent with actual portfolio weights that are constantly changing over time.

So which representation better gauges Magellan's performance over the period? There is no clear-cut answer. The SML benchmark is a better representation of performance relative to the theoretically prescribed passive portfolio, that is, the broadest market index available. On the other hand, style analysis reveals the strategy that most closely tracks the fund's activity and measures performance relative to this strategy. If the strategy revealed by the style analysis method is consistent with the one stated in the fund prospectus, then the performance relative to this strategy is the correct measure of the fund's success.

Figure 24.5 shows the frequency distribution of average residuals across 636 mutual funds from Sharpe's style analysis. The distribution has the familiar bell shape with a slightly negative mean of −.074% per month. This should remind you of Figure 11.7, where we presented the frequency distribution of CAPM alphas for a large sample of mutual funds. As in Sharpe's study, these risk-adjusted returns plot as a bell-shaped curve with a slightly negative mean.

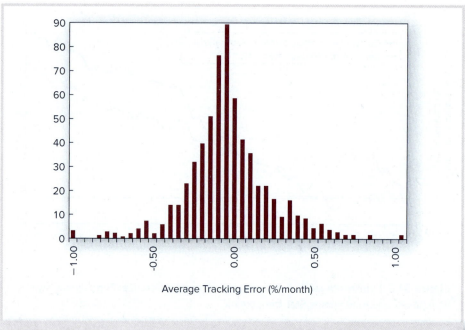

Figure 24.5 Average tracking error for 636 mutual funds, 1985–1989

Source: William F. Sharpe, "Asset Allocation: Management Style and Performance Evaluation," *Journal of Portfolio Management,* Winter 1992, pp. 7–19.

24.3 Performance Measurement with Changing Portfolio Composition

We saw in Section 24.1 that the volatility of stock returns requires a very long observation period to determine performance levels with any precision, even if portfolio returns are distributed with constant mean and variance. Imagine how this problem is compounded when portfolio return distributions are constantly changing.

It may be acceptable to assume that the return distributions of passive strategies have constant mean and variance when the measurement interval is not too long. However, return distributions of active strategies change by design, as the portfolio manager updates the portfolio in accordance with ongoing financial analysis. In such a case, estimating various statistics from a sample period assuming a constant mean and variance may lead to substantial errors. Here is an example.

Example 24.3   Changing Portfolio Risk

Suppose that the Sharpe measure of the market index is .4. In the first year, the portfolio manager executes a low-risk strategy and realizes an (annualized) mean excess return of 1% and standard deviation of 2%. This makes for a Sharpe ratio of .5, which beats the passive strategy. Over the next year, the manager decides that a *high*-risk strategy is optimal and achieves an annual mean excess return of 9% and standard deviation of 18%. Here, again, the Sharpe ratio is .5. Over the 2-year period, our manager consistently maintains a better-than-passive Sharpe measure.

Figure 24.6 shows a pattern of (annualized) quarterly returns that are consistent with our description of the manager's strategy of two years. In the first four quarters the excess returns are −1%, 3%, −1%, and 3%, making for an average of 1% and standard deviation of 2%. In the next four quarters the excess returns are −9%, 27%, −9%, and 27%, making for an average of 9% and standard deviation of 18%. Thus *both* years exhibit a Sharpe measure of .5. However, the mean and standard deviation of the eight quarterly returns are 5% and 13.42%, respectively, making for a Sharpe measure of only .37, apparently inferior to the passive strategy!

What happened in Example 24.3? The shift of the mean from the first four quarters to the next was not recognized as a shift in strategy. Instead, the difference in mean returns in the two years added to the *appearance* of volatility in portfolio returns. The active strategy with shifting means appears riskier than it really is and biases the estimate of the Sharpe measure downward. We conclude that for actively managed portfolios it is necessary to keep track of portfolio composition and changes in portfolio mean and risk. We will see another example of this problem in the next section, which deals with market timing.

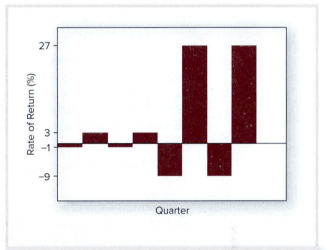

Figure 24.6 Portfolio returns: Returns in last four quarters are more variable than in the first four

Performance Manipulation and the Morningstar Risk-Adjusted Rating

We just saw how time-varying risk and return can distort conventional performance evaluation. The problem can be worse when managers, whose compensation depends on performance, try to game the system. Managers observe how returns unfold over the course of the evaluation period and can adjust portfolio strategies (e.g., either increasing or decreasing risk) in an attempt to manipulate performance measures. Once they do so, portfolio strategy in the latter part of the evaluation period comes to depend on performance in the beginning of the period.

Ingersoll, Spiegel, Goetzmann, and Welch[11] show how the conventional performance measures covered in this chapter can be manipulated. While the details of their model are challenging, the logic is straightforward, and we can illustrate using the Sharpe ratio.

As we saw when analyzing capital allocation (Chapter 6), investment in the risk-free asset (lending or borrowing) does not affect the Sharpe ratio of the portfolio. Put differently, the Sharpe ratio is invariant to the fraction y invested in the risky portfolio rather than in the risk-free asset. The reason is that excess returns are proportional to y and therefore so are both the risk premium and standard deviation, leaving the Sharpe ratio unchanged. But what if y changes during a period?

[11]Jonathan Ingersoll, Matthew Spiegel, William Goetzmann, and Ivo Welch, "Portfolio Performance Manipulation and Manipulation Proof Performance Measures," *Review of Financial Studies* 20 (2007).

Imagine a manager already partway into an evaluation period. While realized excess returns (average return, SD, and Sharpe ratio) are now known for the first part of the evaluation period, the distribution of the remaining future rates is still not determined. The overall Sharpe ratio will be some (complicated) average of the known Sharpe ratio in the first leg and the yet unknown ratio in the second leg of the evaluation period. Increasing leverage during the second leg will increase the influence of the second period on the full-period average performance because leverage will amplify returns, both good and bad. Therefore, managers will wish to increase leverage in the latter part of the period if early returns are poor. Conversely, good first-part performance calls for deleveraging to increase the weight on the initial period. With an extremely good first leg, a manager will shift almost the entire portfolio to the risk-free asset. This strategy induces a (negative) correlation between returns in the first and second legs of the evaluation period.

Investors lose, on average, from this strategy. Arbitrary variation in leverage (and therefore risk) is utility-reducing. It benefits managers only because it allows them to adjust the implicit weighting scheme of the two subperiods over the full evaluation period after observing their initial performance. Hence, investors would like to prohibit or at least eliminate the incentive to pursue this strategy.

Unfortunately, as Ibbotson et al. show, only one performance measure is impossible to manipulate. This is the Morningstar risk-adjusted return (MRAR). Amazingly, Morningstar was not even aiming at a manipulation proof performance measure when it developed its MRAR—it was simply attempting to accommodate investors who wanted a performance measure consistent with constant relative risk aversion. Its measure is defined as follows:

$$\text{Morningstar risk-adjusted return: MRAR}(\gamma) = \left[\frac{1}{T}\sum_{t=1}^{T}\left(\frac{1+r_t}{1+r_{ft}}\right)^{-\gamma}\right]^{\frac{12}{\gamma}} - 1$$

The rating is a sort of harmonic average of excess returns, where $t = 1,\ldots, T$ are monthly observations, and γ measures investor risk aversion. For mutual funds, Morningstar uses $\gamma = 2$, which is considered a reasonable value for an average retail client.[12] The MRAR can be interpreted as the risk-free equivalent excess return of the portfolio for an investor with risk aversion measured by γ.

Panel A of Figure 24.7 shows a scatter of Sharpe ratios versus MRAR of 100 portfolios based on a statistical simulation. Thirty-six excess returns were randomly generated for each portfolio, all with an annual expected return of 7% and SDs varying from 10% to 30%. The correlation between the Sharpe and Morningstar measures was .94, suggesting that in the absence of manipulation, Sharpe ratios track MRAR quite well. Indeed, the scatter is pretty tight along a straight line with a slope of 0.19.

Panel B of Figure 24.7 illustrates the effect of manipulation when one leverage change is allowed after initial performance is observed, specifically in the middle of the 36-month evaluation period.[13] The effect of manipulation is evident from the extreme-value portfolios. When the initial MRAR is high, the switch toward less risky investments preserves

---

[12]The MRAR measure is the *certainty-equivalent geometric average excess return* derived from a more sophisticated utility function than the mean-variance function we used in Chapter 6. The utility function is consistent with *constant relative risk aversion (CRRA)*. When investors have CRRA, their capital allocation (the fraction of the portfolio placed in risk-free versus risky assets) does not change with wealth. The coefficient of risk aversion is: $A = 1 + \gamma$. When $\gamma = 0$ (equivalently, $A = 1$), the utility function is just the geometric average of gross excess returns:

$$\text{MRAR}(0) = \left[\prod_{t=1}^{T}(1 + R_t)\right]^{\frac{12}{T}} - 1$$

[13]To keep the exercise realistic, leverage ratios were capped at 2 (a debt-to-equity ratio of 1.0).

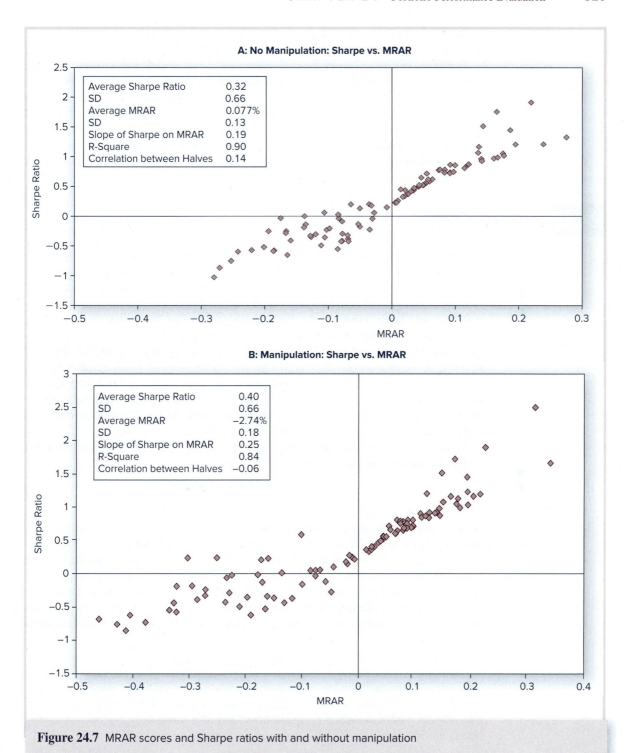

Figure 24.7 MRAR scores and Sharpe ratios with and without manipulation

the first-half high Sharpe ratios that otherwise would be at risk of being reversed in the second half. For initially poor MRARs, leverage ratios are increased, and we see two effects. First, MRARs look worse because of cases where the high leverage backfired and worsened the MRARs (points move to the left). In contrast, Sharpe ratios look better than in Panel A. Indeed, the scatter diagram clearly flattens out in the region of negative performance, showing that *measured* Sharpe ratios for poor performance outcomes are tempered.

The statistics in the box of Panel B quantify the improvement of measured Sharpe ratios; in contrast, MRARs clearly deteriorated from a slight positive value to a certainty-equivalent of −2.74% per year! As predicted, the correlation between average returns in the first and second legs of the period changes from positive to negative. All this happened because of an average increase in leverage from 1.0 to 1.39. Given these results, we conclude that performance manipulation may be an important issue in practice, especially for managers who have the most discretion over investment policy (e.g., hedge fund managers).

24.4 Market Timing

In its pure form, market timing involves shifting funds between a market-index portfolio and a safe asset, depending on whether the market index is expected to outperform the safe asset. In practice, most managers do not shift fully between T-bills and the market. How can we account for partial shifts into the market when it is expected to perform well?

To simplify, suppose that an investor holds only the market-index portfolio and T-bills. If the weight of the market were constant, say, .6, then portfolio beta would also be constant, and the SCL would plot as a straight line with slope .6, as in Figure 24.8, Panel A. If, however, the investor could correctly time the market and shift funds into it in periods when the market does well, the SCL would plot as in Figure 24.8, Panel B. If bull and bear markets can be predicted, the investor will shift more into the market when the market is more likely to go up. The portfolio beta and the slope of the SCL will be higher when r_M is higher, resulting in the curved line that appears in Figure 24.8, Panel B.

Treynor and Mazuy were the first to propose estimating such a line by adding a squared term to the usual linear index model:[14]

$$r_P - r_f = a + b(r_M - r_f) + c(r_M - r_f)^2 + e_P$$

where r_P is the portfolio return, and a, b, and c are estimated by regression analysis. If c turns out to be positive, we have evidence of timing ability, because this last term will make the characteristic line steeper as $r_M - r_f$ is larger. Treynor and Mazuy estimated this equation for a number of mutual funds, but found little evidence of timing ability.

A similar but simpler methodology was proposed by Henriksson and Merton.[15] These authors suggested that the beta of the portfolio takes only two values: a large value if the market is expected to do well and a small value otherwise. Under this scheme the portfolio characteristic line appears as shown in Figure 24.8, Panel C. Such a line appears in regression form as

$$r_P - r_f = a + b(r_M - r_f) + c(r_M - r_f)D + e_P$$

where D is a dummy variable that equals 1 when $r_M > r_f$ and zero otherwise. Hence the beta of the portfolio is b in bear markets and $b + c$ in bull markets. Again, a positive value of c implies market timing ability. They also found little evidence of market timing ability.

---

[14]Jack L. Treynor and Kay Mazuy, "Can Mutual Funds Outguess the Market?" *Harvard Business Review* 43 (July–August 1966).

[15]Roy D. Henriksson and R. C. Merton, "On Market Timing and Investment Performance. II. Statistical Procedures for Evaluating Forecast Skills," *Journal of Business* 54 (October 1981).

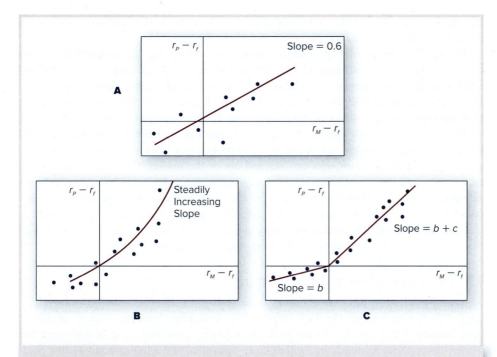

Figure 24.8 Characteristic lines. **Panel A:** No market timing, beta is constant.
Panel B: Market timing, beta increases with expected market excess return.
Panel C: Market timing with only two values of beta.

To illustrate how you might implement a test for market timing, return to Table 24.2, which contains 12 months of excess returns for two managed portfolios, P and Q, and the market index, M. Regress the excess returns of each portfolio on the excess returns of M and the square of these returns as in the following specifications:

$$r_P - r_f = a_P + b_P(r_M - r_f) + c_P(r_M - r_f)^2 + e_P$$
$$r_Q - r_f = a_Q + b_Q(r_M - r_f) + c_Q(r_M - r_f)^2 + e_Q$$

You will derive the following statistics. The numbers in parentheses are included for comparison: They are the regression estimates from the single variable regression reported in Table 24.3.

	Portfolio	
Estimate	**P**	**Q**
Alpha (a)	1.77 (1.63)	−2.29 (5.26)
Beta (b)	0.70 (0.70)	1.10 (1.40)
Timing (c)	0.00	0.10
R-square	0.91 (0.91)	0.98 (0.64)

Portfolio P shows no evidence of attempted timing: Its timing coefficient, c, is estimated to be zero. It is not clear whether this is because no attempt was made at timing or because any effort to time the market was in vain and served only to increase portfolio variance unnecessarily.

The results for portfolio Q, however, reveal that timing has, in all likelihood, been attempted. Here the coefficient, c, is positive, with an estimated value of .10. The evidence thus suggests successful timing, offset by unsuccessful stock selection (negative a). Note that the estimate of alpha, a, is now -2.29% as opposed to the 5.26% estimate derived from the regression equation that did not allow for the possibility of timing activity.

This example illustrates the inadequacy of conventional performance evaluation techniques that assume constant mean returns and constant risk. The market timer constantly shifts beta and mean return, moving into and out of the market. So market timing presents another instance in which portfolio composition and risk change over time, complicating the effort to evaluate performance. Whereas the expanded regression captures this possibility, the simple SCL does not. The important point for performance evaluation is that expanded regressions can capture many of the effects of portfolio composition change that would confound more conventional mean-variance measures.

The Potential Value of Market Timing

Suppose we define perfect market timing as the ability to tell (with certainty) at the beginning of each year whether the S&P 500 portfolio will outperform the strategy of rolling over 1-month T-bills throughout the year. Accordingly, at the beginning of each year, the market timer shifts all funds into either cash equivalents (T-bills) or equities (the S&P portfolio), whichever is predicted to do better. Beginning with $1 on December 31, 1926, how would the perfect timer end an 89-year experiment on December 31, 2015, in comparison with investors who kept their funds in either equity or T-bills for the entire period?

Table 24.5 presents summary statistics for each of the three passive strategies, computed from the historical annual returns of bills and equities. From the returns on stocks and bills, we calculate wealth indexes of the all-bills and all-equity investments and show terminal values for these investors at the end of 2015. The return for the perfect timer in each year is the *maximum* of the return on stocks and the return on bills.

The first row in Table 24.5 shows the terminal value of investing $1 in bills over the 89 years (1926–2015) is $20, while the terminal value of the same initial investment in equities is $3,997. We argued in Chapter 5 that as impressive as the difference in terminal values is, it is best interpreted as no more than fair compensation for the risk borne by equity investors. As we've already seen, the *annual* difference in returns is just about 8%,

Table 24.5

Performance of bills, equities, and perfect (annual) market timers. Initial investment = $1.

Strategy	Bills	Equities	Perfect Timer
Terminal value	$20	$3,997	$534,649
Arithmetic average	3.47%	11.53%	16.54%
Standard deviation	3.15%	20.27%	13.56%
Geometric average	3.42%	9.77%	15.97%
Maximum	14.71%	57.35%	57.35%
Minimum[†]	−0.02%	−44.04%	0.00%
Skew	1.00	−0.40	0.74
Kurtosis	0.93	0.03	−0.12
LPSD	0.00%	13.28%	0.00%

[†]A negative rate on "bills" was observed in 1940. The Treasury security used in the data series in these early years was actually not a T-bill but a T-bond with 30 days to maturity.

which doesn't seem as dramatic. Notice that the standard deviation of the all-equity investor was a hefty 20.27%. This is also why the geometric average of stocks for the period is "only" 9.77%, compared with the arithmetic average of 11.53%. (The difference between the two averages increases with volatility.)

Now observe that the terminal value of the perfect timer is $534,649, a 133-fold increase over the already large terminal value of the all-equity strategy! In fact, this result is even better than it looks, because the return to the market timer is truly risk-free. This is the classic case where a large standard deviation (13.56%) has nothing to do with risk. Because the timer never delivers a return below the risk-free rate, the standard deviation is a measure of *good* surprises only.

The positive skew of the timer's distribution (.74, compared with the negative skew of equities) is a manifestation of the fact that the extreme values are all positive. Other indications of this stellar performance are the minimum and maximum returns—the minimum return for the timer equals zero (in 1940) and the maximum return, 57.35%, is that of equities (in 1933). All negative returns on equities (as low as −44% in 1931) were avoided by the timer. Finally, another clear indication of the advantage of the perfect timer compared to the all-equity portfolio is provided by the lower partial standard deviation, LPSD.[16] The LPSD, which is a measure of the typical amplitude of any return shortfall compared to T-bills, is 13.28% for the all-equity portfolio, but it is necessarily zero for the perfect timer (who always performs *at least* as well as bills).

Valuing Market Timing as a Call Option

The key to valuing market timing ability is to recognize that perfect foresight is equivalent to holding a call option on the equity portfolio—but without having to pay for it! The perfect timer invests 100% in either the safe asset or the equity portfolio, whichever will provide the higher return. The rate of return is *at least* the risk-free rate. This is shown in Figure 24.9.

To see the value of information as an option, suppose that the market index currently is at S_0 and that a call option on the index has an exercise price of $X = S_0(1 + r_f)$. If the market outperforms bills over the coming period, S_T will exceed X; otherwise it will be less than X. Now look at the payoff to a portfolio consisting of this option and S_0 dollars invested in bills:

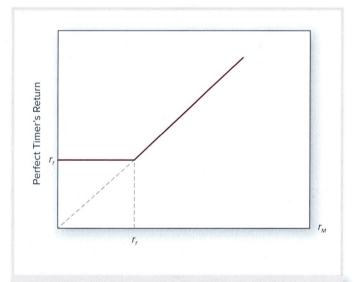

Figure 24.9 Rate of return of a perfect market timer as a function of the rate of return on the market index.

	$S_T < X$	$S_T \geq X$
Bills	$S_0(1 + r_f)$	$S_0(1 + r_f)$
Call	0	$S_T - X$
Total	$S_0(1 + r_f)$	S_T

The portfolio pays the risk-free return when the market is bearish (i.e., the market return is

---

[16]The LPSD is sometimes based on the average squared deviation below the mean. Because the threshold performance in this application is the risk-free rate, we calculate the LPSD for this discussion by taking squared deviations from that rate and the observations are conditional on being below that threshold. It ignores the number of such events.

less than the risk-free rate), and it pays the market return when the market is bullish and outperforms bills. Such a portfolio is a perfect market timer.[17]

Because the ability to predict the better-performing investment is equivalent to acquiring a (free) call option on the market and adding it to a position in bills, we can use option-pricing models to assign a dollar value to perfect timing ability. This value would constitute the fair fee that a perfect timer could charge investors for its services. Placing a value on perfect timing also enables us to assign value to less-than-perfect timers.

The exercise price of the perfect-timer call option on $1 of the equity portfolio is the final value of the T-bill investment. Using continuous compounding, this is $1 \times e^{rT}$. When you use this exercise price in the Black-Scholes formula for the value of the call option, the formula simplifies considerably to[18]

$$\text{MV(Perfect timer per \$ of assets)} = C = 2N(\tfrac{1}{2}\,\sigma_M\,\sqrt{T}) - 1 \qquad \textbf{(24.4)}$$

We have so far assumed annual forecasts, that is, $T = 1$ year. Using $T = 1$, and the standard deviation of stocks from Table 24.5, 20.27%, we compute the value of this call option as 8.07 cents, or 8.07% of the value of the equity portfolio.[19]

If a timer could make the correct choice every month instead of every year, the value of the forecasts would dramatically increase. Of course, making perfect forecasts more frequently requires even better powers of prediction. As the frequency of such perfect predictions increases without bound, the value of the services will increase without bound as well.

Suppose the perfect timer could make perfect forecasts every month. In this case, each forecast would be for a shorter interval, and the value of each individual forecast would be lower, but there would be 12 times as many forecasts, each of which could be valued as another call option. The net result is a big increase in total value. With monthly predictions, the value of each call will be $2N(\tfrac{1}{2} \times .2027 \times \sqrt{1/12}) - 1 = .0233$. Using a monthly T-bill rate of 2%/12, the present value of a 1-year string of such monthly calls, each worth $.0233, is $.28. Thus, the annual value of the monthly perfect timer is 28 cents on the dollar, more than three times as valuable as the 8.07 cent value of an annual timer.

The Value of Imperfect Forecasting

A weather forecaster in Tucson, Arizona, who *always* predicts no rain may be right 90% of the time. But a high success rate for a "stopped-clock" strategy is not evidence of forecasting ability. Similarly, the appropriate measure of market forecasting ability is not the overall proportion of correct forecasts. If the market is up two days out of three and a forecaster always predicts market advance, the two-thirds success rate does not imply forecasting ability. We need to examine the proportion of bull markets ($r_M < r_f$) correctly forecast *and* the proportion of bear markets ($r_M > r_f$) correctly forecast.

If we call P_1 the proportion of the correct forecasts of bull markets and P_2 the proportion for bear markets, then $P_1 + P_2 - 1$ is the correct measure of timing ability. For example, a

---

[17]The analogy between market timing and call options, and the valuation formulas that follow from it, were developed in Robert C. Merton, "On Market Timing and Investment Performance: An Equilibrium Theory of Value for Market Forecasts," *Journal of Business,* July 1981.

[18]Substitute $S_0 = \$1$ for the current value of the equity portfolio and $X = \$1 \times e^{rT}$ in Equation 21.1 of Chapter 21, and you will obtain Equation 24.4.

[19]This is less than the historical-average excess return of perfect timing shown in Table 24.5, reflecting the fact that the actual value of timing is sensitive to fat tails in the distribution of returns, whereas Black-Scholes assumes a log-normal distribution.

forecaster who always guesses correctly will have $P_1 = P_2 = 1$, and will show ability of $P_1 + P_2 - 1 = 1$ (100%). An analyst who always bets on a bear market will mispredict all bull markets ($P_1 = 0$), will correctly "predict" all bear markets ($P_2 = 1$), and will end up with timing ability of $P_1 + P_2 - 1 = 0$.

 Concept Check **24.4**

> What is the market timing score of someone who flips a fair coin to predict the market?

Merton shows that the value of imperfect market timing is equal to a portion of a call option. The value of an imperfect timer is simply the value of the perfect-timing call times our measure of timing ability, $P_1 + P_2 - 1$.[20]

$$\text{MV(Imperfect timer)} = (P_1 + P_2 - 1) \times C = (P_1 + P_2 - 1)[2N(\tfrac{1}{2}\sigma_M \sqrt{T}) - 1] \quad \textbf{(24.5)}$$

24.5   Performance Attribution Procedures

Rather than focus on risk-adjusted returns, practitioners often want simply to ascertain which decisions resulted in superior or inferior performance. Superior investment performance depends on an ability to be in the "right" securities at the right time. Such timing and selection ability may be considered broadly, such as being in equities as opposed to fixed-income securities when the stock market is performing well. Or it may be defined at a more detailed level, such as choosing the relatively better-performing stocks within a particular industry.

Portfolio managers continually make broad-brush asset allocation decisions as well as more detailed sector and security allocation decisions within asset classes. Performance attribution studies attempt to decompose overall performance into discrete components that may be identified with a particular level of the portfolio selection process.

Attribution analysis starts from the broadest asset allocation choices and progressively focuses on ever-finer details of portfolio choice. The difference between a managed portfolio's performance and that of a benchmark portfolio then may be expressed as the sum of the contributions to performance of a series of decisions made at the various levels of the portfolio construction process. For example, one common attribution system decomposes performance into three components: (1) broad asset market allocation choices across equity, fixed-income, and money markets; (2) industry (sector) choice within each market; and (3) security choice within each sector.

The attribution method explains the difference in returns between a managed portfolio, *P,* and a selected benchmark portfolio, *B,* called the **bogey.** The bogey is designed to measure the returns the portfolio manager would earn if he or she were to follow a completely passive strategy. "Passive" in this context has two attributes. First, it means that the allocation of funds across broad asset classes is set in accord with a notion of "usual," or neutral, allocation across sectors. This would be considered a passive asset-market allocation. Second, it means that *within* each asset class, the portfolio manager holds an indexed

---

[20]Notice that Equation 24.5 implies that an investor with a value of $P = 0$ who attempts to time the market would add zero value. The shifts across markets would be no better than a random decision concerning asset allocation.

portfolio, such as the S&P 500 index for the equity sector. In such a manner, the passive strategy used as a performance benchmark rules out asset allocation as well as security selection decisions. Any departure of the manager's return from the passive benchmark must be due to either asset allocation bets (departures from the neutral allocation across markets) or security selection bets (departures from the passive index within asset classes).

While we have already discussed in earlier chapters the justification for indexing within sectors, it is worth briefly explaining the determination of the neutral allocation of funds across the broad asset classes. Weights that are designated as "neutral" will depend on the risk tolerance of the investor and must be determined in consultation with the client. For example, risk-tolerant clients may place a large fraction of their portfolio in the equity market, perhaps directing the fund manager to set neutral weights of 75% equity, 15% bonds, and 10% cash equivalents. Any deviation from these weights must be justified by a belief that one or another market will either over- or underperform its usual risk–return profile. In contrast, more risk-averse clients may set neutral weights of 45%/35%/20% for the three markets. Therefore, their portfolios in normal circumstances will be exposed to less risk than that of the risk-tolerant client. Only intentional bets on market performance will result in departures from this profile.

Suppose that the universe of assets for the managed portfolio P and the bogey portfolio B includes n asset classes such as equities, bonds, and bills. For each asset class, a benchmark index portfolio is determined. The bogey's rate of return is therefore the weighted average of the indexed returns on each asset class with weights equal to the neutral portfolio proportions:

$$r_B = \sum_{i=1}^{n} w_{Bi} r_{Bi}$$

where w_{Bi} is the weight of the bogey in asset class i, and r_{Bi} is the return on the benchmark portfolio of that class.

The portfolio manager chooses weights in each asset class, w_{Pi}, based on his own capital market expectations and chooses a portfolio of securities within each class based on a valuation analysis. Each asset class earns r_{Pi} over the evaluation period, so the return of the managed portfolio is:

$$r_P = \sum_{i=1}^{n} w_{Pi} r_{Pi}$$

The difference between the two rates of return, therefore, is

$$r_P - r_B = \sum_{i=1}^{n} w_{Pi} r_{Pi} - \sum_{i=1}^{n} w_{Bi} r_{Bi} = \sum_{i=1}^{n} (w_{Pi} r_{Pi} - w_{Bi} r_{Bi}) \tag{24.6}$$

Each term in the summation of Equation 24.6 can be rewritten in a way that shows how asset allocation decisions versus security selection decisions contributed to overall performance. We decompose each term of the summation into two terms as follows. The terms we label as contribution from asset allocation and contribution from security selection in the following decomposition do in fact sum to the total contribution of each asset class to overall performance.

Contribution from asset allocation = Excess weight in asset class × Benchmark return =	$(w_{Pi} - w_{Bi})r_{Bi}$
+ Contribution from security selection = Weight in asset class × Excess return	$= w_{Pi}(r_{Pi} - r_{Bi})$
= Total contribution from asset class i	$= w_{Pi} r_{Pi} - w_{Bi} r_{Bi}$

The term on the top line measures the impact of asset allocation because it shows how deviations of the actual weight from the benchmark weight for that asset class added to or subtracted from total performance. The second term measures the impact of security selection because it shows how the manager's excess return *within* the asset class (compared to the benchmark return for that class) added to or subtracted from total performance. Figure 24.10 presents a graphical interpretation of the attribution of overall performance into security selection versus asset allocation.

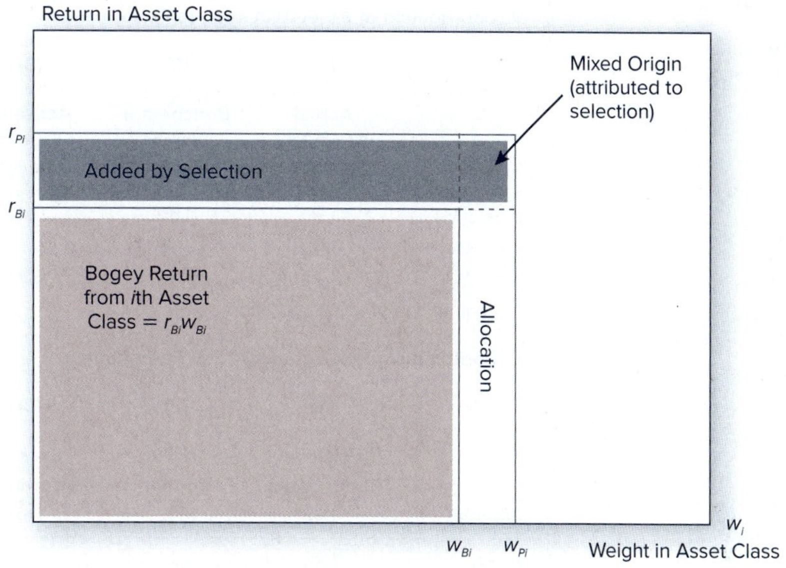

To illustrate, consider the attribution results for a hypothetical portfolio. The portfolio invests in stocks, bonds, and money market securities. An attribution analysis appears in Tables 24.6 through 24.9. The portfolio return over the month is 5.34%.

Figure 24.10 Performance attribution of *i*th asset class. Enclosed area indicates total rate of return.

In Table 24.6, the neutral weights have been set at 60% equity, 30% fixed income, and 10% cash (money market securities). The bogey portfolio, comprised of investments in each index with the 60/30/10 weights, returned 3.97%. The managed portfolio's measure of performance is positive and equal to its actual return less the return of the bogey: $5.34 - 3.97 = 1.37\%$. The next step is to allocate the 1.37% excess return to the separate decisions that contributed to it.

Asset Allocation Decisions

To isolate the effect of the manager's asset allocation choice, we measure the performance of a hypothetical portfolio that would have been invested in the indexes for each market with weights 70/7/23. This return measures the effect of the shift away from the benchmark

Table 24.6

Performance of the managed portfolio

Component	Benchmark Weight	Return of Index during Month (%)
	Bogey Performance and Excess Return	
Equity (S&P 500)	0.60	5.81
Bonds (Barclays Aggregate Index)	0.30	1.45
Cash (money market)	0.10	0.48

Bogey = $(0.60 \times 5.81) + (0.30 \times 1.45) + (0.10 \times 0.48) = 3.97\%$

Return of managed portfolio	5.34%	
− Return of bogey portfolio	3.97	
Excess return of managed portfolio	1.37%	

Table 24.7

Performance
attribution

A. Contribution of Asset Allocation to Performance

	(1)	(2)	(3)	(4)	(5) = (3) × (4)
Market	Actual Weight in Market	Benchmark Weight in Market	Active or Excess Weight	Index Return (%)	Contribution to Performance (%)
Equity	0.70	0.60	0.10	5.81	0.5810
Fixed-income	0.07	0.30	−0.23	1.45	−0.3335
Cash	0.23	0.10	0.13	0.48	0.0624
Contribution of asset allocation					0.3099

B. Contribution of Selection to Total Performance

	(1)	(2)	(3)	(4)	(5) = (3) × (4)
Market	Portfolio Performance (%)	Index Performance (%)	Excess Performance (%)	Portfolio Weight	Contribution (%)
Equity	7.28	5.81	1.47	0.70	1.03
Fixed-income	1.89	1.45	0.44	0.07	0.03
Contribution of selection within markets					1.06

60/30/10 weights without allowing for any effects attributable to active management of the securities selected within each market.

Superior performance relative to the bogey is achieved by overweighting investments in markets that turn out to perform well and by underweighting those in poorly performing markets. The contribution of asset allocation to superior performance equals the sum over all markets of the excess weight (sometimes called the *active weight* in the industry) in each market times the return of the index for each market.

Panel A of Table 24.7 demonstrates that asset allocation contributed 31 basis points to the portfolio's overall excess return of 137 basis points. The major factor contributing to superior performance in this month is the heavy weighting of the equity market in a month when the equity market has an excellent return of 5.81%.

Sector and Security Selection Decisions

If .31% of the excess performance (Table 24.7, Panel A) can be attributed to advantageous asset allocation *across* markets, the remaining 1.06% must be attributable to sector selection and security selection *within* each market. Table 24.7, Panel B, details the contribution of the managed portfolio's sector and security selection to total performance.

Panel B shows that the equity component of the managed portfolio has a return of 7.28% versus a return of 5.81% for the S&P 500. The fixed-income return is 1.89% versus 1.45% for the Barclays Aggregate Bond Index. The superior performance in both equity and fixed-income markets weighted by the portfolio proportions invested in each market sums to the 1.06% contribution to performance attributable to sector and security selection.

Table 24.8 documents the decisions that led to the superior equity market performance. The first three columns detail the allocation of funds within the equity market compared

The performance attribution spreadsheet develops the attribution analysis presented in this section. The model can be used to analyze the performance of mutual funds and other managed portfolios.

You can find this Excel model in Connect.

Excel Questions

1. What would happen to the contribution of asset allocation to overall performance if the actual weights had been 75/12/13 instead of 70/7/23? Explain your result.

2. What would happen to the contribution of security selection to overall performance if the actual return on the equity portfolio had been 6.81% instead of 5.81% and the return on the bond portfolio had been 0.45% instead of 1.45%? Explain your result.

	A	B	C	D	E	F
1	**Performance Attribution**					
2						
3						
4	**Bogey**					
5	**Portfolio**		**Benchmark**	**Return on**	**Portfolio**	
6	**Component**	**Index**	**Weight**	**Index**	**Return**	
7	Equity	S&P 500	0.60	5.8100%	3.4860%	
8	Bonds	Barclays Index	0.30	1.4500%	0.4350%	
9	Cash	Money Market	0.10	0.4800%	0.0480%	
10			Return on Bogey		3.9690%	
11						
12		**Managed**				
13		**Portfolio**	**Portfolio**	**Actual**	**Portfolio**	
14		**Component**	**Weight**	**Return**	**Return**	
15		Equity	0.70	5.8100%	5.0960%	
16		Bonds	0.07	1.4500%	0.1323%	
17		Cash	0.23	0.4800%	0.1104%	
18			Return on Managed		5.3387%	
19			Excess Return		1.3697%	

Sector	(1) Beginning of Month Weights (%)		(3) Active Weight (%)	(4) Sector Return (%)	(5) = (3) × (4) Sector Allocation Contribution
	Portfolio	S&P 500			
Basic materials	1.96	8.3	−6.34	6.9	−0.4375
Business services	7.84	4.1	3.74	7.0	0.2618
Capital goods	1.87	7.8	−5.93	4.1	−0.2431
Consumer cyclical	8.47	12.5	−4.03	8.8	0.3546
Consumer noncyclical	40.37	20.4	19.97	10.0	1.9970
Credit sensitive	24.01	21.8	2.21	5.0	0.1105
Energy	13.53	14.2	−0.67	2.6	−0.0174
Technology	1.95	10.9	−8.95	0.3	−0.0269
Total					1.2898

Table 24.8

Sector selection within the equity market

to their representation in the S&P 500. Column (4) shows the rate of return of each sector. The contribution of each sector's allocation presented in column (5) equals the product of the difference in the sector weight and the sector's performance.

Good performance (a positive contribution) derives from overweighting well-performing sectors such as consumer noncyclicals. The excess return of the equity component of the portfolio attributable to sector allocation alone is 1.29%. Table 24.7, Panel B, column (3), shows that the equity component of the portfolio outperformed the S&P 500 by 1.47%. We conclude that the effect of security selection *within* sectors must have contributed an additional 1.47% − 1.29%, or .18%, to the performance of the equity component of the portfolio.

A similar sector analysis can be applied to the fixed-income portion of the portfolio, but we do not show those results here.

Summing Up Component Contributions

In this particular month, all facets of the portfolio selection process were successful. Table 24.9 details the contribution of each aspect of performance. Asset allocation across the major security markets contributes 31 basis points. Sector and security allocation within those markets contributes 106 basis points, for total excess portfolio performance of 137 basis points.

The sector and security allocation of 106 basis points can be partitioned further. Sector allocation within the equity market results in excess performance of 129 basis points, and security selection within sectors contributes 18 basis points. (The total equity excess performance of 147 basis points is multiplied by the 70% weight in equity to obtain contribution to portfolio performance.) Similar partitioning could be done for the fixed-income sector.

 Concept Check **24.5**

a. Suppose the benchmark weights in Table 24.7 had been set at 70% equity, 25% fixed-income, and 5% cash equivalents. What would have been the contributions of the manager's asset allocation choices?

b. Suppose the S&P 500 return is 5%. Compute the new value of the manager's security selection choices.

Table 24.9

Portfolio attribution: summary

		Contribution (basis points)
1. Asset allocation		31
2. Selection		
a. Equity excess return (basis points)		
i. Sector allocation	129	
ii. Security selection	<u>18</u>	
	147 × 0.70 (portfolio weight) =	102.9
b. Fixed-income excess return	44 × 0.07 (portfolio weight) =	<u>3.1</u>
Total excess return of portfolio		137.0

1. The appropriate performance measure depends on the role of the portfolio to be evaluated. **SUMMARY**
   Appropriate performance measures are as follows:

   a. Sharpe: When the portfolio represents the entire investment fund.
   b. Information ratio: When the portfolio represents the active portfolio to be optimally mixed with the passive portfolio.
   c. Treynor: When the portfolio represents one subportfolio of many.
   d. Jensen (alpha): All of these measures require a positive alpha for the portfolio to be considered attractive.

2. Many observations and long sample periods are required to eliminate the effect of the "luck of the draw" from the evaluation process because portfolio returns commonly are very "noisy."

3. Style analysis uses a multiple regression model where the factors are category (style) portfolios such as bills, bonds, and stocks. The coefficients on the style portfolios indicate a passive strategy that would match the risk exposures of the managed portfolio. These difference in returns between the managed portfolio and the matching portfolio measures performance relative to similar-style funds.

4. Shifting mean and risk of actively managed portfolios make it difficult to assess performance. An important example of this problem arises when portfolio managers attempt to time the market, resulting in ever-changing portfolio betas.

5. Managers can manipulate their performance measures by adjusting their risk-return profile in response to performance in the early part of an evaluation period. The Morningstar risk-adjusted return is the only manipulation-proof performance measure.

6. A simple way to measure timing and selection success simultaneously is to estimate an expanded security characteristic line, with a quadratic term added to the usual index model. Another way to evaluate timers is based on the implicit call option embedded in their performance.

7. Common attribution procedures decompose portfolio performance to asset allocation, sector selection, and security selection decisions. Performance is assessed by calculating departures of portfolio composition from a benchmark or neutral portfolio.

time-weighted average	Sharpe's ratio	information ratio	**KEY TERMS**
dollar-weighted rate of return	Treynor's measure	bogey	
comparison universe	Jensen's alpha		

KEY EQUATIONS

Geometric time-weighted return: $1 + r_G = [(1 + r_1)(1 + r_2) \cdots (1 + r_n)]^{1/n}$

Sharpe ratio: $S_P = \dfrac{r_P - r_f}{\sigma_P}$

M^2 of portfolio P given its Sharpe ratio: $M^2 = \sigma_M(S_P - S_M)$

Treynor measure: $T_P = \dfrac{r_P - r_f}{\beta_P}$

Jensen's alpha: $\alpha_P = \bar{r}_P - [\bar{r}_f + \beta_P(\bar{r}_M - \bar{r}_f)]$

Information ratio: $\dfrac{\alpha_P}{\sigma(e_P)}$

Morningstar risk-adjusted return: $\text{MRAR}(\gamma) = \left[\dfrac{1}{T}\sum_{t=1}^{T}\left(\dfrac{1+r_t}{1+r_{ft}}\right)^{-\gamma}\right]^{\frac{12}{\gamma}} - 1$

PROBLEM SETS   1. A household savings-account spreadsheet shows the following entries:

Date	Additions	Withdrawals	Value
1/1/2016			148,000
1/3/2016	2,500		
3/20/2016	4,000		
7/5/2016	1,500		
12/2/2016	13,460		
3/10/2017		23,000	
4/7/2017	3,000		
5/3/2017			198,000

Calculate the household's dollar-weighted average return between the first and final dates.

2. Is it possible that a positive alpha will be associated with inferior performance? Explain.

3. We know that the geometric average (time-weighted return) on a risky investment is always lower than the corresponding arithmetic average. Can the IRR (the dollar-weighted return) similarly be ranked relative to these other two averages?

4. We have seen that market timing has tremendous potential value. Would it therefore be wise to shift resources to timing at the expense of security selection?

5. Consider the rate of return of stocks ABC and XYZ.

Year	r_{ABC}	r_{XYZ}
1	20%	30%
2	12	12
3	14	18
4	3	0
5	1	−10

a. Calculate the arithmetic average return on these stocks over the sample period.
b. Which stock has greater dispersion around the mean return?
c. Calculate the geometric average returns of each stock. What do you conclude?
d. If you were equally likely to earn a return of 20%, 12%, 14%, 3%, or 1% in each year (these are the five annual returns for stock ABC), what would be your expected rate of return?
e. What if the five possible outcomes were those of stock XYZ?
f. Given your answers to parts (d) and (e), which measure of average return, arithmetic or geometric, appears more useful for predicting future performance?

6. XYZ's stock price and dividend history are as follows:

Year	Beginning-of-Year Price	Dividend Paid at Year-End
2016	$100	$4
2017	120	4
2018	90	4
2019	100	4

An investor buys three shares of XYZ at the beginning of 2016, buys another two shares at the beginning of 2017, sells one share at the beginning of 2018, and sells all four remaining shares at the beginning of 2019.

a. What are the arithmetic and geometric average time-weighted rates of return for the investor?

b. What is the dollar-weighted rate of return? (*Hint:* Carefully prepare a chart of cash flows for the *four* dates corresponding to the turns of the year for January 1, 2016, to January 1, 2019. If your calculator cannot calculate internal rate of return, you will have to use trial and error.)

7. A manager buys three shares of stock today and then sells one of those shares each year for the next three years. His actions and the price history of the stock are summarized below. The stock pays no dividends.

Time	Price	Action
0	$ 90	Buy 3 shares
1	100	Sell 1 share
2	100	Sell 1 share
3	100	Sell 1 share

a. Calculate the time-weighted geometric average return on this "portfolio."
b. Calculate the time-weighted arithmetic average return on this portfolio.
c. Calculate the dollar-weighted average return on this portfolio.

8. Based on current dividend yields and expected capital gains, the expected rates of return on portfolios A and B are 12% and 16%, respectively. The beta of A is .7, while that of B is 1.4. The T-bill rate is currently 5%, whereas the expected rate of return of the S&P 500 index is 13%. The standard deviation of portfolio A is 12% annually, that of B is 31%, and that of the S&P 500 index is 18%.

a. If you currently hold a market-index portfolio, would you choose to add either of these portfolios to your holdings? Explain.
b. If instead you could invest *only* in T-bills and *one* of these portfolios, which would you choose?

9. Consider the two (excess return) index-model regression results for stocks A and B. The risk-free rate over the period was 6%, and the market's average return was 14%. Performance is measured using an index model regression on excess returns.

	Stock A	Stock B
Index model regression estimates	$1\% + 1.2(r_M - r_f)$	$2\% + 0.8(r_M - r_f)$
R-square	0.576	0.436
Residual standard deviation, $\sigma(e)$	10.3%	19.1%
Standard deviation of excess returns	21.6%	24.9%

a. Calculate the following statistics for each stock:
   i. Alpha
   ii. Information ratio
   iii. Sharpe ratio
   iv. Treynor measure
b. Which stock is the best choice under the following circumstances?
   i. This is the only risky asset to be held by the investor.
   ii. This stock will be mixed with the rest of the investor's portfolio, currently composed solely of holdings in the market-index fund.
   iii. This is one of many stocks that the investor is analyzing to form an actively managed stock portfolio.

10. Evaluate the market timing and security selection abilities of four managers whose performances are plotted in the accompanying diagrams.

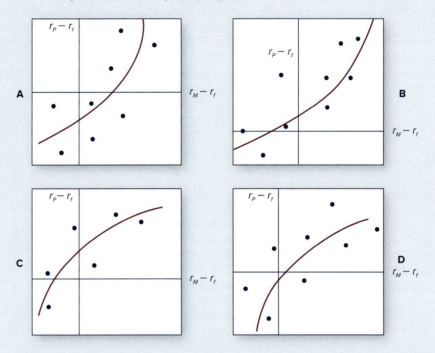

11. Consider the following information regarding the performance of a money manager in a recent month. The table represents the actual return of each sector of the manager's portfolio in column 1, the fraction of the portfolio allocated to each sector in column 2, the benchmark or neutral sector allocations in column 3, and the returns of sector indices in column 4.

	Actual Return	Actual Weight	Benchmark Weight	Index Return
Equity	2%	0.70	0.60	2.5% (S&P 500)
Bonds	1	0.20	0.30	1.2 (Barclay's Aggregate)
Cash	0.5	0.10	0.10	0.5

a. What was the manager's return in the month? What was her overperformance or underperformance?

b. What was the contribution of security selection to relative performance?

c. What was the contribution of asset allocation to relative performance? Confirm that the sum of selection and allocation contributions equals her total "excess" return relative to the bogey.

12. A global equity manager is assigned to select stocks from a universe of large stocks throughout the world. The manager will be evaluated by comparing her returns to the return on the MSCI World Market Portfolio, but she is free to hold stocks from various countries in whatever proportions she finds desirable. Results for a given month are contained in the following table:

Country	Weight in MSCI Index	Manager's Weight	Manager's Return in Country	Return of Stock Index for That Country
U.K.	0.15	0.30	20%	12%
Japan	0.30	0.10	15	15
U.S.	0.45	0.40	10	14
Germany	0.10	0.20	5	12

a. Calculate the total value added of all the manager's decisions this period.

b. Calculate the value added (or subtracted) by her *country* allocation decisions.

c. Calculate the value added from her stock selection ability within countries.

d. Confirm that the sum of the contributions to value added from her country allocation plus security selection decisions equals total over- or underperformance.

13. Conventional wisdom says that one should measure a manager's investment performance over an entire market cycle. What arguments support this convention? What arguments contradict it?

14. Does the use of universes of managers with similar investment styles to evaluate relative investment performance overcome the statistical problems associated with instability of beta or total variability?

15. During a particular year, the T-bill rate was 6%, the market return was 14%, and a portfolio manager with beta of .5 realized a return of 10%.

a. Evaluate the manager based on the portfolio alpha.

b. Reconsider your answer to part (*a*) in view of the Black-Jensen-Scholes finding that the security market line is too flat. Now how do you assess the manager's performance?

16. Bill Smith is evaluating the performance of four large-cap equity portfolios: Funds *A, B, C,* and *D.* As part of his analysis, Smith computed the Sharpe ratio and the Treynor measure for all four funds. Based on his finding, the ranks assigned to the four funds are as follows:

Fund	Treynor Measure Rank	Sharpe Ratio Rank
A	1	4
B	2	3
C	3	2
D	4	1

The difference in rankings for Funds *A* and *D* is most likely due to:

a. A lack of diversification in Fund *A* as compared to Fund *D.*

b. Different benchmarks used to evaluate each fund's performance.

c. A difference in risk premiums.

Use the following information to answer Problems 17 through 20: Primo Management Co. is looking at how best to evaluate the performance of its managers. Primo has been hearing more and more about benchmark portfolios and is interested in trying this approach. As such, the company hired Sally Jones, CFA, as a consultant to educate the managers on the best methods for constructing a benchmark portfolio, how to choose the best benchmark, whether the style of the fund under management matters, and what they should do with their global funds in terms of benchmarking.

For the sake of discussion, Jones put together some comparative 2-year performance numbers that relate to Primo's current domestic funds under management and a potential benchmark.

	Weight		Return	
Style Category	Primo	Benchmark	Primo	Benchmark
Large-cap growth	0.60	0.50	17%	16%
Mid-cap growth	0.15	0.40	24	26
Small-cap growth	0.25	0.10	20	18

As part of her analysis, Jones also takes a look at one of Primo's global funds. In this particular portfolio, Primo is invested 75% in Dutch stocks and 25% in British stocks. The benchmark is invested 50% in Dutch and and 50% in British stocks. On average, the British stocks outperformed the Dutch stocks. The euro appreciated 6% versus the U.S. dollar over the holding period while the pound depreciated 2% versus the dollar. In terms of the local return, Primo outperformed the benchmark with the Dutch investments, but underperformed the index with respect to the British stocks.

17. What is the within-sector selection effect for each individual sector?

18. Calculate the amount by which the Primo portfolio out-(under-)performed the market over the period, as well as the contribution to performance of the pure sector allocation and security selection decisions.

19. If Primo decides to use return-based style analysis, will the R^2 of the regression equation of a passively managed fund be higher or lower than that of an actively managed fund?

20. Which of the following statements about Primo's global fund is most correct? Primo appears to have a positive currency allocation effect as well as

    a. A negative market allocation effect and a positive security allocation effect.
    b. A negative market allocation effect and a negative security allocation effect.
    c. A positive market allocation effect and a negative security allocation effect.

21. Kelli Blakely is a portfolio manager for the Miranda Fund, a core large-cap equity fund. The market proxy and benchmark for performance measurement purposes is the S&P 500. Although the Miranda portfolio generally mirrors the asset class and sector weightings of the S&P, Blakely is allowed a significant amount of leeway in managing the fund. However, her portfolio holds only stocks found in the S&P 500 and cash.

    Blakely was able to produce exceptional returns last year (as outlined in the table below) through her market timing and security selection skills. At the outset of the year, she became extremely concerned that the combination of a weak economy and geopolitical uncertainties would negatively impact the market. Taking a bold step, she changed her market allocation. For the entire year her asset class exposures averaged 50% in stocks and 50% in cash. The S&P's allocation between stocks and cash during the period was a constant 97% and 3%, respectively. The risk-free rate of return was 2%.

One-Year Trailing Returns

	Miranda Fund	S&P 500
Return	10.2%	−22.5%
Standard deviation	37%	44%
Beta	1.10	1.00

    a. What are the Sharpe ratios for the Miranda Fund and the S&P 500?
    b. What are the M^2 measures for Miranda and the S&P 500?
    c. What is the Treynor measure for the Miranda Fund and the S&P 500?
    d. What is the Jensen measure for the Miranda Fund?

22. Go to Kenneth French's data library site at **http://mba.tuck.dartmouth.edu/pages/faculty/ken.french/data_library.html**. Select two industry portfolios of your choice and download 36 months of data. Download other data from the site as needed to perform the following tasks.

    a. Compare the portfolio's performance to that of the market index on the basis of the Sharpe, Jensen, Treynor measures as well as the information ratio. Plot the monthly values of alpha plus residual return.
    b. Now use the Fama-French three-factor model as the return benchmark. Compute plots of alpha plus residual return using the FF model. How does performance change using this benchmark instead of the market index?

1. You and a prospective client are considering the measurement of investment performance, particularly with respect to international portfolios for the past five years. The data you discussed are presented in the following table:

International Manager or Index	Total Return	Country and Security Return	Currency Return
Manager A	−6.0%	2.0%	−8.0%
Manager B	−2.0	−1.0	−1.0
International Index	−5.0	0.2	−5.2

a. Assume that the data for manager A and manager B accurately reflect their investment skills and that both managers actively manage currency exposure. Briefly describe one strength and one weakness for each manager.

b. Recommend and justify a strategy that would enable your fund to take advantage of the strengths of each of the two managers while minimizing their weaknesses.

2. Carl Karl, a portfolio manager for the Alpine Trust Company, has been responsible since 2020 for the City of Alpine's Employee Retirement Plan, a municipal pension fund. Alpine is a growing community, and city services and employee payrolls have expanded in each of the past 10 years. Contributions to the plan in fiscal 2025 exceeded benefit payments by a three-to-one ratio.

The plan board of trustees directed Karl five years ago to invest for total return over the long term. However, as trustees of this highly visible public fund, they cautioned him that volatile or erratic results could cause them embarrassment. They also noted a state statute that mandated that not more than 25% of the plan's assets (at cost) be invested in common stocks.

At the annual meeting of the trustees in November 2025, Karl presented the following portfolio and performance report to the board:

Alpine Employee Retirement Plan

Asset Mix as of 9/30/25	At Cost (millions)		At Market (millions)	
Fixed-income assets:				
Short-term securities	$ 4.5	11.0%	$ 4.5	11.4%
Long-term bonds and mortgages	26.5	64.7	23.5	59.5
Common stocks	10.0	24.3	11.5	29.1
	$41.0	100.0%	$39.5	100.0%

Investment Performance

	Annual Rates of Return for Periods Ending 9/30/25	
	5 Years	1 Year
Total Alpine Fund:		
Time-weighted	8.2%	5.2%
Dollar-weighted (internal)	7.7%	4.8%
Assumed actuarial return	6.0%	6.0%
U.S. Treasury bills	7.5%	11.3%
Large sample of pension funds (average 60% equities, 40% fixed income)	10.1%	14.3%
Common stocks—Alpine Fund	13.3%	14.3%
Alpine portfolio beta coefficient	0.90	0.89
Standard & Poor's 500 stock index	13.8%	21.1%
Fixed-income securities—Alpine Fund	6.7%	1.0%
Broad Investment Grade bond index	4.0%	−11.4%

Karl was proud of his performance and was chagrined when a trustee made the following critical observations:

a. "Our 1-year results were terrible, and it's what you've done for us lately that counts most."

b. "Our total fund performance was clearly inferior compared to the large sample of other pension funds for the last five years. What else could this reflect except poor management judgment?"

c. "Our common stock performance was especially poor for the 5-year period."

d. "Why bother to compare your returns to the return from Treasury bills and the actuarial assumption rate? What your competition could have earned for us or how we would have fared if invested in a passive index (which doesn't charge a fee) are the only relevant measures of performance."

e. "Who cares about time-weighted return? If it can't pay pensions, what good is it?"

Appraise the merits of each of these statements and give counterarguments that Mr. Karl can use.

3. The Retired Fund is an open-ended mutual fund composed of $500 million in U.S. bonds and U.S. Treasury bills. This fund has had a portfolio duration (including T-bills) of between 3 and 9 years. Retired has shown first-quartile performance over the past five years, as measured by an independent fixed-income measurement service. However, the directors of the fund would like to measure the market timing skill of the fund's sole bond investor manager. An external consulting firm has suggested the following three methods:

a. Method I examines the value of the bond portfolio at the beginning of every year, then calculates the return that would have been achieved had that same portfolio been held throughout the year. This return would then be compared with the return actually obtained by the fund.

b. Method II calculates the average weighting of the portfolio in bonds and T-bills for each year. Instead of using the actual bond portfolio, the return on a long-bond market index and T-bill index would be used. For example, if the portfolio on average was 65% in bonds and 35% in T-bills, the annual return on a portfolio invested 65% in a long-bond index and 35% in T-bills would be calculated. This return is compared with the annual return that would have been generated using the indexes and the manager's actual bond/T-bill weighting for each quarter of the year.

c. Method III examines the net bond purchase activity (market value of purchases less sales) for each quarter of the year. If net purchases were positive (negative) in any quarter, the performance of the bonds would be evaluated until the net purchase activity became negative (positive). Positive (negative) net purchases would be viewed as a bullish (bearish) view taken by the manager. The correctness of this view would be measured.

Critique *each* method with regard to market timing measurement problems.

Use the following data to solve CFA Problems 4 and 5: The administrator of a large pension fund wants to evaluate the performance of four portfolio managers. Each portfolio manager invests only in U.S. common stocks. Assume that during the most recent 5-year period, the average annual total rate of return including dividends on the S&P 500 was 14%, and the average nominal rate of return on government Treasury bills was 8%. The following table shows risk and return measures for each portfolio:

Portfolio	Average Annual Rate of Return	Standard Deviation	Beta
P	17%	20%	1.1
Q	24	18	2.1
R	11	10	0.5
S	16	14	1.5
S&P 500	14	12	1.0

4. What is the Treynor performance measure for portfolio P?

5. What is the Sharpe performance measure for portfolio Q?

6. An analyst wants to evaluate portfolio X, consisting entirely of U.S. common stocks, using both the Treynor and Sharpe measures of portfolio performance. The following table provides the average annual rate of return for portfolio X, the market portfolio (as measured by the S&P 500), and U.S. Treasury bills during the past 8 years:

	Average Annual Rate of Return	Standard Deviation of Return	Beta
Portfolio X	10%	18%	0.60
S&P 500	12	13	1.00
T-bills	6	N/A	N/A

a. Calculate the Treynor and Sharpe measures for both portfolio X and the S&P 500. Briefly explain whether portfolio X underperformed, equaled, or outperformed the S&P 500 on a risk-adjusted basis using both the Treynor measure and the Sharpe ratio.

b. On the basis of the performance of portfolio X relative to the S&P 500 calculated in part (a), briefly explain the reason for the conflicting results when using the Treynor measure versus the Sharpe ratio.

7. Assume you invested in an asset for two years. The first year you earned a 15% return, and the second year you earned a negative 10% return. What was your annual geometric return?

8. A portfolio of stocks generates a −9% return in 2016, a 23% return in 2017, and a 17% return in 2018. What is the annualized return (geometric mean) for the entire period?

9. A 2-year investment of $2,000 results in a cash flow of $150 at the end of the first year and another cash flow of $150 at the end of the second year, in addition to the return of the original investment. What is the internal rate of return on the investment?

10. In measuring the performance of a portfolio, the time-weighted rate of return is superior to the dollar-weighted rate of return because:

a. When the rate of return varies, the time-weighted return is higher.
b. The dollar-weighted return assumes all portfolio deposits are made on day 1.
c. The dollar-weighted return can only be estimated.
d. The time-weighted return is unaffected by the timing of portfolio contributions and withdrawals.

11. A pension fund portfolio begins with $500,000 and earns 15% the first year and 10% the second year. At the beginning of the second year, the sponsor contributes another $500,000. What were the time-weighted and dollar-weighted rates of return?

12. During the annual review of Acme's pension plan, several trustees questioned their investment consultant about various aspects of performance measurement and risk assessment.

a. Comment on the appropriateness of using each of the following benchmarks for performance evaluation:
   - Market index.
   - Benchmark normal portfolio.
   - Median of the manager universe.
b. Distinguish among the following performance measures:
   - The Sharpe ratio.
   - The Treynor measure.
   - Jensen's alpha.
   i. Describe how each of the three performance measures is calculated.
   ii. State whether each measure assumes that the relevant risk is systematic, unsystematic, or total. Explain how each measure relates excess return and the relevant risk.

13. Trustees of the Pallor Corp. pension plan ask consultant Donald Millip to comment on the following statements. What should his response be?

a. Median manager benchmarks are statistically unbiased measures of performance over long periods of time.
b. Median manager benchmarks are unambiguous and are therefore easily replicated by managers wishing to adopt a passive/indexed approach.
c. Median manager benchmarks are not appropriate in all circumstances because the median manager universe encompasses many investment styles.

14. James Chan is reviewing the performance of the global equity managers of the Jarvis University endowment fund. Williamson Capital is currently the endowment fund's only

large-capitalization global equity manager. Performance data for Williamson Capital are shown in Table 24A.

Chan also presents the endowment fund's investment committee with performance information for Joyner Asset Management, which is another large-capitalization global equity manager. Performance data for Joyner Asset Management are shown in Table 24B. Performance data for the relevant risk-free asset and market index are shown in Table 24C.

a. Calculate the Sharpe ratio and Treynor measure for both Williamson Capital and Joyner Asset Management.

b. The investment committee notices that using the Sharpe ratio versus the Treynor measure produces different performance rankings of Williamson and Joyner. Explain why these criteria may result in different rankings.

Average annual rate of return	22.1%
Beta	1.2
Standard deviation of returns	16.8%

Table 24A

Williamson Capital performance data, 2004–2015

Average annual rate of return	24.2%
Beta	0.8
Standard deviation of returns	20.2%

Table 24B

Joyner Asset Management performance data, 2004–2015

Risk-Free Asset	
Average annual rate of return	5.0%
Market Index	
Average annual rate of return	18.9%
Standard deviation of returns	13.8%

Table 24C

Risk-free asset and market index performance data, 2004–2015

E-INVESTMENTS EXERCISES

Morningstar has an extensive ranking system for mutual funds, including a screening program that allows you to select funds based on a number of factors. Open the Morningstar Web site at **www.morningstar.com** and click on the *Funds* link. Select the *Mutual Fund Quickrank* link in the Performance section. (Free registration is required to access the site.) Use the Quickrank screener to find a list of large growth stock funds with the highest 1-year returns. Repeat the process to find the funds with the highest 3-year returns. What fraction of funds appear on both lists?

Select three of the funds that appear on both lists. For each fund, click on the ticker symbol to get its Morningstar report and look in the Ratings & Risk section.

1. What is the fund's standard deviation?

2. What is the fund's Sharpe ratio?

3. What is the fund's Treynor ratio?

4. What is the standard index? What is the best-fit index?

5. What are the beta and alpha coefficients using both the standard index and the best-fit index? How do these compare to the fund's parameters?

6. Look at the Management section of the report. Was the same manager in place for the entire 10-year period?

7. Are any of these funds of interest to you? How might your screening choices differ if you were choosing funds for various clients?

✔ SOLUTIONS TO CONCEPT CHECKS

1.

Time	Action	Cash Flow
0	Buy two shares	−40
1	Collect dividends; then sell one of the shares	4 + 22
2	Collect dividend on remaining share, then sell it	2 + 19

a. Dollar-weighted return:

$$-40 + \frac{26}{1+r} + \frac{21}{(1+r)^2} = 0$$

$$r = .1191, \text{ or } 11.91\%$$

b. Time-weighted return:

The rates of return on the stock in the 2 years were:

$$r_1 = \frac{2 + (22 - 20)}{20} = .20$$

$$r_2 = \frac{2 + (19 - 22)}{22} = -.0455$$

Arithmetic time-weighted return: $(r_1 + r_2)/2 = .0773$, or 7.73%

Geometric time-weighted return: $[(1 + r_1)(1 + r_2)]^{1/2} - 1 = .0702 = 7.02\%$

2. Sharpe: $(\bar{r} - \bar{r}_f)/\sigma$

$$S_P = (35 - 6)/42 = .69$$
$$S_M = (28 - 6)/30 = .733$$

Alpha: $\bar{r} - [\bar{r}_f + \beta(r_M - r_f)]$

$$\alpha_P = 35 - [6 + 1.2(28 - 6)] = 2.6$$
$$\alpha_M = 0$$

Treynor: $(\bar{r} - \bar{r}_f)/\beta$

$$T_P = (35 - 6)/1.2 = 24.2$$
$$T_M = (28 - 6)/1.0 = 22$$

Information ratio: $\alpha/\sigma(e)$

$$I_P = 2.6/18 = .144$$
$$I_M = 0$$

Therefore, portfolio P outperformed the market according to the Jensen and Treynor measures, but had an inferior Sharpe measure.

3. The alpha exceeds zero by $.2/2 = .1$ standard deviations. A table of the normal distribution (or, somewhat more appropriately, the distribution of the t-statistic) indicates that the probability of such an event, if the analyst actually has no skill, is approximately 46%.

4. The timer will guess bear or bull markets completely randomly. One-half of all bull markets will be preceded by a correct forecast and similarly for bear markets. Hence $P_1 + P_2 - 1 = \frac{1}{2} + \frac{1}{2} - 1 = 0$.

5. First compute the new bogey performance as $(.70 \times 5.81) + (.25 \times 1.45) + (.05 \times .48) = 4.45$.

   a. Contribution of asset allocation to performance:

Market	(1) Actual Weight in Market	(2) Benchmark Weight in Market	(3) Active or Excess Weight	(4) Market Return (%)	(5) = (3) × (4) Contribution to Performance (%)
Equity	0.70	0.70	0.00	5.81	0.00
Fixed-income	0.07	0.25	−0.18	1.45	−0.26
Cash	0.23	0.05	0.18	0.48	0.09
Contribution of asset allocation					−0.17

   b. Contribution of selection to total performance:

Market	(1) Portfolio Performance (%)	(2) Index Performance (%)	(3) Excess Performance (%)	(4) Portfolio Weight	(5) = (3) × (4) Contribution (%)
Equity	7.28	5.00	2.28	0.70	1.60
Fixed-income	1.89	1.45	0.44	0.07	0.03
Contribution of selection within markets					1.63

International Diversification

25

ALTHOUGH WE IN the United States customarily use a broad index of U.S. equities as the market-index portfolio, the practice is increasingly inappropriate. U.S. equities represent only about 40% of world equities and a far smaller fraction of total world wealth. In this chapter, we look beyond domestic markets to survey issues of international and extended diversification.

In one sense, international investing may be viewed as no more than a straightforward generalization of our earlier treatment of portfolio selection, with a larger menu of assets from which to construct a portfolio. Similar issues of diversification, security analysis, security selection, and asset allocation face the investor. On the other hand, international investments pose some problems not encountered in domestic markets. Among these are the presence of exchange rate risk, restrictions on capital flows across national boundaries, an added dimension of political risk and country-specific regulations, and differing informational transparency in different countries. Therefore, in this chapter we review the major topics covered in the rest of the book, emphasizing their international aspects.

We begin with a brief description of international equity markets, pointing out the wide range of venues available to investors. We then turn to the central concepts of portfolio theory—risk and diversification. We will see how exchange rate fluctuations add another element to the uncertainty surrounding rates of return. However, global diversification offers opportunities for improving portfolio risk–return trade-offs. International investing also entails a range of political risks. We consider several of these risks as well as sources of information pertaining to them. Finally, we show how active asset allocation can be generalized to incorporate country and currency choices in addition to traditional domestic asset class choices and demonstrate performance attribution in an international context.

25.1 Global Markets for Equities

You can easily invest today in the capital markets of nearly 100 countries and obtain up-to-date data about your investments in each of them. By 2015, more than 20 countries had stock markets with market capitalization above $100 billion.

U.S. investors have several avenues through which they can invest internationally. The most obvious method, which is available in practice primarily to larger institutional investors, is to purchase securities directly in the capital markets of other countries. However, even small investors can take advantage of several investment vehicles with an international focus.

Shares of several foreign firms are traded in U.S. markets either directly or in the form of American depositary receipts, or ADRs. A U.S. financial institution such as a bank will purchase shares of a foreign firm in that firm's country and then issue claims to those shares in the United States. Each ADR is then a claim on a given number of the shares of stock held by the bank. Some stocks trade in the U.S. both directly and as ADRs.

There is also a wide array of mutual funds with an international focus. In addition to single-country funds, there are several open-end mutual funds with an international focus. For example, Fidelity offers funds with investments concentrated overseas, generally in Europe, in the Pacific Basin, and in developing economies in an emerging opportunities fund. Vanguard, consistent with its indexing philosophy, offers separate index funds for Europe, the Pacific Basin, and emerging markets. Finally, as noted in Chapter 4, there are many exchange-traded funds known as iShares or WEBS (World Equity Benchmark Shares) that are country-specific index products.

U.S. investors also can trade derivative securities based on prices in foreign security markets. For example, they can trade options and futures on the Nikkei stock index of 225 stocks traded on the Tokyo stock exchange or on FTSE (Financial Times Share Exchange) indexes of U.K. and European stocks.

The investments industry commonly distinguishes between "developed" and "emerging" markets. A typical emerging economy still is undergoing industrialization, is growing faster than developed economies, and has capital markets that usually entail greater risk. We use the FTSE[1] criteria, which emphasize capital market conditions, to classify markets as emerging or developed.

Developed Countries

To appreciate the myopia of an exclusive investment focus on U.S. stocks and bonds, consider the data in Table 25.1. The U.S. accounts for only 40.6% of world stock market capitalization. Clearly, active investors can attain better risk–return trade-offs by extending their search for attractive securities abroad. Developed countries accounted for about 70% of world gross domestic product in 2015 and 78.6% of world market capitalization.

Table 25.1 presents data on both market capitalization and GDP for a sample of developed economies. The United States is by far the largest economy, measured either by GDP or the size of the stock market. However, Switzerland is the leader in GDP per capita, and Hong Kong has the largest stock market compared to GDP. On average, the total stock market capitalization in these countries is about the same magnitude as annual GDP, but there is tremendous variation in these numbers. Capitalization as a fraction of GDP for the counties toward the bottom of the list, with smaller capital markets, is generally far lower than for those counties near the top. This suggests widespread differences in economic structure even across developed nations.

---

[1]FTSE Index Co. (the sponsor of the British FTSE [Financial Times Share Exchange] stock market index) uses 14 specific criteria to divide countries into "developed" and "emerging" lists.

	Market Capitalization ($ billions)	Percent of World (%)	GDP ($ billions)	GDP per Capita ($)	Market Cap as % of GDP
U.S.	$25,068	40.6%	$17,947	$55,837	139.7%
Japan	4,895	7.9	4,123	32,477	118.7
Hong Kong	3,185	5.2	310	42,423	1,027.6
U.K.	2,781	4.4	2,849	43,734	97.6
France	2,088	3.4	2,422	36,248	86.2
Germany	1,716	2.8	3,356	41,219	51.1
Canada	1,593	2.6	1,551	43,249	102.8
Switzerland	1,519	2.5	665	80,215	228.6
Korea	1,231	2.0	1,378	27,222	89.4
Australia	1,187	1.9	1,340	56,328	88.6
Spain	787	1.3	1,199	25,832	65.7
Netherlands	728	1.2	753	44,433	96.8
Italy	587	1.0	1,815	29,847	27.5
Belgium	415	0.7	454	40,231	91.3
Mexico	402	0.7	1,144	9,009	35.2
Israel	244	0.4	296	35,330	82.4
Norway	194	0.3	388	74,735	49.9
Chile	190	0.3	240	13,384	79.2
Turkey	189	0.3	718	9,130	26.3
Poland	138	0.2	475	12,494	29.0
Ireland	128	0.2	238	51,290	53.8
Austria	96	0.2	374	43,439	25.7
New Zealand	74	0.1	174	37,808	42.8
Portugal	60	0.1	199	19,223	30.1
Luxembourg	47	0.1	58	101,450	81.6
Greece	42	0.1	195	18,036	21.6
Hungary	18	0.0	121	12,259	14.7
Slovenia	6	0.0	43	20,713	14.1
All developed countries	49,609	78.6	44,823		110.7
World	63,150	100.0	63,982		98.7

Table 25.1

Market capitalization and GDP of developed countries, 2015

Source: The World Bank, **data.worldbank.org.**

Emerging Markets

For a passive strategy, one could argue that a portfolio of equities of just the six countries with the largest capitalization would make up over 70% (in 2015) of the world portfolio and may be sufficiently diversified. However, this argument will not hold for active portfolios that seek to tilt investments toward promising assets. Active portfolios will naturally include many stocks or indexes of emerging markets.

Surely, active portfolio managers do not want to neglect stocks in markets such as China with an average GDP growth rate in the last five years of 15%. Table 25.2 shows data from

	Market Capitalization ($ billions)	Percent of World (%)	GDP ($ billions)	GDP per Capita (%)	Market Cap as % of GDP
China	$8,188	13.3%	$10,866	7,925%	75.4%
India	1,516	2.5	2,074	1,582	73.1
South Africa	736	1.2	313	5,692	235.3
Singapore	640	1.0	293	52,889	218.6
Brazil	491	0.8	1,775	8,539	27.6
Russia	393	0.6	1,326	9,057	29.7
Malaysia	383	0.6	296	9,766	129.3
Indonesia	353	0.6	862	3,346	41.0
Thailand	349	0.6	395	5,816	88.2
Philippines	239	0.4	292	2,899	81.8
Colombia	86	0.1	292	6,056	29.4
Peru	57	0.1	192	6,122	29.4
Argentina	56	0.1	583	13,432	9.6
Sri Lanka	21	0.0	82	3,926	25.3
Cyprus	3	0.0	19	22,957	13.9
All emerging markets	13,510	21.9	19,660.6		68.7

Table 25.2

Market capitalization of stock exchanges in emerging markets

Source: The World Bank, **data.worldbank.org.**

the largest emerging markets. These markets make up 21% of the world GDP. Per capita GDP in these emerging markets is quite variable, ranging from $1,582 (India) to $52,889 (Singapore). Market capitalization as a percent of GDP in these countries is still below 70%, suggesting that these markets can grow significantly over the coming years, even without spectacular growth in GDP.

Market Capitalization and GDP

A contemporary view of economic development[2] holds that an important requirement for economic advancement is a developed code of business laws, institutions, and regulations that allows citizens to legally own, capitalize, and trade capital assets. As a corollary, we expect that development of equity markets will serve as a catalyst for enrichment of the population.

Figure 25.1 depicts the relationship between per capita GDP and market capitalization (where both variables have been transformed to $\log_{10}$ scale). The positive slope of the regression line through the scatter shows that, on average, countries with larger capital markets also tend to have higher levels of per capita GDP. The slope of the line is .32, which implies that every percentage point increase in total market capitalization predicts an increase of .32% in per capita GDP.[3] Even so, we observe that most of the observations

[2]A highly influential paper in this literature is Rafael La Porta, Florencia Lopez-de-Silanes, Andrei Shleifer, and Robert W. Vishny, "Law and Finance," *Journal of Political Economy* 106 (December 1998), pp. 1113–1155.

[3]This simple single-variable regression is not put forward as a causal model but simply as a way to describe the relation between per capita GDP and the size of markets.

for the developed countries (the circles) lie above the regression line while most of the observations for the emerging markets (the triangles) lie below. This may be evidence that legal, regulatory, and economic institutions in the more advanced economies also contribute to productivity.

Home-Country Bias

We know that purely passive investment strategies would call for risky portfolios that are indexed to a broad market portfolio. In the international context, that market portfolio would include stock markets from all nations, and the market index would be a broadly diversified world portfolio.

Despite this, it is clear that investors everywhere tend to overweight investments in their home countries (relative to representation in the world portfolio) and underweight investments in foreign assets. For example, referring back to Table 25.1, a purely indexed U.S. investor would hold about 41% of the total equity portfolio in U.S. securities with the remaining 59% invested abroad. Yet in practice, we know that U.S. investors hold a large majority of their equity investments in U.S. firms. This pattern is mirrored in the behavior of investors around the world and is commonly called *home-country bias.*

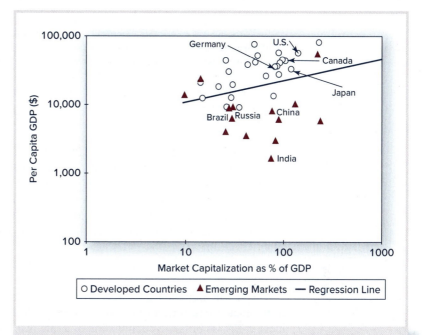

Figure 25.1 Per capita GDP and market capitalization as percent of GDP, 2015

Source: The World Bank, **data.worldbank.org.**

25.2 Exchange Rate Risk and International Diversification

Exchange Rate Risk

When a U.S. investor invests abroad, the dollar-denominated return depends on two factors: first, the performance of the investment in the local currency, and second, the exchange rate at which that investment can be brought back into dollars. We illustrate with the following example.

Example 25.1   Exchange Rate Risk

Consider an investment in risk-free British government bills paying 10% annual interest in British pounds. While these U.K. bills would be the risk-free asset to a British investor, this is not the case for a U.S. investor. Suppose, for example, the current exchange rate is $2 per pound and the U.S. investor starts with $20,000. That amount can be exchanged for £10,000 and invested at a riskless 10% rate in the United Kingdom to provide £11,000 in one year.

What happens if the dollar–pound exchange rate varies over the year? Say that during the year, the pound depreciates relative to the dollar, so that by year-end only $1.80 is required to purchase £1. The £11,000 can be exchanged at the year-end exchange rate for only $19,800 (= £11,000 × $1.80/£), resulting in a loss of $200 relative to the initial $20,000 investment. Despite the positive 10% pound-denominated return, the dollar-denominated return is negative 1%.

We can generalize from Example 25.1. The $20,000 is exchanged for $20,000/$E_0$ pounds, where E_0 denotes the original exchange rate ($2/£). The U.K. investment grows to $(20,000/E_0)[1 + r_f(\text{UK})]$ British pounds, where $r_f(\text{UK})$ is the risk-free rate in the United Kingdom. The pound proceeds ultimately are converted back to dollars at the subsequent exchange rate E_1, for total dollar proceeds of $20,000(E_1/E_0)[1 + r_f(\text{UK})]$. Therefore, the dollar-denominated return on the investment in British bills is

$$1 + r(\text{US}) = [1 + r_f(\text{UK})]E_1/E_0 \tag{25.1}$$

We see in Equation 25.1 that the dollar-denominated return equals the pound-denominated return times the exchange rate "return." For a U.S. investor, the investment in British bills is a combination of a safe investment in the United Kingdom and a risky investment in the performance of the pound relative to the dollar. Here, the pound fared poorly, falling from a value of $2 to only $1.80. The loss on the pound more than offset the earnings on the British bill.

Figure 25.2 illustrates this point. It presents rates of return on stock market indexes in several countries for 2015. The top bar in each pair depicts returns in local currencies, while the bottom bar depicts returns in U.S. dollars, adjusted for exchange rate movements. It's clear that exchange rate fluctuations over this period had large effects on dollar-denominated returns in several countries.

 Concept Check **25.1**

Using the data in Example 25.1, calculate the rate of return in dollars to a U.S. investor holding the British bill if the year-end exchange rate is: (a) $E_1 = \$2.00/£$; (b) $E_1 = \$2.20/£$.

Exchange rate risk arises from uncertainty in exchange rate fluctuations. The investor in safe U.K. bills in Example 25.1 still bears the risk of the U.K./U.S. exchange rate. We can assess the magnitude of exchange rate risk by examining historical rates of change in various exchange rates and their correlations.

Table 25.3, Panel A, presents the annualized standard deviation of monthly percent changes in the exchange rates of major currencies against the U.S. dollar over the period 2011–2016. The data show that currency volatility can be quite high. With the exception of the Chinese RMB, the standard deviation of the percent changes in the exchange rate was around three-quarters that of the S&P 500, with annualized values ranging from 7.47% (Canadian dollar) to 10.01% (Swiss franc). The annualized standard deviation of returns on U.S. large stocks for the same period was 12%. An active investor who believes that a foreign stock is underpriced but has no information about any mispricing of its currency should consider hedging the currency risk exposure when tilting the portfolio toward that stock.

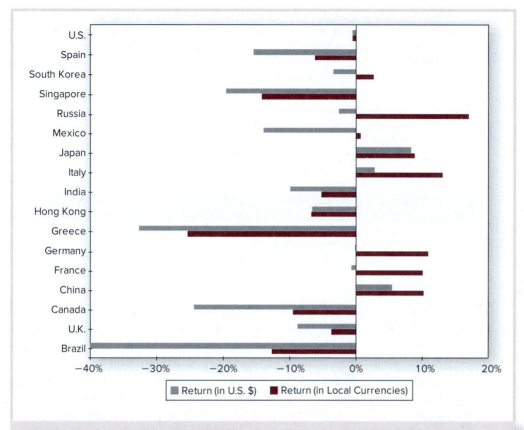

Figure 25.2 Stock market returns, 2015

Source: *The Economist,* January 2, 2016.

A. Monthly Change in Exchange Rate against U.S. Dollar

	Euro (€)	U.K. (£)	Switzerland (SFr)	Japan (¥)	China (RMB)	Canada (C$)
Standard deviation (annualized)	8.19%	8.72%	10.01%	9.47%	2.60%	7.47%
Correlation with S&P 500	−0.095	−0.090	−0.042	0.134	−0.373	−0.453

B. Correlation Matrix of Monthly Changes in Exchange Rate against U.S. Dollar

	Euro (€)	U.K. (£)	Switzerland (SFr)	Japan (¥)	China (RMB)	Canada (C$)
Euro (€)	1.00					
U.K. (£)	0.56	1.00				
Switzerland (SFr)	0.43	0.28	1.00			
Japan (¥)	0.20	0.23	0.28	1.00		
China (RMB)	−0.05	0.27	0.09	−0.10	1.00	
Canada (C$)	0.46	0.44	0.14	0.14	0.29	1.00

Table 25.3

Exchange rate volatility, 2011–2016

Source: Authors' calculations using data downloaded from Datastream.

On the other hand, exchange rate risk may be mostly diversifiable. This is evident both from the low correlation between exchange rate changes and the return on the S&P 500 shown in the second line of Table 25.3, Panel A, as well as the low correlation coefficients among currency pairs that appear in Panel B.

Investors can hedge exchange rate risk using a forward or futures contract in foreign exchange. Recall that such contracts entail delivery or acceptance of one currency for another at a stipulated exchange rate. To illustrate, recall Example 25.1. In this case, to hedge her exposure to the British pound, the U.S. investor would agree to deliver pounds for dollars at a fixed exchange rate, thereby eliminating the risk involved with the eventual conversion of the pound investment back into dollars.

Example 25.2   Hedging Exchange Rate Risk

If the forward exchange rate in Example 25.1 had been $F_0 = \$1.93/£$ when the investment was made, the U.S. investor could have assured a riskless dollar-denominated return by arranging to deliver the £11,000 at the forward exchange rate of $\$1.93/£$. In this case, the riskless U.S. return would have been 6.15%:

$$[1 + r_f(\text{UK})]F_0/E_0 = (1.10)1.93/2.00 = 1.0615.$$

The hedge underlying Example 25.2 is the same strategy at the heart of the spot-futures parity relationship, first discussed in Chapter 22. In both instances, futures or forward markets are used to eliminate the risk of holding another asset. The U.S. investor can lock in a riskless dollar-denominated return either by investing in United Kingdom bills and hedging exchange rate risk or by investing in riskless U.S. assets. Because investments in two riskless strategies must provide equal returns, we conclude that $[1 + r_f(\text{UK})]F_0/E_0 = 1 + r_f(\text{US})$, which can be rearranged to

$$\frac{F_0}{E_0} = \frac{1 + r_f(\text{US})}{1 + r_f(\text{UK})} \tag{25.2}$$

This relationship is called the **interest rate parity relationship** or **covered interest arbitrage relationship,** which we first encountered in Chapter 23.

Unfortunately, such perfect exchange rate hedging usually is not so easy. In our example, we knew exactly how many pounds to sell in the forward or futures market because the pound-denominated return in the United Kingdom was riskless. If the U.K. investment had not been in bills, but instead had been in risky U.K. equity, we would have known neither the ultimate value in pounds of our U.K. investment nor how many pounds to sell forward. The hedging opportunity offered by foreign exchange forward contracts would thus be imperfect.

To summarize, the generalization of Equation 25.1 for unhedged investments is that

$$1 + r(\text{US}) = [1 + r(\text{foreign})]E_1/E_0 \tag{25.3}$$

where $r(\text{foreign})$ is the possibly risky return earned in the currency of the foreign investment and exchange rates are direct quotes ($ per unit of foreign currency). You can set up a perfect hedge only in the special case that $r(\text{foreign})$ is actually known. In that case, you must sell in the forward or futures market an amount of foreign currency equal to $[1 + r(\text{foreign})]$ for each unit of that currency you purchase today.

Concept Check **25.2**

> How many pounds would the investor in Example 25.2 need to sell forward to hedge exchange rate risk if: (a) r(UK) = 20%; and (b) r(UK) = 30%?

Investment Risk in International Markets

While active-strategy managers engage in both individual-market asset allocation as well as security selection, we will restrict our focus to market-index portfolios across countries, keeping us on the side of an enhanced passive strategy. Nevertheless, our analysis illustrates the essential features of extended active management as well.

As we pointed out in Chapter 5, estimates of mean returns are extremely unreliable without very long data series. Little can be learned about average rates of return from periods as short as 5 or even 10 years. This is because estimates of expected return essentially depend on only the initial and final stock price (which fully determine the average rate of increase). Long sample periods are intrinsically necessary for precise estimates of expected return. However, over such long periods, the mean of the return distribution can change. This is a difficult hurdle for empirical research.

In contrast, estimates of volatility can be informed by return variation *within* the sample period. Increasing the frequency of observations therefore can increase the accuracy of risk estimates, meaning that precise estimates are feasible even with relatively short sample periods.

Therefore, we will focus largely on the risk of international investments, where we are more confident in our empirical estimates. We will use monthly data on country index returns for the five years ending in October 2016.

Table 25.4 shows key statistics for the investment risk of various equity indexes during this period. The indexes include most of the world's largest equity markets as well as markets from regions with smaller and less developed capital markets. The first pair of columns show the standard deviation of monthly returns measured both in local currency as well as translated into U.S. dollars, thus reflecting the impact of exchange rate movements in each month.[4]

The U.S. equity market (here taken to be the S&P 500) had the lowest volatility in terms of U.S. dollar-denominated returns over this period, but Canada had the lowest volatility in local currency. Its higher dollar-denominated volatility reflects the added risk attributable to exchange rate movements. But in general, the impact of exchange rate movements on the volatility of dollar-denominated returns is minimal. On average, the volatility of dollar-denominated returns is not much higher than that of local returns. (The mean and median estimates reported in Table 25.4 are computed only over the individual country indexes.)

Correlations with the MSCI World index, shown in the next pair of columns, are also broadly similar for local and dollar-denominated returns. Not surprisingly, given the prominence of the U.S. in the World portfolio and the prominence of its economy in the world economy, the U.S. has the highest correlation with the World index. Similarly, the FTSE index (U.K.) and Euronext index (E.U.), both of which measure returns of large and developed economies, also have very high correlations with the World index, approximately .85

---

[4]Currency-translated returns are not available for the regional indexes. We compute the dollar-denominated return on the MSCI World portfolio as the weighted average of the dollar-denominated returns of the individual country indexes in Table 25.4 where weights are based on the proportion of each country in the World portfolio from Table 25.1. While this sample is not the complete World portfolio, it accounts for over 95% of world market capitalization.

Table 25.4

Stock market volatility using both local and dollar-denominated returns

	Standard Deviation of Monthly Returns		Correlation with $-Denominated MSCI World	
	Local Currency	Dollar-Denominated	Local Currency	Dollar-Denominated
S&P 500	0.032	0.032	0.958	0.905
Nikkei	0.060	0.044	0.696	0.796
FTSE	0.038	0.044	0.863	0.855
Shanghai	0.071	0.072	0.254	0.545
Euronext	0.045	0.048	0.837	0.856
Hang Seng	0.052	0.052	0.653	0.777
Toronto	0.025	0.037	0.711	0.401
Swiss	0.044	0.039	0.726	0.845
India	0.045	0.065	0.614	0.603
Korea	0.035	0.051	0.693	0.743
MSCI-Arabian	0.047		0.494	
MSCI-Latin America	0.070		0.725	
MSCI World	0.035	0.034	0.952	1.000
Mean	0.045	0.048	0.701	0.733
Median	0.045	0.046	0.703	0.786

Source: Authors' calculations using returns downloaded from Datastream.

using either dollar-denominated or local currency returns. The Shanghai index is notable for its low local-currency correlation with the rest of the world.

Table 25.5 shows results for index model regressions of each country's index against the MSCI World portfolio. The betas of each index against the World portfolio appear in the first pair of columns. The beta of the U.S. against the World portfolio is less than 1, as is the median beta of the other indexes in the sample. Betas computed from dollar-denominated returns are on average higher than those using local returns but, with the exception of China, not substantially so.

We do not report country-index alphas in this table because results over 5 years are such unreliable forecasts of future performance. As we noted above, this is a common problem in using an historical sample to estimate expected returns (as opposed to risk measures). It is why many decades of data are commonly used to estimate "normal" returns on the broad market portfolio. Nevertheless, in this sample period, we can report that the median alpha in local currency was only 1 basis point, almost precisely zero. The dollar generally appreciated over this period, so the average dollar-denominated alpha was negative, −32 basis points per month.

The second pair of columns in Table 25.5 show the residual standard deviation for each country index. As discussed in Chapter 8, the regression residual in each month is the portion of the country return that is independent of the return on the World portfolio. The entries in these columns are therefore estimates of the standard deviation of "country-specific returns." The results are consistent with the other risk measures. The U.S. has by far the lowest country-specific risk, reflecting its prominence in the World portfolio, and China has the highest, consistent with its lower correlation with the World portfolio. Indexes for the countries in the Arab world and Latin America have above-average nonsystematic risk despite the fact that these indexes already enjoy some diversification across

Table 25.5

Index model regressions of country indexes against the MSCI World index using both local and dollar-denominated returns

	Beta against MSCI World		Residual Standard Deviation	
	Local Currency	Dollar-Denominated	Local Currency	Dollar-Denominated
S&P 500	0.885	0.847	0.009	0.014
Nikkei	1.207	1.022	0.043	0.027
FTSE	0.955	1.095	0.019	0.023
Shanghai	0.521	1.150	0.069	0.061
Euronext	1.089	1.195	0.025	0.025
Hang Seng	0.975	1.186	0.039	0.033
Toronto	0.512	0.428	0.018	0.033
Swiss	0.919	0.954	0.030	0.021
India	0.804	1.140	0.036	0.052
Korea	0.692	1.109	0.025	0.034
MSCI-Arabian	0.667		0.041	
MSCI-Latin America	1.473		0.049	
World	1.000		0.000	
Mean	0.856	1.013	0.031	0.032
Median	0.902	1.102	0.028	0.030

Source: Authors' calculations using returns downloaded from Datastream.

the countries included in each region. Average country-specific risk is essentially the same regardless of whether returns are measured in local or foreign currency. By and large, country-specific risk is meaningful. Even the U.S. value of 1.4% per month is not trivial. The message is that international diversification is potentially valuable.

By and large, the results in Table 25.4 and Table 25.5 indicate that investment risk is pretty much the same regardless of whether we use local currency or dollar-denominated returns. Therefore, we will focus largely on local returns when we turn to the potential for international diversification in the next section.

International Diversification

In Chapter 7, we looked at the risk of equally weighted portfolios composed of different numbers of U.S. stocks chosen at random and saw the efficacy of naïve diversification. Figure 25.3 presents the results of a similar exercise, but one in which diversification includes stocks from around the world. You can

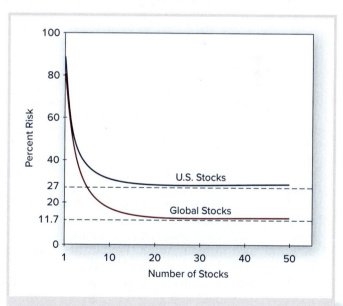

Figure 25.3 International diversification. Portfolio standard deviation as a percentage of the average standard deviation of a one-stock portfolio

Source: B. Solnik, "Why Not Diversify Internationally Rather Than Domestically?" *Financial Analysts Journal*, July/August 1974, pp. 48–54. Copyright 1995, CFA Institute. Reproduced and republished from *Financial Analysts Journal* with permission from the CFA Institute.

Investors' Challenge: Markets Seem Too Linked

It's one of the golden rules of investing: Reduce risk by diversifying your money into a variety of holdings—stock funds, bonds, commodities—that don't move in lockstep with one another. And it's a rule that's getting tougher to obey.

According to recent research, an array of investments whose prices used to rise and fall independently are now increasingly correlated. For an example, look no further than the roller coaster in emerging-markets stocks of recent weeks. The MSCI EAFE index, which measures emerging markets, now shows .96 correlation to the S&P, up from just .32 six years ago.

For investors, that poses a troubling issue: how to maintain a portfolio diversified enough so all the pieces don't tank at once.

The current correlation trend doesn't mean investors should go out and ditch their existing investments. It's just that they may not be "getting the same diversification" they thought if the investment decisions were made some time ago, says Mr. Ezrati, chief economist at money-management firm Lord Abbett & Co. He adds that over long periods of time, going back decades, sometimes varied asset classes tend to converge.

One explanation for today's higher correlation is increased globalization, which has made the economies of various countries more interdependent. International stocks, even with their higher correlations at present, deserve some allocation in a long-term investor's holdings, says Jeff Tjornehoj, an analyst at data firm Lipper Inc. Mr. Tjornehoj is among those who believe these correlations are a temporary phenomenon, and expects that the diversity will return some time down the line—a year or few years.

Source: Shefali Anand, "Investors Challenge: Markets Seem Too Linked," *The Wall Street Journal*, June 2, 2006, p. C1.

---

see that extending the universe of investable assets to foreign stocks allows even greater opportunities for risk reduction.

Of course, as emphasized in the nearby box, the benefits from diversification depend on the correlation structure among securities. The box notes that international correlations have increased over time. Table 25.6 shows correlation pairs (using local currency returns) for our sample of country and regional indexes from a recent five-year period. This correlation matrix can be used to construct the minimum-variance portfolio, which provides a

	S&P 500	Nikkei	FTSE	Shanghai	Euronext	Hang Seng	Toronto	Swiss	India	Korea	Arabian	Latin Am.	World
S&P 500	1.000	0.684	0.832	0.231	0.790	0.555	0.633	0.697	0.562	0.621	0.461	0.677	0.958
Nikkei	0.684	1.000	0.644	0.341	0.621	0.484	0.377	0.636	0.511	0.513	0.283	0.473	0.696
FTSE	0.832	0.644	1.000	0.233	0.844	0.651	0.649	0.724	0.588	0.627	0.353	0.716	0.863
Shanghai	0.231	0.341	0.233	1.000	0.232	0.590	0.231	0.113	0.153	0.360	0.199	0.277	0.254
Euronext	0.790	0.621	0.844	0.232	1.000	0.535	0.559	0.730	0.455	0.578	0.339	0.558	0.837
Hang Seng	0.555	0.484	0.651	0.590	0.535	1.000	0.615	0.393	0.548	0.711	0.486	0.753	0.653
Toronto	0.633	0.377	0.649	0.231	0.559	0.615	1.000	0.484	0.521	0.543	0.442	0.674	0.711
Swiss	0.697	0.636	0.724	0.113	0.730	0.393	0.484	1.000	0.339	0.485	0.272	0.355	0.726
India	0.562	0.511	0.588	0.153	0.455	0.548	0.521	0.339	1.000	0.566	0.266	0.624	0.614
Korea	0.621	0.513	0.627	0.360	0.578	0.711	0.543	0.485	0.566	1.000	0.478	0.692	0.693
Arabian	0.461	0.283	0.353	0.199	0.339	0.486	0.442	0.272	0.266	0.478	1.000	0.472	0.494
Latin Am.	0.677	0.473	0.716	0.277	0.558	0.753	0.674	0.355	0.624	0.692	0.472	1.000	0.725
World	0.958	0.696	0.863	0.254	0.837	0.653	0.711	0.726	0.614	0.693	0.494	0.725	1.000

Table 25.6

Correlation matrix of returns using local currency returns, 2011–2016

Source: Authors' calculations using returns downloaded from Datastream.

	Equally Weighted Portfolio	Minimum Variance Portfolio	Minimum Variance Portfolio (no short sales)
A. Weights			
S&P 500	0.083	0.318	0.114
Nikkei	0.083	−0.034	0.000
FTSE	0.083	0.207	0.000
Shanghai	0.083	0.051	0.024
Euronext	0.083	−0.149	0.000
Hang Seng	0.083	−0.103	0.000
Toronto	0.083	0.696	0.742
Swiss	0.083	−0.107	0.000
India	0.083	0.046	0.000
Korea	0.083	0.308	0.109
Arabian	0.083	0.044	0.012
Latin Am.	0.083	−0.276	0.000
B. Volatility			
Std dev	0.033	0.019	0.024

Table 25.7

Composition and volatility of internationally diversified portfolios

Source: Authors' calculations using returns downloaded from Datastream.

better estimate of the potential benefits from diversification than the naïve diversification exercise conducted in Figure 25.3.

Table 25.7 shows portfolio volatility using equal weights for each country or regional index (column 1), using minimum variance weights (column 2), or using minimum variance weights without allowing short sales (column 3). The equally weighted portfolio is in the spirit of Figure 25.3. Even naïve diversification provides considerable benefit: The standard deviation of the portfolio is 3.3%, which is only 70% of the average of the individual country standard deviations. But we can reduce volatility considerably from this level. The minimum variance portfolio has a standard deviation of only 1.9% when we allow short sales, and 2.4% when we do not. We see here ample evidence for the potential of international diversification to substantially reduce portfolio risk.

What about efficient diversification that achieves the best risk–return trade-off? This is harder to assess because, as we have pointed out several times, sample average returns do not provide reliable estimates of expected returns. However, as an alternative to historical returns, we can estimate expected returns from an international version of the CAPM. Table 25.8 presents such estimates using the MSCI World index as the market portfolio and assuming a risk-free rate of 2% and market risk premium of 8%. Given these expected returns, the standard deviations in Table 25.4, and the correlation matrix in Table 25.6, we can generate the efficient frontier. The results appear in Figure 25.4.

The frontier in Figure 25.4 is drawn without allowing for short sales. This reflects the constraints on shorting imposed on many institutional traders. Even with this restriction, however, the benefits of international diversification are evident. The U.S. portfolio (the S&P 500) appears as the solid dot and is located substantially below the capital allocation line,

Table 25.8

Expected rates of return using local-currency betas against the MSCI World portfolio and an international CAPM

	Beta	Expected Return (%)
S&P 500	0.885	9.1%
Nikkei	1.207	11.7
FTSE	0.955	9.6
Shanghai	0.521	6.2
Euronext	1.089	10.7
Hang Seng	0.975	9.8
Toronto	0.512	6.1
Swiss	0.919	9.3
India	0.804	8.4
Korea	0.692	7.5
MSCI—Arabian	0.667	7.3
MSCI—Latin America	1.473	13.8
World	1.000	10.0

Source: Betas calculated by authors using returns downloaded from Datastream. Expected returns are derived from the CAPM, assuming a risk-free rate of 2% and market risk premium of 8%.

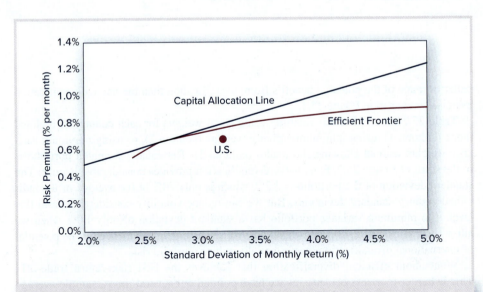

Figure 25.4 Efficient frontier and CAL using country and regional stock indexes

Source: Authors' calculations using data from Tables 25.7 and 25.8.

despite the fact that its weight in the tangency portfolio is nearly 50%. The CAL supported by the U.S. index has a Sharpe ratio (based on monthly returns) of .185, considerably lower than the Sharpe ratio of the tangency portfolio, which is .248. Thus, a U.S. investor who foregoes international equity markets is giving up ample opportunities to improve the risk–return trade-off of his risky portfolio.

Are Benefits from International Diversification Preserved in Bear Markets?

Some studies suggest that correlation in country portfolio returns increases during periods of turbulence in capital markets.[5] If so, benefits from diversification would be lost exactly when they are needed the most. For example, a study by Roll of the crash of October 1987 shows that all 23 country indexes studied declined over the crash period of October 12–26.[6] This correlation is reflected in the movements of regional indexes depicted in Figure 25.5. Roll found that the beta of a country index on the world index (estimated prior to the crash) was the best predictor of that index's response to the October crash of the U.S. stock market. This suggests a common factor underlying the movement of stocks around the world. This model predicts that a macroeconomic shock would affect all countries and that while diversification can mitigate risk, it cannot eliminate exposure to such broad-based events.

The 2008 crash of stock markets around the world allows us to test Roll's prediction. The data in Figure 25.6 include average monthly rates of return for both the 10-year period 1999–2008 and the crisis period corresponding to the last 4 months of 2008, as well as the beta on the U.S. market and monthly standard deviation for several portfolios. The graph shows that both beta against the U.S. and the country-index standard deviation help explain the difference between crisis period returns and overall period averages. Market behavior during the 1987 crisis, that is, larger correlations in extreme bad times, repeated itself in the crisis of 2008, vindicating Roll's prediction.

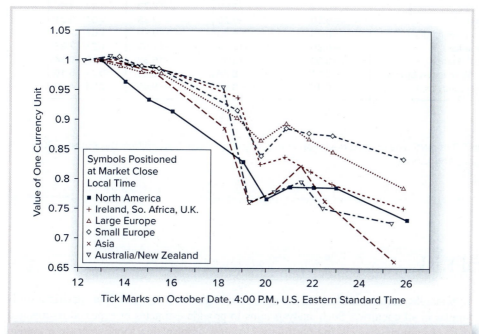

Figure 25.5 Regional indexes around the crash, October 14–October 26, 1987

Source: From Richard Roll, "The International Crash of October 1987," *Financial Analysts Journal,* September–October 1988. Copyright 1995, CFA Institute. Reproduced from *Financial Analysts Journal* with permission from the CFA Institute.

---

[5]F. Longin and B. Solnik, "Is the Correlation in International Equity Returns Constant: 1960–1990?" *Journal of International Money and Finance* 14 (1995), pp. 3–26; and Eric Jacquier and Alan Marcus, "Asset Allocation Models and Market Volatility," *Financial Analysts Journal* 57 (March/April 2001), pp. 16–30.

[6]Richard Roll, "The International Crash of October 1987," *Financial Analysts Journal,* September–October 1988.

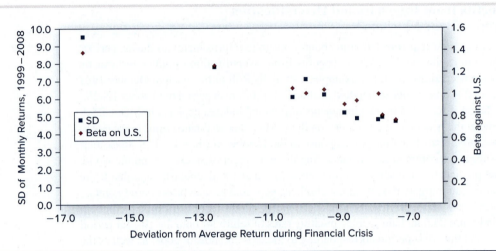

Market	Average Monthly Return 1999–2008	Average Monthly Return 2008: Sept.–Dec.	Deviation from Average	Beta on U.S.	SD
USA	−0.47	−8.31	−7.84	1	4.81
World largest six (non–U.S.) markets	−0.16	−7.51	−7.35	0.77	4.71
EU developed markets	−0.05	−10.34	−10.29	1.06	6.08
Other Europe developed markets	−0.14	−7.59	−7.73	0.82	4.95
Australia + Far East	−0.10	−9.29	−9.38	1.04	6.21
Emerging Far East + South Africa	−0.20	−9.70	−9.90	1.01	7.10
Emerging Latin America	−0.80	−11.72	−12.52	1.27	7.83
Emerging markets in Europe	−0.90	−15.43	−16.32	1.38	9.54
World minus U.S. (48 countries by cap)	−0.01	−8.79	−8.81	0.91	5.19
World portfolio (by country cap)	−0.15	−8.60	−8.45	0.94	4.88

Figure 25.6 Beta and SD of portfolios against deviation of monthly return over September–December 2008 from average return over 1999–2008

Source: Authors' calculations.

25.3 Political Risk

In principle, security analysis at the macroeconomic, industry, and firm-specific level is similar in all countries. Such analysis aims to provide estimates of expected returns and risks of individual assets and portfolios. However, information about assets in a foreign country is by nature more difficult to acquire.

Consider two investors: an American wishing to invest in Indonesian stocks and an Indonesian wishing to invest in U.S. stocks. While each would have to conduct fundamental analysis of each foreign company, the task would be much more difficult for the American investor. The reason is not that investment in Indonesia is *necessarily* riskier than investment in the U.S. You can easily find U.S. stocks that are, in the final analysis, riskier than a number of Indonesian stocks. The difference lies in the fact that U.S. financial markets are more transparent than those of Indonesia.

In addition, **political risk** varies dramatically across countries and its assessment requires expertise in each nation's economic, legal, tax, and political environment. A leading organization providing political risk assessment for investors is the PRS Group (Political Risk Services), and the presentation here follows the PRS methodology.[7]

PRS's country risk analysis results in a country composite risk rating on a scale of 0 (most risky) to 100 (least risky). To illustrate, Table 25.9 shows the rank of a small sample of countries from the January 2015 issue of PRS's *International Country Risk Guide*. It is not surprising to find Switzerland at the top of the low-risk list and small emerging markets at the bottom, with Somalia (ranked 140) closing the list. What may be surprising is the fairly mediocre ranking of the U.S. (ranked 27).

The composite risk rating is a weighted average of three measures: political risk, financial risk, and economic risk. Political risk is measured on a scale of 100–0, while financial risk and economic risk are each measured on a scale of 50–0. The three measures are added and divided by 2 to obtain the composite rating. The variables used by PRS to determine the composite risk rating from the three measures are shown in Table 25.10.

Table 25.11 shows the three risk measures for 11 countries in order of the January 2015 ranking of composite risk. The table shows that the United States was among the best performers in terms of political risk. But it was at the bottom of this (admittedly short) list in terms of financial risk. The surprisingly poor performance of the U.S. in this dimension was probably due to its exceedingly large government and balance-of-trade deficits, which put pressure on its exchange rate. Exchange rate stability, foreign trade imbalance, and foreign indebtedness all enter PRS's computation of financial risk.

Table 25.9

Composite risk ratings for January 2014 and January 2015

Rank	Country	Risk Rating, 2015	Risk Rating, 2014
1	Switzerland	89.8	89.5
6	Canada	83.0	82.3
6	Germany	83.0	85.3
10	Qatar	82.3	82.0
19	Japan	79.5	81.5
27	United States	77.3	75.3
47	China, Peoples' Rep.	72.0	73.3
59	Spain	69.5	69.3
68	Brazil	68.0	69.3
77	Indonesia	67.0	65.5
90	Russia	64.5	69.5
97	Turkey	63.3	59.3
118	Haiti	60.8	58.8
126	Pakistan	58.3	61.3
132	Venezuela	54.8	54.3
138	Liberia	49.3	52.8
139	Syria	41.3	42.0
140	Somalia	37.5	37.5

Source: *International Country Risk Guide*, January 2015, The PRS Group, Inc.

[7]You can find more information on the Web site: **www.prsgroup.com.** We are grateful to the PRS Group for supplying data and guidance.

Political Risk Variables	Financial Risk Variables	Economic Risk Variables
Government stability	Foreign debt (% of GDP)	GDP per capita
Socioeconomic conditions	Foreign debt service (% of exports)	Real annual GDP growth
Investment profile	Current account (% of exports)	Annual inflation rate
Internal conflicts	Net liquidity (months of import cover)	Budget balance (% of GDP)
External conflicts	Exchange rate stability	Current account balance (% GDP)
Corruption		
Military in politics		
Religious tensions		
Law and order		
Ethnic tensions		
Democratic accountability		
Bureaucracy quality		

Table 25.10

Variables used in PRS's political risk score

Table 25.11

Country risk rankings by category, 2015

Country	Political	Financial	Economic	Composite
Pakistan	48.5	37.5	30.5	58.3
Turkey	53.0	37.5	36.0	63.3
Russia	56.5	35.5	37.0	64.5
India	61.0	43.0	33.5	68.8
China, Peoples' Rep.	56.5	47.5	40.0	72.0
United States	82.5	32.5	39.5	77.3
United Kingdom	84.0	35.5	38.0	78.8
Qatar	73.5	42.5	48.5	82.3
Canada	85.0	39.0	42.0	83.0
Germany	84.5	38.0	43.5	83.0
Switzerland	88.0	46.5	45.0	89.8

Source: *International Country Risk Guide*, January 2015, The PRS Group, Inc.

Finally, Table 25.12 shows ratings of political risk by each of its 12 components. The U.S. does well in corruption risk (variable F) and democratic accountability (variable K). China does well in government stability (variable A) but poorly in democratic accountability (variable K).

Each monthly issue of the *International Country Risk Guide* of the PRS Group includes great detail and holds some 250 pages. Other organizations compete in supplying such evaluations. The result is that today's investor can become well equipped to properly assess the risk involved in international investing.

This table lists the total points for each of the following political risk components out of the maximum points indicated. The final column shows the overall political risk rating (the sum of the points awarded to each component).

A	Government stability	12	G	Military in politics	6
B	Socioeconomic conditions	12	H	Religious tensions	6
C	Investment profile	12	I	Law and order	6
D	Internal conflict	12	J	Ethnic tensions	6
E	External conflict	12	K	Democratic accountability	6
F	Corruption	6	L	Bureaucracy quality	4

Country	A	B	C	D	E	F	G	H	I	J	K	L	Risk Rating
Pakistan	6.0	5.5	7.0	6.0	9.0	2.0	1.5	1.0	3.0	1.0	4.5	2.0	48.5
Turkey	7.5	6.0	6.0	7.0	7.0	2.5	2.0	4.0	3.0	2.0	4.0	2.0	53.0
Russia	9.0	5.5	7.5	7.5	7.0	1.5	4.0	5.5	3.0	3.0	2.0	1.0	56.5
China, Peoples' Rep.	9.0	7.0	6.0	7.0	8.0	2.0	3.0	4.0	3.5	3.5	1.5	2.0	56.5
India	8.5	5.0	7.5	6.5	9.0	2.5	4.0	2.5	4.0	2.5	6.0	3.0	61.0
Qatar	10.5	8.0	10.0	9.5	8.5	4.0	4.0	4.0	5.0	6.0	2.0	2.0	73.5
United States	7.5	9.5	12.0	10.0	9.5	4.5	4.0	5.5	5.0	5.0	6.0	4.0	82.5
United Kingdom	7.5	9.5	11.5	10.0	9.5	5.0	6.0	6.0	5.0	4.0	6.0	4.0	84.0
Germany	8.5	9.0	11.0	10.5	10.5	5.0	6.0	5.0	5.0	4.0	6.0	4.0	84.5
Canada	7.5	8.5	12.0	10.0	11.0	5.0	6.0	6.0	5.5	3.5	6.0	4.0	85.0
Switzerland	9.0	10.5	11.5	12.0	10.5	5.0	6.0	4.5	5.0	4.0	6.0	4.0	88.0

Table 25.12

Political risk points by component, January 2015

Source: *International Country Risk Guide,* January 2015, The PRS Group, Inc.

25.4 International Investing and Performance Attribution

Because many security markets may be less efficient than those in highly developed economies such as the U.S., international investing offers greater opportunities for active managers. International investing calls for specialization in additional fields of analysis: currency, country and worldwide industry, as well as a greater universe for stock selection.

Constructing a Benchmark Portfolio of Foreign Assets

Active (as well as passive) international investing requires a benchmark portfolio (called the *bogey*). One widely used international market index is the MSCI World index. MSCI also computes variants on this index that exclude some large markets such as the U.S. Another popular non-U.S. index is the **Europe, Australasia, Far East (EAFE) index** of large and mid-cap securities in 21 developed markets, also computed by MSCI. Other indexes of world equity performance are published by Capital International Indices, Salomon Brothers, Credit Suisse First Boston, and Goldman Sachs. Portfolios designed to mirror or even replicate the country, currency, and company representation of these indexes would be the obvious generalization of the purely domestic passive equity strategy.

An issue that sometimes arises in the international context is the appropriateness of market-capitalization weighting schemes in the construction of international indexes. Capitalization weighting is far and away the most common approach. However, some argue that it might not be the best weighting scheme in an international context. This is in part because different countries have differing proportions of their corporate sector organized as publicly traded firms.

Table 25.13 shows market-capitalization weights versus GDP weights for countries in the EAFE index. These data reveal substantial disparities between the relative sizes of market capitalization and GDP. The countries with smaller stock markets (toward the bottom of the table) tend to have a much smaller share of EAFE total market capitalization than they do of EAFE GDP. For example, while Portugal accounts for 0.5% of total EAFE GDP, it represents only 0.1% of the market cap of the index. At the other extreme, Hong Kong accounts for only 0.7% of GDP, but it represents 6.5% of total EAFE market cap. These disparities indicate that a greater proportion of economic activity is conducted by publicly traded firms in Hong Kong than in the other EAFE countries.

Some argue that it would be more appropriate to weight international indexes by GDP rather than market capitalization. The justification for this view is that an internationally diversified portfolio should purchase shares in proportion to the broad asset base of each country, and GDP might be a better measure of the weight of a country in the international

Table 25.13

Weighting schemes for EAFE countries, 2015

	% of EAFE Market Capitalization	% of EAFE GDP
United States	50.8%	43.1%
Japan	9.9	9.9
Hong Kong	6.5	0.7
United Kingdom	5.6	6.8
France	4.2	5.8
Germany	3.5	8.1
Canada	3.2	3.7
Switzerland	3.1	1.6
Sweden	2.6	1.2
Australia	2.4	3.2
Spain	1.6	2.9
Netherlands	1.5	1.8
Singapore	1.3	0.7
Italy	1.2	4.4
Belgium	0.8	1.1
Norway	0.4	0.9
Denmark	0.4	0.7
Finland	0.3	0.6
Ireland	0.3	0.6
Austria	0.2	0.9
New Zealand	0.2	0.4
Portugal	0.1	0.5
Greece	0.1	0.5

Source: Authors' calculations using data from Tables 25.1 and 25.2.

This Excel model provides an efficient frontier analysis similar to that in Chapter 7. In Chapter 7 the frontier was based on individual securities, whereas this model examines the returns on international exchange-traded funds and enables us to analyze the benefits of international diversification. The Excel spreadsheet is available in Connect or through your course instructor.

Excel Questions

1. Find three points on the efficient frontier corresponding to three different expected returns. What are the portfolio standard deviations corresponding to each expected return?

2. Now assume that the correlation between the S&P 500 and the other country indexes is cut in half. Find the new standard deviations corresponding to each of the three expected returns. Are they higher or lower? Why?

	A	B	C	D	E	F	G	H	I	J
58		Bordered Covariance Matrix for Target Return Portfolio								
59		EWD	EWH	EWI	EWJ	EWL	EWP	EWW	SP 500	
60	Weights	0.00	0.00	0.08	0.38	0.02	0.00	0.00	0.52	
61	0.0000	0.00	0.00	0.00	0.00	0.00	0.00	0.00	0.00	
62	0.0000	0.00	0.00	0.00	0.00	0.00	0.00	0.00	0.00	
63	0.0826	0.00	0.00	4.63	3.21	0.55	0.00	0.00	7.69	
64	0.3805	0.00	0.00	3.21	98.41	1.82	0.00	0.00	53.79	
65	0.0171	0.00	0.00	0.55	1.82	0.14	0.00	0.00	2.09	
66	0.0000	0.00	0.00	0.00	0.00	0.00	0.00	0.00	0.00	
67	0.0000	0.00	0.00	0.00	0.00	0.00	0.00	0.00	0.00	
68	0.5198	0.00	0.00	7.69	53.79	2.09	0.00	0.00	79.90	
69	1.0000	0.00	0.00	16.07	157.23	4.59	0.00	0.00	143.47	
70										
71	Port Via	321.36								
72	Port S.D.	17.93								
73	Port Mean	12.00								
74										
75										
76					Weights					
77	Mean	St. Dev	EWD	EWH	EWI	EWJ	EWL	EWP	EWW	SP 500
78	6	21.89	0.02	0.00	0.00	0.71	0.00	0.02	0.00	0.26
79	9	19.66	0.02	0.00	0.02	0.53	0.02	0.00	0.00	0.41
80	12	17.93	0.00	0.00	0.08	0.38	0.02	0.00	0.00	0.52
81	15	16.81	0.00	0.00	0.14	0.22	0.02	0.00	0.00	0.62
82	18	16.46	0.00	0.00	0.19	0.07	0.02	0.00	0.00	0.73
83	21	17.37	0.00	0.00	0.40	0.00	0.00	0.00	0.00	0.60
84	24	21.19	0.00	0.00	0.72	0.00	0.00	0.00	0.00	0.28
85	27	26.05	0.00	0.00	1.00	0.00	0.00	0.00	0.00	0.00
86										
87										

economy than the value of its outstanding stocks. Others have even suggested weights proportional to the import share of various countries. The argument is that investors who wish to hedge the price of imported goods might choose to hold securities in foreign firms in proportion to the goods imported from those countries.

Performance Attribution

We can measure the contribution of each of the following decisions to portfolio performance following a procedure similar to the performance attribution techniques introduced in Chapter 24.

1. **Currency selection** measures the contribution to total portfolio performance attributable to exchange rate fluctuations relative to the investor's benchmark currency, which we will take to be the U.S. dollar. We might use a benchmark like the EAFE index to compare a portfolio's currency selection for a particular period to that of a

passive benchmark. The benchmark for currency selection would be the weighted average of the appreciation of the currencies represented in the EAFE portfolio using as weights the fraction of that portfolio invested in each currency.

2. **Country selection** measures the contribution to portfolio performance attributable to investing in the better-performing stock markets of the world. It can be assessed from the weighted average of the equity *index* returns of each country using as weights the share of the manager's portfolio in each country. We use index returns to abstract from the effect of security selection within countries. To measure the contribution of country selection, we compare the manager's weighted average to the weighted average of a benchmark passive allocation, for example, the share of the EAFE portfolio in each country.

3. **Stock selection** ability may, as in Chapter 24, be measured as the weighted average of equity returns *in excess of the equity index* in each country. Here, we would use local currency returns and use as weights the investments in each country.

4. **Cash/bond selection** may be measured as the excess return derived from weighting bonds and bills differently from some benchmark weights.

Table 25.14 provides an example of how to measure the contribution of the decisions an international portfolio manager might make.

Table 25.14

Example of performance attribution: International

	EAFE Weight	Return on Equity Index	Currency Appreciation $E_1/E_0 - 1$	Manager's Weight	Manager's Return
Europe	0.30	10%	10%	0.35	8%
Australasia	0.10	5	−10	0.10	7
Far East	0.60	15	30	0.55	18

Overall performance (dollar return = local return + currency appreciation)
EAFE: 0.30(10 + 10) + 0.10(5 − 10) + 0.60(15 + 30) = 32.5%
Manager: 0.35(8 + 10) + 0.10(7 − 10) + 0.55(18 + 30) = 32.4%
Loss of 0.10% relative to EAFE

Currency selection
EAFE: (0.30 × 10%) + (0.10 × (−10%)) + (0.60 × 30%) = 20% appreciation
Manager: (0.35 × 10%) + (0.10 × (−10%)) + (0.55 × 30%) = 19% appreciation
Loss of 1% relative to EAFE

Country selection
EAFE: (0.30 × 10%) + (0.10 × 5%) + (0.60 × 15%) = 12.5%
Manager: (0.35 × 10%) + (0.10 × 5%) + (0.55 × 15%) = 12.25%
Loss of 0.25% relative to EAFE

Stock selection
        (8% − 10%)0.35 + (7% − 5%)0.10 + (18% − 15%)0.55 = 1.15%
Contribution of 1.15% relative to EAFE

Sum of attributions (equal to overall performance)
Currency (−1%) + country (−.25%) + selection (1.15%) = −0.10%

Concept Check **25.3**

Using the data in Table 25.14, compute the manager's country and currency selection if portfolio weights had been 40% in Europe, 20% in Australasia, and 40% in the Far East.

SUMMARY

1. U.S. assets are only a part of the world portfolio. International capital markets offer important opportunities for portfolio diversification with enhanced risk–return characteristics.

2. Exchange rate risk imparts an extra source of uncertainty to investments denominated in foreign currencies. Much of that risk can be hedged in foreign exchange futures or forward markets, but a perfect hedge is not feasible unless the foreign currency rate of return is known.

3. Returns in different countries are far from perfectly correlated. Therefore, there is a benefit from international diversification. The minimum variance global portfolio has considerably lower volatility than almost any individual country index, including that of the U.S. More importantly, single-country stock indexes, again including those of the U.S., plot considerably inside the efficient frontier constructed when foreign equity markets are added to the investment menu. Therefore, international investing offers ample opportunities to improve the risk-reward trade-off.

4. International investing entails an added dimension of political risk, including uncertainty about government and social stability, democratic accountability, macroeconomic conditions, international trade, and legal protections afforded individuals, businesses, and investors. Several services now exist that sell information about political risk to interested parties.

5. Several world market indexes can form a basis for passive international investing. Active international management can be partitioned into currency selection, country selection, stock selection, and cash/bond selection.

KEY TERMS

exchange rate risk
interest rate parity relationship
covered interest arbitrage
relationship

political risk
Europe, Australasia, Far East
(EAFE) index
currency selection

country selection
stock selection
cash/bond selection

KEY EQUATIONS

Interest rate parity (covered interest arbitrage) for direct ($/foreign currency) exchange rates:

$$F_0 = E_0 \frac{1 + r_f(\text{U.S.})}{1 + r_f(\text{foreign})}$$

Interest rate parity for indirect (foreign currency/$) exchange rates:

$$F_0 = E_0 \frac{1 + r_f(\text{foreign})}{1 + r_f(\text{U.S.})}$$

PROBLEM SETS

1. Do you agree with the following claim? "U.S. companies with global operations can give you international diversification." Think about both business risk and foreign exchange risk.

2. In Figure 25.2, we provide stock market returns in both local and dollar-denominated terms. Which of these is more relevant? What does this have to do with whether the foreign exchange risk of an investment has been hedged?

3. Suppose a U.S. investor wishes to invest in a British firm currently selling for £40 per share. The investor has $10,000 to invest, and the current exchange rate is $2/£.

   a. How many shares can the investor purchase?
   b. Fill in the table below for rates of return after one year in each of the nine scenarios (three possible share prices denominated in pounds times three possible exchange rates).

Price per Share (£)	Pound-Denominated Return (%)	Dollar-Denominated Return for Year-End Exchange Rate		
		$1.80/£	$2/£	$2.20/£
£35				
£40				
£45				

   c. When is the dollar-denominated return equal to the pound-denominated return?

4. If each of the nine outcomes in Problem 3 is equally likely, find the standard deviation of both the pound- and dollar-denominated rates of return.

5. Now suppose the investor in Problem 3 also sells forward £5,000 at a forward exchange rate of $2.10/£.

   a. Recalculate the dollar-denominated returns for each scenario.
   b. What happens to the standard deviation of the dollar-denominated return? Compare it to both its old value and the standard deviation of the pound-denominated return.

6. Calculate the contribution to total performance from currency, country, and stock selection for the manager in the example below. All exchange rates are expressed as units of foreign currency that can be purchased with 1 U.S. dollar.

	EAFE Weight	Return on Equity Index	E_1/E_0	Manager's Weight	Manager's Return
Europe	0.30	20%	0.9	0.35	18%
Australasia	0.10	15	1.0	0.15	20
Far East	0.60	25	1.1	0.50	20

7. If the current exchange rate is $1.35/£, the 1-year forward exchange rate is $1.45/£, and the interest rate on British government bills is 3% per year, what risk-free dollar-denominated return can be locked in by investing in the British bills?

8. If you were to invest $10,000 in the British bills of Problem 7, how would you lock in the dollar-denominated return?

9. Much of this chapter was written from the perspective of a U.S. investor. But suppose you are advising an investor living in a small country (choose one to be concrete). How might the lessons of this chapter need to be modified for such an investor?

1. You are a U.S. investor who purchased British securities for £2,000 one year ago when the British pound cost U.S.$1.50. What is your total return (based on U.S. dollars) if the value of the securities is now £2,400 and the pound is worth $1.45? No dividends or interest were paid during this period.

2. The correlation coefficient between the returns on a broad index of U.S. stocks and the returns on indexes of the stocks of other industrialized countries is mostly _____, and the correlation coefficient between the returns on various diversified portfolios of U.S. stocks is mostly _____.

   a. less than .8; greater than .8.
   b. greater than .8; less than .8.
   c. less than 0; greater than 0.
   d. greater than 0; less than 0.

3. An investor in the common stock of companies in a foreign country may wish to hedge against the _____ of the investor's home currency and can do so by _____ the foreign currency in the forward market.

   a. depreciation; selling.
   b. appreciation; purchasing.
   c. appreciation; selling.
   d. depreciation; purchasing.

4. John Irish, CFA, is an independent investment adviser who is assisting Alfred Darwin, the head of the Investment Committee of General Technology Corporation, to establish a new pension fund. Darwin asks Irish about international equities and whether the Investment Committee should consider them as an additional asset for the pension fund.

   a. Explain the rationale for including international equities in General's equity portfolio. Identify and describe three relevant considerations in formulating your answer.
   b. List three possible arguments against international equity investment and briefly discuss the significance of each.
   c. To illustrate several aspects of the performance of international securities over time, Irish shows Darwin the accompanying graph of investment results experienced by a U.S. pension fund in the recent past. Compare the performance of the U.S. dollar and non-U.S. dollar equity and fixed-income asset categories, and explain the significance of the result of the account performance index relative to the results of the four individual asset class indexes.

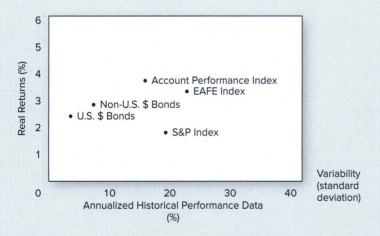

5. You are a U.S. investor considering purchase of one of the following securities. Assume that the currency risk of the Canadian government bond will be hedged, and the 6-month discount on Canadian dollar forward contracts is −.75% versus the U.S. dollar.

Bond	Maturity	Coupon	Price
U.S. government	6 months	6.50%	100.00
Canadian government	6 months	7.50%	100.00

Calculate the expected price change required in the Canadian government bond that would result in the two bonds having equal total returns in U.S. dollars over a 6-month horizon. Assume that the yield on the U.S. bond is expected to remain unchanged.

6. A global manager plans to invest $1 million in U.S. government cash equivalents for the next 90 days. However, she is also authorized to use non-U.S. government cash equivalents, as long as the currency risk is hedged to U.S. dollars using forward currency contracts.

   a. What rate of return will the manager earn if she invests in money market instruments in either Canada or Japan and hedges the dollar value of her investment? Use the data in the following tables.

   b. What must be the approximate value of the 90-day interest rate available on U.S. government securities?

Interest Rates (APR): 90-Day Cash Equivalents

Japanese government	2.52%
Canadian government	6.74%

Exchange Rates: U.S. Dollars per Unit of Foreign Currency

	Spot	90-Day Forward
Japanese yen	0.0119	0.0120
Canadian dollar	0.7284	0.7269

7. The Windsor Foundation, a U.S.-based, not-for-profit charitable organization, has a diversified investment portfolio of $100 million. Windsor's board of directors is considering an initial investment in emerging market equities. Robert Houston, treasurer of the foundation, has made the following comments:

   a. "For an investor holding only developed market equities, the existence of stable emerging market currencies is one of several preconditions necessary for that investor to realize strong emerging market performance."

   b. "Local currency depreciation against the dollar has been a frequent occurrence for U.S. investors in emerging markets. U.S. investors have consistently seen large percentages of their returns erased by currency depreciation. This is true even for long-term investors."

   c. "Historically, the addition of emerging market stocks to a U.S. equity portfolio such as the S&P 500 index has reduced volatility; volatility has also been reduced when emerging market stocks are combined with an international portfolio such as the MSCI EAFE index."

   Discuss whether *each* of Houston's comments is correct or incorrect.

8. After much research on the developing economy and capital markets of the country of Otunia, your firm, GAC, has decided to include an investment in the Otunia stock market in its Emerging Markets Commingled Fund. However, GAC has not yet decided whether to invest actively or by indexing. Your opinion on the active versus indexing decision has been solicited. The following is a summary of the research findings:

   Otunia's economy is fairly well-diversified across agricultural and natural resources, manufacturing (both consumer and durable goods), and a growing finance sector. Transaction costs in securities markets are relatively large in Otunia because of high commissions and government "stamp taxes" on securities trades. Accounting standards and disclosure regulations are quite detailed, resulting in wide public availability of reliable information about companies' financial performance.

Capital flows into and out of Otunia, and foreign ownership of Otunia securities, is strictly regulated by an agency of the national government. The settlement procedures under these ownership rules often cause long delays in settling trades made by nonresidents. Senior finance officials in the government are working to deregulate capital flows and foreign ownership, but GAC's political consultant believes that isolationist sentiment may prevent much real progress in the short run.

a. Briefly discuss aspects of the Otunia environment that favor investing actively, and aspects that favor indexing.
b. Recommend whether GAC should invest in Otunia actively or by indexing. Justify your recommendation based on the factors identified in part (a).

E-INVESTMENTS EXERCISES

A common misconception is that investors can earn excess returns by investing in foreign bonds with higher interest rates than are available in the U.S. Interest rate parity implies that any such interest rate differentials will be offset by premiums or discounts in the forward or futures market for foreign currency.

Interest rates on government bonds in the U.S., U.K., Japan, Germany, and Australia can be found at **www.bloomberg.com/markets/rates/index.html.**

Spot exchange rates on international currencies can be found at **www.bloomberg.com/markets/currencies/fxc.html.**

Forward exchange rates on currency futures contracts can be found at **www.cmegroup.com/trading/fx/index.html.**

1. Select one of these countries and record the yield on a short-term government security from the Bloomberg Web site. Also make note of the U.S. Treasury yield on an instrument with the same (or closest possible) maturity.

2. Record the spot exchange rate from the Bloomberg site and the futures contract exchange rate from the CME Web site for the date closest to the maturity of the investment you chose in the previous question.

3. Calculate the rate of return available on the foreign government security, converting the foreign currency transactions into dollars at the current and forward exchange rates.

4. How well does interest rate parity seem to hold? Are there bargains to be found in other currencies? What factors might account for interest rate parity violation?

✅ SOLUTIONS TO CONCEPT CHECKS

1. $1 + r(\text{US}) = [1 + r_f(\text{UK})] \times (E_1/E_0)$
   a. $1 + r(\text{US}) = 1.1 \times 1.0 = 1.10$. Therefore, $r(\text{US}) = 10\%$.
   b. $1 + r(\text{US}) = 1.1 \times 1.1 = 1.21$. Therefore, $r(\text{US}) = 21\%$.
2. You must sell forward the number of pounds you will end up with at the end of the year. This value cannot be known with certainty, however, unless the rate of return of the pound-denominated investment is known.
   a. $10,000 \times 1.20 = 12,000$ pounds.
   b. $10,000 \times 1.30 = 13,000$ pounds.

3. *Country selection:*

$$(0.40 \times 10\%) + (0.20 \times 5\%) + (0.40 \times 15\%) = 11\%$$

This is a loss of 1.5% (11% versus 12.5%) relative to the EAFE passive benchmark.

Currency selection:

$$(0.40 \times 10\%) + (0.20 \times (-10\%)) + (0.40 \times 30\%) = 14\%$$

This is a loss of 6% (14% versus 20%) relative to the EAFE benchmark.

Hedge Funds

WHILE MUTUAL FUNDS are still the dominant form of investing in securities markets for most individuals, hedge funds enjoyed far greater growth rates in the last two decades, with assets under management increasing from $200 billion in 1997 to about $3 trillion in 2016. Like mutual funds, hedge funds allow private investors to pool assets to be invested by a fund manager. Unlike mutual funds, however, they are commonly organized as private partnerships and thus not subject to many SEC regulations. They typically are open only to wealthy or institutional investors.

Hedge funds touch on virtually every issue discussed in the earlier chapters of the text, including liquidity, security analysis, market efficiency, portfolio analysis, hedging, and option pricing. For example, these funds often bet on the relative mispricing of specific securities but hedge broad market exposure. This sort of pure "alpha seeking" behavior requires a procedure for optimally mixing a hedge fund position with a more traditional portfolio. Other funds engage in aggressive market timing; their risk profiles can shift rapidly and substantially, raising difficult questions for performance evaluation. Many hedge funds take extensive derivatives positions. Even those funds that do not trade derivatives charge incentive fees that resemble the payoff to a call option; an option-pricing background therefore is necessary to interpret both hedge fund strategies and costs. In short, hedge funds raise the full range of issues that one might confront in active portfolio management.

We begin with a survey of various hedge fund orientations. We devote considerable attention to the classic "market-neutral" or hedged strategies that historically gave hedge funds their name. We move on to evidence on hedge fund performance and the difficulties in evaluating that performance. Finally, we consider the implications of their unusual fee structure for investors in and managers of such funds.

26.1   Hedge Funds versus Mutual Funds

Like mutual funds, the basic idea behind **hedge funds** is investment pooling. Investors buy shares in these funds, which then invest the pooled assets on their behalf. The net asset value of each share represents the value of the investor's stake in the portfolio. In this regard, hedge funds operate much like mutual funds. However, there are important differences between the two.

Transparency   Mutual funds are subject to the Securities Act of 1933 and the Investment Company Act of 1940 (designed to protect unsophisticated investors), which require transparency and predictability of strategy. They periodically must provide the public with information on portfolio composition. In contrast, hedge funds usually are set up as limited liability partnerships or limited liability companies and provide minimal information about portfolio composition and strategy to their investors only.

Investors   Hedge funds traditionally are open only to "accredited" or sophisticated investors, in practice usually defined by minimum net worth and income requirements. They generally do not advertise to the general public, and minimum investments often are between $500,000 and $1 million.

Investment Strategies   Mutual funds lay out their general investment approach (e.g., large, value stock orientation versus small-cap growth orientation) in their prospectus. They face pressure to avoid *style drift* (departures from their stated investment orientation), especially given the importance of retirement funds such as 401(k) plans to the industry, and the demand of such plans for predictable strategies. Most mutual funds promise to limit their use of short-selling and leverage, and their use of derivatives is highly restricted. Some so-called 130/30 mutual funds,[1] serving primarily institutional clients, have prospectuses that explicitly allow for more active short-selling and derivatives positions, but even these have less flexibility than hedge funds. In contrast, hedge funds may effectively partake in any investment strategy and may act opportunistically as conditions evolve. For this reason, viewing hedge funds as anything remotely like a uniform asset class would be a mistake. Hedge funds by design are empowered to invest in a wide range of investments, with various funds focusing on derivatives, distressed firms, currency speculation, convertible bonds, emerging markets, merger arbitrage, and so on. Other funds may jump from one asset class to another as perceived investment opportunities shift.

Liquidity   Hedge funds often impose **lock-up periods,** that is, periods as long as several years in which investments cannot be withdrawn. Many also employ redemption notices requiring investors to provide notice weeks or months in advance of their desire to redeem funds. These restrictions limit the liquidity of investors but in turn enable the funds to invest in illiquid assets where returns may be higher, without worrying about meeting unanticipated demands for redemptions.

Compensation Structure   Hedge funds also differ from mutual funds in their fee structure. Whereas mutual funds assess management fees equal to a fixed percentage of assets, for example, between .5% and 1.25% annually for typical equity funds, hedge funds

---

[1]These are funds that may sell short up to 30% of the value of their portfolios, using the proceeds of the sale to increase their positions in invested assets. So for every $100 in net assets, the fund could sell short $30, investing the proceeds to increase its long positions to $130. This gives rise to the 130/30 moniker.

charge a management fee, usually between 1% and 2% of assets, *plus* a substantial *incentive fee* equal to a fraction of any investment profits beyond some benchmark. The incentive fee is often 20%. The threshold return to earn the incentive fee is often a money market rate such as LIBOR. Indeed, some observers only half-jokingly characterize hedge funds as "a compensation scheme masquerading as an asset class."

26.2   Hedge Fund Strategies

Table 26.1 lists most of the common investment themes found in the hedge fund industry. The list contains a wide diversity of styles and suggests how hard it can be to speak generically about hedge funds as a group. We can, however, divide hedge fund strategies into two general categories: directional and nondirectional.

Directional and Nondirectional Strategies

Directional strategies are easy to understand. They are simply bets that one sector or another will outperform other sectors of the market.

In contrast, **nondirectional strategies** are usually designed to exploit temporary misalignments in security valuations. For example, if the yield on corporate bonds seems abnormally high compared to that on Treasury bonds, the hedge fund would buy corporates

Convertible arbitrage	Hedged investing in convertible securities, typically long convertible bonds and short stock.
Dedicated short bias	Net short position, usually in equities, as opposed to pure short exposure.
Emerging markets	Goal is to exploit market inefficiencies in emerging markets. Typically long-only because short-selling is not feasible in many of these markets.
Equity market neutral	Commonly uses long/short hedges. Typically controls for industry, sector, size, and other exposures, and establishes market-neutral positions designed to exploit some market inefficiency. Commonly involves leverage.
Event driven	Attempts to profit from situations such as mergers, acquisitions, restructuring, bankruptcy, or reorganization.
Fixed-income arbitrage	Attempts to profit from price anomalies in related interest rate securities. Includes interest rate swap arbitrage, U.S. versus non-U.S. government bond arbitrage, yield-curve arbitrage, and mortgage-backed arbitrage.
Global macro	Involves long and short positions in capital or derivative markets across the world. Portfolio positions reflect views on broad market conditions and major economic trends.
Long/short equity hedge	Equity-oriented positions on either side of the market (i.e., long or short), depending on outlook. Not meant to be market neutral. May establish a concentrated focus regionally (e.g., U.S. or Europe) or on a specific sector (e.g., tech or health care stocks). Derivatives may be used to hedge positions.
Managed futures	Uses financial, currency, or commodity futures. May make use of technical trading rules or a less structured judgmental approach.
Multistrategy	Opportunistic choice of strategy depending on outlook.
Fund of funds	Fund allocates its cash to several other hedge funds to be managed.

Table 26.1

Hedge fund styles*

*Credit Suisse maintains one of the most comprehensive databases on hedge fund performance. It categorizes hedge funds into these different investment styles.

and short sell Treasury securities. Notice that the fund is *not* betting on broad movements in the entire bond market: It buys one type of bond and sells another. By taking a long corporate–short Treasury position, the fund hedges its interest rate exposure while making a bet on the *relative* valuation across the two sectors. The idea is that when yield spreads revert back to their "normal" relationship, the fund will profit from the realignment regardless of the general trend in the level of interest rates. In this respect, the bet is designed to be **market neutral**—or hedged—with respect to the direction of interest rates, which gives rise to the term "hedge fund."

Nondirectional strategies are sometimes further divided into *convergence* or *relative value* positions. The difference between convergence and relative value is a time horizon at which one can say with confidence that any mispricing ought to be resolved. An example of a convergence strategy would entail mispricing of a futures contract that must be corrected by the time the contract matures. In contrast, the corporate versus Treasury spread we just discussed would be a relative value strategy, because there is no obvious horizon during which the yield spread would "correct" from unusual levels.

Example 26.1   Market-Neutral Positions

We can illustrate a market-neutral position with a strategy used extensively by several hedge funds, which observed that newly issued or "on-the-run" 30-year Treasury bonds regularly sell at higher prices (lower yields) than 29½-year bonds with almost identical duration. The yield spread presumably is a premium due to the greater liquidity of the on-the-run bonds. Hedge funds, which have relatively low liquidity needs, therefore buy the 29½-year bond and sell the 30-year bond. This is a hedged, or market-neutral, position that will generate a profit whenever the yields on the two bonds converge, as typically happens when the 30-year bonds age, are no longer the most liquid on-the-run bond, and are no longer priced at a premium.

This strategy should generate profits regardless of the general direction of interest rates. The long–short position will return a profit as long as the 30-year bonds underperform the 29½-year bonds, as they should when the liquidity premium dissipates. Because the pricing discrepancies between these two securities almost necessarily *must* disappear at a given date, this strategy is an example of convergence arbitrage. While the convergence date in this application is not quite as definite as the maturity of a futures contract, one can be sure that the currently on-the-run T-bonds will lose that status by the time the Treasury next issues 30-year bonds.

Long–short positions such as in Example 26.1 are characteristic of hedged strategies. They are designed to *isolate* a bet on some mispricing without taking on market exposure. Profits are made regardless of broad market movements once prices "converge" or return to their "proper" levels. Hence, use of short positions and derivatives is part and parcel of the industry.

A more complex long–short strategy is *convertible bond arbitrage,* one of the more prominent sectors of the hedge-fund universe. Noting that a convertible bond may be viewed as a straight bond plus a call option on the underlying stock, the market-neutral strategy in this case involves a position in the bond offset by an opposite position in the stock. For example, if the convertible is viewed as underpriced, the fund will buy it and offset its resultant exposure to declines in the stock price by shorting the stock.

Although these market-neutral positions are hedged, they are *not* risk-free arbitrage strategies. Rather, they should be viewed as **pure plays,** that is, bets on *particular* (perceived) mispricing between two sectors or securities, with extraneous sources of risk such as general market exposure hedged away. Moreover, because the funds often operate with considerable leverage, returns can be quite volatile.

 Concept Check **26.1**

Classify each of the following strategies as directional or nondirectional.

  a. The fund buys shares in the India Investment Fund, a closed-end fund that is selling at a discount to net asset value, and sells the MSCI India Index Swap.

  b. The fund buys shares in Petrie Stores and sells Toys "R" Us, which is a major component of Petrie's balance sheet.

  c. The fund buys shares in Generic Pharmaceuticals betting that it will be acquired at a premium by Pfizer.

Statistical Arbitrage

Statistical arbitrage is a version of a market-neutral strategy, but one that merits its own discussion. It differs from pure arbitrage in that it does not exploit risk-free positions based on unambiguous mispricing (such as index arbitrage). Instead, it uses quantitative and often automated trading systems that seek out many temporary and modest misalignments in prices among securities. By taking relatively small positions in many of these opportunities, the law of averages would make the probability of profiting from the collection of apparently positive-value bets very high, ideally almost a "statistical certainty." Of course, this strategy presumes that the fund's modeling techniques can actually identify reliable, if small, market inefficiencies. The law of averages guarantees profits only if the expected return is positive!

Statistical arbitrage often involves trading in hundreds of securities a day with holding periods that can be measured in minutes or less. Such rapid and heavy trading requires extensive use of quantitative tools such as automated trading and mathematical algorithms to identify profit opportunities and efficient diversification across positions. These strategies try to profit from the smallest of perceived mispricing opportunities and require the fastest trading technology and the lowest possible trading costs. They would not be possible without the electronic communication networks discussed in Chapter 3.

One example of statistical arbitrage is **pairs trading,** in which stocks are paired up based on an analysis of either fundamental similarities or market exposures (betas). The general approach is to pair up similar companies whose returns are highly correlated but where one company seems to be priced more aggressively than the other.[2] Market-neutral positions can be formed by buying the relatively cheap firm and selling the expensive one. Many such pairs comprise the hedge fund's overall portfolio. Each pair may have an uncertain outcome, but with many such matched pairs, the presumption is that the large number of long–short bets will provide a very high probability of a positive abnormal return. More general versions of pairs trading allow for positions in clusters of stocks that may be relatively mispriced.

[2]Rules for deciding relative "aggressiveness" of pricing may vary. In one approach, a computer scans for stocks whose prices historically have tracked very closely but have recently diverged. If the differential in cumulative return typically dissipates, the fund will buy the recently underperforming stock and sell the outperforming one. In other variants, pricing aggressiveness may be determined by evaluating the stocks based on some measure of price to intrinsic value.

Statistical arbitrage is commonly associated with **data mining,** which refers to sorting through huge amounts of historical data to uncover systematic patterns in returns that can be exploited by traders. The risk of data mining, and statistical arbitrage in general, is that historical relationships may break down when fundamental economic conditions change or, indeed, that the apparent patterns in the data may be due to pure chance. Enough analysis applied to enough data is sure to produce apparent patterns that do not reflect real relationships that can be counted on to persist in the future.

26.3   Portable Alpha

An important implication of the market-neutral pure play is the notion of **portable alpha.** Suppose that you wish to speculate on a stock that you think is underpriced, but you think that the market is about to fall. Even if you are right about the stock being *relatively* underpriced, it still might decline in response to declines in the broad market. You would like to separate the stock-specific bet from the implicit asset allocation bet on market performance that arises because the stock's beta is positive. The solution is to buy the stock and eliminate the resultant market exposure by selling enough index futures to drive beta to zero. This long stock–short futures strategy gives you a pure play or, equivalently, a *market-neutral* position on the stock.

More generally, you might wish to separate asset allocation from security selection. The idea is to invest wherever you can "find alpha." You would then hedge the systematic risk of that investment to isolate its alpha from the asset market where it was found. Finally, you establish exposure to desired market sectors by using passive products such as indexed mutual funds, ETFs, or index futures. In other words, you have created portable alpha that can be mixed with an exposure to whatever sector of the market you choose. This procedure is also called **alpha transfer** because you transfer alpha from the sector where you find it to the asset class in which you ultimately establish exposure. Finding alpha requires skill. By contrast, beta, or market exposure, is a "standardized commodity" that can be supplied cheaply through index products and does not add value.

An Example of a Pure Play

Suppose you manage a $2.1 million portfolio. You believe that the alpha of the portfolio is positive, $\alpha > 0$, but also that the market is about to fall, that is, that $r_M < 0$. You would therefore try to establish a pure play on the perceived mispricing.

The return on portfolio over the next month may be described by Equation 26.1, which states that the portfolio return will equal its "fair" CAPM return (the first two terms on the right-hand side), plus firm-specific risk reflected in the "residual," e, plus an alpha that reflects perceived mispricing:

$$r_{\text{portfolio}} = r_f + \beta(r_M - r_f) + e + \alpha \tag{26.1}$$

To be concrete, suppose that $\beta = 1.20$, $\alpha = .02$, $r_f = .01$, the current value of the S&P 500 index is $S_0 = 2,016$, and, for simplicity, that the portfolio pays no dividends. You want to capture the positive alpha of 2% per month, but you don't want the positive beta that the stock entails because you are worried about a market decline. So you choose to hedge your exposure by selling S&P 500 futures contracts.

Because the most liquid E-mini S&P futures contracts have a multiplier of $50, and the portfolio has a beta of 1.20, your stock position can be hedged for one month by selling 25 futures contracts:[3]

$$\text{Hedge ratio} = \frac{\$2,100,000}{2,016 \times \$50} \times 1.20 = 25 \text{ contracts}$$

The dollar value of the stock portfolio after one month will be

$$\$2,100,000 \times (1 + r_{\text{portfolio}}) = \$2,100,000 \left[1 + .01 + 1.20 \left(r_M - .01 \right) + .02 + e \right]$$
$$= \$2,137,800 + \$2,520,000 \times r_M + \$2,100,000 \times e$$

The dollar proceeds from your futures position will be:

$25 \times \$50 \times (F_0 - F_1)$	Mark to market on 25 contracts sold
$= \$1,250 \times [S_0(1.01) - S_1]$	Substitute for futures prices from parity relationship
$= \$1,250 \times S_0[1.01 - (1 + r_M)]$	Because $S_1 = S_0(1 + r_M)$ when no dividends are paid
$= \$1,250 \times [S_0(.01 - r_M)]$	Simplify
$= \$25,200 - \$2,520,000 \times r_M$	Because $S_0 = 2,016$

The total value of the stock plus futures position at month's end will be the sum of the portfolio value plus the futures proceeds, which equals

$$\text{Hedged proceeds} = \$2,163,000 + \$2,100,000 \times e \qquad \textbf{(26.2)}$$

Notice that the exposure to the market from your futures position precisely offsets your exposure from the stock portfolio. In other words, you have reduced beta to zero. Your investment is $2.1 million, so your total monthly rate of return is 3% plus the remaining nonsystematic risk (the second term of Equation 26.2). The fair or equilibrium expected rate of return on such a zero-beta position is the risk-free rate, 1%, so you have preserved your alpha of 2%, while eliminating the market exposure of the stock portfolio.

This is an idealized example of a pure play. In particular, it simplifies by assuming a known and fixed portfolio beta, but it illustrates that the goal is to speculate on the stock while hedging out the undesired market exposure. Once this is accomplished, you can establish any desired exposure to other sources of systematic risk by buying indexes or entering index futures contracts in those markets. Thus, you have made alpha portable.

Figure 26.1 is a graphical analysis of this pure play. Panel A shows the excess returns to betting on a positive-alpha stock portfolio "naked," that is, unhedged. Your *expected* return is better than the equilibrium return consistent with your risk, but because of your market exposure you still can lose if the market declines. Panel B shows the characteristic line for the position with systematic risk hedged out. There is no market exposure.

 Concept Check **26.2**

What would be the dollar value and rate of return on the market-neutral position if the value of the residual turns out to be −4%? If the market return in that month is 5%, where would the plot of the strategy return lie in each panel of Figure 26.1?

---

[3]We simplify here by assuming that the maturity of the futures contract precisely equals the hedging horizon, in this case, one month. If the contract maturity were longer, one would have to slightly reduce the hedge ratio in a process called "tailing the hedge."

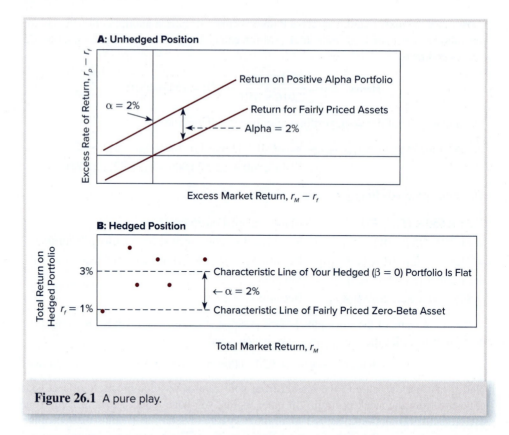

Figure 26.1 A pure play.

A warning: Even market-neutral positions are still bets, and they can go wrong. This is not true arbitrage because your profits still depend on whether your analysis (your perceived alpha) is correct. Moreover, you can be done in by simple bad luck, that is, your analysis may be correct but a bad realization of idiosyncratic risk (negative values of e in Equation 26.1 or 26.2) can still result in losses.

Example 26.2   The Risks of Pure Plays

An apparently market-neutral bet misfired badly in 1998. While the 30- versus 29½-year maturity T-bond strategy (see Example 26.1) worked well over several years, it blew up when Russia defaulted on its debt, triggering massive investment demand for the safest, most liquid assets that drove up the price of the 30-year Treasury relative to its 29½-year counterpart. The big losses that ensued illustrate that even the safest bet—one based on convergence arbitrage—carries risks. Although the T-bond spread had to converge eventually, and in fact it did several weeks later, Long Term Capital Management and other hedge funds suffered large losses on their positions when the spread widened temporarily. The ultimate convergence came too late for LTCM, which was also facing massive losses on its other positions and had to be bailed out.[4]

---

[4]This timing problem is a common one for active managers. We saw other examples of this issue when we discussed limits to arbitrage in Chapter 12. More generally, when security analysts think they have found a mispriced stock, they usually acknowledge that it is hard to know how long it will take for price to converge to intrinsic value.

Even market-neutral bets can result in considerable volatility because most hedge funds use considerable leverage. Most incidents of relative mispricing are fairly minor, and the hedged nature of long–short strategies makes overall volatility low. The hedge funds respond by scaling up their bets. This amplifies gains when their bets work out, but also amplifies losses. In the end, the volatility of the funds is not small.

26.4 Style Analysis for Hedge Funds

While the classic hedge fund strategy may have focused on market-neutral opportunities, as the market has evolved, the freedom to use derivatives contracts and short positions means that hedge funds can in effect follow any investment strategy. While many hedge funds pursue market-neutral strategies, a quick glance at the range of investment styles in Table 26.1 should convince you that many, if not most, funds pursue directional strategies. In these cases, the fund makes an outright bet, for example, on currency movements, the outcome of a takeover attempt, or the performance of an investment sector. These funds are most certainly not hedged, despite their name.

In Chapter 24, we introduced you to style analysis, which uses regression analysis to measure the exposure of a portfolio to various factors or asset classes. The analysis thus measures the implicit asset class exposure of a portfolio. The betas on a series of factors measure the fund's exposure to each source of systematic risk. A market-neutral fund will have no sensitivity to an index for that market. In contrast, directional funds will exhibit significant betas, often called *loadings* in this context, on whatever factors the fund tends to bet on. Observers attempting to measure investment style can use these factor loadings to impute exposures to a range of variables.

We present a simple style analysis for the hedge fund indexes in Table 26.2. The four systematic factors we consider are:

- Interest rates: the return on long-term U.S. Treasury bonds.
- Equity markets: the return on the S&P 500.
- Credit conditions: the difference in the return on Baa-rated bonds over Treasury bonds.
- Foreign exchange: the percentage change in the value of the U.S. dollar against a basket of foreign currencies.

The returns on hedge fund index i in month t may be statistically described by[5]

$$R_{it} = \alpha_i + \beta_{i1} \text{ Factor } 1_t + \cdots + \beta_{i4} \text{ Factor } 4_t + e_{it} \qquad \textbf{(26.3)}$$

The betas (equivalently, factor loadings) measure the sensitivity to each factor. As usual, the residual, e_{it}, measures nonsystematic risk that is uncorrelated with the set of explanatory factors, and the intercept, α_i, measures average performance of fund i net of the impact of these systematic factors.

Table 26.2 presents factor exposure estimates for 13 hedge fund indexes. The results confirm that most funds are in fact directional with very clear exposures to one or more

---

[5]This analysis differs in two important respects from style analysis for mutual funds introduced in Chapter 24. First, in this application, factor loadings are not constrained to be non-negative. This is because, unlike mutual funds, hedge funds easily can take on short positions in various asset classes. Second, portfolio weights are not constrained to sum to 1.0. Again, unlike mutual funds, hedge funds can operate with considerable leverage.

Fund Group*	Alpha	S&P 500	Long T-Bond	Credit Premium	U.S. Dollar
All funds	0.0052	0.2718	0.0189	0.1755	−0.1897
	3.3487	5.0113	0.3064	2.0462	−2.1270
Market neutral	0.0014	0.1677	−0.0163	0.3308	−0.5097
	0.1990	0.6917	−0.0589	0.8631	−1.2790
Short bias	0.0058	−0.9723	0.1310	0.3890	−0.2630
	1.3381	−6.3684	0.7527	1.6113	−1.0476
Event driven	0.0071	0.2335	0.0000	0.2056	−0.1165
	5.1155	4.7858	−0.0002	2.6642	0.1520
Risk arbitrage	0.0034	0.1498	0.0130	−0.0006	−0.2130
	3.0678	3.8620	0.0442	−0.0097	−3.3394
Distressed	0.0068	0.2080	0.0032	0.2521	−0.1156
	5.7697	4.9985	0.0679	3.8318	−1.6901
Emerging markets	0.0082	0.3750	0.2624	0.4551	−0.2169
	2.8867	3.7452	2.2995	2.8748	−1.3173
Fixed income	0.0018	0.1719	0.2284	0.5703	−0.1714
	1.0149	2.8139	3.2806	5.9032	−1.7063
Convertible arbitrage	0.0005	0.2477	0.2109	0.5021	−0.0972
	0.2197	3.1066	2.3214	3.9825	−0.7414
Global macro	0.0079	0.0746	0.0593	0.1492	−0.2539
	3.5217	0.9437	0.6587	1.1938	−1.9533
Long-short equity	0.0053	0.4442	−0.0070	0.0672	−0.1471
	2.5693	6.1425	−0.0850	0.5874	−1.2372
Managed futures	0.0041	0.2565	−0.2991	−0.5223	−0.2703
	0.8853	1.5944	−1.6310	−2.0528	−1.0217
Multistrategy	0.0075	0.2566	−0.0048	0.1781	−0.1172
	4.2180	4.1284	−0.0684	1.8116	−1.1471

Table 26.2

Style analysis for a sample of hedge fund indexes
*Fund definitions are given in Table 26.1.
Note: Top line of each entry is the estimate of the factor beta. Lower line is the *t*-statistic for that estimate.
Source: Authors' calculations. Hedge fund returns are on indexes computed by Credit Suisse/Tremont Index, LLC, available at **www.hedgeindex.com.**

of the four factors. Moreover, the estimated factor betas seem reasonable in terms of the funds' stated style. For example:

- The equity market–neutral funds have uniformly low and statistically insignificant factor betas, as one would expect of a market-neutral posture.
- Dedicated short bias funds exhibit substantial negative betas on the S&P index.
- Distressed-firm funds have significant exposure to credit conditions (more positive credit spreads in this table indicate better economic conditions) as well as to the S&P 500. This exposure arises because restructuring activities often depend on access to borrowing, and successful restructuring depends on the state of the economy.
- Global macro funds show negative exposure to a stronger U.S. dollar, which would make the dollar value of foreign investments less valuable.

We conclude that, by and large, most hedge funds are making very explicit directional bets on a wide array of economic factors.

 Concept Check **26.3**

> Analyze the betas of the fixed-income index in Table 26.2. On the basis of these results, are these funds typically market neutral? If not, do their factor exposures make sense in terms of the markets in which they operate?

26.5 Performance Measurement for Hedge Funds

Table 26.3 shows basic performance data for a collection of hedge fund indexes computed from the standard index model with the S&P 500 used as the market benchmark. The model is estimated using monthly excess returns over the 5-year period ending September 2016. We report for each index the beta relative to the S&P 500, the serial correlation of returns, the alpha, and the Sharpe ratio. Betas tend to be considerably less than 1; not surprisingly, the beta of the short bias index is large and negative. Many of the other betas are near zero, reflecting a widespread strategy of pursuing specific bets without incurring broad exposure to the market index.

By and large, hedge fund performance in this period was not impressive. The average alpha across indexes was slightly negative, and the average Sharpe ratio was less than that of the S&P 500. In earlier periods, however, particularly before 2010, hedge funds generally substantially outperformed passive indexes. Regardless of this variability in outcome, several factors make hedge fund performance difficult to evaluate, and these are important to consider.

	Beta	Serial Correlation	Alpha (%/month)	Sharpe Ratio
Hedge fund composite	0.232	−0.031	−0.17%	0.116
Convertible arbitrage	0.088	0.151	0.12%	0.238
Dedicated short bias	−0.955	−0.113	0.14%	−0.268
Emerging markets	0.497	−0.069	−0.22%	0.157
Equity market neutral	0.169	−0.203	−0.08%	0.097
Event driven	0.313	0.067	−0.31%	0.054
Fixed income arbitrage	0.020	0.104	0.10%	0.244
Global macro	0.125	−0.094	−0.29%	−0.102
Long/short equity	0.501	−0.117	−0.26%	0.195
Managed futures	−0.071	0.000	0.21%	0.037
Multistrategy	0.063	0.123	0.23%	0.448
Average across funds	0.089	−0.017	−0.05%	0.111
S&P 500	1.000	−0.145	0.00%	0.306

Table 26.3

Index model regressions for hedge fund indexes. Estimation period: October 2011–September 2016

Source: Authors' calculations using data downloaded from Credit Suisse Hedge Fund Indexes, **www.hedgeindex.com,** November 2016.

Liquidity and Hedge Fund Performance

Recall from Chapter 9 that one of the more important extensions of the CAPM is a version that allows for the possibility of a return premium for investors willing to hold less liquid assets. Hedge funds tend to hold more illiquid assets than other institutional investors such as mutual funds. They can do so because of restrictions such as the lock-up provisions that commit investors to keep their investment in the fund for some period of time. Therefore, it is important to control for liquidity when evaluating performance. If it is ignored, what may be no more than compensation for illiquidity may appear to be true alpha, that is, risk-adjusted abnormal returns.

Aragon demonstrates that hedge funds with lock-up restrictions do tend to hold less liquid portfolios.[6] Moreover, once he controlled for lock-ups or other share restrictions (such as redemption notice periods), the apparently positive average alpha of those funds turned insignificant. Aragon's work suggests that part of any "alpha" exhibited by hedge funds may in fact be an equilibrium liquidity premium rather than a sign of stock-picking ability—in other words, a "fair" reward for providing liquidity to other investors.

One symptom of illiquid assets is serial correlation in returns. Positive serial correlation means that positive returns are more likely to be followed by positive than by negative returns. Such a pattern is often taken as an indicator of less liquid markets for the following reason. When prices are not available because an asset is not actively traded, the hedge fund must estimate its value to calculate net asset value and rates of return. But such procedures are at best imperfect and, as demonstrated by Getmansky, Lo, and Makarov, tend to result in serial correlation in prices as firms either smooth out their value estimates or only gradually mark prices to true market values.[7] Positive serial correlation is therefore often interpreted as evidence of liquidity problems; in nearly efficient markets with frictionless trading, we would expect serial correlation or other predictable patterns in prices to be minimal.[8]

Hasanhodzic and Lo[9] find that hedge fund returns generally tend to exhibit significant serial correlation. This suggestion of smoothed prices has two important implications. First, it lends further support to the hypothesis that hedge funds are holding less liquid assets and that part of their average returns may reflect liquidity premiums. Second, it implies that their risk-adjusted performance measures are upward-biased because any smoothing in the estimates of portfolio value will reduce measured volatility (thereby increasing the Sharpe ratio) as well as measured covariances and, therefore, betas with systematic factors (thereby increasing measured risk-adjusted alphas). In fact, Figure 26.2 shows that both the alphas and Sharpe ratios of the hedge fund indexes in Table 26.3 increase with the serial correlation of returns. These results are consistent with the fund-specific results of Hasanhodzic and Lo and suggest that price smoothing may account for some part of the apparently superior risk-adjusted hedge fund performance that they found in their sample period.

---

[6]George O. Aragon, "Share Restrictions and Asset Pricing: Evidence from the Hedge Fund Industry," *Journal of Financial Economics* 83 (2007), pp. 33–58.

[7]Mila Getmansky, Andrew W. Lo, and Igor Makarov, "An Econometric Model of Serial Correlation and Illiquidity in Hedge Fund Returns," *Journal of Financial Economics* 74 (2004), pp. 529–609.

[8]With long data series, we find that serial correlations generally are, in fact, small. Of course, in any particular sample period, the point estimate of serial correlation may be positive or negative. In this period, while there is considerable dispersion across funds, the average serial correlation is almost exactly zero.

[9]Jasmina Hasanhodzic and Andrew Lo, "Can Hedge Fund Returns be Replicated? The Linear Case," *Journal of Investment Management* 5 (2007), pp. 5–45.

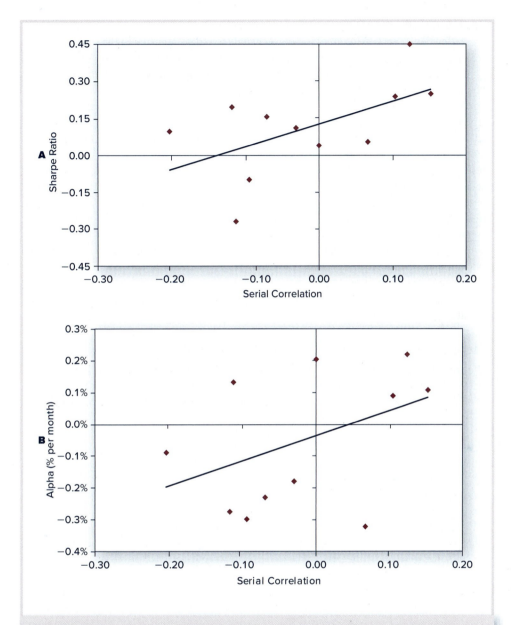

Figure 26.2 Hedge funds with higher serial correlation in returns, an indicator of illiquid portfolio holdings, exhibit higher alphas (**Panel A**) and higher Sharpe ratios (**Panel B**)

Source: Plotted from data in Table 26.3.

Whereas Aragon focuses on the average *level* of liquidity, Sadka addresses the liquidity *risk* of hedge funds.[10] He shows that exposure to unexpected declines in market liquidity is an important determinant of average hedge fund returns, and that the spread in average returns across the funds with the highest and lowest liquidity exposure may be as

---

[10] Ronnie Sadka, "Liquidity Risk and the Cross-Section of Hedge-Fund Returns," *Journal of Financial Economics* 98 (October 2010), pp. 54–71.

much as 6% annually. Hedge fund performance may therefore reflect significant compensation for liquidity risk. Figure 26.3, constructed from data reported in his study, is a scatter diagram relating average return for the hedge funds in each style group of Table 26.2 to the liquidity-risk beta for that group. Average return clearly rises with exposure to changes in market liquidity.

Performance can be even more difficult to interpret if a hedge fund takes advantage of illiquid markets to manipulate returns by purposely misvaluing illiquid assets. In this regard, it is worth noting that, on average, reported hedge fund returns in December are substantially greater than average returns in other months.[11] The pattern is stronger for lower-liquidity funds and funds that are near or beyond the threshold return at which performance incentive fees kick in. It appears that some funds use their discretion in valuing assets to move returns to December when that will enhance their annual incentive fees. It also appears that some hedge funds attempt to manipulate their measured performance by buying additional shares in stocks they already own in an effort to push up their prices.[12] The buying takes place just before market close at the end of the month when hedge fund performance is reported. Moreover, the effort is concentrated in less liquid stocks where the price impact would be expected to be greater. If, as these papers suggest, funds take advantage of illiquid markets to manage returns, then accurate performance measurement becomes almost impossible.

Hedge Fund Performance and Survivorship Bias

We already know that survivorship bias (when only successful funds are included in a database) can affect the estimated performance of a sample of mutual funds. The same problems, as well as related ones, apply to hedge funds. **Backfill bias** arises because hedge

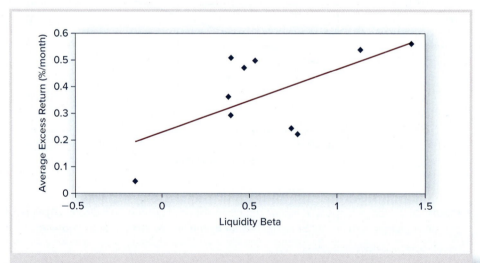

Figure 26.3 Average hedge fund returns as a function of liquidity risk

Source: Plotted from data in Ronnie Sadka, "Liquidity Risk and the Cross-Section of Hedge-Fund Returns," *Journal of Financial Economics* 98 (October 2010), pp. 54–71.

[11]Vikas Agarwal, Naveen D. Daniel, and Narayan Y. Naik, "Do Hedge Funds Manage Their Reported Returns?" *Review of Financial Studies* 24 (2011), pp. 3281–3320.

[12]Itzhak Ben-David, Francesco Franzoni, Augustin Landier, and Rabih Moussawi, "Do Hedge Funds Manipulate Stock Prices?" *Journal of Finance* 68 (December 2013), pp. 2383–2434.

funds report returns to database publishers only if they choose to. Funds started with seed capital will open to the public and therefore enter standard databases only if their past performance is deemed sufficiently successful to attract clients. Therefore, the prior performance of funds that are eventually included in the sample may not be representative of typical performance.

Survivorship bias arises when unsuccessful funds that cease operation stop reporting returns and leave a database, leaving behind only the successful funds. Malkiel and Saha find that attrition rates for hedge funds are far higher than for mutual funds—in fact, commonly more than double the attrition rate of mutual funds—making this an important issue to address.[13] Estimates of survivorship bias in various studies are typically substantial, in the range of 2%–4%.[14]

Hedge Fund Performance and Changing Factor Loadings

In Chapter 24, we pointed out that an important assumption underlying conventional performance evaluation is that the portfolio manager maintains a stable risk profile over time. But hedge funds are designed to be opportunistic and have considerable flexibility to change that profile. This too can make performance evaluation tricky. If risk is not constant, then estimated alphas will be biased if we use a standard, linear index model. And if the risk profile changes systematically with the expected return on the market, performance evaluation is even more difficult.

To see why, look at Figure 26.4, which illustrates the characteristic line of a perfect market timer (see Chapter 24, Section 24.4) who engages in no security selection but moves funds from T-bills into the market portfolio only when the market will outperform bills. The characteristic line is nonlinear, with a slope of 0 when the market's excess return is negative, and a slope of 1 when it is positive. But a naïve attempt to estimate a regression equation from this pattern would result in a fitted line with a slope between 0 and 1, and a positive alpha. Neither statistic accurately describes the fund.

As we noted in Chapter 24, and as is evident from Figure 26.4, an ability to conduct perfect market timing is much like obtaining a call option on the underlying portfolio without having to pay for it. Similar nonlinearities would arise if the fund actually buys or writes options. Figure 26.5, Panel A, illustrates the case of a fund that holds a stock portfolio and writes put options on it, and Panel B

Figure 26.4 Characteristic line of a perfect market timer. The true characteristic line is kinked, with a shape like that of a call option. Fitting a straight line to the relationship will result in misestimated slope and intercept.

[13]Burton G. Malkiel and Atanu Saha, "Hedge Funds: Risk and Return," *Financial Analysts Journal* 61 (2005), pp. 80–88.

[14]For example, Malkiel and Saha estimate the bias at 4.4%; G. Amin and H. Kat, "Stocks, Bonds and Hedge Funds: Not a Free Lunch!" *Journal of Portfolio Management* 29 (Summer 2003), pp. 113–20, find a bias of about 2%; and William Fung and David Hsieh, "Performance Characteristics of Hedge Funds and CTA Funds: Natural versus Spurious Biases," *Journal of Financial and Quantitative Analysis* 35 (2000), pp. 291–307, find a bias of about 3.6%.

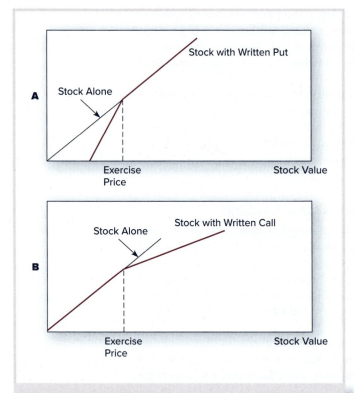

Figure 26.5 Characteristic lines of stock portfolio with written options. **Panel A,** Buy stock, write put. Here, the fund writes fewer puts than the number of shares it holds. **Panel B,** Buy stock, write calls. Here, the fund writes fewer calls than the number of shares it holds.

illustrates the case of a fund that holds a stock portfolio and writes call options. In both cases, the characteristic line is steeper when portfolio returns are poor—in other words, the fund has greater sensitivity to the market when it is falling than when it is rising. This is the opposite profile that would arise from timing ability, which is much like acquiring rather than writing options, and therefore would give the fund greater sensitivity to market advances.[15]

Figure 26.6 presents evidence on these sorts of nonlinearities. A nonlinear regression line is fitted to the scatter diagram of returns on hedge fund indexes plotted against returns on the S&P 500. The fitted lines in each panel suggest that these funds have higher down-market betas (higher slopes) than up-market betas.[16]

This is precisely what investors do *not* want: higher market sensitivity when the market is weak. This is evidence that funds may be *writing* options, either explicitly or implicitly through dynamic trading strategies (see Chapter 21, Section 21.5, for a discussion of such dynamic strategies).

Just as hedge fund betas may be unstable, so may be other aspects of their risk profile, for example, total volatility of returns. Because they have great discretion to use leverage and to trade in derivatives, these funds have tremendous capacity to alter their risk exposures. Recall from Chapter 24 that when portfolio managers change risk within any measurement period, they can induce distortions in standard measures of risk-adjusted return.

Tail Events and Hedge Fund Performance

Imagine a hedge fund whose entire investment strategy is to hold an S&P 500 index fund and write deep out-of-the-money put options on the index. Clearly the fund manager brings no skill to his job. But if you knew only his investment results over limited periods, and not his underlying strategy, you might be fooled into thinking that he is extremely talented. For if the put options are written sufficiently out-of-the-money, they will only rarely end up imposing a loss, and such a strategy can appear over long periods—even over many years—to be consistently profitable. In most periods, the strategy brings in a modest premium from the written puts and therefore outperforms the S&P 500, yielding the impression of consistently superior performance. Every so often, however, such as in the market crash of October 1987, the strategy may lose multiples of its entire gain over

[15]But the fund that writes options would at least receive fair compensation for the unattractive shape of its characteristic line in the form of the premium received when it writes the options.

[16]Not all the hedge fund categories exhibited this sort of pattern. Many showed effectively symmetric up- and down-market betas. However, Figure 26.6, Panel A, shows that the asymmetry affects hedge funds taken as a group.

the last decade. But if you are lucky enough to avoid these rare but extreme *tail events* (so named because they fall in the far-left tail of the probability distribution), the performance of the strategy will appear to be gilded.

The evidence in Figure 26.6 indicating that hedge funds are at least implicitly option writers should make us nervous about taking their measured performance at face value. The problem in interpreting strategies with exposure to extreme tail events (such as short

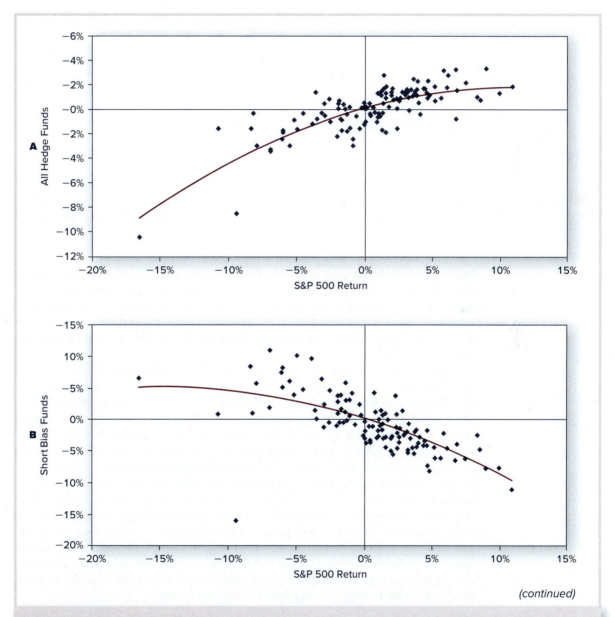

(continued)

Figure 26.6 Monthly return on hedge fund indexes versus return on the S&P 500, 5 years ending September 2016. *Panel A,* composite hedge fund index. *Panel B,* short-bias funds. *Panel C,* multistrategy funds.

Source: Constructed from data downloaded from **www.hedgeindex.com** and **finance.yahoo.com**.

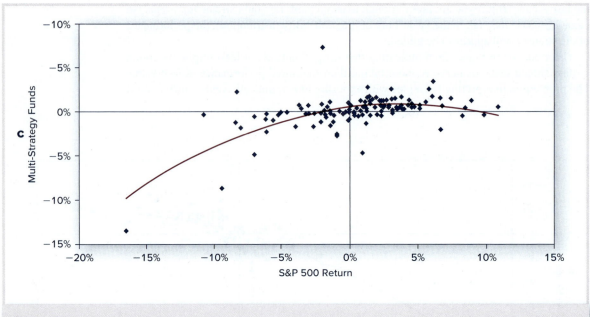

Figure 26.6 (Concluded)

options positions) is that these events by definition occur very infrequently, so *decades* of results may be needed to fully appreciate their true risk and reward attributes. In two influential books, Nassim Taleb, who is a hedge fund operator himself, argues that many hedge funds are analogous to our hypothetical manager, racking up fame and fortune through strategies that make money *most* of the time but expose investors to rare but extreme losses.[17]

Taleb uses the metaphor of the black swan to discuss the importance of highly improbable, but highly impactful, events. Until the discovery of Australia, Europeans believed that all swans were white: they had never encountered swans that were not white. In their experience, the black swan was outside the realm of reasonable possibility—in statistical jargon, an extreme outlier relative to their sample of observations. Taleb argues that the world is filled with black swans, deeply important developments that simply could not have been predicted from the range of accumulated experience to date. While we can't predict which black swans to expect, we nevertheless know that some black swan may be making an appearance at any moment. The October 1987 crash, when the market fell by more than 20% in one day, or the financial crisis of 2008–2009 might be viewed as black swans—events that had never taken place before, ones that most market observers would have dismissed as impossible and certainly not worth modeling, but both with high impact. These sorts of events seemingly come out of the blue, and they caution us to show humility when we use past experience to evaluate the future risk of our actions. With this in mind, consider again the example of Long Term Capital Management.

---

[17]Nassim N. Taleb, *Fooled by Randomness: The Hidden Role of Chance in Life and in the Markets* (New York: TEXERE (Thomson), 2004); and Nassim N. Taleb, *The Black Swan: The Impact of the Highly Improbable* (New York: Random House, 2007).

Example 26.3   Tail Events and Long Term Capital Management

In the late 1990s, Long Term Capital Management was widely viewed as the most successful hedge fund in history. It had consistently provided double-digit returns to its investors, and it had earned hundreds of millions of dollars in incentive fees for its managers. The firm used sophisticated computer models to estimate correlations across assets and believed that its capital was almost 10 times the annual standard deviation of its portfolio returns, presumably enough to withstand any "possible" shock to capital (at least, assuming normal distributions!). But in the summer of 1998, things went badly. On August 17, 1998, Russia defaulted on its sovereign debt and threw capital markets into chaos. LTCM's *1-day* loss on August 21 was $550 million (approximately nine times its estimated *monthly* standard deviation). Total losses in August were about $1.3 billion, despite the fact that LTCM believed that most of its positions were market-neutral relative-value trades. Losses accrued on virtually all of its positions, flying in the face of the presumed diversification of the overall portfolio.

How did this happen? The answer lies in the massive flight to quality and, even more so, to liquidity that was set off by the Russian default. LTCM was typically a seller of liquidity (holding less liquid assets, selling more liquid assets with lower yields, and earning the yield spread) and suffered huge losses. This was a different type of shock from those that appeared in its historical sample/modeling period. In the liquidity crisis that engulfed asset markets, the unexpected commonality of liquidity risk across usually uncorrelated asset classes became obvious. Losses that seemed statistically impossible on past experience had in fact come to pass; LTCM fell victim to a black swan.

26.6   Fee Structure in Hedge Funds

The typical hedge fund fee structure is an annual management fee of 1% to 2% of assets plus an **incentive fee** equal to 20% of investment profits beyond a stipulated benchmark performance. Incentive fees are effectively call options on the portfolio with a strike price equal to current portfolio value times (1 + benchmark return). The manager gets the fee if the portfolio value rises sufficiently, but loses nothing if it falls. Figure 26.7 illustrates the incentive fee for a fund with a 20% incentive fee and a hurdle rate equal to the money market rate, r_f. The current value of the portfolio is denoted S_0 and the year-end value is S_T. The incentive fee is equivalent to .20 call options on the portfolio with exercise price $S_0(1 + r_f)$.

Example 26.4   Black-Scholes Valuation of Incentive Fees

Suppose the standard deviation of a hedge fund's annual rate of return is 30% and the incentive fee is 20% of any investment return over the risk-free money market rate. If the portfolio currently has a net asset value of $100 per share, and the effective annual risk-free rate is 5% (or 4.88% expressed as a continuously compounded rate), then the implicit exercise price on the incentive fee is $105. The Black-Scholes value of a call option with $S_0 = 100$, $X = 105$, $\sigma = .30$, $r_{cc} = .0488$, $T = 1$ year is $11.92, just a shade below 12% of net asset value. Because the incentive fee is worth 20% of the call option, its value is just about 2.4% of net asset value. Together with a typical management fee of 2% of net asset value, the investor in the fund pays annual fees with a total value of 4.4% of assets under management.

The Bernard Madoff Scandal

Bernard Madoff seemed like one of the great success stories in the annals of finance. His asset management firm, Bernard L. Madoff Investment Securities, reported to its clients that their investments of around $20 billion were worth about $65 billion in 2008. But that December, Madoff reportedly confessed to his two sons that he had for years been operating a Ponzi scheme. A Ponzi scheme is an investment fraud in which a manager collects funds from clients, claims to invest those funds on the clients' behalf, reports extremely favorable investment returns, but in fact uses the funds for his own purposes. (The schemes are named after Charles Ponzi, whose success with this scheme in the early 1900s made him notorious throughout the United States.) Early investors who ask to redeem their investments are paid back with the funds coming in from new investors rather than with true earnings. The scheme can continue as long as new investors provide enough funds to cover the redemption requests of the earlier ones—and these inflows are attracted by the superior returns "earned" by early investors and their apparent ability to redeem funds as requested.

As a highly respected member of the Wall Street establishment, Madoff was in a perfect position to perpetrate such a fraud. He was a pioneer in electronic trading and had served as chairman of the NASDAQ Stock Market. Aside from its trading operations, Bernard L. Madoff Investment Securities LLC also acted as a money manager, and it claimed to achieve highly consistent annual returns, between 10% and 12% in good markets as well as bad. Its strategy was supposedly based on option hedging strategies, but Madoff was never precise about his approach. Still, his stature on Wall Street and the prestige of his client list seemed to testify to his legitimacy. Moreover, he played hard to get, and the appearance that one needed connections to join the fund only increased its appeal. The scheme seems to have operated for decades, but in the 2008 stock market downturn, several large clients requested redemptions totaling around $7 billion. With less than $1 billion of assets left in the firm, the scheme collapsed.

Not everyone was fooled and, in retrospect, several red flags should have aroused suspicion. For example, some institutional investors shied away from the fund, objecting to its unusual opacity. Given the magnitude of the assets supposedly under management, the option hedging trades purportedly at the heart of Madoff's investment strategy should have dominated options market trading volume, yet there was no evidence of their execution. Moreover, Madoff's auditor, a small firm with only three employees (including only one active accountant!), seemed grossly inadequate to audit such a large and complex operation. In addition, Madoff's fee structure was highly unusual. Rather than acting as a hedge fund that would charge a percentage of assets plus incentive fees, he claimed to profit instead through trading commissions on the account—if true, this would have been a colossal price break to clients. Finally, rather than placing assets under management with a custodial bank as most funds do, Madoff claimed to keep the funds in-house, which meant that no one could independently verify their existence. In 2000, the SEC received a letter from an industry professional named Harry Markopolos concluding that "Madoff Securities is the world's largest Ponzi scheme," but Madoff continued to operate unimpeded.

Even today, several questions remain unanswered. How much help did Madoff receive from others? Exactly how much money was lost? Most of the "lost" funds represented fictitious profits that had never actually been earned, but some money was returned to early investors. How much was skimmed off to support Madoff's lifestyle? And most important, why didn't the red flags and early warnings prompt a more aggressive response from regulators?

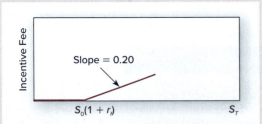

Figure 26.7 Incentive fees as a call option. The current value of the portfolio is denoted S_0 and its year-end value is S_T. The incentive fee is equivalent to .20 call options on the portfolio with exercise price $S_0(1 + r_f)$.

The major complication to this description of the typical compensation structure is the **high water mark.** If a fund experiences losses, it may not be able to charge an incentive fee unless and until it recovers to its previous higher value. With large losses, this may be difficult. High water marks therefore give managers an incentive to shut down funds that have performed poorly, and likely are a cause of the high attrition rate for funds noted above.

A notable fraction of the hedge fund universe is invested in **funds of funds,** which are hedge funds that invest in one or more other hedge funds. Funds of funds are also called *feeder funds,* because they feed assets from the original investor to the ultimate hedge fund. They are marketed as providing investors the capability to diversify across funds, and also as providing the due diligence involved in screening funds for investment worthiness. In principle, this can be a valuable service because many hedge funds are opaque and feeder funds may have greater insight than typical outsiders.

However, when Bernard Madoff was arrested in December 2008 after admitting to a massive Ponzi scheme, many large feeder funds were found to be among his biggest clients, and their "due diligence" may have been, to put it mildly, lacking. At the head of the list was Fairfield Greenwich Advisors, with exposure reported at $7.5 billion, but several other feeder funds and asset management firms around the world were also on the hook for amounts greater than $1 billion. In the end, it appears that some funds had in effect become little more than marketing agents for Madoff. The nearby box presents further discussion of the Madoff affair.

The option-like nature of compensation can have a big impact on expected fees in funds of funds. This is because the fund of funds pays an incentive fee to each underlying fund that outperforms its benchmark, even if the aggregate performance of the fund of funds is poor. In this case, diversification can hurt you![18]

Example 26.5   Incentive Fees in Funds of Funds

Suppose a fund of funds is established with $1 million invested in each of three hedge funds. For simplicity, we will ignore the asset-value-based portion of fees (the management fee) and focus only on the incentive fee. Suppose that the hurdle rate for the incentive fee is a zero return, so each fund charges an incentive fee of 20% of total return. The following table shows the performance of each underlying fund over a year, the gross rate of return, and the return realized by the fund of funds net of the incentive fee. Funds 1 and 2 have positive returns, and therefore earn an incentive fee, but Fund 3 has terrible performance, so its incentive fee is zero.

	Fund 1	Fund 2	Fund 3	Fund of Funds
Start of year (millions)	$1.00	$1.00	$1.00	$3.00
End of year (millions)	$1.20	$1.40	$0.25	$2.85
Gross rate of return	20%	40%	−75%	−5%
Incentive fee (millions)	$0.04	$0.08	$0.00	$0.12
End of year, net of fee	$1.16	$1.32	$0.25	$2.73
Net rate of return	16%	32%	−75%	−9%

Even though the return on the aggregate portfolio of the fund of funds is *negative* 5%, it still pays incentive fees of $.12 for every $3 invested because incentive fees are paid on the first two well-performing funds. The incentive fees amount to 4% of net asset value. As demonstrated in the last column, this reduces the rate of return earned by the fund of funds from −5% to −9%.

The idea behind funds of funds is to spread risk across several different funds. However, investors need to be aware that these funds of funds may operate with considerable leverage, on top of the leverage of the primary funds in which they invest, which can make returns highly volatile. Moreover, if the various hedge funds in which these funds of funds

[18]S. J. Brown, W. N. Goetzmann, and B. Liang, "Fees on Fees in Funds of Funds," *Journal of Investment Management* 2 (2004), pp. 39–56.

invest have similar investment styles, the diversification benefits of spreading investments across several funds may be illusory—but the extra layer of steep management fees paid to the manager of the fund of funds certainly is not.[19]

[19]One small silver lining: While funds of funds pay incentive fees to each of the underlying funds, the incentive fees they charge their own investors tend to be lower, typically around 10% rather than 20%.

SUMMARY

1. Like mutual funds, hedge funds pool the assets of several clients and manage the pooled assets on their behalf. However, hedge funds differ from mutual funds with respect to disclosure, investor base, flexibility and predictability of investment orientation, regulation, and fee structure.

2. Directional funds take a stance on the performance of broad market sectors. Nondirectional funds establish market-neutral positions on relative mispricing. However, even these hedged positions still present idiosyncratic risk.

3. Statistical arbitrage is the use of quantitative systems to uncover many perceived misalignments in relative pricing and ensure profits by averaging over all of these small bets. It often uses data-mining methods to uncover past patterns that form the basis for the investment positions.

4. Portable alpha is a strategy in which one invests in positive-alpha positions, then hedges the systematic risk of that investment, and, finally, establishes market exposure where desired by using passive indexes or futures contracts.

5. Performance evaluation of hedge funds is complicated by survivorship bias, by the potential instability of risk attributes, by the existence of liquidity premiums, and by unreliable market valuations of infrequently traded assets. Performance evaluation is particularly difficult when the fund engages in option positions. Tail events make it hard to assess the true performance of positions involving options without extremely long histories of returns.

6. Hedge funds typically charge investors both a management fee and an incentive fee equal to a percentage of profits beyond some threshold value. The incentive fee is akin to a call option on the portfolio. Funds of hedge funds pay the incentive fee to each underlying fund that beats its hurdle rate, even if the overall performance of the portfolio is poor.

KEY TERMS

hedge funds	statistical arbitrage	survivorship bias
lock-up periods	pairs trading	incentive fee
directional strategy	data mining	high water mark
nondirectional strategy	portable alpha	funds of funds
market neutral	alpha transfer	
pure plays	backfill bias	

PROBLEM SETS

1. Would a market-neutral hedge fund be a good candidate for an investor's entire retirement portfolio? If not, would there be a role for the hedge fund in the overall portfolio of such an investor?

2. How might the incentive fee of a hedge fund affect the manager's proclivity to take on high-risk assets in the portfolio?

3. Why is it harder to assess the performance of a hedge fund portfolio manager than that of a typical mutual fund manager?

4. Which of the following is *most* accurate in describing the problems of survivorship bias and backfill bias in the performance evaluation of hedge funds?

   a. Survivorship bias and backfill bias both result in upwardly biased hedge fund index returns.

   b. Survivorship bias and backfill bias both result in downwardly biased hedge fund index returns.

   c. Survivorship bias results in upwardly biased hedge fund index returns, but backfill bias results in downwardly biased hedge fund index returns.

5. Which of the following would be the *most* appropriate benchmark to use for hedge fund evaluation?

   a. A multifactor model.

   b. The S&P 500.

   c. The risk-free rate.

6. With respect to hedge fund investing, the net return to an investor in a fund of funds would be lower than that earned from an individual hedge fund because of:

   a. Both the extra layer of fees and the higher liquidity offered.

   b. No reason; funds of funds earn returns that are equal to those of individual hedge funds.

   c. The extra layer of fees only.

7. Which of the following hedge fund types is *most likely* to have a return that is closest to risk-free?

   a. A market-neutral hedge fund.

   b. An event-driven hedge fund.

   c. A long/short hedge fund.

8. Is statistical arbitrage true arbitrage? Explain.

9. A hedge fund with $1 billion of assets charges a management fee of 2% and an incentive fee of 20% of returns over a money market rate, which currently is 5%. Calculate total fees, both in dollars and as a percent of assets under management, for portfolio returns of:

   a. −5%

   b. 0

   c. 5%

   d. 10%

10. A hedge fund with net asset value of $62 per share currently has a high water mark of $66. Is the value of its incentive fee more or less than it would be if the high water mark were $67?

11. Reconsider the hedge fund in Problem 10. Suppose it is January 1, the standard deviation of the fund's annual returns is 50%, and the risk-free rate is 4%. The fund has an incentive fee of 20%, but its current high water mark is $66, and net asset value is $62.

    a. What is the value of the annual incentive fee according to the Black-Scholes formula? (Treat the risk-free rate as a continuously compounded value to maintain consistency with the Black-Scholes formula.)

    b. What would the annual incentive fee be worth if the fund had no high water mark and it earned its incentive fee on its total return?

    c. What would the annual incentive fee be worth if the fund had no high water mark and it earned its incentive fee on its return in excess of the risk-free rate?

    d. Recalculate the incentive fee value for part (*b*) assuming that an increase in fund leverage increases volatility to 60%.

12. Log in to Connect and link to Chapter 26 to find a spreadsheet containing monthly values of the S&P 500 index. Suppose that in each month you had written an out-of-the-money put option on one unit of the index with an exercise price 5% lower than the current value of the index.

    a. What would have been the average value of your gross monthly payouts on the puts over the 10-year period October 1977–September 1987? The standard deviation?

    b. Now extend your sample by 1 month to include October 1987, and recalculate the average payout and standard deviation of the put-writing strategy.

    c. What do you conclude about tail risk in naked put writing?

13. Suppose a hedge fund follows the following strategy. Each month it holds $100 million of an S&P 500 index fund and writes out-of-the-money put options on $100 million of the index with exercise price 5% lower than the current value of the index. Suppose the premium it receives for writing each put is $.25 million, roughly in line with the actual value of the puts.

   a. Calculate the Sharpe ratio the fund would have realized in the period October 1982–September 1987. Compare its Sharpe ratio to that of the S&P 500. Use the data from the previous problem, available in Connect, and assume the monthly risk-free interest rate over this period was .7%.
   b. Now calculate the Sharpe ratio the fund would have realized if we extend the sample period by 1 month to include October 1987.
   c. What do you conclude about performance evaluation and tail risk for funds pursuing option-like strategies?

14. The following is part of the computer output from a regression of monthly returns on Waterworks stock against the S&P 500 index. A hedge fund manager believes that Waterworks is underpriced, with an alpha of 2% over the coming month.

Beta	R-square	Standard Deviation of Residuals
0.75	0.65	0.06 (i.e., 6% monthly)

   a. If he holds a $2 million portfolio of Waterworks stock, and wishes to hedge market exposure for the next month using 1-month maturity S&P 500 futures contracts, how many contracts should he enter? Should he buy or sell contracts? The S&P 500 currently is at 2,000 and the contract multiplier is $50.
   b. What is the standard deviation of the monthly return of the hedged portfolio?
   c. Assuming that monthly returns are approximately normally distributed, what is the probability that this market-neutral strategy will lose money over the next month? Assume the risk-free rate is .5% per month.

15. Return to Problem 14.

   a. Suppose you hold an equally weighted portfolio of 100 stocks with the same alpha, beta, and residual standard deviation as Waterworks. Assume the residual returns (the e terms in Equations 26.1 and 26.2) on each of these stocks are independent of each other. What is the residual standard deviation of the portfolio?
   b. Recalculate the probability of a loss on a market-neutral strategy involving equally weighted, market-hedged positions in the 100 stocks over the next month.

16. Return again to Problem 14. Now suppose that the manager misestimates the beta of Waterworks stock, believing it to be .50 instead of .75. The standard deviation of the monthly market rate of return is 5%.

   a. What is the standard deviation of the (now improperly) hedged portfolio?
   b. What is the probability of incurring a loss over the next month if the monthly market return has an expected value of 1% and a standard deviation of 5%? Compare your answer to the probability you found in Problem 14.
   c. What would be the probability of a loss using the data in Problem 15 if the manager similarly misestimated beta as .50 instead of .75? Compare your answer to the probability you found in Problem 14.
   d. Why does the misestimation of beta matter so much more for the 100-stock portfolio than it does for the 1-stock portfolio?

17. Here are data on three hedge funds. Each fund charges its investors an incentive fee of 20% of total returns. Suppose initially that a fund of funds (FF) manager buys equal amounts of each of

these funds, and also charges its investors a 20% incentive fee. For simplicity, assume also that management fees other than incentive fees are zero for all funds.

	Hedge Fund 1	Hedge Fund 2	Hedge Fund 3
Start of year value (millions)	$100	$100	$100
Gross portfolio rate of return	20%	10%	30%

a. Compute the rate of return after incentive fees to an investor in the fund of funds.

b. Suppose that instead of buying shares in each of the three hedge funds, a stand-alone (SA) hedge fund purchases the same *portfolio* as the three underlying funds. The total value and composition of the SA fund is therefore identical to the one that would result from aggregating the three hedge funds. Consider an investor in the SA fund. After paying 20% incentive fees, what would be the value of the investor's portfolio at the end of the year?

c. Confirm that the investor's rate of return in SA is higher than in FF by an amount equal to the extra layer of fees charged by the fund of funds.

d. Now suppose that the return on the portfolio held by hedge fund 3 were −30% rather than +30%. Recalculate your answers to parts (a) and (b).

e. Will either FF or SA charge an incentive fee in the scenario of part (d)?

f. Why then does the investor in FF still do worse than the investor in SA?

 SOLUTIONS TO CONCEPT CHECKS

1. *a.* Nondirectional. The shares in the fund and the short position in the index swap constitute a hedged position. The hedge fund is betting that the discount on the closed-end fund will shrink and that it will profit regardless of the general movements in the Indian market.

   b. Nondirectional. The value of both positions is driven by the value of Toys "R" Us. The hedge fund is betting that the market is undervaluing Petri relative to Toys "R" Us, and that as the *relative* values of the two positions come back into alignment, it will profit regardless of the movements in the underlying shares.

   c. Directional. This is an outright bet on the price that Generic Pharmaceuticals will eventually command at the conclusion of the predicted takeover attempt.

2. The expected rate of return on the position (in the absence of any knowledge about idiosyncratic risk reflected in the residual) is 3%. If the residual turns out to be −4%, then the position will lose 1% of its value over the month and fall to $2.079 million. The excess return on the market in this month over T-bills would be 5% − 1% = 4%, while the excess return on the hedged strategy would be −1% − 1% = −2%, so the strategy would plot in Panel A as the point (4%, −2%). In Panel B, which plots *total* returns on the market and the hedge position, the strategy would plot as the point (5%, −1%).

3. Fixed-income arbitrage portfolios show positive exposure to the long bond and to the credit spread. This pattern suggests that these are *not* hedged arbitrage portfolios, but in fact are directional portfolios.

The Theory of Active Portfolio Management

THIS CHAPTER CONSIDERS practical complexities in the process of constructing optimal portfolios. We've already devoted considerable attention to the principles of portfolio construction, particularly in Chapters 7 and 8. But the execution of these portfolio models presents several problems in implementation. Chief among them is the input list of expected returns (or almost equivalently, of alphas) and covariances. Expected returns are especially difficult to estimate from historical data. Portfolio and security alphas are highly inconsistent from one period to the next. Moreover, as we will see, portfolio weights are exceedingly sensitive to assumed values of alpha. Even apparently reasonable forecasts of alpha can result in optimal risky portfolios calling for extreme positions or short positions in several component securities. These portfolios will be deemed unacceptable by most traders.

Therefore, we need additional guidance as to how to put our models to work in a more realistic setting. Fortunately, theory can provide guidance even for these practical problems. We begin with the Treynor-Black model that we first encountered in Chapter 8, now showing how to handle limited precision in the forecasts of alpha values and the extreme portfolio positions often prescribed by the model. Armed with these insights, we present a prototype organizational chart and discuss the efficacy of adapting the organization to the theoretical underpinning of portfolio management.

In the next section, we present the Black-Litterman model, which allows flexible views about the expected returns of major asset classes to improve asset allocation. Then we look into the potential value of security analysis and end with concluding remarks. An appendix to the chapter presents the mathematics underlying the Black-Litterman model.

27.1 Optimal Portfolios and Alpha Values

In Chapter 8 we showed how to form an optimal risky portfolio with a single-index model. Table 27.1 summarizes the steps in this optimization, commonly known as the Treynor-Black model.[1] The outlined procedure uses the index model that ignores potential

[1] We know from Chapter 10 that a multiple-index model such as that of Fama and French may better describe security returns. In that case, the passive market-index portfolio will be augmented with positions in the additional factor portfolios (e.g., the size and value portfolios in the FF model). However, the rest of the Treynor-Black procedure will remain unchanged.

Table 27.1

Construction and
properties of the
optimal risky portfolio

1. Initial position of security i in the active portfolio	$w_i^0 = \dfrac{\alpha_i}{\sigma^2(e_i)}$
2. Scaled initial positions	$w_i = \dfrac{w_i^0}{\sum_{i=1}^{n} \dfrac{\alpha_i}{\sigma^2(e_i)}}$
3. Alpha of the active portfolio	$\alpha_A = \sum_{i=1}^{n} w_i \alpha_i$
4. Residual variance of the active portfolio	$\sigma^2(e_A) = \sum_{i=1}^{n} w_i^2 \sigma^2(e_i)$
5. Initial position in the active portfolio	$w_A^0 = \dfrac{\dfrac{\alpha_A}{\sigma^2(e_A)}}{\dfrac{E(R_M)}{\sigma_M^2}}$
6. Beta of the active portfolio	$\beta_A = \sum_{i=1}^{n} w_i \beta_i$
7. Adjusted (for beta) position in the active portfolio	$w_A^* = \dfrac{w_A^0}{1 + (1 - \beta_A)w_A^0}$
8. Final weights in passive portfolio and in security i	$w_M^* = 1 - w_A^*; \qquad w_i^* = w_A^* w_i$
9. The beta of the optimal risky portfolio and its risk premium	$\beta_P = w_M^* + w_A^* \beta_A = 1 - w_A^*(1 - \beta_A)$ $E(R_P) = \beta_P E(R_M) + w_A^* \alpha_A$
10. The variance of the optimal risky portfolio	$\sigma_P^2 = \beta_P^2 \sigma_M^2 + [w_A^* \sigma(e_A)]^2$
11. Sharpe ratio of the risky portfolio	$S_P^2 = S_M^2 + \sum_{i=1}^{n} \left(\dfrac{\alpha_i}{\sigma(e_i)}\right)^2$

correlation of residual returns. This is sometimes called the *diagonal model,* because it assumes that the covariance matrix of residuals has nonzero entries only on the diagonals.

For illustration, Spreadsheet 27.1 summarizes the input data we use in this exercise as well as the resulting optimal portfolio. Panel D shows the resulting optimal risky portfolio and the improvement in the Sharpe ratio over the **passive market-index portfolio** offered by adding the **active portfolio** to the mix. To better appreciate this improvement, we have included the *M*-square measure of performance. *M*-square is the incremental expected return of the optimized portfolio compared to the passive alternative once the active portfolio is mixed with bills to provide the same total volatility as the index portfolio (for a review, see Chapter 24).

Forecasts of Alpha Values and Extreme Portfolio Weights

The overriding impression from Spreadsheet 27.1 is the apparently meager improvement in performance: Panel D shows that *M*-square increases by only 19 basis points (equivalent to an improvement of .0136 in the Sharpe ratio). Notice that the Sharpe ratio of the active portfolio is inferior to that of the passive portfolio (due to its large standard deviation), and hence its *M*-square is actually negative. But the active portfolio is mixed with the passive

	A	B	C	D	E	F	G	H	I	J
1										
2										
3	Panel A: Risk Parameters of the Investable Universe (annualized)									
4										
5		SD of Excess Return	Beta	SD of Systematic Component	SD of Residual	Correlation with the S&P 500				
6	S&P 500	0.1358	1.00	0.1358	0	1				
7	HP	0.3817	2.03	0.2762	0.2656	0.72				
8	DELL	0.2901	1.23	0.1672	0.2392	0.58				
9	WMT	0.1935	0.62	0.0841	0.1757	0.43				
10	TARGET	0.2611	1.27	0.1720	0.1981	0.66				
11	BP	0.1822	0.47	0.0634	0.1722	0.35				
12	SHELL	0.1988	0.67	0.0914	0.1780	0.46				
13										
14	Panel B: The Index Model Covariance Matrix									
15										
16			SP 500	HP	DELL	WMT	TARGET	BP	SHELL	
17		Beta	1.00	2.03	1.23	0.62	1.27	0.47	0.67	
18	S&P 500	1.00	0.0184	0.0375	0.0227	0.0114	0.0234	0.0086	0.0124	
19	HP	2.03	0.0375	0.1457	0.0462	0.0232	0.0475	0.0175	0.0253	
20	DELL	1.23	0.0227	0.0462	0.0842	0.0141	0.0288	0.0106	0.0153	
21	WMT	0.62	0.0114	0.0232	0.0141	0.0374	0.0145	0.0053	0.0077	
22	TARGET	1.27	0.0234	0.0475	0.0288	0.0145	0.0682	0.0109	0.0157	
23	BP	0.47	0.0086	0.0175	0.0106	0.0053	0.0109	0.0332	0.0058	
24	SHELL	0.67	0.0124	0.0253	0.0153	0.0077	0.0157	0.0058	0.0395	
25										
26	Panel C: Macro Forecast (S&P 500) and Forecasts of Alpha Values									
27										
28										
29		SP 500	HP	DELL	WMT	TARGET	BP	SHELL		
30	Alpha	0	0.0150	−0.0100	−0.0050	0.0075	0.012	0.0025		
31	Risk premium	0.0600	0.1371	0.0639	0.0322	0.0835	0.0400	0.0429		
32										
33	Panel D: Computation of the Optimal Risky Portfolio									
34										
35		S&P 500	Active Pf A		HP	DELL	WMT	TARGET	BP	SHELL
36				$\sigma^2(e)$	0.0705	0.0572	0.0309	0.0392	0.0297	0.0317
37			0.5505	$\alpha/\sigma^2(e)$	0.2126	−0.1748	−0.1619	0.1911	0.4045	0.0789
38			1.0000	$w_0(i)$	0.3863	−0.3176	−0.2941	0.3472	0.7349	0.1433
39				$[w_0(i)]^2$	0.1492	0.1009	0.0865	0.1205	0.5400	0.0205
40	α_A		0.0222							
41	$\sigma^2(e_A)$		0.0404							
42	w_0		0.1691	Overall						
43	w^*	0.8282	0.1718	Portfolio	0.0663	−0.0546	−0.0505	0.0596	0.1262	0.0246
44	Beta	1	1.0922	1.0158	0.0663	−0.0546	−0.0505	0.0596	0.1262	0.0246
45	Risk premium	0.06	0.0878	0.0648	0.0750	0.1121	0.0689	0.0447	0.0880	0.0305
46	SD	0.1358	0.2497	0.1422	0.3817	0.2901	0.1935	0.2611	0.1822	0.1988
47	Sharpe ratio	0.44	0.35	0.4556						
48	M-square	0	−0.0123	0.0019						
49	Benchmark risk			0.0346						

Spreadsheet 27.1

Active portfolio management with a universe of six stocks

eXcel
Please visit us at
www.mhhe.com/Bodie11e

portfolio, so total volatility is not its appropriate measure of risk. When combined with the passive portfolio, it does offer some improvement in performance, albeit quite modest. This is the best that can be had given the **alpha values** uncovered by the security analysts (see Panel C). Notice that the position in the active portfolio amounts to 17%, financed in part by a combined short position in Dell and Walmart of about 10%. Because the figures in Spreadsheet 27.1 are annualized, this performance is equivalent to a 1-year holding-period return (HPR).

The alpha values we use in Spreadsheet 27.1 are quite modest by the standard of typical analysts' forecasts. Alphas inferred from 1-year-ahead "target" (i.e., forecasted) prices of security analysts are commonly far larger than the values in Panel C. To see how sensitive the optimal risky portfolio can be to assumed alpha, we recompute its composition in

Table 27.2, but with a new set of assumed values of alpha (in the top row of the table) that are more representative of the magnitudes that one might encounter in practice.

Table 27.2 shows the optimal portfolio using these forecasts rather than the original alpha values shown in Panel C in Spreadsheet 27.1. The difference in performance is striking. The Sharpe ratio of the new optimal portfolio has increased from the benchmark's .44 to 2.32, amounting to a huge risk-adjusted return advantage. This shows up in an *M*-square of 25.53%!

However, these results also expose a potential major problem with the Treynor-Black model. The optimal portfolio now calls for extreme long/short positions that may be infeasible for a real-world portfolio manager. For example, the model calls for a position of 5.79 (579%) in the active portfolio (see the bottom row of the top panel), largely financed by a short position of −4.79 in the S&P 500 index. Moreover, the standard deviation of this optimal portfolio is 52.24%, a level of risk that only extremely aggressive hedge funds would be willing to bear. It is important to notice that this risk is largely nonsystematic because the beta of the active portfolio, at .95, is less than 1.0, and the beta of the overall risky portfolio is even lower, only .73, because of the short position in the passive portfolio. Only hedge funds may be interested in this portfolio.

One approach to this problem is to restrict extreme portfolio positions, beginning with short sales. We can rule out short positions in the passive index portfolio (in this example, the S&P 500) by requiring that the weight in the active portfolio must be less than 100%. Imposing this constraint, the active portfolio now comprises the entire risky position and the weight of the S&P 500 is zero. Table 27.3 shows that the optimal portfolio now has a standard deviation of 15.68%, not overwhelmingly greater than the SD of the passive portfolio (13.58%). The beta of the overall risky portfolio is now that of the active portfolio (.95). Despite this severe restriction, the optimization procedure is still powerful, and the *M*-square of the optimal risky portfolio (now the active portfolio) is a very large 16.42%.

Is this a satisfactory solution? This would depend on the organization. For hedge funds, this may be a dream portfolio. For most mutual funds, however, the lack of diversification would rule it out. Notice the positions in the six stocks: Walmart, Target, and British Petroleum alone account for 76% of the portfolio.

Here we have to acknowledge the limitations of our example. Surely, you may be thinking, when the investment company covers more securities, the problem of lack of diversification will largely vanish. But it turns out that the problem with extreme long/short positions typically persists even when we consider a larger number of firms, and this can gut the practical value of the optimization model. Consider this conclusion from an important article by Black and Litterman[2]:

> [T]he mean-variance optimization used in standard asset allocation models is extremely sensitive to expected return assumptions the investor must provide . . . The optimal portfolio, given its sensitivity to the expected returns, often appears to bear little or no relation to the views the investor wishes to express. In practice, therefore, despite obvious conceptual attractions of a quantitative approach, few global investment managers regularly allow quantitative models to play a major role in their asset allocation decisions.

Clearly, the Markowitz mean-variance portfolio selection model (and the Treynor-Black model, which is just a special case of the Markowitz model) must be modified before it can be put into practical use. One approach that has garnered considerable attention is

---

[2]Fischer Black and Robert Litterman, "Global Portfolio Optimization," *Financial Analysts Journal*, September/October 1992. © 1992, CFA Institute. Reprinted with permission from the CFA Institute.

	S&P 500	Active Portfolio A		HP	DELL	WMT	TGT	BP	SHELL
			α	0.1471	0.1753	0.1932	0.2814	0.1797	0.0357
			$\sigma^2(e)$	0.0705	0.0572	0.0309	0.0392	0.0297	0.0317
		25.7562	$\alpha/\sigma^2(e)$	2.0855	3.0641	6.2544	7.1701	6.0566	1.1255
		1.0000	$w_0(i)$	0.0810	0.1190	0.2428	0.2784	0.2352	0.0437
			$[w_0(i)]^2$	0.0066	0.0142	0.0590	0.0775	0.0553	0.0019
α_A		0.2018							
$\sigma^2(e_A)$		0.0078							
w_0		7.9116							
w^*	−4.7937	5.7937		0.4691163	0.6892459	1.4069035	1.6128803	1.3624061	0.2531855
			Overall Portfolio						
Beta	1	0.9538	0.7323	0.4691	0.6892	1.4069	1.6129	1.3624	0.2532
Risk premium	0.06	0.2590	1.2132	0.2692	0.2492	0.2304	0.3574	0.2077	0.0761
SD	0.1358	0.1568	0.5224	0.3817	0.2901	0.1935	0.2611	0.1822	0.1988
Sharpe ratio	0.44	1.65	2.3223						
M-square	0	0.1642	0.2553						
Benchmark risk			0.5146						

Table 27.2

The optimal risky portfolio with the analysts' new forecasts of alpha

	S&P 500	Active Portfolio A		HP	DELL	WMT	TGT	BP	SHELL
			α	0.1471	0.1753	0.1932	0.2814	0.1797	0.0357
			$\sigma^2(e)$	0.0705	0.0572	0.0309	0.0392	0.0297	0.0317
		25.7562	$\alpha/\sigma^2(e)$	2.0855	3.0641	6.2544	7.1701	6.0566	1.1255
		1.0000	$w_0(i)$	0.0810	0.1190	0.2428	0.2784	0.2352	0.0437
			$[w_0(i)]^2$	0.0066	0.0142	0.0590	0.0775	0.0553	0.0019
α_A		0.2018							
$\sigma^2(e_A)$		0.0078							
w_0		7.9116							
w^*	0.0000	1.0000		0.0810	0.1190	0.2428	0.2784	0.2352	0.0437
			Overall Portfolio						
Beta	1	0.9538	0.9538	0.0810	0.1190	0.2428	0.2784	0.2352	0.0437
Risk premium	0.06	0.2590	0.2590	0.2692	0.2492	0.2304	0.3574	0.2077	0.0761
SD	0.1358	0.1568	0.1568	0.3817	0.2901	0.1935	0.2611	0.1822	0.1988
Sharpe ratio	0.44	1.65	1.6515						
M-square	0	0.1642	0.1642						
Benchmark risk			0.0887						

Table 27.3

The optimal risky portfolio with constraint on the active portfolio ($w_A \leq 1$)

the Black-Litterman model, which we will address in Section 27.3. But even the Treynor-Black model can be made far more palatable to practitioners with some straightforward modifications.

Restriction of Benchmark Risk

Black and Litterman point out a related important practical issue. Most investment managers are judged not on their absolute performance, but on performance compared to that of a **benchmark portfolio.** Such commitment raises the importance of **tracking error.** Tracking error is estimated from the time series of differences between the returns on the overall risky portfolio and the benchmark return, that is, $T_E = R_P - R_M$. The portfolio manager must be mindful of benchmark risk, that is, the standard deviation of the tracking error.

The tracking error of the optimized risky portfolio can be expressed in terms of the beta of the portfolio and thus reveals the benchmark risk:

$$\text{Tracking error} = T_E = R_P - R_M$$
$$R_P = w_A^* \alpha_A + [1 - w_A^*(1 - \beta_A)]R_M + w_A^* e_A$$
$$T_E = w_A^* \alpha_A - w_A^*(1 - \beta_A)R_M + w_A^* e_A \tag{27.1}$$
$$\text{Var}(T_E) = [w_A^*(1 - \beta_A)]^2 \text{Var}(R_M) + \text{Var}(w_A^* e_A) = [w_A^*(1 - \beta_A)]^2 \sigma_M^2 + [w_A^* \sigma(e_A)]^2$$
$$\text{Benchmark risk} = \sigma(T_E) = w_A^* \sqrt{(1 - \beta_A)^2 \sigma_M^2 + \sigma(e_A)]^2}$$

Equation 27.1 shows us how to calculate the volatility of tracking error and how to set the position in the active portfolio, w_A^*, to restrict tracking risk to any desired level. For a unit investment in the active portfolio, that is, for $w_A^* = 1$, benchmark risk is

$$\sigma(T_E; w_A^* = 1) = \sqrt{(1 - \beta_A)^2 \sigma_M^2 + [\sigma(e_A)]^2} \tag{27.2}$$

For a desired benchmark risk of $\sigma_0(T_E)$ we would restrict the weight of the active portfolio to

$$w_A(T_E) = \frac{\sigma_0(T_E)}{\sigma(T_E; w_A^* = 1)} \tag{27.3}$$

Obviously, introducing a constraint on tracking risk entails a cost. To limit tracking error, we shift weight from the active to the passive portfolio. Figure 27.1 illustrates the cost of this response. Ignoring tracking error, the portfolio optimization would lead us to portfolio T, the tangency of the capital allocation line (CAL), which is the ray from the risk-free rate to the efficient frontier formed from A and M. Reducing tracking risk by shifting weight from T to M takes us down the efficient frontier, instead of along the CAL, to a lower risk position, reducing the Sharpe ratio and M-square of the constrained portfolio.

Notice that the standard deviation of tracking error using the "meager" alpha forecasts in Spreadsheet 27.1 is only 3.46% because the weight in the active portfolio is only 17%. Using the larger alphas of Table 27.3 with no restriction on portfolio weights, the standard deviation of tracking error is 51.46%, more than any real-life manager who is evaluated against a benchmark would be willing to bear. However, with a weight of 1.0 on the active portfolio, the benchmark risk falls to 8.87% (Table 27.3).

Finally, suppose a manager wishes to restrict benchmark risk to the same level as it was using the original forecasts, that is, to 3.46%. Equations 27.2 and 27.3 instruct us to invest $w_A = .43$ in the active portfolio. We would then obtain the results in Table 27.4. This portfolio is moderate, yet superior in performance: (1) its standard deviation is only slightly higher than that of the passive portfolio, 13.85%; (2) its beta is .98;

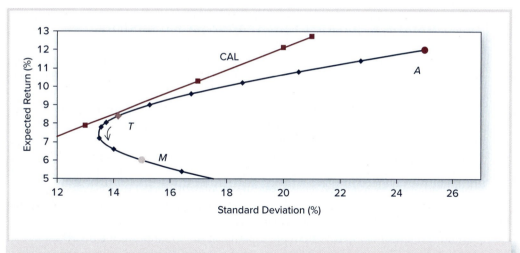

Figure 27.1 Reduced efficiency when benchmark risk is lowered. Reducing tracking error risk results in a shift from the tangency portfolio, *T*, toward the benchmark portfolio, *M*.

(3) the standard deviation of tracking error that we specified is extremely low, 3.85%; (4) given that we have only six securities, the largest position of 12% (in Target, TGT) is quite low and would be lower still if more securities were covered; yet (5) the Sharpe ratio is a whopping 1.06, and the *M*-square is an impressive 8.35%. Thus, by imposing limits on benchmark risk, we can avoid the flaws of the unconstrained portfolio and still maintain superior performance.

	S&P 500	Active Portfolio A		HP	DELL	WMT	TGT	BP	SHELL
			$\sigma^2(e)$	0.0705	0.0572	0.0309	0.0392	0.0297	0.0317
		25.7562	$\alpha/\sigma^2(e)$	2.0855	3.0641	6.2544	7.1701	6.0566	1.1255
		1.0000	$w_0(i)$	0.0810	0.1190	0.2428	0.2784	0.2352	0.0437
			$[w_0(i)]^2$	0.0066	0.0142	0.0590	0.0775	0.0553	0.0019
α_A		0.2018							
$\sigma^2(e_A)$		0.0078							
w_0		7.9116							
w^*	0.5661	0.4339		0.0351	0.0516	0.1054	0.1208	0.1020	0.0190
		Overall Portfolio							
Beta	1	0.9538	0.9800	0.0351	0.0516	0.1054	0.1208	0.1020	0.0190
Risk premium	0.06	0.2590	0.1464	0.0750	0.1121	0.0689	0.0447	0.0880	0.0305
Standard deviation	0.1358	0.1568	0.1385	0.3817	0.2901	0.1935	0.2611	0.1822	0.1988
Sharpe ratio	0.44	1.65	1.0569						
M-square	0	0.1642	0.0835						
Benchmark risk			0.0385						

Table 27.4

The optimal risky portfolio with the analysts' new forecasts (benchmark risk constrained to 3.85%)

27.2   The Treynor-Black Model and Forecast Precision

Suppose the risky portfolio of your 401(k) retirement fund is currently in an S&P 500 index fund, and you are pondering whether you should take some extra risk and allocate some funds to Target's stock. You know that, absent research analysis, you should assume the alpha of any stock is zero. Hence, the mean of your **prior distribution** of Target's alpha is zero. Downloading return data for Target and the S&P 500 reveals a residual standard deviation of 19.8%. Given this volatility, the prior mean of zero, and an assumption of normality, you now have the entire prior distribution of Target's alpha.

One can make a decision using a prior distribution, or refine that distribution by expending effort to obtain additional data. In statistical jargon, this effort is called *the experiment*. The experiment as a stand-alone venture would yield a probability distribution of possible outcomes. The optimal statistical procedure is to combine one's prior distribution for alpha with the information derived from the experiment to form a **posterior distribution** that reflects both. This posterior distribution is then used for decision making.

A "tight" prior, that is, a distribution with a small standard deviation, implies a high degree of confidence in the likely range of possible alpha values even before looking at the data. In this case, the experiment may not be sufficiently convincing to affect your beliefs, meaning that the posterior will be little changed from the prior. In the context of the present discussion, constructing an estimate of alpha and its precision is the experiment that may induce you to update your prior beliefs about its value. The role of the portfolio manager is to form a posterior distribution of alpha that aids portfolio construction.

Adjusting Forecasts for the Precision of Alpha

Imagine that you have just compiled the forecasts we used in Table 27.2, implying that Target's alpha is 28.1%. Should you conclude that the optimal position in Target, before adjusting for beta, is $\alpha/\sigma^2(e) = .281/.198^2 = 7.17$ (717%)? Naturally, before committing to such an extreme position, any reasonable manager would first ask: "How accurate is this forecast?" and "How should I adjust my position to take account of forecast imprecision?"

Treynor and Black[3] asked this question and supplied an answer. The logic of the answer is quite straightforward; you must quantify the uncertainty about this forecast, just as you would the risk of the underlying asset or portfolio. A Web surfer may not have a way to assess the precision of a downloaded forecast, but the employer of the analyst who issued the forecast does. How? By examining the **forecasting record** of previous forecasts issued by the same forecaster.

Suppose that a security analyst provides the portfolio manager with forecasts of alpha at regular intervals, say, the beginning of each month. The portfolio is updated using the forecast and held until the update of next month's forecast. At the end of each month, T, the realized abnormal return of Target's stock is the sum of alpha plus an error term, or "residual":

$$u(T) = R_{TGT}(T) - \beta_{TGT}R_M(T) = \alpha(T) + e(T) \qquad \textbf{(27.4)}$$

where beta is estimated from Target's security characteristic line (SCL) using data for periods prior to T,

$$\text{SCL:} \qquad R_{TGT}(t) = \alpha + \beta_{TGT}R_M(t) + e(t), \qquad t < T \qquad \textbf{(27.5)}$$

---

[3]Jack Treynor and Fischer Black, "How to Use Security Analysis to Improve Portfolio Selection," *Journal of Business,* January 1973.

The 1-month, forward-looking forecast $\alpha^f(T)$ issued by the analyst at the beginning of month T is aimed at the abnormal return, $u(T)$, in Equation 27.4. In order to decide how much credence to place in the forecast for month T, the portfolio manager uses the analyst's forecasting record. The analyst's record is the paired time series of all past forecasts, $\alpha^f(t)$, and realizations, $u(t)$. To assess forecast accuracy, that is, the relationship between forecast and realized alphas, the manager uses this record to estimate the regression:

$$u(t) = a_0 + a_1\alpha^f(t) + \varepsilon(t) \qquad\qquad (27.6)$$

Our goal is to adjust alpha forecasts to properly account for their imprecision. We will form an **adjusted alpha** forecast $\alpha(T)$ for the coming month by using the original forecasts $\alpha^f(T)$ and applying the estimates from the regression Equation 27.6, that is,

$$\alpha(T) = a_0 + a_1\alpha^f(T) \qquad\qquad (27.7)$$

The properties of the regression estimates assure us that the adjusted forecast is the "best linear unbiased estimator" of the abnormal return on Target in the coming month, T. "Best" in this context means it has the lowest possible variance among unbiased forecasts that are linear functions of the original forecast. We show in Appendix A that the value we should use for a_1 in Equation 27.7 is the R-square of the regression Equation 27.6. Because R-square is less than 1, this implies that we "shrink" the forecast toward zero. The lower the precision of the original forecast (the lower its R-square), the more we shrink the adjusted alpha back toward zero. In other words, we pay less attention to noisier forecasts. The coefficient a_0 adjusts the forecast upward if the forecaster has been consistently pessimistic, and downward for consistent optimism.

Distribution of Alpha Values

Equation 27.7 implies that the quality of security analysts' forecasts, as measured by the R-square in regressions of realized abnormal returns on their forecasts, is a critical issue for construction of optimal portfolios and resultant performance. Unfortunately, these numbers are usually impossible to come by.

However, Kane, Kim, and White[4] obtained a unique database of analysts' forecasts from an investment company specializing in large stocks with the S&P 500 as a benchmark portfolio. Their database includes a set of 37 monthly pairs of forecasts of alpha and beta values for between 646 and 771 stocks over the period December 1992 to December 1995—in all, 23,902 forecasts. The investment company policy was to truncate alpha forecasts at $+14\%$ and -12% per month. The histogram of these forecasts is shown in Figure 27.2.

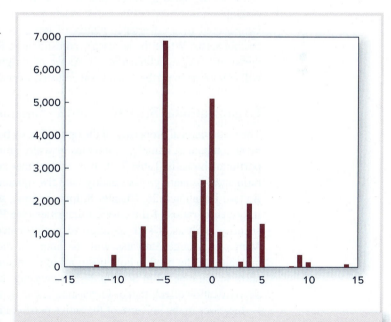

Figure 27.2 Histogram of alpha forecast

[4]Alex Kane, Tae-Hwan Kim, and Halbert White, "Active Portfolio Management: The Power of the Treynor-Black Model," in *Progress in Financial Market Research*, ed. C. Kyrtsou (New York: Nova, 2004).

Returns of large stocks over these years were about average, as shown in the following table, including one average year (1993), one bad year (1994), and one good year (1995):

	1993	1994	1995	1926–1999 Average	SD (%)
Rate of return (%)	9.87	1.29	37.71	12.50	20.39

The histogram shows that the distribution of alpha forecasts was positively skewed, with a larger number of pessimistic forecasts. The adjusted R-square in a regression of these forecasts with actual alphas was .001134, implying a tiny correlation coefficient of .0337.

These results contain "good" and "bad" news. The "good" news is that after adjusting even the wildest forecast, say, an alpha of 12% for the next month, the value to be used by a forecaster when R-square is .001 would be .012%, just 1.2 basis points per month. On an annual basis, this would amount to .14%, which is of the order of the alpha forecasts of the example in Spreadsheet 27.1. With forecasts of this small magnitude, the problem of extreme portfolio weights would never arise. The bad news arises from the same data: The performance of the active portfolio will be no better than in our example—implying an M-square of only 19 basis points.

An investment company that delivers such limited performance will not be able to cover its cost. However, this performance is based on an active portfolio that includes only six stocks. As we show in Section 27.5, even small information ratios of individual stocks can add up (see line 11 in Table 27.1). Thus, when many forecasts of even low precision are used to form a large active portfolio, large profits can be made.

So far we have assumed that forecast errors of various stocks are independent, an assumption that may not be valid. When forecasts are correlated across stocks, precision is measured by a covariance matrix of forecasting errors, which can be estimated from past forecasts. While the necessary adjustment to the forecasts in this case is algebraically messy, it is just a technical detail. As we might guess, correlations among forecast errors will call for us to further shrink the adjusted forecasts toward zero.

Organizational Structure and Performance

The mathematical properties of the optimal risky portfolio reveal a central feature of investment companies, namely, economies of scale. From the Sharpe measure of the optimized portfolio shown in Table 27.1, it is evident that performance as measured by the Sharpe ratio and M-square grows steadily with the squared information ratio of the active portfolio (see Equation 8.26, Chapter 8, for a review), which in turn is the sum of the squared information ratios of the covered securities (see Equation 8.28). Hence, a larger force of security analysts is sure to improve performance, at least before adjustment for cost. Moreover, a larger universe will also improve the diversification of the active portfolio and mitigate the need to hold positions in the neutral passive portfolio. Finally, as we will show in some detail in Section 27.5, increasing the universe of securities creates another diversification effect, that of forecasting errors by analysts.

Increases in the universe of the active portfolio in pursuit of better performance come at a cost, because security analysts of quality do not come cheap. However, the other units of the organization can handle increased activity with little increase in cost. All this suggests economies of scale for larger investment companies provided the organizational structure is efficient.

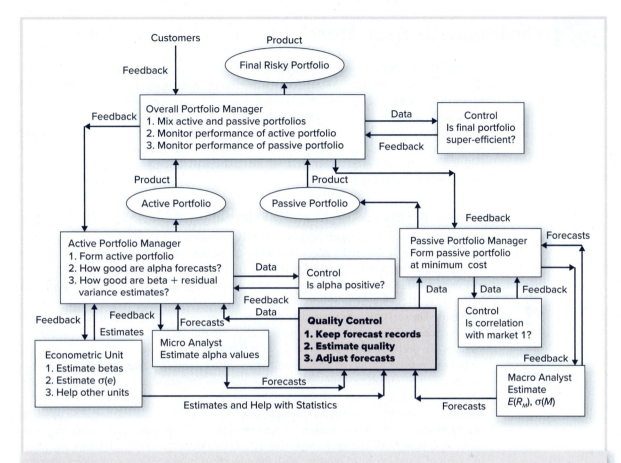

Figure 27.3 Organizational chart for portfolio management

Source: Adapted from Robert C. Merton, *Finance Theory,* Chapter 12, Harvard Business School.

Optimizing the risky portfolio entails a number of tasks of different nature in terms of expertise and need for independence. As a result, the organizational chart of the portfolio management outfit requires a degree of decentralization and proper controls. Figure 27.3 shows an organizational chart designed to achieve these goals. The figure is largely self-explanatory and the structure is consistent with the theoretical considerations worked out in previous chapters. It can go a long way in forging sound underpinnings to the daily work of portfolio management. A few comments are in order, though.

The control units responsible for forecasting records and determining forecast adjustments will directly affect the advancement and bonuses of security analysts and estimation experts. This implies that these units must be independent and insulated from organizational pressures.

An important issue is the conflict between independence of security analysts' opinions and the need for cooperation and coordination in the use of resources and contacts with corporate and government personnel. The relative size of the security analysis unit will further complicate the solution to this conflict. In contrast, the macro forecast unit might become *too* insulated from the security analysis unit. An effort to create an interface and channels of communications between these units is warranted.

27.3 | The Black-Litterman Model

Fischer Black, famous for the Black-Scholes option-pricing formula as well as the Treynor-Black model, teamed up with Robert Litterman to produce another useful model of portfolio construction. The Black-Litterman (BL) model allows portfolio managers to quantify complex forecasts (which they call **views**) and apply these views to portfolio construction.[5] We begin the discussion of the BL model with an illustration of a simple problem of asset allocation. Although we devote the next section to a comparison of the two models, some comments on commonalities of the models will help us better understand the BL model.

Black-Litterman Asset Allocation Decision

Consider a portfolio manager laboring over **asset allocation** to bills, bonds, and stocks for the next month. The risky portfolio will be constructed from bonds and stocks so as to maximize the Sharpe ratio. So far this is no more than the problem described in Section 7.3 of Chapter 7. There, we were concerned with optimizing the portfolio given a set of data inputs. In real life, however, optimization using a given dataset is the least of the manager's problems. The real challenge is how to come by the necessary input data. Black and Litterman propose an approach that uses past data, equilibrium considerations, and the private views of the portfolio manager about the near future.

Data enters the BL model from two sources: history and forecasts, called *views,* about the future. The historical sample is used to estimate the covariance matrix of the asset classes involved in the asset allocation decision. The estimated covariance matrix, combined with a model of equilibrium returns (e.g., the CAPM) is used to produce **baseline forecasts** that would be the basis of a passive strategy. In the next step, views are introduced and quantified. The views represent a departure from the baseline forecast and result in a revised set of expected returns. With the new set of inputs (just as with alpha forecasts in the Treynor-Black model), an optimal risky portfolio is designed to replace the (no-longer-efficient) passive portfolio.

Step 1: The Covariance Matrix from Historical Data

This straightforward task is the first in the chain that makes up the BL model. Suppose step 1 results in the following annualized covariance matrix, estimated from recent historical excess returns:

	Bonds (*B*)		Stocks (*S*)
Standard deviation	0.08		0.17
Correlation (bonds/stocks)		0.3	
Covariance			
Bonds	0.0064		0.00408
Stocks	0.00408		0.0289

Notice that step 1 is common to both the BL and the Treynor-Black (TB) models. This activity appears in the organizational chart in Figure 27.3.

---

[5]Fischer Black and and Robert Litterman, "Global Portfolio Optimization," *Financial Analysts Journal,* September/October 1992, CFA Institute.

Step 2: Determination of a Baseline Forecast

Because past data are of such limited use in inferring expected returns for the next month, BL propose an alternative approach. They start with a baseline forecast derived from the assumption that the market is in equilibrium where current prices of stocks and bonds reflect all available information and, as a result, the theoretical market portfolio with weights equal to market-value proportions is efficient. Suppose that current market values of outstanding bonds and stocks imply that the weight of bonds in the baseline portfolio is $w_B = .25$, and the weight of stocks is $w_S = .75$. When we apply these portfolio weights to the covariance matrix from step 1, the variance of the baseline portfolio emerges as

$$\text{Var}(R_M) = w_B^2 \, \text{Var}(R_B) + w_S^2 \, \text{Var}(R_S) + 2w_B w_S \, \text{Cov}(R_B, R_S)$$

$$= .25^2 \times .0064 \times .75^2 \times .0289 + 2 \times .25 \times .75 \times .00408 = .018186 \qquad (27.8)$$

The CAPM equation (Equation 9.2 in Chapter 9) gives the relationship between the market portfolio risk (variance) and its risk premium (expected excess return) as

$$E(R_M) = \bar{A} \times \text{Var}(R_M) \qquad (27.9)$$

where $\bar{A}$ is the average coefficient of risk aversion. Assuming $\bar{A} = 3$ yields the equilibrium risk premium of the baseline portfolio as: $E(R_M) = 3 \times .018186 = .0546 = 5.46\%$. The equilibrium risk premiums on bonds and stocks can be inferred from their betas on the baseline portfolio:

$$E(R_B) = \frac{\text{Cov}(R_B, R_M)}{\text{Var}(R_M)} E(R_M)$$

$$\text{Cov}(R_B, R_M) = \text{Cov}(R_B, w_B R_B + w_S R_S) = .25 \times .0064 + .75 \times .00408 = .00466$$

$$E(R_B) = \frac{.00466}{.018186} \times 5.46\% = 1.40\% \text{ (bond beta} = 0.26) \qquad (27.10)$$

$$E(R_S) = \frac{.75 \times .0289 + .25 \times .00408}{.018186} \times 5.46\% = 6.81\% \text{ (stock beta} = 1.25)$$

Thus, step 2 ends up with baseline forecasts of a risk premium for bonds of 1.40% and for stocks of 6.81%.

The final element in step 2 is to determine the covariance matrix of the baseline forecasts. This is a statement about the *precision* of these forecasts, which is different from the covariance matrix of realized excess returns on the bond and stock portfolios. We are looking for the precision of the *estimate* of expected return, as opposed to the volatility of actual returns. A conventional rule of thumb in this application is to use a standard deviation that is 10% of the standard deviation of returns (or equivalently, a variance that is 1% of the return variance). To illustrate, imagine that the covariance matrix of actual return was estimated from the returns of the last 100 months. The variance of the average return (which is the forecast of the expected return) would then be 1% of the variance of the actual return. Hence in this case it would be correct to use .01 times the covariance matrix of returns for the expected return. Thus step 2 ends with a forecast and covariance matrix:

	Bonds (*B*)	Stocks (*S*)
Expected return (%)	0.0140	0.0681
Covariance matrix of baseline forecasts		
Bonds	0.000064	0.0000408
Stocks	0.0000408	0.000289

Now that we have backed out market expectations, it is time to integrate the manager's private views into our analysis.

Step 3: Integrating the Manager's Private Views

The BL model allows the manager to introduce any number of views about the baseline forecasts into the optimization process. Appended to the views, the manager specifies his degree of confidence in them. Views in the BL model are expressed as values of various linear combinations of excess returns, and confidence in them is expressed as a covariance matrix of errors in these values.

Example 27.1   Views in the Black-Litterman Model

Suppose the manager takes a contrarian's view concerning the baseline forecasts, that is, he believes that in the next month bonds will outperform stocks by .5%. The following equation expresses this view:

$$1 \times R_B + (-1) \times R_S = .5\%$$

More generally, any view that is a linear combination of the relevant excess returns can be presented as an array (in Excel, an array would be a column of numbers) that multiplies another array (column) of excess returns. In this case, the array of weights is $P = (1, -1)$ and the array of excess returns is (R_B, R_S). The value of this linear combination, denoted Q, reflects the manager's view. In this case, $Q = .5\%$ must be taken into account in optimizing the portfolio.[6]

A view must come with a degree of confidence, that is, a standard deviation to measure the precision of Q. The manager's view is really $Q + \varepsilon$, where ε represents zero-mean error in the view with a standard deviation that reflects the manager's less than perfect confidence. Noticing that the standard deviation of the difference between the expected rates on stocks and bonds is 1.65% (calculated below in Equation 27.13), suppose that the manager assigns a value of $\sigma(\varepsilon) = 1.73\%$.[7] To summarize, if we denote the array of returns by $R = (R_B, R_S)$, then the manager's view, P, applied to these returns is[8]

$$PR^T = Q + \varepsilon$$
$$P = (1, -1)$$
$$R = (R_B, R_S) \tag{27.11}$$
$$Q = .5\% = .005$$
$$\sigma^2(\varepsilon) = .0173^2 = .0003$$

---

[6]A simpler view that bonds will return 3% is also legitimate. In that case $P = (1, 0)$ and the view is really like an alpha forecast in the Treynor-Black model. If all views were like this simple one, there would be no difference between the TB and BL models.

[7]Absent specific information shedding light on the SD of the view, for example, the track record of the source of the view, the SD calculated from the covariance matrix of the baseline forecasts is commonly used. In that case, the SD would be that of Q^E in Equation 27.13: $\sigma(Q^E) = \sqrt{.0002714} = .0165$ (1.65%).

[8]Notice that the view is expressed as a row vector with as many elements as there are risky assets (here, two) applied to the row vector of returns. The manager's view (Q) is obtained from the vector, P, marking the assets included in the view, times their actual returns. We denote the return row vector, R, with a superscript "T" (for transpose—turning a row vector into a column), and therefore compute the "sumproduct" of the two vectors.

Step 4: Revised (Posterior) Expectations

The baseline forecasts of expected returns derived from market values and their covariance matrix comprise the prior distribution of the rates of return on bonds and stocks. The manager's view, together with its confidence measure, provides the probability distribution arising from the "experiment," that is, the additional information that must be optimally integrated with the prior distribution. The result is the posterior: a new set of expected returns, conditioned on the manager's views.

To acquire intuition about the solution, consider what the baseline expected returns imply about the view. The expectations derived from market data are that the expected return on bonds is 1.40% and the expected return on stocks is 6.81%. Therefore, the baseline view is that $E(R_B) - E(R_S) = -5.41\%$. In contrast, the manager thinks this difference is $Q = R_B - R_S = .5\%$. Using the BL linear-equation notation for market expectations:

$$
\begin{aligned}
Q^E &= PR_E^T \\
P &= (1, -1) \\
R_E &= [E(R_B), E(R_S)] = (1.40\%, 6.81\%) \\
Q_E &= 1.40 - 6.81 = -5.41\%
\end{aligned}
$$
(27.12)

The baseline "view" of -5.41% (i.e., that stocks will outperform bonds by 5.41%) is vastly different from the manager's view. The difference, D, and its variance are

$$
\begin{aligned}
D &= Q - Q^E = .005 - (-.0541) = .0591 \\
\sigma^2(D) &= \sigma^2(\varepsilon) + \sigma^2(Q^E) = .0003 + \sigma^2(Q^E) \\
\sigma^2(Q^E) &= \text{Var}[E(R_B) - E(R_S)] = \sigma^2_{E(R_B)} + \sigma^2_{E(R_S)} - 2\text{Cov}[E(R_B), E(R_S)] \\
&= .000064 + .000289 - 2 \times .0000408 = .0002714 \\
\sigma^2(D) &= .0003 + .0002714 = .0005714
\end{aligned}
$$
(27.13)

Given the large difference between the manager's and the baseline views, we would expect a significant change in the conditional expected returns from those of the baseline and, as a result, a very different optimal portfolio.

The expected returns conditional on the view is a function of four elements: the baseline expectations, $E(R)$; the difference, D, between the manager's view and the baseline view (see Equation 27.13); the contribution of the asset return to the variance of D; and the total variance of D. The result is:

$$
E(R|\text{view}) = R + D\frac{\text{Contribution of asset to } \sigma_D^2}{\sigma_D^2}
$$

$$
E(R_B|P) = E(R_B) + \frac{D\left\{\sigma^2_{E(R_B)} - \text{Cov}[E(R_B), E(R_S)]\right\}}{\sigma_D^2}
$$

$$
= .0140 + \frac{.0591(.000064 - .0000408)}{.0005714} = .0140 + .0024 = .0164 \quad (27.14)
$$

$$
E(R_S|P) = E(R_S) + \frac{D\left\{\text{Cov}[E(R_B), E(R_S)] - \sigma^2_{E(R_S)}\right\}}{\sigma_D^2}
$$

$$
= .0681 + \frac{.0591(.0000408 - .000289)}{.0005714} = .0681 - .0257 = .0424
$$

We see that the manager increases his expected returns on bonds by .24% to 1.64%, and reduces his expected return on stocks by 2.57% to 4.24%. The difference between the expected returns on stocks and bonds is reduced from 5.41% to 2.60%. While this is a very large change, we also realize that the manager's private view that $Q = .5\%$ has been greatly tempered by the prior distribution to a value roughly halfway between his private view and the baseline view. In general, the degree of compromise between views will depend on the precision assigned to them.

The example we have described contains only two assets and one view. It can easily be generalized to any number of assets with any number of views about future returns. The views can be more complex than a simple difference between a pair of returns. Views can assign a value to *any* linear combination of the assets in the universe, and the confidence level (the covariance matrix of the set of ε values of the views) can allow for dependence across views. This flexibility gives the model great potential by quantifying a rich set of information that is unique to a portfolio manager. Appendix B to the chapter presents the general BL model.

Step 5: Portfolio Optimization

At this point, the portfolio optimization follows the Markowitz procedure of Chapter 7, with an input list that replaces baseline expectations with the conditional expectations arising from the manager's view.

Spreadsheet 27.2 presents the calculations of the BL model. Panel A shows the calculation of the benchmark forecasts and Panel B incorporates a view to arrive at

	A	B	C	D	E	F	G	H	I
1									
2									
3									
4	**Panel A: Bordered Covariance Matrix from Historical Excess Returns**								
5	**and Market-Value Weights and Calculation of Baseline Forecasts**								
6									
7			Bonds	Stocks					
8		Weights	0.25	0.75					
9	Bonds	0.25	64	40.8					
10	Stocks	0.75	40.8	289					
11		sumproduct	11.65	170.21					
12	Market portfolio variance V(M) = sum(c11,d11) =					181.86			
13	Coefficient of risk aversion of representative investor =					3			
14	Baseline market portfolio risk premium = 0.01A*V(M) =					5.46			
15	Covariance with R_M		46.6	226.95					
16	Baseline risk premiums		1.40	6.81		0.256237542			
17						1.247920819			
18	Proportion of covariance attributed to expected returns					0.01			
19	Covariance matrix of expected returns								
20			Bonds	Stocks					
21		Bonds	0.64	0.408					
22		Stocks	0.408	2.89					
23									
24	**Panel B: Views, Confidence, and Revised (Posterior) Expectations**								
25									
26	View: Difference between returns on bonds and stocks, Q =					0.5			
27	View embedded in baseline forecasts Q^E =					−5.41			
28	Variance of Q^E = Var(R_B − R_S)					2.71			
29	Var[E(R_B)] − Cov[E(R_B),E(R_S)] =					0.23			
30	Cov[E(RB),E(RS)] − Var[E(RB)] =					−2.48			
31	Difference between view and baseline data, D =					5.91			
32	Confidence measured by standard deviation of view Q								
33	Possible SD	0	1	1.73	3.00	6.00			
34	Variance	0	1.5	3	9	36	Baseline		
35	E(R_B|P)	1.90	1.72	1.64	1.52	1.43	1.40		
36	E(R_S|P)	1.40	3.33	4.24	5.56	6.43	6.81		

Spreadsheet 27.2

Sensitivity of the Black-Litterman portfolio to confidence in views

eXcel
Please visit us at
www.mhhe.com/Bodie11e

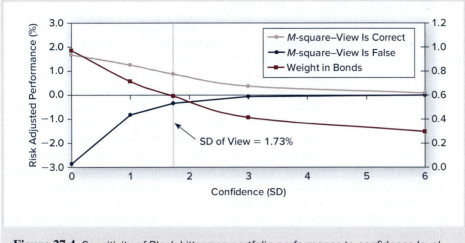

Figure 27.4 Sensitivity of Black-Litterman portfolio performance to confidence level

the revised (conditional) expectations. Figure 27.4 shows portfolio performance measured by M-square for various levels of confidence in the view when the view is correct and incorrect. The weight in bonds declines as the confidence in the view falls (the SD of the view increases). With no confidence in the view (SD very large), the weight in bonds falls to .3, determined by the baseline forecast. At this point, the portfolio is passive; its M-square is zero.

Notice that the M-square profile is asymmetric. With great confidence in the view and the resultant large position in bonds, the gain in M-square when the view is correct is smaller than the loss in M-square when the view is incorrect. With less confidence and therefore a smaller position in bonds, the "game" becomes more symmetric between a correct and incorrect view. Since determination of the SD of a view is quite abstract, the graph tells us that to err on the side of skepticism may well be the prudent choice.

27.4   Treynor-Black versus Black-Litterman: Complements, Not Substitutes

Treynor, Black, and Litterman have earned a place among the important innovators of the investments industry. Wide implementation of their models could contribute much to the industry. The comparative analysis of their models presented here is not aimed at elevating one at the expense of the other—in any case, we find them complementary—but rather to clarify the relative merits of each.

First and foremost, once you reach the optimization stage, the models are identical. Put differently, if users of either model arrive at identical input lists, they will choose identical portfolios and realize identical performance measures. In Section 27.6, we show that these levels of performance should be far superior to passive strategies, as well as to active strategies that do not take advantage of the quantitative techniques of these models. The models differ primarily in the way they arrive at the input list, and analysis of these differences shows that the models are true complements and are best used in tandem.

The BL Model as Icing on the TB Cake

The Treynor-Black (TB) model is really oriented to individual security analysis. This can be seen from the way the active portfolio is constructed. The alpha values assigned to securities must be determined relative to the passive portfolio. This portfolio is the one that would be held if all alpha values turned out to be zero. Now suppose an investment company prospectus mandates a portfolio invested 70% in a U.S. universe of large stocks, say, the S&P 500, and 30% in a well-defined universe of large European stocks. In that case, the macro analysis of the organization would have to be split, and the TB model would have to be run as two separate divisions. In each division, security analysts would compile values of alpha relative to their own passive portfolio. The product of this organization would thus include four portfolios, two passive and two active. This scheme is workable only when the portfolios are optimized separately. That is, the parameters (alpha, beta, and residual variance) of U.S. securities are estimated relative to the U.S. benchmark, while the parameters of European stocks are estimated relative to the European benchmark. Then the final portfolio would be constructed as a standard problem in asset allocation.

The resulting portfolio could be improved using the BL approach. First, views about the relative performance of the U.S. and European markets can be expected to add information to the independent macro forecasts for the two economies. For reasons of specialization, the U.S. and European macro analysts must focus on their respective economies. Obviously, when more country or regional portfolios are added to the company's universe, the need for decentralization becomes more compelling, and the potential of applying the BL model to the TB product greater. Moreover, the foreign-stock portfolios will result in various positions in local currencies. This is a clear area of international finance and the only way to import forecasts from this analysis is with the BL technique.[9]

Why Not Replace the Entire TB Cake with the BL Icing?

This question is raised by the need to use the BL technique if the overall portfolio is to include forecasts from comparative economic and international finance analyses. It is indeed possible to use the BL model for the entire process of constructing the efficient portfolio. The reason is that the alpha compiled for the TB model can be replaced with BL views. To take a simple example, suppose only one security makes up the active portfolio. With the TB model, we have macro forecasts, $E(R_M)$ and σ_M, as well as alpha, beta, and residual variance for the active portfolio. This input list also can be represented in the following form, along the lines of the BL framework:

$$R = [E(R_M), E(R_A) = \beta_A E(R_M)]$$

$$P = \left(0, 1 + \frac{\alpha_A}{\beta_A E(R_M)}\right)$$

$$PR^T = Q + \varepsilon = \alpha_A + \varepsilon$$

$$Q_E = 0$$

$$D = \alpha_A$$

$$\sigma^2(\varepsilon) = \text{Var(forecasting error) in Equation 27.6}$$

$$\sigma^2(D) = \sigma^2(\varepsilon) + \sigma^2(e)$$

(27.15)

where e is the residual in the SCL regression of Equation 27.5. Calculation of the conditional expectations from Equation 27.15 as in Equation 27.13 will bring us to the same adjusted alpha as in Equation 27.7 of the TB model.

---

[9]The BL model can also be used to introduce views about relative performance of various U.S and foreign corporations.

In this light, the BL model can be viewed as a generalization of the TB model. The BL model allows you to adjust expected return from views about alpha values as in the TB model, but it also allows you to express views about *relative* performance that cannot be incorporated in the TB model.

However, this conclusion might produce a false impression that is consequential to investment management. To understand the point, we first discuss the degree of confidence, which is essential to fully represent a view in the BL model. Spreadsheet 27.2 and Figure 27.4 illustrate that the optimal portfolio weights and performance are highly sensitive to the degree of confidence in the BL views. Thus, the validity of the model rests in large part on the way the confidence about views is arrived at.

When a BL view is structured to replace a direct alpha estimate in a TB framework, we must use the variance of the forecasting error taken from Equation 27.7 and applied to Equation 27.15. This is how "confidence" is quantified in the BL model. Whereas in the TB framework one can measure forecast accuracy by computing the correlation between analysts' alpha forecasts and subsequent realizations, such a procedure is not as easily applied to BL views about relative performance. Managers' views may be expressed about different quantities in different time periods, and, therefore, we will not have long forecast histories on a particular variable with which to assess accuracy. To our knowledge, no promotion of how to quantify "confidence" appears in academic or industry publications about the BL model.

This raises the issue of adjusting forecasts in the TB model. We are not aware of actual results where analysts' track records are systematically compiled and used to adjust alpha forecasts, although we cannot assert that such effort is nowhere expended. However, indirect evidence suggests that alphas are usually not adjusted, leading to the common "complaint" that the TB model is not applied in the field because it results in "wild" portfolio weights. Yet, as we saw in Section 27.3, those wild portfolio weights are a consequence of failing to adjust alpha values to reflect forecast precision. Any realistic R-square that can be obtained even by excellent forecasters will result in moderate portfolio weights. Even when "wild" weights do occasionally materialize, they can be "tamed" by a straightforward restriction on the variance of the tracking error.

It is therefore useful to keep the two models separate and distinct; the TB model for the management of security analysis with proper adjustment of forecasts and the BL model for asset allocation where views about relative performance are useful *despite* the fact that the degree of confidence must in practice be inaccurately estimated.

27.5   The Value of Active Management

We showed in Chapter 24 that the value of successful market timing is enormous. Even a forecaster with far-from-perfect predictive power would contribute significant value. Nevertheless, active portfolio management based on security analysis has even greater potential. Even if each individual security analyst has only modest forecasting power, the power of a *portfolio* of analysts is potentially unbounded.

A Model for the Estimation of Potential Fees

The value of market timing was derived from the value of an equivalent number of call options that mimic the return to the timer's portfolio. Thus, we were able to derive an unambiguous market value to timing ability, that is, we could price the implicit call in the timer's services. We cannot get quite that far with valuation of active portfolio management, but we can do the next best thing, namely, we can calculate what a representative investor would pay for such services.

Kane, Marcus, and Trippi[10] derive an annuitized value of portfolio performance measured as a percentage of funds under management. The percentage fee, f, that investors would be willing to pay for active services can be related to the difference between the square of the portfolio Sharpe ratio and that of the passive portfolio as

$$f = (S_P^2 - S_M^2)/2A \tag{27.16}$$

where A is the coefficient of the investor's risk aversion.

The source of the power of the active portfolio is the additive value of the squared **information ratios** $\left(\dfrac{\alpha_i}{\sigma(e_i)}\right)$ and the precision of individual analysts. Recall the expression for the square of the Sharpe ratio of the optimized risky portfolio:

$$S_P^2 = S_M^2 + \sum_{i=1}^{n} \left[\frac{\alpha_i}{\sigma(e_i)}\right]^2$$

Therefore,

$$f = \frac{1}{2A} \sum_{i=1}^{n} \left[\frac{\alpha_i}{\sigma(e_i)}\right]^2 \tag{27.17}$$

Thus, the fee that can be charged, f, depends on three factors: (1) the coefficient of risk aversion, (2) the distribution of the squared information ratio in the universe of securities, and (3) the precision of the security analysts. Notice that this fee is in excess of what an index fund would charge. If an index fund charges about 20 basis points, the active manager could charge incremental fees above that level by the percentage given in Equation 27.17.

Results from the Distribution of Actual Information Ratios

Kane, Marcus, and Trippi investigated the distribution of the squared IR for all S&P 500 stocks over two 5-year periods and estimated that this (annualized) expectation, $E(\text{IR}^2)$, is in the range of .845 to 1.122. With client risk coefficient of risk aversion of 3, a portfolio manager who covers 100 stocks with security analysts whose R-square of forecasts with realized alpha is only .001 would still be able to charge an annual fee 4.88% higher than that of an index fund. This fee is based on the lower end of the range of the expected squared information ratio.

One limitation of this study is that it assumes that the portfolio manager knows the quality of the forecasts, however low they may be. As we have seen, portfolio weights are sensitive to forecast quality, and when that quality is estimated with error, performance will be further reduced.

Results from Distribution of Actual Forecasts

A study of actual forecasts by Kane, Kim, and White (see footnote 4) found the distribution of over 11,000 alpha forecasts for over 600 stocks over 37 months presented in Figure 27.2. The average forecast precision from this database of forecasts provided an R-square of .00108. These are only marginally better than the precision used to interpret the Kane, Marcus, and Trippi study of the distribution of realized information value. Kane, Kim, and White use these R-squares to adjust the forecasts in their database and form optimal portfolios from 105 stocks selected randomly from the 646 covered by the investment company. The annualized M-square measures of performance are quite

---

[10]Alex Kane, Alan Marcus, and Robert R. Trippi, "The Valuation of Security Analysis," *Journal of Portfolio Management* 25 (Spring 1999).

impressive, 2.67% for the index model assuming no correlation across residuals, or 3.01% allowing for correlation.

The key conclusion of this analysis is that even the smallest forecast ability can result in greatly improved performance. Moreover, with better estimation techniques, performance can be further enhanced.

27.6 Concluding Remarks on Active Management

A common concern of students of Investments who encounter a heavy dose of theory laced with math and statistics is whether the analytical approach is necessary or even useful. Here are some observations that should allay any such concern. Investment theory has developed in recent decades at a galloping pace. Yet, perhaps surprisingly, the distance between the basic science of investments and industry practice, one that exists in any field, has actually narrowed in recent years. This trend is due in part to the vigorous growth of the CFA Institute. The CFA designation has become nearly a prerequisite to career success in the industry, and by disseminating research, the Institute contributes to the proximity between investments science and practice.

Yet there is one area in which practice still lags far behind theory, and that is the subject of this chapter—this despite the fact that TB and BL models have been around since 1973 and 1992, respectively. Yet, these models have so far failed to materially penetrate the industry. We hope, however, that this situation will soon be remedied.

Finally, there is little time in the already dense Investments curriculum to discuss the welfare implication of nearly efficient security prices. Prices will approximate these values only when investors optimize portfolios with high-quality analysis and implementation. The value of nearly efficient prices to the welfare of the economy is enormous, competing in importance with advances in technology. High-quality active management therefore can contribute to society even as it enriches its practitioners.

SUMMARY

1. Treynor-Black portfolio weights are sensitive to large alpha values, which can result in practically infeasible long/short portfolio positions. The full-blown Markowitz optimal risky portfolio is also extremely sensitive to assumptions for expected return.

2. Constraining tracking risk (i.e., the variance of the return difference between the managed and the benchmark portfolio) acts to keep the Treynor-Black portfolio within reasonable weights.

3. Alpha forecasts must be shrunk (adjusted toward zero) to account for less-than-perfect forecasting quality. Compiling past analyst forecasts and subsequent realizations allows one to estimate the correlation between realizations and forecasts. Regression analysis can be used to measure the forecast quality and guide the proper adjustment of future forecasts. When alpha forecasts are scaled back to account for forecast imprecision, the resulting portfolio positions become far more moderate.

4. The Black-Litterman model allows the private views of the portfolio manager to be incorporated with market data in the optimization procedure.

5. The Treynor-Black and Black-Litterman models are complementary tools. Both should be used: the TB model is more geared toward security analysis while the BL model more naturally fits asset allocation problems.

6. Even low-quality forecasts are valuable. Almost imperceptible R-squares of only .001 in regressions of realizations on analysts' forecasts can be used to substantially improve portfolio performance.

KEY TERMS

passive market-index portfolio
active portfolio
alpha values
benchmark portfolio
tracking error

prior distribution
posterior distribution
forecasting record
adjusted alphas
views

asset allocation
baseline forecasts
information ratio

PROBLEM SETS

1. How would the application of the BL model to a stock and bond portfolio (per the example in the text) affect security analysis? What does this suggest about the hierarchy of use of the BL and TB models?

2. Figure 27.3 includes a box for the econometrics unit. Item (3) is to "help other units." What sorts of specific tasks might this entail?

3. Make up new alpha forecasts and replace those in Spreadsheet 27.1 in Section 27.1. Find the optimal portfolio and its expected performance.

excel

Please visit us at
www.mhhe.com/Bodie11e

4. Make up a view and replace the one in Spreadsheet 27.2 in Section 27.3. Recalculate the optimal asset allocation and portfolio expected performance.

5. Suppose that sending an analyst to an executive education program will raise the precision of the analyst's forecasts as measured by R-square by .01. How might you put a dollar value on this improvement? Provide a numerical example.

E-INVESTMENTS EXERCISES

Visit **www.blacklitterman.org.** The information on the site can help you answer these questions.

1. What is the difference between a prior and posterior probability distribution?

2. What are some criteria for choosing the asset classes that might be best included in the model?

3. What are some of the problems in applying the model to hedge funds raised in the site?

APPENDIX A: Forecasts and Realizations of Alpha

A linear representation of the process that generates forecasts from the (yet unknown) future values of alpha would be

$$\alpha^f(t) = b_0 + b_1 u(t) + \eta(t) \tag{27A.1}$$

where $\eta(t)$ is the forecasting error and is uncorrelated with the actual $u(t)$. Notice that when the forecast is optimized as in Equation 27.7, the error of the adjusted forecast, $\varepsilon(t)$ in Equation 27.6, is uncorrelated with the optimally adjusted forecast $\alpha(T)$. The coefficients b_0 and b_1 are shift and scale biases in the forecast. Unbiased forecasts would result in $b_0 = 0$ (no shift) and $b_1 = 1$ (no scale bias).

We can derive both the variance of the forecast and the covariance between the forecast and realization from Equation 27A.1:

$$\sigma^2(\alpha^f) = b_1^2 \times \sigma^2(u) + \sigma^2(\eta)$$
$$\text{Cov}(\alpha^f, u) = b_1 \times \sigma^2(u) \tag{27A.2}$$

Therefore the slope coefficient, a_1, in Equation 27.6 is

$$a_1 = \frac{\text{Cov}(u, \alpha^f)}{\sigma^2(\alpha^f)} = \frac{b_1 \times \sigma^2(u)}{b_1^2 \times \sigma^2(u) + \sigma^2(\eta)} \qquad (27A.3)$$

When the forecast has no scale bias, that is, when $b_1 = 1$, a_1 equals the R-square of the regression of forecasts on realizations in Equation 27A.1, which also equals the R-square of the regression of realizations on forecasts in Equation 27.6. When b_1 is different from 1.0, we must adjust the coefficient a_1 to account for the scale bias. Notice also that with this adjustment, $a_0 = -b_0$.

APPENDIX B: The General Black-Litterman Model

The BL model is easiest to write using matrix notation. We describe the model according to the steps in Section 27.3.

Steps 1 and 2: The Covariance Matrix and Baseline Forecasts

A sample of past excess returns of the universe of n assets is used to estimate the $n \times n$ covariance matrix, denoted by $\sum$. It is assumed that the excess returns are normally distributed.

Market values of the universe assets are obtained and used to compute the $1 \times n$ vector of weights w_M in the baseline equilibrium portfolio. The variance of the baseline portfolio is calculated from

$$\sigma_M^2 = w_M \sum w_M^T \qquad (27B.1)$$

A coefficient of risk aversion for the representative investor in the economy, $\overline{A}$, is applied to the CAPM equation to obtain the baseline macro forecast for the market portfolio risk premium,

$$E(R_M) = \overline{A} \sigma_M^2 \qquad (27B.2)$$

The $1 \times n$ vector of baseline forecasts for risk premiums of each security, $E(R)$, is computed from the macro forecast and the covariance matrix by

$$E(R') = E(R_M) \sum w_M^T \qquad (27B.3)$$

The data so far describe the prior (baseline) distribution of the excess rates of return of the asset universe by

$$\widetilde{R} \sim N[E(R), \sum] \qquad (27B.4)$$

The $n \times n$ covariance matrix of the baseline *expected* excess returns, $\tau \sum$, is assumed proportional to the covariance matrix, $\sum$, by the scalar τ.

Step 3: The Manager's Private Views

The $k \times n$ matrix of views, P, includes k views. The ith view is a $1 \times k$ vector that multiplies the $1 \times n$ vector of excess returns, $\widetilde{R}$, to obtain the value of the view, Q_i, with forecasting error ε_i. The entire vector of view values and their forecasting errors is given by

$$RP = Q + \varepsilon \qquad (27B.5)$$

The confidence of the manager in the views is given by the $k \times k$ covariance matrix, Ω, of the vector of errors in views, ε. The views embedded in the baseline forecast, R, are given by Q^E,

$$RP = Q^E$$

Thus, the $1 \times k$ vector of deviation of the view from the baseline view (forecasts) and its covariance matrix S_D is

$$D = Q^E - Q$$
$$S_D = \tau P \sum P^T + \Omega \qquad \text{(27B.6)}$$

Step 4: Revised (Posterior) Expectations

The $1 \times n$ vector of posterior (revised) expectations conditional on the views, as well as the revised covariance matrix, is given by

$$R* = R|P = R + \tau D S_D^{-1} \sum P^T$$
$$\sum* = \sum + M \qquad \text{(27B.7)}$$
$$M = \tau \sum - \tau \sum P^T S_D^{-1} P \tau \sum$$

Step 5: Portfolio Optimization

The vector of revised expectations is used in conjunction with the covariance matrix of excess returns to produce the optimal portfolio weights with the Markowitz algorithm.

Investment Policy and the Framework of the CFA Institute

28

TRANSLATING THE ASPIRATIONS and circumstances of diverse households into appropriate investment decisions is a daunting task. The task is equally difficult for institutions, most of which have many stakeholders and often are regulated by various authorities. The investment process is not easily reduced to a simple or mechanical algorithm.

While many principles of investments are quite general and apply to virtually all investors, some issues are peculiar to the specific investor. For example, tax bracket, age, risk tolerance, wealth, job prospects, and other uncertainties make each investor's circumstances somewhat unique. In this chapter we focus on the process by which investors systematically review their particular objectives, constraints, and circumstances. Along the way, we survey some of the major classes of institutional investors and examine the special issues they must confront.

Of course, there is no unique "correct" investment process. However, some approaches are better than others, and it can be helpful to take one high-quality approach as a useful case study.

For this reason, we will examine the systematic approach suggested by the CFA Institute. Among other things, the Institute administers examinations to certify investment professionals as Chartered Financial Analysts. Therefore, the approach we outline is also one that a highly respected professional group endorses through the curriculum that it requires investment practitioners to master.

The basic framework involves dividing the investment process into four stages: specifying objectives, specifying constraints, formulating policy, and later monitoring and updating the portfolio as needed. We will treat each of these activities in turn. We start with a description of the major types of investors, both individual and institutional, as well as their special objectives. We turn next to the constraints or circumstances peculiar to each investor class, and we consider some of the investment policies that each can choose.

We will examine how the special circumstances of both individuals as well as institutions such as pension funds affect investment decisions. We also will see how the tax system can impart a substantial effect on investment decisions.

28.1   The Investment Management Process

The CFA Institute divides the process of investment management into three main elements that constitute a dynamic feedback loop: planning, execution, and feedback. Figure 28.1 and Table 28.1 describe the steps in that process. As shorthand, you might think of *planning* as focused largely on establishing all the inputs necessary for decision making. These include data about the client as well as the capital market, resulting in very broad policy guidelines (the strategic asset allocation). *Execution* fleshes out the details of optimal asset allocation and security selection. Finally, *feedback* is the process of adapting to changes in expectations and objectives as well as to changes in portfolio composition that result from changes in market prices.

The result of this analysis can be summarized in an investment policy statement addressing the topics specified in Table 28.2. In the next sections we elaborate on the steps leading to such an investment policy statement. We start with the planning phase, the first panel of Table 28.1.

Objectives

Table 28.1 indicates that the management planning process starts off by analyzing one's investment clients—in particular, by considering the objectives and constraints that govern their decisions. Portfolio objectives center on the **risk–return trade-off** between the expected return the investors want (*return requirements* in the first column of Table 28.3)

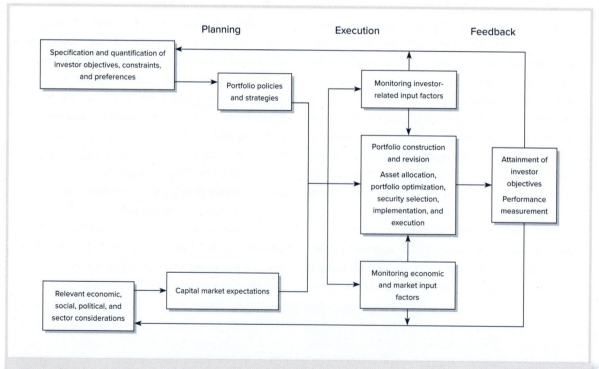

Figure 28.1 CFA Institute investment management process

I.	**Planning**
	A. Identifying and specifying the investor's objectives and constraints
	B. Creating the Investment Policy Statement (see Table 28.2)
	C. Forming capital market expectations
	D. Creating the strategic asset allocation (target minimum and maximum class weights)
II.	**Execution: Portfolio construction and revision**
	A. Asset allocation (including tactical) and portfolio optimization (combining assets to meet risk and return objectives)
	B. Security selection
	C. Implementation and execution
III.	**Feedback**
	A. Monitoring (investor, economic, and market input factors)
	B. Rebalancing
	C. Performance evaluation

Table 28.1

Components of the investment management process

Source: John L. Maginn, Donald L. Tuttle, Dennis W. McLeavey, and Jerald E. Pinto, "The Portfolio Management Process and the Investment Policy Statement," in *Managing Investment Portfolios: A Dynamic Process,* 3rd ed. (CFA Institute, 2007) and correspondence with Tom Robinson, head of educational content.

1. Brief client description
2. Purpose of establishing policies and guidelines
3. Duties and investment responsibilities of parties involved
4. Statement of investment goals, objectives, and constraints
5. Schedule for review of investment performance and the investment policy statement
6. Performance measures and benchmarks
7. Any considerations in developing strategic asset allocation
8. Investment strategies and investment styles
9. Guidelines for rebalancing

Table 28.2

Components of the investment policy statement

Objectives	Constraints	Policies
Return requirements	Liquidity	Asset allocation
Risk tolerance	Horizon	Diversification
	Regulations	Risk positioning
	Taxes	Tax positioning
	Unique needs	Income generation

Table 28.3

Determination of portfolio policies

and how much risk they are willing to assume (*risk tolerance*). Investment managers must know the level of risk that can be tolerated in the pursuit of a higher expected rate of return. The nearby box is an illustration of a questionnaire designed to assess an investor's risk tolerance. Table 28.4 lists factors governing return requirements and risk attitudes for each of the seven major investor categories we will discuss.

Risk Tolerance Questionnaire

Here is an example of a short quiz that may be used by financial institutions to help estimate risk tolerance.

Question	1 Point	2 Points	3 Points	4 Points
1. I plan on using the money I am investing:	Within 6 months.	Within the next 3 years.	Between 3 and 6 years.	No sooner than 7 years from now.
2. My investments make up this share of assets (excluding home):	More than 75%.	50% or more but less than 75%.	25% or more but less than 50%.	Less than 25%.
3. I expect my future income to:	Decrease.	Remain the same or grow slowly.	Grow faster than the rate of inflation.	Grow quickly.
4. I have emergency savings:	No.	No	Yes, but less than I'd like to have.	Yes.
5. I would risk this share of my portfolio in exchange for the same probability of doubling my money:	Zero.	10%.	25%.	50%.
6. I have invested in stocks and stock mutual funds:	No.	Yes, but I was uneasy about it.	No, but I look forward to it.	Yes, and I was comfortable with it.
7. My most important investment goal is to:	Preserve my original investment.	Receive some growth and provide income.	Grow faster than inflation but still provide some income.	Grow as fast as possible. Income is not important today.

Add the number of points for all seven questions. Add one point if you choose the first answer, two if you choose the second answer, and so on. If you score between 25 and 28 points, consider yourself an *aggressive investor*. If you score between 20 and 24 points, your risk tolerance is above average. If you score between 15 and 19 points, consider yourself a *moderate investor*. This means you are willing to accept some risk in exchange for a potential higher rate of return. If you score fewer than 15 points, consider yourself a *conservative investor*. If you have fewer than 10 points, you may consider yourself a very conservative investor.

Source: Securities Industry and Financial Markets Association.

Type of Investor	Return Requirement	Risk Tolerance
Individual and personal trusts	Life cycle (education, children, retirement)	Life cycle (younger are more risk tolerant)
Mutual funds	Variable	Variable
Pension funds	Assumed actuarial rate	Depends on proximity of payouts
Endowment funds	Determined by current income needs and need for asset growth to maintain real value	Generally conservative
Life insurance companies	Should exceed new money rate by sufficient margin to meet expenses and profit objectives; also actuarial rates important	Conservative
Non–life insurance companies	No minimum	Conservative
Banks	Interest-rate spread	Variable

Table 28.4

Matrix of objectives

Individual Investors

The basic factors affecting individual investor return requirements and risk tolerance are life-cycle stage and individual preferences. A middle-aged tenured professor will have a different set of needs and preferences from a retired widow, for example. We will have much more to say about individual investors later in this chapter.

Personal Trusts

Personal trusts are established when an individual confers legal title to property to another person or institution (the trustee) to manage that property for one or more beneficiaries. Beneficiaries customarily are divided into **income beneficiaries,** who receive the interest and dividend income from the trust during their lifetimes, and **remaindermen,** who receive the principal of the trust when the income beneficiary dies and the trust is dissolved. The trustee is usually a bank, a savings and loan association, a lawyer, or an investment professional. Investment of a trust is subject to trust laws, as well as "prudent investor" rules that limit the types of allowable trust investment to those that a prudent person would select.

Objectives for personal trusts normally are more limited in scope than those of the individual investor. Because of their fiduciary responsibility, personal trust managers typically are more risk averse than are individual investors. Certain asset classes such as options and futures contracts, for example, and strategies such as short-selling or buying on margin are ruled out.

Mutual Funds

Mutual funds are pools of investors' money. They invest in ways specified in their prospectuses and issue shares to investors entitling them to a pro rata portion of the income generated by the funds. The return requirement and risk tolerance across mutual funds are highly variable because funds segment the investor market. Various funds appeal to distinct investor groups and will adopt a return requirement and risk tolerance that fit a particular market niche. For example, income funds cater to the conservative investor, while high-growth funds seek out the more risk-tolerant ones. Tax-free bond funds segment the market by tax bracket.

Pension Funds

Pension fund objectives depend on the type of pension plan. There are two basic types: **defined contribution plans** and **defined benefit plans.** Defined contribution plans are in effect tax-deferred retirement savings accounts established by the firm in trust for its employees, with the employee bearing all the risk and receiving all the return from the plan's assets.

In defined benefit plans, by contrast, the employer has an obligation to provide a specified annual retirement benefit. That benefit is defined by a formula that typically takes into account years of service and the level of salary or wages. For example, the employer may pay the retired employee a yearly amount equal to 2% of the employee's final annual salary for each year of service. A 30-year employee would then receive an annual benefit equal to 60% of his or her final salary. The payments are an obligation of the employer, and the assets in the pension fund provide collateral for the promised benefits. If the investment performance of the assets is poor, the firm is obligated to make up the shortfall by contributing additional assets to the fund. In contrast to defined contribution plans, the risk surrounding investment performance in defined benefit plans is borne by the firm. We discuss pension plans more fully later in this chapter.

Endowment Funds

Endowment funds are organizations chartered to use their money for specific nonprofit purposes. They are financed by gifts from one or more sponsors and are typically managed by educational, cultural, and charitable organizations or by independent foundations established solely to carry out the fund's specific purposes. Generally, the investment objectives of an endowment fund are to produce a steady flow of income subject to only a moderate degree of risk. Trustees of an endowment fund, however, can specify other objectives as dictated by the circumstances of the particular endowment fund.

Life Insurance Companies

Life insurance companies generally try to invest so as to hedge their liabilities, which are defined by the policies they write. Thus there are as many objectives as there are distinct types of policies. Until the 1980s, there were for all practical purposes only two types of life insurance policies available for individuals: whole-life and term.

A **whole-life insurance policy** combines a death benefit with a kind of savings plan that provides for a gradual buildup of cash value that the policyholder can withdraw at a later point in life, usually at age 65. **Term insurance,** on the other hand, provides death benefits only, with no buildup of cash value.

The interest rate embedded in the schedule of cash value accumulation promised under a whole-life policy is a fixed rate, and life insurance companies try to hedge this liability by investing in long-term bonds. Often the insured individual has the right to borrow at a prespecified fixed interest rate against the cash value of the policy.

During the inflationary years of the 1970s and early 1980s, when many older whole-life policies carried contractual borrowing rates far lower than those available in the capital markets, policyholders borrowed heavily against the cash value to invest in money market mutual funds paying double-digit yields. In response to these developments the insurance industry came up with two new policy types: **variable life** and **universal life.** Under a variable life policy the insured's premium buys a fixed death benefit plus a cash value that can be invested in a variety of mutual funds from which the policyholder can choose. With a universal life policy, policyholders can increase or reduce the premium or death benefit according to their needs. Furthermore, the interest rate on the cash value component changes with market interest rates. The great advantage of variable and universal life insurance policies is that earnings on the cash value are not taxed until the money is withdrawn.

Non–Life Insurance Companies

Non–life insurance companies such as property and casualty insurers have investable funds primarily because they pay claims *after* they collect policy premiums. Typically, they are conservative in their attitude toward risk. A common thread in the objectives of pension plans and insurance companies is the need to hedge predictable long-term liabilities. Investment strategies typically call for hedging these liabilities with bonds of various maturities.

Banks

The defining characteristic of banks is that most of their investments are loans to businesses and consumers and most of their liabilities are accounts of depositors. Banks earn profit from the interest rate spread between loans extended (the bank's assets) versus deposits and CDs (the bank's liabilities), as well as from fees for services. Managing bank assets calls for balancing the loan portfolio with the portfolio of deposits and CDs. A bank can increase the interest rate spread by lending to riskier borrowers and by increasing the proportion of longer-term loans. However, bank capital regulations are risk-based, so higher-risk strategies will elicit higher capital requirements as well as the possibility of greater regulatory interference in the bank's affairs.

28.2   Constraints

Even with identical attitudes toward risk, different households and institutions might choose different investment portfolios because of their differing circumstances. These circumstances include tax status, requirements for liquidity or a flow of income from the portfolio, or various regulatory restrictions. These circumstances impose constraints on investor choice. Together, objectives and constraints determine investment policy.

As noted, constraints usually have to do with investor circumstances. For example, if a family has children about to enter college, there will be a high demand for liquidity since cash will be needed to pay tuition bills. Other times, however, constraints are imposed externally. For example, banks and trusts are subject to legal limitations on the types of assets they may hold in their portfolios. Finally, some constraints are self-imposed. For example, *social investing* means that investors will not hold shares of firms involved in ethically objectionable activities. Some criteria that have been used to judge firms as ineligible for a portfolio are involvement in countries with human rights abuses, production of tobacco or alcohol, and participation in polluting activities.

Table 28.5 presents a matrix summarizing the main constraints in each category for each of the seven types of investors.

Liquidity

Liquidity is the ease (and speed) with which an asset can be sold and still fetch a fair price. It is a relationship between the time dimension (how long will it take to sell) and the price dimension (any discount from fair market price) of an investment asset. (See the discussion of liquidity in Chapter 9.)

When an actual concrete measure of liquidity is necessary, one thinks of the discount when an immediate sale is unavoidable. Cash and money market instruments such as Treasury bills and commercial paper, where the bid–ask spread is a small fraction of 1%, are the most liquid assets, and real estate is among the least liquid. Office buildings and manufacturing structures can potentially experience a 50% liquidity discount.

Type of Investor	Liquidity	Horizon	Regulations	Taxes
Individuals and personal trusts	Variable	Life cycle	None	Variable
Mutual funds	High	Variable	Few	None
Pension funds	Young, low; mature, high	Long	ERISA	None
Endowment funds	Low	Long	Few	None
Life insurance companies	Low	Long	Complex	Yes
Non–life insurance companies	High	Short	Few	Yes
Banks	High	Short	Changing	Yes

Table 28.5

Matrix of constraints

Both individual and institutional investors must consider how likely they are to dispose of assets at short notice. From this likelihood, they establish the minimum level of liquid assets they want in the investment portfolio.

Investment Horizon

This is the *planned* liquidation date of the investment or substantial part of it. Examples of an individual **investment horizon** could be the time to fund a child's college education or the retirement date for a wage earner. For a university endowment, an investment horizon could relate to the time to fund a major campus construction project. Horizon needs to be considered when investors choose between assets of various maturities, such as bonds, which pay off at specified future dates. For example, the maturity date of a bond might make it a more attractive investment if it coincides with a date on which cash is needed. This idea is analogous to the matching principle from corporate finance: Strive to match financing maturity to the economic life of the financed asset.

Regulations

Professional and institutional investors are constrained by many regulations. First and foremost is the **prudent investor rule.** That is, professional investors who manage other people's money have a responsibility to restrict investment to assets that would have been approved by a prudent investor.

In 2016, the Department of Labor ruled that under ERISA (the Employee Retirement Security Act of 1974), advisers who work with tax-advantaged retirement savings are to be held to a *fiduciary standard,* meaning they they are required to work in the best interest of their clients. Previously, they were required to offer only "suitable" guidance, meaning that investment choices needed to be acceptable, but not necessarily defensible as the best choice for the client. For example, a client's money might be placed in a "suitable" mutual fund even if cheaper funds with nearly identical investment profiles were available. This new rule is meant to reduce conflicts of interest between advisers and clients. The new ruling has not yet been fully implemented, and in the aftermath of the 2016 elections, its timetable (and survival) is not clear.

Also, specific regulations apply to various institutional investors. For instance, U.S. mutual funds are subject to regulations that put upper bounds on the allowed use of leverage or investments in illiquid securities and lower bounds on some measures of diversification.

Tax Considerations

Tax consequences are central to investment decisions. The performance of any investment strategy is measured by how much it yields after taxes. For household and institutional investors who face significant tax rates, tax sheltering and deferral of tax obligations may be pivotal in their investment strategy.

Unique Needs

Virtually every investor faces special circumstances. Imagine husband-and-wife aeronautical engineers holding high-paying jobs in the same aerospace corporation. The entire human capital of that household is tied to a single player in a rather cyclical industry. This couple would need to hedge the risk of a deterioration of the economic well-being of the aerospace industry by investing in assets that will yield more if such deterioration materializes.

Similar issues would confront an executive on Wall Street who owns an apartment near work. Because the value of the home in that part of Manhattan probably depends on the vitality of the securities industry, the individual is doubly exposed to the vagaries of the stock market. Because both job and home already depend on the fortunes of Wall Street, the purchase of a typical diversified stock portfolio would actually increase the exposure to the stock market.

These examples illustrate that the job, or more generally, human capital, is often an individual's biggest "asset," and the unique risk profile that results from employment can play a big role in determining a suitable investment portfolio.

Other unique needs of individuals often center around their stage in the life cycle, as discussed below. Retirement, housing, and children's education constitute three major demands for funds, and investment policy will depend in part on the proximity of these expenditures.

Institutional investors also face unique needs. For example, pension funds will differ in their investment policy, depending on the average age of plan participants. Another example of a unique need for an institutional investor would be a university whose trustees allow the administration to use only cash income from the endowment fund. This constraint would translate into a preference for high-dividend-paying assets.

28.3 Policy Statements[1]

An investment policy statement (IPS) serves as a strategic guide to the planning and implementation of an investment program. When implemented successfully, the IPS anticipates issues related to governance of the investment program, planning for appropriate asset allocation, implementing an investment program with internal and/or external managers, monitoring the results, risk management, and appropriate reporting. The IPS also establishes accountability for the various entities that may work on behalf of an investor. Perhaps most important, the IPS serves as a policy guide that can offer an objective course of action to be followed during periods of disruption when emotional or instinctive responses might otherwise motivate less prudent actions.

The nearby box suggests desirable components of an investment policy statement for use with individual and/or high net worth investors. Not every component will be appropriate for every investor or every situation, and there may be other components that are desirable for inclusion reflecting unique investor circumstances.

Sample Policy Statements for Individual Investors

Perhaps the best way to get a concrete feel for deriving actual policy statements is to consider a sample of such statements for a variety of investors. Therefore, we next present several examples.

1. **Scope and Purpose**

1a. Define the context:

A preamble is often useful to relate information about the investor and/or the source of wealth as a way of establishing the context in which an investment program will be implemented.

> Example: The assets of the Leveaux family trusts trace back to the establishment of Leveaux Vintners in 1902 by Claude Leveaux. In 1979, LVX Industries was

---

[1]This section is adapted from documents of the CFA Institute that were made available to the authors in draft form. They may differ from the final published documents.

Desirable Components of an Investment Policy Statement for Individual Investors

SCOPE AND PURPOSE

- Define the Context
- Define the Investor
- Define the Structure

GOVERNANCE

- Specify responsibility for determining investment policy
- Describe process for review of IPS
- Describe responsibility for engaging/discharging external advisers
- Assign responsibility for determination of asset allocation
- Assign responsibility for risk management

INVESTMENT, RETURN, AND RISK OBJECTIVES

- Describe overall investment objective
- State return, distribution, and risk requirements
- Determine the risk tolerance of the investor
- Describe relevant constraints
- Describe other relevant considerations

RISK MANAGEMENT

- Establish performance measurement accountabilities
- Specify appropriate metrics for risk measurement
- Define a process by which portfolios are rebalanced

---

purchased by the British conglomerate FoodCo. Michelle Leveaux established the Leveaux Foundation with $100 million of the sale proceeds, and much of the remainder constituted the Leveaux Family Trusts which are the subject of this investment policy statement.

1b. Define the investor:

Define who the investor is, be it a natural person or legal/corporate entity.

> Example: "This Investment Policy Statement governs the personal investment portfolios of Mr. Chen Guangping."

1c. Define the structure:

Set forth key responsibilities and actors.

> Example: "Janice Jones, as financial adviser to Sam and Mary Smith, is responsible for coordinating updates to the Investment Policy. Sam and Mary Smith shall be responsible for approving the Investment Policy Statement."

Set forth a "standard of care" for those serving as adviser. Regulations in different jurisdictions may allow for advisers to abide by different standards depending on their preferences, business models, and client preferences. Fiduciary standards generally require that advisers always hold client interests as foremost, whereas suitability standards require recommendations that are suitable for an investor based on the adviser's knowledge of that investor's circumstances.

> Example: "Fuji Advisors acts as a fiduciary in its capacity as adviser to the Takesumi Family Accounts, and acknowledges that all advice and decisions rendered must reflect first and foremost the best interests of its clients."

2. Governance

2a. Specify who is responsible for determining investment policy, executing investment policy, and monitoring the results of implementation of the policy. The IPS documents accountability for all stages of investment policy development and implementation.

2b. Describe the process for review and updating of the IPS. A process for refreshing the IPS as investor circumstances and/or market conditions change should be clearly identified in advance.

> Example: "Wanda Wood is responsible for monitoring the investing requirements of Sam and Susan Smith as well as investment and economic issues, and for suggesting changes to the IPS as necessary, and no less frequently than annually."

2c. Describe the responsibilities for engaging or discharging external advisers. The IPS should set forth who is responsible for hiring and firing external money managers, consultants, or other vendors associated with the investment assets.

2d. Assign responsibility for determination of asset allocation, including inputs used and criteria for development of input assumptions. An asset allocation framework provides strategic context to many of the more tactical investment decisions. The IPS should address the assumptions used in developing and selecting inputs to the asset allocation decision process.

> Example: "At least annually, Tower Advisors shall review the asset allocation of the Family Investment Accounts, and suggest revisions for final approval by James and Jennifer Jensen. Tower Advisors shall consider expected returns and correlation of returns for a broad representation of asset classes in the U.S. capital markets, as well as anticipated changes in the rate of inflation, and changes in marginal tax rates."

2e. Assign responsibility for risk management, monitoring, and reporting. The IPS should document who is responsible for setting risk policy, monitoring the risk profile of the investment portfolio, and reporting on portfolio risk.

3. Investment, Return, and Risk Objectives

3a. Describe overall investment objective. The IPS should relate the purpose of the assets being invested to a broad investment objective.

> Example: "The investment program governed by the IPS is intended to supplement the earned income of Marcel Perrold as well as to provide for funds upon his retirement in 2026."

3b. State the return, distribution, and risk requirements.

State the overall investment performance objective. Careful specification of the overall investment performance objective is likely to incorporate descriptions of general funding needs as well as relations to key factors (such as inflation, spending rate, etc.).

> Example: "The financial plan developed for Margarita Mendez indicates a required real growth rate of 4% to satisfy her future obligations and allow her to retire in 2034 as planned."

Identify performance objectives for each asset class eligible for investment. The investment policy statement should set forth all permissible asset classes in which the portfolio may be invested. Some investors may find benefit in employing techniques to risk-adjust the benchmark return and portfolio return for purposes of comparison.

> Example: "The Family Trust accounts may invest in U.S. equity, U.S. fixed income, U.S. money market, and Developed Country international equity securities. The following benchmarks have been selected for comparison to each asset class: U.S. equity: Russell 3000 index; U.S. fixed income: Barclays U.S. Aggregate Index; U.S. money market: Lipper U.S. Government Money Market Average; Developed Country international equity securities: MSCI EAFE index."

Define distribution/spending assumptions or policies. Spending or distributions from the portfolio should be defined.

> Example: "Based on the overall expected portfolio return of 7.5%, fees of 1.2%, inflation of 2.8%, and an effective tax rate of 32% of total appreciation, the Linzer Trust Portfolio may support an annual spending rate of 1.2% of the portfolio market value while retaining potential for capital preservation or nominal growth."

Define a policy portfolio to serve as a basis for performance and risk assessments. An asset allocation policy should designate target allocations to each asset class, with allowable ranges around the targets.

3c. Determine the risk tolerance of the investor.

Describe the investor's general philosophy regarding tolerance of risk. The IPS should acknowledge the assumption of risk and the potential for returns associated with risk to be both positive and negative over time. Relevant risks are usually myriad, and may include liquidity, legal, political, regulatory, longevity, mortality, business, and/or health risks.

> Example: "Tower Advisors understands that an absolute loss in any 12 month period of more than −33% is intolerable."

3d. Describe relevant constraints.

Investors must address a variety of constraints that affect their investment programs. Such constraints may reflect legal or regulatory imperatives or may reflect internal policies.

Define an evaluation horizon for achievement of performance objectives. Establishing a minimum time horizon for achievement of performance objectives makes clearer when action may need to be taken to resolve underperformance issues.

> Example: "The basis for evaluation of relative success in achieving investment objectives will be on a rolling 8-quarter basis."

Identify any requirements for maintaining liquidity. Investors may have short or medium term needs for cash, which should be specified in the IPS.

> Example: "Up to 15% of the market value of the portfolio should be invested such that it could be liquidated upon 5 days' notice without suffering capital depreciation."

Identify to what extent, if any, tax considerations shall affect investment decision making. The investor's general tax situation as well as specific tax issues should be accounted for in the investment policy statement.

Identify any relevant legal constraints.

> Example: "Management of the Aquilla Family Foundation account is subject to the provisions of the Uniform Prudent Investor Act."

Specify any policies related to leverage. The ability to leverage portfolios may be constrained by policy or relevant statute.

> Example: "At the discretion of Tower Advisors as investment manager, the Xie Weng portfolio may be margined up to 50% of its value."

3e. Describe other considerations relevant to investment strategy.

Identify special factors to be used in including or excluding potential investments from the portfolio. Investors may choose to impose limits on certain investments, consistent with their beliefs in extra-financial factor effects on securities prices.

> Example for an Individual Investor: "Consistent with her personal beliefs, no investments in companies that derive revenue from products or services that are contrary to the teachings of the Catholic Church will be made for Jennifer Jensen's account."

4. Risk Management

4a. Establish performance measurement and reporting accountabilities. The IPS should establish an objective, reliable mechanism for reporting on investment performance.

> Example for an Individual Investor: "Hill Counsel will calculate and report the performance of each investment account by the 15th day of the new quarter. Calculations will be performed consistent with the Global Investment Performance Standards published by CFA Institute."

4b. Specify appropriate metrics for risk measurement and evaluation. Consistent use of metrics to assess and evaluate the risk profile of investment portfolios is important to allow for meaningful comparisons over time.

> Example for an Individual Investor: "In addition to performance reporting, Tower Capital shall report to the Marcel Family Trust trustees indicative risk metrics, such as the standard deviation and information ratio of portfolio returns relative to each portfolio's specified benchmark."

4c. Define a process by which portfolios are rebalanced to target allocations. Boundaries of acceptable variations from target should be specified.

> Example for an Individual Investor: "On the first business day of each new quarter, the investment adviser for the Jensen personal accounts will propose rebalancing transactions to return the accounts to their target allocations, and shall execute these transactions within two business days."

28.4   Asset Allocation

Consideration of their objectives and constraints leads investors to a set of investment policies. The policies column in Table 28.3 lists the various dimensions of portfolio management policymaking—asset allocation, diversification, risk and tax positioning, and income generation. By far the most important part of policy determination is asset allocation, that is, deciding how much of the portfolio to invest in each major asset category.

We can view the process of asset allocation as consisting of the following steps:

1. Specify asset classes to be included in the portfolio. The major classes usually considered are the following:

   a. Money market instruments (usually called *cash*).

   b. Fixed-income securities (usually called *bonds*).

   c. Stocks.

   d. Real estate.

   e. Precious metals.

   f. Other.

   Institutional investors will rarely invest in more than the first four categories, whereas individual investors may include precious metals and other more exotic types of investments in their portfolios.

2. Specify capital market expectations. This step consists of using both historical data and economic analysis to determine your expectations of future rates of return over the relevant holding period on the assets to be considered for inclusion in the portfolio.

When More Is Less

We all would like to reduce the risk of our investment portfolios, at least if it would not come at the expense of lower returns. While economists will tell you there is no such thing as a free lunch, this is an arena where they are at least partially wrong. You *can* get the benefit of lower risk without sacrificing return—by diversifying. It is commonplace to note that adding more securities to your portfolio can reduce risk without necessarily sacrificing return. More risky securities can add up to *less* volatility.

Less appreciated is the fact that you should also think about diversifying your exposure to different kinds of uncertainty. Risk is more than just the volatility surrounding the value of your portfolio. It actually has many dimensions. Here are some to think about.

Market risk: This is the risk that usually gets the most attention. It's the risk that your portfolio will fall in a declining market.

Inflation risk: Even if you invest in "risk-free" Treasury bills with known nominal returns, uncertain inflation will make your real return unpredictable. Some call this exposure the "risk of avoiding risk" because a portfolio too heavily tilted toward safe T-bills can leave you with a loss of purchasing power, especially over long investment horizons.

Interest-rate risk: The systematic risk factor in fixed income markets is interest rate uncertainty. Even "conservative" bond portfolios can suffer big losses when interest rates spike.

Conversely, declines in the rates at which coupon income can be reinvested might reduce the future value of your investment. This is why fixed-income investors are interested in immunization strategies.

Liquidity risk: Buying and selling securities always entails costs, including potential "price concessions," in which you may have to accept an unattractive price in order to get a deal done quickly. Liquidity, the ability to do trades on short notice at fair prices, varies unpredictably over time and entails another source of risk. This can be especially telling when you are unsure about when you will need to cash out your investments.

Political risk: All investments are subject to governmental actions, ranging from taxes on returns to the risk of outright expropriation. Political risk varies enormously across countries but is never fully absent.

Event risk: Low probability but high impact events can affect the whole economy, for example, an earthquake or a tsunami. They can also be firm specific, for example, an accounting fraud or a drug discovery. In both cases, your portfolio may be exposed to "black swans."

The list can go on, including issues such as currency risk, credit risk, energy price risk, and so on. You have to consider your exposure to each of these factors, limiting each of them to a manageable level.

3. Derive the efficient portfolio frontier. This step consists of finding portfolios that achieve the maximum expected return for any given degree of risk.

4. Find the optimal asset mix. This step consists of selecting the efficient portfolio that best meets your risk and return objectives while satisfying the constraints you face.

Taxes and Asset Allocation

Until this point we have glossed over the issue of income taxes in discussing asset allocation. Of course, to the extent that you are a tax-exempt investor such as a pension fund, or if all of your investment portfolio is in a tax-sheltered account such as an individual retirement account (IRA), then taxes may be irrelevant to your portfolio decisions.

But let us say that at least some of your investment income is subject to income taxes at the highest rate under current U.S. law. You are interested in the after-tax holding-period return (HPR) on your portfolio. At first glance it might appear to be a simple matter to figure out what the after-tax HPRs on stocks, bonds, and cash are if you know what they are before taxes. However, there are several complicating factors.

The first is the fact that you can choose between tax-exempt and taxable bonds. We discussed this issue in Chapter 2 and concluded there that you will choose to invest in tax-exempt bonds (i.e., municipal bonds) if your personal tax rate is such that the after-tax rate of interest on taxable bonds is less than the interest rate on "munis."

The second complication is not quite so easy to deal with. It arises from the fact that part of your HPR is in the form of a capital gain or loss. Under the current tax system you pay income taxes on a capital gain only if you *realize* it by selling the asset during the holding period. This applies to bonds as well as stocks, and it makes the after-tax HPR a function of whether the security will actually be sold at the end of the holding period.

Sophisticated investors time the realization of their sales of securities to minimize their tax burden. This often calls for selling securities that are losing money at the end of the tax year and holding on to those that are making money.

Furthermore, because cash dividends on stocks are fully taxable and capital gains taxes can be deferred by not selling stocks that appreciate in value, the after-tax HPR on stocks will depend on the dividend payout policies of the corporations that issued the stock.

28.5   Managing Portfolios of Individual Investors

The overriding consideration in individual investor goal-setting is one's stage in the life cycle. Most young people start their adult lives with only one asset—their earning power. In this early stage of the life cycle an individual may not have much interest in investing in stocks and bonds. The needs for liquidity and preserving safety of principal dictate a conservative policy of putting savings in a bank or a money market fund. The purchase of life and disability insurance will be required to protect the value of human capital.

When labor income grows to the point at which insurance and housing needs are met, saving for retirement may begin, especially if the government provides tax incentives for such savings. Retirement savings typically constitute a family's first pool of investable funds. This is money that can be invested in stocks, bonds, and real estate (other than the primary home).

Human Capital and Insurance

The first significant investment decision for most individuals concerns education, building up their human capital. The major asset most people have during their early working years is the earning power that draws on their human capital. In these circumstances, the risk of illness or injury is far greater than the risk associated with financial wealth.

The most direct way of hedging human capital risk is to purchase insurance. With the combination of your labor income and a disability insurance policy viewed as a portfolio, the rate of return on this portfolio is less risky than the labor income by itself. Life insurance is a hedge against the complete loss of income as a result of death of any of the family's income earners.

Investment in Residence

The first major economic asset many people acquire is their own house. Deciding to buy rather than rent a residence qualifies as an investment decision.

An important consideration in assessing the risk and return aspects of this investment is the value of a house as a hedge against two kinds of risk. The first kind is the risk of increases in rental rates. If you own a house, any increase in rental rates will increase the return on your investment.

The second kind of risk is that the particular house or apartment where you live may not always be available to you. By buying, you guarantee its availability.

Saving for Retirement and the Assumption of Risk

People save and invest money to provide for future consumption and leave an estate. The primary aim of lifetime savings is to allow maintenance of the customary standard of living after retirement. As Figure 28.2 suggests, your retirement consumption depends on your life expectancy at that time. Life expectancy, conditional on retirement at age 65,

FINANCIAL SERVICES

"With your investments, you should enjoy a lifetime of financial security...providing you start drinking, smoking, and eating more fatty foods."

Figure 28.2 Long life expectancy is a double-edged sword

Source: **www.glasbergen.com.** Copyright 2000 by Randy Glasbergen. Reprinted by permission of Randy Glasbergen.

approximates 85 years, so the average retiree needs to prepare a 20-year nest egg and sufficient savings to cover unexpected health care costs. Investment income may also increase the welfare of one's heirs, favorite charity, or both.

Questionnaires suggest that risk aversion increases as investors near retirement age. With age, individuals lose the potential to recover from a disastrous investment performance. When they are young, investors can respond to a loss by working harder and saving more of their income. But as retirement approaches, investors realize there will be less time to recover. Hence the shift to safe assets.

Retirement Planning Models

In recent years, investment companies and financial advisory firms have created a variety of "user-friendly" interactive tools and models for retirement planning. Although they vary in detail, the essential structure behind most of them can be illustrated using the American Saving Education Council's "Ballpark Estimate" worksheet (see Figure 28.3). The worksheet assumes you'll need 70% of current income, that you'll live to age 87, and you'll realize a constant real rate of return of 3% after inflation. The hypothetical client in the worksheet is a 35-year-old working woman with two children, earning $30,000 per year. Seventy percent of her current annual income ($30,000) is $21,000. She would then subtract the income she expects to receive from Social Security ($12,000 in her case) from $21,000, equaling $9,000. This is how much she needs to make up for each retirement year. She expects to retire at age 65, so (using Panel 3 of the worksheet) she multiplies $9,000 × 16.4 equaling $147,600. She has already saved $2,000 in her 401(k) plan and plans to retire in 30 years, so (from Panel 4) she multiplies $2,000 × 2.4 equaling $4,800. She subtracts that from her total, making her projected total savings needed at retirement $142,800. Finally, she multiplies $142,800 × .020 = $2,856 (Panel 6). This is the amount she will need to save annually for her retirement.

 Concept Check **28.1**

a. Think about the financial circumstances of your closest relative in your parents' generation. Write down the objectives and constraints for their investment decisions.

b. Now consider the financial situation of your closest relative who is in his or her 30s. Write down the objectives and constraints that would fit his or her investment decision.

c. How much of the difference between the two statements is due to the age of the investors?

Manage Your Own Portfolio or Rely on Others?

Lots of people have assets such as Social Security benefits, pension and group insurance plans, and savings components of life insurance policies. Yet they exercise limited control, if any, on the investment decisions of these plans. The funds that secure pension and life insurance plans are managed by institutional investors.

BALLPARK ESTIMATE®

1. How much annual income will you want in retirement? (Figure 70% of your current annual income just to maintain your current standard of living. Really.)   **$ 21,000**

2. Subtract the income you expect to receive annually from:
   - Social Security
   If you make under $25,000, enter $8,000; between $25,000 − $40,000, enter $12,000; over $40,000, enter $14,500   **− $ 12,000**
   - Traditional Employer Pension—a plan that pays a set dollar amount for life, where the dollar amount depends on salary and years of service (in today's dollars)   − $ _____
   - Part-time income   − $ _____
   - Other   − $ _____

   This is how much you need to make up for each retirement year   **= $ 9,000**

   Now you want a ballpark estimate of how much money you'll need in the bank the day you retire. So the accountants went to work and devised this simple formula. For the record, they figure you'll realize a constant real rate of return of 3% after inflation, you'll live to age 87, and you'll begin to receive income from Social Security at age 65.

3. To determine the amount you'll need to save, multiply the amount you need to make up by the factor below.   **$147,600**

Age you expect to retire:		Your factor is:	
	55		21.0
	60		18.9
	65		**16.4**
	70		13.6

4. If you expect to retire before age 65, multiply your Social Security benefit from line 2 by the factor below.   + $ _____

Age you expect to retire:		Your factor is:	
	55		8.8
	60		4.7

5. Multiply your savings to date by the factor below (include money accumulated in a 401(k), IRA, or similar retirement plan):   **− $ 4,800**

If you want to retire in:		Your factor is:	
	10 years		1.3
	15 years		1.6
	20 years		1.8
	25 years		2.1
	30 years		**2.4**
	35 years		2.8
	40 years		3.3

   Total additional savings needed at retirement: **= $142,800**

6. To determine the ANNUAL amount you'll need to save, multiply the TOTAL amount by the factor below.   **$ 2,856**

If you want to retire in:		Your factor is:	
	10 years		.085
	15 years		.052
	20 years		.036
	25 years		.027
	30 years		**.020**
	35 years		.016
	40 years		.013

This worksheet simplifies several retirement planning issues such as projected Social Security benefits and earnings assumptions on savings. It also reflects today's dollars; therefore you will need to re-calculate your retirement needs annually and as your salary and circumstances change. You may want to consider doing further analysis, either yourself using a more detailed worksheet or computer software or with the assistance of a financial professional.

Figure 28.3 Sample of American Saving Education Council worksheet

Source: EBRI (Employee Benefit Research Institute)/American Saving Education Council.

Check Out Your Investment Adviser

Before selecting an investment adviser, you should know what services you're paying for, how much those services cost, how the adviser gets paid, and what conflicts of interest the adviser may have when giving you investment advice. If you have a registered investment adviser, review the firm's brochure when you first receive it and when it is updated by the firm—there's a wealth of valuable information in there! And if you don't recall receiving the brochure, request it. You can also find the brochure on the SEC's Investment Adviser Public Disclosure (IAPD) Web site.

Here are some of the questions to ask when evaluating an investment adviser:

1. Are you registered with the SEC, a state, or the Financial Industry Regulatory Authority (FINRA)?

2. Have you or your firm ever been disciplined by any regulator? If yes, for what reasons and how was the matter resolved?

3. Have you ever been sued by a client who was not happy with your work, the services you provided, or the products you recommended?

4. How are you paid for your services? What is your usual hourly rate, flat fee, or commission?

5. What experience do you have, especially with people in my circumstances?

6. Where did you go to school? What is your recent employment history?

7. What products and services do you offer? Are you only supposed to recommend a limited number of products or services to me? If so, why?

Source: http://investor.gov/researching-managing-investments/working-investment-professionals/brokers-advisors/research-advisor.

Outside the "forced savings" plans, however, individuals can manage their own investment portfolios. Managing your own portfolio *appears* to be the lowest-cost solution. However, against the fees and charges that financial planners and professional investment managers impose, you will want to offset the value of your time and energy expended on diligent portfolio management.

Professional managers face two added difficulties. First, getting clients to accurately communicate their objectives and constraints requires considerable skill. This is not a one-time task because objectives and constraints are forever changing. Second, the professional needs to articulate the financial plan and keep the client abreast of outcomes. Professional management of large portfolios is complicated further by the need to set up an efficient organization where decisions can be decentralized and information properly disseminated. The nearby box presents some questions to consider when looking for an investment adviser.

The task of life cycle financial planning is a formidable one for most people. It is not surprising that a whole industry has sprung up to provide personal financial advice.

Tax Sheltering

In this section, we explain three important tax sheltering options that can radically affect optimal asset allocation for individual investors. The first is the tax-deferral option, which arises from the fact that you do not have to pay tax on a capital gain until you choose to realize the gain. The second is tax-deferred retirement plans such as individual retirement accounts, and the third is tax-deferred annuities offered by life insurance companies.

The Tax-Deferral Option   A fundamental feature of the U.S. Internal Revenue Code is that tax on a capital gain on an asset is payable only when the asset is sold; this is its **tax-deferral option.** The investor therefore can control the timing of the tax payment. This conveys a benefit to stock investments.

To see this, compare IBM stock with an IBM bond. Suppose both offer an expected total return of 12%. The stock has a dividend yield of 4% and expected price appreciation of 8%, whereas the bond pays an interest rate of 12%. The bond investor must pay tax on the bond's interest in the year it is earned, whereas the stockholder pays tax only on the dividend and defers paying capital gains tax until the stock is sold.

Suppose one invests $1,000 for five years. Although in reality interest is taxed as ordinary income while capital gains and dividends are taxed at a rate of only 15% for many investors,[2] to isolate the benefit of tax deferral, we will assume that all investment income is taxed at 15%. The bond will earn an after-tax return of $12\% \times (1 - .15) = 10.2\%$. The after-tax accumulation at the end of five years is

$$\$1,000 \times 1.102^5 = \$1,625.20$$

For the stock, the dividend yield after taxes is $4\% \times (1 - .15) = 3.4\%$. Because no taxes are paid on the 8% annual capital gain until year 5, the before-tax accumulation will be

$$\$1,000 \times (1 + .034 + .08)^5 = 1,000(1.114)^5 = \$1,715.64$$

In year 5, when the stock is sold, the (now-taxable) capital gain is

$$\$1,715.64 - \$1,000(1.034)^5 = 1,715.64 - 1,181.96 = \$533.68$$

Taxes due are $80.05, leaving $1,635.59, which is $10.39 more than the bond investment yields. Deferral of the capital gains tax allows the investment to compound at a faster rate until the tax is actually paid. The more of one's total return that is in the form of price appreciation, the greater the value of the tax-deferral option.

Tax-Protected Retirement Plans   Recent years have seen increased use of **tax-protected retirement plans** in which investors can choose how to allocate assets. Such plans include traditional IRAs, Keogh plans, and employer-sponsored "tax-qualified" defined contribution plans such as 401(k) plans. A feature these so-called *traditional plans* have in common is that contributions and earnings are not subject to federal income tax until the individual withdraws them as benefits.

Typically, an individual may have some investment in the form of such qualified retirement accounts and some in the form of ordinary taxable accounts. The basic tax-sheltering principle is to hold whatever bonds you want to hold in the retirement account while holding equities in the ordinary account. You maximize the tax advantage of the retirement account by holding it in the security that is the least tax advantaged.

To see this point, consider an investor who has $200,000 of wealth, of which $100,000 is in a tax-qualified retirement account. She currently invests half of her wealth in bonds and half in stocks, so she allocates half of her retirement account and half of her nonretirement funds to each. She could reduce her tax bill with *no change* in before-tax returns simply by shifting her bonds into the retirement account and holding all her stocks outside the retirement account.

 Concept Check **28.2**

> Suppose our investor earns a 10% per year rate of interest on bonds and a 15% per year return on stocks, with all earnings reinvested. In five years, she will withdraw all her funds and spend them. By how much will she increase her final accumulation if she shifts all bonds into the retirement account and holds all stocks outside the retirement account? Assume the tax rate on interest income is the same as the rate on ordinary income, 28%, while the tax rate on capital gains is 15%. Also assume that equity income is entirely in the form of capital gains, on which taxes are not paid until the investor cashes in the fund in five years.

---

[2]As of 2016, the tax rate on capital gains and dividends is 15% for married couples earning between $73,300 and $466,950. At incomes above $250,000, a 3.8% Medicare surtax on investment income is added, and for incomes above $466,950, the tax rate is 20% (plus the 3.8% surtax).

Traditional IRA and 401(k) plans allow investors to avoid taxes on current income because the funds contributed to the retirement plan are not taxed in the current year. But all the proceeds (both the original contribution *and* the subsequent investment earnings) are taxed at withdrawal. In contrast, *Roth plans* (named after the congressman who proposed them) allow investors to contribute after-tax income to the retirement plan (so there is no tax break in the current year), but they then avoid taxation of future investment income. To compare the plans, think about an employee in a 30% tax bracket with $10,000 in income that will be invested in either a traditional or Roth tax-sheltered plan. Assume that the invested funds will earn 8% per year and be invested for 20 years, at which point the worker will retire.

Suppose first that the $10,000 is put in a traditional IRA or 401(k) plan. The worker actually foregoes only $7,000 in current consumption, as 30% of that money would have been taxed had it not been sheltered in the retirement plan. The $10,000 will grow after 20 years to $10,000 \times 1.08^{20} = \$46,609.57$. But when the worker withdraws the funds, they are fully taxable, so she will net only $\$46,609.57 \times (1 - .30) = \$32,626.70$ after taxes.

In a Roth plan, taxes are paid on the $10,000 of income in the year it is earned. So only $7,000 is available to invest. But the investment earnings are all tax-free, so the funds will grow to $\$7,000 \times 1.08^{20} = \$32,626.70$ with no further tax liability—exactly the same as under the traditional plan. At first glance, it looks like the traditional and Roth plans are equally attractive. In one case, you pay 30% taxes on the original value; in the other, you pay 30% on the final accumulated value. But there are some salient differences.

First, if your tax rate will change over time, you may prefer one plan over the other. For those who believe that their income (and therefore their marginal tax rate) will be significantly lower in retirement, the traditional plan may be preferred, as the tax savings when the contribution is made are greater than the tax rate paid when funds are withdrawn in retirement. On the other hand, if you predict an increase in tax rates, you may prefer the Roth plan.

When the funds that can be put into a plan are limited by law (as is the case in the U.S.), the Roth plan offers a more subtle advantage. Suppose you may put a maximum of $10,000 into a 401(k) plan. Under the traditional plan, you can put aside at most $10,000 in pretax dollars (equivalent to $7,000 in after-tax dollars at a tax rate of 30%). In the Roth plan, you can put aside $10,000 in *after-tax* dollars, equivalent to $13,333 in pretax dollars.

Deferred Annuities   **Deferred annuities** are essentially tax-sheltered accounts offered by life insurance companies. They combine deferral of taxes with the option of withdrawing one's funds in the form of a life annuity. Variable annuity contracts offer the additional advantage of mutual fund investing. One major difference between an IRA and a variable annuity contract is that whereas the amount one can contribute to an IRA is tax-deductible and extremely limited as to maximum amount, the amount one can contribute to a deferred annuity is unlimited, but not tax-deductible.

The defining characteristic of a life annuity is that its payments continue as long as the recipient is alive, although virtually all deferred annuity contracts have several withdrawal options, including a lump sum of cash paid out at any time. You need not worry about running out of money before you die. Like Social Security, therefore, life annuities offer longevity insurance and thus would seem to be an ideal asset for someone in the retirement years. Indeed, theory suggests that where there are no bequest motives, it would be optimal for people to invest heavily in actuarially fair life annuities.[3]

---

[3]For an elaboration of this point, see Laurence J. Kotlikoff and Avia Spivak, "The Family as an Incomplete Annuities Market," *Journal of Political Economy* 89 (April 1981).

There are two types of life annuities: **fixed annuities** and **variable annuities.** A fixed annuity pays a fixed nominal sum of money per period (usually each month), whereas a variable annuity pays a periodic amount linked to the investment performance of some underlying portfolio.

Variable annuities are structured so that the investment risk of the underlying asset portfolio is borne by the recipient, much as shareholders bear the risk of a mutual fund. There are two stages in a variable annuity contract: an accumulation phase and a payout phase. During the *accumulation* phase, the investor contributes money periodically to one or more open-end mutual funds and accumulates shares. The second, or *payout,* stage usually starts at retirement, when the investor typically has several options, including the following:

1. Taking the market value of the shares in a lump sum payment.
2. Receiving a fixed annuity until death.
3. Receiving a variable amount of money each period that depends on the investment performance of the portfolio.

Variable and Universal Life Insurance   Variable life insurance is another tax-deferred investment vehicle offered by the life insurance industry. A variable life insurance policy combines life insurance with the tax-deferred annuities described earlier.

To invest in this product, you pay either a single premium or a series of premiums. In each case there is a stated death benefit, and the policyholder can allocate the money invested to several portfolios, which generally include a money market fund, a bond fund, and at least one common stock fund. The allocation can be changed at any time.

Variable life insurance policies offer a death benefit that is the greater of the stated face value or the market value of the investment base. In other words, the death benefit may rise with favorable investment performance, but it will not drop below the guaranteed face value. Furthermore, the surviving beneficiary is not subject to income tax on the death benefit.

The policyholder can choose from a number of income options to convert the policy into a stream of income, either on surrender of the contract or as a partial withdrawal. In all cases, income taxes are payable on the part of any distribution representing investment gains.

The insured can gain access to the investment without having to pay income tax by borrowing against the cash surrender value. Policy loans of up to 90% of the cash value are available at any time at a contractually specified interest rate.

A universal life insurance policy is similar to a variable life policy except that, instead of having a choice of portfolios to invest in, the policyholder earns a rate of interest that is set by the insurance company and changed periodically as market conditions change. The disadvantage of universal life insurance is that the company controls the rate of return to the policyholder, and, although companies may change the rate in response to competitive pressures, changes are not automatic. Different companies offer different rates, so it often pays to shop around for the best ones.

28.6   Pension Funds

Pension plans are defined by the terms specifying the "who," "when," and "how much," for both the plan benefits and the plan contributions used to pay for those benefits. The *pension fund* of the plan is the cumulation of assets created from contributions and the investment earnings on those contributions, less any payments of benefits from the fund. In the United States, contributions to the fund by either employer or employee are tax-deductible, and investment income of the fund is not taxed. Distributions from the fund, whether to the employer or the employee, are taxed as ordinary income. There are two "pure" types of pension plans: *defined contribution* and *defined benefit.*

Defined Contribution Plans

In a defined contribution plan, a formula specifies contributions made by and on behalf of employees but does not promise the benefits to which they will be entitled. Contribution rules usually are specified as a predetermined fraction of salary (e.g., the employer contributes 5% of the employee's annual wages to the plan), although that fraction need not be constant over the course of an employee's career. The pension fund consists of a set of individual investment accounts, one for each employee. Pension benefits are not specified. The employee often has some choice over both the level of contributions and the way the account is invested.

In principle, contributions could be invested in any security, although in practice most plans limit investment choices to bond, stock, and money market funds. The employee bears all the investment risk, and the employer has no legal obligation beyond making its periodic contributions.

In terms of both taxes and control over investment strategy, a defined contribution plan is nearly identical to a tax-qualified individual retirement account. Indeed, the main providers of investment products for these plans are the same institutions such as mutual funds and insurance companies that serve the general investment needs of individuals. Therefore, in a defined contribution plan much of the task of setting and achieving the income-replacement goal falls on the employee.

 Concept Check **28.3**

An employee is 45 years old. Her salary is $60,000 per year, and she has $100,000 accumulated in her self-directed defined contribution pension plan. Each year she contributes 5% of her salary to the plan, and her employer matches it with another 5%. She plans to retire at age 65.

Her retirement plan offers a choice of two funds: a guaranteed return fund that pays a risk-free real interest rate of 3% per year and a stock index fund that has an expected real rate of return of 6% per year and a standard deviation of 20%. Her current asset mix in the plan is $50,000 in the guaranteed fund and $50,000 in the stock index fund. She plans to reinvest all investment earnings in each fund in that same fund and to allocate her annual contribution equally between the two funds. If her salary grows at the same rate as the cost of living (so her real contributions to each fund will be constant), how much can she expect to have at retirement? How much can she be *sure* of having?

Defined Benefit Plans

Whereas defined contribution plans specify the contributions made on behalf of employees, defined benefit plans specify the retirement *benefits* to which the employee is entitled. The firm is responsible for ensuring that funding will be adequate to provide those benefits. The benefit formula typically takes into account years of service for the employer and level of wages or salary (e.g., an employer might pay an employee for life, beginning at age 65, a yearly amount equal to 2% of his final annual wage for each year of service). The employer (called the *plan sponsor*) or an insurance company hired by the sponsor guarantees the benefits and thus absorbs the investment risk.

As measured by the value of total pension liabilities, the defined benefit form still dominates in most countries around the world. However, the strong trend since the mid-1970s has been for sponsors to choose the defined contribution form when starting new plans. But the two plan types are not mutually exclusive. Some sponsors adopt defined benefit plans as their primary plan, in which participation is mandatory, and supplement them with voluntary defined contribution plans.

With defined benefit plans, there is an important distinction between the pension *plan* and the pension *fund*. The plan is the contractual arrangement setting out the rights and obligations of all parties; the fund is a separate pool of assets set aside to provide collateral for the promised benefits. There may be no separate fund, in which case the plan is said to be unfunded. When there is a separate fund with assets worth less than the present value of the promised benefits, the plan is *underfunded*. And if the plan's assets have a market value that exceeds the present value of the plan's liabilities, it is said to be *overfunded*.

 Concept Check **28.4**

> An employee currently earning $60,000 a year is 40 years old and has been working for the firm for 15 years. The pension plan promises benefits in retirement of 2% of final salary times years of service. If normal retirement age is 65, the interest rate is 8%, and the employee's life expectancy is 85, what is the present value of the accrued pension benefit?

Pension Investment Strategies

The special tax status of pension funds creates the same incentive for both defined contribution and defined benefit plans to tilt their asset mix toward assets with the largest spread between pretax and after-tax rates of return. In a defined contribution plan, because the participant bears all the investment risk, the optimal asset mix also depends on the risk tolerance of the participant.

In defined benefit plans, optimal investment policy may be different because the sponsor absorbs the bulk of downside investment risk. If the sponsor has to share some of the upside potential of the pension assets with plan participants, there is an incentive to simply eliminate investment risk by investing in securities that match the promised benefits. If, for example, the plan sponsor has to pay $100 per year for the next five years, it can provide this stream of benefit payments by buying a set of five zero-coupon bonds each with a face value of $100 and maturing sequentially. By so doing, the sponsor eliminates the risk of a shortfall. This is an example of **immunization** of the pension liability.

If the present value of promised pension benefits exceeds the market value of its assets, FASB Statement 87 requires that the corporation recognize the unfunded liability on its balance sheet. If, however, the pension assets exceed the present value of obligations, the corporation cannot include the surplus on its balance sheet. This asymmetric accounting treatment expresses a deeply held view about defined benefit pension funds. Representatives of organized labor, some politicians, and even a few pension professionals believe that the sponsoring corporation, as guarantor of the accumulated pension benefits, is liable for pension asset shortfalls but does not have a clear right to the entire surplus in case of pension overfunding.

Investing in Equities   If the only goal guiding corporate pension policy were shareholder wealth maximization, it is hard to understand why a financially sound pension sponsor would invest in equities at all. The tax advantage of a pension fund stems from the ability of the sponsor to earn the pretax interest rate on pension investments. To maximize the value of this tax shelter, it is necessary to invest entirely in assets offering the highest pretax interest rate. These will be the most tax *dis*advantaged assets, meaning that corporate pension funds should invest entirely in taxable bonds and other fixed-income investments.

Yet we know that in general, pension funds invest from 40% to 60% of their portfolios in equity securities. Even a casual perusal of the practitioner literature suggests that they do so for a variety of reasons—some, but not all, legitimate. There are three possible correct reasons.

The first possibility is that corporate management views the pension plan as a trust for the employees and manages fund assets as if it were a defined contribution plan. It believes that a successful policy of investment in equities might allow it to pay extra benefits to employees and is therefore worth taking the risk.

The second possible correct reason is that management believes that through superior market timing and security selection it is possible to create value in excess of management fees and expenses. Note that a very weak form of the efficient markets hypothesis would imply that management cannot create shareholder value simply by shifting the pension portfolio out of bonds and into stocks. Even when the entire pension surplus belongs to the shareholders, investing in stocks just moves the shareholders along the capital market line (the market trade-off between risk and return for passive investors) and does not create value. This implies that it makes sense for a pension fund to invest in equities only *if* it is able to pursue an active strategy that beats the market either through superior timing or security selection. A completely passive strategy will add no value to shareholders.

For an underfunded plan of a corporation in financial distress there is another possible reason for investing in stocks and other risky assets—federal pension insurance. Firms in financial distress have an incentive to invest pension fund money in the riskiest assets. They may reason that if the invested assets do well and the firm recovers, it captures the benefit, but if the investment does poorly and the corporation becomes insolvent, the federal insurance program inherits the losses.

Wrong Reasons to Invest in Equities   The illegitimate reasons for a pension fund to invest in equities stem from interrelated fallacies. The first is the notion that stocks are not risky in the long run. This fallacy was discussed at length in Chapter 5. Another related fallacy is the notion that stocks are a hedge against inflation. The reasoning behind this belief is that stocks are an ownership claim over real physical capital. If real profits are either unaffected or enhanced when there is unanticipated inflation, owners of real capital should not be hurt by it. However, empirical studies show that stock returns have demonstrated low or even negative correlation with inflation. Thus, the case for stocks as an inflation hedge is weak.

28.7   Investments for the Long Run

As the aged population around the world grows more rapidly than any other age group, issues of saving for the long run, for the most part surrounding retirement, have come to the fore of the investments industry. Traditionally, the advice for the long run could be summarized by rules of thumb concerning various rates of gradual, age-determined shifts in asset allocation from risky to safe assets. Implications of "modern" portfolio management, now more than 30 years old, originated from Robert Merton's lifetime consumption/ investment model (ICAPM) suggesting that one consider hedge assets to account for extra-market sources of risk, such as inflation, and needs emanating from uncertain longevity.

Making Simple Investment Choices

A target-date retirement fund (TDRF) is a fund composed of other funds, diversified across stocks, bonds, and money market accounts, in which the asset allocation becomes progressively more conservative as the investor approaches his or her retirement date. TDRFs are often advocated as a simple solution to the complex task of determining the appropriate asset allocation among funds in 401(k) plans, IRAs, and other personal investment accounts. TDRFs are marketed as enabling investors to put their investment plans on autopilot. Once you choose a fund with a target year matching your investment horizon, the life cycle manager gradually moves some of your money out of stocks and into bonds as your retirement date nears.

Inflation Risk and Long-Term Investors

While inflation risk is usually low for short horizons, it is a first-order source of risk for retirement planning, where horizons may be extremely long. An inflation "shock" may last for many years and impart substantial uncertainty to the purchasing power of any dollar you (or your client) have saved for retirement.

A conventional answer to the problem of inflation risk is to invest in price-indexed bonds such as TIPS (see Chapter 14 for a review). This is a good first step but is not a full answer to inflation risk. A zero-coupon priced-indexed bond with maturity equal to an investor's horizon would be a riskless investment in terms of purchasing power. This can be achieved with CPI-indexed savings bonds, but the government limits the amount of such bonds one may buy in any year. Unfortunately, market-traded TIPS bonds are not risk-free. As the (real) interest rate changes, the value of those bonds will fluctuate. Moreover, these bonds pay coupons, so the accumulated (real) value of the portfolio is also subject to reinvestment-rate risk. These issues should remind you of our discussion of bond risk in Chapter 16. In this context too, one must balance price risk with reinvestment-rate risk by tailoring the duration of the bond portfolio to the investment horizon. But in this case, we need to calculate duration using the real interest rate and focus on real payoffs from our investments.

1. When the principles of portfolio management are discussed, it is useful to distinguish among seven classes of investors: **SUMMARY**

   a. Individual investors and personal trusts.
   b. Mutual funds.
   c. Pension funds.
   d. Endowment funds.
   e. Life insurance companies.
   f. Non–life insurance companies.
   g. Banks.

   In general, these groups have somewhat different investment objectives, constraints, and portfolio policies.

2. To some extent, most institutional investors seek to match the risk-and-return characteristics of their investment portfolios to the characteristics of their liabilities.

3. The process of asset allocation includes the following steps:

   a. Specifying the asset classes to be included.
   b. Defining capital market expectations.

    c. Specifying the investor's objectives and constraints.

    d. Determining the asset allocation that gives the best risk-return trade-off consistent with the investor's particular circumstances.

4. People living on money-fixed incomes are vulnerable to inflation risk and may want to hedge against it. The effectiveness of an asset as an inflation hedge is related to its correlation with unanticipated inflation.

5. For investors who must pay taxes on their investment income, the process of asset allocation is complicated by the fact that they pay income taxes only on certain kinds of investment income. Interest income on munis is exempt from tax, and high-tax-bracket investors will prefer to hold them rather than short- and long-term taxable bonds. The more complex aspect of taxes is the fact that capital gains are taxable only if realized through the sale of an asset during the holding period. Investment strategies designed to avoid taxes may conflict with the principles of efficient diversification.

6. The life cycle approach to the management of an individual's investment portfolio views the individual as passing through a series of stages, becoming more risk averse in later years. The rationale underlying this approach is that as we age, we use up our human capital and have less time remaining to recoup possible portfolio losses through increased labor supply.

7. People buy life and disability insurance during their prime earning years to hedge against the risk associated with loss of their human capital, that is, their future earning power.

8. There are three ways to shelter investment income from federal income taxes besides investing in tax-exempt bonds: The first is by investing in assets whose returns take the form of appreciation in value, such as common stocks or real estate. As long as capital gains taxes are not paid until the asset is sold, the tax can be deferred indefinitely. The second is through investing in tax-deferred retirement plans such as IRAs. The third is to invest in the tax-advantaged products offered by the life insurance industry—tax-deferred annuities and variable and universal life insurance. They combine the flexibility of mutual fund investing with the tax advantages of tax deferral.

9. When allocating investment funds between tax protected and other accounts, investors will minimize their overall tax burden by holding the least tax-advantage asset (e.g., bonds) in their tax protected accounts [e.g., IRAs or 401(k) plans]. The general investment rule is to hold the least tax-advantaged assets in the tax-protected plan and the most tax-advantaged assets outside of it.

10. Pension plans are either defined contribution plans or defined benefit plans. Defined contribution plans are in effect retirement funds held in trust for the employee by the employer. The employees in such plans bear all the risk of the plan's assets and often have some choice in the allocation of those assets. Defined benefit plans give the employees a claim to a money-fixed annuity at retirement. The annuity level is determined by a formula that takes into account years of service and the employee's wage or salary history.

11. If sponsors viewed their pension liabilities as indexed for inflation, then the appropriate way for them to minimize the cost of providing benefit guarantees would be to hedge using securities whose returns are highly correlated with inflation. Common stocks would not be an appropriate hedge because they have a low correlation with inflation.

KEY TERMS

risk–return trade-off	whole-life insurance policy	tax-deferral option
personal trusts	term insurance	tax-protected retirement plans
income beneficiaries	variable life policy	deferred annuities
remainderman	universal life policy	fixed annuities
defined contribution plans	liquidity	variable annuities
defined benefit plans	investment horizon	immunization
endowment funds	prudent investor rule	

1. Your neighbor has heard that you successfully completed a course in investments and has come to seek your advice. She and her husband are both 50 years old. They just finished making their last payments for their condominium and their children's college education and are planning for retirement. What advice on investing their retirement savings would you give them? If they are very risk averse, what would you advise?

2. What is the least-risky asset for each of the following investors?

   a. A person investing for her 3-year-old child's college tuition.
   b. A defined benefit pension fund with benefit obligations that have an average duration of 10 years. The benefits are not inflation-protected.
   c. A defined benefit pension fund with benefit obligations that have an average duration of 10 years. The benefits are inflation-protected.

3. George More is a participant in a defined contribution pension plan that offers a fixed-income fund and a common stock fund as investment choices. He is 40 years old and has an accumulation of $100,000 in each of the funds. He currently contributes $1,500 per year to each. He plans to retire at age 65, and his life expectancy is age 80.

   a. Assuming a 3% per year real earnings rate for the fixed-income fund and 6% per year for common stocks, what will be George's expected accumulation in each account at age 65?
   b. What will be the expected real retirement annuity from each account, assuming these same real earnings rates?
   c. If George wanted a retirement annuity of $30,000 per year from the fixed-income fund, by how much would he have to increase his annual contributions?

4. The difference between a Roth IRA and a traditional IRA is that in a Roth IRA taxes are paid on the income that is contributed but the withdrawals at retirement are tax-free. In a traditional IRA, however, the contributions reduce your taxable income, but the withdrawals at retirement are taxable. Assume you plan to devote $5,000 to retirement savings in each year. You will retire in 30 years and expect to live for an additional 20 years after retirement.

   a. Assume the before-tax interest rate is 5%. What will be your after-tax 20-year retirement consumption stream if you choose to save in a traditional IRA? Assume your tax rate is fixed at 30%.
   b. What will be your 20-year retirement consumption stream if you choose to save in a Roth IRA?
   c. Which provides better expected results if you expect your tax rate to decrease from 30% today to 25% at retirement?

1. Angus Walker, CFA, is reviewing the defined benefit pension plan of Acme Industries. Based in London, Acme has operations in North America, Japan, and several European countries. Next month, the retirement age for full benefits under the plan will be lowered from age 60 to age 55.

   The median age of Acme's workforce is 49 years. Walker is responsible for the pension plan's investment policy and strategic asset allocation decisions. The goals of the plan include achieving a minimum expected return of 8.4% with expected standard deviation no greater than 16.0%.

   Walker is evaluating the current asset allocation (Table 28A) and selected financial information for the company (Table 28B). There is an ongoing debate within Acme Industries about the pension plan's investment policy statement (IPS). Two investment policy statements under consideration are shown in Table 28C.

International Equities (MSCI World, excluding U.K.)	10%
U.K. bonds	42
U.K. small capitalization equities	13
U.K. large capitalization equities	30
Cash	5

Table 28A

Acme pension plan: Current asset allocation

Acme Industries total assets	£16,000
Pension plan data:	
Plan assets	6,040
Plan liabilities	9,850

Table 28B

Acme Industries selected financial
information (in millions)

	IPS X	IPS Y
Return requirement	Plan's objective is to outperform the relevant benchmark return by a substantial margin.	Plan's objective is to match the relevant benchmark return.
Risk tolerance	Plan has a high risk tolerance because of the long-term nature of the plan and its liabilities.	Plan has a low risk tolerance because of its limited ability to assume substantial risk.
Time horizon	Plan has a very long time horizon because of the plan's infinite life.	Plan has a shorter time horizon than in the past because of plan demographics.
Liquidity	Plan needs moderate level of liquidity to fund monthly benefit payments.	Plan has minimal liquidity needs.

Table 28C

Investment policy statements

a. Determine, for each of the following components, whether IPS X or IPS Y (see Table 28C) has the appropriate language for the pension plan of Acme Industries. Justify each response with one reason.

   i. Return requirement
  ii. Risk tolerance
 iii. Time horizon
 iv. Liquidity

Note: Some components of IPS X may be appropriate, while other components of IPS Y may be appropriate.

b. To assist Walker, Acme has hired two pension consultants, Lucy Graham and Robert Michael. Graham believes that the pension fund must be invested to reflect a low risk tolerance, but Michael believes the pension fund must be invested to achieve the highest possible returns. The fund's current asset allocation and the allocations recommended by Graham and Michael are shown in Table 28D. Select which of the three asset allocations in Table 28D is most appropriate for Acme's pension plan. Explain how your selection meets each of the following objectives or constraints for the plan:

   i. Return requirement
  ii. Risk tolerance
 iii. Liquidity

	Current	Graham	Michael
U.K. large capitalization equities	30%	20%	40%
U.K. small capitalization equities	13	8	20
International equities (MSCI World ex-U.K.)	10	10	18
U.K. bonds	42	52	17
Cash	5	10	5
Total	100%	100%	100%
Expected portfolio return	9.1%	8.2%	10.6%
Expected portfolio volatility (standard deviation)	16.1%	12.8%	21.1%

Table 28D

Asset allocations (in %)

2. Your client says, "With the unrealized gains in my portfolio, I have almost saved enough money for my daughter to go to college in 8 years, but educational costs keep going up." On the basis of this statement alone, which one of the following appears to be least important to your client's investment policy?

   a. Time horizon.
   b. Purchasing power risk.
   c. Liquidity.
   d. Taxes.

3. The aspect least likely to be included in the portfolio management process is

   a. Identifying an investor's objectives, constraints, and preferences.
   b. Organizing the management process itself.
   c. Implementing strategies regarding the choice of assets to be used.
   d. Monitoring market conditions, relative values, and investor circumstances.

4. Sam Short, CFA, has recently joined the investment management firm of Green, Spence, and Smith (GSS). For several years, GSS has worked for a broad array of clients, including employee benefit plans, wealthy individuals, and charitable organizations. Also, the firm expresses expertise in managing stocks, bonds, cash reserves, real estate, venture capital, and international securities. To date, the firm has not utilized a formal asset allocation process but instead has relied on the individual wishes of clients or the particular preferences of its portfolio managers. Short recommends to GSS management that a formal asset allocation process would be beneficial and emphasizes that a large part of a portfolio's ultimate return depends on asset allocation. He is asked to take his conviction an additional step by making a proposal to executive management.

   a. Recommend and justify an approach to asset allocation that could be used by GSS.
   b. Apply the approach to a middle-aged, wealthy individual characterized as a fairly conservative investor (sometimes referred to as a "guardian investor").

5. Jarvis University (JU) is a private, multiprogram U.S. university with a $2 billion endowment fund as of fiscal year-end May 31, 2022. With little government support, JU is heavily dependent on its endowment fund to support ongoing expenditures, especially because the university's enrollment growth and tuition revenue have not met expectations in recent years. The endowment fund must make a $126 million annual contribution, which is indexed to inflation, to JU's general operating budget. The U.S. Consumer Price Index is expected to rise 2.5% annually and the U.S. higher education cost index is anticipated to rise 3% annually. The endowment has also budgeted $200 million due on January 31, 2023, representing the final payment for construction of a new main library.

In a recent capital campaign, JU only met its fund-raising goal with the help of one very successful alumna, Valerie Bremner, who donated $400 million of Bertocchi Oil and Gas common stock at fiscal year-end May 31, 2022. Bertocchi Oil and Gas is a large-capitalization, publicly traded U.S. company. Bremner donated the stock on the condition that no more than 25% of the initial number of shares may be sold in any fiscal year. No substantial additional donations are expected in the future.

Given the large contribution to and distributions from the endowment fund, the endowment fund's investment committee has decided to revise the fund's investment policy statement. The investment committee also recognizes that a revised asset allocation may be warranted. The asset allocation in place for the JU endowment fund as of May 31, 2022, is given in Table 28E.

a. Prepare the components of an appropriate investment policy statement for the Jarvis University endowment fund as of June 1, 2022, based only on the information given.

Note: Each component in your response must specifically address circumstances of the JU endowment fund.

b. Determine the most appropriate revised allocation percentage for each asset in Table 28E as of June 1, 2022. Justify each revised allocation percentage.

6. Susan Fairfax is president of Reston Industries, a U.S.-based company whose sales are entirely domestic and whose shares are listed on the New York Stock Exchange. The following are additional facts concerning her current situation:

- Fairfax is single, aged 58. She has no immediate family, no debts, and does not own a residence. She is in excellent health and covered by Reston-paid health insurance that continues after her expected retirement at age 65.
- Her base salary of $500,000/year, inflation-protected, is sufficient to support her present lifestyle but can no longer generate any excess for savings.
- She has $2,000,000 of savings from prior years held in the form of short-term instruments.
- Reston rewards key employees through a generous stock-bonus incentive plan but provides no pension plan and pays no dividend.
- Fairfax's incentive plan participation has resulted in her ownership of Reston stock worth $10 million (current market value). The stock, received tax-free but subject to tax at a 35% rate (on entire proceeds) if sold, is expected to be held at least until her retirement.
- Her present level of spending and the current annual inflation rate of 4% are expected to continue after her retirement.
- Fairfax is taxed at 35% on all salary, investment income, and realized capital gains. Assume her composite tax rate will continue at this level indefinitely.

Fairfax's orientation is patient, careful, and conservative in all things. She has stated that an annual after-tax real total return of 3% would be completely acceptable to her if it was achieved in a context where an investment portfolio created from her accumulated savings was not subject to a decline of more than 10% in nominal terms in any given 12-month period. To obtain

Asset	Current Allocation (millions)	Current Allocation Percentage	Current Yield	Expected Annual Return	Standard Deviation of Returns
U.S. money market bond fund	$ 40	2%	4.0%	4.0%	2.0%
Intermediate global bond fund	60	3	5.0	5.0	9.0
Global equity fund	300	15	1.0	10.0	15.0
Bertocchi Oil and Gas common stock	400	20	0.1	15.0	25.0
Direct real estate	700	35	3.0	11.5	16.5
Venture capital	500	25	0.0	20.0	35.0
Total	$2,000	100%			

Table 28E

Jarvis University endowment fund asset allocation as of May 31, 2022

the benefits of professional assistance, she has approached two investment advisory firms—HH Counselors ("HH") and Coastal Advisors ("Coastal")—for recommendations on allocation of the investment portfolio to be created from her existing savings assets (the "Savings Portfolio") as well as for advice concerning investing in general.

a. Create and justify an investment policy statement for Fairfax based only on the information provided thus far. Be specific and complete in presenting objectives and constraints. (An asset allocation is not required in answering this question.)

b. Coastal has proposed the asset allocation shown in Table 28F for investment of Fairfax's $2 million of savings assets. Assume that only the current yield portion of projected total return (comprised of both investment income and realized capital gains) is taxable to Fairfax and that the municipal bond income is entirely tax-exempt.

   Critique the Coastal proposal. Include in your answer three weaknesses in the Coastal proposal from the standpoint of the investment policy statement you created for her in part (a).

c. HH Counselors has developed five alternative asset allocations (shown in Table 28G) for client portfolios. Answer the following questions based on Table 28G and the investment policy statement you created for Fairfax in part (a).

   i. Determine which of the asset allocations in Table 28G meet or exceed Fairfax's stated return objective.

   ii. Determine the three asset allocations in Table 28G that meet Fairfax's risk tolerance criterion. Assume a 95% confidence interval is required, with 2 standard deviations serving as an approximation of that requirement.

d. Assume that the risk-free rate is 4.5%.

   i. Calculate the Sharpe ratio for Asset Allocation D in Table 28G.

   ii. Determine the two asset allocations in Table 28G having the best risk-adjusted returns, based only on the Sharpe ratio measure.

e. Recommend and justify the one asset allocation in Table 28G you believe would be the best model for Fairfax's savings portfolio.

7. John Franklin is a recent widower with some experience in investing for his own account. Following his wife's recent death and settlement of the estate, Mr. Franklin owns a controlling interest in a successful privately held manufacturing company in which Mrs. Franklin was formerly active, a recently completed warehouse property, the family residence, and his personal holdings of stocks and bonds. He has decided to retain the warehouse property as a diversifying investment but intends to sell the private company interest, giving half of the proceeds to a medical research foundation in memory of his deceased wife. Actual transfer of this gift is expected to take place

Asset Class	Proposed Allocation (%)	Current Yield (%)	Projected Total Return (%)
Cash equivalents	15.0	4.5	4.5
Corporate bonds	10.0	7.5	7.5
Municipal bonds	10.0	5.5	5.5
Large-cap U.S. stocks	0.0	3.5	11.0
Small-cap U.S. stocks	0.0	2.5	13.0
International stocks (EAFE)	35.0	2.0	13.5
Real estate investment trusts (REITs)	25.0	9.0	12.0
Venture capital	5.0	0.0	20.0
Total	100.0	4.9	10.7
Inflation (CPI), projected			4.0

Table 28F

Susan Fairfax proposed asset allocation, prepared by Coastal Advisors

Asset Class	Projected Total Return	Expected Standard Deviation	Asset Allocation A	Asset Allocation B	Asset Allocation C	Asset Allocation D	Asset Allocation E
Cash equivalents	4.5%	2.5%	10%	20%	25%	5%	10%
Corporate bonds	6.0	11.0	0	25	0	0	0
Municipal bonds	7.2	10.8	40	0	30	0	30
Large-cap U.S. stocks	13.0	17.0	20	15	35	25	5
Small-cap U.S. stocks	15.0	21.0	10	10	0	15	5
International stocks (EAFE)	15.0	21.0	10	10	0	15	10
Real estate investment trusts (REITs)	10.0	15.0	10	10	10	25	35
Venture capital	26.0	64.0	0	10	0	15	5
Total			100	100	100	100	100

Summary Data

	Asset Allocation A	Asset Allocation B	Asset Allocation C	Asset Allocation D	Asset Allocation E
Projected total return	9.9%	11.0%	8.8%	14.4%	10.3%
Projected after-tax total return	7.4%	7.2%	6.5%	9.4%	7.4%
Expected standard deviation	9.4%	12.4%	8.5%	18.1%	10.1%
Sharpe ratio	0.574	0.524	0.506	—	0.574

Table 28G

Alternative asset allocations, prepared by HH Counselors

about 3 months from now. You have been engaged to assist him with the valuations, planning, and portfolio building required to structure his investment program appropriately.

Mr. Franklin has introduced you to the finance committee of the medical research foundation that is to receive his $45 million cash gift 3 months hence (and will eventually receive the assets of his estate). This gift will greatly increase the size of the foundation's endowment (from $10 million to $55 million) as well as enable it to make larger grants to researchers. The foundation's grant-making (spending) policy has been to pay out virtually all of its annual net investment income. As its investment approach has been very conservative, the endowment portfolio now consists almost entirely of fixed-income assets. The finance committee understands that these actions are causing the real value of foundation assets and the real value of future grants to decline due to the effects of inflation. Until now, the finance committee has believed that it had no alternative to these actions, given the large immediate cash needs of the research programs being funded and the small size of the foundation's capital base. The foundation's annual grants must at least equal 5% of its assets' market value to maintain its U.S. tax-exempt status, a requirement that is expected to continue indefinitely. No additional gifts or fund-raising activities are expected over the foreseeable future.

Given the change in circumstances that Mr. Franklin's gift will make, the finance committee wishes to develop new grant-making and investment policies. Annual spending must at least meet the level of 5% of market value that is required to maintain the foundation's tax-exempt status, but the committee is unsure about how much higher than 5% it can or should be. The committee wants to pay out as much as possible because of the critical nature of the research being funded; however, it understands that preserving the real value of the foundation's assets is equally important in order to preserve its future grant-making capabilities. You have been asked to assist the committee in developing appropriate policies.

a. Identify and briefly discuss the three key elements that should determine the foundation's grant-making (spending) policy.

b. Formulate and justify an investment policy statement for the foundation, taking into account the increased size of its assets arising from Mr. Franklin's gift. Your policy statement must encompass all relevant objectives, constraints, and the key elements identified in your answer to part (a).

c. Recommend and justify a long-term asset allocation that is consistent with the investment policy statement you created in part (b). Explain how your allocation's expected return meets the requirements of a feasible grant-making (spending) policy for the foundation. (Hint: Your allocation must sum to 100% and should use the economic/market data presented in Table 28H and your knowledge of historical asset-class characteristics.)

8. Christopher Maclin, aged 40, is a supervisor at Barnett Co. and earns an annual salary of £80,000 before taxes. Louise Maclin, aged 38, stays home to care for their newborn twins. She recently inherited £900,000 (after wealth-transfer taxes) in cash from her father's estate. In addition, the Maclins have accumulated the following assets (current market value):

- £5,000 in cash.
- £160,000 in stocks and bonds.
- £220,000 in Barnett common stock.

The value of their holdings in Barnett stock has appreciated substantially as a result of the company's growth in sales and profits during the past 10 years. Christopher Maclin is confident that the company and its stock will continue to perform well.

The Maclins need £30,000 for a down payment on the purchase of a house and plan to make a £20,000 non–tax deductible donation to a local charity in memory of Louise Maclin's father. The Maclins' annual living expenses are £74,000. After-tax salary increases will offset any future increases in their living expenses.

During their discussions with their financial advisor, Grant Webb, the Maclins express concern about achieving their educational goals for their children and their own retirement goals. The Maclins tell Webb:

- They want to have sufficient funds to retire in 18 years when their children begin their 4 years of university education.
- They have been unhappy with the portfolio volatility they have experienced in recent years and they do not want to experience a loss greater than 12% in any one year.
- They do not want to invest in alcohol and tobacco stocks.
- They will not have any additional children.

After their discussions, Webb calculates that in 18 years the Maclins will need £2 million to meet their educational and retirement goals. Webb suggests that their portfolio be structured to limit shortfall risk (defined as expected total return minus two standard deviations) to no lower than a −12% return in any one year. Maclin's salary and all capital gains and investment income are

	Historic Averages	Intermediate Term Consensus Forecast
U.S. Treasury bills	3.7%	4.2%
Intermediate-term U.S. T-bonds	5.2	5.8
Long-term U.S. T-bonds	4.8	7.7
U.S. corporate bonds (AAA)	5.5	8.8
Non-U.S. bonds (AAA)	N/A	8.4
U.S. common stocks (all)	10.3	9.0
U.S. common stocks (small-cap)	12.2	12.0
Non-U.S. common stocks (all)	N/A	10.1
U.S. inflation	3.1	3.5

Table 28H

Capital markets annualized return data

taxed at 40% and no tax-sheltering strategies are available. Webb's next step is to formulate an investment policy statement for the Maclins.

a. Formulate the risk objective of an investment policy statement for the Maclins.
b. Formulate the return objective of an investment policy statement for the Maclins. Calculate the pretax rate of return that is required to achieve this objective. Show your calculations.
c. Formulate the constraints portion of an investment policy statement for the Maclins, addressing each of the following:
  i. Time horizon
  ii. Liquidity requirements
  iii. Tax concerns
  iv. Unique circumstances

9. Louise and Christopher Maclin (see Problem 8) have purchased their house and made the donation to the local charity. Now that an investment policy statement has been prepared for the Maclins, Grant Webb recommends that they consider the strategic asset allocation described in Table 28I.

a. Identify aspects of the recommended asset allocation in Table 28I that are inconsistent with the Maclins' investment objectives and constraints. Support your responses.
b. After further discussion, Webb and the Maclins agree that any suitable strategic asset allocation will include 5 to 10% in U.K. small-capitalization equities and 10 to 15% in U.K. large-capitalization equities. For the remainder of the portfolio, Webb is considering the asset class ranges described in Table 28J.

Recommend the most appropriate allocation range for each of the asset classes in Table 28J. Justify each appropriate allocation range with a reason based on the Maclins' investment objectives and constraints.

Note: No calculations are required.

Asset Class	Recommended Allocation	Current Yield	Projected Annualized Pretax Total Return	Expected Standard Deviation
Cash	15.0%	1.0%	1.0%	2.5%
U.K. corporate bonds	55.0	4.0	5.0	11.0
U.K. small-capitalization equities	0.0	0.0	11.0	25.0
U.K. large-capitalization equities	10.0	2.0	9.0	21.0
U.S. equities*	5.0	1.5	10.0	20.0
Barnett Co. common stock	15.0	1.0	16.0	48.0
Total portfolio	100.0	—	6.7	12.4

Table 28I

Louise and Christopher Maclin's recommended strategic asset allocation

*U.S. equity data are in British pound terms.

Asset Class	Allocation Ranges		
Cash	0%–3%	5%–10%	15%–20%
U.K. corporate bonds	10%–20%	30%–40%	50%–60%
U.S. equities	0%–5%	10%–15%	20%–25%
Barnett Co. common stock	0%–5%	10%–15%	20%–25%

Table 28J

Louise and Christopher Maclin's asset class ranges

SOLUTIONS TO CONCEPT CHECKS

1. Identify the elements that are life cycle–driven in the two schemes of objectives and constraints.

2. If the investor keeps her present asset allocation, she will have the following amounts to spend after taxes 5 years from now:

Tax-qualified account:

Bonds: $50,000(1.10)^5 \times .72$	= $ 57,978.36
Stocks: $50,000(1.15)^5 \times .72$	= $ 72,408.86
Subtotal	$130,387.22

Nonretirement account:

Bonds: $50,000[1 + (.10 \times .72)]^5$	= $ 70,785.44
Stocks: $50,000(1.15)^5 - .15 \times [50,000(1.15)^5 - 50,000]$	= $ 92,982.68
Subtotal	$163,768.12
Total	$294,155.34

If she shifts all of the bonds into the retirement account and all of the stock into the nonretirement account, she will have the following amounts to spend after taxes 5 years from now:

Tax-qualified account:

Bonds: $100,000(1.10)^5 \times .72$	= $115,956.72

Nonretirement account:

Stocks: $100,000(1.15)^5 - .15 \times [100,000(1.15)^5 - 100,000]$	= $185,965.36
Total	= $301,922.08

Her final accumulation will increase by $7,766.74.

3. The total contribution to each fund (stock and guaranteed return fund) will be $3,000 per year (i.e., 5% of $60,000) in constant dollars. At retirement she will have in her guaranteed return fund:

$$\$50,000 \times 1.03^{20} + \$3,000 \times \text{Future value annuity factor}(3\%, 20 \text{ years}) = \$170,917$$

That is the amount she will have for *sure* because the value of her stock investment can, at least in principle, fall to zero.

In addition, the expected future value of her stock account is:

$$\$50{,}000 \times 1.06^{20} + \$3{,}000 \times \text{Future value annuity factor}\left(6\%, 20 \text{ years}\right) = \$270{,}714$$

4. He has accrued an annuity of $.02 \times 15 \times 60{,}000 = \$18{,}000$ per year that is expected to begin in 25 years (at age 65) and to last for 20 years (from age 65 to 85). The present value of this annuity is $25,805:

$$PV = \$18{,}000 \times \text{Annuity factor}(8\%, 20) \times \text{PV factor}(8\%, 25) = \$25{,}805$$

References to CFA Problems

Each end-of-chapter CFA problem is reprinted with permission from the CFA Institute, Charlottesville, VA. Following is a list of the CFA problems in the end-of-chapter material and the exams and study guides from which they were taken and updated.

Chapter 2
1–3. 1996 Level I CFA Study Guide, © 1996
4. 1994 Level I CFA Study Guide, © 1994
5. 1994 Level I CFA Study Guide, © 1994

Chapter 3
1. 1986 Level I CFA Study Guide, © 1986
2–3. 1986 Level I CFA Study Guide, © 1986

Chapter 5
1. 1992 Level I CFA Study Guide, © 1992
2. 1992 Level I CFA Study Guide, © 1992
3–7. 1993 Level I CFA Study Guide, © 1993

Chapter 6
1–3. 1991 Level I CFA Study Guide, © 1991
4–5. 1991 Level I CFA Study Guide, © 1991
6. 1991 Level I CFA Study Guide, © 1991
7–9. 1993 Level I CFA Study Guide, © 1993

Chapter 7
1–3. 1982 Level III CFA Study Guide, © 1982
4. 1993 Level I CFA Study Guide, © 1993
5. 1993 Level I CFA Study Guide, © 1993
6. 1992 Level I CFA Study Guide, © 1992
7. 1992 Level I CFA Study Guide, © 1992
8–10. 1994 Level I CFA Study Guide, © 1994
11. 2001 Level III CFA Study Guide, © 2001
12. 2001 Level II CFA Study Guide, © 2001
13. 2000 Level II CFA Study Guide, © 2000

Chapter 8
1. 1982 Level I CFA Study Guide, © 1982
2. 1993 Level I CFA Study Guide, © 1993
3. 1993 Level I CFA Study Guide, © 1993
4. 1993 Level I CFA Study Guide, © 1993
5. 1994 Level I CFA Study Guide, © 1994

Chapter 9
1. 2002 Level I CFA Study Guide, © 2002
2. 2002 Level I CFA Study Guide, © 2002
3–5. 1993 Level I CFA Study Guide, © 1993
6. 1992 Level I CFA Study Guide, © 1992
7. 1994 Level I CFA Study Guide, © 1994
8. 1993 Level I CFA Study Guide, © 1993
9. 1994 Level I CFA Study Guide, © 1994
10. 1994 Level I CFA Study Guide, © 1994
11. 2002 Level II CFA Study Guide, © 2002
12. 2000 Level II CFA Study Guide, © 2000

Chapter 10
1. 2001 Level II CFA Study Guide, © 2001
2–8. 1991–1993 Level I CFA Study Guides

Chapter 11
1–5. 1993 Level I CFA Study Guide, © 1993
6. 1992 Level I CFA Study Guide, © 1992
7. 1992 Level I CFA Study Guide, © 1992
8–10. 1996 Level III CFA Study Guide, © 1996

Chapter 12
1. 2000 Level III CFA Study Guide, © 2000
2. 2001 Level III CFA Study Guide, © 2001
3. 2004 Level III CFA Study Guide, © 2004
4. 2003 Level III CFA Study Guide, © 2003
5. 2002 Level III CFA Study Guide, © 2002

Chapter 13
1. 1993 Level I CFA Study Guide, © 1993
2. 1993 Level I CFA Study Guide, © 1993
3. 2002 Level II CFA Study Guide, © 2002

Chapter 14
1. 1993 Level I CFA Study Guide, © 1993
2. 1994 Level I CFA Study Guide, © 1994
3. 1999 Level II CFA Study Guide, © 1999
4. 1992 Level II CFA Study Guide, © 1992
5. 1993 Level I CFA Study Guide, © 1993
6. 1992 Level I CFA Study Guide, © 1992

Chapter 15
1. 1993 Level II CFA Study Guide, © 1993
2. 1993 Level I CFA Study Guide, © 1993
3. 1993 Level II CFA Study Guide, © 1993
4. 1994 Level I CFA Study Guide, © 1994
5. 1994 Level II CFA Study Guide, © 1994
6. 2004 Level II CFA Study Guide, © 2004
7. 1999 Level II CFA Study Guide, © 1999
8. 2000 Level II CFA Study Guide, © 2000
9. 1996 Level II CFA Study Guide, © 1996
10. 2000 Level II CFA Study Guide, © 2000

Chapter 16
1. 1993 Level II CFA Study Guide, © 1993
2. 1992–1994 Level I CFA study guides
3. 1993 Level I CFA Study Guide, © 1993
4. 1993 Level I CFA Study Guide, © 1993
5. 2004 Level II CFA Study Guide, © 2004

Chapter 17 (continued)
6. 1996 Level III CFA Study Guide, © 1996
7. 1998 Level II CFA Study Guide, © 1998
8. From various Level I study guides
9. 1994 Level III CFA Study Guide, © 1994
10. 2000 Level III CFA Study Guide, © 2000
11. 2003 Level II CFA Study Guide, © 2003
12. 2001 Level II CFA Study Guide, © 2001
13. 1992 Level II CFA Study Guide, © 1992

Chapter 17
1. 1993 Level I CFA Study Guide, © 1993
2. 1993 Level I CFA Study Guide, © 1993
3. 1993 Level II CFA Study Guide, © 1993
4. 1993 Level II CFA Study Guide, © 1993
5. 1998 Level II CFA Study Guide, © 1998
6. 1995 Level II CFA Study Guide, © 1995
7. 1993 Level I CFA Study Guide, © 1993

Chapter 18
1. 1995 Level II CFA Study Guide, © 1995
2. 2001 Level II CFA Study Guide, © 2001
3. 2001 Level II CFA Study Guide, © 2001
4. 2001 Level II CFA Study Guide, © 2001
5–6. 2004 Level II CFA Study Guide, © 2004
7. 2001 Level II CFA Study Guide, © 2001
8. 1993 Level I CFA Study Guide, © 1993
9. 2003 Level II CFA Study Guide, © 2003
10. 2003 Level I CFA Study Guide, © 2003
11. 2003 Level II CFA Study Guide, © 2003

Chapter 19
1. 1998 Level II CFA Study Guide, © 1998
2. 1999 Level II CFA Study Guide, © 1999
3. 1994 Level I CFA Study Guide, © 1994
4. 1998 Level II CFA Study Guide, © 1998
5–8. 1992 Level I CFA Study Guide, © 1992
9. 1998 Level I CFA Study Guide, © 1998
10. 1994 Level I CFA Study Guide, © 1994
11. 1992 Level I CFA Study Guide, © 1992
12. 2002 Level II CFA Study Guide, © 2002
13. 1990 Level II CFA Study Guide, © 1990

Chapter 20
1. 2002 Level II CFA Study Guide, © 2002
2. 2000 Level II CFA Study Guide, © 2000
3. 2001 Level II CFA Study Guide, © 2001
4. 2002 Level II CFA Study Guide, © 2002
5. From various Level I study guides

Chapter 21

1. 1998 Level II CFA Study Guide, © 1998
2. 2003 Level II CFA Study Guide, © 2003
3. 1998 Level II CFA Study Guide, © 1998
4. 2000 Level II CFA Study Guide, © 2000
5. 1997 Level III CFA Study Guide, © 1997

Chapter 22

1. 2000 Level II CFA Study Guide, © 2000
2. 1993 Level II CFA Study Guide, © 1993
3. 1986 Level III CFA Study Guide, © 1986
4. 2004 Level II CFA Study Guide, © 2004
5. 2004 Level II CFA Study Guide, © 2004

Chapter 23

1. 2001 Level II CFA Study Guide, © 2001
2. 1995 Level III CFA Study Guide, © 1995

3. 1991 Level III CFA Study Guide, © 1991
4–5. 2003 Level II CFA Study Guide, © 2003
6. 2000 Level III CFA Study Guide, © 2000
7. 1985 Level III CFA Study Guide, © 1985
8. 1996 Level II CFA Study Guide, © 1996

Chapter 24

1. 1995 Level III CFA Study Guide, © 1995
2. 1981 Level I CFA Study Guide, © 1981
3. 1986 Level II CFA Study Guide, © 1986
4–11. From various Level I CFA study guides
12. 2001 Level III CFA Study Guide, © 2001
13. 2000 Level III CFA Study Guide, © 2000
14. 2002 Level III CFA Study Guide, © 2002

Chapter 25

1–3. From various Level I CFA study guides
4. 1986 Level III CFA Study Guide, © 1986
5. 1991 Level II CFA Study Guide, © 1991
6. 1995 Level II CFA Study Guide, © 1995
7. 2003 Level III CFA Study Guide, © 2003
8. 1998 Level II CFA Study Guide, © 1998

Chapter 28

1. 2001 Level III CFA Study Guide, © 2001
2–4. 1988 Level I CFA Study Guide, © 1988
5. 2002 Level III CFA Study Guide, © 2002
6. 1996 Level III CFA Study Guide, © 1996
7. 1993 Level III CFA Study Guide, © 1993
8. 2004 Level III CFA Study Guide, © 2004
9. 2004 Level III CFA Study Guide, © 2004

Glossary

A

abnormal return   Return on a stock beyond what would be predicted by market movements alone. Cumulative abnormal return (CAR) is the total abnormal return for the period surrounding an announcement or the release of information.

accounting earnings   Earnings of a firm as reported on its income statement.

acid test ratio   See *quick ratio*.

active management   Attempts to achieve portfolio returns more than commensurate with risk, either by forecasting broad market trends or by identifying mispriced sectors of a market or particular securities.

active portfolio   In the context of the Treynor-Black model, the portfolio formed by mixing analyzed stocks of perceived nonzero alpha values. This portfolio is ultimately mixed with the passive market-index portfolio.

adjusted alphas   Forecasts for alpha that are modulated to account for statistical imprecision in the analyst's estimate.

agency problem   Conflicts of interest among stockholders, bondholders, and managers.

algorithmic trading   The use of computer programs to make trading decisions.

alpha transfer   A strategy in which you invest in positive alpha positions, hedge the systematic risk of the investment, and finally establish market exposure where you want it using passive indexes. (See *portable alpha*.)

alpha value   The abnormal rate of return on a security in excess of what would be predicted by an equilibrium model like the CAPM.

American depositary receipts (ADRs)   Domestically traded securities representing claims to shares of foreign stocks.

American option   An American option can be exercised before and up to its expiration date. Compare with a *European option*, which can be exercised only on the expiration date.

announcement date   Date on which particular news concerning a given company is announced to the public. Used in *event studies*, which researchers use to evaluate the economic impact of events of interest.

annual percentage rate (APR)   Interest rate is annualized using simple rather than compound interest.

anomalies   Patterns of returns that seem to contradict the efficient market hypothesis.

appraisal ratio   The signal-to-noise ratio of an analyst's forecasts. The ratio of alpha to residual standard deviation.

arbitrage   A zero-risk, zero-net investment strategy that still generates profits.

arbitrage pricing theory (APT)   An asset pricing theory that is derived from a factor model, using diversification and arbitrage arguments. The theory describes the relationship between expected return and factor exposure that follows from the absence of risk-free arbitrage opportunities.

ask price   The price at which a dealer will sell a security.

asset allocation   Allocating a portfolio across broad asset classes such as stocks versus bonds.

at the money   The option's exercise price and the price of the underlying asset are equal.

auction market   A market where all traders in an asset meet (either physically or electronically) at one place to buy and sell.

average collection period   The ratio of accounts receivable to daily sales. Also called *days' receivables*.

B

backfill bias   Bias in the average returns of a sample of funds induced by including past returns on funds that entered the sample only if they happened to be successful.

balance sheet   An accounting statement of a firm's financial position at a specified time.

bank discount yield   An annualized interest rate assuming simple interest, a 360-day year, and using the face value of the security rather than purchase price to compute return per dollar invested.

banker's acceptance   An order to a bank by a customer to pay a sum of money at a future date.

baseline forecasts   Forecast of security returns derived from the assumption that the market is in equilibrium where current prices reflect all available information.

basis   The difference between the futures price and the spot price.

basis risk   Risk attributable to uncertain movements in the spread between a futures price and a spot price.

behavioral finance   Models of financial markets that emphasize implications of psychological factors affecting investor behavior.

benchmark error   Use of an inappropriate proxy for the true market portfolio.

benchmark portfolio   Portfolio against which a manager is to be evaluated.

beta   The measure of the systematic risk of a security. The tendency of a security's returns to respond to swings in the broad market.

bid price   The price at which a dealer is willing to purchase a security.

bid–ask spread The difference between a dealer's bid and ask price.

binomial model An option-valuation model predicated on the assumption that stock prices can move to only two values over any short time period.

Black-Scholes pricing formula An equation to value an option that uses the stock price, the exercise price, the risk-free interest rate, the time to maturity, and the standard deviation of the stock return.

blocks A transaction of more than 10,000 shares of stock. Also referred to as a block sale.

bogey The return an investment manager is compared to for performance evaluation.

bond A security issued by a borrower that obligates the issuer to make specified payments to the holder over a specific period. A *coupon bond* obligates the issuer to make interest payments called coupon payments over the life of the bond, then to repay the *face value* at maturity.

bond equivalent yield Bond yield calculated on an annual percentage rate method. Differs from effective annual yield.

bond indenture The contract between the issuer and the bondholder.

bond reconstitution Combining zero-coupon stripped securities to re-create the original cash flows of a coupon bond.

bond stripping Selling bond cash flows (either coupon or principal payments) as stand-alone zero-coupon securities.

book value The net worth of common equity according to a firm's balance sheet.

book-to-market effect The tendency for stocks of firms with high ratios of book-to-market value to generate abnormal returns.

breadth The extent to which movements in the broad market index are reflected widely in movements of individual stock prices.

brokered market A market where an intermediary (a broker) offers search services to buyers and sellers.

budget deficit The amount by which government spending exceeds government revenues.

bull CD, bear CD A *bull CD* pays its holder a specified percentage of the increase in return on a specified market index while guaranteeing a minimum rate of return. A *bear CD* pays the holder a fraction of any fall in a given market index.

bullish, bearish Words used to describe investor attitudes. *Bullish* means optimistic; *bearish* means pessimistic. Also used in bull market and bear market.

bundling, unbundling Creation of securities either by combining primitive and derivative securities into one composite hybrid or by separating returns on an asset into classes or tranches.

business cycle Repetitive cycles of recession and recovery.

C

calendar spread Buy one option and write another with a different expiration date.

call option The right to buy an asset at a specified exercise price on or before a specified expiration date.

call protection An initial period during which a callable bond may not be called.

callable bond A bond that the issuer may repurchase at a given call price in some specified period.

capital allocation decision Allocation of invested funds between risk-free assets versus the risky portfolio.

capital allocation line (CAL) A graph showing all feasible risk–return combinations of a risky and risk-free asset.

capital gains The amount by which the sale price of a security exceeds the purchase price.

capital market line (CML) The capital allocation line that results when using the market index as the risky portfolio.

capital markets Includes longer-term, relatively riskier securities.

cash equivalents Short-term money-market securities.

cash flow matching A form of immunization, matching cash flows from a bond portfolio with those of an obligation.

cash ratio Measure of liquidity of a firm. Ratio of cash and marketable securities to current liabilities.

cash settlement The provision of some futures contracts that requires not delivery of the underlying assets (as in agricultural futures) but settlement according to the cash value of the asset.

cash/bond selection Asset allocation in which the choice is between short-term cash equivalents and longer-term bonds.

certainty equivalent rate The certain return providing the same utility as a risky portfolio.

certificate of deposit A bank time deposit.

clearinghouse Established by exchanges to facilitate transfer of securities resulting from trades. For options and futures contracts, the clearinghouse may interpose itself as a middleman between two traders.

closed-end (mutual) fund A fund whose shares are traded through brokers at market prices; the fund will not redeem shares at their net asset value. The market price of the fund can differ from the net asset value.

collar An options strategy that brackets the value of a portfolio between two bounds.

collateral A specific asset pledged against possible default on a bond. *Mortgage bonds* are backed by claims on property. *Collateral trust bonds* are backed by claims on other securities. *Equipment obligation bonds* are backed by claims on equipment.

collateralized debt obligation (CDO) A pool of loans sliced into several tranches with different levels of credit risk.

collateralized mortgage obligation (CMO) A mortgage pass-through security that partitions cash flows from underlying mortgages into classes called *tranches* that receive principal payments according to stipulated rules.

commercial paper Short-term unsecured debt issued by large corporations.

common stock Equities, or equity securities, issued as ownership shares in a publicly held corporation. Shareholders have voting rights and may receive dividends based on their proportionate ownership.

comparison universe The set of money managers employing similar investment styles, used for assessing the relative performance of a portfolio manager.

complete portfolio The entire portfolio, including risky and risk-free assets.

conditional tail expectation (CTE) Expectation of a random variable conditional on its falling below some threshold value. Often used as a measure of downside risk.

confidence index Ratio of the yield on top-rated corporate bonds to the yield on intermediate-grade bonds.

conservativism Notion that investors are too slow to update their beliefs in response to new evidence.

constant-growth DDM A special case of the dividend discount model that assumes dividends will grow at a constant rate.

contango theory Holds that the futures price must exceed the expected future spot price.

contingent claim See *derivative asset.*

contingent immunization A mixed passive-active strategy that immunizes a portfolio if necessary to guarantee a minimum acceptable return but otherwise allows active management.

convergence arbitrage A bet that two or more prices are out of alignment and that profits can be made when the prices converge back to proper relationship.

convergence property The convergence of futures prices and spot prices at the maturity of the futures contract.

convertible bond A bond with an option allowing the bondholder to exchange the bond for a specified number of shares of common stock in the firm. The *conversion ratio* specifies the number of shares. The *conversion price* is the current value of the shares for which the bond may be exchanged. The *conversion premium* is the excess of the bond's value over the conversion price.

convexity The curvature of the price-yield relationship of a bond.

corporate bonds Long-term debt issued by private corporations typically paying semiannual coupons and returning the face value of the bond at maturity.

correlation coefficient A statistic in which the covariance is scaled to a value between -1 (perfect negative correlation) and $+1$ (perfect positive correlation).

cost-of-carry relationship See *spot-futures parity theorem.*

country selection Asset allocation in which the investor chooses among investments in different countries.

coupon rate A bond's interest payments per dollar of par value.

covariance A measure of the degree to which returns on two risky assets move in tandem. A positive covariance means that asset returns move together. A negative covariance means they vary inversely.

covered call A combination of selling a call option together with buying the underlying asset.

covered interest arbitrage relationship See *interest rate parity relationship.*

credit default swap (CDS) An insurance policy on the credit risk of a corporate bond or loan.

credit enhancement Purchase of the financial guarantee of another party to reduce the credit risk of a bond or loan.

credit risk The risk that the bond will not make all of its promised payments; default risk.

cross-hedge Hedging a position in one asset using futures contracts on another commodity.

cumulative abnormal return (CAR) See *abnormal return.*

currency selection Asset allocation in which the investor chooses among investments denominated in different currencies.

current ratio Current assets/current liabilities. Measures the ability of the firm to pay off its current liabilities by liquidating current assets.

current yield A bond's annual coupon payment divided by its price. Differs from yield to maturity.

cyclical industries Industries with above-average sensitivity to the state of the economy.

D

dark pools Electronic trading networks where participants can anonymously buy or sell large blocks of securities.

data mining Sorting through large amounts of historical data to uncover systematic patterns that can be used as the basis of a trading strategy.

day order A buy order or a sell order expiring at the close of the trading day.

days' receivables See *average collection period.*

dealer market A market where traders specializing in particular assets buy and sell assets for their own accounts.

debenture bond A bond not backed by specific collateral. Also called an *unsecured bond.*

debt securities Bonds; also called *fixed-income securities.*

dedication strategy Multiperiod cash flow matching.

default premium A differential in promised yield that compensates the investor for the risk inherent in purchasing a corporate bond that entails some risk of default.

defensive industries Industries with below-average sensitivity to the state of the economy.

deferred annuities Tax-advantaged life insurance product. Deferred annuities offer deferral of taxes with the option of withdrawing one's funds in the form of a life annuity.

defined benefit plans Pension plans in which retirement benefits are set according to a fixed formula.

defined contribution plans Pension plans in which the employer is committed to making contributions according to a fixed formula.

degree of operating leverage (DOL) Percentage change in profits for a 1% change in sales.

delta (of option) The number of stocks required to hedge against the price risk of writing one option. Also called the *hedge ratio*.

delta neutral The value of the options portfolio is not affected by changes in the value of the underlying asset.

demand shock An event that affects the demand for goods and services in the economy.

derivative asset Claim whose value is directly dependent on or is contingent on the value of some underlying assets.

derivative security A security whose payoff depends on the value of other financial variables such as stock prices, interest rates, or exchange rates.

direct search market Buyers and sellers seek each other directly and transact directly.

directional strategy Speculation that one sector or another will outperform other sectors of the market.

discount bond A bond selling below par value.

discretionary account An account of a customer who gives a broker the authority to make buy and sell decisions on the customer's behalf.

disposition effect The tendency of investors to hold on to losing investments.

diversifiable risk Nonmarket or firm-specific risk factors that can be eliminated by diversification. Also called *unique risk, firm-specific risk*, or *nonsystematic risk. Nondiversifiable* risk refers to systematic or market risk.

diversification Spreading a portfolio over many investments to avoid excessive exposure to any one source of risk.

dividend discount model (DDM) A formula stating that the intrinsic value of a firm is the present value of all expected future dividends.

dividend payout ratio Percentage of earnings paid out as dividends.

dividend yield The annual dividend payment expressed as a percent of the stock price.

dollar-weighted rate of return The internal rate of return on an investment.

doubling option A sinking fund provision that may allow repurchase of twice the required number of bonds at the sinking fund call price.

DuPont system Decomposition of a firm's profitability measures into component ratios.

duration A measure of the average life of a bond, defined as the weighted average of the times until each payment is made, with weights proportional to the present value of the payment.

dynamic hedging Constant updating of hedge positions as market conditions change.

E

EAFE index The Europe, Australasia, Far East index, computed by Morgan Stanley, is a widely used index of non-U.S. stocks.

earnings management The practice of using flexibility in accounting rules to manipulate the apparent profitability of the firm.

earnings retention ratio The proportion of the firm's earnings reinvested in the business (and therefore not paid out as dividends). Equals 1 minus the dividend payout ratio. Synonym for plowback ratio.

earnings yield The ratio of earnings to price, E/P.

economic earnings The real flow of cash that a firm could pay out without impairing its productive capacity.

economic value added (EVA) The spread between ROA and cost of capital multiplied by the capital invested in the firm. It measures the dollar value of the firm's return in excess of its opportunity cost.

effective annual rate (EAR) Interest rate annualized using compound rather than simple interest.

effective annual yield Annualized interest rate on a security computed using compound interest techniques.

effective duration Percentage change in bond price per change in the level of market interest rates.

efficient diversification The organizing principle of modern portfolio theory, which describes how investors can devise the best possible risk-return trade-off.

efficient frontier Graph representing a set of portfolios that maximize expected return at each level of portfolio risk.

efficient frontier of risky assets The portion of the minimum-variance frontier that lies above the global minimum-variance portfolio.

efficient market hypothesis (EMH) The prices of securities fully reflect available information. Investors buying securities in an efficient market should expect to obtain an equilibrium rate of return. *Weak-form* EMH asserts that stock prices already reflect all information contained in the history of past prices. The *semistrong-form* hypothesis asserts that stock prices already reflect all publicly available information. The *strong-form* hypothesis asserts that stock prices reflect all relevant information, including insider information.

elasticity (of an option) Percentage change in the value of an option accompanying a 1% change in the value of a stock.

electronic communication network (ECN) A computer-operated trading network for trading securities. Some ECNs are registered as formal stock exchanges, and others are considered part of the over-the-counter market.

endowment funds Organizations chartered to invest money for specific purposes.

equity   Ownership share in a firm.

equivalent taxable yield   The pretax yield on a taxable bond providing an after-tax yield equal to the rate on a tax-exempt municipal bond.

Eurodollars   Dollar-denominated deposits at foreign banks or foreign branches of American banks.

Europe, Australasia, Far East (EAFE) index   A widely used index of non-U.S. stocks computed by MSCI.

European option   A European option can be exercised only on the expiration date. Compare with an *American option,* which also can be exercised before its expiration date.

event study   Research methodology designed to measure the impact of an event of interest on stock returns.

event tree   Depicts all possible sequences of events.

excess return   Rate of return in excess of the risk-free rate.

exchange rate   Price of a unit of one country's currency in terms of another country's currency.

exchange rate risk   The uncertainty in dollar-denominated asset returns due to movements in the exchange rates between the dollar and foreign currencies.

exchange-traded funds (ETFs)   Variants of mutual funds that allow investors to trade portfolios of securities just as they do shares of stock.

exchanges   National or regional auction markets providing a facility for members to trade securities.

exercise (or strike) price   Price set for calling (buying) an asset or putting (selling) an asset.

expectations hypothesis (of interest rates)   Theory that forward interest rates are unbiased estimates of expected future interest rates.

expected return   The probability-weighted average of the possible outcomes.

expected return–beta (or mean-beta) relationship   Implication of the CAPM that security risk premiums (expected excess returns) will be proportional to beta.

expected shortfall (ES)   The expected loss on a security *conditional* on returns being in the left tail of the probability distribution.

F

face value   The maturity value of a bond. See *par value of bond.*

factor beta   Sensitivity of security returns to the realization of a systematic factor. Also called *factor loading* and *factor sensitivity.*

factor loading   See *factor beta.*

factor model   A way of decomposing the factors that influence a security's rate of return into common (systematic) and firm-specific influences.

factor portfolio   A well-diversified portfolio constructed to have a beta of 1.0 on one factor and a beta of 0 on any other factor.

factor sensitivity   See *factor beta.*

fair game   An investment prospect that has a zero risk premium.

fair value accounting   Use of current values rather than historic cost in the firm's financial statements.

federal funds   Funds in a bank's reserve account at the Federal Reserve Bank.

FIFO   The first-in first-out accounting method of inventory valuation.

financial assets   Financial assets such as stocks and bonds are claims to the income generated by real assets or claims on income from the government.

financial engineering   Creating and designing securities with custom-tailored characteristics.

financial intermediary   Institutions that "connect" borrowers and lenders by accepting funds from lenders and loaning funds to borrowers.

firm-specific risk   Nonmarket or firm-specific risk factors that can be eliminated by diversification. Also called *unique risk, nonsystematic risk,* or *diversifiable risk.*

first-pass regression   A time series regression to estimate the betas of securities or portfolios.

fiscal policy   The use of government spending and taxation for the specific purpose of stabilizing the economy.

fixed annuities   Annuity contracts in which the insurance company pays a fixed dollar amount of money per period.

fixed-charge coverage ratio   Ratio of earnings to all fixed cash obligations, including lease payments and sinking fund payments.

fixed-income security   A security such as a bond that pays a specified cash flow over a specific period.

flight to quality   Describes the tendency of investors to require larger default premiums on investments under worsening economic conditions.

floating-rate bond   A bond whose interest rate is reset periodically according to a specified market rate.

forced conversion   Use of a firm's call option on a callable convertible bond when the firm knows that bondholders will exercise their option to convert.

forecasting record   The historical record of the forecasting errors of a security analyst.

foreign exchange market   An informal network of banks and brokers that allows customers to enter forward contracts to purchase or sell currencies in the future at a rate of exchange agreed upon now.

foreign exchange swap   An agreement to exchange stipulated amounts of one currency for another at one or more future dates.

forward contract   An agreement calling for future delivery of an asset at an agreed-upon price.

forward interest rate   Rate of interest for a future period that would equate the total return of a long-term bond with that of a strategy of rolling over shorter-term bonds.

framing   Decisions are affected by how choices are described, for example, whether uncertainty is posed as potential gains from a low baseline level, or as losses from a higher baseline value.

fully diluted earnings per share   Earnings per share expressed as if all outstanding convertible securities and warrants have been exercised.

fundamental analysis   Assessment of firm value that focuses on such determinants as earnings and dividends prospects, expectations for future interest rates, and risk evaluation.

fundamental risk   Risk that even if an asset is mispriced, there is still no arbitrage opportunity, because the mispricing can widen before price eventually converges to intrinsic value.

funds of funds   Investment funds that invest in other funds rather than investing directly in securities such as stocks or bonds.

futures contract   Obliges traders to purchase or sell an asset at an agreed-upon price on a specified future date. The *long position* is held by the trader who commits to purchase. The *short position* is held by the trader who commits to sell. Futures differ from forward contracts in their standardization, exchange trading, margin requirements, and daily settling (marking to market).

futures option   The right to enter a specified futures contract at a futures price equal to the stipulated exercise price.

futures price   The price at which a futures trader commits to make or take delivery of the underlying asset.

G

gamma   The curvature of an option pricing function (as a function of the value of the underlying asset).

geometric average   The *n*th root of the product of *n* numbers. It is used to measure the compound rate of return over a given sample period.

globalization   Tendency toward a worldwide investment environment, and the integration of national capital markets.

gross domestic product (GDP)   The market value of goods and services produced in an economy during a particular time period.

H

hedge fund   A private investment pool, open to institutional or wealthy investors, that is largely exempt from SEC regulation and can pursue more speculative policies than mutual funds.

hedge ratio (for futures)   The number of contracts necessary to hedge a particular source of risk.

hedge ratio (of an option)   The shares of stocks required to hedge against the price risk of writing one option. Also called the option's *delta*.

hedging   Investing in an asset or derivative security to offset a specific source of risk.

hedging demands   Demands for securities to hedge particular sources of consumption risk, beyond the usual mean variance diversification motivation.

high water mark   The previous value of a portfolio that must be reattained before a hedge fund can charge incentive fees.

high-frequency trading   A subset of algorithmic trading that relies on computer programs to make rapid trading decisions.

holding-period return   The rate of return over a given period.

home bias   The tendency of investors to allocate a greater share of their portfolios to domestic securities than would be the case under neutral diversification.

homogenous expectations   The assumption that all investors agree on the probability distribution of future returns, so they all use the same input list.

horizon analysis   Forecasting the realized compound yield over various holding periods or investment horizons.

I

illiquidity   Difficulty, cost, and/or delay in selling an asset on short notice without offering substantial price concessions.

illiquidity cost   Costs due to imperfect liquidity of some security.

illiquidity premium   Extra expected return as compensation for limited liquidity.

immunization   A strategy that matches durations of assets and liabilities so as to make net worth unaffected by interest rate movements.

implied volatility   The standard deviation of stock returns that is consistent with an option's market value.

in the money   In the money describes an option whose exercise would produce a positive cash flow. Out of the money describes an option where exercise would result in a negative cash flow.

incentive fee   A fee charged by hedge funds equal to a share of any investment returns beyond a stipulated benchmark performance.

income beneficiary   One who receives income from a trust.

income statement   A financial statement showing a firm's revenues and expenses during a specified period.

indenture   The document defining the contract between the bond issuer and the bondholder.

index arbitrage   An investment strategy that exploits divergences between actual futures prices and their theoretically correct parity values to make a profit.

index fund   A mutual fund holding shares in proportion to their representation in a market index such as the S&P 500.

index model   A model of stock returns using a market index such as the S&P 500 to represent common or systematic risk factors.

index option A call or put option based on a stock market index.

indifference curve A curve connecting all portfolios with the same utility according to their means and standard deviations.

industry life cycle Stages through which firms typically pass as they mature.

inflation The rate at which the general level of prices for goods and services is rising.

information ratio Ratio of alpha to the standard deviation of diversifiable risk.

initial public offering (IPO) Stock issued to the public for the first time by a formerly privately owned company.

input list List of parameters such as expected returns, variances, and covariances necessary to determine the optimal risky portfolio.

inside information Nonpublic knowledge about a corporation possessed by corporate officers, major owners, or other individuals with privileged access to information about a firm.

insider trading Trading by officers, directors, major stockholders, or others who hold private inside information allowing them to benefit from buying or selling stock.

insurance principle The law of averages. The average outcome for many independent trials of an experiment will approach the expected value of the experiment.

interest coverage ratio Measure of financial leverage. Earnings before interest and taxes as a multiple of interest expense.

interest rate The number of dollars earned per dollar invested per period.

interest rate parity relationship (theorem) The relation between spot and forward exchange rates and foreign and domestic interest rates that rules out arbitrage opportunities.

interest rate swaps Contracts between two parties to trade cash flows corresponding to different interest rates.

intermarket spread swap Switching from one segment of the bond market to another (from Treasuries to corporates, for example).

international financial reporting standards (IFRS) Accounting standards used in many non-U.S. markets; compared to U.S. accounting standards, IFRS rely more on principles and less on rules.

intrinsic value (of a firm) The present value of a firm's expected future net cash flows discounted by the required rate of return.

intrinsic value (of a share) The present value of expected future cash flows the firm will provide shareholders on a per share basis.

intrinsic value (of an option) The value the option would have if it were about to expire.

inventory turnover ratio Cost of goods sold as a multiple of average inventory.

investment Commitment of current resources in the expectation of deriving greater resources in the future.

investment bankers Firms specializing in the sale of new securities to the public, typically by underwriting the issue.

investment company Financial intermediaries that pool and invest the funds of individual investors in securities or other assets.

investment horizon Time horizon for purposes of investment decisions.

investment portfolio Set of securities chosen by an investor.

investment-grade bond Bond rated BBB and above or Baa and above. Lower-rated bonds are classified as speculative-grade or junk bonds.

issued shares Shares that have been issued by the company.

J

Jensen's alpha The alpha of an investment.

junk bond A bond rated Ba or lower by Moody's or BB or lower by Standard & Poor's, or an unrated bond. Also called a *speculative-grade bond.*

K

kurtosis Measure of the fatness of the tails of a probability distribution. Indicates probability of observing extreme high or low values.

L

latency The time it takes to accept, process, and deliver a trading order.

Law of One Price The rule stipulating that equivalent securities or bundles of securities must sell at equal prices to preclude arbitrage opportunities.

leading economic indicators Economic series that tend to rise or fall in advance of the rest of the economy.

leverage ratio Ratio of debt to total capitalization of a firm.

LIFO The last-in first-out accounting method of valuing inventories.

limit order An order specifying a price at which an investor is willing to buy or sell a security.

limited liability The fact that shareholders have no personal liability to the creditors of the corporation in the event of bankruptcy.

liquidation value Net amount that could be realized by selling the assets of a firm after paying the debt.

liquidity The speed and ease with which an asset can be converted to cash.

liquidity preference theory Theory that investors demand a risk premium on long-term bonds. Implies that the forward rate generally will exceed the expected future interest rate.

liquidity premium Forward rate minus expected future short interest rate.

load Sales charge on the purchase of some mutual funds.

load fund A mutual fund with a sales commission, or load.

lock-up period Period in which investors cannot redeem investments in the hedge fund.

log-normal distribution The probability distribution that characterizes a variable whose log has a normal (bell-shaped) distribution.

London Interbank Offered Rate (LIBOR) Lending rate among banks in the London market.

long position The futures trader who commits to purchasing the underlying asset.

long position hedge Hedging the future cost of a purchase by taking a long futures position to protect against changes in the price of the asset.

lower partial standard deviation (LPSD) Standard deviation computed using only the portion of the return distribution below a threshold such as the risk-free rate or the sample average.

M

Macaulay's duration Effective maturity of bond, equal to weighted average of the times until each payment, with weights proportional to the present value of the payment.

maintenance, or variation, margin An established value below which a trader's margin may not fall. Reaching the maintenance margin triggers a margin call.

margin Describes securities purchased with money borrowed from a broker. Current maximum allowed margin is 50%.

mark-to-market accounting See *fair value accounting.*

market capitalization rate The market-consensus estimate of the appropriate discount rate for a firm's cash flows.

market model Another version of the index model that breaks down return uncertainty into systematic and nonsystematic components.

market order A buy or sell order to be executed immediately at current market prices.

market portfolio The portfolio encompassing all assets in which each asset is held in proportion to its market value.

market price of risk A measure of the extra return, or risk premium, that investors demand to bear risk. The ratio of the risk premium of the market portfolio to the variance of its return.

market risk Risk factors common to the whole economy; also called *systematic* or *nondiversifiable risk.*

market segmentation The theory that long- and short-maturity bonds are traded in essentially distinct or segmented markets and that prices in one market do not affect those in the other.

market timer An investor who speculates on broad market moves rather than on specific securities.

market timing Asset allocation in which the investment in the market is increased if one forecasts that the market will outperform T-bills.

market-neutral bet A strategy designed to exploit relative mispricing *within* a market but which is hedged to avoid taking a stance on the direction of the broad market.

market-value-weighted index An index of the value of a portfolio of securities computed by calculating a weighted average of the returns of each security in the portfolio, with weights proportional to outstanding market value.

market–book-value (P/B) ratio Ratio of price per share to book value per share.

marking to market Describes the daily settlement of obligations on futures positions.

mean-variance (M-V) criterion The selection of portfolios based on the means and variances of their returns. The choice of the highest expected return portfolio for a given level of variance or the lowest variance portfolio for a given expected return.

mean-variance analysis Evaluation of risky prospects based on the expected value and variance of possible outcomes.

mental accounting Individuals mentally segregate assets into independent accounts rather than viewing them as part of a unified portfolio.

minimum-variance frontier Graph of the lowest possible portfolio standard deviation corresponding to each value of portfolio expected return.

minimum-variance portfolio The portfolio of risky assets with lowest possible variance.

modern portfolio theory (MPT) Principles underlying analysis and evaluation of rational portfolio choices based on risk–return trade-offs and efficient diversification.

modified duration Macaulay's duration divided by 1 + yield to maturity. Measures interest rate sensitivity of bonds.

momentum effect The tendency of poorly performing stocks and well-performing stocks in one period to continue that abnormal performance in following periods.

monetary policy Actions taken by the Board of Governors of the Federal Reserve System to influence the money supply or interest rates.

money market Includes short-term, highly liquid, and relatively low-risk debt instruments.

mortality tables Tables of probability that individuals of various ages will die within a year.

mortgage-backed security Ownership claim in a pool of mortgages or an obligation that is secured by such a pool. Also called a *pass-through,* because payments are passed along from the mortgage originator to the purchaser of the mortgage-backed security.

multifactor CAPM Generalization of the basic CAPM that accounts for extra-market hedging demands.

multifactor model   Model of security returns positing that returns respond to several systematic risk factors as well as firm-specific influences.

municipal bonds   Tax-exempt bonds issued by state and local governments. General obligation bonds are backed by the general taxing power of the issuer. Revenue bonds are backed by the proceeds from the project or agency they are issued to finance.

mutual fund   An investment company pooling and managing funds of investors.

mutual fund theorem   A result associated with the CAPM, asserting that investors will choose to invest their entire risky portfolio in a market-index mutual fund.

N

NAICS codes   North American Industrial Classification System codes that use numerical values to identify industries.

naked option writing   Writing an option without an offsetting stock position.

NASDAQ Stock Market   The computer-linked price quotation and trade execution system on which thousands of securities trade.

neglected-firm effect   That investments in stock of less well-known firms have generated abnormal returns.

net asset value (NAV)   Assets minus liabilities expressed on a per-share basis.

nominal interest rate   The interest rate in terms of nominal (not adjusted for purchasing power) dollars.

nondirectional strategy   A position designed to exploit temporary misalignments in relative pricing. Typically involves a long position in one security hedged with a short position in a related security.

nondiversifiable risk   Risk factors common to the whole economy; also called *market risk* or *systematic risk*.

nonsystematic risk   Nonmarket or firm-specific risk factors that can be eliminated by diversification. Also called *unique risk*, *firm-specific risk*, or *diversifiable risk*. Systematic risk refers to risk factors common to the entire economy.

normal distribution   Bell-shaped probability distribution that characterizes many natural phenomena.

notional principal   Principal amount used to calculate swap payments.

O

on the run   Recently issued bond, selling at or near par value.

on-the-run yield curve   Relationship between yield to maturity and time to maturity for newly issued bonds selling at or near par value.

open interest   The number of futures contracts outstanding.

open-end (mutual) fund   A fund that issues or redeems its own shares at net asset value (NAV).

optimal risky portfolio   An investor's best combination of risky assets; the combination that maximizes the Sharpe ratio.

option elasticity   The percentage increase in an option's value given a 1% change in the value of the underlying security.

original issue discount bond   A bond issued with a low coupon rate that sells at a discount from par value.

out of the money   Out of the money describes an option where exercise would result in a negative cash flow. Out-of-the-money options are therefore never exercised.

outstanding shares   Shares that have been issued by the company and are held by investors.

over-the-counter (OTC) market   An informal network of brokers and dealers where securities can be traded (not a formal exchange).

P

P/E effect   That low P/E stocks have exhibited higher average risk-adjusted returns than high P/E stocks.

pairs trading   A form of statistical arbitrage in which stocks are paired up based on underlying similarities and long/short positions are established to exploit any relative mispricing between each pair.

par value   The face value of the bond. The payment to the bondholder on the bond's maturity date.

pass-through security   Pools of loans (such as home mortgage loans) sold in one package. Owners of pass-throughs receive all principal and interest payments made by the borrowers.

passive investment strategy   Investing in a well-diversified portfolio or market index without attempting to search out mispriced securities.

passive management   Buying a well-diversified portfolio, often a broad-based market index, without attempting to identify mispriced securities.

passive market-index portfolio   A market-index portfolio that can be formed without conducting security analysis.

passive strategy   A portfolio decision that avoids any direct or indirect security analysis. See *passive management*.

peak   The transition from the end of an expansion to the start of a contraction.

personal trust   An interest in an asset held by a trustee for the benefit of another person.

plowback ratio   The proportion of the firm's earnings reinvested in the business (and therefore not paid out as dividends). The plowback ratio equals 1 minus the dividend payout ratio.

political risk   Possibility of the expropriation of assets, changes in tax policy, restrictions on the exchange of foreign currency for domestic currency, or other changes in the business climate of a country.

portable alpha A strategy in which you invest in positive alpha positions, then hedge the systematic risk of that investment, and, finally, establish market exposure where you want it by using passive indexes.

portfolio insurance The practice of using options or dynamic hedge strategies to provide protection against investment losses while maintaining upside potential.

portfolio management Process of combining securities in a portfolio tailored to the investor's preferences and needs, monitoring that portfolio, and evaluating its performance.

portfolio opportunity set The expected return–standard deviation pairs of all portfolios that can be constructed from a given set of assets.

posterior distribution Probability distribution for a variable after adjustment for empirical evidence on its likely value.

preferred habitat theory Holds that investors prefer specific maturity ranges but can be induced to switch if risk premiums are sufficient.

preferred stock Nonvoting shares in a corporation, paying a fixed or variable stream of dividends.

premium (options) The purchase price of an option.

premium bond A bond selling above par value.

present value of growth opportunities (PVGO) Net present value of a firm's future investments.

price value of a basis point The change in the value of a fixed-income portfolio resulting from a 1 basis point change in the yield to maturity.

price-weighted average Weighted average with weights proportional to security prices rather than total capitalization.

price–earnings (P/E) ratio The ratio of a stock's price to its earnings per share. Also referred to as the P/E multiple.

price–earnings multiple Price per share divided by earnings per share.

primary market The market in which new issues of securities are offered to the public.

primitive security, derivative security A *primitive security* is an instrument such as a stock or bond for which cash flows depend only on the financial status of its issuer. A *derivative security* is created from the set of primitive securities to yield returns that depend on factors beyond the characteristics of the issuer and that may be related to prices of other assets.

principal The outstanding balance on a loan.

prior distribution Probability distribution for a variable before adjusting for empirical evidence on its likely value.

private equity Investments in companies whose shares are not publicly traded in a stock market.

private placement Primary offering in which shares are sold directly to a small group of institutional or wealthy investors.

profit margin Operating profits per dollar of sales; also called *return on sales*.

program trading Coordinated buy orders and sell orders of entire portfolios, usually with the aid of computers, often to achieve index arbitrage objectives.

prospect theory Behavioral (as opposed to rational) model of investor utility. Investor utility depends on changes in wealth rather than levels of wealth.

prospectus A description of the firm and the security it is issuing.

protective covenant A provision specifying requirements of collateral, sinking fund, dividend policy, etc., designed to protect the interests of bondholders.

protective put Purchase of an asset combined with a put option on that asset to guarantee proceeds at least equal to the put's exercise price.

proxy An instrument empowering an agent to vote in the name of the shareholder.

prudent investor rule An investment manager must act in accord with the actions of a hypothetical prudent investor.

public offering, private placement A *public offering* consists of securities sold in the primary market to the general public; a *private placement* is sold directly to a limited number of institutional investors.

pure plays Bets on particular mispricing across two or more securities, with extraneous sources of risk such as general market exposure hedged away.

pure yield curve The relationship between yield to maturity and time to maturity for zero-coupon bonds.

pure yield pickup swap Moving to higher-yield, longer-term bonds to capture the liquidity premium.

put bond A bond that the holder may choose either to exchange for par value at some date or to extend for a given number of years.

put option The right to sell an asset at a specified exercise price on or before a specified expiration date.

put-call parity theorem An equation representing the proper relation between put and call prices. Violation of parity implies the existence of arbitrage opportunities.

put/call ratio Ratio of put options to call options outstanding on a stock.

Q

quality of earnings The realism and conservatism of the earnings number and the extent to which we might expect the reported level of earnings to be sustained.

quick ratio A measure of liquidity similar to the current ratio except for exclusion of inventories. It equals cash plus receivables divided by current liabilities.

R

random walk Describes the notion that stock price changes are random and unpredictable.

rate anticipation swap   A switch made between bonds of different durations in response to forecasts of interest rates.

real assets   Assets used to produce goods and services such as land, buildings, and equipment.

real interest rate   The excess of the interest rate over the inflation rate. The growth rate of purchasing power derived from an investment.

realized compound return   Compound rate of return assuming that coupon payments are reinvested until maturity.

rebalancing   Realigning the proportions of assets in a portfolio as needed.

registered bond   A bond whose issuer records ownership and interest payments. Differs from a bearer bond, which is traded without record of ownership and whose possession is its only evidence of ownership.

regression equation   An equation that describes the average relationship between a dependent variable and one or more explanatory variables.

regret avoidance   Notion from behavioral finance that individuals who make decisions that turn out badly will have more regret when that decision was more unconventional.

reinvestment rate risk   The uncertainty surrounding the cumulative future value of reinvested bond coupon payments.

REIT   Real estate investment trust, which is similar to a closed-end mutual fund. REITs invest in real estate or loans secured by real estate and issue shares in such investments.

relative strength   The extent to which a security has outperformed or underperformed either the market as a whole or its particular industry.

remainderman   One who receives the principal of a trust when it is dissolved.

replacement cost   Cost to replace a firm's assets. Also called *reproduction cost*.

representativeness bias   The tendency to believe that a small sample is reliably representative of a broad population and therefore to infer patterns too quickly.

repurchase agreements (repos)   Short-term, often overnight, sales of securities with an agreement to repurchase them at a slightly higher price. A *reverse repo* is a purchase with an agreement to resell at a specified price on a future date.

residual claim   Refers to the fact that shareholders are at the bottom of the list of claimants to assets of a corporation in the event of failure or bankruptcy.

residual income   Another term for economic value added (EVA).

residuals   Parts of stock returns not explained by the explanatory variable (the market-index return). They measure the impact of firm-specific events during a particular period.

resistance level   A price level above which it is supposedly difficult for a stock or stock index to rise.

return on assets (ROA)   A profitability ratio; earnings before interest and taxes divided by total assets.

return on capital (ROC)   EBIT divided by long-term capital.

return on equity (ROE)   Ratio of net profits to common equity.

return on sales (ROS)   Operating profits per dollar of sales; also called *profit margin*.

reversal effect   The tendency of poorly performing stocks and well-performing stocks in one period to experience reversals in following periods.

reversing trade   Entering the opposite side of a currently held futures position to close out the position.

reward-to-volatility or Sharpe ratio   Ratio of excess return to portfolio standard deviation.

riding the yield curve   Buying long-term bonds in anticipation of capital gains as yields fall with the declining maturity of the bonds.

risk arbitrage   Speculation on perceived security mispricing, often in connection with merger and acquisition targets.

risk averse   An investor who will consider risky portfolios only if they provide compensation for risk via a risk premium.

risk lover   An investor who is willing to accept lower expected returns on prospects with higher amounts of risk.

risk neutral   An investor who finds the level of risk irrelevant and considers only the expected return of risk prospects.

risk pooling   Adding uncorrelated, risky investments to the portfolio.

risk premium   An expected return in excess of that on risk-free securities. The premium provides compensation for the risk of an investment.

risk sharing   Spreading risk across many investors so that each investor bears only a fraction of the total risk.

risk-free asset   An asset with a certain rate of return; often taken to be short-term T-bills.

risk-free rate   The interest rate that can be earned with certainty, commonly taken to be the rate on short-term Treasury bills.

risk–return trade-off   Assets with higher expected return entail greater risk.

risky asset   An asset with an uncertain rate of return.

S

scatter diagram   Plot of returns of one security versus returns of another security. Each point represents one pair of returns for a given holding period.

seasoned new issue   Stock issued by companies that already have stock on the market.

second-pass regression   A cross-sectional regression of portfolio returns on betas. The estimated slope is the measurement of the reward for bearing systematic risk during the period.

secondary market Already existing securities are bought and sold on the exchanges or in the OTC market.

sector rotation An investment strategy which entails shifting the portfolio into industry sectors that are forecast to outperform others based on macroeconomic forecasts.

securitization Pooling loans for various purposes into standardized securities backed by those loans, which can then be traded like any other security.

security analysis Determining correct value of a security in the marketplace.

security characteristic line (SCL) A plot of the excess return on a security over the risk-free rate as a function of the excess return on the market.

security market line (SML) Graphical representation of the expected return–beta relationship.

security selection Choice of specific securities within a given asset class.

semistrong-form EMH See *efficient market hypothesis.*

separation property The property that portfolio choice can be separated into two independent tasks: (1) determination of the optimal risky portfolio, which is a purely technical problem, and (2) the personal choice of the best mix of the risky portfolio and the risk-free asset.

Sharpe ratio Reward-to-volatility ratio; ratio of excess return to portfolio standard deviation.

shelf registration Advance registration of securities with the SEC for sale up to 2 years following initial registration.

short position The futures trader committing to deliver the underlying asset.

short rate A one-period interest rate.

short sale The sale of shares not owned by the investor but borrowed through a broker and later repurchased to replace the loan. Profit is earned if the initial sale is at a higher price than the repurchase price.

single-factor model A model of security returns that decomposes the sources of return variability into one systematic economywide factor and firm-specific factors.

single-index model A model of stock returns that decomposes influences on returns into a systematic factor, as measured by the return on a broad market index, and firm-specific factors.

single-stock futures Futures contracts on single stocks rather than an index.

sinking fund A bond indenture that calls for the issuer to periodically repurchase some proportion of the outstanding bonds prior to maturity.

skew Measure of the asymmetry of a probability distribution.

small-firm effect That investments in stocks of small firms appear to have earned abnormal returns.

soft dollars The value of research services that brokerage houses supply to investment managers "free of charge" in exchange for the investment managers' business.

Sortino ratio Excess return divided by lower partial standard deviation.

specialist A trader who makes a market in the shares of one or more firms and who maintains a "fair and orderly market" by dealing personally in the stock.

speculation Undertaking a risky investment with the objective of earning a greater profit than an investment in a risk-free alternative (a risk premium).

speculative-grade bond A bond rated Ba or lower by Moody's or BB or lower by Standard & Poor's , or an unrated bond. Also called a *junk bond.*

spot rate The current interest rate appropriate for discounting a cash flow of some given maturity.

spot-futures parity theorem Describes the theoretically correct relationship between spot and futures prices. Violation of the parity relationship gives rise to arbitrage opportunities. Also called the *cost-of-carry relationship.*

spread (futures) Taking a long position in a futures contract of one maturity and a short position in a contract of different maturity, both on the same underlying asset.

spread (options) A combination of two or more call options or put options on the same stock with differing exercise prices or times to expiration. A *money spread* refers to a spread with different exercise prices; a *time spread* refers to differing expiration dates.

standard deviation Square root of the variance.

statement of cash flows A financial statement showing a firm's cash receipts and cash payments during a specified period.

statistical arbitrage Use of quantitative systems to uncover many perceived misalignments in relative pricing and ensure profit by diversifying across all of these small bets.

stock exchanges Secondary markets where already-issued securities are bought and sold by members.

stock selection An active portfolio management technique that focuses on advantageous selection of particular stocks rather than on broad asset allocation choices.

stock split Issue by a corporation of a given number of shares in exchange for the current number of shares held by stockholders. Splits may go in either direction, either increasing or decreasing the number of shares outstanding. A *reverse split* decreases the number outstanding.

stop-loss order A sell order to be executed if the price of the stock falls below a stipulated level.

straddle A combination of buying both a call and a put on the same asset, each with the same exercise price and expiration date. The purpose is to profit from expected volatility.

straight bond A bond with no option features such as callability or convertibility.

street name Describes securities held by a broker on behalf of a client but registered in the name of the firm.

strike price See *exercise price*.

strip, strap Variants of a straddle. A *strip* is two puts and one call on a stock; a *strap* is two calls and one put, both with the same exercise price and expiration date.

stripped of coupons Describes the practice of some investment banks that create "synthetic" zero-coupon bonds by selling the individual payments made by a coupon-paying Treasury bond.

strong-form EMH See *efficient market hypothesis*.

subordination clause A stipulation that senior bondholders will be paid first in the event of bankruptcy. Claims of *subordinated* or *junior* debtholders are not paid until the senior debt is paid.

substitution swap Exchange of one bond for another more attractively priced bond with similar attributes.

supply shock An event that influences production capacity and costs in the economy.

support level A price level below which it is supposedly difficult for a stock or stock index to fall.

survivorship bias Bias in the average returns of a sample of funds induced by excluding past returns on funds that left the sample because they happened to be unsuccessful.

swaption An option on a swap.

systematic risk Risk factors common to the whole economy; also called *market risk* or *nondiversifiable risk*.

systemic risk Risk of breakdown in the financial system, particularly due to spillover effects from one market into others.

T

tax anticipation notes Short-term municipal debt to raise funds to pay for expenses before actual collection of taxes.

tax swap Swapping two similar bonds to capture a tax benefit.

tax-deferral option The feature of the U.S. Internal Revenue Code that the capital gains tax on an asset is payable only when the gain is realized by selling the asset.

tax-protected retirement plans Employer-sponsored and other plans that protect either contributions or investment earnings from taxes, at least until after retirement.

technical analysis Research to identify mispriced securities that focuses on recurrent and predictable stock price patterns and on proxies for buy or sell pressure in the market.

tender offer An offer from an outside investor to shareholders of a company to purchase their shares at a stipulated price, usually substantially above the market price, so that the investor may amass enough shares to obtain control of the company.

term insurance Provides a death benefit only, with no buildup of cash value.

term premiums Excess of the yields to maturity on long-term bonds over those of short-term bonds.

term structure of interest rates The pattern of interest rates appropriate for discounting cash flows of various maturities. The relation between yield to maturity and time to maturity.

time value (of an option) Difference between an option's price and its intrinsic value. Not to be confused with present value or the time value of money.

time-weighted average An average (often a geometric average) of the period-by-period holding-period returns of an investment.

times interest earned Synonym for interest coverage ratio. Ratio of EBIT to interest expense.

Tobin's q Ratio of market value of the firm to replacement cost.

total asset turnover (ATO) The annual sales generated by each dollar of assets (sales/assets).

tracking error The difference between the return on a managed portfolio and that of a benchmark portfolio against which the manager is evaluated.

tracking portfolio A portfolio constructed to have returns with the highest possible correlation with a systematic risk factor.

tranche See *collateralized mortgage obligation*.

Treasury bill Short-term, highly liquid government debt obligation issued at a discount from the face value and returning the face amount at maturity.

Treasury bond Debt obligation of the federal government with original maturity between 10 and 30 years.

Treasury note Debt obligation of the federal government with original maturity between 1 and 10 years.

treasury stock Stock that has been repurchased by the issuing company and is held in the company's treasury.

Treynor-Black model A special case of the Markowitz model of efficient diversification, derived by assuming returns are generated by the index model.

Treynor's measure Ratio of excess return to beta.

trin statistic Ratio of average trading volume in declining stocks to average volume in advancing stocks. Used in technical analysis.

trough The transition point between recession and recovery.

turnover The ratio of the trading activity of a portfolio to the assets of the portfolio.

12b-1 fees Annual fees charged by a mutual fund to pay for marketing and distribution costs.

two-stage dividend discount model Dividend discount model that allows for an initial high-growth period before the firm settles down to a sustainable growth trajectory.

U

unbundling   See *bundling*.

underwriters   Investment bankers who help companies issue their securities to the public.

underwriting, underwriting syndicate   Underwriters (investment bankers) purchase securities from the issuing company and resell them. Usually a syndicate of investment bankers is organized behind a lead firm.

unemployment rate   The ratio of the number of people classified as unemployed to the total labor force.

unique risk   Nonmarket or firm-specific risk factors that can be eliminated by diversification. Also called *firm-specific risk*, *nonsystematic risk*, or *diversifiable risk*.

unit investment trust   Money invested in a portfolio whose composition is fixed for the life of the fund.

universal life policy   An insurance policy that allows for a varying death benefit and premium level over the term of the policy, with an interest rate on the cash value that changes with market interest rates.

utility   The measure of the welfare or satisfaction of an investor.

utility value   The welfare a given investor assigns to an investment with a particular return and risk.

V

value at risk (VaR)   Measure of downside risk. The loss that will be incurred in the event of an extreme adverse price change with some given, typically low, probability.

variable annuities   Annuity contracts in which the insurance company pays a periodic amount linked to the investment performance of an underlying portfolio.

variable life policy   An insurance policy that provides a fixed death benefit plus a cash value that can be invested in a variety of funds from which the policyholder can choose.

variance   A measure of the dispersion of a random variable. Equals the expected value of the squared deviation from the mean.

variation margin   See *maintenance margin*.

vega   The response of option price to a change in the standard deviation of the underlying asset.

venture capital (VC)   Money invested to finance a new, not yet publicly traded firm.

views   An analyst's opinion on the likely performance of a stock or sector compared to the market-consensus expectation.

volatility risk   The risk in the value of options portfolios due to unpredictable changes in the volatility of the underlying asset.

W

warrant   An option issued by the firm to purchase shares of the firm's stock.

weak-form EMH   See *efficient market hypothesis*.

well-diversified portfolio   A portfolio spread out over many securities in such a way that the weight in any security is close to zero, resulting in negligible diversifiable risk.

whole-life insurance policy   Provides a death benefit and a kind of savings plan that builds up cash value for possible future withdrawal.

workout period   Realignment period of a temporary misaligned yield relationship.

world investable wealth   The part of world wealth that is traded and is therefore accessible to investors.

writing a call   Selling a call option.

Y

yield curve   A graph of yield to maturity as a function of time to maturity.

yield to maturity (YTM)   A measure of the average rate of return that will be earned on a bond if held to maturity.

Z

zero-beta portfolio   The minimum-variance portfolio uncorrelated with a chosen efficient portfolio.

zero-coupon bond   A bond paying no coupons that sells at a discount and provides only payment of face value at maturity.

zero-investment portfolio   A portfolio of zero net value, established by buying and shorting component securities, usually in the context of an arbitrage strategy.

Name Index

Subject Index

Commonly Used Notation

b	Retention or plowback ratio	r_f	The risk-free rate of interest
C	Call option value	r_M	The rate of return on the market portfolio
CF	Cash flow		
D	Duration	ROE	Return on equity, incremental economic earnings per dollar reinvested in the firm
E	Exchange rate		
$E(x)$	Expected value of random variable x	S_p	Sharpe ratio, also called the reward-to-volatility ratio; the excess expected return divided by the standard deviation
F	Futures price		
e	2.718, the base for the natural logarithm, used for continuous compounding		
		t	Time
e_{it}	The firm-specific return, also called the residual return, of security i in period t	T_p	Treynor's measure for a portfolio, excess expected return divided by beta
f	Forward rate of interest		
g	Growth rate of dividends	V	Intrinsic value of a firm, the present value of future dividends per share
H	Hedge ratio for an option, sometimes called the option's delta	X	Exercise price of an option
i	Inflation rate	y	Yield to maturity
k	Market capitalization rate, the required rate of return on a firm's stock	α	Rate of return beyond the value that would be forecast from the market's return and the systematic risk of the security
$\ln$	Natural logarithm function		
M	The market portfolio	β	Systematic or market risk of a security
$N(d)$	Cumulative normal function, the probability that a standard normal random variable will have value less than d	ρ_{ij}	Correlation coefficient between returns on securities i and j
p	Probability	σ	Standard deviation
P	Put value	σ^2	Variance
PV	Present value	$Cov(r_i, r_j)$	Covariance between returns on securities i and j
P/E	Price-to-earnings multiple		
r	Rate of return on a security; for fixed-income securities, r may denote the rate of interest for a particular period		

Useful Formulas

Measures of Risk

Variance of returns: $\sigma^2 = \sum_s p(s)[r(s) - E(r)]^2$

Standard deviation: $\sigma = \sqrt{\sigma^2}$

Covariance between returns: $\text{Cov}(r_i, r_j) = \sum_s p(s)[r_i(s) - E(r_i)][r_j(s) - E(r_j)]$

Beta of security i: $\beta_i = \dfrac{\text{Cov}(r_i, r_M)}{\text{Var}(r_M)}$

Portfolio Theory

Expected rate of return on a portfolio with weights w_i, in each security: $E(r_p) = \sum_{i=1}^{n} w_i E(r_i)$

Variance of portfolio rate of return: $\sigma_p^2 = \sum_{j=1}^{n} \sum_{i=1}^{n} w_j w_i \, \text{Cov}(r_i, r_j)$

Market Equilibrium

The CAPM security market line: $E(r_i) = r_f + \beta_i[E(r_M) - r_f]$

Multifactor security market line (in excess returns): $E(R_i) = \beta_{iM} E(R_M) + \sum_{k=1}^{K} \beta_{ik} E(R_k)$

Fixed-Income Analysis

Present value of $1:

Discrete period compounding: $PV = 1/(1 + r)^T$

Continuous compounding: $PV = e^{-r_{cc}T}$

Forward rate of interest for period T: $f_T = \dfrac{(1 + y_T)^T}{(1 + y_{T-1})^{T-1}} - 1$

Real interest rate: $r_{\text{real}} = \dfrac{1 + r_{\text{nom}}}{1 + i} - 1$

where r_{nom} is the nominal interest rate and i is the inflation rate

Duration of a security: $D = \sum_{t=1}^{T} t \times \dfrac{CF_t}{(1 + y)^t} \Big/ \text{Price}$

Modified duration: $D^* = D/(1 + y)$

Equity Analysis

Constant growth dividend discount model: $V_0 = \dfrac{D_1}{k - g}$

Sustainable growth rate of dividends: $g = \text{ROE} \times b$

Price/earnings multiple: $P/E = \dfrac{1 - b}{k - \text{ROE} \times b}$

$\text{ROE} = (1 - \text{Tax rate})\left[\text{ROA} + (\text{ROA} - \text{Interest rate})\dfrac{\text{Debt}}{\text{Equity}}\right]$

Derivative Assets

Put-call parity: $P = C - S_0 + \text{PV}(X + \text{dividends})$

Black-Scholes formula (with constant dividend yield): $C = Se^{-\delta T}N(d_1) - Xe^{-rT}N(d_2)$

$$d_1 = \frac{\ln(S/X) + (r - \delta + \sigma^2/2)T}{\sigma\sqrt{T}}$$

$$d_2 = d_1 - \sigma\sqrt{T}$$

Spot-futures parity: $F_0 = S_0(1 + r - d)^T$

Interest rate parity (direct exchange rate quotes): $F_0 = E_0\left(\dfrac{1 + r_{\text{US}}}{1 + r_{\text{foreign}}}\right)^T$

Performance Evaluation

Sharpe ratio: $S_p = \dfrac{\bar{r}_p - \bar{r}_f}{\sigma_p}$

Treynor's measure: $T_p = \dfrac{\bar{r}_p - \bar{r}_f}{\beta_p}$

Jensen's alpha: $\alpha_p = \bar{r}_p - [\bar{r}_f + \beta_p(\bar{r}_M - \bar{r}_f)]$

Information ratio: $\dfrac{\alpha_p}{\sigma(e_p)}$

Geometric average return: $r_G = [(1 + r_1)(1 + r_2)\ldots(1 + r_T)]^{1/T} - 1$